PRENTICE HALL
LITERATURE
THE ENGLISH TRADITION

# PRENTICE HALL
# LITERATURE

COPPER

BRONZE

SILVER

GOLD

PLATINUM

THE AMERICAN EXPERIENCE

THE ENGLISH TRADITION

WORLD MASTERPIECES

# PRENTICE HALL
# LITERATURE

# THE ENGLISH TRADITION

SECOND EDITION

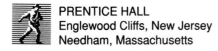

PRENTICE HALL
Englewood Cliffs, New Jersey
Needham, Massachusetts

PRENTICE HALL
A Division of Simon & Schuster
Englewood Cliffs, New Jersey 07632

## STAFF CREDITS FOR PRENTICE HALL LITERATURE

**Editorial:** Eileen Thompson, Ellen Bowler, Philip Fried, Daniel Jackson, Doug McCollum, Jane Standen, Richard Hickox, Carol Schneider, Kelly Ackley

**Design:** Sue Walrath, Nancy Sharkey, Leslie Osher

**Photo Research:** Libby Forsyth

**Production:** Penny Hull, Suse Cioffi, Joan McCulley, Marlys Lehmann, Lisa Meyerhoff, Cleasta Wilburn

**Editorial Systems:** Andrew Grey Bommarito, Ralph O'Brien

**Marketing:** Carol Newman, Mollie Ledwith, Tom Maksym

**Manufacturing:** Laura Sanderson, Denise Herckenrath

**Permissions:** Doris Robinson

## ACKNOWLEDGMENTS

Grateful acknowledgment is made to the following for permission to reprint copyrighted material:

**Edward Arnold (Publishers) Ltd.**
"The Helping Hand" from *The Life to Come and Other Stories* by E.M. Forster. Copyright © 1972 The Trustees of the Late E. M. Forster.

**Broadside Press**
Excerpt from "Ballad of Birmingham" by Dudley Randall from *Poem Counterpoem.* Copyright 1969 by Dudley Randall and Margaret Danner. Reprinted by permission of Broadside Press.

**Jonathan Cape Ltd. and the Estate of Henry Reed**
"Naming of Parts" from *A Map of Verona* by Henry Reed, 1946.

**Carcanet Press Ltd.**
"November Sun" from *Selected Poems* by Elizabeth Daryush, 1972. Reprinted by permission of Carcanet Press Ltd.

**Jonathan Clowes Ltd., London, on behalf of Doris Lessing**
Excerpt from "The Small Personal Voice" from *A Small Per-*

(continued on page 1452)

*vi*

# CONTENTS

# THE SEVENTEENTH CENTURY
## 1625–1660

## The Puritan Age

# THE RESTORATION AND THE EIGHTEENTH CENTURY
## 1660–1798

## The Restoration

## The Age of Pope and Swift

## The Age of Johnson

## Pre-Romantic Poetry

# THE ROMANTIC AGE
## 1798–1832

## Poetry

## Prose

## CONTEMPORARY WRITERS
### 1945–PRESENT

PRENTICE HALL
LITERATURE
THE ENGLISH TRADITION

**BAYEUX (bà yóo′) TAPESTRY: NORMAN CAVALRY CHARGE AT THE SHIELDWALL AT THE BATTLE OF HASTINGS**
*The Granger Collection*

# THE ANGLO-SAXON PERIOD

### 449–1066

When Angles and Saxons came hither from the east,
Sought Britain over the broad-spreading sea,
Haughty war-smiths overcame the Britons,
Valiant earls got for themselves a home.

from The Anglo-Saxon Chronicle

The passage on the previous page comes from a modern translation of *The Anglo-Saxon Chronicle,* an early record of English history. It tells of the attacks staged by warriors from Denmark and Germany on the rock-bound coast of Britain during the fifth century. Most of the fierce "war-smiths" identified themselves as Angles and Saxons, though some belonged to a smaller tribe, the Jutes. At first these pirates sailed their shallow boats across the "broad-spreading" North Sea to raid Britain's low-lying eastern coast. By A.D. 449, however, their raids had turned into a full-scale invasion.

The arrival of the Anglo-Saxons in Britain signaled the beginning of the English language. The "war-smiths" soon drove native Britons from the eastern, central, and southern portions of their island. Those areas became known as "Angles' land," or England. The closely related Germanic languages spoken by the conquering tribes developed into a new language called "Angle-ish," or English. Although that language would change a great deal over the centuries, it was the ancestor of the English we speak today. As the language took shape, so did the literature of Britain, including that of Ireland, Scotland, and Wales.

To put these early times into historical perspective, we must first examine the people whom the Angles and Saxons conquered, the settlers of Britain before 449. As you read about this period, you may want to consult the map on page 7 to locate unfamiliar geographical details.

## BRITAIN BEFORE THE ANGLO-SAXONS

British historian G. M. Trevelyan has compared his country's early history to a battle scene from Shakespeare's *Macbeth* (see page 223): "Prophecy hovers around. Horns are heard blowing in the mist, and a confused uproar of savage tumult and outrage. We catch glimpses of giant figures—mostly warriors at strife. But there are ploughmen, too, it seems, breaking the primeval clod, and we hear the sound of forests crashing to the axe. Around all is the lap of waves and the cry of seamen beaching their ships."

Who were these early warriors and ploughmen? The answer is not entirely clear, for some of them arrived in Britain in the dim recesses before recorded time. Among them were Iberians from present-day Spain and Portugal, who brought late Stone Age weapons to Britain's shores. The last, and by far the most important, of the early conquerors were the Celts, a people from southern Europe who had gradually migrated west. Between 800 and 600 B.C., two groups of Celts invaded the British Isles.

### Arrival of the Celts

One group, who called themselves Brythons (now spelled "Britons"), settled on the largest island, Britain. The other, known as Gaels, settled on the second largest island, known to us as Ireland.

Gaels and Britons spoke different but related languages of the Celtic family. Celtic languages had nothing in common with the Germanic ones later associated with the Angles and Saxons.

The Celts were farmers and hunters. They organized themselves into tightly knit clans, each with a fearsome loyalty to its chieftain. When these clans fell into argument with one another, they often looked to a class of priests known as Druids to settle their disputes. Druids presided over religious rituals including sacrifices and prayers. They also had, as their duty, the memorizing and reciting of long, heroic poems that preserved the people's myths about the past. Some of the poems may have included fables about such leaders as Old King Cole of the nursery rhyme and King Lear of Shakespeare's tragic play.

**RELIGIOUS CEREMONY OF THE DRUIDS**
*Forrest C. Crooks*
Three Lions

# BRITISH EVENTS

Stonehenge

St. Augustine

Buddha Addressing

A Viking Sword

Danes Attacking a British Town

The Coronation of

A Roman Town After the Fall of the Empire

a Disciple

Charles Martel Battling the Moors

William the Conqueror

King Charlemagne

# WORLD EVENTS

**INSIGNIA OF THE ROMAN CIVIL GOVERNOR IN CHARGE OF THE FIVE BRITISH PROVINCES**
*An Early 15th-Century Copy of a Page from the Now-Lost Notitia Dignitatum Utriusque Imperii, a 4th-Century List of Imperial Magistrates, Adorned with the Symbols of their Provinces*
The Granger Collection

## The Roman Conquest

The next conquerors of Britain were the far more sophisticated Romans. In 55 B.C. and again the next year, the Roman general Julius Caesar made hasty invasions. Although he barely penetrated the island, he quickly declared it conquered and returned to what is now France to work on his memoirs. The true conquest of Britain occurred nearly one hundred years later during the reign of the Roman emperor Claudius. Disciplined Roman legions spread out over the island, establishing camps, which soon grew into towns.

The Romans transplanted many comforts of their urban, Mediterranean culture to the distant, rain-drenched north. In perhaps their greatest contribution, they constructed a system of well-paved roads through the woodland wilderness, highways that continued to link the island for centuries. The Romans also brought with them their skills in the art of warfare. Yet they apparently failed to teach the Britons much about self-defense.

The Roman rule of Britain lasted for more than 300 years. It ended only when northern European tribes invaded Italy and increased pressure on Rome itself. The last Roman legions departed from Britain to defend Rome in A.D. 407. By that time, some of their towns were already falling to ruin, and the Britons were easy prey for a new set of invaders.

## THE ANGLO-SAXON CONQUEST

As we have seen, the next invaders were the Anglo-Saxons. Who were these ancient people? Lacking authentic first-hand accounts from the period, historians simply have to guess. Some Anglo-Saxons appear to have been deep-sea fishermen, already accustomed to marauding coasts along the Baltic Sea. Others seem to have been farmers, perhaps seeking soil richer than the sandy or marshy land at home. Ferocious as the Angles and Saxons may have been, they did not perform their piracy merely for plunder—at least not for long. They sought and won territory, apparently by rowing their shallow boats up river into the British heartland and then building camps and waging war on the Britons. Gradually the newcomers gained the upper hand over the island's settlers and took over more and more of what today is England.

### Early Anglo-Saxon Life

The first Angles, Saxons, and Jutes transferred to England their highly organized tribal units. Each tribe was ruled by a king, chosen by a *witan*, or council of elders. Each community had four distinct classes. The *earls* were a hereditary class of ruling warlords who owed their position to the king. The second class, *freemen*, were allowed to own land and engage in commerce. (This class included *thanes*, early barons, who were granted their status as a reward for military service.) Lower on the social scale were *churls*, or serfs, bonded servants who worked the land in return for military protection. Lowest of all were *thralls*, or slaves, usually military prisoners or people being punished.

Invading groups set up numerous small kingdoms, and at first the various kingdoms fought frequently. As time went on, however, many of these tribal differences faded. Anglo-Saxon kingdoms traded with one another. Men married women from different tribes. Kingdoms gradually absorbed one another until seven larger ones remained. As previously mentioned, all this intermingling produced a new language. We call it Anglo-Saxon or Old English to distinguish it from our modern form.

## Anglo-Saxon Beliefs

The Anglo-Saxons brought to Britain their own pagan beliefs. In the world of the sixth century, the ever-present dangers of death by accident or warfare had led these people to take a rather grim view of life. In fact, the early Anglo-Saxons believed that every human life was in the hands of fate. Their attitude was sharply different from the

Christian belief in the freedom of an individual to determine his or her own path.

The early Anglo-Saxons worshiped ancient Germanic gods. They included Tiu, god of war and the sky; Woden, chief of the gods; and Fria, Woden's wife and goddess of the home. These gods were abandoned with the coming of Christianity. Even so, their names survive in our words *Tuesday, Wednesday,* and *Friday.*

### Dispersal of the Britons

In terror of the Anglo-Saxons, the Britons retreated to the edges of their island—and beyond. Some went to Cornwall on the south-western tip of Britain, an area that remained Celtic long after the rest of the island was Anglo-Saxon. Others fled to Britain's hilly western region, an area that became known as Wales. Still others joined the Gaels of Ireland where they formed a splinter group named Scots (from *Scotia,* the Roman word for Ireland). This group then traveled back to Britain and settled in the northern part of the island, Scotland. In all these areas, people spoke Celtic languages —Cornish, Welsh, and Irish and Scottish Gaelic—until modern times. All but Cornish are still spoken today.

**SAXONS, JUTES, AND ANGLES
ARRIVING IN BRITAIN BY SEA**
*English Manuscript Illumination*
The Granger Collection

## THE COMING OF CHRISTIANITY

During the fourth century, the Romans had accepted Christianity and introduced it to Britain. A century later, when the Celts fled the Anglo-Saxons, they took their Christian faith with them. During this period, the faith lived on in Wales. From there it spread to Ireland, assisted by the activities of the legendary St. Patrick.

After Rome fell to barbarian tribes in A.D. 476, communications weakened between Celtic and Roman Christians. While the Roman Church was recovering from political chaos, the Celtic Christian Church continued to thrive. In 563 a group of Irish monks set sail in tiny skiffs for the west coast of Scotland. Led by a soldier and abbot named Columba, they established a Christian monastery on the island of Iona. From this headquarters, Columba and his monks moved across northern Britain in the hope of winning additional souls for the faith. In their travels, they won ready acceptance among many Scots; then among some Saxons and Angles. Their conversions led, in turn, to the establishment of other monasteries in the north.

### Resurgence of the Roman Church

Meanwhile, the Roman Church had reorganized itself and was beginning to send missionaries throughout Europe. In 597, the

Roman cleric Saint Augustine (not the early Christian Church father) arrived in southeast England and quickly converted King Ethelbert of Kent to Christianity. Augustine set up a monastery at Canterbury in Kent and began preaching his faith to other rulers in southern England. To win over a kingdom, Augustine and his followers needed only to convert the king, who would then make Christianity the religion of his realm. By the year 650, they had largely succeeded. Most of England was Christian in name, if not in fact.

The new religion had a profound effect on Anglo-Saxon civilization. It softened the ferocity of a warrior people and improved the conduct of the faithful. No longer could ruling warlords indulge themselves in the belief that they had descended from pagan gods. No longer could freemen think it permissible to treat their wives or children or slaves with cruelty. Christian clerics were now able to end old feuds by denouncing revenge and calling upon a higher law. By providing counsel to quarreling rulers, the Church promoted peace and played a major role in unifying the English people.

## Christianity and Literature

The church also brought to England two elements of civilization that had been missing since the departure of the Romans: education and written literature. Christian leaders established schools at Canterbury and York and supervised the preservation of learning in the island's monasteries. Within their secluded halls, monks often worked as scribes, recording and duplicating *manuscripts,* or books written by hand. At first they worked only in Latin, the language of Church scholarship. Often several monks labored for years to complete a single manuscript. These volumes were elaborately painted and illuminated in gold and silver.

From such monastic training emerged a Northumbrian monk later considered the "father of English history." Today we know him as the Venerable Bede (673–735). Bede was a master of thorough research, tracking down information by studying earlier documents and interviewing people who had witnessed or taken part in past events. His most famous volume was *A History of the English Church and People,* a monumental work that offers the clearest account we have of early Anglo-Saxon times.

Although Christianity did indeed temper Anglo-Saxon civilization, it did not destroy the northerners' spirit. Glimpses of an earlier world lived on in the fragments of epics such as *Beowulf,* a long, narrative poem that depicted great battles between Anglo-Saxon warriors and superhuman monsters. The Anglo-Saxons remained a hardy group, fearless and loyal in their instincts even if less and less predatory in their habits. Now they were about to come face to face with a new peril from a people much like themselves— invasion by the Vikings.

**AN ENGLISH MONK EXACTLY CONTEMPORARY WITH BEDE**
*Illumination from an early 8th-century Northumbrian Codex*
The Granger Collection

# THE FIRST DANISH INVASION

Between the eighth and twelfth centuries, a great restlessness overtook the region of northern Europe known as Scandinavia. Beset with a rising population and limited farmland, the people of Norway, the Norse, and of Denmark, the Danes, followed old traditions and took to the seas. In some of their most adventurous voyages, the Vikings (warriors) carried their piracy to the British Isles. The Norse set their sights on Northumbria, Scotland, Wales, and Ireland, whereas the Danes targeted eastern and southern England.

## Viking Raids

Viking invaders sacked and plundered monasteries, destroyed manuscripts, and stole sacred religious objects. They burned entire communities and put villagers to the sword. Wherever the Vikings went, the sight of their square-sailed ships stirred specters of terror and destruction. One Anglo-Saxon prayer of the day reflected the fear that the Danish pirates inspired: "From the fury of the Northmen, O Lord, deliver us."

**THE 9TH-CENTURY OSEBERG VIKING SHIP**
*The Granger Collection*

Although the English fought back valiantly, the Danes made broad inroads. By the middle of the ninth century, most of northern, eastern, and central England had fallen to the invaders. They called their territory the Danelaw. Only the Saxon kingdom of Wessex managed to fight the Danes to a standstill.

## Alfred the Great

In 871 a king ascended to the Wessex throne who would become the only ruler in England's history ever to be honored with the epithet "the Great." His name was Alfred, and he earned the title partly by resisting further Danish encroachment. Under a truce concluded in 886, England was formally divided: the Saxons acknowledged Danish rule in the east and north, but the Danes agreed to respect Saxon rule in the south. As the king of a much-expanded Wessex, Alfred the Great became a national hero.

Alfred's achievements went far beyond the field of battle, however. Not only was he instrumental in preserving the remnants of pre-Danish civilization in Britain, but he encouraged a rebirth of learning and education. To make literature and other documents more readily available, he himself translated Bede's *History* and other works from Latin into Anglo-Saxon, the everyday language of the people. In this way he fostered the growth of the English language and its literature. He also began to keep records of English history in *The Anglo-Saxon Chronicle,* today among our principal sources of information on early English life.

## Danish Contributions

Gradually the Danes became more peaceful, and old animosities subsided. A once war-obsessed people settled into the workaday world of farming, beer-brewing, and moving goods to market. Even before their arrival in England, many Danes had been accustomed to the merchant's trade, however crudely it may have existed in northern Europe at the time. Now they built their Danelaw communities not only as military fortresses but as trading centers, and one result was the growth of English towns.

Like the Anglo-Saxons, the Danes spoke a Germanic language, so they were able to communicate easily with the English. In fact, many Norse words slowly crept into the English vocabulary. The word *law* is Danish, for example. Its use reflected the Danes' interest in legal procedures.

## THE SECOND DANISH INVASION AND THE NORMAN CONQUEST

The peace and stability that began with Alfred's reign lasted more than a century. Immigration from Scandinavia dwindled, and

**ALFRED THE GREAT ACKNOWLEDGED AS KING BY ALL MEN OF ENGLAND, 871 A.D.**
*Three Lions*

**PAGE FROM AN EARLY 12TH-CENTURY MANUSCRIPT OF THE *ANGLO-SAXON CHRONICLE* DESCRIBING THE NORMAN CONQUEST**
*The Granger Collection*

the descendants of Alfred the Great were able to regain much conquered territory. Toward the close of the tenth century, however, a new series of onslaughts began as more Danes from Europe attempted to recapture and widen the Danelaw. Once they had succeeded, they forced the Saxon witan to select a succession of Danish kings.

## Edward the Confessor and the Normans

Then, in 1042, the line of succession returned to a descendant of Alfred the Great. This king, Edward, had gained the title "the Confessor" because he was a deeply religious Christian. He had spent many of his early years in Normandy, a region once settled by Scandinavians and now a part of France. Norman on his mother's side, Edward had developed a close friendship with his cousin William, Normandy's ruler. Once Edward took the English throne, his association with the Normans further weakened Saxon power. His death in 1066 led directly to a Norman conquest of England and brought the end of the Anglo-Saxon period of literature, as we shall see in the next unit.

## ANGLO-SAXON LITERATURE

Scholars now believe that the literature of the British Isles began with Celtic Druids. These priests assumed the function of storytellers, memorizing and reciting long, heroic poems about Celtic leaders and their deeds. In the same way, Anglo-Saxon literature began not with books, but with spoken verse and incantations. Their purpose was to pass along tribal history and values to an audience that could not read.

To be sure, some Anglo-Saxons were familiar with the written word. In the third century in northern Europe, they had devised an alphabet of letters called runes. When they came to Britain, they brought this alphabet with them and used it until the Latin alphabet we have today superseded it. Yet they employed runes chiefly for inscriptions on important buildings, on statues, and the like. Few early Anglo-Saxons could read or write.

## Origins of Anglo-Saxon Poetry

The reciting of poems often occurred on ceremonial occasions such as the celebration of a military victory. A warrior's comrades would gather in his hall or castle, and the performance would begin. The performers were usually professional minstrels, known as *scops,* and their assistants, called *gleemen.* The scops and gleemen recited for hours and, in some instances, even for days.

Scholars now suppose that these recitations took place to the accompaniment of a harp. The poems followed a set formula of composition, which probably made them easier to memorize. A formal, rigid pattern of word stresses gave the lyrics a terse,

THE BAYEUX TAPESTRY: EDWARD THE CONFESSOR SPEAKS TO HAROLD OF WESSEX
*The Granger Collection*

sing-song effect. A mid-line pause, called a *caesura,* occurred in many lines. Another part of the pattern was *alliteration,* the repetition of sounds, especially initial consonant sounds.

## Types of Anglo-Saxon Verse

Only about 30,000 lines of Anglo-Saxon verse still exist. Almost all of it is found in four works dating from about A.D. 975 to 1050. The early verse falls mainly into two categories. One is heroic poetry, which recounts the achievements of warriors involved in great battles. The other is elegiac poetry, sorrowful laments that mourn the deaths of loved ones and the loss of the past.

Copied many years after their composition, the poems have obviously undergone many changes. Later scops may have adapted them, and so may have monastic scribes. Nevertheless, pagan elements remain, particularly in the ever-present sense of an ominous fate, or *wyrd.* Consider, for example, these lines from one of the elegiac poems, "The Wanderer":

> He then, wise in soul, with weighty
> thought thinks deeply upon this dark-
> some life, this fallen fastness. . . .

## The Beowulf Legend

Of the heroic poetry, the most important work is *Beowulf,* the story of a great pagan warrior renowned for his courage, strength, and dignity. *Beowulf* is an *epic,* a long heroic poem. Because it is the first such work to be composed in the English language, it is considered the national epic of England.

Like most Anglo-Saxon poets, the author of *Beowulf* is unknown. Although versions of the poem were probably recited as early as the sixth century, the text that we have today was composed in the eighth century and not written down until the eleventh. Thus, the poem includes many references to Christian ideas and Latin classics. Clearly evident in *Beowulf,* however, are the values of a warrior society, especially such values as dignity, bravery, and prowess in battle:

> And Beowulf was ready, firm with our
> Lord's
> High favor and his own bold courage and
> strength.

Emphasis on such values did not disappear in Christian times. It appeared in later Anglo-Saxon poems such as *The Battle of Maldon,* which commemorates a great military defeat of the Danes.

## Poets of the Christian Era

Among the few known poets of the Christian era, two are worthy of mention—Caedmon and Cynewulf. Caedmon, who apparently

**A PAGE FROM THE CAEDMON MANUSCRIPT, c. 1000**
*The Granger Collection*

lived in the seventh century, is mentioned in Bede's *History*. The poet's only authenticated verse consists of a few lines that Bede recorded, called "Caedmon's Hymn." Nevertheless, the term *Caedmonian verse* is often used to identify other early Christian poetry in English. Scholars believe that Cynewulf lived around the turn of the ninth century. He is known because he "signed" his name, spelling it out in runes, on four poems that survive today.

## Anglo-Saxon Prose

Before the reign of Alfred the Great, all important prose written in the British Isles was composed in Latin. The monks who transcribed these works regarded the vernacular, the language of the common people, as a "vulgar tongue." The greatest of England's Latin scholars was the Venerable Bede, as mentioned earlier. His *History* gives an account of England from the Roman invasion to his own time.

Bede's *History* concerns itself mostly with northern England, but it is not simply the story of Northumbria or the people who settled there. The monk couples his view of the Roman Church as a universal force with a distinctly nationalistic view of a unified English people. Although Bede wrote in Latin, his *History* may nevertheless be considered the first truly English prose work. From it we derive much of what we know about early Anglo-Saxon times.

Bede's successor as the leading English scholar was Alcuin (735–804), another monk who, like Bede, won fame throughout Europe. Trained at York, Alcuin traveled widely in Europe and eventually headed the palace school of the powerful European emperor Charlemagne. By the time of his death, Alcuin had produced many major works in philosophy, religion, and Latin grammar.

## Alfred the Great and His Successors

Historians usually credit Alfred the Great with having changed the course of British literature. The spur he gave to the English language was evident in its more widespread use among scholars after his death. Of these scholars, the foremost were Aelfric and Wulfstan, who lived in the second half of the tenth century. Aelfric, a monk of Wessex, wrote many works in the vernacular, including a series of *homilies,* or sermons, based on Bible stories. Though in prose, these sermons employ a great deal of the sort of alliteration more commonly associated with Anglo-Saxon poetry. Wulfstan, an archbishop of York, also wrote several sermons in Old English, including a famous speech on the devastation of the Danish raids.

After the Normans occupied England, they gradually transformed the English that the Anglo-Saxons spoke. Old English or Anglo-Saxon evolved into what we now call Middle English, whose literature we will explore in the next unit.

I sing of myself, a sorrowful woman.
> **Anonymous,** "A Wife's Lament," translated by Kemp Malone

This tale is true, and mine. It tells
How the sea took me, swept me back
And forth, in sorrow and fear and pain.
> **Anonymous,** "The Seafarer," translated by Burton Raffel

It is better never to begin a good work than, having begun it, to stop.
> **Bede,** *A History of the English Church and People*

Out from the marsh, from the foot of misty
Hills and bogs, bearing God's hatred,
Grendel came.

Beowulf spoke, in spite of the swollen
Livid wound, knowing he'd unwound
His string of days on earth. . . .
                              My days
Have gone by as fate willed, waiting
For its word to be spoken.
> **Anonymous,** *Beowulf,* translated by Burton Raffel

Light was first
Through the Lord's word
Named day:
Beauteous, bright creation!
> **Caedmon,** *Creation. The First Day,* translated by Benjamin Thorpe

And those people should not be listened to who keep saying the voice of the people is the voice of God, since the riotousness of the crowd is always very close to madness.
> **Alcuin** in a letter to Charlemagne

Alcuin was my name; learning I loved.
> **Alcuin** in his own epitaph

Thought shall be the harder, heart the keener, courage the greater, as our might lessens.
> **Anonymous,** *The Battle of Maldon,* translated by R. K. Gordon

# READING CRITICALLY

## The Literature of 449–1066

When you read literature, it is important to know its historical context. Doing so will help you to understand the writer's ideas and techniques.

**Historical Context**

In 449 the island of Britain was invaded by warlike Germanic peoples known as Angles and Saxons. These invaders brought with them their pagan beliefs and traditions, which appear in Anglo-Saxon poetry and legends. They also brought with them a grim, fatalistic view of the world. These Germanic invaders were followed by Roman missionaries, who converted Britain to Christianity. During this time, different kinds of literature developed, including the oral poetry of the Anglo-Saxons and written historical and religious prose. The literature of the time shows both pagan and Christian influences.

**Literary Movements**

Very few people were able to read during this period. Therefore, an oral tradition flourished. The Anglo-Saxons were fond of poetry, which was developed and passed on by scops, or poet-singers. Eventually, some of this oral literature was written down by monks in monasteries, who are largely responsible for having preserved oral material.

**Writers' Techniques**

Because most literature was oral, it was composed in such a way that it was easily memorized. Lines of poetry with regular rhythms were easier to remember than was prose. Poets used alliteration for the same reason. In addition, Anglo-Saxon poets were fond of the kenning, a compound metaphorical name for something, such as "whale's home" for the sea. The Anglo-Saxon poetry that has been preserved illustrates these techniques.

On the following pages is an Anglo-Saxon poem, "The Seafarer." The notes in the side column point out features of the poem that show the historical context or the literary techniques of the period.

# The Seafarer

translated by Burton Raffel

**Literary Movement:** Because this poem was passed on in the oral tradition, different versions of it exist.

This tale is true, and mine. It tells
How the sea took me, swept me back
And forth in sorrow and fear and pain,
Showed me suffering in a hundred ships,
5 In a thousand ports, and in me. It tells
Of smashing surf when I sweated in the cold
Of an anxious watch, perched in the bow
As it dashed under cliffs. My feet were cast
In icy bands, bound with frost,
10 With frozen chains, and hardship groaned
Around my heart. Hunger tore
At my sea-weary soul. No man sheltered
On the quiet fairness of earth can feel
How wretched I was, drifting through winter
15 On an ice-cold sea, whirled in sorrow,
Alone in a world blown clear of love,
Hung with icicles. The hailstorms flew.
The only sound was the roaring sea,
The freezing waves. The song of the swan
20 Might serve for pleasure, the cry of the sea-fowl,
The death-noise of birds instead of laughter,
The mewing of gulls instead of mead.
Storms beat on the rocky cliffs and were echoed
By icy-feathered terns and the eagle's screams;
25 No kinsman could offer comfort there,
To a soul left drowning in desolation.
        And who could believe, knowing but
The passion of cities, swelled proud with wine
And no taste of misfortune, how often, how wearily,
30 I put myself back on the paths of the sea.
Night would blacken; it would snow from the north;
Frost bound the earth and hail would fall,
The coldest seeds. And how my heart
Would begin to beat, knowing once more
35 The salt waves tossing and the towering sea!
The time for journeys would come and my soul
Called me eagerly out, sent me over
The horizon, seeking foreigners' homes.

**Historical Background:** The poet's subject is the sea. The sea is a common subject because the British are an island people.

**Writer's Technique:** Anglo-Saxon poetry frequently uses a line divided by a caesura, a pause. Alliteration joins the two parts: an important word in the first part of the line has the same initial consonant sound as an important word in the second part of the line.

**Writer's Technique:** "coldest seeds" is a kenning, a metaphorical name, for "hail."

**SHIPS WITH THREE MEN, FISH**
*Bodleian Library, Oxford*

**Historical Context:** The Anglo-Saxons saw Fate as grim and overpowering.

But there isn't a man on earth so proud,
40   So born to greatness, so bold with his youth,
Grown so brave, or so graced by God,
That he feels no fear as the sails unfurl,
Wondering what Fate has willed and will do.
No harps ring in his heart, no rewards,
45   No passion for women, no worldly pleasures,
Nothing, only the ocean's heave;
But longing wraps itself around him.
Orchards blossom, the towns bloom,
Fields grow lovely as the world springs fresh,
50   And all these admonish that willing mind

Leaping to journeys, always set
In thoughts traveling on a quickening tide.
So summer's sentinel, the cuckoo, sings
In his murmuring voice, and our hearts mourn
55  As he urges. Who could understand,
In ignorant ease, what we others suffer
As the paths of exile stretch endlessly on?
      And yet my heart wanders away,
My soul roams with the sea, the whales'
60  Home, wandering to the widest corners
Of the world, returning ravenous with desire,
Flying solitary, screaming, exciting me
To the open ocean, breaking oaths
On the curve of a wave.
      Thus the joys of God
65  Are fervent with life, where life itself
Fades quickly into the earth. The wealth
Of the world neither reaches to Heaven nor remains.
No man has ever faced the dawn
Certain which of Fate's three threats
70  Would fall: illness, or age, or an enemy's
Sword, snatching the life from his soul.
The praise the living pour on the dead
Flowers from reputation: plant
An earthly life of profit reaped
75  Even from hatred and rancor, of bravery
Flung in the devil's face, and death
Can only bring you earthly praise
And a song to celebrate a place
With the angels, life eternally blessed
80  In the hosts of Heaven.
      The days are gone
When the kingdoms of earth flourished in glory;
Now there are no rulers, no emperors,
No givers of gold, as once there were,
When wonderful things were worked among them
85  And they lived in lordly magnificence.
Those powers have vanished, those pleasures are dead.
The weakest survives and the world continues,
Kept spinning by toil. All glory is tarnished.
The world's honor ages and shrinks,
90  Bent like the men who mold it. Their faces
Blanch as time advances, their beards
Wither and they mourn the memory of friends.
The sons of princes, sown in the dust.

**Historical Context:** Fear of Fate was balanced with a firm reliance on God.

The soul stripped of its flesh knows nothing
95  Of sweetness or sour, feels no pain,
Bends neither its hand nor its brain. A brother
Opens his palms and pours down gold
On his kinsman's grave, strewing his coffin
With treasures intended for Heaven, but nothing
100  Golden shakes the wrath of God
For a soul overflowing with sin, and nothing
Hidden on earth rises to Heaven.
                    We all fear God. He turns the earth,
He set it swinging firmly in space,
105  Gave life to the world and light to the sky.
Death leaps at the fools who forget their God.
He who lives humbly has angels from Heaven
To carry him courage and strength and belief.
A man must conquer pride, not kill it,
110  Be firm with his fellows, chaste for himself,
Treat all the world as the world deserves,
With love or with hate but never with harm,
Though an enemy seek to scorch him in hell,
Or set the flames of a funeral pyre
115  Under his lord. Fate is stronger
And God mightier than any man's mind.
Our thoughts should turn to where our home is,
Consider the ways of coming there,
Then strive for sure permission for us
120  To rise to that eternal joy,
That life born in the love of God
And the hope of Heaven. Praise the Holy
Grace of Him who honored us,
Eternal, unchanging creator of earth. Amen.

**Literary Movement:** The prayerful ending may have been added by Christian monks in recording the oral poem.

"The Seafarer" was composed by an unknown poet, probably in the eighth century. It is one of relatively few poems that survive from the oral tradition in pre-Christian Britain. Preserved by Christian copyists in monasteries, it first appeared in the *Exeter Book*, a famous collection of Anglo-Saxon poems copied around 975 and donated to Exeter Cathedral, where it remains today.

## THINKING ABOUT THE SELECTION

### Recalling

1. What are three images the poet uses in the first stanza to convey his sense of isolation?
2. The poet names "Fate's three threats." What are they?
3. (a) What happens to "fools who forget their God"? (b) What happens to those who "live humbly"?

### Interpreting

4. How might you explain the mixed feelings about the sea that the poet seems to feel?
5. Pagans in Anglo-Saxon England—that is, non-Christians—felt themselves at the mercy of forces utterly beyond their control, while Christians put their trust in salvation and heaven. In what way do lines 39 through 43 show the influence of both beliefs?
6. Explain lines 66 and 67: "The wealth / Of the world neither reaches to Heaven nor remains."
7. "The Seafarer" is a poem of contrasts. What contrast is implied in lines 80 through 102?
8. What does the poet mean by the word *home* in line 117?

### Applying

9. Explain how a person can dislike something as much as the sailor dislikes life at sea and yet keep going back to it.

## ANALYZING LITERATURE

### Understanding Anglo-Saxon Poetry

A **lyric poem** is one that expresses intense personal emotions. "The Seafarer" mixes pagan with Christian beliefs and expresses sorrow for something lost or past. At times the poet's feelings seem to border on despair.

1. What deep personal feelings does the poet express in the first part of "The Seafarer" that show this to be a lyric poem?
2. "The Seafarer" has two distinct parts, the second of which begins at line 64. What are some of the strong emotions expressed in the second part of the poem?

## CRITICAL THINKING AND READING

### Comparing and Contrasting Attitudes

To **compare** two ideas or attitudes is to point out similarities. To **contrast** them is to point out differences. Most people have mixed feelings on certain subjects.

Explain what accounts for the poet's state of mind at the beginning of the poem and at the end.

## UNDERSTANDING LANGUAGE

### Appreciating Old English

Old English is the English language as it existed from about 500 to about 1150. Our language has changed so much since then that Anglo-Saxon poems like "The Seafarer" must be translated, just as if they came from a foreign language, if modern readers are to appreciate them. Here are lines 42 and 43 from "The Seafarer" in Old English:

> þæt he a his sæfore    sorge næbbe.
> to hwon hine Dryhten    gedon wille.

A few Old English words still appear in dictionaries but are seldom used any more. Find the meanings of the following words.

1. churl
2. thane
3. tor
4. yare
5. yclept

## THINKING AND WRITING

### Writing About Anglo-Saxon Beliefs

"The Seafarer" is not an easy poem to understand. One critic has said that almost any theory can be made to explain its meaning. What is *your* theory? What main idea do you think the poet intends to convey? In your prewriting, list the various thoughts and feelings the poet expresses in the poem. Use these notes as the basis for a thesis statement in which you summarize what you think the main idea of the poem is. In writing a first draft, support your thesis statement with evidence from the poem. When you revise, be sure you have made clear the reasons for your conclusion.

# BEOWULF

## 700 [?]

Composed by an unknown poet who lived more than twelve hundred years ago, *Beowulf* marks the beginning of English literature. Minstrels called scops recited this poem to audiences in England for about three hundred years before it was first written down. Only one original manuscript of the complete 3128-line poem survives, but *Beowulf* is in no danger of becoming extinct. Not only does it have lasting historical importance as a record of the Angles, Saxons, and Jutes in England, but it also tells a hair-raising tale that has electrified readers and listeners through the centuries.

Beowulf, a Geat from a region that is today southern Sweden, sets sail from his homeland to try to free Danish King Hrothgar's great banquet hall, Herot, of a monster that has been ravaging it for twelve years. This monster, Grendel, is a terrifying swampland creature of enormous size whose eyes burn "with a gruesome light." The struggle between Beowulf, a young adventurer eager for fame, and Grendel, a fierce and bloodthirsty foe, is the first of three mortal battles in the long poem. The first battle is the one described in this book. The second struggle pits Beowulf against Grendel's "water-hag" mother, and the third, fifty years later, against a dragon.

Although the action takes place in sixth century Scandinavia, the poem is unmistakably English. Recited originally in Old English, *Beowulf* is based on legends and chronicles of the various Northern Europeans who migrated to England.

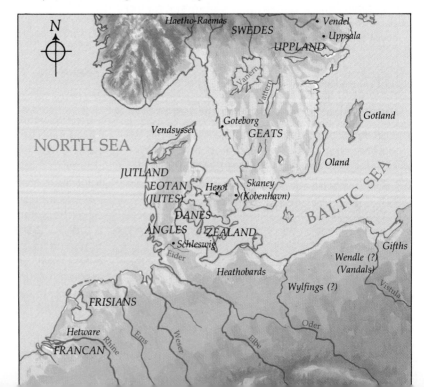

# GUIDE FOR INTERPRETING

## *from* Beowulf

**Literary Forms**

**Anglo-Saxon Epic Poetry.** An epic is a long narrative poem, sometimes developed orally, that celebrates the deeds of a legendary or heroic figure. A few epics predate the Anglo-Saxon *Beowulf.* Well-known epics from earlier times include the Greek *Iliad* and *Odyssey* by Homer and the Roman *Aeneid* by Virgil. Typically, an epic, featuring a hero who is larger than life, concerns eternal human problems such as the struggle between good and evil. An epic is presented in a serious way, often through the use of elevated language. The hero of an epic represents widespread national, cultural, or religious values.

*Beowulf* is one of the oldest European epics. Its hero, Beowulf, embodies the highest ideals of his time and place: loyalty, valor, unselfishness, and a sense of justice. He represents good, while Grendel represents evil. Throughout *Beowulf* there is a prevailing yet somewhat uneasy blend of Christian ethics and pagan morality. Against a backdrop of gloom that reflects the Anglo-Saxons' stoic acceptance of fate, the story applauds the highest virtues of human nature—courage, generosity, faithfulness. Despite its blood and horror, *Beowulf* is a deeply idealistic narrative.

Anglo-Saxon epic poetry, of which *Beowulf* is the great example, has certain distinctive features. One is the two-part line. Each line is separated by a pause, known as a caesura, and there are generally two strong beats per part. Another feature is the kenning, a colorful, indirect way of naming something: The sea is a *whalepath;* a battle is *spear play;* the sun is the *candle of the skies.*

**Commentary**

*Beowulf* belongs to the present as well as the past. Perhaps the most popular contemporary works it inspired are a series of epics about the fantasy world of Middle Earth. Beginning in 1937 with *The Hobbit,* Oxford don J. R. R. Tolkien wove imaginative tales about good and evil. The enthusiastic response to his trilogy *The Lord of the Rings* (1954–1955—*The Fellowship of the Ring, The Two Towers, The Return of the King*) prompted him to continue the saga in *The Silmarillion* (1977), an account of the origins of Middle Earth. Tolkien, however, was originally far more famous for completely changing the way we read *Beowulf.* In his 1936 article "Beowulf: The Monsters and the Critics," he saw *Beowulf* as poetry rather than history, and modern *Beowulf* scholarship began.

**Writing**

At the time *Beowulf* was composed, the ideals of the Anglo-Saxons included loyalty, valor, unselfishness, and a sense of justice. Those are still highly regarded ideals, but they are not the only ones. List four other ideals that are important to Americans today.

# *from* Beowulf

## translated by Burton Raffel

*The selection opens during an evening of celebration at Herot, the banquet hall of the Danish king Hrothgar (hroth' gär). Outside in the darkness, however, lurks the monster Grendel, a murderous creature who poses a great danger to the people inside the banquet hall.*

## The Wrath of Grendel

A powerful monster, living down
In the darkness, growled in pain, impatient
As day after day the music rang
Loud in that hall,[1] the harp's rejoicing

5   Call and the poet's clear songs, sung
Of the ancient beginnings of us all, recalling
The Almighty making the earth, shaping
These beautiful plains marked off by oceans,
Then proudly setting the sun and moon

10   To glow across the land and light it;
The corners of the earth were made lovely with trees
And leaves, made quick with life, with each
Of the nations who now move on its face. And then
As now warriors sang of their pleasure:

15   So Hrothgar's men lived happy in his hall
Till the monster stirred, that demon, that fiend,
Grendel, who haunted the moors, the wild
Marshes, and made his home in a hell
Not hell but earth. He was spawned in that slime,

20   Conceived by a pair of those monsters born
Of Cain,[2] murderous creatures banished
By God, punished forever for the crime
Of Abel's death. The Almighty drove
Those demons out, and their exile was bitter,

25   Shut away from men; they split
Into a thousand forms of evil—spirits
And fiends, goblins, monsters, giants,
A brood forever opposing the Lord's
Will, and again and again defeated.

30     Then, when darkness had dropped, Grendel
Went up to Herot, wondering what the warriors
Would do in that hall when their drinking was done.

**1. hall:** Herot.

**2. Cain:** The oldest son of Adam and Eve, who murdered his brother Abel.

**THE DRAGON FOR "THE HIGH KINGS"**
*George Sharp*

He found them sprawled in sleep, suspecting
Nothing, their dreams undisturbed. The monster's
35 Thoughts were as quick as his greed or his claws:
He slipped through the door and there in the silence
Snatched up thirty men, smashed them
Unknowing in their beds and ran out with their bodies,
The blood dripping behind him, back
40 To his lair, delighted with his night's slaughter.
      At daybreak, with the sun's first light, they saw
How well he had worked, and in that gray morning
Broke their long feast with tears and laments
For the dead. Hrothgar, their lord, sat joyless
45 In Herot, a mighty prince mourning
The fate of his lost friends and companions,
Knowing by its tracks that some demon had torn
His followers apart. He wept, fearing
The beginning might not be the end. And that night
50 Grendel came again, so set
On murder that no crime could ever be enough,
No savage assault quench his lust
For evil. Then each warrior tried
To escape him, searched for rest in different
55 Beds, as far from Herot as they could find,
Seeing how Grendel hunted when they slept.
Distance was safety; the only survivors
Were those who fled him. Hate had triumphed.
      So Grendel ruled, fought with the righteous,
60 One against many, and won; so Herot
Stood empty, and stayed deserted for years,
Twelve winters of grief for Hrothgar, king
Of the Danes, sorrow heaped at his door
By hell-forged hands. His misery leaped
65 The seas, was told and sung in all
Men's ears: how Grendel's hatred began,
How the monster relished his savage war
On the Danes, keeping the bloody feud
Alive, seeking no peace, offering
70 No truce, accepting no settlement, no price
In gold or land, and paying the living
For one crime only with another. No one
Waited for reparation from his plundering claws:
That shadow of death hunted in the darkness,
75 Stalked Hrothgar's warriors, old
And young, lying in waiting, hidden
In mist, invisibly following them from the edge
Of the marsh, always there, unseen.
      So mankind's enemy continued his crimes,

80  Killing as often as he could, coming
    Alone, bloodthirsty and horrible. Though he lived
    In Herot, when the night hid him, he never
    Dared to touch king Hrothgar's glorious
    Throne, protected by God—God,
85  Whose love Grendel could not know. But Hrothgar's
    Heart was bent. The best and most noble
    Of his council debated remedies, sat
    In secret sessions, talking of terror
    And wondering what the bravest of warriors could do.
90  And sometimes they sacrificed to the old stone gods,
    Made heathen vows, hoping for Hell's
    Support, the Devil's guidance in driving
    Their affliction off. That was their way,
    And the heathen's only hope, Hell
95  Always in their hearts, knowing neither God
    Nor His passing as He walks through our world, the Lord
    Of Heaven and earth; their ears could not hear
    His praise nor know His glory. Let them
    Beware, those who are thrust into danger,
100 Clutched at by trouble, yet can carry no solace
    In their hearts, cannot hope to be better! Hail
    To those who will rise to God, drop off
    Their dead bodies and seek our Father's peace!

## The Coming of Beowulf

        So the living sorrow of Healfdane's son[3]
105 Simmered, bitter and fresh, and no wisdom
    Or strength could break it: that agony hung
    On king and people alike, harsh
    And unending, violent and cruel, and evil.
        In his far-off home Beowulf, Higlac's[4]
110 Follower and the strongest of the Geats—greater
    And stronger than anyone anywhere in this world—
    Heard how Grendel filled nights with horror
    And quickly commanded a boat fitted out,
    Proclaiming that he'd go to that famous king,
115 Would sail across the sea to Hrothgar,
    Now when help was needed. None
    Of the wise ones regretted his going, much
    As he was loved by the Geats: the omens were good,
    And they urged the adventure on. So Beowulf
120 Chose the mightiest men he could find,
    The bravest and best of the Geats, fourteen
    In all, and led them down to their boat;
    He knew the sea, would point the prow
    Straight to that distant Danish shore.

**3. Healfdane's** (hă′ alf
den′nəz) **son:** Hrothgar.

**4. Higlac's** (hig′ laks):
Higlac was the king of the
Geats (gā′ ats) and
Beowulf's feudal lord and
uncle.

**ARTHUR GOING TO AVALON FOR "THE HIGH KINGS"**
*George Sharp*

125     Then they sailed, set their ship
        Out on the waves, under the cliffs.
        Ready for what came they wound through the currents,
        The seas beating at the sand, and were borne
        In the lap of their shining ship, lined
130     With gleaming armor, going safely
        In that oak-hard boat to where their hearts took them.
        The wind hurried them over the waves,
        The ship foamed through the sea like a bird
        Until, in the time they had known it would take,
135     Standing in the round-curled prow they could see
        Sparkling hills, high and green,
        Jutting up over the shore, and rejoicing
        In those rock-steep cliffs they quietly ended
        Their voyage. Jumping to the ground, the Geats
140     Pushed their boat to the sand and tied it
        In place, mail shirts and armor rattling
        As they swiftly moored their ship. And then
        They gave thanks to God for their easy crossing.
                High on a wall a Danish watcher
145     Patrolling along the cliffs saw
        The travelers crossing to the shore, their shields
        Raised and shining; he came riding down,
        Hrothgar's lieutenant, spurring his horse,
        Needing to know why they'd landed, these men
150     In armor. Shaking his heavy spear
        In their faces he spoke:
                                "Whose soldiers are you,
        You who've been carried in your deep-keeled ship
        Across the sea-road to this country of mine?
        Listen! I've stood on these cliffs longer
155     Than you know, keeping our coast free
        Of pirates, raiders sneaking ashore
        From their ships, seeking our lives and our gold.
        None have ever come more openly—
        And yet you've offered no password, no sign
160     From my prince, no permission from my people for your
            landing
        Here. Nor have I ever seen,
        Out of all the men on earth, one greater
        Than has come with you; no commoner carries
        Such weapons, unless his appearance, and his beauty,
165     Are both lies. You! Tell me your name,
        And your father's; no spies go further onto Danish
        Soil than you've come already. Strangers,
        From wherever it was you sailed, tell it,
        And tell it quickly, the quicker the better,
170     I say, for us all. Speak, say
        Exactly who you are, and from where, and why."

Their leader answered him, Beowulf unlocking
Words from deep in his breast:
                              "We are Geats,
Men who follow Higlac. My father
175 Was a famous soldier, known far and wide
As a leader of men. His name was Edgetho.
His life lasted many winters;
Wise men all over the earth surely
Remember him still. And we have come seeking
180 Your prince, Healfdane's son, protector
Of this people, only in friendship: instruct us,
Watchman, help us with your words! Our errand
Is a great one, our business with the glorious king
Of the Danes no secret; there's nothing dark
185 Or hidden in our coming. You know (if we've heard
The truth, and been told honestly) that your country
Is cursed with some strange, vicious creature
That hunts only at night and that no one
Has seen. It's said, watchman, that he has slaughtered
190 Your people, brought terror to the darkness. Perhaps
Hrothgar can hunt, here in my heart,
For some way to drive this devil out—
If anything will ever end the evils
Afflicting your wise and famous lord.
195 Here he can cool his burning sorrow.
Or else he may see his suffering go on
Forever, for as long as Herot towers
High on your hills."
                              The mounted officer
Answered him bluntly, the brave watchman:
200     "A soldier should know the difference between words
And deeds, and keep that knowledge clear
In his brain. I believe your words, I trust in
Your friendship. Go forward, weapons and armor
And all, on into Denmark. I'll guide you
205 Myself—and my men will guard your ship,
Keep it safe here on our shores,
Your fresh-tarred boat, watch it well,
Until that curving prow carries
Across the sea to Geatland a chosen
210 Warrior who bravely does battle with the creature
Haunting our people, who survives that horror
Unhurt, and goes home bearing our love."
          Then they moved on. Their boat lay moored,
Tied tight to its anchor. Glittering at the top
215 Of their golden helmets wild boar heads gleamed,
Shining decorations, swinging as they marched,
Erect like guards, like sentinels, as though ready

To fight. They marched, Beowulf and his men
And their guide, until they could see the gables
220 Of Herot, covered with hammered gold
And glowing in the sun—that most famous of all dwellings,
Towering majestic, its glittering roofs
Visible far across the land.
Their guide reined in his horse, pointing
225 To that hall, built by Hrothgar for the best
And bravest of his men; the path was plain,
They could see their way . . .

    *Beowulf and his men arrive at Herot and are about to be*
*escorted in to see King Hrothgar.*

                Beowulf arose, with his men
230 Around him, ordering a few to remain
With their weapons, leading the others quickly
Along under Herot's steep roof into Hrothgar's
Presence. Standing on that prince's own hearth,
Helmeted, the silvery metal of his mail shirt
235 Gleaming with a smith's high art, he greeted
The Danes' great lord:
                "Hail, Hrothgar!
Higlac is my cousin[5] and my king; the days
Of my youth have been filled with glory. Now Grendel's
Name has echoed in our land: sailors
240 Have brought us stories of Herot, the best
Of all mead-halls, deserted and useless when the moon
Hangs in skies the sun had lit,
Light and life fleeing together.
My people have said, the wisest, most knowing
245 And best of them, that my duty was to go to the Danes'
Great king. They have seen my strength for themselves,
Have watched me rise from the darkness of war,
Dripping with my enemies' blood. I drove
Five great giants into chains, chased
250 All of that race from the earth. I swam
In the blackness of night, hunting monsters
Out of the ocean, and killing them one
By one; death was my errand and the fate
They had earned. Now Grendel and I are called
255 Together, and I've come. Grant me, then,
Lord and protector of this noble place,
A single request! I have come so far,
Oh shelterer of warriors and your people's loved friend,
That this one favor you should not refuse me—
260 That I, alone and with the help of my men,
May purge all evil from this hall. I have heard,
Too, that the monster's scorn of men

**5. cousin:** Here, used as a general term for relative.

Is so great that he needs no weapons and fears none.
Nor will I. My lord Higlac

265 Might think less of me if I let my sword
Go where my feet were afraid to, if I hid
Behind some broad linden[6] shield: my hands
Alone shall fight for me, struggle for life
Against the monster. God must decide

270 Who will be given to death's cold grip.
Grendel's plan, I think, will be
What it has been before, to invade this hall
And gorge his belly with our bodies. If he can,
If he can. And I think, if my time will have come,

275 There'll be nothing to mourn over, no corpse to prepare
For its grave: Grendel will carry our bloody
Flesh to the moors, crunch on our bones
And smear torn scraps of our skin on the walls
Of his den. No, I expect no Danes

280 Will fret about sewing our shrouds, if he wins.
And if death does take me, send the hammered
Mail of my armor to Higlac, return
The inheritance I had from Hrethel, and he
From Wayland.[7] Fate will unwind as it must!''

**6. linden:** A very sturdy type of wood.

**7. Wayland:** From Germanic folklore, an invisible blacksmith.

## The Battle with Grendel

*That night Beowulf and his men take the places of Hrothgar and the Danes inside Herot. While his men sleep, Beowulf lies awake, eager to meet with Grendel.*

285     Out from the marsh, from the foot of misty
Hills and bogs, bearing God's hatred,
Grendel came, hoping to kill
Anyone he could trap on this trip to high Herot.
He moved quickly through the cloudy night,

290 Up from his swampland, sliding silently
Toward that gold-shining hall. He had visited Hrothgar's
Home before, knew the way—
But never, before nor after that night,
Found Herot defended so firmly, his reception

295 So harsh. He journeyed, forever joyless,
Straight to the door, then snapped it open,
Tore its iron fasteners with a touch
And rushed angrily over the threshold.
He strode quickly across the inlaid

300 Floor, snarling and fierce: his eyes
Gleamed in the darkness, burned with a gruesome
Light. Then he stopped, seeing the hall
Crowded with sleeping warriors, stuffed
With rows of young soldiers resting together.

305 And his heart laughed, he relished the sight,
Intended to tear the life from those bodies
By morning; the monster's mind was hot
With the thought of food and the feasting his belly
Would soon know. But fate, that night, intended
310 Grendel to gnaw the broken bones
Of his last human supper. Human
Eyes were watching his evil steps,
Waiting to see his swift hard claws.
Grendel snatched at the first Geat
315 He came to, ripped him apart, cut
His body to bits with powerful jaws,
Drank the blood from his veins and bolted
Him down, hands and feet; death
And Grendel's great teeth came together,
320 Snapping life shut. Then he stepped to another
Still body, clutched at Beowulf with his claws,
Grasped at a strong-hearted wakeful sleeper
—And was instantly seized himself, claws
Bent back as Beowulf leaned up on one arm.
325     That shepherd of evil, guardian of crime,
Knew at once that nowhere on earth
Had he met a man whose hands were harder;
His mind was flooded with fear—but nothing
Could take his talons and himself from that tight
330 Hard grip. Grendel's one thought was to run
From Beowulf, flee back to his marsh and hide there:
This was a different Herot than the hall he had emptied.
But Higlac's follower remembered his final
Boast and, standing erect, stopped
335 The monster's flight, fastened those claws
In his fists till they cracked, clutched Grendel
Closer. The infamous killer fought
For his freedom, wanting no flesh but retreat,
Desiring nothing but escape; his claws
340 Had been caught, he was trapped. That trip to Herot
Was a miserable journey for the writhing monster!
     The high hall rang, its roof boards swayed,
And Danes shook with terror. Down
The aisles the battle swept, angry
345 And wild. Herot trembled, wonderfully
Built to withstand the blows, the struggling
Great bodies beating at its beautiful walls;
Shaped and fastened with iron, inside
And out, artfully worked, the building
350 Stood firm. Its benches rattled, fell
To the floor, gold-covered boards grating
As Grendel and Beowulf battled across them.

Hrothgar's wise men had fashioned Herot
To stand forever; only fire,
355 They had planned, could shatter what such skill had put
Together, swallow in hot flames such splendor
Of ivory and iron and wood. Suddenly
The sounds changed, the Danes started
In new terror, cowering in their beds as the terrible
360 Screams of the Almighty's enemy sang
In the darkness, the horrible shrieks of pain
And defeat, the tears torn out of Grendel's
Taut throat, hell's captive caught in the arms
Of him who of all the men on earth
365 Was the strongest.

That mighty protector of men
Meant to hold the monster till its life
Leaped out, knowing the fiend was no use
To anyone in Denmark. All of Beowulf's
Band had jumped from their beds, ancestral
370 Swords raised and ready, determined
To protect their prince if they could. Their courage
Was great but all wasted: they could hack at Grendel

From every side, trying to open
A path for his evil soul, but their points
375 Could not hurt him, the sharpest and hardest iron
Could not scratch at his skin, for that sin-stained demon
Had bewitched all men's weapons, laid spells
That blunted every mortal man's blade.
And yet his time had come, his days
380 Were over, his death near; down
To hell he would go, swept groaning and helpless
To the waiting hands of still worse fiends.
Now he discovered—once the afflictor
Of men, tormentor of their days—what it meant
385 To feud with Almighty God: Grendel
Saw that his strength was deserting him, his claws
Bound fast, Higlac's brave follower tearing at
His hands. The monster's hatred rose higher,
But his power had gone. He twisted in pain,
390 And the bleeding sinews deep in his shoulder
Snapped, muscle and bone split
And broke. The battle was over, Beowulf

**HEAD OF CARVED POST FROM THE SHIP BURIAL AT OSEBERG**
*Werner Forman Archive*

**HELMET**
*Statens Historiska Museet, Stockholm*
*Werner Forman Archive*

**GOLDEN HORN**
*National Museet Copenhagen*

from *Beowulf* 35

Had been granted new glory: Grendel escaped,
But wounded as he was could flee to his den,
395 His miserable hole at the bottom of the marsh,
Only to die, to wait for the end
Of all his days. And after that bloody
Combat the Danes laughed with delight.
He who had come to them from across the sea,
400 Bold and strong-minded, had driven affliction
Off, purged Herot clean. He was happy,
Now, with that night's fierce work; the Danes
Had been served as he'd boasted he'd serve them; Beowulf,
A prince of the Geats, had killed Grendel,
405 Ended the grief, the sorrow, the suffering
Forced on Hrothgar's helpless people
By a bloodthirsty fiend. No Dane doubted
The victory, for the proof, hanging high
From the rafters where Beowulf had hung it, was the
    monster's
410 Arm, claw and shoulder and all.

---

## THINKING ABOUT THE SELECTION

### Recalling

1. (a) When does Grendel first go to Herot? (b) Explain what the warriors are doing when he arrives. (c) What does he do to them?
2. Why is Grendel afraid of touching Hrothgar's throne?
3. (a) What is Beowulf's plan for fighting Grendel? (b) Why does he choose this plan?
4. How does Grendel die?

### Interpreting

5. At the beginning of the poem, Hrothgar's warriors are happy, while Grendel is consumed by hatred. What causes these differences in attitude?
6. How does Beowulf's remark, "Fate will unwind as it must," reflect the Anglo-Saxons' attitude toward fate?
7. What traits of Beowulf and Grendel raise the fight between them to an epic struggle between two great opposing forces in the world?

### Applying

8. Beowulf is thought to be a perfect hero for his times. (a) What qualities should a modern hero have? (b) In what situations might a modern hero demonstrate these heroic qualities? (c) Give examples of modern heroes or of heroic behavior.

## ANALYZING LITERATURE

### Understanding the Anglo-Saxon Epic

An **epic** is a long, narrative poem, presented in an elevated style, that celebrates episodes in a people's heroic tradition.

The Anglo-Saxon epic *Beowulf* has two distinctive features. One feature is the two-part line in which the two parts are separated by a caesura. Each part has two strong beats.

Till the *mon*ster *stirred* / that *de*mon, that *fiend*

The kenning is another feature in *Beowulf*. A kenning is a colorful, roundabout way of naming something.

That *shepherd of evil, guardian of crime*

1. What are the two parts and the four strong beats in each of the following lines?

As day after day the music rang
Loud in that hall, the harp's rejoicing

2. In addition to the example given, find another kenning in Beowulf.
3. Explain why you do or do not find the use of kenning effective.

## CRITICAL THINKING AND READING
### Making Inferences About Ideals

An **inference** is a conclusion you reach from stated information in literature. The hero in an epic embodies the highest ideals of the times. The Anglo-Saxon epic *Beowulf* reflects the values of the plundering Anglo-Saxon warriors. Beowulf himself is a fighting man, eager for challenging personal encounters in a good cause.

From Beowulf's description of his previous heroic feats (lines 247–254), you can infer that his listeners respected and admired the qualities that enabled Beowulf to accomplish such deeds. In addition, you can infer that they believed that such qualities enabled Beowulf to take on the evil Grendel.

1. In what specific way does Beowulf demonstrate loyalty to his lord and king?
2. In what specific ways does he demonstrate his valor?

3. In lines 378–380, Grendel realizes that he has been beaten:

Now he discovered—once the afflictor
Of men, tormentor of their days—what it meant
To feud with Almighty God.

What inference about Anglo-Saxon beliefs can you make from these lines?

## UNDERSTANDING LANGUAGE
### Using a Glossary

A **glossary** is a small, specialized dictionary designed to help you with unfamiliar words. Which of the following are included in the glossary entries in the back of this book?
1. pronunciation
2. part of speech
3. etymology
4. inflected forms
5. cross references
6. variant spellings

## THINKING AND WRITING
### Writing About Character Traits

Write a composition for your classmates in which you tell the incidents in *Beowulf* from Grendel's point of view. Begin by jotting down notes about Grendel's thoughts and feelings during his final, fatal visit to Hrothgar's hall. Then arrange these notes in a logical order to create a working outline. Next, write a draft, keeping in mind that you are giving Grendel's version of events, not your own or Beowulf's. Finally, revise your draft, improving your content and organization and correcting any errors you find in grammar or mechanics.

# GUIDE FOR INTERPRETING

## *from* Beowulf

**Pagan and Christian Elements.** The eighth-century poet who composed *Beowulf* lived in a civilization that had become Christian only a hundred or so years before. It is not surprising, therefore, that for the characters and events of his story, he drew on pagan legends and folk tales. The magnificent monsters of *Beowulf*, for example, derive from the trolls of Scandinavian mythology, shadowy creatures who lurked around waterfalls or caves.

However, the Christian beliefs of the poets of England also penetrate the poem. For example, the poet disguises the true lineage of Grendel and his mother, giving them instead a Biblical origin:

. . . He [Grendel] was spawned in that slime,
Conceived by a pair of those monsters born
Of Cain, murderous creatures banished
By God, punished forever for the crime
Of Abel's death . . .

In battling Grendel, Beowulf is not only a brave pagan warrior, but also a Christian hero challenging the forces of evil, the first such hero in a line that includes Sir Galahad of the Round Table and the legendary Saint George, dragon slayer and patron saint of England.

The combat with Grendel's mother, described on the following pages, also reflects the weaving together of pagan and Christian elements. The creature's underwater lair and the magic sword found by the hero are familiar from many pagan folk tales. However, in *Beowulf* God plays a role in the battle: "and Holy/God, who sent him victory, gave judgment/For truth and right . . ."

The Christian influence on the poem is not limited to specific references to the Bible and God. As Charles W. Kennedy points out, the spirit of the newly victorious religion is evident throughout the epic: "The *Beowulf* is a tale of the pagan past in which the endurance, the loyalty, the courage, and the strength of the heroic age are tempered by union with Christian virtues. . . ." Alert readers will find this "welding of pagan heroism with Christian virtue" in the depiction of Beowulf as a young warrior and an aging king.

In his battle with Grendel's mother and later with a dragon, Beowulf faces the possibility of failure. Briefly describe a time when you had to confront the chance that you might fail. Tell how you struggled with this feeling and overcame it.

# *from* Beowulf

## translated by Burton Raffel

*Hrothgar and his host celebrate Beowulf's victory over the
monster Grendel. That night, however, Grendel's mother
kidnaps and kills Hrothgar's closest friend and carries off
the claw that Beowulf tore from her child. The next day
the horrified king tells Beowulf about the two monsters
and their underwater lair.*

### The Monsters' Lair

"I've heard that my people, peasants working
In the fields, have seen a pair of such fiends
Wandering in the moors and marshes, giant
Monsters living in those desert lands.
415 And they've said to my wise men that, as well as they
    could see,
One of the devils was a female creature.
The other, they say, walked through the wilderness
Like a man—but mightier than any man.
They were frightened, and they fled, hoping to find
    help
420 In Herot. They named the huge one Grendel:
If he had a father no one knew him,
Or whether there'd been others before these two,
Hidden evil before hidden evil.
They live in secret places, windy
425 Cliffs, wolf-dens where water pours
From the rocks, then runs underground, where mist
Steams like black clouds, and the groves of trees
Growing out over their lake are all covered
With frozen spray, and wind down snakelike
430 Roots that reach as far as the water
And help keep it dark. At night that lake
Burns like a torch. No one knows its bottom,
No wisdom reaches such depths. A deer,
Hunted through the woods by packs of hounds,
435 A stag with great horns, though driven through the
    forest
From faraway places, prefers to die
On those shores, refuses to save its life
In that water. It isn't far, nor is it
A pleasant spot! When the wind stirs

440 And storms, waves splash toward the sky,
As dark as the air, as black as the rain
That the heavens weep. Our only help,
Again, lies with you. Grendel's mother
Is hidden in her terrible home, in a place
445 You've not seen. Seek it, if you dare! Save us,
Once more, and again twisted gold,
Heaped-up ancient treasure, will reward you
For the battle you win!''


## The Battle with Grendel's Mother

*Beowulf resolves to kill the "lady monster." Arriving at the lake under which she lives, Beowulf and his companions see serpents in the water and sea beasts on the rocks. The young hero kills one of the beasts with an arrow and then prepares to fight with Grendel's mother.*

Then Edgetho's brave son[1] spoke:

"Remember,

450 Hrothgar, Oh knowing king, now
When my danger is near, the warm words we uttered,
And if your enemy should end my life
Then be, oh generous prince, forever
The father and protector of all whom I leave
455 Behind me, here in your hands, my belovèd
Comrades left with no leader, their leader
Dead. And the precious gifts you gave me,
My friend, send them to Higlac. May he see
In their golden brightness, the Geats' great lord
460 Gazing at your treasure, that here in Denmark
I found a noble protector, a giver
Of rings whose rewards I won and briefly
Relished. And you, Unferth,[2] let
My famous old sword stay in your hands:
465 I shall shape glory with Hrunting, or death
Will hurry me from this earth!''

As his words ended
He leaped into the lake, would not wait for anyone's
Answer; the heaving water covered him
Over. For hours he sank through the waves;
470 At last he saw the mud of the bottom.
And all at once the greedy she-wolf
Who'd ruled those waters for half a hundred
Years discovered him, saw that a creature
From above had come to explore the bottom
475 Of her wet world. She welcomed him in her claws,
Clutched at him savagely but could not harm him,

**1. Edgetho's brave son:** Beowulf. Elsewhere he is identified by such phrases as 'the Geats' proud prince" and "the Geats' brave prince." These different designations add variety and interest to the poem.

**2. Unferth:** A Danish warrior who had questioned Beowulf's bravery before the battle with Grendel.

Tried to work her fingers through the tight
Ring-woven mail on his breast, but tore
And scratched in vain. Then she carried him, armor
480 And sword and all, to her home; he struggled
To free his weapon, and failed. The fight
Brought other monsters swimming to see
Her catch, a host of sea beasts who beat at
His mail shirt, stabbing with tusks and teeth
485 As they followed along. Then he realized, suddenly,
That she'd brought him into someone's battle-hall,
And there the water's heat could not hurt him,
Nor anything in the lake attack him through
The building's high-arching roof. A brilliant
490 Light burned all around him, the lake
Itself like a fiery flame.
                              Then he saw
The mighty water witch and swung his sword,
His ring-marked blade, straight at her head;
The iron sang its fierce song,
495 Sang Beowulf's strength. But her guest
Discovered that no sword could slice her evil
Skin, that Hrunting could not hurt her, was useless
Now when he needed it. They wrestled, she ripped
And tore and clawed at him, bit holes in his helmet,
500 And that too failed him; for the first time in years
Of being worn to war it would earn no glory;
It was the last time anyone would wear it. But
    Beowulf
Longed only for fame, leaped back
Into battle. He tossed his sword aside,
505 Angry; the steel-edged blade lay where
He'd dropped it. If weapons were useless he'd use
His hands, the strength in his fingers. So fame
Comes to the men who mean to win it
And care about nothing else! He raised
510 His arms and seized her by the shoulder; anger
Doubled his strength, he threw her to the floor.
She fell, Grendel's fierce mother, and the Geats'
Proud prince was ready to leap on her. But she rose
At once and repaid him with her clutching claws,
515 Wildly tearing at him. He was weary, that best
And strongest of soldiers; his feet stumbled
And in an instant she had him down, held helpless.
Squatting with her weight on his stomach, she drew
A dagger, brown with dried blood, and prepared
520 To avenge her only son. But he was stretched
On his back, and her stabbing blade was blunted
By the woven mail shirt he wore on his chest.

SLAYING OF A BULL ON THE BASE OF A
CAULDRON (CELTIC ARTIFACT, 100 B.C.)
*National Museum, Copenhagen*
Werner Forman Archive

The hammered links held; the point
Could not touch him. He'd have traveled to the bottom
   of the earth,
525 Edgetho's son, and died there, if that shining
Woven metal had not helped—and Holy
God, who sent him victory, gave judgment
For truth and right, Ruler of the Heavens,
Once Beowulf was back on his feet and fighting.

530    Then he saw, hanging on the wall, a heavy
Sword, hammered by giants, strong
And blessed with their magic, the best of all weapons
But so massive that no ordinary man could lift
Its carved and decorated length. He drew it
535 From its scabbard, broke the chain on its hilt,
And then, savage, now, angry
And desperate, lifted it high over his head
And struck with all the strength he had left,
Caught her in the neck and cut it through,
540 Broke bones and all. Her body fell
To the floor, lifeless, the sword was wet
With her blood, and Beowulf rejoiced at the sight.
   The brilliant light shone, suddenly,
As though burning in that hall, and as bright as
   Heaven's
545 Own candle, lit in the sky. He looked
At her home, then following along the wall
Went walking, his hands tight on the sword,
His heart still angry. He was hunting another
Dead monster, and took his weapon with him
550 For final revenge against Grendel's vicious
Attacks, his nighttime raids, over
And over, coming to Herot when Hrothgar's
Men slept, killing them in their beds,
Eating some on the spot, fifteen
555 Or more, and running to his loathsome moor
With another such sickening meal waiting
In his pouch. But Beowulf repaid him for those visits,
Found him lying dead in his corner,
Armless, exactly as that fierce fighter
560 Had sent him out from Herot, then struck off
His head with a single swift blow. The body
Jerked for the last time, then lay still.
   The wise old warriors who surrounded Hrothgar,
Like him staring into the monsters' lake,
565 Saw the waves surging and blood
Spurting through. They spoke about Beowulf,
All the graybeards, whispered together

**CELTIC FIGURE FROM THE SIDE OF A
BOWL FROM A BURIAL MOUND (NORWAY,
9TH CENTURY)**
*Werner Forman Archive*

And said that hope was gone, that the hero
Had lost fame and his life at once, and would never
570 Return to the living, come back as triumphant
As he had left; almost all agreed that Grendel's
Mighty mother, the she-wolf, had killed him.
The sun slid over past noon, went further
Down. The Danes gave up, left
575 The lake and went home, Hrothgar with them.
The Geats stayed, sat sadly, watching,
Imagining they saw their lord but not believing
They would ever see him again.
                          —Then the sword
Melted, blood-soaked, dripping down
580 Like water, disappearing like ice when the world's
Eternal Lord loosens invisible
Fetters and unwinds icicles and frost
As only He can, He who rules
Time and seasons, He who is truly
585 God. The monsters' hall was full of
Rich treasures, but all that Beowulf took
Was Grendel's head and the hilt of the giants'
Jeweled sword; the rest of that ring-marked
Blade had dissolved in Grendel's steaming
590 Blood, boiling even after his death.
And then the battle's only survivor
Swam up and away from those silent corpses;
The water was calm and clean, the whole
Huge lake peaceful once the demons who'd lived in it
595 Were dead.
        Then that noble protector of all seamen
Swam to land, rejoicing in the heavy
Burdens he was bringing with him. He
And all his glorious band of Geats
Thanked God that their leader had come back
    unharmed;
600 They left the lake together. The Geats
Carried Beowulf's helmet, and his mail shirt.
Behind them the water slowly thickened
As the monsters' blood came seeping up.
They walked quickly, happily, across
605 Roads all of them remembered, left
The lake and the cliffs alongside it, brave men
Staggering under the weight of Grendel's skull,
Too heavy for fewer than four of them to handle—
Two on each side of the spear jammed through it—
610 Yet proud of their ugly load and determined
That the Danes, seated in Herot, should see it.
Soon, fourteen Geats arrived

DETAIL OF A DRAGON-HEAD ON THE
MAMMEN HORSE COLLAR (VIKING
ARTIFACT, 10TH CENTURY)
*National Museum, Denmark*
Werner Forman Archive

At the hall, bold and warlike, and with Beowulf,
Their lord and leader, they walked on the mead-hall
615 Green. Then the Geats' brave prince entered
Herot, covered with glory for the daring
Battles he had fought; he sought Hrothgar
To salute him and show Grendel's head.
He carried that terrible trophy by the hair,
620 Brought it straight to where the Danes sat,
Drinking, the queen among them. It was a weird
And wonderful sight, and the warriors stared.

## The Last Battle

*After being honored by Hrothgar, Beowulf and his fellow
Geats return home. He is welcomed by the king, his uncle
Higlac, and later becomes king himself when Higlac and
his son have died. Beowulf rules Geatland for fifty years.
Then a dragon menaces his kingdom. Although he is an
old man, Beowulf determines to slay the beast. Before
going into battle, he tells the men who have accompanied
him about the history of the royal house and his exploits
in its service.*

And Beowulf uttered his final boast:
"I've never known fear, as a youth I fought
625 In endless battles. I am old, now,
But I will fight again, seek fame still,
If the dragon hiding in his tower dares
To face me."
Then he said farewell to his followers,
Each in his turn, for the last time:
630 "I'd use no sword, no weapon, if this beast
Could be killed without it, crushed to death
Like Grendel, gripped in my hands and torn

GILT-BRONZE WINGED DRAGON
(SWEDISH ARTIFACT, 8TH CENTURY)
*Statens Historiska Museet,
Stockholm*
Werner Forman Archive

Limb from limb. But his breath will be burning
Hot, poison will pour from his tongue.
635   I feel no shame, with shield and sword
And armor, against this monster: when he comes to
      me
I mean to stand, not run from his shooting
Flames, stand till fate decides
Which of us wins. My heart is firm,
640   My hands calm: I need no hot
Words. Wait for me close by, my friends.
We shall see, soon, who will survive
This bloody battle, stand when the fighting
Is done. No one else could do
645   What I mean to, here, no man but me
Could hope to defeat this monster. No one
Could try. And this dragon's treasure, his gold
And everything hidden in that tower, will be mine
Or war will sweep me to a bitter death!''
650      Then Beowulf rose, still brave, still strong,
And with his shield at his side, and a mail shirt on
      his breast,
Strode calmly, confidently, toward the tower, under
The rocky cliffs: no coward could have walked there!
And then he who'd endured dozens of desperate
655   Battles, who'd stood boldly while swords and shields
Clashed, the best of kings, saw
Huge stone arches and felt the heat
Of the dragon's breath, flooding down
Through the hidden entrance, too hot for anyone
660   To stand, a streaming current of fire
And smoke that blocked all passage. And the Geats'
Lord and leader, angry, lowered
His sword and roared out a battle cry,
A call so loud and clear that it reached through
665   The hoary rock, hung in the dragon's
Ear. The beast rose, angry,
Knowing a man had come—and then nothing
But war could have followed. Its breath came first,
A steaming cloud pouring from the stone,
670   Then the earth itself shook. Beowulf
Swung his shield into place, held it
In front of him, facing the entrance. The dragon
Coiled and uncoiled, its heart urging it
Into battle. Beowulf's ancient sword
675   Was waiting, unsheathed, his sharp and gleaming
Blade. The beast came closer; both of them
Were ready, each set on slaughter. The Geats'
Great prince stood firm, unmoving, prepared

Behind his high shield, waiting in his shining
680 Armor. The monster came quickly toward him,
Pouring out fire and smoke, hurrying
To its fate. Flames beat at the iron
Shield, and for a time it held, protected
Beowulf as he'd planned; then it began to melt,
685 And for the first time in his life that famous prince
Fought with fate against him, with glory
Denied him. He knew it, but he raised his sword
And struck at the dragon's scaly hide.
The ancient blade broke, bit into
690 The monster's skin, drew blood, but cracked
And failed him before it went deep enough, helped
    him
Less than he needed. The dragon leaped
With pain, thrashed and beat at him, spouting
Murderous flames, spreading them everywhere.
695 And the Geats' ring-giver did not boast of glorious
Victories in other wars: his weapon
Had failed him, deserted him, now when he needed it
Most, that excellent sword. Edgetho's
Famous son stared at death,
700 Unwilling to leave this world, to exchange it
For a dwelling in some distant place—a journey
Into darkness that all men must make, as death
Ends their few brief hours on earth.
    Quickly, the dragon came at him, encouraged
705 As Beowulf fell back; its breath flared,
And he suffered, wrapped around in swirling
Flames—a king, before, but now
A beaten warrior. None of his comrades
Came to him, helped him, his brave and noble
710 Followers; they ran for their lives, fled
Deep in a wood. And only one of them
Remained, stood there, miserable, remembering,
As a good man must, what kinship should mean.

    His name was Wiglaf, he was Wexstan's son
715 And a good soldier; his family had been Swedish,
Once. Watching Beowulf, he could see
How his king was suffering, burning. Remembering
Everything his lord and cousin had given him,
Armor and gold and the great estates
720 Wexstan's family enjoyed, Wiglaf's
Mind was made up; he raised his yellow
Shield and drew his sword—an ancient
Weapon that had once belonged to Onela's
Nephew, and that Wexstan had won, killing

725 The prince when he fled from Sweden, sought safety
With Herdred, and found death.[3] And Wiglaf's father
Had carried the dead man's armor, and his sword,
To Onela, and the king had said nothing, only
Given him armor and sword and all,

730 Everything his rebel nephew had owned
And lost when he left this life. And Wexstan
Had kept those shining gifts, held them
For years, waiting for his son to use them,
Wear them as honorably and well as once

735 His father had done; then Wexstan died
And Wiglaf was his heir, inherited treasures
And weapons and land. He'd never worn
That armor, fought with that sword, until Beowulf
Called him to his side, led him into war.

740 But his soul did not melt, his sword was strong;
The dragon discovered his courage, and his weapon,
When the rush of battle brought them together.
    And Wiglaf, his heart heavy, uttered
The kind of words his comrades deserved:

745 "I remember how we sat in the mead-hall, drinking
And boasting of how brave we'd be when Beowulf
Needed us, he who gave us these swords
And armor: all of us swore to repay him,
When the time came, kindness for kindness

750 —With our lives, if he needed them. He allowed us to
        join him,
Chose us from all his great army, thinking
Our boasting words had some weight, believing
Our promises, trusting our swords. He took us
For soldiers, for men. He meant to kill

755 This monster himself, our mighty king,
Fight this battle alone and unaided,
As in the days when his strength and daring dazzled
Men's eyes. But those days are over and gone
And now our lord must lean on younger

760 Arms. And we must go to him, while angry
Flames burn at his flesh, help
Our glorious king! By almighty God,
I'd rather burn myself than see
Flames swirling around my lord.

765 And who are we to carry home
Our shields before we've slain his enemy
And ours, to run back to our homes with Beowulf
So hard-pressed here? I swear that nothing
He ever did deserved an end

770 Like this, dying miserably and alone,
Butchered by this savage beast: we swore

**3. Onela's/Nephew . . . found death:** When Onela seized the throne of Sweden, his two nephews sought shelter with the king of Geatland, Herdred. Wiglaf's father, Wexstan, killed the older nephew for Onela.

**GILT-SILVER BROOCH FROM GOTLAND (PRE-VIKING SCANDINAVIA)**
*Statens Historiska Museet, Stockholm*
Werner Forman Archive

from *Beowulf* 47

That these swords and armor were each for us all!"
    Then he ran to his king, crying encouragement
As he dove through the dragon's deadly fumes.


## The Spoils

*Together, Wiglaf and Beowulf kill the dragon, but the old
king is mortally wounded. As a last request, Beowulf asks
Wiglaf to bring him the treasure that the dragon was
guarding.*

775     Then Wexstan's son went in, as quickly
As he could, did as the dying Beowulf
Asked, entered the inner darkness
Of the tower, went with his mail shirt and his sword.
Flushed with victory he groped his way,
780   A brave young warrior, and suddenly saw
Piles of gleaming gold, precious
Gems, scattered on the floor, cups
And bracelets, rusty old helmets, beautifully
Made but rotting with no hands to rub
785   And polish them. They lay where the dragon left
        them;
It had flown in the darkness, once, before fighting
Its final battle. (So gold can easily
Triumph, defeat the strongest of men,
No matter how deep it is hidden!) And he saw,
790   Hanging high above, a golden
Banner, woven by the best of weavers
And beautiful. And over everything he saw
A strange light, shining everywhere,
On walls and floor and treasure. Nothing
795   Moved, no other monsters appeared;
He took what he wanted, all the treasures
That pleased his eye, heavy plates
And golden cups and the glorious banner,
Loaded his arms with all they could hold.
800   Beowulf's dagger, his iron blade,
Had finished the fire-spitting terror
That once protected tower and treasures
Alike; the gray-bearded lord of the Geats
Had ended those flying, burning raids
805   Forever.
                Then Wiglaf went back, anxious
To return while Beowulf was alive, to bring him
Treasure they'd won together. He ran,
Hoping his wounded king, weak
And dying, had not left the world too soon.

SILVER PENDANT SHOWING THE HELMET
OF THE VENDEL (EARLY VIKING PERIOD,
10TH CENTURY)
*Statens Historiska Museet,
Stockholm*
Werner Forman Archive

**THE OSEBERG SHIP (VIKING ARTIFACT, C. A.D. 850)**
*Viking Ship Museum, Bygdoy, Oslo*
Werner Forman Archive

810    Then he brought their treasure to Beowulf, and found
      His famous king bloody, gasping
      For breath. But Wiglaf sprinkled water
      Over his lord, until the words
      Deep in his breast broke through and were heard.
815    Beholding the treasure he spoke, haltingly:
        "For this, this gold, these jewels, I thank
      Our Father in Heaven, Ruler of the Earth—
      For all of this, that His grace has given me,
      Allowed me to bring to my people while breath
820    Still came to my lips. I sold my life
      For this treasure, and I sold it well. Take
      What I leave, Wiglaf, lead my people,
      Help them; my time is gone. Have
      The brave Geats build me a tomb,
825    When the funeral flames have burned me, and build
        it
      Here, at the water's edge, high
      On this spit of land, so sailors can see
      This tower, and remember my name, and call it
      Beowulf's tower, and boats in the darkness

830    And mist, crossing the sea, will know it."
       Then that brave king gave the golden
Necklace from around his throat to Wiglaf,
Gave him his gold-covered helmet, and his rings,
And his mail shirt, and ordered him to use them well:
835    "You're the last of all our far-flung family.
Fate has swept our race away,
Taken warriors in their strength and led them
To the death that was waiting. And now I follow
       them."
       The old man's mouth was silent, spoke
840    No more, had said as much as it could;
He would sleep in the fire, soon. His soul
Left his flesh, flew to glory.


## The Farewell

*Wiglaf denounces the soldiers who deserted Beowulf in*
*his combat with the dragon. The Geats burn their king's*
*body on a great funeral pyre and bitterly lament his death.*

            Then the Geats built the tower, as Beowulf
       Had asked, strong and tall, so sailors
845    Could find it from far and wide; working
For ten long days they made his monument,
Sealed his ashes in walls as straight
And high as wise and willing hands
Could raise them. And the riches he and Wiglaf
850    Had won from the dragon, rings, necklaces,
Ancient, hammered armor—all
The treasures they'd taken were left there, too,
Silver and jewels buried in the sandy
Ground, back in the earth, again
855    And forever hidden and useless to men.
And then twelve of the bravest Geats
Rode their horses around the tower,
Telling their sorrow, telling stories
Of their dead king and his greatness, his glory,
860    Praising him for heroic deeds, for a life
As noble as his name. So should all men
Raise up words for their lords, warm
With love, when their shield and protector leaves
His body behind, sends his soul
865    On high. And so Beowulf's followers
Rode, mourning their beloved leader,
Crying that no better king had ever
Lived, no prince so mild, no man
So open to his people, so deserving of praise.

# THINKING ABOUT THE SELECTION

## Recalling

1. Briefly summarize the battle between Beowulf and Grendel's mother.
2. Describe what occurs when Beowulf attempts to fight the dragon alone.
3. The poet writes, "So gold can easily/Triumph, defeat the strongest of men,/No matter how deep it is hidden!" Explain the symbolic significance of the dragon's treasure.

## Interpreting

4. Critics have praised the *Beowulf* poet's skill in describing various settings. (a) Find a passage in which the poet displays this skill. (b) Explain what makes the description so effective.
5. (a) Compare and contrast the three battles described in these excerpts. (b) How are all three battles different versions of the poem's main conflict?
6. (a) Identify the figure of speech that the poet uses in lines 578–583. (b) Explain how the figure of speech adds to the meaning of the poem.

## Applying

7. Many critics claim that *Beowulf* contains themes that are relevant to modern life. Do you agree or disagree? Why?

# ANALYZING LITERATURE

## Tracing Pagan and Christian Elements

In *Beowulf,* we can see evidence of the Anglo-Saxon warrior culture, with its stress on heroism, and Christianity's emphasis on brotherly love and God's care for creation. For example, in the combat with the dragon, Beowulf seeks "fame" like any self-respecting warrior. As he is dying, however, he thanks "Our Father in Heaven" for the opportunity to give his people the treasure.

1. Reread the tribute to Beowulf in the last eight lines of the poem. Identify pagan and Christian influences in the qualities for which the king is praised. Give reasons for your conclusions.
2. A prominent Germanic pagan belief is that fame is the only thing that will survive a human being's death. (a) What evidence do you find in this poem of the importance placed on public esteem or reputation? (b) What value do you feel contemporary society places on fame?
3. The poem contains many references to the blind and mysterious power of *Wyrd,* or Fate, as in line 836. Do such references suggest pagan or Christian influence? Explain.

# UNDERSTANDING LANGUAGE

## Identifying Old English Words

Old English is the bedrock on which our language is established. Words like *sword, blood, cup,* and *flesh*—all derived from Old English and all appearing in this translation—give our language a down-to-earth, nitty-gritty quality. They contrast sharply with fancy, Latin-derived words like *perception* and *speculation.*

Scan this excerpt from *Beowulf* and find five more words that you think are Anglo-Saxon in origin. Then look up these words in a dictionary to see whether you were correct.

# THINKING AND WRITING

## Responding to Criticism

Burton Raffel, who made this translation, remarked that, "of all the many-sided excellences of *Beowulf,*" one of the most satisfying "is the poet's insight into people." Respond to this observation, expressing your agreement or disagreement. First gather evidence. Identify instances where the poet does or does not show insight into human nature. Then write a thesis statement setting forth your point of view. Back up this statement with references to specific passages in the poem. As you revise your essay, see whether you can find other passages that support your thesis. Remember that descriptions of action can reveal character as effectively as direct statements.

# COMPARING TRANSLATIONS

## Beowulf

### TRANSLATION: "A THANKLESS AND DESOLATE UNDERTAKING"

The twentieth century poet Ezra Pound once remarked that "all translation is a thankless, or at least most apt to be a thankless and desolate undertaking." Although translating *Beowulf* has proven to be an especially challenging task, an impressive number of scholars have tried their hands at it. Currently, well over half a dozen translations of *Beowulf* are in print, and a score of others are available in libraries. But judging from the problems these scholars encountered—and the criticism they received—Pound may well have had a point about the translator's task!

### THE DISASTROUS FATE OF THE *BEOWULF* MANUSCRIPT

Most translators of *Beowulf* start with the *Beowulf* manuscript. This manuscript, however, is far from perfect. It represents the work of two tenth-century scribes copying from an older manuscript. However the text is in prose, not verse. It contains spotty punctuation and vowel markings, apparently resulting from the uncertainty of the unlearned scribes. In addition, the manuscript is damaged—a disastrous fire in 1731 scorched the manuscript, hastening its disintegration. It was sheer good fortune that Danish scholar Thorkelin made the first translation in 1787 before the manuscript crumbled further. Subsequent work showed that letters visible when Thorkelin worked have become illegible or even disappeared completely. Although steps were taken to preserve the manuscript from further harm, precious passages had already been lost forever.

### THE PECULIAR PROBLEMS OF TRANSLATING *BEOWULF*

Aside from the dilemma of working with a damaged text, *Beowulf* presents special problems for the translator. Most notable is the metrical puzzle, for the form of Old English verse is very different from that of modern poetry. Most poetry composed after the Norman Conquest in 1066 depends on the regular pattern of stressed and unstressed syllables. Old English poetry, in contrast, is held together by four stresses and alliteration. If this dilemma is not enough to give pause to even the most determined translator, consider *Beowulf*'s content. How can a translator make the remote, unfamiliar past of a long gone civilization come alive for today's readers?

### THE KENNEDY VERSUS RAFFEL TRANSLATIONS

Of all the translations now available, scholars generally agree that Charles Kennedy and Burton Raffel have produced the most useful works. That's about all they agree on, however, for each translator has his staunch defenders—and detractors.

Kennedy called his 1940 poetic translation an example of "authentic modern verse." However, he has been criticized for using such artificial expressions as "Lo! I ween" and "smote him sore." But critics

## THE CASE OF THE FIRST THREE LINES

Openings set the stage for what's to follow. Which of the following two openings do you think best captures the excitement and grandeur of *Beowulf*?

### Kennedy's translation
Lo! we have listened to many a lay
Of the Spear-Danes' fame, their splendor of
old,
Their mighty princes, and martial deeds!

### Raffel's translation
HEAR ME! We've heard of Danish heroes,
Ancient kings and the glory they cut
For themselves, swinging mighty swords!

What difference in tone do you detect between Kennedy's literal translation of the Old English "lā" into "lo" and Raffel's use of the more modern phrase "Hear me"? Is Kennedy's translation more dignified? Is Raffel's more assertive? Why might Kennedy have used the alliterative *l* (*lo, listened,* and *lay*) but Raffel the *h* (*hear, heard, heroes*) in the same first line? Why do you think Kennedy translated the original as "splendor of old" but Raffel used "glory they cut"? Notice how Raffel used *enjambment,* running the second line into the third, to set a swing to the passage, while Kennedy used a list to create a feeling of nobility and stateliness.

That two scholars can produce such different versions of only three lines shows the challenges and excitement of translation!

**Manuscript page from BEOWULF**
*The British Museum*

have condemned the modern idiom Raffel used in his 1963 version as "too physical," and panned the entire work for creating "a new art rather than making available the old."

# CROSS CURRENTS

## Beowulf and John Gardner's Grendel

Let's face it—against heroic Beowulf, evil Grendel just didn't stand a chance. And if Beowulf didn't kill the monster, the bad press surely would have! This situation changed recently, however, when contemporary novelist John Gardner decided to tell the monster's side of the story in his novel *Grendel*. And what a story it is! *Newsweek* called Gardner's *Grendel* "a marvelous novel, absolutely marvelous: witty, intelligent, delightful."

### BEOWULF BECOMES GRENDEL?

How much of the Anglo-Saxon tale of *Beowulf* did Gardner use in his novel? Is *Grendel* simply the Beowulf legend retold from the monster's point of view? Let's start with the form of each. *Beowulf* can be divided into four parts: the episode with Grendel, the battle with Grendel's mother, the return voyage, and the dragon fight. Each part ends before the next begins, and Beowulf rules successfully for fifty years between the dragon fight and his victory over Grendel and his mother. The order of events in *Grendel* is very different, however. The novel begins with the monster attacking Hrothgar's meadhall and men, and ends right after the fight with Beowulf, as Grendel is about to die. This particular section is only about a quarter of the Anglo-Saxon poem. There is also a difference in characters. Although both Grendel's mother and the dragon appear in *Grendel*, Gardner gives each new roles.

### A MONSTER WITH A NAPKIN TUCKED UNDER HIS CHIN

The main difference between the Anglo-Saxon poem and the modern "retelling,"  however, lies in the development of Grendel as a character. In *Beowulf*, the monster is static, his actions predictable. In *Grendel*, the monster is dynamic, his awareness growing as the action unfolds. Compare Grendel's attack in this excerpt from Gardner's novel to lines 285–324 of the poem (pages 32–33).

"I am swollen with excitement, bloodlust and joy and a strange fear that mingle in my chest like the twisting rage of a bone-fire," Grendel begins. "I step onto the brightly shining floor and angrily advance onto them. They're all asleep, the whole company! I can hardly believe my luck and my wild heart laughs, but I let out no sound. Swiftly, softly, I will move from bed to bed and destroy them all, swallow every man. I am blazing, half-crazy with joy. For pure, mad prank, I snatch a cloth from the nearest table and tie it around my neck to make a napkin. I delay no longer. I seize up a sleeping man, tear at him hungrily, bite through his bone-locks and suck hot, slippery blood. He goes down in huge morsels, head, chest, hips, legs, even the hands and feet. My face and arms are wet, matted. The napkin is sopping. The dark floor steams. I move on at once and I reach for another one . . . and I seize a wrist. A shock goes through me. Mistake!"

A monster tying a napkin around his neck? This is not the Grendel we've encountered in *Beowulf*! Gardner's use of the first-person point of view helps him remake Grendel from the Anglo-Saxon incarnation of blind evil, unthinking and senseless, to a conscious, rational force.

## BEOWULF TAUNTS GRENDEL

Gardner plays equally sly tricks with Beowulf. In place of the noble hero of Anglo-Saxon lore we get a man who is strangely mechanical, even mad. Beowulf taunts Grendel as he kills him, demanding songs that amount to the playground surrender of "enough." See how Grendel describes it in this passage:

> And now something worse. He's whispering—spilling words like showers of sleet, his mouth three inches from my ear. I will not listen. I continue whispering. As long as I whisper to myself I need not hear. His syllables lick at me, chilly fire . . . I do not listen. I am sick at heart. I have been betrayed by talk like that. "Mama!" I bawl . . . And still he whispers.
> Grendel, Grendel! You make the world by whispers, second by second. Are you blind to that? Whether you make it a grave or a garden of roses is not the point. Feel the wall: is it not hard? He smashes me against it, breaks open my forehead. Hard, yes! . . . Now sing of walls! Sing!
> I howl.
> Sing!
> "I'm singing!"
> Sing words! Sing raving hymns!
> "You're crazy! Ow!"

**GRENDEL (Frontispiece from BEOWULF)**
*Patten Wilson*
*The British Library*

> Sing!
> "I sing of walls," I howl. "Hooray for the hardness of walls!"

## AN EXTRAORDINARY ACHIEVEMENT

What *The New York Times* called John Gardner's "extraordinary achievement" is far more than *Beowulf* retold from Grendel's view. It's a funny, intriguing, and ultimately touching examination of the way we look at monsters, heroes, and the world we create with both.

# GUIDE FOR INTERPRETING

## The Wanderer

**The Theme of Exile.** Exile means separation or banishment from one's native country, region, or home. The theme of exile recurs throughout world literature—the medieval Italian poet Dante wrote his *Divine Comedy* after being banished from his beloved city of Florence—but this theme is expressed with memorable sadness and pain in Anglo-Saxon poetry.

We cannot understand what exile meant to an Anglo-Saxon warrior until we understand what he meant by home. While we identify ourselves as citizens of a certain country, an Anglo-Saxon viewed himself as the follower of a particular lord or king. The notion of loyalty toward one's country, called patriotism today, did not exist. It was the lord himself who commanded allegiance, and of course there were many lords in what is now called England. The Anglo-Saxon word for "lord," *hlaford,* came from the word *hlaf-weard,* which means "guardian of the loaf." The lord was the dispenser of bread and the source of sustenance. He was also the dispenser of the booty won in raids and skirmishes, a "gold-lord." Perhaps even more important, he guaranteed the security of his followers in a dangerous and uncertain world. In return, he expected loyalty in war. His followers would form his great shield-wall in the thick of battle.

The most important symbol of home was the mead hall (mead was an alcoholic beverage made of fermented honey and water), where the lord and his followers shared the warmth of fire, the comfort of food and drink, and the pleasures of hearing poetry recited. The pleasures of poetry were especially welcome when the *scop* praised the heroism of the listening warriors. Since we tend to identify home with individual families living in a house or an apartment, it is useful to keep in mind the image of the mead hall while reading "The Wanderer." Enlivened with a feeling of masculine fellowship, the mead hall was smoky, noisy, smelly, and crowded. It was home.

Imagine what it meant for a warrior to lose his lord and his place in the mead hall. The Anglo-Saxon exile was indeed a *wraecca,* a word meaning "wretch, stranger, unhappy man, and wanderer."

Suppose that you were forced to leave your home for an indefinite period of time. List some of the things that you would miss the most. What effect would the loss of these things eventually have on you?

# The Wanderer

**translated by Charles W. Kennedy**

**RECONSTRUCTED HELMET, SUTTON HOO SHIP BURIAL (A.D. 7TH CENTURY)**
*The Granger Collection*

Oft to the wanderer,   weary of exile,
Cometh God's pity,   compassionate love,
Though woefully toiling   on wintry seas
With churning oar   in the icy wave,
5  Homeless and helpless   he fled from fate.
Thus saith the wanderer   mindful of misery,
Grievous disasters,   and death of kin:
   "Oft when the day broke,   oft at the dawning,
Lonely and wretched   I wailed my woe.
10  No man is living,   no comrade left,
To whom I dare fully   unlock my heart.
I have learned truly   the mark of a man
Is keeping his counsel   and locking his lips,
Let him think what he will!   For, woe of heart
15  Withstandeth not fate;   a failing spirit
Earneth no help.   Men eager for honor
Bury their sorrow   deep in the breast.
   "So have I also,   often in wretchedness
Fettered[1] my feelings,   far from my kin,
20  Homeless and hapless,[2]   since days of old,
When the dark earth   covered my dear lord's face,
And I sailed away   with sorrowful heart,
Over wintry seas,   seeking a gold-lord,
If far or near   lived one to befriend me
25  With gift in the mead-hall   and comfort for grief.
   "Who bears it, knows   what a bitter companion,
Shoulder to shoulder,   sorrow can be,
When friends are no more.   His fortune is exile,
Not gifts of fine gold;   a heart that is frozen,
30  Earth's winsomeness[3] dead.   And he dreams of the hall-men,
The dealing of treasure,   the days of his youth,

---

**1. Fettered** (Fet′ ərd): Chained, restrained.
**2. hapless** (hap′ lis): Unlucky.
**3. winsomeness** (win′ səm nəs): Pleasantness, delightfulness.

When his lord bade welcome   to wassail[4] and feast.
But gone is that gladness,   and never again
Shall come the loved counsel   of comrade and king.
35   "Even in slumber   his sorrow assaileth,
And, dreaming he claspeth   his dear lord again,
Head on knee, hand on knee,   loyally laying,
Pledging his liege[5]   as in days long past.
Then from his slumber   he starts lonely-hearted,
40   Beholding gray stretches   of tossing sea,
Sea-birds bathing,   with wings outspread,
While hailstorms darken,   and driving snow.
Bitterer then   is the bane of his wretchedness,
The longing for loved one:   his grief is renewed.
45   The forms of his kinsmen   take shape in the silence;
In rapture he greets them;   in gladness he scans
Old comrades remembered.   But they melt into air
With no word of greeting   to gladden his heart.
Then again surges   his sorrow upon him;
50   And grimly he spurs   his weary soul
Once more to the toil   of the tossing sea.
   "No wonder therefore,   in all the world,
If a shadow darkens   upon my spirit
When I reflect   on the fates of men—
55   How one by one   proud warriors vanish
From the halls that knew them,   and day by day
All this earth ages   and droops unto death.
No man may know wisdom   till many a winter
Has been his portion.   A wise man is patient,
60   Not swift to anger,   nor hasty of speech,
Neither too weak,   nor too reckless, in war,
Neither fearful nor fain,[6]   nor too wishful of wealth,
Nor too eager in vow—   ere he know the event.
A brave man must bide[7]   when he speaketh his boast
65   Until he know surely   the goal of his spirit.
   "A wise man will ponder   how dread is that doom
When all this world's wealth   shall be scattered and waste

---

**4. wassail** (wäs' əl): A toast in drinking a person's
health, or a celebration at which such toasts are
made.
**5. liege** (lēj): Loyalty.
**6. fain** (fān): An archaic word meaning "eager"; in
this context it means "too eager."
**7. bide** (bīd): Wait.

iuitas syrie que nunc tyrus dicit̃. olim
serra uocabat̃ a pisce quodam quj illic
abundabat. quem sua lingua sar apellãt
ex quo diriuatũ est huı̃ similitudinis pis
ciculos sardas. sardinas        q̃ uocari.

**SERRA FLYING OVER A BOAT: ILLUMINA-
TION FROM AN ENGLISH BESTIARY
(C. 1185)**
*The Granger Collection*

As now, over all,   through the regions of earth,
Walls stand rime-covered[8]   and swept by the winds.
70  The battlements crumble,   the wine-halls decay;
Joyless and silent   the heroes are sleeping
Where the proud host fell   by the wall they defended.
Some battle launched   on their long, last journey;
One a bird bore   o'er the billowing sea;
75  One the gray wolf slew;   one a grieving earl
Sadly gave   to the grave's embrace.
The Warden of men   hath wasted this world
Till the sound of music   and revel is stilled,
And these giant-built structures   stand empty of life.
80    ''He who shall muse   on these moldering ruins,
And deeply ponder   this darkling life,
Must brood on old legends   of battle and bloodshed,
And heavy the mood   that troubles his heart:
'Where now is the warrior?   Where is the war horse?
85  Bestowal of treasure,   and sharing of feast?
Alas! the bright ale-cup,   the byrny-clad[9] warrior,
The prince in his splendor   —those days are long sped
In the night of the past,   as if they never had been!'
And now remains only,   for warriors' memorial,
90  A wall wondrous high   with serpent shapes carved.
Storms of ash-spears   have smitten the earls,
Carnage of weapon,   and conquering fate.
    ''Storms now batter   these ramparts of stone;
Blowing snow   and the blast of winter
95  Enfold the earth;   night-shadows fall
Darkly lowering,   from the north driving
Raging hail   in wrath upon men.
Wretchedness fills   the realm of earth,
And fate's decrees   transform the world.
100  Here wealth is fleeting,   friends are fleeting,
Man is fleeting,   maid is fleeting;
All the foundation of earth   shall fail!''
    Thus spake the sage   in solitude pondering.
Good man is he   who guardeth his faith.
105  He must never too quickly   unburden his breast
Of its sorrow, but eagerly   strive for redress;
And happy the man   who seeketh for mercy
From his heavenly Father,   our fortress and strength.

---

**8. rime** (rīm) **-covered:** Covered with frost.
**9. byrny** (bər' nē) **-clad:** Dressed in a coat of
chain-mail armor.

## THINKING ABOUT THE SELECTION

### Recalling

1. (a) What event causes the wanderer to go into exile? (b) What is the goal of his search?
2. Name three things from the past that he misses the most.
3. Identify a brief passage in which he expresses his outlook on life.

### Interpreting

4. "The Wanderer" has been called an elegy, meaning a poem of mourning and lament. (a) Identify three vivid details that evoke in you a mood of mourning and lament. (b) Explain why these details are effective.
5. How does the poet's use of repetition contribute to the mood?
6. Explain the wanderer's attitude toward wisdom. Find details to support your interpretation.
7. **Tone** refers to a writer's attitude toward his subject or theme. (a) Choose two adjectives to describe the tone of this poem. (b) Give reasons for your choices.

### Applying

8. What does this poem suggest about the role of women in the Anglo-Saxon world?
9. What would a modern wanderer be like? Briefly describe the causes of such a person's exile and the goal of his or her search.

## ANALYZING LITERATURE

### Understanding Exile

As a poem about exile, the loss of one's home, "The Wanderer" works primarily through contrast. For instance, the vivid dream-image in which the wanderer once again clasps his king, "Head on knee, hand on knee," contrasts with the waking image of the monotonous "gray stretches" of sea and the "Seabirds . . . with wings outspread." The first image conveys closeness and enfolded intimacy, while the second communicates the far-flung emptiness of exile and desolation.

1. Identify two other pairs of contrasting images in the poem and explain how they contribute to the theme of exile.
2. In addition to using contrasting images, the poet also juxtaposes his personal experience with broad generalities about human life. Would the poem be more effective or less effective if the poet's generalizations (lines 100–103) preceded his account of his exile? Why?

## CRITICAL THINKING AND READING

### Appreciating a Poem's Structure

Critics often seek to understand a poem by analyzing its structure, the major units of meaning into which it is divided. "The Wanderer," for example, is framed by opening (lines 1–5) and closing (lines 104–108) passages that refer to God's "pity" and "mercy." These religious invocations are clearly different from the soliloquy in the rest of the poem. The body of the poem itself, however, can also be divided into distinct parts.

1. Identify the units of meaning into which you think the poem should be divided. Indicate the lines where each begins and ends.
2. Explain why you divide the poem as you do. Consider such factors as a change in pronouns or a shift from an individual's experience to generalities.

## THINKING AND WRITING

### Responding to Criticism

The scholar Michael Alexander argues that the mournful mood of "The Wanderer" is not diminished by the more comforting religious passages that appear at the beginning and end of the poem. Write an essay in which you agree or disagree with this assertion. Begin by identifying all the passages and phrases that contribute most to the poem's mood. Then write a thesis statement expressing your opinion of Alexander's critical comment. In revising your work, test your thesis by rereading the poem several times and being receptive to the mood it evokes in you.

# BEDE

## 673–735

Much of what the world knows about England before A.D. 700 is based on a history written in Latin by a Benedictine monk, Bede, who is often called the father of English history. Bede was the most learned scholar of his day not only in England but in all of Western Europe. Although he wrote forty books on a variety of subjects, his reputation would be secure on the basis of a single book—his *Historia Ecclesiastica Gentis Anglorum,* or, in English, *A History of the English Church and People.*

Bede was born in Wearmouth (now the city of Sunderland) on the northeast coast of England. As a child of seven, he entered the nearby monastic school of Jarrow on the river Tyne. A diligent student, he took full advantage of the library at Jarrow, in time becoming a priest, teacher, and scholar at the monastery. He remained at Jarrow for the rest of his life.

A contemporary of the unknown author of *Beowulf,* Bede was fascinated by a broad range of ideas. His writings summarize much of the thought and learning of his time. As the earliest important English prose writer, he concentrated on the Bible but did not neglect science and history. One of his innovations was the dating of events from the birth of Christ, a system that other scholars began to follow. It was through Bede's work that the Christian chronology in use today became common throughout Europe.

Bede had a deep love for his native island and its people, which led him to write his *History of the English Church and People.* In working on his history, Bede gathered information from many kinds of documents, interviewed knowledgeable monks, and, in general, proceeded very much like a modern historian, although he accepted as fact some miracles that a modern historian would not.

In the *History,* Bede describes the conquests of the Anglo-Saxon tribes and the fortunes of the various small fiefdoms that spread across the land. His primary concern, however, was the expansion of Christianity and the growth of the Church in England. He wrote in Latin, the language of scholarship in his age. There are several surviving manuscripts, however, that have the Old English text in addition to Bede's Latin version. He became famous throughout the land as one of the most learned scholars of his age, despite the fact that he never ventured beyond Northumbria.

In the century after his death, King Alfred translated Bede's history from Latin into English. In the same century, the word *Venerable* was first applied to his name to honor his wisdom and achievements. The honor was well deserved. The Venerable Bede was largely responsible for what is sometimes called the Christian renaissance in eighth-century England.

# GUIDE FOR INTERPRETING

## *from* A History of the English Church and People

**Historical Writing.** A history is a factual narrative or record of past events. Unless a historian has actually observed the events being described, he or she must rely on outside sources. These sources include testimony from living witnesses, accounts in letters or memoirs, records from courts, businesses, churches, armies, or other groups. Today's historian has libraries of books, newspapers, films, and other items to consult, as well as unwritten records such as buildings, artworks, and various physical remains of bygone days. An enormous amount of historical material exists.

That was not the case in Bede's time. English monastic libraries had modest collections of documents that Bede read, cross-checked, and evaluated. He made excellent use of the limited sources of his time. Bede was an innovator among historical writers, and if he sometimes accepted unlikely tales as truth, he did so far less often than did most scholars of his era.

If you were writing a history of your community, you would have to find and use a number of different sources. List at least five specific sources that might be helpful.

The end of a man's life is often compared to the winding up of a well-written play, where the principal persons still act in character, whatever the fate is which they undergo. **JOSEPH ADDISON**, *The Spectator*

Bede's own death was certainly in character, and it became the subject of historical writing in the hands of Cuthbert, a former student: "At the ninth hour, Bede said to me, 'I have a few valuables in my cask—pepper, vestments, and incense. Run quickly and bring the priests of our monastery, so that I may share among them little gifts, such as God has granted me.' And I did so with trembling. When they were all present, he addressed each and every one, urging them, imploring them they should say prayers and masses for him—which they freely promised. But they all kept weeping and sorrowing, especially because he said they must not think to see his face much longer in this world. But they rejoiced because he said, 'It is time for me, if my Maker sees fit, to be freed from the flesh and go to Him who made me out of nothing, at the time when I was nothing. I have lived a long time, and my merciful Judge has ordered my life well . . . This and much else he said for our instruction, and passed his last day happily until evening . . . upon the floor of his little cell, chanting . . . his spirit passed from the body.''

# A History of the English Church and People

**Bede** translated by Leo Sherley-Price

## The Situation of Britain and Ireland: Their Earliest Inhabitants

Britain, formerly known as Albion, is an island in the ocean, facing between north and west, and lying at a considerable distance from the coasts of Germany, Gaul, and Spain, which together form the greater part of Europe. It extends 800 miles northwards, and is 200 in breadth, except where a number of promontories stretch farther, the coastline round which extends to 3675 miles. To the south lies Belgic Gaul,[1] from the nearest shore of which travelers can see the city known as Rutubi Portus, which the English have corrupted to Reptacestir.[2] The distance from there across the sea to Gessoriacum,[3] the nearest coast of the Morini, is 50 miles or, as some write it, 450 furlongs. On the opposite side of Britain, which lies open to the boundless ocean, lie the isles of the Orcades.[4] Britain is rich in grain and timber; it has good pasturage for cattle and draft animals,[5] and vines are cultivated in various localities. There are many land and sea birds of various species, and it is well known for its plentiful springs and rivers abounding in fish. There are salmon and eel fisheries, while seals, dolphins, and some-times whales are caught. There are also many varieties of shellfish, such as mussels, in which are often found excellent pearls of several colors: red, purple, violet, and green, but mainly white. Cockles are abundant, and a beautiful scarlet dye is extracted from them which remains unfaded by sunshine or rain; indeed, the older the cloth, the more beautiful its color. The country has both salt and hot springs, and the waters flowing from them provide hot baths, in which the people bathe separately according to age and sex. As Saint Basil says: "Water receives its heat when it flows across certain metals, and becomes hot, and even scalding." The land has rich veins of many metals, including copper, iron, lead, and silver. There is also much black jet[6] of fine quality, which sparkles in firelight. When burned, it drives away snakes, and, like amber, when it is warmed by friction, it clings to whatever is applied to it. In old times, the country had twenty-eight noble cities, and innumerable castles, all of which were guarded by walls, towers, and barred gates.

Since Britain lies far north toward the pole, the nights are short in summer, and at midnight it is hard to tell whether the evening twilight still lingers or whether dawn is approaching; for in these northern latitudes the sun does not remain long below the horizon at night. Consequently both sum-

---

1. **Belgic Gaul:** France.
2. **Reptacestir:** Richborough, part of the city of Sandwich.
3. **Gessoriacum:** Boulogne, France.
4. **Orcades:** The Orkney Isles.
5. **draft animals:** Animals used for pulling loads.

6. **jet** *n*.: A type of coal.

mer days and winter nights are long, and when the sun withdraws southwards, the winter nights last eighteen hours. In Armenia,[7] Macedonia,[8] and Italy, and other countries of that latitude, the longest day lasts only fifteen hours and the shortest nine.

At the present time there are in Britain, in harmony with the five books of the divine law, five languages and four nations —English, British, Scots, and Picts. Each of these have their own language, but all are united in their study of God's truth by the fifth, Latin, which has become a common medium through the study of the scriptures. The original inhabitants of the island were the Britons, from whom it takes its name, and who, according to tradition, crossed into Britain from Armorica,[9] and occupied the southern parts. When they had spread northwards and possessed the greater part of the islands, it is said that some Picts from Scythia[10] put to sea in a few long ships and were driven by storms around the coasts of Britain, arriving at length on the north

---

**7. Armenia:** Now part of the Soviet Union.
**8. Macedonia:** Now a region divided among Greece, Yugoslavia, and Bulgaria.

**9. Armorica:** Brittany, France.
**10. Scythia** (siťh' ē ə): An ancient region in southeastern Europe.

**MONKS**
*Bodleian Library, Oxford*

coast of Ireland. Here they found the nation of the Scots, from whom they asked permission to settle, but their request was refused. Ireland is the largest island after Britain, and lies to the west. It is shorter than Britain to the north, but extends far beyond it to the south towards the northern coasts of Spain, although a wide sea separates them. These Pictish seafarers, as I have said, asked for a grant of land to make a settlement. The Scots replied that there was not room for them both, but said: "We can give you good advice. There is another island not far to the east, which we often see in the distance on clear days. Go and settle there if you wish; should you meet resistance, we will come to your help." So the Picts crossed into Britain, and began to settle in the north of the island, since the Britons were in possession of the south. Having no women with them, these Picts asked wives of the Scots, who consented on condition that, when any dispute arose, they should choose a king from the female royal line rather than the male. This custom continues among the Picts to this day. As time went on, Britain received a third nation, that of the Scots, who migrated from Ireland under their chieftain Reuda, and by a combination of force and treaty, obtained from the Picts the settlements that they still hold. From the name of this chieftain, they are still known as Dalreudians, for in their tongue *dal* means a division.

Ireland is broader than Britain, and its mild and healthy climate is superior. Snow rarely lies longer than three days, so that there is no need to store hay in summer for winter use or to build stables for beasts. There are no reptiles, and no snake can exist there, for although often brought over from Britain, as soon as the ship nears land, they breathe its scented air and die. In fact, almost everything in this isle enjoys immunity to poison, and I have heard that folk suffering from snakebite have drunk water in which scrapings from the leaves of books from Ireland had been steeped, and that this remedy checked the spreading poison and reduced the swelling. The island abounds in milk and honey, and there is no lack of vines, fish, and birds, while deer and goats are widely hunted. It is the original home of the Scots, who, as already mentioned, later migrated and joined the Britons and Picts in Britain. There is a very extensive arm of the sea, which originally formed the boundary between the Britons and the Picts. This runs inland from the west for a great distance as far as the strongly fortified British city of Alcuith.[11] It was to the northern shores of this firth that the Scots came and established their new homeland.

---

**11. Alcuith** (al kü′ əth): Dumbarton, Scotland.

## THINKING ABOUT THE SELECTION

### Recalling

1. What countries formed the greater part of Europe at the time of Bede's history?
2. (a) In Bede's time, what were the four nations in Britain. (b) What united them?
3. What animals does Bede say were widely hunted in Ireland?

### Interpreting

4. What does the explanation about scarlet dye imply about the lifestyle of the people?
5. Bede states that Britain once "had twenty-eight noble cities . . . guarded by walls, towers, and barred gates." What does this statement suggest about the political situation at the time?
6. What is one unlikely tale that Bede includes in his history?

### Applying

7. If you wanted to read a reliable history of early England, you would probably choose something other than Bede's work. Why? What kind of source might you choose?

## ANALYZING LITERATURE

### Understanding Historical Writing

A history provides factual information about the past. This information comes from a variety of sources, including books and other printed materials, public records, and, if possible, personal letters, memoirs, and interviews. A good historian like Bede does more than just list facts, however. Bede presents his facts as part of an understandable whole.

1. Accuracy is very important in historical writing. Read the quotation from the Scots on page 66 (a) Do you think the statement is an exact quotation? (b) If not, does it cast doubt on the accuracy of Bede's history? Explain.
2. Bede sometimes relies on people's oral statements for his information. On page 66 he makes a specific reference to such a source. What is it?

## CRITICAL THINKING AND READING

### Making Inferences About Attitudes

Bede's history reflects his own attitudes and those of the people he is writing about. Since these attitudes tend to be revealed indirectly, you must make inferences, or draw conclusions about them. For example, Bede states that the people of England are "united in their study of God's truth." From this statement you can infer that religion played an important role in the life of the people.

1. From Bede's comments on page 66 what do you think the general attitude was in Britain toward snakes?
2. Do you think the Picts and Scots got along well with each other? Cite the evidence on which you base your inference.

## UNDERSTANDING LANGUAGE

### Tracing Word Histories

An **etymology** explains the origin and history of a word. It usually appears in brackets in a dictionary entry.

> **amber** *n.* [ME. *aumbre,* amber, ambergris <OFr. *ambre* < Ar. '*anbar,* ambergris]

The present English word *amber* is derived from the Middle English word *aumbre,* which came from Old French, and originally from Arabic.

Trace the history of the following words.

1. promontory     3. migrate
2. furlong        4. cockle

## THINKING AND WRITING

### Writing a Critical Review

Give your opinion of this excerpt from Bede's history. First, jot down your answers to the following questions: Does the history seem accurate? Is it clearly written? What do you find to be its most striking fact? Next, write a topic sentence that states your opinion clearly. Then write a draft, using examples to support your opinion. Finally, revise your draft, making sure that its sentences are in logical order.

# THE CHANGING ENGLISH LANGUAGE

## Old English 449–1066

### "ENGLISC"

The story of English is the story of roamings and settling, invasions and war. What we call *Anglo-Saxon* or *Old English* developed through the contributions of many different peoples, including the Jutes (from Danish Jutland), the Saxons (from the region of Germany still called Lower Saxony), and scatterings of other groups. Old English began with the *Angles,* a people who originated in a section of Denmark still called *Angeln,* a word that means "an angle in the coast." The Celts called their German conquerors *Saxons* but by degrees the terms *Anglii* and *Anglia* entered their speech. Soon, people were referring to their language as *Englisc* and themselves as *Angelcynn;* literally, the relatives (*cynn* as "kin") of the Angles. By A.D. 1000 they called their country *Englisc.*

### THE HUNDRED MOST COMMON WORDS

The Anglo-Saxons were farmers—when they were not at war—and they soon settled down and took over all the good farming country, chasing the Celts to the hilltops or to Wales and Ireland. Although more than half the vocabulary of modern English is borrowed, and more than half the words of Old English (some say as much as 85 percent) have vanished, the language of these Anglo-Saxon farmers became the basis of modern English. Of the hundred most common words in our speech today, every one derives from Old English; of the next hundred, eighty-three are native. Some Old English words hardly need translation—*mann* and *hus* for example—although of course we spell them differently today (man and

house). It is nearly impossible to write a modern English sentence without using a wealth of Old English vocabulary. All the words in Roosevelt's famous comforting phrase—"The only thing we have to fear is fear itself"—come from Old English. Francis Scott Key used words derived from Old English in 1814 when he saw the flag waving over Fort McHenry: "Oh say, can you see, by the dawn's early light, what so proudly we hailed at the twilight's last gleaming?" "Proud" is the only borrowing, and it's nearly a thousand years old!

### RIDDLES

The Anglo-Saxons delighted in word play, riddles, and ambiguity in language. Few people could read or write, and so they had to rely on their memories. As a result, the Anglo-Saxons developed their oral tradition very fully. They liked stating their ideas in subtle, original ways, and especially admired poems that went in circles. This love of word play, which characterizes English to the present, can be seen especially in *The Exeter Book of Riddles,* a collection of Old English verse. Can you solve this one-line riddle? "On the way a miracle: water becomes bone." Ice!

### THE INFLUENCE OF CHRISTIANITY

Although the English people already knew about *heofon* (heaven), *synne* (sin) and *hel* (hell), the language received a huge boost in A.D. 597, when Christianity arrived with its enormous Latin vocabulary, more than 400 words of which survive to this day. For example, the Latin *evangelium* (good news) became the English *god-spell* which has become the modern word *gospel*. Even more importantly, words from Latin gave English speakers the ability to express abstract thoughts, including such concepts as *angel* and *discipline*. Further, Old English rejuvenated itself by giving new meaning to old words. *God, heaven,* and *hell* all assumed deeper meanings upon the arrival of Christianity.

## THE VIKINGS SIMPLIFY ENGLISH

Superior numbers and literacy assured the victory of English over Danish, but the Danes left a lasting influence on English nonetheless. First, they contributed at least 900 words, such as *husbondi (house-master* or *husband)* and *syster*(sister). Second, the Danes added pronouns to English, filling a real linguistic need. Most importantly, before the arrival of the Danes, Old English conveyed meaning through word endings rather than word order. The Danes simplified language by eliminating some of the word change, called inflection, although the process would not be completed until Middle English developed.

## THE SPELLING DILEMMA

Written English, however, confronted the language with a problem that still confounds us today: spelling. Almost all writing is based on symbols that stand for the sounds of the language they record. The early scribes used the Roman alphabet to record Old English. Now, the Roman alphabet did a fine job representing the sounds of Latin, for which it had been created. But Old English included a number of decidedly un-Roman sounds, such as the sound we now write as *TH*. The scribes solved the problem by borrowing two symbols from the runic alphabet, þ and ð. Unfortunately, they used the two symbols interchangeably. This continued with other sounds, and spelling problems abounded.

So begun, English would continue to develop over the next four hundred years, becoming ever richer and more flexible.

**THE ANGLO SAXON CHRONICLE**
*The British Library*

# YOU THE WRITER

**Assignment**

**1.** Imagine that you have been lost for many days in the north Atlantic Ocean in a small boat. At last you reach land. Write a narrative poem in which you describe the hardships, both physical and mental, that you endured. Use any verse form you feel is suitable.

 **Prewriting.** First list several of the main sufferings you endured. Then make notes on the details of each. Think of ways to make your narrative as vivid and concrete as possible.

 **Writing.** Write your first draft in chronological order, using description to expand on each of the basic hardships you are recounting.

 **Revising.** When you revise, first see if you need to adjust the overall narrative structure of your poem. Then look to improve the details of each piece of description. Read your poem aloud. Can you improve its musical quality?

**Assignment**

**2.** Many notable works of literature are based on characters or incidents from earlier works. Select any character or incident from Anglo-Saxon literature and write a brief prose monologue or narrative based on the character or incident you have chosen.

 **Prewriting.** First use your imagination to think up a new view of the character or incident. Then plan the structure and details of your monologue or narrative.

 **Writing.** Your first draft should contain, in rough form, all the contents of your work—either your character's remarks or the details of the incident you are narrating.

 **Revising.** When you revise, improve the organization and structure of your work. Then try to polish and perfect the details.

**Assignment**

**3.** Imagine that you have gone back in time to Anglo-Saxon England and, twenty-four hours later, have returned to the present. Write a brief magazine article whose purpose is to convey your discovery of the differences between the Anglo-Saxon world and the modern world.

 **Prewriting.** List the details of what you saw, heard, and experienced. Then fit them into an outline that will enable you to convey a clear, vivid picture of your day in the past.

 **Writing.** Following your outline, write fully developed paragraphs, each of which focuses on a single impression or experience. Conclude by summarizing the differences.

 **Revising.** Can you replace one of the impressions or experiences with a better, more revealing one? Can you alter your structure or style for greater expressiveness? Revise according to these questions.

# YOU THE CRITIC

**Assignment**

**1.** Write a critical evaluation of any one of the selections from the Anglo-Saxon period. The purpose of your evaluation should be to indicate what interest the work holds for a contemporary reader.

**Prewriting.** Answer these questions: What is my general opinion of this work? What specifically did I admire or dislike about it? What is the basic opinion I wish to share with readers who have not yet read the work?

**Writing.** Write an essay in which you first state in a topic sentence your critical judgment. Then offer your reasons. Refer to details of the work to clarify and support your argument.

**Revising.** Revise in the light of these questions: Is my opinion fair, objective, and clearly expressed? Can I make my argument more forceful and persuasive by citing other details or aspects of the work?

**Assignment**

**2.** Some readers suppose that the earliest literature of a people tends to be crude and primitive. Write a brief essay in which you point out the literary artistry—the imaginative power, sophisticated design, or stylistic appeal—of any one of the Anglo-Saxon selections you have read.

**Prewriting.** First decide what you liked about the work. Then analyze it to determine the methods the writer used to make it artistically effective.

**Writing.** First state or describe clearly the kind of literary excellence you see in the work. Then refer to specific aspects and details of the work to embody and clarify your view.

**Revising.** When you revise keep in mind the question, "Have I demonstrated and illustrated the artistic excellence I see in ———?" Make changes that help you show, not just talk about, the virtues of the literary work.

**Assignment**

**3.** Write an essay with the title "Anglo-Saxon Literature: Mirror of the Times." Show how the literature you have read reflects what you have learned about Anglo-Saxon history and life.

**Prewriting.** Review the introduction to the Anglo-Saxon period and any other information you have gathered about it. Which work that you have read comes to mind in the course of your review? What brings this work to mind?

**Writing.** Write a first draft based on this last question. Tell how Anglo-Saxon history or life reveals itself in the work you have selected. Your basic approach should be a descriptive comparison of the historical background and the literary expression of it.

**Revising.** Concentrate on increasing the clarity and precision of your description of the link between the literature and its historical setting.

**PILGRIMS TO CANTERBURY: DETAIL OF AN ENGLISH ILLUMINATED MANUSCRIPT, c.1400**
*The Granger Collection*

# THE MEDIEVAL PERIOD

## 1066–1485

A Knyght ther was, and that a worthy man
That fro the tyme that he first bigan
To riden out, he loved chivalrie,
Trouthe and honour, fredom and curteisie

**Geoffrey Chaucer**

**THE BAYEUX TAPESTRY: DUKE WILLIAM ENCOURAGES HIS MEN AT HASTINGS**
*The Granger Collection*

The famous description on the preceding page comes from an English literary masterpiece, *The Canterbury Tales,* by Geoffrey Chaucer (1340?–1400). The passage reflects many of the ideas and attitudes held by Europeans during the fourteenth century. In these years knights lived by the code of chivalry, which stressed truth, honor, and courtesy off the battlefield and valor on it. The Roman Catholic Church had become the only force uniting most of Western Europe. Religion pervaded daily life, and to be a devout Christian —a worthy man—was important not only to knights but to all members of English society.

During these years the English language changed from its Anglo-Saxon form to one called Middle English, far more familiar to modern readers. Looking at Chaucer's words above, we can readily recognize their modern English counterparts—"knyght" is *knight,* "ther" is *there,* "fro" is *from,* "riden" is *ride,* "chivalrie" is *chivalry,* and so on. The change from Old English to Middle English took place gradually. Yet this change can be traced to one riveting event—the Norman invasion of 1066.

## THE NORMAN CONQUEST

The Normans, or "north men," were descendants of Vikings who had invaded the coast of France in the ninth century. Over the years, these people had adopted many French ways. They had become devout Christians. They had accustomed themselves to speaking a dialect of the French language. They had also organized themselves according to the French political and economic system of the times—feudalism.

William, Duke of Normandy, had family ties to Edward the Confessor, the English king. When Edward died in 1066, the Saxon witan—the council of elders—chose Harold II as king. William of Normandy, meanwhile, claimed that Edward had promised him the throne. William thereupon led a few thousand Norman and French troops across the English Channel to assert his claim by force.

He met King Harold at the Battle of Hastings near a seaside village in southern England. Harold was killed, and William emerged victorious. He then headed for London, brutally crushing all resistance. At Westminster Abbey on Christmas Day, William "the Conqueror" took the throne of England as King William I.

Over the next five years, William consolidated his victory. He suppressed the Anglo-Saxon nobility and confiscated their lands. He saw to it that Normans controlled government at all levels. The Normans conducted their business in Norman French or Latin. They gradually remade England along feudal lines.

### The Rise of Feudalism

Feudalism had taken root on the European continent at a time when no central government was strong enough to keep order.

Under the circumstances, nobles had to rely on their own warriors for help. The system they created was an exchange of property for personal service. The person who granted the property was the lord or overlord. The person who received it was the vassal. The vassal promised service to his lord in a ceremony called the act of homage. At the same time, the vassal usually pledged his faithfulness by taking the Christian vow of fealty.

In theory, all the land belonged to the ruler. The king kept some of it for his personal use, granted some to the church, and parceled out the rest among his powerful supporters. He gave these supporters noble titles—usually baron—and the special privileges that went with them. The parcels of land granted to the barons were known as fiefs.

As a vassal of his overlord, each baron was obliged to pay certain fees or taxes. He was also expected to supply a specified number of knights, or professional soldiers, should the king require them. In return for their services, knights usually received smaller parcels of land, called manors. The peasants who worked these manors were the lowest class in the feudal system, the serfs. Manors became the basic community of the feudal system. Most were self-sufficient, using their own craftsmen to provide nearly all their needs.

In the eleventh century, Europe had no nation-states with firm political boundaries. William and the Norman kings who followed him—William II, Henry I, and Stephen of Blois—held feudal domains in both England and France. Since they had two realms, Norman kings had far wider responsibilities than Saxon kings had faced. The situation also meant that English barons dissatisfied with their overlord could cross the English Channel and stir up trouble on the other side.

## A Shifting Language

Like a great many of history's conquerors, the Normans thought themselves vastly superior to the people they had conquered. The invaders treated the Saxons and Danes as not quite human and sniffed at their language as unworthy of respect. The Normans substituted their dialect of French in the law courts as well as in the conduct of business in general. To this day, French words such as *bail* and *sergeant* remain embedded in the language of English law.

Traces of Norman discrimination against the Saxons have lingered for centuries. In his nineteenth-century novel *Ivanhoe,* Sir Walter Scott noted one aspect of Norman superiority. In the field, he wrote, a domestic animal is often referred to by its Saxon name —swine, sheep, or ox. When the same animal appears on a dinner table, however, it takes a French name—pork, mutton, or beef. In other words, the raising of farm animals was considered a Saxon activity, whereas the more elegant pursuit, dining, befitted the Normans.

**A BALIFF SUPERVISING THE HARVEST (THE MONTH OF AUGUST): MANUSCRIPT ILLUMINATION, ENGLISH, EARLY 14TH CENTURY**
*The Granger Collection*

| | |
|---|---|
| 1066 | Saxons defeated at Hastings. |
| 1073 | Canterbury becomes England's religious center. |
| c. 1075 | Construction on Tower of London begins. |
| 1100 | Henry I becomes king. |
| 1110 | First recorded miracle play performed at Dunstable. |
| c. 1130 | Oxford becomes a center for learning. |
| c. 1136 | Geoffrey of Monmouth writes *Historia Regum Britanniae*. |
| 1151 | Chess introduced to England. |
| 1170 | Thomas Becket, Archbishop of Canterbury, murdered. |
| 1171 | Henry II conquers southeastern Ireland. |
| 1176 | First Eisteddfod, Welsh festival of poetry and music. |
| 1180 | Glass windows first used in private homes. |
| c. 1190 | Beginning of legendary era of Robin Hood. |
| 1215 | King John forced to sign Magna Carta. |
| 1218 | First Newgate Prison built in London. |
| 1233 | First coal mined at Newcastle. |
| 1258 | First commoners allowed in Parliament. |
| c. 1265 | Roger Bacon writes *Opus Majus*. |

The Murder of Thomas Becket

King John Signs the Magna Carta

Roger Bacon

Pope Gregory IX

Manuscript of

The Siege of Jerusalem During the First Crusade

Genghis Khan

The Song of Roland

Twelfth-century Chess Piece

# WORLD EVENTS

# BRITISH EVENTS

| | |
|---|---|
| 1272 | Edward I becomes king. |
| c. 1281 | Cambridge University founded. |
| 1282 | England conquers Wales. |
| c. 1285 | The legendary Patrick Spens's ship wrecked off Aberdeen, Scotland. |
| 1295 | Edward I assembles Model Parliament. |
| 1337 | Beginning of Hundred Years' War with France. |
| 1348 | Black death begins sweeping through England. |
| 1372 | Bible first translated into English. |
| c. 1375 | Surviving version of *Sir Gawain and the Green Knight* written. |
| 1381 | Peasants' Revolt. |
| 1386 | **Chaucer** begins writing *The Canterbury Tales*. |
| c. 1450 | *The Second Shepherds' Play* first performed. |
| 1455 | Beginning of Wars of the Roses. |
| 1460 | Richard of York killed at Battle of Wakefield. |
| c. 1470 | **Thomas Malory** writes *Morte D' Arthur*. |
| 1476 | William Caxton builds first English printing press. |

François Villon

Joan of Arc

Printer's Device Used by Caxton

Black Death

Marco Polo

Johann Gutenburg Printing First Bible

Sweeps Through England

*Canterbury Tales*

Battle During the Hundred Years' War

# WORLD EVENTS

## Reign of the Plantagenets

Although Norman influence continued for centuries, Norman rule ended in 1154 when Henry Plantagenet, Count of Anjou, came to the throne as Henry II. Henry founded the royal house of Plantagenet, otherwise known as the Angevin (from Anjou) line of English monarchs. A strongly committed ruler, Henry established a record as one of England's ablest kings. He had an avid interest in government and a keen understanding of the law.

## Henry II and the Church

Henry's concern with legal matters led him into direct conflict with the Church. By the twelfth century, the Church had grown ever more powerful, obtaining the authority to put clergymen on trial in Church-run courts. Henry sought to curb some abuses connected with this privilege. When the archbishop's seat at Canterbury fell vacant, he appointed his friend Thomas Becket to the position, expecting Becket to go along with royal policy. Instead, Becket defied the king and appealed to the Pope in Rome. The Pope sided with Becket, provoking Henry to rage.

Some of Henry's knights misunderstood the royal wrath. In 1170, four of them went to Canterbury and murdered Becket in his cathedral. Henry quickly condemned the crime and tried to atone for it by making a holy journey, or pilgrimage, to Becket's tomb. Thereafter a pilgrimage to Becket's shrine at Canterbury became a common English means of showing religious devotion. The characters in Chaucer's *The Canterbury Tales,* for example, make just such a pilgrimage.

## Origins of Constitutional Government

The next king, Richard I, spent most of his reign staging military expeditions overseas. His activities proved costly, and his successor, King John, inherited the debts. John tried to raise money by ordering new taxes on the barons and saved money by curtailing services such as the sending of judges to local districts to settle quarrels. The barons resisted these measures, bringing England to the edge of civil war. To avert further trouble, King John at last agreed to certain of the barons' conditions by putting his seal to the Magna Carta (Latin for "Great Charter").

In this document, the king promised not to tax land without first meeting with the barons. He also said he would choose as his officers only those "who know the law of the realm and mean to observe it well." The Magna Carta produced no radical changes in government. Yet many historians believe that the document's restrictions on royal power marked the beginning of constitutional government in England.

Constitutional government continued to develop under subsequent kings. During the reign of Henry III, the Great Council of barons who advised the king came to be called Parliament. Henry's successor, Edward I, became the first king to summon a Parliament partly elected by "free men"—a term that included some ordinary townspeople as well as barons. By the end of the thirteenth century, then, Parliament had already been established as a cornerstone of government in the British Isles.

## The Growth of Towns

It was no accident that some members of Parliament now represented townspeople. In the thirteenth century, towns were becoming increasingly important in English life. The Crusades, a series of religious wars in the twelfth and thirteenth centuries, had stimulated trade between Europe and the Middle East. As trade expanded, so did Europe's trading centers. The largest of these centers in England was London, originally built by the Romans. Four times more populous than any other English community, London had already achieved status as a city.

In London and elsewhere, townspeople organized themselves into guilds, or associations, of various sorts. The two most significant types were merchant guilds and craft guilds. Merchant guilds were formed in an effort to promote business within a town, often at the expense of other towns nearby. As these guilds became more powerful, some of them virtually took over town governments. Craft guilds, like our modern labor unions, sought to protect the interests of workers such as weavers, carpenters, and tanners. They also tried to assure the quality of the work these craftspeople produced. Such organizations operated in a world in which advancement was tightly controlled. A young person typically entered a craft as an apprentice, or beginner, and worked his way up the ladder, sometimes reaching the highest rung as master craftsman.

The growth of towns meant that wealth was no longer restricted to land ownership, which remained a privilege of the nobility.

Unfortunately, it also meant that people lived much closer together, often under conditions that were far from sanitary. When infectious diseases came to England, they spread havoc in the towns. The worst epidemic, a great plague called the Black Death, swept the island in 1348 and 1349, killing a third of the population.

## THE LATER MIDDLE AGES

By the time of the Black Death, England had already passed into the period known as the Later Middle Ages. This period lasted from the beginning of the fourteenth century to the end of the fifteenth. During these years, the house of Lancaster replaced the Plantagenets on the throne, only to be replaced in turn by the house of York. The Lancastrian kings were Henry IV, Henry V, and Henry VI, all of whom later became central figures in the historical dramas of Shakespeare.

During the Later Middle Ages, the feudal system went into a steep decline. As new towns appeared, feudal notions of land tenure seemed more and more outdated. After the Black Death swept across England, a massive labor shortage increased the value of a peasant's work. More and more land owners began paying their farmers in cash, giving these workers a greater sense of freedom. Along with freedom went frustration, as peasants began complaining about discriminatory laws and onerous taxation. Finally, in 1381, peasants in southern England staged a revolt, demanding, among other things, an end to serfdom. Although the revolt was eventually crushed, many of its causes continued, and so did the peasants' discontent.

## An Attack on the Church

At about the time of the peasants' revolt, other complaints were being directed at the church. They came from an outspoken scholar, John Wycliffe (c. 1320–84), who thought that religion had traveled far from its roots. Wycliffe opposed all forms of wealth among the clergy. He showed only scorn for monks, calling them men with "red and fat cheeks and great bellies." He believed that all religious authority sprang from the Bible, not from the Church.

Wycliffe directed the translation of the Bible into English in the hope of making it more accessible to the people. He also helped to organize an order of "poor priests" known as Lollards. Eventually, the archbishop of Canterbury moved against the Lollards as heretics, people who attack Church doctrine and undermine Church authority. Yet the Lollards continued to spread Wycliffe's teachings for a number of years after the scholar's death.

## Wars of the Roses

Just as the English Middle Ages had opened with a struggle for power, they closed with a similar conflict. This one began in 1453, when King Henry VI suffered the first of many bouts of madness. Parliament appointed his cousin Richard of York as temporary head of government. When Henry recovered briefly, Richard was forced from office, and Henry returned to the throne. Richard would not depart without a fight, however. The resulting civil war became known as the first War of the Roses, for it pitted the house of York, whose symbol was a white rose, against the house of Lancaster, whose symbol was a red rose.

In 1461, a Yorkist victory put Richard's son, Edward, on the throne. As Edward IV, he ruled England until his death in 1483, when his eldest son, still a boy, became Edward V. Soon afterward, Edward V and his brother died mysteriously in the Tower of London while under the supposed protection of their uncle, Richard of Gloucester. Richard, accused by many people of these "Tower murders," then proclaimed himself King Richard III.

Two years later, Henry Tudor, a distant cousin and supporter of the Lancastrian kings, led a rebellion against the unpopular King Richard and killed him. Tudor, crowned Henry VII, later married Richard's niece. By doing so, he united the houses of York and Lancaster and ended the Wars of the Roses. By the time Henry had established a new royal line, the house of Tudor, the English Middle Ages had ended.

## CHIVALRY AND ROMANCE

Most societies have lived by a well-established set of ideals, and England of the Middle Ages was no exception. One set of standards by which people measured themselves during these years was the code of knightly behavior known as chivalry. The idea of chivalry first arose on the European continent at the time of the

**KING HENRY VII OF ENGLAND**
*Panel, 1505, by Michiel Sittow*
The Granger Collection

Crusades. Although the Crusades often involved brutality and bloodshed, they encouraged warriors to search for higher rules of conduct.

At first the code dealt mainly with loyalty and valor, both on and off the battlefield. By the thirteenth century, however, chivalry had grown considerably more complex. Every knight was supposed to pledge his service to a lady. He might also be expected to joust for his lady's favor or to rescue maidens in distress.

French poets known as troubadours popularized this tradition in songs of gallant knights. Originally these songs were written in Romance, or Roman-influenced, languages rather than Latin, and so they were called romances. At the French court, it became important for knights to treat ladies with a respect that bordered on reverence. Gradually the same ideal took root in the English court.

## The Legend of King Arthur

One example illustrating the development of chivalry originated with the Celts. For centuries after their defeat by the Anglo-Saxons, the Celts had told stories of a great hero, King Arthur. Inasmuch as historians cannot say for certain whether Arthur actually lived or not, tales about him are considered legends, a blend of fiction and fact. When the Normans were battling the Anglo-Saxons, they became interested in the old Celtic legends. In about 1136, a Welsh-born scholar, Geoffrey of Monmouth (c. 1100–54), drew upon his knowledge of Celtic legends and his readings of Bede to produce a *History of the Kings of Britain*. This fanciful history, though written in Latin, quickly popularized the early Celtic king.

Because of the Normans' French ties, the tales of Arthur spread not only in England but also in France. There they were influenced

**SIR GALAHAD, 1864 (WATERCOLOR)**
*Dante Gabriel Rossetti*
The Granger Collection

by other romances, often involving the French hero Charlemagne. New versions of the Arthur legend, though usually set in the past, began to depict Arthur as more modern in his practices. His Knights of the Round Table became paragons of chivalry, as adept in courtly love as they were in fighting battles. The legend also inspired *Sir Gawain and the Green Knight,* a fourteenth-century narrative poem by an anonymous author. In the poem an Arthurian knight, Sir Gawain, displays all the virtues of chivalry in his battles with the Green Knight, a supernatural figure.

Arthurian romance reached its height with *La Morte d' Arthur (The Death of Arthur),* a fifteenth-century prose work by Sir Thomas Malory (d. 1471). Translating from French sources, Malory created the most complete Middle English compilation of the various legends involving Arthur and his court. *La Morte d' Arthur* was printed in twenty-one volumes.

## LEARNING AND LITERATURE

Although the Normans and French eventually had great influence on English letters, that development did not begin in 1066. To the contrary, the Norman invasion put a temporary halt to scholarship and literature in the British Isles. After the turbulence of conquest subsided, however, England experienced a "little renaissance," a small rebirth of learning, in the twelfth century. Although monasteries continued their scholastic traditions, new centers of learning emerged. Scholars flocked to the religious community at Oxford to hear lectures by noted visitors; then colleges were built to house the scholars, and the first English university was born. A second university at Cambridge followed some years later.

Probably the most famous scholar that Oxford produced in the Middle Ages was Roger Bacon (c. 1214–94), a scientist and mathematician now considered the father of English philosophy. A member of the Franciscan brotherhood, Bacon created his *Opus Majus* (Major Work), a Latin study of science, grammar, mathematics, and philosophy, at the request of the Pope. Later, however, the Church condemned Bacon as a heretic. The scholar died in obscurity, probably at Oxford, but his ideas were taken up a century later by another Franciscan, William Ockham (d. 1349). Like Bacon, Ockham attempted to use a scientific approach in exploring the universe; he, too, was accused of heresy.

While Latin remained the language of Church and university scholarship, Norman French was frequently used in government. Both languages contributed to what came to be called Middle English. Latin literature gradually gave way to literature written in the vernacular, or the language of the people. The use of the vernacular increased after 1372, when John Wycliffe began directing the English translation of the Bible. Wycliffe's work proved a major advance for literature, inasmuch as it encouraged more people to learn to read.

Another important invention of the period, printing from movable type, also encouraged literacy. In 1454 a German silversmith, Johann Gutenberg, devised a printing process with individual metal letters that could be used again and again. Printing spread rapidly from Germany to other parts of Europe, and further improvements were made. In 1476 a London merchant, William Caxton (c. 1422–91) set up the first movable-type press in England. This invention meant that English literature no longer needed to be hand copied by church scribes. Now it could be produced far more quickly and made available to a much wider circle of readers.

## POETRY OF THE ENGLISH MIDDLE AGES

One of Caxton's first projects was the printing of *The Canterbury Tales.* His enthusiasm for this verse showed the importance that he and others placed on poetry in general. Two key poets of the period, William Langland and Geoffrey Chaucer, lived during the later Middle Ages. Their writings reveal the changes that were taking place in the English language and in society as a whole.

### William Langland

Scholars know very little about the poet they usually call William Langland. He appears to have come from western England and to have been a country boy. In his masterpiece, *Piers Plowman,* he followed a tradition of the Middle Ages by writing in the form of an allegory, a work in which most of the characters, settings, and events are arranged in a symbolical pattern. He also took a typically Anglo-Saxon delight in alliteration.

Like John Wycliffe, Langland was greatly concerned with the ways the wealthy oppress the poor. He left little doubt that his sympathies went out to those who had been treated harshly by the world. His most vivid writing concerned events he may have witnessed—tavern squabbles, for instance, or the misery of people suffering from the plague. Some scholars judge *Piers Plowman* one of the most deeply felt poems in all of English literature.

### Geoffrey Chaucer

The towering figure of Middle English verse is Geoffrey Chaucer. In many estimates he ranks second only to Shakespeare as England's greatest writer. Chaucer owed much of his early sophistication to his training as an attendant to King Edward III. The poet also traveled widely and familiarized himself with important Italian poets, including Dante and Petrarch.

Chaucer's major works include a number of narrative poems, such as the verse romance *Troilus and Criseyde* (1372–86) and several shorter poems. Yet his finest achievement was *The Canterbury Tales,* a series of verse stories told by different pilgrims on their

A PAGE FROM THE LANSDOWNE MS OF
GEOFFREY CHAUCER'S
CANTERBURY TALES
*The Granger Collection*

way to the tomb of Thomas Becket. The pilgrims represent many walks of life—a knight, a squire, a clerk, a friar, a nun, a miller, a merchant, and so on. In Chaucer's deft hands, each storyteller emerges as a vivid personality in his or her own right. Some of the tales have religious themes; others are humorous or satiric. All in all, they provide a remarkable portrait of life in the later Middle Ages.

## Lyrics and Ballads

Europeans of the Middle Ages had a fondness for a harplike instrument called the lyre. In palaces and castles, poets often strummed lyres as they recited their verse. From this custom English lyric poetry developed.

Lyric poems of this period fall into two main categories, secular and religious. The usual topics of the secular poetry are love or nature; many of them celebrate the renewal of spring or the joys of summer:

> Sumer is icumen in;
> Lhude° sing cuccu!                                    °Loudly

Religious lyrics might consist of a hymn praising God or a prayer of supplication. One of the most famous religious lyrics in Middle English celebrates the Virgin Mary:

> I syng of myden
>     That is makeles;°                               °matchless
> Kyng of alle kynges
>     To here son che ches.                          °she chose

Another includes the Latin line *Timor mortis conturbat me* ("The fear of death disturbs me") to teach the lesson that in the midst of life there is death:

> In what state that ever I be,
>     *Timor mortis conturbat me.*

> As I me walked in on° morning                        °one
> I hard a birde both wepe and synge;
> This was the tenor of her talkynge:
>     *Timor mortis conturbat me.*

Another popular poetic form was the ballad, a folk song that told a story. Experts find most surviving ballads impossible to date. Those from the Scottish border probably arose long after the Middle Ages, and those from before 1485 have most likely changed a good deal over the centuries.

One surviving series of ballads concerns Robin Hood, a legendary hero who may have existed around the turn of the thirteenth century. Robin, an outlaw, lives in the woods with his band of "merrye" men, robbing from the rich and helping the poor. He and his lady friend, Maid Marian, eventually became part of traditional

**ROBIN HOOD**
*Richard Dadd*
*Center for British Art,*
*Paul Mellon Collection*

May Day festivities. These folk celebrations honoring the coming of spring took place each year on the first day of May.

## DRAMA OF THE MIDDLE AGES

The theater of William Shakespeare had its roots in the dramas of the Middle Ages. During early Norman times, the Church often sponsored plays as part of religious services. In time, these plays moved from the church to the churchyard and then to the marketplace. The earliest dramas were miracle plays, in England sometimes also called mystery plays. They retold stories from the Bible or dealt with some aspect of the lives of saints.

Over the years the theater gained in popularity among English townspeople. Several communities became famous for performing a particular series of plays, or cycle, which presented a Biblical history of humankind. York, the religious capital of northern England, had one of the largest cycles. Chester and Wakefield also staged multi-play productions. Clergymen usually wrote the plays, and actors performed them on wagons or fixed scaffolds. Each of the town's craft guilds would take turns producing one play.

During the turbulent years of the fifteenth century, a new kind of drama arose—the morality play. Morality plays depicted the life of an ordinary person, sometimes from birth to death. Along the way the hero meets characters who symbolize abstract qualities, such as Vice or Virtue. The purpose of these allegorical dramas was to teach a moral lesson.

The most famous surviving morality play is *Everyman,* which had its origin in the Netherlands and was not adapted for English audiences until about 1500. By that time, Middle English was giving way to modern English, the form of the language we speak today. Even so, *Everyman* is usually studied as part of Middle English literature, for it is one of the most powerful examples of the kinds of morality plays performed in the later Middle Ages.

Subsequent generations of writers owe a great debt to the literature of the English Middle Ages. In Chaucer, the era produced the first major writer in English to be known and respected for his craft. With works such as *Everyman,* the period produced the foundations of the great English dramatic tradition. In addition, the romantic adventures of King Arthur and his knights became a source to which future writers would turn again and again.

## Quotations by Prominent Figures of the Period

Manners maketh man.
> **William of Wykeham,** Motto of two colleges at Oxford

It behooves us to place the foundations of knowledge in mathematics.
> **Roger Bacon,** *Opus Majus*

Who pulleth out this sword of this stone and anvil, is rightwise king born of all England.
> **Sir Thomas Malory,** *Morte d' Arthur*

> In a somer seson whan soft was the sonne
> Who will bell the cat?
> **William Langland,** *Piers Plowman*

A foule may ek° a wys-man often gide.°   °also   °guide
> **Geoffrey Chaucer,** *Troilus and Criseyde*

Looke who that is moost vertuous alway,
Pryvee° and apert, and most entendeth ay   °private, secret
To do the gentil dedes that he kan;
Tak him for the grettest gentil man.
> **Geoffrey Chaucer,** "The Wife of Bath's Tale," *The Canterbury Tales*

Pacience is an heigh vertu, certeyn.
> **Geoffrey Chaucer,** "The Franklin's Tale," *The Canterbury Tales*

> When captains couragious, whom death could not daunte
> Did march to the seige of the city of Gaunt,
> They mustered their soldiers by two and by three
> And the foremost in battle was Mary Ambree.
> **Anonymous,** "Mary Ambree"

> Come listen to me, you gallants so free,
> All you that loves mirth for to hear,
> And I will you tell of a bold outlaw
> That lived in Nottinghamshire.
> **Anonymous,** "Robin Hood and Allen a Dale"

# The Literature of 1066–1485

When you read literature, it is important to place it in its historical context. Doing so will help you to understand influences on the writer's ideas and techniques.

**Historical Context**

In 1066 the Normans conquered England by defeating the Anglo-Saxons at the Battle of Hastings. Although many Anglo-Saxon traditions and attitudes survived the invasion, the Normans dramatically changed English life by introducing a social, economic, and political system called feudalism. Under this system, land was divided among noble overlords. Controlling large, self-sufficient feudal manors, the overlords were served by knights, who provided protection, and serfs, who farmed the land and herded animals. Although it was an ideal that few of them may have actually attained, the knights tried to live according to the code of chivalry, which required them to be honorable, courteous, brave, and skillful. Toward the later part of this period, gun power was replacing swords and the feudal order was being replaced by the aristocratic code.

**Literary Movements**

The concept of chivalry played an important role in shaping the literature of the Medieval Period. When chivalry was blended with such magical elements as giants, wizards, sorcerers, and dragons, the form of literature known as the romance was created. Filled with fantasy, adventure, and courtly love, romances were one of the most popular literary forms of the period. Apart from romantic literature, most of the literature of the period reflected the influence of religion. This influence is most noticeable in the two forms of drama that were popular during the period: mystery plays and morality plays.

**Writers' Techniques**

Although the first printing press was established toward the end of the Medieval Period, much of the literature of the period was composed orally. Folk ballads were sung or recited by common people and passed down from generation to generation. These ballads, along with most other medieval literature, were written in verse and told a story. Toward the end of the period, however, a number of writers began writing prose.

On the following pages is a selection by Thomas Malory, the first English writer to compile and arrange the numerous legends of King Arthur. The notes in the side column should help you to place the selection in its historical context.

# *from* Morte d'Arthur

Sir Thomas Malory

**Historical Context:**
Malory's Morte d'Arthur was completed around 1470. The legend of a king who adheres to the principles of chivalry is a fitting subject for this period during which feudalism was dying. The legend itself may be based on the life of a Celtic Chieftain who lived during the sixth century.

*This selection begins after King Arthur has traveled to France at the insistence of his nephew, Gawain, to besiege his former friend and knight, Lancelot, for his involvement with Queen Guenevere. However, the king's attempts to punish are halfhearted, and he is soon forced to abandon them altogether when he learns that his nephew, Mordred, has seized control of England. Arthur leads his forces back to England, and Mordred attacks them upon their landing. Gawain is killed in the fighting, but before he dies, he manages to send word to Lancelot that Arthur is in need of assistance.*

*So upon Trinity Sunday at night King Arthur dreamed a wonderful dream, and in his dream him seemed*[1] that he saw upon a chafflet[2] a chair, and the chair was fast to a wheel, and thereupon sat King Arthur in the richest cloth of gold that might be made. And the King thought there was under him, far from him, an hideous deep black water, and therein was all manner of serpents, and worms, and wild beasts, foul and horrible. And suddenly the King thought that the wheel turned upside down, and he fell among the serpents, and every beast took him by a limb. And then the King cried as he lay in his bed, "Help, help!"

And then knights, squires, and yeomen awaked the King, and then he was so amazed that he wist[3] not where he was. And then so he awaked until it was nigh day, and then he fell on slumbering again, not sleeping nor thoroughly waking. So the King seemed[4] verily that there came Sir Gawain unto him with a number of fair ladies with him. So when King Arthur saw him, he said, "Welcome, my sister's son. I weened ye had been dead. And now I see thee on-live, much am I beholden

**Literary Movement:** King Arthur was a common subject of medieval romances.

**Literary Movement:** Strange, unnatural beasts such as serpents are often depicted in medieval romances.

---

1. **him seemed:** It seemed to him.
2. **chafflet:** Platform.
3. **wist:** Knew.
4. **the King seemed:** It seemed to the King.

unto Almighty Jesu. Ah, fair nephew and my sister's son, what been these ladies that hither be come with you?"

**Literary Movement:** In medieval romances chivalrous knights fought for and protected women.

"Sir," said Sir Gawain, "all these be ladies for whom I have foughten for when I was man living. And all these are those that I did battle for in righteous quarrels, and God hath given them that grace, at their great prayer, because I did battle for them for their right, that they should bring me hither unto you. Thus much hath given me leave God, for to warn you of your death. For and ye fight as tomorn[5] with Sir Mordred, as ye both have assigned, doubt ye not ye must be slain, and the most party of your people on both parties. And for the great grace and goodness that Almighty Jesu hath unto you, and for pity of you and many more other good men there shall be slain, God hath sent me to you of his special grace to give you warning that in no wise ye do battle as tomorn, but that ye take a treaty for a month from today. And proffer you largely,[6] so that tomorn ye put in a delay. For within a month shall come Sir Lancelot with all his noble knights and rescue you worshipfully and slay Sir Mordred and all that ever will hold with him."

Then Sir Gawain and all the ladies vanished. And anon the King called upon his knights, squires, and yeomen, and charged them wightly[7] to fetch his noble lords and wise bishops unto him. And when they were come the King told them of his avision,[8] that Sir Gawain had told him and warned him that, and he fought on the morn, he should be slain. Then the King commanded Sir Lucan the Butler and his brother Sir Bedivere the Bold, with two bishops with them, and charged them in any wise to take a treaty for a month from today with Sir Mordred. "And spare not: proffer him lands and goods as much as ye think reasonable."

So then they departed and came to Sir Mordred where he had a grim host of an hundred thousand, and there they entreated Sir Mordred long time. And at the last Sir Mordred was agreed for to have Cornwall and Kent by King Arthur's days, and after that, all England, after the days of King Arthur.

---

**5. and . . . tomorn:** If you fight tomorrow.
**6. proffer you largely:** Make generous offers.
**7. wightly:** Quickly.
**8. avision:** Dream.

Then were they condescended[9] that King Arthur and Sir Mordred should meet betwixt both their hosts, and each of them should bring fourteen persons. And so they came with this word unto Arthur. Then said he, "I am glad that this is done," and so he went into the field.

And when King Arthur should depart, he warned all his host that, and they see any sword drawn, "Look ye come on fiercely and slay that traitor Sir Mordred, for I in no wise trust him." In like wise Sir Mordred warned his host that "And ye see any manner of sword drawn, look that ye come on fiercely, and so slay all that ever before you standeth, for in no wise I will not trust for this treaty." And in the same wise said Sir Mordred unto his host, "For I know well my father will be avenged upon me."

And so they met as their pointment[10] was and were agreed and accorded thoroughly. And wine was fetched and they drank together. Right so came an adder out of a little heathbush, and it stung a knight in the foot. And so when the knight felt him so stung, he looked down and saw the adder. And anon he drew his sword to slay the adder, and thought none other harm. And when the host on both parties saw that sword drawn, then they blew beams,[11] trumpets, and horns, and shouted grimly. And so both hosts dressed them together. And King Arthur took his horse and said, "Alas, this unhappy day!" and so rode to his party, and Sir Mordred in like wise.

And never since was there never seen a more dolefuller battle in no Christian land, for there was but rushing and riding, lunging and striking; and many a grim word was there spoken of either to other, and many a deadly stroke. But ever King Arthur rode throughout the battle[12] of Sir Mordred many times and did full nobly, as a noble king should do, and at all times he fainted never. And Sir Modred did his devoir that day and put himself in great peril.

And thus they fought all the long day, and never stinted[13] till the noble knights were laid to the cold earth. And ever

**Historical Context:** Bravery and skill in battle were important aspects of chivalry.

---

**9. condescended:** Agreed.
**10. pointment:** Arrangement.
**11. beams:** A type of trumpet.
**12. battle:** Battalion.
**13. stinted:** Stopped.

**THE NINE HEROES TAPESTRIES. CHRISTIAN HEROES: ARTHUR (Detail)**
*Probably Nicolas Bataille, Paris*
The Metropolitan Museum of Art

they fought still till it was near night, and by then was there an hundred thousand laid dead upon the down. Then was King Arthur wood-wroth[14] out of measure when he saw his people so slain from him. And so he looked about him and could see no more of all his host, and good knights left no more on-live, but two knights: the t'one was Sir Lucan the Butler and the other his brother Sir Bedivere. And yet they were full sore wounded.

"Jesu, mercy," said the King, "where are all my noble knights become? Alas that ever I should see this doleful day! For now," said King Arthur, "I am come to mine end. But would to God," said he, "that I wist now where were that traitor Sir Mordred that has caused all this mischief."

Then King Arthur looked about and was ware where stood Sir Mordred leaning upon his sword among a great heap of dead men.

"Now give me my spear," said King Arthur unto Sir Lucan, "for yonder I have espied the traitor that all this woe hath wrought."

"Sir, let him be," said Sir Lucan, "for he is unhappy. And if ye pass this unhappy day ye shall be right well revenged upon him. And, good lord, remember ye of your night's dream, and what the spirit of Sir Gawain told you tonight, and yet God of his great goodness hath preserved you hitherto. And for God's sake, my lord, leave off by this, for, blessed be God, ye have won the field: for yet we been here three on-live, and with Sir Mordred is not one on-live. And therefore if ye leave off now, this wicked day of destiny is past."

"Now, tide[15] me death, tide me life," said the King, "now I see him yonder alone, he shall never escape mine hands. For at a better avail shall I never have him."

"God speed you well!" said Sir Bedivere.

Then the King got his spear in both his hands and ran toward Sir Mordred, crying and saying, "Traitor, now is thy deathday come!"

And when Sir Mordred saw King Arthur he ran until him with his sword drawn in his hand, and there King Arthur smote Sir Mordred under the shield, with a thrust of his spear, throughout the body more than a fathom. And when

**Writer's Technique:** King Arthur is motivated by his love for his slain knights to confront Mordred.

**Historical Context:** Sir Lucan demonstrates his loyalty to King Arthur. Loyalty to one's king or overlord was an important medieval virtue.

---

**14. wood-wroth:** Wild with rage.
**15. tide:** Befall.

Sir Mordred felt that he had his death's wound, he thrust himself with the might that he had up to the burr[16] of King Arthur's spear, and right so he smote his father King Arthur with his sword holden in both his hands, upon the side of the head, that the sword pierced the helmet and the casing of the brain. And therewith Sir Mordred dashed down stark dead to the earth.

And noble King Arthur fell in a swough to the earth, and there he swooned oftentimes, and Sir Lucan and Sir Bedivere ofttimes heaved him up. And so, weakly betwixt them, they led him to a little chapel not far from the seaside, and when the King was there, him thought him reasonably eased. Then heard they people cry in the field. "Now go thou, Sir Lucan," said the King, "and do me to wit[17] what betokens that noise in the field."

So Sir Lucan departed, for he was grievously wounded in many places. And so as he walked he saw and harkened by the moonlight how that pillagers and robbers were come into the field to pill and to rob many a full noble knight of brooches and bracelets and of many a good ring and many a rich jewel. And who that were not dead all out there they slew them for their harness and their riches. When Sir Lucan understood this work, he came to the King as soon as he might and told him all what he had heard and seen. "Therefore by my read,"[18] said Sir Lucan, "it is best that we bring you to some town."

"I would it were so," said the King, "but I may not stand, my head works so. Ah, Sir Lancelot," said King Arthur, "this day have I sore missed thee. And alas that ever I was against thee, for now have I my death, whereof Sir Gawain me warned in my dream."

Then Sir Lucan took up the King the t'one party[19] and Sir Bedivere the other party; and in the lifting up the King swooned and in the lifting Sir Lucan fell in a swoon that part of his guts fell out of his body, and therewith the noble knight's heart burst. And when the King awoke he beheld Sir Lucan how he lay foaming at the mouth and part of his guts lay at his feet.

---

**16. burr:** Hand guard.
**17. me to wit:** Let me know.
**18. read:** Advice.
**19. party:** Side.

"Alas," said the King, "this is to me a full heavy sight to see this noble duke so die for my sake, for he would have helped me that had more need of help than I. Alas that he would not complain him for his heart was so set to help me. Now Jesu have mercy upon his soul."

Then Sir Bedivere wept for the death of his brother.

"Now leave this mourning and weeping, gentle knight," said the King, "for all this will not avail me. For wit thou well, and I might live myself, the death of Sir Lucan would grieve me evermore. But my time passeth on fast," said the King. "Therefore," said King Arthur unto Sir Bedivere, "take thou here Excalibur my good sword and go with it to yonder water's side; and when thou comest there I charge thee throw my sword in that water and come again and tell me what thou sawest there."

"My lord," said Sir Bedivere, "your commandment shall be done, and I shall lightly[20] bring you word again."

So Sir Bedivere departed. And by the way he beheld that noble sword, that the pommel and the haft[21] was all precious stones. And then he said to himself, "If I throw this rich sword in the water, thereof shall never come good, but harm and loss." And then Sir Bedivere hid Excalibur under a tree. And so, as soon as he might, he came again unto the King and said he had been at the water and had thrown the sword into the water.

"What saw thou there?" said the King.

"Sir," he said, "I saw nothing but waves and winds."

"That is untruly said of thee," said the King. "And therefore go thou lightly again and do my commandment; as thou art to me loved and dear, spare not, but throw it in."

Then Sir Bedivere returned again and took the sword in his hand. And yet him thought sin and shame to throw away that noble sword. And so eft[22] he hid the sword and returned again and told the King that he had been at the water and done his commandment.

"What sawest thou there?" said the King.

"Sir," he said, "I saw nothing but waters wap and waves wan."[23]

**Writer's Technique:**
Notice the dilemma here. A knight's first duty is to obey his king, but Sir Bedivere sees the value of the sword and cannot bring himself to carry out King Arthur's command.

---

**20. lightly:** Quickly.
**21. pommel . . . haft:** Hilt and hand guard.
**22. eft:** Again.
**23. waters . . . wan:** Waters lap and waves grow dark.

"Ah, traitor unto me and untrue," said King Arthur, "now hast thou betrayed me twice. Who would have weened that thou that has been to me so loved and dear, and thou art named a noble knight, and would betray me for the riches of this sword. But now go again lightly, for thy long tarrying putteth me in great jeopardy of my life, for I have taken cold. And but if thou do now as I bid thee, if ever I may see thee I shall slay thee mine own hands, for thou wouldest for my rich sword see me dead."

**Literary Movement:** Magic was an important element of medieval romances.

Then Sir Bedivere departed and went to the sword and lightly took it up, and so he went to the water's side; and there he bound the girdle about the hilts, and threw the sword as far into the water as he might. And there came an arm and an hand above the water and took it and clutched it, and shook it thrice and brandished; and then vanished away the hand with the sword into the water. So Sir Bedivere came again to the King and told him what he saw.

"Alas," said the King, "help me hence, for I dread me I have tarried overlong."

Then Sir Bedivere took the King upon his back and so went with him to that water's side. And when they were at the water's side, even fast[24] by the bank floated a little barge with many fair ladies in it; and among them all was a queen; and all they had black hoods, and all they wept and shrieked when they saw King Arthur.

"Now put me into that barge," said the King; and so he did softly. And there received him three ladies with great mourning, and so they set them down. And in one of their laps King Arthur laid his head, and then the queen said, "Ah, my dear brother, why have ye tarried so long from me? Alas, this wound on your head hath caught overmuch cold." And anon they rowed fromward the land, and Sir Bedivere beheld all tho ladies go froward him.

Then Sir Bedivere cried and said, "Ah, my lord Arthur, what shall become of me, now ye go from me and leave me here alone among mine enemies?"

"Comfort thyself," said the King, "and do as well as thou mayest, for in me is no trust for to trust in. For I must into the vale of Avilion[25] to heal me of my grievous wound. And if thou hear nevermore of me, pray for my soul."

---

**24. fast:** Close.
**25. Avilion:** A legendary island.

But ever the queen and ladies wept and shrieked, that it was pity to hear. And as soon as Sir Bedivere had lost sight of the barge he wept and wailed, and so took the forest and went all that night.

And in the morning he was ware, betwixt two bare woods, of a chapel and an hermitage. Then was Sir Bedivere glad, and thither he went, and when he came into the chapel he saw where lay an hermit groveling on all fours, close thereby a tomb was new dug. When the hermit saw Sir Bedivere he knew him well, for he was but little tofore Bishop of Canterbury, that Sir Mordred put to flight.

"Sir," said Sir Bedivere, "what man is there here interred that you pray so fast for?"

"Fair son," said the hermit. "I wot not verily but by guessing. But this same night, at midnight, here came a number of ladies and brought here a dead corpse and prayed me to inter him. And here they offered an hundred tapers, and gave me a thousand gold coins."

"Alas," said Sir Bedivere, "that was my lord King Arthur, which lieth here buried in this chapel."

Then Sir Bedivere swooned, and when he awoke he prayed the hermit that he might abide with him still, there to live with fasting and prayers:

"For from hence will I never go," said Sir Bedivere, "by my will, but all the days of my life here to pray for my lord Arthur."

"Sir, ye are welcome to me," said the hermit, "for I know you better than ye think that I do: for ye are Sir Bedivere the Bold, and the full noble duke Sir Lucan the Butler was your brother."

Then Sir Bedivere told the hermit all as you have heard tofore, and so he stayed with the hermit that was beforehand Bishop of Canterbury. And there Sir Bedivere put upon him poor clothes, and served the hermit full lowly in fasting and in prayers.

Thus of Arthur I find no more written in books that been authorized, neither more of the very certainty of his death heard I nor read, but thus was he led away in a ship wherein were three queens; that one was King Arthur's sister, Queen Morgan le Fay, the other was the Queen of North Galis, and the third was the Queen of the Waste Lands.

Now more of the death of King Arthur could I never find, but that these ladies brought him to his grave, and such one was interred there which the hermit bare witness that was

**Writer's Technique:** Sir Bedivere's request conveys his undying devotion to King Arthur.

**Writer's Technique:** Malory's reference to the "books that been authorized" makes his account seem factual.

once Bishop of Canterbury. But yet the hermit knew not in certain that he was verily the body of King Arthur; for this tale Sir Bedivere, a knight of the Table Round, made it to be written.

Yet some men say in many parts of England that King Arthur is not dead, but carried by the will of our Lord Jesu into another place; and men say that he shall come again, and he shall win the Holy Cross. Yet I will not say that it shall be so, but rather I would say: here in this world he changed his life. And many men say that there is written upon the tomb this:

HIC IACET ARTHURUS, REX
QUONDAM, REXQUE FUTURUS[26]

---

**26. Hic . . . futurus:** Here lies Arthur, who was once king and king will be again.

---

Sir Thomas Malory 1405[?]–1471 wrote *Morte d'Arthur* by compiling and giving order to a collection of French, English, and Latin tales about King Arthur and the Knights of the Round Table. The work was first published in 1485 by William Caxton, after Caxton had established the first printing press in England.

Although Malory seems to have stayed on the right side of the law while young, his arrest in 1451 for damaging a monastery in Lincolnshire signalled the beginning of his lifelong battles with authority. He was also brought up on charges of breaking out of jail, twice for looting the Abbey of Coombe, and for extortion—as well as various other crimes. He denied all the charges against him, but was convicted and jailed nonetheless. Malory spent most of his later years in prison, probably because he supported the Lancasters while the Yorkists ruled England during the War of the Roses. In fact, it was in prison that he wrote *Morte d' Arthur.*

Malory lived in a wild, unruly time, torn by the strife of the War of the Roses. Harassed by those in power, perhaps he defended taking the law into his own hands as a political necessity. Scholars have suggested, however, that he had a fierce temper and was not against confrontations. Malory most likely died in jail, after King Edward IV, a Yorkist, expressly barred him from two amnesties he allowed the other Lancaster supporters.

## THINKING ABOUT THE SELECTION

### Recalling

1. What warning does King Arthur receive in his dream?
2. (a) What instruction does Arthur give his men before he leaves to meet Mordred? (b) What does Mordred tell his men?
3. (a) How does Arthur slay Mordred? (b) What does Mordred do just before he dies?
4. (a) What does Sir Lucan observe when Arthur sends him back to the battlefield? (b) How does Sir Lucan die?
5. (a) What does Sir Bedivere learn on the morning after the battle? (b) What does he decide to do as a result of his discovery?

### Interpreting

6. (a) How would you characterize Arthur? (b) How would you characterize Mordred?
7. What do you think are Sir Bedivere's reasons for twice failing to obey Arthur's request to throw Excalibur in the water?
8. What is ironic, or unexpected, about the way the battle begins?
9. How does the ending add to the mysterious, magical quality of the tale?

### Applying

10. Why do you think the legend of King Arthur has retained its popularity for so long?

## ANALYZING LITERATURE

### Recognizing Legends

Legends are anonymous traditional stories popularly believed to be based on history. Generally, legends reflect the attitudes and values of the society that created them, and the heroes of legends usually possess qualities that the people of that society consider admirable. Legends also often involve evil characters who possess qualities considered undesirable.

1. What qualities does King Arthur possess that would have been considered admirable during medieval times?

2. What qualities does Mordred possess that would be considered undesirable?

## CRITICAL THINKING AND READING

### Recognizing Elements of Fantasy

Although legends are popularly believed to be based on history, they often involve characters with superhuman powers and contain fantastic events.

1. What incident occurs in this selection that is clearly an example of fantasy?
2. What makes the women who come for Arthur at the end of the selection seem magical and mysterious?

## UNDERSTANDING LANGUAGE

### Appreciating Word Origins

As a result of the Norman conquest, many French words were introduced into the English language. For example, Malory uses the word *quarrel,* which comes from the French word *querele,* meaning "complaint."

The words below are of French origin. Use your dictionary to find the French word and meaning from which each word comes.

1. vanish
2. preserve
3. rescue
4. depart

## THINKING AND WRITING

### Writing About Character

Write an essay in which you discuss what this excerpt reveals about King Arthur's character. Reread the selection, focusing on Arthur's comments and behavior. Also take note of how the other characters react to him. When you write your essay, use evidence from the selection to support your argument. When you finish writing, revise and proofread your essay.

# GUIDE FOR INTERPRETING

## English And Scottish Folk Ballads

Long before most people in Britain could read or write, they were familiar with the stories told in ballads. A **ballad** is a narrative poem, usually brief, that is meant to be sung. When the writer is unknown, the ballad is called a **folk** ballad, or sometimes a **popular** or **traditional** ballad. Such ballads as "Barbara Allan" have been recited, chanted, or sung from their earliest appearance down to the present day.

No one knows when the first folk ballads appeared in Britain, but it was probably during the twelfth century. Since the ballads were unwritten, they were passed along orally for many centuries. Most of the earliest ballads we know about probably date from the fifteenth century. Even at that time, no one paid much attention to them as literature. Not until 1765, with the publication of Bishop Thomas Percy's *Reliques of Ancient English Poetry,* did ballads come to be recognized as a fascinating part of Britain's literary heritage.

Sir Walter Scott, the author of *Ivanhoe,* was one of a number of famous writers whose interest in old ballads was sparked by Percy's *Reliques.* Scott often traveled to the Scottish-English border region to collect material on the subject. His *Minstrelsy of the Scottish Border,* published in 1803, is a pioneer work of scholarship on the background and variations of Scottish ballads.

The four ballads in this unit originated in the wild, rugged border country between England and Scotland. Their language is the Scots dialect of English. As they were passed along from person to person, place to place, and generation to generation, these ballads often acquired new words and new verses. There is no such thing as a standard version of a folk ballad, because every balladeer feels free to make alterations. Literally hundreds of versions of "Barbara Allan" have appeared in print.

Many ballads handed down to us in English have counterparts in other languages. This is because the incidents they describe are shared by much of European folklore. Both "Barbara Allan" and "The Twa Corbies" are found in other languages, for example, as is "Sir Patrick Spens," although not in its present form.

Folk ballads, with their familiar melodies, are truly songs of the people. Later writers, including Sir Walter Scott, produced literary ballads in imitation of the traditional ones. But few literary ballads have had the power of the old folk ballads to capture and hold the imagination.

# Sir Patrick Spens; Get Up and Bar the Door; The Twa Corbies; Barbara Allan

**Folk Ballad.** It is not surprising that folk ballads appeared on the rugged English-Scottish border. Folk ballads are typically found in areas where a formal, written literature has yet to develop, or where people's lives do not permit books and reading.

A folk ballad usually presents a single dramatic episode. It is told impersonally, through action and dialogue, with very little characterization, description, or motivation. The story seems to be simple and direct, yet because it often begins in the middle, lacks transitions, and skips over incidents without explanation, it can convey an air of mystery. Ballads deal with many subjects: adventure, love, jealousy, heroism, disaster, revenge. A few folk ballads are humorous.

Most ballads have quatrains, or four-line stanzas, in which the second and fourth lines rhyme. Often, but not always, there are eight syllables in the first and third lines and six syllables in the second and fourth lines. Ballads frequently have a refrain—a regularly repeated phrase or line at the end of a stanza, or sometimes a whole separate stanza. The general effect is musical, as you would expect in poems meant to be sung.

Most popular music has a brief life span. Songs from a few years ago tend to sound dated and sentimental to listeners today. Yet folk ballads have been sung for centuries and in some places are still performed for appreciative audiences. Why? What is it that can make a song so enduring? Freewrite about the qualities that you think make a song become a long-lasting popular classic.

One of the most enduring modern ballads is "Taxi," Harry Chapin's haunting lament of lost love and opportunity. The story begins with the chance meeting between a down-and-out taxi driver and his seemingly successful former girl friend:

> It was raining one night in 'Frisco.
> I needed one more fare to make my night.
> A lady up ahead waved to flag me down
> She got in at the light.

"Through the too many miles and the too little smiles," the narrator remembers their dreams. By the end of the song, he realizes that neither he nor his former love are happy. What other modern ballads do you know that are meant to be sung?

# Sir Patrick Spens

*This version of "Sir Patrick Spens" is in the original
Middle English.*

The king sits in Dumferling[1] toune,
    Drinking the blude-reid wine:
"O whar will I get guid sailor,
    To sail this schip of mine?"

5  Up and spak an eldern knicht,
    Sat at the kings richt kne:
"Sir Patrick Spens is the best sailor,
    That sails upon the se."

The king has written a braid letter,
10    And signd it wi his hand,
And sent it to Sir Patrick Spens,
    Was walking on the sand.

The first line that Sir Patrick red,
    A loud lauch lauchèd he;
15  The next line that Sir Patrick red,
    The teir blinded his ee.

"O wha is this has don this deid,
    This ill deid don to me,
To send me out this time o' the yeir,
20    To sail upon the se!

"Mak hast, mak hast, my mirry men all
    Our guid schip sails the morne:"
"O say na sae, my master deir,
    For I feir a deadlie storme.

25  "Late, late yestreen I saw the new moone,
    Wi the auld moone in hir arme,
And I feir, I feir, my deir master,
    That we will cum to harme."

O our Scots nobles wer richt laith
30    To weet their cork-heild schoone,
Bot lang owre a' the play wer playd,
    Thair hats they swam aboone.

**MEDIEVAL BARON DINING; FROM BREVIARIUM GRIMARI,
15TH CENTURY**
*The Bettmann Archive*

---

**1. Dumferling:** A town in Scotland near
Edinburgh.

# Sir Patrick Spens

*This version of "Sir Patrick Spens" is in modern English.*

The king sits in Dumferling town,
    Drinking the blood-red wine:
"O where will I get a good sailor,
    To sail this ship of mine?"

5  Up and spoke an ancient knight,
    Sat at the king's right knee:
"Sir Patrick Spens is the best sailor,
    That sails upon the sea."

The king has written a broad letter,
10    And signed it with his hand,
And sent it to Sir Patrick Spens,
    Was walking on the sand.

The first line that Sir Patrick read,
    A loud laugh laughed he;
15 The next line that Sir Patrick read,
    The tear blinded his eye.

"O who is this has done this deed,
    This ill deed done to me,
To send me out this time of the year,
20    To sail upon the sea!

"Make haste, make haste, my merry men all
    Our good ship sails the morn:"
"O say not so, my master dear,
    For I fear a deadly storm.

25 "Late, late yesterday evening I saw the new moon,
    With the old moon in her arm,
And I fear, I fear, my dear master,
    That we will come to harm."

O our Scots nobles were right loath
30    To wet their cork-heeled shoes,
But long before the play were played,
    Their hats they swam above.

O lang, lang may their ladies sit,
    Wi thair fans to their hand,
35  Or eir they se Sir Patrick Spens
    Cum sailing to the land.

O lang, lang may the ladies stand,
    Wi thair gold kems in their hair,
Waiting for thar ain deir lords,
40      For they'll se thame na mair.

Half owre, half owre to Aberdour,[1]
    It's fiftie fadom deip,
And thair lies guid Sir Patrick Spens,
    Wi the Scots lords at his feit.

---

1. **Aberdour:** A town near Edinburgh.

---

## THINKING ABOUT THE SELECTION
### Recalling

1. What problem does the king face at the beginning of the ballad?
2. From whom does the king get the idea of having Sir Patrick Spens sail for him?
3. How does Sir Patrick Spens react to the king's letter?

### Interpreting

4. Why do you think the king's wine is described as "blood-red"?
5. Why does Sir Patrick Spens view the king's request as an "ill deed"?
6. In the seventh stanza, why does the sailor think the voyage is ill-fated?
7. (a) What happens to the Scots lords who dislike the idea of getting their "cork-heeled shoes" wet? (b) How do you know? (c) How is this outcome ironic?
8. In what way does Sir Patrick Spens seem to embody Medieval ideals of duty?

### Applying

9. Sir Patrick Spens does his duty despite serious—and his well-founded—misgivings. What might he have done to avoid sailing? How wise would such a course of action have been?

## ANALYZING LITERATURE
### Understanding Folk Ballads

"Sir Patrick Spens," like most folk ballads, is short and deals with a single episode. Abrupt transitions and the absence of characterization and description force the audience to make assumptions about characters, places, and events. Dialogue moves the story along.

1. (a) How many characters are directly quoted in the poem? (b) Who are they?
2. What are some of the missing details in "Sir Patrick Spens" that, if included, would make the ballad easier to understand?

O long, long may their ladies sit,
    With their fans into their hand,
35  Or ever they see Sir Patrick Spens
    Come sailing to the land.

O long, long may the ladies stand,
    With their gold combs in their hair,
Waiting for their own dear lords,
40    For they'll see them no more.

Halfway over, halfway over to Aberdour,
    It's fifty fathoms deep
And there lies good Sir Patrick Spens,
    With the Scots lords at his feet.

---

## UNDERSTANDING LANGUAGE
### Recognizing Language Change

A centuries-old ballad like "Sir Patrick Spens" looks different today from how it looked when it first appeared in print. Not only is the old Scots dialect unfamiliar to most modern readers, so is much of the spelling and vocabulary of the standard English of that day.

1. What are five words in the first stanza whose spellings have changed over the years?

2. In the fifth stanza, note that the *ei* spelling has changed in two different ways. What are the two ways?
3. How is each of the following words written in modern English?
   a. knicht      d. owre
   b. lauch      e. kems
   c. schoone

---

**Commentary**

Many serious ballads reveal that love and bravery, however great, are not enough to prevent doom. In humorous ballads, in contrast, people use wit to successfully counter evil and misfortune. Sometimes humorous ballads are built around riddles as a device to outwit an opponent and defuse a dangerous situation. "The Riddle Song" illustrates this. Before you read the last stanza, see if you can guess the answer to the riddles.

1. I gave my love a cherry that has no stones,
   I gave my love a chicken that has no bones,
   I gave my love a ring that has no end.
   I gave my love a baby that's no cryen.
2. How can there be a cherry that has no stones?
   How can there be a chicken that has no bones?
   How can there be a ring that has no end?
   How can there be a baby that's no cryen?
3. A cherry when it's blooming, it has no stones,
   A chicken when it's pipping [hatching], it has no bones,
   A ring when it's rolling, it has no end,
   A baby when it's sleeping, it's no cryen.

# Get Up and Bar the Door

It fell about the Martinmas[1] time,
    And a gay time it was then,
When our goodwife got puddings to make,
    She's boild them in the pan.

5  The wind sae cauld blew south and north.
    And blew into the floor;
Quoth our goodman to our goodwife,
    "Gae out and bar the door."

"My hand is in my hussyfskap,[2]
10     Goodman, as ye may see;
An it should nae be barrd this hundred year,
    It's no be barrd for me."[3]

They made a paction[4] tween them twa.
    They made it firm and sure.
15  That the first word whaeer shoud speak,
    Shoud rise and bar the door.

Then by there came two gentlemen,
    At twelve o'clock at night,
And they could neither see house nor hall,
20     Nor coal nor candlelight.

"Now whether is this a rich man's house,
    Or whether it is a poor?"
But neer a word wad ane o' them[5] speak,
    For barring of the door.

25  And first they[6] ate the white puddings,
    And then they ate the black:
Tho muckle[7] thought the goodwife to hersel,
    Yet neer a word she spake.

Then said the one unto the other,
30     "Here, man, take ye my knife;
Do ye tak aff the auld man's beard,
    And I'll kiss the goodwife."

1. **Martinmas time:** November 11.

2. **hussyfskap:** Household duties.

3. **"it should . . . me":** It will not be barred in a hundred years if it has to be barred by me."
4. **paction:** Agreement.

5. **them:** The man and his wife.

6. **they:** The strangers.

7. **muckle:** Much.

"But there's nae water in the house,
    And what shall we do than?"
35 "What ails ye at the pudding broo,[8]
    That boils into[9] the pan?"

O up then started our goodman,
    An angry man was he:
"Will ye kiss my wife before my een,
40    And scad[10] me wi pudding bree?"[11]

Then up and started our goodwife,
    Gied three skips on the floor:
"Goodman, you've spoken the foremost word;
    Get up and bar the door."

**8. "What . . . broo:**
"What's the matter with
pudding water?
**9. into:** In.

**10. scad:** Scald.
**11. bree:** Broth.

---

## THINKING ABOUT THE SELECTION
### Recalling

1. Why does the goodwife refuse to bar the door when her husband first asks?
2. What agreement do the husband and wife reach about barring the door?
3. To whom does the word *one* refer in line 29?
4. What do the two strangers plan to do to (a) the goodman? (b) the goodwife?
5. (a) Who wins the battle of wills between husband and wife? (b) How?

### Interpreting

6. Why does the goodman want the door barred?

7. When do the goodman and his wife first become aware of the presence of the strangers?
8. In lines 25–29, the goodwife is thinking to herself. What might she be thinking?
9. What do you think the stranger means when he suggests taking "aff the auld man's beard"?
10. What serious point does this humorous ballad make?

### Applying

11. Can people be hurt by stubbornness—their own or someone else's? Explain your answer.

# The Twa Corbies[1]

1. **Twa Corbies:** Two ravens.

As I was walking all alane,
I heard twa corbies making a mane.[2]
The tane unto the tither did say,
"Whar sall we gang and dine the day?"

2. **mane:** Moan.

5   "In behint yon auld fail dyke,[3]
I wot[4] there lies a new-slain knight;
And naebody kens[5] that he lies there
But his hawk, his hound, and his lady fair.

3. **fail dyke:** Bank of earth.
4. **wot:** know.
5. **kens:** knows.

"His hound is to the hunting gane,
10  His hawk to fetch the wild-fowl hame,
His lady's ta'en anither mate,
So we may mak our dinner sweet.

"Ye'll sit on his white hause-bane,[6]
And I'll pike out his bonny blue e'en;[7]
15  Wi' ae lock o' his gowden hair
We'll theek[8] our nest when it grows bare.

6. **hause-bane:** Neck-bone.
7. **e'en:** Eyes.

8. **theek:** Thatch.

"Mony a one for him maks mane,
But nane sall ken whar he is gane.
O'er his white banes, when they are bare,
20  The wind sall blaw for evermair."

---

## THINKING ABOUT THE SELECTION

### Recalling

1. (a) Where is the knight lying? (b) In what condition is he?
2. Who besides the ravens knows what has happened to the knight?
3. Why is the knight's lady not interested in his fate?
4. What does one of the ravens suggest doing with the knight's golden hair?

### Interpreting

5. (a) How would you describe the tone of the ballad? (b) How does the tone add to the ballad's impact?
6. What effect would be lost if the incident were described by a human speaker rather than as a conversation between two ravens?

### Applying

7. Stories told from the point of view of an animal are unusual but by no means rare. What other story or stories do you recall that present the viewpoint of an animal?

# Barbara Allan

It was in and about the Martinmas time,[1]
    When the green leaves were a-fallin';
That Sir John Graeme in the West Country
    Fell in love with Barbara Allan.

5  He sent his man down through the town
    To the place where she was dwellin':
"O haste and come to my master dear,
    Gin[2] ye be Barbara Allan."

O slowly, slowly rase[3] she up,
10    To the place where he was lyin',
And when she drew the curtain by:
    "Young man, I think you're dyin'."

"O it's I'm sick, and very, very sick,
    And 'tis a' for Barbara Allan."
15  "O the better for me ye sal[4] never be,
    Though your heart's blood were a-spillin'.

"O dinna ye mind,[5] young man," said she,
    "When ye the cups were fillin',
That ye made the healths gae round and round,
20    And slighted Barbara Allan?"

He turned his face unto the wall,
    And death with him was dealin':
"Adieu, adieu, my dear friends all,
    And be kind of Barbara Allan."

25  And slowly, slowly rase she up,
    And slowly, slowly left him;
And sighing said she could not stay,
    Since death of life had reft[6] him.

She had not gane a mile but twa,[7]
30    When she heard the dead-bell knellin',
And every jow[8] that the dead-bell ga'ed[9]
    It cried, "Woe to Barbara Allan!"

"O mother, mother, make my bed,
    O make it soft and narrow:
35 Since my love died for me today,
    I'll die for him tomorrow."

---

**1. Martinmas time:** November 11.

**2. gin:** If.

**3. rase:** Rose.

**4. sal:** Shall.

**5. dinna ye mind:** Don't you remember.

**6. reft:** Deprived.

**7. not . . . twa:** Gone but two miles.

**8. jow:** Stroke.

**9. ga'ed:** Made.

**VERONICA VERONESE**
*Dante Gabriel Rossetti*
Delaware Art Museum

## THINKING ABOUT THE SELECTION

### Recalling

1. Why does Sir John Graeme want Barbara Allan to visit him?
2. What are Barbara Allan's first words when she sees Sir John?
3. According to Sir John, why is he "sick, and very, very sick"?
4. What reason does Barbara Allan give for acting unconcerned about his plight?
5. (a) When does Barbara Allan admit how she feels about Sir John? (b) How does she feel?

### Interpreting

6. (a) At what point does the ballad make you critical of Barbara Allan? (b) When does it make you sympathize with her?
7. One critic thinks that Sir John acts "like a spineless lover who gave up the ghost without a struggle." How would you answer that criticism?

### Applying

8. "Barbara Allan," like most ballads, leaves out things you might like to know. If you were adding a stanza to it (not necessarily at the end), what information would you include?

## CRITICAL THINKING AND READING

### Interpreting Symbols in Folk Ballads

Ballads are generally concise and direct, but sometimes their words and phrases function as symbols, thereby suggesting more than is immediately evident. A **symbol** is a word, person, or object that stands for something beyond itself. For example, the events in "Barbara Allan" (as well as in "Get Up and Bar the Door") occur "about the Martinmas time." Martinmas, a Christian festival on November 11 in honor of St. Martin, gradually came to symbolize both revelry and a warm, Indian-summer break in the autumn weather. A balladeer, by making use of a well-understood symbol like Martinmas, could add

meaning to a brief story without adding an excessive number of words.

1. The literal meaning of line 18, "When ye the cups were fillin'," is that Sir John was filling people's glasses with drinks. What is the symbolic meaning?
2. When Barbara Allan asks her mother to "make my bed . . . soft and narrow," in lines 33 and 34, what kind of "bed" is probably being symbolized?

## SPEAKING AND LISTENING

### Sharing Folk Ballads

"Barbara Allan" is one of the most widely recorded ballads in history, sometimes under the name "Bawbie Allan," "Bonnie Barbara Allan," or a similar title. It was brought to America in the earliest days of settlement. Today there are many recorded American versions as well as many English and Scottish versions of the song. As a class project, find at least five recorded versions of "Barbara Allan" and bring them to class. Play them all, noting the differences in wording from one recording to another. Decide which version the class prefers, and why.

Then look through some poetry anthologies or collections of ballads to find a ballad you like. Read it to the class. Try to give your reading the expression and intonation it would have been given by the balladeers who first sang it.

## THINKING AND WRITING

### Writing About a Folk Ballad

Choose one of the four folk ballads you have read. Reread it until you are sure you understand it fully. Make notes. Write the first draft of a composition, explaining the events in the ballad and noting any details that are implied but not directly stated. Point out the literary techniques —such as rhyme, dialogue, repetition—that heighten the dramatic effect of the ballad. Go over your first draft carefully, paying close attention to what you have written. Make any changes needed. Then write the final draft.

# GEOFFREY CHAUCER

## 1343[?]–1400

In his own lifetime Geoffrey Chaucer was considered the greatest English poet, and the centuries have not dimmed his reputation. With the single exception of William Shakespeare, no English writer has surpassed Chaucer's achievements. His unfinished master-piece, *The Canterbury Tales,* ranks as one of the world's finest works of literature. It also provides the best contemporary picture we have of fourteenth century England.

Although the exact date of Geoffrey Chaucer's birth is unknown, official records furnish many of the details of his active life as a public servant. His father was a well-to-do wine merchant in London, a man with sufficient influence to get young Geoffrey a position as a page in a household connected to that of King Edward III. As a page Chaucer's duties were humble, but the job provided him an opportunity to observe the ruling aristocracy, thus broaden-ing his knowledge of the various classes of society. In 1359, while serving in the English army in France, he was captured and held prisoner. The king paid a £16 (sixteen pounds) ransom for his release. In 1366 Chaucer married a lady-in-waiting to the queen. His marriage to Philippa de Roet lasted until her death in 1387. Scholars believe that Chaucer and his wife had three children. Their eldest, Thomas, was apparently ambitious and advanced higher in the world than his father had. Little is known about a son, probably called Lewis, and a daughter called Elizabeth.

Throughout his life Chaucer served in key government posi-tions. He was a controller of customs, a justice of the peace, and a one-term member of Parliament. He spent time in France and Italy on diplomatic missions, served as a supervisor of construction and repairs at Westminster Abbey and the Tower of London, and, late in life, acted as a subforester of the king's forest.

It might seem as if Chaucer would have had little time for writing, but in fact he wrote a great deal. He began producing poetry in his twenties and continued to do so for the rest of his life. Moreover, as he grew older, his literary works showed increasing depth and sophistication. In *Troilus and Criseyde,* a long poem dealing with themes from classical antiquity, he displays the dramatic flair and penetrating insight into human character that are his hallmarks. *The Canterbury Tales,* of which only 24 of the projected 124 tales were completed, shows Chaucer's absolute mastery of the storyteller's art.

Chaucer was the first person to be buried in what is now the Poet's Corner of Westminster Abbey.

# THE CANTERBURY TALES

People in medieval England sometimes made pilgrimages to sacred shrines. One such shrine was the cathedral in Canterbury, a town about fifty miles southeast of London, where archbishop Thomas à Becket had been murdered in 1170. The pilgrims often traveled in groups for the sake of companionship and protection. Chaucer's masterpiece, *The Canterbury Tales,* introduces a group of "nine and twenty" pilgrims, one of whom is Chaucer himself. These pilgrims appear first at the Tabard Inn in Southwark, near London, and later on the road to Canterbury.

*The Canterbury Tales* is a frame story; that is, a story that includes, or frames, another story or stories. Chaucer's frame is the pilgrimage, which he originally planned as a round trip but which remained incomplete at his death. Within this frame are the 24 individual stories the pilgrims tell. Chaucer did not invent the frame-story device. The same structural scheme had been used centuries earlier in *The Thousand and One Nights;* and Boccaccio, an Italian contemporary of Chaucer, used it in the *Decameron,* published about 1350.

Chaucer's handling of his pilgrimage frame is brilliant. The stories are mostly old familiar ones, superbly retold. Perhaps even more impressive than the stories are the storytellers. Chaucer's pilgrims, all of whom are introduced briefly in his Prologue, are memorable, vividly drawn individuals whose personalities are unique but whose character traits are universal. The pilgrims interact with one another. Clashes erupt among them as one pilgrim takes offense at another's tale and proceeds to retaliate with his or her own story.

By using the vehicle of the pilgrimage, Chaucer brings together people from the three main segments of medieval society—the church, the court, and the common people. His pilgrims are drawn from the class structure of feudalism (a knight, a squire, a reeve, for example) as well as from the more open classes in the emerging cities (a merchant, an innkeeper) and the powerful, hierarchical church of the time (a nun, a friar, a pardoner). Chaucer's interest in all these people and the shrewd but affectionate pictures he draws of them make them stand out in such distinct detail that they seem real, alive, and almost modern in their foibles and concerns.

Chaucer wrote only the "Tale of Melibeus" and the "Parson's Tale" in prose. With the exception of the "Monk's Tale," he told his story in either rhymed couplets or in stanzas of seven lines. His use of iambic pentameter couplets was a forerunner of the heroic couplets perfected in the 1700's by Alexander Pope.

# GUIDE FOR INTERPRETING

## The Prologue *from* The Canterbury Tales

Writer's Techniques

**Characterization.** Characterization refers to the personality of a fictional character as well as to the methods by which a writer creates that personality. Writers use a number of methods of characterization. Sometimes a writer makes a direct statement about a person: "Phil was hard to get to know, but those who knew him liked him." More often an author reveals character in an indirect way, through action, thoughts, and dialogue: "I should really study harder," Joan thought, laying the novel aside. "If I did, I could probably pass the test." Character can also be revealed through comments about the person by others in the story: "He's the kind of guy," said Linda, "who thinks football is the most important thing in life." A character's physical appearance and habits can help to reveal personality: "Doris wore the same threadbare dress she had worn to the party, but today she stood straighter, her shoulders squared." In defining a character, a writer will often combine these techniques to create a lifelike picture.

Writing

Jot down a few notes for a physical description of a fictional character. Choose a name for your character. Then note the following details: (1) facial features, (2) typical expression, (3) body structure, (4) typical posture, (5) clothing, (6) physical surroundings. Try to list details that not only describe the character but also help to reveal personality.

Primary Source

What was it like to live during the Middle Ages? In *The Life and Times of Chaucer,* the contemporary writer John Gardner creates a vivid picture.

> But in small things, too, we might be bothered, at least at first, by life in the Middle Ages—for instance, by Chaucer's annoying habit (or any other well-educated man's) of always reading to himself aloud, never silently, "barking on books," as one fifteenth-century playwright puts it; or, to speak of things less petty, we might be bothered by the general manners of the better class of people in the fourteenth century. They ate with their fingers, except for the occasional employment of a knife or soup spoon, and even the fingers of courtly ladies were not impeccably clean.

# The Prologue

Geoffrey Chaucer
translated by Nevill Coghill

Whan that Aprill with his shourës sootë
The droghte of March hath percëd to the rootë
And bathëd every veyne in swich licour
Of which vertu engendrëd is the flour,
5  Whan Zephirus eek with his sweetë breeth
Inspirëd hath in every holt and heeth
The tendrë croppës, and the yongë sonnë
Hath in the Ram his half cours y-ronnë,
And smalë fowelës maken melodyë
10  That slepen al the nyght with open eye,
So priketh hem Nature in hir corages,
Than longen folk to goon on pilgrymages,
And palmeres for to seken straungë strondës,
To fernë halwës kouthe in sondry londës.
15  And specially, from every shirës endë
Of Engelond, to Caunterbury they wendë,
The holy, blisful martir for to seke
That hem hath holpen whan that they were seekë.

When in April the sweet showers fall
And pierce the drought of March to the root, and all
The veins are bathed in liquor of such power
As brings about the engendering of the flower,
5  When also Zephyrus[1] with his sweet breath
Exhales an air in every grove and heath
Upon tender shoots, and the young sun
His half-course in the sign of the Ram[2] has run,
And the small fowl are making melody
10  That sleep away the night with open eye
(So nature pricks them and their heart engages)
Then people long to go on pilgrimages
And palmers[3] long to seek the stranger strands[4]
Of far-off saints, hallowed in sundry lands,
15  And specially, from every shire's end
In England, down to Canterbury they wend
To seek the holy blissful martyr,[5] quick
To give his help to them when they were sick.

1. **Zephyrus** (zef' ər əs): The west wind.

2. **Ram:** Aries, the first sign of the zodiac. The pilgrimage began on April 11, 1387.

3. **palmers:** Pilgrims who wore two crossed palm leaves to show that they had visited the Holy Land.

4. **strands:** Shores.

5. **martyr:** St. Thomas à Becket, the Archbishop of Canterbury, who was murdered in the Canterbury Cathedral in 1170.

**THE TABARD INN**
*Arthur Szyk for the Canterbury Tales*
The George Macy Companies

It happened in that season that one day
20  In Southwark[6], at The Tabard,[7] as I lay
Ready to go on pilgrimage and start
For Canterbury, most devout at heart,
At night there came into that hostelry
Some nine and twenty in a company
25  Of sundry folk happening then to fall
In fellowship, and they were pilgrims all
That towards Canterbury meant to ride.

**6. Southwark** (sut͡h′ ərk):
A suburb of London at the time.
**7. The Tabard** (ta′ bərd):
An inn.

The rooms and stables of the inn were wide;
They made us easy, all was of the best.
30 And shortly, when the sun had gone to rest,
By speaking to them all upon the trip
I soon was one of them in fellowship
And promised to rise early and take the way
To Canterbury, as you heard me say.
35      But nonetheless, while I have time and space,
Before my story takes a further pace,
It seems a reasonable thing to say
What their condition was, the full array
Of each of them, as it appeared to me
40 According to profession and degree,
And what apparel they were riding in;
And at a Knight I therefore will begin.
There was a *Knight,* a most distinguished man,
Who from the day on which he first began
45 To ride abroad had followed chivalry,
Truth, honor, generousness and courtesy.
He had done nobly in his sovereign's war
And ridden into battle, no man more,
As well in Christian as heathen places,
50 And ever honored for his noble graces.
     When we took Alexandria,[8] he was there.
He often sat at table in the chair
Of honor, above all nations, when in Prussia.
In Lithuania he had ridden, and Russia,
55 No Christian man so often, of his rank.
When, in Granada, Algeciras sank
Under assault, he had been there, and in
North Africa, raiding Benamarin;
In Anatolia he had been as well
60 And fought when Ayas and Attalia fell,
For all along the Mediterranean coast
He had embarked with many a noble host.
In fifteen mortal battles he had been
And jousted for our faith at Tramissene
65 Thrice in the lists, and always killed his man.
This same distinguished knight had led the van
Once with the Bey of Balat, doing work
For him against another heathen Turk;
He was of sovereign value in all eyes.
70 And though so much distinguished, he was wise
And in his bearing modest as a maid.
He never yet a boorish thing had said
In all his life to any, come what might;
He was a true, a perfect gentle-knight.

**8. Alexandria:** The site of one of the campaigns fought by Christians against groups who posed a threat to Europe during the fourteenth century. The place names that follow refer to other battlesites in these campaigns, or crusades.

75    Speaking of his equipment, he possessed
      Fine horses, but he was not gaily dressed.
      He wore a fustian[9] tunic stained and dark
      With smudges where his armor had left mark;
      Just home from service, he had joined our ranks
80    To do his pilgrimage and render thanks.
          He had his son with him, a fine young *Squire*,
      A lover and cadet, a lad of fire
      With locks as curly as if they had been pressed.
      He was some twenty years of age, I guessed.
85    In stature he was of a moderate length,
      With wonderful agility and strength.
      He'd seen some service with the cavalry
      In Flanders and Artois and Picardy[10]
      And had done valiantly in little space
90    Of time, in hope to win his lady's grace.
      He was embroidered like a meadow bright
      And full of freshest flowers, red and white.
      Singing he was, or fluting all the day;
      He was as fresh as is the month of May.
95    Short was his gown, the sleeves were long and wide;
      He knew the way to sit a horse and ride.
      He could make songs and poems and recite,
      Knew how to joust and dance, to draw and write.
      He loved so hotly that till dawn grew pale
100   He slept as little as a nightingale.
      Courteous he was, lowly and serviceable,
      And carved to serve his father at the table.
          There was a *Yeoman*[11] with him at his side,
      No other servant; so he chose to ride.
105   This Yeoman wore a coat and hood of green,
      And peacock-feathered arrows, bright and keen
      And neatly sheathed, hung at his belt the while
      —For he could dress his gear in yeoman style,
      His arrows never drooped their feathers low—
110   And in his hand he bore a mighty bow.
      His head was like a nut, his face was brown.
      He knew the whole of woodcraft up and down.
      A saucy brace[12] was on his arm to ward
      It from the bow-string, and a shield and sword
115   Hung at one side, and at the other slipped
      A jaunty dirk,[13] spear-sharp and well-equipped.
      A medal of St. Christopher[14] he wore
      Of shining silver on his breast, and bore
      A hunting-horn, well slung and burnished clean,
120   That dangled from a baldric[15] of bright green.
      He was a proper forester I guess.

**9. fustian** (fus' chən): A coarse cloth of cotton and linen.

**10. Flanders . . . Picardy:** Regions in Belgium and France.

**11. Yeoman** (yō' mən) *n*.: Attendant.

**12. brace:** Bracelet.

**13. dirk** *n*.: A short, straight dagger.

**14. St. Christopher:** The patron saint of forests and travelers.

**15. baldric** *n*.: A belt worn over one shoulder and across the chest to support a sword.

There also was a *Nun*, a Prioress.[16]
Her way of smiling very simple and coy.
Her greatest oath was only "By St. Loy!"[17]
125 And she was known as Madam Eglantyne.
And well she sang a service,[18] with a fine
Intoning through her nose, as was most seemly,
And she spoke daintily in French, extremely,
After the school of Stratford-atte-Bowe;[19]
130 French in the Paris style she did not know.
At meat her manners were well taught withal;
No morsel from her lips did she let fall,
Nor dipped her fingers in the sauce too deep;
But she could carry a morsel up and keep
135 The smallest drop from falling on her breast.
For courtliness she had a special zest,
And she would wipe her upper lip so clean
That not a trace of grease was to be seen
Upon the cup when she had drunk; to eat,
140 She reached a hand sedately for the meat.
She certainly was very entertaining,
Pleasant and friendly in her ways, and straining
To counterfeit a courtly kind of grace,
A stately bearing fitting to her place,
145 And to seem dignified in all her dealings.
As for her sympathies and tender feelings,
She was so charitably solicitous
She used to weep if she but saw a mouse
Caught in a trap, if it were dead or bleeding.
150 And she had little dogs she would be feeding
With roasted flesh, or milk, or fine white bread.
And bitterly she wept if one were dead
Or someone took a stick and made it smart;
She was all sentiment and tender heart.
155 Her veil was gathered in a seemly way,
Her nose was elegant, her eyes glass-gray;
Her mouth was very small, but soft and red,
Her forehead, certainly, was fair of spread,
Almost a span[20] across the brows, I own;
160 She was indeed by no means undergrown.
Her cloak, I noticed, had a graceful charm.
She wore a coral trinket on her arm,
A set of beads, the gaudies[21] tricked in green,
Whence hung a golden brooch of brightest sheen
165 On which there first was graven a crowned A,
And lower, *Amor vincit omnia.*[22]
    Another *Nun*, the chaplain at her cell,
Was riding with her, and *three Priests* as well.

**16. Prioress** *n.*: In an abbey, the nun ranking just below the abbess.
**17. St. Loy:** St. Eligius, patron saint of goldsmiths and courtiers.
**18. service:** Daily prayer.

**19. Stratford-atte-Bowe:** A nunnery near London.

**THE YEOMAN**
*Arthur Szyk for the Canterbury Tales*
The George Macy Companies

**20. span:** Nine inches.

**21. gaudies:** Large green beads that marked certain prayers on a set of prayer beads.
**22. *Amor vincit omnia*** (ä môr′ wink′ it ôm′ nē ä): "Love conquers all" (Latin).

A *Monk* there was, one of the finest sort
170 Who rode the country; hunting was his sport.
A manly man, to be an Abbot able;
Many a dainty horse he had in stable.
His bridle, when he rode, a man might hear
Jingling in a whistling wind as clear,
175 Aye, and as loud as does the chapel bell
Where my lord Monk was Prior of the cell.
The Rule of good St. Benet or St. Maur[23]
As old and strict he tended to ignore;
He let go by the things of yesterday
180 And took the modern world's more spacious way.
He did not rate that text at a plucked hen
Which says that hunters are not holy men
And that a monk uncloistered is a mere
Fish out of water, flapping on the pier,
185 That is to say a monk out of his cloister.
That was a text he held not worth an oyster;
And I agreed and said his views were sound;
Was he to study till his head went round
Poring over books in cloisters? Must he toil
190 As Austin[24] bade and till the very soil?
Was he to leave the world upon the shelf?
Let Austin have his labor to himself.
   This Monk was therefore a good man to horse;
Greyhounds he had, as swift as birds, to course.
195 Hunting a hare or riding at a fence
Was all his fun, he spared for no expense.
I saw his sleeves were garnished at the hand
With fine gray fur, the finest in the land,
And on his hood, to fasten it at his chin
200 He had a wrought-gold cunningly fashioned pin;
Into a lover's knot it seemed to pass.
His head was bald and shone like looking-glass;
So did his face, as if it had been greased.
He was a fat and personable priest;
205 His prominent eyeballs never seemed to settle.
They glittered like the flames beneath a kettle;
Supple his boots, his horse in fine condition.
He was a prelate fit for exhibition,
He was not pale like a tormented soul.
210 He liked a fat swan best, and roasted whole.
His palfrey[25] was as brown as is a berry.
   There was a *Friar*, a wanton[26] one and merry,
A Limiter,[27] a very festive fellow.
In all Four Orders[28] there was none so mellow
215 So glib with gallant phrase and well-turned speech.

**23. St. Benet or St. Maur:** St. Benedict, author of monastic rules, and St. Maurice, one of his followers. Benet and Maur are French versions of Benedict and Maurice.

**24. Austin:** English version of St. Augustine, who criticized lazy monks.

**25. palfrey:** Saddle horse.
**26. wanton:** Jolly.
**27. Limiter:** A friar who is given begging rights for a certain limited area.
**28. Four Orders:** There were four orders of friars who supported themselves by begging: Dominicans, Franciscans, Carmelites, and Augustinians.

**THE MONK**
*Arthur Szyk for the Canterbury Tales*
The George Macy Companies

He'd fixed up many a marriage, giving each
Of his young women what he could afford her.
He was a noble pillar to his Order.
Highly beloved and intimate was he
220  With County folk within his boundary,
And city dames of honor and possessions;
For he was qualified to hear confessions,
Or so he said, with more than priestly scope;
He had a special license from the Pope.
225  Sweetly he heard his penitents at shrift[29]
With pleasant absolution, for a gift.
He was an easy man in penance-giving
Where he could hope to make a decent living;
It's a sure sign whenever gifts are given
230  To a poor Order that a man's well shriven,[30]
And should he give enough he knew in verity
The penitent repented in sincerity.
For many a fellow is so hard of heart
He cannot weep, for all his inward smart.
235  Therefore instead of weeping and of prayer
One should give silver for a poor Friar's care.
He kept his tippet[31] stuffed with pins for curls,
And pocket-knives, to give to pretty girls.
And certainly his voice was gay and sturdy,
240  For he sang well and played the hurdy-gurdy.[32]
At sing-songs he was champion of the hour.
His neck was whiter than a lily-flower
But strong enough to butt a bruiser down.
He knew the taverns well in every town
245  And every innkeeper and barmaid too
Better than lepers, beggars and that crew,
For in so eminent a man as he
It was not fitting with the dignity
Of his position, dealing with a scum
250  Of wretched lepers; nothing good can come
Of dealings with the slum-and-gutter dwellers,
But only with the rich and victual-sellers.
But anywhere a profit might accrue
Courteous he was and lowly of service too.
255  Natural gifts like his were hard to match.
He was the finest beggar of his batch,
And, for his begging-district, payed a rent;
His brethren did no poaching where he went.
For though a widow mightn't have a shoe,
260  So pleasant was his holy how-d'ye-do
He got his farthing from her just the same
Before he left, and so his income came

**29. shrift:** Confession.

**30. well shriven:** Absolved of his sins.

**31. tippet:** Hood.

**32. hurdy-gurdy:** A stringed instument played by cranking a wheel.

To more than he laid out. And how he romped,
Just like a puppy! He was ever prompt
265   To arbitrate disputes on settling days
(For a small fee) in many helpful ways,
Not then appearing as your cloistered scholar
With threadbare habit hardly worth a dollar,
But much more like a Doctor or a Pope.
270   Of double-worsted was the semi-cope[33]
Upon his shoulders, and the swelling fold
About him, like a bell about its mold
When it is casting, rounded out his dress.
He lisped a little out of wantonness
275   To make his English sweet upon his tongue.
When he had played his harp, or having sung,
His eyes would twinkle in his head as bright
As any star upon a frosty night.
This worthy's name was Hubert, it appeared.
280       There was a *Merchant* with a forking beard
And motley dress; high on his horse he sat,
Upon his head a Flemish[34] beaver hat
And on his feet daintily buckled boots.
He told of his opinions and pursuits
285   In solemn tones, and how he never lost.
The sea should be kept free at any cost
(He thought) upon the Harwich-Holland range,[35]
He was expert at currency exchange.
This estimable Merchant so had set
290   His wits to work, none knew he was in debt,
He was so stately in negotiation,
Loan, bargain and commercial obligation.
He was an excellent fellow all the same;
To tell the truth I do not know his name.
295       An *Oxford Cleric*, still a student though,
One who had taken logic long ago,
Was there; his horse was thinner than a rake,
And he was not too fat, I undertake,
But had a hollow look, a sober stare;
300   The thread upon his overcoat was bare.
He had found no preferment in the church
And he was too unworldly to make search
For secular employment. By his bed
He preferred having twenty books in red
305   And black, of Aristotle's[36] philosophy,
To having fine clothes, fiddle or psaltery.[37]
Though a philosopher, as I have told,
He had not found the stone for making gold.[38]
Whatever money from his friends he took

**33. semi-cope:** Cape.

**34. Flemish:** From Flanders.

**35. Harwich-Holland range:** The North Sea between England and Holland.

**36. Aristotle's** (ar' is tot' əlz): Referring to the Greek philosopher (384–322 B.C.).

**37. psaltery** (sôl' tər ē): An ancient stringed instrument.

**38. stone . . . gold:** At the time alchemists believed that a "philosopher's stone" existed that could turn base metals into gold.

**THE STUDENT**
*Arthur Szyk for the Canterbury Tales*
The George Macy Companies

310　He spent on learning or another book
　　And prayed for them most earnestly, returning
　　Thanks to them thus for paying for his learning.
　　His only care was study, and indeed
　　He never spoke a word more than was need,
315　Formal at that, respectful in the extreme,
　　Short, to the point, and lofty in his theme.
　　The thought of moral virtue filled his speech
　　And he would gladly learn, and gladly teach.
　　　A *Sergeant at the Law* who paid his calls,
320　Wary and wise, for clients at St. Paul's[39]
　　There also was, of noted excellence.
　　Discreet he was, a man to reverence,
　　Or so he seemed, his sayings were so wise.
　　He often had been Justice of Assize
325　By letters patent, and in full commission.
　　His fame and learning and his high position
　　Had won him many a robe and many a fee.
　　There was no such conveyancer[40] as he;
　　All was fee-simple[41] to his strong digestion,
330　Not one conveyance could be called in question.
　　Nowhere there was so busy a man as he;
　　But was less busy than he seemed to be.
　　He knew of every judgment, case and crime
　　Recorded, ever since King William's time.
335　He could dictate defenses or draft deeds;
　　No one could pinch a comma from his screeds,
　　And he knew every statute off by rote.
　　He wore a homely parti-colored coat
　　Girt with a silken belt of pin-stripe stuff;
340　Of his appearance I have said enough.
　　　There was a *Franklin*[42] with him, it appeared;
　　White as a daisy-petal was his beard.
　　A sanguine man, high-colored and benign,
　　He loved a morning sop[43] of cake in wine.
345　He lived for pleasure and had always done,
　　For he was Epicurus'[44] very son,
　　In whose opinion sensual delight
　　Was the one true felicity in sight.
　　As noted as St. Julian[45] was for bounty
350　He made his household free to all the County.
　　His bread, his ale were the finest of the fine
　　And no one had a better stock of wine.
　　His house was never short of bake-meat pies,
　　Of fish and flesh, and these in such supplies
355　It positively snowed with meat and drink
　　And all the dainties that a man could think.

**39. St. Paul's:** A London cathedral near which lawyers often met to discuss their cases.

**40. conveyancer:** One who draws up documents for transferring ownership of property.

**41. fee-simple:** Restricted ownership.

**42. *Franklin*:** Wealthy landowner.

**43. sop:** Piece.

**44. Epicurus'** (ep′ i kyoor′ əs): Referring to a Greek philosopher (342?–370 B.C.) who believed that happiness is the most important goal in life.

**45. St. Julian:** Patron saint of hospitality.

According to the seasons of the year
Changes of dish were ordered to appear.
He kept fat partridges in coops, beyond,
360 Many a bream and pike were in his pond.
Woe to the cook whose sauces had no sting
Or who was unprepared in anything!
And in his hall a table stood arrayed
And ready all day long, with places laid.
365 As Justice at the Sessions[46] none stood higher;
He often had been Member for the Shire.[47]
A dagger and a little purse of silk
Hung at his girdle, white as morning milk.
As Sheriff he checked audit, every entry.
370 He was a model among landed gentry.
    A *Haberdasher*, a *Dyer*, a *Carpenter*,
A *Weaver* and a *Carpet-maker* were
Among our ranks, all in the livery
Of one impressive guild-fraternity.
375 They were so trim and fresh their gear would pass
For new. Their knives were not tricked out with brass
But wrought with purest silver, which avouches
A like display on girdles and on pouches.
Each seemed a worthy burgess,[48] fit to grace
380 A guild-hall with a seat upon the dais.
Their wisdom would have justified a plan
To make each one of them an alderman;
They had the capital and revenue,
Besides their wives declared it was their due.
385 And if they did not think so, then they ought;
To be called "*Madam*" is a glorious thought,
And so is going to church and being seen
Having your mantle carried like a queen.
    They had a *Cook* with them who stood alone
390 For boiling chicken with a marrow-bone,
Sharp flavoring-powder and a spice for savor.
He could distinguish London ale by flavor,
And he could roast and seethe and broil and fry,
Make good thick soup and bake a tasty pie.
395 But what a pity—so it seemed to me,
That he should have an ulcer on his knee.
As for blancmange,[49] he made it with the best.
    There was a *Skipper* hailing from far west;
He came from Dartmouth, so I understood.
400 He rode a farmer's horse as best he could,
In a woolen gown that reached his knee.
A dagger on a lanyard[50] falling free
Hung from his neck under his arm and down.
The summer heat had tanned his color brown,

**46. Sessions:** Court sessions.
**47. Member . . . Shire:** Parliamentary representative for the county.

**48. burgess:** A member of a legislative body.

**49. blancmange** (bləmänj'): At the time, a creamy chicken dish.

**50. lanyard:** A loose rope around the neck.

405 And certainly he was an excellent fellow.
Many a draught of vintage, red and yellow,
He'd drawn at Bordeaux, while the trader snored.
The nicer rules of conscience he ignored.
If, when he fought, the enemy vessel sank,
410 He sent his prisoners home; they walked the plank.
As for his skill in reckoning his tides,
Currents and many another risk besides,
Moons, harbors, pilots, he had such dispatch
That none from Hull to Carthage was his match.
415 Hardy he was, prudent in undertaking;
His beard in many a tempest had its shaking,
And he knew all the havens as they were
From Gottland to the Cape of Finisterre,
And every creek in Brittany and Spain;
420 The barge he owned was called *The Maudelayne.*
        A *Doctor* too emerged as we proceeded;
No one alive could talk as well as he did
On points of medicine and of surgery,
For, being grounded in astronomy,
425 He watched his patient's favorable star
And, by his Natural Magic, knew what are
The lucky hours and planetary degrees
For making charms and magic effigies.
The cause of every malady you'd got
430 He knew, and whether dry, cold, moist or hot;[51]
He knew their seat, their humor and condition.
He was a perfect practicing physician.
These causes being known for what they were,
He gave the man his medicine then and there.
435 All his apothecaries[52] in a tribe
Were ready with the drugs he would prescribe,
And each made money from the other's guile;
They had been friendly for a goodish while.
He was well-versed in Esculapius[53] too
440 And what Hippocrates and Rufus knew
And Dioscorides, now dead and gone,
Galen and Rhazes, Hali, Serapion,
Averroes, Avicenna, Constantine,
Scotch Bernard, John of Gaddesden, Gilbertine.[54]
445 In his own diet he observed some measure;
There were no superfluities for pleasure,
Only digestives, nutritives and such.
He did not read the Bible very much.
In blood-red garments, slashed with bluish-gray
450 And lined with taffeta,[55] he rode his way;
Yet he was rather close as to expenses
And kept the gold he won in pestilences.

**51. The cause . . . hot:** It was believed that the body was composed of four "humors" (cold and dry, hot and moist, hot and dry, cold and moist) and that diseases resulted from a disturbance of one of these "humors."

**52. apothecaries** (ə päth′ ə ker′ ēz): Persons who prepared drugs.

**53. Esculapius** (es′ kyoo lā′ pē əs): In Roman mythology, the god of medicine and healing.

**54. Hippocrates . . . Gilbertine:** Famous physicians and medical authorities.

**55. taffeta** (taf′ i tə): A fine silk fabric.

Gold stimulates the heart, or so we're told.
He therefore had a special love of gold.

455     A worthy *woman* from beside *Bath*[56] city
Was with us, somewhat deaf, which was a pity.
In making cloth she showed so great a bent
She bettered those of Ypres and of Ghent.[57]
In all the parish not a dame dared stir
460   Towards the altar steps in front of her,
And if indeed they did, so wrath was she
As to be quite put out of charity.
Her kerchiefs were of finely woven ground;[58]
I dared have sworn they weighed a good ten pound,
465   The ones she wore on Sunday, on her head.
Her hose were of the finest scarlet red
And gartered tight; her shoes were soft and new.
Bold was her face, handsome, and red in hue.
A worthy woman all her life, what's more
470   She'd had five husbands, all at the church door,
Apart from other company in youth;
No need just now to speak of that, forsooth.
And she had thrice been to Jerusalem,
Seen many strange rivers and passed over them;
475   She'd been to Rome and also to Boulogne,
St. James of Compostella and Cologne,[59]
And she was skilled in wandering by the way.
She had gap-teeth, set widely, truth to say.
Easily on an ambling horse she sat
480   Well wimpled[60] up, and on her head a hat
As broad as is a buckler[61] or a shield;
She had a flowing mantle that concealed
Large hips, her heels spurred sharply under that.
In company she liked to laugh and chat
485   And knew the remedies for love's mischances,
An art in which she knew the oldest dances.

        A holy-minded man of good renown
There was, and poor, the *Parson* to a town,
Yet he was rich in holy thought and work.
490   He also was a learned man, a clerk,
Who truly knew Christ's gospel and would preach it
Devoutly to parishioners, and teach it.
Benign and wonderfully diligent,
And patient when adversity was sent
495   (For so he proved in great adversity)
He much disliked extorting tithe[62] or fee,
Nay rather he preferred beyond a doubt
Giving to poor parishioners round about
From his own goods and Easter offerings.
500   He found sufficiency in little things.

**56. *Bath*:** An English resort city.

**57. Ypres** (ē′ prə) **and of Ghent** (gent): Flemish cities known for wool making.

**58. ground:** A composite fabric.

**59. Jerusalem . . . Rome . . . Boulogne . . . St. James of Compostella . . . Cologne:** Famous pilgrimage sites at the time.

**60. wimpled:** Wearing a scarf covering the head, neck, and chin.

**61. buckler:** A small, round shield.

**62. tithe** (tīth): One tenth of a person's income, paid as a tax to support the church.

Wide was his parish, with houses far asunder,
Yet he neglected not in rain or thunder,
In sickness or in grief, to pay a call
  On the remotest, whether great or small,
505 Upon his feet, and in his hand a stave.
This noble example to his sheep he gave,
First following the word before he taught it,
And it was from the gospel he had caught it.
This little proverb he would add thereto
510 That if gold rust, what then will iron do?
For if a priest be foul in whom we trust
No wonder that a common man should rust;
And shame it is to see—let priests take stock—
A soiled shepherd and a snowy flock.
515 The true example that a priest should give
Is one of cleanness, how the sheep should live.
He did not set his benefice to hire[63]
And leave his sheep encumbered in the mire
Or run to London to earn easy bread
520 By singing masses for the wealthy dead,
Or find some Brotherhood and get enrolled.
He stayed at home and watched over his fold
So that no wolf should make the sheep miscarry.
He was a shepherd and no mercenary.
525 Holy and virtuous he was, but then
Never contemptuous of sinful men,
Never disdainful, never too proud or fine,
But was discreet in teaching and benign.
His business was to show a fair behavior
530 And draw men thus to Heaven and their Savior,
Unless indeed a man were obstinate;
And such, whether of high or low estate,
He put to sharp rebuke to say the least.
I think there never was a better priest.
535 He sought no pomp or glory in his dealings,
No scrupulosity had spiced his feelings.
Christ and His Twelve Apostles and their lore
He taught, but followed it himself before.
  There was a *Plowman* with him there, his brother.
540 Many a load of dung one time or other
He must have carted through the morning dew.
He was an honest worker, good and true,
Living in peace and perfect charity,
And, as the gospel bade him, so did he,
545 Loving God best with all his heart and mind
And then his neighbor as himself, repined
At no misfortune, slacked for no content,
For steadily about his work he went

**THE WIFE OF BATH**
*Arthur Szyk for the Canterbury Tales*
*The George Macy Companies*

**63. set . . . hire:** Pay
someone else to perform
his parish duties.

To thrash his corn, to dig or to manure
550  Or make a ditch; and he would help the poor
For love of Christ and never take a penny
If he could help it, and, as prompt as any,
He paid his tithes in full when they were due
On what he owned, and on his earnings too.
555  He wore a tabard[64] smock and rode a mare.
         There was a *Reeve*,[65] also a *Miller*, there,
A College *Manciple*[66] from the Inns of Court,
A papal *Pardoner*[67] and, in close consort,
A Church-Court *Summoner*,[68] riding at a trot,
560  And finally myself—that was the lot.
         The *Miller* was a chap of sixteen stone,[69]
A great stout fellow big in brawn and bone.
He did well out of them, for he could go
And win the ram at any wrestling show.
565  Broad, knotty and short-shouldered, he would boast
He could heave any door off hinge and post,
Or take a run and break it with his head.
His beard, like any sow or fox, was red
And broad as well, as though it were a spade;
570  And, at its very tip, his nose displayed
A wart on which there stood a tuft of hair,
Red as the bristles in an old sow's ear.
His nostrils were as black as they were wide.
He had a sword and buckler at his side,
575  His mighty mouth was like a furnace door.
A wrangler and buffoon, he had a store
Of tavern stories, filthy in the main.
His was a master-hand at stealing grain.
He felt it with his thumb and thus he knew
580  Its quality and took three times his due—
A thumb of gold, by God, to gauge an oat!
He wore a hood of blue and a white coat.
He liked to play his bagpipes up and down
And that was how he brought us out of town.
585      The *Manciple* came from the Inner Temple;
All caterers might follow his example
In buying victuals; he was never rash
Whether he bought on credit or paid cash.
He used to watch the market most precisely
590  And go in first, and so he did quite nicely.
Now isn't it a marvel of God's grace
That an illiterate fellow can outpace
The wisdom of a heap of learned men?
His masters—he had more than thirty then—
595  All versed in the abstrusest legal knowledge,
Could have produced a dozen from their College

**64. tabard:** A loose jacket.

**65. *Reeve*:** An estate manager.

**66. *Manciple*:** A buyer of provisions.

**67. *Pardoner*:** One who dispenses papal pardons.

**68. *Summoner*:** One who serves summonses to church courts.

**69. sixteen stone:** 224 pounds. A stone equals 14 pounds.

Fit to be stewards in land and rents and game
To any Peer in England you could name,
And show him how to live on what he had
600 Debt-free (unless of course the Peer were mad)
Or be as frugal as he might desire,
And they were fit to help about the Shire
In any legal case there was to try;
And yet this Manciple could wipe their eye.
605      The *Reeve* was old and choleric and thin;
His beard was shaven closely to the skin,
His shorn hair came abruptly to a stop
Above his ears, and he was docked on top
Just like a priest in front; his legs were lean,
610 Like sticks they were, no calf was to be seen.
He kept his bins and garners[70] very trim;
No auditor could gain a point on him.
And he could judge by watching drought and rain
The yield he might expect from seed and grain.
615 His master's sheep, his animals and hens,
Pigs, horses, dairies, stores and cattle-pens
Were wholly trusted to his government.
And he was under contract to present
The accounts, right from his master's earliest years.
620 No one had ever caught him in arrears.
No bailiff, serf or herdsman dared to kick,
He knew their dodges, knew their every trick;
Feared like the plague he was, by those beneath.
He had a lovely dwelling on a heath,
625 Shadowed in green by trees above the sward.[71]
A better hand at bargains than his lord,
He had grown rich and had a store of treasure
Well tucked away, yet out it came to pleasure
His lord with subtle loans or gifts of goods,
630 To earn his thanks and even coats and hoods.
When young he'd learnt a useful trade and still
He was a carpenter of first-rate skill.
The stallion-cob he rode at a slow trot
Was dapple-gray and bore the name of Scot.
635 He wore an overcoat of bluish shade
And rather long; he had a rusty blade
Slung at his side. He came, as I heard tell,
From Norfolk, near a place called Baldeswell.
His coat was tucked under his belt and splayed.
640 He rode the hindmost of our cavalcade.
     There was a *Summoner* with us in the place
Who had a fire-red cherubinnish face,[72]
For he had carbuncles. His eyes were narrow,
He was as hot and lecherous as a sparrow.

**70. garners** n.: Buildings for storing grain.

**71. sward** n.: Turf.

**72. fire–red . . . face:** In the art of the Middle Ages, the faces of cherubs, or angels, were often painted red.

*The Prologue* from *The Canterbury Tales*   133

645 Black, scabby brows he had, and a thin beard.
Children were afraid when he appeared.
No quicksilver, lead ointments, tartar creams,
Boracic, no, nor brimstone, so it seems,
Could make a salve that had the power to bite,
650 Clean up or curve his whelks of knobby white.
Or purge the pimples sitting on his cheeks.
Garlic he loved, and onions too, and leeks,
And drinking strong wine till all was hazy.
Then he would shout and jabber as if crazy,
655 And wouldn't speak a word except in Latin
When he was drunk, such tags as he was pat in;
He only had a few, say two or three,
That he had mugged up out of some decree;
No wonder, for he heard them every day.
660 And, as you know, a man can teach a jay
To call out "Walter" better than the Pope.
But had you tried to test his wits and grope
For more, you'd have found nothing in the bag.
Then *Questio quid juris*[73] was his tag.
665 He was a gentle varlet and a kind one,
No better fellow if you went to find one.
He would allow—just for a quart of wine—
Any good lad to keep a concubine
A twelvemonth and dispense it altogether!
670 Yet he could pluck a finch to leave no feather:
And if he found some rascal with a maid
He would instruct him not to be afraid
In such a case of the Archdeacon's curse
(Unless the rascal's soul were in his purse)
675 For in his purse the punishment should be.
"Purse is the good Archdeacon's Hell," said he.
But well I know he lied in what he said;
A curse should put a guilty man in dread,
For curses kill, as shriving brings, salvation.
680 We should beware of excommunication.
Thus, as he pleased, the man could bring duress
On any young fellow in the diocese.
He knew their secrets, they did what he said.
He wore a garland set upon his head
685 Large as the holly-bush upon a stake
Outside an ale-house, and he had a cake,
A round one, which it was his joke to wield
As if it were intended for a shield.
　　　He and a gentle *Pardoner* rode together,
690 A bird from Charing Cross of the same feather,
Just back from visiting the Court of Rome.
He loudly sang "*Come hither, love, come home!*"

**73. "Questo quid juris":** "The question is, what is the point of the law?" (Latin).

The Summoner sang deep seconds to this song,
No trumpet ever sounded half so strong.
695 This Pardoner had hair as yellow as wax,
Hanging down smoothly like a hank of flax.
In driblets fell his locks behind his head
Down to his shoulders which they overspread;
Thinly they fell, like rat-tails, one by one.
700 He wore no hood upon his head, for fun;
The hood inside his wallet had been stowed,
He aimed at riding in the latest mode;
But for a little cap his head was bare
And he had bulging eyeballs, like a hare.
705 He'd sewed a holy relic on his cap;
His wallet lay before him on his lap,
Brimful of pardons come from Rome all hot.
He had the same small voice a goat has got.
His chin no beard had harbored, nor would harbor,
710 Smoother than ever chin was left by barber.
I judge he was a gelding, or a mare.
As to his trade, from Berwick down to Ware
There was no pardoner of equal grace,
For in his trunk he had a pillowcase
715 Which he asserted was Our Lady's veil.
He said he had a gobbet[74] of the sail
Saint Peter had the time when he made bold
To walk the waves, till Jesu Christ took hold.
He had a cross of metal set with stones
720 And, in a glass, a rubble of pigs' bones.
And with these relics, any time he found
Some poor up-country parson to astound,
On one short day, in money down, he drew
More than the parson in a month or two,
725 And by his flatteries and prevarication
Made monkeys of the priest and congregation.
But still to do him justice first and last
In church he was a noble ecclesiast.
How well he read a lesson or told a story!
730 But best of all he sang an Offertory,[75]
For well he knew that when that song was sung
He'd have to preach and tune his honey-tongue
And (well he could) win silver from the crowd.
That's why he sang so merrily and loud.
735     Now I have told you shortly, in a clause,
The rank, the array, the number and the cause
Of our assembly in this company
In Southwark, at that high-class hostelry
Known as *The Tabard,* close beside *The Bell.*
740 And now the time has come for me to tell

**74. gobbet:** Piece.

**75. Offertory:** The song that accompanies the collection of the offering at a church service.

How we behaved that evening; I'll begin
After we had alighted at the inn,
Then I'll report our journey, stage by stage,
All the remainder of our pilgrimage.
745   But first I beg of you, in courtesy,
Not to condemn me as unmannerly
If I speak plainly and with no concealings
And give account of all their words and dealings,
Using their very phrases as they fell.
750   For certainly, as you all know so well,
He who repeats a tale after a man
Is bound to say, as nearly as he can,
Each single word, if he remembers it,
However rudely spoken or unfit,
755   Or else the tale he tells will be untrue,
The things invented and the phrases new.
He may not flinch although it were his brother,
If he says one word he must say the other.
And Christ Himself spoke broad[76] in Holy Writ,

**76. broad:** Bluntly.

760   And as you know there's nothing there unfit,
And Plato[77] says, for those with power to read,
"The word should be as cousin to the deed."
Further I beg you to forgive it me
If I neglect the order and degree

**77. Plato:** A Greek philosopher (427?–347? B.C.).

765   And what is due to rank in what I've planned.
I'm short of wit as you will understand.
       Our *Host* gave us great welcome; everyone
Was given a place and supper was begun.
He served the finest victuals you could think,
770   The wine was strong and we were glad to drink.
A very striking man our Host withal,
And fit to be a marshal in a hall.
His eyes were bright, his girth a little wide;
There is no finer burgess in Cheapside.[78]

**78. Cheapside:** A district in London.

775   Bold in his speech, yet wise and full of tact,
There was no manly attribute he lacked,
What's more he was a merry-hearted man.
After our meal he jokingly began
To talk of sport, and, among other things
780   After we'd settled up our reckonings,
He said as follows: "Truly, gentlemen,
You're very welcome and I can't think when
—Upon my word I'm telling you no lie—
I've seen a gathering here that looked so spry,
785   No, not this year, as in this tavern now.
I'd think you up some fun if I knew how.
And, as it happens, a thought has just occurred
And it will cost you nothing, on my word.

You're off to Canterbury—well, God speed!
790 Blessed St. Thomas answer to your need!
And I don't doubt, before the journey's done
You mean to while the time in tales and fun.
Indeed, there's little pleasure for your bones
Riding along and all as dumb as stones.
795 So let me then propose for your enjoyment,
Just as I said, a suitable employment.
And if my notion suits and you agree
And promise to submit yourselves to me
Playing your parts exactly as I say
800 Tomorrow as you ride along the way,
Then by my father's soul (and he is dead)
If you don't like it you can have my head!
Hold up your hands, and not another word.''
        Well, our consent of course was not deferred,
805 It seemed not worth a serious debate;
We all agreed to it at any rate
And bade him issue what commands he would.
''My lords,'' he said, ''now listen for your good,
And please don't treat my notion with disdain.
810 This is the point. I'll make it short and plain.
Each one of you shall help to make things slip
By telling two stories on the outward trip
To Canterbury, that's what I intend,
And, on the homeward way to journey's end
815 Another two, tales from the days of old;
And then the man whose story is best told,
That is to say who gives the fullest measure
Of good morality and general pleasure,
He shall be given a supper, paid by all,
820 Here in this tavern, in this very hall,
When we come back again from Canterbury.
And in the hope to keep you bright and merry
I'll go along with you myself and ride
All at my own expense and serve as guide.
825 I'll be the judge, and those who won't obey
Shall pay for what we spend upon the way.
Now if you all agree to what you've heard
Tell me at once without another word,
And I will make arrangements early for it.''
830     Of course we all agreed, in fact we swore it
Delightedly, and made entreaty too
That he should act as he proposed to do,
Become our Governor in short, and be
Judge of our tales and general referee,
835 And set the supper at a certain price.
We promised to be ruled by his advice

Come high, come low; unanimously thus
We set him up in judgment over us.
More wine was fetched, the business being done;
840   We drank it off and up went everyone
To bed without a moment of delay.
        Early next morning at the spring of day
Up rose our Host and roused us like a cock,
Gathering us together in a flock,
845   And off we rode at slightly faster pace
Than walking to St. Thomas' watering-place;[79]
And there our Host drew up, began to ease
His horse, and said, "Now, listen if you please,
My lords! Remember what you promised me.
850   If evensong and matins will agree[80]
Let's see who shall be first to tell a tale.
And as I hope to drink good wine and ale
I'll be your judge. The rebel who disobeys,
However much the journey costs, he pays.
855   Now draw for cut and then we can depart;
The man who draws the shortest cut shall start."

**79. St. Thomas' watering-place:** A brook two miles from the inn.

**80. If evensong . . . agree:** If what you said last night holds true this morning.

<hr>

**Primary Source**

Seventeenth-century poet and dramatist John Dryden called Chaucer the "father of English poetry," a ranking still considered valid today. Dryden ranked Chaucer with the "same degree of veneration as the Grecians held Homer or the Romans held Virgil," and found in his work "a perpetual fountain of good sense." Writing about a hundred years later, poet and essayist Samuel Taylor Coleridge found: " . . . unceasing delight in Chaucer. His cheerfulness is especially delicious to me in my old age. How exquisitely tender he is, and yet how perfectly free from the least touch of sickly melancholy or morbid drooping. The sympathy of the poet with the subjects of his poetry is particularly remarkable in Shakespeare and Chaucer; but what Shakespeare effects by a strong act of imagination and mental changing, Chaucer does without any effort, merely by the inborn kindly joyousness of his nature. How well we seem to know Chaucer! How absolutely nothing do we know of Shakespeare!"

## THINKING ABOUT THE SELECTION

### Recalling

1. What does Chaucer say that people long to do when spring comes?
2. Which pilgrim is described as being (a) "modest as a maid"? (b) "all sentiment and tender heart"? (c) "a very festive fellow"?
3. Which pilgrim is described as having (a) "a special love of gold"? (b) "gap-teeth"? (c) "a store of tavern stories"?
4. How does Chaucer say he will report the events of the pilgrimage?
5. What entertainment on the journey does the host propose?

### Interpreting

6. Chaucer pokes gentle fun at some of the pilgrims. What is his opinion of the Nun's singing voice and of her French?
7. Although the Friar and the Parson are both religious men, they are very different. What are some of the ways in which they differ?
8. What, if anything, does Chaucer seem to dislike about (a) the Skipper? (b) the Doctor?

### Applying

9. If Chaucer were writing *The Canterbury Tales* today, what three kinds of pilgrims do you think he might consider adding to the group?

## ANALYZING LITERATURE

### Understanding Characterization

Chaucer sometimes makes direct statements about a character: "He was an honest worker, good and true." More often he reveals character indirectly, often through action: "She used to weep if she but saw a mouse/Caught in a trap." There is not much dialogue in the Prologue, but Chaucer frequently uses physical appearance to suggest character. Compare the appearance of the Miller ("A great stout fellow big in brawn and bone") with that of the Reeve ("old and choleric and thin"). Their looks match their personalities.

1. What nouns does Chaucer use to characterize the Squire?

2. How does Chaucer mainly characterize (a) the Doctor? (b) the Host?

## CRITICAL THINKING AND READING

### Making Inferences About Characters

If you are to understand fictional characters fully, you must make inferences about them. You must draw conclusions based on what the writer has told you about their actions, thoughts, words, and appearance. When Chaucer writes of the Parson, "That if gold rust, what will iron do?" you can infer that the Parson realizes he should be a model of behavior for his parishioners. What can you infer about the Pardoner from the information in lines 714–720?

## UNDERSTANDING LANGUAGE

### Using Similes

A **simile** is a comparison of two unlike things using *like* or *as:*

His mighty mouth was *like* a furnace door.
White *as* a daisy-petal was his beard.

The usual purpose of a simile is to give the reader an apt and striking picture of the person or object being described.

1. What four similes appear in lines 695–704 of the sketch of the Pardoner?
2. Try to find at least five other similes in the Prologue. What are they?

## THINKING AND WRITING

### Writing a Pilgrim's Tale

Now that you know something about each of Chaucer's pilgrims, write a tale you think one of them might tell. Choose a pilgrim and study his or her sketch carefully. When you are sure you understand the pilgrim's character, write a tale that he or she might tell. You may modernize the tale, if you wish, setting it in the present. But make sure the message of the tale fits the character of the pilgrim.

# GUIDE FOR INTERPRETING

## The Nun's Priest's Tale

**Writer's
Techniques**

**The Mock-Heroic Style.** Writers use a **mock-heroic style** when they write about trivial matters in a style that would be more appropriate for great and important events. The disparity between content and style results in comic effects. For example, imagine describing a vain young man in front of his mirror as if he were participating in a solemn, religious ritual: With total devotion and concentration and hardly breathing at all, Tom carefully applied the comb to the curl that had violated the upper part of his ear . . .

In "The Nun's Priest's Tale," Chaucer uses the mock-heroic style to transform a popular animal fable into a masterpiece of comedy. He describes the barnyard interactions of animals as if he were writing an epic poem. Among the epic elements he borrows are the hero's elaborate boasts, the vivid accounts of battles, and the intervention of supernatural forces. To make his tale even more ridiculous, he includes barnyard debates about controversial issues of the day: fate versus free will and woman as the source of man's misfortune. The contrast between these lofty concerns and the animal debaters is ludicrous but appealing.

Chaucer casts a rooster and hen as his romantic leads, presenting them as if they were the lord and lady of a castle. As master of all he surveys, the rooster Chanticleer is pompous, naive, and thoroughly charming. He struts and preaches, displaying his male ego and sprinkling his conversation with learned classical allusions. Meanwhile, his hen-wife Pertelote is a comically practical heroine. She gives her lord and master advice about his health and, for all his strutting, wields emotional power over him.

The mock-heroic style works best when ridicule is tempered with affection. Chaucer certainly succeeds in this respect. His fondness for his characters, even at their most absurd, comes through in the pleasant and cheerful tone of the tale.

**Writing**

Think about the many little things you do every day: brushing your teeth, tying your shoe laces, opening a box of cereal. Use the mock-heroic style to describe a trivial chore or activity that is part of your daily routine. Remember to stress the contrast between style and subject matter in order to heighten the humor. After you have finished, exchange descriptions with a classmate.

# The Nun's Priest's Tale

Geoffrey Chaucer

Once, long ago, there dwelt a poor old widow
In a small cottage, by a little meadow
Beside a grove and standing in a dale.
This widow-woman of whom I tell my tale
5   Since the sad day when last she was a wife
Had led a very patient, simple life.
Little she had in capital or rent,
But still, by making do with what God sent,
She kept herself and her two daughters going.
10  Three hefty sows—no more—were all her showing,
Three cows as well; there was a sheep called Molly.
   Sooty her hall, her kitchen melancholy,
And there she ate full many a slender meal;
There was no *sauce piquante*[1] to spice her veal,
15  No dainty morsel ever passed her throat,
According to her cloth she cut her coat.
Repletion[2] never left her in disquiet
And all her physic was a temperate diet,
Hard work for exercise and heart's content.
20  And rich man's gout did nothing to prevent
Her dancing, apoplexy[3] struck her not;
She drank no wine, nor white nor red had got.
Her board was mostly served with white and black,
Milk and brown bread, in which she found no lack;
25  Broiled bacon or an egg or two were common,
She was in fact a sort of dairy-woman.
   She had a yard that was enclosed about
By a stockade and a dry ditch without,
In which she kept a cock called Chanticleer.
30  In all the land for crowing he'd no peer;
His voice was jollier than the organ blowing
In church on Sundays, he was great at crowing.
Far, far more regular than any clock
Or abbey bell the crowing of this cock.
35  The equinoctial wheel and its position[4]
At each ascent he knew by intuition;
At every hour—fifteen degrees of movement—
He crowed so well there could be no improvement.

1. *sauce piquante*
(pē′ kənt): French for a
pleasantly sharp sauce,
used for fancy and
expensive meals.
2. **Repletion** (ri plē′ shən)
*n.*: The state of having
eaten too much.

3. **apoplexy:** An old-
fashioned term for a
stroke.

4. **equinoctial . . .
position:** Chaucer and his
contemporaries accounted
for changes in the
positions of stars and
planets by imagining that
the heavens circled the
earth once a day, moving
fifteen degrees each hour.

His comb was redder than fine coral, tall
40 And battlemented like a castle wall,
His bill was black and shone as bright as jet,
Like azure were his legs and they were set
On azure toes with nails of lily white,
Like burnished gold his feathers, flaming bright.
45      This gentlecock was master in some measure
Of seven hens, all there to do his pleasure.
They were his sisters and his paramours,
Colored like him in all particulars;
She with the loveliest dyes upon her throat
50 Was known as gracious Lady Pertelote.
Courteous she was, discreet and debonair,
Companionable too, and took such care
In her deportment, since she was seven days old
She held the heart of Chanticleer controlled,
55 Locked up securely in her every limb;
O such happiness his love to him!
And such a joy it was to hear them sing,
As when the glorious sun began to spring,
In sweet accord *My love is far from land*[5]
60 —For in those far off days I understand
All birds and animals could speak and sing.
    Now it befell, as dawn began to spring,
When Chanticleer and Pertelote and all
His wives were perched in this poor widow's hall
65 (Fair Pertelote was next him on the perch),
This Chanticleer began to groan and lurch
Like someone sorely troubled by a dream,
And Pertelote who heard him roar and scream
Was quite aghast and said, "O dearest heart,
70 What's ailing you? Why do you groan and start?
Fie, what a sleeper! What a noise to make!"
"Madam," he said, "I beg you not to take
Offense, but by the Lord I had a dream
So terrible just now I had to scream;
75 I still can feel my heart racing from fear.
God turn my dream to good and guard all here.
And keep my body out of durance vile![6]
I dreamt that roaming up and down a while
Within our yard I saw a kind of beast,
80 A sort of hound that tried or seemed at least
To try and seize me . . . would have killed me dead!
His color was a blend of yellow and red,
His ears and tail were tipped with sable fur
Unlike the rest; he was a russet cur.
85 Small was his snout, his eyes were glowing bright.

**5. *My love is far from land:*** The refrain of a popular song.

**6. durance vile:** Long imprisonment.

**ENGLISH TRAVELERS SETTING FORTH FROM THE CANTERBURY TALES**
*The British Library*

It was enough to make one die of fright.
That was no doubt what made me groan and swoon.''
    ''For shame,'' she said, ''you timorous poltroon!⁷
Alas, what cowardice! By God above,

90  You've forfeited my heart and lost my love.
I cannot love a coward, come what may.
For certainly, whatever we may say,
All women long—and O that it might be!—
For husbands tough, dependable and free,

95  Secret, discreet, no niggard,⁸ not a fool
That boasts and then will find his courage cool
At every trifling thing. By God above,
How dare you say for shame, and to your love,
That anything at all was to be feared?

100  Have you no manly heart to match your beard?
And can a dream reduce you to such terror?
Dreams are a vanity, God knows, pure error.
Dreams are engendered in the too-replete
From vapors in the belly, which compete

105  With others, too abundant, swollen tight.
    ''No doubt the redness in your dream tonight
Comes from the superfluity and force
Of the red choler in your blood. Of course.
That is what puts a dreamer in the dread

110  Of crimsoned arrows, fires flaming red,
Of great red monsters making as to fight him,
And big red whelps and little ones to bite him;
Just so the black and melancholy vapors
Will set a sleeper shrieking, cutting capers

115  And swearing that black bears, black bulls as well,
Or blackest fiends are haling him to Hell.
And there are other vapors that I know
That on a sleeping man will work their woe,
But I'll pass on as lightly as I can.

120      ''Take Cato⁹ now, that was so wise a man,
Did he not say, 'Take no account of dreams'?
Now, sir,'' she said, ''on flying from these beams,
For love of God do take some laxative;
Upon my soul that's the advice to give

125  For melancholy choler; let me urge
You free yourself from vapors with a purge.
And that you may have no excuse to tarry
By saying this town has no apothecary,
I shall myself instruct you and prescribe

130  Herbs that will cure all vapors of that tribe,
Herbs from our very farmyard! You will find
Their natural property is to unbind

**7. poltroon** (päl trōōn′)
*n.*: Coward.

**8. niggard:** Stingy person.

**9. Cato:** A Roman statesman and philosopher (95–46 B.C.) with a reputation for wisdom.

And purge you well beneath and well above.
Now don't forget it, dear, for God's own love!
135 Your face is choleric and shows distension;
Be careful lest the sun in his ascension
Should catch you full of humors,[10] hot and many.
And if he does, my dear, I'll lay a penny
It means a bout of fever or a breath
140 Of tertian ague.[11] You may catch your death.
   "Worms for a day or two I'll have to give
As a digestive, then your laxative.
Centaury, fumitory, caper-spurge
And hellebore will make a splendid purge;
145 And then there's laurel or the blackthorn berry,
Ground-ivy too that makes our yard so merry;
Peck them right up, my dear, and swallow whole.
Be happy, husband, by your father's soul!
Don't be afraid of dreams. I'll say no more."
150    "Madam," he said, "I thank you for your lore,
But with regard to Cato all the same,
His wisdom has, no doubt, a certain fame,
But though he said that we should take no heed
Of dreams, by God in ancient books I read
155 Of many a man of more authority
Than ever Cato was, believe you me,
Who say the very opposite is true
And prove their theories by experience too.
Dreams have quite often been significations
160 As well of triumphs as of tribulations
That people undergo in this our life.
This needs no argument at all, dear wife,
The proof is all too manifest indeed.
   "One of the greatest authors one can read
165 Says thus: there were two comrades once who went
On pilgrimage, sincere in their intent.
And as it happened they had reached a town
Where such a throng was milling up and down
And yet so scanty the accommodation,
170 They could not find themselves a habitation,
No, not a cottage that could lodge them both.
And so they separated, very loath,
Under constraint of this necessity
And each went off to find some hostelry,
175 And lodge whatever way his luck might fall.
   "The first of them found refuge in a stall
Down in a yard with oxen and a plow.
His friend found lodging for himself somehow
Elsewhere, by accident or destiny,

**10. humors:** People in Chaucer's time believed that bodily fluids called humors were responsible for one's health and disposition. An excess of the fluid called yellow bile resulted in a choleric, or quick-tempered, personality. In lines 108 and 125, Chaucer seems to use the word *choler* as a synonym for the term *humor.*

**11. tertian ague** (tur' shən ā' gyo͞o): A malarial fever.

180    Which governs all of us and equally.
       "Now it so happened, long ere it was day,
    This fellow had a dream, and as he lay
    In bed it seemed he heard his comrade call,
    'Help! I am lying in an ox's stall
185    And shall tonight be murdered as I lie.
    Help me, dear brother, help or I shall die!
    Come in all haste!' Such were the words he spoke;
    The dreamer, lost in terror, then awoke.
    But once awake he paid it no attention,
190    Turned over and dismissed it as invention,
    It was a dream, he thought, a fantasy.
    And twice he dreamt this dream successively.
       "Yet a third time his comrade came again,
    Or seemed to come, and said, 'I have been slain.
195    Look, look! my wounds are bleeding wide and deep,
    Rise early in the morning, break your sleep

And go to the west gate. You there shall see
A cart all loaded up with dung,' said he,
'And in that dung my body has been hidden.
200  Boldly arrest that cart as you are bidden.
It was my money that they killed me for.'
     "He told him every detail, sighing sore,
And pitiful in feature, pale of hue.
This dream, believe me, Madam, turned out true;
205  For in the dawn, as soon as it was light,
He went to where his friend had spent the night
And when he came upon the cattle-stall
He looked about him and began to call.
     "The innkeeper, appearing thereupon,
210  Quickly gave answer, 'Sir, your friend has gone.
He left the town a little after dawn.'
The man began to feel suspicious, drawn
By memories of his dream—the western gate,
The dung-cart—off he went, he would not wait,
215  Towards the western entry. There he found,
Seemingly on its way to dung some ground,
A dung-cart loaded on the very plan
Described so closely by the murdered man.
So he began to shout courageously
220  For right and vengeance on the felony,
'My friend's been killed! There's been a foul attack,
He's in that cart and gaping on his back!
Fetch the authorities, get the sheriff down
—Whosever job it is to run the town—
225  Help! My companion's murdered, sent to glory!'
     "What need I add to finish off the story?
People ran out and cast the cart to ground,
And in the middle of the dung they found
The murdered man. The corpse was fresh and new.
230  "O blessed God, that art so just and true,
Thus thou revealest murder! As we say,
'Murder will out.' We see it day by day.
Murder's a foul, abominable treason,
So loathsome to God's justice, to God's reason,
235  He will not suffer its concealment. True,
Things may lie hidden for a year or two,
But still 'Murder will out,' that's my conclusion.
     "All the town officers in great confusion
Seized on the carter and they gave him hell,
240  And then they racked the innkeeper as well,
And both confessed. And then they took the wrecks
And there and then they hanged them by their necks.
     "By this we see that dreams are to be dreaded.

And in the self-same book I find embedded,
245  Right in the very chapter after this
(I'm not inventing, as I hope for bliss)
The story of two men who started out
To cross the sea—for merchandise no doubt—
But as the winds were contrary they waited.
250  It was a pleasant town, I should have stated,
Merrily grouped about the haven-side.
A few days later with the evening tide
The wind veered round so as to suit them best;
They were delighted and they went to rest
255  Meaning to sail next morning early. Well,
To one of them a miracle befell.
     "This man as he lay sleeping, it would seem,
Just before dawn had an astounding dream.
He thought a man was standing by his bed
260  Commanding him to wait, and thus he said:
'If you set sail tomorrow as you intend
You will be drowned. My tale is at an end.'
     "He woke and told his friend what had occurred
And begged him that the journey be deferred
265  At least a day, implored him not to start.
But his companion, lying there apart,
Began to laugh and treat him to derision.[12]                    **12. derision** (di rizh′ ən)
'I'm not afraid,' he said, 'of any vision,                       *n.*: Contempt or ridicule.
To let it interfere with my affairs;
270  A straw for all your dreamings and your scares.
Dreams are just empty nonsense, merest japes;[13]               **13. japes:** Jokes.
Why, people dream all day of owls and apes,
All sorts of trash that can't be understood,
Things that have never happened and never could.
275  But as I see you mean to stay behind
And miss the tide for wilful sloth of mind,
God knows I'm sorry for it, but good day!'
And so he took his leave and went his way.
     "And yet, before they'd covered half the trip
280  —I don't know what went wrong—there was a rip
And by some accident the ship went down,
Her bottom rent,[14] all hands aboard to drown                  **14. Rent:** Torn.
In sight of all the vessels at her side,
That had put out upon the self-same tide.
285  "So, my dear Pertelote, if you discern
The force of these examples, you may learn
One never should be careless about dreams,
For, undeniably, I say it seems
That many are a sign of trouble breeding.
290  "Now, take St. Kenelm's life which I've been reading;

He was Kenulphus' son, the noble King
Of Mercia. Now, St. Kenelm dreamt a thing
Shortly before they murdered him one day.
He saw his murder in a dream, I say.
295 His nurse expounded it and gave her reasons
On every point and warned him against treasons
But as the saint was only seven years old
All that she said about it left him cold.
He was so holy how could visions hurt?
300     "By God, I willingly would give my shirt
To have you read his legend as I've read it;
And, Madam Pertelote, upon my credit,
Macrobius wrote of dreams and can explain us
The vision of young Scipio Africanus,[15]
305 And he affirms that dreams can give a due
Warnings of things that later on come true.
    "And then there's the Old Testament—a manual
Well worth your study; see the *Book of Daniel.*
Did Daniel think a dream was vanity?
310 Read about Joseph too and you will see
That many dreams—I do not say that all—
Give cognizance of what is to befall.
    "Look at Lord Pharaoh, king of Egypt! Look
At what befell his butler and his cook.
315 Did not their visions have a certain force?
But those who study history of course
Meet many dreams that set them wondering.
    "What about Croesus too, the Lydian king,
Who dreamt that he was sitting in a tree,
320 Meaning he would be hanged? It had to be.
    "Or take Andromache, great Hector's wife;[16]
The day on which he was to lose his life
She dreamt about, the very night before,
And realized that if Hector went to war
325 He would be lost that very day in battle.
She warned him; he dismissed it all as prattle
And sallied forth to fight, being self-willed,
And there he met Achilles and was killed.
The tale is long and somewhat overdrawn,
330 And anyhow it's very nearly dawn,
So let me say in very brief conclusion
My dream undoubtedly foretells confusion,
It bodes me ill, I say. And, furthermore,
Upon your laxatives I set no store,
335 For they are venomous. I've suffered by them
Often enough before and I defy them.
    "And now, let's talk of fun and stop all this.

**15. Scipio Africanus**
(sip′ ē ō af′ ri kā′ nəs):
A famous Roman general
(237–183 B.C.).

**16. Andromache** (an
dräm′ ə kē) **. . . wife:** She
was the wife of the
greatest warrior in Troy,
Hector, at the time of the
Trojan War.

Dear Madam, as I hope for Heaven's bliss,
Of one thing God has sent me plenteous grace,
340　For when I see the beauty of your face,
That scarlet loveliness about your eyes,
All thought of terror and confusion dies.
For it's as certain as the Creed, I know,
*Mulier est hominis confusio*
345　(A Latin tag, dear Madam, meaning this:
'Woman is man's delight and all his bliss'),
For when at night I feel your feathery side,
Although perforce I cannot take a ride
Because, alas, our perch was made too narrow,
350　Delight and solace fill me to the marrow
And I defy all visions and all dreams!''
　　And with that word he flew down from the beams,
For it was day, and down his hens flew all,
And with a chuck he gave the troupe a call
355　For he had found a seed upon the floor.
Royal he was, he was afraid no more.
He feathered Pertelote in wanton play
And trod her twenty times ere prime of day.
Grim as a lion's was his manly frown
360　As on his toes he sauntered up and down;
He scarcely deigned to set his foot to ground
And every time a seed of corn was found
He gave a chuck, and up his wives ran all.
Thus royal as a prince who strides his hall
365　Leave we this Chanticleer engaged on feeding
And pass to the adventure that was breeding.
　　Now when the month in which the world began,
March, the first month, when God created man,
Was over, and the thirty-second day
370　Thereafter ended, on the third of May
It happened that Chanticleer in all his pride,
His seven wives attendant at his side,
Cast his eyes upward to the blazing sun,
Which in the sign of *Taurus* then had run
375　His twenty-one degrees and somewhat more,
And knew by nature and no other lore
That it was nine o'clock. With blissful voice
He crew triumphantly and said, ''Rejoice,
Behold the sun! The sun is up, my seven.
380　Look, it has climbed forty degrees in heaven,
Forty degrees and one in fact, by this.
Dear Madam Pertelote, my earthly bliss,
Hark to those blissful birds and how they sing!
Look at those pretty flowers, how they spring!

385 Solace and revel fill my heart!'' He laughed.
   But in that moment Fate let fly her shaft;
Ever the latter end of joy is woe,
God knows that worldly joy is swift to go.
A rhetorician[17] with a flair for style
390 Could chronicle this maxim in his file
Of Notable Remarks with safe conviction.
Then let the wise give ear; this is no fiction
My story is as true, I undertake,
As that of good Sir Lancelot du Lake[18]
395 Who held all women in such high esteem.
Let me return full circle to my theme.
   A coal-tipped fox of sly iniquity[19]
That had been lurking round the grove for three
Long years, that very night burst through and passed
400 Stockade and hedge, as Providence forecast,
Into the yard where Chanticleer the Fair
Was wont, with all his ladies, to repair.
Still, in a bed of cabbages, he lay
Until about the middle of the day
405 Watching the cock and waiting for his cue,
As all these homicides so gladly do
That lie about in wait to murder men.
O false assassin, lurking in thy den!
O new Iscariot, new Ganelon!
410 And O Greek Sinon,[20] thou whose treachery won
Troy town and brought it utterly to sorrow!
O Chanticleer, accursed be that morrow
That brought thee to the yard from thy high beams!
Thou hadst been warned, and truly, by thy dreams

**17. rhetorician** (ret′ ə rish′ ən) *n.*: A person skilled in public speaking or writing.

**18. Sir Lancelot du Lake:** The most celebrated of King Arthur's knights of the Round Table.
**19. iniquity** (i nik′ wi tē) *n.*: Wickedness.

**20. Iscariot . . . Ganelon . . . Sinon:** Each of these men was famous for betrayal. Judas Iscariot betrayed Jesus Christ; Ganelon betrayed Charlemagne's greatest knight, Roland; and Sinon convinced King Priam to bring the Trojan horse, filled with Greek troops, into Troy.

THE NUN'S PRIEST
DETAIL FROM THE ELLESMERE
MANUSCRIPT
*The Huntington Library, San Marino, California*

415 That this would be a perilous day for thee.
  But that which God's foreknowledge can foresee
Must needs occur, as certain men of learning
Have said. Ask any scholar of discerning;
He'll say the Schools are filled with altercation
420 On this vexed matter of predestination[21]
Long bandied by a hundred thousand men.
How can I sift it to the bottom then?
The Holy Doctor St. Augustine shines
In this, and there is Bishop Bradwardine's
425 Authority, Boethius'[22] too, decreeing
Whether the fact of God's divine foreseeing
Constrains me to perform a certain act
  —And by ''constraint'' I mean the simple fact
Of mere compulsion by necessity—
430 Or whether a free choice is granted me
To do a given act or not to do it
Though, ere it was accomplished, God foreknew it,
Or whether Providence is not so stringent
And merely makes necessity contingent.
435   But I decline discussion of the matter;
My tale is of a cock and of the clatter
That came of following his wife's advice
To walk about his yard on the precise
Morning after the dream of which I told.
440   O woman's counsel is so often cold!
A woman's counsel brought us first to woe,
Made Adam out of Paradise to go
Where he had been so merry, so well at ease.
But, for I know not whom it may displease
445 If I suggest that women are to blame,
Pass over that; I only speak in game.
Read the authorities to know about
What has been said of women; you'll find out.
These are the cock's words, and not mine, I'm giving;
450 I think no harm of any woman living.
  Merrily in her dust-bath in the sand
Lay Pertelote. Her sisters were at hand
Basking in sunlight. Chanticleer sang free,
More merrily than a mermaid in the sea
455 (For *Physiologus*[23] reports the thing
And says how well and merrily they sing).
And so it happened as he cast his eye
Towards the cabbage at a butterfly
It fell upon the fox there, lying low.
460 Gone was all inclination then to crow.
''Cok cok,'' he cried, giving a sudden start,

**21. predestination** (prē des' tə nā' shən) *n.*: The idea that God arranges beforehand everything that will happen.

**22. Bishop Bradwardine's . . . Boethius'** (bō ē' thē əs): Bishop Bradwardine was a well-known theologian of Chaucer's time. Boethius (A.D. 480–524) was a famous Roman philosopher.

**23. *Physiologus:*** A book on nature written in Latin meter.

As one who feels a terror at his heart,
For natural instinct teaches beasts to flee
The moment they perceive an enemy,
465 Though they had never met with it before.
　　This Chanticleer was shaken to the core
And would have fled. The fox was quick to say
However, "Sir! Whither so fast away?
Are you afraid of me, that am your friend?
470 A fiend, or worse, I should be, to intend
You harm, or practice villainy upon you;
Dear sir, I was not even spying on you!
Truly I came to do no other thing
Than just to lie and listen to you sing.
475 You have as merry a voice as God has given
To any angel in the courts of Heaven;
To that you add a musical sense as strong
As had Boethius who was skilled in song.
My Lord your Father (God receive his soul!),
480 Your mother too—how courtly, what control!—
Have honored my poor house, to my great ease;
And you, sir, too, I should be glad to please.
For, when it comes to singing, I'll say this
(Else may these eyes of mine be barred from bliss),
485 There never was a singer I would rather
Have heard at dawn than your respected father.
All that he sang came welling from his soul
And how he put his voice under control!
The pains he took to keep his eyes tight shut
490 In concentration—then the tip-toe strut,
The slender neck stretched out, the delicate beak!
No singer could approach him in technique
Or rival him in song, still less surpass.
I've read the story in *Burnel the Ass*,[24]
495 Among some other verses, of a cock
Whose leg in youth was broken by a knock
A clergyman's son had given him, and for this
He made the father lose his benefice.
But certainly there's no comparison
500 Between the subtlety of such an one
And the discretion of your father's art
And wisdom. Oh, for charity of heart,
Can you not emulate your sire and sing?"
　　This Chanticleer began to beat a wing
505 As one incapable of smelling treason,
So wholly had this flattery ravished reason.
Alas, my lords! there's many a sycophant[25]
And flatterer that fill your courts with cant

**CHAUCER RECITING TROILUS &
CRESSIDA BEFORE A COURT GATHERING
(FRONTISPIECE)**
*Corpus Christi College*

**24. Burnel the Ass:** A
twelfth-century poem in
which a rooster gains
revenge after being
mistreated by a priest's
son.

**25. sycophant** (sik' ə fənt)
*n.*: A person who seeks
favor by flattering
influential people.

And give more pleasure with their zeal forsooth
510 Than he who speaks in soberness and truth.
Read what *Ecclesiasticus*[26] records
Of flatterers. 'Ware treachery, my lords!

This Chanticleer stood high upon his toes,
He stretched his neck, his eyes began to close,
515 His beak to open; with his eyes shut tight
He then began to sing with all his might.

Sir Russel Fox then leapt to the attack,
Grabbing his gorge he flung him o'er his back
And off he bore him to the woods, the brute,
520 And for the moment there was no pursuit.

O Destiny that may not be evaded!
Alas that Chanticleer had so paraded!
Alas that he had flown down from the beams!
O that his wife took no account of dreams!
525 And on a Friday too to risk their necks!
O Venus, goddess of the joys of sex,
Since Chanticleer thy mysteries professed
And in thy service always did his best,
And more for pleasure than to multiply
530 His kind, on thine own day is he to die?

O Geoffrey, thou my dear and sovereign master[27]
Who, when they brought King Richard to disaster
And shot him dead, lamented so his death,
Would that I had thy skill, thy gracious breath,
535 To chide a Friday half so well as you!
(For he was killed upon a Friday too.)
Then I could fashion you a rhapsody
For Chanticleer in dread and agony.

Sure never such a cry or lamentation

**26. *Ecclesiasticus:*** Not Ecclesiastes, but a book of proverbs included with the Apocrypha in the Authorized Version of the Bible.

**27. O Geoffrey . . . master:** Geoffrey de Vinsauf, twelfth-century author of a book on rhetoric.

**CHAUCER'S CANTERBURY PILGRIMS**
*William Blake*
*The Huntington Library, San Marino, California*

540     Was made by ladies of high Trojan station,
        When Ilium fell and Pyrrhus with his sword
        Grabbed Priam by the beard, their king and lord,
        And slew him there as the *Aeneid* tells,[28]
        As what was uttered by those hens. Their yells
545     Surpassed them all in palpitating fear
        When they beheld the rape of Chanticleer.
        Dame Pertelote emitted sovereign shrieks
        That echoed up in anguish to the peaks
        Louder than those extorted from the wife
550     Of Hasdrubal,[29] when he had lost his life
        And Carthage all in flame and ashes lay.
        She was so full of torment and dismay
        That in the very flames she chose her part
        And burnt to ashes with a steadfast heart.
555     O woeful hens, louder your shrieks and higher
        Than those of Roman matrons when the fire
        Consumed their husbands, senators of Rome,
        When Nero burnt their city and their home,
        Beyond a doubt that Nero was their bale![30]
560        Now let me turn again to tell my tale;
        This blessed widow and her daughters two
        Heard all these hens in clamor and halloo
        And, rushing to the door at all this shrieking,
        They saw the fox towards the covert streaking
565     And, on his shoulder, Chanticleer stretched flat.
        "Look, look!" they cried, "O mercy, look at that!
        Ha! Ha! the fox!" and after him they ran,
        And stick in hand ran many a serving man,
        Ran Coll our dog, ran Talbot, Bran and Shaggy,
570     And with a distaff in her hand ran Maggie,
        Ran cow and calf and ran the very hogs
        In terror at the barking of the dogs;
        The men and women shouted, ran and cursed,
        They ran so hard they thought their hearts would burst,
575     They yelled like fiends in Hell, ducks left the water
        Quacking and flapping as on point of slaughter,
        Up flew the geese in terror over the trees,
        Out of the hive came forth the swarm of bees;
        So hideous was the noise—God bless us all,
580     Jack Straw and all his followers in their brawl[31]
        Were never half so shrill, for all their noise,
        When they were murdering those Flemish boys,
        As that day's hue and cry upon the fox.
        They grabbed up trumpets made of brass and box,
585     Of horn and bone, on which they blew and pooped,
        And therewithal they shouted and they whooped

**28. Sure never . . .
Aeneid tells:** A
reference to the
destruction of Troy as
described in the Roman
poet Virgil's *Aeneid*.

**29. Hasdrubal** (haz' dro͞o
bəl): A Carthaginian
general.

**30. bale:** Evil, harm.

**31. Jack Straw . . .
brawl:** Jack Straw was
one of the leaders of the
Peasants' Revolt (1381).

So that it seemed the very heavens would fall.
    And now, good people, pay attention all.
See how Dame Fortune quickly changes side
590 And robs her enemy of hope and pride!
This cock that lay upon the fox's back
In all his dread contrived to give a quack
And said, "Sir Fox, if I were you, as God's
My witness, I would round upon these clods
595 And shout, 'Turn back, you saucy bumpkins all!
A very pestilence upon you fall!
Now that I have in safety reached the wood
Do what you like, the cock is mine for good;
I'll eat him there in spite of every one.'"
600     The fox replying, "Faith, it shall be done!"
Opened his mouth and spoke. The nimble bird,
Breaking away upon the uttered word,
Flew high into the tree-tops on the spot.
And when the fox perceived where he had got,
605 "Alas," he cried, "alas, my Chanticleer,
I've done you grievous wrong, indeed I fear
I must have frightened you; I grabbed too hard
When I caught hold and took you from the yard.
But, sir, I meant no harm, don't be offended,
610 Come down and I'll explain what I intended;
So help me God I'll tell the truth—on oath!
"No," said the cock, "and curses on us both,
And first on me if I were such a dunce
As let you fool me oftener than once.
615 Never again, for all your flattering lies,
You'll coax a song to make me blink my eyes;
And as for those who blink when they should look,
God blot them from his everlasting Book!"
"Nay, rather," said the fox, "his plagues be flung
620 On all who chatter that should hold their tongue."
    Lo, such it is not to be on your guard
Against the flatterers of the world, or yard,
And if you think my story is absurd,
A foolish trifle of a beast and bird,
625 A fable of a fox, a cock, a hen,
Take hold upon the moral, gentlemen.
    St. Paul himself, a saint of great discerning,
Says that all things are written for our learning;
So take the grain and let the chaff be still.
630 And, gracious Father, if it be thy will
As saith my Savior, make us all good men,
And bring us to his heavenly bliss.
                        Amen.

## THINKING ABOUT THE SELECTION

### Recalling

1. Describe the living conditions of the widow who owns Chanticleer.
2. Which physical features of Chanticleer and Pertelote are presented as especially attractive?
3. What is Pertelote's advice to Chanticleer when he tells her his dream?
4. How does the fox capture Chanticleer and how does Chanticleer escape?

### Interpreting

5. (a) Compare and contrast the methods of argument that Pertelote and Chanticleer use to defend their interpretations of dreams. (b) What are the fallacies in each argument?
6. The first story that Chanticleer tells has the three-part structure typical of medieval tales: an exposition describing the characters and setting, a complication or problem, and a climax. Does "The Nun's Priest's Tale" as a whole follow this pattern? Why or why not?
7. (a) What is the moral of this fable? (b) How seriously do you think the narrator takes this moral? Explain.
8. What does this tale suggest about its teller, the nun's priest?

### Applying

9. What does this tale reveal about the concerns of people in medieval times? Do we share similar concerns today? Explain.

## ANALYZING LITERATURE

### Understanding the Mock-Heroic Style

Chaucer uses the **mock-heroic style** in "The Nun's Priest's Tale," portraying the domestic animals in a barnyard as if they were the heroes and heroines of a great epic. He describes Chanticleer, for example, in terms that seem more appropriate for a mighty warrior: "His comb was redder than fine coral, tall/And battlemented like a castle wall/ . . . Like burnished gold his feathers, flaming bright."

1. Epic heroes are often boastful. (a) How does the narrator portray Chanticleer's boastfulness through his words and behavior? (b) Why does this boastfulness strike a humorous note?
2. Which words and phrases in the description of Pertelote would be more suitable for a noble lady than for a hen?
3. Epics often depict the intervention of gods or goddesses in the affairs of humans. Where does Chaucer imitate this convention?

## CRITICAL THINKING AND READING

### Understanding Courtly Love

According to the tradition of courtly love, popular in medieval times, a knight and a noble lady could only experience love at a distance. The goal was not marriage, or even physical contact, but admiration from afar. The lady's role was to believe in the knight's heroism and to inspire him with a token of her love, like a scarf or belt. His role was to show courage and total devotion.

Does the romance between Pertelote and Chanticleer follow the rules of courtly love? Why or why not?

## THINKING AND WRITING

### Writing a Beast Fable

The beast epic and fable were very popular forms during the medieval period. Write your own beast fable in which you use the mock-heroic style that characterizes "The Nun's Priest's Tale." Select a situation or theme that your classmates will recognize, and decide on the moral lesson that your story will illustrate. Then choose appropriate animal characters. Before writing, briefly outline the exposition, complication, and climax of your tale. As you write, remember to describe the doings of your beasts in lofty, mock-heroic terms. Test the success of your fable by reading it aloud to a group of classmates.

## The Pardoner's Tale *from* The Canterbury Tales

**Writer's Techniques**

**Exemplum.** An anecdote is a brief account of an incident or event. Although "The Pardoner's Tale" may seem rather long for an anecdote, it is a special kind of anecdote—a 238-line anecdote within a sermon, something the Pardoner would have called an *exemplum,* or example. While anecdotes are often personal or biographical, the *exemplum* in "The Pardoner's Tale" is intended to establish the truth of a moral.

The idea for "The Pardoner's Tale" did not originate with Chaucer; it goes back to antiquity. The Pardoner uses this simple but powerful anecdote as an *exemplum* to prove the maxim, *"Radix malorum est cupiditas,"* or "Greed is the root of all evil."

**Writing**

You have heard many sayings similar to "Greed is the root of evil." List at least five such sayings. Try to think of ones for which a good exemplum might be written.

**Primary Source**

In "The Pardoner's Tale," Chaucer drew from traditional stories, such as this exemplum on swearing by Thomas of Cantimpre. Preachers added detail to such exemplums to illustrate their themes more vividly. This exemplum was written before 1263.

> In the city of Louvain, within the boundaries of Brabant we saw a noble and worthy citizen who, rising to go to matins on the holy night of Good Friday, passed in front of a tavern in which dissolute young men were sitting, playing at dice and vying with one another in blasphemies and oaths. Continuing on his way, this citizen found men in the street near the tavern who were making a loud lamentation over a certain stranger who was badly wounded and bleeding. When he asked the men who had inflicted these wounds they answered: 'Those young men who are playing dice.' Entering the tavern, the citizen upbraided the young men for playing on that night and asked them sternly why they had so cruelly beaten the stranger who had been with them. Much astonished, the young men denied that anyone had come in since they had sat down, and protested that they had wounded no one either by word or blow. Going forth quickly with the citizen, they sought for the bleeding stranger but could not find him. Having now recovered their senses, each of them realized that by their terrible oaths they had again insulted the Lord Christ and by their taunts had crucified him afresh.

# *from* The Pardoner's Tale

Geoffrey Chaucer

translated by Nevill Coghill

*During their journey to Canterbury, each of the pilgrims
tells a tale. After the Knight, the Miller, the Reeve, the Nun,
and the narrator have finished, the Pardoner entertains the
others with a tale that supports his claim that "greed is the
root of all evil."*

It's of three rioters I have to tell
Who long before the morning service bell[1]
Were sitting in a tavern for a drink.
And as they sat, they heard the hand-bell clink
5  Before a coffin going to the grave;
One of them called the little tavern-knave[2]
And said "Go and find out at once—look spry!—
Whose corpse is in that coffin passing by;
And see you get the name correctly too."
10  "Sir," said the boy, "no need, I promise you;
Two hours before you came here I was told.
He was a friend of yours in days of old,
And suddenly last night, the man was slain,
Upon his bench, face up, dead drunk again.
15  There came a privy[3] thief, they call him Death,
Who kills us all round here, and in a breath
He speared him through the heart, he never stirred.
And then Death went his way without a word.
He's killed a thousand in the present plague,[4]
20  And, sir, it doesn't do to be too vague
If you should meet him; you had best be wary.
Be on your guard with such an adversary,
Be primed to meet him everywhere you go,
That's what my mother said. It's all I know."
25  The publican[5] joined in with, "By St. Mary.
What the child says is right; you'd best be wary,
This very year he killed, in a large village
A mile away, man, woman, serf at tillage,[6]
Page in the household, children—all there were.
30  Yes, I imagine that he lives round there.
It's well to be prepared in these alarms,
He might do you dishonor." "Huh, God's arms!"

**1. long before . . . bell:**
Long before 9:00 A.M.

**2. tavern-knave:** Serving
boy.

**3. privy:** Secretive.

**4. plague:** The Black
Death, which killed over a
third of the population of
England in 1348 and 1349.

**5. publican:** Innkeeper.

**6. tillage:** Plowing.

The rioter said, "Is he so fierce to meet?
I'll search for him, by Jesus, street by street.
35 God's blessed bones! I'll register a vow!
Here, chaps! The three of us together now,
Hold up your hands, like me, and we'll be brothers
In this affair, and each defend the others,
And we will kill this traitor Death, I say!
40 Away with him as he has made away
With all our friends. God's dignity! To-night!"
     They made their bargain, swore with appetite,
These three, to live and die for one another
As brother-born might swear to his born brother.
45 And up they started in their drunken rage
And made towards this village which the page
And publican had spoken of before.
Many and grisly were the oaths they swore,
Tearing Christ's blessed body to a shred;[7]
50 "If we can only catch him, Death is dead!"
     When they had gone not fully half a mile,
 Just as they were about to cross a stile,
They came upon a very poor old man
Who humbly greeted them and thus began,
55 "God look to you, my lords, and give you quiet!"
To which the proudest of these men of riot
Gave back the answer, "What, old fool? Give place!
Why are you all wrapped up except your face?
Why live so long? Isn't it time to die?"
60     The old, old fellow looked him in the eye
And said, "Because I never yet have found,
Though I have walked to India, searching round
Village and city on my pilgrimage,
One who would change his youth to have my age.
65 And so my age is mine and must be still
Upon me, for such time as God may will.
     "Not even Death, alas, will take my life;
So, like a wretched prisoner at strife
Within himself, I walk alone and wait
70 About the earth, which is my mother's gate,
Knock-knocking with my staff from night to noon
And crying, 'Mother, open to me soon!
Look at me, mother, won't you let me in?
See how I wither, flesh and blood and skin!
75 Alas! When will these bones be laid to rest?
Mother, I would exchange—for that were best—
The wardrobe in my chamber, standing there
So long, for yours! Aye, for a shirt of hair[8]
To wrap me in!' She has refused her grace,
80 Whence comes the pallor of my withered face.

"But it dishonored you when you began
To speak so roughly, sir, to an old man,
Unless he had injured you in word or deed.
It says in holy writ, as you may read,
85  'Thou shalt rise up before the hoary head
And honor it,' And therefore be it said
'Do no more harm to an old man than you,
Being now young, would have another do
When you are old'—if you should live till then.
90  And so may God be with you, gentlemen,
For I must go whither I have to go."

"By God," the gambler said, "you shan't do so,
You don't get off so easy, by St. John!
I heard you mention, just a moment gone,
95  A certain traitor Death who singles out
And kills the fine young fellows hereabout.
And you're his spy, by God! You wait a bit.
Say where he is or you shall pay for it,
By God and by the Holy Sacrament!
100  I say you've joined together by consent
To kill us younger folk, you thieving swine!"

"Well, sirs," he said, "if it be your design
To find out Death, turn up this crooked way
Towards that grove. I left him there today
105  Under a tree, and there you'll find him waiting.
He isn't one to hide for all your prating.
You see that oak? He won't be far to find.
And God protect you that redeemed mankind,
Aye, and amend you!" Thus that ancient man.
110  At once the three young rioters began
To run, and reached the tree, and there they found
A pile of golden florins[9] on the ground,
New-coined, eight bushels of them as they thought.
No longer was it Death those fellows sought,
115  For they were all so thrilled to see the sight,
The florins were so beautiful and bright,
That down they sat beside the precious pile.
The wickedest spoke first after a while.
"Brothers," he said, "you listen to what I say.
120  I'm pretty sharp although I joke away.
It's clear that Fortune has bestowed this treasure
To let us live in jollity and pleasure.
Light come, light go! We'll spend it as we ought.
God's precious dignity! Who would have thought
125  This morning was to be our lucky day?

"If one could only get the gold away,
Back to my house, or else to yours, perhaps—
For as you know, the gold is ours, chaps—
We'd all be at the top of fortune, hey?

**9. florins:** Coins.

130 But certainly it can't be done by day.
   People would call us robbers—a strong gang,
   So our own property would make us hang.
   No, we must bring this treasure back by night
   Some prudent way, and keep it out of sight.
135 And so as a solution I propose
   We draw for lots and see the way it goes.
   The one who draws the longest, lucky man,
   Shall run to town as quickly as he can
   To fetch us bread and wine—but keep things dark—
140 While two remain in hiding here to mark
   Our heap of treasure. If there's no delay,
   When night comes down we'll carry it away,

**THE PARDONER**
*Arthur Szyk for the Canterbury Tales*
The George Macy Companies

All three of us, wherever we have planned.''

He gathered lots and hid them in his hand
145 Bidding them draw for where the luck should fall.
It fell upon the youngest of them all,
And off he ran at once towards the town.

As soon as he had gone, the first sat down
And thus began a parley[10] with the other:
150 ''You know that you can trust me as a brother;
Now let me tell you where your profit lies;
You know our friend has gone to get supplies
And here's a lot of gold that is to be
Divided equally amongst us three.
155 Nevertheless, if I could shape things thus
So that we shared it out—the two of us—
Wouldn't you take it as a friendly turn?''

''But how!'' the other said with some concern,
''Because he knows the gold's with me and you;
160 What can we tell him? What are we to do?'

''Is it a bargain,'' said the first, ''or no?
For I can tell you in a word or so
What's to be done to bring the thing about.''

''Trust me,'' the other said, ''you needn't doubt
165 My word. I won't betray you, I'll be true.''

''Well,'' said his friend, ''you see that we are two,
And two are twice as powerful as one.
Now look; when he comes back, get up in fun
To have a wrestle; then, as you attack,
170 I'll up and put my dagger through his back
While you and he are struggling, as in game;
Then draw your dagger too and do the same.
Then all this money will be ours to spend,
Divided equally of course, dear friend.
175 Then we can gratify our lusts and fill
The day with dicing at our own sweet will.''
Thus these two miscreants[11] agreed to slay
The third and youngest, as you heard me say.

The youngest, as he ran towards the town,
180 Kept turning over, rolling up and down
Within his heart the beauty of those bright
New florins, saying, ''Lord, to think I might
Have all that treasure to myself alone!
Could there be anyone beneath the throne
185 Of God so happy as I then should be?''

And so the Fiend,[12] our common enemy,
Was given power to put it in his thought
That there was always poison to be bought,
And that with poison he could kill his friends.

**10. parley** (pär' lē): Discussion.

**11. miscreants** (mis' krē ənts): Villains.

**12. Fiend:** Satan.

190 To men in such a state the Devil sends
Thoughts of this kind, and has a full permission
To lure them on to sorrow and perdition;[13]
For this young man was utterly content
To kill them both and never to repent.

195     And on he ran, he had no thought to tarry,
Came to the town, found an apothecary
And said, "Sell me some poison if you will,
I have a lot of rats I want to kill
And there's a polecat too about my yard
200 That takes my chickens and it hits me hard;
But I'll get even, as is only right,
With vermin that destroy a man by night."
    The chemist answered, "I've a preparation
Which you shall have, and by my soul's salvation
205 If any living creature eat or drink
A mouthful, ere he has the time to think,
Though he took less than makes a grain of wheat,
You'll see him fall down dying at your feet;
Yes, die he must, and in so short a while
210 You'd hardly have the time to walk a mile,
The poison is so strong, you understand."
    This cursed fellow grabbed into his hand
The box of poison and away he ran
Into a neighboring street, and found a man
215 Who lent him three large bottles. He withdrew
And deftly poured the poison into two.
He kept the third one clean, as well he might,
For his own drink, meaning to work all night
Stacking the gold and carrying it away.
220 And when this rioter, this devil's clay,
Had filled his bottles up with wine, all three,
Back to rejoin his comrades sauntered he.
    Why make a sermon of it? Why waste breath?
Exactly in the way they'd planned his death
225 They fell on him and slew him, two to one.
Then said the first of them when this was done,
"Now for a drink. Sit down and let's be merry,
For later on there'll be the corpse to bury."
And, as it happened, reaching for a sup,
230 He took a bottle full of poison up
And drank; and his companion, nothing loth,
Drank from it also, and they perished both.
    There is, in Avicenna's long relation[14]
Concerning poison and its operation,
235 Trust me, no ghastlier section to transcend
What these two wretches suffered at their end.
Thus these two murderers received their due,
So did the treacherous young poisoner too.

**13. perdition:** Damnation.

**14. Avicenna's** (aʹ vǝ senʹ ǝz) **long relation:** A book on medicines written by Avicenna (980–1037), an Arab physician, which contains a chapter on poisons.

# THINKING ABOUT THE SELECTION

## Recalling

1. What do the three rioters pledge to do?
2. (a) What does the old man tell the rioters they will find under a tree? (b) What do they actually find there?
3. How do the two rioters decide to increase their share of the gold? Explain their plan.
4. What does the youngest rioter do when he goes to town for bread and wine?

## Interpreting

5. In line 39, Death is presented as a traitor. Do you think this description appropriate? Explain you answer.
6. Do the rioters keep the pledge they made in the tavern? Why or why not?
7. Does the old man know that in directing the three rioters to the oak tree he is sending them to their deaths? Explain.

## Applying

8. What person in the news today, or in the recent past, has shown character traits similar to those of the Pardoner?

# ANALYZING LITERATURE

## Understanding an Anecdote (Exemplum)

"The Pardoner's Tale" is an *exemplum,* a brief moral story that the Pardoner tells the pilgrims. In medieval times an *exemplum* was often included in a sermon.

1. How does the young rioter's dialogue with the chemist help to characterize both the rioter and his two companions?
2. What moral does this exemplum establish?
3. In what ways does "The Pardoner's Tale" differ from a short story?

# CRITICAL THINKING AND READING

## Making Inferences

In the Prologue Chaucer makes the point that he is reporting the pilgrims' tales, "using their very phrases." Therefore, although the narrator of *The Canterbury Tales* is Chaucer, the narrator of each individual tale is a particular pilgrim. You can make judgments about the Pardoner based on his own narration. Since Chaucer has already commented in the Prologue on the Pardoner's character, you have a chance to compare Chaucer's view of the Pardoner with the Pardoner's view of himself.

1. Does the topic the Pardoner chooses for his *exemplum* reflect his own interests? Explain.
2. Considering Chaucer's Prologue, how seriously do you think the Pardoner takes his moral that "Greed is the root of evil"? Explain.

# SPEAKING AND LISTENING

## Reading Middle English Aloud

After the Norman conquest of England in 1066, there were two languages in daily use: the French of the invaders and the Old English of the natives. As time passed, the English language began to change. By about 1150 the changes in English were notable enough for later scholars to identify the start of a new period; Middle English lasted roughly from 1150 to 1500.

Middle English is much easier to read than is Old English, but there are differences between it and the language we use today. In reading Middle English, you pronounce every syllable: *bathed* is /bath′ ed/; *soote* is /sō′ tə/. Some consonants that today are silent were sounded in Middle English: *k* in *k*nyght; *g* in *g*nawe; *l* in fo*l*k; and *gh* in drou*gh*te.

Read aloud lines 1–25 on page 159.

# THINKING AND WRITING

## Writing an Analysis

Write an essay analyzing "The Pardoner's Tale." An analysis is not a plot summary; it is an explanation of how the various elements in a literary work fit together. In analyzing Chaucer's tale, consider at least three of these elements: characters, plot, dialogue, moral, rhyme scheme, similes, symbolism.

# CROSS CURRENTS

## Travel Writing

Travel became important during the Middle Ages and many travelers—both fictional and real-life—kept records of their journeys. Chaucer's pilgrims set off for Canterbury, King Arthur and his knights encountered strange creatures on their quests, and the real-life Marco Polo visited the court of Kublai Khan.

Writing about travel has been important throughout the ages and across cultures. For example, traveling along the Silk Road to India in the year 648, Prince Tripitaka stopped at the oasis of Kharashahr to describe an unusual custom. "The children born of common parents," he wrote, "have their heads flattened by the pressure of a wooden board." Not all travel diaries note such remarkable customs, but then again, not all travelers encounter waters "bluish-black in color, salty and bitter in taste" in whose depths "dragons and fishes swim together; scaly monsters rise to the surface,

**WORLD MAP: CATHAY AND THE EMPIRE OF THE GREAT KHAN, 1459**
*Mauro*
Biblioteca Nazionale Marciana, Venice

and passing travelers pray to them for good fortune."

## EDUCATIONAL ACCOUNTS?

Whether the things travelers encounter on their journeys are exciting or commonplace, an astonishing number of people are moved to record their voyages in diaries. Many justify their accounts by claiming that travel is educational. E. S. Bates, for example, describes the "educational" sights people saw on the Continent in the 1600's:

> Torture accompanying execution was common, and branding and mutilation things that no traveller could well avoid seeing. But none seemed to want to avoid them: Evelyn [author of a famous diary] went to the Chatelet prison at Paris to look on while a prisoner underwent legal torture. The only occasions that seem to have struck them as too horrible was when the headsman bungled matters: a Dutchman at Paris saw one try sixteen times and then have to be assisted.

It appears that education, like beauty, may be in the eye of the beholder!

## DIGNITY AND DECORUM

A travel diary allows one to record one's thoughts after the fact, and still maintain one's dignity. Few people were as famous for their dignity as Queen Victoria of England. Notice how she maintained her pride even as her carriage tumbled over, spilling her and Princess Alice to the ground.

**A MEDIEVAL VIEW OF THE UNIVERSE**
*Ronald Sheridan Ancient Art and Architecture Collection*

There was an awful pause, during which Alice said: "We are upsetting." In another moment—during which I had time to reflect whether we should be killed or not, and thought there were still things I had not settled and wanted to—the carriage turned over on its side, and we were all precipitated to the ground!"

According to Victoria's account, she "precipitated" from the carriage. No "fall" or "drop" here!

## "OPEN THE HEART'S STORE"

A travel diary gives us a way to say that this is what I, not the camera, saw. This is how Clara Milburn, an ordinary Englishwoman, voiced it in her travel diary: "There is so much background, one can't be dull, but can just open the heart's store, look round the shelves, take down the memory and live it over again. Grand!"

## 1375[?]

Audiences in the Middle Ages enjoyed tales of adventure and fantasy, featuring heroes and rogues, magicians and monsters. One of the finest of these medieval romances, *Sir Gawain and the Green Knight,* was written by an unknown bard who lived at the time of Chaucer. "Master Anonymous," as the *Gawain* poet has been called, tells an unforgettable tale about one of the legendary knights of King Arthur's Round Table.

Although the poet is unknown, the *Gawain* manuscript (of which the British Museum owns the only copy) suggests something of its creator's background. The poet probably lived in northwestern England, judging by the poem's dialect and by its old-fashioned alliterative verse, neither of which reflects the fashion in Chaucer's London. Nevertheless, the poet is familiar with life at court and, like Chaucer, may have been connected to an aristocratic household. The poet also seems to have read widely in Latin and French as well as in English.

*Sir Gawain's* plot elements date back many centuries. In ancient vegetation myths, beheading is a ritual death intended to ensure the return of spring and the growth of new crops. More in line with Sir Gawain's adventure, a ninth century Irish narrative recounts a beheading contest as the supreme test of courage. Twelfth century French romances tell a similar tale, while the temptations faced by young Gawain may owe something to early French stories.

Arthurian legends, popular throughout Europe, developed orally over a long period of time. Despite this lengthy tradition, *Sir Gawain* is an original and masterful work. Not only is it excitingly told, but the poet introduces a high degree of realism into the setting. Most medieval romances take place with Camelot shimmering in the bright days of spring or summer. Not this poem. Sir Gawain's adventures occur in the bleakness of winter, with the chill desolation reinforcing the hero's trials. Nor is the hero himself without fault, as he is in so many other tales of knights and ladies. Sir Gawain is admirable but not invulnerable, which lends a psychological dimension to this medieval story. As one critic put it, the hero "gains in human credibility what he loses in ideal perfection."

# *from* Sir Gawain and the Green Knight

**Literary Forms**

**Medieval Romance.** From the twelfth to the fifteenth century, medieval romances were the popular literature of England. Based on the feudal ideal of chivalry and imbued with adventure, love, and the supernatural, medieval romances typically feature kings, knights, and damsels in distress. The earliest romances were always in verse, but later ones were sometimes in prose.

The enduring popularity of these tales of romance stems in part from their glamorous portrayal of castle life—the festivals, the feasts, the knights in armor, the courtly love. Medieval romances were for many generations the stock in trade of professional storytellers, some of whom were employed in noble households, others of whom made the rounds of modest inns and taverns. As literacy increased, the status of the minstrel declined, but the romances, preserved in written form, continue to have appeal even today.

Of all the medieval romances, the best known are those about King Arthur and his Knights of the Round Table. Arthur, who may have been a Welsh chieftain in the fifth or sixth century, is the central figure in early Arthurian romances. In later ones King Arthur's knights, such as Sir Gawain and Sir Lancelot, assume the principal roles.

**Writing**

In a few sentences, comment on the following statement by Charles Kingsley, nineteenth century English historian and writer: "Some say that the spirit of chivalry is past, that the spirit of romance is dead. The age of chivalry is never past, so long as there is a wrong left unredressed on earth."

**Primary Source**

Many authors have retold the Arthurian legend, perhaps the most spellbinding of all medieval romances. One of the most famous versions is T. H. White's *The Once and Future King*. Here, White describes some of the glories of the age:

> For there, under the window in Arthur's Gramarye, the sun's rays flamed from a hundred jewels of stained glass in monasteries and convents, or danced from the pinnacles of cathedrals and castles, which their builders had actually loved . . . Think of the glass itself, with its five grand colors stained right through. It was rougher than ours, thicker, fitted in smaller pieces . . . Picture the insides of those ancient churches . . . insides blazing with color, plastered with frescoes in which all the figures stood on tiptoe, fluttering with tapestry or with brocades from Bagdad.

# *from* Sir Gawain and the Green Knight

## translated by Marie Borroff

*The work begins at the start of a New Year's Eve feast at King Arthur's Court in Camelot. Before anyone has started eating, the festivities are interrupted by an immense green knight who suddenly appears at the hall door. The knight rides a green horse and is armed with a gigantic ax.*

This horseman hurtles in, and the hall enters;
Riding to the high dais,[1] recked he no danger;
Not a greeting he gave as the guests he o'erlooked,
Nor wasted his words, but "Where is," he said,
5  "The captain of this crowd? Keenly I wish
To see that sire with sight, and to himself say my say."
    He swaggered all about
    To scan the host so gay;
    He halted, as if in doubt
10    Who in that hall held sway.

There were stares on all sides as the stranger spoke,
For much did they marvel what it might mean
That a horseman and a horse should have such a hue,
Grow green as the grass, and greener, it seemed.
15  Then green fused on gold more glorious by far.
All the onlookers eyed him, and edged nearer,
And awaited in wonder what he would do,
For many sights had they seen, but such a one never,
So that phantom and fairy the folk there deemed it,
20  Therefore chary[2] of answer was many a champion bold,
And stunned at his strong words stone-still they sat
In a swooning silence in the stately hall.
As all were slipped into sleep, so slackened their speech
  apace.
    Not all, I think, for dread,
25    But some of courteous grace
    Let him who was their head
    Be spokesman in that place.

Then Arthur before the high dais that entrance beholds,
And hailed him, as behooved, for he had no fear,

**1. dais** (dā' is) *n.*: Platform.

**2. chary** (cher' ē) *adj.*: Not giving freely.

**FROM THE ROMANCE OF KING ARTHUR
AND HIS KNIGHTS OF THE ROUND TABLE**
*Arthur Rackham*
*Weathervane Books*

from *Sir Gawain and the Green Knight*    171

30 And said "Fellow, in faith you have found fair welcome;
The head of this hostelry Arthur am I;
Leap lightly down, and linger, I pray,
And the tale of your intent you shall tell us after."
"Nay, so help me," said the other, "He that on high sits,
35 To tarry here any time, 'twas not mine errand;
But as the praise of you, prince, is puffed up so high,
And your court and your company are counted the best,
Stoutest under steel-gear on steeds to ride,
Worthiest of their works the wide world over,
40 And peerless to prove in passages of arms,
And courtesy here is carried to its height,
And so at this season I have sought you out.
You may be certain by the branch that I bear in hand
That I pass here in peace, and would part friends,
45 For had I come to this court on combat bent,
I have a hauberk[3] at home, and a helm beside,
A shield and a sharp spear, shining bright,
And other weapons to wield, I ween well, to boot,
But as I willed no war, I wore no metal.
50 But if you be so bold as all men believe,
You will graciously grant the game that I ask by right."
　　　　Arthur answer gave
　　　　And said, "Sir courteous knight,
　　　　If contest here you crave,
55 　　　　You shall not fail to fight."

"Nay, to fight, in good faith, is far from my thought;
There are about on these benches but beardless children,
Were I here in full arms on a haughty[4] steed,
For measured against mine, their might is puny.
60 And so I call in this court for a Christmas game,
For 'tis Yule, and New Year, and many young bloods about;
If any in this house such hardihood claims,
Be so bold in his blood, his brain so wild,
As stoutly to strike one stroke for another,
65 I shall give him as my gift this gisarme[5] noble,
This ax, that is heavy enough, to handle as he likes,
And I shall bide the first blow, as bare as I sit.
If there be one so wilful my words to assay,
Let him leap hither lightly, lay hold of this weapon;
70 I quitclaim it forever, keep it as his own,
And I shall stand him a stroke, steady on this floor,
So you grant me the guerdon to give him another, sans
　　blame.[6]
　　　　In a twelvemonth[7] and a day
　　　　He shall have of me the same;
75 　　　　Now be it seen straightway
　　　　Who dares take up the game."

**3. hauberk** (hô′ bərk) *n.*: Coat of armor.

**4. haughty** (hôt′ ē) *adj.*: Lofty.

**5. gisarme** (gi zärm′) *n.*: Battle-ax.

**6. I . . . blame:** I will stand firm while he strikes me with the ax provided that you reward me with the opportunity to do the same to him without being blamed for it.

**7. twelvemonth:** A year.

If he astonished them at first, stiller were then
All that household in hall, the high and the low;
The stranger on his green steed stirred in the saddle,
80  And roisterously his red eyes he rolled all about,
Bent his bristling brows, that were bright green,
Wagged his beard as he watched who would arise.
When the court kept its counsel he coughed aloud,
And cleared his throat coolly, the clearer to speak:
85  "What, is this Arthur's house," said that horseman then,
"Whose fame is so fair in far realms and wide?
Where is now your arrogance and your awesome deeds,
Your valor and your victories and your vaunting words?
Now are the revel and renown of the Round Table
90  Overwhelmed with a word of one man's speech,
For all cower and quake, and no cut felt!"
With this he laughs so loud that the lord grieved;
The blood for sheer shame shot to his face, and pride.
        With rage his face flushed red,
95          And so did all beside.
        Then the king as bold man bred
        Toward the stranger took a stride.


And said, "Sir, now we see you will say but folly,
Which whoso has sought, it suits that he find.
100  No guest here is aghast of your great words.
Give to me your gisarme, in God's own name,
And the boon you have begged shall straight be granted."
He leaps to him lightly, lays hold of his weapon;
The green fellow on foot fiercely alights.
105  Now has Arthur his ax, and the haft grips,
And sternly stirs it about, on striking bent.
The stranger before him stood there erect,
Higher than any in the house by a head and more;
With stern look as he stood, he stroked his beard,
110  And with undaunted countenance drew down his coat,
No more moved nor dismayed for his mighty dints
Than any bold man on bench had brought him a drink of
  wine.
        Gawain by Guenevere
        Toward the king doth now incline:
115         "I beseech, before all here,
        That this melee may be mine."


"Would you grant me the grace," said Gawain to the king,
"To be gone from this bench and stand by you there,
If I without discourtesy might quit this board,
120  And if my liege lady[8] misliked it not,
I would come to your counsel before your court noble.

**8. liege** (lēj) **lady:**
Guenevere, the wife of the lord, Arthur, to whom Gawain is bound to give service and allegiance.

from *Sir Gawain and the Green Knight*  173

For I find it not fit, as in faith it is known,
When such a boon is begged before all these knights,
Though you be tempted thereto, to take it on yourself
125 While so bold men about upon benches sit,
That no host under heaven is hardier of will,
Nor better brothers-in-arms where battle is joined;
I am the weakest, well I know, and of wit feeblest;
And the loss of my life would be least of any;
130 That I have you for uncle is my only praise;
My body, but for your blood, is barren of worth;
And for that this folly befits not a king,
And 'tis I that have asked it, it ought to be mine,
And if my claim be not comely let all this court judge in
sight."
135       The court assays the claim,
      And in counsel all unite
      To give Gawain the game
      And release the king outright.

Then the king called the knight to come to his side,
140 And he rose up readily, and reached him with speed,
Bows low to his lord, lays hold of the weapon,
And he releases it lightly, and lifts up his hand,
And gives him God's blessing, and graciously prays
That his heart and his hand may be hardy both.
145 "Keep, cousin," said the king, "what you cut with this day,
And if you rule it aright, then readily, I know,
You shall stand the stroke it will strike after."
Gawain goes to the guest with gisarme in hand,
And boldly he bides there, abashed not a whit.
150 Then hails he Sir Gawain, the horseman in green:
"Recount we our contract, ere you come further.
First I ask and adjure you, how you are called
That you tell me true, so that trust it I may."
"In good faith," said the good knight, "Gawain am I
155 Whose buffet befalls you,[9] whate'er betide after,
And at this time twelvemonth take from you another
With what weapon you will, and with no man else alive."
      The other nods assent:
      "Sir Gawain, as I may thrive,
160       I am wondrous well content
      That you this dint[10] shall drive."

"Sir Gawain," said the Green Knight, "By God, I rejoice
That your fist shall fetch this favor I seek,
And you have readily rehearsed, and in right terms,
165 Each clause of my covenant with the king your lord,

**9. Whose . . . you:** Whose blow you will receive.

**10. dint:** Blow.

Save that you shall assure me, sir, upon oath,
That you shall seek me yourself, wheresoever you deem
My lodgings may lie, and look for such wages[11]

**11. wages:** A blow.

As you have offered me here before all this host."
170 "What is the way there?" said Gawain, "Where do you
        dwell?"
I heard never of your house, by Him that made me,
Nor I know you not, knight, your name nor your court.
But tell me truly thereof, and teach me your name,
And I shall fare forth to find you, so far as I may,
175 And this I say in good certain, and swear upon oath."
"That is enough in New Year, you need say no more,"
Said the knight in the green to Gawain the noble,
"If I tell you true, when I have taken your knock,
And if you handily have hit, you shall hear straightway
180 Of my house and my home and my own name;
Then follow in my footsteps by faithful accord.
And if I spend no speech, you shall speed the better:
You can feast with your friends, nor further trace my
        tracks.[12]

**12. If I tell you . . . tracks** (lines 178–183): The Green Knight tells Gawain that he will let him know where he lives after he has taken the blow. If he is unable to speak following the blow, there will be no need for Gawain to know.

            Now hold your grim tool steady
185         And show us how it hacks."
            "Gladly, sir; all ready,"
            Says Gawain; he strokes the ax.

The Green Knight upon ground girds him with care:
Bows a bit with his head, and bares his flesh:
190 His long lovely locks he laid over his crown,
Let the naked nape for the need be shown.
Gawain grips to his ax and gathers it aloft—
The left foot on the floor before him he set—
Brought it down deftly upon the bare neck,
195 That the shock of the sharp blow shivered the bones
And cut the flesh cleanly and clove it in twain,[13]

**13. clove it in twain:** Split it in two.

That the blade of bright steel bit into the ground.
The head was hewn off and fell to the floor;
Many found it at their feet, as forth it rolled;
200 The blood gushed from the body, bright on the green,
Yet fell not the fellow, nor faltered a whit,
But stoutly he starts forth upon stiff shanks,
And as all stood staring he stretched forth his hand,
Laid hold of his head and heaved it aloft,
205 Then goes to the green steed, grasps the bridle,
Steps into the stirrup, bestrides his mount,
And his head by the hair in his hand holds,
And as steady he sits in the stately saddle
As he had met with no mishap, nor missing were his head.

210         His bulk about he haled,
                  That fearsome body that bled;
                  There were many in the court that quailed
                  Before all his say was said.

     For the head in his hand he holds right up;
215  Toward the first on the dais directs he the face,
     And it lifted up its lids, and looked with wide eyes,
     And said as much with its mouth as now you may hear:
     "Sir Gawain, forget not to go as agreed,
     And cease not to seek till me, sir, you find,
220  As you promised in the presence of these proud knights.
     To the Green Chapel come, I charge you, to take
     Such a dint as you have dealt—you have well deserved
     That your neck should have a knock on New Year's morn.
     The Knight of the Green Chapel I am well-known to many,
225  Wherefore you cannot fail to find me at last;
     Therefore come, or be counted a recreant knight."
     With a roisterous rush he flings round the reins,
     Hurtles out at the hall door, his head in his hand,
     That the flint fire flew from the flashing hooves.
230  Which way he went, not one of them knew
     Nor whence he was come in the wide world so fair.
               The king and Gawain gay
               Make a game of the Green Knight there,
               Yet all who saw it say
235            'Twas a wonder past compare.

     Though high-born Arthur at heart had wonder,
     He let no sign be seen, but said aloud
     To the comely queen, with courteous speech,
     "Dear dame, on this day dismay you no whit;
240  Such crafts are becoming at Christmastide,
     Laughing at interludes, light songs and mirth,
     Amid dancing of damsels with doughty knights.
     Nevertheless of my meat now let me partake,
     For I have met with a marvel, I may not deny."
245  He glanced at Sir Gawain, and gaily he said,
     "Now, sir, hang up your ax, that has hewn enough,"
     And over the high dais it was hung on the wall
     That men in amazement might on it look,
     And tell in true terms the tale of the wonder.
250  Then they turned toward the table, those two together,
     The good king and Gawain, and made great feast,
     With all dainties double, dishes rare,
     With all manner of meat and minstrelsy both,
     Such happiness wholly had they that day in hold.

Now take care, Sir Gawain,
That your courage wax not cold
When you must turn again
To your enterprise foretold.

*The following November, Sir Gawain sets out to fulfill his promise to the Green Knight. For weeks he travels alone through the cold, threatening woods of North Wales. Then, after he prays for shelter, he comes upon a wondrous castle on Christmas Eve, where he is greeted warmly by the lord of the castle and his lady. Sir Gawain inquires about the location of the Green Chapel, and the lord assures him that it is nearby and promises to provide him with a guide to lead him there on New Year's Day. Before the lord and Sir Gawain retire for the night, they agree to exchange whatever they receive during the next three days. Sir Gawain keeps his pledge for the first two days, but on the third day he does not give the lord the magic green girdle that the lady gives him because she promises that the girdle will protect him from any harm. The next day, Gawain sets out for the Green Chapel. His guide urges him not to proceed, but Gawain refuses to take this advice. He feels that it would be dishonorable not to fulfill his pledge. He is determined to accept his fate; however, he does wear the magic green girdle that the lady had given him.*

**"SIR GAWAIN AND THE GREEN KNIGHT"**
*The Bodleian Library, Oxford*

He puts his heels to his horse, and picks up the path;
260   Goes in beside a grove where the ground is steep,
Rides down the rough slope right to the valley;
And then he looked a little about him—the landscape was
    wild,
And not a soul to be seen, nor sign of a dwelling,
But high banks on either hand hemmed it about,
265   With many a ragged rock and rough-hewn crag;
The skies seemed scored by the scowling peaks.
Then he halted his horse, and hoved there a space,
And sought on every side for a sight of the Chapel,
But no such place appeared, which puzzled him sore,
270   Yet he saw some way off what seemed like a mound,
A hillock high and broad, hard by the water,
Where the stream fell in foam down the face of the steep
And bubbled as if it boiled on its bed below.
The knight urges his horse, and heads for the knoll;
275   Leaps lightly to earth; loops well the rein
Of his steed to a stout branch, and stations him there.
He strides straight to the mound, and strolls all about,
Much wondering what it was, but no whit the wiser;
It had a hole at one end, and on either side,
280   And was covered with coarse grass in clumps all without,
And hollow all within, like some old cave,
Or a crevice of an old crag—he could not discern aright.
        "Can this be the Chapel Green?
        Alack!" said the man, "Here might
285         The devil himself be seen
        Saying matins[14] at black midnight!"

"Now by heaven," said he, "it is bleak hereabouts;
This prayer house is hideous, half covered with grass!
Well may the grim man mantled in green
290   Hold here his orisons,[15] in hell's own style!
Now I feel it is the Fiend, in my five wits,
That has tempted me to this tryst,[16] to take my life;
This is a Chapel of mischance, may the mischief take it!
As accursed a country church as I came upon ever!"
295   With his helm on his head, his lance in his hand,
He stalks toward the steep wall of that strange house.
Then he heard, on the hill, behind a hard rock,
Beyond the brook, from the bank, a most barbarous din:
Lord! it clattered in the cliff fit to cleave it in two,
300   As one upon a grindstone ground a great scythe!
Lord! it whirred like a mill-wheel whirling about!
Lord! it echoed loud and long, lamentable to hear!
Then "By heaven," said the bold knight, "That business up
    there
Is arranged for my arrival, or else I am much misled.

**14. matins** *n.*: Morning prayers.

**15. orisons** *n.*: Prayers.

**16. tryst** (trist) *n.*: Meeting.

305                Let God work! Ah me!
                    All hope of help has fled!
                    Forfeit my life may be
                    But noise I do not dread."

Then he listened no longer, but loudly he called,
310   "Who has power in this place, high parley to hold?
For none greets Sir Gawain, or give him good day;
If any would a word with him, let him walk forth
And speak now or never, to speed his affairs."
"Abide," said one on the bank above over his head,
315   "And what I promised you once shall straightway be
       given."
Yet he stayed not his grindstone, nor stinted its noise,
But worked awhile at his whetting before he would rest,
And then he comes around a crag, from a cave in the rocks,
Hurtling out of hiding with a hateful weapon,
320   A Danish ax[17] devised for that day's deed,
With a broad blade and bright, bent in a curve,
Filed to a fine edge—four feet it measured
By the length of the lace that was looped round the haft.
And in form as at first, the fellow all green,
325   His lordly face and his legs, his locks and his beard,
Save that firm upon two feet forward he strides,
Sets a hand on the ax-head, the haft to the earth;
When he came to the cold stream, and cared not to wade,
He vaults over on his ax, and advances amain
330   On a broad bank of snow, overbearing and brisk of mood.
             Little did the knight incline
             When face to face they stood;
             Said the other man, "Friend mine,
             It seems your word holds good!"

**17. Danish ax:** A long-bladed ax.

335   "God love you, Sir Gawain!" said the Green Knight then,
"And well met this morning, man, at my place!
And you have followed me faithfully and found me betimes,
And on the business between us we both are agreed:
Twelve months ago today you took what was yours,
340   And you at this New Year must yield me the same.
And we have met in these mountains, remote from all eyes:
There is none here to halt us or hinder our sport;
Unhasp your high helm, and have here your wages;
Make no more demur than I did myself
345   When you hacked off my head with one hard blow."
"No, by God," said Sir Gawain, "that granted me life,
I shall grudge not the guerdon,[18] grim though it prove;
And you may lay on as you like till the last of my part be
     paid."

**18. guerdon:** Reward.

350           He proffered, with good grace,
              His bare neck to the blade,
              And feigned a cheerful face:
              He scorned to seem afraid.

Then the grim man in green gathers his strength,
355  Heaves high the heavy ax to hit him the blow.
With all the force in his frame he fetches it aloft,
With a grimace as grim as he would grind him to bits;
Had the blow he bestowed been as big as he threatened,
A good knight and gallant had gone to his grave.
360  But Gawain at the great ax glanced up aside
As down it descended with death-dealing force,
And his shoulders shrank a little from the sharp iron.
Abruptly the brawny man breaks off the stroke,
And then reproved with proud words that prince among
     knights.
365  "You are not Gawain the glorious," the green man said,
"That never fell back on field in the face of the foe,
And now you flee for fear, and have felt no harm:
Such news of that knight I never heard yet!
I moved not a muscle when you made to strike,
370  Nor caviled at the cut in King Arthur's house;
My head fell to my feet, yet steadfast I stood,
And you, all unharmed, are wholly dismayed—
Wherefore the better man I, by all odds, must be."
            Said Gawain, "Strike once more;
375            I shall neither flinch nor flee;
            But if my head falls to the floor
            There is no mending me!"

"But go on, man, in God's name, and get to the point!
Deliver me my destiny, and do it out of hand,
380  For I shall stand to the stroke and stir not an inch
Till your ax has hit home—on my honor I swear it!"
"Have at thee then!" said the other, and heaves it aloft,
And glares down as grimly as he had gone mad.
He made a mighty feint, but marred not his hide;
385  Withdrew the ax adroitly before it did damage.
Gawain gave no ground, nor glanced up aside,
But stood still as a stone, or else a stout stump
That is held in hard earth by a hundred roots.
Then merrily does he mock him, the man all in green:
390  "So now you have your nerve again, I needs must strike;
Uphold the high knighthood that Arthur bestowed,
And keep your neck-bone clear, if this cut allows!"
Then was Gawain gripped with rage, and grimly he said.

"Why, thrash away, tyrant, I tire of your threats;
395 You make such a scene, you must frighten yourself."
Said the green fellow, "In faith, so fiercely you speak
That I shall finish this affair, nor further grace allow."
      He stands prepared to strike
      And scowls with both lip and brow;
400      No marvel if the man mislike
      Who can hope no rescue now.

He gathered up the grim ax and guided it well:
Let the barb at the blade's end brush the bare throat;
He hammered down hard, yet harmed him no whit
405 Save a scratch on one side, that severed the skin;
The end of the hooked edge entered the flesh,
And a little blood lightly leapt to the earth.
And when the man beheld his own blood bright on the
    snow,
He sprang a spear's length with feet spread wide,
410 Seized his high helm, and set it on his head,
Shoved before his shoulders the shield at his back,
Bares his trusty blade, and boldly he speaks—
Not since he was a babe born of his mother
Was he once in this world one half so blithe—
415 "Have done with your hacking—harry me no more!
I have borne, as behooved, one blow in this place;
If you make another move I shall meet it midway
And promptly, I promise you, pay back each blow with
    brand.
      One stroke acquits me here;
420      So did our covenant stand
      In Arthur's court last year—
      Wherefore, sir, hold your hand!"

He lowers the long ax and leans on it there,
Sets his arms on the head, the haft on the earth,
425 And beholds the bold knight that bides there afoot,
How he faces him fearless, fierce in full arms,
And plies him with proud words—it pleases him well.
Then once again gaily to Gawain he calls,
And in a loud voice and lusty, delivers these words:
430 "Bold fellow, on this field your anger forbear!
No man has made demands here in manner uncouth,
Nor done, save as duly determined at court.
I owed you a hit and you have it; be happy therewith!
The rest of my rights here I freely resign.
435 Had I been a bit busier, a buffet, perhaps,
I could have dealt more directly; and done you some harm.

First I flourished with a feint, in frolicsome mood,
And left your hide unhurt—and here I did well
By the fair terms we fixed on the first night;
440 And fully and faithfully you followed accord:
Gave over all your gains as a good man should.
A second feint, sir, I assigned for the morning
You kissed my comely wife—each kiss you restored.
For both of these there behooved but two feigned blows by
   right.
445            True men pay what they owe;
               No danger then in sight.
               You failed at the third throw,
               So take my tap, sir knight.


"For that is my belt about you, that same braided girdle,
450 My wife it was that wore it; I know well the tale,
And the count of your kisses and your conduct too,
And the wooing of my wife—it was all my scheme!
She made trial of a man most faultless by far
Of all that ever walked over the wide earth;
455 As pearls to white peas, more precious and prized,
So is Gawain, in good faith, to other gay knights.
Yet you lacked, sir, a little in loyalty there,
But the cause was not cunning, nor courtship either,
But that you loved your own life; the less, then, to blame."
460 The other stout knight in a study stood a long while,
So gripped with grim rage that his great heart shook.
All the blood of his body burned in his face
As he shrank back in shame from the man's sharp speech.
The first words that fell from the fair knight's lips:
465 "Accursed be a cowardly and covetous heart!
In you is villainy and vice, and virtue laid low!"
Then he grasps the green girdle and lets go the knot,
Hands it over in haste, and hotly he says:
"Behold there my falsehood, ill hap betide it!
470 Your cut taught me cowardice, care for my life,
And coveting came after, contrary both
To largesse and loyalty belonging to knights.
Now am I faulty and false, that fearful was ever
Of disloyalty and lies, bad luck to them both! and greed.
475            I confess, knight, in this place,
               Most dire is my misdeed;
               Let me gain back your good grace,
               And thereafter I shall take heed."


Then the other laughed aloud, and lightly he said,
480 "Such harm as I have had, I hold it quite healed.

**GAWAIN RECEIVING THE GREEN GIRDLE**
*Woodcut by Fritz Kredel from Gardner*
*The Complete Works of the Gawain Poet, 1965*
The University of Chicago

from *Sir Gawain and the Green Knight*   **183**

You are so fully confessed, your failings made known,
And bear the plain penance of the point of my blade,
I hold you polished as a pearl, as pure and as bright
As you had lived free of fault since first you were born.
485 And I give you, sir, this girdle that is gold-hemmed
And green as my garments, that, Gawain, you may
Be mindful of this meeting when you mingle in throng
With nobles of renown—and known by this token
How it chanced at the Green Chapel, to chivalrous knights.
490 And you shall in this New Year come yet again
And we shall finish out our feast in my fair hall, with
  cheer.''

## Commentary

Humorist Samuel Clemens took a lighter look at the King Arthur legend in his 1889 novel, *A Connecticut Yankee in King Arthur's Court.* A Hartford munitions maker, clunked on the head ''during a misunderstanding conducted with crowbars,'' wakes up to find himself in Camelot, England, in the year 513. ''The Boss,'' as he comes to be called, has opinions on everything. Here he discusses the proper medieval attire for following Sir Gawaine:

''I was to have an early breakfast, and start at dawn, for that was the usual way; but I had the demon's own time with my armor, and this delayed me a little. It is troublesome to get into, and there is so much detail. First you wrap a layer or two of blanket around your body, for a sort of cushion and to keep off the cold iron; then you put on your sleeves and a shirt of chain mail—these are made of small steel links woven together, and they form a fabric so flexible that if you toss your shirt onto the floor, it slumps into a pile like a peck of wet fishnet; it is very heavy and is nearly the most uncomfortablest material in the world for a nightshirt . . . then you put on your shoes—flat-boats roofed over the interleaving bands of steel . . . and you begin to feel crowded; then you hitch onto the breastplate the half-petticoat of broad overlapping bands of steel which hangs down in front but is scalloped out behind you so you can sit down, and isn't any real improvement on an inverted coalscuttle, either for looks or for wear, or to wipe your hands on; next you belt on your sword; then you put your stove-pipe joints onto your arms, your iron gauntlets onto your hands, your iron rat-trap onto your head . . . This is no time to dance. Well, a man that is packed away like that is a nut that isn't worth the cracking, there is so little of the meat, when you get down to it, by comparison to the shell.'' Imagine getting on the horse!

## THINKING ABOUT THE SELECTION

### Recalling

1. What kind of challenge does King Arthur at first think the Green Knight has in mind?
2. The Green Knight's challenge has two parts. (a) What is Sir Gawain to do immediately? (b) What is he to do a year later?
3. What does Sir Gawain do at the Green Chapel to cause the Green Knight to question his valor?
4. Why does the Green Knight only scratch Sir Gawain with his ax?

### Interpreting

5. The Green Knight laughs at the members of the Round Table in line 92. Why?
6. When Sir Gawain sees the Green Chapel, who does he think the Green Knight may be?
7. In lines 465–477 why is Sir Gawain upset?

### Applying

8. What modern occupation do you think comes closest to matching the duties and ideals of the Knights of the Round Table? Explain your answer.

## ANALYZING LITERATURE

### Understanding Medieval Romances

Most medieval romances
- Embody the ideals of chivalry
- Are set in a remote time or place
- Emphasize rank and social distinctions
- Convey a sense of the supernatural
- Present a hero engaged in pure adventure
- Have a loose structure, lacking in unity
- Include love as a major plot element
- Feature spontaneous, unmotivated fighting

1. Which of these characteristics does *Sir Gawain and the Green Knight* NOT display?
2. In medieval romances, a hero seldom admits failure. Does Sir Gawain follow this tradition? Explain.

## CRITICAL THINKING AND READING

### Making Inferences About Chivalry

Human actions and motivations reflect the ideals of the society in which people live. Today a community leader might laugh off the kind of challenge the Green Knight hurls at King Arthur. You can infer from the way Arthur and Sir Gawain react, however, that in the age of chivalry one took seriously such challenges to one's courage.

1. What ideals of medieval society can you infer from Sir Gawain's offer to accept the challenge made to Arthur?
2. What ideals can you infer from Sir Gawain's distress at the end of the poem, even after he has withstood the blow of the ax?

## UNDERSTANDING LANGUAGE

### Using Abstract Words

An **abstract word** expresses a quality that cannot be directly perceived through the senses. For example, although you can see a *knight* or an *ax* (concrete words), you cannot see, hear, touch, taste, or smell *chivalry, courage,* or *loyalty.* Often the best way to define an abstract word is with a specific example:

Sir Gawain set out for the Green Chapel even though he was certain it meant death. That is what I call *bravery.*

Write a specific example that shows the meaning of each of the following abstract words.
1. grandeur
2. temerity
3. perspicacity
4. flightiness

## THINKING AND WRITING

### Evaluating the Medieval Romance

One of the world's most famous novels, *Don Quixote* by Miguel de Cervantes, satirizes medieval romances like *Sir Gawain and the Green Knight.* What aspects of the medieval romance do you think Cervantes may have felt deserved satire? Jot down your answers to this question. Arrange your answers in a logical order for development in an essay. Write the essay. Make any revisions that seem necessary.

## 1475 [?]

English theater began with what are called miracle plays, sometimes referred to as mystery plays. The aim of a miracle play is to dramatize an incident from the Bible. Morality plays, which came later, deal with the human struggle between virtues and vices. They feature characters that represent abstract qualities such as Beauty, Good Deeds, Knowledge, and Death. The most famous and sophisticated of the morality plays is *Everyman,* written by an unknown playwright.

The English theater originated in the medieval church. To make religious services more meaningful and impressive, the clergy began inserting bits of dialogue into the mass. These miniature dramas, much expanded, became miracle plays. The plays moved outdoors, lost their direct connection with the church, and became a popular form of entertainment. The miracle plays were performed on wagons that moved from place to place within a town or city. Each wagon stopped at designated stations, presenting the same play over and over. A viewer could sometimes see as many as fifty miracle plays by staying in one place throughout the day and watching as the procession of wagons passed by.

Morality plays such as *Everyman* grew out of these miracle plays and also out of medieval allegories, not all of them English, in which the characters are abstractions—Fear, Courtesy, Greed, Delight, and so on. *Everyman* resembles an earlier Dutch morality play, *Elckerlijk,* but since the subject matter of the two plays, the summoning of death, is so common, both may come from a single source. The theme of *Everyman* is the salvation of the soul as death approaches. When Everyman is summoned by Death, he finds that none of his friends and relatives—Fellowship, Cousin, Kindred, or Goods—will keep him company. As he makes his descent into the grave, only Good Deeds will go with him.

This play has enjoyed extraordinary success since its appearance in the fifteenth century. The allegory has been translated into many languages, has been used by later writers as the basis of their plays, and has often been performed, both as an academic revival and a commercial production, on the twentieth-century stage.

## *from* Everyman

**Morality Play.** Medieval morality plays have a singleness of purpose, to dramatize the conflict between the power of good and evil for control of one's soul. Although the plays are intended to entertain audiences, they also seek to teach strict lessons of right and wrong. Essentially religious, morality plays are allegories in which characters appear as abstract virtues and vices. By their very nature the characters are one-dimensional, lacking the complexity found in characters in more sophisticated drama. The plays were originally produced for a middle-class town audience, many of whose members could neither read nor write. For the most part the plays are anonymously written. This may seem strange to you, because *Everyman* and other moralities came into being at a time when records were kept. A main reason for the anonymity of writers is (as the morality plays teach) that worldly ambition counted for little in the Church-dominated culture of that era. Lack of credit for individual achievement was the order of the day. No one knows, for instance, who designed the magnificent Gothic cathedrals or created the stained glass and statues that adorn them. The medieval architect and sculptor, like the medieval playwright, worked primarily for the glory of God.

Four different copies of *Everyman* survive—two whole, one damaged, one fragmentary. It is thought that all four texts were printed between 1508 and 1537. The text used most often now, known as the Britwell copy, is the one reprinted in 1904. The title page of this slender volume is printed with the well-known wood-cut of Everyman. In this picture he sports a small, round hat with a feather sticking jauntily out of the brim and a short open cape with broad lapels. He holds his hands up sadly, palms turned outward. His expression is upset as he turns toward the skeletal, eerie figure of Death, who is sternly summoning him. The background is dotted with what look like graveyard crosses; Death holds what appears to be a huge scroll, probably the list of those to be summoned next. If you were preparing an edition of *Everyman,* what cover illustration would you provide?

Assume you are writing a play to dramatize a principle such as "Honesty is the best policy" or "Haste makes waste." Write the principle. Then list at least five characters you would cast in the play. Give them abstract names like Deceit or Punctuality.

# *from* Everyman

*Here beginneth a treatise[1] how the High Father of Heaven sendeth* DEATH *to summon every creature to come and give account of their lives in this world, and is in manner of a moral play.*

[*Enter* MESSENGER.]

**MESSENGER.** I pray, you all give your audience,
 And hear this matter with reverence,
 By figure[2] a moral play.
 *The Summoning of Everyman* called it is,
5 That of our lives and ending shows
 How transitory we be all day.[3]
 The matter is wonder precious,
 But the intent of it is more gracious
 And sweet to bear away.
10 The story saith: Man, in the beginning
 Look well, and take good heed to the ending,
 Be you never so gay.
 You think sin in the beginning full sweet,
 Which in the end causeth the soul to weep,
15 When the body lieth in clay.
 Here shall you see how fellowship and jollity,
 Both strength, pleasure, and beauty,
 Will fade from thee as flower in May.
 For ye shall hear how our Heaven-King
20 Calleth Everyman to a general reckoning.
 Give audience and hear what he doth say.

[*Exit* MESSENGER. *Enter* GOD.]

**GOD.** I perceive, here in my majesty,
 How that all creatures be to me unkind,[4]
 Living without dread in worldly prosperity.
25 Of ghostly[5] sight the people be so blind,
 Drowned in sin, they know me not for their God.
 In worldly riches is all their mind:
 They fear not of my righteousness the sharp rod;
 My law that I showed when I for them died
30 They forget clean, and shedding of my blood red.
 I hanged between two,[6] it cannot be denied:
 To get them life I suffered to be dead.
 I healed their feet, with thorns hurt was my head.
 I could do no more than I did, truly—
35 And now I see the people do clean forsake me.

**1. treatise:** Narrative.

**2. by figure:** In form.

**3. all day:** Always.

**4. unkind:** Thoughtless.

**5. ghostly:** Spiritual.

**6. two:** The two thieves between whom Christ was crucified.

They use the seven deadly sins damnable,
As pride, coveitise,[7] wrath, and gluttony
Now in the world be made commendable.
And thus they leave of angels the heavenly company.

40 Every man liveth so after his own pleasure,
And yet of their life they be nothing sure.
I see the more that I them forbear,
The worse they be from year to year:
All that liveth appaireth[8] fast.

45 Therefore I will, in all the haste,
Have a reckoning of every man's person.
For, and[9] I leave the people thus alone
In their life and wicked tempests,
Verily they will become much worse than beasts;

50 For now one would by envy another up eat.
Charity do they all clean forgeet.
I hoped well that every man
In my glory should make his mansion,
And thereto I had them all elect.[10]

55 But now I see, like traitors deject,[11]
They thank me not for the pleasure that I to[12] them
    meant,
Nor yet for their being that I them have lent.
I proffered the people great multitude of mercy,
And few there be that asketh it heartily.[13]

60 They be so cumbered[14] with worldly riches
That needs on them I must do justice—
On every man living without fear.
Where art thou, Death, thou mighty messenger?

[*Enter* DEATH.]

DEATH. Almighty, God, I am here at your will,
65 Your commandment to fulfull.
GOD. Go thou to Everyman,
And show him, in my name,
A pilgrimage he must on him take,
Which he in no wise may escape;

70 And that he bring with him a sure reckoning
Without delay or any tarrying.
DEATH. Lord, I will in the world go run over all,[15]
And cruelly out-search both great and small.

[*Exit* GOD.]

Everyman will I beset that liveth beastly
75 Out of God's laws, and dreadeth not folly.
He that loveth riches I will strike with my dart,
His sight to blind, and from heaven to depart[16]—
Except that Almsdeeds[17] be his good friend—
In hell for to dwell, world without end.

**7. coveitise:** Avarice.

**8. appaireth:** Degenerates.

**9. and:** If.

**10. elect:** Chosen.
**11. deject:** Abased.
**12. to:** For.

**13. heartily:** Sincerely.
**14. cumbered:** Encumbered.

**15. over all:** Everywhere.

**16. depart:** Separate.
**17. Almsdeeds:** Deeds of mercy; good deeds.

80　　Lo, yonder I see Everyman walking:
　　　Full little he thinketh on my coming;
　　　His mind is on fleshly lusts and his treasure,
　　　And great pain it shall cause him to endure
　　　Before the Lord, Heaven-King.

　　　[*Enter* EVERYMAN.]

85　　Everyman, stand still! Whither art thou going
　　　Thus gaily? Hast thou thy Maker forgeet?
　　　EVERYMAN. Why askest thou?
　　　Why wouldest thou weet?[18]                                    **18. weet:** Know.
　　　DEATH. Yea, sir, I will show you:
　　　In great haste I am sent to thee
　　　From God out of his majesty.
　　　EVERYMAN. What! sent to me?
　　　DEATH. Yea, certainly.
　　　Though thou have forgot him here,
95　　He thinketh on thee in the heavenly sphere,
　　　As, ere we depart, thou shalt know.
　　　EVERYMAN. What desireth God of me?
　　　DEATH. That shall I show thee:
　　　A reckoning he will needs have
100　 Without any longer respite.
　　　EVERYMAN. To give a reckoning longer leisure I crave.
　　　This blind[19] matter troubleth my wit.                        **19. blind:** Unexpected.
　　　DEATH. On thee thou must take a long journay:
　　　Therefore thy book of count[20] with thee thou bring,          **20. count:** Accounts.
105　 For turn again thou cannot by no way.
　　　And look thou be sure of thy reckoning,
　　　For before God thou shalt answer and shew
　　　Thy many bad deeds and good but a few—
　　　How thou hast spent thy life and in what wise,
110　 Before the Chief Lord of Paradise.
　　　Have ado that we were in that way,[21]                         **21. Have ado . . . way:** Let
　　　For weet thou well thou shalt make none attornay.[22]          us get started.
　　　　　　　　　　　　　　　　　　　　　　　　　　　　**22. none attornay:** None
　　　EVERYMAN. Full unready I am such reckoning to give.            appear in your place.
　　　I know thee not. What messenger art thou?
115　 DEATH. I am Death that no man dreadeth,[23]                     **23. that no man**
　　　For every man I 'rest,[24] and no man spareth;                 **dreadeth:** That fears no
　　　For it is God's commandment                                    one.
　　　That all to me should be obedient.                             **24. 'rest:** Arrest.
　　　EVERYMAN. O Death, thou comest when I had thee least in
　　　　mind.
120　 In thy power it lieth me to save:
　　　Yet of my good[25] will I give thee, if thou will be kind,     **25. good:** Goods.
　　　Yea, a thousand pound shalt thou have—
　　　And defer this matter till another day.
　　　DEATH. Everyman, it may not be, by no way.

| | |
|---|---|
| 125 | I set nought by[26] gold, silver, nor riches, |
| | Nor by pope, emperor, king, duke, nor princes, |
| | For, and I would receive gifts great, |
| | All the world I might get. |
| | But my custom is clean contrary: |
| 130 | I give thee no respite. Come hence and not tarry! |

**26. set nought by:** Care nothing for.

**EVERYMAN.** Alas, shall I have no longer respite?
I may say Death giveth no warning.
To think on thee it maketh my heart sick,
For all unready is my book of reckoning.

| | |
|---|---|
| 135 | But twelve year and I might have a biding,[27] |
| | My counting-book I would make so clear |
| | That my reckoning I should not need to fear. |
| | Wherefore, Death, I pray thee, for God's mercy, |
| | Spare me till I be provided of remedy. |

**27. twelve year . . . biding:** If I might have a twelve-year delay.

| | |
|---|---|
| 140 | **DEATH.** Thee availeth not to cry, weep, and pray; |
| | But haste thee lightly[28] that thou were gone that journay, |
| | And prove[29] thy friends, if thou can. |
| | For weet thou well the tide[30] abideth no man, |
| | And in the world each living creature |
| 145 | For Adam's sin must die of nature.[31] |

**28. lightly:** Quickly.
**29. prove:** Test.
**30. tide:** Time.

**31. of nature:** Naturally.

**EVERYMAN.** Death, if I should this pilgrimage take
And my reckoning surely make,
Show me, for saint[32] charity,
Should I not come again shortly?

**32. saint:** Holy.

| | |
|---|---|
| 150 | **DEATH.** No, Everyman. And thou be once there, |
| | Thou mayst never more come here, |
| | Trust me verily. |

**EVERYMAN.** O gracious God in the high seat celestial,
Have mercy on me in this most need!

| | |
|---|---|
| 155 | Shall I have company from this vale terrestrial |
| | Of mine acquaintance that way me to lead? |

**DEATH.** Yea, if any be so hardy
That would go with thee and bear thee company.
Hie[33] thee that thou were gone to God's magnificence,

**33. Hie:** Hasten.

| | |
|---|---|
| 160 | Thy reckoning to give before his presence. |
| | What, weenest[34] thou thy life is given thee, |
| | And thy worldly goods also? |

**34. weenest:** Suppose.

**EVERYMAN.** I had weened so, verily.

**DEATH.** Nay, nay, it was but lent thee.

| | |
|---|---|
| 165 | For as soon as thou art go, |
| | Another a while shall have it and then go therefro, |
| | Even as thou hast done. |
| | Everyman, thou art mad! Thou hast thy wits[35] five, |
| | And here on earth will not amend thy live![36] |
| 170 | For suddenly I do come. |

**35. wits:** Senses.
**36. thy live:** In thy life.

**EVERYMAN.** O wretched caitiff! Whither shall I flee
That I might 'scape this endless sorrow?

Now, gentle Death, spare me till tomorrow,
That I may amend me
175    With good advisement.[37]

**DEATH.** Nay, thereto I will not consent,
Nor no man will I respite,
But to the heart suddenly I shall smite,
Without any advisement.
180    And now out of thy sight I will me hie:
See thou make thee ready shortly,
For thou mayst say this is the day
That no man living may 'scape away.

[*Exit* DEATH.]

*Everyman calls on Fellowship, Cousin, Kindred, and
Goods (his friends, relatives, and wealth) to accompany him
on his journey, but they all refuse and desert him. Everyman then summons his Good Deeds and Knowledge, and
Knowledge leads him to Confession, who comforts him.
Following his meeting with Confession, Everyman is assisted by Good Deeds, Knowledge, Beauty, Strength, Five-Wits
(Five Senses), and Discretion (the attributes that make up an
integrated person) in making up his book of accounts. Then
each one, except for Good Deeds and Knowledge, leaves
him as he makes final preparations for his journey to the
grave.*

**EVERYMAN.** O Jesu, help, all hath forsaken me!
185    **GOOD DEEDS.** Nay, Everyman, I will bide with thee:
I will not forsake thee indeed;
Thou shalt find me a good friend at need.
**EVERYMAN.** Gramercy,[38] Good Deeds! Now may I true friends
    see.
They have forsaken me every one—
190    I loved them better than my Good Deeds alone.
Knowledge, will ye forsake me also?
**KNOWLEDGE.** Yea, Everyman, when ye to Death shall go,
But not yet, for no manner of danger.
**EVERYMAN.** Gramercy, Knowledge, with all my heart!
195    **KNOWLEDGE.** Nay, yet will I not from hence depart
Till I see where ye shall become.[39]
**EVERYMAN.** Methink, alas, that I must be gone
To make my reckoning and my debts pay,
For I see my time is nigh spent away.
200    Take example, all ye that this do hear or see,
How they that I best loved do forsake me,
Except my Good Deeds that bideth truly.
**GOOD DEEDS.** All earthly things is but vanity.

**37. advisement:**
Preparation.

**38. Gramercy:** Good
thanks.

**39. where ye shall
become:** What shall
become of you.

Beauty, Strength, and Discretion do man forsake,
205 Foolish friends and kinsmen that fair spake—
All fleeth save Good Deeds, and that am I.
**EVERYMAN.** Have mercy on me, God most mighty,
And stand by me, thou mother and maid, holy Mary!
**GOOD DEEDS.** Fear not: I will speak for thee.
210 **EVERYMAN.** Here I cry God mercy!
**GOOD DEEDS.** Short our end, and 'minish our pain.[40]
Let us go, and never come again.
**EVERYMAN.** Into thy hands, Lord, my soul I commend:
Receive it, Lord, that it be not lost.
215 As thou me boughtest,[41] so me defend,
And save me from the fiend's boast,
That I may appear with that blessed host
That shall be saved at the day of doom.
*In manus tuas,* of mights most,
220 Forever *commendo spiritum meum.*[42]

[EVERYMAN *and* GOOD DEEDS *descend into the grave.*]

**KNOWLEDGE.** Now hath he suffered that we all shall endure,
The Good Deeds shall make all sure.
Now hath he made ending,
Methinketh that I hear angels sing
225 And make great joy and melody
Where Everyman's soul received shall be.
**ANGEL.** [*within*] Come, excellent elect spouse to Jesu![43]
Here above thou shalt go
Because of thy singular virtue.
230 Now the soul is taken the body fro,
Thy reckoning is crystal clear:
Now shalt thou into the heavenly sphere—
Unto the which all ye shall come
That liveth well before the day of doom.

[*Enter Doctor.*[44]]

235 **DOCTOR.** This memorial[45] men may have in mind:
Ye hearers, take it of worth, old and young,
And forsake Pride, for he deceiveth you in the end.
And remember Beauty, Five-Wits, Strength, and
 Discretion,
They all at the last do Everyman forsake,
240 Save his Good Deeds there doth he take—
But beware, for and they be small,
Before God he hath no help at all—
None excuse may be there for Everyman.
Alas, how shall he do than?[46]
245 For after death amends may no man make,
For then mercy and pity doth him forsake.

**40. Short . . . pain:** Make our death quick and diminish our pain.

**41. boughtest:** Redeemed.

**42. *In manus . . . meum:*** "Into thy hands, O greatest of powers, I commend my spirit forever." (Latin)

**43. spouse to Jesu:** Everyman's soul is referred to as the bride of Jesus.

**44. doctor:** A learned theologian.
**45. memorial:** Reminder.

**46. than:** Then.

If his reckoning be not clear when he doth come,
God will say, "*Ite, maledicti, in ignem eternum!*"[47]
And he that hath his account whole and sound,

250 High in heaven he shall be crowned,
Unto which place God bring us all thither,
That we may live body and soul togither.
Thereto help, the Trinity!
Amen, say ye, for saint charity.

**47. *Ite . . . eternum:***
"Depart, ye cursed, into everlasting fire." (Latin)

**THE OLD MAN AND DEATH, C.1774**
*Joseph Wright of Derby*
Wadsworth Atheneum, Hartford

## THINKING ABOUT THE SELECTION

### Recalling

1. On what mission does God send Death?
2. What does Everyman request when he first learns the purpose of Death's visit?
3. (a) How does Good Deeds respond to Everyman's plea for companionship? (b) How does Knowledge respond?
4. According to the Doctor, what can be done after death to make up for mistakes or oversights in life? Explain.

### Interpreting

5. What is God's main complaint about the way people on earth are behaving?
6. Death repeatedly refuses to give Everyman any additional time. Why?
7. What does Death tell Everyman about the ownership of worldly goods?

### Applying

8. How do you account for the fact that stage productions of *Everyman* have continued to be successful up to the present day?

## ANALYZING LITERATURE

### Understanding a Morality Play

The basic question in a morality play is, "What must I do to be saved?" A struggle occurs between good and evil, virtues and vices, for the possession of one's soul. The characters are persons presented as abstractions: Death, Pride, Strength, Beauty, Knowledge. *Everyman's* plot is restricted to the last part of a typical morality play—the arrival of Death.

1. Find two places in *Everyman* (not at the very beginning or end) where a line or lines directly express the play's message. Write the lines.
2. Which characters represent categories of people rather than abstract qualities?

## CRITICAL THINKING AND READING

### Interpreting Names as Symbols

The name of a character in literature can be used as a symbol. A **symbol** is a word, person, or object that stands for something beyond itself. For example, a star can stand for achievement. In a morality play like *Everyman,* a character is simply called Achievement, but the star symbol can be used as a character's name for the same purpose—e.g., Brenda Starr. Achievement can also be suggested by a name like Mark Winner. Choose two of the following fictional names and make them into appropriate morality play names. (Example: Mr. Bumble = Stupidity) (1) Mr. Gradgrind (2) Holly Golightly (3) Jack Armstrong (4) Lady Sneerwell (5) Tess Truehart (6) Flem Snopes (7) Daddy Warbucks.

## SPEAKING AND LISTENING

### Performing in a Play

When you act in a play, you must fully understand your part as the playwright intends it. You must go beyond a mere reading of lines. What is the character's personality? What is his or her motivation?

Go to the library and borrow a recording of a play for which you can also borrow the text. Choose a scene and read it a few times. Then listen to the professional actor read it. Note the stress, the pauses, the emotion. Compare the professional performance with your own.

Next, select a passage from *Everyman* and read it until you understand its meaning and purpose completely. Rehearse it until you know how you want to say every word. If possible, practice it with a tape recorder. Be prepared to read the passage in class.

## THINKING AND WRITING

### Discussing a Morality Play

Write an essay in which you discuss the playwright's answer in *Everyman* to the morality play question about the conduct of life. Give your opinion of the play's effectiveness. Is the play dramatic? Persuasive? Would it be better if Everyman escaped Death? Explain. When you revise, make sure you have supplied adequate support for your opinion.

# THE CHANGING ENGLISH LANGUAGE

## Middle English 1066–1485

### THE NORMAN CONQUEST

In the long run, the Norman Conquest may have benefited the English language; in the short run, it was a disaster. As Normans took over the country, so they took over the language, replacing English with French. Norman clergymen ruled the English church, Norman clerks ran the English government, Norman merchants regulated English commerce—and they all spoke French. In effect, the Norman Conquest transformed England virtually overnight into a bilingual country. While most of the English still spoke English at home and among themselves, to survive many learned to understand French if not to speak it. Likewise, many of the French-speaking upper classes understood English, even if they could not speak it.

The immediate changes in English reflect the influence of the conquerors on the conquered. The English lived in a humble *cot* (cottage); the Normans, in a French *maneir* (manor or mansion) or *castel*. The English did the *werc;* the Normans relished the *leisir* and *profit.* Life for the Normans was *asie;* for the English, *hard.* In writing, Latin became the language of business. In 1154, the English monks abandoned their work on the *Anglo-Saxon Chronicle* and a great silence fell on English writing. The victory of Norman French seemed complete. Had things continued in this way, England might well have assumed the language of its conquerors.

Why did English survive? First, English was simply too well rooted to die. It was one thing for writing, controlled by a small group of educated clerks, to adopt Latin and French; it was quite another for the established daily speech of regular people to change. Second, the two cultures quickly intermarried. Thus as early as 1177, a chronicler could write that "the two nations have become so mixed that it is scarcely possible today, speaking of free men, to tell who is English, who is of Norman race." Third, around 1200 King John lost nearly all of his land in France to the French crown. In effect, this forced the Norman lords to make up their minds whether to be French or English.

### ENGLISH MAKES A COMEBACK

The appearance of church sermons, prayers, and carols in English in the early part of the thirteenth century heralded the recovery of the language. English words began to sneak into Latin documents. By 1300, almost everyone in England spoke English but only a few also spoke French. A poet of the age, writing in English, was able to report that:

Lewede men cune Ffrensch non
Among an hondryd, unne pis on.

**Bayeux Tapestry—Normans Attack the English**

(Of French the common men know none/Among a hundred, scarcely one.)

Anti-French sentiment during The Hundred Years War with France (1337–1454) greatly encouraged people to speak English rather than French. The Black Death, by causing so many deaths in monasteries and churches, gave rise to a new generation of non-French and -Latin speakers who took over as abbots and prioresses.

## MIDDLE ENGLISH

English had survived, but it had changed. It had become what scholars now call Middle English, a term coined in the nineteenth century to describe English from A.D. 1150 to 1500. The category is somewhat artificial, though, for much of what has come to be called Middle English is simply a written record of what had already happened to the spoken language. Therefore, while spoken English had almost certainly shed most of its inflections (word changes that indicate meaning) by 1066, it is not until the language was written down that these changes were recorded. Another important simplification in the language was the adoption of prepositions to replace the Old English word endings, a process that we know began earlier. Still another key change was the loss of grammatical gender in the vast majority of words. Today we use gender in a few pronouns, such as *he* and *she* for male and female people, and *it* to refer to everything else. Further, words were no longer formed in the Old English style, by adding complex prefixes and suffixes. To some extent this was replaced by the use of Latin prefixes (dis-, trans-, and re-). Overall,

these changes resulted in a vast simplification of the language.

## GEOFFREY CHAUCER

Chaucer's career illustrates the triumph of English. By deliberately writing in English, he represented the rebirth of English as a national language. His work integrates the changes English had undergone in the preceding centuries, the richness of Middle English, Latinized and Frenchified by Christianity and Conquest.

## THE TRIUMPH OF ENGLISH

Seventeen years after Chaucer's death, Henry V became the first English king since Harold to use English in his official documents, including his will. In 1415, Henry crossed the Channel to fight the French. In the first letter he dictated in France he decided to write in English. This national statement indicates a turning point. English had triumphed.

# YOU THE WRITER

**Assignment**

**1.** Many English poets have written imitations of medieval ballads and narratives. Write your own imitation of a poem in this unit. Make your poem medieval in content as well as in form and style.

**Prewriting.** First think of the "medieval" plot, characters, and setting you will use in your poem. Prepare a map outlining these features. Then examine your model for the structure, verse form, and other literary aspects you will imitate.

**Writing.** When you write your first draft, concentrate on getting the story down on paper in a clear, interesting, well-organized way. Write in verse, but do not try to refine the poetry yet.

**Revising.** You may now concentrate on emulating the style and form of your model. Work on your poem until it could almost pass for an authentic medieval ballad or narrative. Read it aloud. How would it sound if it were accompanied by a musical instrument?

**Assignment**

**2.** Write a monologue in prose or verse in which one of the characters you have encountered in medieval literature presents his or her thoughts about the kind of life he or she has led or about life in general.

**Prewriting.** First select your character. Then decide what main idea or ideas your character will express. Then think of the references to medieval experience your character will use to illustrate and support these ideas.

**Writing.** Try to make your monologue sound authentically medieval by modeling it on the selections you have read in this unit. Make sure your narrator's personality shines clearly through his or her words.

**Revising.** Try to improve the details of the monologue so they both aptly convey the speaker's ideas and create the impression that a medieval character is speaking. Finally, make any improvements you can in the organization and style of the monologue.

**Assignment**

**3.** Imagine that you are a medieval man or woman who has witnessed any episode presented in the selections of this unit. Write a letter to a friend or relative in which you tell what you witnessed.

**Prewriting.** First establish your viewpoint: Where were you in relation to the characters and events? What exactly did you observe?

**Writing.** Try to think of yourself as a medieval person as you write your letter. Base your style of writing on the selections in this unit. Apart from the style, your letter should be a conventional personal letter.

**Revising.** Can you in any way express more vividly the details of what you witnessed? Can you give the letter a more medieval flavor? Revise in the light of these questions.

# YOU THE CRITIC

**Assignment**

**1.** The literature of past societies provides clues to what life might have been like for the ordinary person. Write an essay in which you present your impressions of medieval life based on the selections in this unit.

**Prewriting.** Ask yourself, "Judging by the literature I have read, how would I have felt living in medieval England? What would have been the troubles and the advantages of living in those days?"

**Writing.** Your essay should basically answer the preceding questions. Be sure you refer to the clues you found in the selections you read.

**Revising.** First check that your essay is faithful to your sense of how you would have responded to life in the Middle Ages. Then revise it for organization, style, and grammatical correctness.

**Assignment**

**2.** The literature of the past sometimes presents ideas, values, or customs that would be useful to life today. Write an essay in which you explain how one such medieval idea, value, or custom would enhance present-day life.

**Prewriting.** First decide what the details of the literature you have read reveal about life and how they illustrate the quality about which you are concerned. Then list your reasons for wanting to see this quality revived or maintained today.

**Writing.** Write an essay that first describes the idea, value, or custom; then illustrates it by reference to literature; and finally argues for its relevance to the present.

**Revising.** Make sure the organization of your essay allows for adequate treatment of the description, illustration, and argumentation mentioned above. Check for lapses in style and usage.

**Assignment**

**3.** Choose the selection from medieval literature that you liked best, and write an essay in which you explain why you consider it superior to other selections in the unit.

**Prewriting.** First choose one or two other works of medieval literature with which you can appropriately compare the selection you have chosen. Then list your reasons for preferring it to the others.

**Writing.** Write an essay based on your prewriting work. Illustrate and support your reasons by apt references to the literature. Aim to make your reader see the excellence you perceive in the work of your choice.

**Revising.** Concentrate on making your evaluation fair and balanced. Tone down any excessive claims for the preferred work or against the others. Finally, look for and correct any errors in grammar or lapses in style.

**QUEEN ELIZABETH AND SIR WALTER RALEIGH**
*Charles Edouard Boutibonne*
Three Lions

# THE ENGLISH RENAISSANCE
## 1485–1625

This royal throne of kings, this sceptered isle,
This earth of majesty, this seat of Mars,
This other Eden, demi-paradise,
This fortress built by Nature for herself
Against infection and the hand of war,
This happy breed of men, this little world,
This precious stone set in the silver sea,
Which serves it in the office of a wall,
Or as a moat defensive to a house,
Against the envy of less happier lands,
This blessed plot, this earth, this realm, this England.

**William Shakespeare**

The ending of the Wars of the Roses and the founding of the Tudor dynasty in 1485 opened a new era in English life. Monarchs assured stability by increasing their own power and undercutting the strength of the nobles. At the same time, they dramatically changed England's religious practices. They also helped to transform England from a small, insular nation into one of the world's great powers. In this way the English people gained a new pride and sense of nationhood, clearly reflected in the patriotic lines by William Shakespeare (1564–1616) on the previous page.

## THE COMING OF THE RENAISSANCE

The Renaissance was a flowering of literary, artistic, and intellectual development that began in Italy in the fourteenth century. The movement was inspired by the arts and scholarship of ancient Greece and Rome, which were rediscovered during the Crusades. Classical learning lived again as new generations of scholars and artists explored and extended the achievements of the ancients. Among the key characteristics of the Renaissance were:

- The religious devotion of the Middle Ages, with its emphasis on the afterlife, gave way to a new interest in the human being's place here on earth.
- Universities introduced a new curriculum called the humanities, which included history, geography, poetry, and modern languages.
- The invention of printing from movable type made books available to more people than ever before. A German printer, Johann Gutenberg, published a Bible in the 1450's that is believed to be the first book printed in the new manner.
- While scholars used Greek and Latin to study the ancients and students learned those languages in school, more and more writers began working in the vernacular—the local language. In England, the English language shed some of its regional differences and became increasingly standardized.

### The Slow Spread of Renaissance Ideas

The Renaissance did not jump the Channel into England until the final two decades of the fifteenth century. At that time, Renaissance ideas had already been spreading across the European continent for more than a century. Because the Renaissance began in Italy, many of the leading Renaissance figures were Italian. Among them were the poet Dante Alighieri (1265–1321), author of *The Divine Comedy;* Francesco Petrarca, known as Petrarch (1304–1374), who wrote lyric poetry in a new fourteen-line form called the sonnet; and the painter, sculptor, architect, engineer, and scientist Leonardo da Vinci (1452–1519). Because of the scope of his interests and talents, Da Vinci typifies what we call the Renaissance man—a person of broad education and interests whose curiosity knew no bounds.

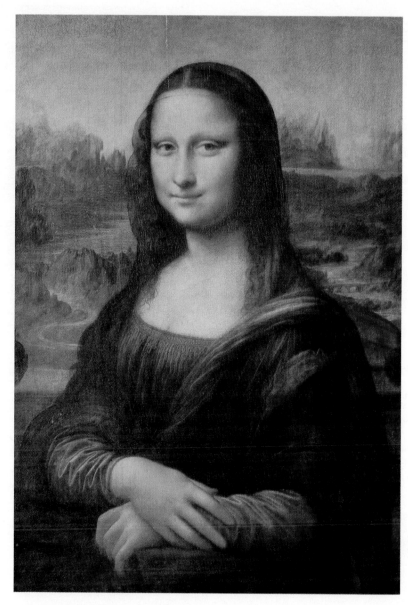

**MONA LISA**
*Leonardo Da Vinci*
Three Lions

## The Age of Exploration

The Renaissance thirst for knowledge had many practical consequences, one of which was a great burst of exploration. The Crusades had opened routes to Asia, but the merchants of the Italian city-states quickly monopolized trade over the new routes by sea and land. Seeking their own path to the riches of Asia, navigators representing Portugal and Spain began seeking an all-sea route. Aided by the development of the compass and by advances in astronomy, which freed them from the need to cling closely to the ocean's shores, these navigators ventured far and

# BRITISH EVENTS

Sir Thomas More with His Family

Queen Elizabeth I

The Last Supper

Copernicus's Treatise of Astronomy

Columbus Sets Sail from Spain

English Navy Attacking Spanish Armada

London c. 1558

Francisco Pizarro

# WORLD EVENTS

| | |
|---|---|
| 1490 | Italy: Ballet introduced. |
| 1492 | Columbus lands in New World. |
| 1495 | Italy: Leonardo da Vinci paints *The Last Supper*. |
| 1497 | North America: John Cabot explores north-eastern coast. |
| | Africa: Vasco da Gama rounds Cape of Good Hope. |
| 1500 | Italy: Michelangelo sculpts *David*. |
| 1503 | Italy: Leonardo da Vinci paints *Mona Lisa*. |
| 1506 | Italy: Construction on St. Peter's Cathedral begins. |
| 1509 | Italy: Michelangelo paints ceiling of Sistine Chapel. |
| 1510 | Japan: Ports opened to European ships. |
| 1513 | North America: Ponce de Leon explores Florida. |
| | Balboa sights Pacific Ocean. |
| 1518 | Africa: Algiers and Tunisia founded. |
| 1519-1522 | Magellan sails around the world. |
| 1520 | Spain: Chocolate first introduced to Europe. |
| 1521 | Mexico: Cortez conquers Aztecs. |
| | Italy: Pope Leo X excommunicates Martin Luther. |
| 1530 | Poland: Copernicus completes treatise on astronomy. |
| 1532 | Peru: Pizarro conquers Incas. |
| | France: Rabelais publishes *Gargantua and Pantagruel*, Book I. |

*Introduction* 205

# BRITISH EVENTS

**Globe Theatre**

1590   **Edmund Spenser** publishes *The Faerie Queene*, Part I.

1594   **Shakespeare** composes *Romeo and Juliet*.

1595   **Shakespeare's** *A Midsummer Night's Dream* first performed.

1599   Globe Theatre opens.

1600   East India Company founded.

1602   Bodeleian Library opens at Oxford.

1603   Elizabeth I dies; James I becomes king.

1605   Guy Fawkes executed for Gunpowder Plot.

       **Shakespeare's** *Macbeth* first performed.

1606   **Ben Jonson** publishes *Volpone*.

1609   **Shakespeare's** *Sonnets* published.

1611   King James Bible published.

1616   *Collected Works of Ben Jonson* published.

1620   **Francis Bacon** publishes *Novum Organum*.

1623   First patent laws passed.

1625   James I dies.

**Galileo**

**Cervantes**

**The Pilgrims Land at Plymouth Rock**

William Shakespeare

*The Wedding Dance*

Abkar the Great

1534    Spain: St. Ignatius Loyola founds Jesuit brotherhood.

1554    Italy: Cellini completes bronze statue of Perseus.

1556    India: Akbar the Great comes to power.

1565    Malta: Knights of St. John fight off Turkish invasion.

1566    Belgium: Bruegel paints *The Wedding Dance*.

1567    South America: 2,000,000 Indians die of typhoid.

       Brazil: Rio de Janeiro founded by Portuguese.

1580    France: Montaigne's *Essays* published.

1582    Italy: Pope Gregory XIII introduces new calendar.

1595    South America: Sir Walter Raleigh explores Orinoco River.

1605    Spain: Cervantes publishes Part I of *Don Quixote*.

1607    North America: British colony established at Jamestown.

1609    Italy: Galileo builds first telescope.

       North America: French colony of Quebec established.

1618    Germany: Kepler proposes laws of planetary motion.

1620    North America: Pilgrims land at Plymouth Rock.

**PORTRAIT OF ERASMUS**
*Hans Holbein*
*National Gallery, Parma*
*Scala/Art Resource*

wide. Their explorations culminated in Columbus's discovery of the New World in 1492. Soon, European powers were establishing colonies in the Americas and extracting great wealth from the new lands.

England's participation in this Age of Exploration began in 1497, when the Italian-born explorer John Cabot, sailing for an English company, reached Newfoundland (an island off the east coast of what is now Canada) and perhaps also the mainland. Cabot thus laid the basis for future English claims in North America. However, English leaders would not exploit those claims until near the end of the English Renaissance.

## The Protestant Reformation

Hand in hand with commercial expansion came a growing sense of nationalism, which, along with the new Renaissance spirit, led many Europeans to question the universal authority of the Roman Catholic Church. Many people had grievances against the Church. Some objected to the sale of indulgences—remissions of punishment for sins, for which people made payments that often went straight into the pockets of corrupt Church officials. Critics also objected to other forms of payment to the Church, viewing them as a form of taxation. Other people argued that Church leaders played favorites by supporting Mediterranean powers against more northerly countries. Still others—scholars who were influenced by the growth of independent thinking in the universities—questioned Church teachings and the church hierarchy.

One critical scholar was the great Dutch thinker Desiderius Erasmus (1466–1536), whose edition of the New Testament raised serious questions about standard Church interpretations of the Bible. Erasmus studied and taught in England. Through his friendship with such English writers as Thomas More (1478–1535), Erasmus focused attention on issues of morality and religion, which remained as central concerns of the English Renaissance, often overshadowing the artistic concerns that dominated the Italian Renaissance.

Although Erasmus himself remained a Roman Catholic, he helped to pave the way for a split in the Roman Church that began in 1517, when a German monk named Martin Luther (1483–1546) nailed a list of dissenting beliefs (his "ninety-five theses") to the door of a German church. Luther's protest was aimed only at reforming the Roman Catholic Church, but it ended by dividing that Church and introducing a new Christian denomination known as Protestantism. The process that Luther started has come to be called the Protestant Reformation.

Fueled by political discontent, the Protestant Reformation swept through much of Europe. It led to frequent wars between European nations whose rulers had opposing religious beliefs. Protestants and Catholics both suffered persecution, depending on where they happened to live and which religion their ruler supported. Protestants themselves were divided, and in Germany the followers of Luther (called Lutherans) persecuted the followers of another Protestant reformer, John Calvin of Geneva. Calvin's ideas (called Calvinism) found a foothold in Switzerland, England, and Scotland, however, and helped bring about the establishment of the Puritan and Presbyterian sects.

## ENGLAND UNDER THE TUDORS

The Tudor dynasty ruled England from 1485 to 1603. Looking back, we see this period as a time of stability and economic expansion. English wool growers were finding new markets abroad. English investors were forming trading companies to tap the riches of far-off places like India. London had grown into a metropolis of more than 180,000 people. However, those who lived in Tudor times often saw economic changes as a threat to the old familiar ways, and memories of the Wars of the Roses caused many people to fear new outbreaks of civil strife.

### Henry VII and Henry VIII

The first Tudor monarch, Henry VII, inherited an England that had been depleted and exhausted by years of civil war. By the time he died in 1509, he had rebuilt the nation's treasury and established law and order. In doing so, he had restored the prestige of the monarchy and had set the stage for his successors.

Henry VII was succeeded by his handsome and athletic son,

**MARTIN LUTHER FASTENING HIS 95 THESES ON THE DOOR OF ALL SAINTS CHURCH, WITTENBURG, GERMANY, ON 31 OCTOBER, 1517**
*19th-Century Engraving*
The Granger Collection

Henry VIII. Like his father, Henry VIII was a practicing Catholic. He even wrote a book against Luther, for which a grateful Pope granted him the title "Defender of the Faith."

Henry VIII's relationship with the Pope did not last, however. Because his marriage with Catherine of Aragon had not produced a son, Henry tried to obtain an annulment from the Pope so that he could marry Anne Boleyn. When the Pope refused, Henry remarried anyway. This defiance of papal authority led to an open break with the Roman Catholic Church. Under the Act of Supremacy (1534), the king assumed full control of the Church in England and severed all ties with Rome. Henry became supreme head of the new Church of England (or Anglican Church). He seized the Catholic Church's English property and dissolved the powerful monasteries, selling some of their lands to benefit the royal treasury and granting the rest as gifts to loyal friends.

Although the Protestant Reformation was not directly responsible for Henry's break with Rome, it helped to pave the way. Many people in England had resented Roman dominance, and the break helped to stir new feelings of national pride. Henry used ruthless measures to suppress opposition among monks, friars, and a few others. He even had his former friend and leading advisor, Thomas More, executed, because More had refused to renounce his faith.

Henry married six times in all. His first two marriages produced two daughters, Mary and Elizabeth. His third wife, Jane Seymour, bore a son, Edward, who was but a frail child when Henry died in 1547.

**KING HENRY VIII OF ENGLAND**
*Hans Holbein*
The Granger Collection

## Edward VI and Mary I

Henry VIII's son, Edward VI, became king at the age of nine and died at the age of fifteen. During his brief reign, a series of parliamentary acts were instituted that dramatically changed the nation's religious practices. English replaced Latin in church ritual, and the Anglican prayer book, or *Book of Common Prayer,* became required in public worship. By Edward's death in 1553, England was well on its way to becoming a Protestant nation.

Roman Catholicism made a turbulent comeback, however, when Edward's half-sister, Mary, took the throne. Mary I was herself Catholic, and she restored Roman practices to the Church of England. She also restored the authority of the Pope over the English Church and insisted on marrying her Spanish cousin, Philip II, thus seeming to make England a minor appendage to the powerful Spanish state. In a time of growing national feeling, many people found these acts extremely unpatriotic. People were also disturbed by Mary's violent repression of Protestants. Ordering the execution of some 200 Protestants, she earned the nickname Bloody Mary and strengthened anti-Catholic sentiment within England.

## Elizabeth I

When Mary I died after a five-year reign, her half-sister, Elizabeth I, came to the throne. She would be the last of the Tudors, dying unmarried and childless, after a long and successful reign.

Strong and clever, Elizabeth was probably England's ablest monarch since William the Conqueror. She received a Renaissance education and read widely in the Greek and Latin classics. She became a great patron of the arts, gathering around her a flock of courtiers that included most of the best writers of her day. Many of the era's greatest literary works bear a dedication to the queen, and the word *Elizabethan* has come to signify the English Renaissance at its height.

Elizabeth also put an end to the religious turmoil that had existed during Mary I's reign. She reestablished the monarch's supremacy in the Church of England and restored the *Book of Common Prayer,* and she instituted a policy of religious moderation that enjoyed great popular support, although it failed to please many devout Catholics and Protestants.

Often working with England's Catholic factions were France and Spain, Europe's strongest powers at the start of Elizabeth's reign. Both nations sought to dominate England, but each was anxious that the other should not. Elizabeth and her counselors adroitly played one side against the other, dangling offers of marriage to the queen as bait. Elizabeth's clever maneuvering of French and Spanish royalty allowed England a period of peace during which commercial and maritime interests prospered.

If Elizabeth had one outstanding problem, it was her Catholic cousin Mary Stuart, queen of Scotland by birth and (as great-granddaughter of Henry VII) next in line for the throne of England. Because Catholics did not recognize Henry VIII's marriage to Elizabeth's mother, Anne Boleyn, they considered Mary Stuart the queen of England. As a prisoner in England for nineteen years, Mary became the center of numerous Catholic plots against Elizabeth. While punishing the plotters, Elizabeth let her royal cousin live. Finally, however, a court convicted Mary of plotting to murder Elizabeth, and Parliament insisted on Mary's execution. Mary went to the block in 1587, a Catholic martyr. Her famous motto, "In my end is my beginning," took on new meaning when her death led Catholic Spain to declare war on England.

## Defeat of the Spanish Armada

The quarrels between Spain and England went beyond the execution of Mary. Spain rejected most English claims to territory in the Americas and resented the fact that English adventurers, known as privateers, had been attacking and plundering Spanish ships. In theory, privateers like John Hawkins and Francis Drake operated on their own, but in reality they acted on the authority of Queen Elizabeth.

**QUEEN ELIZABETH I OF ENGLAND** *c.* **1588**
*by or after George Gower*
The Granger Collection

**QUEEN ELIZABETH I KNIGHTING FRANCIS
DRAKE ON BOARD THE *GOLDEN HIND* AT
DEPTFORD, 4 APRIL, 1581**
*19th-Century Engraving*
The Granger Collection

Spain's King Philip II, already infuriated by the sea pirates, considered Mary's execution the last straw. He prepared a Spanish fleet, or armada, of 130 warships and sent it to attack England. In an eight-day battle in the English Channel in 1588, English sailors outfought and outmaneuvered the Spanish fleet. The defeat of the Spanish armada marked the decline of Spain and the emergence of England as a great sea power.

## STUARTS AND PURITANS

The English Renaissance continued after Elizabeth died in 1603, although a new dynasty—the Stuarts—came to the throne of England. Determined that the end of the Tudor line should not bring a dispute over the throne and a return of civil strife, Elizabeth named Scotland's King James VI as her successor. James's claim to England's throne rested on his descent from King Henry VII through his mother, Mary Stuart, Elizabeth's old antagonist. Unlike Mary, however, James was a Protestant.

**THE LAUNCHING OF FIRESHIPS AGAINST THE SPANISH ARMADA**
*National Maritime Museum, Greenwich, England*

The years of the new Stuart king (1603–25), who became England's James I, are sometimes described as the Jacobean era, from *Jacobus,* the Latin word for *James.* On the surface, the era seemed to be merely an extension of the Elizabethan age. Like his predecessor, James I was a strong supporter of the arts. He also took measures to further England's position as a world power, sponsoring the establishment of England's first successful American colony—Jamestown, Virginia.

During James's reign, however, a conflict began developing that would later erupt into war. Guided by the medieval idea of the "divine right of kings," James I often treated the Parliament with contempt. He and Parliament became involved in a power struggle, quarreling over taxes and foreign wars. James I also persecuted the Puritans, who were strongly represented in the House of Commons. Prompted by James's religious intolerance, a group of Puritans migrated to America, and established the Plymouth Colony in 1621.

## ACHIEVEMENTS OF THE ENGLISH RENAISSANCE

The Elizabethan Age produced an explosion of cultural energy. English architects designed and constructed beautiful mansions. Composers turned out new hymns to fit the Anglican service and popularized the English madrigal, a love song sung without musical accompaniment, often by several harmonizing voices. Painters and sculptors were busy, too. While the Renaissance masters generally were not English, some—like the German artist Hans Holbein the Younger (1497?–1543), court painter to Henry VIII—did move to England.

Meanwhile, the Renaissance spurred the growth of English educational institutions. Instead of depending on tutors, wealthy families began sending their sons to public schools (that is, schools outside the home—they were actually what Americans call private secondary schools). At the same time, the universities at Oxford and Cambridge were improved and expanded.

### Literature in Early Tudor Times

The years from 1485 to 1558 served as a prelude to the great age of Elizabethan literature. Many major writers, such as Thomas More, continued to work in Latin. More's *Utopia* (1516) is a powerful vision of a society free of medieval superstition and prejudice. More and more writers, however, were using the vernacular—English.

The poet Thomas Wyatt (1503–42), who had traveled widely on the continent, introduced the sonnet to England. Wyatt translated or adapted many of the sonnets of the Italian Renaissance poet Petrarch. A second early Tudor poet, Henry Howard, Earl of Surrey (1517–47), experimented with the sonnet form and was the first to use blank verse, the unrhymed ten-syllable lines that would later be the tool of the great Elizabethan dramatists.

## Elizabethan Poetry

During the lengthy reign of Elizabeth I, English literature came of age. Many of the most significant literary developments came in the area of poetry. Favoring lyric poetry, rather than the narrative poems favored by their medieval predecessors, the Elizabethan poets perfected the sonnet and began experimenting with other poetic forms.

One of the most popular literary forms during the Elizabethan age was the sonnet cycle, a series of sonnets that fit loosely together to form a story. The first of the great Elizabethan sonnet cycles was *Astrophel and Stella* by Philip Sidney (1554–86). As a member of a poetry club called Areopagus, Sidney also helped to adapt classical verse forms to fit the English language.

Another major Elizabethan poet was Edmund Spenser (1552?–99). Spenser wrote intricate verse filled with rich imagery. Although Spenser wrote many fine sonnets, his most famous work, *The Faerie Queene,* is an imaginative epic, or long heroic poem, dedicated to Queen Elizabeth. Spenser wrote his epic in complex nine-line units, now called Spenserian stanzas.

Christopher Marlowe (1564–93), a noted playwright, was also a gifted lyric poet. Marlowe helped popularize pastoral verse, which idealizes the rustic simplicity of rural life, in such poems as "The Passionate Shepherd to His Love."

Marlowe's poem inspired Sir Walter Raleigh (1552?–1618) to write a famous response, "The Nymph's Reply to the Shepherd." Poet, historian, courtier, soldier, and explorer, Raleigh was a typical Renaissance man whose adventurous life mirrored the restless spirit of his day.

Another brilliant lyric poet, William Shakespeare, brought the Elizabethan sonnet to new heights. In composing his sonnets, Shakespeare changed the pattern and rhyme scheme of the Petrarchan, or Italian, sonnet, employing a form now known as the English, or Shakespearean, sonnet.

## Elizabethan Drama

During the Elizabethan age, English drama also came into full bloom. Playwrights turned away from religious subjects and began

SIR WALTER RALEIGH
*N. Hilliard*
Three Lions

writing more complex and sophisticated plays. Drawing upon the classical models of ancient Greece and Rome, writers reintroduced tragedies—plays in which disaster befalls a hero or heroine—and comedies—originally, plays in which a humorous situation leads to a happy resolution. Playwrights also began writing their plays in carefully crafted blank verse, using rich language, filled with vivid imagery.

Since Elizabethan dramas were almost entirely in verse, it is not surprising that many of the age's best poets were also its leading playwrights. Christopher Marlowe became the first major Elizabethan dramatist in the 1580s, writing such plays as *Tamburlaine the Great* and *The Tragical History of Doctor Faustus*. Had Marlowe lived past the age of thirty, he might well have rivaled Shakespeare as England's greatest playwright.

Shakespeare began his involvement with the theater as an actor. By 1592 he was a popular playwright, his works even having been performed at Elizabeth's court. After the Globe Theater was built in 1599, many of Shakespeare's plays were performed there. Shakespeare wrote thirty-seven plays, among them many of the greatest plays of all time. He wrote nine tragedies, including *Romeo and Juliet, Hamlet,* and *Macbeth*; several comedies, including *A Merchant of Venice* and *A Midsummer Night's Dream;* ten histories, including *Richard II, Richard III,* and *Henry V*; and a number of plays often classified as "romances" or "tragic comedies." Filled with powerful and beautiful language, his plays display his deep understanding of human nature and his compassion for all types and classes of people. Because of their eloquent language and their depth and complexity, Shakespeare's plays have retained their popularity for centuries. As the seventeenth-century writer Ben Jonson said of Shakespeare: "He was not of an age but for all time."

**WILLIAM SHAKESPEARE**
*Artist Unknown*
Three Lions

## Elizabethan and Jacobean Prose

Prose took a back seat to poetry and drama in the English Renaissance. Scholars still preferred to write in Latin, and their English prose had a Latin flavor. Because they used long words and ornate sentences their work is often difficult to read today.

Several Elizabethan poets contributed major works of prose however. Philip Sidney's *Defence of Poesie* (about 1582) is one of the earliest works of English literary criticism. Thomas Nashe's *Unfortunate Traveler* (1594), a fictional adventure, was a forerunner of the novel. Another important work of prose, *History of the World,* was written by Walter Raleigh during his years of confinement in the Tower of London (for allegedly plotting against James I).

Perhaps the leading prose writer of the English Renaissance was Francis Bacon, a high government official under James I. "I

**TITLE PAGE OF THE FIRST EDITION OF THE KING JAMES *BIBLE***
*London, 1611*
*The Granger Collection*

have taken all knowledge to be my province," Bacon wrote, and his literary output reflects his scholarship in many fields. His greatest work, the *Novum Organum* (1620), written in Latin, made major contributions to natural science and philosophy. Bacon is also known for his formal essays—short prose works focusing on single topics. His essays, including "Of Studies" and "Of Ambition," highlight the rational detachment of his clever, inquiring mind.

The most monumental prose achievement of the entire English Renaissance is undoubtedly the English translation of the Bible commissioned by King James on the advice of Protestant clergymen. Fifty-four scholars labored for three years to bring this magnificent work to fruition. The King James Bible, or Authorized Version, is among the most widely quoted and influential works in the English language.

The English Renaissance moved England out of its medieval past and into the modern world. No writers since have surpassed the literary achievements of Shakespeare or the majestic language of the King James Bible. These provide the standard against which all English literature has been judged right down to the present time.

# ENGLISH VOICES

## Quotations by Prominent Figures of the Period

They (in Utopia) wonder much to hear that gold, which in itself
is so useless a thing, should be everywhere so much esteemed.
   **Sir Thomas More,** *Utopia*

I know I have the body of a weak and feeble woman, but I have
the heart and stomach of a king, and of a king of England too.
   **Elizabeth I,** speech to the troops on the approach of the
      Armada

Was this the face that launched a thousand ships,
And burnt the topless towers of Ilium?
   **Christopher Marlowe,** *The Tragical History of Doctor Faustus*

Now is the winter of our discontent
Made glorious summer by this sun of York.
   **William Shakespeare,** *Richard III*

The quality of mercy is not strained,
It droppeth as the gentle rain from heaven
Upon the place beneath: it is twice blessed;
It blesseth him that gives and him that takes. . . .
   **William Shakespeare,** *The Merchant of Venice*

The fault, dear Brutus, is not in our stars,
But in ourselves, that we are underlings.
   **William Shakespeare,** *Julius Caesar*

Something is rotten in the state of Denmark.
   **William Shakespeare,** *Hamlet*

The world's mine oyster.
   **William Shakespeare,** *The Merry Wives of Windsor*

Of one that loved not wisely but too well.
   **William Shakespeare,** *Othello*

How sharper than a serpent's tooth it is
To have a thankless child!
   **William Shakespeare,** *King Lear*

# READING CRITICALLY

# The Literature of 1485–1625

**Historical Context**

During the years from 1485 to 1625, English life changed dramatically. The feudal system disappeared, and overseas commerce transformed England into a wealthy and powerful nation. The English navy became one of the world's strongest military forces, and through exploration and colonization Britain developed into a large, rapidly expanding empire. Religious life in England also underwent a major transformation during this period. Refusing to accept the Pope's decision not to allow him to divorce his wife, King Henry VIII severed the country's connection with the Roman Catholic Church and established the Church of England, appointing himself as the church's leader.

**Literary Movements**

It was during this period that English literature came into full bloom. A cultural movement known as the Renaissance swept through the European continent, eventually making its way into England. Responding to this movement, Queen Elizabeth I actively supported education, science, and the arts. Her support helped to generate a tremendous amount of literary activity. Influenced by the classical works of ancient Rome and Greece, writers explored new literary forms and created some of the finest works the country has ever produced.

**Writers' Techniques**

The most significant developments of the period came in the areas of poetry and drama. Turning away from the long narrative poems of the Middle Ages, poets introduced a new poetic form, the lyric, into English literature. Lyrics are short, tightly structured poems in which the speaker generally focuses on conveying his or her thoughts or feelings. Most often, during this period lyrics were written in sonnet form, and they frequently dealt with the subject of love. Sonnets were often written in sequences and were generally filled with energetic, musical language. Dramas during this period were also known for their beautiful language. Written in carefully crafted verse, these dramas delve into complex characters and themes, frequently offering important insights about human nature.

On the following pages is a selection by poet Sir Thomas Wyatt. The notes in the side column should help you to place the selection in its historical context.

**VIEW OF A PARK, WITH HUNTSMEN AND DEER**
*Peter Tillemans*

# Whoso List¹ to Hunt

## Sir Thomas Wyatt

Whoso list to hunt, I know where is an hind,²
But as for me, alas, I may no more:
The vain travail hath wearied me so sore.

> **Writer's Technique:** This poem is a Petrarchan sonnet with an *abbaabba cddcee* rhyme scheme.

---

**1. Whoso list:** Whoever wants.
**2. hind:** Doe.

**Literary Movement:** The deer represents a woman whom the speaker loves. During this period literature frequently explored the subject of love.

**Writer's Technique:** Wyatt uses lively, musical language.

**Historical Context:** The woman to whom Wyatt is referring is Anne Boleyn, who soon became King Henry VIII's second wife.

I am of them that farthest cometh behind;
5  Yet may I, by no means, my wearied mind
Draw from the deer, but as she fleeth afore,
Fainting I follow. I leave off therefore,
Since in a net I seek to hold the wind.
Who list her hunt, I put him out of doubt,
10  As well as I, may spend his time in vain.
And graven with diamonds in letters plain
There is written, her fair neck round about,
*"Noli me tangere,*[3] for Caesar's I am,[4]
And wild for to hold, though I seem tame."

———————

**3. *Noli me tangere***: "Don't touch me"; words spoken by the resurrected Jesus in John 20:17.
**4. Caesar's I am:** At the time in which the poem was written, it was believed that Caesar attached collars inscribed with the words "Do not touch me, for I am Caesar's" to his deer to protect them from hunters.

**Sir Thomas Wyatt** (1503?–1542) was a diplomat and courtier in the service of King Henry VIII as well as a poet. Born in Kent, Wyatt lived an eventful and sometimes dangerous life. In 1527 while on a government mission in Italy, he became deeply interested in the works of Petrarch, the great fourteenth-century Italian poet. Already a master of traditional English lyrics, Wyatt became, under Petrarch's influence, a skillful writer of sonnets and introduced this form into England.

Wyatt was born in Kent in the castle of his father, a member of Henry's Privy Council and an executor of his will. Following in his father's footsteps, young Thomas took his place in court as a page at Princess Mary's christening. He entered Cambridge University in 1516, and married Elizabeth Brook, the daughter of Lord Cobden, in 1520.

Wyatt's poetry has been praised for its vigor and drama but is sometimes criticized for its roughness of meter. He was fortunate to have found in Petrarch an excellent form—the sonnet—which gave artistic shape to the sincerity and depth of emotion he felt when writing about love. The sonnet "Whoso List to Hunt," illustrates both the virtues of his poetry and his debt to Petrarch. It also has a special biographical interest, for it is almost certainly about his relationship with Anne Boleyn, later the wife of Henry VIII.

Sir Thomas Wyatt was the first important poet of the English Renaissance. He introduced to England a poetic form used by numerous great poets, including Shakespeare, for nearly five centuries. He ushered in the first great age of English lyric poetry. Finally, he wrote a number of poems that have a permanent place in English literature.

## THINKING ABOUT THE SELECTION

### Recalling

1. On the literal level, what realization has the speaker come to?
2. Tell why you think his feelings are or are not in complete harmony with this realization.
3. What are his cautionary remarks to other hunters?

### Interpreting

4. (a) If this poem on the figurative level is about the poet's love for Anne Boleyn, then what does hunting a hind represent? (b) Whom does Caesar stand for?
5. What special meaning does "Noli me tangere" have?

### Applying

6. Wyatt lived and wrote four and a half centuries ago. Do the feelings in "Whoso List to Hunt" seem to be outdated? Tell why you think that this poem does or does not speak to people today.

## ANALYZING LITERATURE

### Understanding the Petrarchan Sonnet

A sonnet is a fourteen-line poem in iambic pentameter with a fixed rhyme scheme. In the **Petrarchan sonnet** you have just read, the rhyme scheme of the octave is *abbaabba;* that of the sestet is *cddcee.*

1. To what extent is the two-part structure of the sonnet reflected in the thought content?
2. The sonnet was originally used almost exclusively for love poetry. Is there something about the sonnet form that makes it more suitable for this subject than for others? Explain your answer.

## CRITICAL THINKING AND READING

### Interpreting the Figurative Meaning

A poet will sometimes write a poem that has both a literal and a **figurative meaning.** "Whoso List to Hunt" is such a poem. On the literal level it is about hunting a hind. On the figurative level it is about the speaker's frustrated love for a lady. In general, you should view a poem as having a figurative meaning only when there is either internal or external evidence for such a view. Internal evidence refers to the details of a poem that clearly suggest an intended meaning beyond the literal one. External evidence refers to knowledge about the poet's life, artistic beliefs, and so on, that likewise suggests a meaning beyond the literal.

1. What external evidence do you have for interpreting Wyatt's poem as an account of his love for Anne Boleyn?
2. What internal evidence indicates that the sonnet is a love poem?

## SPEAKING AND LISTENING

### Reading Aloud Classic British Poems

Reading aloud older British poems may be more difficult than reading more recent poems. In older poetry you will encounter more archaic, obsolete, and unfamiliar words. The sentence structure may be more complicated and twisted. Historical references may be obscure. Such difficulties impede reading.

Practice reading "Whoso List to Hunt" aloud.

## THINKING AND WRITING

### Responding to Criticism

A critic of Wyatt's, J. W. Lever, remarked in his book *The Elizabethan Love Sonnet* that "Wyatt's best love poetry was really out-of-love poetry." In a brief essay, show why you think that "Whoso List to Hunt" could or could not be used as evidence to support Lever's statement.

First go over the poem carefully looking for details that help you answer the question "Is this a love poem or an out-of-love poem?" Then decide on an effective order in which to present your analyses and conclusions. When you revise, be sure you have relied on what is actually in the poem and have not read anything into it. Assume that you are writing for people who enjoy reading intelligent, well-written literary criticism.

# SIR PHILIP SIDNEY

## 1554–1586

Sir Philip Sidney wrote the first great sonnet sequence in English, *Astrophel and Stella*. Before Sidney, Sir Thomas Wyatt and the Earl of Surrey had written excellent sonnets, but Sidney was the first to write a series of sonnets linked by subject matter and theme. In addition, his *Defence of Poesy* marks the beginning of English literary criticism.

Sidney was born at Penshurst, the country home of his aristocratic family. After studying at Oxford and Cambridge he traveled extensively in Europe. Back in England he became a favorite at court, where his charm, intelligence, and good judgment were recognized and admired. In 1575 he made the acquaintance of Penelope Devereux, the daughter of Lord Essex. She was then thirteen. They became engaged, but the engagement was later broken off and Penelope became the wife of Lord Rich. She is the Stella of *Astrophel and Stella*.

In 1580 he fell out of favor with the court for writing a letter to Queen Elizabeth urging her not to marry the Duke of Anjou. He then retired to his sister's home, where he wrote part of *Arcadia,* a pastoral romance. Eventually he regained his status with the queen and was knighted in 1583. In 1586 during a military engagement against the Spanish Catholics in Holland, Sidney was wounded. As he lay on the ground, he refused the water offered him, insisting that it be given to another wounded soldier. Twenty-six days later Sidney died, to the great grief of his country.

As the nephew of the influential Earl of Leicester and the son of the highly respected Elizabethan statesman Sir Henry Sidney, young Philip was early groomed for success. Yet throughout his life he carried himself with modesty. Former schoolmate Fulke Greville captured Sidney's innate dignity in a line from the biography he wrote twenty-five years after his friend's death: "though I . . . knew him from a child, yet I never knew him other than a man—with such staidness of mind, lovely and familiar gravity, as carried grace and reverence above greater years."

During his life Sir Philip Sidney was widely revered as a courtier, soldier, scholar, and poet—a model gentleman of the English Renaissance. Today he is acknowledged as the first important literary critic in English. He is also recognized as the poet who inspired the sonnet sequences of later Renaissance poets and as the author of a number of eloquent sonnets that stand with the best poetry of this period.

# GUIDE FOR INTERPRETING

## Sonnet 31; Sonnet 39

Literary Forms

**The Sonnet Sequence.** A sonnet sequence is a group of sonnets linked by theme or subject. The form was brought to perfection by the fourteenth-century Italian poet Petrarch, whose *Sonnets to Laura* directly or indirectly inspired the sequences of later poets.

Again and again certain conventions appear in sonnet sequences: The lady is golden-haired, with cheeks like roses or lilies. She is proud. She cruelly rebuffs her poet-lover. The lover is unfailingly faithful. He fears her scorn and rejection but hopes for her love. Hence he describes himself as alternately freezing and burning. He is like a ship tossed by the sea. He calls upon sleep to ease his cares. Through his poetry his lady will be given eternal fame.

The widespread reliance of English Renaissance poets on such conventions makes their poetry seem somewhat artificial. In real life, love is seldom as it is depicted in poetry that makes use of Petrarchan conventions. Nevertheless, the sonnet sequences were enormously popular in their day, and the best of them are still read today.

**Writing**

Do love stories of today (in books, films, and TV shows) make use of widely recurring conventional ideas about men, women, and the course of love? List as many as you can recall.

**Primary Source**

In Sonnet 31 the speaker refers to "wit." This was one of the most important qualities of a Renaissance courtier and writer. Although the speaker here refers to intelligence rather than humor, Sonnet 31—as with much of Sidney's work—is shot through with clever, often humorous wordplays. J. C. A. Rathmell believes that Sidney's poetry "is characterized by the frequent appearance of a sly and subtle wit that is always threatening into question, albeit affectionately, the heroic and romantic values it ostensibly celebrates." Although Sidney's sonnets can be marred by over-elaboration, he continues, "what is immediately discernible, however, is his critical awareness of these elements in his work and his readiness to subject them to a good-humored scrutiny . . . an often disconcertingly dry and caustic wit are crucial components of Sidney's style, and it is their alliance with other quite contrary elements —vulnerability, sensibility, and a lingering attachment to the old high ways of romance and chivalry—that combine to make his writing so distinctive, and so winning." What examples of wit can you find in life today?

# Sonnet 31

## Sir Philip Sidney

With how sad steps, O Moon, thou climb'st the skies!
   How silently, and with how wan a face!
   What, may it be that even in heavenly place
That busy archer[1] his sharp arrows tries?
5 Sure, if that long-with-love-acquainted eyes
   Can judge of love, thou feel'st a lover's case.
   I read it in thy looks, thy languished grace,
To me, that feel the like, thy state descries.[2]
   Then even of fellowship, O Moon, tell me
10    Is constant love deemed there but want of wit?[3]
Are beauties there as proud as here they be?
Do they above love to be loved, and yet
   Those lovers scorn whom that love doth possess?
   Do they call virtue there ungratefulness?

---

**1. busy archer:** Cupid, the Roman god of love.
**2. descries:** Reveals.
**3. wit:** Intelligence.

## THINKING ABOUT THE SELECTION

### Recalling

1. What four lover's complaints are expressed in the sestet?
2. Describe the appearance of the moon.

### Interpreting

3. What is the connection between the appearance of the moon and the thoughts the speaker utters?

4. Paraphrase lines 3–4 and lines 5–8.
5. Judging by what is said in the sonnet, what do you infer about the speaker's relationship with his lady?

### Applying

6. How would you answer the speaker's question to the moon: "O Moon, tell me/Is constant love deemed there but want of wit"? How is constancy in love viewed in the modern world? Explain your answer.

**SHEPHERDS UNDER A FULL MOON**
*Samuel Palmer*
Ashmolean Museum, Oxford

## Primary Source

London in Sidney's day held little of the beauties of nature that he described in his sonnets. Here is how Alfred H. Bill describes what the city was like when Sidney was a teenager:

"There were the aisles of the cathedral, filled with bargaining hucksters and strutting loungers. The streets were thronged with grave merchants, apprentices dodging on their errands, groups of idle serving men badged with blue and gold, whose swords and bucklers might clash at any moment in some bloody outbreak of their noble masters' rivalry at court. Gallants swaggered through the press, so extravagant in the width of their ruffs and the lengths of their swords and daggers that a law had to be passed to regulate them . . . There was the stirring of cutpurses at night. There were stage plays; and even a sensitive boy had been so toughened by the brutal sights common at the time that he could look on at a bull-baiting or a bear-baiting with as much enjoyment as one of the present day gets out of a boxing match. Criminals were strung up publicly and as nearly as might be on the scene of their wrong-doing. Dead pirates clanked on their chains in the gallows on the river-bank. With a litte luck one might see at Tyburn the ghastly business of a traitor's disembowelment alive. The heads and quarters of such, all shiny-black with the tar that preserved them from the weather, decorated the spikes above London Bridge and Temple Bar."

From this description, what picture do you get of London in Sidney's day? Would you have like to have lived there? Why or why not?

# Sonnet 39

## Sir Philip Sidney

Come sleep, O sleep, the certain knot of peace,
The baiting place[1] of wit, the balm of woe,
The poor man's wealth, the prisoner's release,
The indifferent judge between the high and low;
5  With shield of proof[2] shield me from out the prease[3]
Of those fierce darts Despair at me doth throw:
O make in me those civil wars to cease;
I will good tribute pay, if thou do so.
Take thou of me smooth pillows, sweetest bed,
10  A chamber deaf to noise, and blind to light,
A rose garland, and a weary head:
And if these things, as being thine by right,
Move not thy heavy grace, thou shalt in me,
Livelier then elsewhere, Stella's image see.

---

1. **baiting place:** A place for refreshment.
2. **proof:** Proven strength.
3. **prease:** Crowd.

## Commentary

"Come sleep," the speaker cries in the first line of Sonnet 39. But what exactly causes sleep? And what purpose does it serve? Scientists have made enormous strides in identifying the chemicals our brain releases to make us sleep and have described several kinds of sleep. D-sleep, for example, is so called because people awakened during these periods often report that they have been *dreaming*. S-sleep, in contrast, seems not to be marked by dreaming, although it is also a deep stage of sleep.

Despite this progress understanding the nature of sleep, no one is really sure what function sleep provides. Some scientists claim that sleep has no biological function at all—that it is simply a sort of habit! Others, however, believe that sleep does indeed play a very important role in our survival. We have more S-sleep after exercise, starvation, and other times of metabolic stress, for example. This suggests that S-sleep most likely helps rebuild the body and the brain. D-sleep appears to function in much the same way, but on a more complex level, restoring the higher-level brain functions.

The need for sleep varies tremendously. An infant sleeps 16 to 18 hours a day, at least half of which is D-sleep. A teenager, though, sleeps only 7 to 8 hours, of which 1.5 hours are spent in D-sleep. You've probably heard stories of people who do not need sleep, but such reports are unproven; everyone needs at least 4 or 5 hours of sleep a night.

# THINKING ABOUT THE SELECTION

## Recalling

1. What six benefits does the speaker attribute to sleep in lines 1–4?

## Interpreting

2. Literally, what are the fierce darts that Despair hurls (line 6)?
3. What might the metaphor "civil wars" (line 7) signify?
4. In what sense could sleep see Stella's image in the speaker?
5. Why is the speaker addressing sleep?

## Applying

6. What psychological truth about people's desire for sleep is the basis for the speaker's calling upon sleep?

# ANALYZING LITERATURE

## Understanding a Sonnet Sequence

The names Astrophel and Stella mean "star-lover" and "star." Since it is known that Sidney's sequence of 108 sonnets plus 11 songs is based on his love for Penelope Devereux, we know that Astrophel represents Sidney and Stella represents Penelope. The 108 sonnets do not present a love story in narrative form. Rather, they offer reflections on the course of Astrophel's love. A reader, however, can detect the story that underlies the sequence.

Since *Astrophel and Stella* makes extensive use of the love-poem conventions present in Petrarch's *Sonnets to Laura,* the sequence seems to mix the artificial and the real, convention and sincerity. In the best of Sidney's poems, the Petrarchan conventions produce an effect of courtly grace and charm, while allowing the lover's real feelings to show through.

1. Do Sidney's two sonnets seem to you primarily sincere or primarily artificial? Give reasons for your opinion.
2. Why do you suppose a poet would decide to use an elaborate set of conventional ideas and images in love poetry, rather than write of love in a realistic way?

# THINKING AND WRITING

## Writing a Letter of Response

If Stella had received Sonnets 31 and 39 as a gift from Sidney, how might she have responded to them? What might she have said to him in a letter acknowledging that she had received and read the sonnets? Write the letter you think Stella might have written.

First reread the material in the Guide for Reading to review the way ladies were depicted in sonnet sequences. Then decide what Stella would have said in her letter. Assume that she "got the message" Sidney's poems contain. How would she have expressed her thanks for the poems? What might she have said about what the poems imply about her and her treatment of Astrophel? When you revise, make the style of your letter as suitable as you can to the courtly, Petrarchan love depicted in Sidney's sonnets.

# CHRISTOPHER MARLOWE

## 1564–1593

Though not the first English poet to write in blank verse (unrhymed iambic pentameter), Christopher Marlowe's brilliant use of it in his plays established blank verse as the preeminent meter for verse drama and ultimately for epic poetry in English. Marlowe is the author of one of the world's immortal tragedies, *Dr. Faustus,* as well as several other notable plays and poems.

Born in Canterbury, Marlowe was the son of a shoemaker. He went to Cambridge University on a scholarship usually awarded to students studying for the ministry. However, he spent much of his time writing plays and serving as a government agent. He never took holy orders. He is, indeed, reputed to have been an atheist, or at least to have held highly unorthodox religious views.

While at Cambridge Marlowe wrote *Tamburlaine,* the play that made the public aware of his dazzling abilities. It dramatizes the exploits of a fourteenth-century Scythian shepherd who conquered much of the known world. As Marlowe portrays him, Tamburlaine personifies energy and ambition and is thus a character eminently suited for the dramatist's powerful blank verse. In the remaining six years of his life, Marlowe wrote five more plays, including *Dr. Faustus* and a sequel to *Tamburlaine.* On May 30, 1593, he was killed by a dagger thrust in a tavern. His death may have been the result of a fight over the bill, or it may have been a political assassination.

Was Marlowe a spy? Hints that he may have been for a time a spy for Queen Elizabeth's secret service rest on an astonishing letter the Queen's Privy council wrote to the authorities at Cambridge in June of 1587. The letter seeks to suppress rumors that Marlowe planned to go to Rheims. "It was not in her Majesty's pleasure that anyone employed as he had been in matters touching the benefit of his country should be defamed by those who are ignorant in the affairs he went about," they wrote. Such official concern for a young divinity student suggests that Marlowe had performed an unusual service for the government.

Marlowe's fame rests primarily on his plays, especially on his "mighty line," as Ben Jonson described his dramatic blank verse. *Dr. Faustus* has been a classic of dramatic literature for four hundred years. However, Marlowe's nondramatic poetry alone would be enough to secure him a permanent place in English literature. His *Hero and Leander* is one of the finest narrative poems ever written in English, and "The Passionate Shepherd to His Love" is one of the best-known and most popular lyrics of the English Renaissance.

# GUIDE FOR INTERPRETING

## The Passionate Shepherd to His Love

**Pastoral Poetry.** A lyric poem is a poem that expresses personal thoughts and feelings. As the word lyric suggests, such a poem may have some of the characteristics of a song. It is often brief and written in rhymed verse with a pronounced rhythm. Many lyric poems have, in fact, been set to music, such as the one you are about to read. Ballads, sonnets, odes, songs, and elegies are some of the more common types of lyric poetry.

"The Passionate Shepherd to His Love" is one of the most famous examples of pastoral poetry. A *pastoral poem* is a lyric that celebrates the beauty and pleasures of country life. As a tradition in English literature, pastoral poetry often makes use of a number of conventions. The speaker in a pastoral poem is frequently a shepherd. He either addresses or speaks about a shepherdess or other country maiden with whom he is in love. The world of nature is idealized. The goodness and happiness of a life in harmony with such a world are valued above all else. Pastoral poetry was especially popular during the English Renaissance, but the tradition extends from the classical era of Greece and Rome to the present.

Think of the most appealing country place you know. If you wanted to persuade a friend to visit the place, which features would you mention? List five or six and briefly describe them.

Perhaps because of his own experience wrestling with words, Renaissance critic, university president, and baseball commissioner A. Bartlett Giamatti had this to say about Marlowe's use of language: "Renaissance man felt he had the power to transform himself because he had the power of language. Words were units of energy. Through words man could assume forms and aspire to shapes and states otherwise beyond his reach." But "words, like men, were fallen; . . . they contained, as we do, shapes of evil within them. Fallen words . . . are unstable elements; thus they are, as we are, such dangers to us. As we must always check that impulse to deformation in ourselves, so we must constantly be aware of the beast in language—Spencer calls it the Blatant Beast, whose rabid bite is vicious slander—and we must know that when we unleash a word and let it soar, we run the risk of loosing an evil force as well, one that we cannot control. We, as men using words, must stay within our limits, or what we master may master and misshape us." What power does language give you? What limits does it impose on you?

# The Passionate Shepherd to His Love

Christopher Marlowe

Come live with me, and be my love,
And we will all the pleasures prove[1]
That hills and valleys, dales and fields,
And all the craggy mountains yields.

5    And we will sit upon the rocks,
Seeing the shepherds feed their flocks,
By shallow rivers, to whose falls
Melodious birds sing madrigals.

---

**1. prove:** Experience.

**THE HIRELING SHEPHERD**
*William Holman Hunt*
*The Manchester City Art Galleries*

And I will make thee beds of roses,
10 And a thousand fragrant posies,
A cap of flowers and a kirtle[2]
Embroidered all with leaves of myrtle;

A gown made of the finest wool,
Which from our pretty lambs we pull;
15 Fair lined slippers for the cold,
With buckles of the purest gold;

A belt of straw and ivy buds,
With coral clasps and amber studs;
And if these pleasures may thee move,
20 Come live with me, and be my love.

The shepherd swains shall dance and sing
For thy delight each May morning;
If these delights thy mind may move,
Then live with me, and be my love.

---

**2. kirtle:** Skirt.

## THINKING ABOUT THE SELECTION
### Recalling

1. Describe the kind of life the shepherd is offering his love.

### Interpreting

2. How realistic is his representation of the kind of life he and his love will lead? Explain.

### Applying

3. If a poet of today were to write a contemporary version of this poem, how might the details differ from Marlowe's?

## ANALYZING LITERATURE
### Appreciating Pastoral Poems

A **pastoral poem** idealizes the rustic life. Such poetry often contains an implied contrast between the good life of nature and the corrupt life of a court or city.

1. Read Marlowe's poem aloud. What qualities of it might inspire someone to set it to music?
2. Since a shepherd, not Marlowe, is the speaker, in what sense can the poem be said to express personal thoughts and feelings?
3. Would you infer from "The Passionate Shepherd to His Love" that Marlowe's Elizabethan readers valued the pastoral life because England was becoming more urbanized? Why or why not?

# GUIDE FOR INTERPRETING

## *from* The Tragical History of the Life and Death of Doctor Faustus

**Historical Context**

**The Faust Legend.** The Faust legend is one of the most important legends of western civilization. Numerous writers have seen it as a profound revelation of the consequences of aspiring to rise above the ordinary human condition.

The legend derives from the life and activities of an actual German scholar and magician, Johann Faust (or Faustus), who lived from about 1480 to 1540. He traveled widely, performed magic, and died under mysterious circumstances. Many Germans of the time considered him a fraud, but Martin Luther, the founder of Protestantism, believed that he had Satanic powers. Even during Faust's life he was the subject of legends. According to many of them, he had sold his soul to the devil for youth, knowledge, and magical powers.

In 1587 a crude, unreliable biography of Faust appeared. The unknown author incorporated into it many legends of other magicians. The biography concludes with Faust going to hell at the end of his life. This volume appeared in an English translation titled *The History of the Damnable Life and Deserved Death of Doctor John Faustus*. It is the immediate source of Marlowe's play, which was probably written in 1588.

**Commentary**

What effect did *The Tragical History of the Life and Death of Doctor Faustus* have on Elizabethan audiences? Witches and devils were very real to Elizabethans, and when Faustus signed his soul away, their blood froze. Indeed, Elizabethans often attributed to witchcraft any unexplained occurrence. Many contemporary legends sprang up about performances of *Doctor Faustus,* just as today stories will often spring up when a horror movie is made. One story concerns a performance of the play in Exeter. As Faustus summoned the devils, the actors counted one more devil than the scene called for and feared that Satan himself was in their midst. Terrified, they stopped the play, the audience ran from their seats, and the actors bolted from town early the next morning.

**Writing**

Create an imaginary experience you would anticipate with dread— for example, a test of some kind, a visit to a doctor or dentist, or a confrontation. What would be your thoughts and feelings as the time of the experience neared? Write a monologue that presents your thoughts as they pass through your mind. Try to write the monologue in a way that expresses your feelings without naming them.

*from* # The Tragical History of the Life and Death of Doctor Faustus

Christopher Marlowe

> *Early in the play, Dr. Faustus, the main character, contracts his soul to the devil for special powers of the mind. Now, facing death, he makes a desperate attempt to repent and save his soul.*

**FAUST.** Ah, Faustus,
  Now hast thou but one bare hour to live
  And then thou must be damned perpetually!
  Stand still, you ever-moving spheres of heaven,
5  That time may cease and midnight never come;
  Fair Nature's eye, rise, rise again, and make
  Perpetual day; or let this hour be but
  A year, a month, a week, a natural day,
  That Faustus may repent and save his soul!
10  *O lente lente currite noctis equi.*[1]
  The stars move still,[2] time runs, the clock will strike,
  The devil will come, and Faustus must be damned.
  O, I'll leap up to my God! Who pulls me down?
  See, see, where Christ's blood streams in the firmament!
15  One drop would save my soul—half a drop! ah, my Christ!
  Rend not my heart for naming of my Christ;
  Yet will I call on him—O, spare me, Lucifer!
  Where is it now? 'Tis gone; and see where God
  Stretcheth out his arm and bends his ireful brows.
20  Mountains and hills, come, come and fall on me
  And hide me from the heavy wrath of God,
  No, no—
  Then will I headlong run into the earth:
  Earth, gape! O no, it will not harbor me.
25  You stars that reigned at my nativity,
  Whose influence hath allotted death and hell,
  Now draw up Faustus like a foggy mist

---

**1. *O lente . . . equi:*** "Slowly, slowly run, O horses of the night," adapted from a line in Ovid's *Amores.*
**2. still:** Always.

Into the entrails of yon laboring cloud
That when you vomit forth into the air,
30  My limbs may issue from your smoky mouths,
So that my soul may but ascend to heaven.

[*The watch strikes.*]

Ah, half the hour is past; 'twill all be past anon.
O God,
If thou wilt not have mercy on my soul,
35  Yet for Christ's sake whose blood hath ransomed me
Impose some end to my incessant pain:
Let Faustus live in hell a thousand years,
A hundred thousand, and at last be saved!
O, no end is limited to damnèd souls!
40  Why wert thou not a creature wanting soul?
Or why is this immortal that thou hast?
Ah, Pythagoras' *metempsychosis*[3]—were that true,
This soul should fly from me, and I be changed
Unto some brutish beast. All beasts are happy,
45  For when they die
Their souls are soon dissolved in elements,
But mine must live still to be plagued in hell.
Cursed be the parents that engendered me!
No, Faustus, curse thyself, curse Lucifer
50  That hath deprived thee of the joys of heaven.

[*The clock strikes twelve.*]

---

**3. metempsychosis:** The supposed passing of the soul at death into
another body; from the philosophy of Pythagoras, an ancient Greek
philosopher and mathematician, who lived in the sixth century B.C.

**FAUST CONJURING UP THE DEVIL (WOODCUT)**
*Artist Unknown*
*The Bettmann Archive*

It strikes, it strikes! Now, body, turn to air
Or Lucifer will bear thee quick[4] to hell!

[*Thunder and lightning.*]

O soul, be changed to little water drops
And fall into the ocean, ne'er be found.
55  My God, my God, look not so fierce on me!

[*Enter* DEVILS.]

Adders and serpents, let me breathe awhile!
Ugly hell, gape not—come not, Lucifer—
I'll burn my books—ah, Mephistophilis!

[*Exit* DEVILS *with* FAUSTUS.]

---

**4. quick:** Alive.

---

## THINKING ABOUT THE SELECTION
### Recalling

1. What vain hopes and longings pass through Faustus's mind as midnight approaches?

### Interpreting

2. Explain his exclamation "O, I'll leap up to my God! Who pulls me down? / See, see, where Christ's blood streams in the firmament!"
3. What does Faustus request of the stars in lines 25–31?
4. Paraphrase lines 40–46.
5. Analyze Marlowe's poetic technique in the excerpt. How does he convey Faustus's terror and despair?

### Applying

6. Can you imagine another situation that would cause someone to feel terror and despair equal to Faustus's? Explain why you do or do not think that Faustus's terror and despair are unsurpassable.

## ANALYZING LITERATURE
### Understanding Historical Context

Marlowe's *Dr. Faustus* is the first great literary treatment of the Faust legend. In the centuries that have followed, a number of major writers have used the legend as the basis for literary works. The greatest of these is Goethe's poetic drama *Faust.*

The importance of the Faust legend is that it embodies what some thinkers see as an enduring impulse in Western civilization from the Renaissance to the present: the drive to go beyond ordinary bounds of knowledge and power, even at the cost of one's own soul.

1. What impression do you get of Faustus's character and personality from his speech?
2. What moral values and attitudes does the speech implicitly uphold?
3. Name one character from history who could be termed "Faustian." Explain the similarity between this character and Faust.
4. Explain why the quest for knowledge would be an appropriate theme during the English Renaissance.

# SIR WALTER RALEIGH

## 1552–1618

Most people remember Sir Walter Raleigh as the courtier who supposedly covered a puddle with his cloak so that Queen Elizabeth I would not get her feet wet. Raleigh was much more than a dashing gallant, however. He is renowned as the founder of the colony of Virginia and the man who introduced tobacco to Europe. In his own time he was honored as a soldier, an explorer, and a poet. Today his actions often receive more attention than his words, but Raleigh's poems, few of which have survived, are rich and complex, reflecting the vicissitudes of his own life.

Raleigh, born into a well to-do family in Devonshire, served as a soldier for the Huguenots in France, attended Oxford briefly, and then, with others, outfitted a fleet purportedly for exploration but in fact to attack Spanish shipping. Returning to England in 1581, he gained an introduction to court and, making the most of his proud, handsome bearing and forceful personality, quickly became a favorite of Queen Elizabeth I. She showered him with honors, bestowed upon him vast estates in Ireland, and put him in charge of expeditions to colonize America, including the one that ended with the "Lost Colony" at Roanoke, Virginia.

Trouble began for Raleigh when the queen learned of his secret marriage to one of her maids of honor. His brief imprisonment at that time foreshadowed a much longer imprisonment under King James I. Accused by James of treason and convicted in an unfair trial, Raleigh spent many of the last years of his life in the Tower of London. There, surrounded by family and servants, he wrote his *History of the World,* a work intended to show God's judgment on the wicked. Released when he was past sixty, he made one final voyage to South America in search of gold. The expedition failed, and upon his return the Spanish ambassador accused him of burning a Spanish settlement. The old charge of treason was revived. Raleigh was convicted, and after calmly composing his own epitaph on October 28, 1618, he went to his execution the next day. He is reported to have run his hand along the edge of the executioner's axe and said, "Think you I fear the shadow of the axe, when I fear not the axe itself?"

Raleigh's reputation as a writer is difficult to assess because so little of his work has survived. What does survive suggests a mature poetic talent. His lyrics convey realism, humor, and largeness of spirit, with occasional flashes of bitterness that his cruel fate would seem to have warranted.

# GUIDE FOR INTERPRETING

## The Nymph's Reply to the Shepherd; To His Son

**Writer's Techniques**

**The Speaker.** The speaker in a poem is comparable to the narrator in prose fiction. He or she is the one—not usually the poet—who presumably is delivering the lines of the poem. In Marlowe's "The Passionate Shepherd to His Love," for instance, the speaker is a love-obsessed shepherd, not the historical and very unrustic Christopher Marlowe. This distinction is important. It is easy to make the mistake of regarding the poet as the speaker when in fact poets use all sorts of speakers in their poems: kings, knights, shepherds, lovers, Greek gods, mythological heroes, and historical figures, not to mention clouds, animals, and so on. Identifying the speaker and evaluating the purpose of the speaker in a poem can help you understand poetry better.

**Writing**

Think of an issue or event about which you have strong feelings. It may be the lyrics of a song you dislike. It may be an aspect of school that you think could be improved. It may be a political situation that you think presents problems for your community, state, or nation. Using the cluster technique, jot down your thoughts on the issue.

**Primary Source**

Sir Walter Raleigh was a dynamic speaker as well as a writer. Over and over Raleigh's contemporaries commented upon the power of his eloquence and personal magnetism to move even his enemies to his side. Nowhere is this more evident than when he was fighting for his very life. His speech during his first trial, in 1603, provides an example of his remarkable appeal. An eyewitness reported that Raleigh answered his accusers with "that temper, wit, learning, courage, and judgment, that, save it went with the hazard of his life, it was the happiest day that ever he spent. In one word, never was a man so hated and so popular in so short a time." Another observer said, "Never man spoke so well in the time past, nor would in the time to come." When he first heard Raleigh speak, the man was "so led with the common hatred that he would have gone a hundred miles to see him hanged," yet he would, before they parted, "have gone a thousand to save his life."

Raleigh's persuasive eloquence characterizes his writing as well. He urges his son, for example, not to allow his passion to overcome his reason, "for that way lies misery." He ends by warning his son, "Have therefore ever more care that thou be beloved of thy wife, rather than thyself besotted [captivated] on her." Do you think Raleigh is correct in saying it is better to be loved than to love? Why or why not?

# The Nymph's Reply to the Shepherd

Sir Walter Raleigh

*This poem was written by Raleigh as a response to the invitation presented in Christopher Marlowe's "The Passionate Shepherd to His Love."*

If all the world and love were young,
And truth in every shepherd's tongue,
These pretty pleasures might me move
To live with thee, and be thy love.

5    Time drives the flocks from field to fold,
When rivers rage and rocks grow cold,
And Philomel[1] becometh dumb,
The rest complains of cares to come.

The flowers do fade, and wanton fields
10    To wayward winter reckoning yields;
A honey tongue, a heart of gall,
Is fancy's spring, but sorrow's fall.

Thy gowns, thy shoes, thy beds of roses,
Thy cap, thy kirtle,[2] and thy posies
15    Soon break, soon wither, soon forgotten,
In folly ripe, in reason rotten.

Thy belt of straw and ivy buds,
Thy coral clasps and amber studs,
All these in me no means can move
20    To come to thee and be thy love.

But could youth last and love still breed,
Had joys no date[3] nor age no need,
Then these delights my mind might move,
To live with thee and be thy love.

---

1. **Philomel:** The nightingale.
2. **kirtle:** Skirt.
3. **date:** Ending.

## THINKING ABOUT THE SELECTION

### Recalling

1. (a) Who is the speaker in this poem? (b) Who is the person being addressed? (c) From what literary work are these two characters taken?
2. How does the speaker first suggest that the shepherd may be making unrealistic promises?

### Interpreting

3. What does the speaker think about the gifts being offered her in the previous poem?
4. Under what circumstances might the speaker accept the shepherd's offer?
5. In what ways does the form of Raleigh's poem resemble that of Marlowe's?

### Applying

6. If the shepherd and the nymph were to debate the question "What is love?" whose side would you take? Why?


## ANALYZING LITERATURE

### Identifying the Speaker in a Poem

The **speaker** in a poem is the character portrayed as delivering the lines. In "The Nymph's Reply to the Shepherd," the speaker is a nymph—the same nymph whom Marlowe's shepherd addresses in "The Passionate Shepherd to His Love" (page 230). The speaker in a poem should not be confused with the poet. In Raleigh's poem the nymph is the speaker; she is obviously not Raleigh himself. Sometimes the beliefs and attitudes of the speaker are the same as those of the poet, but not always.

1. (a) What is the speaker's attitude toward the shepherd's proposal? (b) How would you describe her emotional state?
2. Do you think Sir Walter Raleigh's own view of the shepherd's proposal is probably the same as or different from that of the nymph? Support your answer.


## CRITICAL THINKING AND READING

### Making Inferences About Tone

**Tone** is the attitude shown by a writer toward his or her subject, characters, or audience. It is often expressed as an adjective: cheerful, sarcastic, amused, lofty, sad, or any of dozens of other possibilities. The tone of "The Passionate Shepherd to His Love" might be described as optimistic. Tone is created through choice of words and details.

1. How would you describe the tone of "The Nymph's Reply to the Shepherd"?
2. What words in the poem help to convey this tone? Find at least five words.


## THINKING AND WRITING

### Writing an Invitation in Verse

Write a four-line or eight-line poem to invite a group of friends to a picnic in the country. Use a four-beat line and an *aabb* rhyme scheme. First think of some of the most appealing aspects of the picnic, such as the guests, the foods that will be served, and the scenic features of the picnic area. Then describe them in verse. You might conclude your invitation by repeating all or part of your opening line.

When you revise, try to make the tone of your verses lighthearted and pleasant. If you wish, idealize the pleasures of the picnic. Read the invitation aloud to check that the rhythm and rhyme sound right.


## THINKING AND WRITING

### Writing Your Own Reply

Using either Marlowe's (page 230) or Raleigh's poem as a model, write a poetic response of your own to one or both of the poets' views of love. Begin by making notes on what the poet says; then make a few notes on what you will say. Write your poem trying to match the form of Marlowe's or Raleigh's poem. As you revise your poem, be sure you have made your views clear. The tone of your poem can be humorous, if you wish.

# To His Son

## Sir Walter Raleigh

Three things there be that prosper up apace
And flourish, whilst they grow asunder far,
But on a day, they meet all in one place,
And when they meet, they one another mar;
5   And they be these: the wood, the weed, the wag.[1]
The wood is that which makes the gallow tree;
The weed is that which strings the hangman's bag;
The wag, my pretty knave, betokeneth thee.
Mark well, dear boy, whilst these assemble not,
10   Green springs the tree, hemp grows, the wag is wild,
But when they meet, it makes the timber rot;
It frets the halter, and it chokes the child.
Then bless thee, and beware, and let us pray
We part not with thee at this meeting day.

---

**1. wag** *n.*: A mischievous young boy.

## THINKING ABOUT THE SELECTION

### Recalling

1. (a) Who is the speaker in this poem? (b) Who is the person being spoken to?
2. What happens when the wood, the weed, and the wag meet?
3. Who is the wag in the poem?
4. What is the speaker's main concern?

### Interpreting

5. Given the speaker's concern, what conclusion can you draw about the behavior of the speaker's son? Explain.
6. How would you describe the poem's tone?

### Applying

7. The German writer Goethe wrote, "Behavior is the mirror in which everyone displays his own image." Discuss the meaning of this quotation.

## CRITICAL THINKING AND READING

### Making Inferences About Purpose

A poet's purpose in writing a poem involves more than just subject and theme. **Purpose** is a broad term that covers whatever the writer intends to communicate to the reader. To infer purpose, you must understand the poem's central idea and you must experience its emotional impact. When you fully understand the meaning of "The Nymph's Reply to the Shepherd," for instance, you can infer that Raleigh's purpose is to refute Marlowe's idealistic and simplistic view of love and to present a more realistic view.

What do you think was Raleigh's purpose in writing this poem to his son?

# EDMUND SPENSER

## 1552–1599

Edmund Spenser, the "poet's poet," is one of the very greatest poets of the English Renaissance. An imaginative experimenter in verse forms, he invented the Spenserian stanza and the Spenserian sonnet, which exerted a powerful influence on the poets who followed him.

Unlike many poets of the time, Edmund Spenser was born into a working-class family. His father was a clothmaker, and Edmund attended the Merchant Taylors' School on a scholarship for a poor man's son. He went on to Cambridge University as a "sizar," a student who was required to work his way through school. During Spenser's first year at Cambridge, his earliest poems were published.

Graduating with an M.A. degree in 1576, Spenser served in a variety of positions with wealthy noblemen, including that of secretary to the Earl of Leicester, a favorite of Queen Elizabeth I. While in Leicester's service, he became friends with Sir Philip Sidney, and the two of them formed the core of a select literary group.

In 1580 Spenser took a position as secretary to the Lord Deputy of Ireland. Thereafter he spent most of his life in Ireland, acquiring Kilcolman Castle, an Irish estate, where he did much of his writing. Sir Walter Raleigh visited him at Kilcolman Castle and was so impressed by Spenser's unfinished *The Faerie Queene* that he persuaded Spenser to take the first three books to London for publication.

*The Faerie Queene* established Spenser's reputation as the leading poet of his day. This great work, intentionally written in an archaic style, combines two literary forms, the romance and the epic, into an allegory about "the twelve moral virtues." Dedicated to Queen Elizabeth I, *The Faerie Queene* brought Spenser a small pension but no position at court.

In 1594 Spenser married Elizabeth Boyle, whom his sonnet sequence *Amoretti* commemorates. *Amoretti,* which means "little cupids" or "little love poems," is unique in the English Renaissance for being addressed to the poet's wife.

Irish rebels destroyed Spenser's castle during an uprising, and Spenser returned to London. He died on January 13, 1599, and is buried in what is now the Poet's Corner of Westminster Abbey.

# GUIDE FOR INTERPRETING

## *from* The Faerie Queen; Sonnet 1; Sonnet 26; Sonnet 75

**Writer's Techniques**

**Spenserian Poetry.** Edmund Spenser had a lifelong interest in theories of poety, and he is recognized as one of the great innovators in English verse forms. Two of his innovations are especially notable.

When Spenser wrote *The Faerie Queene,* he created a new type of stanza that was named for him. A *Spenserian stanza* consists of nine lines, the first eight of which are in iambic pentamenter. The ninth line has two additional syllables and is called an *alexandrine.* The rhyme scheme of a Spenserian stanza is *ababbcbcc.*

Although most sonnets follow either the Petrarchan or the Shakespearean form, there is a third type called the Spenserian sonnet. A *Spenserian sonnet* has fourteen lines, but its rhyme scheme differs from that of other sonnets. The rhyme scheme is *abab bcbc cdcd ee.* Often there is no break in a Spenserian sonnet between the octave (first eight lines) and sestet (last six lines).

**Writing**

Spenser intended *The Faerie Queene,* a lengthy allegory, to consist of twelve books, but he completed only six. In each a hero representing a moral virtue was to have a series of adventures, fighting off such enemies as Envy, Pride, and Despair. Among the virtues in Spenser's plan are Holiness, Friendship, Justice, and Courtesy. All twelve books were to be unified by the presence of the legendary Prince Arthur and by Gloriana, who represents Queen Elizabeth I. Select either a virtue such as truth or honesty or a fault such as pride or envy. Freewrite about it.

**Primary Source**

Even in Elizabethan days poets had trouble getting paid. *The Oxford Book of Literary Anecdotes* records the following event:

Queen Elizabeth ordered that Spenser be given one hundred pounds in payment for some poems he had written in her honor. Lord Treasurer Burleigh objected to the payment, scorning Spenser's work with the comment, "What, all this for a song?" The Queen replied, "Then give him a reason" [for not being paid]. After waiting some time and receiving neither reason nor money, Spenser decided to remind the Queen of her promise. He sent her the following poem: I was promised on a time/To have reason for my rhime./From that time, unto this season,/I received nor rhime, nor reason.

The paper produced the intended effect, and the Queen, after sharply criticizing the Treasurer, immediately ordered that Spenser be paid the hundred pounds she had promised.

# from The Faerie Queene

## Edmund Spenser

*This excerpt from Spenser's epic,* The Faerie Queene, *is a description of the Redcrosse Knight, the hero of Book 1, who represents the virtue of holiness.*

A Gentle Knight was pricking[1] on the plaine,
Ycladd in mightie armes[2] and silver shielde,
Wherein old dints of deepe wounds did remaine,
The cruell markes of many a bloudy fielde;
5  Yet armes till that time did he never wield:[3]
His angry steede did chide his foming bitt,
As much disdayning to the curbe to yield:
Full jolly[4] knight he seemd, and faire did sitt,
As one for knightly giusts[5] and fierce encounters fitt.

---

**1. pricking:** Cantering.
**2. armes:** Armor.
**3. Wherein . . . wield:** The knight wears the armor of the Christian man, which bears the dents of every Christian's fight against evil. However, Redcrosse is wearing the armor for the first time.
**4. jolly:** Gallant.
**5. giusts:** Jousts.

---

## THINKING ABOUT THE SELECTION

### Recalling

1. (a) What is the knight wearing? (b) What is he carrying? (c) What is he doing?

### Interpreting

2. What is strange about the knight's armor?
3. The knight is described as gentle and jolly (gallant). What one adjective do you think might sum up the knight's character?

### Applying

4. If you were to pick a character to represent the moral virtue of truth, what kind of person would you choose?

## ANALYZING LITERATURE

### Understanding the Spenserian Stanza

The first eight lines of a Spenserian stanza are in iambic pentameter, or ten syllables with a pattern of alternating stressed and unstressed syllables. The ninth line, called the alexandrine, has two additional syllables.

1. Choose three lines of the stanza from *The Faerie Queene,* and mark them for stressed and unstressed syllables and for feet. Use ∪ to indicate an unstressed syllable and / to indicate a stressed syllable.
2. What is the rhyme scheme of this stanza?

# Sonnet 1

## Edmund Spenser

Happy ye leaves when as those lily hands,
which hold my life in their dead doing[1] might,
Shall handle you and hold in love's soft bands,
Like captives trembling at the victor's sight,
5  And happy lines, on which with starry light,
Those lamping[2] eyes will deigne sometimes to look
And read the sorrows of my dying spright,[3]
Written with tears in heart's close[4] bleeding book.
And happy rhymes bathed in the sacred brook
10  Of Helicon[5] whence she derived is,
When ye behold that angel's blessed look,
My soul's long lacked food, my heaven's bliss.
Leaves, lines, and rhymes, seek her to please alone,
Whom if ye please, I care for other none.

---

**1. doing:** Killing.
**2. lamping:** Flashing.
**3. spright:** Spirit.
**4. close:** Secret.
**5. sacred . . . Helicon:** From Greek mythology, the Hippocrene, the fountain from which the waters of poetic inspiration flowed, located on Mt. Helicon, the sacred home of the Muses.

## THINKING ABOUT THE SELECTION

### Recalling

1. What three listeners does the speaker address in Sonnet 1?

### Interpreting

2. Who is *she* in line 10 and *her* in line 13?
3. What is the speaker asking the listeners to do?
4. (a) To what objects does Spenser give human qualities? (b) How does Spenser tie this personification to the main idea of the sonnet?

### Applying

5. What animal would you choose to personify pride? Why?

## ANALYZING LITERATURE

### Understanding the Spenserian Sonnet

The rhyme scheme of a Spenserian sonnet differs from that of the more familiar Petrarchan sonnet. The Spenserian rhyme Scheme is *abab bcbc cdcd ee*. Does this rhyme Scheme seem easier or harder for a poet to work with? Explain.

## UNDERSTANDING LANGUAGE

### Interpreting Personification

A writer who attributes human qualities to objects or animals is using **personification.** When Spenser calls the leaves in line 1 "happy," he is personifying them. In allegory, personification even extends to abstract words. Find two other examples of personification in Sonnet 1.

# Sonnet 26

## Edmund Spenser

Sweet is the rose, but grows upon a briar;
Sweet is the juniper, but sharp his bough;
Sweet is the eglantine,[1] but pricketh near;
Sweet is the fir bloom, but his branches rough;
5   Sweet is the cypress, but his rynd is tough,
Sweet is the nut, but bitter is his pill;[2]
Sweet is the broom flower, but yet sour enough;
And sweet is moly, but his root is ill.
So every sweet with sour is tempered still,[3]
10  That maketh it be coveted the more:
For easy things that may be got at will,
Most sorts of men do set but little store.
Why then should I account of little pain,
That endless pleasure shall unto me gain.

---

**1. eglantine:** A European rose with hooked spines.
**2. pill:** Core.
**3. still:** Always.

---

## THINKING ABOUT THE SELECTION

### Recalling

1. In what ways are the lines in the octave of Sonnet 26 similar?
2. According to Spenser, what is the effect of tempering every "sweet with sour"?

### Interpreting

3. How would you express in today's English what Spenser says in the closing couplet?

### Applying

4. List other examples from life where the sweet is offset by the sour.
5. Find information on the Chinese principle of yin and yang.

# Sonnet 75

## Edmund Spenser

BODEGO BAY, CALIFORNIA, PACIFIC OCEAN
© Peter Arnold

One day I wrote her name upon the strand,[1]
But came the waves and washèd it away:
Again I wrote it with a second hand,
But came the tide, and made my pains his prey.
5   "Vain man," said she, "that dost in vain assay,
A mortal thing so to immortalize,
For I myself shall like to this decay,
And eek[2] my name be wipèd out likewise."
"Not so," quod[3] I, "let baser things devise.
10   To die in dust, but you shall live by fame:
My verse your virtues rare shall eternize,
And in the heavens write your glorious name.
Where whenas death shall all the world subdue,
Our love shall live, and later life renew."

---

**1. strand:** Beach.
**2. eek:** Also.
**3. quod:** Said.

## THINKING ABOUT THE SELECTION
### Recalling

1. What two events occur twice in the first quatrain of Sonnet 75?
2. (a) Who begins speaking in line 5? (b) Who begins speaking in line 9?

### Interpreting

3. (a) Why does the poet believe his love's name will not be washed away by the tide? (b) Has time proven him right?

### Applying

4. How do the three sonnets from Spenser's *Amoretti*—1, 26, and 75—fit the definition of a sonnet sequence?

## THINKING AND WRITING
### Comparing and Contrasting Sonnets

Reread Sonnet 26 and Sonnet 75 noting their similarities and differences. Write a composition in which you compare and contrast the form, tone, and meaning of the two sonnets. Begin with a chart:

|           | Form | Tone | Meaning |
|-----------|------|------|---------|
| Sonnet 26 |      |      |         |
| Sonnet 75 |      |      |         |

Use the chart as a basis for writing the first draft of your composition. Remember that to **compare** means to examine similarities; to **contrast** means to discuss differences. When you have finished, read your first draft carefully for organization, content, grammar, mechanics, and style. Revise it as necessary.

# THOMAS NASHE

## 1567–1601

Although Thomas Nashe is best known today for his novel *The Unfortunate Traveler,* the Elizabethans knew him better as a brash, opinionated writer of pamphlets. His personality made him stand out from his contemporaries. While they were writing lyrical poetry or plays, he was carrying on violent written arguments with the Puritans, whom he despised. In addition to his notoriety as a warring pamphleteer, he acquired a modest literary reputation as a poet, novelist, and playwright.

Nashe, the sheltered son of an English churchman, attended Cambridge as a sizar—a scholarship student who worked to defray expenses. Upon graduation he traveled briefly in France and Italy, then settled in London as a writer. He soon began turning out breezy but acidic criticisms of current literary trends and Puritan pamphleteers. At one point his running argument with Gabriel Harvey, a satirical versifier, became so heated that the government ordered both men to cease and desist.

Using material from daily life, Nashe wrote novels and roguish adventures that are filled with spirit and wit. *The Unfortunate Traveler,* published in 1594, is a remarkable work of its kind and helped to establish the adventure novel in England. As a dramatist, often in collaboration with other writers, Nashe achieved less success. One of his comedies, *The Isle of Dogs,* the text of which is now lost, so angered the authorities that Nashe was sent to Fleet prison for a time. Nashe's poetry is not as sensational as his prose, but like his prose it relies on everyday life for inspiration.

As a lyric poet Nashe is often linked with certain other sixteenth-century writers who are not widely read today. Among these excellent but less familiar poets are John Skelton, Sir Edward Dyer, Robert Southwell, and Thomas Campion. Except for the prolific Campion, most of them, like Nashe, are known for only a few poems.

Although Nashe's writing abounds with clever plays on language, he often got carried away by his own eloquence. *Pierce Penilesse his supplication to the divells* (1592), for example, is one of Nashe's most successful works. Nonetheless, it shows both the strengths and failings that characterize his writing. While the language is clever and smooth, the work lacks a consistent direction and structure. As a result the book drifts from its point. In much the same way, *The Terrors of the Night,* an attack on demonology, is frequently confusing. This resulted in an uneven quality in his work, leading one critic to label him "the first of the English prose eccentrics, an extraordinary inventor of verbal hybrids."

# GUIDE FOR INTERPRETING

## A Litany in Time of Plague

**Writer's Techniques**

**Litany.** Strictly speaking, the word *litany* is a religious rather than a literary term. A litany is a prayer that consists of a series of alternating appeals by a minister or priest and responses by the congregation or choir. The term is sometimes applied to a poem, chant, or other recital that is echoic and repetitive.

As you read "A Litany in Time of Plague," decide which lines would be read by the minister or priest and which ones are a response by the congregation. Why is a litany particularly appropriate for a time of plague?

**Commentary**

Physicians could offer little help against the plague. Since many doctors thought that the plague was caused by foul air, they advised people to build bonfires to restore the atmosphere. Some suggested that "No poultry should be eaten, no waterfowl, no suckling pig . . . Cold, moist, and watery foods are generally harmful and should be avoided." People believed that the body was composed of four elements or "humors": blood (hot, moist), yellow bile (hot, dry), phlegm (cold, moist), and black bile (cold, dry). Disease resulted when the humors got unbalanced. Avoiding certain foods, they felt, would stabilize the body. Bleeding and purging were also used. Others turned to magic. Besides "magical" charms and garlic, many repeated the word "abracadabra" to ward off plague and fever.

In London's streets, children played a game to protect against the plague. Holding hands, they circled clockwise as they sang a rhyme to the "plague-stricken" child in the middle: Ring a ring of rosies,/A pocket full of posies,/Ashes, ashes,/All fall down.

The "ring of rosies" might have been the hair garland the children wore or the rash that characterized the disease. "Posies" were the bouquets people carried to ward off the stench of death. "Ashes" might have referred to dust from which everyone came and to which they would return upon death, presumably after falling down and dying from the plague.

**Writing**

At the time Nashe was writing, the bubonic plague and black plague (or Black Death), two forms of the same infection, had ravaged Europe periodically. The mortality rate ran as high as 90 percent among those infected. The causes of the plague were unknown, and even the quarantining of victims had only limited effectiveness against the frightening menace. Jot down two or three threats to modern life for which a litany might be an appropriate literary form. Freewrite briefly about one of them.

*Guide for Interpreting* 249

# A Litany in Time of Plague

## Thomas Nashe

Adieu, farewell earth's bliss,
This world uncertain is;
Fond[1] are life's lustful joys,
Death proves them all but toys,[2]
5  None from his darts can fly.
I am sick, I must die.
  Lord, have mercy on us!

Rich men, trust not in wealth,
Gold cannot buy you health;
10  Physic[3] himself must fade,
All things to end are made.
The plague full swift goes by;
I am sick, I must die.
  Lord, have mercy on us!

15  Beauty is but a flower
Which wrinkles will devour;
Brightness falls from the air,
Queens have died young and fair,
Dust hath closed Helen's[4] eye.
20  I am sick, I must die.
  Lord, have mercy on us!

Strength stoops unto the grave,
Worms feed on Hector[5] brave,
Swords may not fight with fate.
25  Earth still holds ope her gate;
Come! come! the bells do cry.
I am sick, I must die.
  Lord, have mercy on us!

Wit with his wantonness
30  Tasteth death's bitterness;
Hell's executioner
Hath no ears for to hear
What vain art can reply.
I am sick, I must die.
35    Lord, have mercy on us!

Haste, therefore, each degree,
To welcome destiny.
Heaven is our heritage,
Earth but a player's stage;
40  Mount we unto the sky.
I am sick, I must die.
  Lord, have mercy on us!

---

**1. fond:** Foolish.
**2. toys:** Trifles.
**3. physic:** Doctor.
**4. Helen's:** Referring to Helen of Troy,
the legendary wife of the king of Sparta, whose
abduction led to the start of the Trojan War.

---

**5. Hector:** A Trojan hero killed by
Achilles in Homer's *Iliad*.

## THINKING ABOUT THE SELECTION

### Recalling

1. (a) What does the speaker believe must inevitably happen to him? (b) What line states the basis for this belief?
2. According to the speaker, what is the fate of (a) beauty? (b) strength?

### Interpreting

3. After beginning a stanza with a general statement, how does the poet emphasize the truth of the statement?
4. (a) Is the speaker in despair because he must die? (b) Why or why not?
5. Do you think the speaker is suggesting that nothing on earth endures? Explain.

### Applying

6. "A Litany in Time of Plague" was presented before the Archbishop of Canterbury in 1592. How does this fact indicate that the speaker in the poem—the "I"—is not Thomas Nashe himself?

## ANALYZING LITERATURE

### Understanding a Litany

A **litany** is a form of prayer in which appeals to God alternate with responses by the congregation. The word *litany,* when applied to a literary work, often has a meaning defined by the work itself, one that may differ from the religious meaning. In "A Litany in Time of Plague," however, there does appear to be a statement–response pattern in each stanza.

1. When this poem was presented to the Archbishop of Canterbury, it was as part of a play. What lines in each stanza do you think would be spoken in the play as a response to the "priest"?

2. What features of the poem make it appropriate for presentation as a statement–response litany?

## CRITICAL THINKING AND READING

### Generalizing from a Set of Assumptions

A **generalization** is a general idea, principle, or rule that you assume to be true. It is based on inductive reasoning. To make a generalization, you must look at a number of specific cases and draw conclusions from them. A *valid generalization* is one based on a sufficient amount of supporting evidence. The more evidence you have, the more reliable your generalization will be, but sometimes generalizations must be made on limited evidence or on a set of assumptions. Any assumptions you make—any guesses based on evidence—must be as sound and sensible as possible if the generalization you draw from them is to be valid.

1. What generalization can you make about the concerns of the people in London at the time Nashe wrote this poem?
2. What assumptions did you make that led you to this generalization?

## THINKING AND WRITING

### Writing About the Concerns of a People

What was London like in the late sixteenth century? What did people worry about? Based on your reading of "A Litany in Time of Plague" and your answers in the Critical Thinking and Reading section, write a composition explaining your answers. Use quotes from the poem to support your conclusion, and find additional evidence if you can.

# WILLIAM SHAKESPEARE

## 1564–1616

Because of his profound understanding of the many aspects of human nature, his compassion toward all types and classes of people, and the power and beauty of his language, William Shakespeare is generally regarded as the greatest writer of English literature. More than 350 years after his death, Shakespeare's plays continue to be read widely and produced frequently throughout the world. His plays have the same powerful impact on audiences today as they did when they were first staged.

Shakespeare was born in a small country town, Stratford-on-Avon, in April (probably April 23) 1564. His father was a successful businessman who held a number of positions in the town government. Presumably educated at the Stratford grammar school, Shakespeare acquired a basic understanding of Latin, but he did not attend a university. Shakespeare married Anne Hathaway in 1582, and the couple had a daughter, Susanna, in 1583 and twins, Hamnet and Judith, in 1585. Very little is known about Shakespeare's life from the date the twins were born to his appearance in a London acting company seven years later.

By that time, however, he had already developed a reputation as an actor and had written several plays. It was not unusual for members of theater companies to do a number of different jobs, from writing to acting to designing costumes to taking care of advertising, theater arrangements, and finances. By 1594 Shakespeare was a part owner and the principal playwright of the Lord Chamberlain's Men, one of the most successful theater companies in London. In 1599 the company built the famous Globe Theater, where most of Shakespeare's plays were performed. When James I became king in 1603, following Queen Elizabeth I's death, he took control of the Lord Chamberlain's Men and renamed the company The King's Men. In about 1610 Shakespeare retired to Stratford, though he continued to write plays. Six years later, on April 23, he died and was buried in Holy Trinity Church in Stratford.

Because Shakespeare wrote his plays to be performed, not published, no one knows exactly when each of the plays was written. However, through extensive research, scholars have been able to chart several periods in Shakespeare's development as a playwright. During his early years (through most of the 1590's) Shakespeare wrote a number of comedies (including *The Comedy of Errors, Love's Labor's Lost, The Merchant of Venice,* and *A Midsummer Night's Dream*), several histories (including *Richard II, Richard III,* and *Henry IV*), and two tragedies *(Titus Andronicus and Romeo and Juliet).* Shakespeare then wrote several of his finest romantic comedies *(As You Like It, Twelfth Night,* and *Much Ado About Nothing)* just before the turn of the century. During the first decade of the seventeenth century, Shakespeare created his greatest tragedies *(Hamlet, Othello, King Lear, Macbeth, Antony and Cleopatra,* and *Coriolanus).* Finally, toward the end of his life, Shakespeare wrote several plays referred to as "romances" or "tragicomedies" *(The Winter's Tale, Cymbeline,* and *The Tempest).*

In addition to his 37 plays, Shakespeare wrote 154 sonnets and two narrative poems. He probably worked on his sonnets from 1592 through 1598, a time when sonneteering was in vogue in London. It is likely that he wrote many of them in 1592, when the London theater was closed because of a plague.

Below is a list of Shakespeare's poems and plays in roughly chronological order.

**Poems**

*Venus and Adonis*
*The Rape of Lucrece*
*Sonnets*
*The Phoenix and the Turtle*

**Plays**

*The Comedy of Errors*
*Love's Labor's Lost*
*2 Henry VI*
*3 Henry VI*
*1 Henry VI*
*Richard III*
*Titus Andronicus*
*The Taming of the Shrew*
*The Two Gentlemen of Verona*
*The Tragedy of Romeo and Juliet*
*Richard II*
*A Midsummer Night's Dream*
*King John*
*The Merchant of Venice*
*1 Henry IV*
*2 Henry IV*
*Much Ado About Nothing*
*Henry V*
*The Tragedy of Julius Caesar*

*As You Like It*
*Twelfth Night*
*Hamlet*
*The Merry Wives of Windsor*
*Troilus and Cressida*
*All's Well That Ends Well*
*Othello*
*Measure for Measure*
*King Lear*
*Macbeth*
*Antony and Cleopatra*
*Timon of Athens*
*Coriolanus*
*Pericles*
*Cymbeline*
*The Winter's Tale*
*The Tempest*
*Henry VIII*

# GUIDE FOR INTERPRETING

## Sonnet 29; Sonnet 73; Sonnet 116; Sonnet 130

**Writer's Techniques**

**Shakespearean Sonnet.** During the Elizabethan period, the sonnet sequence, a group of sonnets unified by a common theme, became a popular literary form. Shakespeare's 154 sonnets, like those in other sonnet sequences, are numbered and fit loosely together to form a story. Most of the sonnets are addressed to a handsome, talented young man, urging him at first to marry and have children who can carry on his talents. The speaker also warns the young man about the destructive powers of time, age, and moral weakness. Midway through the sequence, the sonnets focus on a rival poet who has also addressed poems to the young man. Twenty-five of the later sonnets are addressed to a "dark lady," who is romantically involved with both the speaker and the young man. The focus of these later sonnets is on the grief she causes by her betrayal of the speaker.

Scholars fiercely debate the identity of the young man (Mr. W.H.), the "dark lady," and the rival poet to whom the sonnets are addressed. Leading candidates for the role of Mr. W.H. are Henry Wriothesley, third earl of Southampton, to whom Shakespeare dedicated his narrative poems, and William Herbert, third earl of Pembroke. Those favoring Southampton claim Mrs. John Davenant was the "dark lady," but the Pembroke side goes with Mary Fitton, a woman of doubtful reputation. The many nominees for the rival poet include Edmund Spenser, Christopher Marlowe, Ben Jonson, and John Donne, all Shakespeare's contemporaries—but even Chaucer, who had been dead for 200 years, has been proposed!

William Shakespeare did not invent what is now called the Shakespearean sonnet (Sir Thomas Wyatt and the Earl of Surrey did), but Shakespeare is its greatest master. A Shakespearean sonnet, fourteen lines in iambic pentameter, consists of three quatrains and a rhyming couplet. The usual rhyme scheme is *abab cdcd efef gg*. Shakespeare's sonnets ordinarily present a problem or premise in the first twelve lines and offer a solution or conclusion (sometimes a statement of the theme) in the final couplet.

**Writing**

Shakespeare's sonnets reflect on various aspects of life, such as personal relationships, the passing of time, and the relationship between human beings and nature. Jot down your thoughts on three aspects of life that you might consider writing about in a sonnet. Then list some of the ideas and emotions you associate with each one.

# Sonnet 29

## William Shakespeare

When in disgrace with fortune and men's eyes,
I all alone beweep my outcast state,
And trouble deaf heaven with my bootless[1] cries,
And look upon myself and curse my fate,
5  Wishing me like to one more rich in hope,
Featured like him, like him with friends possessed,
Desiring this man's art, and that man's scope,
With what I most enjoy contented least.
Yet in these thoughts myself almost despising,
10  Haply I think on thee, and then my state,
Like to the lark at break of day arising
From sullen earth, sings hymns at heaven's gate;
    For thy sweet love remembered such wealth brings
    That then I scorn to change my state with kings.

---

**1. bootless:** Futile.

---

## THINKING ABOUT THE SELECTION

### Recalling

1. With whom or what is the speaker in disfavor?
2. What are three things the speaker wishes for?
3. When the speaker thinks of the person to whom the sonnet is addressed, how does his attitude change?

### Interpreting

4. How would you describe the mood (a) of the first eight lines of this sonnet? (b) of the last six lines?
5. Why is the comparison with the lark an appropriate one for the speaker to make?
6. How do the last two lines summarize the theme of the sonnet?

### Applying

7. If you were to give this sonnet a title, what would it be?

## ANALYZING LITERATURE

### Understanding Shakespearean Sonnets

Sonnet 29 is a Shakespearean sonnet consisting of three quartains and a couplet. It has the usual rhyme scheme of such a sonnet, *abab cdcd efef gg*. In a Shakespearean sonnet, the poet typically presents a problem or premise in the first twelve lines followed by a solution or conclusion in the last two. In Sonnet 29, however, a change in direction occurs at line 9, as it does in a Petrarchan sonnet.

1. Each of the first two quatrains expresses a distinct but related thought. In your own words, what are these two thoughts?
2. What rhyming words represent (a) the *b*'s in the rhyme scheme? (b) the *e*'s? (c) the *g*'s?
3. How does the thought expressed in the last two lines of the sonnet relate to what is said in the first eight lines?
4. What is your reaction to this sonnet's theme?

**THE SONNET**
*William Mulready*

256   *The English Renaissance*

# Sonnet 73

## William Shakespeare

That time of year thou mayst in me behold
When yellow leaves, or none, or few, do hang
Upon those boughs which shake against the cold,
Bare ruined choirs where late the sweet birds sang.
5  In me thou see'st the twilight of such day
As after sunset fadeth in the west,
Which by and by black night doth take away,
Death's second self that seals up all in rest.
In me thou see'st the glowing of such fire,
10  That on the ashes of his youth doth lie,
As the deathbed whereon it must expire,
Consumed with that which it was nourished by.[1]
> This thou perceivest, which makes thy love more
>     strong,
> To love that well which thou must leave ere long.

---

**1. Consumed . . . by:** Choked by the ashes of that which fueled its flame.

## THINKING ABOUT THE SELECTION

### Recalling

1. To what season of the year does the speaker compare himself?
2. To what time of day does the speaker compare himself?
3. What comparison does the speaker make in the third quatrain?

### Interpreting

4. How does the speaker resemble the three things to which he compares himself?

5. In the "bare ruin'd choirs" of line 4, the word *choirs* refers literally to the loft where church singers perform. What does it mean as Shakespeare uses it here?
6. Explain the meaning of "Death's second self" in line 8.
7. How does the thought in the final couplet relate to the rest of the sonnet?

### Applying

8. Many people regret growing old. How do you think the speaker in this sonnet feels about it? Support your answer with details from the sonnet.

# Sonnet 116

## William Shakespeare

Let me not to the marriage of true minds
Admit impediments.[1] Love is not love
Which alters when it alteration finds,
Or bends with the remover to remove.
5  O, no! It is an ever-fixèd mark
That looks on tempests and is never shaken;
It is the star to every wandering bark,[2]
Whose worth's unknown, although his height be taken.
Love's not Time's fool, though rosy lips and cheeks
10  Within his bending sickle's compass come;
Love alters not with his brief hours and weeks,
But bears it out even to the edge of doom.[3]
    If this be error, and upon me proved,
    I never writ, nor no man ever loved.

---

**1. impediments:** Reasons why a marriage should not be allowed to take place.
**2. star . . . bark:** The star that guides every wandering ship; the North Star.
**3. doom:** Judgment Day.

---

## THINKING ABOUT THE SELECTION

### Recalling

1. According to the speaker, what are three things that love is not?
2. To what is love compared in the second quatrain?

### Interpreting

3. What are the points of similarity between true love and the North Star?
4. The speaker notes that "Love's not Time's fool." (a) What does he mean? (b) How does this idea fit in with the central theme of the sonnet?
5. Ordinarily, the final couplet in a Shakespearean sonnet offers a summary or solution. This final couplet is a bit different. What point does it make about the content of the rest of the sonnet?

### Applying

6. What is your opinion of the speaker's concept of true love? Explain your answer.

# Sonnet 130

## William Shakespeare

My mistress' eyes are nothing like the sun;
Coral is far more red than her lips' red;
If snow be white, why then her breasts are dun;
If hairs be wires, black wires grow on her head.
5  I have seen roses damasked,[1] red and white,
But no such roses see I in her cheeks;
And in some perfumes is there more delight
Than in the breath that from my mistress reeks.[2]
I love to hear her speak. Yet well I know
10  That music hath a far more pleasing sound.
I grant I never saw a goddess go;[3]
My mistress, when she walks, treads on the ground.
    And yet, by heaven, I think my love as rare
    As any she belied with false compare.

---

**1. damasked:** Variegated.
**2. reeks:** Emanates.
**3. go:** Walk.

## THINKING ABOUT THE SELECTION

### Recalling

1. What is less than perfect about the mistress's (a) lips? (b) cheeks? (c) breath? (d) voice?

### Interpreting

2. "Sonnet 130" is often called an anti-Petrarchan sonnet. What do you think is meant by "anti-Petrarchan"?
3. There are indications even before the final couplet that the speaker loves his mistress despite her supposed imperfections. What is one such indication?

### Applying

4. Would you like to have this kind of sonnet written about you, or would you prefer the more traditional kind with its idealized comparisons? Give your reasons.

## THINKING AND WRITING

### Comparing and Contrasting Sonnets

Choose the Shakespeare sonnet you like best. Then choose a sonnet by another writer —Wyatt, Sidney, or Spenser. Write an essay in which you compare and contrast the form, tone, and meaning of the two sonnets. Set up a chart for taking notes. Write the first draft of your essay, keeping in mind that to **compare** means to examine similarities; to **contrast** means to discuss differences.

As you write, try to incorporate direct quotations from the sonnets into your paper. When you have finished your first draft, reread it, paying special attention to the way you have punctuated direct quotations. Make any changes needed before completing your final draft. Then share it with your classmates.

# GUIDE FOR INTERPRETING

## Tell Me Where Is Fancy Bred? It Was a Lover and His Lass; Fear No More the Heat o' the Sun

**Writer's Techniques**

**Shakespearean Songs.** Music and song were important aspects of life during the English Renaissance. Serenades, street songs, pastoral invitations, nonsense songs, ballads—all were popular at every level of English society. Shakespeare included 124 songs in his plays. The songs serve specific purposes in the plays in which they appear; they were not added merely to capitalize on the appeal of music. Although Shakespeare's songs were sung on stage as part of the productions, none of the original printed versions of the plays includes the music. As a consequence, much of the original music has been lost. Nevertheless, the lyrics can be enjoyed as poems without music. They can also be appreciated outside the context of the plays. William Shakespeare, unparalleled playwright and poet, was also one of England's great songwriters.

**Writing**

Take the lyrics of a popular song and rewrite them in your own way. Your song can be as playful or as serious as you wish.

**Primary Source**

> But supper being ended, and Musicke bookes, according to the custome being brought to the table; the mistresse of the house presented mee with a part, earnestly requesting mee to sing. But when after manie excuses, I protested unfainedly that I could not: everie one began to wonder. Yea, some whispered to others, demaunding how I was brought up . . .

Few of us today have been embarrassed by being unable to sing unfamiliar music at the dinner table! Yet young people in Shakespeare's day were expected to be able to do just that, according to Elizabethan composer Thomas Morely's account of how a young man of his acquaintance came to study music. Young men learned Latin, Greek, and French in school, but music was not taught in the classroom, for there was no need to teach music in a country where "every christening, wedding, and funeral went to the strains of flutes and trumpets and the sound of drums and singing; where May Day games and the feast of St. Nicholas resounded with music, and travelers reported everywhere the beautiful playing of violas and pandoras and that 'even in small villages the musicians wait on you for a small fee.'" At what occasions do we expect music now? How do we learn music today?

# Tell Me Where Is Fancy[1] Bred

William Shakespeare

*This song is sung in* The Merchant of Venice *(Act III, Scene ii) while Bassanio is trying to choose among the caskets of gold, silver, and lead, knowing that only by making the correct choice will he be able to win Portia as his wife.*

Tell me where is fancy bred,
Or in the heart or in the head?
How begot, how nourishèd?
    Reply, reply.
5 It is engendered in the eyes,
With gazing fed; and fancy dies
In the cradle where it lies.
    Let us all ring fancy's knell:
I'll begin it—Ding, dong, bell.
10 Ding, dong, bell.

---

**1. Fancy:** Love.

---

## THINKING ABOUT THE SELECTION

### Recalling

1. What two possible sources of fancy are mentioned at the beginning of the song?
2. Where does the reply to the two questions place the origin of fancy?

### Interpreting

3. The word *fancy* is central to the meaning of the poem. It means "love," to be sure, but a superficial kind of love—a love based only on outward appearances. Why is this distinction important?

4. What is it that helps fancy flourish?
5. Why do you think the speaker says that fancy dies in the cradle?
6. What does it mean to "ring fancy's knell"?

### Applying

7. Bassanio must choose the correct one of three caskets if he is to win Portia. Two of the caskets are of glittering gold and silver; one is of plain lead. Bassanio chooses the lead casket. Using the words of the song as clues, why do you think he makes that choice?

# It Was a Lover and His Lass

## William Shakespeare

*This song, from* As You Like It *(Act V, Scene iii), is sung by two pages to Touchstone, a clown, and Audrey, a country maid, on the day before their marriage.*

It was a lover and his lass,
    With a hey, and a ho, and a hey nonino,
That o'er the green cornfield did pass
    In the springtime, the only pretty ringtime,[1]
5  When birds do sing, hey ding a ding, ding.
Sweet lovers love the spring.

Between the acres of the rye,
    With a hey, and a ho, and a hey nonino,
These pretty country folks would lie,
10    In the springtime, the only pretty ringtime,
When birds do sing, hey ding a ding, ding.
Sweet lovers love the spring.

This carol they began that hour,
    With a hey, and a ho, and a hey nonino,
15  How that life was but a flower
    In the springtime, the only pretty ringtime,
When birds do sing, hey ding a ding, ding.
Sweet lovers love the spring.

And therefore take the present time,
20    With a hey, and a ho, and a hey nonino,
For love is crownèd with the prime
    In the springtime, the only pretty ringtime,
When birds do sing, hey ding a ding, ding.
Sweet lovers love the spring.

---

**1. ringtime:** Wedding season.

**THE WOODCUTTER COURTING THE MILKMAID**
*Thomas Gainsborough*
Woburn Abbey

## THINKING ABOUT THE SELECTION

### Recalling

1. What do lovers love?
2. To what do lovers compare life?

### Interpreting

3. Why do you think springtime is called "the only pretty ringtime"?
4. What recommendation about love is made in the last stanza?

### Applying

5. Love songs have always been popular. What modern love song do you think comes closest to having the same message as "It Was a Lover and His Lass"?

## CRITICAL THINKING AND READING
### Finding Details That Develop Mood

The **mood** of a piece of writing is the atmosphere or emotion it conveys. Mood can be created through descriptive details and word choice. For example, a dark sky, rolling thunder, and howling wind can create an eerie mood. Such words as *shivering, aghast, oppressive,* and *helplessness* can add to it.

1. How would you describe the mood in this song?
2. (a) What descriptive details help convey the mood? (b) What words help convey it?

# Fear No More the Heat o' the Sun

## William Shakespeare

*This song, from* Cymbeline *(Act IV, Scene ii), is a lament for Imogen, the heroine, who is supposed to be dead.*

Fear no more the heat o' the sun,
 Nor the furious winter's rages;
Thou thy worldly task hast done,
 Home art gone, and ta'en thy wages.
5 Golden lads and girls all must,
As[1] chimney sweepers, come to dust.

Fear no more the frown o' the great;
 Thou art past the tyrant's stroke;
Care no more to clothe and eat;
10  To thee the reed is as the oak:
The scepter, learning, physic,[2] must
All follow this, and come to dust.

Fear no more the lightning flash,
 Nor the all-dreaded thunder stone;[3]
15 Fear not slander, censure rash;
 Thou hast finished joy and moan:
All lovers young, all lovers must
Consign to thee, and come to dust.

No exorciser harm thee!
20 Nor no witchcraft charm thee!
Ghost unlaid forbear thee!
Nothing ill come near thee!
Quiet consummation have;
And renownèd be thy grave!

---

**1. As:** Like.
**2. scepter, learning, physic:** Kings, scholars, doctors.
**3. thunder stone:** At the time it was believed that the sound of thunder was caused by falling meteorites.

## THINKING ABOUT THE SELECTION

### Recalling

1. What are five aspects of life that the deceased no longer has to worry about?
2. What will happen to young lovers?

### Interpreting

3. In the last stanza, what do the three concerns mentioned have in common?
4. Judging by the things the deceased no longer has to fear, what status in life do you think she held?

### Applying

5. If this song were to be sung today, where would a person be most likely to hear it? Explain your answer.

## ANALYZING LITERATURE

### Understanding Shakespeare's Songs

The songs in Shakespeare's plays are functional; that is, each serves a specific purpose. In "Fear No More the Heat o' the Sun," the purpose is to convince the audience to look upon Imogen's death as a release from the pain and sorrow of life. The details in the song all stress the idea that Imogen has no further need to fear these troubling aspects of existence.

1. What are some of the details that support the purpose of the song?
2. Suppose the lament were to take exactly the opposite approach—with the details chosen to emphasize life's vanished joys. What might some of the specific details be?

## THINKING AND WRITING

### Writing About Shakespeare's Songs

Write an essay about Shakespeare's songs, commenting on their themes, tone, and language. Explain how the songs do or do not match your general impression of Shakespeare's works. Begin by rereading the songs and making notes on them. Then write a thesis sentence that states the main idea you intend to develop. In writing your first draft, try to work in appropriate quotations from the songs. Reread the first draft making sure the paper is logically developed and reads smoothly. Write a final draft incorporating all changes and corrections.

---

### Commentary

In the United States it is hard to find an inn in the thirteen original states dating back to the Revolutionary period that doesn't claim "Washington Slept Here." In England a similar situation exists in regard to Shakespeare. Although there is a lack of sure information about Shakespeare's life, traditions about the poet have become attached to places and objects. For example, tradition identifies the pew in Stratford's Guild Chapel in which Shakespeare worshiped. In 1877 the head of the grammar school proudly displayed Shakespeare's desk to visitors.

"William was a studious lad and selected that corner of the room so that he might not be disturbed by the other boys," he said, with no proof whatsoever to back up his claim. Although Shakespeare left no personal papers behind, tradition has identified and enshrined an absurd assortment of his personal effects: his pencil-case, walking stick, gloves, brooch, table, spoon, and wooden salt cellars. The owner of the Shakespeare Hotel proudly showed off Shakespeare's clock before selling it at public auction in 1880; not to be bested, the nearby Falcon Inn boasted the shovel-board at which he played.

# THE ELIZABETHAN THEATER

English drama came of age during the reign of Elizabeth I, developing into a sophisticated and very popular art form. While playwrights like Shakespeare were mainly responsible for the great theatrical achievements of the time, the importance of actors, audiences, and theater buildings should not be underestimated.

Before the reign of Elizabeth I, theater companies traveled about the country putting on plays wherever they could find an audience, often performing in the open courtyards of inns. Spectators watched from the ground or from the inn windows. The system persisted for years, but inns as theaters had a number of disadvantages. A permanent building solely for the production of plays was sorely needed.

## England's First Playhouse

When Shakespeare was twelve years old, an actor named James Burbage built London's first theater, called The Theater, just beyond the city walls in Shoreditch. Actors—even prominent and well-to-do actors like Burbage—occupied an anomalous place in society. Despite the growing popularity of plays, actors of the time, however prosperous, were widely regarded as rogues and vagabonds. An act of Parliament in 1572 required acting companies to operate under the patronage of a respectable person or organization, and a London ordinance two years later imposed a number of licensing restrictions on theatrical groups and productions. Burbage's acting company enjoyed the patronage of the Earl of Leicester, but Burbage financed the new theater himself. His theater, once completed, proved a success, and its design set the pattern for the theaters that followed, including the famous Globe Theater in Southwark, built in 1599, where many of Shakespeare's plays were performed.

## The Globe Theater

The Globe was an octagonal structure with an unroofed yard in the center where the "groundlings" stood. Groundlings were members of the audience who paid a mere penny to attend. Three tiers of seats, the galleries, rose around the perimeter of the yard and were protected by a thatched roof. Theatergoers in the galleries looked down on a rectangular wooden stage, raised a few feet off the ground, that jutted out into the yard. The groundlings were closer to the stage than were members of the gallery audience, but they had a less satisfactory view.

Permanence, however, allowed many refinements. At the back of the main stage were two doors that led to a dressing room and were used for most of the actors' entrances and exits. Built into the main stage were one or more trapdoors leading to an area below the stage. Actors playing ghosts or witches would appear and disappear through the trapdoors. Behind the main stage was a curtained recess, or inner stage, that was used (with the curtain opened) for the presentation of indoor scenes. Directly over the inner stage was an upper stage, often used as a bedroom or a balcony. Above that—at the height of the top tier of seats—was a small building known as "the heavens" where the stage crew could produce thunder and other sound effects.

Although the Globe was not a large theater, it could accommodate more than two thousand spectators, about eight hundred of whom stood in the yard. Performances were given in the afternoon, the stage being lit by daylight. Costumes were colorful and often expensive, but the sets were simple, and scenery as we think of it today was hardly used at all. The companies strove for special effects, however, such as birds and goddesses descending from the roof by means of ropes and pulleys.

Women's roles in the plays were acted by men or, more commonly, by boys. Partly because of the absence of scenery to change and the absence of a curtain across the main stage, the plays proceeded at a brisk pace. Actors spoke their lines more rapidly than they do today. A good voice and excellent diction were imperative, and Elizabethan audiences spoke of "hearing" plays rather than "seeing" them. To a theatergoer of the time, the vocabulary of Shakespeare was familiar and easily grasped. Even so, the plays had to have dramatic power to hold a popular and sometimes unruly audience. Shakespeare's plays surely had that power. They still do.

# SHAKESPEAREAN TRAGEDY

# The Tragedy of Macbeth

*Macbeth* is one of Shakespeare's great tragedies, a compelling and timeless drama about the success, treachery, and disintegration of a brave but flawed human being. Its diagnosis of evil is as apt today as it was when The King's Men first presented the play.

Shakespeare completed *Macbeth* in 1606, not long after the appearance of his other great tragedies—*Hamlet, Othello,* and *King Lear.* Intended as a tribute to King James I, *Macbeth* may have been first performed before the royal family at Hampton Court, a palace twelve miles from the center of London. King James, who already wore the crown of Scotland when he ascended the throne of England, would have found *Macbeth* especially intriguing. The play is set in Scotland in the eleventh century, when James's family, the Stuarts, first came to the Scottish throne. One of the strongest and most virtuous characters in the play, Banquo, is said to have been the father of the first of the Stuart kings.

Shakespeare derived the basic plot for *Macbeth* from an account of eleventh-century Scottish history in Raphael Holinshed's *Chronicles of England, Scotland, and Ireland.* In writing his play, Shakespeare altered and expanded Holinshed's history, reshaped the personalities, and invented some new characters.

The central character in *Macbeth,* as in other Elizabethan (and Greek) tragedies, is a tragic hero, a person of high rank and personal quality. Because of a fatal weakness, a tragic flaw, the hero becomes involved in a series of events that lead to his eventual downfall and destruction.

At the beginning of Shakespeare's play, the hero, Macbeth, is pictured as courageous, trustworthy, and loyal. By the end of the play, his ambition has driven him to commit a series of horrendous acts that, once begun, he is powerless to stop. While the audience is repelled by Macbeth's actions, it also pities him, understanding Macbeth's anguish and knowing how easy it is to fall prey to uncontrolled ambition or greed.

The temptations Macbeth faces are ones that have confronted people throughout time. These universal lures—along with Shakespeare's suspense-filled plot, superbly drawn characters, and masterly use of language—have contributed to the play's continuing popularity from Elizabethan days to the present.

## The Whole Play

A great play like *Macbeth* weaves a variety of elements into a unified whole. No matter how impressive the individual speeches or how memorable the incidents, the play must be judged on its total effect. If the playwright has successfully blended plot, character, setting, atmosphere, diction, and imagery—and if the actors have then captured the entire rich tapestry on stage—the result is an intensely satisfying drama.

## Plot

Basic to every plot is conflict, or struggle. External conflict occurs when a character struggles against another person or an outside force. In *Macbeth* there is external conflict between Macbeth and Macduff. Internal conflict is that which occurs within the mind of a character. Macbeth's agonizing over whether or not to kill Duncan is an example of internal conflict.

## Character

Nothing is more important in a work of literature than the portrayal of character. *Macbeth* is a masterpiece of characterization. Macbeth, the tragic hero, is shown as being destroyed because of a tragic flaw.

## Setting

Setting is the time and place in which the events in a literary work take place. The general setting of *Macbeth* is Scotland (and briefly England) in the tenth and eleventh centuries. Specific scenes are set at Inverness, on a desolate heath, in the royal palace at Forres, and so on. Because of the limited scenery in Elizabethan drama, Shakespeare often has his characters describe their surroundings.

## Atmosphere

The atmosphere in *Macbeth* is one of doom and foreboding. Much of the action takes place in foul weather or in the "thick night" of darkened castles. The witches and apparitions cast a pall whenever they appear. Except for the porter's brief speech, there is little in the play resembling lightheartedness.

## Diction

The term *diction* has two meanings. It can mean the pronunciation of words by an actor or other speaker. It can also mean the writer's choice of words, which in a play are delivered by the actors. A writer chooses words with care, making sure they are appropriate to the character, theme, and atmosphere of the literary work. For example, King Duncan in *Macbeth* uses language suitable for a king, while the porter speaks in a more earthy style.

## Imagery

Imagery is usually visual, but it can evoke responses from any of the senses. Images, wrote one critic, like those of ". . . pouring the sweet milk of concord into hell; of the earth shaking in fever; . . . of the tale told by an idiot . . . —all keep the imagination moving 'on a wild and violent sea.' . . ."

# GUIDE FOR INTERPRETING

## The Tragedy of Macbeth, Act I

**Blank Verse.** Like all of Shakespeare's plays, *Macbeth* is written mainly in blank verse. Blank verse is composed of unrhymed lines of iambic pentameter. Iambic pentameter has five feet, or beats, per line, and every other syllable is stressed. The following two lines are an example of blank verse from Act I of *Macbeth*.

    U   /   U   /   U / U  /   U    /
    Your face, my Thane, is as a book where men
    U   /   U    / U  / U  /  U  /
    May read strange matters. To beguile the time,

Blank verse, which was introduced into English literature by the Earl of Surrey, can be stately and dignified, but it can also produce an effect of smooth, natural speech more effectively than most other metrical patterns. It is one of the most flexible and versatile verse forms, a favorite not only of the poets during the English Renaissance, but of many later poets.

**Writing**

Because of its versatility, blank verse can be used to reproduce all kinds of speech. Listen carefully to a discussion, or think of a conversation you have recently had. Reshape this speech into dialogue written in blank verse. Try to make it sound as natural as possible.

**Commentary**

Unlike many of Shakespeare's other plays, *Macbeth* was easy to date. Most scholars believe it was sparked by the shattering Gunpowder Plot of November 5, 1605. In writing *Macbeth* Shakespeare quickly seized on the sympathy generated by the failed conspiracy to kill James I and the Parliament. The plot originated with a group of Catholics seeking revenge against James's severe anti-Catholic laws. With the help of many, including soldier-of-fortune Guy Fawkes, the rebels planned to blow up Parliament. They rented a cellar directly beneath the House of Lords where they stored thirty-six barrels of gunpowder. Fawkes was to ignite the gunpowder on November 5 and then escape to Flanders. But one of the rebels exposed the plot and Fawkes was arrested early that day as he emerged from the cellar. After officials found fuses hidden on his person and the barrels of gunpowder, he was tortured on the rack until he confessed and revealed his associates, nearly all of whom were hanged with him on January 31, 1606. The Gunpowder Plot is celebrated in Great Britain on November 5th, when people hang effigies of Guy Fawkes.

# The Tragedy of Macbeth

## William Shakespeare

---

### CHARACTERS

**Duncan,** King of Scotland
**Malcolm** } his sons
**Donalbain**
**Macbeth**
**Banquo**
**Macduff**
**Lennox** } noblemen of Scotland
**Ross**
**Menteith**
**Angus**
**Caithness**
**Fleance,** son to Banquo
**Siward,** Earl of Northumberland,
   general of the English forces
**Young Siward,** his son

**Seyton,** an officer attending on Macbeth
**Son to Macduff**
**An English Doctor**
**A Scottish Doctor**
**A Porter**
**An Old Man**
**Three Murderers**
**Lady Macbeth**
**Lady Macduff**
**A Gentlewoman attending**
   **on Lady Macbeth**
**Hecate**
**Witches**
**Apparitions**
**Lords, Officers, Soldiers, Attend-**
   **ants, and Messengers**

---

Setting: Scotland; England

# Act I

**Scene i.** *An open place.*
[*Thunder and lightning. Enter* THREE WITCHES.]

    **FIRST WITCH.** When shall we three meet again?
      In thunder, lightning, or in rain?

    **SECOND WITCH.** When the hurlyburly's done,
      When the battle's lost and won.

5    **THIRD WITCH.** That will be ere the set of sun.

    **FIRST WITCH.** Where the place?

    **SECOND WITCH.**               Upon the heath.

    **THIRD WITCH.** There to meet with Macbeth.

**THE THREE WITCHES**
*Henry Fuseli*
*Courtauld Institute Galleries, London*

**FIRST WITCH.** I come, Graymalkin.[1]

**SECOND WITCH.** Paddock[2] calls.

**THIRD WITCH.** Anon![3]

10   **ALL.** Fair is foul, and foul is fair.
      Hover through the fog and filthy air.      [*Exit.*]

**1. Graymalkin:** The first witch's helper, a gray cat.
**2. Paddock:** The second witch's helper, a toad.
**3. Anon:** At once.

**Scene ii.** *A camp near Forres, a town in northeast Scotland.*
[*Alarum within.*[1] *Enter* KING DUNCAN, MALCOLM, DONALBAIN, LENNOX, *with* ATTENDANTS, *meeting a bleeding* CAPTAIN.]

    **KING.** What bloody man is that? He can report,
      As seemeth by his plight, of the revolt
      The newest state.

**1. Alarum within:** Trumpet call offstage.

**MALCOLM.**                    This is the sergeant[2]
Who like a good and hardy soldier fought
5    'Gainst my captivity. Hail, brave friend!
Say to the king the knowledge of the broil[3]
As thou didst leave it.

**CAPTAIN.**                    Doubtful it stood,
As two spent swimmers, that do cling together
And choke their art.[4] The merciless Macdonwald—
10   Worthy to be a rebel for to that
The multiplying villainies of nature
Do swarm upon him—from the Western Isles[5]
Of kerns and gallowglasses[6] is supplied;
And fortune, on his damnèd quarrel[7] smiling,
15   Showed like a rebel's whore:[8] but all's too weak:
For brave Macbeth—well he deserves that name—
Disdaining fortune, with his brandished steel,
Which smoked with bloody execution,
Like valor's minion[9] carved out his passage
20   Till he faced the slave;
Which nev'r shook hands, nor bade farewell to him,
Till he unseamed him from the nave to th' chops,[10]
And fixed his head upon our battlements.

**KING.** O valiant cousin! Worthy gentleman!

25   **CAPTAIN.** As whence the sun 'gins his reflection[11]
Shipwracking storms and direful thunders break,
So from that spring whence comfort seemed to come
Discomfort swells. Mark, King of Scotland, mark:
No sooner justice had, with valor armed,
30   Compelled these skipping kerns to trust their heels
But the Norweyan lord,[12] surveying vantage,[13]
With furbished arms and new supplies of men,
Began a fresh assault.

**KING.**                    Dismayed not this
Our captains, Macbeth and Banquo?

**CAPTAIN.**                    Yes;
35   As sparrows eagles, or the hare the lion.
If I say sooth,[14] I must report they were
As cannons overcharged with double cracks;[15]
So they doubly redoubled strokes upon the foe.
Except[16] they meant to bathe in reeking wounds,
40   Or memorize another Golgotha,[17]
I cannot tell—
But I am faint; my gashes cry for help.

**2. sergeant:** Officer.

**3. broil:** Battle.

**4. choke their art:** prevent each other from swimming.

**5. Western Isles:** The Hebrides, off Scotland.
**6. Of kerns and gallowglasses:** With lightly armed Irish foot soldiers and heavily armed soldiers.
**7. damnèd quarrel:** Accursed cause.
**8. Showed . . . whore:** Falsely appeared to favor Macdonwald.
**9. minion:** Favorite.
**10. unseamed . . . chops:** Split him open from the navel to the jaws.

**11. 'gins his reflection:** Rises.

**12. Norweyan lord:** King of Norway.
**13. surveying vantage:** Seeing an opportunity.

**14. sooth:** Truth.
**15. cracks:** Explosives.
**16. except:** Unless.
**17. memorize . . . Golgotha** (gol' gə thə): Make the place as memorable for slaughter as Golgotha, the place where Christ was crucified.

**KING.** So well thy words become thee as thy wounds;
They smack of honor both. Go get him surgeons.

[*Exit* CAPTAIN, *attended.*]

[*Enter* ROSS *and* ANGUS.]

Who comes here?

45 **MALCOLM.**                    The worthy Thane[18] of Ross.

**LENNOX.** What a haste looks through his eyes! So
should he look
That seems to[19] speak things strange.

**ROSS.**                              God save the king!

**KING.** Whence cam'st thou, worthy Thane?

**ROSS.**                              From Fife, great King;
Where the Norweyan banners flout the sky
50    And fan our people cold.
Norway[20] himself, with terrible numbers,
Assisted by that most disloyal traitor
The Thane of Cawdor, began a dismal[21] conflict;
Till that Bellona's bridegroom, lapped in proof,[22]
55    Confronted him with self-comparisons,[23]
Point against point, rebellious arm 'gainst arm,
Curbing his lavish[24] spirit: and, to conclude,
The victory fell on us.

**KING.**                    Great happiness!

**ROSS.**                              That now
Sweno, the Norways' king, craves composition;[25]
60    Nor would we deign him burial of his men
Till he disbursèd, at Saint Colme's Inch,[26]
Ten thousand dollars to our general use.

**KING.** No more that Thane of Cawdor shall deceive
Our bosom interest:[27] go pronounce his present[28]
death,
65    And with his former title greet Macbeth.

**ROSS.** I'll see it done.

**KING.** What he hath lost, noble Macbeth hath won.

[*Exit.*]

**Scene iii.** *A heath near Forres.*
[*Thunder. Enter the* THREE WITCHES.]

**FIRST WITCH.** Where hast thou been, sister?

**SECOND WITCH.** Killing swine.[1]

**THIRD WITCH.** Sister, where thou?

---

**18. Thane:** A Scottish title of nobility.

**19. seems to:** Seems about to.

**20. Norway:** The King of Norway.
**21. dismal:** Threatening.
**22. Bellona's . . . proof:** Macbeth is called the mate of Bellona, the goddess of war, clad in tested armor.
**23. self-comparisons:** Counter movements.
**24. lavish:** Insolent.

**25. composition:** Terms of peace.
**26. St. Colme's Inch:** Island near Edinburgh, Scotland.

**27. our bosom interest:** My heart's trust.
**28. present:** Immediate.

**1. Killing swine:** It was commonly believed that witches killed domestic animals.

**FIRST WITCH.** A sailor's wife had chestnuts in her lap,
And mounched, and mounched, and mounched.
5       "Give me," quoth I.
"Aroint thee,[2] witch!" the rump-fed ronyon[3] cries.
Her husband's to Aleppo[4] gone, master o' th' Tiger:
But in a sieve[5] I'll thither sail,
And, like a rat without a tail,[6]
10   I'll do, I'll do, and I'll do.

**SECOND WITCH.** I'll give thee a wind.

**FIRST WITCH.** Th' art kind.

**THIRD WITCH.** And I another.

**FIRST WITCH.** I myself have all the other;
15     And the very ports they blow,[7]
All the quarters that they know
I' th' shipman's card.[8]
I'll drain him dry as hay:
Sleep shall neither night nor day
20     Hang upon his penthouse lid;[9]
He shall live a man forbid:[10]
Weary sev'nights[11] nine times nine
Shall he dwindle, peak,[12] and pine:
Though his bark cannot be lost,
25     Yet it shall be tempest-tossed.
Look what I have.

**SECOND WITCH.** Show me, show me.

**FIRST WITCH.** Here I have a pilot's thumb,
Wracked as homeward he did come.
                [*Drum within.*]

30   **THIRD WITCH.** A drum, a drum!
Macbeth doth come.

**ALL.** The weird[13] sisters, hand in hand,
Posters[14] of the sea and land,
Thus do go about, about:
35     Thrice to thine, and thrice to mine,
And thrice again, to make up nine.
Peace! The charm's wound up.

[*Enter* MACBETH *and* BANQUO.]

**MACBETH.** So foul and fair a day I have not seen.

**BANQUO.** How far is 't called to Forres? What are these
40     So withered, and so wild in their attire,
That look not like th' inhabitants o' th' earth,
And yet are on 't? Live you, or are you aught

**2. Aroint thee:** Be off.
**3. rump-fed ronyon:** Fat-rumped, scabby creature.
**4. Aleppo:** A trading center in Syria.
**5. sieve:** It was commonly believed that witches often sailed in sieves.
**6. rat . . . tail:** According to popular belief, witches could assume the form of any animal, but the tail would always be missing.
**7. they blow:** To which the winds blow.
**8. card:** Compass.

**9. penthouse lid:** Eyelid.
**10. forbid:** Cursed.
**11. sev'nights:** Weeks.
**12. peak:** Waste away.

**13. weird:** Destiny-serving.
**14. Posters:** Swift travelers.

That man may question? You seem to understand
    me,
By each at once her choppy[15] finger laying
45    Upon her skinny lips. You should be women,
And yet your beards forbid me to interpret
That you are so.

**MACBETH.**              Speak, if you can: what are you?

**FIRST WITCH.** All hail, Macbeth! Hail to thee, Thane of
    Glamis!

**SECOND WITCH.** All hail, Macbeth! Hail to thee, Thane of
    Cawdor!

**THIRD WITCH.** All hail, Macbeth, that shalt be King
50    hereafter!

**BANQUO.** Good sir, why do you start, and seem to fear
Things that do sound so fair? I' th' name of truth,
Are you fantastical,[16] or that indeed
Which outwardly ye show? My noble partner
55    You greet with present grace[17] and great prediction
Of noble having[18] and of royal hope,
That he seems rapt withal:[19] to me you speak not.
If you can look into the seeds of time,
And say which grain will grow and which will not,
60    Speak then to me, who neither beg nor fear
Your favors nor your hate.

**FIRST WITCH.** Hail!

**SECOND WITCH.** Hail!

**THIRD WITCH.** Hail!

65    **FIRST WITCH.** Lesser than Macbeth, and greater.

**SECOND WITCH.** Not so happy,[20] yet much happier.

**THIRD WITCH.** Thou shalt get kings, though thou be
    none.
So all hail, Macbeth and Banquo!

**FIRST WITCH.** Banquo and Macbeth, all hail!

70    **MACBETH.** Stay, you imperfect[21] speakers, tell me more:
By Sinel's[22] death I know I am Thane of Glamis;
But how of Cawdor? The Thane of Cawdor lives,
A prosperous gentleman; and to be King
Stands not within the prospect of belief,
75    No more than to be Cawdor. Say from whence
You owe[23] this strange intelligence?[24] Or why
Upon this blasted heath you stop our way
With such prophetic greeting? Speak, I charge you.
                      [WITCHES *vanish.*]

**15. choppy:** chapped.

**16. fantastical:** Imaginary.
**17. grace:** Honor.
**18. having:** Possession.
**19. rapt withal:** Entranced by it.

**20. happy:** Fortunate.

**21. imperfect:** Incomplete.
**22. Sinel's** (si′ nəlz): Macbeth's father's.

**23. owe:** Own.
**24. intelligence:** Information.

**MACBETH AND THE WITCHES**
*Clarkson Stanfield*
Leicestershire Museums

*Macbeth, Act I, Scene iii*   *277*

**BANQUO.** The earth hath bubbles as the water has,
80     And these are of them. Whither are they vanished?

**MACBETH.** Into the air, and what seemed corporal[25] melt-
    ed
    As breath into the wind. Would they had stayed!

**BANQUO.** Were such things here as we do speak about?
    Or have we eaten on the insane root[26]
85     That takes the reason prisoner?

**MACBETH.** Your children shall be kings.

**BANQUO.**                    You shall be King.

**MACBETH.** And Thane of Cawdor too. Went it not so?

**BANQUO.** To th' selfsame tune and words. Who's here?

[*Enter* ROSS *and* ANGUS.]

**ROSS.** The King hath happily received, Macbeth,
90     The news of thy success; and when he reads[27]
    Thy personal venture in the rebels' fight,
    His wonders and his praises do contend
    Which should be thine or his.[28] Silenced with that,
    In viewing o'er the rest o' th' selfsame day,
95     He finds thee in the stout Norweyan ranks,
    Nothing afeard of what thyself didst make,
    Strange images of death.[29] As thick as tale
    Came post with post,[30] and every one did bear
    Thy praises in his kingdom's great defense,
    And poured them down before him.

100 **ANGUS.**                 We are sent
    To give thee, from our royal master, thanks;
    Only to herald thee into his sight,
    Not pay thee.

**ROSS.** And for an earnest[31] of a greater honor,
105     He bade me, from him, call thee Thane of Cawdor;
    In which addition,[32] hail, most worthy Thane!
    For it is thine.

**BANQUO.** [*Aside*] What, can the devil speak true?

**MACBETH.** The Thane of Cawdor lives: why do you
    dress me
    In borrowed robes?

**ANGUS.**            Who was the thane lives yet,
110     But under heavy judgment bears that life
    Which he deserves to lose. Whether he was
    combined[33]

**25. corporal:** Real.

**26. insane root:** Henbane
or hemlock, believed to
cause insanity.

**27. reads:** Considers.
**28. His wonders . . . his:**
His admiration contends
with his desire to praise
you.
**29. Nothing . . . death:**
Killing, but not being
afraid of being killed.
**30. As thick . . . post:** As
fast as could be counted
came messenger after mes-
senger.

**31. earnest:** Pledge.

**32. In which addition:**
With this new title.

**33. combined:** Allied.

With those of Norway, or did line[34] the rebel
With hidden help and vantage,[35] or that with both
He labored in his country's wrack,[36] I know not;
115    But treasons capital, confessed and proved,
Have overthrown him.

**MACBETH.**          [*Aside*] Glamis, and Thane of Cawdor:
The greatest is behind.[37] [*To* ROSS *and* ANGUS]
     Thanks for your pains.
[*Aside to* BANQUO] Do you not hope your children
     shall be kings,
When those that gave the Thane of Cawdor to me
Promised no less to them?

120    **BANQUO.** [*Aside to* MACBETH] That, trusted home,[38]
Might yet enkindle you unto[39] the crown,
Besides the Thane of Cawdor. But 'tis strange:
And oftentimes, to win us to our harm,
The instruments of darkness tell us truths,
125    Win us with honest trifles, to betray 's
In deepest consequence.
Cousins,[40] a word, I pray you.

**MACBETH.**               [*Aside*] Two truths are told,
As happy prologues to the swelling act
Of the imperial theme.[41]—I thank you,
     gentlemen.—
130    [*Aside*] This supernatural soliciting
Cannot be ill, cannot be good. If ill,
Why hath it given me earnest of success,
Commencing in a truth? I am Thane of Cawdor:
If good, why do I yield to that suggestion[42]
135    Whose horrid image doth unfix my hair
And make my seated[43] heart knock at my ribs,
Against the use of nature?[44] Present fears
Are less than horrible imaginings.
My thought, whose murder yet is but fantastical
140    Shakes so my single[45] state of man that function
Is smothered in surmise, and nothing is
But what is not.

**BANQUO.**          Look, how our partner's rapt.
**MACBETH.** [*Aside*] If chance will have me King, why,
     chance may crown me,
Without my stir.

**BANQUO.**          New honors come upon him,
Like our strange[46] garments, cleave not to their
145         mold
But with the aid of use.

34. **line:** support.
35. **vantage:** Assistance.
36. **wrack:** Ruin.

37. **behind:** Still to come.

38. **home:** fully.
39. **enkindle you unto:** Encourage you to hope for.

40. **Cousins:** Often used as a term of courtesy between fellow noblemen.

41. **swelling . . . theme:** Stately idea that I will be King.

42. **suggestion:** Thought of murdering Duncan.
43. **seated:** Fixed.
44. **Against . . . nature:** In an unnatural way.

45. **single:** Unaided, weak.

46. **strange:** New.

**MACBETH.** [*Aside*] Come what come may,
Time and the hour runs through the roughest day.

**BANQUO.** Worthy Macbeth, we stay upon your leisure.⁴⁷

**MACBETH.** Give me your favor.⁴⁸ My dull brain was
wrought
150  With things forgotten. Kind gentlemen, your pains
Are registered where every day I turn
The leaf to read them. Let us toward the King.
[*Aside to* BANQUO] Think upon what hath chanced,
and at more time,
The interim having weighed it,⁴⁹ let us speak
Our free hearts⁵⁰ each to other.

155  **BANQUO.**                          Very gladly.

**MACBETH.** Till then, enough. Come, friends.          [*Exit.*]

**Scene iv.** *Forres. The palace.*
[*Flourish.¹ Enter* KING DUNCAN, LENNOX, MALCOLM, DONALBAIN, *and*
ATTENDANTS.]

**KING.** Is execution done on Cawdor? Are not
Those in commission² yet returned?

**MALCOLM.**                          My liege,
They are not yet come back. But I have spoke
With one that saw him die, who did report
5  That very frankly he confessed his treasons,
Implored your Highness' pardon and set forth
A deep repentance: nothing in his life
Became him like the leaving it. He died
As one that had been studied³ in his death,
10  To throw away the dearest thing he owed⁴
As 'twere a careless⁵ trifle.

**KING.**                          There's no art
To find the mind's construction⁶ in the face:
He was a gentleman on whom I built
An absolute trust.

[*Enter* MACBETH, BANQUO, ROSS, *and* ANGUS.]

O worthiest cousin!
15  The sin of my ingratitude even now
Was heavy on me: thou art so far before,
That swiftest wing of recompense is slow
To overtake thee. Would thou hadst less deserved,
That the proportion both of thanks and payment
20  Might have been mine!⁷ Only I have left to say,
More is thy due than more than all can pay.

---

**47. stay upon your leisure:** Await your convenience.
**48. favor:** Pardon.

**49. The interim . . . it:** When we have had time to think about it.
**50. Our free hearts:** Our minds freely.

**1. Flourish:** Trumpet fanfare.

**2. in commission:** Commissioned to oversee the execution.

**3. studied:** Rehearsed.
**4. owed:** Owned.
**5. careless:** Worthless.

**6. mind's construction:** A person's character.

**7. Would . . . mine:** If you had been less worthy, my thanks and payment could have exceeded the rewards you deserve.

**MACBETH.** The service and the loyalty I owe,
In doing it, pays itself.[8] Your Highness' part
Is to receive our duties: and our duties
25 Are to your throne and state children and servants;
Which do but what they should, by doing every thing
Safe toward[9] your love and honor.

**KING.**                                   Welcome hither.
I have begun to plant thee, and will labor
To make thee full of growing. Noble Banquo,
30 That hast no less deserved, nor must be known
No less to have done so, let me enfold thee
And hold thee to my heart.

**BANQUO.**                         There if I grow,
The harvest is your own.

**KING.**                         My plenteous joys,
Wanton[10] in fullness, seek to hide themselves
35 In drops of sorrow. Sons, kinsmen, thanes,
And you whose places are the nearest, know,
We will establish our estate upon
Our eldest, Malcolm,[11] whom we name hereafter
The Prince of Cumberland: which honor must
40 Not unaccompanied invest him only,
But signs of nobleness, like stars, shall shine
On all deservers. From hence to Inverness,[12]
And bind us further to you.

**MACBETH.** The rest is labor, which is not used for you.[13]
45 I'll be myself the harbinger,[14] and make joyful
The hearing of my wife with your approach;
So, humbly take my leave.

**KING.**                         My worthy Cawdor!

**MACBETH.** [*Aside*] The Prince of Cumberland! That is a
    step
On which I must fall down, or else o'erleap,
50 For in my way it lies. Stars, hide your fires;
Let not light see my black and deep desires:
The eye wink at the hand;[15] yet let that be
Which the eye fears, when it is done, to see.   [*Exit.*]

**KING.** True, worthy Banquo; he is full so valiant,
55 And in his commendations I am fed;
It is a banquet to me. Let's after him,
Whose care is gone before to bid us welcome.
It is a peerless kinsman.                [*Flourish. Exit.*]

**8. pays itself:** Is its own reward.

**9. Safe toward:** With sure regard for.

**10. Wanton:** Unrestrained.

**11. Establish . . . Malcolm:** Make Malcolm the heir to my throne.

**12. Inverness:** Macbeth's castle.

**13. The rest . . . you:** Anything not done for you is laborious.
**14. harbinger:** An advance representative of the army or royal party who makes arrangements for a visit.

**15. wink at the hand:** Be blind to the hand's deed.

**Scene v.** *Inverness. Macbeth's castle.*
[*Enter* MACBETH'S WIFE. *alone, with a letter.*]

LADY MACBETH. [*Reads*] "They met me in the day of
success; and I have learned by the perfect'st report
they have more in them than mortal knowledge.
When I burned in desire to question them fur-
5　ther, they made themselves air, into which they vanished. Whiles I stood rapt in the wonder of it, came
missives[1] from the King, who all-hailed me 'Thane
of Cawdor'; by which title, before, these weird sisters
saluted me, and referred me to the coming on
10　of time, with 'Hail, King that shalt be!' This have I
thought good to deliver thee,[2] my dearest partner of
greatness, that thou mightst not lose the dues of
rejoicing, by being ignorant of what greatness is
promised thee. Lay it to thy heart, and farewell."

15　Glamis thou art, and Cawdor, and shalt be
What thou art promised. Yet do I fear thy nature;
It is too full o' th' milk of human kindness
To catch the nearest[3] way. Thou wouldst be great,
Art not without ambition, but without
20　The illness[4] should attend it. What thou wouldst
highly,
That wouldst thou holily; wouldst not play false,
And yet wouldst wrongly win. Thou'dst have, great
Glamis,
That which cries "Thus thou must do" if thou have
it;
And that which rather thou dost fear to do
25　Than wishest should be undone.[5] Hie thee hither,
That I may pour my spirits in thine ear,
And chastise with the valor of my tongue
All that impedes thee from the golden round[6]
Which fate and metaphysical aid doth seem
To have thee crowned withal.

[*Enter* MESSENGER.]

30　　　　　　　　　　　　　　What is your tidings?

MESSENGER. The King comes here tonight.

LADY MACBETH.　　　　　　Thou'rt mad to say it!
Is not thy master with him, who, were't so,
Would have informed for preparation?

MESSENGER. So please you, it is true. Our thane is
coming.
35　One of my fellows had the speed of him,[7]
Who, almost dead for breath, had scarcely more
Than would make up his message.

**1. missives:** Messengers.

**2. deliver thee:** Report to you.

**3. nearest:** Quickest.

**4. illness:** Wickedness.

**5. that which . . . undone:** What you are afraid of doing you would not wish undone once you have done it.
**6. round:** Crown.

**7. had . . . him:** Overtook him.

**LADY MACBETH.**            Give him tending;
He brings great news.      [*Exit* MESSENGER.]
              The raven himself is hoarse
That croaks the fatal entrance of Duncan
40   Under my battlements. Come, you spirits
That tend on mortal[8] thoughts, unsex me here,
And fill me, from the crown to the toe, top-full
Of direst cruelty! Make thick my blood,
Stop up th' access and passage to remorse[9]
45   That no compunctious visitings of nature[10]
Shake my fell[11] purpose, nor keep peace between
Th' effect[12] and it! Come to my woman's breasts,
And take my milk for gall,[13] you murd'ring minis-
     ters,[14]
Wherever in your sightless[15] substances
50   You wait on[16] nature's mischief! Come, thick night,
And pall[17] thee in the dunnest[18] smoke of hell,
That my keen knife see not the wound it makes,
Nor heaven peep through the blanket of the dark,
To cry "Hold, hold!"

[*Enter* MACBETH.]

           Great Glamis! Worthy Cawdor!
Greater than both, by the all-hail hereafter!
55   Thy letters have transported me beyond
This ignorant[19] present, and I feel now
The future in the instant.[20]

**MACBETH.**           My dearest love,
Duncan comes here tonight.

**LADY MACBETH.**        And when goes hence?

**MACBETH.** Tomorrow, as he purposes.

**LADY MACBETH.**         O, never
60   Shall sun that morrow see!
Your face, my Thane, is as a book where men
May read strange matters. To beguile the time,[21]
Look like the time; bear welcome in your eye,
Your hand, your tongue: look like th' innocent flower,
65   But be the serpent under 't. He that's coming
Must be provided for: and you shall put
This night's great business into my dispatch;[22]
Which shall to all our nights and days to come
Give solely sovereign sway and masterdom.

**MACBETH.** We will speak further.

70   **LADY MACBETH.**        Only look up clear.[23]
To alter favor ever is to fear.[24]
Leave all the rest to me.         [*Exit.*]

**8. mortal:** Deadly.
**9. remorse:** Compassion.
**10. compunctious . . . nature:** Natural feelings of pity.
**11. fell:** Savage.
**12. effect:** Fulfillment.
**13. milk for gall:** Kindness in exchange for bitterness.
**14. ministers:** Agents.
**15. sightless:** Invisible.
**16. wait on:** Assist.
**17. pall:** Enshroud.
**18. dunnest:** Darkest.

**19. ignorant:** Unknowing.
**20. instant:** Present.

**21. beguile the time:** Deceive the people tonight.

**22. dispatch:** Management.

**23. look up clear:** Appear innocent.
**24. To alter . . . fear:** To show a disturbed face will arouse suspicion.

**Scene vi.** *Before Macbeth's castle.*

[*Hautboys.*[1] *Torches. Enter* KING DUNCAN, MALCOLM, DONALBAIN, BANQUO, LENNOX, MACDUFF, ROSS, ANGUS, *and* ATTENDANTS.]

KING. This castle hath a pleasant seat;[2] the air
Nimbly and sweetly recommends itself
Unto our gentle[3] senses.

BANQUO.                    This guest of summer,
The temple-haunting martlet,[4] does approve[5]
5    By his loved mansionry[6] that the heaven's breath
Smells wooingly here. No jutty,[7] frieze,
Buttress, nor coign of vantage,[8] but this bird
Hath made his pendent bed and procreant cradle.[9]
Where they most breed and haunt,[10] I have observed
The air is delicate.

[*Enter* LADY MACBETH.]

10   KING.                    See, see, our honored hostess!
The love that follows us sometime is our trouble,
Which still we thank as love. Herein I teach you
How you shall bid God 'ield us for your pains
And thank us for your trouble.[11]

LADY MACBETH.                    All our service
15   In every point twice done, and then done double,
Were poor and single business[12] to contend
Against those honors deep and broad wherewith
Your Majesty loads our house: for those of old,
And the late dignities heaped up to them,
We rest your hermits.[13]

20   KING.                    Where's the Thane of Cawdor?
We coursed[14] him at the heels, and had a purpose
To be his purveyor:[15] but he rides well,
And his great love, sharp as his spur, hath holp[16] him
To his home before us. Fair and noble hostess,
We are your guest tonight.

25   LADY MACBETH.                    Your servants ever
Have theirs, themselves, and what is theirs, in
     compt,[17]
To make their audit at your Highness' pleasure,
Still[18] to return your own.

KING.                    Give me your hand.
Conduct me to mine host: we love him highly,
30   And shall continue our graces towards him.
By your leave, hostess.                    [*Exit.*]

1. **Hautboys:** Oboes announcing the arrival of royalty.
2. **seat:** Location.

3. **gentle:** Soothed.

4. **temple-haunting martlet:** The martin, a bird that usually nests in churches. In Shakespeare's time *martin* was a slang term for a person who is easily deceived.
5. **approve:** Show.
6. **mansionry:** Nests.
7. **jutty:** Projection.
8. **coign of vantage:** Advantageous corner.
9. **procreant** (prō′ krē ənt) **cradle:** Nest where the young are hatched.
10. **haunt:** Visit.

11. **The love . . . trouble:** Though my visit inconveniences you, you should ask God to reward me for coming, because it was my love for you that prompted my visit.
12. **single business:** Feeble service.

13. **rest your hermits:** Remain your dependents bound to pray for you. Hermits were often paid to pray for another person's soul.
14. **coursed:** Chased.
15. **purveyor:** Advance supply officer.
16. **holp:** Helped.

17. **compt:** Trust.

18. **Still:** Always.

## Scene vii. *Macbeth's castle.*

[*Hautboys. Torches. Enter a* SEWER,[1] *and diverse* SERVANTS *with dishes and service over the stage. Then enter* MACBETH.]

MACBETH. If it were done[2] when 'tis done, then 'twere well
It were done quickly. If th' assassination
Could trammel up the consequence, and catch,
With his surcease, success;[3] that but this blow
5    Might be the be-all and the end-all—here,
But here, upon this bank and shoal of time,
We'd jump the life to come.[4] But in these cases
We still have judgment here; that we but teach
Bloody instructions, which, being taught, return
10   To plague th' inventor: this even-handed[5] justice
Commends[6] th' ingredients of our poisoned chalice[7]
To our own lips. He's here in double trust:
First, as I am his kinsman and his subject,
Strong both against the deed; then, as his host,
15   Who should against his murderer shut the door,
Not bear the knife myself. Besides, this Duncan
Hath borne his faculties[8] so meek, hath been
So clear[9] in his great office, that his virtues
Will plead like angels trumpet-tongued against
20   The deep damnation of his taking-off;
And pity, like a naked newborn babe,
Striding the blast, or heaven's cherubin[10] horsed
Upon the sightless couriers[11] of the air,
Shall blow the horrid deed in every eye,
25   That tears shall drown the wind. I have no spur
To prick the sides of my intent, but only
Vaulting ambition, which o'erleaps itself
And falls on th' other—

[*Enter* LADY MACBETH.]

How now! What news?

LADY MACBETH. He has almost supped. Why have you
left the chamber?

MACBETH. Hath he asked for me?

30   LADY MACBETH.                    Know you not he has?

MACBETH. We will proceed no further in this business:
He hath honored me of late, and I have bought[12]
Golden opinions from all sorts of people,
Which would be worn now in their newest gloss,
Not cast aside so soon.

35   LADY MACBETH.                    Was the hope drunk

---

**1. sewer:** Chief butler.

**2. done:** Over and done with.

**3. If . . . success:** If the assassination could be done successfully and with-out consequence.
**4. We'd . . . come:** I would risk life in the world to come.

**5. even-handed:** Impartial.
**6. commends:** Offers.
**7. chalice:** Cup.

**8. faculties:** Powers.
**9. clear:** Blameless.

**10. cherubin:** Angels.
**11. sightless couriers:** Unseen messengers (the wind).

**12. bought:** Acquired.

Wherein you dressed yourself? Hath it slept since?
And wakes it now, to look so green and pale
At what it did so freely? From this time
Such I account thy love. Art thou afeard

40  To be the same in thine own act and valor
As thou art in desire? Wouldst thou have that
Which thou esteem'st the ornament of life,[13]
And live a coward in thine own esteem,
Letting "I dare not" wait upon[14] "I would,"
Like the poor cat i' th' adage? [15]

45  **MACBETH.**                              Prithee, peace!
I dare do all that may become a man;
Who dares do more is none.

**LADY MACBETH.**                     What beast was 't then
That made you break[16] this enterprise to me?
When you durst do it, then you were a man;

50  And to be more than what you were, you would
Be so much more the man. Nor time nor place
Did then adhere,[17] and yet you would make both.
They have made themselves, and that their[18] fitness now
Does unmake you. I have given suck, and know

55  How tender 'tis to love the babe that milks me:
I would, while it was smiling in my face,
Have plucked my nipple from his boneless gums,
And dashed the brains out, had I so sworn as you
Have done to this.

**MACBETH.**                     If we should fail?

**LADY MACBETH.**                     We fail?

60  But[19] screw your courage to the sticking-place[20]
And we'll not fail. When Duncan is asleep—
Whereto the rather shall his day's hard journey
Soundly invite him—his two chamberlains
Will I with wine and wassail[21] so convince,[22]

65  That memory, the warder of the brain,
Shall be a fume, and the receipt of reason
A limbeck only:[23] when in swinish sleep
Their drenchèd natures lies as in a death,
What cannot you and I perform upon

70  Th' unguarded Duncan, what not put upon
His spongy[24] officers, who shall bear the guilt
Of our great quell? [25]

**MACBETH.**                     Bring forth men-children only;
For thy undaunted mettle[26] should compose
Nothing but males. Will it not be received,

75  When we have marked with blood those sleepy two

**13. ornament of life:** The crown.

**14. wait upon:** Follow.
**15. poor . . . adage:** From an old proverb about a cat who wants to eat fish but is afraid of getting its paws wet.

**16. break:** Reveal.

**17. Did then adhere:** Was then suitable (for the assassination).
**18. that their:** Their very.

**19. But:** Only.
**20. sticking-place:** The notch that holds the bowstring of a taut crossbow.

**21. wassail:** Carousing.
**22. convince:** Overpower.

**23. That . . . only:** That memory, the guardian of the brain, will be confused by the fumes of the drink, and the reason become like a still, distilling confused thoughts.
**24. spongy:** Sodden.
**25. quell:** Murder.

**26. mettle:** Spirit.

**SCENE FROM MACBETH**
*Cattermole*
By permission of The Folger Shakespeare Library

## Commentary

Shakespeare was grateful to King James I for doubling the payment for court performances, more than doubling the number of performances, and elevating Shakespeare and his players in rank. Much of the play, then, is a tribute to the King and one of his chief interests, demonology, on which he had written a book. James's fascination with witches no doubt grew with his own brush with witchcraft. Shakespearean scholar A. L. Rowse recounts how in 1589 James suffered a stormy voyage across the North Sea on his way to Oslo to marry Anne, daughter of King Frederick of Denmark. Soon after he and his bride returned to Scotland, a number of women were arrested for witchcraft. One "witch" claimed that she and the others had gone to sea in sieves to raise a storm to wreck the ship in which James had been sailing. James conducted the first investigations of the women. One of the accused, Agnes Sampson, told him the details of a private conversation James had had with his wife on their marriage night. Soon after James began to work on his book.

Of his own chamber, and used their very daggers,
That they have done 't?

LADY MACBETH.                    Who dares receive it other,[27]
As we shall make our griefs and clamor roar
Upon his death?

MACBETH.                    I am settled, and bend up
80    Each corporal agent to this terrible feat.
Away, and mock the time[28] with fairest show:
False face must hide what the false heart doth know.
                                    [*Exit.*]

27. **other:** Otherwise.

28. **mock the time:** Mislead the world.

---

## THINKING ABOUT THE SELECTION

### Recalling

1. (a) What does the Captain tell King Duncan about Macbeth's battlefield deeds? (b) What does the King learn from Ross about the Thane of Cawdor's activities? (c) What reward for victory does Macbeth receive almost immediately from the King?
2. What do the three witches predict (a) for Macbeth? (b) for Banquo?
3. How does Macbeth react to the witches' hailing him as Thane of Cawdor?
4. (a) What happens to the Thane of Cawdor? (b) Why, despite the witches' predictions, does Macbeth have reason to doubt he will succeed Duncan as king?
5. (a) How does Lady Macbeth first learn of the witches' predictions regarding Macbeth? (b) What in Macbeth's personality does she fear may thwart his ambition?
6. (a) What action does Lady Macbeth plan to take during the King's visit? (b) How does she intend to accomplish it? (c) How does she advise Macbeth to act in King Duncan's presence?

### Interpreting

7. Both the witches and Macbeth make statements about "foul" and "fair." (a) What are two possible meanings for the witches' words? (b) What does Macbeth mean by his remark?
8. Macbeth and Banquo respond differently to the witches' predictions. (a) After becoming Thane of Cawdor, how does Macbeth react to the thought of becoming king? (b) How does Banquo view the witches' predictions?
9. In Scene vi, what is the irony in the description of the air surrounding Macbeth's castle?
10. Why is Macbeth indecisive about the idea of killing the King?
11. How does Lady Macbeth's knowledge of her husband's character help her to convince him that the murder plot should be carried out?

### Applying

12. How do you think that Macbeth should have answered Lady Macbeth when, speaking of the planned murder, she said, "What beast was't then / That made you break this enterprise to me?"

## ANALYZING LITERATURE

### Understanding Blank Verse

Most of the lines in Shakespeare's plays are written in **blank verse,** or unrhymed iambic pentameter. Each line has ten syllables, with the stress falling on every second syllable.

U / U / U/U / U /
The King hath happily received, Macbeth,

U / U / U / U / U
The news of thy success; and when he

/
reads

Blank verse approximates the rhythm of spoken conversation. To keep the lines from becoming monotonous, Shakespeare sometimes varies the pattern of unstressed and stressed syllables or writes a shorter or longer line. Pauses at different places in the lines also help to prevent a singsong rhythm from developing.

1. *Scansion* is the analysis of verse according to its meter. Write the following lines marking stressed and unstressed syllables.

   But here, upon this bank and shoal of time,
   We'd jump the life to come. But in these cases

2. What variation does the second line show?
3. Find two successive lines in Act 1 that are in perfect iambic pentameter. Write them marking stressed and unstressed syllables.

## CRITICAL THINKING AND READING
### Making Inferences About Characters

When you read or see a play by Shakespeare, you must make inferences about the major characters. You have to draw your own conclusions about their personalities and motivations. Since Shakespeare's characters are complex, you should avoid hasty conclusions. For instance, Macbeth at first appears to be brave, resolute, and loyal. But later in Act I you begin to see him in a different light. Always wait until you have sufficient evidence before making inferences about an important Shakespearean character.

1. In Scene iii, from line 70 to the end, Shakespeare presents a vivid picture of Macbeth. Based on the accumulating evidence, what inferences can you draw about Macbeth's character?
2. What can you infer about Banquo from the more limited evidence in Scene iii, lines 120–126?

## SPEAKING AND LISTENING
### Reading Blank Verse Aloud

Since the blank-verse pattern of stressed and unstressed syllables is a natural one, you are likely to find it easier and more comfortable to read Shakespeare's plays aloud than to read rigidly rhymed verse. With blank verse you will not be tempted into the singsong trap set by rhyme. When reading blank verse, allow the meaning of the passage—and its punctuation —to guide your reading. Listening to professional actors reading Shakespeare can be highly valuable.

Choose a passage of about ten lines from Act I. Read it until you understand it fully. Then practice reading it aloud. Stop at the end of a line only when the punctuation calls for it. When you are ready, read the passage in class so that the meaning comes through clearly to your audience.

## THINKING AND WRITING
### Comparing and Contrasting Characters

Write a composition comparing and contrasting the character of Macbeth with that of Lady Macbeth. Find at least two passages spoken by each character that illustrate and support the points you intend to make. Include these in your first draft. When you revise, make sure the quoted passages fit logically into what you have written.

# GUIDE FOR INTERPRETING

## Writer's Techniques

## Macbeth, Act II

**Atmosphere.** The atmosphere in a work of literature is its general mood or feeling. Atmosphere can often be described in one word: *fateful,* for example, or *melancholy* or *cheerful.* A writer creates atmosphere mainly through setting, word choice, and selection of specific details. Since realistic scenery was minimal and since lighting could not be controlled on the Elizabethan stage, Shakespeare often had to rely on dialogue to describe settings. His precise wording and choice of details help build the prevailing mood in each play. A great deal of the atmosphere in *Macbeth* and other Elizabethan plays depends on speech—on what the characters say. Shakespeare, like most great writers, is a master at creating atmosphere.

## Writing

Choose an adjective that describes mood—*lively, dismal,* or *scary,* for example—and freewrite a passage that creates the intended atmosphere. Choose words that help to emphasize the mood. You may find it helpful to look in a thesaurus.

## Primary Source

Nineteenth-century Shakespearean scholar A. C. Bradley commented on the central effect of atmosphere in *Macbeth.*

> A Shakespearean tragedy, as a rule, has a special tone or atmosphere of its own, quite as perceptible, however difficult to describe. The effect of this atmosphere is marked with unusual strength in *Macbeth.* It is due to a variety of influences . . . so that, acting and reacting, they form a whole; and the desolation of the blasted heath, the design of the Witches, the guilt in the hero's soul, the darkness of the night, seem to emanate from one and the same source. . . . Darkness, we may even say blackness, broods over this tragedy. It is remarkable that almost all the scenes which at once recur to the memory take place either at night or in some dark spot. The vision of the dagger, the murder of Duncan, the sleepwalking of Lady Macbeth, are all night scenes. The witches dance in the thick air of a storm, or, 'black and midnight hags' receive Macbeth in a cavern. The blackness of the night is to the hero a thing of fear, even of horror; and that which he feels becomes the spirit of the play . . . The atmosphere of *Macbeth,* is not that of unrelieved blackness . . . it is really the impression of a black night broken by flashes of light and color, sometimes vivid and even glaring.

# Act II

**Scene i.** *Inverness. Court of Macbeth's castle.*
[*Enter* BANQUO, *and* FLEANCE, *with a torch before him.*]

**BANQUO.** How goes the night, boy?

**FLEANCE.** The moon is down; I have not heard the clock.

**BANQUO.** And she goes down at twelve.

**FLEANCE.**                                            I take't, 'tis later, sir.

**BANQUO.** Hold, take my sword. There's husbandry[1] in
    heaven.
5    Their candles are all out. Take thee that[2] too.
    A heavy summons[3] lies like lead upon me,
    And yet I would not sleep. Merciful powers,
    Restrain in me the cursèd thoughts that nature
    Gives way to in repose!

[*Enter* MACBETH, *and a* SERVANT *with a torch.*]

               Give me my sword!
10   Who's there?

**MACBETH.** A friend.

**BANQUO.** What, sir, not yet at rest? The King's a-bed:
    He hath been in unusual pleasure, and
    Sent forth great largess to your offices:[4]
15   This diamond he greets your wife withal,
    By the name of most kind hostess; and shut up[5]
    In measureless content.

**MACBETH.**                                       Being unprepared,
    Our will became the servant to defect,
    Which else should free have wrought.[6]

**BANQUO.**                                              All's well.
20   I dreamt last night of the three weird sisters:
    To you they have showed some truth.

**MACBETH.**                                          I think not of them.
    Yet, when we can entreat an hour to serve,
    We would spend it in some words upon that business,
    If you would grant the time.

**BANQUO.**                                       At your kind'st leisure.

25   **MACBETH.** If you shall cleave to my consent, when 'tis,[7]
    It shall make honor for you.

---

1. **husbandry:** Thrift.

2. **that:** Probably his sword belt.
3. **summons:** Weariness.

4. **largess . . . offices:** Gifts to your servants' quarters.
5. **shut up:** Retired.

6. **Being . . . wrought:** Because we did not have enough time to prepare, we were unable to entertain as lavishly as we wanted to.

7. **cleave . . . 'tis:** Join my cause when the time comes.

**BANQUO.**                                   So[8] I lose none
In seeking to augment it, but still keep
My bosom franchised[9] and allegiance clear,
I shall be counseled.

**MACBETH.**                          Good repose the while!

30    **BANQUO.** Thanks, sir. The like to you!
                              [*Exit* BANQUO *with* FLEANCE.]

**MACBETH.** Go bid thy mistress, when my drink is ready,
She strike upon the bell. Get thee to bed.
                                          [*Exit* SERVANT.]

Is this a dagger which I see before me,
The handle toward my hand? Come, let me clutch
    thee.
35    I have thee not, and yet I see thee still.
Art thou not, fatal vision, sensible[10]
To feeling as to sight, or art thou but
A dagger of the mind, a false creation,
Proceeding from the heat-oppressèd brain?
40    I see thee yet, in form as palpable
As this which now I draw.
Thou marshal'st[11] me the way that I was going;
And such an instrument I was to use.
Mine eyes are made the fools o' th' other senses,
45    Or else worth all the rest. I see thee still;
And on thy blade and dudgeon[12] gouts[13] of blood,
Which was not so before. There's no such thing.
It is the bloody business which informs[14]
Thus to mine eyes. Now o'er the one half-world
50    Nature seems dead, and wicked dreams abuse[15]
The curtained sleep; witchcraft celebrates
Pale Hecate's offerings;[16] and withered murder,
Alarumed by his sentinel, the wolf,
Whose howl's his watch, thus with his stealthy pace,
With Tarquin's[17] ravishing strides, towards his de-
55        sign
Moves like a ghost. Thou sure and firm-set earth,
Hear not my steps, which way they walk, for fear
Thy very stones prate of my whereabout,
And take the present horror from the time,
60    Which now suits with it.[18] Whiles I threat, he lives:
Words to the heat of deeds too cold breath gives.
[*A bell rings.*]
I go, and it is done: the bell invites me.
Hear it not, Duncan, for it is a knell
That summons thee to heaven, or to hell.        [*Exit.*]

**8. So:** Provided that.

**9. bosom franchised:** Heart free (from guilt).

**10. sensible:** Able to be felt.

**11. marshal'st:** Leads.

**12. dudgeon:** Wooden hilt.
**13. gouts:** Large drops.
**14. informs:** Takes shape.
**15. abuse:** Deceive.

**16. Hecate's** (hĕk'ə tēz) **offerings:** Offerings to Hecate, the Greek goddess of witchcraft.
**17. Tarquin's:** Of Tarquin, a Roman tyrant.

**18. take . . . it:** Remove the horrible silence which suits this moment.

**ELLEN TERRY AS LADY MACBETH**
*John Singer Sargent*
Tate Gallery, on Loan to National Portrait Gallery, London

### Scene ii. *Macbeth's castle.*

[*Enter* LADY MACBETH.]

    **LADY MACBETH.** That which hath made them drunk hath
        made me bold;
    What hath quenched them hath given me fire. Hark!
        Peace!
    It was the owl that shrieked, the fatal bellman,
    Which gives the stern'st good-night.[1] He is about it.
5    The doors are open, and the surfeited grooms[2]
    Do mock their charge with snores. I have drugged
        their possets,[3]
    That death and nature do contend about them,
    Whether they live or die.

**1. bellman . . . good-night:** It was customary for a bell to be rung at midnight outside a condemned person's cell on the night before an execution.

**2. surfeited grooms:** Overfed servants.

**3. possets:** Warm bedtime drinks.

MACBETH.                    [*Within*] Who's there? What, ho?

LADY MACBETH. Alack, I am afraid they have awaked
10      And 'tis not done! Th' attempt and not the deed
        Confounds[4] us. Hark! I laid their daggers ready;         **4. Confounds:** Ruins.
        He could not miss 'em. Had he not resembled
        My father as he slept, I had done 't.

[*Enter* MACBETH.]

                                    My husband!

MACBETH. I have done the deed. Didst thou not hear a
        noise?

LADY MACBETH. I heard the owl scream and the crickets
15          cry.
        Did not you speak?

MACBETH.                    When?

LADY MACBETH.               Now.

MACBETH.                        As I descended?

LADY MACBETH. Ay.

MACBETH. Hark!
        Who lies i' th' second chamber?

LADY MACBETH.                   Donalbain.

20  MACBETH. This is a sorry[5] sight.                            **5. sorry:** Miserable.

LADY MACBETH. A foolish thought, to say a sorry sight.

MACBETH. There's one did laugh in 's sleep, and one
            cried "Murder!"
        That they did wake each other. I stood and heard
            them.
        But they did say their prayers, and addressed them
        Again to sleep.

25  LADY MACBETH. There are two[6] lodged together.              **6. two:** Malcolm and Do-
                                                                  nalbain, Duncan's sons.

MACBETH. One cried "God bless us!" and "Amen" the
            other,
        As they had seen me with these hangman's hands:
        List'ning their fear, I could not say "Amen,"
        When they did say "God bless us!"

LADY MACBETH.                    Consider it not so deeply.

MACBETH. But wherefore could not I pronounce
30          "Amen"?
        I had most need of blessing, and "Amen"
        Stuck in my throat.

**LADY MACBETH.**　　　These deeds must not be thought
After these ways; so, it will make us mad.

**MACBETH.** Methought I heard a voice cry "Sleep no more!
35　Macbeth does murder sleep"—the innocent sleep,
Sleep that knits up the raveled sleave[7] of care,
The death of each day's life, sore labor's bath,
Balm of hurt minds, great nature's second course,[8]
Chief nourisher in life's feast—

**LADY MACBETH.**　　　　　　What do you mean?

40　**MACBETH.** Still it cried "Sleep no more!" to all the house:
"Glamis hath murdered sleep, and therefore Cawdor
Shall sleep no more: Macbeth shall sleep no more."

**LADY MACBETH.** Who was it that thus cried? Why, worthy
　　Thane,
You do unbend[9] your noble strength, to think
45　So brainsickly of things. Go get some water,
And wash this filthy witness[10] from your hand.
Why did you bring these daggers from the place?
They must lie there: go carry them, and smear
The sleepy grooms with blood.

**MACBETH.**　　　　　　I'll go no more.
50　I am afraid to think what I have done;
Look on 't again I dare not.

**LADY MACBETH.**　　　　　Infirm of purpose!
Give me the daggers. The sleeping and the dead
Are but as pictures. 'Tis the eye of childhood
That fears a painted devil. If he do bleed,
55　I'll gild[11] the faces of the grooms withal,
For it must seem their guilt.　[*Exit. Knock within.*]

**MACBETH.**　　　　　　Whence is that knocking?
How is 't with me, when every noise appalls me?
What hands are here? Ha! They pluck out mine eyes!
Will all great Neptune's ocean wash this blood
60　Clean from my hand? No; this my hand will rather
The multitudinous seas incarnadine,[12]
Making the green one red.

[*Enter* LADY MACBETH.]

**LADY MACBETH.** My hands are of your color, but I shame
To wear a heart so white. [*Knock.*] I hear a knocking
65　At the south entry. Retire we to our chamber.
A little water clears us of this deed:
How easy is it then! Your constancy
Hath left you unattended.[13] [*Knock.*] Hark! more
　　knocking.

**7. knits . . . sleave:**
Straightens out the tangled
threads.
　**8. second course:** The
main course; sleep.

**9. unbend:** Relax.

**10. witness:** Evidence.

**11. gild:** Paint.

**12. incarnadine** (in kär′
nə din): Redden.

**13. Your constancy . . .
unattended:** Your firmness
of purpose has left you.

70 Get on your nightgown, lest occasion call us
And show us to be watchers.[14] Be not lost
So poorly in your thoughts.

**MACBETH.** To know my deed, 'twere best not know
myself. [*Knock.*]
Wake Duncan with thy knocking! I would thou
couldst!                                                    [*Exit.*]

**14. watchers:** Up late.

**Scene iii.** *Macbeth's castle.*
[*Enter a* PORTER.[1] *Knocking within.*]

**1. porter:** Doorkeeper.

**PORTER.** Here's a knocking indeed! If a man were porter
of hell gate, he should have old[2] turning the key.
[*Knock.*] Knock, knock, knock! Who's there, i' th'
name of Beelzebub?[3] Here's a farmer, that
5 hanged himself on th' expectation of plenty.[4] Come
in time! Have napkins enow[5] about you; here you'll
sweat for 't. [*Knock.*] Knock, knock! Who's there, in
th' other devil's name? Faith, here's an equivocator,
that could swear in both the scales against
10 either scale;[6] who committed treason enough for
God's sake, yet could not equivocate to heaven. O,
come in, equivocator. [*Knock.*] Knock, knock, knock!
Who's there? Faith, here's an English tailor come
hither for stealing out of a French hose:[7]
15 come in, tailor. Here you may roast your goose.[8]
[*Knock.*] Knock, knock; never at quiet! What are you?
But this place is too cold for hell. I'll devil-porter it no
further. I had thought to have let in some of all
professions that go the primrose way to th'
20 everlasting bonfire. [*Knock.*] Anon, anon! [*Opens an
entrance.*] I pray you, remember the porter.

[*Enter* MACDUFF *and* LENNOX.]

**MACDUFF.** Was it so late, friend, ere you went to bed,
That you do lie so late?

**PORTER.** Faith, sir, we were carousing till the second
25 cock:[9] and drink, sir, is a great provoker of three
things.

**MACDUFF.** What three things does drink especially
provoke?

**PORTER.** Marry, sir, nose-painting, sleep, and urine.
30 Lechery, sir, it provokes and unprovokes; it provokes
the desire, but it takes away the performance: therefore much drink may be said to be an equivocator with lechery: it makes him and it mars him; it

**2. should have old:**
Would have plenty of.
**3. Beelzebub** (bē el' zə
bub): The chief devil.
**4. A farmer . . . plenty:**
A farmer who hoarded
grain, hoping that the prices would come up as a re-
sult of a bad harvest.
**5. enow:** Enough.
**6. an equivocator . . .
scale:** A liar who could
make two contradictory
statements and swear that
both were true.
**7. stealing . . . hose:**
Stealing some cloth from
the hose while making
them.
**8. goose:** Pressing iron.

**9. second cock:** 3:00
A.M.

35 sets him on and it takes him off; it per-
suades him and disheartens him; makes him stand
to and not stand to; in conclusion, equivocates him
in a sleep, and giving him the lie, leaves him.

**MACDUFF.** I believe drink gave thee the lie[10] last night.

10. **gave thee the lie:**
Laid you out.

40 **PORTER.** That it did, sir, i' the very throat on me: but I
requited him for his lie, and, I think, being too strong
for him, though he took up my legs some-
time, yet I make a shift to cast[11] him.

11. **cast:** Vomit.

**MACDUFF.** Is thy master stirring?

[*Enter* MACBETH.]

Our knocking has awaked him; here he comes.

**LENNOX.** Good morrow, noble sir.

45 **MACBETH.**                    Good morrow, both.

**MACDUFF.** Is the king stirring, worthy Thane?

**MACBETH.**                              Not yet.

**MACDUFF.** He did command me to call timely[12] on him:
I have almost slipped the hour.

12. **timely:** Early.

**MACBETH.**                         I'll bring you to him.

**MACDUFF.** I know this is a joyful trouble to you;
50 But yet 'tis one.

**MACBETH.** The labor we delight in physics pain.[13]
This is the door.

13. **labor . . . pain:** Labor
that we enjoy cures discomfort.

**MACDUFF.**           I'll make so bold to call,
For 'tis my limited service.[14]           [*Exit* MACDUFF.]

14. **limited service:** Assigned duty.

**LENNOX.** Goes the king hence today?

**MACBETH.**                    He does: he did appoint so.

55 **LENNOX.** The night has been unruly. Where we lay,
Our chimneys were blown down, and, as they say,
Lamentings heard i' th' air, strange screams of
death,
And prophesying with accents terrible
Of dire combustion[15] and confused events
60 New hatched to th' woeful time: the obscure bird[16]
Clamored the livelong night. Some say, the earth
Was feverous and did shake.

15. **combustion:** Confusion.
16. **obscure bird:** Bird of
darkness, the owl.

**MACBETH.**                    'Twas a rough night.

**LENNOX.** My young remembrance cannot parallel
A fellow to it.

**LADY MACBETH SEIZING THE DAGGERS**
*Henry Fuseli*
The Tate Gallery, London

[*Enter* MACDUFF.]

65     **MACDUFF.** O horror, horror, horror! Tongue nor heart
        Cannot conceive nor name thee.

     **MACBETH AND LENNOX.**                What's the matter?

     **MACDUFF.** Confusion[17] now hath made his masterpiece.
        Most sacrilegious murder hath broke ope
        The Lord's anointed temple,[18] and stole thence
        The life o' th' building.

70     **MACBETH.**                 What is 't you say? The life?

     **LENNOX.** Mean you his Majesty?

     **MACDUFF.** Approach the chamber, and destroy your
        sight

**17. Confusion:** Destruction.

**18. The Lord's anointed temple:** The King's body.

With a new Gorgon:[19] do not bid me speak;
See, and then speak yourselves. Awake, awake!

[*Exit* MACBETH *and* LENNOX.]

75  Ring the alarum bell. Murder and Treason!
Banquo and Donalbain! Malcolm! Awake!
Shake off this downy sleep, death's counterfeit,
And look on death itself! Up, up, and see
The great doom's image![20] Malcolm! Banquo!
80  As from your graves rise up, and walk like sprites,[21]
To countenance[22] this horror. Ring the bell.

[*Bell rings. Enter* LADY MACBETH.]

LADY MACBETH. What's the business,
That such a hideous trumpet calls to parley[23]
The sleepers of the house? Speak, speak!

MACDUFF.                                    O gentle lady,
85  'Tis not for you to hear what I can speak:
The repetition, in a woman's ear,
Would murder as it fell.

[*Enter* BANQUO.]

                        O Banquo, Banquo!
Our royal master's murdered.

LADY MACBETH.                        Woe, alas!
What, in our house?

BANQUO.                        Too cruel anywhere.
90  Dear Duff, I prithee, contradict thyself,
And say it is not so.

[*Enter* MACBETH, LENNOX, *and* ROSS.]

MACBETH. Had I but died an hour before this
    chance,
I had lived a blessèd time; for from this instant
There's nothing serious in mortality:[24]
95  All is but toys.[25] Renown and grace is dead,
The wine of life is drawn, and the mere lees[26]
Is left this vault[27] to brag of.

[*Enter* MALCOLM *and* DONALBAIN.]

DONALBAIN. What is amiss?

MACBETH.                        You are, and do not know 't.
The spring, the head, the fountain of your blood
100  Is stopped; the very source of it is stopped.

MACDUFF. Your royal father's murdered.

MALCOLM.                                    O, by whom?

**19. Gorgon:** Medusa, a
mythological monster
whose appearance was so
ghastly that those who
looked at it turned to
stone.

**20. great doom's image:**
Likeness of Judgment Day.
**21. sprites:** Spirits.
**22. countenance:** Be in
keeping with.

**23. parley:** A war conference.

**24. serious in mortality:**
Worthwhile in mortal life.
**25. toys:** Trifles.
**26. lees:** Dregs.
**27. vault:** World.

**LENNOX.** Those of his chamber, as it seemed, had
    done 't:
  Their hands and faces were all badged[28] with blood;
  So were their daggers, which unwiped we found
105  Upon their pillows. They stared, and were distracted.
  No man's life was to be trusted with them.

**MACBETH.** O, yet I do repent me of my fury,
  That I did kill them.

**MACDUFF.**           Wherefore did you so?

**MACBETH.** Who can be wise, amazed, temp'rate and
    furious,
110  Loyal and neutral, in a moment? No man.
  The expedition[29] of my violent love
  Outrun the pauser, reason. Here lay Duncan,
  His silver skin laced with his golden blood,
  And his gashed stabs looked like a breach in nature
115  For ruin's wasteful entrance: there, the murderers,
  Steeped in the colors of their trade, their daggers
  Unmannerly breeched with gore.[30] Who could
    refrain,
  That had a heart to love, and in that heart
  Courage to make 's love known?

**LADY MACBETH.**         Help me hence, ho!

**MACDUFF.** Look to the lady.

**MALCOLM.** [*Aside to* DONALBAIN] Why do we hold our
120    tongues,
  That most may claim this argument for ours?[31]

**DONALBAIN.** [*Aside to Malcolm*] What should be spoken
    here,
  Where our fate, hid in an auger-hole,[32]
  May rush, and seize us? Let's away:
  Our tears are not yet brewed.

125  **MALCOLM.** [*Aside to* DONALBAIN] Nor our strong sorrow
  Upon the foot of motion. [33]

**BANQUO.**         Look to the lady.
          [LADY MACBETH *is carried out.*]
  And when we have our naked frailties hid,[34]
  That suffer in exposure, let us meet
  And question[35] this most bloody piece of work,
130  To know it further. Fears and scruples[36] shake us.
  In the great hand of God I stand, and thence
  Against the undivulged pretense[37] I fight
  Of treasonous malice.

**MACDUFF.**        And so do I.

**28. badged:** Marked.

**29. expedition:** Haste.

**30. breeched with gore:**
Covered with blood.

**31. That most . . . ours:**
Who are the most con-
cerned with this topic.

**32. auger-hole:** Tiny hole,
an unsuspected place be-
cause of its size.

**33. Our tears . . .
motion:** We have not yet
had time for tears nor to
turn our sorrow into ac-
tion.
**34. when . . . hid:** When
we have put on our clothes.
**35. question:** Investigate.
**36. scruples:** Doubts.

**37. undivulged pretense:**
Hidden purpose.

**ALL.** So all.

**MACBETH.** Let's briefly[38] put on manly readiness,
And meet i' th' hall together.

135 **ALL.** Well contented.
*[Exit all but* MALCOLM *and* DONALBAIN.]

**MALCOLM.** What will you do? Let's not consort with
them.
To show an unfelt sorrow is an office[39]
Which the false man does easy. I'll to England.

**DONALBAIN.** To Ireland, I; our separated fortune
140 Shall keep us both the safer. Where we are
There's daggers in men's smiles; the near in blood,
The nearer bloody.[40]

**MALCOLM.** This murderous shaft that's shot
Hath not yet lighted,[41] and our safest way
Is to avoid the aim. Therefore to horse;
145 And let us not be dainty of leave-taking,
But shift away. There's warrant[42] in that theft
Which steals itself[43] when there's no mercy left.
*[Exit.]*

**Scene iv.** *Outside Macbeth's castle.*
*[Enter* ROSS *with an* OLD MAN.]

**OLD MAN.** Threescore and ten I can remember well:
Within the volume of which time I have seen
Hours dreadful and things strange, but this sore[1]
night
Hath trifled former knowings.

**ROSS.** Ha, good father,
5 Thou seest the heavens, as troubled with man's act,
Threatens his bloody stage. By th' clock 'tis day,
And yet dark night strangles the traveling lamp:[2]
Is 't night's predominance, or the day's shame,
That darkness does the face of earth entomb,
When living light should kiss it?

10 **OLD MAN.** 'Tis unnatural,
Even like the deed that's done. On Tuesday last
A falcon, tow'ring in her pride of place,[3]
Was by a mousing owl hawked at and killed.

**ROSS.** And Duncan's horses—a thing most strange
and certain—
15 Beauteous and swift, the minions of their race,
Turned wild in nature, broke their stalls, flung out,
Contending 'gainst obedience, as they would make
War with mankind.

**38. briefly:** Quickly.

**39. office:** Function.

**40. the near ... bloody:** The closer we are in blood relationship to Duncan, the greater our chance of being murdered.
**41. lighted:** Reached its target.
**42. warrant:** Justification
**43. that theft ... itself:** stealing away.

**1. sore:** Grievous.

**2. traveling lamp:** The sun.

**3. tow'ring ... place:** Soaring at its summit.

**OLD MAN.**                              'Tis said they eat[4] each other.

**ROSS.** They did so, to th' amazement of mine eyes,
That looked upon 't.

[*Enter* MACDUFF.]

20                              Here comes the good Macduff.
How goes the world, sir, now?

**MACDUFF.**                              Why, see you not?

**ROSS.** Is 't known who did this more than bloody deed?

**MACDUFF.** Those that Macbeth hath slain.

**ROSS.**                              Alas, the day!
What good could they pretend?[5]                    **5. pretend:** Hope for.

**MACDUFF.**                              They were suborned:[6]                    **6. suborned:** Bribed.
25    Malcolm and Donalbain, the king's two sons,
Are stol'n away and fled, which puts upon them
Suspicion of the deed.

**ROSS.**                              'Gainst nature still.
Thriftless ambition, that will ravin up[7]                    **7. ravin up:** Devour
Thine own life's means! Then 'tis most like                    greedily.
30    The sovereignty will fall upon Macbeth.

**MACDUFF.** He is already named, and gone to Scone[8]                    **8. Scone** (sko͞on): Where
To be invested.                    Scottish kings were
                    crowned.

**ROSS.**                              Where is Duncan's body?

**MACDUFF.** Carried to Colmekill,
The sacred storehouse of his predecessors
And guardian of their bones.

35    **ROSS.**                              Will you to Scone?

**MACDUFF.** No, cousin, I'll to Fife.[9]                    **9. Fife:** Where Macduff's
                    castle is located.

**ROSS.**                              Well, I will thither.

**MACDUFF.** Well, may you see things well done there.
Adieu,
Lest our old robes sit easier than our new!

**ROSS.** Farewell, father.

40    **OLD MAN.** God's benison[10] go with you, and with those                    **10. benison:** Blessing.
That would make good of bad, and friends of foes!
                              [*Exit.*]

## THINKING ABOUT THE SELECTION
### Recalling

1. (a) What is it that Macbeth thinks he sees in his "fatal vision"? (b) When the bell rings at the end of Scene i, what does Macbeth do?
2. (a) Why, according to Lady Macbeth, did she not kill the King herself? (b) What does Macbeth do with the daggers after the murder? (c) Why does this bother Lady Macbeth? (d) What action does she take?
3. (a) What does the drunken porter imagine he is doing in response to the knocking at the door? (b) What does Macbeth wish the knocking could do? (c) Who is doing the knocking? Why?
4. (a) Who first learns that a murder has taken place? (b) What action does Macbeth take against the grooms? (c) Why do Malcolm and Donalbain leave Macbeth's castle?
5. (a) Who does Macduff say has killed King Duncan? Why do Malcolm and Donalbain fall under suspicion, according to Macduff?

### Interpreting

6. What does Macbeth mean by saying he has "murdered sleep"?
7. What is ironic about Lady Macbeth's remark "A little water clears us of this deed"?
8. (a) Why do you think critics consider the porter's speech to be comic relief? (b) How do the porter's comments on the people arriving at "hell gate" mirror Macbeth's dilemma?
9. What do you think causes Lady Macbeth to faint?
10. (a) Why does Ross have doubts about accepting the grooms as the murderers? (b) Why is Macduff concerned that "our old robes" may fit "easier than our new"?

### Applying

11. In his soliloquy in Scene i, Macbeth speaks of "vaulting ambition." (a) How can vaulting ambition bring with it great success? (b) How can it bring with it destruction?

## ANALYZING LITERATURE
### Understanding Atmosphere

**Atmosphere** is the general mood or feeling in a literary work. In *Macbeth* the murder of the King occurs on an unusually dark, moonless night. The blackness of the night, which is conveyed through dialogue, matches the blackness of the deed. The grim, foreboding atmosphere reinforces the emotional states of the characters.

1. What is eerie about Macbeth's soliloquy in Scene i?
2. Reread Lennox's description of the night, Scene iii, lines 43–50. How does this description add to the atmosphere of the scene?
3. (a) How do the strange natural occurrences mentioned in Scene iv affect the atmosphere? (b) How do they relate to the night's events at Inverness Castle?

## CRITICAL THINKING AND READING
### Interpreting Symbols

A **symbol** is a word, person, object, or action that stands for something beyond itself. A flag, for example, is more than a piece of cloth; it stands for a country, its people, its ideals. Similarly, the ringing of the bell in Scene i is more than just a sound. It symbolizes an imminent death, much like the bell announcing an execution at London's Newgate prison or the small handbell that was rung outside a condemned person's cell at midnight to urge repentance.

1. In Scene ii, Lady Macbeth compares an owl's shriek to the "fatal bellman." How does this comparison extend the symbol of the bell?
2. Blood and water function as symbols in Scene ii, lines 44–68. (a) What does each symbolize? (b) What indication is there that Macbeth is less impressed by this symbolism than his wife is?
3. It has been suggested that the Old Man in Scene iv is a symbol for the people of Scotland. What is there about the Old Man that makes this suggestion plausible?

# GUIDE FOR INTERPRETING

## Macbeth, Act III

**Irony.** In general, irony is a contrast between what is said and what is meant or between what is expected and what occurs. There are three kinds of irony in literature, all of which occur in *Macbeth.*

*Dramatic irony* exists when the words or acts of a character in a play carry a meaning the character does not understand but the audience does. An example of dramatic irony occurs in *Macbeth* at the beginning of Act I, Scene vi, when Banquo and Duncan discuss the pleasant and delicate air as they arrive at Inverness. The audience knows, but Banquo and Duncan do not, that a murderous plot is being hatched behind the castle walls.

*Situational irony* occurs when the expected results of an action or situation differ from the actual results.

*Verbal irony* exists when a speaker says one thing and means the opposite. In a famous speech in Shakespeare's *Julius Caesar,* for example, when Mark Antony says of the assassins of Caesar, "So are they all, all honorable men," he means exactly the opposite of what he says. To him, the assassins are *not* honorable men. Antony's words are therefore verbal irony.

The Elizabethans believed that ghosts of dead people could return to earth. Spirits could appear to whomever they wanted, whenever they wanted, so that one person in a crowd might see a ghost while the others did not. Ghosts were especially likely to return when they were troubled. In Shakespeare's plays, ghosts often return to haunt a murderer. Although clergymen preached that the belief in ghosts was wicked and sinful, people remained convinced that ghosts were real, and well-stocked Elizabethan households boasted a stockpile of charms to ward off ghosts.

Perhaps William Shakespeare had his country folks' belief in ghosts in mind when he chose this epitaph for his own grave:

> Good friend, for Jesus' sake forbare
> To dig the dust encloséd here.
> Blest be the man that spares these stones,
> And curst be he that moves my bones.

At this point in *Macbeth,* you know a great deal about the major characters—more, in fact, than they know about themselves. Based on your knowledge, make notes on what you think will happen to the following characters by the end of the play: Macbeth, Lady Macbeth, Banquo, Macduff.

# Act III

**Scene i.** *Forres. The palace.*
[*Enter* BANQUO.]

     **BANQUO.** Thou hast it now: King, Cawdor, Glamis, all,
       As the weird women promised, and I fear
       Thou play'dst most foully for 't. Yet it was said
       It should not stand[1] in thy posterity,
5      But that myself should be the root and father
       Of many kings. If there come truth from them—
       As upon thee, Macbeth, their speeches shine—
       Why, by the verities on thee made good,
       May they not be my oracles as well
10    And set me up in hope? But hush, no more!

[*Sennet[2] sounded. Enter* MACBETH *as King,* LADY MACBETH,
LENNOX, ROSS, LORDS, *and* ATTENDANTS.]

     **MACBETH.** Here's our chief guest.

     **LADY MACBETH.**              If he had been forgotten,
       It had been as a gap in our great feast,
       And all-thing[3] unbecoming.

     **MACBETH.** Tonight we hold a solemn[4] supper, sir,
       And I'll request your presence.

15    **BANQUO.**                 Let your Highness
       Command upon me, to the which my duties
       Are with a most indissoluble tie
       For ever knit.

     **MACBETH.** Ride you this afternoon?

     **BANQUO.**               Ay, my good lord.

20    **MACBETH.** We should have else desired your good advice
       (Which still hath been both grave and prosperous[5])
       In this day's council; but we'll take tomorrow.
       Is 't far you ride?

     **BANQUO.** As far, my lord, as will fill up the time
25    'Twixt this and supper. Go not my horse the better,[6]
       I must become a borrower of the night
       For a dark hour or twain.

     **MACBETH.**               Fail not our feast.

     **BANQUO.** My lord, I will not.

     **MACBETH.** We hear our bloody cousins are bestowed
30    In England and in Ireland, not confessing
       Their cruel parricide, filling their hearers
       With strange invention.[7] But of that tomorrow,

**1. stand:** Continue.

**2. Sennet:** Trumpet call.

**3. all-thing:** Altogether.

**4. solemn:** Ceremonious.

**5. grave and prosperous:**
Weighty and profitable.

**6. Go not . . . better:** Unless my horse goes faster than I expect.

**7. invention:** Lies.

When therewithal we shall have cause of state
Craving us jointly.[8] Hie you to horse. Adieu,
35     Till you return at night. Goes Fleance with you?

**BANQUO.** Ay, my good lord: our time does call upon 's.

**MACBETH.** I wish your horses swift and sure of foot,
And so I do commend you to their backs.
Farewell.                                    [*Exit* BANQUO.]
40     Let every man be master of his time
Till seven at night. To make society
The sweeter welcome, we will keep ourself
Till suppertime alone. While[9] then, God be with you!

[*Exit* LORDS *and all but* MACBETH *and a* SERVANT.]

Sirrah,[10] a word with you: attend those men
45     Our pleasure?

**ATTENDANT.** They are, my lord, without the palace gate.

**MACBETH.** Bring them before us.          [*Exit* SERVANT.]
To be thus[11] is nothing, but[12] to be safely thus—
Our fears in Banquo stick deep,
50     And in his royalty of nature reigns that
Which would be feared. 'Tis much he dares;
And, to[13] that dauntless temper of his mind,
He hath a wisdom that doth guide his valor
To act in safety. There is none but he
55     Whose being I do fear: and under him
My genius is rebuked,[14] as it is said
Mark Antony's was by Caesar. He chid[15] the sisters,
When first they put the name of King upon me,
And bade them speak to him; then prophetlike
60     They hailed him father to a line of kings.
Upon my head they placed a fruitless crown
And put a barren scepter in my gripe,[16]
Thence to be wrenched with an unlineal hand,
No son of mine succeeding. If 't be so,
65     For Banquo's issue have I filed[17] my mind;
For them the gracious Duncan have I murdered;
Put rancors in the vessel of my peace
Only for them, and mine eternal jewel[18]
Given to the common enemy of man,[19]
70     To make them kings, the seeds of Banquo kings!
Rather than so, come, fate, into the list,
And champion me to th' utterance![20] Who's there?

[*Enter* SERVANT *and* TWO MURDERERS.]

Now go to the door, and stay there till we call.
                                    [*Exit* SERVANT.]
Was it not yesterday we spoke together?

8. **cause . . . jointly:**
Matters of state demanding
our joint attention.

9. **While:** Until.

10. **Sirrah:** A common address to an inferior.

11. **thus:** King.
12. **but:** Unless.

13. **to:** Added to.

14. **genius is rebuked:**
Guardian spirit is cowed.
15. **chid:** Scolded.

16. **gripe:** Grip.

17. **filed:** Defiled.

18. **eternal jewel:** Soul.
19. **common . . . man:**
The Devil.

20. **champion me to th'
utterance:** Fight against
me to the death.

**MURDERERS.** It was, so please your Highness.

75 **MACBETH.**                               Well then, now
Have you considered of my speeches? Know
That it was he in the times past, which held you
So under fortune,[21] which you thought had been
Our innocent self: this I made good to you
In our last conference; passed in probation[22] with
80       you,
How you were born in hand,[23] how crossed, the
       instruments,
Who wrought with them, and all things else that
       might
To half a soul[24] and to a notion[25] crazed
Say "Thus did Banquo."

**FIRST MURDERER.**            You made it known to us.

85 **MACBETH.** I did so; and went further, which is now
Our point of second meeting. Do you find
Your patience so predominant in your nature,
That you can let this go? Are you so gospeled,[26]
To pray for this good man and for his issue,
90 Whose heavy hand hath bowed you to the grave
And beggared yours for ever?

**FIRST MURDERER.**                 We are men, my liege.

**MACBETH.** Ay, in the catalogue ye go for[27] men;
As hounds and greyhounds, mongrels, spaniels,
       curs,
Shoughs, water-rugs[28] and demi-wolves, are clept[29]
95 All by the name of dogs: the valued file[30]
Distinguishes the swift, the slow, the subtle,
The housekeeper, the hunter, every one
According to the gift which bounteous nature
Hath in him closed,[31] whereby he does receive
100 Particular addition,[32] from the bill
That writes them all alike: and so of men.
Now if you have a station in the file,[33]
Not i' th' worst rank of manhood, say 't,
And I will put that business in your bosoms
105 Whose execution takes your enemy off,
Grapples you to the heart and love of us,
Who wear our health but sickly in his life,[34]
Which in his death were perfect.

**SECOND MURDERER.**              I am one, my liege,
Whom the vile blows and buffets of the world
110 Hath so incensed that I am reckless what
I do to spite the world.

**21. held . . . fortune:** Kept you from good fortune.
**22. passed in probation:** Reviewed the proofs.
**23. born in hand:** Deceived.

**24. half a soul:** A halfwit.
**25. notion:** Mind.

**26. gospeled:** Ready to forgive.

**27. go for:** Pass as.
**28. Shoughs** (sḣuks), **water-rugs:** Shaggy dogs, long-haired dogs.
**29. clept:** Called.
**30. valued file:** Classification by valuable traits.

**31. closed:** Enclosed.
**32. addition:** Distinction (to set it apart from other dogs).
**33. file:** Ranks.

**34. wear . . . life:** Are sick as long as he lives.

**FIRST MURDERER.**              And I another
So weary with disasters, tugged with fortune,
That I would set[35] my life on any chance,
To mend it or be rid on 't.

**MACBETH.**                    Both of you
Know Banquo was your enemy.

115    **BOTH MURDERERS.**              True, my lord.

**MACBETH.** So is he mine, and in such bloody distance[36]
That every minute of his being thrusts
Against my near'st of life:[37] and though I could
With barefaced power sweep him from my sight
120    And bid my will avouch[38] it, yet I must not,
For certain friends that are both his and mine,
Whose loves I may not drop, but wail his fall[39]
Who I myself struck down: and thence it is
That I to your assistance do make love,
125    Masking the business from the common eye
For sundry weighty reasons.

**SECOND MURDERER.**              We shall, my lord,
Perform what you command us.

**FIRST MURDERER.**              Though our lives—

**MACBETH.** Your spirits shine through you. Within this
      hour at most
I will advise you where to plant yourselves,
130    Acquaint you with the perfect spy o' th' time,
The moment on 't;[40] for 't must be done tonight,
And something[41] from the palace; always thought[42]
That I require a clearness:[43] and with him—
To leave no rubs[44] nor botches in the work—
135    Fleance his son, that keeps him company,
Whose absence is no less material to me
Than is his father's, must embrace the fate
Of that dark hour. Resolve yourselves apart:[45]
I'll come to you anon.

**MURDERERS.**              We are resolved, my lord.

140    **MACBETH.** I'll call upon you straight.[46] Abide within.
It is concluded: Banquo, thy soul's flight,
If it find heaven, must find it out tonight.      [*Exit.*]

### Scene ii. *The palace.*
[*Enter* MACBETH'S LADY *and a* SERVANT.]

**LADY MACBETH.** Is Banquo gone from court?

**SERVANT.** Ay, madam, but returns again tonight.

**35. set:** Risk.

**36. distance:** Disagreement.

**37. near'st of life:** Most vital parts.

**38. avouch:** Justify.

**39. wail his fall:** (I must) bewail his death.

**40. the perfect . . . on 't:** The exact information of the exact time.

**41. something:** Some distance.

**42. thought:** Remembered.

**43. clearness:** Freedom from suspicion.

**44. rubs:** Flaws.

**45. Resolve yourselves apart:** Make your own decision.

**46. straight:** Immediately.

**LADY MACBETH.** Say to the King, I would attend his
    leisure
    For a few words.

**SERVANT.**                Madam, I will.          [*Exit.*]

**LADY MACBETH.**             Nought's had, all's spent,
5     Where our desire is got without content:
    'Tis safer to be that which we destroy
    Than by destruction dwell in doubtful joy.

[*Enter* MACBETH.]

    How now, my lord! Why do you keep alone,
    Of sorriest fancies your companions making,
10     Using those thoughts which should indeed have died
    With them they think on? Things without all remedy
    Should be without regard: what's done is done.

**MACBETH.** We have scotched[1] the snake, not killed it:
    She'll close[2] and be herself, whilst our poor malice
15     Remains in danger of her former tooth.[3]
    But let the frame of things disjoint,[4] both the worlds[5]
        suffer,
    Ere we will eat our meal in fear, and sleep
    In the affliction of these terrible dreams
    That shake us nightly: better be with the dead,
20     Whom we, to gain our peace, have sent to peace,
    Than on the torture of the mind to lie
    In restless ecstasy.[6] Duncan is in his grave;
    After life's fitful fever he sleeps well.
    Treason has done his worst: nor steel, nor poison,
25     Malice domestic, foreign levy,[7] nothing,
    Can touch him further.

**LADY MACBETH.**              Come on.
    Gentle my lord, sleek o'er your rugged looks;
    Be bright and jovial among your guests tonight.

**MACBETH.** So shall I, love; and so, I pray, be you:
30     Let your remembrance apply to Banquo;
    Present him eminence,[8] both with eye and tongue:
    Unsafe the while, that we must lave[9]
    Our honors in these flattering streams
    And make our faces vizards[10] to our hearts,
    Disguising what they are.

35 **LADY MACBETH.**           You must leave this.

**MACBETH.** O, full of scorpions is my mind, dear wife!
    Thou know'st that Banquo, and his Fleance, lives.

**LADY MACBETH.** But in them nature's copy's not eterne.[11]

---

1. **scotched:** Wounded.
2. **close:** Heal.
3. **in . . . tooth:** In as much danger as before.
4. **frame of things disjoint:** Universe collapse.
5. **both the worlds:** Heaven and earth.

6. **ecstasy:** Frenzy.

7. **Malice . . . levy:** Civil and foreign war.

8. **Present him eminence:** Honor him.
9. **Unsafe . . . lave:** We are unsafe as long as we have to wash.
10. **vizards** (viz′ ərdz): Masks.

11. **nature's . . . eterne:** Nature's lease is not eternal.

**BANQUO AT THE GATE, WOOD ENGRAVING AFTER SIR JOHN GILBERT**
*The Granger Collection*

**MACBETH.** There's comfort yet; they are assailable.
40     Then be thou jocund. Ere the bat hath flown
    His cloistered flight, ere to black Hecate's summons
    The shard-borne[12] beetle with his drowsy hums
    Hath rung night's yawning peal, there shall be done
    A deed of dreadful note.

**LADY MACBETH.**           What's to be done?

45 **MACBETH.** Be innocent of the knowledge, dearest
      chuck,[13]
    Till thou applaud the deed. Come, seeling[14] night,
    Scarf up[15] the tender eye of pitiful day,
    And with thy bloody and invisible hand
    Cancel and tear to pieces that great bond[16]
50     Which keeps me pale! Light thickens, and the crow
    Makes wing to th' rooky[17] wood.
    Good things of day begin to droop and drowse,
    Whiles night's black agents to their preys do rouse.
    Thou marvel'st at my words: but hold thee still;
55     Things bad begun make strong themselves by ill:
    So, prithee, go with me.          [*Exit.*]

**12. shard-borne:** Borne on scaly wings.

**13. chuck:** A term of endearment.
**14. seeling:** Eye-closing. Falconers sometimes sewed a hawk's eyes closed in order to train it.
**15. Scarf up:** Blindfold.
**16. great bond:** Between Banquo and fate.
**17. rooky:** Full of rooks, or crows.

**Scene iii.** *Near the palace.*

[*Enter* THREE MURDERERS.]

FIRST MURDERER. But who did bid thee join with us?

THIRD MURDERER.                                    Macbeth.

SECOND MURDERER. He needs not our mistrust; since he delivers
Our offices[1] and what we have to do
To the direction just.[2]

FIRST MURDERER.              Then stand with us.
5     The west yet glimmers with some streaks of day.
Now spurs the lated traveler apace
To gain the timely inn, and near approaches
The subject of our watch.

THIRD MURDERER.              Hark! I hear horses.

BANQUO. [*Within*] Give us a light there, ho!

SECOND MURDERER.                   Then 'tis he. The rest
10    That are within the note of expectation[3]
Already are i' th' court.

FIRST MURDERER.              His horses go about.[4]

THIRD MURDERER. Almost a mile: but he does usually—
So all men do—from hence to th' palace gate
Make it their walk.

[*Enter* BANQUO *and* FLEANCE, *with a torch.*]

SECOND MURDERER. A light, a light!

THIRD MURDERER.              'Tis he.

15    FIRST MURDERER.              Stand to 't.

BANQUO. It will be rain tonight.

FIRST MURDERER.              Let it come down.

[*They set upon* BANQUO.]

BANQUO. O, treachery! Fly, good Fleance, fly, fly, fly!
                                   [*Exit* FLEANCE.]

              Thou mayst revenge. O slave! [*Dies.*]

THIRD MURDERER. Who did strike out the light?

FIRST MURDERER.                   Was 't not the way?[5]

20    THIRD MURDERER. There's but one down; the son is fled.

SECOND MURDERER. We have lost best half of our affair.

FIRST MURDERER. Well, let's away and say how much is
done.                                   [*Exit.*]

1. **offices:** Duties.
2. **direction just:** Exact detail.

3. **within . . . expectations:** On the list of expected guests.
4. **His . . . about:** His horses have been taken to the stable.

5. **way:** Thing to do.

**Scene iv.** *The palace.*

[*Banquet prepared. Enter* MACBETH, LADY MACBETH, ROSS, LENNOX, LORDS, *and* ATTENDANTS.]

MACBETH. You know your own degrees;¹ sit down:
At first and last, the hearty welcome.

LORDS. Thanks to your Majesty.

MACBETH. Ourself will mingle with society²
5    And play the humble host.
Our hostess keeps her state,³ but in best time
We will require⁴ her welcome.

LADY MACBETH. Pronounce it for me, sir, to all our
    friends,
For my heart speaks they are welcome.

[*Enter* FIRST MURDERER.]

MACBETH. See, they encounter thee with their hearts'
10    thanks.
Both sides are even: here I'll sit i' th' midst:
Be large in mirth; anon we'll drink a measure⁵
The table round. [*Goes to* MURDERER] There's blood
    upon thy face.

MURDERER. 'Tis Banquo's then.

15  MACBETH. 'Tis better thee without than he within.⁶
Is he dispatched?

MURDERER. My lord, his throat is cut; that I did for him.

MACBETH. Thou art the best o' th' cutthroats.
Yet he's good that did the like for Fleance;
20    If thou didst it, thou art the nonpareil.⁷

MURDERER. Most royal sir, Fleance is 'scaped.

MACBETH. [*Aside*] Then comes my fit again: I had else
    been perfect,
Whole as the marble, founded as the rock,
As broad and general as the casing⁸ air:
25    But now I am cabined, cribbed, confined, bound in
To saucy⁹ doubts and fears.—But Banquo's safe?

MURDERER. Ay, my good lord: safe in a ditch he bides,
With twenty trenchèd¹⁰ gashes on his head,
The least a death to nature.¹¹

MACBETH.               Thanks for that.
[*Aside*] There the grown serpent lies; the worm
30    that's fled

**1. degrees:** Ranks. At state banquets guests were seated according to rank.

**2. society:** The company.

**3. keeps her state:** Remains seated on her throne.
**4. require:** Request.

**5. measure:** Toast.

**6. thee . . . within:** You outside than he inside.

**7. nonpareil:** Without equal.

**8. as . . . casing:** As unrestrained as the surrounding.
**9. saucy:** Insolent.

**10. trenchèd:** Trenchlike.
**11. nature:** Natural life.

Hath nature that in time will venom breed,
No teeth for th' present. Get thee gone. Tomorrow
We'll hear ourselves[12] again.     [*Exit* MURDERER.]

**LADY MACBETH.**         My royal lord,
You do not give the cheer.[13] The feast is sold
35   That is not often vouched, while 'tis a-making,
'Tis given with welcome.[14] To feed were best at home;
From thence, the sauce to meat is ceremony;[15]
Meeting were bare without it.

[*Enter the* GHOST OF BANQUO, *and sits in* MACBETH'*s place.*]

**MACBETH.**                Sweet remembrancer!
Now good digestion wait on appetite,
And health on both!

40  **LENNOX.**            May 't please your Highness sit.

**MACBETH.** Here had we now our country's honor roofed,[16]
Were the graced person of our Banquo present—
Who may I rather challenge for unkindness
Than pity for mischance![17]

**ROSS.**               His absence, sir,
Lays blame upon his promise. Please 't your
45     Highness
To grace us with your royal company?

**MACBETH.** The table's full.

**LENNOX.**           Here is a place reserved, sir.

**MACBETH.** Where?

**LENNOX.** Here, my good lord. What is 't that moves your
Highness?

**MACBETH.** Which of you have done this?

50  **LORDS.**              What, my good lord?

**MACBETH.** Thou canst not say I did it. Never shake
Thy gory locks at me.

**ROSS.** Gentlemen, rise, his Highness is not well.

**LADY MACBETH.** Sit, worthy friends. My lord is often thus,
55   And hath been from his youth. Pray you, keep seat.
The fit is momentary; upon a thought[18]
He will again be well. If much you note him,
You shall offend him and extend his passion.[19]
Feed, and regard him not.—Are you a man?

60  **MACBETH.** Ay, and a bold one, that dare look on that
Which might appall the devil.

**12. hear ourselves:** Talk it over.

**13. give the cheer:** Make the guests feel welcome.

**14. The feast . . . welcome:** The feast at which the host fails to make the guests feel welcome while the food is being prepared is no more than a bought dinner.

**15. From . . . ceremony:** Ceremony adds a pleasant flavor to the food.

**16. our . . . roofed:** The most honorable men in the country under one roof.

**17. Who . . . mischance:** Whom I hope I may reproach for being absent due to discourtesy rather than pity because he has had an accident.

**18. upon a thought:** In a moment.

**19. passion:** Suffering.

**LADY MACBETH.**                         O proper stuff!
This is the very painting of your fear.
This is the air-drawn dagger which, you said,
Led you to Duncan. O, these flaws[20] and starts,
65  Impostors to true fear, would well become
A woman's story at a winter's fire,
Authorized[21] by her grandam. Shame itself!
Why do you make such faces? When all's done,
You look but on a stool.

**MACBETH.**                         Prithee, see there!
70  Behold! Look! Lo! How say you?
Why, what care I? If thou canst nod, speak too.
If charnel houses[22] and our graves must send
Those that we bury back, our monuments
Shall be the maws of kites.[23]          [*Exit* GHOST.]

**LADY MACBETH.**          What, quite unmanned in folly?

**MACBETH.** If I stand here, I saw him.

75  **LADY MACBETH.**                         Fie, for shame!

**MACBETH.** Blood hath been shed ere now, i' th' olden
          time,
Ere humane statute purged the gentle weal;[24]
Ay, and since too, murders have been performed
Too terrible for the ear. The times has been
80  That, when the brains were out, the man would die,
And there an end; but now they rise again,
With twenty mortal murders on their crowns,[25]
And push us from our stools. This is more strange
Than such a murder is.

**LADY MACBETH.**                         My worthy lord,
Your noble friends do lack you.

85  **MACBETH.**                         I do forget.
Do not muse at me, my most worthy friends;
I have a strange infirmity, which is nothing
To those that know me. Come, love and health to all!
Then I'll sit down. Give me some wine, fill full.

[*Enter* GHOST.]

90  I drink to th' general joy o' th' whole table,
And to our dear friend Banquo, whom we miss;
Would he were here! To all and him we thirst,[26]
And all to all.

**LORDS.**          Our duties, and the pledge.

**20. flaws:** Gusts of wind; outbursts of emotion.

**21. Authorized:** Vouched for.

**22. charnel houses:** Vaults containing human bones dug up in making new graves.
**23. our . . . kites:** Our tombs shall be the bellies of birds of prey.

**24. Ere . . . weal:** Before humane laws civilized the state and made it gentle.

**25. mortal . . . crowns:** Deadly wounds on their heads.

**26. thirst:** Drink.

**MACBETH.** Avaunt![27] and quit my sight! Let the earth
  hide thee!
95 Thy bones are marrowless, thy blood is cold;
  Thou hast no speculation[28] in those eyes
  Which thou dost glare with.

**LADY MACBETH.**     Think of this, good peers,
  But as a thing of custom, 'tis no other.
  Only it spoils the pleasure of the time.

100 **MACBETH.** What man dare, I dare.
  Approach thou like the rugged Russian bear,
  The armed rhinoceros, or th' Hyrcan[29] tiger;
  Take any shape but that,[30] and my firm nerves
  Shall never tremble. Or be alive again,
105 And dare me to the desert[31] with thy sword.
  If trembling I inhabit[32] then, protest me
  The baby of a girl. Hence, horrible shadow!
  Unreal mock'ry, hence!    [*Exit* GHOST.]
      Why, so: being gone,
  I am a man again. Pray you, sit still.

**LADY MACBETH.** You have displaced the mirth, broke the
110 good meeting,
  With most admired[33] disorder.

**MACBETH.**      Can such things be,
  And overcome us[34] like a summer's cloud,
  Without our special wonder? You make me strange
  Even to the disposition that I owe,[35]
115 When now I think you can behold such sights,
  And keep the natural ruby of your cheeks,
  When mine is blanched with fear.

**ROSS.**      What sights, my lord?

**LADY MACBETH.** I pray you, speak not: He grows worse
  and worse;
  Question enrages him: at once, good night.
120 Stand not upon the order of your going,[36]
  But go at once.

**LENNOX.**   Good night; and better health
  Attend his Majesty!

**LADY MACBETH.**   A kind good night to all!
      [*Exit* LORDS.]

**MACBETH.** It will have blood, they say: blood will have
  blood.
  Stones have been known to move and trees to
  speak;

**27. Avaunt:** Be gone!

**28. speculation:** sight.

**29. Hyrcan** (hər′ kən):
From Hyrcania, a province
of the ancient Persian and
Macedonian empires south
of the Caspian Sea.
**30. that:** Banquo's shape.
**31. desert:** A place where
neither of us could escape.
**32. inhabit:** Remain indoors.

**33. admired:** Amazing.

**34. overcome us:** Come
over us.

**35. disposition . . . owe:**
My own nature.

**36. Stand . . . going:** Do
not wait to depart in order
of rank.

125     Augures and understood relations[37] have
    By maggot-pies and choughs[38] and rooks brought
       forth
    The secret'st man of blood.[39] What is the night?

**LADY MACBETH.** Almost at odds[40] with morning, which is
    which.

**MACBETH.** How say'st thou, that Macduff denies his
    person
    At our great bidding?

130   **LADY MACBETH.**           Did you send to him, sir?

**MACBETH.** I hear it by the way, but I will send:
    There's not a one of them but in his house
    I keep a servant fee'd.[41] I will tomorrow,
    And betimes[42] I will, to the weird sisters:
135     More shall they speak, for now I am bent[43] to know
    By the worst means the worst. For mine own good
    All causes shall give way. I am in blood
    Stepped in so far that, should I wade no more,
    Returning were as tedious as go o'er.
140     Strange things I have in head that will to hand,
    Which must be acted ere they may be scanned.[44]

**LADY MACBETH.** You lack the season of all natures,[45]
    sleep.

**MACBETH.** Come, we'll to sleep. My strange and self-
    abuse[46]
    Is the initiate fear that wants hard use.[47]
145     We are yet but young in deed.        *[Exit.]*

*Scene v.* *A witches' haunt.*
*[Thunder. Enter the* THREE WITCHES, *meeting* HECATE.]

**FIRST WITCH.** Why, how now, Hecate! you look angerly.

**HECATE.** Have I not reason, beldams[1] as you are,
    Saucy and overbold? How did you dare
    To trade and traffic with Macbeth
5     In riddles and affairs of death;
    And I, the mistress of your charms,
    The close contriver[2] of all harms,
    Was never called to bear my part,
    Or show the glory of our art?
10     And, which is worse, all you have done
    Hath been but for a wayward son,
    Spiteful and wrathful; who, as others do,
    Loves for his own ends, not for you.
    But make amends now: get you gone,

**37. Augures and understood relations:** Omens and the relationship between the omens and what they represent.
**38. maggot-pies and choughs** (chufs): Magpies and crows.
**39. man of blood:** Murderer.
**40. at odds:** Disputing.

**41. fee'd:** Paid to spy.
**42. betimes:** Quickly.
**43. bent:** Determined.

**44. scanned:** Examined.
**45. season . . . natures:** Preservative of all living creatures.
**46. My . . . self-abuse:** My strange delusion.
**47. initiate . . . use:** Beginner's fear that will harden with experience.

**1. beldams:** Hags.

**2. close contriver:** secret inventor.

15 And at the pit of Acheron[3]
Meet me i' th' morning: thither he
Will come to know his destiny.
Your vessels and your spells provide,
Your charms and everything beside.
20 I am for th' air; this night I'll spend
Unto a dismal and a fatal end:
Great business must be wrought ere noon.
Upon the corner of the moon
There hangs a vap'rous drop profound;
25 I'll catch it ere it come to ground:
And that distilled by magic sleights[4]
Shall raise such artificial sprites[5]
As by the strength of their illusion
Shall draw him on to his confusion.[6]
30 He shall spurn fate, scorn death, and bear
His hopes 'bove wisdom, grace, and fear:
And you all know security[7]
Is mortals' chiefest enemy.

[*Music and a song.*]

Hark! I am called; my little spirit, see,
35 Sits in a foggy cloud and stays for me.     [*Exit.*]

[*Sing within,* "Come away, come away," *etc.*]

**FIRST WITCH.** Come, let's make haste; she'll soon be back
again.                                  [*Exit.*]

**Scene vi.** *The palace.*
[*Enter* LENNOX *and another* LORD.]

**LENNOX.** My former speeches have but hit[1] your
thoughts,
Which can interpret farther.[2] Only I say
Things have been strangely borne.[3] The gracious
Duncan
Was pitied of Macbeth: marry, he was dead.
5 And the right-valiant Banquo walked too late;
Whom, you may say, if 't please you, Fleance killed,
For Fleance fled. Men must not walk too late.
Who cannot want the thought,[4] how monstrous
It was for Malcolm and for Donalbain
10 To kill their gracious father? Damnèd fact![5]
How it did grieve Macbeth! Did he not straight,
In pious rage, the two delinquents tear,
That were the slaves of drink and thralls[6] of sleep?
Was not that nobly done? Ay, and wisely too;
15 For 'twould have angered any heart alive
To hear the men deny 't. So that I say

**3. Acheron** (ak′ ə ron′):
Hell; in Greek mythology
the river of Hades.

**4. sleights:** Devices.
**5. artificial sprites:** Spirits created by magic.

**6. confusion:** Ruin.

**7. security:** Overconfidence.

**1. hit:** Coincided.

**2. Which . . . farther:**
From which you can draw
your own conclusions.
**3. borne:** Managed.

**4. cannot . . . thought:**
Can fail to think.

**5. fact:** Deed.

**6. thralls:** slaves.

He has borne all things well: and I do think
That, had he Duncan's sons under his key—
As, an 't[7] please heaven, he shall not—they should find
20   What 'twere to kill a father. So should Fleance.
But, peace! for from broad[8] words, and 'cause he failed
His presence at the tyrant's feast, I hear,
Macduff lives in disgrace. Sir, can you tell
Where he bestows himself?

**LORD.**                         The son of Duncan,
25   From whom this tyrant holds the due of birth,[9]
Lives in the English court, and is received
Of the most pious Edward[10] with such grace
That the malevolence of fortune nothing
Takes from his high respect.[11] Thither Macduff
30   Is gone to pray the holy King, upon his aid[12]
To wake Northumberland and warlike Siward;[13]
That by the help of these, with Him above
To ratify the work, we may again
Give to our tables meat, sleep to our nights,
35   Free from our feasts and banquets bloody knives,
Do faithful homage and receive free honors:[14]
All which we pine for now. And this report
Hath so exasperate the King that he
Prepares for some attempt of war.

**LENNOX.**                       Sent he to Macduff?

40   **LORD.** He did: and with an absolute "Sir, not I,"
The cloudy[15] messenger turns me his back,
And hums, as who should say "You'll rue the time
That clogs[16] me with this answer."

**LENNOX.**                    And that well might
Advise him to a caution, t' hold what distance
45   His wisdom can provide. Some holy angel
Fly to the court of England and unfold
His message ere he come, that a swift blessing
May soon return to this our suffering country
Under a hand accursed!

**LORD.**                   I'll send my prayers with him.
                                 [*Exit.*]

**7. an 't:** If it.

**8. broad:** Unguarded.

**9. due of birth:** Birthright, claim to the throne.
**10. Edward:** Edward the Confessor, King of England 1042–1066.
**11. with . . . respect:** Does not diminish the high respect he is given.
**12. upon his aid:** To aid Malcolm.
**13. To . . . Siward:** To call to arms the commander of the English forces, the Earl of Northumberland, and his son Siward.
**14. free honors:** Honors given to free men.

**15. cloudy:** Disturbed.

**16. clogs:** Burdens.

## THINKING ABOUT THE SELECTION
### Recalling

1. (a) In Scene i, what are Banquo's thoughts about the witches' prophecies? (b) What are Macbeth's thoughts about the prophecies?
2. (a) What two people are the murderers told to kill? (b) Why is it necessary to kill both?
3. What goes wrong with the murderers' plans?
4. (a) In Scene iv, why does Macbeth not sit down at the banquet table? (b) How does Lady Macbeth explain his behavior?
5. (a) Why does Macbeth want to see the witches again? (b) What does Lady Macbeth think Macbeth needs most?
6. (a) In Scene vi, what reason does Lennox give for Macduff's being in disgrace? (b) What is Macduff trying to accomplish in England?

### Interpreting

7. Macbeth's soliloquy in Scene i shows that his attitude toward those who stand in his way has changed. Recall the soliloquy prior to Duncan's murder. What change or changes have occurred?
8. How does Macbeth's technique of persuading the murderers resemble Lady Macbeth's earlier method of persuading Macbeth?
9. How has the relationship between Macbeth and Lady Macbeth changed?
10. Events at the banquet show that Macbeth can no longer pretend to be innocent. What evidence is there that he will continue to kill those who threaten him?

### Applying

11. By the end of Act III, Macbeth is in desperate trouble. What advice would you give him concerning his best course of action?

## ANALYZING LITERATURE
### Understanding Irony

In *verbal irony* there is a contrast between what is said and what is meant. An example of verbal irony occurs in Act III, Scene i, when Macbeth says to Banquo, "Here's our chief guest," knowing that Banquo will be murdered on his orders before the great feast begins.

1. What three additional examples of verbal irony can you find in the conversation in Scene i between Macbeth and Banquo?
2. In Scene vi Lennox appears to accept Macbeth's version of the various murders. (a) How can you tell from what Lennox says that he does not really believe in Macbeth's innocence? (b) What are three examples of verbal irony in Lennox's opening speech?

## CRITICAL THINKING AND READING
### Interpreting Connotative Meanings

The **connotation** of a word is what is suggested by the word in addition to its literal meaning, or denotation. For instance, the denotation of the word *home* is "the place where one lives." The associations of *home* give the word its *connotative meanings*: "warmth, love, peace." Shakespeare, like all good writers, chooses words for their connotative meanings.

1. When the ghost of Banquo exits (Scene iv, line 108), Macbeth says, "I am a man again." What are the connotative meanings of *man*?
2. When Macbeth is talking to the murderers (Scene i, lines 90–91), he says, "Whose heavy hand hath bowed you to the grave / And *beggared* yours forever?" What are the connotative meanings of *beggared*?

## THINKING AND WRITING
### Who Is the Third Murderer?

Shakespeare never reveals the identity of the third murderer. Who do you think the third murderer might be? Write an essay supporting your theory of his or her identity. Reread Scene iii carefully. Then build a logical case using facts and lines from the play to support your theory. Use the process of elimination to exonerate some of the major characters. Remember, though, that the third murderer may have been sent by someone—even the witches—for a specific purpose (perhaps the killing of Banquo or the escape of Fleance). In revising your paper, make sure you have left no logical holes in your argument. Proofread and prepare a final draft.

# GUIDE FOR INTERPRETING

## Writer's Techniques

## Macbeth, Act IV

**Plot Development.** The plot of a literary work is the sequence of related events that create and then resolve a conflict. Conflict is the struggle, or interplay of forces, that takes place within the story. The main character may be in conflict with another person, with a value system, with fate, or with nature. Certain background information is necessary for an understanding of the action. This information is called **exposition,** and it usually appears early in the story. The plot movement at the beginning is one of *rising action* toward a climax. The *climax,* or *crisis,* is the peak of tension, a dramatic turning point. In a tragedy like *Macbeth,* the climax often occurs near the middle of the play. Then comes a period of *falling action,* which, in tragedy, shows the downfall of the tragic hero. The falling action leads finally to the *resolution,* or *denouement,* the point at which the conflict ends and the outcome is made clear.

## Writing

Plot is closely intertwined with character. Indeed, in a work of literary merit, you will find that character largely drives the plot, not the other way around. Make some notes analyzing that character of Macbeth. List his virtues as well as his faults, for the complexity of Macbeth's character lies at the heart of his difficulties.

## Commentary

Although Shakespeare began with Holinshed's account of two different murders, he transformed these historical tales into an entirely original plot. The first influence was the story of Duncan's assassination (c. 1040) by Macbeth and several rebels—including the treacherous Banquo, a detail Shakespeare obviously changed. He combined this with the earlier murder of another Scottish monarch, King Duff. As in *Macbeth,* the King was murdered on orders of his host while at his home; unlike the murder of Duncan in *Macbeth,* the King was killed by servants. The Bard also added parts of Holinshed's tale of King Kenneth. To Lady Macbeth went the King's inability to sleep and terrifying guilt at being part of a murder, but the playwright rejected the murder itself (of a nephew) and the haunting by a mysterious voice promising divine punishment. He also compressed the events of Macbeth's seventeen year reign into as many weeks. Finally, two of the greatest scenes in *Macbeth* are both original to Shakespeare. Both have to do with guilt: the banquet scene (III, iii) and the sleepwalking scene (V,i). Many critics feel that Shakespeare's most brilliant invention in the play is the banquet scene, which draws together the plot by dramatizing many of the ideas previously implied.

# Act IV

**Scene i.** *A witches' haunt.*
[*Thunder. Enter the* THREE WITCHES.]

> **FIRST WITCH.** Thrice the brinded[1] cat hath mewed.
>
> **SECOND WITCH.** Thrice and once the hedge-pig[2] whined.
>
> **THIRD WITCH.** Harpier[3] cries. 'Tis time, 'tis time.
>
> **FIRST WITCH.** Round about the caldron go:
> 5    In the poisoned entrails throw.
>     Toad, that under cold stone
>     Days and nights has thirty-one
>     Swelt'red venom sleeping got,[4]
>     Boil thou first i' th' charmèd pot.
>
> 10  **ALL.** Double, double, toil and trouble;
>     Fire burn and caldron bubble.
>
> **SECOND WITCH.** Fillet of a fenny snake,
>     In the caldron boil and bake;
>     Eye of newt and toe of frog,
> 15  Wool of bat and tongue of dog,
>     Adder's fork[5] and blindworm's[6] sting,
>     Lizard's leg and howlet's[7] wing,
>     For a charm of pow'rful trouble,
>     Like a hell-broth boil and bubble.
>
> 20  **ALL.** Double, double, toil and trouble;
>     Fire burn and caldron bubble.
>
> **THIRD WITCH.** Scale of dragon, tooth of wolf,
>     Witch's mummy, maw and gulf[8]
>     Of the ravined[9] salt-sea shark,
> 25  Root of hemlock digged i' th' dark,
>     Liver of blaspheming Jew,
>     Gall of goat, and slips of yew
>     Slivered in the moon's eclipse,
>     Nose of Turk and Tartar's lips,[10]
> 30  Finger of birth-strangled babe
>     Ditch-delivered by a drab,
>     Make the gruel thick and slab:[11]
>     Add thereto a tiger's chaudron,[12]
>     For th' ingredience of our caldron.
>
> 35  **ALL.** Double, double, toil and trouble;
>     Fire burn and caldron bubble.
>
> **SECOND WITCH.** Cool it with a baboon's blood,
>     Then the charm is firm and good.

[*Enter* HECATE *and the other* THREE WITCHES.]

---

1. **brinded:** Striped.
2. **hedge-pig:** Hedgehog.
3. **Harpier:** One of the spirits attending the witches.
4. **Swelt'red . . . got:** Venom sweated out while sleeping.
5. **fork:** Forked tongue.
6. **blindworm's:** Small, limbless lizard's.
7. **howlet's:** A small owl's.
8. **maw and gulf:** Stomach and gullet.
9. **ravined:** Ravenous.
10. **blaspheming Jew . . . Tartar's lips:** For many in Shakespeare's audience, the words "Jew," "Turk," and "Tartar" evoked stereotypical enemies of Christianity.
11. **slab:** sticky.
12. **chaudron** (shô′ drən): Entrails.

**HECATE.** O, well done! I commend your pains;
40     And every one shall share i' th' gains:
    And now about the caldron sing,
    Like elves and fairies in a ring,
    Enchanting all that you put in.

[*Music and a song:* "Black Spirits," *etc. Exit* HECATE
*and the other* THREE WITCHES.]

**SECOND WITCH.** By the pricking of my thumbs,
45     Something wicked this way comes:
    Open, locks,
    Whoever knocks!

[*Enter* MACBETH.]

**MACBETH.** How now, you secret, black, and midnight
    hags!
    What is 't you do?

**ALL.**             A deed without a name.

50 **MACBETH.** I conjure you, by that which you profess,
    Howe'er you come to know it, answer me:
    Though you untie the winds and let them fight
    Against the churches; though the yesty[13] waves
    Confound[14] and swallow navigation up;
55     Though bladed corn be lodged[15] and trees blown
      down;
    Though castles topple on their warders' heads;
    Though palaces and pyramids do slope[16]
    Their heads to their foundations; though the treas-
      ure
    Of nature's germens[17] tumble all together,
60     Even till destruction sicken, answer me
    To what I ask you.

**FIRST WITCH.**       Speak.

**SECOND WITCH.**       Demand.

**THIRD WITCH.**       We'll answer.

**FIRST WITCH.** Say, if th' hadst rather hear it from our
    mouths,
    Or from our masters?

**MACBETH.**       Call' em, let me see 'em.

**FIRST WITCH.** Pour in sow's blood, that hath eaten
65     Her nine farrow;[18] grease that's sweaten
    From the murderer's gibbet[19] throw
    Into the flame.

**ALL.**       Come, high or low,

---

**13. yesty:** Foamy.
**14. Confound:** Destroy.
**15. lodged:** Beaten down.

**16. slope:** Bend.

**17. nature's germens:** Seeds of all life.

**18. farrow:** Young pigs.
**19. gibbet** (jib' it): Gallows.

Thyself and office[20] deftly show!

[*Thunder.* FIRST APPARITION: *an Armed Head.*[21]]

**MACBETH.** Tell me, thou unknown power—

**FIRST WITCH.**                         He knows thy thought:
70      Hear his speech, but say thou nought.

**FIRST APPARITION.** Macbeth! Macbeth! Macbeth! Beware
        Macduff!
        Beware the Thane of Fife. Dismiss me: enough.
                                    [*He descends.*]

**MACBETH.** Whate'er thou art, for thy good caution
        thanks:
        Thou hast harped[22] my fear aright. But one word
        more—

**FIRST WITCH.** He will not be commanded. Here's
75      another,
        More potent than the first.

[*Thunder.* SECOND APPARITION: *a Bloody Child.*[23]]

**SECOND APPARITION.** Macbeth! Macbeth! Macbeth!

**MACBETH.** Had I three ears, I'd hear thee.

**SECOND APPARITION.** Be bloody, bold, and resolute! Laugh
        to scorn
80      The pow'r of man, for none of woman born
        Shall harm Macbeth.            [*Descends.*]

**MACBETH.** Then live, Macduff: what need I fear of thee?
        But yet I'll make assurance double sure,
        And take a bond of fate.[24] Thou shalt not live;
85      That I may tell pale-hearted fear it lies,
        And sleep in spite of thunder.

[*Thunder.* THIRD APPARITION: *a Child Crowned, with a
tree in his hand.*[25]]

                            What is this,
        That rises like the issue of a king,
        And wears upon his baby-brow the round
        And top of sovereignty? [26]

**ALL.**                         Listen, but speak not to 't.

90    **THIRD APPARITION.** Be lion-mettled, proud, and take no
        care
        Who chafes, who frets, or where conspirers are:
        Macbeth shall never vanquished be until
        Great Birnam Wood to high Dunsinane Hill
        Shall come against him.            [*Descends.*]

**20. office:** Function.

**21. an Armed Head:** A symbol of Macduff.

**22. harped:** Hit upon.

**23. a Bloody Child:** A symbol of Macduff at birth.

**24. take . . . fate:** Get a guarantee from fate (by killing Macduff).

**25. a Child . . . hand:** A symbol of Malcolm.

**26. top of sovereignty:** Crown.

**MACBETH.**                              That will never be.

95     Who can impress[27] the forest, bid the tree
    Unfix his earth-bound root? Sweet bodements,[28]
      good!
    Rebellious dead, rise never, till the Wood
    Of Birnam rise, and our high-placed Macbeth
    Shall live the lease of nature,[29] pay his breath
100     To time and mortal custom.[30] Yet my heart
    Throbs to know one thing. Tell me, if your art
    Can tell so much: shall Banquo's issue ever
    Reign in this kingdom?

**ALL.**                              Seek to know no more.

**MACBETH.** I will be satisfied. Deny me this,
105     And an eternal curse fall on you! Let me know.
    Why sinks that caldron? And what noise is this?

[*Hautboys.*]

**FIRST WITCH.** Show!

**SECOND WITCH.** Show!

**THIRD WITCH.** Show!

110    **ALL.** Show his eyes, and grieve his heart;
    Come like shadows, so depart!

[*A show of eight* KINGS *and* BANQUO, *last* KING *with a glass*[31] *in his hand.*]

**MACBETH.** Thou art too like the spirit of Banquo. Down!
    Thy crown does sear mine eyelids. And thy hair,
    Thou other gold-bound brow, is like the first.
115     A third is like the former. Filthy hags!
    Why do you show me this? A fourth! Start, eyes!
    What, will the line stretch out to th' crack of doom?
    Another yet! A seventh! I'll see no more.
    And yet the eighth appears, who bears a glass
120     Which shows me many more; and some I see
    That twofold balls and treble scepters[32] carry:
    Horrible sight! Now I see 'tis true;
    For the blood-boltered[33] Banquo smiles upon me,
    And points at them for his.[34] What, is this so?

125    **FIRST WITCH.** Ay, sir, all this is so. But why
    Stands Macbeth thus amazedly?
    Come, sisters, cheer we up his sprites,
    And show the best of our delights:
    I'll charm the air to give a sound,
130     While you perform your antic round,[35]
    That this great king may kindly say
    Our duties did his welcome pay.

**27. impress:** Force into service.
**28. bodements:** Prophecies.

**29. lease of nature:** Natural lifespan.
**30. mortal custom:** Natural death.

**31. glass:** Mirror.

**32. twofold . . . scepters:** Coronation emblems and insignia of the kingdoms of England, Scotland, and Ireland, united in 1603 when James VI of Scotland became James I of England.
**33. blood-boltered:** With his hair matted with blood.
**34. his:** His descendants.
**35. antic round:** Grotesque circular dance.

**MACBETH AND THE WITCHES**
*Engraved by Thew after Reynolds*
*Royal Academy of Arts, London*

[*Music.* THE WITCHES *dance, and vanish.*]

> **MACBETH.** Where are they? Gone? Let this pernicious
> hour
> Stand aye accursèd in the calendar!
> Come in, without there!

[*Enter* LENNOX.]

135     **LENNOX.**                 What's your Grace's will?

> **MACBETH.** Saw you the weird sisters?

> **LENNOX.**                  No, my lord.

> **MACBETH.** Came they not by you?

> **LENNOX.**              No indeed, my lord.

> **MACBETH.** Infected be the air whereon they ride,
> And damned all those that trust them! I did hear
140    The galloping of horse. Who was 't came by?

**LENNOX.** 'Tis two or three, my lord, that bring you word
Macduff is fled to England.

**MACBETH.**                              Fled to England?

**LENNOX.** Ay, my good lord.

**MACBETH.** [*Aside*] Time, thou anticipat'st[36] my dread
exploits.
145    The flighty purpose never is o'ertook
Unless the deed go with it.[37] From this moment
The very firstlings of my heart[38] shall be
The firstlings of my hand. And even now,
To crown my thoughts with acts, be it thought and
done:
150    The castle of Macduff I will surprise;
Seize upon Fife; give to th' edge o' th' sword
His wife, his babes, and all unfortunate souls
That trace[39] him in his line. No boasting like a fool;
This deed I'll do before this purpose cool:
155    But no more sights!—Where are these gentlemen?
Come, bring me where they are.                    [*Exit.*]

*Scene ii. Macduff's castle.*
[*Enter* MACDUFF'S WIFE, *her* SON, *and* ROSS.]

**LADY MACDUFF.** What had he done, to make him fly the
land?

**ROSS.** You must have patience, madam.

**LADY MACDUFF.**                              He had none:
His flight was madness. When our actions do not,
Our fears do make us traitors.

**ROSS.**                              You know not
5    Whether it was his wisdom or his fear.

**LADY MACDUFF.** Wisdom! To leave his wife, to leave his
babes,
His mansion and his titles,[1] in a place
From whence himself does fly? He loves us not;
He wants the natural touch:[2] for the poor wren,
10    The most diminutive of birds, will fight,
Her young ones in her nest, against the owl.
All is the fear and nothing is the love;
As little is the wisdom, where the flight
So runs against all reason.

**ROSS.**                              My dearest coz,[3]
15    I pray you, school[4] yourself. But, for your husband,
He is noble, wise, judicious, and best knows

**36. anticipat'st:** Foretold.

**37. The flighty . . . it:**
The fleeting plan is never
fulfilled unless it is carried
out at once.
**38. firstlings . . . heart:**
First thoughts, impulses.

**39. trace:** Succeed.

**1. titles:** possessions.

**2. wants . . . touch:**
Lacks natural affection.

**3. coz:** Cousin.
**4. school:** Control.

The fits o' th' season.[5] I dare not speak much further:
But cruel are the times, when we are traitors
And do not know ourselves;[6] when we hold rumor
20 From what we fear,[7] yet know not what we fear,
But float upon a wild and violent sea
Each way and move. I take my leave of you.
Shall not be long but I'll be here again.
Things at the worst will cease, or else climb upward
25 To what they were before. My pretty cousin,
Blessing upon you!

**LADY MACDUFF.** Fathered he is, and yet he's fatherless.

**ROSS.** I am so much a fool, should I stay longer,
It would be my disgrace and your discomfort.[8]
I take my leave at once.                    [*Exit* ROSS.]

30 **LADY MACDUFF.**            Sirrah, your father's dead;
And what will you do now? How will you live?

**SON.** As birds do, mother.

**LADY MACDUFF.**            What, with worms and flies?

**SON.** With what I get, I mean; and so do they.

**LADY MACDUFF.** Poor bird! thou'dst never fear the net nor
lime,[9]
35 The pitfall nor the gin.[10]

**SON.** Why should I, mother? Poor birds they are not set
for.
My father is not dead, for all your saying.

**LADY MACDUFF.** Yes, he is dead: how wilt thou do for a
father?

**SON.** Nay, how will you do for a husband?

40 **LADY MACDUFF.** Why, I can buy me twenty at any market.

**SON.** Then you'll buy 'em to sell[11] again.

**LADY MACDUFF.** Thou speak'st with all thy wit, and yet
i' faith,
With wit enough for thee.[12]

**SON.** Was my father a traitor, mother?

45 **LADY MACDUFF.** Ay, that he was.

**SON.** What is a traitor?

**LADY MACDUFF.** Why, one that swears and lies.[13]

**SON.** And be all traitors that do so?

**5. fits o' th' season:** Disorders of the time.

**6. when . . . ourselves:** When we are treated as traitors but do not know of any treason.

**7. when . . . fear:** Believe rumors based on our fears.

**8. It . . . discomfort:** I would disgrace myself and embarrass you by weeping.

**9. lime:** Birdlime, a sticky substance smeared on branches to catch birds.
**10. gin:** Trap.

**11. sell:** Betray.

**12. for thee:** For a child.

**13. swears and lies:** Takes an oath and breaks it.

**WOOD ENGRAVING AFTER SIR JOHN GILBERT**
*The Granger Collection*

**LADY MACDUFF.** Every one that does so is a traitor, and
    must be hanged.

50  **SON.** And must they all be hanged that swear and lie?

**LADY MACDUFF.** Every one.

**SON.** Who must hang them?

**LADY MACDUFF.** Why, the honest men.

**SON.** Then the liars and swearers are fools; for there are
55      liars and swearers enow[14] to beat the honest men
       and hang up them.

**LADY MACDUFF.** Now, God help thee, poor monkey! But
       how wilt thou do for a father?

**SON.** If he were dead, you'd weep for him. If you would
60      not, it were a good sign that I should quickly have a
       new father.

**LADY MACDUFF.** Poor prattler, how thou talk'st!

[*Enter a* MESSENGER.]

**MESSENGER.** Bless you, fair dame! I am not to you known,
       Though in your state of honor I am perfect.[15]
65      I doubt[16] some danger does approach you nearly:
       If you will take a homely[17] man's advice,
       Be not found here; hence, with your little ones.
       To fright you thus, methinks I am too savage;
       To do worse to you were fell[18] cruelty,
70      Which is too nigh your person. Heaven preserve you!
       I dare abide no longer.          [*Exit* MESSENGER.]

**LADY MACDUFF.**          Whither should I fly?
       I have done no harm. But I remember now
       I am in this earthly world, where to do harm
       Is often laudable, to do good sometime
75      Accounted dangerous folly. Why then, alas,
       Do I put up that womanly defense,
       To say I have done no harm?—What are these faces?

[*Enter* MURDERERS.]

**MURDERER.** Where is your husband?

**LADY MACDUFF.** I hope, in no place so unsanctified
       Where such as thou mayst find him.

80   **MURDERER.**                    He's a traitor.

**SON.** Thou li'st, thou shag-eared[19] villain!

**MURDERER.**                    What, you egg!

                    [*Stabbing him.*]

       Young fry[20] of treachery!

**SON.**               He has killed me, mother:
       Run away, I pray you! [*Dies.*]

                    [*Exit* LADY MACDUFF *crying "Murder!"*
                         *followed by* MURDERERS.]

14. **enow:** Enough.

15. **in . . . perfect:** I am
fully informed of your honorable rank.
16. **doubt:** Fear.
17. **homely:** Simple.

18. **fell:** Fierce.

19. **shag-eared:** Hairy-
eared.

20. **fry:** Offspring.

**Scene iii.** *England. Before the King's palace.*
[*Enter* MALCOLM *and* MACDUFF.]

    **MALCOLM.** Let us seek out some desolate shade, and
        there
      Weep our sad bosoms empty.

    **MACDUFF.**                 Let us rather
      Hold fast the mortal[1] sword, and like good men
      Bestride our down-fall'n birthdom.[2] Each new morn
5    New widows howl, new orphans cry, new sorrows
      Strike heaven on the face, that it resounds
      As if it felt with Scotland and yelled out
      Like syllable of dolor.[3]

    **MALCOLM.**             What I believe, I'll wail;
      What know, believe; and what I can redress,
10   As I shall find the time to friend,[4] I will.
      What you have spoke, it may be so perchance.
      This tyrant, whose sole[5] name blisters our tongues,
      Was once thought honest:[6] you have loved him well;
      He hath not touched you yet. I am young; but some-
        thing
15   You may deserve of him through me;[7] and wisdom[8]
      To offer up a weak, poor, innocent lamb
      T' appease an angry god.

    **MACDUFF.** I am not treacherous.

    **MALCOLM.**                But Macbeth is.
      A good and virtuous nature may recoil
20   In an imperial charge.[9] But I shall crave your pardon;
      That which you are, my thoughts cannot
        transpose:[10]
      Angels are bright still, though the brightest[11] fell:
      Though all things foul would wear[12] the brows of
        grace,
      Yet grace must still look so.[13]

    **MACDUFF.**             I have lost my hopes.

    **MALCOLM.** Perchance even there where I did find my
25      doubts.
      Why in that rawness[14] left you wife and child,
      Those precious motives, those strong knots of love,
      Without leave-taking? I pray you,
      Let not my jealousies[15] be your dishonors.
30   But mine own safeties.[16] You may be rightly just
      Whatever I shall think.

    **MACDUFF.**          Bleed, bleed, poor country:
      Great tyranny, lay thou thy basis sure,

**1. mortal:** Deadly.

**2. Bestride . . . birthdom:** Protectively stand over our native land.

**3. Like . . . dolor:** A similar cry of anguish.

**4. to friend:** Be friendly.

**5. sole:** Very.
**6. honest:** Good.

**7. deserve . . . me:** Earn by betraying me to Macbeth.
**8. wisdom:** It is wise.

**9. recoil . . . charge:** Give way to a royal command.
**10. transpose:** Transform.
**11. the brightest:** Lucifer.
**12. would wear:** Desire to wear.
**13. so:** Like itself.

**14. rawness:** Unprotected state or condition.

**15. jealousies:** Suspicions.
**16. safeties:** Protections.

For goodness dare not check thee: wear thou thy
 wrongs:
The title is affeered.[17] Fare thee well, lord:
35 I would not be the villain that thou think'st
For the whole space that's in the tyrant's grasp
And the rich East to boot.

**MALCOLM.**       Be not offended:
I speak not as in absolute fear of you.
I think our country sinks beneath the yoke;
40 It weeps, it bleeds, and each new day a gash
Is added to her wounds. I think withal
There would be hands uplifted in my right;[18]
And here from gracious England[19] have I offer
Of goodly thousands: but, for all this,
45 When I shall tread upon the tyrant's head,
Or wear it on my sword, yet my poor country
Shall have more vices than it had before,
More suffer, and more sundry ways than ever,
By him that shall succeed.

**MACDUFF.**      What should he be?

50 **MALCOLM.** It is myself I mean, in whom I know
All the particulars of vice so grafted[20]
That, when they shall be opened,[21] black Macbeth
Will seem as pure as snow, and the poor state
Esteem him as a lamb, being compared
With my confineless harms. [22]

55 **MACDUFF.**      Not in the legions
Of horrid hell can come a devil more damned
In evils to top Macbeth.

**MALCOLM.**      I grant him bloody,
Luxurious,[23] avaricious, false, deceitful,
Sudden,[24] malicious, smacking of every sin
60 That has a name: but there's no bottom, none,
In my voluptuousness: your wives, your daughters,
Your matrons and your maids, could not fill up
The cistern of my lust, and my desire
All continent impediments[25] would o'erbear,
65 That did oppose my will. Better Macbeth
Than such an one to reign.

**MACDUFF.**     Boundless intemperance
In nature[26] is a tyranny; it hath been
Th' untimely emptying of the happy throne,
And fall of many kings. But fear not yet
70 To take upon you what is yours: you may
Convey[27] your pleasures in a spacious plenty,

**17. affeered:** Legally confirmed.

**18. in my right:** On behalf of my claim.
**19. England:** The King of England.

**20. grafted:** Implanted.
**21. opened:** In bloom.

**22. confineless harms:** Unbounded evils.

**23. luxurious:** Lecherous.
**24. Sudden:** Violent.

**25. continent impediments:** Restraints.

**26. nature:** Man's nature.

**27. Convey:** Secretly manage.

And yet seem cold, the time you may so hoodwink.
We have willing dames enough. There cannot be
That vulture in you, to devour so many
As will to greatness dedicate themselves,
Finding it so inclined.

**MALCOLM.**                    With this there grows
In my most ill-composed affection[28] such
A stanchless[29] avarice that, were I King,
I should cut off the nobles for their lands,
Desire his jewels and this other's house:
And my more-having would be as a sauce
To make me hunger more, that I should forge
Quarrels unjust against the good and loyal,
Destroying them for wealth.

**MACDUFF.**                    This avarice
Sticks deeper, grows with more pernicious root
Than summer-seeming[30] lust, and it hath been
The sword of[31] our slain kings. Yet do not fear.
Scotland hath foisons[32] to fill up your will
Of your mere own.[33] All these are portable,[34]
With other graces weighed.

**MALCOLM.** But I have none: the king-becoming graces,
As justice, verity, temp'rance, stableness,
Bounty, perseverance, mercy, lowliness,
Devotion, patience, courage, fortitude,
I have no relish of them, but abound
In the division of each several crime,[35]
Acting it many ways. Nay, had I pow'r, I should
Pour the sweet milk of concord into hell,
Uproar the universal peace, confound[36]
All unity on earth.

**MACDUFF.**                    O Scotland, Scotland!

**MALCOLM.** If such a one be fit to govern, speak:
I am as I have spoken.

**MACDUFF.**                    Fit to govern!
No, not to live. O nation miserable!
With an untitled[37] tyrant bloody-sceptered,
When shalt thou see thy wholesome days again,
Since that the truest issue of thy throne[38]
By his own interdiction[39] stands accursed,
And does blaspheme his breed?[40] Thy royal father
Was a most sainted king: the queen that bore thee,
Oft'ner upon her knees than on her feet,
Died[41] every day she lived. Fare thee well!
These evils thou repeat'st upon thyself

**28. affection:** Character.
**29. stanchless:** Never-ending.

**30. summer-seeming:** Summerlike.
**31. of:** That killed.
**32. foisons** (foi′ zǝnz): Plenty.
**33. mere own:** Own property.
**34. portable:** Bearable.

**35. division . . . crime:** Variations of each kind of crime.

**36. confound:** Destroy.

**37. untitled:** Having no right to the throne.
**38. truest . . . throne:** Child of the true king.
**39. interdiction:** Exclusion.
**40. blaspheme his breed:** Slander his ancestry.
**41. Died:** Prepared for heaven.

Hath banished me from Scotland. O my breast,
Thy hope ends here!

**MALCOLM.**                Macduff, this noble passion,
115       Child of integrity, hath from my soul
Wiped the black scruples, reconciled my thoughts
To thy good truth and honor. Devilish Macbeth
By many of these trains[42] hath sought to win me
Into his power; and modest wisdom[43] plucks me
120       From over-credulous haste: but God above
Deal between thee and me! For even now
I put myself to thy direction, and
Unspeak mine own detraction,[44] here abjure
The taints and blames I laid upon myself,
125       For[45] strangers to my nature. I am yet
Unknown to woman, never was forsworn,
Scarcely have coveted what was mine own,
At no time broke my faith, would not betray
The devil to his fellow, and delight
130       No less in truth than life. My first false speaking
Was this upon myself. What I am truly,
Is thine and my poor country's to command:
Whither indeed, before thy here-approach,
Old Siward, with ten thousand warlike men,
135       Already at a point,[46] was setting forth.
Now we'll together, and the chance of goodness
Be like our warranted quarrel![47] Why are you silent?

**MACDUFF.** Such welcome and unwelcome things at once
'Tis hard to reconcile.

*[Enter a* DOCTOR.*]*

**MALCOLM.** Well, more anon. Comes the King forth, I pray
140       you?

**DOCTOR.** Ay, sir. There are a crew of wretched souls
That stay[48] his cure: their malady convinces
The great assay of art;[49] but at his touch,
Such sanctity hath heaven given his hand,
They presently amend.[50]

145    **MALCOLM.**                I thank you, doctor.
                                 *[Exit* DOCTOR.*]*

**MACDUFF.** What's the disease he means?

**MALCOLM.**                 'Tis called the evil:[51]
A most miraculous work in this good King,
Which often since my here-remain in England
I have seen him do. How he solicits heaven,
150       Himself best knows: but strangely-visited people,

**42. trains:** Enticements.
**43. modest wisdom:** Prudence.

**44. detraction:** Slander.

**45. For:** As.

**46. at a point:** Prepared.

**47. the chance . . . quarrel:** May our chance of success equal the justice of our cause.

**48. stay:** Wait for.
**49. convinces . . . art:** Defies the efforts of medical science.
**50. presently amend:** Immediately recover.

**51. evil:** Scrofula (skrof′ yə lə), a skin disease called "the king's evil" because it was believed that it could be cured by the king's touch.

All swoll'n and ulcerous, pitiful to the eye,
The mere[52] despair of surgery, he cures,
Hanging a golden stamp[53] about their necks,
Put on with holy prayers: and 'tis spoken,
155  To the succeeding royalty he leaves
The healing benediction. With this strange virtue
He hath a heavenly gift of prophecy,
And sundry blessings hang about his throne
That speak him full of grace.

**52. mere:** Utter.
**53. stamp:** Coin.

[*Enter* ROSS.]

**MACDUFF.**                                    See, who comes here?

160  **MALCOLM.** My countryman; but yet I know him not.

**MACDUFF.** My ever gentle[54] cousin, welcome hither.

**54. gentle:** Noble.

**MALCOLM.** I know him now: good God, betimes[55] remove
The means that makes us strangers!

**55. betimes:** Quickly.

**ROSS.**                                    Sir, amen.

**MACDUFF.** Stands Scotland where it did?

**ROSS.**                                    Alas, poor country!
165  Almost afraid to know itself! It cannot
Be called our mother but our grave, where nothing[56]
But who knows nothing is once seen to smile;
Where sighs and groans, and shrieks that rent the
       air,
Are made, not marked, where violent sorrow seems
170  A modern ecstasy.[57] The dead man's knell
Is there scarce asked for who,[58] and good men's lives
Expire before the flowers in their caps,
Dying or ere they sicken.

**56. nothing:** No one.

**57. modern ecstasy:** Ordinary emotion.
**58. The dead . . . who:** People can no longer keep track of Macbeth's victims.

**MACDUFF.**                                    O, relation
Too nice,[59] and yet too true!

**59. nice:** Exact.

**MALCOLM.**                                    What's the newest grief?

175  **ROSS.** That of an hour's age doth hiss the speaker;[60]
Each minute teems[61] a new one.

**60. That . . . speaker:** The report of the grief of an hour ago is hissed as stale news.
**61. teems:** Gives birth to.

**MACDUFF.**                                    How does my wife?

**ROSS.** Why, well.

**MACDUFF.**        And all my children?

**ROSS.**                                    Well too.

**MACDUFF.** The tyrant has not battered at their peace?

**ROSS.** No; they were well at peace when I did leave 'em.

180  **MACDUFF.** Be not a niggard of your speech: how goes 't?

**ROSS.** When I came hither to transport the tidings,
Which I have heavily borne, there ran a rumor
Of many worthy fellows that were out;[62]
Which was to my belief witnessed[63] the rather,
185  For that I saw the tyrant's power[64] afoot.
Now is the time of help. Your eye in Scotland
Would create soldiers, make our women fight,
To doff[65] their dire distresses.

**MALCOLM.**                              Be 't their comfort
We are coming thither. Gracious England hath
190  Lent us good Siward and ten thousand men;
An older and a better soldier none
That Christendom gives out.

**ROSS.**                              Would I could answer
This comfort with the like! But I have words
That would be howled out in the desert air,
Where hearing should not latch[66] them.

195  **MACDUFF.**                              What concern they?
The general cause or is it a fee-grief[67]
Due to some single breast?

**ROSS.**                              No mind that's honest
But in it shares some woe, though the main part
Pertains to you alone.

**MACDUFF.**                    If it be mine,
200  Keep it not from me, quickly let me have it.

**ROSS.** Let not your ears despise my tongue for ever,
Which shall possess them with the heaviest sound
That ever yet they heard.

**MACDUFF.**                    Humh! I guess at it.

**ROSS.** Your castle is surprised; your wife and babes
205  Savagely slaughtered. To relate the manner,
Were, on the quarry[68] of these murdered deer,
To add the death of you.

**MALCOLM.**                    Merciful heaven!
What, man! Ne'er pull your hat upon your brows;
Give sorrow words. The grief that does not speak
210  Whispers the o'er-fraught[69] heart and bids it break.

**MACDUFF.** My children too?

**ROSS.**                              Wife, children, servants, all
That could be found.

62. **out:** In rebellion.
63. **witnessed:** Confirmed.
64. **power:** Army.

65. **doff:** Put off.

66. **latch:** Catch.

67. **fee-grief:** Personal grief.

68. **quarry:** Heap of game slain in a hunt.

69. **o'er-fraught:** Overburdened.

**MACDUFF.** And I must be from thence!
My wife killed too?

**ROSS.** I have said.

**MALCOLM.** Be comforted.
Let's make us med'cines of our great revenge,
215 To cure this deadly grief.

**MACDUFF.** He has no children. All my pretty ones?
Did you say all? O hell-kite![70] All?
What, all my pretty chickens and their dam
At one fell swoop?

**MALCOLM.** Dispute it[71] like a man.

220 **MACDUFF.** I shall do so;
But I must also feel it as a man.
I cannot but remember such things were,
That were most precious to me. Did heaven look on,
And would not take their part? Sinful Macduff,
225 They were all struck for thee! Naught[72] that I am,
Not for their own demerits but for mine
Fell slaughter on their souls. Heaven rest them now!

**MALCOLM.** Be this the whetstone of your sword. Let grief
Convert to anger; blunt not the heart, enrage it.

230 **MACDUFF.** O, I could play the woman with mine eyes,
And braggart with my tongue! But, gentle heavens,
Cut short all intermission; front to front[73]
Bring thou this fiend of Scotland and myself;
Within my sword's length set him. If he 'scape,
Heaven forgive him too!

**MALCOLM.** This time goes manly.
Come, go we to the King. Our power is ready;
Our lack is nothing but our leave.[74] Macbeth
Is ripe for shaking, and the pow'rs above
Put on their instruments.[75] Receive what cheer you
may.
240 The night is long that never finds the day. [*Exit.*]

---

**70. hell-kite:** Hellish bird of prey.

**71. Dispute it:** Counter your grief.

**72. Naught:** Wicked.

**73. front to front:** Face to face.

**74. Our . . . leave:** We need only to take our leave.
**75. Put . . . instruments:** Urge us onward as their agents.

## THINKING ABOUT THE SELECTION

### Recalling

1. (a) What does the first apparition tell Macbeth? (b) How does the prophecy of the second apparition seem to contradict that of the first? (c) What does the third apparition promise?
2. (a) What question do the witches refuse to answer? (b) What vision do they parade before Macbeth?
3. (a) Where does Lennox say Macduff has gone? (b) On learning of Macduff's absence, what does Macbeth decide to do to Macduff's family?
4. (a) In his conversation with Macduff, why does Malcolm pretend to have all of Macbeth's vices and more? (b) What convinces Malcolm that Macduff is trustworthy?
5. (a) What good news about "gracious England" does Ross bring Malcolm? (b) What bad news does Ross bring Macduff?

### Interpreting

6. Why does Macbeth readily accept the predictions made by the second and third apparitions?
7. (a) In the witches' procession of kings, why do some kings carry double and triple scepters? (b) Why does Banquo carry a mirror?
8. (a) What is Macbeth's reason for killing Macduff's wife and child? (b) How do these murders differ from the previous ones?
9. How would you describe Macbeth's character at this point in the play?
10. How is Malcolm's character revealed in the dialogue with Macduff in Scene iii?
11. Based on Macduff's reaction to the murder of his wife and son, how would you describe Macduff's character?

### Applying

12. In staging *Macbeth*, some producers eliminate Scene ii, the murder of Lady Macduff and her son. (a) What reasons do you think they give for doing so? (b) What is your reaction to that kind of cut?

## ANALYZING LITERATURE

### Understanding Plot Development

**Plot** is a series of related incidents progressing through a period of *rising action* to a *climax*.
1. How do the apparitions' prophecies in Scene i prepare the audience for the plot developments to follow?
2. By the end of Act IV, the character of each major living participant—Macbeth, Lady Macbeth, Malcolm, Macduff, even Ross—has been made clear. How has this portrayal of character laid the groundwork for later events?

## CRITICAL THINKING AND READING

### Reading Between the Lines

In a play as carefully crafted as *Macbeth*, there are very few insignificant lines. For instance, in Act IV when one of the witches says, "'Tis time, 'tis time," the reader should think, "Time for what? Time for the witches to exact their price from Macbeth?"

Even today, critics have differing opinions about the character of Ross, a man who can be evaluated only by reading between the lines. What is your opinion of Ross's character—is he a toadying politician, a loyal Scot, or something else? Defend your assessment.

## THINKING AND WRITING

### Writing About Macbeth's Tragic Flaw

Macbeth is a tragic hero, a person of high rank who is brought to eventual ruin by a flaw in his character. Macbeth's tragic flaw is his ambition, which leads him into a series of bloody and increasingly indefensible acts. Write a composition in which you relate Macbeth's character to the plot development of the play. First make some notes on how Macbeth's personality and motivations get him into trouble and prevent him from getting out. Then write a first draft. When you revise, make sure each of your major points ties Macbeth's character to a plot element.

# GUIDE FOR INTERPRETING

## Macbeth, Act V

**Theme.** The theme of a literary work is its central idea, an idea that can usually be expressed as a general statement about life. Every element in a work of literature—plot, character, setting, and so on—contributes to the theme. In many works of literature, including *Macbeth,* the theme pertains not only to the lives of the characters on stage but also, and more importantly, to the lives of the members of the audience. Sometimes it is possible to state a theme in one sentence, although complex literary works may require a lengthier explanation. A theme may be directly stated, but more commonly it is implied.

Jot down a few lines from Act V of *Macbeth* (and perhaps from earlier acts) that seem to imply the theme of the play. While the theme is not directly stated, the dialogue gives many indications that you will find helpful. Remember that the theme cannot be expressed in a single word or phrase. It requires at least a complete sentence and often more.

The theme of *Macbeth* is reinforced by the imagery of blood that permeates the play. Critic Mark Von Doren claimed,

> Never in a play has there been so much of this substance, and never has it been so sickening . . . The second scene opens with a messenger running in to Duncan red with wounds. And blood darkens every scene thereafter. It is not bright red, nor does it run freely and wash away . . . It is so real that we see, feel, and smell it on everything. And it sticks. "This is a sorry sight," says Macbeth as he comes from Duncan's murder, staring at his hands. He had not thought there would be so much blood on them, or that it would stay like that. Lady Macbeth is for washing the "filthy witness" off, but Macbeth knows that all great Neptune's oceans will not make him clean; rather his hand, plunged into the green, will make it all one red. The blood of the play is everywhere physical in its looks and gross in its quantity.

# Act V

**Scene i.** *Dunsinane. In the castle.*
[*Enter a* DOCTOR OF PHYSIC *and a* WAITING-GENTLEWOMAN.]

**DOCTOR.** I have two nights watched with you, but can perceive no truth in your report. When was it she last walked?

5   **GENTLEWOMAN.** Since his Majesty went into the field.[1] I have seen her rise from her bed, throw her nightgown upon her, unlock her closet,[2] take forth paper, fold it, write upon 't, read it, afterwards seal it, and again return to bed; yet all this while in a most fast sleep.

10   **DOCTOR.** A great perturbation in nature, to receive at once the benefit of sleep and do the effects of watching![3] In this slumb'ry agitation, besides her walking and other actual performances, what, at any time, have you heard her say?

15   **GENTLEWOMAN.** That, sir, which I will not report after her.

**DOCTOR.** You may to me, and 'tis most meet[4] you should.

**GENTLEWOMAN.** Neither to you nor anyone, having no witness to confirm my speech.

[*Enter* LADY MACBETH, *with a taper.*]

20   Lo you, here she comes! This is her very guise,[5] and, upon my life, fast asleep! Observe her; stand close.[6]

**DOCTOR.** How came she by that light?

**GENTLEWOMAN.** Why, it stood by her. She has light by her continually. 'Tis her command.

25   **DOCTOR.** You see, her eyes are open.

**GENTLEWOMAN.** Ay, but their sense[7] are shut.

**DOCTOR.** What is it she does now? Look, how she rubs her hands.

30   **GENTLEWOMAN.** It is an accustomed action with her, to seem thus washing her hands: I have known her continue in this a quarter of an hour.

**LADY MACBETH.** Yet here's a spot.

**DOCTOR.** Hark! She speaks. I will set down what comes from her, to satisfy[8] my remembrance the more
35   strongly.

**1. field:** Battlefield.

**2. closet:** Chest.

**3. effects of watching:** Deeds of one awake.

**4. meet:** Suitable.

**5. guise:** Custom.

**6. close:** Hidden.

**7. sense:** Powers of sight.

**8. satisfy:** Support.

**MRS. SIDDONS AS LADY MACBETH**
*G. H. Harlow*
*Garrick Club*
*E. T. Archive*

**LADY MACBETH.** Out, damned spot! Out, I say! One: two: why, then 'tis time to do 't. Hell is murky. Fie, my lord, fie! A soldier, and afeard? What need we fear who knows it, when none can call our pow'r to accompt?[9] Yet who would have thought the old man to have had so much blood in him?

40

**9. to accompt:** Into account.

**DOCTOR.** Do you mark that?

**LADY MACBETH.** The Thane of Fife had a wife. Where is she now? What, will these hands ne'er be clean? No more o' that, my lord, no more o' that! You mar all with this starting.

**DOCTOR.** Go to, go to! You have known what you should not.

**GENTLEWOMAN.** She has spoke what she should not, I am sure of that. Heaven knows what she has known.

**LADY MACBETH.** Here's the smell of the blood still. All the perfumes of Arabia will not sweeten this little hand. Oh, oh, oh!

**DOCTOR.** What a sigh is there! The heart is sorely charged.[10]

    **10. charged:** Burdened.

**GENTLEWOMAN.** I would not have such a heart in my bosom for the dignity[11] of the whole body.

    **11. dignity:** Worth.

**DOCTOR.** Well, well, well—

**GENTLEWOMAN.** Pray God it be, sir.

**DOCTOR.** This disease is beyond my practice. Yet I have known those which have walked in their sleep who have died holily in their beds.

**LADY MACBETH.** Wash your hands; put on your nightgown; look not so pale! I tell you yet again, Banquo's buried. He cannot come out on 's[12] grave.

    **12. on 's:** Of his.

**DOCTOR.** Even so?

**LADY MACBETH.** To bed, to bed! There's knocking at the gate. Come, come, come, come, give me your hand! What's done cannot be undone. To bed, to bed, to bed!     [*Exit* LADY MACBETH.]

**DOCTOR.** Will she go now to bed?

**GENTLEWOMAN.** Directly.

**DOCTOR.** Foul whisp'rings are abroad. Unnatural deeds
Do breed unnatural troubles. Infected minds
To their deaf pillows will discharge their secrets.
More needs she the divine than the physician.
God, God forgive us all! Look after her;
Remove from her the means of all annoyance,[13]

    **13. annoyance:** Injury.

And still keep eyes upon her. So good night.
My mind she has mated[14] and amazed my sight:

    **14. mated:** Baffled.

I think, but dare not speak.

**GENTLEWOMAN.**            Good night, good doctor.
                         [*Exit.*]

**Scene ii.** *The country near Dunsinane.*
[*Drum and colors. Enter* MENTEITH, CAITHNESS, ANGUS, LENNOX,
SOLDIERS.]

MENTEITH. The English pow'r[1] is near, led on by
    Malcolm,
    His uncle Siward and the good Macduff.
    Revenges burn in them; for their dear causes
    Would to the bleeding and the grim alarm
    Excite the mortified man.[2]

5  ANGUS.                Near Birnam Wood
    Shall we well meet them; that way are they coming.

CAITHNESS. Who knows if Donalbain be with his
    brother?

LENNOX. For certain, sir, he is not. I have a file[3]
    Of all the gentry: there is Siward's son,
10    And many unrough[4] youths that even now
    Protest[5] their first of manhood.

MENTEITH.              What does the tyrant?

CAITHNESS. Great Dunsinane he strongly fortifies.
    Some say he's mad; others, that lesser hate him,
    Do call it valiant fury: but, for certain,
15    He cannot buckle his distempered cause
    Within the belt of rule.[6]

ANGUS.            Now does he feel
    His secret murders sticking on his hands;
    Now minutely revolts upbraid his faith-breach.[7]
    Those he commands move only in command,
20    Nothing in love. Now does he feel his title
    Hang loose about him, like a giant's robe
    Upon a dwarfish thief.

MENTEITH.          Who then shall blame
    His pestered[8] senses to recoil and start,
    When all that is within him does condemn
    Itself for being there?

25  CAITHNESS.         Well, march we on,
    To give obedience where 'tis truly owed.
    Meet we the med'cine of the sickly weal,[9]
    And with him pour we, in our country's purge,
    Each drop of us.[10]

LENNOX.          Or so much as it needs
30    To dew the sovereign flower and drown the weeds.[11]
    Make we our march towards Birnam.

                       [*Exit, marching.*]

---

**1. pow'r:** Army.

**2. Would . . . man:** Would incite a dead man to join the bloody and grim call to arms.

**3. file:** List.

**4. unrough:** Beardless.
**5. Protest:** Assert.

**6. rule:** Self-control.

**7. minutely . . . faith-breach:** Every minute revolts rebuke his disloyalty.

**8. pestered:** Tormented.

**9. med'cine . . . weal:** Malcolm and his supporters are "the med'cine" that will heal "the sickly" commonwealth.
**10. Each . . . us:** Every last drop of our blood.

**11. dew . . . weeds:** Water the royal flower (Malcolm) and drown the weeds (Macbeth).

**Scene iii.** *Dunsinane. In the castle.*
[*Enter* MACBETH, DOCTOR, *and* ATTENDANTS.]

MACBETH. Bring me no more reports; let them fly all![1]
    Till Birnam Wood remove to Dunsinane
    I cannot taint[2] with fear. What's the boy Malcolm?
    Was he not born of woman? The spirits that know
5    All mortal consequences[3] have pronounced me thus:
    "Fear not, Macbeth; no man that's born of woman
    Shall e'er have power upon thee." Then fly, false thanes,
    And mingle with the English epicures.[4]
    The mind I sway[5] by and the heart I bear
10    Shall never sag with doubt nor shake with fear.

[*Enter* SERVANT.]

    The devil damn thee black, thou cream-faced loon.[6]
    Where got'st thou that goose look?

SERVANT. There is ten thousand—

MACBETH.                    Geese, villain?

SERVANT.                       Soldiers, sir.

MACBETH. Go prick thy face and over-red thy fear.
15    Thou lily-livered boy. What soldiers, patch?[7]
    Death of thy soul! Those linen[8] cheeks of thine
    Are counselors to fear. What soldiers, whey-face?

SERVANT. The English force, so please you.

MACBETH. Take thy face hence.         [*Exit* SERVANT.]
              Seyton!—I am sick at heart.
20    When I behold—Seyton, I say!—This push[9]
    Will cheer me ever, or disseat[10] me now.
    I have lived long enough. My way of life
    Is fall'n into the sear,[11] the yellow leaf,
    And that which should accompany old age,
25    As honor, love, obedience, troops of friends,
    I must not look to have; but, in their stead,
    Curses not loud but deep, mouth-honor, breath,
    Which the poor heart would fain deny, and dare not.
    Seyton!

[*Enter* SEYTON.]

SEYTON. What's your gracious pleasure?

30  MACBETH.                   What news more?

SEYTON. All is confirmed, my lord, which was reported.

1. **let . . . all:** Let them all desert me!

2. **taint:** Become infected

3. **mortal consequences:** Future human events.

4. **epicures:** Gluttons.
5. **sway:** Move.

6. **loon:** Fool.

7. **patch:** Fool.
8. **linen:** Pale as linen.

9. **push:** Effort.
10. **disseat:** Unthrone.

11. **the sear:** A withered state.

**MACBETH.** I'll fight, till from my bones my flesh be
hacked.
Give me my armor.

**SEYTON.**                      'Tis not needed yet.

**MACBETH.** I'll put it on.
35    Send out moe[12] horses, skirr[13] the country round.
Hang those that talk of fear. Give me mine armor.
How does your patient, doctor?

**DOCTOR.**                           Not so sick, my lord,
As she is troubled with thick-coming fancies
That keep her from her rest.

**MACBETH.**                            Cure her of that.
40    Canst thou not minister to a mind diseased,
Pluck from the memory a rooted sorrow,
Raze out[14] the written troubles of the brain,
And with some sweet oblivious antidote
Cleanse the stuffed bosom of that perilous stuff
Which weighs upon the heart?

45  **DOCTOR.**                             Therein the patient
Must minister to himself.

**MACBETH.** Throw physic[15] to the dogs, I'll none of it.
Come, put mine armor on. Give me my staff.
Seyton, send out.—Doctor, the thanes fly from
me.—
50    Come, sir, dispatch. If thou couldst, doctor, cast
The water[16] of my land, find her disease
And purge it to a sound and pristine health,
I would applaud thee to the very echo,
That should applaud again.—Pull 't off,[17] I say.—
55    What rhubarb, senna, or what purgative drug,
Would scour these English hence? Hear'st thou of
them?

**DOCTOR.** Ay, my good lord; your royal preparation
Makes us hear something.

**MACBETH.**                           Bring it[18] after me.
I will not be afraid of death and bane[19]
60    Till Birnam Forest come to Dunsinane.

**DOCTOR.** [*Aside*] Were I from Dunsinane away and clear,
Profit again should hardly draw me here.      [*Exit.*]

*Scene iv.* *Country near Birnam Wood.*
[*Drum and colors. Enter* MALCOLM, SIWARD, MACDUFF, SIWARD's SON,
MENTEITH, CAITHNESS, ANGUS, *and* SOLDIERS, *marching.*]

**12. moe:** More.
**13. skirr:** Scour.

**14. Raze out:** Erase.

**15. physic:** Medicine.

**16. cast the water:** Diagnose the illness.

**17. Pull 't off:** Pull off a piece of armor which has been put on incorrectly in Macbeth's haste.

**18. it:** His armor.
**19. bane:** Destruction.

**MALCOLM.** Cousins, I hope the days are near at hand
    That chambers will be safe.[1]

**MENTEITH.**                        We doubt it nothing.

**SIWARD.** What wood is this before us?

**MENTEITH.**                   The Wood of Birnam.

**MALCOLM.** Let every soldier hew him down a bough
5    And bear 't before him. Thereby shall we shadow[2]
    The numbers of our host, and make discovery[3]
    Err in report of us.

**SOLDIERS.**              It shall be done.

**SIWARD.** We learn no other but the confident tyrant
    Keeps still in Dunsinane, and will endure
    Our setting down before 't.[4]

10 **MALCOLM.**                'Tis his main hope,
    For where there is advantage to be given
    Both more and less[5] have given him the revolt,
    And none serve with him but constrainèd things
    Whose hearts are absent too.

**MACDUFF.**             Let our just censures
15    Attend the true event,[6] and put we on
    Industrious soldiership.

**SIWARD.**             The time approaches,
    That will with due decision make us know
    What we shall say we have and what we owe.[7]
    Thoughts speculative their unsure hopes relate,
20    But certain issue strokes must arbitrate:[8]
    Towards which advance the war.[9] [*Exit, marching.*]

---

**Scene v.** *Dunsinane. Within the castle.*
[*Enter* MACBETH, SEYTON, *and* SOLDIERS, *with drum and colors.*]

**MACBETH.** Hang out our banners on the outward walls.
    The cry is still "They come!" Our castle's strength
    Will laugh a siege to scorn. Here let them lie
    Till famine and the ague[1] eat them up.
5    Were they not forced[2] with those that should be ours,
    We might have met them dareful,[3] beard to beard,
    And beat them backward home.
               [*A cry within of women.*]
                      What is that noise?

**SEYTON.** It is the cry of women, my good lord.    [*Exit.*]

---

1. **That . . . safe:** That people will be safe in their own homes.

2. **shadow:** Conceal.

3. **discovery:** Those who see us.

4. **setting down before 't:** Laying siege to it.

5. **more and less:** People of high and low rank.

6. **our . . . event:** True judgment await the actual outcome.

7. **owe:** Own.

8. **strokes . . . arbitrate:** Fighting must decide.
9. **war:** Army.

1. **ague:** Fever.
2. **forced:** Reinforced.
3. **dareful:** Boldly.

**MACBETH.** I have almost forgot the taste of fears:
10    The time has been, my senses would have cooled
      To hear a night-shriek, and my fell⁴ of hair
      Would at a dismal treatise⁵ rouse and stir
      As life were in 't. I have supped full with horrors.
      Direness, familiar to my slaughterous thoughts,
      Cannot once start⁶ me.

[*Enter* SEYTON.]

15                                    Wherefore was that cry?

**SEYTON.** The Queen, my lord, is dead.

**MACBETH.** She should⁷ have died hereafter;
      There would have been a time for such a word.⁸
      Tomorrow, and tomorrow, and tomorrow
20    Creeps in this petty pace from day to day,
      To the last syllable of recorded time;
      And all our yesterdays have lighted fools
      The way to dusty death. Out, out, brief candle!
      Life's but a walking shadow, a poor player
25    That struts and frets his hour upon the stage
      And then is heard no more. It is a tale
      Told by an idiot, full of sound and fury
      Signifying nothing.

[*Enter a* MESSENGER.]

      Thou com'st to use thy tongue; thy story quickly!

30    **MESSENGER.** Gracious my lord,
      I should report that which I say I saw,
      But know not how to do 't.

**MACBETH.**                      Well, say, sir.

**MESSENGER.** As I did stand my watch upon the hill,
      I looked toward Birnam, and anon, methought,
      The wood began to move.

35    **MACBETH.**               Liar and slave!

**MESSENGER.** Let me endure your wrath, if 't be not so.
      Within this three mile may you see it coming;
      I say a moving grove.

**MACBETH.**               If thou speak'st false,
      Upon the next tree shalt thou hang alive,
40    Till famine cling⁹ thee. If thy speech be sooth,¹⁰
      I care not if thou dost for me as much.
      I pull in resolution, and begin
      To doubt th' equivocation of the fiend
      That lies like truth: "Fear not, till Birnam Wood

**4. fell:** Scalp.
**5. treatise:** Story.

**6. start:** Startle.

**7. should:** Inevitably would.
**8. word:** Message.

**9. cling:** Wither.
**10. sooth:** Truth.

45  Do come to Dunsinane!" And now a wood
    Comes toward Dunsinane. Arm, arm, and out!
    If this which he avouches[11] does appear,
    There is nor flying hence nor tarrying here.
    I 'gin to be aweary of the sun,
50  And wish th' estate o' th' world were now undone.
    Ring the alarum bell! Blow wind, come wrack!
    At least we'll die with harness[12] on our back. [*Exit.*]

**11. avouches:** Asserts.

**12. harness:** Armor.

**Scene vi.** *Dunsinane. Before the castle.*
[*Drum and colors. Enter* MALCOLM, SIWARD, MACDUFF, *and their army, with boughs.*]

MALCOLM. Now near enough. Your leavy[1] screens throw
    down,
    And show like those you are. You, worthy uncle,
    Shall, with my cousin, your right noble son,
    Lead our first battle.[2] Worthy Macduff and we
5   Shall take upon 's what else remains to do,
    According to our order.[3]

**1. leavy:** Leafy.

**2. battle:** Battalion.

**3. order:** Plan.

SIWARD.                              Fare you well.
    Do we but find the tyrant's power[4] tonight,
    Let us be beaten, if we cannot fight.

**4. power:** Forces.

MACDUFF. Make all our trumpets speak; give them all
    breath,
10  Those clamorous harbingers of blood and death.
                    [*Exit. Alarums continued.*]

**Scene vii.** *Another part of the field.*
[*Enter* MACBETH.]

MACBETH. They have tied me to a stake; I cannot fly,
    But bearlike I must fight the course.[1] What's he
    That was not born of woman? Such a one
    Am I to fear, or none.

**1. bearlike . . . course:** Like a bear chained to a stake being attacked by dogs, I must fight until the end.

[*Enter* YOUNG SIWARD.]

YOUNG SIWARD. What is thy name?

5   MACBETH.                     Thou'lt be afraid to hear it.

YOUNG SIWARD. No; though thou call'st thyself a hotter
    name
    Than any is in hell.

MACBETH.                     My name's Macbeth.

YOUNG SIWARD. The devil himself could not pronounce a
    title
    More hateful to mine ear.

MACBETH.                     No, nor more fearful.

**YOUNG SIWARD.** Thou liest, abhorrèd tyrant; with my
10       sword
         I'll prove the lie thou speak'st.
                    [*Fight, and* YOUNG SIWARD *slain.*]

**MACBETH.**                    Thou wast born of woman.
         But swords I smile at, weapons laugh to scorn,
         Brandished by man that's of a woman born.   [*Exit.*]

[*Alarums. Enter* MACDUFF.]

**MACDUFF.** That way the noise is. Tyrant, show thy face!
15       If thou be'st slain and with no stroke of mine,
         My wife and children's ghosts will haunt me still.
         I cannot strike at wretched kerns, whose arms
         Are hired to bear their staves.[2] Either thou, Macbeth,
         Or else my sword, with an unbattered edge,
20       I sheathe again undeeded.[3] There thou shouldst be;
         By this great clatter, one of greatest note
         Seems bruited.[4] Let me find him, Fortune!
         And more I beg not.                [*Exit. Alarums.*]

[*Enter* MALCOLM *and* SIWARD.]

**SIWARD.** This way, my lord. The castle's gently
         rend'red:[5]
25       The tyrant's people on both sides do fight;
         The noble thanes do bravely in the war;
         The day almost itself professes yours,
         And little is to do.

**MALCOLM.**              We have met with foes
         That strike beside us.[6]

**SIWARD.**                    Enter, sir, the castle.
                         [*Exit. Alarum.*]

**Scene viii.** *Another part of the field.*
[*Enter* MACBETH.]

**MACBETH.** Why should I play the Roman fool, and die
         On mine own sword?[1] Whiles I see lives,[2] the gashes
         Do better upon them.

[*Enter* MACDUFF.]

**MACDUFF.**              Turn, hell-hound, turn!

**MACBETH.** Of all men else I have avoided thee.
5        But get thee back! My soul is too much charged
         With blood of thine already.

**MACDUFF.**              I have no words:
         My voice is in my sword, thou bloodier villain
         Than terms can give thee out![3]
                    [*Fight. Alarum.*]

2. **staves:** Spears.

3. **undeeded:** Unused.

4. **bruited:** Reported.

5. **gently rend'red:** Easily
surrendered.

6. **strike . . . us:** Deliberately miss us.

1. **play . . . sword:** Die like
Brutus or Cassius, who
killed themselves with their
own swords in the moment
of defeat.
2. **Whiles . . . lives:** So
long as I see living men.

3. **terms . . . out:** Words
can describe you.

**MACBETH.** Thou losest labor:
As easy mayst thou the intrenchant[4] air
10    With thy keen sword impress[5] as make me bleed:
Let fall thy blade on vulnerable crests;
I bear a charmèd life, which must not yield
To one of woman born.

**MACDUFF.** Despair thy charm,
And let the angel[6] whom thou still hast served
15    Tell thee, Macduff was from his mother's womb
Untimely ripped.[7]

**MACBETH.** Accursèd be that tongue that tells me so,
For it hath cowed my better part of man![8]
And be these juggling fiends no more believed,
20    That palter[9] with us in a double sense;
That keep the word of promise to our ear,
And break it to our hope. I'll not fight with thee.

**MACDUFF.** Then yield thee, coward,
And live to be the show and gaze o' th' time:[10]
25    We'll have thee, as our rarer monsters[11] are,
Painted upon a pole,[12] and underwrit,
"Here may you see the tyrant."

**MACBETH.** I will not yield,
To kiss the ground before young Malcolm's feet,
And to be baited with the rabble's curse.
30    Though Birnam Wood be come to Dunsinane,
And thou opposed, being of no woman born,
Yet I will try the last. Before my body
I throw my warlike shield. Lay on, Macduff;
And damned be him that first cries "Hold, enough!"
                [*Exit, fighting. Alarums.*]

[*Re-enter fighting, and* MACBETH *slain. Exit* MACDUFF, *with* MACBETH. *Retreat and flourish.*[13] *Enter, with drum and colors,* MALCOLM, SIWARD, ROSS, THANES, *and* SOLDIERS.]

35   **MALCOLM.** I would the friends we miss were safe arrived.

**SIWARD.** Some must go off;[14] and yet, by these I see,
So great a day as this is cheaply bought.

**MALCOLM.** Macduff is missing, and your noble son.

**ROSS.** Your son, my lord, has paid a soldier's debt:
40    He only lived but till he was a man;
The which no sooner had his prowess confirmed
In the unshrinking station[15] where he fought,
But like a man he died.

**SIWARD.** Then he is dead?

**4. intrenchant:** Incapable of being cut.
**5. impress:** Make a dent in.

**6. angel:** Fallen angel, fiend.

**7. his . . . ripped:** Macduff's mother died before giving birth to him.

**8. better . . . man:** Courage.
**9. palter:** Juggle.

**10. gaze o' th' time:** Spectacle of the age.
**11. monsters:** Freaks.
**12. Painted . . . pole:** Pictured on a banner stuck on a pole by a showman's booth.

**13. Retreat and flourish:** Trumpet call to withdraw and fanfare.

**14. go off:** Die.

**15. unshrinking station:** Place where he stood firmly.

**ROSS.** Ay, and brought off the field. Your cause of sorrow
45    Must not be measured by his worth, for then
       It hath no end.

**SIWARD.**                    Had he his hurts before?

**ROSS.** Ay, on the front.

**SIWARD.**                         Why then, God's soldier be he!
       Had I as many sons as I have hairs,
       I would not wish them to a fairer death:
       And so his knell is knolled.

50    **MALCOLM.**                         He's worth more sorrow,
       And that I'll spend for him.

**SIWARD.**                         He's worth no more:
       They say he parted well and paid his score:
       And so God be with him! Here comes newer comfort.

[*Enter* MACDUFF, *with* MACBETH'S *head.*]

**MACDUFF.** Hail, King! for so thou art: behold, where
              stands
55    Th' usurper's cursèd head. The time is free.[16]
       I see thee compassed with thy kingdom's pearl,[17]
       That speak my salutation in their minds,
       Whose voices I desire aloud with mine:
       Hail, King of Scotland!

**ALL.**                         Hail, King of Scotland!

[*Flourish.*]

60    **MALCOLM.** We shall not spend a large expense of time
       Before we reckon with your several loves,[18]
       And make us even with you.[19] My thanes and kins-
              men,
       Henceforth be earls, the first that ever Scotland
       In such an honor named. What's more to do,
65    Which would be planted newly with the time[20]—
       As calling home our exiled friends abroad
       That fled the snares of watchful tyranny,
       Producing forth the cruel ministers
       Of this dead butcher and his fiendlike queen,
70    Who, as 'tis thought, by self and violent hands
       Took off her life—this, and what needful else
       That calls upon us, by the grace of Grace
       We will perform in measure, time, and place:[21]
       So thanks to all at once and to each one,
       Whom we invite to see us crowned at Scone.

                         [*Flourish. Exit all.*]

**16. The . . . free:** Our
country is liberated.
**17. compassed . . . pearl:**
Surrounded by the noblest
people in the kingdom.

**18. reckon . . . loves:** Reward each of you for your
devotion.
**19. make . . . you:** Pay
what we owe you.

**20. What's . . . time:**
What remains to be done at
the beginning of this new
age.

**21. in measure . . . place:**
Fittingly at the appropriate
time and place.

## THINKING ABOUT THE SELECTION
### Recalling

1. (a) Why are the doctor and the gentlewoman watching Lady Macbeth? (b) What does the gentlewoman refuse to tell the doctor?
2. (a) While Lady Macbeth is sleepwalking, to to what three prior events does she refer? (b) To which event does she keep coming back?
3. (a) In Scene ii what are the four Scottish lords preparing to do? (b) Where will they meet the English forces?
4. (a) What news does Seyton bring Macbeth in Scene v? (b) What in the messenger's report makes Macbeth fear that the apparitions' second prophecy is coming true?
5. (a) In Scene viii why does Macbeth tell Macduff he does not wish to fight him? (b) What does Macduff tell Macbeth concerning the apparitions' third prophecy?
6. (a) Whom does Macbeth kill in the encounter with the English forces? (b) Whom does Macduff kill? (c) At the end of the play, who is to be crowned King of Scotland?

### Interpreting

7. Why do you think it is an "accustomed action" for Lady Macbeth to wash her hands while sleepwalking?
8. (a) Why does Macbeth remain confident of surviving the battle with Malcolm's army despite his own troops' desertion? (b) Judging by the way Macbeth behaves in Scene iii, describe his state of mind.
9. What changes in his personality is Macbeth describing in Scene v, lines 9–14?
10. Why does Macbeth say, "She should have died hereafter," upon learning of the death of Lady Macbeth?
11. Macbeth, mad and murderous though he is, shows certain admirable traits to the very end. What are some of his better traits?

### Applying

12. If Macbeth had defeated Malcolm's forces and remained King of Scotland, what actions do you think he would have taken in regard to (a) Malcolm? (b) the rebellious Scottish lords? (c) the witches?

## ANALYZING LITERATURE
### Understanding Theme

**Theme** is the central or dominating idea in a literary work. In a tragedy the theme is based on the actions of a tragic hero—a basically moral person, often of noble stature, whose downfall usually results from a bad choice. The bad choice stems from a tragic flaw in the hero's character.

1. What is the tragic flaw in Macbeth's character? Support your answer.
2. What is the theme of *Macbeth*? State the theme. Your statement should be in the form of a universal truth, not restricted to Macbeth's tragic flaw and its consequences.
3. What events in Act V show Macbeth's downfall to be complete and irreversible?

## UNDERSTANDING LANGUAGE
### Reading Shakespearean English

The language of Shakespeare is Early Modern English, the direct ancestor of our own Modern English. Around the year 1500, Middle English, the language of Chaucer, began to undergo a number of gradual, systematic changes. One was the elimination of the vowel sound at the end of many words. The word *name,* for example, had two syllables in Middle English but only one by Shakespeare's time. Other changes occurred. The so-called "Great Vowel Shift" resulted in many changes in pronunciation: *he* in Middle English had sounded like *hey, mouse* like *moose,* and *moon* like *moan.* The renewed interest in Greek and Latin added many words of classical origin to the language. Certain consonants, such as the *l* in *would* and *could,* were still pronounced in Shakespeare's day. The pronouns *thou* and *thee* were in common use, as were the verbs *hath* and *doth* and the expressions *anon, prithee,* and *fie.*

1. In Scene iii, lines 35–37, find and list three examples of how Shakespearean English differs from today's.
2. In Scene v, lines 38–41, find and list three more examples of these differences.

# GREAT WORKS

## HAMLET
## by William Shakespeare

**DELACROIX AS HAMLET**
*Delacroix*
*le Louvre, Paris*

### "What a Sensational Story!"

"*Hamlet* is the most wonderful play ever written," claims critic A. C. Bradley. "What a sensational story! Why, there are some eight violent deaths, not to speak of a ghost, a mad woman, and a fight in a grave!" Whether we agree with Bradley's assessment or not, no one can deny that *Hamlet* is certainly among the most enthralling plays in the world. From the very first scene, we are plunged into a dark world of mystery and excitement.

### "Something Is Rotten in the State of Denmark"

The play opens at midnight on the battlements of Elsinore Castle. The soldiers on duty are tired and edgy, for unnerving things have been happening lately. Moments later, the uneasy quiet is shattered by the appearance of a ghost, the very image of the former King of Denmark, down to his majestic presence and full armor. The guards and Horatio, Hamlet's friend, beg the ghost to tell them why it has been haunting the battlements, but it refuses to answer, and vanishes. The men decide to tell Hamlet, the dead king's son, what they have seen that night. If things weren't bad enough, we

**OPHELIA**
*Sir John Everett Millais*
The Tate Gallery, London

learn that Norway is poised to attack Denmark, as young Fortinbras is intent on getting revenge on Denmark for his father's death in battle. There is profound trouble afoot in Denmark.

## "Frailty, Thy Name Is Woman!"

Yet in the next scene it appears that matters are well in hand—at least on the surface. Claudius, charming and smooth, has assumed the throne after his brother's death, and married his wife, to boot. The only thing disturbing about this picture of domestic and political bliss is the presence of Prince Hamlet. In contrast to the colorful clothing of the royal couple and the courtiers, Hamlet is dressed entirely in the "inky cloak" of deep black mourning and stands well apart from the jovial mood of the others. "O! that this too too solid flesh would melt,/ Thaw and resolve itself into a dew," he exclaims in his first soliloquy, pouring out his bitterness at his uncle's falsity. His anger is directed especially at his mother's hasty remarriage to her former brother-in-law—less than two months after the death of her tender and loving husband.

Hamlet bravely sets out to the battlements at midnight to confront the ghost and learn what it is, if he can. But Shakespeare keeps us in suspense as he introduces us to Claudius's chief advisor, Polonius, and Polonius's two children, Laertes and Ophelia. We learn that Hamlet has declared his love to Ophelia, but Polonius doubts the sincerity of his words and has forbidden

**HAMLET AND HORATIO**
*Delacroix*
le Louvre, Paris

## "Though This Be Madness, Yet There Is Method in 't"

Ophelia, at least, is convinced of his madness when he appears soon after in her room and acts most strangely. Polonius, too, is persuaded, but Claudius is not as certain, and sets spies on his stepson. Hamlet makes a mockery of the clumsy spies, his former friends Rosencrantz and Guildenstern, and has a great deal of fun tweaking Polonius as well. But his melancholy hangs on him as his black cloak, as he must find a way to verify the ghost's claim and achieve his revenge. "O! what a rogue and peasant slave am I," he exclaims, vowing to take action at once.

## "The Play's the Thing, Wherein I'll Catch the Conscience of the King"

Just then the troop of traveling players arrive on its annual visit. To verify Claudius's guilt, Hamlet decides to insert a reenactment of the murder in one of the plays. But his sadness has grown so deep that he cannot help but reproach himself. In his most famous soliloquy, Hamlet cries:

> To be, or not to be: that is the
>     question:
> Whether 'tis nobler in the mind to
>     suffer
> The slings and arrows of
>     outrageous fortune,
> Or to take arms against a sea of
>     troubles,
> And by opposing, end them.

Claudius's violent reaction leaves no doubt of his guilt, and his later confession seals his fate. Mistaking Polonius for Claudius, Hamlet kills him, sending Ophelia into madness. Claudius arranges to have Hamlet killed, but he escapes and returns to Denmark's shores. He achieves his revenge brilliantly, but at a terrible price.

Ophelia to have anything more to do with Hamlet.

But it is to the eerie night air that our attention turns. What will happen when Hamlet confronts the ghost?

### Murder Most Foul!

As the men talk of Claudius's lavish parties, the ghost suddenly appears. It beckons Hamlet to follow him. Is the ghost sent to bring Hamlet crashing down the battlements to his doom? His friends try to hold him back, but Hamlet insists on following the ghost to a secluded spot. There, the ghost tells him that it is indeed his father's spirit, poisoned by his brother Claudius. He entreats Hamlet to "revenge his foul and most unnatural murder." Hamlet swears to do so. But how? He vows to "put on an antic disposition"—to feign madness—to better accomplish his mission. Can we trust him? Is this an act, or reality?

## Shakespeare Today

Why then do we continue to read Shakespeare 400 years after his death? According to writer Pablo Neruda, it is because we see ourselves—our hopes, uncertainties, terrors—so clearly in his works.

One reason more, then, to love William Shakespeare, the greatest of all human beings. There will always be time and space to explore in Shakespeare, to lose ourselves, or begin the long journey around his statue, like the Lilliputians around Gulliver. And though we may go a long way without reaching the end, we always return with hands filled with fragrance and blood, with flowers and sorrows, with mortal treasures.

At this solemn moment, it is my pleasure to open the door of tributes, raising the curtain so the dazzling, pensive figure of the Bard may appear. And across four centuries I would say to him: "Greetings, Prince of Light! Good health, sir itinerant actor! We are the heirs to your great dreams; we dream them still. Your words do honor to the entire world."

And, more quietly, I would whisper into his ear: "My friend, I thank you."

**THE PLAY SCENE IN HAMLET**
*Daniel Maclise*
*The Tate Gallery, London*

# GUIDE FOR INTERPRETING

## *from* Novum Organum: Idols of the Cave

**Sir Francis Bacon** (1561–1626) was born in London, the son of Sir Nicholas Bacon, Lord Keeper of the Great Seal. Although he made no discoveries in natural science and proposed no new scheme of philosophy, he gave to the seventeenth century something that it lacked, a "science of science" and a "philosophy of philosophy." Bacon's *Essays,* fifty-eight in all, appeared between 1597 and 1625. Full of practical wisdom and noted for their style, they reflect the experiences of Bacon's own life.

An account of Sir Francis Bacon's last days survives in a report by his friend, John Aubrey. According to Aubrey, Bacon was riding in a coach through the snow on the way to Highgate. With him was Dr. Witherborne, the King's physician. Looking at the snow, Bacon got the idea that meat might be preserved in cold, as it was in salt. Bacon and the doctor decided to try the experiment at once. They stopped the coach in front of a poor woman's home in Highgate, bought a hen from her and had her kill it and removed its innards. The two men then stood in the frigid air and stuffed the dead fowl with snow. Sir Francis got so chilled that he immediately fell deathly ill. Unable to complete the journey home, he went to a friend's house at Highgate. The only bed available was very damp, for it had not been used for about a year. Although Bacon's host warmed the bed with a pan, the bed was still so damp that the scientist's symptoms worsened. He died two or three days later.

## Writer's Techniques

**Aphorism.** An aphorism is a short statement that expresses a wise or clever observation about life. The term comes from Hippocrates's *Aphorisms,* a collection of tersely worded medical principles written by the early Greek physician. Hippocrates's opening sentence is a famous example of an aphorism: "Life is short, art is long, opportunity fleeting, experimenting dangerous, reasoning difficult."

As you read Bacon's "Idols of the Cave" from *Novum Organum,* look for the aphorisms. What insights about life do they provide?

## Writing

Write the following headings across the top of a piece of paper: *Being a teenager, Being a student, Being a friend, Being a son or daughter.* Under each heading write two or more observations you have made or facts you have learned from your experience.

*from* # Novum Organum[1]
## Idols[2] of the Cave

### Sir Francis Bacon

#### 53

The *Idols of the Cave* take their rise in the peculiar constitution, mental or bodily, of each individual; and also in education, habit and accident. Of this kind there is a great number and variety; but I will instance those the pointing out of which contains the most important caution, and which have most effect in disturbing the clearness of the understanding.

#### 54

Men become attached to certain particular sciences[3] and speculations, either because they fancy themselves the authors and inventors thereof, or because they have bestowed the greatest pains upon them and become most habituated to them. But men of this kind, if they betake themselves to philosophy and contemplations of a general character, distort and color them in obedience to their former fancies; a thing especially to be noticed in Aristotle,[4] who made his natural philosophy a mere bondservant to his logic, thereby rendering it contentious and well nigh useless. The race of chemists[5]

again out of a few experiments of the furnace have built up a fantastic philosophy, framed with reference to a few things; and Gilbert[6] also, after he had employed himself most laboriously in the study and observation of the loadstone,[7] proceeded at once to construct an entire system in accordance with his favorite subject.

#### 55

There is one principal and, as it were, radical distinction between different minds, in respect of philosophy and the sciences, which is this: that some minds are stronger and apter to mark the differences of things, others to mark their resemblances. The steady and acute mind can fix its contemplations and dwell and fasten on the subtlest distinctions: the lofty and discursive mind recognizes and puts together the finest and most general resemblances. Both kinds however easily err in excess, by catching the one at gradations, the other in shadows.

#### 56

There are found some minds given to an extreme admiration of antiquity, others to an extreme love and appetite for novelty; but few so duly tempered that they can hold the mean, neither carping at what has been well

---

**1. Novum Organum:** The New Instrument of Learning.
**2. Idols:** Misleading images of truth.
**3. sciences:** Ideas.
**4. Aristotle:** Ancient Greek philosopher (384–322 B.C.).
**5. chemists:** Alchemists; people who practiced alchemy, an early form of chemistry, involving the study of philosophical and magical associations.

**6. Gilbert:** William Gilbert (1540?–1603), an English physician, known for his studies of magnetic force.
**7. loadstone** *n*: A strongly magnetic variety of the mineral magnetite.

laid down by the ancients, nor despising what is well introduced by the moderns. This however turns to the great inquiry of the sciences and philosophy; since these affectations of antiquity and novelty are the humors of partisans rather than judgments; and truth is to be sought for not in the felicity of any age, which is an unstable thing, but in the light of nature and experience, which is eternal. These factions therefore must be abjured, and care must be taken that the intellect be not hurried by them into assent.

### 57

Contemplations of nature and of bodies in their simple form break up and distract the understanding, while contemplations of nature and bodies in their composition and configuration overpower and dissolve the understanding:[8] a distinction well seen in the school of Leucippus and Democritus[9] as compared with the other philosophies. For

---

**8. contemplations . . . understanding:** Neither reducing nature to the most basic principles nor trying to observe all of nature's particulars can produce a true understanding of it.
**9. Leucippus and Democritus:** Ancient Greek philosophers.

that school is so busied with the particles that it hardly attends to the structure; while the others are so lost in admiration of the structure that they do not penetrate to the simplicity of nature. These kinds of contemplation should therefore be alternated and taken by turns; that so the understanding may be rendered at once penetrating and comprehensive, and the inconveniences above mentioned with the idols which proceed from them, may be avoided.

### 58

Let such then be our provision and contemplative prudence for keeping off and dislodging the *Idols of the Cave*, which grow for the most part either out of the predominance of a favorite subject, or out of an excessive tendency to compare or to distinguish, or out of partiality for particular ages, or out of the largeness or minuteness of the objects contemplated. And generally let every student of nature take this as a rule —that whatever his mind seizes and dwells upon with peculiar satisfaction is to be held in suspicion, and that so much the more care is to be taken in dealing with such questions to keep the understanding even and clear.

---

## THINKING ABOUT THE SELECTION
### Recalling

1. In 53 what four sources of the "Idols of the Cave" does Bacon identify?
2. What two reasons are mentioned in 54 for people becoming attached to certain ideas?
3. What is the main distinction noted in 55 between different minds?
4. According to Bacon in 57, what is the main fault with the philosophy of Leucippus and Democritus?

### Interpreting

5. In your own words, what does Bacon think is wrong with Aristotle's philosophy?

6. (a) If Bacon were to put himself into one of the two categories in 55, which one would it be? (b) Why?
7. In both 55 and 56, Bacon warns against going to extremes. How does he suggest doing it?
8. What purpose does the advice in 58 serve?

### Applying

9. (a) In your own words, what is the rule Bacon recommends in 58 for a "student of nature"? (b) What is your opinion of the rule? (c) What, if any, instances can you think of in your personal experience where it might apply?

## ANALYZING LITERATURE
### Understanding Aphorism

An **aphorism** is a concise statement expressing a wise or clever observation about life. In a very few words it summarizes a great deal of information or experience. Explaining the meaning of an aphorism requires many more words than those in the aphorism. Sometimes an example helps to make the meaning of an aphorism clear. In your own words, give the meaning of each of the following aphorisms from the works of Sir Francis Bacon.

1. "Revenge is a kind of wild justice, which the more man's nature seems to run to, the more ought law to weed it out."
2. "Virtue is like a rich stone—best plain set."
3. "There is no excellent beauty that hath not some strangeness in the proportion."
4. "Prosperity is not without many fears and distastes; and adversity is not without comforts and hopes."

## CRITICAL THINKING AND READING
### Reasoning

Before Bacon's time, science was based on *deductive reasoning*—the process of applying an already accepted general principle to specific facts. Bacon considered that method to be backwards. He argued that true science requires *inductive reasoning*—the process of examining specific facts in order to derive a general principle. From "some good quantity of observation" Bacon created his aphorisms in *Novum Organum*. Bacon's aphorisms therefore demonstrate in style as well as content the method of inductive reasoning.

When inductive reasoning is carried out logically, it results in a *valid generalization*—a statement, supported by evidence, that holds true in a large number of cases. If you make a generalization on the basis of only a few examples, without taking exceptions or qualifying facts into account, you produce a *hasty generalization*. A hasty generalization may be valid but only by accident, since the process of reaching it is flawed.

Read the following examples and decide which are valid generalizations and which are hasty generalizations.

1. I did worse on today's calculus test than I did on the three previous ones. I'm going to get a bad grade in calculus.
2. In the ninth inning I struck out with the bases loaded. I'll never be a good baseball player.
3. I helped my aunt run her day-care center for six toddlers this summer. I worked every day for two months. It takes skill and patience to care for young children.
4. It rained on my birthday for the last two years. It's almost sure to rain on it this year, too.

## UNDERSTANDING LANGUAGE
### Words from Latin Roots

Many words in the English language came from Latin. Sometimes the entire word was borrowed—*senator,* for example—but more often the Latin base, or root, was used in combination with something else to create a new word.

Use each of the following Latin roots to make at least two English words. If necessary, use a dictionary. You may have to change the spelling of the Latin root when you write the English word. For example, the Latin root *aer* (air) gives us *airplane* and *airmail.*

1. *omni* (all)
2. *viv* (live)
3. *flex* (bend)
4. *avis* (bird)
5. *sect* (cut)
6. *fid* (faith)
7. *rupt* (break)
8. *aqua* (water)
9. *grat* (thank)
10. *locut* (speak)

## THINKING AND WRITING
### Writing Aphorisms

Choose three of the observations that you made for the Writing assignment. Rewrite each observation in the form of an aphorism. Be sure that your aphorism, like those of Sir Francis Bacon, is a valid generalization. This requires that your observation be based on sufficient evidence to make the resulting aphorism express a general truth, one that cannot be easily disproved.

## The Elizabethan World View

### ORDER IN THE LAND!

The Elizabethans viewed the world as an ordered, rational place. Each person occupied a specific rung on the social ladder. With each rank came understood responsibilities to those above and below in the chain. Everyone understood and accepted this hierarchy, and it was constantly reinforced in daily life. On Sunday, during compulsory services at the Established Church of England, for example, ministers explained that "Every degree of people . . . hath appointed to them, their duty and order. Some are in high degree, some are in low, some kings and princes, some inferiors and subjects. Almighty God hath created and appointed all things . . . in a most excellent and perfect order."

The social ranking of people extended to everything in the universe, as each element, creature, and spiritual being occupied a fixed place in the universe.

### HEAVENLY BODIES

This divinely directed order began with the heavens themselves. To the Elizabethans, the entire universe was enclosed by a sphere called the *primum mobile*. Beneath it lay the fixed stars. Next came the planets, whose motion was directed by the primum mobile. While opinion differed on exactly how many planets made up the universe— was it nine? ten? eleven?—no one with any sense doubted that these spheres circled around a fixed earth. Copernicus had a wild idea that the sun, not the earth, was the center of the universe. He even went so far as to claim that the earth was actually in motion, not fixed in place!

The angels too obeyed a strict hierarchy. The three different classes ranged from the highest, the Seraphs, to the lowest, the angels. Shakespeare commented on this order in *Troilus and Cressida* when Ulysses remarked that "The heavens themselves, the planets, and this center/Observe degree, priority, and place."

THE FIRST BOOKE OF THE

THE PRIMUM MOBILE from THE COSMOGRAPHICAL GLASS, 1559
*from William Cuningham*
The Huntington Library, San Marino, California

## THE GREAT CHAIN OF BEING

Heaven and its inhabitants were linked to the rest of the universe through a belief called The Great Chain of Being. It stretched from the humblest thing in the universe all the way up to God, and the order of each world was reflected in all others. England's rulers, fc. example, were arranged in order, which corresponded to the order of the rest of creation. The Sovereign was analogous to fire, the chief element; the sun, the chief planet; and the eagle, the chief bird, for instance.

Naturally, humans with their superior intellect were expected to exceed the other worlds. A woman in *A Comedy of Errors* points this out while lecturing to her sister:

> The beasts, the fishes, and the
>     winged fowl,
> Are their males' subjects and at
>     their controls.
> Man, more divine, the master of all
>     these,
> Lord of the wide world and wilde
>     watery seas,
> Endued with intellectual sense and
>     souls,
> Of more preeminence than fish and
>     fowls,
> Are masters to their females, and
>     their lords;
> Then let your will attend on their
>     accords.

Although her sister resents being told she ought to be submissive to men, the Elizabethans saw the dominance of the man within the family as a model for the broader world order.

## FATHER KNOWS BEST

As the king ruled over the kingdom, so the man of the family ruled over his wife and children. He had absolute right to dispose of his daughters in marriage, for example. Old Capulet would be considered an extremely considerate father to the Elizabethans, for when the question of Juliet's marriage to Paris is first discussed, he is willing to let her refuse. It is not until she defies him that he gives commands. Children were brought up to fear and respect their parents. They called their father "Sir" and stood in his presence. The power and authority of the father was recognized as part of the social order.

## DRESS FOR SUCCESS

This rigid hierachy was even seen in the clothing laws, which decreed who was allowed to wear what. Clothing Acts were passed to halt the "intolerable abuse and unmeasurable disorder" caused by the poorer people dressing as their betters. No one under the rank of knight, for example, could wear velvet cloaks or silk stockings; only countesses and higher appeared in purple silk; gold and silver cloth were allowed only for nobles. But most people ignored the laws, much to the dismay of the lawmakers.

## THE LINKS WEAKEN

Dramatic advances in knowledge prompted some to stress the old idea of hierarchy. But the quickening pace combined with the avalanche of invention and discovery, relentlessly undermined the previously accepted notions of order.

# THE KING JAMES BIBLE

## 1611

King James I, son of Mary Queen of Scots, ascended the English throne upon the death of Queen Elizabeth I. One of the first demands the new king faced was that of the Puritans for a uniform English version of the Bible. At the Hampton Court Conference in 1604, James accepted their demand. He commissioned fifty-four English scholars and clergymen to compare all extant texts of the Bible and to produce a definitive English edition. They succeeded perhaps beyond their expectations. The King James Version of the Holy Bible, published in 1611, has been called "the only classic ever created by a committee." From its earliest appearance until the present day it has been regarded as one of the great works of English literature.

The Bible, a collection of books developed over a period of more than twelve hundred years, consists of two main parts, the Old Testament and the New Testament. The Old Testament was originally written in Hebrew, the New Testament in Greek. In A.D. 382, St. Jerome translated the Bible into Latin, and his translation, called the Vulgate Version, remained the standard Bible in the West for centuries. An English reformer, John Wyclif, along with his followers, produced the first English translation from Latin in the late 1300's.

It was the Reformation in the 1500's, however—and the growing use of Gutenberg's movable type—that increased the demand for a Bible in the vernacular, or common language of the people. William Tyndale, a Protestant chaplain and tutor, decided to prepare a new English translation from Hebrew and Greek. Faced with clerical opposition at home, he went to Germany, where he translated and printed the New Testament in English. Arrested for heresy while at work on the Old Testament, Tyndale was executed near Brussels, Belgium, in 1536. The importance of Tyndale's New Testament is that the King James committee, impressed by its diction and rhythm, followed it more closely than any other translation in working on their 1611 masterpiece.

Other Bibles preceded the King James Version. None had the immense impact of the King James or Authorized Version, which in fact was never officially "authorized." It won its acceptance through use. Generations of people in Great Britain and the United States grew up reading its text and adding its wisdom to the common store of knowledge. Hundreds of expressions—"swords into plowshares," "fat of the land," "out of the mouths of babes"—are familiar to nearly every English-speaking person, while the magnificent rhythms of the Bible have influenced English prose and poetry throughout its history.

# GUIDE FOR INTERPRETING

## Literary Forms

## Psalm 23; The Parable of the Prodigal Son; I Corinthians 13

**Psalm and Parable.** The Bible, particularly the Old Testament, contains a wide variety of literary forms in both prose and poetry. Many of them are already familiar to you, but two may not be. A psalm is a song or lyric poem in praise of God. Psalms were originally meant to be sung to the accompaniment of a stringed instrument. Today the word *psalm* generally refers to one of the 150 poetic pieces in the Old Testament Book of Psalms. Although the Hebrew authors of the psalms are mostly unknown, King David is often credited with having composed a few of them. The subject matter of the psalms varies widely. Some are hymns for public worship; others tell of historical events; still others portray everyday life in the Holy Land.

A parable is a short, simple story, usually about a common kind of occurrence, from which a moral or religious lesson can be drawn. Some parables, such as that of the unproductive vineyard, appear in the Old Testament. In the New Testament, Jesus often answers a question by telling a brief story based on an experience familiar to his listeners. Among the best known New Testament parables are those of the good Samaritan, the mustard seed, and the prodigal son.

## Commentary

The *King James Bible* was published the same year that Shakespeare began his last play, *The Tempest*. While both works are masterpieces of the English language, there is one significant difference between them—words. Shakespeare nearly turned the language on its ear in his search for words. This is evident in the stunning array of different words he used in *The Tempest* (as well as his other works). The authors of the *King James Bible,* in contrast, used but 8,000 different words to convey their message. Noting this contrast moved one critic to remark that "from that day to this, the Shakespearean cornucopia and the biblical iron rations represent, as it were, the North and South poles of the language, reference points for writers and speakers throughout the world, from the Shakespearean splendor of a Joyce or Dickens to the biblical rigor of a Bunyan or Hemingway."

## Writing

Think of an incident that would make a good parable. It should be an everyday occurrence whose outcome conveys a moral lesson. Jot down some notes about what happened. Indicate why you think the incident you have chosen fits the requirements for a parable.

# Psalm 23

The Lord is my shepherd; I shall not want.

He maketh me to lie down in green pastures: he leadeth me
beside the still waters.

He restoreth my soul: he leadeth me in the paths of
righteousness for his name's sake.

Yea, though I walk through the valley of the shadow of
death, I will fear no evil: for thou art with me; thy rod and
thy staff they comfort me.

5    Thou preparest a table before me in the presence of mine
enemies; thou anointest my head with oil; my cup
runneth over.

Surely goodness and mercy shall follow me all the days of
my life: and I will dwell in the house of the Lord forever.

---

## THINKING ABOUT THE SELECTION

### Recalling

1. In the first part of the psalm, what images carry out the idea of the Lord as a shepherd?
2. At what point does the psalmist change from speaking of the Lord as a shepherd to viewing Him as a host preparing a feast?

### Interpreting

3. Why would the Lord's (shepherd's) rod and staff comfort the psalmist (sheep)?
4. Why is it significant that the table is prepared "in the presence of mine enemies"?

### Applying

5. Two years before the King James Bible appeared, the Douay Version, an English translation from Latin, was published in France. Following are the last three lines of Psalm 23 in the Douay Bible. What stylistic features of the King James Version distinguish it from the Douay Version?

Thou hast fatted my head with oil,
and my chalice inebriating how
goodly is it!
And thy mercy shall follow me
all the days of my life
And that I may dwell in the house
of the Lord in longitude of days.

## ANALYZING LITERATURE

### Recognizing a Psalm

A **psalm** is a sacred song or lyric poem. The psalms in the Book of Psalms, originally in Hebrew, were meant to be sung to the accompaniment of a stringed instrument. Since none of the Biblical translations really advanced that purpose, the paraphrasing of psalms into metrical verse began during the Reformation. This rephrasing, which permitted the psalms to be sung by congregations, emphasized the lyrical nature of the original compositions.

What qualities of Psalm 23 make it especially lyrical?

# Luke 15:11–32

## The Parable of the Prodigal Son

A certain man had two sons. And the younger of them said to his father, "Father, give me the portion of goods that falleth to me." And he divided unto them his living.

And not many days after the younger son gathered all together, and took his journey into a far country, and there wasted his substance with riotous living. And when he had spent all, there arose a mighty famine in that land; and he began to be in want. And he went and joined himself to a citizen of that country; and he sent him into his fields to feed swine. And he would fain[1] have filled his belly with the husks that the swine did eat and no man gave unto him.

And when he came to himself, he said, "How many hired servants of my father's have bread enough and to spare, and I perish with hunger! I will arise and go to my father, and will say unto him, "Father, I have sinned against heaven, and before thee, and am no more worthy to be called thy son. Make me as one of thy hired servants.""

And he arose, and came to his father. But when he was yet a great way off, his father saw him, and had compassion and ran, and fell on his neck, and kissed him. And the son said unto him, "Father, I have sinned against heaven, and in thy sight, and am no more worthy to be called thy son."

**KING JAMES BIBLE, 1611**
*Title page of the New Testament*
The Folger Shakespeare Library

---

**1. fain** *adv.*: Gladly.

But the father said to his servants, "Bring forth the best robe, and put it on him; and put a ring on his hand, and shoes on his feet; and bring hither the fatted calf, and kill it; and let us eat, and be merry: for this my son was dead, and is alive again; he was lost, and is found." And they began to be merry.

Now his elder son was in the field; and as he came and drew nigh to the house, he heard music and dancing. And he called one of the servants, and asked what these things meant. And he said unto him, "Thy brother is come; and thy father hath killed the fatted calf, because he hath received him safe and sound."

And he was angry, and would not go in: therefore came his father out, and entreated him. And he answering said to his father, "Lo, these many years do I serve thee, neither transgressed I at any time thy commandment; and yet thou never gavest me a kid, that I might make merry with my friends; but as soon as this thy son was come, which hath devoured thy living, thou hast killed for him the fatted calf."

And he said unto him, "Son, thou art ever with me, and all that I have is thine. It was meet[2] that we should make merry, and be glad: for this thy brother was dead, and is alive again; and was lost, and is found."

---

2. **meet** *adj.*: Fitting.

## THINKING ABOUT THE SELECTION

### Recalling

1. What happens to the younger son's money?
2. (a) Why does the younger son decide to return home? (b) What does he intend to say to his father?
3. How does the father react to the return of his younger son?
4. (a) Why is the older son angry? (b) How does his father answer the complaint?

### Interpreting

5. From the limited evidence given in the parable, how repentant do you think the younger son is?

6. Why is the father happy rather than unhappy at the sight of his younger son?
7. To what extent do you think the older son is justified in being angry at the treatment given his brother?

### Applying

8. A parable is meant to teach a moral or spiritual lesson. What lesson do you draw from this one?
9. Sometimes this parable is called "The Parable of the *Lost* Son." How might that title affect your reaction to it?

# I Corinthians 13

Though I speak with the tongues of men and of angels, and have not charity, I am become as sounding brass, or a tinkling cymbal. And though I have the gift of prophecy, and understand all mysteries, and all knowledge; and though I have all faith, so that I could remove mountains, and have not charity, I am nothing. And though I bestow all my goods to feed the poor, and though I give my body to be burned, and have not charity, it profiteth me nothing. Charity suffereth long, and is kind; charity envieth not; charity vaunteth not itself, is not puffed up, doth not behave itself unseemly, seeketh not her own, is not easily provoked, thinketh no evil; rejoiceth not in iniquity, but rejoiceth in the truth; beareth all things, believeth all things, hopeth all things, endureth all things. Charity never faileth: but whether there be prophecies, they shall fail; whether there be tongues, they shall cease; whether there be knowledge, it shall vanish away. For we know in part, and we prophesy in part. But when that which is perfect is come, then that which is in part shall be done away. When I was a child, I spake as a child, I understood as a child, I thought as a child: but when I became a man, I put away childish things. For now we see through a glass darkly; but then face to face: now I know in part; but then shall I know even as also I am known. And now abideth faith, hope, charity, these three; but the greatest of these is charity.

---

## THINKING ABOUT THE SELECTION

### Recalling

1. In each of the first three sentences, the apostle Paul mentions some impressive personal achievements. (a) What are they? (b) In each case, if he lacks charity, what is the result?
2. The sentence beginning "Charity suffereth long" describes the nature of charity. (a) What does charity do? (b) What does it not do?
3. This passage is a letter to the Corinthians. In it Paul advises them to prepare for the coming perfect times with God. What analogy does he use to make his point clear?

### Interpreting

4. Knowing what Paul means by *charity* is vital to an understanding of the passage. He does *not* mean "human kindness" or "doing good." What does the word *charity* mean, as Paul uses it? Context clues can help, but you may also need to consult a dictionary.
5. (a) Given this definition of *charity,* how do faith and hope relate to charity? (b) Why is charity "the greatest of these"?
6. (a) Find two uses of parallelism. (b) Does the use of parallelism make the writing more or less effective? Explain.

### Applying

7. The apostle Paul is giving advice to the Corinthians on how to live a spiritual life. How, if at all, do you think it would be possible to know whether a person is following Paul's advice concerning charity?

# THE CHANGING ENGLISH LANGUAGE

## Shakespearean English 1485–1625

### A BLOODLESS INVASION

After the Normans invaded England in 1066, there were no more major assaults by foreign armies, but there did come another invasion of a kind—the onslaught of European culture.

Throughout the reign of the Tudors, England quarreled with her neighbors on the continent. Henry VIII severed allegiance with Rome. His daughter Elizabeth constantly sparred with the superpowers of the day, France and Spain. Through these skirmishes came the increasing interchange of words. Sailors returning from France brought cargo in the holds and *bigot* and *detail* on their lips. From Italy came *cupola* and *stucco;* the Dutch countries contributed *smuggle* and *reef.* Spenser's poetry even contains slang from the sailors who defeated the Armada!

### WHAT SHALL WE CALL IT?

When they weren't off negotiating, exploring, or trading, the English were inventing and discovering wondrous new things, which all had to be named. From physics came *paradox* and *chronology;* from biology, *skeleton.* Through Vesalius's work with anatomy we learned how *strenuous* activity could be. Soon, people needed an *encyclopedia* to learn about *gravity!*

### LATIN AND GREEK ENTER THE MIX

The renewed focus on scholarship also helped the English language to grow. This interest in learning sparked a new class of scholars concerned with the refinement of writing style. Such writers as Thomas More and Francis Bacon rebelled against what they saw as the awkwardness of English. Bacon, for example, preferred to write in Latin, which was still the language of scholarship. English, he sneered, will "play the bankrupts with books." When forced to write in English, these men decorated their sentences with Latinate words they had gleaned from classical texts. From Latin they took *agile, capsule, habitual,* for instance; from Greek, *catastrophe, lexicon,* and *thermometer.*

### A RETURN TO BASICS?

Not everyone was enthusiastic about the deluge of new words pouring into the language. Elizabeth's subjects felt as proud of their native tongue as they did of their land —and took both very seriously. Thomas Chaloner is often cited for his attack on writers who "serche . . . out of some rotten Pamphlet foure or fyve disused woords of antiquitee, therewith to darken the sence unto the reader." But others endorsed the importation of foreign terms: "Seeing that we borrow (and not shamefully) from the Dutch, the Breton, the Roman, the Dane, and French, Italian, and Spaniard, how can our stock be other than exceeding plentiful?" The battle between these two camps spilled over onto the stage. One of Ben Jonson's plays shows a poet cleansed of such borrowed Latin words as *retrograde* and *inflate.* Despite such protests, this mix of domestic and foreign words resulted in a language that one critic has called "of unsurpassed richness and beauty, which, however, defies all the rules."

## AND NOW TO THOSE RULES . . .

This rich outpouring of foreign words into English did have its drawbacks, however—chief among them, the matter of consistent rules for the different parts of speech. During the Renaissance, almost any English word could be used as almost every part of speech. Adverbs could become verbs, for example, and nouns could become adjectives; nouns and adjectives could even take the place of verbs and adverbs. In Elizabethan English you could *happy* your friend, *malice* or *foot* your enemy, or *fall* an axe on his neck. Words could be spelled any number of different ways—even within the same sentence! Nouns didn't have to match their verbs. The order of words in a sentence was up for grabs as well: Objects could come before verbs and adjectives could come after nouns, for example. Despite the linguistic model of Latin, the order of the day was disorder. In general, people felt that it was more important for language to be strong and interesting than logical.

## IT LOOKS FAMILIAR . . .

Since the language of the Renaissance was shaped to appeal to listeners, why does it seem hard to understand today? It is simply that language changes. As it grew during the Renaissance, so it has developed through the centuries, and many words used in the past have long been discarded, replaced by terms that describe our life now. Someone from the Renaissance who arrived in America today would be baffled by "television" and "computer," as we are by their "chopine" (a high-heeled shoe) and "kecksey" (a wild plant). Even more perilous are the words that look familiar—those we think we know but that mean something entirely different today. For example, when someone in a Shakespearean play remarks, "I love not the *humor* of it," he is talking about the general tone of a situation, not its amusing aspects.

But it is only through such change that language remains fascinating—even challenging—and always alive.

**Letter from Patent granted by Elizabeth I to Francis Drake**

# YOU THE WRITER

**Assignment**

**1.** Write a sonnet modeled on any one contained in this unit. Your poem should have fourteen five-beat lines and the same rhyme scheme as your model.

**Prewriting.** Before you write, make a list of subjects that interest you—places, sports, hobbies, people you know, and so on. Then, from this list, choose the topic that appeals to you most and freewrite about it.

**Writing.** Write the first draft of your sonnet. You might devote the octave to one main idea and use the sestet to comment on it.

**Revising.** When you revise, check to see that your sonnet has fourteen five-beat lines and a rhyme scheme like that of one of the sonnets you have read.

**Assignment**

**2.** Write a scene modeled on the dramatic literature of this period, showing two individuals in conflict. As the characters talk, have them reveal the nature of the conflict between them and aspects of their personalities.

**Prewriting.** Before you write, make notes on the conflict between the characters. What is it about? How will it develop? How will it conclude?

**Writing.** Start the scene off slowly and gradually build the conflict. Although you need not use blank verse, try to emulate the style of the speeches in Marlowe or Shakespeare.

**Revising.** See if you can improve the way you developed and concluded the conflict. Then read the dialogue aloud. Can you improve the style of the speeches? Have you followed the conventions of drama in writing your scene?

**Assignment**

**3.** One of the most effective types of figurative language is personification. When a poet uses personification, he or she speaks about a nonhuman thing as if it were a person, maybe by saying something like "The sun is smiling." Write ten examples of personification modeled on the use of this figure of speech in Elizabethan poetry that you have read.

**Prewriting.** Before you write, look around you at the objects in your room, on the street outside your window, in your back yard. Let your imagination picture some of the objects you see doing things that human beings might do—singing, dancing, smiling, and so on.

**Writing.** Now, using the ideas you obtained by letting your imagination work, write your ten examples of personification.

**Revising.** When you revise, be sure that each of your examples is expressed in a complete sentence and that the personification is appropriate and clear.

**Assignment**

**1.** Choose a character from a play in this unit and write an essay discussing the changes he or she undergoes. Tell (1) what the character was like at first, (2) what caused him or her to change, and (3) what he or she was like after the change.

**Prewriting.** Scan the play of your choice for a character who undergoes a change. When you have found this character, divide a sheet of paper into three columns and make notes on the three focal points mentioned above.

**Writing.** In your opening paragraph, state your main idea about the change the character undergoes. In the paragraphs that follow, discuss each of the focal points. In your concluding paragraph, restate your main idea in an interesting way.

**Revising.** When you revise, see if you can improve the organization and style of your essay.

**Assignment**

**2.** The theme of a poem is the central idea or insight the poem presents. Choose two poems from this section and write an essay stating the theme of each. In addition, identify the images, lines, and figures of speech that helped the author of each poem to express the theme.

**Prewriting.** Reread two of the poems you liked best. As you read each poem, ask yourself this question: What is the main idea this poem is expressing? The answer to this question is the theme. Now ask yourself how the poet developed and expressed the theme by using images, figures of speech, and other poetic devices.

**Writing.** Discuss each poem separately. For each poem state the theme and identify the specific devices that the poet used to develop it.

**Revising.** When revising, check that your remarks are clear and well supported by apt references to the literature.

**Assignment**

**3.** Write an essay about a sonnet from this section, discussing the following: (1) the subject of the sonnet, (2) the poet's attitude toward this subject, and (3) the passages in the poem where this attitude is revealed most clearly.

**Prewriting.** Reread the poem and try to grasp the author's tone of voice, for this tone reveals the poet's attitude. Where do you hear this tone most clearly—in what lines, words, images?

**Writing.** In your opening paragraph, identify the subject of the poem and the author's attitude toward it. Then in the body paragraphs, discuss in detail the specific lines in the poem where this attitude is revealed most clearly.

**Revising.** Revise to improve the clarity and organization of your essay. Then correct any errors in grammar and style that you find.

**THE THAMES AT WESTMINSTER STAIRS**
*Claude de Jongh, c. 1631 or 1637*
Yale Center for British Art, Paul Mellon Collection

# THE SEVENTEENTH CENTURY

## 1625–1660

During the time men live without a common power to keep them all in awe, they are in that condition which is called war, and such a war as is of every man against every man. . . . In such condition there is no place for industry, because the fruit thereof is uncertain, and consequently no culture of the earth; no navigation, nor use of the commodities that may be imported by sea; no commodious building; . . . no arts; no letters; no society; and, which is worst of all, continual fear, and danger of violent death; and the life of man, solitary, poor, nasty, brutish, and short.

**Thomas Hobbes**

In the passage above, Thomas Hobbes pictures the terrible condition of people who lived before there were kings to bring order to society. Without rulers to keep people "in awe," Hobbes insisted, society would dissolve in chaos, and life would be "poor, nasty, brutish, and short." Hobbes claimed he was writing about a "state of nature" that existed before the dawn of history. But, in 1651, he had good reason to worry about the breakdown of society. The English had shocked the world by beheading their king in 1649 and abolishing the monarchy. Perhaps England had not quite reverted to the state of nature Hobbes imagined. But Hobbes, like many conservatives, believed that the violence would continue until the English again had "a common power to keep them all in awe."

It is difficult to believe that civil war followed so closely on the Golden Age of Elizabeth, with its triumphant defeat of the Spanish Armada and its brilliant literary achievements. Looking back, we see the English Renaissance as a time of unsurpassed accomplishments, but to people at the time, the age was one of frightening doubts as well as great expectations.

In science, philosophy, religion, and politics, long-held beliefs and ideas were discredited. The Ptolemaic world view—according to which Earth is the center of a finite universe—was giving way to the Copernican theory of an infinite universe in which the Earth is merely one planet in one of countless solar systems, and not even at the center of its own solar system. William Gilbert's studies of magnetism and William Harvey's discovery of the circulation of the blood opened new realms to the human imagination as well as to the human understanding. Sir Francis Bacon's writings popularized a reliance on observation and experimentation, as opposed to ancient authority, in scientific and intellectual pursuits. And, later in the century, Sir Isaac Newton created the classical physics that remained unchallenged until our own century. The triumph of the modern scientific spirit in the seventeenth century is symbolized by the establishment of the Royal Society in 1662.

Moreover, religious and political grievances, masked by the brilliance of Elizabeth I, began to emerge in the reign of the first Stuart king, James I. During the reign of Charles I, they led to a full-scale civil war. The Civil War unleashed new forces in English society, challenging the most basic ideas of order, even the monarchy itself. It swept away the rigid structure of the old society, in which the court was the center of political power and literary activity. In its place grew a new, competitive society, with a looser social structure and greater freedom in religion and politics.

## THE ROOTS OF CIVIL CONFLICT

The roots of the religious and political conflicts that underlay the Civil War stretched back many years. Under Elizabeth the Anglican

Church held to a middle course between Catholicism and Calvinism. Puritans still worshiped and held positions in the Anglican Church, even though they disagreed with some of the Church's practices. That situation started to change after James I became king in 1603. James made no secret of his hostility toward Calvinism. He used his power as head of the Anglican Church to dismiss Puritan clergymen.

## Charles I

In 1625, Charles I inherited all the religious problems his father had faced—and made them worse. He was married to the daughter of the king of France, a Catholic. That fact alone alarmed the people of England, most of whom were firmly Protestant.

Like his father, Charles had little love for Puritans. The king wholeheartedly supported Archbishop Laud, the reactionary leader of the anti-Puritans. Laud insisted that clergymen "conform," or observe all the church ceremonies, including those the Puritans disliked. In this way, Laud pulled the Anglican Church back toward Catholicism. Laud retreated so far from Protestantism, in fact, that the Pope offered to make him a Catholic bishop. Laud refused, but many Protestants still saw him as a Catholic in all but name.

## Money Troubles

Charles I was like his father in another way. He was determined, in the words of Charles Dickens, "to be a high and mighty king not to be called to account by anybody." This attitude put Charles on a collision course with Parliament, and the crash came quickly over a basic question: money.

Charles had instigated wars against Spain and France and needed money to fight both enemies. Under English law, the money had to be granted to him by Parliament. But Parliament supported neither venture, and the king had to turn elsewhere. From his wealthy subjects Charles extorted loans by threatening them with prison. Charles lost popularity with commoners by pressing the poor into service as soldiers and sailors.

The king's abuse of his power angered many subjects. When Parliament met in 1628, its members boldly stood up to the king by passing the Petition of Right. This document spelled out the basic rights of Englishmen—at the time women had no political rights. Charles unhappily accepted the Petition of Right in order to get approval for new revenues. He soon showed that he had no intention of abiding by it. When leaders of Parliament protested, Charles had them arrested and then dissolved Parliament. For the next eleven years, Charles ruled without so much as calling Parliament into session.

# BRITISH EVENTS

1625    Full-bottomed wigs come into fashion.

1627    **Sir Francis Bacon** publishes *The New Atlantis*.

1628    William Harvey explains blood circulation.

1633    **John Donne's** *Poems* published.

       **George Herbert's** *The Temple* published.

1634    Covent Garden Market opens.

1635    Public mail service established.

1637    Charles I summons Long Parliament.

       **John Milton** publishes *Lycidas.*

1640    **John Donne's** *Devotions upon Emergent Occasions* published.

1642    English Civil War begins.

       Puritans close theaters.

1644    **John Milton** writes *Areopagitica.*

1645    **John Milton** publishes *Poems.*

1646    **John Suckling** publishes *Fragmenta Aurea.*

1647    First newspaper ad appears.

1648    George Fox founds Society of Friends (Quakers).

       **Robert Herrick** publishes *Hesperides.*

1649    Charles I beheaded.

       **Richard Lovelace** publishes *Lucasta.*

1651    Thomas Hobbes publishes *Leviathan.*

1653    Oliver Cromwell becomes Lord Protector.

1658    Oliver Cromwell dies.

1659    Puritan government collapses.

1660    Monarchy restored.

       Theaters reopened.

Sir Francis Bacon

Execution of Charles I

The Night Watch

John Milton

Covent Garden Market

New Amsterdam

Molière

King Louis XIV

Andrew Marvell

# WORLD EVENTS

**1626**  North America: Dutch found New Amsterdam.

**1630**  France: Beginning of public advertising.

North America: William Bradford begins writing *Of Plymouth Plantation*.

Boston founded by John Winthrop.

**1636**  North America: Rhode Island founded by Roger Williams.

Harvard University founded.

France: Corneille publishes *Le Cid*.

**1637**  Japan: All Europeans expelled.

**1639**  India: English settlement established at Madras.

**1640**  North America: *Bay Psalm Book* published in Massachusetts.

Italy: First European cafe opens in Venice.

Holland: Rembrandt paints *Self-Portrait*.

**1642**  Holland: Rembrandt paints *Night Watch*.

North America: Education becomes compulsory in Massachusetts.

**1643**  France: Molière founds Comédie Française.

**1644**  France: Descartes publishes *Principia Philosophicae*.

China: Ming Dynasty ends.

**1647**  North America: Massachusetts establishes free public schools.

**1651**  North America: William Bradford finishes *Of Plymouth Plantation*.

**1654**  France: Louis XIV becomes king.

**1657**  France: First stockings manufactured.

**1659**  France: Molière publishes *The Flying Doctor*.

**1660**  South Africa: First Dutch settlers arrive.

**PORTRAIT OF CHARLES I**
*Anthony van Dyck*
The Louvre, Paris

## Conflict with the Puritans

Many English subjects were disgusted with Charles, but none more so than the Puritans. The king's ally, Archbishop Laud, had stepped up his persecution of these Calvinist "dissenters." In brutal public ceremonies, Puritan leaders had their noses slit, their cheeks branded, and their ears cropped off. The Puritans often displayed such faith and resolve during these mutilations that they won the hearts of onlookers. "The more I am beaten down, the more I am lifted up!" exclaimed one Puritan as a torturer finished his work.

It was no accident that Laud and the "High Church" Anglicans supported the king, while most Puritans opposed him. The Puritan religious outlook had implications for politics. Radical Puritans wanted to do away with bishops and the whole hierarchy of the Anglican Church. They believed that each congregation, or group of worshipers, had the right to choose its own minister. As you can see, this belief resembled democracy in politics.

Most Puritans were dead set against the idea of a king's "divine right" to rule, on which Charles I insisted. One Puritan put the matter plainly: "A King is a thing men have made for their own sakes." It was only a short step further to the idea that men could unmake a king. James I had understood this danger and summed it up in the curt phrase, "No bishop, no king."

## The Long Parliament

The policies of Charles and Archbishop Laud were unpopular enough in England. But when the king and archbishop tried to force conformity on Scottish Calvinists, the Scots rose up in defiance. In 1639, King Charles had to lead an army north to put down the rebellion. With the war stalemated, Charles returned to London, once again desperate for funds.

Parliament, however, was in no mood to grant the king's request without guarantees in return. Among other things, Parliament demanded the trial of Laud and Thomas Wentworth, the hated leader of the king's army. Both were tried and later executed. The legislators also insisted on reforms to limit the power of the king. As the session went on in the stormy atmosphere of London, one demand led to another. At last, in 1642, Parliament condemned Charles as a tyrant.

Charles struck back by sending armed men into Parliament to seize the opposition leaders. The leaders escaped, and Parliament began raising its own army. Charles fled north, rallying loyalists to his side. For the next eleven years, the "Long Parliament" ruled England. The Civil War had begun.

## The Civil War

When war came, the people of England were forced to choose sides. The king's supporters were called Cavaliers, since many of

THE EXECUTION OF KING CHARLES I OF
ENGLAND AT WHITEHALL, LONDON, JANUARY
30, 1649
*Colored woodcut from Contemporary*
*Ballad-Sheet*
*The Granger Collection*

these aristocrats were skilled horsemen, or cavalry. They generally lived in the countryside. Parliament drew its followers from London and the towns, where Puritanism ran strong. Because these austere Calvinists cut their hair short, they were known as Roundheads.

The same grit Puritans had shown under the torturer's hand made them fierce enemies. The dour Puritan leader Oliver Cromwell took charge of Parliament's forces. He drilled them into an unparalleled fighting machine called the New Model Army. At the Battle of Marston Moor, the New Model Army showed the power of its training. The next year, in 1645, Cromwell's troops defeated a Cavalier army and captured Charles I.

Meanwhile, a battle of another kind was going on in Parliament. There, members of the different Protestant factions were struggling for power. Gradually, the most radical Puritans won out. In 1648, they shut the doors on moderate members. Then the radicals brought Charles I to trial. With no moderates to oppose them, the radical Puritans found the king guilty of treason. Charles I was beheaded on January 1, 1649. Parliament, or the few members who remained, declared that the monarchy was over and that England was a republic.

## From Commonwealth to Protectorate

The monarchy was gone, but what would replace it? Oliver Cromwell became leader of the new English Commonwealth, as the new government was called. Cromwell, ruling with the radicals left in Parliament, faced the hopeless task of uniting a nation divided not into two but numerous factions. Many subjects had turned against Parliament after the execution of Charles I. A popular poem of the time lamented:

> On Tuesday last his Grace,
>     Cheerfully, cheerfully,
> Went to his dying place,
>     to end all strife,
> Where many a weeping eye,
> With groans unto the skie,
>     To see his Majesty,
>     There end his life.

Discontent among the English people was fueled by the severe policies of the Puritans. They outlawed gambling, horse racing, newspapers, fancy clothes, public dancing, and theater. Cromwell faced perils from outside England, too. In Scotland, rebels rallied to Charles II, son of the executed king. In Ireland, Catholics had risen against Protestant landowners. Cromwell himself led the force that savagely repressed that rebellion. In addition, England was at war against Spain and Holland.

These disorders forced Cromwell to give up even the pretense of republican government. In 1653, he dissolved Parliament and named himself Lord Protector. He ruled as a virtual dictator until his death in 1658, when his son became Lord Protector. By then the English people were thoroughly sick of the endless taxations, violence, and disorder. Parliament reconvened and asked Charles II to become king. In 1660, the monarchy was restored. Though Cromwell inspired as much fear and hatred as love and reverence, he always remained true to his own high moral purposes. The measures he resorted to as ruler of England were stern and painful, yet they were probably necessary to achieve order in such a troubled, disorderly period of English history.

## LITERATURE OF A TURBULENT AGE

The reign of Charles I and the Interregnum, or period between reigns, that followed were a time of intense religious and political conflict. Under Charles I, the court remained the center of literary life. Poets upheld the traditional courtly values of loyalty to crown and church and the strict code of honor. Not surprisingly, the poets often fought on the side of the king.

The literature of the turbulent years from 1625 to 1660 in part continues the styles of the Renaissance and in part reflects changing conditions. Although Ben Jonson and others wrote plays that were more popular than Shakespeare's, the period is not remembered for its drama. Rather, it is an age that produced some of the best-loved poems in English—Jonson's crystalline lyrics and dignified longer poems modeled after classical precedents; John Donne's brilliant, intellectually ingenious amorous and religious verses; and Andrew Marvell's lyrics combining the classical polish of Jonson and the intellectual brilliance of Donne. Appropriate to a society cleft by civil war, the literature of the age had another side. The Puritan writers John Milton and John Bunyan produced deeply religious works very much different in style and substance from those of Jonson, Donne, and their followers.

## Jonson's Life

The most influential writer of the early 1600s was Ben Jonson. Jonson's life is a mirror of the tensions of his time. Jonson rose from humble origins—his stepfather was a bricklayer. The family lived near Westminster Abbey, however, and Jonson was lucky enough to attend its school. There he read the Greek and Latin authors that shaped so much of his own later writing. Although he hoped to attend college, the young Jonson found himself laying bricks. But he refused to give up his ambitions. One friend described him as having "a trowel in his hand . . . and a book in his pocket."

Jonson set down his trowel to become a soldier, and later turned up as an actor in London. One of his earliest works, a satirical play, was condemned as slanderous and landed Jonson in jail. A later play was well received, but Jonson had little chance to bask in the praise. He argued with an actor, killed him in a duel, and was once again imprisoned. There Jonson converted to Catholicism, though he later returned to the Anglican church—another sign of the changeable times he lived in.

Ultimately, Jonson became a great favorite of James I and was friendly with many noblemen and with other writers—including Shakespeare, who acted in one of Jonson's earliest plays and is the subject of one of his finest poems. By the 1620s Jonson was the best-known poet in a city of poets. As one admirer said, Jonson was the "fairest light in no darke time."

# THE SCHOOLS OF JONSON AND DONNE

## Jonson's Work

In Jonson's life we can see the turmoil of his age—violence, persecution, religious conflict. But in his writing Jonson strove for the perfection and harmony he found in his beloved classical authors, turning away from the ornate style of Elizabethan times. Although Jonson was steeped in, and greatly influenced by, the classics, he was not an imitator. He created his own voice, which people of the time recognized as distinctively modern and strong.

**BEN JONSON**
*The Granger Collection*

Jonson took seriously the role of poet. He believed, in fact, that no other profession could compare to it. Poets, he wrote, encourage "young men to all good disciplines, inflame grown men to all great virtues, [and] keep old men in their best and supreme state." A person could not be "the good poet without first being a good man," he asserted. Jonson lived up to this moral duty in several ways: by giving good advice in some poems; by honoring worthy men and women in others; and, in his plays, by satirizing corruption and immorality.

## The School of Donne

The other great poet of the early 1600's was John Donne (1572?–1631). Whereas Jonson did all he could to raise the prestige of poets, and personally oversaw the printing of his poems, Donne never tried to make writing a career. His poems, in fact, were not published until two years after his death. But manuscripts of his work circulated at court, and his witty, cerebral poems created a widely admired style in English literature: metaphysical poetry.

Donne's life, like Jonson's, reflected his turbulent age. Donne was raised a Roman Catholic. After studying at Oxford, he traveled abroad, fighting against the Spanish in the 1590's. As a young man, Donne took an active part in the life of the court and composed many fine love poems. (According to Ben Jonson, Donne wrote "all his best pieces ere he was twenty-five.") Later, Donne turned to the Protestant faith. In 1615, he was ordained as an Anglican minister. His sermons in St. Paul's Cathedral, which often lasted for hours, held hundreds of listeners at rapt attention. They are among the finest prose works of the century. After the death of his wife, Donne withdrew from society. In contrast to the fervent love poems of his youth, Donne's later poetry expresses intense religious feeling, often penitential in character. Given Donne's evolution from courtier to minister, it is not surprising that his poetry often embodies the conflict between the spirit and the world.

More than any other poet, Donne is associated with the metaphysical school of poetry. Metaphysical poetry is characterized by an unusual degree of intellectualism. Even in his love poems, Donne will base his images and figures of speech on material drawn from law, medieval theology and philosophy, natural science, metallurgy, medicine, astronomy, old legends, and other sources that more conventional poets seldom make use of. Moreover, Donne's poems are frequently structured like ingenious, subtle arguments involving complicated—and often witty—reasoning. Finally, they often employ a type of metaphor termed a *conceit*. A conceit is a comparison in which the subject is likened to something that would never normally be associated with it. In Donne's most famous conceit, for example, he likens his and his beloved's souls to the legs of a geometrician's compass:

> If they be two, they are two so
>   As stiff twin compasses are two;
> Thy soul, the fixed foot, makes no show
>   To move, but doth if the other do.
>
> And though it in the center sit,
>   Yet, when the other far doth roam,
> It leans and hearkens after it,
>   And grows erect as that comes home.

### The Sons of Ben

Jonson and Donne were the dominant poets of their age. Later poets of the seventeenth century are usually classified as being

**JOHN DONNE**
*The Granger Collection*

disciples of either Jonson or Donne. Like all such categorizations, these are only partly correct. The "Sons of Ben" were influenced by Donne's work, and the "School of Donne" read and admired Ben Jonson. The basic distinction is useful nonetheless.

Among the best-known sons of Ben were Robert Herrick, Sir John Suckling, and Richard Lovelace. These Sons of Ben are also called Cavalier poets, since they are identified with the king's cause. Robert Herrick (1591–1674) was probably closest to Jonson in style and temperament. Although he lived through the Civil War and Interregnum, Herrick's poetry gives little evidence of these worldly disturbances. He concentrated instead on things that could not be touched by war: "I sing of Brooks, of Blossomes, Birds, and Bowers; /Of April, May, of June and July-Flowers." Herrick, who became an Anglican minister, also wrote graceful religious poems.

Sir John Suckling (1609–1642), an admirer of Jonson's style but not of his moral severity, was also influenced by Donne's early love poems. Suckling, the perfect courtier, was everything the Puritans despised. A gambler, cardsharp, and pleasure seeker, he is remembered today for his love poems. In 1639, Suckling marched north with Charles I to put down the Scottish rebellion. He fled England two years later after becoming involved in a political intrigue and died in France at a young age.

Richard Lovelace (1618–1656?) was, like Suckling, a luminary of Charles I's court. A strikingly handsome man, Lovelace wrote about themes near the heart of the Cavaliers: honor, bravery, true love, and stoical resolve. Lovelace also fought for the king's cause and went to prison for it. It was there that he wrote many of his finest poems.

## The School of Donne

The most notable followers of John Donne were George Herbert (1593–1633) and Andrew Marvell (1621–1678). Herbert's mother was a friend of Donne's, and in many ways the life of Herbert parallels Donne's. He keenly felt the tension between religious and worldly drives. At first intending to enter the church, Herbert was tempted for a time to enjoy the sparkling life at the court of James I. Later Herbert became an Anglican deacon and gave himself to the care of his parish. Like Donne, Herbert excelled at the conceit and the other stylistic features of metaphysical poetry. However, Herbert's best poems are almost all religious lyrics. When read together, in his volume *The Temple*, they reveal a greater range of religious feelings than are found in Donne's religious verse.

Andrew Marvell was born later than the other metaphysical and Cavalier poets and is in many ways a figure of transition. Marvell was still a young man when the Civil War began and had little connection with the court. In fact, for three years Marvell tutored the daughter of a Puritan leader. Later Marvell became the assistant of John Milton, the greatest of the Puritan poets. When the monarchy was restored in 1660, Marvell used his influence at court to prevent Milton's execution for treason.

Marvell's best lyrics blend the metaphysical brilliance of Donne and Herbert and the classical finish of Jonson and Herrick. They offer observations on nature, love, and God that, at first, seem urbane and conventional but, on closer inspection, prove profound and problematical. His best-known poem, "To His Coy Mistress," is one of the very best lyrics in English literature.

## THE PURITAN WRITERS

So far we have been looking at poets connected with the court of the Stuarts. But perhaps the greatest poet of the seventeenth century was a Puritan, not a Cavalier: John Milton. The Puritan movement also produced the best-selling prose writer of the century, John Bunyan. Only the Bible sold more copies than Bunyan's religious narrative *The Pilgrim's Progress*.

## John Milton

In John Milton (1608–1674) the streams of the Renaissance and the Reformation flow together. Like Ben Jonson, he was a learned disciple of the Greek and Latin authors. But unlike Elizabethan humanists and the Cavalier poets, Milton was a profound Calvinist who studied the Old Testament in Hebrew.

Milton was born in London to a prosperous middle-class family. He got a good basic education, studied at Cambridge, and spent six years after college reading and studying on his own. In the 1640's, Milton was working as a private tutor in London. As the battle between Charles I and Parliament grew hotter, Milton began writing political pamphlets for the Roundhead cause. His part in the "pamphlet wars" produced *Areopagitica,* a ringing call for freedom of the press.

Milton supported the Commonwealth and Protectorate and even defended the execution of Charles I. As Cromwell's rule turned to a dictatorship, however, Milton lost hope in the possibility of forming a just society on earth. Milton, who went completely blind by 1652, set about composing an epic that would offer a poetic explanation as to why God allows suffering and unhappiness in this world.

*Paradise Lost,* published in 1667, reflects Milton's humanistic love of poetry and his Puritan devotion to God. In Book I of *Paradise Lost,* Milton voices his poetic ambition: to create "things unattempted yet in Prose or Rhyme." A few lines later he asserts his religious aim: to "justify the ways of God to men." The poem is both a heroic epic that recounts the expulsion of Adam and Eve from Eden and a vindication of God's wisdom.

## John Bunyan

After decades of political activity, Milton concluded that the best humans could hope for was to lead their individual lives blamelessly. That was the premise that John Bunyan began with. Unlike Milton, Bunyan had little education beyond reading the Bible, but what his reading and studies lacked in variety they made up for in profundity. A tinker by trade, Bunyan wandered from town to town in rural England, preaching wherever people would listen. After the restoration of Charles II, Bunyan was imprisoned, and it was there he wrote *The Pilgrim's Progress.*

The simplicity of the work in form and style was no small factor in its success. The allegory tells the story of a man who flees sin to lead a holy life. In his "apology" for the work Bunyan tells his readers:

> This book will make a traveller of thee,
> If by its counsel thou wilt ruled be;
> It will direct thee to the Holy Land,
> If thou wilt its directions understand.

Bunyan and Milton produced the greatest literary works of the Puritan revolution. The Commonwealth had failed, but left behind a new culture that was neither courtly nor Puritan. The next age would belong to professional writers, journalists, and playwrights, not to courtly poets or Puritan proselytizers. The revolution that had begun in the mid-seventeenth century would continue in the eighteenth.

# ENGLISH VOICES

## Quotations by Prominent Figures of the Period

No man is an Island, entire of itself; . . . any man's death diminishes me, because I am involved in Mankind; and therefore never send to know for whom the bell tolls; it tolls for thee.
**John Donne,** "Meditation XVII"

Art hath an enemy called Ignorance.
**Ben Jonson,** "Every Man Out of His Humor"

Drink to me only with thine eyes
And I will pledge with mine.
**Ben Jonson,** "To Celia"

Gather ye rosebuds while ye may,
Old Time is still a-flying.
**Robert Herrick,** "To the Virgins, to Make Much of Time"

They also serve who only stand and wait.
**John Milton,** "Sonnet: On His Blindness"

But at my back I always hear
Time's winged chariot hurrying near.
**Andrew Marvell,** "To His Coy Mistress"

I have laid aside business, and gone a-fishing.
**Izaak Walton,** *The Compleat Angler*

Stone walls do not a prison make,
Nor iron bars a cage.
**Richard Lovelace,** "To Althea, from Prison"

# The Literature of 1625–1660

When you read literature, it is important to place it in its historical context. Doing so will help you to understand influences on the writer's ideas and techniques.

**Historical Context**

During the years from 1625 to 1660, England suffered from tremendous political and religious unrest. Shortly after Charles I inherited the throne in 1625, he became involved in a power struggle with the Parliament, whose members strongly objected to his efforts to limit Parliamentary authority. Charles I's continuing suppression of Puritans also aroused a great deal of anger among certain members of the Parliament, many of whom were Puritans. This controversy resulted in a civil war that began in 1642 and brought about the temporary downfall of the monarchy in 1649. Oliver Cromwell, a Puritan member of Parliament, ruled the nation for nine years before dying in 1658 and leaving the country in the hands of his son, Richard. Richard proved to be an ineffective ruler, however, and in 1660 the monarchy was restored.

**Literary Movements**

The writers from this period can be divided essentially into two groups: the metaphysical poets and the Sons of Ben. A group consisting of John Donne and several of his followers, the metaphysical poets are known for their intellectual verse filled with complex, elaborate, and striking comparisons. In contrast, the Sons of Ben, led by the influential poet Ben Jonson, are known for their precise, witty, and elegant poetry. However, John Milton, probably the most significant writer of the period, did not fit into either of these categories. Drawing upon a variety of literary traditions, Milton produced a range of different types of works.

**Writers' Techniques**

Among the metaphysical poets, the conceit, an especially striking type of metaphor, was a popular literary device. Influenced by the works of the ancient Greeks and Romans, the Sons of Ben relied on classical poetic forms and often used allusions in their works. Milton, on the other hand, made extensive use of both metaphors and allusions.

On the following pages is a poem by Ben Jonson. The notes in the side column should help you to place the poem in its historical context.

# To the Memory of My Beloved Master, William Shakespeare

Ben Jonson

To draw no envy, Shakespeare, on thy name,
Am I thus ample[1] to thy book and fame:
While I confess thy writings to be such
As neither man nor Muse can praise too much.
5 'Tis true, and all men's suffrage.[2] But these ways
Were not the paths I meant unto thy práise:
For silliest[3] ignorance on these may light,
Which, when it sounds at best, but echoes right;
Or blind affection,[4] which doth ne'er advance
10 The truth, but gropes, and urgeth all by chance;
Or crafty malice, might pretend this praise,
And think to ruin, where it seemed to raise . . .
But thou art proof against them, and indeed
Above the ill fortune of them, or the need.
15 I, therefore will begin. Soul of the age!
The applause! delight! the wonder of our stage!
My Shakespeare, rise; I will not lodge thee by
Chaucer, or Spenser, or bid Beaumont[5] lie
A little further, to make thee a room:
20 Thou art a monument, without a tomb,
And art alive still, while thy book doth live,
And we have wits to read, and praise to give.

**Historical Context:** This poem first appeared in the opening pages of the first edition of Shakespeare's collected plays, published in 1623.

**Literary Movement:** Jonson stresses a rational, intellectual examination of Shakespeare's achievements.

**Writer's Technique:** Jonson uses apostrophe, directly addressing Shakespeare in the poem.

**Literary Movement:** Jonson uses the type of strong and elegant yet simple and precise language that characterized the poetry of the Sons of Ben.

---

**1. ample:** Liberal.
**2. suffrage:** Agreement.
**3. silliest:** Simplest.
**4. blind affection:** Prejudice.
**5. Beaumont:** Francis Beaumont (1584–1616), a playwright who was one of Shakespeare's contemporaries. Chaucer, Spenser, and Beaumont were buried in Westminster Abbey; Shakespeare was buried in Stratford. Jonson believes that it is proper for Shakespeare to be buried apart from these other important writers.

**SHAKESPEARE AND BEN JONSON AT CHESS**
*Karel van Mander*

*Writer's Technique:*
Jonson uses regular
rhyme and rhythm
throughout the poem.

*Writer's Technique:*
Jonson alludes to
classical Greek and
Roman tragic playwrights.

That I not mix thee so, my brain excuses,
I mean with great, but disproportioned[6] Muses;
25   For, if I thought my judgment were of years,
I should commit thee surely with thy peers,
And tell, how far thou didst our Lyly outshine,
Or sporting Kyd, or Marlowe's[7] mighty line.
And though thou hadst small[8] Latin, and less Greek,
30   From thence to honor thee, I would not seek
For names; but call forth thund'ring Aeschylus,
Euripides, and Sophocles to us,
Paccuvius, Accius,[9] him of Cordova dead,[10]
To life again, to hear thy buskin[11] tread,
35   And shake a stage: Or, when thy socks[12] were on,

---

   **6. disproportioned:** Not comparable.
   **7. Lyly . . . Kyd . . . Marlowe:** Elizabethan playwrights who
influenced Shakespeare.
   **8. small:** A limited knowledge of.
   **9. Aeschylus** (es′ kə ləs)**, Euripides** (yoo rip′ ə dēz′) **. . . Sophocles**
(sof′ ə klēz′) **. . . Paccuvius** (pə kōō′ vē əs)**, Accius** (ak′ ē əs)**:** Classical
Greek and Roman tragic playwrights.
   **10. him . . . dead:** Classical Roman playwright, Seneca, born in
Cordova, Spain.
   **11. buskin:** Symbolizes tragedy. Tragic actors wore shoes with thick
"buckskin" soles.
   **12. socks:** Symbolize comedy. Comic actors wore thin-soled shoes
called "socks."

Leave thee alone, for the comparison
Of all, that insolent Greece, or haughty Rome
Sent forth, or since did from their ashes come.
Triumph, my Britain, thou hast one to show,
40   To whom all scenes[13] of Europe homage owe.
He was not of an age, but for all time!
And all the Muses still were in their prime,
When like Apollo[14] he came forth to warm
Our ears, or like a Mercury[15] to charm!
45   Nature herself was proud of his designs,
And joyed to wear the dressing of his lines!
Which were so richly spun, and woven so fit,[16]
As, since, she will vouchsafe no other wit.
The merry Greek, tart Aristophanes,
50   Neat Terence, witty Plautus,[17] now not please,
But antiquated, and deserted lie
As they were not of Nature's family.
Yet must I not give Nature all; thy art,
My gentle Shakespeare, must enjoy a part.
55   For though the poet's matter nature be,
His art doth give the fashion.[18] And, that he
Who casts[19] to write a living line, must sweat,
(Such as thine are) and strike the second heat
Upon the Muse's anvil; turn the same,
60   (And himself with it) that he thinks to frame,
Or for the laurel[20] he may gain a scorn;
For a good poet's made, as well as born.
And such wert thou. Look how the father's face
Lives in his issue, even so, the race
65   Of Shakespeare's mind, and manners brightly shines
In his well torned, and true filèd[21] lines;
In each of which, he seems to shake a lance,[22]
As brandished at the eyes of ignorance.

**Writer's Technique:** Jonson alludes to figures from Greek and Roman mythology.

**Writer's Technique:** Jonson alludes to classical Greek and Roman comic dramatists. Jonson's frequent use of allusions to classical Greece and Rome reflects the influence of classical writing and ideas on his work.

**Writer's Technique:** Jonson uses the work of a blacksmith as a metaphor for the tasks of a poet.

**Literary Movement:** Jonson stresses the importance of education and hard work in shaping a poet's talent.

---

**13. scenes:** Stages.
**14. Apollo:** In Greek and Roman mythology, the god of light, music, and poetry.
**15. Mercury:** In Roman mythology, the messenger of the gods and the god of cleverness.
**16. fit:** Appropriately.
**17. Aristophanes** (ar′ is tof′ ə nēz′) **. . . Terence** (ter′ əns) **. . . Plautus** (plô′ təs): Classical Greek and Roman comic playwrights.
**18. fashion:** Form.
**19. casts:** Undertakes.
**20. laurel:** Fame.
**21. true filèd:** Accurately polished.
**22. shake a lance:** A pun on Shakespeare's name.

Sweet swan of Avon![23] what a sight it were

70  To see thee in our waters yet appear,
And make those flights upon the banks of Thames
That so did take Eliza and our James![24]
But stay, I see thee in the hemisphere
Advanced, and made a constellation there!

75  Shine forth, thou star of poets, and with rage[25]
Or influence, chide, or cheer the drooping stage,
Which, since thy flight from hence, hath mourned like
    night,
And despairs day, but for thy volume's light.

_____

**23. Avon:** The river on which Shakespeare's home town, Stratford, is located.
**24. Eliza . . . James:** Queen Elizabeth I and King James I.
**25. rage:** Poetic inspiration.

**Historical Context:**
Jonson refers to Queen Elizabeth I and King James I, who encouraged and supported Shakespeare and other writers.

---

## THINKING ABOUT THE SELECTION
### Recalling

1. According to lines 1–12, what are the wrong reasons for praising Shakespeare?
2. According to the final two lines, how has the stage reacted since Shakespeare's death?

### Interpreting

3. What does Jonson mean when he comments that Shakespeare was "not of an age, but for all time"?
4. What is the meaning of the metaphor in lines 57–59?
5. (a) What does this poem reveal about Jonson's attitude toward Shakespeare? (b) What does it reveal about his attitudes concerning the art of writing?
6. (a) How does your awareness of the meaning of the allusions contribute to your overall understanding of Jonson's poem? (b) How does Jonson's use of allusions help to give you a sense of Shakespeare's place in literary history?

7. How do Jonson's allusions reflect his interest in classical Greek and Roman literature?

### Applying

8. In this poem, Jonson expresses the idea that a writer can be immortalized through his or her work. Explain whether you agree with this suggestion.

## THINKING AND WRITING
### Writing a Letter

Write a letter to Ben Jonson in which you tell him whether you agree with the attitudes he expresses concerning Shakespeare and the art of writing. Reread the poem, focusing on Jonson's attitudes. Brainstorm about your own attitudes on these subjects. Then express your opinions in a personal letter. Use an informal, conversational writing style, but be sure to support your opinions. When you revise, make sure you have not included any unnecessary information. Proofread your letter and prepare a final draft.

# The Schools of
# Donne and Jonson

**GREENWICH PALACE FROM THE NORTHEAST WITH A MAN-OF-WAR AT ANCHOR (detail)** *c.* 1630
*National Maritime Museum*

# JOHN DONNE

## 1572(?)–1631

John Donne's reputation has changed over time. He was very popular during his own lifetime, but his writings went out of favor soon after his death. At the beginning of the twentieth century, however, interest in his works revived. Now Donne occupies a major position in literature. Modern critics place him with William Shakespeare and John Milton at the very pinnacle of English poetry.

Donne was raised by his widowed mother, who was a devout Catholic and a member of the family of St. Thomas More. At the time, being Catholic was difficult, for Roman Catholics were severely discriminated against in Queen Elizabeth's England. Indeed, Donne later recanted his Catholicism and joined the Anglican Church. Scholars are divided as to his motives. They wonder whether he experienced a genuine conversion or made a shrewd move to try to gain advancement in courtly society.

Donne's life is generally described as falling into two parts. The first is often thought of as the "wild youth of Jack Donne, ambitious man about town." Bright, clever, and charming, Donne was welcomed into the most exclusive courtly circles and served as private secretary to one of the Queen's highest-ranking officials. He was so charming that he wooed and won the hand in marriage of Anne More, his employer's niece.

As with his religious conversion, some scholars have questioned Donne's motives. Cynics thought that through this marriage Donne had made a shrewd move to advance his career. However, the marriage did not work out that way. Because of the opposition of Anne's father, Donne's marriage ruined his chances for advancement. As a consequence, the devoted couple and their many children experienced seventeen years of poverty, illness, and despair. During these years Donne eked out a living as a writer of religious tracts and as the temporary secretary of several aristocrats. He also became during this difficult period one of the most widely read and influential poets of the age.

Later Donne was ordained and made dean of St. Paul's Cathedral in London. He now entered the second part of his life, which has been described as the "sacred calling of Dr. John Donne, Dean of St. Paul's." From this time until his death, Donne was the most popular preacher in England; his meditations and sermons were published during his life and went through several editions.

We should not, however, emphasize too much the differences between the younger and older Donne. All of his writings, whether on love or faith, were written with the same intensity and wit.

# GUIDE FOR INTERPRETING

## Song, Holy Sonnet 10, Holy Sonnet 14

Donne was a leading writer of what has come to be called *metaphysical poetry* because of its concern with philosophical and religious issues. This kind of poetry is characterized by the extensive use of paradoxes and conceits.

**Paradox.** In literature, a paradox is an apparent self-contradiction that reveals a kind of truth. One of the most famous literary paradoxes is present in Donne's "Holy Sonnet 14": "Take me to You, imprison me, for I, / Except You enthral me, never shall be free." Finding "freedom" in prison or in slavery would seem to many people a contradiction. But here, "prison" and "enthral" (enslave) are metaphors for submissive devotion to God, which to the deeply religious person represents true freedom.

**Metaphysical Conceit.** A conceit is an extended, fanciful metaphor that makes a surprising or unexpected comparison. In the sixteenth century, the Elizabethans fell in love with long, elaborate conceits, as in Sir Philip Sidney's comparison of the moon with a languishing lover in "Sonnet 31." The metaphysical poets, such as John Donne and Andrew Marvell, wrote ingenious, often shocking conceits in which very dissimilar objects are compared.

Sir George Moore was so furious that his seventeen-year-old daughter Anne married John Donne against his wishes that he not only threw her and his son-in-law out of his home, but also convinced Lord Chancellor Egerton to fire Donne from his position as Secretary to the Great Seal and arranged to have the young poet imprisoned. Donne and his wife found sanctuary in a house in Pyrford, but near Anne's father, who lived in Surrey. Legend has it that one of the first actions Donne took upon his arrival in Pyrford was to write the following lines on a pane of glass in his new home:

John Donne

An Donne

Undone.

Was Donne really "undone"? According to what he says in "Song," what did he lose—and what did he win?

Write a short composition in which you use metaphors to explain yourself. Try to convince someone of an unusual experience you have had. Find objects, ideas, or common experiences that you can compare with your own experience and explain the connections.

# Song

### John Donne

Sweetest love, I do not go,
    For weariness of thee,
Nor in hope the world can show
    A fitter love for me;
5        But since that I
Must die at last, 'tis best
To use[1] myself in jest,
        Thus by feigned[2] deaths to die.

Yesternight the sun went hence,
10       And yet is here today;
He hath no desire nor sense,
    Nor half so short a way;
        Then fear not me,
But believe that I shall make
15   Speedier journeys, since I take
        More wings and spurs than he.

O how feeble is man's power,
    That if good fortune fall,
Cannot add another hour,
20       Nor a lost hour recall!
        But come bad chance,
And we join to it our strength,
And we teach it art and length,
        Itself o'er us to advance.

25   When thou sigh'st, thou sigh'st not wind,
    But sigh'st my soul away;
When thou weep'st, unkindly kind,
    My life's blood doth decay.
        It cannot be
30   That thou lovest me as thou say'st,
If in thine my life thou waste,
        That art the best of me.

---

**1. use:** Condition.
**2. feigned:** Imagined.

                    Let not thy divining heart
                    Forethink me any ill,
35              Destiny may take thy part,
                    And may thy fears fulfill;
                    But think that we
                Are but turned aside to sleep.
                They who one another keep
40              Alive, ne'r parted be.

---

## THINKING ABOUT THE SELECTION
### Recalling

1. What are the speaker's reasons for leaving his beloved?
2. What does the speaker say happens when "bad chance" comes (ll. 21–24)?
3. How do the beloved's sighs and tears affect the speaker?
4. How does the speaker suggest that his beloved think of their parting?

### Interpreting

5. To what is the sun in stanza 2 compared?
6. Of what is the speaker trying to convince his beloved? How would you outline the speaker's argument?
7. What is the tone of the poem? Is it angry, beseeching, reassuring, uncertain, mocking?

### Applying

8. The speaker in this poem resorts to exaggeration as an instrument of persuasion. Do you think that exaggerating in order to win is a valid persuasive technique? Explain your answer.

9. Although this is a love poem, it is cast in the form of an argument. Why is that appropriate?

## ANALYZING LITERATURE
### Understanding Paradox

A paradox is an apparent self-contradiction that reveals a truth. A very well-known one is the statement of Jesus in Matthew 16:25, "For whosoever will save his life shall lose it." A related paradox can be found in Donne's Holy Sonnet 10: ". . . poor death, nor yet canst thou kill me." In this example, the speaker says death cannot kill him because as a devout Christian he will have eternal life. Our very puzzlement adds zest to our understanding once we have figured out the meaning of the paradox, which is why religious leaders and writers so often employ them.

Donne's "Song" contains a couple of paradoxes. Explain why the following quote is a paradox, what it means, and how it works in the poem: "When thou weep'st, unkindly kind" (line 27).

# Holy Sonnet 10

John Donne

Death be not proud, though some have called thee
Mighty and dreadful, for thou art not so;
For those whom thou think'st thou dost overthrow,
Die not, poor death, nor yet canst thou kill me.
5  From rest and sleep, which but thy pictures[1] be,
Much pleasure; then from thee much more must flow,
And soonest our best men with thee do go,
Rest of their bones, and soul's delivery[2]
Thou art slave to fate, chance, kings, and desperate men,
10  And dost with poison, war, and sickness dwell,
And poppy,[3] or charms can make us sleep as well
And better than thy stroke; why swell'st[4] thou then?
One short sleep past, we wake eternally,
And death shall be no more; Death, thou shalt die.

---

**1. pictures:** Images.
**2. And . . . delivery:** Our best men go with you to rest their bones
and find freedom for their souls.
**3. poppy:** Opium.
**4. swell'st:** Swell with pride.

---

## THINKING ABOUT THE SELECTION

### Recalling

1. In the first four lines, why does the speaker say that death should not be proud?
2. Why does the speaker say in lines 5–8 that death is pleasant? What within these lines indicates that death is a source of pleasure?
3. How does the speaker characterize death in lines 9–12?
4. Why does the speaker say that death shall be no more?

### Interpreting

5. (a) What does the speaker mean when he says in lines 3–4: "For those whom thou think'st thou dost overthrow, / Die not, poor death, nor yet canst thou kill me"? (b) In what way is this meaning reinforced by the last two lines?
6. (a) What does the paradox "Death, thou shalt die" mean? What makes it paradoxical? (b) In what way does the final paradox serve as the conclusion to the argument of the poem?

### Applying

7. In the poem, the speaker gives human characteristics to death. This is called *personification.* Death has often been personified in art and literature, sometimes as the grim reaper carrying a scythe, at other times as an angel with black wings and a net, and at still other

**SIR THOMAS ASTON AT THE DEATHBED OF HIS WIFE**
*John Souch*
Manchester City Art Galleries

times as a fierce horseman whose head is often a skull. Think of other ways you may have seen death personified in literature or art. Discuss with your classmates what each of these images implies about our attitudes toward death. How does Donne's poem address these attitudes?

## ANALYZING LITERATURE
### Understanding Metaphysical Conceit

The term *conceit* comes from the Italian word *concetto,* meaning "conception." Meta-physical poets often worked out complex, far-fetched conceits, and Donne's are among the best of them. Sometimes a metaphysical conceit is an elaborate image; sometimes it can be just a line or two. What is essential to all metaphysical conceits, however, is the startling conjunction of dissimilar concepts, ideas, images, or objects. The underlying conceit of Holy Sonnet 10 is the likening of death to a proud but ultimately ineffectual tyrant.

1. What are the images in the poem that illustrate the conceit?
2. How do they relate with each other to form a single image of a powerless Death?

# Holy Sonnet 14

## John Donne

Batter my heart, three-personed God;[1] for You
As yet but knock, breathe, shine, and seek to mend;
That I may rise, and stand, o'erthrow me, and bend
Your force, to break, blow, burn and make me new.
5　I, like an usurped town, to another due,
　Labor to admit You, but O, to no end,
Reason Your viceroy[2] in me, me should defend,
But is captived, and proves weak or untrue.
Yet dearly I love You, and would be loved fain,
10　But am betrothed unto Your enemy.
Divorce me, untie, or break that knot again;
Take me to You, imprison me, for I,
Except You enthral[3] me, never shall be free,
Nor ever chaste, except You ravish me.

---

**1. three-personed God:** The Trinity:
the Father, the Son, and the Holy Ghost.
**2. viceroy:** Deputy.
**3. enthral:** Enslave.

## THINKING ABOUT THE SELECTION

### Recalling

1. In the first four lines what does the speaker ask God to do?
2. (a) To what does the speaker compare himself in line 5? (b) Of what does the speaker complain in lines 6–8? (c) How is reason characterized in lines 7 and 8?
3. (a) How does the speaker describe his condition in lines 9 and 10? (b) What does the speaker ask God to do in lines 11–12? (c) What reason does he give for his request in lines 13–14?

### Interpreting

4. In line 2 why does the speaker complain of God's gentleness? Why does the speaker want God to treat him violently?
5. What are the paradoxes in lines 3, 13, and 14? What do they mean? How do they affect you, the reader?
6. Who is the "enemy" to whom the speaker is "betrothed"?
7. What is the tone in this poem? Is it belligerent, argumentative, pleading, arrogant, or contemptuous?

### Applying

8. In the poem the speaker wants to be overwhelmed with emotion. There are many instances when a person might want to experience a deep emotion. What are some of these instances?

## CRITICAL THINKING AND READING

### Following an Argument

Metaphysical poets were said to combine "passion with reason." Reason is the chief tool of philosophy, and arguments are the chief tools of reason. A philosophical argument—which is much different from the shouting match we usually think of—is a logical or reasonable demonstration of how certain facts or ideas can or must lead to a conclusion. When you say, "I believe such and such because of this, that, and the other," you are offering an *argument* for your beliefs.

But of course, few if any literary works display their "arguments" as nakedly as we have just done. For example, if we think of Holy Sonnet 14 as an argument—rather than as a prayer or an appeal, which is another way to view the poem—then we might ask why the speaker is saying, in effect, "God, please beat down my resistance so that I can worship you." After reflection, we might come up with the proposition: "Suffering overwhelms doubt and leads to the love of God."

Reread Holy Sonnet 14 and support the proposition with the images and metaphors of the poem. First state the proposition or thesis, then give evidence supporting the proposition. Finally restate the proposition as a conclusion in such a way as to indicate it follows from the evidence.

## THINKING AND WRITING

### Writing a Philosophical Argument

Take your argument—thesis or proposition, supporting evidence, and conclusion—for Donne's poem and discuss it in a 500-word composition. Make sure you express your opinion of Donne's argument. Include in your discussion evidence supporting your opinion.

Take off from Donne's poem and write your own philosophical argument. For example, Holy Sonnet 14 might suggest questions about the difficulty of making a commitment or of feeling an attachment to a transcendent or abstract idea. Freewrite, exploring your answer to this question. After you have arrived at an answer to your question, take that as your thesis or proposition. Develop supporting evidence; take into account opposing views, if there are any; answer them; and present your conclusion. When you revise, keep in mind that when writing an argumentative essay, you have to persuade your readers that your views are correct. Are your supporting details arranged so that they will have a powerful effect? Have you provided enough support? Proofread your essay and prepare a final draft.

# GUIDE FOR INTERPRETING

## Meditation 17

**Theme.** The central or main idea of a literary work is its *theme*. In some works, the theme is stated directly. At the beginning of Sir Francis Bacon's "Idols of the Cave," for example, he says that prejudices derived from "education, habit, and accident" may interfere with the ability to understand things clearly. More often, though, the theme of a literary work is presented indirectly. An example of this can be found in John Donne's "Song." We can say the theme of the poem is something like: "Separation may seem like death, but it is really more like sleep, and lovers would suffer less if they viewed their separation this way."

Many works of literature have more than one theme. When they do, there is usually one dominant or controlling idea and several secondary or subordinate ones. For example, the major theme of *Macbeth* is the effects of ruthless ambition. This is not, however, the only theme in the play. To it can be added as secondary themes: cruelty by rulers causes rebellion; illegitimate power will be overthrown; and evil deeds bring their own punishment.

No matter the kind of writing, themes arise from the elements of the work. In a poem, for example, metaphor, image, and choice of words frequently develop the theme; in a play or novel, plot, character, and dialogue usually illustrate the theme; and in an essay, subordinate ideas and the ways in which language is used.

**Commentary**

In 1940, Ernest Hemingway sparked a run on copies of "Meditation 17" when he used a phrase from it for the title of his bestselling novel, *For Whom the Bell Tolls*. To underscore the parallel between the theme of Donne's meditation and that of his book, Hemingway also quoted a portion of the meditation on the book's inside front cover. Hemingway used the theme of Donne's "Meditation 17" as a call for personal involvement in the Spanish Civil War, the subject of his novel, and by extension, World War II.

Publishers rushed to reissue "Meditation 17." The Oxford Press, for example, reported that all its editions of Donne's poetry sold out, while "fifteen hundred sheets [of 'Meditation 17'] ordered by Random House were bombed out of existence."

What do you think there was in Donne's theme in "Meditation 17" that captured the mood of the war years?

**Writing**

Jot down ideas as they come to you while reading Donne's meditation. Then assign numbers to your jottings according to their importance to you. Number one will be your main theme.

# Meditation 17

## John Donne

*Nunc lento sonitu dicunt, Morieris.*

(Now, this bell tolling softly for another, says to me, Thou must die.)

Perchance he for whom this bell tolls may be so ill as that he knows not it tolls for him; and perchance I may think myself so much better than I am as that they who are about me and see my state may have caused it to toll for me, and I know not that. The church is catholic, universal, so are all her actions; all that she does belongs to all. When she baptizes a child, that action concerns me; for that child is thereby connected to that head which is my head too, and ingrafted into that body[1] whereof I am a member. And when she buries a man, that action concerns me: all mankind is of one author and is one volume; when one man dies, one chapter is not torn out of the book, but translated[2] into a better language; and every chapter must be so translated. God employs several translators; some pieces are translated by age, some by sickness, some by war, some by justice; but God's hand is in every translation, and his hand shall bind up all our scattered leaves again for that library where every book shall lie open to one another. As therefore the bell that rings to a sermon calls not upon the preacher only, but upon the congregation to come, so this bell calls us all; but how much more me, who am brought so near the door by this sickness. There was a contention as far as a suit[3] (in which both piety and dignity, religion and estimation,[4] were mingled) which of the religious orders should ring to prayers first in the morning; and it was determined that they should ring first that rose earliest. If we understand aright the dignity of this bell that tolls for our evening prayer, we would be glad to make it ours by rising early, in that application, that it might be ours as well as his whose indeed it is. The bell doth

---

**3. suit:** Lawsuit.
**4. estimation:** Self-esteem.

**1. body:** The Church
**2. translated:** Carried across on a spiritual level from one sphere to another.

toll for him that thinks it doth; and though it intermit again, yet from that minute that that occasion wrought upon him, he is united to God. Who casts not up his eye to the sun when it rises? but who takes off his eye from a comet when that breaks out? Who bends not his ear to any bell which upon any occasion rings? but who can remove it from that bell which is passing a piece of himself out of this world? No man is an island, entire of itself; every man is a piece of the continent, a part of the main.[5] If a clod be washed away by the sea, Europe is the less, as well as if a promontory were, as well as if a manor of thy friend's or of thine own were. Any man's death diminishes me because I am involved in mankind, and therefore never send to know for whom the bell tolls; it tolls for thee. Neither can we call this a begging of misery or a borrowing of misery, as though we were not miserable enough of

ourselves but must fetch in more from the next house, in taking upon us the misery of our neighbors. Truly it were an excusable covetousness if we did; for affliction is a treasure, and scarce any man hath enough of it. No man hath affliction enough that is not matured and ripened by it, and made fit for God by that affliction. If a man carry treasure in bullion, or in a wedge of gold, and have none coined into current money, his treasure will not defray him as he travels. Tribulation is treasure in the nature of it, but it is not current money in the use of it, except we get nearer and nearer our home, heaven, by it. Another man may be sick too, and sick to death, and this affliction may lie in his bowels as gold in a mine and be of no use to him; but this bell that tells me of his affliction digs out and applies that gold to me, if by this consideration of another's danger, I take mine own into contemplation and so secure myself by making my recourse to my God, who is our only security.

---

**5. main:** Mainland.

---

### Primary Source

Poet and critic T. S. Eliot ignited a literary bonfire in 1921 when he set about establishing Donne as the speaker for the twentieth-century mood. Eliot believed that:

"In the seventeenth century a dissociation of sensibility set in, from which we have never recovered; and this dissociation . . . was aggravated by the influence of the two most poweful poets of the century, Milton and Dryden.

"Each of these men performed certain poetic functions so magnificently well that the magnitude of the effect concealed the absence of others. The language went on and in some respects improved; the best verse of Collins, Gray, Johnson, and even Goldsmith satisfies some of our fastidious demands better than that of Donne or Marvell or

King. But while the language became more refined, the feeling became more crude. The feeling, the sensibility, expressed in the 'Country Churchyard' is cruder than that in 'Coy Mistress' . . .

"We can only say that it appears likely that poetry in our civilization, as it exists at present, must be *difficult*. Our civilization comprehends great variety and complexity, and this variety and complexity, playing upon a refined sensibility, must produce more . . . complex results. The poet must become more and more comprehensive, more allusive, more indirect, in order to force, to dislocate if necessary, language into his meaning."

His remarks set the standard for a generation of students: Donne soared; Milton and Dryden plummeted.

## THINKING ABOUT THE SELECTION

### Recalling

1. In "Meditation 17," what are the circumstances that cause church bells to toll?
2. Why does Donne say the tolling bell applies to him as well as to others?
3. At the conclusion, why does Donne say that contemplation of the tolling bell brings one close to God?

### Interpreting

4. To what do the metaphors "chapter," "book," "language," and "translated" refer?
5. What is meant by "No man is an island entire of itself; every man is a piece of the continent"?

### Applying

6. At the beginning of the Second World War, Donne's phrase "No man is an island" became widely used as a slogan by those fighting Nazi Germany. It served to explain why Great Britain went to war in defense of Poland and France, and why the United States helped Britain in its most difficult times. Given this historical context, how did the meaning of the phrase match the meaning intended by Donne?
7. What is Donne's attitude toward death in "Meditation 17"? How does it compare with his view of death in Holy Sonnet 10?

## ANALYZING LITERATURE

### Recognizing Themes

**Themes** are the central ideas of literary works. Some works have several themes in the same piece, one dominant and others subordinate. The subordinate ideas usually play a supporting role by backing up or reinforcing the main idea.

1. In the following list of ideas from "Meditation 17," which one is central and which are secondary?
   a. Death comes to everyone.
   b. There is life after death.
   c. All humans share the same experiences.
   d. Contemplation of another's death and suffering can prepare one for life after death.
   e. By empathizing with another's suffering, we recognize our common humanity.
   f. No individual exists alone.
2. Explain how the secondary ideas support the main one, and show how Donne's theme controls the other ideas.

## CRITICAL THINKING AND READING

### Arguing Through Analogy

An **analogy** is a comparison pointing up the resemblance between two or more things, ideas, or people. For example, one might draw an analogy between a teacher, who takes students through the difficulties of a subject, and a guide who takes travelers over some difficult or dangerous terrain.

Analogies are often used to explain complicated ideas or argue difficult points. As a rule, an analogy compares an unusual or abstract concept to something familiar or concrete. A frequent analogy, for example, is the comparison of the effect of a person's attractiveness to the action of a magnet on metal, as when we talk of an individual's "magnetism."

To "prove" that there is an afterlife and that death is not final, Donne draws an analogy. What is that analogy? How does this analogy contribute to the overall argument of "Meditation 17"?

## THINKING AND WRITING

### Writing About the Theme of a Work

Take the idea that you chose in Analyzing Literature as central to "Meditation 17" and discuss how Donne developed it. Show how he hammered away at certain ideas through repetition. Also show how one idea supported another in an almost pyramidal fashion, with Donne's major theme at the apex.

# GEORGE HERBERT

## 1593–1633

Herbert was born to a wealthy and influential aristocratic family. Instead of becoming a high-ranking official at the English court, however, he became a country parson at one of the smallest rural churches in England. There he served the poor and wrote the poems that gained him fame.

Like many wealthy young men, George Herbert first looked toward worldly success. He served as spokesman for Cambridge University, usually a steppingstone to high public office, and became a favorite of King James I. It was during this period of great promise that Herbert also served for two years as a Member of Parliament. With the deaths of his mother and several patrons, he withdrew from London. In 1630 he accepted a parish assignment in a remote part of England. For the remaining three years of his life he devoted himself to his church: He restored the church buildings at his own expense, tended to his parishioners, performed music for his congregation, and composed his devotional poems.

In many ways, Herbert's poetry shows the influence of John Donne. This is understandable, since Donne was older and a good family friend. Herbert's temperament, however, was very different from that of his doubt-ridden, anxious mentor. The poetry Herbert wrote is graceful, pious verse intended to instill devotion by giving pleasure. As he himself put it: "A verse may find him who a sermon flies, / And turn delight into a sacrifice."

Herbert organized his poems in a particular sequence and called his collection *The Temple*. Just before his death, he sent the manuscript of *The Temple* to a profoundly religious friend named Nicholas Ferrar with a special request. If Ferrar found the poems worthy, then he should have them published; if not, they should be burned. Fortunately, Ferrar found the poems worthy. *The Temple,* as it turned out, was enormously popular throughout the seventeenth century.

Herbert had carefully given his collection of 160 very different poems a unifying concept. Taken together, all the poems represent the experience of attending church. *The Temple* opens with the rather long poem "The Church Porch" and then, in a wide variety of verse forms, represents parts of a church building, religious services, sacred objects, and private devotions. We can glimpse the large assortment of forms and themes present in Herbert's collection of poems by examining the three reprinted in this volume.

# GUIDE FOR INTERPRETING

## Virtue, Easter Wings, Man

**Emblematic Images.** Emblems were usually pictures accompanied by mottoes or labels and poems connecting or explaining the pictures and the mottoes. In some instances the poem itself was shaped so as to serve as picture, motto, and explanation. George Herbert's "Easter Wings" is such a poem. Verses of this type are called *emblematic images* or *emblem poems.*

Emblem poems were written so that visual image and verbal image could reinforce one another. "Easter Wings," for example, is concerned with the resurrection of the spirit, and angelic wings may well help the troubled soul to rise and take flight. When this poem was first published, it was printed on its side. In this way, the poem *looked* as if an angel or bird were flying, wings spread apart.

Shaped poems, such as "Easter Wings," have been produced intermittently since ancient times. An ancient Roman, writing about a sea fight, had the lines of his poems written so that they made pictures of ships at battle. Shaped poems were not produced after the classical period until their revival at the beginning of the Renaissance. Then they became popular. One Renaissance poet wrote a drinking song shaped like a bottle. Other poets wrote their verses so as to make shapes of crosses, altars, hearts, tears, and so forth. Shaped poems are still being written today, and they often still serve a kind of emblematic purpose.

**Writing**

Write the name of a picture that appeals to you. For example, you might choose the painting, *Mona Lisa,* by Leonardo da Vinci, or the photograph of the Beatles dressed as *Sergeant Pepper's Lonely Hearts Club Band.* Use the name as the motto and write a short comment for motto and picture.

**Primary Source**

What kind of preacher was Herbert? Were his sermons full of the clever word plays that characterize his verse? One source tells us that Herbert delivered his first sermon "after a most florid manner, both with great learning and eloquence," but promised that "since Almighty God does not intend to lead men to heaven by hard questions, he would not therefore fill their heads with unnecessary notions; but that for their sakes, his language and his expressions should be more plain and practical in his future sermons . . . He often tells them, that sermons are dangerous things, that none goes out of church as he came in, but either better or worse; that none is careless before his Judge, and that the word of God shall judge us. By these and other means the parson procures attention; but the character of his sermon is holiness; he is not witty, or learned, or eloquent, but holy."

# Virtue

George Herbert

Sweet day, so cool, so calm, so bright,
The bridal of the earth and sky;
The dew shall weep thy fall tonight;
        For thou must die.

5   Sweet rose, whose hue angry and brave[1]
Bids the rash gazer wipe his eye:
Thy root is ever in its grave,
        And thou must die.

Sweet spring, full of sweet days and roses,
10  A box where sweets[2] compacted lie;
My music shows ye have your closes,[3]
        And all must die.

Only a sweet and virtuous soul,
Like seasoned timber, never gives;
15  But though the whole world turn to coal,[4]
        Then chiefly lives.

---

**1. angry and brave:** Red (the hue of anger) and splendid.
**2. sweets:** Perfumes.
**3. closes:** The concluding sounds.
**4. turn to cinder:** Be reduced to cinder and ash by the fires of the
Last Judgment (see II Peter 3:10).

---

## THINKING ABOUT THE SELECTION

### Recalling

1. In the first three stanzas of "Virtue," what happens to "sweet day," "sweet rose," and "sweet spring"?
2. In the last stanza, what happens to the "sweet and virtuous soul"?

### Interpreting

3. (a) What do the last lines of each of the four stanzas say? (b) How is the last line in the fourth stanza different from the other three? (c) When combined, what additional meaning do they gain?
4. How is the thought that all of nature dies but the soul lives eternally shown in this poem?
5. If death means a permanent end to existence, in what sense can one say that *days, roses,* and *spring* actually die?
6. Mark the rhyme scheme of the poem. What rhyming sound is most often repeated? What rhyming sound replaces this in the last stanza? In what way does the rhyme emphasize the theme or main point of the poem?

## Applying

7. Basically, this poem says that the virtuous soul need not fear death. What other poem in this book imparts a similar message?

## ANALYZING LITERATURE

### Understanding Emblematic Images

Although emblematic images are usually associated with pictures and shaped verse, it is sometimes possible to see a kind of emblematic impulse in more traditionally formed poems. To see the emblematic image in a poem such as "Virtue," for example, we need to probe the meaning of the word *emblem*. The word comes into English from the Latin meaning "inlaid," as in mosaic pictures, which are made of little pieces of stone put together according to a pattern that forms an image. From this use it came to mean "symbol," one thing standing for another.

In early Renaissance emblems, poems were written to comment on or explain pictorial symbols. After a while, poems and pictures became separated and the reader of an emblematic poem had to imagine the symbolic picture to which it related.

Explain the symbolism of "sweet day," "sweet rose," and "sweet spring." Then explain what "seasoned timber" might represent and how it relates to the sweet day, rose, and spring symbols. Describe the pictorial image you think this poem might fit.

# Easter Wings

George Herbert

Lord, who createdst man in wealth and store,[1]
  Though foolishly he lost the same,
    Decaying more and more,
      Till he became
5         Most poor:
        With thee
      O let me rise
    As larks, harmoniously,
  And sing this day thy victories:
10 Then shall the fall further the flight in me.

My tender age in sorrow did begin.
  And still with sickness and shame
    Thou didst so punish sin,
      That I became
15         Most thin.
        With thee
      Let me combine
    And feel this day thy victory:
  For, if I imp[2] my wing on thine,
Affliction shall advance the flight in me.

----

**1. store:** Abundance.
**2. imp:** Graft.

## THINKING ABOUT THE SELECTION
### Recalling

1. At the end of the poem, why does the speaker say he wants to "combine" with God? In what way does this echo lines 6–10?

### Interpreting

2. (a) In line 11, what does the speaker mean when he says: "My tender age in sorrow did begin"? Why should he have begun in sorrow? (b) How does this line echo lines 1–5?

3. In what way is line 10 a paradox?
4. How are the title and shape of the poem appropriate to its meaning or theme?

### Applying

5. George Herbert was sickly as a child and remained in frail health throughout his rather short life. He also moved from the pomp of the royal court to the poverty of a rural church. In what way are these personal experiences reflected in "Easter Wings"?

# Man

### George Herbert

> My God, I heard this day,
> That none doth build a stately habitation,
>     But he that means to dwell therein.
>     What house more stately hath there been,
> Or can be, than is man? to whose creation
>     All things are in decay.[1]
>
>     For Man is every thing,
> And more: He is a tree, yet bears more fruit;
>     A beast, yet is, or should be more:[2]
>     Reason and speech we only bring.[3]
> Parrots may thank us, if they are not mute,
>     They go upon the score.[4]
>
>     Man is all symmetry,
> Full of proportions, one limb to another,
>     And all to all the world besides:
>     Each part may call the furthest, brother:
> For head with foot hath private amity,
>     And both with moons and tides.
>
>     Nothing hath got so far,
> But man hath caught and kept it, as his prey.
>     His eyes dismount the highest star:
>     He is in little all the sphere.
> Herbs gladly cure our flesh; because that they
>     Find their acquaintance there.
>
>     For us the winds do blow,
> The earth doth rest, heaven move, and fountains flow.
>     Nothing we see, but means our good,
>     As our delight, or as our treasure:
> The whole is, either our cupboard of food,
>     Or cabinet of pleasure.

---

**1. to . . . decay:** In comparison to created man, all other things are in decay.

**2. For . . . more:** Man has an animal, vegetable, and spiritual nature.

**3. Reason . . . bring:** Man alone is capable of speaking and using reason.

**4. Parrots . . . score:** Parrots may also seem to be able to speak, but only because man has taught them how.

The stars have us to bed;
Night draws the curtain, which the sun withdraws;
Music and light attend our head.
All things unto our flesh are kind
35 In their descent and being; to our mind
In their ascent and cause.

Each thing is full of duty:
Waters united are our navigation;
Distinguished, our habitation;
40 Below, our drink; above, our meat;
Both are our cleanliness. Hath one such beauty?
Than how are all things neat?[5]

More servants wait on man,
Than he'll take notice of: in every path
45 He treads down that which doth befriend him,
When sickness makes him pale and wan.[6]
Oh mighty love! Man is one world, and hath
Another to attend him.

Since then, my God, thou hast
50 So brave a palace built; O dwell in it,
That it may dwell with thee at last!
Till then, afford us so much wit;
That, as the world serves us, we may serve thee,
And both thy servants be.

---

**5. Each . . . neat:** Each element serves man in a number of ways.
Water is used as an example. Oceans are used for navigation; dividing
waters created the earth that man inhabits (Genesis 1:6-7); water
provides man with food and drink; and water allows man to cleanse
himself. If one element can serve man so well, how beautiful is the
sum of the elements.
**6. He . . . won:** Man treads down the herb that can cure him when he
is sick.

## THINKING ABOUT THE SELECTION

### Recalling

1. In the first stanza of "Man," what question does the speaker ask?
2. How is man described in lines 7–24?
3. In lines 25–42, what does the speaker say is the relation of nature to man?
4. As shown in the next-to-last stanza, how does man behave toward nature?
5. In the final stanza, what are the two requests the speaker makes?

### Interpreting

6. To what specific categories do the items mentioned in lines 7–10 belong? In broad general terms, how is man characterized in these lines?
7. To what does the "brave palace" of line 50 refer? In what way does this metaphor recall lines 4 and 5? How does this echoing serve to conclude or "close" the poem?

### Applying

8. In a certain sense, this poem can be read as a criticism of human disregard for the rich bounties of nature. If modern environmentalists were to make the same criticism, as they often do, what would they say? To whom would they address their pleas? How would they present their position or viewpoint?

## CRITICAL THINKING AND READING

### Analyzing Herbert's Style

The word *style* refers to the characteristic way in which an individual does something, such as dressing, swimming, painting a picture, or writing a poem. In literature, style refers specifically to the way an individual uses language.

When we analyze a literary style, we examine a writer's characteristic choice of words, use of figures of speech, arrangement of sentences, organization of paragraphs, and, in poetry, treatment of rhythm and rhyme. Sometimes we also look at an author's use of certain literary devices —such as paradox, imagery, or symbolism —and his or her seeming preference for certain subjects or themes. John Donne, for example, seems to prefer themes that reflect anxiety, uncertainty, or suffering. He often uses exaggerated language when treating these difficult matters, thereby creating discomfort and heightening the emotional response to his writing. Donne's style could thus be described as highly provocative.

George Herbert stands in marked contrast to Donne. The poems Herbert wrote tend to make the reader feel comfortable, perhaps even soothed, as if listening to the gentle murmur of continuous prayer. Herbert's diction, or vocabulary, is essentially quiet, never clangorous as is Donne's on many occasions. Even when dealing with so potentially traumatic a subject as the Fall of Man, or his own approaching death, Herbert's words are mild, almost as if spoken in a whisper.

Reread "Easter Wings" and look closely at the way Herbert uses language. For example, notice the way he uses rhyme (in Herbert's day, "poor" rhymed with "more" and "store"); notice also that in the second half of each stanza, the only perfect rhyme for "thee" is "me," and "thee" of course refers to God. Describe Herbert's style in this poem and show how it complements his main idea. In addition to his use of rhyme, take into account his choice of words, his changes in line lengths, and his treatment of metaphors and similes.

## THINKING AND WRITING

### Writing About Emblematic Images

Properly speaking, an emblem consisted of a picture, a motto, and a poem. Over time, however, picture and poem came to be separated. As a result, many poems were written as if they contained their own picture, as in "Easter Wings," for example, or as if they were written to explain or comment on a picture in the poet's mind, as might be said of "Virtue" or of "Man."

Reread "Man" and describe the picture that might have been in Herbert's mind or that could accompany the poem today. Explain your description by referring to the details of the poem. When you revise, make sure you have included

# ANDREW MARVELL

## 1621–1678

Although seemingly easy and relaxed in style, Andrew Marvell was actually tough in poetry and politics. Beneath his graceful lyrics lie somber ideas and rigorous structures. Alongside his ready adaptability resided a firm attachment to his friends and beliefs.

Marvell was the son of a Puritan minister who was appointed to a church in Hull, a small town on the Humber River in northern England. There young Andrew remained until he entered Cambridge University at the age of twelve. While at Cambridge, he wrote several poems in Greek and Latin that were published by the university in a volume dedicated to King Charles I. After his father's death, Marvell traveled in Europe, where he learned to speak several modern European languages.

During his stay in Europe, the English Parliament, dominated by Puritans, rebelled against the king. On first returning to England, Marvell established friendships with royalist supporters of Charles I. At this time he wrote several verses commemorating these friends, among whom was the poet Richard Lovelace. Somewhat later, he was hired by Lord Fairfax, the commanding general of the anti-royalist Parliamentary army, to teach his daughter foreign languages. Marvell held this position for about two years, at which time he may have written most of the poems for which he is now famous.

Several years after ceasing to teach Fairfax's daughter, Marvell became tutor to the ward of Oliver Cromwell, leader of the Puritan rebellion and ruler of England. Shortly afterward, Marvell served as unofficial court poet to Cromwell himself. Obviously capable, Marvell gained the attention and sponsorship of the great English poet John Milton, who was at the time Latin Secretary to Cromwell's Council of State. Several years later, Marvell became Milton's assistant. Throughout this period, Marvell wrote several political and commemorative poems.

In 1659, after Cromwell's death and shortly before the monarchy was restored, Marvell was elected the Member of Parliament from Hull. He was regularly returned to Parliament until his death, almost twenty years later. It is believed that while a member, he was mainly responsible for saving Milton from a long imprisonment and possible death sentence.

Marvell showed an extraordinary ability to adjust to the realities of his time. He also displayed, however, an equal firmness of principle. After the Restoration of Charles II, Marvell wrote political satires and prose pamphlets attacking the abuses of monarchy and defending democratic concepts.

# GUIDE FOR INTERPRETING

## To His Coy Mistress, The Picture of Little T. C. in a Prospect of Flowers

**Writer's Techniques**

**Couplets and Quatrains.** Two of the most common structural elements in poetry are couplets and quatrains. Two lines rhyming together are called a *couplet,* and four lines rhyming in various ways are called a *quatrain.* Here is an example of a couplet and a quatrain. The verses are by Andrew Marvell, who used these forms in an early poem that he wrote as a debate between the Soul and Pleasure.

| | | |
|---|---|---|
| **Quatrain:** | PLEASURE | |
| | Wilt thou all the glory crave | a |
| | That war or peace commend? | b |
| | Half the world shall be thy slave, | a |
| | The other half they friend. | b |
| **Couplet:** | SOUL | |
| | What friends, if to my self untrue! | c |
| | What slaves, unless I captive you! | c |

Although both the couplet and the quatrain are often used as complete stanzas by themselves, they are also frequently used as parts of longer stanzas.

**Writing**

Write two lines that rhyme, then write several more two-line rhymes. If four of these rhyming lines seem related, perhaps because they deal with the same subject or central idea, join them together. Now write four new lines in which the rhymes alternate. You might then have one quatrain rhyming *a b a b* and another rhyming *a a b b.*

**Primary Source**

Charles II decided to show his respect for Marvell's wit and intelligence as well as buy his allegiance. He sent a messenger who told Marvell that the king would grant him a favor. When Marvell refused, the messenger offered a thousand gold pieces. With a smile Marvell replied, "Surely, my good Lord, you do not mean to treat me ludicrously by these munificent offers, which seem to interpret a poverty on my part. Pray, my Lord Treasurer, do these apartments wear in the least the air and mark of need? And as for my living, that is plentiful and good, which you shall have from the mouth of the servant. —Pray, what had I to dinner yesterday? —'A shoulder of mutton, sir.'" The messenger left with a smile, and Marvell went to ask his bookseller for a loan.

How do you see Marvell's independent streak in these poems?

# To His Coy Mistress

**Andrew Marvell**

Had we but world enough, and time,
This coyness lady were no crime.
We would sit down, and think which way
To walk, and pass our long love's day.
5    Thou by the Indian Ganges' side
Should'st rubies find; I by the tide
Of Humber[1] would complain. I would
Love you ten years before the Flood,
And you should if you please refuse
10   Till the conversion of the Jews.[2]
My vegetable love should grow
Vaster than empires, and more slow;
An hundred years should go to praise
Thine eyes, and on thy forehead gaze;
15   Two hundred to adore each breast,
But thirty thousand to the rest;
An age at least to every part,
And the last age should show your heart.
For, lady, you deserve this state,[3]
20   Nor would I love at lower rate.
     But at my back I always hear
Time's winged chariot hurrying near:
And yonder all before us lie
Deserts of vast eternity.
25   Thy beauty shall no more be found,
Nor, in thy marble vault, shall sound
My echoing songs; then worms shall try
That long-preserved virginity,
And your quaint honor turn to dust,
30   And into ashes all my lust:
The grave's a fine and private place,
But none I think do there embrace.
     Now therefore, while the youthful hew
Sits on thy skin like morning dew,
35   And while thy willing soul transpires[4]
At every pore with instant fires,

---

**1. Humber:** River flowing through Hull, Marvell's home town.
**2. conversion of the Jews:** According to Christian tradition, the
Jews were to be converted immediately before the Last Judgment.
**3. state:** Dignity.
**4. transpires:** Breathes out.

Now let us sport us while we may,
And now, like amorous birds of prey,
Rather at once our time devour

40 Than languish in his slow-chapped[5] power.
Let us roll all our strength, and all
Our sweetness, up into one ball,
And tear our pleasures with rough strife
Thorough[6] the iron gates of life:

45 Thus, though we cannot make our sun
Stand still, yet we will make him run.

---

**5. slow-chapped:** Slow-jawed.
**6. thorough:** Through.

## THINKING ABOUT THE SELECTION
### Recalling

1. According to line 1 of "To His Coy Mistress," under what conditions would the lady's coyness not be a crime?
2. In lines 3–7, what would the lady and the speaker each do, separately and together?
3. Starting at the end of line 7 and continuing to line 20, how does the speaker express his love?
4. In lines 21–24, what does the speaker hear at his back, and what lies before him and the lady?
5. In what place does the action described in lines 25–32 occur?
6. In lines 33–40, why does the speaker urge the lady to act "now"?
7. In conclusion (lines 41–46), what does the speaker say that he and the lady should do?

### Interpreting

8. If you had to state the speaker's objections to the lady's resistance in one sentence, what would that sentence be?
9. Since time is central to the poem, how is it expressed? Point to the word pictures or images and to the comparisons or metaphors that stand for and represent time.

### Applying

10. The lines "But at my back I always hear / Time's winged chariot hurrying near" have a great deal of meaning. What is the modern experience that these lines express?

## ANALYZING LITERATURE
### Recognizing Couplets and Quatrains

Couplets are two lines that rhyme and quatrains are four lines that rhyme in various ways. One of the ways to make a quatrain is to join two couplets that deal with one idea, word picture, or comparison. This is sometimes done in long poems, although the quatrain may thus be "hidden."

There are indeed several hidden quatrains in this poem made up entirely of couplets. For example, look at lines 21–24.

These four lines make a single unit, a quatrain. The preceding lines all deal with praising the beauty of the lady; the following lines describe what happens to the body after death. By contrast, the quatrain deals directly with the experience of time.

Find at least one other hidden quatrain. Explain how Marvell's ideas, word pictures, and comparisons move through his couplets.

# The Picture of Little T. C. in a Prospect[1] of Flowers

Andrew Marvell

See with what simplicity
This nymph begins her golden days!
In the green grass she loves to lie,
And there with her fair aspect tames
5  The wilder flowers and gives them names,
But only with the roses plays,
　　　　And them does tell
What color best becomes them, and what smell.
Who can foretell for what high cause
10  This darling of the gods was born!
Yet this is she whose chaster laws
The wanton love shall one day fear,
And, under her command severe
See his bow broke and ensigns[2] torn.
15  　　　　Happy who can
Appease this virtuous enemy of man!
O then let me in time compound
And parley with those conquering eyes
Ere they have tried their force to wound,
20  Ere, with their glancing wheels, they drive
In triumph over hearts that strive,
And them that yield but more despise:
　　　　Let me be laid,
Where I may see thy glories from some shade.
25  Meantime, whilst every verdant[3] thing
Itself does at thy beauty charm,
Reform the errors of the spring;
Make that the tulips may have share
Of sweetness, seeing they are fair;
30  And roses of their thorns disarm:
　　　　But most procure

---

**1. prospect:** Landscape.
**2. ensigns:** Flags.
**3. verdant** *adj.*: Green.

That violets may a longer age endure.
But O, young beauty of the woods,
Whom nature courts with fruits and flowers,
35   Gather the flowers, but spare the buds,
Lest Flora[4] angry at thy crime
To kill her infants in their prime,
Do quickly make th' example yours;
      And ere we see,
40   Nip in the blossom all our hopes and thee.

---

**4. Flora:** The Roman goddess of flowers.

---

## THINKING ABOUT THE SELECTION

### Recalling

1. What is the nymph doing in stanza 1?
2. In stanza 2, what will Love fear?
3. Why does the speaker, in stanza 3, want to converse with "those conquering eyes"?
4. To whom are stanzas 4 and 5 addressed?
5. What is asked for in the fourth stanza?
6. Of what is the "young beauty" warned in the last stanza?

### Interpreting

7. Nymphs are pretty young nature goddesses from classical mythology. They were often depicted in art and literature as rejecting ardent lovers, many of whom were gods. What details in the poem identify little T.C. with a wood nymph?
8. The speaker at first addresses someone outside the poem, then suddenly shifts and addresses directly little T.C. Where in the poem does this shift occur? What word signals the shift?

### Applying

9. Each stanza of this poem ends in a couplet, two lines that rhyme together. What other poems that you have read in this volume end their stanzas with couplets?
10. In a sense, "The Picture of Little T. C. in a Prospect of Flowers" can be thought of as an emblem poem such as George Herbert might have written. Emblems were pictures with mottoes and poems. What sort of picture do you think would be appropriate for this poem by Marvell?

## THINKING AND WRITING

### Comparing and Contrasting Styles

A literary style is a distinctive use of language. Individual writers have their own style, true enough, but sometimes groups of writers also share a common style. The metaphysical poets were such a group. Among the stylistic traits shared by these poets were a fondness for conceits (extended, farfetched comparisons), paradoxes (apparent contradictions), arguments (efforts at persuasion), and obscure bits of knowledge. Choose two metaphysical writers. List the characteristics of their style. Write an essay comparing and contrasting their styles. When you revise make sure you have included details from their poems to support your ideas.

# BEN JONSON

## 1572–1637

From bricklayer to literary dictator, Ben Jonson's life story is the perfect tale of rags to riches. Not only does his life suggest myth, his physique does too. He was a large man with boundless energy and enormous courage. Friend of Shakespeare and Donne, Jonson was their chief rival in drama and lyric. In addition, Jonson was a classical scholar, an astute critic, a superb prose stylist, a skillful translator, and the chief arbiter of taste for an entire generation of writers.

Adopted when an infant by a bricklayer, Jonson worked for his stepfather a number of years while attending the equivalent of high school under one of the leading teachers of the age. Too poor to pursue his education further, Jonson enlisted in the army and fought in the wars for Dutch independence from Spain. At one point as a soldier, he fought in single combat the champion of the enemy before the massed armies of Holland and Spain. Jonson won.

On returning to England, Jonson went on the stage as an actor. His early years in the theater were stormy ones: He was jailed one time for taking part in a "seditious and slanderous" play; another time he was almost hanged for killing a fellow actor in a duel; and still later he was suspected of having a part in a plot on the life of King James I. Despite the turbulence of his life, however, Jonson learned his stagecraft well and became a major dramatist in his own right. His first play had William Shakespeare in a major role, and his later plays were performed by the chief acting companies of the day, including Shakespeare's.

Jonson was so successful he was granted a handsome pension by King James I and treated as if he were poet laureate of England. Over many years he had written masques, elaborate entertainments, for the royal court, where he was a favorite writer. During these years he was enormously influential, functioning as virtual dictator over the literary efforts of the day.

A number of the brightest and best of the young courtly writers flocked about Jonson and called themselves the "Sons" or "Tribe of Ben." Among the outstanding Sons of Ben can be counted Robert Herrick and John Suckling. Although not himself one of the "Sons," Richard Lovelace was also much influenced by Jonson. Indeed, Jonson's direct influence extended beyond these poets to the end of the seventeenth century and into the eighteenth. It is still felt today. What Jonson said of Shakespeare can be said of him as well: "He was not of an age, but for all time."

# GUIDE FOR INTERPRETING

## Writer's Techniques

### On My First Son, Song: To Celia, Still to Be Neat

**Apostrophe.** An apostrophe is a figure of speech in which an abstract idea or quality, a place or inanimate thing, or a dead or absent person is addressed as if present and able to hear and understand what is said. Ben Jonson used an apostrophe when he directly addressed William Shakespeare, who had been dead for several years, in his poem "To the Memory of My Beloved Master, William Shakespeare."

Apostrophes have been used since very early times by the ancient Greeks and Romans. Here is the opening line to Homer's *Odyssey:*

Tell me, Muse, of the man of many ways. . . .

Although it is rare to find a modern poet apostrophizing, it does sometimes occur. Dylan Thomas apostrophized part of his anatomy in his poem "All All and All the Dry World's Lever."

Know, O my bone, the jointed lever.

For the most part, though, use of the apostrophe today sounds old-fashioned, which brings to mind an ancient Roman apostrophe.

O time! O custom!

## Writing

Often people have unfinished conversations with others, conversations that they complete many times over in the privacy of their homes. Complete an unfinished conversation.

## Primary Source

Few comments have been as controversial as Jonson's remarks about Shakespeare: "I remember, the players have often mentioned it as an honor to Shakespeare, that in his writing . . . he never blotted out a line. My answer hath been, would he had blotted a thousand. Which they thought was a malevolent speech . . . And to justify mine own candor (for I loved the man, and do honor his memory, on this side of idolatry, as much as any). He was (indeed) honest, and of an open, and free nature: he had an excellent fancy; brave notions, and gentle expressions . . . But he redeemed his vices, with his virtues. There was ever more in him to be praised, than to be pardoned." How do you think Jonson really felt about Shakespeare? As you read, look for the feelings Jonson expresses about the person in each poem.

# On My First Son

**Ben Jonson**

Farewell, thou child of my right hand,[1] and joy;
    My sin was too much hope of thee, loved boy,
Seven years thou wert lent to me, and I thee pay,
    Exacted by thy fate, on the just[2] day.
5 O, could I lose all father,[3] now. For why
    Will man lament the state he should envy?
To have so soon scaped world's, and flesh's rage,
    And, if no other misery, yet age?
Rest in soft peace, and, asked, say here doth lie
10     Ben Jonson his best piece of poetry.
For whose sake, henceforth, all his vows be such,
    As what he loves may never like too much.

---

**1. child . . . hand:** The literal translation of the Hebrew name
Benjamin. Jonson's son was born in 1596 and died in 1603.
**2. just:** Exact.
**3. lose . . . father:** Give up all thoughts of being a father.

## THINKING ABOUT THE SELECTION

### Recalling

1. What is the epitaph Jonson has composed for his son in lines 9–12? What vow does Jonson make as part of the epitaph?

### Interpreting

2. How would you rephrase the "sin" Jonson attributes to himself in line 2? What details in the poem support this reading?
3. Why does Jonson say in line 6 that his son's death is enviable?

### Applying

4. Compare Jonson's poem on his son's death with Donne's meditation and sonnet. Does Jonson express as much anguish or suffering as Donne?

## ANALYZING LITERATURE

### Understanding Apostrophes

The apostrophe is a literary convention that allows an author to bring vividly to the mind of a reader the subject of the apostrophe. It endows that subject with a degree of life it might not otherwise have and thereby makes it easier for the reader to share the writer's emotion.

1. To whom is this poem addressed?
2. What question does Jonson ask in lines 5–8?
3. Explain how the device of the apostrophe allows him to clearly express his emotions.

# Song: To Celia

Ben Jonson

Drink to me only with thine eyes,
And I will pledge with mine;
Or leave a kiss but in the cup,
And I'll not look for wine.
5  The thirst that from the soul doth rise,
Doth ask a drink divine:
But might I of Jove's[1] nectar sup,
I would not change for thine.

I sent thee late[2] a rosy wreath,
10  Not so much honoring thee,
As giving it a hope, that there
It could not withered be.
But thou thereon did'st only breathe,
And sent'st it back to me;
15  Since when it grows and smells, I swear,
Not of itself, but thee.

---

**1. Jove's:** Jupiter's. In Roman mythology, Jupiter
is the ruler of the gods.
**2. late:** Recently.

---

## THINKING ABOUT THE SELECTION

### Recalling

1. What does the speaker ask for in the first four lines of "Song: To Celia"?
2. In the next four lines, what does the speaker say the soul requires and what substitutes does it desire?
3. (a) Why, according to lines 11–12, did the speaker send the "rosy wreath" to Celia? (b) In lines 14–16, what does the speaker say happened to the wreathe?

### Interpreting

4. The speaker says a number of times that he prefers expressions of love to drink, whether wine or nectar. (a) What does love give him that drink cannot? (b) In which lines does he say this?

### Applying

5. Many of Jonson's songs were updated versions of classical Latin and Greek poems. If you were asked to update "Song: To Celia," how would you do so?
6. In your opinion, why has this song been so popular down through the centuries?

# Still to Be Neat

Ben Jonson

> Still to be neat, still to be dressed,
> As, you were going to a feast;
> Still to be powdered, still perfumed:
> Lady, it is to be presumed,
> 5   Though arts hid causes are not found,
> All is not sweet, all is not sound.
>
> Give me a look, give me a face,
> That makes simplicity a grace;
> Robes loosely flowing, hair as free:
> 10   Such sweet neglect more taketh me,
> Then all th'adulteries of art.
> They strike mine eyes, but not my heart.

---

## THINKING ABOUT THE SELECTION
### Recalling

1. To whom is the first stanza of "Still to Be Neat" addressed?
2. In stanza 1, what is the speaker saying about the Lady's appearance?
3. What does the speaker ask for in the second stanza?

### Interpreting

4. The speaker's tone in the first stanza is one of complaint and criticism. What words convey this tone?

5. Where does the speaker say that art raises questions about the good and the true?
6. Essentially, the poem says that art is false, and that naturalness is both more truthful and more appealing. What statements in the poem support this theme or main idea?

### Applying

7. A modern writer once said, "Nature imitates art." What does this statement reveal about modern attitudes toward art and nature, and how does it contrast with the attitude expressed by Jonson?

**MARRIAGE À LA MODE IV:
THE COUNTESS'S MORNING LEVÉE**
*William Hogarth*
National Gallery, London

## THINKING AND WRITING
### Responding to Criticism

Imagine that you are either the Lady or the Lady's friend and are called upon to respond to the speaker's criticism. Write a letter to the speaker defending the Lady, the virtue of neatness, and the truthfulness of art. Remember, you do not want to offend the speaker; if possible, you would like to persuade him that he is mistaken. It would be a nice touch if you could write your letter as a poem, but prose will do as well.

# ROBERT HERRICK

## 1591–1674

Called the greatest songwriter of the English language, Herrick's verses please the ear more than the mind. Although he lived through one of the most controversial periods of English history, little of this is reflected in his poetry. His poems are light, whimsical, highly polished, and extremely artificial. They are also a joy to read and hear.

Born to a wealthy goldsmith in London who died when Robert was young, Herrick was apprenticed to his even wealthier uncle, who was also a goldsmith. Although there are no records of his early education, Herrick went up to Cambridge when he was 22 and graduated when he was 29 with a master's degree. Shortly afterward he was ordained a minister and served as a chaplain with English troops fighting in France. On his return from France he was assigned a rural parish in southwestern England. At first unhappy at his "internal exile," Herrick soon adjusted to the lovely countryside and easy life of a country parson. There he wrote his charming verse that celebrated equally the passage of time, the beauty of nature, the joys of love, the pleasures of paganism, and the modesty of Christian devotion.

Although not politically active, Herrick was evicted from his parish by triumphant Puritans after the final defeat of Charles I. Returning to his native and much-loved London, Herrick published his poems in a single, thick little volume with two titles: *Hesperides* and *Noble Numbers*. *Hesperides,* which is the classical Greek name for a mythological garden at the western edge of the world, contained Herrick's secular poems, for which he is best known today. *Noble Numbers* contained his religious verse. Published at a politically turbulent time in London, Herrick's light and graceful poems were ignored by his contemporaries. Interest in them was revived in the nineteenth century, and they are highly regarded today.

With the Restoration in 1660, Herrick went back to his parish in the west country and remained there until his death. When he was young, he had been one of the most ardent disciples of Ben Jonson. From the older poet, Herrick had learned the virtues of a light touch, of a polished surface, and of a restrained manner. He carried his lessons well into his exile, where he sang "of brooks, of blossoms, birds, and bowers: / Of April, May, of June, and July flowers."

# GUIDE FOR INTERPRETING

## An Ode for Him, To the Virgins, to Make Much of Time

**Writer's Techniques**

**Symbols.** A symbol stands for something other than itself while at the same time making us aware of itself. For example, although we realize that the American flag is a piece of cloth, we also recognize that it stands for the United States, its system of government, and the kinds of freedom that are enjoyed here. Writers often use symbols because they are such economical ways of expressing complex ideas. For example, the rose is used frequently to express the idea of the swift passage of time and the short duration of beauty and freshness. Feasts or meals often symbolize sharing, affection, community, and close companionship. The rose and the feast are central symbols in the following two poems by Herrick.

**Commentary**

In "To the Virgins, to Make Much of Time," Herrick advises young women to marry while they can. How does Herrick's advice relate to the reality of marriage-making in the seventeenth century?

Marriages were essentially economic, not romantic, affairs. In most cases, the parents made all the arrangements. A daughter would almost always agree to marry the man that her parents had selected, for she was usually still a teenager and had been brought up to expect her parents to select her husband. Often, as with the very wealthy, the negotiations for marriage began when the prospective brides were still infants. Sometimes, however, girls flatly refused to accept their parents' choices.

Fourteen-year-old Mary Boyle, the daughter of the Earl of Cork, for example, stood her ground against the match her parents had arranged. In turning down James Hamilton, she wrote, "My aversion for him was extraordinary. I could never be brought by fair means or foul to it." Dorothy Osborn was equally determined to marry for love rather than for social and economic advantage. Although the family estates were ruined by the Civil War, her father's health was declining, and her mother was dead, she steadily refused the stream of prospective husbands that her brother provided. "I am certain," she wrote, "I could not love the most perfect person in the world unless I did first believe he had a passion for me."

In light of the realities of the seventeenth-century marriage mart, why do you think Herrick advises women to marry young?

**Writing**

Write the name of an object, such as a flag, a flower, a football, a catcher's mitt, a sewing needle, or a rolling pin. First describe the object as it actually exists: the way it looks, what it is used for. Then write down all the associations you have with the object.

# An Ode for Him (Ben Jonson)

Robert Herrick

Ah Ben!
Say how, or when
Shall we thy guests
Meet at those lyric feasts,
5        Made at the Sun,
The Dog, the Triple Tun?[1]
Where we such clusters had,
As made us nobly wild, not mad;
And yet each verse of thine
10  Outdid the meat, outdid the frolic wine.

My Ben
Or[2] come again:
Or send to us,
Thy wits great overplus;
15        But teach us yet
Wisely to husband[3] it;
Lest we that talent spend:
And having once brought to an end
That precious stock; the store
20  Of such a wit the world should have no more.

---

**1. Sun . . . Dog . . . Triple Tun:** The names of taverns where "The Tribe of Ben" (see p. 444) would gather.
**2. or:** Either.
**3. husband:** Conserve.

## THINKING ABOUT THE SELECTION

### Recalling

1. What question is asked in the first six lines?
2. In lines 7–10, what does the speaker say took place at Ben Jonson's favorite taverns?
3. (a) In lines 11–16, what does the speaker ask of Ben? (b) In lines 17–20, what risks does the speaker describe if Ben does not respond?

### Interpreting

4. In what way were the speaker and others Ben Jonson's guests?
5. The tone of this poem is melancholy. What words, phrases, and thoughts contribute to setting this melancholy tone?

### Applying

6. "An Ode for Him" is a poem praising Ben Jonson. Today, there are many occasions when we speak words of praise. What are those occasions and how would you express yourself on such occasions?

## CRITICAL THINKING AND READING
### Knowing Differences Among Synonyms

A **synonym** is a word that has the same or similar meaning as another word, as, for example, *error* and *mistake*. Sometimes, several words are synonyms, such as *error, mistake, slip-up,* and *blunder.* They all mean "incorrectness" or "inaccuracy," but there are slight differences among them. *Error* often implies that the incorrectness is the result of *stubborness,* as when we say, "That was an error in judgment." In contrast, *mistake* is much less harsh in implication. It does not, for example, suggest *willfulness,* as does *error.* The word *mistake* also often suggests that the incorrectness or inaccuracy is minor, as when we say, "Oh well, he just made a mistake." We would never use the word *error* in that sentence.

We might, though, use the word *slip-up* if we felt the mistake was a result of carelessness. *Slip-up* is even less formal than *mistake* and would not be used in a report to the top boss of a corporation, for instance. On the other hand, *blunder,* which is far more formal than *slip-up* and *mistake,* is much farther from *error* in its associated meanings than the other two. The senses of *stupidity, clumsiness,* and *sloppiness* are part of the meaning of *blunder.*

If we were to arrange our three words according to how close they are to the word *error,* we would put them in the following order: *error,* (1) *mistake,* (2) *slip-up,* and (3) *blunder.* Do the same with the following synonyms taken from "An Ode for Him." Look each word up in the dictionary, number them according to how close they are to the main word, and explain how they differ from one another.

1. *feast:* meal, banquet, religious celebration
2. *wild:* uncivilized, uncontrolled, impassioned
3. *teach:* guide, train, instruct

## THINKING AND WRITING
### Writing About Thinking

Imagine that you are writing a letter to a friend explaining how you arranged the synonyms. In your letter, answer the following questions. What was the basis for the order in which you placed the synonyms? Did you first look in the dictionary to find out what the words mean? How did you know the dictionary definition was correct? Did you try to make up sentences to fit the definitions? Did you try out the definitions and sentences on people you know? What was their reaction? Did you check out the order of the synonyms with these people? How did they react to that? Did they confirm your judgment? If not, what did you do? At the end of your letter, ask your friend what he thinks the order of the synonyms should be and why. Revise your letter and prepare a final draft.

# To the Virgins, to Make Much of Time

Robert Herrick

Gather ye rosebuds while ye may,
    Old time is still a-flying;
And this same flower that smiles today
    Tomorrow will be dying.

5    The glorious lamp of heaven, the sun,
    The higher he's a-getting,
The sooner will his race be run,
    And nearer he's to setting.

That age is best which is the first,
10    When youth and blood are warmer;
But being spent, the worse, and worst
    Times still succeed the former.

Then be not coy, but use your time,
    And, while ye may, go marry;
15    For, having lost but once your prime,
    You may forever tarry.[1]

---

**1. tarry** (tar′ē) *v*.: Delay.

## THINKING ABOUT THE SELECTION
### Recalling

1. In stanza 1, why does the speaker advise the girls to gather the rosebuds while they may?
2. In the second stanza, what happens to the sun as it gets higher in the sky?
3. According to the third stanza, what is the best age and what happens when it is passed?
4. In stanza 4, why does the speaker suggest that the young girls stop delaying and marry?

### Interpreting

5. The central theme or idea of this poem is the swift passage of time. What images express this theme?

### Applying

6. This poem is in one sense advice to young women to marry while still young. In what way does it also express the "carpe diem" or "seize the day" tradition? Why do you think

**THREE LADIES ADORNING A TERM OF HYMEN**
*Sir Joshua Reynolds*
The Tate Gallery, London

this tradition was so popular during the seventeenth century?

## ANALYZING LITERATURE

### Understanding Symbols

Symbols are at the same time themselves and stand for something else. The poets of the sixteenth and seventeenth centuries loved playing with the conventions of their art. One of the most popular conventions of the period was the combination of a swiftly passing time and an urgent need to love. Robert Herrick was one of the most successful players of this conventional game.

1. Point to all the symbols of time in "To the Virgins, to Make Much of Time."
2. How do these symbols work together to suggest "blossoming youth" and "decaying age"?

# BIOGRAPHIES

## Sir John Suckling (1609–1642)
## Richard Lovelace (1618–1657)

The works of Suckling and Lovelace have been linked together as the prime examples of the courtly lyrics known as *Cavalier poetry.* Both poets wrote a light and easy kind of verse associated with the court of Charles I. Both affected a tone of gentlemanly nonchalance in their poems; both were courtiers under Charles.

Suckling came from an extremely wealthy family and used up his inheritance in extravagant living. At one point he hired one hundred fighting men, dressed them up in fancy uniforms, went off to fight for the king in Scotland, and was roundly beaten by the sullen, unfashionably dressed Scots. When he was not engaged in futile fights, he wasted his wealth in gambling. However, he was also a serious patron of many excellent poets, wrote four plays that were spectacularly staged and published at his own exorbitant cost, and composed the delicate lyrics that have gained him fame for over 300 years. As Parliament rebelled against King Charles and gained control of the government, Suckling joined in a conspiracy to free a Royalist leader from the Tower of London. The plot was exposed and Suckling fled to France. There he died impoverished and in despair.

Also from an extremely wealthy family, Lovelace was the pretty boy of Cavalier poetry. He was so handsome that the king and queen ordered that he be granted a master's degree before he completed his studies at Oxford. He was, however, also talented. While at Oxford he wrote a play, painted some fine pictures, and performed credibly on several musical instruments. Perhaps because he was so attractive, Lovelace was chosen by the Royalists to present to Parliament a demand for the restoration of the king's right to absolute authority. Lovelace was immediately arrested. It was while imprisoned that he wrote "To Althea" as a justification for siding with the king even though it meant being confined in jail. After his release from prison, he rejoined Charles's forces in the civil war and spent most of his fortune to help equip the king's army. Upon Charles's defeat in 1645, Lovelace went to France and fought against Holland. Returning to England some while later, he was once again imprisoned by the Puritans. It was during this second imprisonment that he prepared for publication the volume of poems that included "To Lucasta." Although no one knows for certain, it is believed that he died in poverty.

# GUIDE FOR INTERPRETING

## The Constant Lover; Song; To Lucasta, on Going to the Wars; To Althea, from Prison

**Writer's Techniques**

**Tone.** In literature, *tone* refers to the attitude expressed by an author toward his or her subject or audience. A writer's attitude is conveyed through language, characterization, setting, point of view, and details of appearance, voice, location, and the like. Whether in prose or poetry, recognizing the writer's tone is essential to an understanding of the work. Without this recognition, we cannot tell if an author is serious or playful, mocking or admiring, angry or joking, laughing or crying. Very often the tone of a piece of writing can shift from one quality to another.

**Writing**

Describe the way you feel about something. Your subject can be either serious or trivial. The important thing about your writing is that you reveal how you feel through the words and details you choose. Do not say directly how you feel; do not say, "I am angry," "I am amused," "I am proud," or "I am sorry."

**Primary Source**

A man investigating prison conditions in the seventeenth century wrote, "Lord Bless me! What a Sight is here! I do not think there had been so much cruelty in the Hearts of Englishmen, to use Englishmen in this manner." What he saw was appalling indeed.

Prisoners were herded together, without privacy or comfort. They slept on piles of straw, usually directly on the cold ground. Since there was no indoor plumbing, bathing was virtually impossible. A few prisons had fireplaces and jailers might provide coals for a fee, but more than a century later the majority of English prisons still did not have heating or baths. Prisoners were given only a quarter of a loaf of bread daily, supplemented by what their family and friends could supply. Scores perished from jail fever. For this, prisoners paid five pounds a year!

Because jailers had to pay a tax on windows, fresh air was scarcer than water and heat. One eyewitness wrote, "The most pernicious infection next to the plague is the smell of a jail, whereof we have had, in our time, experience once or twice." One visitor protected himself by "smelling to vinegar, while I was in those places, and changing my apparel afterwards."

How does the tone of "To Althea, from Prison" reflect prison life in the seventeenth century?

# The Constant Lover

## Sir John Suckling

Out upon it! I have loved
    Three whole days together;
And am like to love three more,
    If it prove fair weather.

5  Time shall molt away his wings,
    Ere he shall discover
In the whole wide world again
    Such a constant lover.

But the spite on 't is, no praise
10    Is due at all to me:
Love with me had made no stays,
    Had it any been but she.

Had it any been but she,
    And that very face,
15  There had been at least ere this
    A dozen dozen in her place.

**THE INTERRUPTED SLEEP**
*François Boucher*
*The Metropolitan Museum of Art*

---

## THINKING ABOUT THE SELECTION

### Recalling

1. In the first stanza of "The Constant Lover," how long has the speaker loved?
2. According to lines 3 and 4, what conditions are necessary for the speaker to continue to love?
3. In the second stanza, how long will it be before Time will find a lover as faithful as the speaker?
4. According to stanza 3, why is praise not due the speaker?
5. In the last stanza, what reason does the speaker give for not leaving his lady for another "dozen dozen" women?

### Interpreting

6. The poem is an elaborate compliment to a lady. What are the elements that contribute to this compliment?
7. When an inanimate object or an abstract idea, such as Time or Death, is given human characteristics, it is called *personification*. What is personified in stanza 2 and how does it work in the poem?
8. (a) What attitude toward love and the woman are evident? (b) In what way is the word *constant* in the title ironic?

### Applying

9. What qualities do you think characterize a *constant* lover?

# Song

### Sir John Suckling

**FAIR IS MY LOVE**
*Edwin A. Abbey*
The Harris Museum and Art Gallery, Preston

Why so pale and wan, fond lover?
    Prithee, why so pale?
Will, when looking well can't move her,
    Looking ill prevail?
5        Prithee, why so pale?

Why so dull and mute, young sinner?
    Prithee, why so mute?
Will, when speaking well can't win her,
    Saying nothing do't?
10      Prithee, why so mute?

Quit, quit, for shame; this will not move,
    This cannot take her.
If of herself she will not love,
    Nothing can make her:
15      The devil take her!

## THINKING ABOUT THE SELECTION

### Recalling

1. In the first stanza of "Song," how does the lover look?
2. What is the question the speaker asks in the second stanza?
3. What advice to the lover does the speaker give in the third stanza?

### Interpreting

4. The third stanza is different from the two preceding ones. In what way is it different?
5. What has caused the "fond" lover to look and behave in the way described by the speaker?
6. What do you think is the lover's emotional state? Explain your answer.

### Applying

7. This poem is in a sense an early example of advice to the lovelorn. If a good friend broke up with a loved one, what sort of advice would you give? What would you say and how would you say it?

## THINKING AND WRITING

### Writing About Tone

Write an essay in which you discuss the tone of Suckling's "Song." Imagine that you will deliver this paper to a scholarly audience. For this audience you will want to discuss the use of irony and wit as instruments for expressing the poet's attitude toward his subject.

# To Lucasta, on Going to the Wars

## Richard Lovelace

**GOING TO THE BATTLE**
*Edward Burne-Jones*
Fitzwilliam Museum, Cambridge

Tell me not, Sweet, I am unkind,
    That from the nunnery
Of thy chaste breast, and quiet mind,
    To war and arms I fly.

5    True, a new mistress now I chase,
    The first foe in the field;
And with a stronger faith embrace
    A sword, a horse, a shield.

Yet this inconstancy is such,
10    As you too shall adore;
I could not love thee, Dear, so much,
    Loved I not honor more.

## THINKING ABOUT THE SELECTION

### Recalling

1. In the first stanza of "To Lucasta, on Going to the Wars," from whom is the speaker going and toward what is he "flying"?
2. In the second stanza, whom does the speaker chase and what will he embrace?
3. According to the last stanza, why will the abandoned lady "adore" the speaker's "inconstancy"?

### Interpreting

4. What is the "new mistress" the speaker refers to in the second stanza?
5. What do you believe is the "stronger faith" mentioned by the speaker in line 7?
6. What does the speaker mean when he says in lines 11–12, "I could not love thee, Dear, so much / Loved I not honor more"?
7. This poem is an argument made by the speaker to his lady-love in an effort to convince her to accept his leaving her for war. What details in the poem support this interpretation?

### Applying

8. If you were to leave a loved one to go off to fight, what would you say to convince that person to accept your departure?
9. In "Song" (pages 420–421), John Donne also wrote an argument trying to persuade his beloved to accept his leaving her. Compare the poems by Donne and Lovelace. How do they differ? In what one respect are they similar?

# To Althea, from Prison

### Richard Lovelace

When love with unconfined wings
    Hovers within my gates,
And my divine Althea brings
    To whisper at the grates;
5  When I lie tangled in her hair
    And fettered to her eye,
The gods[1] that wanton[2] in the air
    Know no such liberty.

When flowing cups run swiftly round,
10    With no allaying Thames,[3]
Our careless heads with roses bound,
    Our hearts with loyal flames;
When thirsty grief in wine we steep,
    When healths[4] and drafts[5] go free,
15  Fishes that tipple in the deep,
    Know no such liberty.

When, like committed linnets,[6] I
    With shriller throat shall sing
The sweetness, mercy, majesty,
20    And glories of my King;
When I shall voice aloud how good
    He is, how great should be,
      Enlarged[7] winds that curl the flood,
    Know no such liberty.

---

**1. gods:** The word *gods* is replaced by *birds* in some versions of this poem.
**2. wanton:** Play.
**3. cups . . . Thames** (temz): Wine that has not been diluted by water (from the river Thames).
**4. healths:** Toasts.
**5. drafts:** Drinks.
**6. committed linnets:** Caged finches.
**7. enlarged:** Released.

25  Stone walls do not a prison make,
        Nor iron bars a cage;
    Minds innocent and quiet take
        That for an hermitage;
    If I have freedom in my love,
30      And in my soul am free,
    Angels alone that soar above,
        Enjoy such liberty.

---

## THINKING ABOUT THE SELECTION

### Recalling

1. (a) According to lines 1–4, where is the god Love hovering? (b) Where is the "divine Althea" whispering?
2. (a) In lines 5–8, what does the speaker say gives him the greatest freedom? (b) What conditions does the speaker describe in the second stanza as yielding the greatest freedom?
3. In the third stanza, when will the speaker know the greatest "liberty"?
4. (a) What, in the last stanza, does the speaker say is required to enable him to enjoy the maximum freedom? (b) What or who does the speaker say in the first three stanzas will experience no greater freedom than he? (c) To what does the speaker compare his freedom in the last stanza?

### Interpreting

5. (a) The conditions for the speaker's freedom form a progressive movement in the first three stanzas. What is that movement? (b) Summarize the speaker's conception of freedom.
6. In seventeenth-century England, part of the conflict between King Charles I and his rebellious Parliament was over freedom. Charles wanted to rule by "divine right," which meant basically that he could do as he wished. Parliament wished to take that right away from him. To Charles, this meant a loss of freedom. The Puritans in Parliament, on the other hand, felt that Charles had tried to take away their freedom of religion. From their point of view, it was either his freedom or their freedom that was at stake.

    (a) In what way does Lovelace's poem, "To Althea," reflect this issue? (b) Why does each stanza turn on the idea of "liberty"?
7. Some critics have called "To Althea" a love poem; others have said it was an expression of devotion to King Charles. Which interpretation do you believe is right and why?

### Applying

8. The first two lines of the fourth stanza of "To Althea" are very famous. They have been repeated down through the ages, often by people who did not know their source. Aside from their poignancy, why, in your opinion, have these lines been so very popular?

# The Puritan Age

**THE FARRIER'S SHOP, c. 1620–1687**
*Gael Barend*
*Guildhall Art Gallery, London*

# JOHN MILTON

## 1608–1674

Ranked with William Shakespeare and Geoffrey Chaucer as one of the greatest poets of the English language, John Milton actually produced comparatively few poems. The major part of his life he spent either studying literature or writing political tracts. Yet *Paradise Lost* by itself would have been enough to earn him a place among the immortals of English literature.

Born in London to a middle-class family, Milton grew up in a highly cultured environment. His father was a composer and musician of considerable ability as well as a professional scribe or notary. Milton's father was also deeply religious and devoted to the Protestant cause. Educated first at home by tutors, Milton started his formal education in the equivalent of high school when he was about thirteen. While a student at this school he mastered Greek, Latin, and Hebrew as well as several modern European languages. Then he went on to college.

It was while at Cambridge University that Milton decided to prepare himself for a career as a great poet ("God's poet," was how he described it). From this point onward until the English Civil War broke out, Milton devoted himself to a life of study. After earning his degrees from Cambridge, he withdrew to his father's house at Horton for five years, where he is reputed to have read everything that was written in the ancient and modern languages that he knew. It was during this long period of study that Milton wrote "L'Allegro," "Il Penseroso," and "Lycidas," which by themselves would have earned him a lasting position as a major poet. Following his stay at Horton, he went on the Grand European Tour for two years.

While Milton was in Europe, Parliament rebelled against King Charles I; learning of the revolt, Milton cut short his trip and rushed back to England. There, he immediately took up the cudgels in defense of the Parliamentary and Puritan cause. It was in this role that he took part in the pamphlet war of the time and became a leading exponent of republican principles. As a result of his brilliant writings, Oliver Cromwell made Milton Latin Secretary of the Commonwealth. It was in this job that he went blind. Upon restoration of the monarchy, he was at first imprisoned and then released. Andrew Marvell, his former assistant and now Member of Parliament, may have argued in his behalf.

After Milton's release and the loss of most of his property, he withdrew into his blindness and poverty to write *Paradise Lost,* the greatest epic of the English language.

# GUIDE FOR INTERPRETING

## When I Consider How My Light Is Spent; On His Having Arrived at the Age of Twenty-Three

**Writer's Techniques**

**The Italian Sonnet.** The sonnet is one of the major forms of English poetry, but it was invented by the Italians in the thirteenth century. It was imported into England by Wyatt and Surrey in the middle of the sixteenth century. The Italian sonnet is a fourteen-line lyric poem. It is usually divided into two segments, an octave of eight lines and a sestet of six lines. According to the sonnet convention, the octave is supposed to present a situation or problem and the sestet is supposed to offer an answer or response. The rhyme scheme also follows a fairly strict pattern. The octave rhymes *abbaabba* and the sestet usually varies, although within a fairly narrow range. In English, sonnets, whether Italian or not, are written in ten-syllable lines, five beats to the line with a stress pattern that goes like this:

U / U / U / U / U /
*open unto the fields and to the sky.*

**Commentary**

In "On His Having Arrived at the Age of Twenty-Three," Milton assesses his life. People completing their education today sometimes assess their lives as they prepare to embark on a career. Some people even feel that they should have acccomplished more. Imagine how they would feel hearing the stories of child prodigies who have already achieved a lifetime of accomplishments before reaching their teens!

Wolfgang Amadeus Mozart (1756–1791), for example, began music lessons at age four, and by five was composing minuets. A year later his ability to sight read music caused a sensation throughout Europe. He wrote his first symphony at eight; at twelve, he wrote two operas and a mass. His achievements grew as he matured, and today he is considered a musical genius.

John Stuart Mill (1806–1873) was fluent in Greek at three, Latin at eight—not to mention history and mathematics. By twelve he had read the classics in the original. He became an important theorist and writer in politics, economics, and philosopy who dedicatd himself to justice and the public good.

According to the poem, how does Milton believe he will accomplish his goals?

**Writing**

Jot down some ideas on reaching whatever age you might now be—16, 17, 18. Try to include some ideas reflecting your view of your accomplishments to date and what you expect from the future.

# When I Consider How My Light Is Spent

John Milton

When I consider how my light is spent
    Ere half my days, in this dark world and wide,
    And that one talent[1] which is death to hide,
    Lodged with me useless, though my soul more bent
5  To serve therewith my Maker, and present
    My true account, lest he returning chide;
    "Doth God exact day labor, light denied?"
    I fondly[2] ask; but Patience to prevent
That murmur, soon replies, "God doth not need
10    Either man's work or his own gifts; who best
    Bear his mild yoke, they serve him best. His state
Is kingly. Thousands[3] at his bidding speed
    And post[4] o'er land and ocean without rest:
    They also serve who only stand and wait."

---

**1. talent:** An allusion to the parable of the talents (Matthew 25:14-30).
**2. fondly:** Foolishly.
**3. thousands:** Thousands of angels.
**4. post:** Travel.

## THINKING ABOUT THE SELECTION

### Recalling

1. According to lines 1–2, at what point in the speaker's life does his eyesight fail?
2. What three qualities does the second speaker attribute to God?

### Interpreting

3. The first speaker in this poem expresses a sense of failure. What is the nature of that failure?

4. Why, in your opinion, might Milton have felt that his blindness made his talent useless?
5. Explain the last line of the poem: "They also serve who only stand and wait."
6. This sonnet, unlike most other sonnets, is like the dialogue in a play. How does this unusual formal arrangement affect your understanding of the poem?

### Applying

7. Do you feel it is necessary for people to use their talents? Explain your answer.

## ANALYZING LITERATURE

### Understanding Italian Sonnets

The rhyme scheme of Milton's sonnet on his blindness is *abbaabba cdecde,* which is common to the Italian sonnet. To emphasize their rhyme scheme, most sonneteers end-stop their lines. When a natural pause occurs at the end of a line, the line is called *end-stopped.* An example of end stopping is the third line of Milton's "When I Consider . . . " This can be contrasted with the next line, the normal reading of which carries one over to the following or fifth line. This kind of carry-over is called *enjambment* or a *run-on line.* Run-on lines tend to obscure end rhymes and thereby make the rhyme scheme more subtle than it might otherwise be. There are a number of run-on lines in Milton's poem.

Another characteristic of the sonnet is the change that takes place between the first eight lines, or octave, and the followig six lines, or sestet. Most often the change is very subtle in the Italian sonnet. In Milton's "When I Consider . . ." it is very obvious.

1. Which rhyme sounds are end-stopped and which run-on in the octave?
2. How many end-stopped lines are there in the sestet?
3. Did you read the run-on lines as if you were reading prose? Explain your answer.
4. Which seemed more natural to you, the end-stopped lines or the run-on ones? Which more artificial?
5. What shift in tone did you experience between the octave and sestet when reading aloud? How do you account for this shift?

## UNDERSTANDING LANGUAGE

### Understanding Multiple Meanings

Most words have more than one meaning. Picking the word *friend* at random, one dictionary indicates five different meanings; another indicates seven.

Poets often use words in such a way as to exploit several meanings of a word at the same time. In this way they enrich an image or a poem.

1. What are the two meanings of the word *talent*?
2. Which is the primary one in the poem?
3. How does the secondary one reinforce the meaning of the primary sense of *talent*?
4. In Milton's mind, what was his chief, perhaps only, talent? What had he spent most of his early life preparing for?
5. What kind of "death" might Milton have experienced if he "hid" or did not use his talent?

---

### Primary Source

Milton's essay, "The Second Defense of the English People," written in 1654, offers an intriguing glimpse into his life. In the following excerpt, he discusses his childhood and describes what he sees as the cause for his later blindness:

"I will now mention who and whence I am. I was born at London, of an honest family; my father was distinguished by the undeviating integrity of his life; my mother, by the esteem in which she was held, and the alms which she bestowed. My father destined me from a child to the pursuits of literature; and my appetite for knowledge was so voracious, that, from twelve years of age, I hardly ever left my studies, or went to bed before midnight. This primarily led to my loss of sight. My eyes were naturally weak, and I was subject to frequent head-aches; which, however, could not chill the ardor of my curiosity, or retard the progress of my improvement."

# On His Having Arrived at the Age of Twenty-Three

John Milton

How soon hath Time, the subtle thief of youth,
    Stolen on his wing my three and twentieth year!
    My hasting days fly on with full career,[1]
    But my late spring no bud or blossom showeth.
5  Perhaps my semblance might deceive[2] the truth,
    That I to manhood am arrived so near,
    And inward ripeness doth much less appear,
    That some more timely-happy spirits[3] endueth.[4]
Yet be it less or more, or soon or slow,
10    It shall be still[5] in strictest measure even,
    To that same lot,[6] however mean or high,
Toward which Time leads me, and the will of Heaven;
    All is, if I have grace to use it so,
    As ever in my great Taskmaster's eye.

---

1. **career:** Speed.
2. **deceive:** Prove false.
3. **timely-happy spirits:** Other people who seem to be more accomplished poets at the age of twenty-three.
4. **endueth:** Endoweth.
5. **still:** Always.
6. **lot:** Fate.

# THINKING ABOUT THE SELECTION

## Recalling

1. According to the first line, who or what is the "subtle thief of youth"?
2. According to the second line, what was stolen?
3. What, according to line 3, flies on swiftly?
4. In line 4, what is not shown?
5. In lines 5–6, what is the speaker's image that "might deceive the truth"?
6. According to lines 7–8, what does not appear that others seem to have?
7. According to lines 8–12, to what will the speaker's accomplishments eventually conform?
8. What, according to lines 13–14, is forever in the "great Taskmaster's eye"?

## Interpreting

9. A metaphor is a comparison of two unlike things. In line 4, Milton uses two metaphors: one for the advanced stage of his youth, the other to represent the early or full development of his poetic ability. Which words are the metaphors?
10. Compare and contrast the concerns of the first four and second four lines of the poem.
11. Overall, what concerns the speaker in the first eight lines?
12. How do the last six lines answer the concern expressed in the first eight lines?

## Applying

13. One reason Milton may have felt he hadn't achieved much is that he hadn't yet decided on a career. He had first thought of entering the church and becoming a minister, but by the time he was twenty-three had decided against it. How many people do you know who have made career decisions by the time they were twenty-three? Why do you think it is so difficult to do this?

# THINKING AND WRITING

## Comparing and Contrasting Sonnets

Write an essay comparing and contrasting the Italian and English sonnets. Imagine you are writing this explanation for your school newspaper.

The English sonnet, which is also commonly known as the Shakespearean sonnet, is markedly different from the Italian form. The sonnet was first developed by the Italians as a fourteen-line love poem with a strict rhyme scheme and structure. The structure is divided into an eight-line octave and a six-line sestet.

The English sonnet, which derives from the Italian, has an entirely different structure and rhyme scheme. In this instance, the sonnet is divided into three four-line quatrains and a concluding two-line couplet. Each of these units has a different set of rhymes and a slightly different thought or image.

Use Shakespeare's "Sonnet 73" (page 257) and Milton's "On His Having Arrived at the Age of Twenty-Three" as your models. Analyze the ryhme scheme for both poems and explain the shifts in thought and image for both poems. Also describe the subjects of both poems. In what way are the subjects similar? How are they different? When you revise, make sure you have arranged your information in logical order. Proofread your essay and prepare a final draft.

# GUIDE FOR INTERPRETING

## Writer's Techniques

## *from* **Paradise Lost**

**Epic Poetry.** An epic is a long narrative poem written in an elevated style. It tells the story of a major cultural hero and reflects the values of the society in which it was produced. The early English epic *Beowulf* exhibits the values of the Anglo-Saxon warriors for whom it was composed. John Milton's epic *Paradise Lost* expresses the values of Christian England in the late seventeenth century. It also expresses, however, ideas that are so universal that the poem has become *the* epic of the English-speaking world.

Milton based his poem on the Biblical story of Adam and Eve and his style on the classical epics of ancient Greece and Rome. Like the *Aeneid,* the epic of classical Rome, Milton divided *Paradise Lost* into twelve books. He wrote the poem in blank verse, which no one writing in English had done before except in plays. Milton chose blank verse, which uses an unrhymed iambic pentameter line, because the great epics of ancient Greece and Rome did not rhyme.

## Commentary

*Paradise Lost* had to be licensed by the Archbishop of Canterbury before it could be published. As was the practice, the Archbishop passed the manuscript to a deputy. In this case the deputy was a chaplain named Tomkyns who had written pamphlets against the dissenters. Fortunately, Tomkyns did not wish to direct attention to himself and so chose to ignore anti-monarchy passages in the manuscript that might even have gotten Milton hanged. Tomkyns might also have thought that *Paradise Lost* was religious verse that would never be read at court, and therefore its contents were not important. He passed it on.

After his manuscript was licensed by the Archbishop, Milton found a publisher for it in Aldersgate, which had not been destroyed in the recent Great Fire. The contract, still preserved in the national museum, records that the agreement was drawn up between the author "John Milton, gent. of the one parte, and Samuel Symons, printer, of the other parte." For his work Milton received five pounds down and was to receive a second five pounds each for the sale of the first, second, and third editions, respectively.

Milton earned only five more pounds for the sale of the first edition. All told, he received ten pounds for his masterpiece. Do you think the market has changed today for serious literature?

## Writing

Jot down all the information you remember of the Biblical story of the fall of Adam and Eve.

# *from* Paradise Lost

## John Milton

Of man's first disobedience, and the fruit
Of that forbidden tree, whose mortal[1] taste
Brought death into the world, and all our woe,
With loss of Eden, till one greater Man[2]
5   Restore us, and regain the blissful seat,
Sing Heavenly Muse,[3] that on the secret top
Of Oreb, or of Sinai,[4] didst inspire
That shepherd, who first taught the chosen seed,
In the beginning how the Heavens and Earth
10   Rose out of Chaos: or if Sion hill[5]
Delight thee more, and Siloa's brook[6] that flowed
Fast[7] by the oracle of God, I thence
Invoke thy aid to my adventurous song,
That with no middle flight intends to soar
15   Above the Aonian mount,[8] while it pursues
Things unattempted yet in prose or rhyme.
And chiefly thou O Spirit,[9] that dost prefer
Before all temples the upright heart and pure,
Instruct me, for thou know'st; thou from the first
20   Wast present, and with mighty wings outspread
Dovelike sat'st brooding on the vast abyss
And mad'st it pregnant: what in me is dark
Illumine, what is low raise and support;
That to the height of this great argument[10]

---

**1. mortal:** Deadly.

**2. one . . . Man:** Christ.

**3. Heavenly Muse:** Urania, the muse of astronomy and sacred poetry in Greek mythology. Here, Milton associates Urania with the holy spirit that inspired Moses ("That shepherd,") to receive and interpret the word of God for the Jews ("the chosen seed"). To convey the message of God to his people, Moses wrote the first five books of the Bible, including Genesis. Genesis is the book on which *Paradise Lost* is based.

**4. Oreb** (ôr′ ĕb) **. . . Sinai** (sī′ nī′): Alternate names for the mountain where God communicated the laws to Moses.

**5. Sion** (sī′ ən) **hill:** The hill near Jerusalem on which the temple ("the oracle of God,") stood.

**6. Siloa's** (sī lō′ əz) **brook:** A stream near Sion hill.

**7. fast:** Close.

**8. Aonian** (ā ō′ nē ən) **Mount:** Mount Helicon in Greek mythology, home of the Muses. Milton is drawing a comparison between the epic he is now presenting and the epics written by the classical Greek poets, Homer and Virgil.

**9. Spirit:** The Holy Spirit, the voice that provided inspiration for the Hebrew prophets.

**10. argument:** Theme.

25    I may assert Eternal Providence,
    And justify the ways of God to men.
        Say first, for Heaven hides nothing from thy view
    Nor the deep tract of Hell, say first what cause
    Moved our grand[11] parents in that happy state,
30    Favored of Heaven so highly, to fall off
    From their Creator, and transgress his will
    For[12] one restraint,[13] lords of the world besides?[14]
    Who first seduced them to that foul revolt?
    The infernal Serpent; he it was, whose guile
35    Stirred up with envy and revenge, deceived
    The mother of mankind, what time his pride
    Had cast him out from Heaven, with all his host
    Of rebel angels, by whose aid aspiring
    To set himself in glory above his peers,
40    He trusted to have equaled the Most High,
    If he opposed; and with ambitious aim
    Against the throne and monarchy of God
    Raised impious war in Heaven and battle proud
    With vain attempt. Him the Almighty Power
45    Hurled headlong flaming from the ethereal sky
    With hideous ruin and combustion down
    To bottomless perdition, there to dwell
    In adamantine[15] chains and penal fire.
    Who durst defy the Omnipotent to arms.
50    Nine times the space that measures day and night
    To mortal men, he with his horrid crew
    Lay vanquished, rolling in the fiery gulf,
    Confounded though immortal. But his doom
    Reserved him to more wrath; for now the thought
55    Both of lost happiness and lasting pain
    Torments him; round he throws his baleful eyes
    That witnessed[16] huge affliction and dismay,
    Mixed with obdurate pride and steadfast hate.
    At once as far as angels' ken,[17] he views
60    The dismal situation waste and wild:
    A dungeon horrible, on all sides round,
    As one great furnace flamed, yet from those flames
    No light, but rather darkness visible
    Served only to discover sights of woe,
65    Regions of sorrow, doleful shades, where peace

---

**11. grand:** First in importance and in time.
**12. for:** Because of.
**13. one restraint:** That Adam and Eve should not eat of the fruit of the tree of knowledge.
**14. besides:** In every other respect.
**15. adamantine** (ad′ ə man′ tēn) *adj:* Unbreakable.
**16. witnessed:** Gave evidence of.
**17. ken:** Can see.

And rest can never dwell, hope never comes
That comes to all; but torture without end
Still urges,[18] and a fiery deluge, fed
With ever-burning sulfur unconsumed:
70 Such place eternal justice had prepared
For these rebellious, here their prison ordained
In utter darkness, and their portion set
As far removed from God and light of Heaven
As from the center thrice to the utmost pole.[19]
75 O how unlike the place from whence they fell!
There the companions of his fall, o'erwhelmed
With floods and whirlwinds of tempestuous fire,
He soon discerns, and weltering by his side
One next himself in power, and next in crime,
80 Long after known in Palestine, and named
Beelzebub.[20] To whom the archenemy,
And thence in Heaven called Satan, with bold words
Breaking the horrid silence thus began:
        "If thou beest he; but O how fallen! how changed
85 From him, who in the happy realms of light
Clothed with transcendent brightness didst outshine
Myriads though bright: if he whom mutual league,
United thoughts and counsels, equal hope
And hazard in the glorious enterprise,
90 Joined with me once, now misery hath joined
In equal ruin: into what pit thou seest
From what height fallen, so much the stronger proved
He with his thunder:[21] and till then who knew
The force of those dire arms? Yet not for those,
95 Nor what the potent Victor in his rage
Can else inflict, do I repent or change,
Though changed in outward luster, that fixed mind
And high disdain, from sense of injured merit,
That with the Mightiest raised me to contend,
100 And to the fierce contention brought along
Innumerable force of spirts armed
That durst dislike his reign, and me preferring,
His utmost power with adverse power opposed
In dubious battle on the plains of Heaven,
105 And shook his throne. What though the field be lost?
All is not lost; the unconquerable will,

---

**18. urges:** Afflicts.
**19. center . . . pole:** Three times the distance from the center of the
universe (earth) to the outermost sphere of the universe.
**20. Beelzebub** (bē el' zə bub'): Traditionally, the chief devil, or
Satan. In this poem, Satan's chief lieutenant among the fallen angels.
**21. He . . . thunder:** God.

And study[22] of revenge, immortal hate,
And courage never to submit or yield:
And what is else not to be overcome?
110 That glory never shall his wrath or might
Extort from me. To bow and sue for grace
With suppliant knee, and deify his power
Who from the terror of this arm so late
Doubted[23] his empire, that were low indeed,
115 That were an ignominy and shame beneath
This downfall; since by fate the strength of gods
And this empyreal substance[24] cannot fail,
Since through experience of this great event,
In arms not worse, in foresight much advanced,
120 We may with more successful hope resolve
To wage by force or guile eternal war
Irreconcilable, to our grand Foe,
Who now triumphs, and in the excess of joy
Sole reigning holds the tyranny of Heaven."
125     So spake the apostate angel, though in pain,
Vaunting aloud, but racked with deep despair;
And him thus answered soon his bold compeer.[25]
    "O prince, O chief of many throned Powers,
That led the embattled Seraphim[26] to war
130 Under thy conduct, and in dreadful deeds
Fearless, endangered Heaven's perpetual King,
And put to proof his high supremacy,
Whether upheld by strength, or chance, or fate!
Too well I see and rue the dire event[27]
135 That with sad overthrow and foul defeat
Hath lost us Heaven, and all this mighty host
In horrible destruction laid thus low,
As far as gods and heavenly essences
Can perish: for the mind and spirit remains
140 Invincible, and vigor soon returns,
Though all our glory extinct, and happy state
Here swallowed up in endless misery.
But what if he our conqueror (whom I now
Of force[28] believe almighty, since no less
145 Than such could have o'erpowered such force as ours)
Have left us this our spirit and strength entire
Strongly to suffer and support our pains,

---

**22. study:** Pursuit.
**23. doubted:** Feared for.
**24. empyreal** (em pir′ ē əl) **substance:** The indestructible substance of which Heaven, or the empyrean, is composed.
**25. compeer:** Comrade, equal.
**26. Seraphim** (sĕr′ ə fim): The highest order of angels.
**27. event:** Outcome.
**28. of force:** Necessarily.

That we may so suffice[29] his vengeful ire,
Or do him mightier service as his thralls
150 By right of war, whate'er his business be
Here in the heart of Hell to work in fire,
Or do his errands in the gloomy deep?
What can it then avail though yet we feel
Strength undiminished, or eternal being
155 To undergo eternal punishment?"
Whereto with speedy words the Archfiend replied:
      "Fallen cherub, to be weak is miserable,
Doing or suffering:[30] but of this be sure,
To do aught[31] good never will be our task,
160 But ever to do ill our sole delight,
As being the contrary to his high will
Whom we resist. If then his providence
Out of our evil seek to bring forth good,
Our labor must be to pervert that end,
165 And out of good still[32] to find means of evil;
Which oft times may succeed, so as perhaps
Shall grieve him, if I fail not,[33] and disturb
His inmost counsels from their destined aim.
But see the angry Victor[34] hath recalled
170 His ministers of vengeance and pursuit
Back to the gates of Heaven: the sulfurous hail
Shot after us in storm, o'erblown hath laid
The fiery surge, that from the precipice
Of Heaven received us falling, and the thunder,
175 Winged with red lightning and impetuous rage,
Perhaps hath spent his shafts, and ceases now
To bellow through the vast and boundless deep.
Let us not slip[35] the occasion, whether scorn,
Or satiate[36] fury yield it from our Foe.
180 Seest thou yon dreary plain, forlorn and wild,
The seat of desolation, void of light,
Save what the glimmering of these livid flames
Casts pale and dreadful? Thither let us tend
From off the tossing of these fiery waves,
185 There rest, if any rest can harbor there,
And reassembling our afflicted powers,[37]
Consult how we may henceforth most offend

---

**29. suffice:** Satisfy.
**30. doing or suffering:** Whether one is active or passive.
**31. aught:** Anything.
**32. still:** Always.
**33. if . . . not:** Unless I am mistaken.
**34. angry Victor:** God.
**35. slip:** Fail to take advantage of.
**36. satiate:** Satisfied.
**37. afflicted powers:** Overthrown armies.

Our Enemy, our own loss how repair,
How overcome this dire calamity,
190   What reinforcement we may gain from hope,
If not what resolution from despair.''
        Thus Satan talking to his nearest mate,
With head uplift above the wave, and eyes
That sparkling blazed; his other parts besides,
195   Prone on the flood, extended long and large,

**PARADISE LOST, 1688**
*From the British Library*

Lay floating many a rood,[38] in bulk as huge
As whom the fables name of monstrous size,
Titanian, or Earthborn, that warred on Jove,
Briareos or Typhon,[39] whom the den
200 By ancient Tarsus[40] held, or that sea beast
Leviathan,[41] which God of all his works
Created hugest that swim the ocean stream:
Him haply slumbering on the Norway foam
The pilot of some small night-foundered skiff,
205 Deeming some island, oft, as seamen tell,
With fixed anchor in his scaly rind
Moors by his side under the lee, while night
Invests[42] the sea, and wished morn delays:
So stretched out huge in length the Archfiend lay
210 Chained on the burning lake, nor ever thence
Had risen or heaved his head, but that the will
And high permission of all-ruling Heaven
Left him at large to his own dark designs,
That with reiterated crimes he might
215 Heap on himself damnation, while he sought
Evil to others, and enraged might see
How all his malice served but to bring forth
Infinite goodness, grace and mercy shown
On man by him seduced, but on himself
220 Treble confusion, wrath and vengeance poured.
Forthwith upright he rears from off the pool
His mighty stature; on each hand the flames
Driven backward, slope their pointing spires, and rolled
In billows leave in the midst a horrid vale.
225 Then with expanded wings he steers his flight
Aloft, incumbent[43] on the dusky air
That felt unusual weight, till on dry land
He lights, if it were land that ever burned
With solid, as the lake with liquid fire;
230 And such appeared in hue, as when the force
Of subterranean wind transports a hill
Torn from Pelorus, or the shattered side

---

**38. rood:** An old unit of measure, equal to seven or eight yards.
**39. Titanian** (tī tā′ nē ən) **. . . Earthborn . . . Briareos** (brī är′ ē
əs) **. . . Typhon** (tī′ fən): In classical mythology, both the Titans, led
by Briareos, who had a hundred hands, and the Giants (Earthborn),
led by Typhon, a hundred-headed serpent monster, fought with Jove.
As punishment for their rebellion, both Briareos and Typhon were
thrown into the underworld.
**40. Tarsus** (tär′ səs): The capital of Cilicia (sə lish′ ə). Typhon is said
to have lived in Cilicia near Tarsus.
**41. Leviathan** (lə vī′ ə thən): A great sea monster.
**42. invests:** Covers.
**43. incumbent:** Lying.

Of thundering Etna,[44] whose combustible
And fueled entrails thence conceiving fire,
235 Sublimed[45] with mineral fury, aid the winds,
And leave a singed bottom all involved[46]
With stench and smoke: such resting found the sole
Of unblessed feet. Him followed his next mate,
Both glorying to have scaped the Stygian[47] flood
240 As gods, and by their own recovered strength,
Not by the sufferance[48] of supernal[49] power.
      "Is this the region, this the soil, the clime,"
Said then the lost Archangel, "this the seat
That we must change[50] for Heaven, this mournful gloom
245 For that celestial light? Be it so, since he
Who now is sovereign can dispose and bid
What shall be right: farthest from him is best,
Whom reason hath equaled, force hath made supreme
Above his equals. Farewell happy fields,
250 Where joy forever dwells. Hail horrors! Hail
Infernal world! and thou, profoundest Hell
Receive thy new possessor, one who brings
A mind not to be changed by place or time.
The mind is its own place, and in itself
255 Can make a Heaven of Hell, a Hell of Heaven.
What matter where, if I be still the same,
And what I should be, all but less than he
Whom thunder hath made greater? Here at least
We shall be free; the Almighty hath not built
260 Here for his envy, will not drive us hence:
Here we may reign secure, and in my choice
To reign is worth ambition though in Hell:
Better to reign in Hell than serve in Heaven.
But wherefore[51] let we then our faithful friends,
265 The associates and copartners of our loss
Lie thus astonished[52] on the oblivious[53] pool,
And call them not to share with us their part
In this unhappy mansion, or once more
With rallied arms to try what may be yet
270 Regained in Heaven, or what more lost in Hell?"

---

**44. Pelorus** (pə lôr′ əs) **. . . Etna:** Volcanic mountains in Sicily.
**45. sublimed:** Vaporized.
**46. involved:** Enveloped.
**47. Stygian** (stĭj′ ē ən): Of the river Styx, which, in Greek mythology, encircled Hades, the home of the dead.
**48. sufferance:** Permission.
**49. supernal:** Heavenly.
**50. change:** Exchange.
**51. wherefore:** Why.
**52. astonished:** Stunned.
**53. oblivious:** Causing forgetfulness.

# THINKING ABOUT THE SELECTION

## Recalling

1. The first five lines of *Paradise Lost* allude to the Biblical story of Adam and Eve and their expulsion from Paradise. What are the five elements of the story that Milton chooses to emphasize?
2. Lines 6–26 are the invocation to the muse. Which lines state the help that Milton is seeking?
3. In lines 29–36, Milton fills out a bit of the story of Adam and Eve. What new element does he introduce here?
4. (a) Lines 34–53 tell of another, earlier fall from grace. Who fell that earlier time? (b) What caused that earlier fall?
5. Lines 59–74 describe Hell. What are its main features?
6. (a) In lines 84–155 Satan addresses Beelzebub and speaks of eternal rebellion and war against God. What are his motives for continuing the war? (b) Explain Beelzebub's advice.
7. From lines 193 to 209, Milton describes the size of Satan. To what creatures is Satan compared?

## Interpreting

8. Throughout his invocation, from the first line to the twenty-sixth, Milton mixes references to the Hebrew Bible and classical mythology. What effect is created by Milton's combination of Hebrew and Greek-Roman elements?
9. In what ways are the Fall of Adam and Eve paralleled by the Fall of Satan and his cohorts? Point out the parallels in the poem.
10. Between lines 200 and 208 Milton uses an epic simile in which he compares Satan to the sea beast Leviathan. How does Milton convey the huge size of Leviathan, the point of the comparison?
11. From lines 242 until the end of this excerpt at line 270, Satan expresses simultaneously his despair at losing heaven and his resolve to glory in his lost condition. What words, phrases, and lines show Satan's feelings?
12. How would you describe Satan's character? Is he petty, mean, grand, self-pitying, heroic, stubborn, weak, or rebellious? You may combine several of these characterizations, but support your choices with references to the poem.

## Applying

13. The eighteenth-century poet William Blake said "Milton was of the Devil's party." What do you think this statement means? Explain why you agree or disagree with this statement. Find evidence from the poem to support your answer.

# ANALYZING LITERATURE

## Understanding Epic Poetry

Epic poems express the values of their cultures through stories of heroes and villains in conflict. As in any other kind of story, the conflict is central and can be of many different kinds. Some conflicts are between characters, some are between a character and the environment, and some are within a character's mind.

The conflict in *Paradise Lost* is essentially between Satan and God, and the arena in which the struggle takes place is in the heart and mind first of Eve and then of Adam. The most illuminating insights into the struggle, however, come from the mind of Satan, which is always conscious of the beauty of goodness as it plans evil.

1. What causes Satan the greatest mental anguish?
2. How does he view Heaven? Contrast this to his view of Hell.
3. Interpret his statement: "The mind is its own place, and in itself / Can make a Heaven of Hell, a Hell of Heaven."

# CROSS CURRENTS

## Views of Paradise

You're plodding through the gray slush, an icy wind tearing at your eyes. Your cheeks are flushed crimson, your fingers nearly frozen. Suddenly a car veers too close to the curb, an angry face glares out, and a blast of icy slush dives into your shoes. In desperation, your thoughts drift to a lush green garden overflowing with sweet fruit. Peace and freedom reign, as people live in harmony with each other and their animal companions. The birds sing lyrically, the flowers sway softly, and a fresh breeze wafts gently over all. Paradise!

The word *paradise* came from the Old Persian word *pairidaeza,* which meant a "walled enclosure, pleasure park, garden." Curiously, the description of paradise differs little among various cultures. Cross-culturally and throughout the ages, it is seen as a beautiful garden free from violence or pain.

### CUNEIFORM TABLETS

An early account of paradise appears on tablets produced by the Sumer tribe in southern Mesopotamia around the year 5000 B.C. The inscription opens with praise for the plain of Babylon, called "Edinn." In this innocent, clean, and sun-filled land, gods are forever young, healthy, and amiable. The only thing lacking is water, but this is soon brought by the sun god Utu at the command of the water god Enki. Water completes paradise by creating a lush garden bursting with fruit.

### THE GARDEN OF EDEN

In *Paradise Lost,* Milton gives the traditional description of the Garden of Eden. Again we have a garden: this time, an en-closed area on the top level of a steep hill whose sides are covered with rows of shrubs. The entire scene is illuminated by the glorious light of the sun. The image suggests the power of humanity as well as the beauty and security of paradise.

Milton's account owes much to the traditional seventeenth-century European gardens. These were private estates and parks, carefully and cleverly planted in geometrical patterns, and stocked for their wealthy owners. These lavish formal gardens were an idealized setting for thought and learning.

### THE GOLDEN APPLES OF THE SUN

In Greek mythology, paradise is the garden of the Hesperides, the home of the daughters of Atlas, the evening star. Assisted by a dragon, the inhabitants guard the tree that gives the golden apples. The tree, with branches and leaves of gold, had been a wedding gift to the goddess Hera from Gaea, Mother Earth. The apples were so closely guarded that theft was thought impossible; in fact, one of the hero Hercules' twelve labors was to bring back the golden apples of the Hesperides.

### AFRICAN, BUDDHIST, AND HINDU TALES OF PARADISE

Although every culture has a different word for "paradise," the tales are curiously alike. In African tales, for example, paradise is a beautiful garden with ample food and leisure. There is no death or disease. Humans live in harmony with animals, able to understand their language. But something happened that ended paradise, making life what it is today.

**THE GARDEN OF EDEN**
*Erastus S. Field*

To the Buddhists, India will become paradise when the next Buddha, called "Maitreya," appears. Evil will vanish and people will be strong and healthy. The earth will effortlessly yield an abundance of rice. Calm, broad rivers will nourish a wonderful variety of fruits and flowers.

Perhaps the most striking example of paradise is the Hindu belief in the world ages, called "yugas." There are four world ages in each cycle, all related to the ages of the life of the god Brahma. The "krtayuga" is the golden age, equivalent to paradise, where equality, prosperity, and fulfillment rein. This is followed by three ages of increasing decay, climaxing in the dark age, when people and the world are at their worst. By some Buddhist accounts, we are now unfortunately in the dark age, slated to last 432,000 human years.

## PARADISE ON EARTH?

People have long searched the four corners of the globe for paradise. The Guarani Indians of South America provide perhaps the best recorded instance of an actual quest. They believe that paradise really exists on earth, but that it is cleverly concealed. For more than four hundred years, the tribe has conducted numerous voyages to find what they call the "land without evil."

Christopher Columbus claimed that the freshwater tides he found in the Gulf of Paria between Trinidad and the coast of South America originated in the four rivers that flow out of Eden. He took as proof the area's sweet climate, fragrant flowers, and lush vegetation. But paradise has also been "discovered" in less logical places, such as the North Pole!

# JOHN BUNYAN

## 1628–1688

Perhaps the most widely read book by any English author, *The Pilgrim's Progress* was written by an ill-educated traveling tinker or mender of pots, pans, and other household utensils. John Bunyan's father had been a tinker before him and had trained him in his craft. As a child John received some education at the local grammar school. After marriage, Bunyan educated himself by reading two religious tracts that his wife brought as a dowry and the Bible. On the basis of this background he wrote a great many religious books and tracts, culminating in the most popular, *The Pilgrim's Progress.*

Born and raised near Bedford in central England, he left there at sixteen to join the Parliamentary army and did not return until a number of years later. At twenty-one he married and at twenty-five he started to preach after several years of an intense spiritual struggle in the dark night of the soul. Bunyan had joined a nonconformist sect and was an unlicensed preacher to its congregation at Bedford. Upon the restoration of the Stuart monarchy, Bunyan, as well as many other nonconformist preachers, was arrested. Refusing to renounce his faith, he remained imprisoned for twelve years, during which time he wrote a fairly large number of religious works. Upon his release as a result of a general amnesty, Bunyan returned to Bedford as a licensed preacher. Except for a short period during which he was imprisoned again, Bunyan remained in Bedford for the rest of his life. There he preached to his congregation and an increasing audience in the barn that served as his church and continued to work at his trade as a tinker. During his second imprisonment, Bunyan wrote the first part of *The Pilgrim's Progress.* Several years later he wrote the second part of this work and a number of other fairly successful books. Altogether Bunyan wrote and published nearly sixty works, yet at his death he was almost as poor as when he was born.

From the seventeenth century through the nineteenth, *The Pilgrim's Progress* was the most successful Christian text written by an Englishman. It was translated into well over 100 languages. Once you have read it, you can understand why the book was so popular. Bunyan was a superb storyteller. He wrote with humor; drew vivid, easily understandable characters; provided suspense and action; and sent a clear, unambiguous message. Moreover, his language, though simple and colloquial, is charged with echoes of the Bible. In essence, Bunyan's tale reflected the main cultural values of his audience.

# GUIDE FOR INTERPRETING

## from *The Pilgrim's Progress*

**Allegory.** When the plot, characters, and setting of a story clearly represent abstract ideas, the narrative is called an *allegory*. An allegory can be prose or poetry. It operates on at least two levels: an on-the-surface level and a beneath-the-surface level.

The interest in allegory goes back very far in human history. In fact, the word itself comes from ancient Greece. However, allegory as a way of creating literature hit its stride in the Middle Ages. There are several kinds of allegories. *The Faerie Queene,* for example, is primarily a social allegory, although it has religious, moral, and political elements as well. *Everyman,* on the other hand, is almost entirely a moral allegory, and *The Pilgrim's Progress* is almost entirely a religious one.

The purpose of all allegory is to teach entertainingly. As Bunyan put it in his preface to *The Pilgrim's Progress:*

> [Fish] must be groped for, and tickled too,
> Or they will not be catch'd, whate'er you do.

To make their instruction clear, writers of allegories draw simple, one-dimensional characters and settings, which are then assigned the names of their governing traits. For example, *The Pilgrim's Progress* is an allegory of Christian redemption and salvation. The hero's name is Christian. He leaves the City of Destruction (this world) and goes toward the Celestial City (the place of salvation or heaven). Some of the characters on his journey are Obstinate, Faithful, and Mr. Worldly Wiseman.

**Writing**

Jot down the names of several traits, such as Happy, Dour, Mr. Cynic, or Miss Know-it-All. Then write little scenes in which characters bearing these names display the traits.

**Primary Source**

"Vanity Fair" is an allegorical version of a country fair. Fairs were common in Bunyan's day. A disgruntled seventeenth-century shopper, annoyed at the price and quality offered, reports that "There are (as I take it) few great towns in England that have not their weekly markets . . . where all manner of provisions for household is to be bought and sold, for ease and benefit of the country round about . . . And, as these have been in times past erected for the benefit of the realm, so are they in many places too, too much abused: for the relief and ease of the buyer is not so much intended in them as the benefit of the seller . . . For, in most of these markets, neither . . . bread nor . . . sweetness of grain are any whit looked unto, but each one suffered to sell or set up what and how himself listeth."

# from The Pilgrim's Progress

John Bunyan

## Vanity Fair

*This is probably the best-known episode of* The Pilgrim's Progress. *The book's hero, Christian, and his companion, Faithful, pass through the town of Vanity during the season of the local fair. Local fairs were an important British tradition, giving people the opportunity to buy wares sold by merchants from all over Europe. At the same time, these fairs involved a good deal of eating and drinking and offered a wide variety of entertainment. In this selection, Bunyan uses the fair to demonstrate how worldly attractions can corrupt religious life.*

Then I saw in my dream, that when they were got out of the wilderness, they presently saw a town before them, and the name of that town is Vanity; and at the town there is a fair kept, called Vanity Fair. It is kept all the year long. It beareth the name of Vanity Fair, because the town where it is kept, is lighter than vanity, and also, because all that is there sold, or that cometh thither, is vanity; as is the saying of the wise, "All that cometh is vanity" (Ecclesiastes 1:2, 14; 2:11, 7; 11:8; Isaiah 11:17).

This fair is no new-erected business, but a thing of ancient standing. I will show you the original of it.

Almost five thousand years ago, there were pilgrims walking to the Celestial City,[1] as these two honest persons are; and Beelzebub,[2] Apollyon,[3] and Legion,[4] with their companions, perceiving by the path that the pilgrims made, that their way to the city lay through this town of Vanity, they contrived here to set up a fair; a fair wherein should be sold all sorts of vanity, and that it should last all the year long. Therefore at this fair are all such merchandise sold as houses, lands, trades, places, honors, preferments,[5] titles, countries, kingdoms, lusts, pleasures, and delights of all sorts, as harlots, wives, husbands, children, masters, servants, lives, blood, bodies, souls, silver, gold, pearls, precious stones, and what not.

And moreover, at this fair there is at all times to be seen jugglings, cheats, games, plays, fools, apes, knaves, and rogues, and that of every kind.

Here are to be seen, too, and that for nothing, thefts, murders, adulteries, false swearers, and that of a blood-red color.

And as, in other fairs of less moment, there are the several rows and streets under

---

**1. Celestial City:** The source of salvation.
**2. Beelzebub** (bē el′ zə bub): Prince of the devils (Matthew 12:24).
**3. Apollyon** (a pol′ yən): The angel of the bottomless pit (Revelation 9:11).
**4. Legion:** The unclean spirit (Mark 5:9).

---

**5. preferments:** Appointments and promotions to political or ecclesiastical positions.

their proper names, where such and such wares are vended; so here likewise you have the proper places, rows, streets (namely, countries and kingdoms), where the wares of this fair are soonest to be found. Here is the Britain Row, the French Row, the Italian Row, the Spanish Row, the German Row, where several sorts of vanities are to be sold. But as in other fairs some one commodity is as the chief of all the fair, so the ware of Rome and her merchandise is greatly promoted in this fair; only our English nation, with some others, have taken a dislike thereat.

Now, as I said, the way to the Celestial City lies just through this town where this lusty[6] fair is kept; and he that would go to the city, and yet not go through this town, "must needs go out of the world" (I Corinthians 5:10). The Prince of princes himself, when here, went through this town to his own country, and that upon a fair day too;[7] yea, and, as I think, it was Beelzebub, the

6. **lusty:** Merry.
7. **The Prince . . . too:** Refers to the temptation of Christ in the wilderness (Matthew 4:1–11).

PILGRIM'S PROGRESS
Angels/Pilgrim/Knight Figures
*John Bunyan*
*The British Library*

chief lord of this fair, that invited him to buy of his vanities; yea, would have made him lord of the fair, would he but have done him reverence as he went through the town. Yea, because he was such a person of honor, Beelzebub had him from street to street, and showed him all the kingdoms of the world in a little time, that he might, if possible, allure that Blessed One to cheapen[8] and buy some of his vanities; but he had no mind to the merchandise, and, therefore, left the town without laying out so much as one farthing upon these vanities. This fair, therefore, is an ancient thing of long standing, and a very great fair.

Now these pilgrims, as I said, must needs go through this fair. Well, so they did; but, behold, even as they entered into the fair, all the people in the fair were moved, and the town itself, as it were, in a hubbub about them, and that for several reasons: for

First, the pilgrims were clothed with such kind of raiment[9] as was diverse from the raiment of any that traded in that fair. The people, therefore, of the fair made a great gazing upon them: some said they were fools, some they were bedlams[10] and some they were outlandish men[11] (I Corinthians 2:7,8).

Secondly, and as they wondered at their apparel, so they did likewise at their speech; for few could understand what they said. They naturally spoke the language of Canaan,[12] but they that kept the fair were the men of this world; so that, from one end of the fair to the other, they seemed barbarians each to the other (Job 12:4; I Corinthians 4:9).

Thirdly, but that which did not a little amuse the merchandisers was that these pilgrims set very light by their wares; they cared not so much as to look upon them; and if they called upon them to buy, they would put their fingers in their ears, and cry, "Turn away mine eyes from beholding vanity," and look upwards, signifying that their trade and traffic was in heaven (Psalms 129:37; Philippians 3:19, 20).

One chanced mockingly, beholding the carriages of the men, to say unto them, "What will ye buy?" But they, looking gravely upon him, said, "We buy the truth" (Proverbs 23:23). At that there was an occasion taken to despise the men the more; some mocking, some taunting, some speaking reproachfully, and some calling upon others to smite them. At last things came to a hubbub and great stir in the fair, insomuch that all order was confounded. Now was word presently brought to the great one of the fair, who quickly came down, and deputed some of his most trusty friends to take these men into examination, about whom the fair was almost overturned. So the men were brought to examination; and they that sat upon[13] them, asked them whence they came, whither they went, and what they did there, in such an unusual garb? The men told them that they were pilgrims and strangers in the world, and that they were going to their own country, which was the Heavenly Jerusalem (Hebrews 11:13–16); and that they had given no occasion to the men of the town, nor yet to the merchandisers, thus to abuse them, and to let[14] them in their journey, except it was for that, when one asked them what they would buy, they said they would buy the truth. But they that were appointed to examine them did not believe them to be any other than bedlams and mad, or else such as came to put all things into a confusion in the fair. Therefore they took them and beat them, and besmeared them with dirt, and then put them into the cage, that they might be made a spectacle to all the men of the fair.

---

**8. cheapen:** Ask the price of.
**9. raiment:** Clothing.
**10. bedlams:** Lunatics from Bethlehem Hospital, the insane asylum in London.
**11. outlandish men:** Foreigners.
**12. Canaan:** The Promised Land. The "language of Canaan" is the language of the Bible.

---

**13. sat upon:** Interrogated and tried them.
**14. let:** Hinder.

# THINKING ABOUT THE SELECTION

## Recalling

1. In *The Pilgrim's Progress,* on what path or route is the town of Vanity located?
2. When in time was the fair established at Vanity?
3. Who were the ones that first set up the fair?
4. What can be seen at the fair?
5. Which individuals *must* go through the town and hence through the fair as well?
6. What were the three reasons the two pilgrims caused such a stir at the fair?
7. What did the pilgrims say that led to their being examined by "the great one's trusty friends"?

## Interpreting

8. Why do the travelers have to pass through the fair to reach their destination?
9. What does the fair represent?
10. Why were the pilgrims so uppity toward the inhabitants of the fair?

## Applying

11. "Vanity Fair," as well as the whole of *The Pilgrim's Progress,* represents a level and type of writing that is no longer common. If you were to write something like "Vanity Fair" today, how would you go about it?

# ANALYZING LITERATURE

## Recognizing Allegory

Everything in an **allegory** is geared toward delivering a message. The plot, characters, dialogue, and setting all contribute to the same end—to make the author's ideas immediately understandable.

1. How does the allusion to the temptation of Jesus in the wilderness relate to the purpose of the fair at Vanity?
2. Why is the town and its fair astride the path the true Christian must follow?
3. Why is the fair run by Beelzebub?
4. In relation to Christian virtue, what does the fair represent?

# CRITICAL THINKING AND READING

## Interpreting the Author's Point of View

Point of view refers to the way a story is told. Stories are told by *someone* and that someone or narrator is represented by a grammatical form or person. The first-person narrator is the character in the story who says "I," like the dreamer in *The Pilgrim's Progress.* The third-person narrator is the one who says "he," "she," or "it." In *The Pilgrim's Progress* the dreamer is also a third-person narrator.

In this excerpt from the "Vanity Fair" episode, there is a first-person and third-person narrator.

1. Point out where each occurs and what the function of the narrator is in any one circumstance.
2. Describe which kind of third-person narrator is being used.
3. Discuss the effect that using two kinds of narrators has on Bunyan's story.
4. In what way might this device suit Bunyan's purpose and allow him the freedom to express his own point of view?

# THINKING AND WRITING

## Writing an Allegory for Today's World

Allegories generally use one-dimensional characters and situations to present clear ideas about religious, moral, political, or social issues. Write an allegory about the modern world for your fellow students. Remember, allegories are stories, and all stories have conflict. In allegories, this conflict is between characters representing abstract ideas. You should have one central character that the reader can identify with. Do not forget to choose a particular point of view when writing your narrative. You may wish to use a first-person or third-person narrator, or you may wish to alternate between the two, as Bunyan did.

# THE CHANGING ENGLISH LANGUAGE

## New Worlds, New Words

The Renaissance had sparked the rebirth of spoken and written English. The language continued to grow and spread during the reign of James I. As the seventeenth century opened, English was poised on the edge of worldwide recognition.

The story of English in the seventeenth century is largely the story of the New World. Sparked by a combination of optimism,

**CAPTAIN JOHN SMITH**
*The Granger Collection*

faith, and self-interest, thousands of people undertook the brutal voyage to America. Captain John Smith established the first permanent British colony in Jamestown, Virginia, in 1607; the Puritans anchored the Mayflower at Plymouth Bay in December, 1620. With these voyages, the English language was planted—and took root—in an entirely new land.

Initially, the majority of people who braved the terrors of the unknown were Puritans from a section of England called East Anglia, the Puritan stronghold. Cromwell himself was from East Anglia and had trained his New Model Army there. Throughout the period, Puritans from East Anglia would continue to pour into the New World, seeking to establish a stronghold of their faith and better their lot in life. As they brought their dreams across the ocean, so they brought their language.

### SEVENTEENTH-CENTURY ENGLISH LINGERS TODAY

This mass immigration to the New World had an exciting effect on the English language. Thomas Jefferson commented on the results of this movement nearly two hundred years after the first settlers established their fragile beachheads on the shores of the New World. "New circumstances," he said, "call for new words, new phrases, and the transfer of old words to new objects."

Even today, visitors from England can hear distinctive traces of seventeenth-century British speech in American English. To the ears of the British, these words are clearly archaic. For example, today in American English we use "gotten"—a term commonplace in England until the late eighteenth century—in place of "got." American speakers still use the term "mad" to mean "angry," another remnant of seventeenth-century English. In England today, "sick" means "nausea," not illness in general, as is the case in modern America, where we have retained the older definition. "Platter," meaning "dish," is a commonplace term in America; it is largely unknown in contemporary England. Another frequently used American term carried over on those first ships is "I guess"; scholars have identified it as dating back as far as Chaucer's age. The English use "autumn" to refer to the season before winter; we interchange it with the seventeenth-century word "fall."

## YOU SAY POTATO . . .

And how did all this sound? Despite the growing discontent with monarchy in the beginning of the seventeenth century, the speech of the court still set the standard for "proper" spoken and written English throughout the land. The sound of this "standard English" was different enough from the speech of the villages to be discernible, however. A country visitor to the court was easily able to identify what he called a "true kynde of pronunciation," one of the first references to what was to become standard English. As we can tell from this remark, those who spoke in courtly tones thought themselves vastly superior to those who used country dialect. Another contemporary noted this elitist attitude when he wrote:

> There be gentlemen and other that speake, but specially write, as good Southerne as we of Middlesex or Surrey do, but not the common people or every shire, of whome the gentlemen, and also their learned clarkes, do for the most part condescend.

Since Johnson had yet to write his dictionary, people tended to spell words as they sounded, which offers us clues as to their pronunciation. From the above quotation, for example, we can see that "clerkes" was pronounced "clarkes" because of the way it was spelled. Many of the rhymes found in poetry of the age—such as "tea" with "tay," and "sea" with "say"—also offer hints. From these clues and others, scholars believe that seventeenth-century standard English most likely sounded like a combination of the Irish and West Country speech of today.

## CALLS FOR LANGUAGE REFORM

Carried across the vast ocean by eager pilgrims, English took firm root in the fertile linguistic soil of the new land. But back home in England, many people were beginning to feel that language matters had gotten out of hand. English, perhaps like the bulk of English society itself, was willful and coarse. In the decades to come, writers and scholars would be increasingly concerned with reining in the unruly mother tongue.

# YOU THE WRITER

**Assignment**

**1.** Several poems in this unit are addressed to a person. Select one of these poems and turn it into a personal letter such as the poet might have conceivably written.

**Prewriting.** Write a line-by-line paraphrase of the poem. Then decide how this material should be developed in prose.

**Writing.** When you write the letter, use modern English, but try to capture the personality and tone of your seventeenth-century author.

**Revising.** Think of the purpose or main point of your letter. What changes can you make to improve the letter's effectiveness? See if you can add to its seventeenth-century style and tone.

**Assignment**

**2.** Many of the authors in this unit led adventurous lives. Write a brief short story in which the main character is an author from this unit.

**Prewriting.** Review the author's biography and his works. Jot down notes about this author. List details that make him come alive. Then use your imagination. In what scene or situation can you picture him? What other characters are present? How does the scene or situation conclude? Make a map outlining the events in your short story.

**Writing.** Write the first draft of your short story. Aim to give the reader a glimpse of the author's personality and style. Your narrative should have a beginning, middle, and end. Arrange events in chronological order.

**Revising.** Make whatever changes will enhance the seventeenth-century character of your narrative. Does the dialogue sound appropriate to the time and place? Then see if you can improve the narrative flow and style.

**Assignment**

**3.** Several poems in this unit are about specific people. Write a poem about a person you know, modeling your verses on one of the seventeenth-century poems.

**Prewriting.** Think of the person your poem will be about and jot down whatever comes to mind about him or her. Then select thoughts and images that can be linked in a poem structured like your seventeenth-century model.

**Writing.** You might first write a prose passage that contains all the ideas you wish to express. Then turn the passage into verse, following the rhythm, rhyme scheme, and stanza pattern of your model.

**Revising.** Rewrite your verses until they can stand alone as a satisfactory imitation of seventeenth-century poetry. Read it aloud. Listen to the way it sounds.

# YOU THE CRITIC

**Assignment**

**1.** Jacobean poetry is distinguished by the presence of striking, highly imaginative figures of speech. Write an essay in which you develop this point by citing and analyzing such figures in the work of three Jacobean poets.

**Prewriting.** Review the poems you have read and scan them for figures of speech. Analyze the figures to determine what makes them effective vehicles of meaning.

**Writing.** Write the first draft of your essay. Discuss the figures of speech in a systematic way to prove and illustrate the idea that striking and imaginative figures of speech are a distinctive characteristic of seventeenth-century poetry.

**Revising.** First check that your separate analyses all relate to and support your main point. Then look for and correct lapses in grammar and style.

**Assignment**

**2.** Write an essay in which you compare one humorous and one serious love poem from this unit. Show how each presents a distinctive attitude toward love or the poet's beloved.

**Prewriting.** Once you have chosen the poems you plan to write about, find the lines, words, ideas, and images that create the humorous or serious tone of each poem.

**Writing.** Begin with a topic sentence that sums up the different attitude toward love seen in each poem. Then write about each poem separately, supporting your thesis sentence with the evidence you gathered in your prewriting work.

**Revising.** First check that you have compared the poems in a way that shows clearly the different feelings and attitudes they express. Then look for and correct errors in grammar and style.

**Assignment**

**3.** How does seventeenth-century English literature in general differ from the literature of earlier periods? Write an essay in which you answer this question.

**Prewriting.** First think of one or two differences in subject matter between seventeenth-century and earlier English literature. Then think of one or two differences in style or artistic technique. What specific works or parts of works would you cite to support your views?

**Writing.** You might first discuss the differences in subject matter and then the differences in style or technique. Be sure to refer to specific works or passages to support your ideas.

**Revising.** Pay particular attention to improving the organization of your essay so that the characteristics you are concerned with emerge clearly and vividly.

**MORVILLE HALL, SHROPSHIRE**
*John Inigo Richards*
Roy Miles Fine Paintings, London

# THE RESTORATION AND THE EIGHTEENTH CENTURY

## 1660–1798

All Nature is but art, unknown to thee,
All chance, direction which thou canst not see;
All discord, harmony not understood;
All partial evil, universal good.

**Alexander Pope**

In 1660, England stood at the threshold of a new age. The religious conflicts that had brought on the Civil War had been settled, and a king once again sat on the throne. The people of England could look forward to a period of stability, order, and progress.

This happy prospect was reinforced by the ideas of a scientific revolution then sweeping Europe. From their close observation of nature, Isaac Newton and other scientists concluded that harmony and order underlay all the events in the world. They also believed that human beings were capable of discovering and understanding that order.

The Scientific Revolution ushered in a new era called the Age of Reason, or the Enlightenment. During the Enlightenment, confidence in human reason spread beyond the realm of science. In the verses quoted on page 471, for example, Alexander Pope asserted that everything in nature has a design and purpose. Disharmony is an illusion—no more than "harmony not understood." Like scientists, Pope believed, poets must struggle to see beneath the superficial chaos and grasp the underlying harmony of the world.

The Enlightenment thus put great emphasis on order, harmony, and stability. At the same time, however, it was an age that believed in progress, and progress meant change. Great changes indeed overtook England between 1660 and the late 1700's. As Parliament restricted the power of the monarch, England improved what was already an admirably democratic political system in Europe. Even more profound changes took place in the economic sphere. English merchants were accumulating great wealth, in part because of their trade with England's colonial empire. In the late 1700's they began to invest in the first factories of the Industrial Revolution. By 1800, Britain had surpassed its ancient rival, France, as the foremost military and economic power in Europe.

From 1660 to the late 1700's, British literature continued to exhibit order and harmony in spite of, or perhaps because of, the rapid transformation of British society. Before discussing the literature of the period, however, it will be helpful to look in more detail at the political, social, and economic developments that took place in England from 1660 to the end of the 1700's.

## THE GROWTH OF ENGLISH DEMOCRACY

### The Restoration of Monarchy

Soon after Oliver Cromwell's death, in 1658, Parliament offered the crown to the exiled son of Charles I. In 1660, he became Charles II. Most English people fervently hoped that the restoration of the House of Stuart would end the fighting between Puritans and Anglicans and between Parliament and the Crown.

The omens in the first years of Charles II's reign were not good. In 1665, a plague swept the city of London, killing 70,000 people. A year later, the Great Fire destroyed over half the city's houses. Yet these calamities were quickly overcome. London was rebuilt on a grander scale under the direction of the brilliant architect Christopher Wren (1632–1723). Profits from the global trade carried on by British merchants furthered London's growth.

Charles II had lived in Paris during Cromwell's Protectorship. In sharp contrast to the drab Puritan leaders, Charles II enjoyed elegance. His court copied the plush clothing, rich jewelry, and elaborate wigs of Paris. An avid patron of the arts, Charles also invited Italian composers and Dutch painters to live and work in London. In 1662 he advanced the scientific spirit of the age by chartering the Royal Society, devoted to the study of natural science.

Although some critics said Charles cared more about pleasure than power, he was a shrewd ruler. He kept his Catholic convictions to himself even while accepting money from the Catholic king of France. The problem of having a Catholic king rule a Protestant nation could not, however, be kept in check forever. After Charles II died, James, son of Charles I, became king. James II was a stubborn ruler and a devout Catholic. Trouble loomed when James appointed Catholics to high offices and dismissed Parliament for failing to obey his wishes.

## A Glorious Revolution

The crisis came in 1688, when James II's wife gave birth to a son. To the people of England, this meant that another Catholic king would someday sit on the throne. Parliament reacted quickly. Several leaders invited Mary, the Protestant daughter of James II, to rule England jointly with her husband, William of Orange. William was a prince of Holland and a champion of Protestantism in Europe.

When William and Mary arrived in England, they were prepared to fight for the throne if necessary. But James, recalling the fate of his father, escaped to France. The people of England hailed the event as a "Glorious Revolution," since not a drop of blood had been shed. The next year, William and Mary agreed to respect a Bill of Rights passed by Parliament. Among other things, it guaranteed Parliament the right to approve all taxes and said that a king could not suspend the law. With the Bill of Rights, England attained a limited, or constitutional, monarchy. Although it was far from being a democracy in the modern sense, England was among the most democratic nations of Europe.

## Political Parties Emerge

After William of Orange followed his wife Mary to the grave in 1702, Mary's sister Anne, a Protestant, became queen. Under Queen Anne, England grew stronger and more united. One important act of her reign was the joining of the realms of England and Scotland. The Act of Union, passed in 1707, created the nation of Great Britain, with a central government in London.

# BRITISH EVENTS

1660    **Samuel Pepys** begins *Diary*.

1662    Royal Society chartered.

1663    Drury Lane Theater opens.

1666    Great Fire of London.

       First cheddar cheese produced.

1667    **John Milton's** *Paradise Lost* published.

1668    **John Dryden** publishes *An Essay of Dramatic Poesy*.

1685    James II becomes king.

1687    Isaac Newton publishes *Philosophiae Naturalis Principia Mathematica*.

1688    Glorious Revolution.

1689    Bill of Rights becomes law.

1690    John Locke publishes *Essay Concerning Human Understanding*.

1700    William Congreve publishes *The Way of the World*.

1701    Act of Settlement.

1702    England enters War of the Spanish Succession.

       First daily newspaper begins publication.

1707    Great Britain created by Act of Union.

1709    First Copyright Act.

       First literary magazine, *The Tatler*, begins publication.

1712    **Alexander Pope** publishes *The Rape of the Lock*.

1714    George I becomes king.

1719    First organized cricket match takes place.

       **Daniel Defoe** publishes *Robinson Crusoe*.

Palace at Versailles

The Syndics

Samuel Pepys        John Locke

The Great Fire of London

La Salle Visits Indian Village

AMACAO.
Major Port for Trade with China

Johann Sebastian Bach

# WORLD EVENTS

1661    Holland: Rembrandt paints *The Syndics*.

1662    France: Louis XIV begins palace at Versailles.

1664    North America: Britain seizes New Netherlands.

1665    Holland: Vermeer paints *The Artist's Studio*.

1666    Italy: Stradivari labels first violin.

1669    France: Molière's *Tartuffe* first performed.

1677    France: Racine's *Phèdre* first performed.

1678    North America: La Salle explores Great Lakes.

1680    Dodo becomes extinct.

1685    China: All ports opened to foreign trade.

1690    India: Calcutta founded by British.

1700    Japan: Kabuki Theater developed.

1703    Russia: Peter the Great begins building St. Petersburg.

1714    Holland: Fahrenheit constructs mercury thermometer.

1715    France: Louis XV succeeds to throne.

1721    Germany: Bach composes *Brandenburg Concertos*.

1727    Brazil: First coffee planted.

1728    Pacific: Behring explores Alaskan waters.

1735    Russia: Ballet school opens in St. Petersburg.

1740    Prussia: Frederick the Great succeeds to throne.

1748    France: Montesquieu publishes *The Spirit of the Law*.

1749    Portugal: Sign language invented.

# BRITISH EVENTS

1726    **Jonathan Swift** publishes *Gulliver's Travels*.

1735    William Hogarth paints *The Rake's Progress*.

1745    Last Jacobite rebellion in Scotland.

1749    Henry Fielding publishes *Tom Jones*.

1750    **Thomas Gray** publishes "Elegy in a Country Churchyard".

1755    **Samuel Johnson** publishes *Dictionary of the English Language*.

1756    Britain enters Seven Years' War.

1766    **Oliver Goldsmith** publishes *The Vicar of Wakefield*.

1775    Actress Sarah Siddons debuts at Drury Lane Theater.

1786    **Robert Burns** publishes *Poems Chiefly in Scottish Dialect*.

1789    **William Blake** publishes *Songs of Innocence*.

1791    **James Boswell** publishes *The Life of Samuel Johnson*.

1793    England goes to war with France.

1798    Admiral Nelson defeats French at Aboukir Bay.

Illustration from *Gulliver's Travels*

The American Revolution Begins

Robert Burns

Johnson and Boswell

Captain Cook Explores the South Pacific

The Storming of the Bastille

Benjamin Franklin

Mozart

The Boston Tea Party

# WORLD EVENTS

| | |
|---|---|
| 1752 | North America: Benjamin Franklin invents lightning rod. |
| 1759 | Canada: British troops capture Québec. |
| 1765 | North America: Stamp Act imposed. |
| 1769 | Pacific: Captain Cook explores New Zealand and Australia (to 1770). |
| 1772 | France: Diderot publishes *Encyclopédie*. |
| 1773 | Austria: Waltz introduced. |
| | North America: Boston Tea Party. |
| 1774 | France: Louis XVI succeeds to throne. |
| | Germany: Goethe publishes *The Sorrows of Young Werther*. |
| 1775 | United States: Revolution begins. |
| 1776 | United States: Thomas Jefferson writes Declaration of Independence. |
| 1780 | Peru: Rebellion against Spanish rule. |
| 1781 | France: Rousseau's *Confessions* published. |
| | Germany: Kant publishes *Critique of Pure Reason*. |
| 1784 | France: First school for the blind established. |
| 1786 | Austria: Mozart's *Marriage of Figaro* first performed. |
| 1789 | France: Revolution begins with storming of Bastille. |
| 1791 | Austria: Haydn composes *Surprise Symphony*. |
| 1793 | France: Reign of Terror begins. |
| 1795 | Africa: Mungo Park explores Niger River. |

During Anne's reign, there was another important political development. Once again, France and Britain were at war. The war helped to crystallize two political factions in Parliament, the Tories and the Whigs. The Tories included aristocrats and lesser landowners. As a group, they were conservatives who were against the changes taking place in Britain. Most Tories opposed the war with France as a waste of tax money. Whigs, on the other hand, supported the war. Many Whigs came from Britain's growing class of merchants, who made handsome profits supplying war goods. They also wanted Britain to crush France once and for all and become the undisputed trade leader of Europe. The split between Tories and Whigs would remain a basic fact of British politics for many decades.

Favoring the Tories, Queen Anne signed a treaty to end the war in 1713, the same year she fell ill. Earlier, Parliament had passed a law stipulating that only a Protestant could inherit the throne. When Anne died in 1714, the throne passed to a little-known relative of James I who ruled a small principality in Hanover, Germany.

**QUEEN ANNE AND THE KNIGHTS OF THE GARTER, 1713**
*Peter Angelis*
*The Granger Collection*

## A Cabinet and Prime Minister

The new king, George I, spoke no English and had little interest in the affairs of Britain. He seemed an unlikely figure to advance democracy in Britain, but in fact he did. George I relied on ministers, chosen from Parliament, to run the country. This group of ministers was called the cabinet, and the chief among them came to be known as the prime minister. Robert Walpole, a brilliant and energetic Whig was the first man to unify the cabinet government in the person of the prime minister. Thus began the cabinet system still used in Britain today. Through the cabinet, Parliament gained a greater voice in the nation's policies.

In 1760, another Hanoverian king came to the British throne. Born in Britain, George III thought of himself as an Englishman, not a German. He was a strong-willed man who took his mother seriously when she said, "George, be a king." Using his wealth and influence, the king packed Parliament with men loyal to him. He then set about pursuing his own policies. His strong-headed handling of the American colonies helped bring about the American Revolution.

The king's disastrous policies toward America angered Parliament. In 1782, a fiery twenty-four-year-old became prime minister. William Pitt, the youthful Tory leader, had great plans for reform of the British government. Before he had a chance to put them into effect, however, France erupted in revolution. Soon thereafter, Britain and France were at war again, putting off any chance of reform.

KING GEORGE III OF ENGLAND, c. 1760
*Allan Ramsay*
*The Granger Collection*

## THE TRANSFORMATION OF BRITAIN'S ECONOMY

### An Agricultural Revolution

After the Restoration, Britain's system of government became gradually more democratic. Gradual changes also occurred in the economic life of the nation.

In 1660, the vast majority of the British people were farmers. Most either rented their fields from a landlord or cultivated a patch of common land. By the late 1600's, however, new economic forces were changing life in the countryside. New farm tools made it possible for farmers to plant and harvest a much bigger crop. As a result, landlords began to fence in the land they had once rented out, hiring laborers to work the land for them.

Bigger, more efficient estates replaced the small holdings of earlier times. By the mid-1700's, British farms were producing much more food. With more food available, the population of the small island surged upward. Since fewer farmhands were needed, many people left the countryside. In the growing towns, they became the factory hands who ran the machines of the early Industrial Revolution.

## The Industrial Age Dawns

The Industrial Revolution began in Britain. A series of British inventions after 1750 made the spinning and weaving of cloth much more efficient. At the same time, the steam engine was perfected and adapted to run a power loom. These machines were brought together in factories, which were soon producing vast quantities of cotton cloth. Merchants sold the goods all over the world, adding more gold to the nation's coffers.

Although the Industrial Revolution happened first in England, the nation did not become predominantly industrial until the 1800's. As late as the 1790's, a majority of British people still earned their living as farmers. Yet the economic changes of the 1700's had major significance. They profoundly affected ways of thinking about the world.

## NEW IDEAS FOR A NEW AGE

### The Enlightenment

In a sense, the Industrial Revolution began when British inventors found practical ways to apply the ideas of the Scientific Revolution. The Scientific Revolution led to other developments as well. Works by Enlightenment thinkers in many other fields can all be considered its offspring.

In 1687, Sir Isaac Newton published his monumental study of gravity and the movement of the planets. Popular awareness of Newton's achievement is reflected in this couplet from a poem by Alexander Pope:

> Nature and Nature's laws lay hid in night:
> God said, Let Newton be! and all was light.

Each breakthrough in astronomy, physics, and chemistry seemed to affirm the hope that human beings would someday perfect their knowledge of the world. Thinkers in other fields tried to make their studies as orderly and rational as the studies of a scientist. In *The Wealth of Nations,* for example, Adam Smith suggested that economic life is ruled by laws as discoverable as scientific laws.

One of the greatest figures of the Enlightenment was John Locke, a British philosopher and political theorist. After the Glorious Revolution, Locke brought the rationalism of the age to his study of government. Kings, said Locke, did not have a "divine right" to hold power. Rather, a monarch's authority came from the consent of the people. If the monarch abuses his subjects, they "are thereupon absolved from any further obedience." Locke's enlightened ideas about government helped shape the arguments of the American colonists during their disputes with George III.

The scientific advances of the Enlightenment established the basis for the new technology of the Industrial Revolution. But beyond that, a new confidence in human ability encouraged inventors to experiment with new devices, and capitalists to risk their money on untested ideas. Hence, the Industrial Revolution both grew out of and reinforced the new scientific spirit.

## The Neoclassical Ideal

Everywhere they looked, the Enlightenment thinkers discerned what they took to be evidence of the world's harmony and order. When Alexander Pope and others sought kindred spirits in the past, they often found them among the writers of ancient Greece and Rome. In the works of Homer, Virgil, Horace, and other classical authors, Enlightenment thinkers and artists discovered harmony, restraint, and clarity—the very qualities they admired most.

English writers of the Enlightenment are often called *neoclassical* because they emulated classical styles. The features of neoclassicism are easy to identify. One feature is the frequent use of classical allusions—that is, references to the myths, gods, and heroes of ancient times. Another is an inclination to generalize about the world rather than to describe it from a particular individual's point of view. John Dryden, Alexander Pope, and Samuel Johnson often put their generalizations about the world in the form of *aphorisms*—short, quotable sentences, such as "The proper study of mankind is man." (See the quotations on page 487.)

One other feature of neoclassicism makes the work of Pope and others lively and amusing: a fondness for satire, the literary ridicule of the vices, follies, and stupidities of society. Such classical poets as Horace, Juvenal, and Martial provided the English poets of the eighteenth century with superb models of the genre.

Most of the satires of the time were mild and inoffensive, usually written in a formal, neoclassical style. Pope, for example, wrote a long poem, *The Dunciad,* in a high-flown, heroic style—but the poem is a satirical celebration of stupidity. Other satirists, such as Jonathan Swift, were less polite. His *Gulliver's Travels* includes savage attacks on lawyers, princes, and mankind in general. In *A Modest Proposal,* Swift suggests a way "for preventing the children of poor people in Ireland from being a burden to their parents or country." Swift's ironic solution—to eat them—is the modest proposal at the heart of a bitter satire directed against the English absentee landlords who were destroying Ireland.

## The Literary World Expands

As Britain grew wealthier, more men and women could afford an education. The number of people who could read grew, as did the number who could spend money on books. This change had several results. Daily newspapers began to appear. The first real magazine, the *Gentleman's Magazine,* began publication in 1731. The first private lending libraries, which charged their members a fee, also opened in the early 1700's.

In London, coffeehouses and clubs became popular places for middle-class men to stop in, read the newspapers, and chat about politics. Expanding literacy presented writers with a real opportunity. No longer did they have to rely on a few wealthy patrons for their livelihood. For the first time, writers could at least survive on the money they made from their books and articles. The modern world of publishers, copyright laws, and royalties began to take shape in London during the 1700's.

## THREE LITERARY AGES

The literature of the Restoration and eighteenth century may be thought of as comprising three broad divisions, or "ages": the Age of Dryden, the Age of Pope and Swift, and the Age of Johnson.

## The Age of Dryden

The Age of Dryden in literature extends from the year of the restoration of Charles II, 1660, to 1700, the year of Dryden's death. In history, this forty-year period is called the Restoration. Dryden, whose works included poems, plays, and essays, dominated the period. He was named poet laureate, England's official poet, by Charles II.

Among Dryden's most famous works are his satirical poems,

especially *MacFlecknoe,* written in 1682. These satires included unflattering portraits of real people of his time. Although the poems employ lofty, heroic language, they actually ridicule their "heroes." For this reason they are often called mock heroic poems, or mock epics. Dryden also created several celebratory poems for royal and other public events. These poems, in true Enlightenment spirit, hail the achievements of humanity. A famous example is "A Song for St. Cecilia's Day," an ode in honor of music.

The Restoration was also noted for its drama, especially comedies. When he became king, Charles II reopened the London theaters, which the disapproving Puritans had closed. The Restoration theaters, fancier and more costly than those of Shakespeare's time, did a thriving business. Dryden himself wrote the best tragedy of the period. Entitled *All for Love,* it recounts the ill-fated romance of Antony and Cleopatra.

Prose writing also flourished in the Restoration. Dryden wrote a series of essays about drama that laid the foundation for British literary criticism. These, along with his translations of Plutarch and other prose compositions, represent what many literary historians consider the first modern prose. They are clear, plain, direct, colloquial in tone, and—for people of today—easy to read. Probably the most fascinating prose work of the period, however, was the diary kept by Samuel Pepys (1633–1703). Pepys kept his journal for nine years, beginning in 1660. With remarkable frankness he recorded the daily events in London during those turbulent years, including the deadly plague of 1665 and the Great Fire.

## The Age of Pope and Swift

During the reign of Queen Anne in the early 1700's, one of the most admired writers in London was Alexander Pope. Pope's poetry is a shining example of neoclassical style, exhibiting wit, elegance, and moderation. All these qualities show forth in his most famous work, *The Rape of the Lock,* a mock-heroic poem that satirizes the absurdities of a war between the sexes.

Pope also had enormous influence as a literary critic. His principles found eloquent expression in *An Essay on Criticism,* a long verse essay in heroic couplets. Many well-known aphorisms can be traced to that work, including the following couplet:

True wit is Nature to advantage dress'd;
What oft was thought, but ne'er so well express'd.

Pope, a Tory, was a special favorite of Queen Anne. When George I came to power in 1714, the Tories fell out of favor, and Pope retired to his country house. There he wrote *An Essay on Man,* a long poem that asserts the essential order and goodness of the universe and the rightness of humanity's place in it.

Another Tory writer of the time was Jonathan Swift (1667–1745). Swift, a close friend of Pope's, wrote mild satires while Queen Anne reigned. After her death and the fall of the Tories, Swift grew increasingly bitter. The behavior of the rising merchants, whom he viewed as shameless money grubbers, enraged Swift. *Gulliver's Travels* and *A Modest Proposal* date from this later period. Swift stood apart from many of his contemporaries by his antagonism to the idea that human nature is essentially good. In his great satires he presents the older view that human nature is deeply flawed, and that improvement must begin with a recognition of our intellectual and moral limitations.

One book that enjoyed a huge success at the time told about a shipwrecked British sailor struggling to survive on a deserted island. The work, *Robinson Crusoe,* has been called the first novel in English. It was such a success that its author, Daniel Defoe, immediately set to work on other novels. Defoe's experiments with the novel opened up a new form of fiction that, in the 1800's, would become the favorite reading matter of the middle classes.

England's first literary periodicals, *The Tatler* and *The Spectator,* also appeared in the early 1700's. Written by Joseph Addison (1672–1719) and Richard Steele (1672–1729), these one-page papers included crisply written reflective essays and news. The essays quickly became models for other prose writers.

## The Age of Johnson

Alexander Pope died in 1744, and Jonathan Swift the following year. The dominant literary figure of the next generation was Samuel Johnson. Like many young writers after him, Johnson honed his writing style by working as a journalist. He later published his own magazine, *The Rambler.* Johnson also wrote poetry, literary criticism, and a novel. His most important work, however, was the *Dictionary of the English Language,* published in 1755. It was the first dictionary that could be considered a standard and authoritative reference work on English.

Samuel Johnson dominated his age not only by his writings but also by his conversation and acquaintanceships. A brilliant and inexhaustible talker, he was friendly with most of the writers, painters, and actors of his time. His wise advice helped nurture the careers of many younger talents.

One reason we know so much about Samuel Johnson is that one of those younger talents, James Boswell (1740–1795), wrote his biography. Boswell followed his friend and mentor from club to coffeehouse to dinner party, faithfully recording Johnson's comments and witticisms. The result, Boswell's *Life of Samuel Johnson,* was the first modern biography written in English. It gives a vivid portrait not only of Johnson but of life in London in the 1700's.

The Age of Johnson saw other literary accomplishments. On the stage, the Restoration tradition of satire was carried on by Oliver Goldsmith and other comic playwrights. Among the many important works of prose, Edward Gibbon's history of Rome stands out. And novelists, working in the tradition begun by Defoe, produced a spate of popular books. Among the best were Samuel Richardson's *Pamela* and *Clarissa*, Fanny Burney's *Evelina,* Henry Fielding's *Tom Jones* and *Joseph Andrews*, and Lawrence Sterne's *Tristram Shandy.*

## THE ECLIPSE OF THE ENLIGHTENMENT

By 1750 Britain was launched on a course of rapid industrialization. In the new industrial towns, mills and factories belched smoke into the country air. Inside the factories, men, women, and children toiled at machines for twelve and fourteen hours a day. Every year

**SIR ISAAC NEWTON, c. 1726**
*Attributed to John Vanderbank*
The Granger Collection

more poor people crowded into the towns and cities, unable to find regular work and barely able to survive.

As a result of these changes, writers and intellectuals began to lose faith in the ability of human reason to solve every problem. The thinkers in the Age of Reason looked to science to make life better for humanity. Yet by the late 1700's, "progress" seemed to be bringing misery to millions.

As they began to doubt the basic assumptions of the Enlightenment, writers turned away from the standards of neoclassicism. Instead of using the impersonal, high-flown style of the early 1700's, some wrote in the common language of everyday life. Departing from the spirit of rationalism, they charged their poems with powerful emotions. Thomas Gray's *Elegy Written in a Country Churchyard,* completed in 1750, exemplifies the transition from the formal, classical poetic styles of the early eighteenth century to the more emotional manner of the Romantic era.

William Blake broke even more sharply with the ideas and attitudes of Pope and the neoclassicists. In simple language, he conveyed mystical ideas and biting attacks on what England was becoming. In one poem he derided those who held to a complacent faith in human rationality, while ignoring the spiritual side of human existence:

> You don't believe—I won't attempt to make ye;
> You are asleep—I won't attempt to wake ye.
> Sleep on! Sleep on! while in your pleasant dreams
> Of Reason you may drink of Life's clear streams.
> Reason and Newton, they are quite two things;
> For so the swallow and the sparrow sings.

The Age of Reason, with its unbounded faith in human intelligence, was coming to an end. New voices were being raised, and they no longer spoke in the clipped and polished language of rationalist neoclassicism. They would make the 1800's a new literary age.

# ENGLISH VOICES
## Quotations by Prominent Figures of the Period

Errors, like straws, upon the surface flow;
He who would search for pearls must dive below.
    **John Dryden,** *All for Love*

Titles are shadow, crowns are empty things,
The good of subjects is the end of kings.
    **Daniel Defoe,** *The True-Born Englishman*

Satire is a sort of glass, wherein beholders do generally discover
everybody's face but their own.
    **Jonathan Swift,** "The Battle of the Books"

Proper words in proper places, make the true definition of a
style.
    **Jonathan Swift,** "Letter to a Young Clergyman"

Sweet are the slumbers of the virtuous man.
    **Joseph Addison,** *Cato*

Reading is to the mind what exercise is to the body.
    **Richard Steele,** *The Tatler*

The noblest motive is the public good.
    **Richard Steele,** *The Spectator*

To err is human, to forgive divine.
    **Alexander Pope,** *An Essay on Criticism*

Fools rush in where angels fear to tread.
    **Alexander Pope,** *An Essay on Criticism*

When a man is tired of London, he is tired of life.
    **Samuel Johnson,** Quoted by James Boswell in *The Life of
      Samuel Johnson*

The paths of glory lead but to the grave.
    **Thomas Gray,** "Elegy Written in a Country Churchyard"

The best laid plans o' mice and men
Gang aft a-gley.
    **Robert Burns,** "To a Mouse."

# READING CRITICALLY

# The Literature of 1660–1798

When you read literature, it is important to place it in its historical context. Doing so will help you to see how it was shaped by the dominant attitudes of the period and to appreciate the techniques the writer used to convey these attitudes.

## Historical Context

During the years from 1660 to 1798, English life was dominated by a desire for social and political stability. The nation had been severely shaken by the events of the civil war and the Puritan dictatorship and sought to reestablish a sense of order and security. Although the monarchy had been restored, the Parliament developed into the nation's supreme ruling force. Despite this shift in power, the English people generally remained complacent. The nation prospered financially and its citizens tended to be patriotic and optimistic. This sense of optimism resulted in part from scientific and philosophical advances that helped create a belief that everything in the universe could be explained.

## Literary Movements

The literature written between 1660 and 1798 generally reflects the faith in reason and the desire for stability that characterized English life at the time. Strongly influenced by the works of classical Greek and Roman writers, writers generally displayed their intelligence, education, and sense of discipline in their works. Their works also conveyed their faith in English traditions and captured the elegance of English aristocratic life at the time. Toward the end of the eighteenth century, however, some poets, who are often referred to as Preromantics, began to react against the emphasis on reason and the intellect.

## Writer's Techniques

During this period English prose flourished. Writers wrote formal essays on a variety of subjects, presenting logical, scientific arguments. The literary letter became a popular form; the first modern biography was written; and literary criticism and fiction flourished. In poetry, writers generally turned away from the lyric and wrote formally structured poems, often filled with classical allusions. Writers often displayed their wit by satirizing the society of their day in both poems and essays. The Preromantic poets, however, disregarded the tastes of the time and reestablished the lyric.

On the following page is a poem by William Blake, a Preromantic poet. The notes in the side column should help you to place the selection in its historical context.

# Holy Thursday

## William Blake

Is this a holy thing to see,
In a rich and fruitful land,
Babes reduced to misery,
Fed with cold and usurious[1] hand?

5  Is that trembling cry a song?
Can it be a song of joy?
And so many children poor?
It is a land of poverty!

And their sun does never shine,
10  And their fields are bleak and bare,
And their ways are filled with thorns;
It is eternal winter there.

For where-e'er the sun does shine,
And where-e'er the rain does fall,
15  Babe can never hunger there,
Nor poverty the mind appall.

**Historical Context:**
Although England was a wealthy and prosperous nation during the · eighteenth century, the poor were generally neglected.

**Literary Movement:**
Unlike most writers of the time, the Preromantic poets often wrote about lower-class people.

**Writer's Technique:** This poem is a lyric in which the speaker expresses his thoughts and feelings concerning the poor.

**Literary Movement:**
Blake appeals to both the reader's emotions and sense of reason.

---

**1. usurious** (yōō zhoor′ ē əs) *adj.*: Lending money at a high rate of interest.

# THINKING ABOUT THE SELECTION

## Recalling

1. (a) How does Blake characterize England in the first stanza? (b) How does he characterize the country in the second stanza?
2. What observations about the poor does Blake make in the third stanza?
3. According to the final stanza, what can never happen "where-e'er the sun does shine" and "the rain does fall"?

## Interpreting

4. Holy Thursday is another name for Ascension Day, the day on which Jesus' ascension into heaven is celebrated. Why do you think Blake used this name as the title of his poem?
5. (a) Find one example of Blake's use of parallelism—the repetition of phrases, clauses, or sentences that are similar in meaning or structure? (b) How does his use of parallelism reinforce the meaning of the poem?
6. (a) What is the theme, or main point, of the poem? (b) What was Blake's purpose in writing the poem?

## Applying

7. Do you think this poem could be applied to contemporary American society? Why or why not?

# ANALYZING LITERATURE

## Using Sound Devices

Alliteration, consonance, and assonance are three sound devices used in poetry. **Alliteration** is the repetition of consonant sounds at the beginnings of words or accented syllables. For example, the *th* sound is repeated in line 1 of "Holy Thursday": "Is *th*is a holy *th*ing to see." **Consonance** is the repetition of consonant sounds at the ends of words or accented syllables. Notice the repetition of the *d* sound in line 4 of Blake's poem: "Fe*d* with col*d* an*d* usurious han*d*." **Assonance** is the repetition of vowel sounds. For example, the short *i* sound is repeated in "*i*s," "th*i*s," "*i*n," and "r*i*ch" in the first two lines of "Holy Thursday."

1. Find another example of alliteration in "Holy Thursday."
2. Find another example of consonance.
3. Find another example of assonance.

# CRITICAL THINKING AND READING

## Analyzing the Effect of Sound Devices

Sound devices cause poetry to have a musical quality. The repetition of sounds also adds emphasis to certain words and reinforces the meaning of a poem.

1. Find two cases in which Blake's use of a sound device adds emphasis to important words.
2. How does the emphasis of these words reinforce the meaning of the poem?

# THINKING AND WRITING

## Responding to Criticism

A critic has stated that Blake had "the ability to establish direct contact with readers, however remote in time or space." Write an essay in which you discuss this comment in relation to "Holy Thursday." Consider the meaning of the critic's comment. Reread the poem with the critic's statement in mind. Prepare a thesis statement. Then write your essay, using evidence from the poem to support your thesis. When you revise, make sure you have not included any unnecessary information.

# The Restoration

**THE ELECTION—THE POLLING**
*William Hogarth*
Sir John Soane's Museum, London

# JOHN DRYDEN

## 1631–1700

John Dryden dominated the literary scene in the last quarter of the seventeenth century. The most accomplished poet of the period, he also ranks high in English letters as a dramatist, essayist, satirist, and critic. His versatility and professionalism helped to establish writing as a legitimate career in England. The poet T. S. Eliot has maintained that Dryden "is the ancestor of nearly all that is best in the poetry of the eighteenth century," while the poet Matthew Arnold observed, "Here at last we have the true English prose, a prose such as we would all gladly use if only we knew how."

Born at the vicarage of Aldwinkle All Saints, Northamptonshire, where his father was a country gentleman, young Dryden studied at Westminster School. He graduated from Trinity College, Cambridge, in 1654, and five years later published his first important poem, *Heroic Stanzas*. The poem commemorates the death of Oliver Cromwell, under whose protectorate Dryden seems to have held a minor political post. A year later, in *Astraea Redux,* he did a political about-face and hailed the return to the throne of King Charles II. While in his fifties, Dryden, who had once been a Puritan and then an Anglican, became a convert to Roman Catholicism.

Dryden first came to prominence as a playwright, producing blank-verse tragedies and comedies. He was appointed poet laureate in 1668, a position that was supposed to pay an annual salary of two hundred pounds, but because of problems in the Royal Treasury, he received only half. His best play, *All for Love* (1677), is a rewriting of Shakespeare's *Antony and Cleopatra* in a clear, simple style. He displays his full power in *Absalom and Achitophel,* a political poem published in 1681. This poem was followed a year later by the equally impressive *The Medall,* also on politics.

After the Revolution of 1688 in England, which brought the Protestants William and Mary to the throne, Dryden lost his laureateship. He was replaced by Thomas Shadwell, whom Dryden had satirized a few years earlier in the poem *MacFlecknoe.* To compensate for his lost income, Dryden increased his literary output, translating classical writers and writing prologues and miscellaneous pieces. The last of these efforts, his *Fables, Ancient and Modern*—translations from Chaucer, Boccaccio, and Ovid —appeared the year he died.

As a writer, Dryden was uniquely a man of his era. He expressed himself on virtually every important issue of the day. His friend William Congreve, a fellow playwright, pays tribute to Dryden's talents, saying that "no man hath written in our language so much . . . and in so various manners so well. . . ."

# GUIDE FOR INTERPRETING

## *from* **An Essay of Dramatic Poesy**

**Literary Forms**

**Essay.** An essay is a prose composition that expresses the writer's viewpoint on a limited topic. Essays vary in length from several paragraphs to the equivalent of an entire book. Modern essays are generally short, but in the eighteenth century, when the essay flourished as a popular literary form, essays were considerably longer. Dryden's complete essay on dramatic poesy—about thirty-five printed pages—is of average length for the time. Essays can be classified as formal or informal. A *formal essay* is one that deals with a serious subject in a carefully organized and often lofty way. An *informal essay,* or *personal essay,* is lighter and less structured than a formal essay. It may be humorous, and—even though classified as nonfiction—it may stretch the truth considerably or abandon it entirely. An informal essay is generally written in a conversational tone, reflecting the personality of the author and displaying distinctly personal touches.

**Commentary**

Writing style, as with style in fashion, changes throughout the years. Dryden's style of writing, however, has become "classic"—the standard by which we measure all other writing—because it is clear, direct, and elegant. To Samuel Johnson, for example, Dryden does not appear "to have any other art than that of expressing with clearness what he thinks with vigor. His style could not easily be imitated, either seriously or ludicrously; for, being always equable and always varied, it has no prominent or discriminative characters." What are the qualities of Dryden's style?

His sentences are basically subject-verb-object, with just enough variety to avoid monotony. While his sentences are usually longer than was fashionable in the seventeenth century, they are still not overly long, when judged by earlier standards. Clear and concise, they have a conversational tone and avoid excessive figurative language. What other elements of style can you find in the following essay that contribute to Dryden's concise, clear, and dignified writing?

**Writing**

When you read a work of fiction, what do you look for? An exciting plot? Well-developed, believable characters? Insights into human nature? List at least five characteristics that you think a work of fiction should have. Then make a second list in which you include the characteristics that detract from a work of fiction—for example, dull characters or an unbelievable plot.

# *from* An Essay of Dramatic Poesy

John Dryden

## Shakespeare and Ben Jonson Compared

To begin, then, with Shakespeare. He was the man who of all modern, and perhaps ancient poets, had the largest and most comprehensive soul. All the images of nature were still present to him, and he drew them, not laboriously, but luckily; when he describes anything, you more than see it, you feel it too. Those who accuse him to have wanted[1] learning, give him the greater commendation: he was naturally learned; he needed not the spectacles of books to read nature; he looked inwards, and found her there. I cannot say he is everywhere alike; were he so, I should do him injury to compare him with the greatest of mankind. He is many times flat, insipid; his comic wit degenerating into clenches,[2] his serious swelling into bombast. But he is always great, when some great occasion is presented to him; no man can say he ever had a fit subject for his wit, and did not then raise himself as high above the rest of poets,

*Quantum lenta solent inter viburna cupressi*[3]

The consideration of this made Mr. Hales of Eton say that there was no subject of which any poet ever writ, but he would produce it much better done in Shakespeare; and however others are now generally preferred before him, yet the age wherein he lived, which had contemporaries with him Fletcher[4] and Jonson, never equaled them to him in their esteem: and in the last king's court, when Ben's reputation was at highest, Sir John Suckling, and with him the greater part of the courtiers, set our Shakespeare far above him. . . .

As for Jonson, to whose character I am now arrived, if we look upon him while he was himself (for his last plays were but his dotages), I think him the most learned and judicious writer which any theater ever had. He was a most severe judge of himself, as well as others. One cannot say he wanted wit, but rather that he was frugal of it. In his works you find little to retrench[5] or alter. Wit, and language, and humor also in some measure, we had before him; but something of art was wanting to the drama till he came.

---

**1. wanted:** Lacked.
**2. clenches:** Puns.
**3. *Quantum . . . cupressi:*** As do cypresses among the bending shrubs. From Virgil's *Eclogues* 1:25.

**4. Fletcher:** John Fletcher (1579–1625), an Elizabethan playwright.
**5. retrench:** Delete.

He managed his strength to more advantage than any who preceded him. You seldom find him making love in any of his scenes or endeavoring to move the passions; his genius was too sullen and saturnine[6] to do it gracefully, especially when he knew he came after those who had performed both to such a height. Humor was his proper sphere: and in that he delighted most to represent mechanic people.[7] He was deeply conversant in the ancients, both Greek and Latin, and he borrowed boldly from them: there is scarce a poet or historian among the Roman authors of those times whom he has not translated in *Sejanus* and *Catiline*.[8] But he has done his robberies so openly, that one may see he fears not to be taxed by any law. He invades authors like a monarch; and what would be theft in other poets is only victory in him. With the spoils of these writers he so represents old Rome to us, in its rites, ceremonies, and customs, that if one of their poets had written either of his tragedies, we had seen less of it than in him. If there was any fault in his language, 'twas that he weaved it too closely and laboriously, in his serious plays; perhaps, too, he did a little too much Romanize our tongue, leaving the words which he translated almost as much Latin as he found them, wherein, though he learnedly followed the idiom of their language, he did not enough comply with the idiom of ours. If I would compare him with Shakespeare, I must acknowledge him the more correct poet, but Shakespeare the greater wit. Shakespeare was the Homer, or father of our dramatic poets; Jonson was the Virgil, the pattern of elaborate writing; I admire him, but I love Shakespeare. . . .

---

6. **saturnine:** Heavy.
7. **mechanic people:** Artisans.
8. ***Sejanus*** and ***Catiline*:** Two of Jonson's plays.

---

## THINKING ABOUT THE SELECTION
### Recalling

1. How does Dryden respond to the criticism that Shakespeare lacked learning?
2. What was the opinion of Shakespeare held by Mr. Hales of Eton?
3. According to Dryden, what was missing from English drama before Ben Jonson started writing?
4. Far from accusing Jonson of theft, what does Dryden say about his borrowing from classical writers?

### Interpreting

5. In your own words, what does Dryden mean by saying that Shakespeare "had the largest and most comprehensive soul"?

6. Dryden uses a Latin quotation from Virgil to describe Shakespeare's achievement. How does this quotation relate to the comment that immediately precedes it?
7. In what sense does Dryden mean that Shakespeare was not a "correct poet"?

### Applying

8. Assume that the virtues of Shakespeare and Jonson represent the qualities Dryden admired in all writers. (a) What qualities would Dryden's perfect writer have? (b) What writer, in your opinion, comes closest to having those qualities? Explain the reasons for your choice.

## ANALYZING LITERATURE
### Understanding an Essay

An **essay** is a prose composition, usually short, that deals with one topic. Typically, the writer of an essay states his or her personal views on the topic. A formal essay is serious and dignified. An informal essay is lighter and more conversational. Dryden's "Essay of Dramatic Poesy," written more than three hundred years ago, may not seem like an informal essay, but it is. It is written in the form of a conversation among four friends as they are boating on the Thames. One of them, named Neander, represents Dryden. He is the person speaking in the excerpt included in this book.

1. Two signs of informality in writing are (a) the occasional use of sentence fragments and (b) the occasional use of a conjunction to start a sentence. Find an example of each of these in the excerpt from Dryden's essay.
2. Compare Dryden's essay with Bacon's "Idols of the Cave" (pages 357–358). What are three noticeable differences in prose style between the two essays. (In examining prose style, look at sentence structure, sentence length, rhetorical devices, word choice, and so on.)

## CRITICAL THINKING AND READING
### Charting an Analysis

Dryden's "An Essay of Dramatic Poesy" is an analysis of the literary merits of William Shakespeare and Ben Jonson. The essay contains a number of specific statements praising, criticizing, or comparing the two writers. On a sheet of paper, list as many properties of a writer as you can find in Dryden's essay. These properties can be good or bad. Beside each property on your list, state in a phrase or short sentence how Dryden rates each writer in regard to it. For example, you might list "Education" as a property. Your entry for Shakespeare might then read, "Lacked formal education but was thoroughly self-educated."

| Property | Shakespeare | Jonson |
|---|---|---|
| 1. Education | Lacked formal education but was thoroughly self-educated | |

If nothing is said about one of the two writers in regard to a particular property, write, "No comment." Complete your chart with a statement summarizing Dryden's overall opinion of Shakespeare and Jonson as writers.

## THINKING AND WRITING
### Writing an Evaluation of an Analysis

Review the chart you prepared on Shakespeare and Jonson. Also review the lists you made before reading. Use these materials as the basis for an essay in which you evaluate Dryden's analysis of the literary merits of Shakespeare and Jonson. Take into account your own opinion of Shakespeare and Jonson as well. Is Dryden fair to Shakespeare? Does Dryden overrate Jonson? These and other questions should occur to you as you write the first draft. When you are ready to revise, reread the Dryden excerpt to be sure you are interpreting his opinions accurately. Be sure you have supported your own opinions well. Make any needed changes. Then write your final draft.

# GUIDE FOR INTERPRETING

## Literary Forms

## A Song for St. Cecilia's Day

**Ode.** An ode is a lyric poem, usually rhymed, that addresses and praises a person, an object, or a quality. Most odes are dignified or exalted in subject matter and style. The word *ode* comes from a Greek word meaning "song." The earliest odes, dating back to ancient Greece, were elaborate chants with themes and responses sung by a divided choir. Pindar, a Greek poet of the fifth century B.C., refined the form, becoming one of its great masters. The form he devised has been considerably changed over the centuries. Although Dryden patterned his odes loosely on classical models, later writers varied the form in many ways. Once recognizable by its shape, the ode today is more a matter of tone and intention than of structure.

## Commentary

In his day it was common knowledge among literary circles that Dryden was a solemn, dignified person who was not much given to making amusing remarks. He admitted this himself on numerous occasions. One of his witty rejoinders, however, has been passed down.

According to many reports, he and his wife, Lady Elizabeth, do not seem to have been on very friendly terms with each other. If we trust the gossip of his day, the relationship got off to a rocky start when Dryden had been forced into marriage with the woman by one of her brothers. Regardless of the reason, the union was less than cordial.

One day, so the story goes, Lady Elizabeth began to feel more than usually neglected by her husband, who spent a great deal of time alone with his books and papers. Marching into the study, she burst out, "Lord, Mr. Dryden, how can you always be pouring over those musty books? I wish I were a book, and then I should have more of your company." Dryden was ready with a quick answer. "Pray, my dear," he replied, "if you do become a book let it be an almanack, for then I shall change you every year."

What contrast do you see between "A Song for St. Cecilia's Day" and Dryden's domestic situation?

## Writing

Jot down some thoughts on a person, thing, or event you think deserves to be honored. Then freewrite a short tribute, either in a paragraph or in a few lines of poetry, in which you make clear the qualities of the person, thing, or event that you believe justify the tribute.

# A Song for St. Cecilia's Day[1]

## John Dryden

### 1

From harmony, from heavenly harmony
    This universal frame[2] began;
    When Nature underneath a heap
    Of jarring atoms[3] lay,
5     And could not heave her head,
The tuneful voice was heard from high,
    "Arise, ye more than dead."

Then cold and hot and moist and dry[4]
    In order to their stations leap,
10     And Music's power obey.
From harmony, from heavenly harmony
    This universal frame began:
    From harmony to harmony
Through all the compass of the notes it ran,
15 The diapason[5] closing full in Man.

### 2

What passion cannot Music raise and quell?
    When Jubal[6] struck the chorded shell,
    His listening brethren stood around,
    And, wondering, on their faces fell
20     To worship that celestial sound.

---

**1.** "A Song for St. Cecilia's Day" was composed for the Festival of St. Cecilia on November 22, 1687. According to legend, St. Cecilia was an early Christian martyr, who became the patron saint of music.
**2. universal frame:** The structure of the universe.
**3. jarring atoms:** The chaos that preceded the creation of the universe.
**4. cold . . . dry:** Earth, fire, water, and air, the four elements out of which everything was composed, according to the ancient Greeks.
**5. diapason** (dī′ ə pā′ zən): The entire range of tones on a musical scale. Dryden is also making reference to the Chain of Being, the ordered creation from inanimate nature up to man.
**6. Jubal:** In Genesis 4:21, Jubal is said to be the inventor of the lyre and the pipe.

**THE MUSIC OF A BYGONE AGE**
*John Melhuish Strudwick*
Art Resource

Less than a god they thought there could not dwell
      Within the hollow of that shell
      That spoke so sweetly, and so well.
What passion cannot Music raise and quell?

### 3

25       The trumpet's loud clangor
        Excites us to arms
      With shrill notes of anger
        And mortal alarms.
      The double double double beat
30         Of the thundering drum
        Cries, "Hark! the foes come:
Charge, charge, 'tis too late to retreat."

### 4

      The soft complaining flute
      In dying notes discovers[7]
35       The woes of hopeless lovers,
Whose dirge is whispered by the warbling lute.

### 5

      Sharp violins proclaim
Their jealous pangs and desperation.
Fury, frantic indignation,
40       Depth of pains and height of passion,
      For the fair, disdainful dame.

### 6

      But Oh! What art can teach,
      What human voice can reach
        The sacred organ's praise?
45         Notes inspiring holy love,
Notes that wing their heavenly ways
      To mend the choirs above.

### 7

Orpheus[8] could lead the savage race,
And trees unrooted left their place,
50       Sequacious of the lyre:
      But bright Cecilia raised the wonder higher:

---

**7. discovers:** Reveals.
**8. Orpheus** (ôr′ fē əs): In Greek mythology, a poet and musician
whose magic musical powers enabled him to charm rocks, trees, and
wild beasts by playing his lyre.

When to her organ vocal breath was given,
An angel heard, and straight appeared
   Mistaking earth for heaven.

GRAND CHORUS

55   *As from the power of sacred lays*[9]
    *The spheres began to move.*[10]
*And sung the great Creator's praise*
    *To all the blessed above;*
    *So when the last and dreadful hour*
60   *This crumbling pageant*[11] *shall devour,*
*The trumpet shall be heard on high,*[12]
*The dead shall live, the living die,*
*And Music shall untune the sky.*

---

**9. lays:** Songs.
**10. spheres . . . move:** According to legend, the celestial bodies
(spheres) were put into motion by angelic song. The motion of the
spheres was believed to produce harmonious music, a hymn of
"praise" for the "Creator," sung by the created.
**11. pageant:** The universe.
**12. trumpet . . . high:** From I Corinthians 15:52, the last trumpet
that will announce the Last Judgment, or the end of the universe.

---

**Primary Source**

    For people in the eighteenth century, music was a social as well as an intellectual pastime. In the summer concerts were offered in public gardens, where people strolling among the "regular rows of young trees" feasted on fruit tarts, almond cheesecakes, and fine Epping butter. Sometimes there were fireworks as well, brilliant displays "splendid beyond conception." The following contemporary advertisement promised exotically named fireworks as well as music:

    "Marybone Gardens.—This day, June 2, will be performed a Concert of Vocal and Instrumental Music. In the course of which will be sung for the first time this season an Entertainment of Music called 'The MAGNET.' The Vocal Parts by Mr. Reinhold, Miss Wilde, and Miss Wewitzer. The celebrated Mons. Ladell, Musician to the King of Portugal, will perform a Concert on the German Flute. Admittance Two Shillings and Sixpence. The Doors will be opened at Five o'clock. The Concert will begin at Half Past Six o'clock . . . To-morrow Sig. Torre's Second Exhibition; when he will repeat the Forge of Vulcan, as it was performed at the Marriage of his Royal Highness the Count d'Artois.

    "Marybone Gardens will open To-morrow Evening immediately after Five o'clock for Company to walk in. Tea, Coffee, and other Refreshments may be had at the Bar. To prevent Improper company each Person to pay sixpence at the Door."

## THINKING ABOUT THE SELECTION

### Recalling

1. According to the first stanza, what was the condition of Nature when the universe took shape?
2. In addition to the corded shell, what musical instruments are mentioned in the poem?
3. What does Dryden claim an angel did upon hearing Cecilia play the organ?
4. What instrument will announce Judgment Day?

### Interpreting

5. The word *harmony* dominates the first stanza. What meaning, or meanings, does it have as Dryden uses it?
6. (a) What musical instrument does Dryden suggest is the most heavenly? (b) In view of the day the poem celebrates, why is this praise especially appropriate?
7. Why will music "untune the sky" in "the last and dreadful hour"?

### Applying

8. Dryden is often called an "occasional" poet, because he wrote in response to major news events, literary developments, and, as in this poem, to celebrate special days. Occasional poetry is no longer popular. What do people do today to commemorate special events and heroes?

## ANALYZING LITERATURE

### Recognizing an Ode

An **ode** is a lyrical poem that pays homage to a person, thing, or quality. The earliest odes are from classical times, such as those of the Greek poet Pindar (522?–443 B.C.) and the Latin poet Horace (65–8 B.C.). The Greek ode, which is the ancestor of the odes written by Dryden, is composed of three-part stanzas called *triads*. Each triad is made up of a *strophe* (sung by one half the singers in a choir), an *antistrophe* (sung by the other half), and an *epode* (sung by the entire choir). Dryden and other poets of the seventeenth century use a much looser prosodic system than Pindar's, as do later writers.

1. In "A Song for St. Cecilia's Day," how many lines are (a) in each numbered stanza? (b) in the Grand Chorus?
2. (a) Which stanzas have regular patterns of rhyme? (b) What are these patterns? (Use *a, b, c,* and so on, to show patterns.)
3. Why do you think Dryden uses such an irregular stanza and rhyme scheme for his poem?

## CRITICAL THINKING AND READING

### Understanding the Effect of Sound

Dryden's words carry meaning not only in a lexical, or dictionary, sense but also through their sound. For example, in the third stanza, the word *shrill* echoes—that is, imitates the sound of—the insistent cry of the trumpet. The word *double,* while not in itself echoic of a drum, becomes so when repeated like a drumbeat—"double, double, double."

1. What word in the third stanza besides *double* has a sound that echoes the pounding of the drum?
2. What words in the fourth stanza have sounds that echo the melodic flute and lute?
3. What sounds in the fifth stanza echo the piercing tone of the violin?

## THINKING AND WRITING

### Writing an Ode

Choose one of the following topics and write an ode concerning it. You may decide on the number of stanzas and the length of lines, but try to follow at least two of the rhyme patterns used by Dryden in "A Song for St. Cecilia's Day." Also, use as many echoic, or sound-imitative, devices as you can. Read your ode aloud to judge its effect. After revising, proofread it and prepare a final draft.

1. The United States
2. A season of the year
3. A brother or sister
4. Honesty

# SAMUEL PEPYS

## 1633–1703

Samuel Pepys (pēps) is an unusual figure in English literature, not so much because his fame rests on a single work but rather the one work, his *Diary,* was never intended for publication. This *Diary,* which Pepys kept in shorthand and in his own private code, was not deciphered until the nineteenth century.

The man who painted this vivid portrait of his times was a "very worthy, industrious, and curious person," according to his friend John Evelyn. Born in London, the son of a tailor, Pepys studied at St. Paul's School and Magdalene (mag′ də lēn) College, Cambridge. Upon graduation in 1653, he became secretary to his influential cousin, Edward Montagu, later the Earl of Sandwich. Two years later he married Elizabeth St. Michel, a girl of fifteen. The *Diary* contains many details of their strife-ridden union, which survived Pepys countless infidelities and lasted until her early death in 1669.

Pepys began his career as a naval man—as well as his famous *Diary*—in 1660, when he was appointed clerk of the King's ships and clerk of the privy seal. His advancement, as the *Diary* notes, was rapid, and with each new position, Pepys grew richer. Yet his life was not without its tragedies. In the same year his wife died, Pepys's failing eyesight caused him to stop keeping the *Diary.* In 1679 he was imprisoned briefly in the Tower of London, accused of popery and treason, and in 1690 he once again spent some time in prison on charges of intrigue.

The *Diary,* originally in six manuscript volumes, remained in cipher until 1819 when a student at Magdalene College, Cambridge, began transcribing it. Published in 1825, the *Diary* proved a fascinating mix of candid private revelations and keenly observed public scenes. The 1660's, during which the diary was kept, saw Pepys' personal rise in the world from obscure clerk to highly regarded public servant. It also saw—and through Pepys's eyes modern readers can see—the coronation of King Charles II, the devastating London plague of 1665, and the Great Fire of 1666.

In the centuries since his death, some readers have dismissed Pepys as a shallow figure and his observations as mere gossip. But the Samuel Pepys who emerges from between the lines of the *Diary* is more than just a government careerist with a roving eye. He is a man of intelligence and great diplomacy, much admired by the people of his time, and evidently deserving of that admiration. He is also a diarist of exceptional honesty and perception. Readers of today who wish to know about life in seventeenth-century London are greatly in his debt.

# GUIDE FOR INTERPRETING

## Literary Forms

### *from* The Diary

**Diary.** A diary is a personal day-by-day record of events, experiences, and observations. Perhaps you think of a diary as simply a collection of notes about the small details in one's life, such as what the diarist had for breakfast. Many diaries fit that definition but not all. The diaries that become literature are usually those that provide insights into important historical events or periods. *The Diary of Anne Frank,* for instance, gives readers a poignant glimpse of a young Jewish girl's ultimately futile attempt to escape Nazi persecution by hiding with her family in Nazi-occupied Netherlands in World War II. The events have an importance beyond Anne Frank's individual fate. Moreover, as with most diaries that are regarded as literature, it is exceptionally well written.

## Commentary

Pepys's diary gives us first-hand information about life in London. As we know from Pepys's account, there was considerable danger from fire in the town and countryside. Once started, fires spread with terrible speed. Water could be obtained only by great difficulty through pumps and conduits. Homes in town were supplied through a huge water wheel at London Bridge, but people in the country had to rely on well water or store rainwater in huge lead casks. By the beginning of the eighteenth century, with memories of the Great Fire still fresh, stronger measures were being taken against the threat of fire.

In 1708, for example, an Act was passed "for the better preventing of mischiefs that may happen by fire." Some shops carried rope ladders and other devices to help people escape from burning buildings. Most noteworthy, perhaps, was the establishment of the first insurance companies. These included the symbolically named "Phoenix," "The Friendly Society," and "The Amicable Contributors." The firms all had offices in London coffeehouses, centers for the exchange of news and views, and meeting places for businessmen, wits, and idlers. The fire insurance companies could be easily identified by their own specially uniformed firemen.

What evidence do you have from Pepys's account that adequate measures were not yet in place to combat the fires?

## Writing

Make some notes about an especially memorable event you have experienced. These notes can be in the form of a diary entry; that is, they do not have to be written in grammatically complete sentences or arranged in an orderly sequence.

# from The Diary

## Samuel Pepys

### The Plague

*Sept. 3, 1665.* (Lord's Day.) Church being done, my Lord Bruncker, Sir J. Minnes, and I up to the vestry[1] at the desire of the Justices of the Peace, Sir Theo. Biddulph and Sir W. Boreman and Alderman Hooker, in order to the doing something for the keeping of the plague from growing; but Lord! to consider the madness of the people of the town, who will (because they are forbid) come in crowds along with the dead corps[2] to see them buried; but we agreed on some orders for the prevention thereof.[3] Among other stories, one was very passionate, methought, of a complaint brought against a man in the town for taking a child from London from an infected house. Alderman Hooker told us it was the child of a very able citizen in Gracious Street, a saddler,[4] who had buried all the rest of his children of the plague, and himself and wife now being shut up and in despair of escaping, did desire only to save the life of this little child; and so prevailed to have it received stark-naked into the arms of a friend, who brought it (having put it into new fresh clothes) to Greenwich; where upon hearing the story,

we did agree it should be permitted to be received and kept in the town. Thence with my Lord Bruncker to Captain Cocke's, where we mighty merry and supped, and very late I by water to Woolwich, in great apprehensions of an ague. . . .

*Sept. 14, 1665.* When I come home I spent some thoughts upon the occurrences of this day, giving matter for as much content on one hand and melancholy on another, as any day in all my life. For the first; the finding of my money and plate,[5] and all safe at London, and speeding in my business of money this day. The hearing of this good news to such excess, after so great a despair of my Lord's doing anything this year; adding to that, the decrease of 500 and more, which is the first decrease we have yet had in the sickness since it begun: and great hopes that the next week it will be greater. Then, on the other side, my finding that though the bill[6] in general is abated, yet the city within the walls is increased, and likely to continue so, and is close to our house there. My meeting dead corpses of the plague, carried to be buried close to me at noonday through the city in Fanchurch Street. To see a person sick of the sores, carried close by me by Grace church in a

---

**1. vestry** (ves′ trē) *n.*: A church meeting room.
**2. corps:** corpses.
**3. but we . . . thereof:** Funeral processions were forbidden in London during the plague. However, the law was often ignored.
**4. saddler** *n.*: A person who makes, sells, and repairs saddles.

---

**5. plate:** Valuable serving dishes and flatware.
**6. bill:** Weekly list of burials.

hackney coach.[7] My finding the Angell Tavern at the lower end of Tower Hill, shut up, and more than that, the alehouse at the Tower Stairs, and more than that, the person was then dying of the plague when I was last there, a little while ago, at night, to write a short letter there, and I overheard the mistress of the house sadly saying to her husband somebody was very ill, but did not think it was of the plague. To hear that poor Payne, my waiter, hath buried a child, and is dying himself. To hear that a laborer I sent but the other day to Dagenhams, to know how they did there, is dead of the plague; and that one of my own watermen, that carried me daily, fell sick as soon as he had landed me on Friday morning last, when I had been all night upon the water (and I believe he did get his infection that day at Brainford), and is now dead of the plague. To hear that Captain Lambert and Cuttle are killed in the taking these ships; and that Mr. Sidney Montague is sick of a desperate fever at my Lady Carteret's, at Scott's Hall. To hear that Mr. Lewes hath another daughter sick. And, lastly, that both my servants, W. Hewer and Tom Edwards, have lost their fathers, both in St. Sepulcher's parish, of the plague this week, do put me into great apprehensions of melancholy, and with good reason. But I put off the thoughts of sadness as much as I can, and the rather to keep my wife in good heart and family also. After supper (having eat nothing all this day) upon a fine tench[8] of Mr. Shelden's taking, we to bed.

## The Fire of London

*Sept. 2, 1666.* (Lord's day.) Some of our maids sitting up late last night to get things ready against our feast today, Jane called us up about three in the morning, to tell us of a great fire they saw in the city. So I rose and slipped on my night-gown, and went to her window, and thought it to be on the back side of Mark Lane at the farthest; but, being unused to such fires as followed, I thought it far enough off; and so went to bed again and to sleep. About seven rose again to dress myself, and there looked out at the window, and saw the fire not so much as it was and farther off. So to my closet to set things to rights after yesterday's cleaning. By and by Jane comes and tells me that she hears that above 300 houses have been burned down tonight by the fire we saw, and that it is now burning down all Fish Street, by London Bridge. So I made myself ready presently, and walked to the Tower,[9] and there got up upon one of the high places, Sir J. Robinson's little son going up with me; and there I did see the houses at that end of the bridge all on fire, and an infinite great fire on this and the other side the end of the bridge; which, among other people, did trouble me for poor little Michell and our Sarah on the bridge. So down, with my heart full of trouble, to the Lieutenant of the Tower, who tells me that it begun this morning in the King's baker's house in Pudding Lane, and that it hath burned St. Magnus's Church and most part of Fish Street already. So I down to the waterside, and there got a boat and through bridge, and there saw a lamentable fire. Poor Michell's house, as far as the Old Swan, already burned that way, and the fire running farther, that in a very little time it got as far as the steel yard, while I was there. Everybody endeavoring to remove their goods, and flinging into the river or bringing them into lighters that lay off; poor people staying in their houses as long as till the very fire touched them, and then running into boats, or clambering from one pair of stairs by the waterside to another. And among other things, the poor pigeons, I perceive, were loth to leave their houses, but hovered about the windows and balconies

---

**7. hackney coach:** A carriage for hire.
**8. tench** *n.*: A type of fish.

**9. Tower:** The Tower of London.

**THE GREAT FIRE OF LONDON, 1666**
*The Museum of London*

till they were, some of them burned, their wings, and fell down. Having stayed, and in an hour's time seen the fire rage every way, and nobody, to my sight, endeavoring to quench it, but to remove their goods, and leave all to the fire, and having seen it get as far as the steel yard, and the wind mighty high and driving it into the city; and everything, after so long a drought, proving combustible, even the very stones of churches, and among other things the poor steeple by which pretty Mrs.— lives, and whereof my old schoolfellow Elborough is parson, taken fire in the very top, and there burned till it fell down. I to Whitehall (with a gentleman with me who desired to go off from the Tower, to see the fire, in my boat), and there up to the King's closet in the chapel, where people come about me, and I did give them an account dismayed them all, and word was carried in to the King. So I was called for, and did tell the King and Duke of York what I saw, and that unless his Majesty did command houses to be pulled down nothing could stop the fire. They seemed much troubled, and the King commanded me to go to my Lord Mayor from him, and command him to spare no houses, but to pull down before the fire every way. The Duke of York bid me tell him that if he would have any more soldiers he shall; and so did my Lord Arlington afterwards, as a great secret. Here meeting with Captain Cocke, I in his coach, which he lent me, and Creed with me to Paul's,[10] and there walked along Watling Street, as well as I could, every creature coming away loaden with goods to save, and here and there sick people carried away in beds. Extraordinary good goods carried in carts and on backs. At last met my Lord Mayor in Canning Street, like a man spent,

---

**10. Paul's:** St. Paul's Cathedral.

with a handkerchief about his neck. To the King's message he cried, like a fainting woman, "Lord! what can I do? I am spent: people will not obey me. I have been pulling down houses; but the fire overtakes us faster than we can do it." That he needed no more soldiers; and that, for himself, he must go and refresh himself, having been up all night. So he left me, and I him, and walked home, seeing people all almost distracted, and no manner of means used to quench the fire. The houses, too, so very thick thereabouts, and full of matter for burning, as pitch and tar, in Thames Street; and warehouses of oil, and wines, and brandy, and other things. Here I saw Mr. Isaake Houblon, the handsome man, prettily dressed and dirty, at his door at Dowgate, receiving some of his brothers' things, whose houses were on fire; and, as he says, have been removed twice already; and he doubts (as it soon proved) that they must be in a little time removed from his house also, which was a sad consideration. And to see the churches all filling with goods by people who themselves should have been quietly there at this time. By this time it was about twelve o'clock; and so home. Soon as dined, and walked through the city, the streets full of nothing but people and horses and carts loaden with goods, ready to run over one another, and removing goods from one burned house to another. They now removing out of Canning Street (which received goods in the morning) into Lumbard Street, and farther; and among others I now saw my little goldsmith, Stokes, receiving some friend's goods, whose house itself was burned the day after. I to Paul's Wharf, where I had appointed a boat to attend me, and took in Mr. Carcasse and his brother, whom I met in the street, and carried them below and above bridge to and again to see the fire, which was now got farther, both below and above, and no likelihood of stopping it. Met with the King and Duke of York in their barge, and with them to Queenhithe, and there called Sir Richard Browne

to them. Their order was only to pull down houses apace, and so below bridge at the waterside; but little was or could be done, the fire coming upon them so fast. Good hopes there was of stopping it at the Three Cranes above, and at Buttolph's Wharf below bridge, if care be used; but the wind carries it into the city, so as we know not by the waterside what it do there. River full of lighters and boats taking in goods, and good goods swimming in the water, and only I observed that hardly one lighter or boat in three that had the goods of a house in, but there was a pair of virginals[11] in it. Having seen as much as I could now, I away to Whitehall by appointment, and there walked to St. James's Park, and there met my wife and Creed and Wood and his wife, and walked to my boat; and there upon the water again, and to the fire up and down, it still increasing, and the wind great. So near the fire as we could for smoke; and all over the Thames, with one's face in the wind, you were almost burned with a shower of firedrops. This is very true; so as houses were burned by these drops and flakes of fire, three or four, nay, five or six houses, one from another. When we could endure no more upon the water, we to a little alehouse on the Bankside, over against the Three Cranes, and there stayed till it was dark almost, and saw the fire grow; and, as it grew darker, appeared more and more, and in corners and upon steeples, and between churches and houses, as far as we could see up the hill of the city, in a most horrid malicious bloody flame, not like the fine flame of an ordinary fire. Barbary and her husband away before us. We stayed till, it being darkish, we saw the fire as only one entire arch of fire from this to the other side the bridge, and in a bow up the hill for an arch of above a mile long: it made me weep to see it. The churches, houses, and all on fire and flaming at once; and a horrid noise the flames made, and the cracking of houses

---

**11. virginals** *n.*: Small, legless harpsichords.

at their ruin. So home with a sad heart, and there find everybody discoursing and lamenting the fire; and poor Tom Hater come with some of his few goods saved out of his house, which is burned upon Fish Street Hill. I invited him to lie at my house, and did receive his goods, but was deceived in his lying there, the news coming every moment of the growth of the fire; so as we were forced to begin to pack up our own goods, and prepare for their removal; and did by moonshine (it being brave dry, and moonshine, and warm weather) carry much of my goods into the garden, and Mr. Hater and I did remove my money and iron chests into my cellar, as thinking that the safest place. And got my bags of gold into my office, ready to carry away, and my chief papers of accounts also there, and my tallies into a box by themselves. So great was our fear, as Sir W. Batten hath carts come out of the country to fetch away his goods this night. We did put Mr. Hater, poor man, to bed a little; but he got but very little rest, so much noise being in my house, taking down of goods.

3rd. About four o'clock in the morning, my Lady Batten sent me a cart to carry away all my money, and plate, and best things, to Sir W. Rider's at Bednall Green. Which I did, riding myself in my nightgown in the cart; and, Lord! to see how the streets and the highways are crowded with people running and riding, and getting of carts at any rate to fetch away things. I find Sir W. Rider tired with being called up all night, and receiving things from several friends. His house full of goods, and much of Sir W. Batten's and Sir W. Pen's. I am eased at my heart to have my treasure so well secured. Then home, with much ado to find a way, nor any sleep all this night to me nor my poor wife.

---

## THINKING ABOUT THE SELECTION

### Recalling

1. In his entry for September 3, 1665, Pepys tells a story of a saddler's family. What is the story of the last living child?
2. In his entry for September 14, 1665, Pepys gives two reasons for feeling content. One is that his valuables are safe. What is the other?
3. (a) When does Pepys first learn of the great fire? (b) When Pepys looks out his window at seven in the morning on September 2, 1666, what does he observe about the fire?
4. (a) What does Pepys recommend to the King and the Duke of York? (b) What is the reply?
5. Summarize Pepys's actions on September 3, 1666.

### Interpreting

6. In the entry for September 14, 1665, Pepys states that he has despaired "of my Lord's doing anything this year." (a) What does he mean by the statement? (b) What does it show about Pepys's beliefs?
7. On September 2, 1666, Pepys sees "the churches all filling with goods by people who themselves should have been quietly there at this time." (a) Why do you think people are storing goods in churches? (b) Why do you think they themselves should have been there at the time?
8. From the evidence of these diary entries, how would you describe Pepys's character and personality?

### Applying

9. (a) In Pepys's London, which do you think was the greater disaster—the plague or the great fire? Explain. (b) What disasters in modern times, if any, compare with the London plague of 1665 and the great fire of 1666?

# The Age of Pope and Swift

**CONVERSATION IN A PARK**
*Thomas Gainsborough*
The Louvre, Paris

# DANIEL DEFOE

## 1660–1731

Although Daniel Defoe produced an impressive number of pamphlets, essays, and poems throughout his life, he was nearly sixty years old before he began writing the novels that established him as a writer of genius. Defoe's *Robinson Crusoe,* a book that recounts the mostly imaginary adventures of a real person, marked the beginning of the modern English novel. Defoe's realistic, almost documentary narrative of a man marooned on a desert island was something new in English literature. It established a genre.

Defoe's life was an odd mixture of business, politics, religion, and journalism. Born to a middle-class family named Foe (he added the "De" later), Defoe attended a school run by the Dissenters, a loosely knit group that refused to accept the principles set down by the Church of England. He considered entering the Presbyterian ministry but instead turned his attention to commerce. He invested heavily and not always well in a variety of ventures—a ship, diving bells, wines, civet cats. The scope of his activities is shown by the size of his debt. When he declared bankruptcy in 1692, he owed his creditors 17,000 pounds.

At that point, he turned to writing (and to patrons for his writing) to try to improve his fortunes. His pen, however, also got him into trouble. After enjoying brief success with *The True-Born Englishman* (1701), a defense of King William III against his detractors, he wrote an ill-advised satire, *The Shortest Way with the Dissenters* (1702), that landed him in jail and in the pillory. Published anonymously, this pamphlet condemned the very religious group Defoe favored. Its irony amused neither the Dissenters nor members of the Church of England, but Defoe had enough popularity to attract cheering supporters rather than rock throwers at his pillory appearance.

Late in life Defoe turned to writing books that purported to be memoirs, among them *Robinson Crusoe* (1719) and *Moll Flanders* (1722). As published, these books were not novels in the strict sense, since they were sold as nonfiction. Although Defoe has been accused "of forging a story, and imposing it on the world for truth," these books are generally regarded as novels today—and as outstanding novels at that.

Defoe's journalistic talents served him well in writing *A Journal of the Plague Year* (1722). He studied official documents, interviewed survivors of the plague, and may have drawn upon his own memories as a young child. The vivid historical re-creation of the plague is a triumph of Defoe's energetic, detailed style in a genre that set English fiction upon a new path.

# GUIDE FOR INTERPRETING

**Writer's Techniques**

**First-person Narrative.** Fiction is written from one of two main points of view—first person or third person. The narrator's perspective can vary somewhat in each of them. A third-person narrator, for example, can be *omniscient* (all-knowing) or *limited* (restricted to the mind of one character). A first-person narrator ("I") can be a *participant* (directly involved in the action) or an *observer* (reporting on the actions of another, as Watson reports on Sherlock Holmes). From a writer's standpoint, first-person narration imposes severe limitations. The narrator must be physically present at all times and involved in most of the important action. Everything must be observed through the eyes and mind of that narrator; there can be no omniscience, no multiple viewpoints. If the first-person narrator is a participant, the story will sound very much like a personal memoir or an autobiography. If the writing is highly realistic and plausible, you may think (unless told otherwise) that you are reading nonfiction. In *A Journal of the Plague Year,* that is exactly what Defoe had in mind.

**Writing**

Choose an imaginary setting for a description, such as a new planet inhabited by an unfamiliar species or your own community at a time in the distant past or future. Using that setting, list some of the specific details you would include in a first-person narrative.

**Primary Source**

Plague struck with terrifying frequency, but it was only one of a series of epidemics that ravaged England in the seventeenth century. More frequent were outbreaks of smallpox, dysentery, and measles. Herbal and folk remedies were passed down through the generations. Every area had its treatments, and both men and women took an active interest in doctoring.

To relieve measles, for example, people advised that a live sheep be laid on the bed of the afflicted one, "because these creatures are easily infected and draw the venom to themselves, by which means some ease may happen to the sick person." To treat plague, you were advised:

> "Take halfe a handfull of Rew, likewise of Mandragories, Featherfew, Sorrell Burnet, and a quantity of the Crops and rootes of Dragons, and wash them clean, and seeth them with a soft fire in running water for a potle to a quart, and then straine them together through a cleane cloth, and if it be bitter, put thereto a quantity of sugar-candy, and if this medicine be used before the Purples do arise, yee shall be whole by God's grace."

# *from* A Journal of the Plague Year

## Daniel Defoe

The face of London was now indeed strangely altered, I mean the whole mass of buildings, city, liberties, suburbs, Westminster, Southwark, and altogether; for as to the particular part called the city, or within the walls, that was not yet much infected.

**THE DEAD CART**
*The British Library*

But in the whole the face of things, I say, was much altered; sorrow and sadness sat upon every face; and though some parts were not yet overwhelmed, yet all looked deeply concerned; and as we saw it apparently coming on, so everyone looked on himself and his family as in the utmost danger. Were it possible to represent those times exactly to those that did not see them, and give the reader due ideas of the horror that everywhere presented itself, it must make just impressions upon their minds and fill them with surprise. London might well be said to be all in tears; the mourners did not go about the streets indeed, for nobody put on black or made a formal dress of mourning for their nearest friends; but the voice of mourning was truly heard in the streets. The shrieks of women and children at the windows and doors of their houses, where their dearest relations were perhaps dying, or just dead, were so frequent to be heard as we passed the streets, that it was enough to pierce the stoutest heart in the world to hear them. Tears and lamentations were seen almost in every house, especially in the first part of the visitation; for toward the latter end men's hearts were hardened, and death was so always before their eyes, that they did not so much concern themselves for the loss of their friends, expecting that themselves should be summoned the next hour. . . .

I went all the first part of the time freely

about the streets, though not so freely as to run myself into apparent danger, except when they dug the great pit in the churchyard of our parish of Aldgate. A terrible pit it was, and I could not resist my curiosity to go and see it. As near as I may judge, it was about forty feet in length, and about fifteen or sixteen feet broad, and, at the time I first looked at it, about nine feet deep; but it was said they dug it near twenty feet deep afterwards in one part of it, till they could go no deeper for the water; for they had, it seems, dug several large pits before this. For though the plague was long a-coming to our parish, yet, when it did come, there was no parish in or about London where it raged with such violence as in the two parishes of Aldgate and Whitechapel.

I say they had dug several pits in another ground, when the distemper began to spread in our parish, and especially when the dead carts began to go about, which was not, in our parish, till the beginning of August. Into these pits they had put perhaps fifty or sixty bodies each; then they made larger holes, wherein they buried all that the cart brought in a week, which, by the middle to the end of August, came to from 200 to 400 a week; and they could not well dig them larger, because of the order of the magistrates confining them to leave no bodies within six feet of the surface; and the water coming on at about seventeen or eighteen feet, they could not well, I say, put more in one pit. But now, at the beginning of September, the plague raging in a dreadful manner, and the number of burials in our parish increasing to more than was ever buried in any parish about London of no larger extent, they ordered this dreadful gulf to be dug, for such it was rather than a pit.

They had supposed this pit would have supplied them for a month or more when they dug it, and some blamed the churchwardens for suffering[1] such a frightful thing,

telling them they were making preparations to bury the whole parish, and the like; but time made it appear the churchwardens knew the condition of the parish better than they did, for the pit being finished the 4th of September, I think, they began to bury in it the 6th, and by the 20th, which was just two weeks, they had thrown into it 1114 bodies, when they were obliged to fill it up, the bodies being then come to lie within six feet of the surface. I doubt not but there may be some ancient persons alive in the parish who can justify the fact of this, and are able to show even in what place of the churchyard the pit lay better than I can. The mark of it also was many years to be seen in the churchyard on the surface, lying in length parallel with the passage which goes by the west wall of the churchyard out of Houndsditch, and turns east again into Whitechapel, coming out near the Three Nuns' Inn.

It was about the 10th of September that my curiosity led, or rather drove, me to go and see this pit again, when there had been near 400 people buried in it; and I was not content to see it in the daytime, as I had done before, for then there would have been nothing to have been seen but the loose earth; for all the bodies that were thrown in were immediately covered with earth by those they called the buriers, which at other times were called bearers; but I resolved to go in the night and see some of them thrown in.

There was a strict order to prevent people coming to those pits, and that was only to prevent infection. But after some time that order was more necessary, for people that were infected and near their end, and delirious also, would run to those pits, wrapped in blankets or rugs, and throw themselves in, and, as they said, bury themselves. I cannot say that the officers suffered any willingly to lie there; but I have heard that in a great pit in Finsbury, in the parish of Cripplegate, it lying open then to the fields, for it was not then walled about,

---

**1. suffering:** Allowing.

[some] came and threw themselves in, and expired there, before they threw any earth upon them; and that when they came to bury others, and found them there, they were quite dead, though not cold.

This may serve a little to describe the dreadful condition of that day, though it is impossible to say anything that is able to give a true idea of it to those who did not see it, other than this, that it was indeed very, very, very dreadful, and such as no tongue can express.

I got admittance into the churchyard by being acquainted with the sexton who attended, who, though he did not refuse me at all, yet earnestly persuaded me not to go, telling me very seriously, for he was a good, religious, and sensible man, that it was indeed their business and duty to venture, and to run all hazards, and that in it they might hope to be preserved; but that I had no apparent call to it but my own curiosity, which, he said, he believed I would not pretend was sufficient to justify my running that hazard. I told him I had been pressed in my mind to go, and that perhaps it might be an instructing sight, that might not be without its uses. "Nay," says the good man, "if you will venture upon that score, name of God go in; for, depend upon it, 't will be a sermon to you, it may be, the best that ever you heard in your life. 'T is a speaking sight," says he, "and has a voice with it, and a loud one, to call us all to repentance"; and with that he opened the door and said, "Go, if you will."

His discourse had shocked my resolution a little, and I stood wavering for a good while, but just at that interval I saw two links[2] come over from the end of the Minories, and heard the bellman, and then appeared a dead cart, as they called it, coming over the streets; so I could no longer resist my desire of seeing it, and went in. There was nobody, as I could perceive at first, in the church-yard, or going into it, but the buriers and the fellow that drove the cart, or rather led the horse and cart; but when they came up to the pit they saw a man go to and again,[3] muffled up in a brown cloak, and making motions with his hands under his cloak, as if he was in a great agony, and the buriers immediately gathered about him, supposing he was one of those poor delirious or desperate creatures that used to pretend, as I have said, to bury themselves. He said nothing as he walked about, but two or three times groaned very deeply and loud, and sighed as he would break his heart.

When the buriers came up to him they soon found he was neither a person infected and desperate, as I have observed above, or a person distempered in mind, but one oppressed with a dreadful weight of grief indeed, having his wife and several of his children all in the cart that was just come in with him, and he followed in an agony and excess of sorrow. He mourned heartily, as it was easy to see, but with a kind of masculine grief that could not give itself vent by tears; and calmly defying the buriers to let him alone, said he would only see the bodies thrown in and go away, so they left importuning him. But no sooner was the cart turned round and the bodies shot into the pit promiscuously, which was a surprise to him, for he at least expected they would have been decently laid in, though indeed he was afterwards convinced that was impracticable; I say, no sooner did he see the sight but he cried out aloud, unable to contain himself. I could not hear what he said, but he went backward two or three steps and fell down in a swoon. The buriers ran to him and took him up, and in a little while he came to himself, and they led him away to the Pie Tavern over against the end of Houndsditch, where, it seems, the man was known, and where they took care of him. He looked into the pit again as he went away,

2. links: Torches.

3. to and again: To and fro.

but the buriers had covered the bodies so immediately with throwing in earth, that though there was light enough, for there were lanterns, and candles in them, placed all night round the sides of the pit, upon heaps of earth, seven or eight, or perhaps more, yet nothing could be seen.

This was a mournful scene indeed, and affected me almost as much as the rest; but the other was awful and full of terror. The cart had in it sixteen or seventeen bodies; some were wrapped up in linen sheets, some in rags, some little other than naked, or so loose that what covering they had fell from them in the shooting out of the cart, and they fell quite naked among the rest; but the matter was not much to them, or the indecency much to anyone else, seeing they were all dead, and were to be huddled together into the common grave of mankind, as we may call it, for here was no difference made, but poor and rich went together; there was no other way of burials, neither was it possible there should, for coffins were not to be had for the prodigious numbers that fell in such a calamity as this.

## THINKING ABOUT THE SELECTION

### Recalling

1. (a) Describe the great pit in the churchyard of Aldgate parish. (b) What was the purpose of the pit?
2. (a) What limited the depth to which the pit could be dug? (b) What restriction did an order of the magistrates put on the use of the pit?
3. How many bodies does the narrator say were buried in the great pit between September 6 and September 20?
4. (a) What prompts the narrator to visit the pit? (b) Why does he go at night?
5. (a) What kind of person did the buriers at first suppose the man in the brown cloak to be? (b) Summarize the incident concerning the man in the brown cloak.

### Interpreting

6. Why do you think the narrator describes the great pit in such a specific and detailed way?
7. Judging by the tone of this excerpt and the narrator's reason for visiting the pit, what kind of person do you think the narrator is?
8. Why does the sexton at the churchyard say that visiting the pit will "be a sermon to you . . . a voice . . . to call us all to repentence"?

9. What causes the "masculine grief" of the man in the brown cloak to turn suddenly to anguish?

### Applying

10. Many writers have written fictional accounts of great disasters or have used disasters as backgrounds for their fiction. Why do you think disasters have this fictional appeal?

## ANALYZING LITERATURE

### Recognizing First-person Narrative

A **first-person narrative** is one told by an "I" narrator—a person present at the events being described. A first-person narrator can be either a participant or an observer in the main action. Defoe's *A Journal of the Plague Year* claims to be a first-person narrative of a London resident, one "H. F.," written during the great plague of 1665. In reality, it is a fictional reconstruction written by Defoe more than fifty years later.

1. Why do you think Defoe chose a first-person narrator, an "eyewitness," to present this account of the plague year?
2. Defoe has been called the father of modern journalism. (a) If "H. F.'s" first-person account of the plague were true, what features would qualify it as good journalism? (b) What features would you not find in the usual modern news story?

# JONATHAN SWIFT

## 1667–1745

The life of Jonathan Swift is a tale of thwarted ambition coupled with brilliant literary achievement. In the Church of England and in British politics, he sometimes seemed on the verge of great success, only to have an unkind fate baffle his expectations. In literature, on the other hand, he achieved an almost unparalleled triumph with *Gulliver's Travels,* a book that can be read—and has been read since its publication—as a children's story, a fantasy, a parody of travel books, and a sophisticated satire on English politics.

Jonathan Swift was born in Dublin, Ireland, to English parents. His father died before he was born, and young Jonathan, through the assistance of relatives, attended Kilkenny Grammar School and Trinity College, Dublin. Later he joined the household of Sir William Temple, a retired diplomat, who lived at Moor Park, Surrey, England. Swift read, studied, and wrote for the next few years. Receiving none of the hoped-for political support from Sir William, he decided on a career in the church.

After Temple's death in 1699, Swift was given a small parish near London. The satirical writing he had done while in the Temple household was somewhat out of character for a clergyman, but its brilliance was widely acknowledged when it appeared as two separate books in 1704. Published anonymously, *A Tale of a Tub* satirizes excesses in religion and learning, while *The Battle of the Books* describes a comic encounter between ancient and modern literature.

Although *A Tale of a Tub* dashed his hopes for advancement to the rank of bishop in the Church of England, Swift remained a defender of the Anglican faith. In 1710, he changed his political allegiance from the conservative Whig party to the Tory party favored by Queen Anne. He benefited immediately from this switch. As the leading party writer for the government, he wrote many pamphlets and wielded considerable political influence. The glory was short-lived, however. Anne died in 1714; the Whigs regained power; and Swift, embittered, returned to Ireland as dean of St. Patrick's Cathedral, a position he held for more than thirty years.

Back in Ireland, he continued to write satires, including *Drapier Letters* (1724) and *A Modest Proposal* (1729), which championed the Irish cause. With the publication of *Gulliver's Travels* (1726), he reached the height of his literary power. In his later years, he suffered what was probably Ménière's disease, marked by a serious loss of memory and balance. His death in 1745 deprived the world of one of its great writers—a generous and learned man who despised the fanaticism, selfishness, and pride of people in general but admired individual human beings.

# GUIDE FOR INTERPRETING

## *from* Gulliver's Travels

**Satire.** Satire is writing that uses wit and humor to ridicule vices, follies, stupidities, and abuses. Irony is often an element in satire, as is sarcasm. Satire can take the form of prose, poetry, or drama. Satirists, by directing their barbs toward those they view as offenders, hope to improve the situation—to reform individuals, groups, or humanity as a whole. Satire may be gentle and amusing, or it may be cruel and even vicious. Whatever its tone, satire is usually subtle enough to require the reader to make at least a small mental leap to connect it with its target.

Think about current social or political problems or situations that might be suitable subjects for satire. Try to suggest at least two. Jot these ideas down. After each subject, give one aspect of it that is particularly open to ridicule.

The allure of distant lands is timeless. In Swift's day, as in our own, writers offered advice to would-be travelers. Perhaps these "Hints for Travellers," from the late seventeenth century, would have helped Gulliver in his voyages!

In such a one going to travel; there is required–
First. A competent age. That he be above eighteen or twenty years old: although the years of fourteen or fifteen are more proper for learning the true accent of any language . . .
Secondly. That he hath the Latin tongue.
Thirdly. That he be skillful in architecture: able so well to limn or paint, as to take in paper the situation of a castle or a city, or a platform [plan] of a fortification.
Fourthly. That he be well grounded in the true religion: lest he be seduced and perverted.
Fifthly. He should be first well acquainted with his own country, before he go abroad; as to the places and government.
Sixthly. It were of use to inform himself, before he undertakes his voyage, by the best . . . map of . . . the country he goes to; both in itself, and relatively to the universe.
Men that travel must be very cautious both of speech and demeanor. The Italian proverb saith, "For a man to travel safely through the world; it behoveth him to have a falcon's eye, an ass's ears, a monkey's face, a merchant's words, a camel's back, a hog's mouth, and a deer's feet."

# from Gulliver's Travels

## Jonathan Swift

*In* Gulliver's Travels, *Swift exposes the corruption and defects in England's political, social, and economic institutions. The work centers on the four imaginary voyages of Lemuel Gulliver, the narrator, a well-educated but unimaginative ship's surgeon. Each of these voyages takes Gulliver to a different remarkable and bizarre world. During his stays in these imaginary lands, Gulliver is led toward realizations about the flawed nature of the society from which he had come, and he returns to England filled with disillusionment.*

## *from* A Voyage to Lilliput

*After being shipwrecked, Gulliver swims to shore and drifts off to sleep. When he awakens, he finds that he has been tied down by the Lilliputians (lil' ə py$\overline{oo}$' shənz), a race of people who are only six inches tall. Though he is held captive and his sword and pistols are taken from him, Gulliver gradually begins to win the Lilliputians' favor because of his mild disposition, and he is eventually granted his freedom. Through Gulliver's exposure to Lilliputian politics and court life, the reader becomes increasingly aware of the remarkable similarities between the English and Lilliputian affairs of state. The following excerpt begins during a discussion between the Lilliputian Principal Secretary of Private Affairs and Gulliver concerning the affairs of the Lilliputian empire.*

We are threatened with an invasion from the island of Blefuscu,[1] which is the other great empire of the universe, almost as large and powerful as this of his Majesty. For as to what we have heard you affirm, that there are other kingdoms and states in the world, inhabited by human creatures as large as yourself, our philosophers are in much doubt, and would rather conjecture that you dropped from the moon, or one of the stars; because it is certain, that an hundred mortals of your bulk would, in a short time, destroy all the fruits and cattle of his Majesty's dominions. Besides, our histories of six thousand moons make no mention of any other regions, than the two great empires of Lilliput and Blefuscu. Which two mighty powers have, as I was going to tell you, been engaged in a most obstinate war for six and thirty moons past. It began upon the following occasion. It is allowed on all hands, that the primitive way of breaking eggs before we eat them, was upon the larger end; but his present Majesty's grandfather, while he was a boy, going to eat an egg, and breaking it according to the ancient practice, happened to cut one of his fingers. Whereupon the Emperor, his father, published an edict,

---

1. **Blefuscu:** Represents France.

commanding all his subjects, upon great penalties, to break the smaller end of their eggs. The people so highly resented this law that our histories tell us there have been six rebellions raised on that account; wherein one emperor lost his life, and another his crown.[2] These civil commotions were constantly fomented by the monarchs of Blefuscu; and when they were quelled, the exiles always fled for refuge to that empire. It is computed that eleven thousand persons have, at several times, suffered death rather than submit to break their eggs at the smaller end. Many hundred large volumes have been published upon this controversy; but the books of the Big-Endians have been long forbidden, and the whole party rendered incapable by law of holding employments.[3] During the course of these troubles, the emperors of Blefuscu did frequently expostulate by their ambassadors, accusing us of making a schism in religion, by offending against a fundamental doctrine of our great prophet Lustrog, in the fifty-fourth chapter of the *Brundecral* (which is their Alcoran[4]). This, however, is thought to be a mere strain upon the text, for the words are these: That all true believers shall break their eggs at the convenient end; and which is the convenient end, seems, in my humble opinion, to be left to every man's conscience, or at least in the power of the chief magistrate[5] to determine. Now the Big-Endian exiles have found so much credit in the Emperor of Blefuscu's court, and so much private assistance and encouragement from their party here at home, that a bloody war hath been carried on between the two empires for six and thirty moons with various success; during which time we have lost forty capital ships, and a much greater number of smaller vessels, together with thirty thousand of our best seamen and soldiers; and the damage received by the enemy is reckoned to be somewhat greater than ours. However, they have now equipped a numerous fleet, and are just preparing to make a descent upon us; and his Imperial Majesty, placing great confidence in your valor and strength, hath commanded me to lay this account of his affairs before you.

I desired the Secretary to present my humble duty to the Emperor, and to let him know, that I thought it would not become me, who was a foreigner, to interfere with parties; but I was ready, with the hazard of my life, to defend his person and state against all invaders.

The empire of Blesfuscu is an island situated to the north-northeast side of Lilliput, from whence it is parted only by a channel of eight hundred yards wide. I had not yet seen it, and upon this notice of an intended invasion, I avoided appearing on that side of the coast, for fear of being discovered by some of the enemy's ships, who had received no intelligence of me, all intercourse between the two empires having been strictly forbidden during the war, upon pain of death, and an embargo laid by our Emperor upon all vessels whatsoever. I communicated to his Majesty a project I had formed of seizing the enemy's whole fleet; which, as our scouts assured us, lay at anchor in the harbor ready to sail with the first fair wind. I consulted the most experienced seamen upon the depth of the channel, which they had often plumbed, who told me, that in the middle at high water it was seventy *glumgluffs* deep (which is about six feet of European measure), and the rest of it fifty *glumgluffs* at most. I walked to the northeast coast over against Blefuscu, where, lying down behind a hillock, I took out my small pocket perspective-glass, and

---

**2. It is allowed . . . crown:** Here, Swift satirizes the dispute in England between the Catholics (Big-Endians) and Protestants (Little-Endians). King Henry VIII who "broke" with the Catholic church, King Charles I who "lost his life," and King James who lost his "crown" are each referred to in the passage.

**3. the whole party . . . employments:** The Test Act (1673) prevented Catholics from holding office.

**4. Alcoran:** Koran, the sacred book of the Moslems.

**5. chief magistrate:** Ruler.

viewed the enemy's fleet at anchor, consisting of about fifty men of war, and a great number of transports. I then came back to my house and gave order (for which I had a warrant) for a great quantity of the strongest cable and bars of iron. The cable was about as thick as packthread, and the bars of the length and size of a knitting-needle. I trebled the cable to make it stronger, and for the same reason I twisted three of the iron bars together, bending the extremities into a hook. Having thus fixed fifty hooks to as many cables, I went back to the northeast coast and, putting off my coat, shoes, and stockings, walked into the sea in my leathern jerkin, about half an hour before high water. I waded with what haste I could, and swam in the middle about thirty yards until I felt ground; I arrived at the fleet in less than half an hour. The enemy was so frightened when they saw me, that they leaped out of their ships, and swam to shore, where there could not be fewer than thirty thousand souls. I then took my tackling, and, fastening a hook to the hole at the prow of each, I tied all the cords together at the end. While I was thus employed, the enemy discharged several thousand arrows, many of which struck in my hands and face and, besides the excessive smart, gave me much disturbance in my work. My greatest apprehension was for my eyes, which I should have infallibly lost, if I had not suddenly thought of an expedient. I kept among other little necessaries a pair of spectacles in a private pocket, which, as I observed before, had escaped the Emperor's searchers. These I took out and fastened as strongly as I could upon my nose and thus armed went on boldly with my work in spite of the enemy's arrows, many of which struck against the glasses of my spectacles, but without any other effect further than a little to discompose them. I had now fastened all the hooks

*Illustration for* Gulliver's Travels, *by Willy Pogany*
The Donnell Library Children's Room, New York Public Library

and, taking the knot in my hand, began to pull; but not a ship would stir, for they were all too fast held by their anchors, so that the boldest part of my enterprise remained. I therefore let go the cord, and, leaving the hooks fixed to the ships, I resolutely cut with my knife the cables that fastened the anchors, receiving above two hundred shots in my face and hands; then I took up the knotted end of the cables to which my hooks were tied and, with great ease, drew fifty of the enemy's largest men-of-war after me.

The Blefuscudians, who had not the least imagination of what I intended, were at first confounded with astonishment. They had seen me cut the cables and thought my design was only to let the ships run adrift or fall foul on each other; but when they perceived the whole fleet, moving in order, and saw me pulling at the end, they set up such a scream of grief and despair that it is almost impossible to describe or conceive. When I had got out of danger, I stopped a while to pick out the arrows that stuck in my hands and face, and rubbed on some of the same ointment that was given me at my first arrival, as I have formerly mentioned. I then took off my spectacles, and, waiting about an hour until the tide was a little fallen, I waded through the middle with my cargo and arrived safe at the royal port of Lilliput.

The Emperor and his whole court stood on the shore expecting the issue of this great adventure. They saw the ships move forward in a large half-moon but could not discern me, who was up to my breast in water. When I advanced to the middle of the channel, they were yet more in pain, because I was under water to my neck. The Emperor concluded me to be drowned, and that the enemy's fleet was approaching in a hostile manner; but he was soon eased of his fears; for, the channel growing shallower every step I made, I came in a short time within hearing, and holding up the end of the cable by which the fleet was fastened, I cried in a loud voice, Long live the most puissant[6] Emperor of Lilliput! This great prince received me at my landing with all possible encomiums and created me a *Nardac* upon the spot, which is the highest title of honor among them.

His Majesty desired I would take some other opportunity of bringing all the rest of his enemy's ships into his ports. And so unmeasurable is the ambition of princes, that he seemed to think of nothing less than reducing the whole empire of Blesfuscu into a province and governing it by a viceroy; of destroying the Big-Endian exiles and compelling that people to break the smaller end of their eggs, by which he would remain sole monarch of the whole world. But I endeavored to divert him from this design by many arguments drawn from the topics of policy as well as justice, and I plainly protested that I would never be an instrument of bringing a free and brave people into slavery. And when the matter was debated in council, the wisest part of the ministry were of my opinion.

This open bold declaration of mine was so opposite to the schemes and politics of his Imperial Majesty that he could never forgive me; he mentioned it in a very artful manner at council, where I was told that some of the wisest appeared, at least, by their silence, to be of my opinion; but others, who were my secret enemies, could not forbear some expressions, which by a sidewind reflected on me. And from this time began an intrigue between his Majesty and a junta of ministers maliciously bent against me, which broke out in less than two months and had like to have ended in my utter destruction. Of so little weight are the greatest services to princes when put into the balance with a refusal to gratify their passions.

### *from* A Voyage to Brobdingnag

*Gulliver's second voyage leads him to*

---

**6. puissant** (pyōō′ i sənt): Powerful.

*Brobdingnag (brob' ding nag'), an island located near Alaska that is inhabited by giants twelve times as tall as Gulliver. After being sold to the Queen of Brobdingnag, Gulliver describes the English social and political institutions to the king, who reacts to his description with contempt and disgust.*

It is the custom that every Wednesday (which, as I have before observed, was their Sabbath), the King and Queen, with the royal issue of both sexes, dine together in the apartment of his Majesty, to whom I was now become a favorite; and at these times my little chair and table were placed at his left hand before one of the saltcellars. This prince took a pleasure in conversing with me, inquiring into the manners, religion, laws, government, and learning of Europe, wherein I gave him the best account I was able. His apprehension was so clear, and his judgment so exact, that he made very wise reflections and observations upon all I said. But I confess, that after I had been a little too copious in talking of my own beloved country, of our trade, and wars by sea and land, of our schisms in religion, and parties in the state, the prejudices of his education prevailed so far, that he could not forbear taking me up in his right hand, and stroking me gently with the other, after an hearty fit of laughing, asked me whether I were a Whig or a Tory.[7] Then turning to his first minister, who waited behind him with a white staff, near as tall as the mainmast of the *Royal Sovereign*,[8] he observed how contemptible a thing was human grandeur, which could be mimicked by such diminutive insects as I. And yet, said he, I dare engage, those creatures have their titles and distinctions of honor, they contrive little nests and burrows, that they call houses and cities; they make a figure in dress and equipage;[9] they

love, they fight, they dispute, they cheat, they betray. And thus he continued on, while my color came and went several times, with indignation to hear our noble country, the mistress of arts and arms, the scourge of France, the arbitress of Europe, the seat of virtue, piety, honor and truth, the pride and envy of the world, so contemptuously treated. . . .

He laughed at my odd kind of arithmetic (as he was pleased to call it) in reckoning the numbers of our people by a computation drawn from the several sects among us in religion and politics. He said he knew no reason why those who entertain opinions prejudicial to the public should be obliged to change or should not be obliged to conceal them. And, as it was tyranny in any government to require the first, so it was weakness not to enforce the second; for, a man may be allowed to keep poisons in his closets, but not to vend them about as cordials.

He observed, that among the diversions of our nobility and gentry[10] I had mentioned gaming.[11] He desired to know at what age this entertainment was usually taken up, and when it was laid down. How much of their time it employed; whether it ever went so high as to affect their fortunes. Whether mean vicious people by their dexterity in that art might not arrive at great riches, and sometimes keep our very nobles in dependence, as well as habituate them to vile companions, wholly take them from the improvment of their minds, and force them, by the losses they received, to learn and practice that infamous dexterity upon others.

He was perfectly astonished with the historical account I gave him of our affairs during the last century, protesting it was only an heap of conspiracies, rebellions, murders, massacres, revolutions, banishments, the very worst effects that avarice,

---

**7. Whig . . . Tory:** British political parties.
**8. *Royal Sovereign*:** One of the largest ships in the British Navy.
**9. equipage** (ek' wə pij): Horses and carriages.

**10. gentry:** The class of landowning people ranking just below the nobility.
**11. gaming:** Gambling.

faction, hypocrisy, perfidiousness, cruelty, rage, madness, hatred, envy, lust, malice, and ambition could produce.

His Majesty in another audience was at the pains to recapitulate the sum of all I had spoken; compared the questions he made with the answers I had given; then taking me into his hands, and stroking me gently, delivered himself in these words, which I shall never forget, nor the manner he spoke them in. "My little friend Grildrig, you have made a most admirable panegyric upon your country. You have clearly proved that ignorance, idleness, and vice are the proper ingredients for qualifying a legislator. That laws are best explained, interpreted, and applied by those whose interest and abilities lie in perverting, confounding, and eluding them. I observe among you some lines of an institution, which in its original might have been tolerable, but these half erased, and the rest wholly blurred and blotted by corruptions. It doth not appear from all you have said how any one perfection is required toward the procurement of any one station among you, much less that men are ennobled on account of their virtue, that priests are advanced for their piety or learning, soldiers for their conduct or valor, judges for their integrity, senators for the love of their country, or counselors for their wisdom. As for yourself, continued the King, who have spent the greatest part of your life in traveling, I am well disposed to hope you may hitherto have escaped many vices of your country. But, by what I have gathered from your own relation, and the answers I have with much pains wringed and extorted from you, I cannot but conclude the bulk of your natives to be the most pernicious race of little odious vermin that nature ever suffered to crawl upon the surface of the earth."

Nothing but an extreme love of truth could have hindered me from concealing this part of my story. It was in vain to discover my resentments, which were always turned into ridicule; and I was forced to rest with patience while my noble and most beloved country was so injuriously treated. I am heartily sorry as any of my readers can possibly be that such an occasion was given, but this prince happened to be so curious and inquisitive upon every particular that it could not consist either with gratitude or good manners to refuse giving him what satisfaction I was able. Yet thus much I may be allowed to say in my own vindication that I artfully eluded many of his questions and gave to every point a more favorable turn by many degrees than the strictness of truth would allow. For I have always borne that laudable partiality to my own country, which Dionysius Halicarnassensis[12] with so much justice recommends to an historian. I would hide the frailties and deformities of my political mother and place her virtues and beauties in the most advantageous light. This was my sincere endeavor in those many discourses I had with that mighty monarch, although it unfortunately failed of success.

But great allowances should be given to a king who lives wholly secluded from the rest of the world, and must therefore be altogether unacquainted with the manners and customs that most prevail in other nations: the want of which knowledge will ever produce many prejudices, and a certain narrowness of thinking, from which we and the politer countries of Europe are wholly exempted. And it would be hard indeed, if so remote a prince's notions of virtue and vice were to be offered as a standard for all mankind.

To confirm what I have now said, and further to show the miserable effects of a confined education, I shall here insert a passage which will hardly obtain belief. In hopes to ingratiate myself farther into his Majesty's favor, I told him of an invention discovered between three and four hundred

---

**12. Dionysius** (dī′ ə nish′ əs) **Halicarnassensis** (hal′ ə kär na sen′ sis): A Greek writer who lived in Rome and attempted to persuade the Greeks to submit to their Roman conquerors.

years ago, to make a certain powder, into an heap of which the smallest spark of fire falling, would kindle the whole in a moment, although it were as big as a mountain, and make it all fly up in the air together, with a noise and agitation greater than thunder. That a proper quantity of this powder rammed into an hollow tube of brass or iron, according to its bigness, would drive a ball of iron or lead with such violence and speed as nothing was able to sustain its force. That the largest balls, thus discharged, would not only destroy whole ranks of an army at once, but batter the strongest walls to the ground, sink down ships, with a thousand men in each, to the bottom of the sea; and when linked together by a chain, would cut through masts and rigging, divide hundreds of bodies in the middle, and lay all waste before them. That we often put this powder into large hollow balls of iron, and discharged them by an engine into some city we were besieging, which would rip up the pavement, tear the houses to pieces, burst and throw splinters on every side, dashing out the brains of all who came near. That I knew the ingredients very well, which were cheap, and common; I understood the manner of compounding them, and could direct his workmen how to make those tubes of a size proportionable to all other things in his Majesty's kingdom, and the largest need not be above two hundred foot long; twenty or thirty of which tubes, charged with the proper quantity of powder and balls, would batter down the walls of the strongest town

*Illustration for* Gulliver's Travels, *by Willy Pogany*
*The Donnell Library Children's Room, New York Public Library*

in his dominions in a few hours, or destroy the whole metropolis, if ever it should pretend to dispute his absolute commands. This I humbly offered to his Majesty as a small tribute of acknowledgment in return of so many marks that I had received of his royal favor and protection.

The King was struck with horror at the description I had given of those terrible engines and the proposal I had made. He was amazed how so impotent and groveling an insect as I (these were his expressions) could entertain such inhuman ideas, and in so familiar a manner as to appear wholly unmoved at all the scenes of blood and desolation which I had painted as the common effects of those destructive machines; whereof he said some evil genius, enemy to mankind, must have been the first contriver. As for himself, he protested that although few things delighted him so much as new discoveries in art or in nature, yet he would rather lose half his kingdom than be privy to such a secret, which he commanded me, as I valued my life, never to mention any more.

## THINKING ABOUT THE SELECTION
### Recalling

1. (a) Describe the conflict between Lilliput and Blefuscu over the breaking of eggs. (b) How many people have died as a result?
2. (a) How does Gulliver capture the Blefuscudian fleet? (b) What problem do the enemy arrows cause him? (c) How does he solve the problem?
3. (a) What are some of the words the king of Brobdingnag uses to describe English history over the preceding hundred years? (b) How does he describe the English people?
4. (a) What invention does Gulliver describe to the King of Brobdingnag? (b) What is the King's reaction to the invention?

### Interpreting

5. In the dispute between English Catholics and Protestants, what does Swift's attitude seem to be? Explain.
6. Why does Gulliver lose favor with the Lilliputian King in spite of having captured the Blefuscudian fleet?

7. If the views of the King of Brobdingnag represent Swift's own views, what is Swift's general opinion of recent English history and politics?
8. (a) Why do you think Gulliver supposes that his gunpowder proposal to the King of Brobdingnag will be regarded favorably? (b) How is it regarded? (c) Why?

### Applying

9. Why do you think Swift makes one of the races Gulliver visits tiny in comparison with him and the other race gigantic?

## ANALYZING LITERATURE
### Understanding Satire

**Satire** is writing that uses wit and humor to expose and ridicule human vice and folly. Instead of praising the ideal, the satirist focuses on what is false, despicable, or foolish. Since people perceive things differently, not everyone will agree on what deserves to be satirized. Yet effective satire is so ingenious in its presentation and, at the same time, so clear in its purpose that most readers will appreciate the writing and grasp the point, regardless of their personal views. Satire can be light and good-humored, or it can be bitter and unsparing. An important ingredient of much satire is irony—that is, a contrast between what is said and what is meant. For example, when Gulliver says that his "color came and went several times, with indignation to hear our noble country . . . the seat of virtue, piety, honor . . . the pride and envy of the world, so contemptuously treated," you can be quite sure that Swift is being ironic.

1. What is Swift satirizing in *Gulliver's Travels?*
2. From the excerpts you have read, how would you describe the tone of Swift's prose?
3. Point out at least three examples of irony in the excerpts from *Gulliver's Travels.*

## CRITICAL THINKING AND READING

### Understanding Generalizations

A **generalization** is a conclusion based on the accumulation of evidence. This evidence may come in the form of facts, statistics, incidents, and so on. In the excerpt from "A Voyage to Lilliput," Gulliver uses a single striking example as the basis for this generalization: "Of so little weight are the greatest services to princes when put into the balance with a refusal to gratify their passions." In "A Voyage to Brobdingnag," the King makes a number of generalizations about the English and other Europeans based on what Gulliver tells him.

1. What generalization does the King make to his first minister after Gulliver, sitting at a little table and chair . . . before one of the salt cellars," has told him about European manners, religion, laws, government, and learning? Is the generalization valid, or sound in light of the information the king has? Explain your answer.
2. After listening to Gulliver's historical account of "our affairs during the last century," what generalization does the King make about each of the following groups?
   a. legislators
   b. priests
   c. soldiers
   d. judges
   e. senators
3. What broader generalization does the King make about *all* the groups listed above?

## UNDERSTANDING LANGUAGE

### Using Words from Literature

Sometimes the names invented by writers become so closely associated with certain character traits or behaviors that they enter the language as standard English words. The word *lilliputian,* for example, can be found in most dictionaries. Several other words from *Gulliver's Travels* have joined the mainstream of modern English. Look up each of the following words in a standard dictionary. On a sheet of paper, write (a) each word you find and (b) its definition(s). Indicate capitalization where needed.

1. yahoo     2. lilliputian     3. brobdingnagian

## THINKING AND WRITING

### Writing a New Adventure for Gulliver

In addition to his trips to Lilliput and Brobdingnag, Lemuel Gulliver journeys to a place called Laputa and to the land of the Houyhnhnms. In Laputa, Swift's satire is directed against learned fools, impractical professors who, among other silly enterprises, are trying to extract sunshine from cucumbers. In the land of the Houyhnhnms, he encounters a race of noble, intelligent horses that are served by vile, human-like Yahoos. Create a fifth land for Gulliver to visit. Remember the types of creatures he has already encountered and the things he has learned along the way. In a narrative passage of a page or two, write your version of a new voyage by Gulliver. Give the land a name. Give its inhabitants names and characteristics. Include the truths about humans that Gulliver hears uttered by his hosts in this strange land. When you revise, make sure you have told your tale in chronological order.

# GUIDE FOR INTERPRETING

**Writer's
Techniques**

## *from* Thoughts on Various Subjects

**Epigram.** The word *epigram* has two meanings. An epigram can be a short poem with a witty or satirical point, or it can be a brief, clever statement that often pairs opposite thoughts. This pairing of opposite thoughts is called *antithesis.* In an epigram terseness is vital—the writer must state the point as concisely as possible.

As you read the excerpts from Swift's "Thoughts on Various Subjects," note the humor in the epigrams. Also look for examples of antithesis.

**Commentary**

Swift did not confine his sense of humor only to witty epigrams and satires; it spilled over into his daily life as well. One example of his keen wit concerns a joke he played on Lady Berkeley.

While visiting London, Swift stayed with the Berkeley family, acting as their chaplain. At Lady Berkeley's request Swift read Boyle's *Meditations* to her, which he found unbearably dull. He decided to end the readings. Sneaking into the room, he inserted his own "Meditation on a Broom-stick," and replaced the book.

When Lady Berkeley next asked him to read one of the meditations, he opened to the page he had inserted, and calmly read the title. Astonished, she exclaimed, "A Meditation on a Broom-stick! Bless me, what a strange subject! But there is no knowing what useful lessons of instruction this wonderful man may draw from things apparently the most trivial. Pray let us hear what he says upon it." Swift solemnly read the silly piece. Lady Berkeley was convinced that she was indeed hearing a serious meditation.

As the room filled with others, Swift left. Lady Berkeley praised Boyle, saying, "The Doctor has been just reading one to me which surprised me more than all the rest . . . the excellent 'Meditation on a Broom-stick.' When everyone protested that they had never heard of it, she urged them to look for themselves.

When they found the meditation written in Swift's handwriting, everyone burst out laughing. History has recorded that Lady Berkeley was a good sport. Laughing along with the rest, she said, "What a vile trick has the rogue played on me. But it is his way, he never baulks [restrains] his humor in anything." The affair ended with general good feelings–and Swift never had to read Boyle's *Meditations* again.

**Writing**

Think of a well-known short story or choose one of the stories in this book. Consider the theme of the story. Then write a one-sentence summary of the theme. Make it as concise and epigrammatic as possible.

# *from* Thoughts on Various Subjects

### Jonathan Swift

*Thoughts on Various Subjects developed out of an agreement between Alexander Pope and Swift to record their passing thoughts. The following are some of Swift's ideas and impressions, which were included in his commonplace book, or book of collected passages.*

We have just enough religion to make us hate, but not enough to make us love one another.

When we desire or solicit anything, our minds run wholly on the good side or circumstances of it; when 'tis obtained, our minds run wholly on the bad ones.

When a true genius appears in the world, you may know him by this sign: that the dunces are all in confederacy against him.

It is in disputes as in armies where the weaker side sets up false lights and makes a great noise to make the enemy believe them more numerous and strong than they really are.

I have known some men possessed of good qualities which were very serviceable to others but useless to themselves, like a sundial on the front of a house, to inform the neighbors and passengers but not the owner within.

If a man would register all his opinions upon love, politics, religion, learning, etc. beginning from his youth, and so go on to old age, what a bundle of inconsistencies and contradictions would appear at last.

Ambition often puts men upon doing the meanest offices; so climbing is performed in the same posture with creeping.

Ill company is like a dog who dirts those most whom he loves best.

No wise man ever wished to be younger.

The common fluency of speech in many men and most women is owing to a scarcity of matter and scarcity of words; for whoever is a master of language and hath a mind full of ideas, will be apt, in speaking, to hesitate upon the choice of both; whereas common speakers have only one set of ideas and one set of words to clothe them in, and these are always ready at the mouth: So people come faster out of a church when it is almost empty than when a crowd is at the door.

Dignity, high station, or great riches are in some sort necessary to old men in order to keep the younger at a distance who are otherwise too apt to insult them upon the score of their age.

Every man desires to live long, but no man would be old.

Most sorts of diversion in men, children, and other animals are an imitation of fighting.

Very few men, properly speaking, live at present but are providing to live another time.

## THINKING ABOUT THE SELECTION
### Recalling

1. To what does Swift compare armies that attempt to confuse the enemy by means of false lights and great noise?
2. According to Swift, what does a wise man never wish?
3. What does Swift say that most forms of play resemble?

### Interpreting

4. The American writer Ralph Waldo Emerson observed, "A foolish consistency is the hobgoblin of little minds." Of which Swift epigram does Emerson's thought remind you?
5. In your own words, what is Swift's view of the difference between the speaking habits of a master of language and a common speaker?

### Applying

6. Using a standard book of quotations arranged by subject matter, find other epigrams on three of the subjects dealt with by Swift.

## THINKING AND WRITING
### Writing Epigrams

In an epigram, as in lyric poetry, every word counts. The aim is to express an original thought in a brief, witty, memorable way. Review the epigrams from Swift's *Thoughts on Various Subjects,* paying close attention to how Swift uses wit and antithesis. Then write three epigrams of your own. Take your time in planning and writing the epigrams. Revise carefully. Although a good epigram looks simple, it requires considerable thought and imagination.

## ROBINSON CRUSOE
### by Daniel Defoe

**Illustration from ROBINSON CRUSOE**
*N. C. Wyeth*
*The Granger Collection*

Around 1742, so the story goes, a certain village in England was without a place of worship—the closest parish church being more than five miles away. Although the village also lacked a Bible, the inhabitants did have a Testament and a Common Prayer-book, bound together, that they shared. This valuable possession belonged to the innkeeper, who kept it safely tucked away on a kitchen shelf with her other prize, a copy of *Robinson Crusoe*.

Surprised by a sudden, fierce thunderstorm one summer's afternoon, a group of villagers made a wild dash for the inn's kitchen, the closest shelter. The terrified people decided prayers were in order and called for Jack, the innkeeper's helper, who had the rare good fortune to know how to read. Dropping to their knees in the large dining room, the villagers sent Jack back into the kitchen to get the one-volume Testament and Prayer-book, which was, you will recall, kept next to *Robinson Crusoe*. What with all the screaming and moaning, Jack took down the wrong book.

Rushing back into the dining room, he fell to his knees and began reading as quickly as he could. In his own fright, he mispronounced many words, and thus continued reading for quite some time until the villagers began to realize that they were not listening to prayers at all. Finally, when he read the name of Robinson Crusoe's servant, Friday, the innkeeper cried out, "Why, Jock! thee hast got the wrong book! sure thee'st reading prayers out of *Robinson Crusoe!*" The lad, taking this comment as an insult, stubbornly continued to read, declaring that *"Robinson Crusoe* would as soon stop the thunder as the prayer-book."

## The Masterpiece of the Age

Whether *Robinson Crusoe* did indeed have the power to stop the thunder has not been recorded, but the astonishing popularity of Defoe's book can easily be verified. Upon its publication in 1719, *Robinson Crusoe* was hailed as the masterpiece of the century. No less a critic than Samuel Johnson asserted that Defoe's fictional story of a sailor shipwrecked on a desert isle was sufficient alone to establish Defoe's reputation. "How few books are there of which one ever can possibly arrive at the last page!" he exclaimed. "Was there ever yet anything written by a mere man that was wished longer by its readers, excepting *Don Quixote, Robinson Crusoe,* and the *Pilgrim's*

## "The Wonders of this Man's Life"

*Robinson Crusoe* claims to be the auto-biography of a young man who throws all warning aside to lead a life of adventure on the high seas. In the short opening, Crusoe tells about his life before he is shipwrecked on a distant island. The rest of the book is his firsthand journal of his experiences on the island.

Eight years after defying his parents by going to sea, Crusoe's ship runs aground during a fierce storm somewhere in the West Indies. His crew lost, only he makes it to shore, barely alive. For the next eleven days he ransacks the ship for supplies, until it is swallowed up by another storm. Practical, independent, and resourceful, he sets about building shelter, finding food, and keeping a record of his new life. Despite serious illness and extreme loneliness, Crusoe's faith and common sense see him through. By his eleventh year on the island, our hero has everything he could need—food, utensils, even pets—except human companionship. This too is solved; his twenty five years of solitude come to a dramatic end with the arrival of a man he calls "Friday" (to commemorate the day they met), a native destined to become his servant and friend. Will Crusoe and Friday survive? Will they be rescued?

**Illustration from ROBINSON CRUSOE**
*N. C. Wyeth*
*The Granger Collection*

*Progress?"* An 1810 critic was equally lavish in his praise, writing: "Perhaps there exists no work, either of instruction or entertainment, in the English language, which has been more generally read, and more universally admired, than the *Life and Adventures of Robinson Crusoe*. . . . Society is forever indebted to the memory of Defoe for his production of a work, in which the ways of Providence are simply and pleasingly vindicated, and a lasting and useful moral is conveyed through the channel of an interesting and delightful story."

### Alexander Selkirk

Eighteenth-century readers relished travel, escape, and adventure books, as we do today. Defoe had copies of all the popular books of the day, including the one on which he based *Robinson Crusoe:* Captain Roger's *Cruising Voyage Around the World.* This is the true story of Alexander Selkirk, the Scottish sailor marooned on a Pacific island for four years. Most of Defoe's readers assumed that *The Life and Strange Surprising Adventures of Robinson Crusoe, of*

*York, Mariner* was also a true account. Defoe kept mum on the issue, for it boosted sales.

## Storytelling at Its Best

But ultimately the appeal of the novel lies with Defoe's skill in making the impossible seem possible. At his hands, wild storms, pirate attacks, shipwrecks, cannibalism, and the attack of five hundred savage wolves all seem realistic. As a storyteller Defoe has few rivals; as an adventure tale *Robinson Crusoe* enthralls us today as it did in 1719.

**Illustration from ROBINSON CRUSOE**
*N. C. Wyeth*
*The Granger Collection*

# BIOGRAPHIES

## Joseph Addison (1672–1719)
## Sir Richard Steele (1672–1729)

Although great writing seldom results from a team effort, the collaboration of Joseph Addison and Richard Steele is an exception to the general rule. Addison and Steele's work on two precedent-setting periodicals, *The Tatler* and *The Spectator,* has earned both authors a permanent place in literary history.

The two men, born a few weeks apart, were opposites in many ways. Joseph Addison, dignified, shy, and rather cold, enjoyed a reputation as a Latin scholar. Richard Steele, energetic, witty, and outgoing, was a man-about-town. Nevertheless, for most of their lives they were close friends, temperamentally different but sharing similar aims and values. Addison, born in a village in Wiltshire, England, and Steele, born in Dublin, Ireland, met as classmates at the Charterhouse School in London. They then went on to Oxford, where Addison graduated but Steele did not.

Instead, Steele took a commission in the army and immersed himself in the London literary scene. Steele had a tendency to live beyond his means, and in 1709, to earn some extra money, he started *The Tatler,* a periodical dealing with "gallantry, pleasure and entertainment." *The Tatler* proved highly popular in London coffee-houses, appearing three times a week from April 1709 to January 1711.

Since his undergraduate days, Addison had pursued a different path from that of Steele. An outstanding student, he became a Fellow of Magdalen College, Oxford, and was invited by John Dryden to do translations of Virgil. After four years of European study and travel, he produced a hugely successful epic poem, "The Campaign," celebrating the Duke of Marlborough's victory at the Battle of Blenheim. In 1706 Addison was named undersecretary of state, and two years later was elected to the House of Commons, where he remained until his death.

In 1709, while serving briefly as secretary to the Lord Lieutenant of Ireland, he began reading the newly published *Tatler.* Despite Steele's pen name, "Isaac Bickerstaff," Addison recognized the writing as that of his old friend, and he began to submit contributions, notes, and suggestions. *The Tatler,* mostly the work of Steele, was succeeded by *The Spectator,* issued daily except Sunday from March 1711 to December 1712, and revived briefly in 1714. *The Spectator* was mostly the work of Addison, although Steele contributed regularly.

# GUIDE FOR INTERPRETING

## Literary Forms

## Country Manners;
## Thoughts in Westminster Abbey

**Informal Essay.** An *informal essay,* like a formal essay, presents the observations and opinions of its author, but it does so in a more relaxed and conversational manner. The informal essay is sometimes called a *familiar essay,* a *personal essay,* or, when printed in a magazine or newspaper, a *periodical essay.* The eighteenth century was a time in which the formal essay flourished. The formal essay was first used in England by Sir Francis Bacon. The informal essay, introduced by the sixteenth-century French writer Michel de Montaigne, had a great influence on English writers through the vigorous translation of John Florio. An informal essay, less structured than a formal essay, is written in a personal, often anecdotal, sometimes humorous way.

The informal essays of Addison and Steele were published regularly in *The Tatler* and *The Spectator.* These two publications are notable for their wide-ranging, nonpolitical content and their graceful tone and style. Steele was the more imaginative writer, Addison the better craftsman. Both set a high standard for later periodical essayists and journalists.

## Commentary

How were the periodicals of Addison and Steele different from the newspapers of the day? The newspapers recorded events; *The Spectator* and *The Tatler* transformed journalism into literature.

Influential men employed writers to provide them with news of the Court in their absence. By the beginning of the seventeenth century, this expanded into the news-book, sixteen pages of foreign news, much of it scurrilous, including torrents of abuse and outright lies. This led to years of suppression, but the pamphlets flourished, and by the middle of the century the newspaper was firmly entrenched. Advertisements appeared in 1655. These ads seem meek by today's standards; coffee, for instance, was promoted as "a simple Innocent thing incomparable good for those that are troubled with melancholy." By 1715 the newspaper was established, and the press was a power recognized by every political party.

## Writing

Think of a topic on which opinion varies. It should be a topic about which you have strong opinions of your own. Jot down notes about this topic. These notes should include not only support for your own viewpoint but also evidence that helps to refute the opposing viewpoint. Save these notes for later use.

# Country Manners

## Joseph Addison

### The Spectator, July 17, 1711

The first and most obvious reflections which arise in a man who changes the city for the country are upon the different manners of the people whom he meets with in those two different scenes of life. By manners I do not mean morals, but behavior and good breeding as they show themselves in the town and in the country.

And here, in the first place, I must observe a very great revolution that has happened in this article of good breeding. Several obliging deferences, condescensions, and submissions, with many outward forms and ceremonies that accompany them, were first of all brought up among the politer part of mankind, who lived in courts and cities and distinguished themselves from the rustic part of the species (who on all occasions acted bluntly and naturally) by such a mutual complaisance and intercourse of civilities. These forms of conversation by degrees multiplied and grew troublesome; the modish world found too great a constraint in them, and have therefore thrown most of them aside. Conversation was so encumbered with show and ceremony that it stood in need of a reformation to retrench its superfluities and restore its natural good sense and beauty. At present, therefore, an unconstrained carriage and a certain openness of behavior are the height of good breeding. The fashionable world is grown free and easy; our manners sit more loose upon us; nothing is so modish as an agreeable negligence. In a word, good breeding shows itself most where to an ordinary eye it appears the least.

If after this we look on the people of mode in the country, we find in them the manners of the last age. They have no sooner fetched themselves up to the fashion of a polite world, but the town has dropped them, and are nearer to the first stage of nature than to those refinements which formerly reigned in the court and still prevail in the country. One may now know a man that never conversed in the world by his excess of good breeding. A polite country squire[1] shall make you as many bows in half an hour as would serve a courtier[2] for a week. There is infinitely more to do about place and precedency in a meeting of justices' wives than in an assembly of duchesses.

This rural politeness is very troublesome to a man of my temper who generally takes the chair that is next me and walks first or last, in the front or in the rear, as chance directs. I have known my friend Sir Roger's dinner almost cold before the company could adjust the ceremonial and be prevailed upon to sit down; and have heartily pitied my old friend when I have seen him forced to pick and cull his guests, as they sat at the several parts of his table, that he might drink their healths according to their respective ranks and qualities. Honest Will Wimble, who I should have thought had

---

**1. squire** n.: A country gentleman or landed proprietor.
**2. courtier** (kôr′ tē ər) n.: An attendant at a royal court.

been altogether uninfected with ceremony, gives me abundance of trouble in this particular. Though he has been fishing all the morning, he will not help himself at dinner till I am served. When we are going out of the hall, he runs behind me; and last night, as we were walking in the fields, stopped short at a stile till I came up to it and, upon my making signs to him to get over, told me, with a serious smile, that sure I believed they had no manners in the country.

There has happened another revolution in the point of good breeding which relates to the conversation among men of mode and which I cannot but look upon as very extraordinary. It was certainly one of the first distinctions of a well-bred man to express everything that had the most remote appearance of being obscene in modest terms and distant phrases; whilst the clown, who had no such delicacy of conception and expression, clothed his ideas in those plain homely terms that are the most obvious and natural. This kind of good manners was perhaps carried to an excess so as to make conversation too stiff, formal, and precise; for which reason (as hypocrisy in one age is generally succeeded by atheism in another) conversation is in a great measure relapsed into the first extreme; so that at present several of our men of the town, and particularly those who have been polished in France, make use of the most coarse, uncivilized words in our language and utter themselves often in such a manner as a clown would blush to hear.

This infamous piece of good breeding, which reigns among the coxcombs[3] of the town, has not yet made its way into the country; and as it is impossible for such an irrational way of conversation to last long among a people that makes any profession of religion or show of modesty, if the country gentlemen get into it, they will certainly be left in the lurch. Their good breeding will come too late to them, and they will be thought a parcel of lewd clowns, while they fancy themselves talking together like men of wit and pleasure.

As the two points of good breeding, which I have hitherto insisted upon, regard behavior and conversation, there is a third which turns upon dress. In this too the country are very much behindhand. The rural beaus are not yet got out of the fashion that took place at the time of the Revolution[4] but ride about the country in red coats and laced hats; while the women in many parts are still trying to outvie one another in the height of their headdresses.

But a friend of mine, who is now upon the western circuit, having promised to give me an account of the several modes and fashions that prevail in the different parts of the nation through which he passes, I shall defer the enlarging upon this last topic till I have received a letter from him, which I expect every post.

---

**3. coxcombs** *n.:* Silly, vain men; dandies.
**4. the Revolution:** The "Glorious Revolution" of 1688, during which James II was expelled from the throne.

## THINKING ABOUT THE SELECTION

### Recalling

1. (a) What happened in the first "great revolution . . . of good breeding"? (b) Where did the revolution occur? (c) What brought about the change?
2. How did "country gentlemen" react to the change in city manners?
3. What annoys the writer about the behavior of (a) Sir Roger? (b) Honest Will Wimble?
4. (a) What did the second revolution in good breeding involve? (b) Where did it occur? (c) Why might its effects make "a clown . . . blush"?
5. (a) How has the country reacted to the revolution in conversation? (b) In what other area of good breeding may country gentlemen someday react?

### Interpreting

6. Why do you think the country lags behind the city in manners?
7. Why would a city dweller who had once expected an "excess of good breeding" now be annoyed by it?
8. (a) To which group mentioned in the essay does the writer belong? (b) Why must he await a letter before he can comment on the fashion prevailing in the country?

### Applying

9. In the United States today, what are the differences, if any, between country manners and city manners? Explain.
10. In nineteenth-century America, Walt Whitman wrote, "To the real artist in humanity, what are called bad manners are often the most picturesque and significant of all."

How do you think Addison and Steele would have reacted to Whitman's comment? Explain your answer.

## ANALYZING LITERATURE

### Understanding Informal Essay

As its name implies, an informal essay expresses the observations and opinions of its author in a personal, conversational way. The informal essay is less rigid than the formal essay. The views stated can be highly individual, even outrageous. Although Addison and Steele are seldom outrageous, they do express unequivocal, thought-provoking opinions.

1. For each of the three "points of good breeding" in "Country Manners," find one statement that you consider highly opinionated.
2. A personal essay shows clear signs of having been written by the specific individual whose opinions it expresses. What are three such signs in "Country Manners"?

## THINKING AND WRITING

### Writing an Informal Essay

Use the topic that you chose for Writing, page 537, or else select a new topic on which opinions vary. Possible general topic areas include politics, sports, arts, and leisure. If you are using the topic you chose earlier, you have existing notes for it. If not, begin by stating your opinion clearly in one sentence. Then jot down notes before you start to write. When writing the first draft of your informal essay, use a personal, conversational style. In revising the first draft, pay close attention to tone. A good conversational style is friendly and down-to-earth but not overly clever.

# Thoughts in Westminster Abbey[1]

### Joseph Addison

## The Spectator, March 30, 1711

When I am in a serious humor, I very often walk by myself in Westminster Abbey; where the gloominess of the place, and the use to which it is applied, with the solemnity of the building, and the condition of the people who lie in it, are apt to fill the mind with a kind of melancholy, or rather thoughtfulness, that is not disagreeable. I yesterday passed a whole afternoon in the churchyard, the cloisters, and the church, amusing myself with the tombstones and inscriptions that I met with in those several regions of the dead. Most of them recorded nothing else of the buried person, but that he was born upon one day, and died upon another: the whole history of his life being comprehended in those two circumstances, that are common to all mankind. I could not but look upon these registers of existence, whether of brass or marble, as a kind of satire upon the departed persons; who had left no other memorial of them, but that they were born and that they died. They put me in mind of several persons mentioned in the battles of heroic poems, who have sounding names given them, for no other reason but that they may be killed, and are celebrated for nothing but being knocked on the head.

Upon my going into the church, I entertained myself with the digging of a grave; and saw in every shovelful of it that was thrown up, the fragment of a bone or skull intermixed with a kind of fresh moldering earth that some time or other had a place in the composition of a human body. Upon this I began to consider with myself what innumerable multitudes of people lay confused together under the pavement of that ancient cathedral; how men and women, friends and enemies, priests and soldiers, monks and prebendaries,[2] were crumbled amongst one another, and blended together in the same common mass; how beauty, strength, and youth, with old age, weakness, and deformity, lay undistinguished in the same promiscuous heap of matter.

After having thus surveyed this great magazine of mortality, as it were, in the lump; I examined it more particularly by the accounts which I found on several of the monuments which are raised in every quarter of that ancient fabric. Some of them were covered with such extravagant epitaphs that, if it were possible for the dead person to be acquainted with them, he would blush at the praises which his friends have bestowed upon him. There are others so excessively modest, that they deliver the character of the person departed in Greek or

---

**1. Westminster Abbey:** A famous church in Westminster, England, where English monarchs are crowned, and where English monarchs and many famous writers and statesmen are buried.

**2. prebendaries** (preb′ ən der′ ēz) *n.*: In the Church of England, honorary clergymen.

Hebrew, and by that means are not understood once in a twelvemonth. In the poetical quarter, I found there were poets who had no monuments, and monuments which had no poets. I observed, indeed, that the present war[3] had filled the church with many of these uninhabited monuments, which had been erected to the memory of persons whose bodies were perhaps buried in the plains of Blenheim,[4] or in the bosom of the ocean.

I could not but be very much delighted with several modern epitaphs, which are written with great elegance of expression and justness of thought, and therefore do honor to the living as well as to the dead. As a foreigner is very apt to conceive an idea of the ignorance or politeness of a nation, from the turn of their public monuments and inscriptions, they should be submitted to the perusal of men of learning and genius, before they are put in execution. Sir Cloudesly Shovel's[5] monument has very often given me great offense: instead of the brave rough English admiral, which was the distinguishing character of that plain gallant man, he is represented on his tomb by the figure of a beau, dressed in a long periwig,[6] and reposing himself upon velvet cushions under a canopy of state. The inscription is answerable to the monument; for instead of celebrating the many remarkable actions he had performed in the service of his country, it acquaints us only with the manner of his death, in which it was impossible for him to reap any honor. The Dutch,

---

**3. the present war:** The War of the Spanish Succession, in which England and several other European nations fought against an alliance led by the French and Spanish.
**4. Blenheim** (blen′ əm): Village in western Bavaria that was the site of an important battle (1704) during the War of the Spanish Succession.

**5. Sir Cloudesly Shovel** (1650–1707): English admiral and commander of the British fleet.
**6. periwig** (per′ ə wig′) *n*.: A type of wig often worn by men during the seventeenth and eighteenth centuries.

ST. EDMUND'S CHAPEL, WESTMINSTER ABBEY
*John Fulleylove*

whom we are apt to despise for want of genius, show an infinitely greater taste of antiquity and politeness in their buildings and works of this nature, than what we meet with in those of our own country. The monuments of their admirals, which have been erected at the public expense, represent them like themselves; and are adorned with rostral crowns and naval ornaments, with beautiful festoons of seaweed, shells, and coral.

But to return to our subject. I have left the repository of our English kings for the contemplation of another day, when I shall find my mind disposed for so serious an amusement. I know that entertainments of this nature are apt to raise dark and dismal thoughts in timorous minds and gloomy imaginations; but for my own part, though I am always serious, I do not know what it is to be melancholy; and can therefore take a view of nature in her deep and solemn scenes, with the same pleasure as in her most gay and delightful ones. By this means I can improve myself with those objects which others consider with terror. When I look upon the tombs of the great, every emotion of envy dies in me; when I read the epitaphs of the beautiful, every inordinate desire goes out; when I meet with the grief of parents upon a tombstone, my heart melts with compassion; when I see the tomb of the parents themselves, I consider the vanity of grieving for those whom we must quickly follow: when I see kings lying by those who deposed them, when I consider rival wits placed side by side, or the holy men that divided the world with their contests and disputes, I reflect with sorrow and astonishment on the little competitions, factions, and debates of mankind. When I read the several dates of the tombs, of some that died yesterday, and some six hundred years ago, I consider that great day when we shall all of us be contemporaries, and make our appearance together.

## THINKING ABOUT THE SELECTION
### Recalling

1. (a) At what times does the author say he visits Westminster Abbey? (b) Why does he go then?
2. (a) Who was Sir Cloudsley Shovel? (b) What kind of man was he? (b) Why does the author object to Shovel's monument?
3. On what does the author reflect with "sorrow and astonishment"?

### Interpreting

4. What two kinds of epitaphs seem to offend the author most?

5. The author states that some modern epitaphs "do honor to the living as well as to the dead." (a) What does he mean? (b) Why does he think proposed monuments and epitaphs should be reviewed by "men of learning and genius"?
6. What does the author mean by "that great day when we shall all of us be contemporaries"?

### Applying

7. At the end of the essay the author lists a number of ironies he sees in Westminster Abbey. (a) Which of them seems the most poignant to you? (b) What ironies can you think of that might be added to the list?

## Literary Magazines Today

Editor Reginald Gibbons recently observed in the *Chicago Tribune*, "It's no accident that almost every writer of our century who is now regarded as the author of great and enduring work was first published in the little literary magazines, some of which, like T. S. Eliot's famous *Criterion*, had as few as 700 subscribers."

Many literary magazines from the early part of the twentieth century have passed into legend, but not before leaving an indelible mark on literature and culture. *The Masses, The Pagan, The Dial,* and *The Fugitive* published the early works of T. S. Eliot, Ezra Pound, Wallace Stevens, as well as many other landmark writers. The mass-market magazines, in contrast, published the long-forgotten verse of such authors as Anne Bunner and Fannie Stearns Davis. But before we can consider the effect of today's literary magazines, we have to be sure we know how to recognize one!

### WHAT IS A LITERARY MAGAZINE?

The Council of Literary Magazines and Presses includes among its members 380 literary magazines. They define a literary magazine as "a noncommercial magazine in which fiction, poetry, or literary essay comprises at least 50% of the editorial material." Yet many of these journals are indeed published for a profit. *Granta,* for instance, is published by Penguin Books. This notable magazine, begun by students at Cambridge University in 1888, has showcased the work of A. A. Milne (of Winnie the Pooh fame), E. M. Forster, Sylvia Plath, Graham Greene, and Saul Bellow, to mention just a few. In a similar fashion, the publishing house of W. W. Norton supports the literary magazine *Antaeus,* and Vintage Books publishes *The Quarterly.*

According to this definition, mass-market literary magazines are an entirely different kettle of literature. Yet *The New Yorker, Atlantic, Harper's, The New York Review of Books, The Times Literary Supplement,* and *Partisan Review* devote the majority of their editorial space to publishing some of today's most important fiction, poetry, and literary essays. Twenty-five percent of the 155 short stories published in single volumes in 1987 were first published in *The New Yorker; The Atlantic* came in a laudable second. Virtually all the stories published in these magazines, however, were by already-famous writers.

But whether they are published for profit or not, literary magazines offer an astonishing diversity of style and content. At one end of the spectrum are the long-established publications such as *The Paris Review.* Founded as a journal where undiscovered writers could gain public notice, *The Paris Review* has enjoyed the same fate as many of its original contributors: It has gone mainstream. Now they publish the work of such well-known writers as Nadine Gordimer and John Irving. At the other end of the scale are such "hip lit" publications as *Bomb* and *Between C & D.* The latter, for example, has rejected the understated in favor of shock: The entire print run of 600 copies, printed directly from a home computer, is distributed with sprocket holes still attached and the pages connected in a single, long accordion of folded pages. The content is as offbeat as the style.

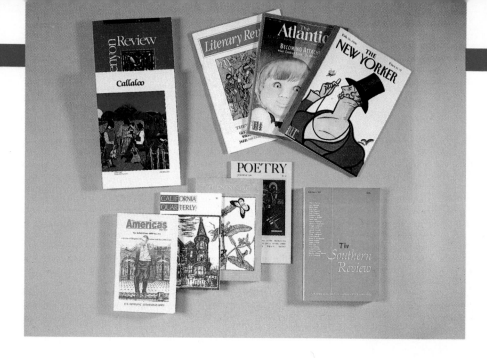

## HOW ARE LITERARY MAGAZINES DISTRIBUTED?

How do people hear about literary magazines? Many are distributed through universities and colleges; others are publicized through word of mouth. A surprising number of literary magazines are distributed through bookstores. These include the more famous titles—*Antioch Review, VLS (Voice Literary Supplement), Yale Literary Magazine, Hudson Review, TriQuarterly, American Poetry Review, Hornbook, Paris Review, American Book Review, American Poetry Review,* and *October*—as well as the often colorfully named newer productions —*Coyote's Journal, Callaloo, Southpaw, Sulphur, Zyzzyva, Alcatraz, Imagine,* and *ACM (Another Chicago Magazine).*

Often, bookstores alert their customers to new literary magazines through poetry readings, book signings, and fancy receptions. Although literary magazines often sell only a handful of copies, they are surprisingly profitable to bookstore owners. Richard Bray, owner of Guild Books in Chicago, remarked, "We don't lose money on them. It's profitable from the standpoint that people who buy and browse these magazines are probably, more than any other category, book buyers. Just as magazines in general are a draw to help sell books, I'd say literary magazines are—and more so."

## THE IMPORTANCE OF LITERARY MAGAZINES

Although the number of people reading literary magazines is limited, these publications nonetheless play a very significant role in the literary scene. They give famous writers a chance to take a chance and try a new writing style or topic, but, even more important, they allow readers to see new and unusual literary experiments by writers who are still developing a career. You might be the one to discover the next "classic" writer!

# ALEXANDER POPE

## 1688–1744

From the age of eight or nine, Alexander Pope knew that he wanted to become not just a poet but a great poet. Before he was twenty-one, his *Essay on Criticism* had brought him to the attention of the leading literary figures of England. His satiric *The Rape of the Lock,* probably the best mock-epic poem in English, followed when he was twenty-four. Despite a crippling childhood disease and persistent ill health, Pope triumphantly achieved his boyhood ambition. A brilliant satirist in verse, he gave his name (the Age of Pope and Swift) to the literary era in which he lived and wrote.

Born into the Roman Catholic family of a London linen merchant, Pope had to struggle for position. After the expulsion of King James II, English Catholics could not legally vote, hold office, attend a university, or live within ten miles of London. To comply with the rule of residency, his family moved to Binfield, near Windsor Forest, a rural setting where Pope spent his formative years writing poetry, studying the classics, and becoming broadly self-educated. Pope's physical problems were as severe as his religious ones. Deformed by tuberculosis of the spine, Pope stood only about four and a half feet tall—"the little Alexander whom the women laugh at," he said—and he suffered from nervousness and excruciating headaches throughout his life. In 1718 Pope moved to a five-acre estate at Twickenham (twit′ nam), a village on the Thames, where he lived until his death.

Although Pope, "the Wasp of Twickenham," is more often remembered for his quarrels than for his cordiality, he became friends, and remained so for life, with members of a Tory group that included Jonathan Swift, John Gay, and Lord Bolingbroke. Pope instigated the formation of the Scriblerus Club, the purpose of which was to ridicule what its members regarded as "false tastes in learning." The satiric emphasis of the club probably gave some impetus to the writing of Swift's *Gulliver's Travels,* Gay's *Beggar's Opera,* and Pope's *The Dunciad*—a "burlesque heroick" attack on Pope's literary enemies (most of whom are now forgotten).

In the 1730's Pope's writing turned increasingly philosophical. He embarked on a massive work concerning morality and government, but completed only *An Essay on Man* and *Moral Essays.* Nevertheless, the entire body of his work is sufficient for critics today to accord him exceptionally high praise. The twentieth-century poet Edith Sitwell calls Pope "perhaps the most flawless artist our race has yet produced."

## *from* The Rape of the Lock

**Literary Forms**

**Mock Epic.** A mock epic is a long, humorous narrative poem that treats a trivial subject in the grand, elevated style of a true epic such as the *Odyssey* or *Paradise Lost*. Sometimes called a *mock-heroic* poem, this literary form reached the height of its popularity in the eighteenth century. The *conventions,* or standard elements, of an epic require both the characters and the action to be of heroic proportions. The theme of a true epic concerns fundamental human problems. In a classical epic, gods and goddesses oversee and sometimes intervene in human affairs. When these conventions of an epic are satirically applied to a subject of little consequence, the result can be highly amusing.

**Writing**

Freewrite about an incident you have heard or read about that you think has been magnified beyond its importance. In your writing, carry the incident to an illogical extreme, as the writer of a mock epic would do.

**Primary Source**

Concerned that the publication of his poem could cause greater hard feelings, Pope wrote a dedication to Arabella Fermor, the model for Belinda, intended to coax her into a good mood. After you read the following excerpt, decide whether Pope succeeded.

Madam,
It will be in vain to deny that I have some Regard for this Piece, since I Dedicate it to You. Yet . . . it was intended only to divert a few young ladies, who have good Sense and good Humor enough, to laugh not only at their Sex's little unguarded Follies, but at their own. But as it was communicated with the Air of A Secret, it soon found its Way into the World. . . .

As to the following Cantos, all the Passages in them are as Fabulous, as the Vision at the Beginning, or the Transformation at the end; (except the Loss of your Hair, which I always mention with Reverence). The Human Persons are as Fictitious as the Airy ones; and the Character of Belinda, as it is now manag'd, resembles you in nothing but in Beauty.

If this Poem had as many Graces as there are in Your Person, or in Your Mind, yet I could never hope it would pass thro' the World half so Uncensured as You have done. But let its Fortune be what it will, mine is happy enough, to have given you this Occasion of assuring You that I am, with the truest Esteem . . . A. Pope

# *from* The Rape of the Lock

Alexander Pope

*The Rape of the Lock, a mock epic, or a humorous poem written in the style of and recalling situations from the famous epic poems of Homer, Virgil, and Milton, is based on an actual incident. When Lord Petre, a wealthy baron, cut a lock of hair from the head of the beautiful Arabella Fermor, a great quarrel developed between the lady's family and the family of Lord Petre. Following the incident, Pope's friend John Caryll suggested that Pope write a poem mocking the trivial incident to point out the absurdity of the families' reactions. In writing* The Rape of the Lock, *however, Pope went far beyond the ridiculous incident that inspired it. The poem, filled with allusions to the great literary works of the past, is a poignant appraisal of the social manners and human behavior of the time.*

*The first of the poem's five cantos opens with a formal statement of theme and an invocation to the Muse for poetic inspiration. Then Belinda, the poem's heroine, receives a warning from the sylph Ariel that a dreadful event will take place in her immediate future. In Canto II, during a boat ride on the Thames, an adventurous baron admires Belinda's hair and is determined to cut two bright locks from her head and keep them as a prize. Aware of the baron's desires, Ariel urges the spirits to protect Belinda.*

## Canto III

Close by those meads, forever crowned with flowers,
Where Thames with pride surveys his rising towers,
There stands a structure of majestic frame,[1]
Which from the neighboring Hampton takes its name.
5  Here Britain's statesmen oft the fall foredoom
Of foreign tyrants, and of nymphs at home;
Here thou, great Anna![2] whom three realms obey,

---

**1. structure . . . frame:** Hampton Court, a royal palace near London.
**2. Anna:** Queen Anne, who ruled England, Ireland, and Scotland from 1702 through 1714.

Dost sometimes counsel take—and sometimes tea.
   Hither the heroes and the nymphs resort,
10  To taste awhile the pleasures of a court;
   In various talk th' instructive hours they passed,
   Who gave the ball, or paid the visit last;
   One speaks the glory of the British Queen,
   And one describes a charming Indian screen;
15  A third interprets motions, looks, and eyes;
   At every word a reputation dies.

from *The Rape of the Lock*   **549**

Snuff, or the fan,[3] supply each pause of chat,
With singing, laughing, ogling, and all that.
          Meanwhile, declining from the noon of day,
20   The sun obliquely shoots his burning ray;
The hungry judges soon the sentence sign,
And wretches hang that jurymen may dine;
The merchant from th' Exchange[4] returns in peace,
And the long labors of the toilet[5] cease.
25   Belinda now, whom thirst of fame invites,
Burns to encounter two adventurous knights,
At omber[6] singly to decide their doom;
And swells her breast with conquests yet to come.
Straight the three bands prepare in arms to join,
30   Each band the number of the sacred nine.[7]
Soon as she spreads her hand, th' aerial guard
Descend, and sit on each important card:
First Ariel perched upon a Matadore,[8]
Then each, according to the rank they bore;
35   For sylphs, yet mindful of their ancient race,
Are, as when women, wondrous fond of place.
          Behold, four kings in majestry revered,
With hoary whiskers and a forky beard;
And four fair queens whose hands sustain a flower,
40   Th' expressive emblem of their softer power;
Four knaves in garbs succinct,[9] a trusty band,
Caps on their heads, and halberts[10] in their hand;
And particolored troops, a shining train,
Draw forth to combat on the velvet plain.
45        The skilful nymph reviews her force with care:
Let spades be trumps! she said, and trumps they were.
          Now move to war her sable Matadores,
In show like leaders of the swarthy Moors.
Spadillio[11] first, unconquerable Lord!
50   Led off two captive trumps, and swept the board.
As many more Manillio[12] forced to yield,
And marched a victor from the verdant field.[13]

---

**3. snuff . . . fan:** At the time, gentlemen commonly took snuff, and ladies usually carried a fan.
**4. Exchange:** The London financial center where merchants, bankers, and brokers conducted business.
**5. toilet:** Dressing tables.
**6. omber:** A popular card game.
**7. sacred nine:** A reference to the nine Muses of Greek mythology.
**8. Matadore:** A powerful card that could take a trick.
**9. succinct** (sək siŋkt′): Belted.
**10. halberts:** Long-handled weapons.
**11. Spadillio:** The ace of spades.
**12. Manillio:** The two of spades.
**13. verdant field:** The card table, covered with a green cloth.

Him Basto[14] followed, but his fate more hard
Gained but one trump and one plebeian card.
55 With his broad saber next, a chief in years,
The hoary majesty of spades appears,
Puts forth one manly leg, to sight revealed,
The rest, his many-colored robe concealed.
The rebel knave, who dares his prince engage,
60 Proves the just victim of his royal rage.
Even mighty Pam,[15] that kings and queens o'erthrew
And mowed down armies in the fights of loo,
Sad chance of war! now destitute of aid,
Falls undistinguished by the victor spade!
65      Thus far both armies to Belinda yield;
Now to the baron fate inclines the field.
His warlike Amazon her host invades,
Th' imperial consort of the crown of spades.
The club's black tyrant first her victim died,
70 Spite of his haughty mien, and barbarous pride.
What boots[16] the regal circle on his head,
His giant limbs, in state unwieldy spread;
That long behind he trails his pompous robe,
And, of all monarchs, only grasps the globe?
75      The baron now his diamonds pours apace;
Th' embroidered king who shows but half his face,
And his refulgent queen, with powers combined
Of broken troops an easy conquest find.
Clubs, diamonds, hearts, in wild disorder seen,
80 With throngs promiscuous strew the level green.
Thus when dispersed a routed army runs,
Of Asia's troops, and Afric's sable sons,
With like confusion different nations fly,
Of various habit, and of various dye,
85 The pierced battalions disunited fall,
In heaps on heaps; one fate o'erwhelms them all.
      The knave of diamonds tries his wily arts,
And wins (oh shameful chance!) the queen of hearts.
At this, the blood the virgin's cheek forsook,
90 A livid paleness spreads o'er all her look;
She sees, and trembles at th' approaching ill,
Just in the jaws of ruin, and codille.[17]
And now (as oft in some distempered state)
On one nice trick depends the general fate.

**14. Basto:** The ace of clubs.
**15. Pam:** The knave of clubs, the highest card in the game called
"100."
**16. what boots:** Of what benefit is.
**17. codille:** A term meaning the defeat of a hand of cards.

95 An ace of hearts steps forth; the king unseen
Lurked in her hand, and mourned his captive queen.
He springs to vengeance with an eager pace,
And falls like thunder on the prostrate ace.
The nymph exulting fills with shouts the sky;
100 The walls, the woods, and long canals reply.
Oh thoughtless mortals! ever blind to fate,
Too soon dejected, and too soon elate.
Sudden, these honors shall be snatched away,
And cursed forever this victorious day.

**THE RAPE OF THE LOCK, 1895–96**
*Aubrey Beardsley*

105       Fo lo! the board with cups and spoons is crowned,
       The berries crackle, and the mill turns round;[18]
       On shining altars of Japan[19] they raise
       The silver lamp; the fiery spirits blaze;
       From silver spouts the grateful liquors glide,
110      While China's earth[20] receives the smoking tide.
       At once they gratify their scent and taste,
       And frequent cups prolong the rich repast.
       Straight hover round the fair her airy band;
       Some, as she sipped, the fuming liquor fanned,
115      Some o'er her lap their careful plumes displayed,
       Trembling, and conscious of the rich brocade.
       Coffee (which makes the politician wise,
       And see through all things with his half-shut eyes)
       Sent up in vapors to the baron's brain
120      New stratagems, the radiant lock to gain.
       Ah cease, rash youth! desist ere 'tis too late,
       Fear the just gods, and think of Scylla's fate![21]
       Changed to a bird, and sent to flit in air,
       She dearly pays for Nisus' injured hair!
125        But when to mischief mortals bend their will,
       How soon they find fit instruments of ill!
       Just then, Clarissa drew with tempting grace
       A two-edged weapon from her shining case:
       So ladies in romance assist their knight,
130      Present the spear, and arm him for the fight.
       He takes the gift with reverence, and extends
       The little engine[22] on his fingers' ends;
       This just behind Belinda's neck he spread,
       As o'er the fragrant steams she bends her head.
135      Swift to the lock a thousand sprites repair,
       A thousand wings, by turns, blow back the hair;
       And thrice they twitched the diamond in her ear;
       Thrice she looked back, and thrice the foe drew near.
       Just in that instant, anxious Ariel sought
140      The close recesses of the virgin's thought;
       As on the nosegay in her breast reclined,
       He watched th' ideas rising in her mind,
       Sudden he viewed, in spite of all her art,
       An earthly lover lurking at her heart.[23]

---

**18. the berries . . . round:** The coffee beans are ground in a hand mill at the table.
**19. altars of Japan:** Small imported lacquer tables.
**20. China's earth:** Earthenware cups imported from China.
**21. Scylla's** (sĭl′ əz) **fate:** Scylla, the daughter of King Nisus, was turned into a sea bird because she cut off the lock of her father's hair on which his safety depended and sent it to his enemy.
**22. engine:** Instrument.
**23. earthly lover . . . heart:** If in her heart Belinda wants the baron to succeed, they cannot protect her.

145    Amazed, confused, he found his power expired,
      Resigned to fate, and with a sigh retired.
          The peer now spreads the glittering forfex[24] wide,
      T' enclose the lock; now joins it, to divide.
      Even then, before the fatal engine closed,
150    A wretched sylph too fondly interposed;
      Fate urged the shears, and cut the sylph in twain,
      (But airy substance soon unites again).
      The meeting points the sacred hair dissever
      From the fair head, forever, and forever!
155        Then flashed the living lightning from her eyes,
      And screams of horror rend th' affrighted skies.
      Not louder shrieks to pitying heaven are cast,
      When husbands, or when lap dogs breathe their last;
      Or when rich China vessels fallen from high,
160    In glittering dust, and painted fragments lie!
          "Let wreaths of triumph now my temples twine,"
      The victor cried, "the glorious prize is mine!"
      While fish in streams, or birds delight in air,
      Or in a coach and six the British Fair,
165    As long as *Atalantis*[25] shall be read,
      Or the small pillow grace a lady's bed,
      While visits shall be paid on solemn days,
      When numerous wax lights in bright order blaze,
      While nymphs take treats, or assignations give,
170    So long my honor, name, and praise shall live!
      What time would spare, from steel receives its date,[26]
      And monuments, like men, submit to fate!
      Steel could the labor of the gods destroy,
      And strike to dust th' imperial towers of Troy;
175    Steel could the works of mortal pride confound,
      And hew triumphal arches to the ground.
      What wonder then, fair nymph! thy hairs should feel,
      The conquering force of unresisted steel?

### *from* Canto V

*In* Canto IV, *after Umbriel, "a dusky, melancholy sprite,"
empties a bag filled with "the force of female lungs, sighs,
sobs, and passions, and the war of tongues" onto Belinda's
head, the lady erupts over the loss of her lock. Then she
"bids her beau," Sir Plume, to "demand the precious hairs,"
but Plume is unable to persuade the baron to return the hair.*

---

**24. forfex:** Scissors.
**25. Atalantis:** A popular book of scandalous gossip.
**26. receives its date:** Is destroyed.

*In the beginning of* Canto V, *Clarissa, a level-headed nymph, tries to bring an end to the commotion, but rather than being greeted with applause, her speech is followed by a battle cry.*

"To arms, to arms!" the fierce virago[27] cries,
And swift as lightning to the combat flies.
All side in parties, and begin th' attack;
Fans clap, silks rustle, and tough whalebones crack;
5 Heroes' and heroines' shouts confusedly rise,
And bass and treble voices strike the skies.
No common weapons in their hands are found,
Like gods they fight, nor dread a mortal wound.
　　　　So when bold Homer makes the gods engage,
10 And heavenly breasts with human passions rage;
'Gainst Pallas, Mars, Latona, Hermes[28] arms;
And all Olympus[29] rings with loud alarms:
Jove's[30] thunder roars, heaven trembles all around,
Blue Neptune[31] storms, the bellowing deeps resound;
15 Earth shakes her nodding towers, the ground gives way,
And the pale ghosts start at the flash of day!
　　　　Triumphant Umbriel on a sconce's height[32]
Clapped his glad wings, and sat to view the fight;
Propped on their bodkin spears,[33] the sprites survey
20 The growing combat, or assist the fray.
　　　　While through the press enraged Thalestris[34] flies,
And scatters death around from both her eyes,
A beau and witling[35] perished in the throng,
One died in metaphor, and one in song.
25 "O cruel nymph! a living death I bear,"
Cried Dapperwit, and sunk beside his chair.
A mournful glance Sir Fopling[36] upwards cast,
"Those eyes are made so killing"—was his last.

---

**27. virago** (və rā′ gō): Scolding woman.
**28. Pallas . . . Hermes:** Gods who directed the Trojan War. Pallas and Hermes supported the Greeks, while Mars and Latona sided with the Trojans.
**29. Olympus:** The mountain which was supposed to be the home of the gods.
**30. Jove's:** Referring to Jupiter, the ruler of the Gods in Roman mythology; identified with Zeus in Greek mythology.
**31. Neptune:** The Roman god of the sea; identified with Poseidon in Greek mythology.
**32. sconce's height:** A candleholder attached to the wall.
**33. bodkin spears:** Large needles.
**34. Thalestris** (thə lĕs′ trĭs): An Amazon (a race of female warriors supposed to have lived in Scythia) who played a role in the medieval tales of Alexander the Great.
**35. witling:** A person who fancies himself or herself a wit.
**36. Dapperwit, Sir Fopling:** Names of amusing characters in comedies of the time.

Thus on Maeander's[37] flowery margin lies

30 Th' expiring swan, and as he sings he dies.

When bold Sir Plume had drawn Clarissa down,
Chloe[38] stepped in, and killed him with a frown;
She smiled to see the doughty hero slain,
But, at her smile, the beau revived again.

35 Now Jove suspends his golden scales in air,
Weighs the men's wits against the lady's hair;
The doubtful beam long nods from side to side;
At length the wits mount up, the hairs subside.

See, fierce Belinda on the baron flies,

40 With more than usual lightning in her eyes;
Nor feared the chief th' unequal fight to try,
Who sought no more than on his foe to die.
But this bold lord with manly strength endued,
She with one finger and a thumb subdued:

45 Just where the breath of life his nostrils drew,
A charge of snuff the wily virgin threw;
The gnomes direct, to every atom just,
The pungent grains of titillating dust.
Sudden with starting tears each eye o'erflows,

50 And the high dome re-echoes to his nose.

"Now meet thy fate," incensed Belinda cried,
And drew a deadly bodkin[39] from her side . . .

"Boast not my fall," he cried, "insulting foe!
Thou by some other shalt be laid as low.

55 Nor think, to die dejects my lofty mind;
All that I dread is leaving you behind!
Rather than so, ah let me still survive,
And burn in Cupid's flames—but burn alive."

"Restore the lock!" she cries; and all around

60 "Restore the lock!" the vaulted roofs rebound.
Not fierce Othello in so loud a strain
Roared for the handkerchief that caused his pain.[40]
But see how oft ambitious aims are crossed,
And chiefs contend till all the prize is lost!

65 The lock, obtained with guilt, and kept with pain,
In every place is sought, but sought in vain.
With such a prize no mortal must be blessed,
So Heaven decrees! with Heaven who can contest?

---

**37. Maeander's:** Referring to a river in Asia.

**38. Chloe** (klō′ ē): The heroine of the ancient Greek pastoral romance, *Daphnis and Chloe*.

**39. bodkin:** An ornamental pin shaped like a dagger.

**40. not . . . pain:** In Shakespeare's *Othello*, the hero is convinced that his wife is being unfaithful to him when she cannot find the handkerchief that he had given her. Actually, the handkerchief had been taken by the villain, Iago, who uses it as part of his evil plot.

**THE BATTLE OF THE BEAUX AND BELLES**
*Aubrey Beardsley*

Some thought it mounted to the lunar sphere,
70    Since all things lost on earth are treasured there.
There heroes' wits are kept in ponderous vases,
And beaux' in snuffboxes and tweezer cases.
There broken vows and deathbed alms are found,
And lovers' hearts with ends of riband bound . . .
75        But trust the Muse—she saw it upward rise,
Though marked by none but quick, poetic eyes . . .
A sudden star, it shot through liquid[41] air
And drew behind a radiant trail of hair . . .[42]
    Then cease, bright Nymph! to mourn thy ravished hair,
80    Which adds new glory to the shining sphere!
Not all the tresses that fair head can boast,
Shall draw such envy as the lock you lost.
For, after all the murders of your eye,[43]
When, after millions slain, yourself shall die;
85    When those fair suns shall set, as set they must,
And all those tresses shall be laid in dust,
This lock, the Muse shall consecrate to fame,
And midst the stars inscribe Belinda's name.

---

**41. liquid:** Clear.
**42. trail of hair:** The word "comet" comes from a Greek word meaning "long-haired."
**43. murders . . . eye:** Lovers struck down by her glances.

## THINKING ABOUT THE SELECTION

### Recalling

1. (a) In what activity is Belinda engaged during the first half of Canto III? (b) What is the outcome?
2. (a) What is the group doing when the "berries crackle, and the mill turns round"?
3. (a) What is the "two-edged weapon" that Clarissa gives the baron? (b) How many times does the baron fail to get the lock of hair? (c) How does Belinda respond when he does get it? (d) How does the baron react?
4. (a) In Canto V, what noises accompany the attack that follows Belinda's cry of "To arms, to arms!"? (b) With what weapon does Belinda threaten the baron's life? (c) What does she demand that he do?
5. (a) Who has possession of the lock at the end of Canto V? (b) What do some people think has happened to it?

### Interpreting

6. Why do you think Pope precedes the trivial episodes in Canto III with such a grisly image as "wretches hang that jurymen may dine"?
7. What similarity is there between Pope's description of the omber game and his description of the events following the theft of the lock?

8. Lines 79–88 in Canto V are "elegant spoofing," according to one critic. Yet in a sense Pope made the poem's extravagant claim come true. How did he do it?

## Applying

9. Pope based *The Rape of the Lock* on an actual incident. What incident in the news today might provide the basis for a similar mock epic? (Your freewriting on page 547 may supply an answer to this question.)

## ANALYZING LITERATURE
### Understanding Mock Epic

A **mock epic** is a humorous narrative poem done in the manner of a true epic. It may resemble classical epics such as the *Odyssey* or the *Iliad.* It may contain elements of English epics such as *Beowulf* or *Paradise Lost.* Or, as in *The Rape of the Lock,* a mock epic may show traces of both types. In either case it will have characters who perform what appear to be heroic deeds. It may also contain references from mythology and include impossible or supernatural events.

1. (a) What are three trivial incidents in *The Rape of the Lock* that Pope presents in a heroic manner? (b) What are three characteristics of the heroic manner that the poem exhibits?
2. What are some of the mythical creatures, including deities and muses, mentioned in the poem? Try to find at least seven.

## CRITICAL THINKING AND READING
### Inferring the Author's Purpose

Up to a point, you know the author's purpose in writing *The Rape of the Lock.* Pope is mocking the overwrought reaction of two noble families to a hair-cutting prank. In his own words, Pope is "using a vast force to lift a feather." But that is not his only intent. The author has a more serious purpose than just memorializing a silly incident. To understand what it is, you have to read between the lines—to infer—what Pope believes about human behavior and social manners. The following lines from the poem give clues to the author's purpose. First interpret the lines in your own words. Then write a general statement expressing what you believe to be Pope's purpose in writing the poem.

1. "Oh thoughtless mortals! ever blind to fate,/ Too soon dejected, and too soon elate." (Canto III, lines 101–102)
2. "But when to mischief mortals bend their will,/How soon they find fit instruments of ill!" (Canto III, lines 125–126)
3. "But see how oft ambitious aims are crossed,/ And chiefs contend till all the prize is lost!" (Canto V, lines 63–64)

## THINKING AND WRITING
### Writing About Tone

Tone is sometimes easier to recognize than to describe. You can easily see that the tone of *The Rape of the Lock* is high-flown and heroic. But what are the features of Pope's language that lend the poem its distinctive tone? Ask yourself these questions. You will find it helpful to take notes in answering them.

1. How do the words in the poem differ from the words you use in ordinary speaking and writing? (Consider figurative as well as literal meanings of words.)
2. How does the arrangement of words in sentences differ from that in most sentences in everyday English? (Pay attention to inverted elements, modifier placement, parallelism, and so on.)
3. More broadly, what is the total effect of Pope's language? (Look at his overstatement, allusions, choice of details—indeed, anything that makes the poem high-flown and mock heroic.)

Use your answers to these questions to write a composition on the tone of *The Rape of the Lock.* Begin by stating what you believe the tone of the poem to be. Support that statement by citing examples from the poem. Use quotations. Revise, checking especially your organization and coherence.

# GUIDE FOR INTERPRETING

## *from* An Essay on Man

**Writer's Techniques**

**Heroic Couplet.** A heroic couplet is a rhyming pair of lines in iambic pentameter. Since it requires the clear thought and precise wording admired by classically inspired writers, it was a favorite verse form among Restoration and eighteenth-century poets. Dryden, Swift, and Pope are among the best-known users of the form. The heroic couplet, concise and quotable, is often used in satire. The following lines from Pope's *The Rape of the Lock* are a heroic couplet.

```
U  /   U /   U   /  / U / U   /
He springs to vengeance with an eager pace,

U   /  U  /  U  / U  /  U   /
And falls like thunder on the prostrate ace.
```

**Writing**

Many of Pope's heroic couplets are closed couplets—that is, their two lines represent a complete thought.

> True wit is Nature to advantage dress'd,
> What oft was thought, but ne'er so well expressed.

That couplet, a complete thought, is from Pope's *Essay on Criticism.* Create a closed couplet; it will consist of two rhyming lines with ten syllables each, the stress falling on every second syllable. As a closed couplet, it will make a complete, understandable statement, ideally in an effective and memorable way.

**Primary Source**

The form of the heroic couplet makes it an easy form to mock and makes Pope, because of his tendency to quarrel with others, an easy target as well. The following is an excerpt of a parody of Pope's style from *A Pipe of Tobacco* (1736) by Isaac Hawkins Browne.

The parody is agreeable and skillful, and though it lacks any bite, was very much admired in its own day, as was its author. Although sensitive about his work, Pope spoke highly of Browne and his parody, remarking: "Browne is an excellent copyist, and those who talk ill of him are very much in the wrong."

> . . . Nor less, the critic owns thy genial aid,
> While supperless he plies the piddling trade.
> What tho' to love and soft delights a foe,
> By ladies hated, hated by the beau,
> Yet social freedom, long to courts unknown,
> Fair health, fair truth, and virtue are thy own.
> Come to thy poet, come with healing wings,
> And let me taste thee unexcis'd by kings.

# *from* An Essay on Man

## Alexander Pope

*An Essay on Man is an examination of human nature, society, and morals. In describing the work, Pope comments that it is "a general map of man, marking out . . . the greater parts, their extent, their limits, and their connection." The following excerpt is from the second epistle, in which Pope attempts to show how it is possible for man to achieve a psychological harmony through self-understanding and self-love.*

Know then thyself, presume not God to scan;
The proper study of mankind is man.
Placed on this isthmus of a middle state,
A being darkly wise, and rudely great:
5  With too much knowledge for the skeptic side,
With too much weakness for the stoic's pride,
He hangs between; in doubt to act, or rest;
In doubt to deem himself a god, or beast;
In doubt his mind or body to prefer;
10  Born but to die, and reasoning but to err;
Alike in ignorance, his reason such,
Whether he thinks too little, or too much:
Chaos of thought and passion, all confused;
Still by himself abused, or disabused;
15  Created half to rise, and half to fall;
Great lord of all things, yet a prey to all;
Sole judge of truth, in endless error hurled:
The glory, jest, and riddle of the world!

## THINKING ABOUT THE SELECTION
### Recalling

1. What does Pope say should be the object of man's study?
2. According to Pope, what prevents man from being (a) a skeptic? (b) a stoic?
3. What word, repeated three times, suggests the world of chaos and error in which human beings exist?

### Interpreting

4. Pope writes that man stands on an "isthmus of a middle state." He describes the middle state in detail. In a single word, what is (a) at one end of the isthmus? (b) at the other end?
5. What do you think Pope means by the line, "In doubt his mind or body to prefer"?
6. "Know then thyself," writes Pope. How can a person "in mindless error hurled" achieve that goal?

### Applying

7. Most writers today reject the idea of literature presenting an obvious moral. Pope believed just the opposite. He felt that poetry has a didactic, or instructional, role to play. What do you think?

## ANALYZING LITERATURE
### Understanding a Heroic Couplet

A heroic couplet is a pair of rhymed lines in iambic pentameter. An *iamb* is a metrical foot consisting of one short syllable followed by one long syllable or one unstressed syllable followed by one stressed syllable. The word *apply* (ə plī'), for instance, could function as an iamb:

$$\cup \; / $$
apply

1. Find one word that functions as an iamb in each of the following lines: 1, 2, 7, 8, 11.
2. Since it is a heroic couplet, lines 7–8 should rhyme, but they seem not to. (a) What explanation can you suggest for this apparent mistake? (Hint: Look up in a dictionary the pronunciation of the adjective *bestial*.) (b) Find five similarly nonrhyming pairs of words in *The Rape of the Lock*. How can you explain them?

## CRITICAL THINKING AND READING
### Generalizing

To some extent—except for stable religious convictions—each era sets its own moral and intellectual standards. What is viewed as acceptable in one century may seem outrageous in another. For example, the word *leg* (referring to that part of the human anatomy) was considered so scandalous by Victorians that even chairs and tables were said to have *limbs*. Today the word *leg* seems innocuous.

1. If Pope's observations represent the thought of his day, how did people in the eighteenth century view the relationship between the intellect and the emotions?
2. What differences, if any, do you see in that relationship today?

## THINKING AND WRITING
### Responding to Neoclassical Criticism

In the preface to his poem "Religio Laici," John Dryden offers his critical opinion of how poetry should be written:

> The expressions of a poem designed purely for instruction ought to be plain and natural, and yet majestic; for the poet is . . . a kind of lawgiver, and those three qualities which I have named are proper to the legislative style.

In an essay of no more than one page, state (1) whether you agree with Dryden as to how a poem "purely for instruction" should be written, and (2) whether you think *An Essay on Man* (based on the excerpt you have read) has the three elements named. Draw freely from the poem to support your opinion. When you revise, make sure you have provided adequate support for your opinion.

# The Age of Johnson

Oliver Goldsmith, James Boswell,
And Samuel Johnson At The
Mitre Tavern
*Nineteenth-century colored engraving*
*The Granger Collection*

# SAMUEL JOHNSON

## 1709–1784

Many readers know Samuel Johnson only through the biography written by his contemporary and ardent admirer, James Boswell. That is unfortunate, because the Samuel Johnson who is revealed through his own writings is a man with much to say on a variety of subjects—a man who, despite the excellence of Boswell's portrait, is best read firsthand. During his own lifetime, Johnson was widely recognized as the most influential literary figure of his day as well as a brilliant and witty conversationalist. Indeed, the second half of the eighteenth century is often called the Age of Johnson.

Johnson's success was hard-won. The son of a bookseller in Lichfield, a small town north of Birmingham, he grew up in poverty. He described himself as a "poor diseased infant." A series of childhood illnesses left him physically weak and facially disfigured. A brilliant child who read *Hamlet* at the age of eight, Johnson feared that insanity would deprive him of his single advantage, his intellect. He entered Pembroke College, Oxford, in 1728, but was forced to leave after fourteen months because of a lack of funds. For six years thereafter, until deciding to pursue a literary career in earnest, he was a Lichfield bookseller and schoolmaster, reading widely and occasionally working on translations. At the age of twenty-six he married a widow much older than he, to whom he remained devoted until her death.

In 1737 he moved to London. Despite critical praise for his early writing, he failed to gain a large audience. It was Johnson's *Dictionary of the English Language,* published in 1755, that earned him a permanent place in English letters. For the next two years, he wrote *The Idler,* a series of articles for a weekly newspaper, in addition to completing one of his best-loved works, *Rasselas,* a moral romance.

Johnson was awarded an annual pension of three hundred pounds in 1762, which made him something of a man of leisure. The next year he and twenty-three-year-old James Boswell met for the first time in the back parlor of Tom Davis's bookshop. It was a fateful meeting, one that led, after many further meetings, to Boswell's *Life of Johnson,* a book generally regarded as the finest biography in English.

In 1765 Johnson published an acclaimed edition of Shakespeare. His last important work, *The Lives of the Poets,* appeared in ten volumes between 1779 and 1781. It is a group of fifty-two critical biographies that cover about two hundred years of English literary history. Late in life Johnson received honorary degrees from Oxford and from Trinity College, Dublin—thus the "Dr." that often precedes his name. He is buried in Westminster Abbey.

# GUIDE FOR INTERPRETING

## Letter to Lord Chesterfield; *from* The Preface to A Dictionary of the English Language; *from* A Dictionary of the English Language

**Writer's Techniques**

**Diction and Style.** In written communication, *diction* means word choice. A careful writer chooses words that are clear, correct, and effective. The words that are chosen are at the same time combined in phrases, sentences, and paragraphs. The distinctive way in which words are combined is called *style*. Diction and style change over the years, just as fashion changes. Writing tends to be more casual today than it was two hundred years ago, although formal situations still require formal diction and style. The intended audience for a piece of writing helps to determine appropriate diction and style.

**Commentary**

According to contemporary reports, Johnson was enthralled by words, especially their histories. No doubt this led to his keen interest in diction and style. The following story sheds light on the process of compiling a dictionary—as well as on Samuel Johnson's character.

The story has it that an anonymous source once sent Johnson a letter containing his derivation of "curmudgeon," an ill-tempered person. The unknown donor claimed that the word came from the French *coeur méchant;* literally, "heart wicked," or wicked heart. This wild guess so pleased Johnson that he used it in his *Dictionary,* giving due credit to the "unknown correspondent."

The matter came up again twenty years later, when Dr. John Ash, compiling his own dictionary, came across the entry in Johnson's *Dictionary.* He, too, found it interesting and decided to use it. Unlike Johnson, however, Ash wanted to claim full credit for discovering the word's history, so he wrote that "curmudgeon" was created from *coeur,* meaning "unknown," and *méchant,* meaning "correspondent." Do you think it is necessary to give credit for a word's history? Can anyone "own" a word?

**Writing**

In your local newspaper, find a letter to the editor with which you disagree. Jot down your points of disagreement. Then write the opening paragraph of a response. Try to match your diction and style to that of the published letter you have chosen.

# Letter to Lord Chesterfield

## Samuel Johnson

*Shortly after the completion of the* Dictionary, *Lord Chesterfield published two articles praising it. He had earlier ignored Johnson's appeals for financial assistance for the writing of the* Dictionary.

To the Right Honorable
the Earl of Chesterfield

February 7, 1755

My Lord:

I have been lately informed by the proprietor of the *World*[1] that two papers in which my *Dictionary* is recommended to the public were written by your Lordship. To be so distinguished is an honor which, being very little accustomed to favors from the great, I know not well how to receive, or in what terms to acknowledge.

When upon some slight encouragement I first visited your Lordship, I was overpowered like the rest of mankind by the enchantment of your address,[2] and could not forbear to wish that I might boast myself *"Le vainqueur du vainqueur de la terre"*;[3] that I might obtain that regard for which I saw the world contending, but I found my attendance so little encouraged that neither pride nor modesty would suffer me to continue it. When I had once addressed your Lordship in public, I had exhausted all the art of pleasing which a retired and uncourtly scholar can possess. I had done all that I could; and no man is well pleased to have his all neglected, be it ever so little.

Seven years, my Lord, have now passed since I waited in your outward rooms or was repulsed from your door, during which time I have been pushing on my work through difficulties of which it is useless to complain and have brought it at last to the verge of publication without one act of assistance, one word of encouragement, or one smile of favor. Such treatment I did not expect, for I never had a patron before.

The shepherd in Virgil grew at last acquainted with love, and found him a native of the rocks.[4] Is not a patron, my Lord, one who looks with unconcern on a man struggling for life in the water and when he has reached ground encumbers him with help. The notice which you have been pleased to take of my labors, had it been early, had been kind; but it has been delayed till I am indifferent and cannot enjoy it, till I am solitary and cannot impart it, till I am known and do not want[5] it.

---

**1. the *World*:** A newspaper in which Lord Chesterfield had praised Johnson's *Dictionary.*
**2. address:** Conversation.
**3. *Le vainqueur du vainqueur de la terre*** (lə van kər' dyo͞o van kər' də lä ter'): French for "the conqueror of the conqueror of the earth."

**4. The shepherd . . . rocks:** In Virgil's *Eclogue,* a shepherd complains that love must have been born among jagged rocks.
**5. want:** Need.

I hope it is no very cynical asperity not to confess obligation where no benefit has been received, or to be unwilling that the public should consider me as owing that to a patron which Providence has enabled me to do for myself.

Having carried on my work thus far with so little obligation to any favorer of learning, I shall not be disappointed though I should conclude it, if less be possible, with less; for I have been long wakened from that dream of hope, in which I once boasted myself with so much exultation, my Lord,

Your Lordship's most humble,
most obedient servant,
Samuel Johnson

---

## THINKING ABOUT THE SELECTION

### Recalling

1. (a) How did Johnson learn of Lord Chesterfield's articles in the *World*? (b) Why does he feel the need to respond?
2. How much time has passed since Johnson first tried to get financial assistance from Lord Chesterfield for work on the *Dictionary*?
3. What does Johnson say will not cause him any disappointment at this point?

### Interpreting

4. How does the definition of a patron in the fourth paragraph apply to Johnson's experience with Lord Chesterfield?
5. From Johnson's remarks in the next to last paragraph, what misinformation do you think Chesterfield may have conveyed in his *World* articles concerning his relationship with Johnson?

### Applying

6. Suppose Lord Chesterfield had assisted Johnson throughout the development of his dictionary. How do you think Johnson would then have responded to the articles in the *World*?

## ANALYZING LITERATURE

### Diction and Style

**Diction** in writing is word choice. **Style** is the overall effect of a writer's choice and arrangement of words. In fact, Lord Chesterfield once called style "the dress of thought." Diction and style are influenced by purpose, audience, and the period in which the writing is done. In his "Letter to Lord Chesterfield," Samuel Johnson intends his diction and style to deliver an unmistakable message.

1. (a) What is the purpose of the letter? (b) What is its audience? (c) How does Johnson feel about the audience?
2. What are ten words that you consider to be especially well chosen for the point Johnson wants to make and the way in which he wants to make it?
3. What are three stylistic devices that Johnson uses effectively? Give one example of each from the letter. (Among the possibilities, consider parallelism, understatement, overstatement, and quotation.)

# *from* The Preface to A Dictionary of the English Language

## Samuel Johnson

It is the fate of those who toil at the lower employments of life, to be rather driven by the fear of evil, than attracted by the prospect of good; to be exposed to censure, without hope of praise; to be disgraced by miscarriage, or punished for neglect, where success would have been without applause, and diligence without reward.

Among these unhappy mortals is the writer of dictionaries; whom mankind have considered, not as the pupil, but the slave of science, the pioneer of literature, doomed only to remove rubbish and clear obstructions from the paths through which learning and genius press forward to conquest and glory, without bestowing a smile on the humble drudge that facilitates their progress. Every other author may aspire to praise; the lexicographer can only hope to escape reproach, and even this negative recompense has been yet granted to very few.

I have, notwithstanding this discouragement, attempted a dictionary of the English language, which, while it was employed in the cultivation of every species of literature, has itself been hitherto neglected; suffered to spread under the direction of chance, into wild exuberance; resigned to the tyranny of time and fashion: and exposed to the corruptions of ignorance and caprices of innovation.

When I took the first survey of my undertaking, I found our speech copious without order and energetic without rule: wherever I turned my view, there was perplexity to be disentangled and confusion to be regulated; choice was to be made out of boundless variety, without any established principle of selection; adulterations were to be detected, without a settled test of purity; and modes of expression to be rejected or received, without the suffrages of any writers of classical reputation or acknowledged authority.

Having therefore no assistance but from general grammar, I applied myself to the perusal of our writers; and noting whatever might be of use to ascertain or illustrate any word or phrase, accumulated in time the materials of a dictionary, which, by degrees, I reduced to method, establishing to myself, in the progress of the work, such rules as experience and analogy suggested to me; experience, which practice and observation were continually increasing; and analogy, which, though in some other words obscure, was evident in others . . .

In hope of giving longevity to that which its own nature forbids to be immortal, I have devoted this book, the labor of years, to the honor of my country, that we may no longer yield the palm of philology, without a contest to the nations of the continent. The chief glory of every people arises from its authors. Whether I shall add anything by my own writings to the reputation of English literature, must be left to time. Much of my life has been lost under the pressures of disease; much has been trifled away; and much has always been spent in provision for the day that was passing over me; but I shall not think my employment useless or ignoble, if by my assistance foreign nations and distant ages gain access to the propagators of knowledge, and understand the teachers of truth; if my labors afford light to the repositories of science, and add celebrity to Bacon, to Hooker, to Milton, and to Boyle.[1]

When I am animated by this wish, I look with pleasure on my book, however defective, and deliver it to the world with the spirit of a man that has endeavored well. That it will immediately become popular, I have not promised to myself. A few wild blunders, and risible absurdities, from which no work of such multiplicity was ever free, may for a time furnish folly with laughter, and harden ignorance into contempt; but useful diligence will at last prevail, and there never can be wanting some who distinguish desert; who will consider that no dictionary of a living tongue ever can be perfect, since, while it is hastening to publication, some words are budding, and some falling away; that a whole life cannot be spent upon syntax and etymology, and that even a whole life would not be sufficient; that he, whose design includes whatever language can express, must often speak of what he does not understand; that a writer will sometimes be hurried by eagerness to the end, and sometimes faint with weariness under a task which Scaliger[2] compares to the labors of the anvil and the mine; that what is obvious is not always known, and what is known is not always present; that sudden fits of inadvertency will surprise vigilance, slight avocations[3] will seduce attention, and casual eclipses of the mind will darken learning; and that the writer shall often in vain trace his memory at the moment of need, for that which yesterday he knew with intuitive readiness, and which will come uncalled into his thoughts tomorrow.

In this work, when it shall be found that much is omitted, let it not be forgotten that much likewise is performed; and though no book was ever spared out of tenderness to the author, and the world is little solicitous to know whence proceed the faults of that which it condemns; yet it may gratify curiosity to inform it, that the *English Dictionary* was written with little assistance of the learned, and without any patronage of the great; not in the soft obscurities of retirement, or under the shelter of academic bowers, but amidst inconvenience and distraction, in sickness and in sorrow. It may repress the triumph of malignant criticism to observe that if our language is not here fully displayed, I have only failed in an attempt which no human powers have hitherto completed. If the lexicons of ancient tongues, now immutably fixed and comprised in a few volumes, be yet, after the toil of successive ages, inadequate and delusive; if the aggregated knowledge and cooperating diligence of the Italian academicians did not secure them from the censure of Beni;[4] if the embodied critics of France, when fifty years had been spent upon their work, were obliged to change its economy[5] and give their second edition another form, I may surely be contented without the praise of perfection, which, if I could obtain, in this gloom of solitude, what would it avail me? I have protracted my work till most of those whom I wished to please have sunk into the grave,[6] and success and miscarriage are empty sounds: I therefore dismiss it with frigid tranquility, having little to fear or hope from censure or from praise.

---

**1. Bacon . . . Boyle:** Writers quoted by Johnson in the *Dictionary.*
**2. Scaliger:** Joseph Justus Scaliger (1540–1609), a scholar who suggested that criminals should be condemned to writing dictionaries.
**3. avocation:** Something that calls one away or distracts one from something.

**4. Beni:** Paolo Beni severely criticized the first Italian dictionary.
**5. economy:** Organization.
**6. sunk . . . grave:** Johnson's wife had died three years earlier.

## THINKING ABOUT THE SELECTION

### Recalling

1. (a) Among what class of workers does Johnson place writers of dictionaries? (b) What is the lexicographer's "negative recompense"?
2. (a) When Johnson "took the first survey," what did he find English speech to be lacking? (b) What gave him his only assistance?
3. To whom or what does Johnson say he has "devoted this book"?
4. Why, according to "The Preface," can "no dictionary of a living tongue ever be perfect"?

### Interpreting

5. (a) What is Johnson's reason for having undertaken the task of writing a dictionary of English? (b) What can you conclude about prior dictionary-making in England?
6. How did Johnson collect the words for his dictionary?
7. Johnson seems to have mixed feelings about his efforts. (a) Do you think he is hopeful or pessimistic (or perhaps both) about the fate of his dictionary? Explain. (b) How have his efforts held up against the test of time?

### Applying

8. What opinion do you think Johnson would have of today's unabridged English dictionaries?

9. How have computers changed the role of dictionary makers?

## THINKING AND WRITING

### Comparing and Contrasting Styles

A **writer's style** is the distinctive way that he or she uses language. No two writers have exactly the same style, although you may notice obvious similarities, especially among writers of the same era. Think about other writers' works that you have read so far in this book. Which writer has a style the most like—or, if you prefer, the least like—that of Samuel Johnson? To answer the question, you will need to consider diction, sentence structure, tone, and point of view. Style is a complex matter; parallels can be difficult. Once you have made your choice, write a short essay in which you compare and contrast the style of Johnson with that of the other writer you have chosen. Take notes before you start to do your first draft. Be specific as to the similarities and differences between the two styles you are comparing. When you revise for your final draft, go back to make sure that your observations about style are accurate and that your quoted excerpts are correct.

*from* # A Dictionary of the English Language

### Samuel Johnson

**athle'tick.** Strong of body; vigorous; lusty; robust.

> Science distinguishes a man of honor from one of those *athletick* brutes, whom underservedly we call heroes. Dryden.

**bang.** A blow; a thump; a stroke: a low word.

> I am a bachelor. That's to say, they are fools that marry; you'll bear me a *bang* for that. Shakespeare, *Julius Caesar.*

**to ba'rbecue.** A term used in the West Indies for dressing a hog whole; which, being split to the backbone, is laid flat upon a large gridiron, raised about two foot above a charcoal fire, with which it is surrounded.

> Oldfield, with more than harpy throat endu'd,
> Cries, send me, gods, a whole hog *barbecu'd.* Pope.

**bu'ffleheaded.** A man with a large head, like a buffalo; dull; stupid; foolish.

**cream.** The unctuous or oily part of milk, which, when it is cold, floats on the top, and is changed by the agitation of the churn into butter; the flower of milk.

**electri'city.** A property in some bodies, whereby, when rubbed so as to grow warm, they draw little bits of paper, or such like substances, to them. Quincy.

> Such was the account given a few years ago of electricity; but the industry of the present age, first excited by the experiments of Gray, has discovered in electricity a multitude of philosophical wonders. Bodies electrified by a sphere of glass, turned nimbly round, not only emit flame, but may be fitted with such a quantity of the electrical vapor as, if discharged at once upon a human body, would endanger life. The force of this vapor has hitherto appeared instantaneous, persons at both ends of a long chain seeming to be struck at once. The philosophers are now endeavoring to intercept the strokes of lightning.

**to fu'rnace.** To throw out as sparks from a furnace. A bad word.

> He *furnaces*
> The thick sighs from him. Shakespeare's *Cymbeline.*

**gang.** A number herding together; a troop; a company; a tribe; a herd. It is seldom used but in contempt or abhorrence.

**ha'tchet-face.** An ugly face; such, I suppose, as might be hewn out of a block by a hatchet.

An ape his own dear image will em-
brace;
An ugly beau adores a *hatchet-face.*
Dryden.

**lifegua'rd.** The guard of a king's person.

**mo'dern.** In Shakespeare, vulgar; mean;
common.
> We have our philosophical persons to
> make *modern* and familiar things su-
> pernatural and causeless. Shakespeare.

**pa'tron.** One who countenances, supports
or protects. Commonly a wretch who supports with insolence, and is paid with
flattery.

**pi'ckle.** Condition; state. A word of contempt and ridicule.
> How cam'st though in this *pickle?*
> Shakespeare.

**plu'mper.** Something worn in the mouth to
swell out the cheeks.
> She dex'trously her *plumpers* draws,
> That serve to fill her hollow jaws. Swift's
> *Miscellanies.*

**shill-I-shall-I.** A corrupt reduplication of
*shall I?* The question of a man hesitating.
To stand *shill-I-shall-I,* is to continue hesitating and procrastinating.
> I am somewhat dainty in making a reso-
> lution, because when I make it, I keep it;
> I don't stand *shill-I-shall-I* then; if I
> say't, I'll do't. Congreve's *Way of the
> World.*

**to sneeze.** To emit wind audibly by the
nose.

**wi'llow.** A tree worn by forlorn lovers.

**to wipe.** To cheat; to defraud.
> The next bordering lords commonly en-
> croach one upon another, as one is
> stronger, or lie still in wait to *wipe* them
> out of their lands. Spenser, *On Ireland.*

**you'ngster, you'nker.** A young person. In
contempt.

**youth.** The part of life succeeding to childhood and adolescence; the time from fourteen to twenty-eight.

# THINKING ABOUT THE SELECTION

## Recalling

1. What is Johnson's definition of (a) *lifeguard* and (b) *modern?*
2. According to Johnson, what is (a) a "tree worn by forlorn lovers"? (b) a person "from fourteen to twenty-eight"?

## Interpreting

3. How does Johnson indicate that a word is a verb?
4. Why do you think the word *electricity* receives such a long definition?
5. Given what you know of Johnson's life, how do you account for his comment about *patron:* "a wretch who supports with insolence, and is paid with flattery"?
6. (a) In a modern dictionary, how is the entry for *shill-I-shall-I* spelled? (b) What inferences do you make about Johnson based on his definition?

## Applying

7. Dictionaries are generally scientific, objective works. Johnson's dictionary, however, is filled with opinions and value judgments. What are three conspicuous examples of the kind of wording that would not appear in a modern dictionary?

# CRITICAL THINKING AND READING

## Making Inferences About Tone

**Tone,** the manner in which a writer communicates, shows the writer's attitude toward his or her subject. It often displays traces of the writer's personality or set of values. When tone seems to be completely straightforward, as in a newspaper report, a reader will tend to accept the writer's message at face value. If tone appears to be ironic or sarcastic, as in a satirical essay, a reader will be on guard for less obvious meanings. Tone can usually be described by one or two adjectives. Review Johnson's definitions of the following words. Then, in a brief paragraph, tell what you can infer from them about Johnson's tone.

1. bang
2. cream
3. to furnace
4. hatchet-face
5. youngster

# THINKING AND WRITING

## Writing Johnsonian Dictionary Entries

Take a look once again at the entries from Johnson's *Dictionary.* Pay close attention to exactly how they are written. Then search through a standard modern dictionary of the English language and find at least five words that might be imaginatively redefined through Johnson's eyes. Finally, write Johnsonian definitions for these words. Follow his style in every way possible, including accenting, diction, and outspokenness.

# JAMES BOSWELL

## (1740–1795)

Not until the twentieth century did James Boswell rise from the fringes of literary history to take his place as perhaps the greatest biographer in English literature. Best known for his biography of Samuel Johnson, Boswell wrote with vigor, training his eye now on the picturesque, now on the grotesque.

Born into an aristocratic family in Edinburgh, Scotland, Boswell was educated at the University of Glasgow, the University of Edinburgh, and the University of Utrecht. Although he received his degree in law and was admitted to the bar in both Scotland and England, Boswell's true passion was literature. His father, a prominent judge, was angered by what he saw as his son's "shallow" values. The extremely sensitive young Boswell interpreted this dissatisfaction as rejection, which led in turn to feelings of inferiority. In an effort to overcome his low self-esteem and at the same time find a suitable father figure, Boswell became a celebrity chaser, seeking out the acquaintanceship of the great men and women of his day. To his credit, many of them became his lifelong friends.

Among these was the writer Samuel Johnson, whom Boswell met while visiting London in 1763. After his acceptance into the prestigious Literary Club, Boswell devoted thirty years to compiling detailed records of Johnson's activities and conversations. From these assorted bits and pieces he distilled his famous work, *The Life of Samuel Johnson,* a precise yet wonderfully intimate portrait of the colorful poet. "The great art of biography," Boswell wrote, "is to keep the person whose life we are giving always in the reader's view." This he does by depicting Johnson variously as "a rhinoceros, in a kind of good humoured growl," and as "blowing out his breath like a whale" following an argument.

In addition to his portrait of Johnson, Boswell wrote numerous personal journals. *An Account of Corsica* (1768) is a sympathetic report of his meeting with the Corsican patriot Paoli and of Corsica's struggle for independence. His *Journal of a Tour in the Hebrides* (1785), published after Johnson's death, tells of the trip he made with the sage to Scotland.

During his lifetime Boswell's popularity was stifled by the biting criticism leveled at his work by the poet Thomas Gray, who caustically noted that "any fool may write a valuable book by chance, if he will only tell what he heard and saw. . . ." It is only since the 1920's, in fact, when a batch of Boswell's private papers were discovered in Malahide Castle, that the reading public has had any real awareness of this often rowdy, often vain young gentleman who gave the world its closest look at Samuel Johnson.

# GUIDE FOR INTERPRETING

## *from* The Life of Samuel Johnson

**Biography.** A biography is an account of a person's life, usually written, though sometimes communicated orally, by another person. Effective biography will represent the subject's life accurately and thoroughly. A good biography, in other words, paints a complete portrait, giving as much space to the subject's flaws and limitations as to his or her most admirable traits. An important milestone in the writing of biography was James Boswell's *The Life of Samuel Johnson.* In his work Boswell displayed an impressive grasp of Johnson's character by presenting countless particular details rather than a distant and generalized view of the man. The art of the biography has continued into the present century with such monumental works as Carl Sandburg's massive work on the life of Abraham Lincoln, which spans several volumes.

Boswell claimed that his biography of Johnson would be the most complete life of a person ever penned, but in a curious way he was proven wrong: The one he wrote about himself is far more complete. When his eighteen volumes of journals were published after his death, he became, according to critic J. W. Krutch, "perhaps the best self-documented man in all history."

Boswell began jotting down occasional notes in 1758. By 1762 he was writing in his journal regularly, a practice he continued until about thirteen months before he died. He published only a few excerpts from his journals during his life. As he did not intend the bulk of the material for public eyes, the *Journals* are free and open expressions of his feelings and clearly reveal his decision to write the truth about himself.

Since he had no intention of publishing his journals, why did he spend so much time on them? As he wrote, "Know thyself, for surely this knowledge is of all the most important." And what better way for a person to gain self-awareness than by "attending to the feelings of his heart and to his external actions. . . . I have therefore determined to keep a daily journal in which I shall set down my various conduct, which will be not only useful but very agreeable."

What do Boswell's accounts of Johnson reveal about himself?

Imagine that you were able to interview a person whom you greatly admire. The person in question may be an athlete, film star, author, or the like. Prepare a list of questions that you think would reveal the individual behind the public mask.

# from The Life of Samuel Johnson

### James Boswell

## Boswell Meets Johnson

## 1763

This is to me a memorable year; for in it I had the happiness to obtain the acquaintance of that extraordinary man whose memoirs I am now writing; an acquaintance which I shall ever esteem as one of the most fortunate circumstances in my life. Though then but two-and-twenty, I had for several years read his works with delight and instruction, and had the highest reverence for their author, which had grown up in my fancy into a kind of mysterious veneration, by figuring to myself a state of solemn elevated abstraction, in which I supposed him to live in the immense metropolis of London. . . .

Mr. Thomas Davies[1] the actor, who then kept a bookseller's shop in Russel Street, Covent Garden, told me that Johnson was very much his friend, and came frequently to his house, where he more than once invited me to meet him; but by some unlucky accident or other he was prevented from coming to us.

At last, on Monday the 16th day of May, when I was sitting in Mr. Davies's back parlor, after having drunk tea with him and Mrs. Davies, Johnson unexpectedly came into the shop; and Mr. Davies having perceived him through the glass door in the room in which we were sitting, advancing towards us—he announced his aweful[2] approach to me, somewhat in the manner of an actor in the part of Horatio, when he addresses Hamlet on the appearance of his father's ghost, "Look, my Lord, it comes,"[3] I found that I had a very perfect idea of Johnson's figure, from the portrait of him painted by Sir Joshua Reynolds[4] soon after he had published his *Dictionary,* in the attitude of sitting in his easy chair in deep meditation, which was the first picture his friend did for him, which Sir Joshua very kindly presented to me, and from which an engraving has been made for this work. Mr. Davies mentioned my name, and respectfully introduced me to him. I was much agitated; and recollecting his prejudice against the Scotch, of which I had heard much, I said to Davies, "Don't tell where I come from." "From Scotland," cried Davies roguishly. "Mr. Johnson," said I, "I do indeed come from Scotland, but I cannot help it." I am willing to flatter myself that I meant this as light pleasantry to sooth and conciliate him, and not as an humiliating abasement at the expense of my country. But however that might be, this speech was somewhat

1. **Thomas Davies:** An English bookseller and unsuccessful actor (1712–1785).

2. **aweful:** Awe-inspiring.
3. **Horatio " . . . it comes":** From Shakespeare's *Hamlet* (Act I, Scene iv).
4. **Sir Joshua Reynolds:** A celebrated portrait painter at the time (1723–1792).

from *The Life of Samuel Johnson* 577

unlucky; for with that quickness of wit for which he was so remarkable, he seized the expression "come from Scotland," which I used in the sense of being of that country; and, as if I had said that I had come away from it, or left, retorted, "That, Sir, I find, is what a very great many of your countrymen cannot help." This stroke stunned me a good deal; and when we had sat down, I felt myself not a little embarrassed, and apprehensive of what might come next. He then addressed himself to Davies: "What do you think of Garrick?[5] He has refused me an order for the play for Miss Williams, because he knows the house will be full, and that an order would be worth three shillings." Eager to take any opening to get into conversation with him, I ventured to say, "O, Sir, I cannot think Mr. Garrick would grudge such a trifle to you." "Sir," said he, with a stern look, "I have known David Garrick longer than you have done: and I know no right you have to talk to me on the subject." Perhaps I deserved this check; for it was rather presumptuous in me, an entire stranger, to express any doubt of the justice of his animadversion upon his old acquaintance and pupil. I now felt myself much mortified, and began to think that the hope which I had long indulged of obtaining his acquaintance was blasted. And, in truth, had not my ardor been uncommonly strong, and my resolution uncommonly persevering, so rough a reception might have deterred me forever from making any further attempts. Fortunately, however, I remained upon the field not wholly discomfited; and was soon rewarded by hearing some of his conversation, of which I preserved the following short minute,[6] without marking the questions and observations by which it was produced.

"People," he remarked, "may be taken in once, who imagine that an author is greater in private life than other men. Uncommon parts require uncommon opportunities for their exertion."

"In barbarous society, superiority of parts is of real consequence. Great strength or great wisdom is of much value to an individual. But in more polished times there are people to do everything for money; and then there are a number of other superiorities, such as those of birth and fortune, and rank, that dissipate men's attention, and leave no extraordinary share of respect for personal and intellectual superiority. This is wisely ordered by Providence, to preserve some equality among mankind."

"Sir, this book (*The Elements of Criticism*,[7] which he had taken up) is a pretty essay, and deserves to be held in some estimation, though much of it is chimerical."

Speaking of one[8] who with more than ordinary boldness attacked public measures and the royal family, he said, "I think he is safe from the law, but he is an abusive scoundrel; and instead of applying to my Lord Chief Justice to punish him, I would send half a dozen footmen and have him well ducked."[9]

"The notion of liberty amuses the people of England, and helps to keep off the *taedium vitae*.[10] When a butcher tells you that his heart bleeds for his country, he has, in fact, no uneasy feeling."

"Sheridan[11] will not succeed at Bath with his oratory. Ridicule has gone down before him, and, I doubt,[12] Derrick[13] is his enemy."

---

**5. Garrick:** David Garrick (1717–1779), a famous actor who had been educated by Johnson. Garrick was also one of the managing partners of the Drury Lane Theater in London.
**6. minute:** Note.

**7. *Elements of Criticism*:** One of the works of Scottish philosophical writer Henry Home (1696–1782).
**8. one:** John Wilkes (1727–1797), an English political agitator.
**9. ducked:** Tied to a chair at the end of a plank and plunged into water.
**10. *taedium vitae*** (tī′dē əm vē′ tī): Boredom.
**11. Sheridan:** Thomas Sheridan (1719–1788), an Irish actor and author. At the time, Sheridan was reading lectures at the Oratory at Bath.
**12. doubt:** Fear.
**13. Derrick:** The Master of Ceremonies of the Oratory at Bath.

"Derrick may do very well, as long as he can outrun his character; but the moment his character gets up with him, it is all over."

It is, however, but just to record, that some years afterwards, when I reminded him of this sarcasm, he said, "Well, but Derrick has now got a character that he need not run away from."

I was highly pleased with the extraordinary vigor of his conversation, and regretted that I was drawn away from it by an engagement at another place. I had, for a part of the evening, been left alone with him, and had ventured to make an observation now and then, which he received very civilly; so that I was satisfied that though there was a roughness in his manner, there was no ill nature in his disposition. Davies followed me to the door, and when I complained to him a little of the hard blows which the great man had given me he kindly took upon him to console me by saying, "Don't be uneasy. I can see he likes you very well."

## Johnson's Character

The character of Samuel Johnson has, I trust, been so developed in the course of this work, that they who have honored it with a perusal, may be considered as well acquainted with him. As, however, it may be expected that I should collect into one view the capital and distinguishing features of this extraordinary man, I shall endeavor to acquit myself of that part of my biographical undertaking, however difficult it may be to do that which many of my readers will do better for themselves.

His figure was large and well formed, and his countenance of the cast of an ancient statue; yet his appearance was rendered strange and somewhat uncouth by convulsive cramps, by the scars of that distemper[14] which it was once imagined the royal touch could cure,[15] and by a slovenly mode of dress. He had the use only of one eye; yet so much does mind govern and even supply the deficiency of organs, that his visual perceptions, as far as they extended, were uncommonly quick and accurate. So morbid was his temperament, that he never knew the natural joy of a free and vigorous use of his limbs: when he walked, it was like the struggling gait of one in fetters; when he rode, he had no command or direction of his horse, but was carried as if in a balloon. That with his constitution and habits of life he should have lived seventy-five years, is a proof that an inherent *vivida vis*[16] is a powerful preservative of the human frame.

Man is, in general, made up of contradictory qualities; and these will ever show themselves in strange succession, where a consistency in appearance at least, if not in reality, has not been attained by long habits of philosophical discipline. In proportion to the native vigor of the mind, the contradictory qualities will be the more prominent, and more difficult to be adjusted; and, therefore, we are not to wonder that Johnson exhibited an eminent example of this remark which I have made upon human nature. At different times, he seemed a different man, in some respects; not, however, in any great or essential article, upon which he had fully employed his mind, and settled certain principles of duty, but only in his manners and in the display of argument and fancy in his talk. He was prone to superstition, but not to credulity. Though his imagination might incline him to a belief of the marvelous and the mysterious, his vigorous reason examined the evidence with jealousy.[17] He was a sincere and zealous Christian, of high Church of England and monarchical princi-

---

14. **distemper** *n*.: Scrofula, a type of tuberculosis that causes swelling and scarring of the neck.

15. **royal touch . . . cure:** It was at one time believed that the touch of an English monarch had the power to heal. As a child Johnson was taken to Queene Anne to receive her touch in the hope that it would cure him.
16. *vivida vis:* Lively force.
17. **jealousy:** Suspicion.

ples, which he would not tamely suffer to be questioned; and had, perhaps, at an early period, narrowed his mind somewhat too much, both as to religion and politics. His being impressed with the danger of extreme latitude in either, though he was of a very independent spirit, occasioned his appearing somewhat unfavorable to the prevalence of that noble freedom of sentiment which is the best possession of man. Nor can it be denied, that he had many prejudices; which, however, frequently suggested many of his pointed sayings that rather show a playfulness of fancy than any settled malignity. He was steady and inflexible in maintaining the obligations of religion and morality; both from a regard for the order of society, and from a veneration for the Great Source of all order; correct, nay, stern in his taste; hard to please, and easily offended; impetuous and irritable in his temper, but of a most humane and benevolent heart, which showed itself not only in a most liberal charity, as far as his circumstances would allow, but in a thousand instances of active benevolence. He was afflicted with a bodily disease, which made him often restless and fretful; and with a constitutional melancholy, the clouds of which darkened the brightness of his fancy, and gave a gloomy cast to his whole course of thinking: we, therefore, ought not to wonder at his sallies of impatience and passion at any time; especially when provoked by obtrusive ignorance, or presuming petulance; and allowance must be made for his uttering hasty and satirical sallies even against his best friends. And, surely, when it is considered, that, "amidst sickness and sorrow," he exerted his faculties in so many works for the benefit of mankind, and particularly that he achieved the great and admirable Dictionary of our language, we must be astonished at his resolution. The solemn text, "of him to whom much is given, much will be required," seems to have been ever present to his mind, in a rigorous sense, and to have made him dissatisfied with his labors and

acts of goodness, however comparatively great; so that the unavoidable consciousness of his superiority was, in that respect, a cause of disquiet. He suffered so much from this, and from the gloom which perpetually haunted him and made solitude frightful, that it may be said of him, "If in this life only he had hope, he was of all men most miserable."[18] He loved praise, when it was brought to him; but was too proud to seek for it. He was somewhat susceptible of flattery. As he was general and unconfined in his studies, he cannot be considered as master of any one particular science; but he had accumulated a vast and various collection of learning and knowledge, which was so arranged in his mind, as to be ever in readiness to be brought forth. But his superiority over other learned men consisted chiefly in what may be called the art of thinking, the art of using his mind; a certain continual power of seizing the useful substance of all that he knew and exhibiting it in a clear and forcible manner; so that knowledge, which we often see to be no better than lumber[19] in men of dull understanding, was, in him, true, evident, and actual wisdom. His moral precepts are practical; for they are drawn from an intimate acquaintance with human nature. His maxims carry conviction; for they are founded on the basis of common sense, and a very attentive and minute survey of real life. His mind was so full of imagery, that he might have been perpetually a poet; yet it is remarkable, that, however rich his prose is in this respect, his poetical pieces, in general, have not much of that splendor, but are rather distinguished by strong sentiment and acute observation, conveyed in harmonious and energetic verse, particularly in heroic couplets. Though usually grave, and even aweful, in his deportment, he possessed uncommon and peculiar powers of wit and humor; he frequently indulged himself in colloquial pleasantry; and the hearti-

---

**18. "If . . . miserable":** From I Corinthians 15:19.
**19. lumber:** Rubbish.

est merriment was often enjoyed in his company; with this great advantage, that as it was entirely free from any poisonous tincture of vice or impiety, it was salutary to those who shared in it. He had accustomed himself to such accuracy in his common conversation, that he at all times expressed his thoughts with great force, and an elegant choice of language, the effect of which was aided by his having a loud voice, and a slow deliberate utterance. In him were united a most logical head with a most fertile imagination, which gave him an extraordinary advantage in arguing: for he could reason close or wide, as he saw best for the moment. Exulting in his intellectual strength and dexterity, he could, when he pleased, be the greatest sophist[20] that ever contended in the lists of declamation; and, from a spirit of contradiction and a delight in showing his powers, he would often maintain the wrong side with equal warmth and ingenuity; so that, when there was an audience, his real opinions could seldom be gathered from his talk; though when he was in company with a single friend, he would discuss a subject with genuine fairness: but he was too conscientious to make error permanent and pernicious, by deliberately writing it; and, in all his numerous works, he earnestly inculcated what appeared to him to be the truth; his piety being constant, and the ruling principle of all his conduct.

Such was Samuel Johnson, a man whose talents, acquirements, and virtues, were so extraordinary, that the more his character is considered the more he will be regarded by the present age, and by posterity, with admiration and reverence.

---

**20. sophist** (säf′ ist) *n.*: One who makes misleading arguments.

## THINKING ABOUT THE SELECTION

### Recalling

1. What aspects of Johnson's appearance prompt Boswell to describe him as "strange and somewhat uncouth"?
2. (a) What, according to the selection, was Johnson's position on superstition? (b) On religion? (c) On praise? (d) On flattery?

### Interpreting

3. (a) What details of Johnson's personality described in this excerpt explain his sarcastic remark about Scotland in "Boswell Meets Johnson"? (b) His desire to obtain a free theater ticket for a friend? (c) His harsh reply to Boswell's comment on Garrick?
4. What do you learn about Boswell himself from this passage? Support your comments with evidence.

### Applying

5. (a) Which of the observations presented in this excerpt do you think apply more or less to most people? (b) Do you think the inclusion of these details detracts from the integrity of Boswell's biography? Explain your answer.
6. (a) What similarities do you detect between the lifestyles and habits of celebrities of the eighteenth century and those of our own age? (b) What differences do you detect?

## ANALYZING LITERATURE

### Understanding Biography

A **biography** is a history of a person told or written by others. A good biography meets several criteria. It presents (1) the subject in an impartial light; (2) a complete and unified picture of the subject; (3) the subject against the backdrop of the times in which he or she lived. Based on the excerpt from Boswell's The Life of Samuel Johnson, state how well you think the work meets these criteria. In making your assessment, consider the following questions.

1. Can Boswell's statement that he "was much agitated" upon meeting Johnson be taken as an admission that he was not in a frame of mind to report facts impartially? Why?
2. On page 578, Boswell notes that he preserved Johnson's observations "without marking the questions and observations" that led up to them. Does this suggest a lack of completeness? Why?

## CRITICAL THINKING AND READING

### Recognizing Subjective Information

**Subjective** information is information colored by a person's own attitudes and feelings. Objective information is information that preserves some widely held truth. The statement "I like to eat chicken" is a piece of subjective information. The statement "Chicken is a source of protein" is a piece of objective information. Biography, if it is interesting, will usually contain a mixture of subjective and objective statements.

Bearing in mind what you read about Boswell in the biographical sketch of him on page 574, which of the details presented in this excerpt do you suspect of being the most subjective? Explain your answer.

## THINKING AND WRITING

### Writing from Johnson's Point of View

Write an account of the meeting described in this excerpt from Samuel Johnson's point of view. Before beginning, review Boswell's quotations of Johnson in order to help you form an impression of the older man's prose style and general attitude toward life. Feel free to add original details that may have escaped Boswell's attention.

# Pre-Romantic Poetry

HAYMAKERS, 1785
*George Stubbs*
The Granger Collection

# THOMAS GRAY

## (1716–1771)

Although Thomas Gray produced precious little poetry during his lifetime, his scant output was more a result of his perfectionism than it was of any lack of ideas. Gray was a scholar, with interests ranging from literature to art to science and beyond. Had he lived in an era more compatible with the romantic yearnings of his soul, he might, as the poet Matthew Arnold suggested, have been capable of far greater things.

Gray was born in the Cornhill section of London. Gray himself suffered from convulsions, a condition that forced his mother on at least one occasion to open a vein in his head to relieve pressure on his brain. He was educated at Eton and Cambridge and, after completing his studies, traveled through Europe with his friend Horace Walpole.

At the end of three years, Gray returned to England and lived for a time with his mother and sister in the village of Stoke Poges. It was in this sleepy hamlet during the summer of 1742 that he wrote his first important poems—"On the Spring," "On a Distant Prospect of Eton College," and "Hymn to Adversity." It was also around this time that Gray penned his most famous poetic work, "Elegy Written in a Country Churchyard." A copy of the elegy that he sent to Walpole accidentally fell into the hands of a dishonest editor. Ultimately it was retrieved, though only after a great struggle, which adds a touch of irony to Gray's having refused to accept payment for the poem when at last it was published.

After reaching the age of thirty, Gray lived an increasingly quiet country life, becoming something of a hermit. A confirmed bachelor, he busied himself with books and experimented with new poetic forms, while conducting private studies in classical literature at Cambridge. His work of this period, which includes the odes "The Bard" (1757) and "The Descent of Odin" (1761), reflects his love of Celtic and Norse mythology and his interest in history and language. In 1771 while planning a visit to a friend in Switzerland, the poet suffered a violent attack of gout and died on July 30. Seven years after his death, a monument honoring him was erected in Westminster Abbey.

Although Gray was a less than energetic poet, the small body of works that he left behind is notable for its juxtaposing of established forms and novel sentiments. His "Elegy Written in a Country Churchyard," in particular, skillfully combines the neoclassical style of his own century with the Romantic ideals of the next one.

# GUIDE FOR INTERPRETING

## Literary Forms

## Elegy Written in a Country Churchyard

**Elegy.** An elegy is a lyric poem or musical composition that laments a death. The form, which dates back to ancient Greece and Rome, flourished during the European Renaissance that spanned the fourteenth through the sixteenth centuries. Although an elegy usually mourns the death of an individual, it may also address the ravages of time or may function as a meditation on the nature of loss. The elegy, while conforming to no rigid structural guidelines, often opens with an expression of grief and moves gradually toward a philosophical acceptance of the loss. Thomas Gray's "Elegy Written in a Country Churchyard," inspired by the death of the poet's close friend Richard West, marks one of three highpoints of the elegiac form in English literature, the other being Milton's "Lycidas" and Tennyson's *In Memoriam*.

## Writing

Gray's elegy ends with an epitaph, a poetic inscription intended to appear on a gravestone. Often an epitaph mentions a property or trait of the deceased for which he or she might best be remembered. Write an epitaph for yourself or for a friend. Focus, using as few words as possible, on the individual's most memorable quality.

## Primary Source

Whether Gray wrote his own epitaph has not been recorded, but several other writers of the time did leave behind the poems they wanted inscribed on their gravestones. Alexander Pope, for example, left the following lines for his gravestone:

> Under this marble, or under the sill,
> Or under this turf, or e'en what they will;
> Whatever an heir, or a friend in his stead,
> Or any good creature shall lay o'er my head;
> Lies he who ne'er car'd, and still cares not a pin,
> What they said, or may say of the mortal within.
> But who living and dying, serene still and free,
> Trusts in God, that as well as he was, he shall be.

Several years later, Coleridge penned this epitaph for himself:

> Here sleeps at length poor Col., and without screaming;
> Who died as he lived, a-dreaming:
> Shot dead, while sleeping, by the gout within—
> All alone and unknown, at Edinbro' in an inn.

As you read, look for the differences between the epitaph that ends Gray's elegy and the ones Pope and Coleridge wrote for themselves.

# Elegy Written in a Country Churchyard

Thomas Gray

The curfew tolls the knell of parting day,
    The lowing herd winds slowly o'er the lea,[1]
The plowman homeward plods his weary way,
    And leaves the world to darkness and to me.

5  Now fades the glimmering landscape on the sight,
    And all the air a solemn stillness holds,
Save where the beetle wheels his droning flight,
    And drowsy tinklings lull the distant folds;

Save that from yonder ivy-mantled tower,
10    The moping owl does to the moon complain
Of such as, wandering near her secret bower,
    Molest her ancient solitary reign.

Beneath those rugged elms, that yew tree's shade,
    Where heaves the turf in many a moldering heap,
15  Each in his narrow cell forever laid,
    The rude[2] forefathers of the hamlet sleep.

The breezy call of incense-breathing morn,
    The swallow twittering from the straw-built shed,
The cock's shrill clarion, or the echoing horn,[3]
20    No more shall rouse them from their lowly bed.

For them no more the blazing hearth shall burn,
    Or busy housewife ply her evening care;
No children run to lisp their sire's return,
    Or climb his knees the envied kiss to share.

---

**1. lea:** Meadow.
**2. rude:** Uneducated.
**3. horn:** The hunter's horn.

25   Oft did the harvest to their sickle yield,
       Their furrow oft the stubborn glebe[4] has broke;
  How jocund did they drive their team afield!
       How bowed the woods beneath their sturdy stroke!

  Let not Ambition mock their useful toil,
30        Their homely joys, and destiny obscure;
  Nor Grandeur hear with a disdainful smile
       The short and simple annals of the poor.

  The boast of heraldry,[5] the pomp of power,
       And all that beauty, all that wealth e'er gave,
35   Awaits alike the inevitable hour.
       The paths of glory lead but to the grave.

---

**4. glebe:** Soil.
**5. heraldry:** Noble descent.

Nor you, ye proud, impute to these the fault,
    If memory o'er their tomb no trophies[6] raise,
Where through the long-drawn aisle and fretted vault[7]
40    The pealing anthem swells the note of praise.

Can storied urn,[8] or animated[9] bust,
    Back to its mansion call the fleeting breath?
Can honor's voice provoke[10] the silent dust,
    Or Flattery soothe the dull cold ear of Death?

45 Perhaps in this neglected spot is laid
    Some heart once pregnant with celestial fire;
Hands, that the rod of empire might have swayed,
    Or waked to ecstasy the living lyre.

But Knowledge to their eyes her ample page
50    Rich with the spoils of time did ne'er unroll;
Chill Penury repressed their noble rage,
    And froze the genial current of the soul.

Full many a gem of purest ray serene
    The dark unfathomed caves of ocean bear:
55 Full many a flower is born to blush unseen,
    And waste its sweetness on the desert air.

Some village Hampden,[11] that, with dauntless breast,
    The little tyrant of his fields withstood,
Some mute inglorious Milton[12] here may rest,
60    Some Cromwell[13] guiltless of his country's blood.

The applause of listening senates to command,
    The threats of pain and ruin to despise,
To scatter plenty o'er a smiling land,
    And read their history in a nation's eyes,

65 Their lot forbade: nor circumscribed alone
    Their growing virtues, but their crimes confined
Forbade to wade through slaughter to a throne,
    And shut the gates of mercy on mankind,

---

**6. trophies:** Symbolic figures or pictures depicting the achievements of the dead man.
   **7. fretted vault:** A church ceiling decorated with intersecting lines.
   **8. storied urn:** A funeral urn with an epitaph inscribed on it.
   **9. animated:** Lifelike.
**10. provoke:** Call forth.
**11. Hampden:** John Hampden (1594–1643), an English statesman who defied King Charles I by resisting the king's efforts to revive the obsolete tax of ship-money without the authority of Parliament.
**12. Milton:** English poet, John Milton (1608–1674).
**13. Cromwell:** Oliver Cromwell (1599–1658), English revolutionary leader and Lord Protector of the Commonwealth from 1653 to 1658.

The struggling pangs of conscious truth to hide,
70      To quench the blushes of ingenuous shame,
Or heap the shrine of Luxury and Pride
        With incense kindled at the Muse's flame.

Far from the madding[14] crowd's ignoble strife,
        Their sober wishes never learned to stray;
75  Along the cool sequestered vale of life
        They kept the noiseless tenor of their way.

Yet even these bones from insult to protect
        Some frail memorial still erected nigh,
With uncouth rhymes and shapeless sculpture decked,[15]
80      Implores the passing tribute of a sigh.

Their name, their years, spelt by the unlettered Muse,[16]
        The place of fame and elegy supply:
And many a holy text around she strews,
        That teach the rustic moralist to die.

85  For who, to dumb Forgetfulness a prey,
        This pleasing anxious being e'er resigned,
Left the warm precincts of the cheerful day,
        Nor cast one longing lingering look behind?

On some fond breast the parting soul relies,
90      Some pious drops[17] the closing eye requires;
Even from the tomb the voice of Nature cries,
        Even in our ashes live their wonted fires.

For thee,[18] who, mindful of the unhonored dead,
        Dost in these lines their artless tale relate;
95  If chance, by lonely contemplation led,
        Some kindred spirit shall enquire thy fate,

Haply[19] some hoary-headed[20] swain may say,
        "Oft have we seen him at the peep of dawn
Brushing with hasty steps the dews away,
100     To meet the sun upon the upland lawn.

---

**14. madding:** Frenzied.
**15. Some . . . decked:** Contrasts with "the storied urn[s] or animated bust[s]" (line 41) inside the church.
**16. the unlettered Muse:** The uneducated gravestone carver.
**17. drops:** Tears.
**18. thee:** Grav himself.
**19. haply:** Perhaps.
**20. hoary-headed:** White-haired.

"There at the foot of yonder nodding beech,
　　That wreathes its old fantastic roots so high,
His listless length at noontide would he stretch,
　　And pore upon the brook that babbles by.

105 "Hard by yon wood, now smiling as in scorn,
　　Muttering his wayward fancies he would rove;
Now drooping, woeful wan, like one forlorn,
　　Or crazed with care, or crossed in hopeless love.

"One morn I missed him on the customed hill,
110　　Along the heath, and near his favorite tree;
Another came; nor yet beside the rill,[21]
　　Nor up the lawn, nor at the wood was he;

"The next, with dirges due in sad array
　　Slow through the churchway path we saw him borne.
115 Approach and read (for thou canst read) the lay
　　Graved on the stone beneath yon aged thorn."[22]


**The Epitaph**

*Here rests his head upon the lap of Earth*
　　*A youth, to Fortune and to Fame unknown.*
*Fair Science[23] frowned not on his humble birth,*
120　　*And melancholy marked him for her own.*

*Large was his bounty, and his soul sincere,*
　　*Heaven did a recompense as largely send:*
*He gave to misery (all he had) a tear,*
　　*He gained from Heaven ('twas all he wished) a friend.*

125 *No farther seek his merits to disclose,*
　　*Or draw his frailties from their dread abode*
*(There they alike in trembling hope repose),*
　　*The bosom of his Father and his God.*

---

**21. rill:** Brook.
**22. thorn:** Hawthorn tree.
**23. Science:** Learning.

## THINKING ABOUT THE SELECTION
### Recalling

1. The first four stanzas establish the setting of the poem. (a) Where is the speaker? (b) What time of day is it?
2. According to lines 21–25, what pleasure will these "rude forefathers" no longer partake of?
3. What sorts of lives does the speaker speculate, in lines 57–60, that these people might have led under other circumstances?
4. To whom is "The Epitaph" in the last three stanzas dedicated?

### Interpreting

5. (a) What do you think is meant by "the inevitable hour" in line 35? (b) By "its mansion" in line 42?
6. (a) How would you summarize the sentiment expressed in lines 53–56? (b) In lines 77–92?

### Applying

7. (a) Tell who or what the poet is elegizing. (b) State whether you share his sense of loss, giving reasons for your answer.

## ANALYZING LITERATURE
### Understanding an Elegy

An **elegy** is a lyric poem that expresses mourning. Usually the object of this mourning is the death of an individual, though an elegy can also grieve the toll that time's passage takes on youth or beauty. Typically the elegy begins solemnly, with the poet's expression of sadness over his or her loss, and ends with an insight that enables the poet to cope with this loss.

1. (a) Whom does the poet grieve in "Elegy Written in a Country Churchyard"? (b) What do these people seem to represent to the poet? (c) What words express the poet's sadness?
2. (a) Does the poet come to accept his loss by the end of the poem? Explain your answer. (b) What insight helps him to reach this acceptance? (c) What ideas or thoughts bridge his grief and his acceptance?

## CRITICAL THINKING AND READING
### Evaluating Inverted Sentences

In English the most common sentence structure is subject-verb-object. That is, the "doer" of the action is usually named first, the word specifying the action appears second, and the recipient of the action comes last. In poetry the parts of the sentence are sometimes **inverted,** or reversed, to emphasize a particular idea. In line 90, for example, the poet places the object *some pious drops* before both the subject and verb of the sentence, to focus the reader's attention on the idea of tears. Locate the following lines, and identify the order of the sentence parts. Then tell what idea is being stressed.

1. Line 5
2. Lines 13–16
3. Lines 49–50
4. Lines 81–82

## UNDERSTANDING LANGUAGE
### Appreciating Vivid Verbs

The words a poet uses can help convey the poem's mood and can influence the feelings the poem arouses in the reader. In the opening stanzas of Gray's "Elegy," the mood is one of quiet solemnity. To carry this feeling across to the reader, the poet chooses **vivid,** or highly descriptive, verbs. Notice, for instance, Gray's use of the verb *plod* in line 3, to suggest slow and weary movement. Imagine how bland the line would have seemed if the poet had instead chosen the verb *goes*.

Find five vivid verbs in this elegy and explain the effect of each.

## THINKING AND WRITING
### Writing an Elegy

Using the epitaph you created for the Writing activity on page 585 as a starting point, write an elegy. Imitate as many of the features of Gray's "Elegy" as you can, including inverted sentence structure and vivid verbs. Remember to begin your elegy with an expression of your grief and to end it with a statement of acceptance.

# GUIDE FOR INTERPRETING

## Woman

**Oliver Goldsmith** (1728–1774) was generally regarded as an essayist of the highest standing. Much of what is known of the first half of Goldsmith's life is known through his own accounts. In 1766, four years after the publication of an important collection of essays titled *The Citizen of the World,* he produced his only novel, *The Vicar of Wakefield.* Later, Goldsmith turned to poetry and enjoyed both critical and financial success

Goldsmith's early years gave no indication of his future success. As a child, he was badly scarred by smallpox and was ill-suited for sports. He was an unmotivated student whom others judged lazy and thick. Nonetheless, his clergyman father enrolled him in Trinity College, Dublin, as a scholarship student. Although he received his degree in 1749, he still had no clear idea of what path he wished to pursue. A relative paid his way to medical college in Scotland, but he found the study not to his liking and instead roamed through Europe for several years. After somehow procuring a medical degree, he returned to England when he was twenty-eight years old but was unable to make a living as a doctor. He ended up trying his hand at writing. He had found his niche.

His writings are remarkable for their quality and variety, including such brilliant comedies as the play *She Stoops to Conquer* and the elegant poem "The Deserted Village."

**Writer's Technique**

**Poetic Structure.** Poetic structure is the pattern or formal design of a poem. Several factors determine a poem's structure: number of stressed syllables per line, line length, and rhyme scheme. Also grouped under the heading of structure are such considerations as the size and shape of the stanzas and the relationship among ideas, images, and sound devices used by the poet. Generally poems are categorized, in terms of their structure, as either closed-pattern or open-pattern. Closed-pattern poems are those that exhibit some or all of the properties of a well-defined traditional poetic form; sonnets and ballads are two examples of closed-pattern poems. Open-pattern poems exhibit no such properties. Oliver Goldsmith's "Woman" is an example of an open-pattern poem.

**Writing**

Imagine that you write an advice column for a local newspaper. You have received a letter from a young man or woman who is heartbroken. Write a response in the form of a poem offering original suggestions that will help the person get through this difficult period.

# Woman

## Oliver Goldsmith

When lovely woman stoops to folly,
    And finds too late that men betray,
What charm can soothe her melancholy?
    What art can wash her tears away?

5   The only art her guilt to cover,
    To hide her shame from every eye,
To give repentance to her lover,
    And wring his bosom is—to die.

## THINKING ABOUT THE SELECTION

### Recalling

1. What has made the woman in the poem melancholy?
2. (a) What question does the speaker ask? (b) What answer does he give?

### Interpreting

3. Judging from its usage in lines 4 and 5, what do you think is meant by the term "art"?
4. Do you think the poet is being serious in his solution for melancholy of the sort described in the poem? Explain why you feel as you do?

### Applying

5. What does the poet's addressing this poem exclusively to women suggest about the values of his era?

## ANALYZING LITERATURE

### Understanding Poetic Structure

**Poetic structure** is the shape or general pattern of a poem. The elements that determine a poem's structure include the number of beats per line, line length, rhyme scheme, and stanza size. Depending on their structure, poems fall into either the closed-pattern or open-pattern category. Closed-pattern poems are those that follow a well-defined set of structural rules. The sonnet, which is required among other things to have exactly fourteen lines, is an example of a closed-pattern poetic form. Open-pattern poems, by contrast, are free of such rigid constraints. The structure a poet chooses for a particular poem is often a function of the poem's content and theme.

1. (a) What aspects of the content and theme in "Woman" do you think led the poet to choose an open pattern for the poem? (b) Why do you think he wrote his poem in a total of two four-line stanzas?
2. What effect is created by the short, almost abrupt, lines?
3. What other factors can you think of that may have led to the poet's use of rhyming lines and a regular number of stressed syllables? Support your answer.

# ROBERT BURNS

## 1759–1796

No other name is more synonymous with the title "The voice of Scotland" than that of the poet Robert Burns. A farmer and a farmer's son, Burns was born at Alloway, in Ayrshire, and spent his early years in the two-room clay cottage his father had built. Although poverty prevented Burns from receiving a formal education, with his father's encouragement he read widely, studying the Bible, Shakespeare, and Alexander Pope on his own. His mother, though herself illiterate, instilled in him a love of Scottish folk songs, legends, and proverbs.

In 1786 Burns published his first collection of poems at a small local press. Although the collection, which included "To a Mouse," was successful, Burns only first came to the attention of the public at large the following year when a fuller collection, *Poems: Chiefly in Scottish,* was published at Edinburgh. He was invited to the Scottish capital, where he was swept into the social scene, if only as something of a rustic curiosity. He left Edinburgh in 1788, to explore the English border region and the Highlands.

Later that year he married Jean Armour, his sweetheart of many years, and returned to the farm to work the land. The soil proved unproductive, however, and so to supplement his income he took a position with the Excise Service—Scotland's department of taxation. All the while he continued to refine his poetic style, turning out some of his finest verses. At the outbreak of the French Revolution, he became an outspoken supporter of the republican cause, a move that threatened his job and alienated many of his friends. His spirits low and his health taxed by a weak heart he had had since childhood, Burns contracted a fever from which he never recovered. Thousands of people from all social levels followed his coffin to the grave, and he was acclaimed the national poet of Scotland.

Burns's numerous adventures produced many lyrics that figure among the most natural and spontaneous the English language has produced. His poems, written for the most part in dialect, are characterized by innocence, honesty, and simplicity. First and last a people's poet, Burns crafted poetic "melodies" that speak to "the sons and daughters of labor and poverty"—and for them. Though some of the poet's work had its origins in folk tunes, "it is not," as James Douglas wrote, "easy to tell where the vernacular ends and the personal magic begins."

# GUIDE FOR INTERPRETING

## To a Mouse; To a Louse; Afton Water; John Anderson, My Jo

**Writer's Technique**

**Dialect.** Dialect is the language, and particularly the speech habits, of a particular social class, region, or group. A dialect may vary from the standard form of a language in grammar, in pronunciation, and in the use of certain expressions. In literature it can serve to establish character, tone, and setting. The use of dialect by a writer or poet can also add to the immediacy and familiarity of a piece of literature.

In the eighteenth century, the belief was widespread among writers that only formal diction was acceptable in poetry. Rules were thus developed concerning the subjects and styles that were thought to be appropriate for poetry. Common life and colloquial language were almost always excluded from the poet's domain. Robert Burns rebelled against these rules, both with his use of Scottish dialect and his celebration of the rural and working life. Like so many poets of the age that ushered in the Romanticism of the next generation, Burns strived to capture in words the language and experiences of the human heart.

**Writing**

Write an account titled A Day in the Life of a _____, filling in the blank with one of the following: dog, cat, bird, squirrel, goldfish, or gerbil. Try to get inside the mind of the subject of your narrative, imagining the triumphs, defeats, fears, and hopes your creature experiences on a typical day.

**Primary Source**

As with many writers, Burns kept a Commonplace Book, a place to record scraps of lyrics, topics for poetry, and various thoughts and ideas on numerous different topics. A number of his entries reveal that he had long considered using dialect and adapting legendary Scotch songs in his poetry. In one entry, he remarked:

> There is a degree of wild irregularity in many of the compositions & Fragments which are daily sung to them by my compeers, the common people—a certain happy arrangement of old Scotch syllables, & yet, very frequently, nothing, not even like rhyme, or sameness of jingle at the ends of the lines. —This has made me sometimes imagine that perhaps, it might be possible for a Scotch Poet, with a nice, judicious ear, to set compositions to many of our favorite airs, particularly the class of them mentioned above, independent of rhyme altogether.—

# To a Mouse

On Turning Her up in Her Nest with
the Plow, November, 1785

Robert Burns

Wee, sleekit,[1] cow'rin', tim'rous beastie,
O, what a panic's in thy breastie!
Thou need na start awa sae hasty,
    Wi' bickering brattle![2]
5  I wad be laith[3] to rin an' chase thee
    Wi' murd'ring pattle![4]

---

1. **sleekit:** Sleek.
2. **Wi' . . . brattle:** In sudden flight.
3. **wad be laith:** Would be loath.
4. **pattle:** Paddle for cleaning a plow.

I'm truly sorry man's dominion
Has broken Nature's social union,
An' justifies that ill opinion,
10         Which makes thee startle,
At me, thy poor, earth-born companion,
            An' fellow-mortal!

I doubt na, whyles,[5] but thou may thieve;
What then? poor beastie, thou maun[6] live!
15   A daimen icker in a thrave[7]
            'S a sma' request:
I'll get a blessin' wi' the lave,[8]
            And never miss't!

Thy wee bit housie, too, in ruin!
20   Its silly wa's[9] the win's are strewin'!
An' naething, now, to big[10] a new ane,
            O' foggage[11] green!
An' bleak December's winds ensuin',
            Baith snell[12] an keen!

25   Thou saw the fields laid bare and waste,
An' weary winter comin' fast,
An' cozie here, beneath the blast,
            Thou thought to dwell,
Till crash! the cruel coulter[13] past
30         Out through thy cell.

That wee bit heap o' leaves an' stibble,
Has cost thee mony a weary nibble!
Now thou's turned out, for a' thy trouble,
            But[14] house or hald,[15]
35   To thole[16] the winter's sleety dribble,
            An' cranreuch[17] cauld!

---

5. **whyles:** At times.
6. **maun:** Must.
7. **A . . . thrave:** An occasional ear of grain in a bundle.
8. **lave:** Rest.
9. **silly wa's:** Feeble walls.
10. **big:** Build.
11. **foggage:** Rough grass.
12. **snell:** Sharp.
13. **coulter:** Plow blade.
14. **But:** Without.
15. **hald:** Property.
16. **thole:** Withstand.
17. **cranreuch** (krən' rəkh): Frost.

But, Mousie, thou art no thy lane,[18]
In proving foresight may be vain:
The best laid schemes o' mice an' men
    Gang aft a-gley,[19]
40
An' lea'e us nought but grief an' pain,
    For promised joy.

Still thou art blest, compared wi' me!
The present only toucheth thee:
45
But, och! I backward cast my e'e
    On prospects drear!
An' forward, though I canna see,
    I guess an' fear!

---

**18. no thy lane:** Not alone.
**19. Gang aft a-gley:** Go often awry.

## THINKING ABOUT THE SELECTION

### Recalling

1. What is the setting of the poem?
2. For what reason does the speaker apologize to the mouse?
3. Why is the mouse unable to build a new home?
4. Why does the speaker say that, compared with him, the mouse is blessed?

### Interpreting

5. To what "social union" do you think the speaker is referring in line 7?
6. What does the sentiment in lines 13–14 suggest about the speaker's own moral code?
7. (a) What famous line in the poem carries the poem's theme? (b) How might you state this theme in your own words?

### Applying

8. What value do you place on foresight? Explain your answer.

## ANALYZING LITERATURE

### Recognizing Dialect

**Dialect** is a collection of speech habits and patterns belonging to a specific group, class, or region. Often, a dialect will possess its own unique grammar, pronunciation, and vocabulary. One of the first poets to write using the Scottish dialect of English, Robert Burns placed himself in direct opposition to the poetic standards of the eighteenth century.

1. (a) What does the use of dialect in this poem suggest about the speaker's social station? (b) How does it help carry across the poem's theme?
2. Like the standard language, dialects of a language follow rules. Find at least two examples in the poem of each of the following pronunciation rules for Scottish English. (a) Final consonants are dropped. (b) The letter *o* is replaced by either *ae* or *a*.
3. How would the effect of this poem have been different if it had been written in standard English?

# To a Louse

## On Seeing One on a Lady's Bonnet at Church

### Robert Burns

Ha! whare ye gaun, ye crowlin' ferlie![1]
Your impudence protects you sairly:[2]
I canna say but ye strunt[3] rarely,
     Owre gauze and lace;
5  Though faith! I fear ye dine but sparely
     On sic a place.

Ye ugly, creepin', blastit wonner,[4]
Detested, shunned by saunt an' sinner,
How dare ye set your fit[5] upon her,
10     Sae fine a lady?
Gae somewhere else, and seek your dinner
     On some poor body.

Swith![6] in some beggar's haffet[7] squattle;[8]
There ye may creep, and sprawl, and sprattle[9]
15  Wi' ither kindred, jumping cattle,
     In shoals and nations:
Whare horn nor bane[10] ne'er dare unsettle
     Your thick plantations.

Now haud[11] ye there, ye're out o' sight,
20  Below the fatt'rels,[12] snug an' tight;
Na, faith ye yet![13] ye'll no be right
     Till ye've got on it,
The vera tapmost, tow'ring height
     O' Miss's bonnet.

---

1. **crowlin' ferlie:** Crawling wonder.
2. **sairly:** Sorely.
3. **strunt:** Strut.
4. **blastit wonner:** Blasted wonder.
5. **fit:** Foot.
6. **swith:** Swift.
7. **haffet:** Locks.
8. **squattle:** Sprawl.
9. **sprattle:** struggle.
10. **horn nor bane:** Comb nor poison.
11. **haud:** Hold.
12. **fatt'rels:** Ribbon ends.
13. **Na faith ye yet!:** Confound you!

25    My sooth! right bauld ye set your nose out,
      As plump and gray as onie grozet;[14]
      O for some rank, mercurial rozet,[15]
          Or fell,[16] red smeddum,[17]
      I'd gie you sic a hearty dose o't,
30            Wad dress your droddum![18]

      I wad na been surprised to spy
      You on an auld wife's flannen toy;[19]
      Or aiblins some bit duddie boy,[20]
          On's wyliecoat;[21]
35    But Miss's fine Lunardi![22] fie,
          How daur ye do't?

      O, Jenny, dinna toss your head,
      An' set your beauties a' abread![23]
      Ye little ken what cursèd speed
40            The blastie's[24] makin'!
      Thae[25] winks and finger-ends, I dread,
          Are notice takin'!

      O wad some Pow'r the giftie gie us
      To see oursels as ithers see us!
45    It wad frae monie a blunder free us
          And foolish notion:
      What airs in dress an' gait wad lea'e us,
          And ev'n devotion!

---

**14. onie grozet** (grŏz′ it): Any gooseberry.
**15. rozet** (rŏz′ it): Rosin.
**16. fell:** Sharp.
**17. smeddum:** Powder.
**18. Wad . . . droddum:** Would put an end to you.
**19. flannen toy:** Flannel cap.
**20. Or . . . boy:** Or perhaps on some little ragged boy.
**21. wyliecoat** (wī′ lē kōt′): Undershirt.
**22. Lunardi:** A balloon-shaped bonnet, named for Vincenzo Lunardi, a balloonist of the late 1700's.
**23. abread:** Abroad.
**24. blastie's:** Creature's.
**25. Thae:** Those.

## THINKING ABOUT THE SELECTION
### Recalling

1. (a) What is the louse doing? (b) What does the speaker command it to do instead?
2. What does the speaker say he would like to do in lines 27–30?
3. (a) Whom does the speaker address in the seventh stanza? (b) What does he warn her against?

### Interpreting

4. (a) What conclusions can you draw about Jenny's character? (b) What evidence supports these assumptions?
5. What is the poet's tone—that is, his attitude toward his subject?
6. Like "To a Mouse," this poem contains a famous line that suggests the poem's theme. (a) What is that line? (b) What is the poem's theme?

### Applying

7. William Hazlitt wrote, "Life is the art of being well deceived." How do you think Burns would respond to this statement? Explain your answer.

## CRITICAL THINKING AND READING
### Recognizing Satire

**Satire** is writing that uses humor and wit to expose folly and flaws of humans or institutions.

Popular since ancient Greek and Roman times, satire has long been an effective tool of both writers and reformers. In order to recognize the target of the poet's satire, reread the brief biography of Robert Burns on page 594. Based on information you find there and on the poem itself, answer the following questions about "To a Louse."

1. (a) What do you imagine to be the social class of the speaker? Why? (b) Of Jenny? Why?
2. (a) What is the louse's "crime"? What does the speaker have in common with those to whom he seems to feel the louse belongs? (b) What is ironic about this?

## THINKING AND WRITING
### Comparing and Contrasting Two Poems

"To a Mouse" and "To a Louse" are often considered to be companion poems. Indeed, both poems address creatures of nature, and both are written in the Scottish dialect. Apart from these obvious similarities, consider other traits the poems share in common, as well as features that set the two apart. Consider in particular the theme of the poems and the attitude of the poet toward society. Discuss your findings with your classmates. Then write an essay comparing and contrasting the two poems. When you revise, make sure you have presented both similarities and differences. Proofread your essay and prepare a final draft.

# Afton[1] Water

## Robert Burns

Flow gently, sweet Afton, among thy green braes,[2]
Flow gently, I'll sing thee a song in thy praise;
My Mary's asleep by thy murmuring stream,
Flow gently, sweet Afton, disturb not her dream.

5   Thou stock-dove whose echo resounds through the glen,
Ye wild whistling blackbirds in yon thorny den,
Thou green-crested lapwing, thy screaming forbear,
I charge you, disturb not my slumbering fair.

How lofty, sweet Afton, thy neighboring hills,
10  Far marked with the courses of clear, winding rills;
There daily I wander as noon rises high,
My flocks and my Mary's sweet cot[3] in my eye.

---

**1. Afton:** The Afton is a river in Ayrshire, a former county in Southwestern Scotland.
**2. braes** (brāz): Slopes.
**3. cot:** Cottage.

How pleasant thy banks and green valleys below,
Where wild in the woodlands the primroses blow;
15  There oft as mild evening weeps over the lea,[4]
The sweet-scented birk[5] shades my Mary and me.

Thy crystal stream, Afton, how lovely it glides,
And winds by the cot where my Mary resides;
How wanton thy waters her snowy feet lave,
20  As gathering sweet flowerets she stems thy clear wave.

Flow gently, sweet Afton, among thy green braes,
Flow gently, sweet river, the theme of my lays;
My Mary's asleep by thy murmuring stream,
Flow gently, sweet Afton, disturb not her dream.

---

**4. lea:** Meadow.
**5. birk:** Birch.

## THINKING ABOUT THE SELECTION

### Recalling

1. (a) Why does the speaker ask the Afton to "flow gently"? (b) What other three things does he command to be silent?
2. What is the speaker's occupation?

### Interpreting

3. (a) What is the poem's mood—the feeling it conveys to the reader? (b) What words and phrases help achieve this mood?
4. (a) What assumptions can you make about Mary based on the poem? (b) About the speaker's feelings toward her?
5. Do you think the author, in composing these lines, had any purpose in mind other than to entertain? Explain your answer.

### Applying

6. What songs or lullabies are you familiar with that carry the same message as this poem?

# John Anderson, My Jo[1]

Robert Burns

John Anderson, my jo, John,
    When we were first acquent,
Your locks were like the raven,
    Your bonnie[2] brow was brent;[3]
5  But now your brow is beld,[4] John,
    Your locks are like the snow;
But blessings on your frosty pow,[5]
    John Anderson, my jo.

John Anderson, my jo, John,
10    We clamb[6] the hill thegither;
And monie[7] a canty[8] day, John,
    We've had wi' ane anither:
Now we maun[9] totter down, John,
    And hand in hand we'll go,
15  And sleep thegither at the foot,
    John Anderson, my Jo.

---

1. **jo:** Joy.
2. **bonnie:** Pretty.
3. **brent:** Unwrinkled.
4. **beld:** Bald.
5. **pow:** Head.
6. **clamb:** Climbed.
7. **monie:** Many.
8. **canty:** Cheerful.
9. **maun:** Must.

## THINKING ABOUT THE SELECTION
### Recalling

1. (a) How does the speaker say John Anderson looked when she and he first met? (b) How does he look now?
2. What does the speaker say she and John Anderson will do now?

### Interpreting

3. What do you suppose to be the relationship between the speaker and John Anderson? Explain your assumption.
4. (a) How would you paraphrase what the speaker is saying in the first four lines of the second stanza? (b) In the last four lines?

### Applying

5. It has been noted that "John Anderson, My Jo" reveals Robert Burns's great talent for writing romantic poetry. Explain why you agree or disagree with this observation.

## THINKING AND WRITING
### Writing About Dialect

Three of the four poems you have read by Robert Burns are written in dialect. In an essay, explain how you believe the impact of these poems would have been altered had the poet chosen to write them instead in standard English. Before writing consider the following questions. What factors do you think influenced Burns's decision to use dialect? What qualities of tone are communicated through the use of dialect? Of theme? What aspects of the message in "Afton Waters" may have prompted the poet to write in standard English?

# WILLIAM BLAKE

## 1757–1827

When William Blake was four years old, he screamed because he saw God at his window. At age eight, while walking in the fields, he saw a tree filled with angels. To outside observers, Blake's "spells" might have seemed a cause for grave concern. In the home of his parents—themselves followers of the mystical teachings of Emanuel Swedenborg—the boy's "gift of vision" was something to be revered and nurtured. At least partly as a result of the family's way of life, the century and the world received a painter and a poet whose contributions are as rare as they are brilliant.

Blake was born in London, where his father ran a hosiery shop. He was never sent to school but instead, after expressing a desire to become a painter, was apprenticed to an engraver. Ultimately self-taught, he found his way into art and literature.

Between the ages of twelve and twenty, Blake wrote a series of poems, *Poetical Sketches,* that followed the tradition of English lyric poetry, while bringing a new innocence to his subject matter. When he was thirty-two, he published his *Songs of Innocence,* which he had composed when he was younger, and which explored his favorite subject—the destiny of the human spirit. Instead of printing the collection, he developed a unique process whereby the words and illustrations were etched on metal plates with varnish, then painted in by hand. Because the process was time-consuming, few books could be produced, and so to support himself, Blake hired himself out to other authors as an illustrator and sold what he could of his own works for one pound apiece. He also continued to write and in 1794 brought out a companion to *Songs of Innocence* titled *Songs of Experience.*

In *Songs of Innocence* Blake had suggested that by recapturing the imagination and wonderment of childhood, we could achieve the goal of self-awareness. The poems thus present views of the world as filtered through the eyes and mind of a child. In *Songs of Experience* he now insisted that a return to innocence was not, at least by itself, sufficient for us to attain an awareness of our true identity—that we must also recognize and attempt to understand the evils around us. Thus Blake's credo was that there must be a union of opposites, a fusion of innocence and experience.

Unrecognized by his peers and living only slightly above poverty level, Blake spent his seventy years in constant creative activity. Only later, many years after his death, was the system behind his work understood. His poetry operates on two levels, one of them symbolic, the other literal. Both of them address a single purpose—the renewal of the human spirit.

# GUIDE FOR INTERPRETING

## The Lamb; The Tiger; The Human Abstract; Infant Sorrow; A Poison Tree

**Symbolism.** Symbolism is the use of a person, an object, a place, or an idea to represent itself and something beyond itself at the same time. Two well-known examples of symbolism are the use of the Stars and Stripes to represent the United States and the use of a skull and crossbones to represent something poisonous. While symbolism occurs in all types of literature, poetry, by virtue of its purity as an art form, is an especially natural vehicle for the presentation of ideas in symbolic form. Symbolism also permits the poet to introduce in relatively little space concepts and ideas that would ordinarily require more extensive treatment. In "The Tiger," William Blake uses the jungle cat as a symbol for the savage and untamed forces in the world that prompt human beings to perform evil actions.

Imagine that suddenly you are four or five years old again. Look around you, at the people and objects in your presence, and describe what you see. Use words that you believe would be appropriate to a small child, and remember that much which you take for granted would seem new and wonderful to a younger you.

To realize Blake's importance in the history of engraving, it is important to know that since the masterpieces of Albrecht Dürer, the sixteenth-century German engraver/printer, engraving on metal had been abandoned. It was replaced by the easier method of etching, which did not involve as much labor and training.

Much attention has been focused on Blake's mastery of this difficult art form. The following excerpt is from the famous description of Blake's process of engraving and the explanation of its discovery that appeared the year after he died:

> Blake, after deeply perplexing himself as to the mode of accomplishing the publication of his illustrated songs, without their being subject to the expense of letter-press, his brother Robert stood before him in one of his visionary imaginations, and so decidedly directed him in the way in which he thought he ought to proceed, that he immediately followed his advice, by writing his poetry, and drawing his marginal subjects of embellishments in outline upon the copper-plate with an impervious liquid, and then eating the plain parts or lights away with aqua fortis considerably below them, so that the outlines were left as a stereotype.

# The Lamb

## William Blake

Little Lamb, who made thee?
Dost thou know who made thee?
Gave thee life, and bid thee feed,
By the stream and o'er the mead;
5 Gave thee clothing of delight,
Softest clothing, woolly, bright;
Gave thee such a tender voice,
Making all the vales rejoice?
Little Lamb, who made thee?
10 Dost thou know who made thee?

Little Lamb, I'll tell thee,
Little Lamb, I'll tell thee.
He is called by thy name,
For He calls Himself a Lamb.
15 He is meek, and He is mild;
He became a little child.
I a child, and thou a lamb,
We are callèd by His name.
Little Lamb, God bless thee!
20 Little Lamb, God bless thee!

## THINKING ABOUT THE SELECTION
### Recalling

1. (a) What questions does the speaker ask in the first stanza? (b) What answer does he give in the second?
2. How does the speaker identify himself in the second stanza?

### Interpreting

3. Blake uses repetition to create a mood, or overall feeling, in this poem. (a) What types of words does he repeat? (b) What feeling is created?
4. (a) How would you characterize the creator imagined in this poem? (b) Find at least three words that support your opinion.

### Applying

5. Assume that you were asked to illustrate this poem. (a) What kinds of images would you use to represent the words? (b) What style of drawing might you use?

## ANALYZING LITERATURE
### Recognizing Symbolism

A **symbol** is a thing, idea, person, or place that has a meaning in and of itself but also stands for more. An old, bent man with a scythe symbolizes the end of the year. In poetry, symbolism—the systematic use of symbols —adds particular clarity to a poet's point. In "The Lamb," Blake offers two separate but related symbolic representations for the animal named in the title.

1. What two things does the lamb symbolize? What properties of the lamb suggest its use as a symbol? What is the origin of the symbolic interpretation of the lamb in the second stanza?
2. Restate "The Lamb" in purely literal language. What is the poet's message? How is that message altered, if at all, by restating the poem in literal terms?

The Lamb

Little Lamb who made thee!
Dost thou know who made thee
Gave thee life & bid thee feed.
By the stream & o'er the mead;
Gave thee clothing of delight,
Softest clothing wooly bright;
Gave thee such a tender voice,
Making all the vales rejoice;
    Little Lamb who made thee
    Dost thou know who made thee

    Little Lamb I'll tell thee,
    Little Lamb I'll tell thee;
He is called by thy name,
For he calls himself a Lamb:
He is meek & he is mild,
He became a little child:
I a child & thou a lamb,
We are called by his name.
    Little Lamb God bless thee.
    Little Lamb God bless thee.

*From a manuscript of ``The Lamb,'' by William Blake*
Lessing J. Rosenwald Collection, Library of Congress,
Washington, D. C.

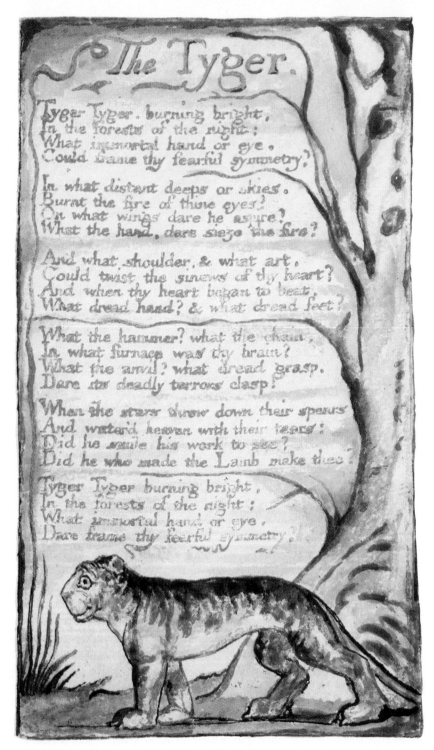

*From a manuscript of "The Tiger," by William Blake*
The Metropolitan Museum of Art

# The Tiger

## William Blake

Tiger! Tiger! burning bright
In the forests of the night,
What immortal hand or eye
Could frame thy fearful symmetry?

5  In what distant deeps or skies
Burnt the fire of thine eyes?
On what wings dare he aspire?
What the hand dare seize the fire?

And what shoulder, and what art,
10  Could twist the sinews of thy heart?
And when thy heart began to beat,
What dread hand? and what dread feet?

What the hammer? what the chain?
In what furnace was thy brain?
15  What the anvil? what dread grasp
Dare its deadly terrors clasp?

When the stars threw down their spears,
And watered heaven with their tears,
Did he smile his work to see?
20  Did he who made the Lamb make thee?

Tiger! Tiger! burning bright
In the forests of the night,
What immortal hand or eye
Dare frame thy fearful symmetry?

## THINKING ABOUT THE SELECTION
### Recalling

1. (a) What question is raised in the first stanza? (b) In the second stanza? (c) In the fifth stanza?

### Interpreting

2. (a) What properties of the tiger are suggested by the images mentioned in the fourth stanza? (b) What emotional impact is created by those images?
3. (a) What do you suppose to be the answer to the central question of the poem? (b) Is it the same answer as that given in "The Lamb"? Explain.

### Applying

4. "The Lamb" was included in *Songs of Innocence,* "The Tiger" in *Songs of Experience.* What does the use of the tiger as a symbol of the world of experience suggest about Blake's view of that world?

# The Human Abstract

## William Blake

Pity would be no more,
If we did not make somebody Poor;
And Mercy no more could be,
If all were as happy as we;

5 And mutual fear brings peace,
Till the selfish loves increase;
Then Cruelty knits a snare,
And spreads his baits with care.

He sits down with holy fears,
10 And waters the ground with tears;
Then Humility takes its root
Underneath his foot.

Soon spreads the dismal shade
Of Mystery over his head;
15 And the Caterpillar and Fly
Feed on the Mystery.

And it bears the fruit of Deceit,
Ruddy and sweet to eat;
And the Raven his nest has made
20 In its thickest shade.

The Gods of the earth and sea,
Sought through Nature to find this Tree,
But their search was all in vain:
There grows one in the Human Brain.

---

## THINKING ABOUT THE SELECTION

### Recalling

1. (a) What, according to the first stanza, would happen if no one in the world were poor? (b) If everyone were happy?
2. A tree is described in the third and following stanzas? Where is this tree said to grow?

### Interpreting

3. In the fifth stanza Blake writes of "the fruit of Deceit." (a) What do you think this phrase is intended to symbolize? (b) What other symbols are present in the poem? (c) How do they expand the poem's meaning?

### Applying

4. (a) What does the title suggest about the poet's outlook? (b) Do you agree with the view he presents here? Explain your answer.

# Infant Sorrow

## William Blake

My mother groaned, my father wept,
Into the dangerous world I leapt;
Helpless, naked, piping loud,
Like a fiend hid in a cloud.

5   Struggling in my father's hands,
Striving against my swaddling bands,
Bound and weary, I thought best
To sulk upon my mother's breast.

## THINKING ABOUT THE SELECTION

### Recalling

1. (a) How does the speaker describe each of his parents in the opening stanza? (b) The world?
2. What event has just occurred?

### Interpreting

3. How would you describe this poem's tone —the feelings it awakens in the reader? What words contribute to these feelings?
4. (a) In what sense do you think the speaker is "bound," as he describes himself in line 7? (b) Where do you suppose he would prefer to be?

### Applying

5. In which of the two volumes, *Songs of Innocence* or *Songs of Experience,* do you think this poem was included? Explain your assumption.

# A Poison Tree

## William Blake

I was angry with my friend:
I told my wrath, my wrath did end.
I was angry with my foe:
I told it not, my wrath did grow.

5   And I watered it in fears,
Night and morning with my tears;
And I sunnèd it with smiles,
And with soft deceitful wiles.

And it grew both day and night,
10   Till it bore an apple bright.
And my foe beheld it shine,
And he knew that it was mine,

And into my garden stole
When the night had veiled the pole;[1]
15   In the morning glad I see
My foe outstretched beneath the tree.

---

**1. pole:** Sky.

*From a manuscript of "A Poison Tree," by William Blake*
Lessing J. Rosenwald Collection, Library of Congress,
Washington, D. C.

## THINKING ABOUT THE SELECTION

### Recalling

1. (a) What does the speaker say occurred when he revealed his anger? (b) When he did not?
2. What "grows" out of the speaker's anger?

### Interpreting

3. What sort of person do you find the speaker of this poem to be? What evidence can you find in support of your view?
4. (a) What symbols are used in the poem? (b) How effective do you find them to be?

### Applying

5. In what other famous piece of literature does an apple appear as a symbol? What relationship can you detect between its symbolic value there and here?
6. (a) Which of the four other poems by Blake printed here is this one most reminiscent of in theme, structure, and symbolism? (b) Which of the two poems do you think states its message most clearly? Give your reasons.

## THINKING AND WRITING

### Writing About Symbolism

Blake wrote to communicate his deeply mystical belief that coming of age forces a child to leave "Eden and struggle with a world that has lost its Paradise." For Blake, the uniting of innocence and experience carries with it an awareness of the inseparability of good and evil. His poems make extensive use of symbolism to convey that notion. List the symbols used by Blake in the six poems to represent these opposing forces of good and evil. Then in an essay discuss how these symbols clarify and add dimension to the notion underlying the poems. When you revise, make sure you have included adequate examples. Proofread your essay and prepare a final draft.

### Primary Source

Why do people come to respect each other? It is intriguing to speculate on the interactions of great contemporaries and to wonder why this one or that one could not plainly see the merits of the other—which seem so clear to us from a distance of two centuries! An article that appeared in *The Examiner* in 1809, for example, described Blake as "an unfortunate lunatic whose personal inoffensiveness secures him from confinement." His now-famous *Descriptive Catalogue* was blasted as "the wild effusions of a distempered brain." At least one well-regarded peer did recognize Blake's talent, however.

In a letter dated May 24, writer Charles Lamb described Blake as "a most extraordinary man. . . . [His] wild designs accompany a splendid folio edition of the Night Thoughts. . . . He paints in water colors marvelous strange pictures, visions of his brain, which he asserts that he has seen. They have great merit. He has *seen* the Old Welsh bards on Snowdon . . . and has painted them from memory (I have seen his paintings). . . . His Pictures—one in particular, the Canterbury Pilgrims (far above Stothard's)—have great merit, but hard, dry, yet with grace. He has written a Catalogue of them, with a most spirited criticism on Chaucer, but mystical and full of Vision. . . . There is one [song] to a tiger, which I have heard recited . . . which is glorious, but alas! I have not the book; for the man is flown, whither I know not. . . . But I must look on his as one of the most extraordinary persons of the age."

# THE CHANGING ENGLISH LANGUAGE

## The Restoration and the Eighteenth Century 1660–1798

### A CALL FOR ORDER

The spirit of adventure, independence, and individualism that had characterized the sixteenth and early seventeenth centuries gave way in the eighteenth century to a desire for order, regularity, and certainty in all aspects of life. "How barbarously we yet write and speak," exclaimed John Dryden, uttering a commonly held view. Different versions of English were still used in different regions, including, for example, the Scots dialect Robert Burns immortalized. As with society itself, English had simply gotten out of hand! From 1660 to the end of the eighteenth century, one of the most important concerns facing the literary establishment was the reform of English.

### LATIN PROVIDES A MODEL

Many looked back to Latin, the language of mathematics and theology, for a model of regular grammar, spelling, and style. Dryden, for example, confessed that at times he had to translate an idea into Latin in order to decide on the correct way to express it in English! It seemed to some that English, in its current wild state, could not last. Latin, on the other hand, had prevailed because it had a definite set of rules.

### "A PROPOSAL FOR CORRECTING, IMPROVING, AND ASCERTAINING THE ENGLISH TONGUE"

Jonathan Swift was a particularly strong voice in the call for language reform. For example, he objected to words being shortened. While many of these words—such as *rep* for "reputation" and *incog* for "incognito"—have passed out of use, we have retained *mob* for "mobile," as well as inventing scores of new ones, such as *taxi, bus,* and *phone.* He equally detested the shortening of verbs, calling such words as *rebuk'd* and *disturb'd* "the disgrace of our language." He also proposed an end to slang terms, condemning "all the modern terms of art, *sham, banter, mob, bubble, bully, cutting, shuffling,* and *palming.*"

His 1712 call for the establishment of an English Academy—"A Proposal for Correcting, Improving, and Ascertaining the English Tongue"—was echoed in many quarters. Some gathered support from Italian and French models of language improvement. The Italians, for example, had specifically commissioned an Academy to order their language. In France Cardinal Richelieu had founded the Académie Française to purify French. Their task was "to labor with all possible care and diligence to give definite rules to our language, and to render it pure, eloquent and capable of treating the arts and sciences."

Nonetheless, the idea of an English Academy never gathered enough support to become a reality. Writer Daniel Defoe, for example, lent his voice to those opposing the idea, for he felt that if an official Academy was established to dictate correct grammar, "it would be as criminal to coin words as money."

### THE QUESTION OF GRAMMAR AND SPELLING

But more and more educated people seriously examined English. They began with grammar, but to their dismay, they discovered that English had no grammar. Latin had rules; English had none. Even the notion that there should be a right way of spelling was foreign to many letter writers and printers, as the uneven spelling of their books and papers shows. Swift had this to say about the turmoil of English spelling:

> Another Cause . . . which hath contributed not a little to the maiming of our Language, is a foolish Opinion, advanced of late Years, that we ought to spell exactly as we speak; which besides the obvious Inconvenience of utterly destroying our Etymology, would be a thing we should never see an End of. Not only the several Towns and Countries of England have a different way of Pronouncing, but even here in London, they clip their Words after one Manner about the Court, another in the City, and a third in the Suburbs. . . .

The practice of spelling as you spoke had produced such monstrosities as "sartinly" (certainly), "gine" (join), and "byled" (boiled). Things had gotten even more confusing when writers had changed words based on mistaken derivations, so that *iland* became "island," *sissors*, "scissors." The time had come for a standardized source book.

## SAMUEL JOHNSON'S *DICTIONARY*

While there had been other dictionaries, none approached the scope of Johnson's *Dictionary*. Johnson and his six assistants worked nine years, filling eighty large notebooks with the practical definitions of more than 40,000 words. His resulting two-volume work is a landmark that stood unrivalled for more than a century. In Boswell's words the *Dictionary* "conferred stability on the language of his country."

As the century drew to a close, English became increasingly refined and standardized as the language of power and learning.

**Allegory of the Royal Society by Hollar**
*The Mansell Collection*

# YOU THE WRITER

**Assignment**

**1.** Select a poem from this unit and write a stanza or two that could be added onto the end as a continuation of the original. Your additional lines should follow the verse form and style of the original.

**Prewriting.** Freewrite, exploring the meaning of the original poem. Decide what you might say that would be in harmony with the content of the original. Then study the meter and rhyme of this poem.

**Writing.** Write your lines in verse, trying to keep to the meter and rhyme of the original. Your first concern, however, should be with the content.

**Revising.** Refine your verse. Have you followed your model's meter and rhyme? Is the style of your lines appropriate? Finally, check over the content. Does it seem in keeping with that of the original?

**Assignment**

**2.** Write a prose narrative or essay modeled on one of the selections in this unit. The content should reflect the ideas and beliefs of the period. The style should closely follow that of your model.

**Prewriting.** Reread the selection you have chosen. Decide what subject matter, ideas, and viewpoint would make your narrative or essay a close imitation of the original.

**Writing.** When you write your first draft, try to keep within the mind and outlook of the author whose work you are following. As well as you can, follow his style.

**Revising.** First check that the content of your writing is in keeping with the era of the original. Then check that the style is also appropriate. Finally, look for and correct any lapses in grammar and style.

**Assignment**

**3.** Imagine you are a young lady or gentleman of the eighteenth century. Write a letter to a friend in which you express your thoughts on any major event or concern of the day.

**Prewriting.** Review the introduction to this unit and any other information you have gathered about the era. Select your subject from this material. Then outline what you will say to your friend. Remember that you are an eighteenth-century person and your comments should reflect the standards and concerns of this time.

**Writing.** When you write your letter, concentrate on expressing your thoughts in a clear, well-organized way. Try, however, to maintain an eighteenth-century outlook.

**Revising.** See if you can enhance the eighteenth-century character and flavor of your letter. Although your letter is to a friend, it should have a somewhat formal tone. Make sure your language is appropriate. Then correct any errors in grammar that you notice.

# YOU THE CRITIC

**Assignment**

**1.** The era called Restoration and the Eighteenth century makes up one of the great periods of English prose. Write a descriptive essay in which you compare and contrast the prose of the period with the prose you find in magazines and newspapers of today.

**Prewriting.** First decide what you find especially admirable in one or two of the selections you have read. What adjectives would you use to describe this quality? What passages would you cite to illustrate it? How is the prose of today different?

**Writing.** Write an essay based on your prewriting work. Strive to be clear and precise in your descriptions.

**Revising.** Ask yourself, "Am I conveying clearly the qualities I see in the prose? Am I using comparison and contrast effectively to differentiate eighteenth-century prose from the prose of today?"

**Assignment**

**2.** A line from Alexander Pope, "What oft was thought, but ne'er so well expressed," could be applied to some of the best literature of this period. Choose at least two works from this unit and show how they express traditional ideas both elegantly and memorably.

**Prewriting.** Review selections you have read and find statements or passages that could stand alone as memorable quotations. Jot down notes about the meaning of each passage. Then decide in what order you will quote and comment on them.

**Writing.** First write a topic sentence that sums up your general opinion of the style and content of the lines and passages you are concerned with. Then present your quotations with comments on their literary effectiveness.

**Revising.** Look for and correct any lapses in the style and organization of your essay or in grammar.

**Assignment**

**3.** Literature reflects the times in which it is created. Write an essay showing how the literature you have read in this unit reflects the historical developments and trends of the period.

**Prewriting.** Review the introduction to the unit and any other related knowledge you may have. Which of the selections you have read comes to mind during your review? How do they reflect their times? Freewrite, exploring your answers.

**Writing.** Write an essay based on your prewriting work. You might first mention a historical development or trend and then describe how it is reflected in one of the works you have read.

**Revising.** Check that your essay is well organized and unified by a topic sentence, and that your explanations are clear and well developed. Finally, correct any errors in grammar or style.

**VIEW IN HAMPSHIRE**
*Patrick Nasmyth*

# THE ROMANTIC AGE
## 1798–1832

One impulse from a vernal wood
   May teach you more of man,
Of moral evil and of good,
   Than all the sages can.

Sweet is the lore which Nature brings;
   Our meddling intellect
Misshapes the beauteous forms of things—
   We murder to dissect.

Enough of Science and of Art;
   Close up those barren leaves;
Come forth, and bring with you a heart
   That watches and receives.

from "The Tables Turned"
**William Wordsworth**

**CAPTURE OF THE BASTILLE, JULY 14, 1789**
*Claude Cholat*
The Granger Collection

The preceding stanzas from "The Tables Turned," written in 1798, capture some of the main sentiments of a new age in British literature, an age in which writers "turned the tables" on eighteenth century thinking, insisting that the world be viewed through the heart, not the mind. During this period, which was named the Romantic Age by historians during the late 1800's, nearly all the attitudes and tendencies of eighteenth-century classicism and rationalism were redefined or changed dramatically. To understand how these changes occurred, it is necessary to examine not only the impact of events in Britain, but also the effects of the social and political upheaval that began taking place in other parts of the world.

## REVOLUTION AND REACTION

Toward the end of the eighteenth century, two revolutions occurred outside England that indirectly threatened the stability of the British political and social systems. During the 1770's the American colonies revolted against British rule, eventually winning their independence and forming a government based on the principles of freedom and equality. While the American Revolution divided British public opinion and aroused some awareness of the need for reform, its impact on British society was not nearly as great as that of the French Revolution, which demonstrated that it was possible for a long-standing government to be successfully challenged on its own soil.

The French Revolution began on July 14, 1789, when a group of French citizens stormed the Bastille, a Paris prison for political prisoners. In the weeks that followed, the revolutionaries placed limits on the powers of King Louis XVI, established a new government, and approved a document called the Declaration of the Rights of Man, affirming the principles of "liberty, equality, and fraternity." France became a constitutional monarchy.

### Opposing Views

From the start, the revolution evoked strong reactions from both liberals and conservatives throughout the rest of Europe. In England the ruling class felt threatened by the implications of the events in France, while most intellectuals, including several of the most important and influential writers of the Romantic Age, enthusiastically supported the revolution and the democratic ideals on which it was grounded. One ardent supporter of the revolution was Charles James Fox, leader of the Whig party, who declared, "How much the greatest event it is that ever happened in the world! and how much the best!" Poet William Wordsworth also spoke out in support of the revolution, and philosopher and novelist William Godwin (1756–1836) reacted to the revolution by writing *An Enquiry Concerning Social Justice* (1793), in which he predicted that British society would evolve peacefully into a nation characterized by freedom and equality. In contrast, Whig political thinker Edmund Burke (1729–1797), who had sympathized with the American Revolution, condemned the events in France. In *Reflections on the Revolution in France* (1790), he argued that the French, unlike the Americans, were attacking the very fabric of their society with complete disregard for their roots and ancestry. Burke warned that the revolution was bound to grow violent and mourned that "the age of chivalry is gone . . . and the glory of Europe is extinguished forever."

## THE REIGN OF TERROR

Burke's views did not win wide acceptance in Britain until his dire predictions began coming true. As royalists, moderates, and radicals jockeyed for power, the French Revolution became more and more chaotic. In 1792, France declared war on Austria, touching off an invasion by Austrian and Prussian troops, whose leader proclaimed the intention of restoring the French king to full authority. Fuming with patriotic indignation, a radical group called the Jacobins gained control of the French legislative assembly, abolished the monarchy, and declared the nation a republic. Mobs attacked and killed many prisoners—including former aristocrats and priests—and soon French refugees began pouring into England with tales of these bloody "September massacres." Within weeks the revolutionaries had tried and convicted Louis XVI on a charge of treason. When Louis XVI went to the guillotine early in 1793, a revolutionary leader, Georges Danton, exclaimed: "The kings of Europe would challenge us. We throw them the head of a king!"

Following the execution, revolutionary violence reached its peak, as the Jacobins, under the leadership of Maximilien Robespierre, began what is called the Reign of Terror. Before the terror ended in the summer of 1794, revolutionary authorities had imprisoned thousands of royalists, moderates, and even radicals, sending some 4000 of them—including Danton and finally Robespierre himself—to the guillotine.

### British Reaction

The September massacres and the Reign of Terror were so shocking that even Britons who had sympathized with the French Revolution now turned against it. Conservative Britons, already hostile to the Revolution, demanded a crackdown on reformers within Britain, whom they denounced as dangerous Jacobins. Adding to British alarm was the success of France's new "citizen army," which expelled the Austrian and Prussian invaders and then set out to "liberate" other European nations from despotic rule. British leaders did not want France or any other nation to win dominance on the European continent. In 1793, France took the initiative by declaring war on Britain. Thus began a series of wars

# BRITISH EVENTS

**1798**    **William Wordsworth** and **Samuel Taylor Coleridge** publish *Lyrical Ballads*.

Wolfe Tone Rebellion in Ireland.

**1801**    Act of Union creates United Kingdom of Great Britain and Ireland.

Union Jack becomes official flag.

**1802**    J.M.W. Turner's *Calais Pier* exhibited in London.

**1803**    Henry Shrapnel invents exploding shell.

**1805**    Battle of Trafalgar.

**1807**    Thomas Moore writes *Irish Melodies*.

**1811**    King George III declared permanently insane.

**1812**    **Byron** publishes *Childe Harold's Pilgrimage*.

**1813**    Waltz becomes acceptable in London ballrooms.

**Jane Austen** publishes *Pride and Prejudice*.

**1814**    George Stephenson constructs first successful steam locomotive.

Walter Scott publishes *Waverley*.

**1815**    John MacAdam constructs roads of crushed stone.

**1817**    **William Hazlitt** writes *Characters of Shakespeare's Plays*.

**1818**    Thomas Bowdler publishes censored edition of Shakespeare's plays.

**Mary Wollstonecraft Shelley** publishes *Frankenstein, or the Modern Prometheus*.

William Wordsworth

George Stephenson's

Union Jack

Jane Austen

Rosetta Stone

Sir Walter Scott and Robert Burns

Locomotive

Napoleon

Beethoven

Robert Fulton's Steamboat

## WORLD EVENTS

1799  France: Napoleon becomes head of revolutionary government.

Egypt: Rosetta Stone, key to deciphering hieroglyphics, discovered.

1800  Italy: Volta builds first electric battery.

Spain: Goya paints *The Two Majas*.

1802  Haiti: Toussaint L'Ouverture leads rebellion against French rule.

1803  United States: Louisiana Territory purchased from France.

Germany: French occupy Hanover.

1804  Germany: Beethoven composes *Symphony No. 3*.

France: Napoleon crowns himself emperor.

1805  Eastern Europe: Napoleon defeats allies at Austerlitz.

1807  United States: Fulton's steamboat navigates Hudson River.

1808  Italy: Excavation of Pompeii begins.

Germany: Goethe publishes *Faust*, Part I.

1809  United States: Washington Irving writes "Rip Van Winkle."

1810  South America: Simón Bolívar leads rebellions against Spanish rule.

1812  Russia: Napoleon loses hundreds of thousands of troops in retreat from Moscow.

Spain: Wellington drives French from Madrid.

United States: War with Britain declared.

1813  Germany: Allies defeat Napoleon at Leipzig.

Mexico: Independence declared.

# BRITISH EVENTS

**1819** Peterloo Massacre in Manchester.

**Percy Bysshe Shelley** publishes "Ode to the West Wind".

**1820** King George III dies.

**John Keats** publishes "Ode on a Grecian Urn".

**1821** *Manchester Guardian* begins publication.

John Constable paints *The Grove*

**1823** **Charles Lamb** publishes *Essays of Elia.*

**1824** First labor unions permitted.

**1825** Horse-drawn buses begin operating in London.

John Nash completes rebuilding of Buckingham Palace.

**1827** System for purifying London water installed.

**1829** Catholic Emancipation Act passed.

Robert Peel establishes Metropolitan Police in London.

**1830** Liverpool-Manchester railway opens.

**1831** Michael Faraday demonstrates electromagnetic induction.

**1832** First Reform Act extends voting rights.

John Keats

The Grove

London in the 1820's

Charles Lamb

Liverpool-Manchester

The Peterloo Massacre

THE

# LAST OF THE MOHICANS.

BY

JAMES FENIMORE COOPER.

NEW YORK:
D. APPLETON AND COMPANY, PUBLISHERS.

*The Last of the Mohicans*

*Savannah,* the First Steamer to Cross the Atlantic

Railway

Edgar Allan Poe

## WORLD EVENTS

| | |
|---|---|
| **1814** | France: Napoleon abdicates and is exiled to Elba. |
| **1815** | France: Napoleon returns for "Hundred Days." |
| | Belgium: Napoleon defeated at Waterloo. |
| | France: Napoleon exiled to St. Helena. |
| **1816** | Italy: Rossini composes *The Barber of Seville*. |
| **1817** | United States: William Cullen Bryant publishes "Thanatopsis." |
| | Germany: Hegel publishes *Encyclopedia of the Philosophical Sciences*. |
| **1818** | First steamship crosses Atlantic. |
| **1821** | Greece: War with Turkey begins. |
| | Germany: Heinrich Heine publishes *Poems*. |
| **1822** | Austria: Schubert begins *Symphony No. 8* ("Unfinished Symphony"). |
| | Russia: Aleksandr Pushkin publishes *Eugene Onegin*. |
| **1823** | United States: Monroe Doctrine closes Americas to further European colonization. |
| **1825** | Russia: Bolshoi Ballet established. |
| **1826** | Germany: Mendelssohn composes *Overture to A Midsummer Night's Dream*. |
| | United States: James Fenimore Cooper publishes *The Last of the Mohicans*. |
| **1827** | France: Alexandre Dumas publishes *The Three Musketeers*. |
| **1830** | France: Stendhal publishes *The Red and the Black*. |
| **1831** | United States: Edgar Allan Poe publishes *Poems*. |
| | France: Victor Hugo publishes *The Hunchback of Notre Dame*. |

that would drag on for twenty-two years, creating fear and rigidity within Britain and effectively squelching during that time all hope of reform within British society.

The Tory government led by William Pitt (the Younger) began the reaction by outlawing all talk of parliamentary reform outside the halls of Parliament, banning public meetings, and suspending certain basic rights. Later, Pitt's government crushed a rebellion in Ireland. Liberal-minded Britons had no political outlet for their hopes and dreams. Many turned to literature and art as a way to find in the pristine world of romanticized nature the source of beauty and truth.

## The Napoleonic Wars

Britain's battles against France took a new turn after 1799, when a military leader named Napoleon Bonaparte came to power in Paris. Napoleon had grandiose plans for French military expansion, and he was an able leader. After a brief break in French-British hostilities in 1802–03, war resumed in earnest. Napoleon, who had declared himself emperor of France, planned an invasion of Britain, but had to abandon the plan after a British fleet under Lord Nelson defeated the French fleet at the Battle of Trafalgar, off Spain, in 1805. Napoleon's armies fought well against Britain's European allies, however, and by 1807 they controlled almost all of Europe as far east as the borders of Russia. Britain ruled the ocean, but Napoleon ruled Europe.

In 1812 Napoleon finally overextended himself by invading Russia. There his armies suffered a series of bloody defeats. At the same time, Napoleon was experiencing reverses in the west. His forces were defeated in the Peninsular War (1808–13) in Portugal

**THE BATTLE OF TRAFALGAR**
*J. M. W. Turner*
The Granger Collection

and Spain and, in 1814, British and allied armies closed in on him and forced him to abandon his crown. Napoleon was not finished, however. Exiled to the Mediterranean island of Elba, he plotted a return, and in 1815 he managed to escape to France, assemble an army, and resume rule for a period known as the Hundred Days. Napoleon's attempt to regain his former glory ended on the battle-field at Waterloo, Belgium, in 1815, when the Duke of Wellington, British hero of the Peninsular War, led an allied army to a decisive victory.

All over Britain, people celebrated the end of the Napoleonic Wars with bonfires and other festivities. Royalists hailed the restoration of monarchical authority throughout Europe, while radicals mourned the failure of the revolutionary ideals of liberty and equality.

**NAPOLEON (THE CAMPAIGN IN FRANCE, 1814)**
*J. L. E. Meissonier*
*The Granger Collection*

## COPING WITH SOCIETY'S PROBLEMS

Throughout the long wars with France, Britain's government kept a tight lid on domestic dissent. It ignored the problems caused by the Industrial Revolution—including the overcrowding of factory towns, the unpleasant and unsafe working conditions in the factories, and the long working hours, and low pay experienced by the workers—and the problems only got worse.

### Rumblings Among the People

Britain's government claimed to be following a hands-off policy, but in fact it sided openly with employers against workers even helping to crush the workers' attempts to form unions. Meanwhile, the working class grew steadily larger and more restless. In the factory towns of northern England, workers protested the loss of jobs to new machinery in the violent Luddite Riots (1811–13). In Manchester, mounted soldiers charged a peaceful mass meeting of cotton workers and killed several of them in what came to be known as the Peterloo Massacre (1819). To many, it seemed that British society was splitting into two angry camps—the working classes, who demanded reform, and the ruling classes, who resisted fiercely.

**KING WILLIAM IV OF ENGLAND**
*Sir Martin Archer Shee*
*The Granger Collection*

### Beginnings of Reform

During this time, Britain had a series of weak and ineffective royal heads. George III, long subject to bouts of insanity, went irretrievably mad in 1811. His eldest son, the scandal-plagued and unpopular George, Prince of Wales, ruled as Regent from 1811 to 1820—a period known as the Regency. Then the old king died and the Regent became George IV. When he died in 1830, his brother took over as William IV—an old and weak but amiable king, who ruled until 1837.

The weakness of these kings helped to enhance the power of the prime ministers—in theory named by the king, but in practice

**SKETCH FOR HADLEIGH CASTLE,** *c.* **1828–9**
*John Constable*
*The Granger Collection*

chosen by the strongest party in Parliament. The Tory leaders who held power during and immediately after the Napoleonic Wars rejected all suggestions of reform. A new generation of Tories emerged in the 1820's, however, and a trickle of reforms began. However, a law was passed in 1824 permitting Britain's first labor unions to organize; and in 1829 the Catholic Emancipation Act restored economic and religious freedoms to Roman Catholics.

The trickle grew into a stream of reforms following a Whig victory in the election of 1830. The Reform Law of 1832 brought sweeping changes to British political life. By extending voting rights to the small but important middle class (males only), this law threatened the traditional dominance of land-owning aristocrats in Parliament. Moreover, in 1833 Parliament passed the first law governing factory safety. That same year, it also abolished slavery.

## THE BEGINNINGS OF ROMANTICISM

Writers of the Romantic Age reacted strongly to the events of their time. They felt stirrings of excitement or repulsion as they contemplated the French Revolution. They saw the dramatic changes being wrought by the Industrial Revolution and longed for the simplicity and purity of the past. They sensed the rumblings of discontent and desperation that could not be silenced, even by the repressive measures of the war years. Those who had applauded the French Revolution, envisioning a new age of democracy and equality in Britain, were left in a state of bitter disappointment. They turned their attention to literary endeavors, creating a Romantic style that offered a new perspective on the world—a perspective that focused on nature and "the common people."

### New Literary Concerns

Just as the French revolutionaries had at first discarded the customs and procedures that had traditionally governed French society, the Romantic writers abandoned many of the dominant attitudes and principles of eighteenth-century literature. New literary concerns emerged, many of which had been shaped either by the French revolutionary spirit or by the effects of the Industrial Revolution. The Romantic writers' interest in the trials and dreams of common people and their desire for radical change developed out of the democratic idealism that characterized the early part of the French Revolution, while their deep attachment to nature was a response to the consequences of industrialization. These and other characteristics of Romantic literature represent a distinct departure from the concerns associated with eighteenth-century classicism and rationalism. Because of this dichotomy, the prevailing ideas and attitudes of Romanticism are most easily grasped when viewed in contrast to those of the eighteenth century. The following chart identifies some of the contrasting tendencies.

| | CLASSICISM AND RATIONALISM | ROMANTICISM |
|---|---|---|
| **SOURCES OF INSPIRATION** | scientific observation of the outer world; logic | examination of inner feelings, emotions; imagination |
| | classical Greek and Roman literature | the literature of the Middle Ages |
| **ATTITUDES AND INTERESTS** | pragmatic | idealistic |
| | interested in science, technology | interested in the mysterious and supernatural |
| | concerned with general, universal experiences | concerned with the particular |
| | believed in following standards and traditions | sought to develop new forms of expression |
| | felt optimistic about the present | romanticized the past |
| | emphasized moderation and self-restraint | tended toward excess and spontaneity |
| | appreciated elegance, refinement | appreciated folk traditions |
| **SOCIAL CONCERNS** | valued stability and harmony | desired radical change |
| | favored a social hierarchy | favored democracy |
| | interested in maintaining the aristocracy | concerned with common people |
| | concerned with society as a whole | concerned with the individual |
| | believed that nature should be controlled by humans | felt that nature should be untamed |

It is customary to set the beginning of Britain's Romantic Age in 1798, the year in which William Wordsworth and Samuel Taylor Coleridge published the *Lyrical Ballads,* establishing the Romantic principles that would dominate British literature for several decades. However, the ideas of Romanticism arose on continental Europe well before the turn of the century. Even in Britain a handful of poets—most notably Thomas Gray, Robert Burns, and William Blake—had displayed some of the characteristics of Romantic thinking before *Lyrical Ballads* was published.

## Jean-Jacques Rousseau

Though he died before the start of the Romantic Age, Swiss-born writer Jean-Jacques Rousseau (1712–1778), a leading philosopher of eighteenth-century France, planted one of the seeds from

**RAIN, STEAM, AND SPEED—THE GREAT WESTERN RAILWAY 1844**
*J. M. W. Turner*
The Granger Collection

which Romanticism grew. Rousseau saw society as a force of evil that infringed on personal liberty and human happiness. "Man is born free," he wrote, "and everywhere he is in chains." He reasoned that humanity should revert to its natural state, abandoning its stifling social institutions and outworn philosophies and listening instead to nature, instinct, and intuition.

Rousseau prepared the way for political revolution. The Americans who declared their independence in 1776 quoted Rousseau often, and the French revolutionaries of 1789 quoted him even more frequently. Rousseau also prepared the way for a new artistic movement, Romanticism. During the latter part of the eighteenth century, in the German-speaking areas of Europe, which were not yet a unified nation and often suffered from the repressive policies of powerful Prussia and Austria, a group of nationalistically minded writers began incorporating Rousseau's ideas into major works of poetry, drama, and fiction.

## Johann Wolfgang von Goethe

The most influential of this group was Johann Wolfgang von Goethe (1749–1832). In search of inspiration, Goethe turned to the German literature of the Middle Ages, early vernacular works filled with myth and superstition, adventure and passion, not unlike the Anglo-Saxon *Beowulf.* In these works Goethe found not only a source of pride for a new generation of German writers but also a primitive simplicity much in keeping with Rousseau's ideas and values. A fascination with medieval times—the same Middle Ages that "enlightened" thinkers had despised—soon became characteristic of the emerging artistic movement. In fact, the movement would later be named the Romantic Age because of its interest in medieval *romances*—imaginary tales of adventure written in one of the Roman dialects, the early forms of languages derived from Latin.

## THE ROMANTIC AGE IN BRITISH POETRY

Romanticism was a movement that affected not only literature but all the arts. In music, it produced such brilliant European composers as Germany's Ludwig van Beethoven (1770–1827) and Austria's Franz Schubert (1797–1828), but no one of comparable stature in Britain. In painting, it influenced the intensely personal and warmly spontaneous rural landscapes of Britain's John Constable (1776–1837) and J. M. W. Turner (1775–1851). However, it is for literature, and especially for poetry, that Britain's Romantic Age is most famous.

### Wordsworth and Coleridge: A Break with the Past

When William Wordsworth (1770–1850) asked his friend Samuel Taylor Coleridge (1772–1834) to collaborate with him in the publication of *Lyrical Ballads,* he was well aware that their collection

**CALAIS PIER: AN ENGLISH PACKET ARRIVING**
*J. M. W. Turner*
The Granger Collection

of poetry would make a distinct break with the past. To underscore that break, Wordsworth included in the second (1800) and third (1802) editions of *Lyrical Ballads* a preface explaining the new poetic principles he and Coleridge had employed. That preface defined poetry as "the spontaneous overflow of powerful feelings" and explained that poetry "takes its origin from emotion recollected in tranquillity." An emphasis on the emotions, then, was central to the new Romantic poetry the two men were creating.

Equally important was subject matter. According to the preface, poetry should deal with "incidents and situations from common life" over which the poet throws "a certain coloring of imagination, whereby ordinary things should be presented . . . in an unusual way." Wordsworth's poems gave "the charm of novelty to things of every day," as Coleridge later said. Coleridge, on the other hand, provided the "coloring of imagination," creating imaginative settings and mysterious sequences of events.

Finally, Wordsworth's preface spoke about incorporating human passions with "the beautiful and permanent forms of nature." An emphasis on nature would become another important characteristic of British Romantic verse, and Wordsworth would frequently be described as a "nature poet."

The Romantic view of nature was quite different from that of most eighteenth-century literature. Nature was not a force to be tamed and analyzed scientifically; rather, it was a wild, free force that could inspire poets to instinctive spiritual understanding. In "The Tables Turned," Wordsworth advised readers to

> Come forth into the light of things,
> Let Nature be your Teacher.

**SAMUEL TAYLOR COLERIDGE**
*Peter Vandyke*
The Granger Collection

In idealizing unspoiled nature, Wordsworth and the other Romantics were not merely abandoning the philosophies of classicism and rationalism; they were condemning the Industrial Revolution and its encroachment on the English countryside.

*Lyrical Ballads* met a cool reception at first, but with time it came to be regarded as the cornerstone of Britain's Romantic Age. Also with time, Wordsworth and Coleridge became respected members of Britain's literary establishment. Their literary ideas began to seem less radical than they once had, and their political thinking—deeply marked by events in France—grew more conservative.

## The Second Generation of Romantic Poets

Wordsworth and Coleridge blazed the way for a new generation of British Romantic poets—the so-called "second generation" of poets, which included Byron, Shelley, and Keats. Coming of age during the Napoleonic era and the Regency, these younger poets rebelled even more strongly than Wordsworth and Coleridge against the British conservatism of the time. All three died abroad after tragically short lives, and their viewpoints were those of disillusioned outsiders.

George Gordon, Lord Byron (1788–1824), did not begin life as an outsider. On the contrary, he was part of the British aristocracy —a member of the House of Lords, an intimate of high-born men and women. Although critics responded unfavorably to his early poetry, Byron persisted and finally achieved success when he published *Childe Harold's Pilgrimage* (1812). Handsome, egotistical, and aloof, Byron became the darling of elegant society—but not for long. Shocked by Byron's radical politics and scandalous love affairs, London hostesses began to shun him, and Byron left Britain in 1816, never to return. He died of a fever while fighting with Greek revolutionaries in their struggle to win independence from Turkey.

Because they had abandoned their democratic ideals, Byron wrote scornfully about Wordsworth and Coleridge. However much of his work reflects their Romantic style. His long narrative poems often feature brooding, passionate, rebellious figures. Such "Byronic" heroes and heroines became a common feature of the literature of the Romantic Age. On the other hand, some of Byron's work —such as his poem *Don Juan* (1819–24)—owes more to eighteenth-century mock epics than it does to Wordsworth and Coleridge.

Byron's friend Percy Bysshe Shelley (1792–1822) was also well-born and politically radical—more consistently radical, in fact, than Byron. In poems such as "Song to the Men of England" (1819), Shelley urged England's lower classes to rebel.

Like Byron, Shelley was shunned for his radical ideas; he left Britain for good in 1818. Unlike Byron, however, Shelley did not attain fame in his own lifetime. Yet he is now remembered for the fervor he brought to lyric poetry in such intensely personal and emotional verses as "To a Skylark" (1821).

John Keats (1795–1821), the third great figure in the second generation of Romantic poets, was also a master of lyrical poetry. Unlike Byron and Shelley, Keats was born outside elegant society, the son of a London stable keeper. Keats trained to be a doctor, then abandoned his medical career to pursue his passion for poetry. He produced many of his greatest poems in a burst of creativity during the first nine months of 1819—works like *The Fall of Hyperion* and "Ode on a Grecian Urn." Unfortunately, however, Keats was already struggling against tuberculosis. Hoping to recuperate in a warmer climate he traveled to Italy, where he died at the age of twenty-five. By his own request, his epitaph reads: "Here lies one whose name was writ in water."

**JOHN KEATS**
*Joseph Severn*
The Granger Collection

## THE ROMANTIC AGE IN BRITISH PROSE

Poetry was the dominant literary form during the Romantic Age, but not the only one. Many significant prose works also appeared, mainly in the form of essays and novels. This was a dry period for drama; only two theaters were licensed to produce plays, and they tended to feature popular spectacles rather than serious plays. However, Shelley and other poets did write closet dramas, verse works intended to be read rather than produced on the stage.

### The Romantic Essayists

British readers of the Romantic Age could find brilliant literary criticism and topical essays in a variety of new periodicals. The earliest of these periodicals reflected the conservative and neoclassical ideals of an earlier age; they roundly condemned the Romantic poets and their work. In time, however, periodicals that were more sympathetic to the Romantics came into being. One such publication, *The London Magazine,* although it appeared only from 1820 to 1829, attracted major contributions from the three greatest essayists of the era: Charles Lamb (1775–1834), William Hazlitt (1778–1830), and Thomas De Quincey (1785–1859). Lamb, in particular, transformed the informal essay of the eighteenth century into a more personal, more introspective Romantic composition.

### The Romantic Novelists

Unlike the Romantic poets, the novelists of the Romantic Age did not make a sharp break with the past. In fact, the three main types of Romantic novels—the Gothic novel, the novel of manners, and the historical romance—all represented elaborations on earlier forms.

The Gothic novel first appeared in the middle of the eighteenth

SIR WALTER SCOTT/ABBOTSFORD FAMILY,
1804
*Sir David Wilkie*
The Granger Collection

century. It featured a number of standard ingredients, including brave heroes and heroines, threatening scoundrels, vast eerie castles, and ghosts. The Romantic fascination with mystery and the supernatural made such novels quite popular during the Romantic Age. One of the most successful was *Frankenstein, or the Modern Prometheus* (1818), written by Shelley's wife, Mary Wollstonecraft Shelley (1797–1851).

The Romantic novel of manners carried on in the tradition of earlier writers by turning a satirical eye on British customs. The most highly regarded writer of novels of manners was Jane Austen (1775–1817) whose works include *Sense and Sensibility* (1811) and *Pride and Prejudice* (1813). Her incisive portrayals of character are more reflective of the classical sensibility of the eighteenth century than the Romantic notions of the new age.

Historical romances—imaginative works of fiction built around a real person or historical event—had appeared long before the Romantic Age, but they attained their peak of popularity in the work of Sir Walter Scott (1771–1832). Passionately devoted to his native Scotland, Scott wrote about the days of knights and chivalry. Although he expressed a Scottish nationalism not unlike the nationalism of Germany's Romantic writers, Scott remained popular with England's ruling class, who apparently did not view his tales of a bygone age as a threat to the status quo.

The close of Britain's Romantic Age is usually set in 1832, the year of the passage of the First Reform Bill. However, the ideas of Romanticism remained a strong influence on many writers from following generations. In fact, even today we can detect elements of Romanticism in many major works of contemporary fiction and poetry as well as in TV dramas, movies, and popular songs.

## Quotations by Prominent Figures of the Period

Bliss was it on that dawn to be alive . . .
France standing on the top of golden hours
And human nature seemed born again.
    **William Wordsworth,** *The Prelude*

But yet I know, where'er I go.
That there hath past away a glory from the earth . . .
    nothing can bring back the hour
Of splendor in the grass, of glory in the flower.
    **William Wordsworth,** "Ode: Intimations of Immortality from
        Recollections of Early Childhood"

Poetry is not the proper antithesis to prose, but to science.
    **Samuel Taylor Coleridge,** *Definitions of Poetry*

One half the world cannot understand the pleasures of the
other.
    **Jane Austen,** *Emma*

It is a truth universally acknowledged that a man in possession
of a good fortune must be in want of a wife.
    **Jane Austen,** *Pride and Prejudice*

Clear writers, like fountains, do not seem so deep as they are.
    **Charles Lamb,** *Imaginary Conversation*

I love not man the less, but Nature more.
    **George Gordon, Lord Byron,** *Childe Harold's Pilgrimage*

If Winter comes, can Spring be far behind?
    **Percy Bysshe Shelley,** "Ode to the West Wind"

The poetry of earth is never dead.
    **John Keats,** "Sonnet: On the Grasshopper and the Cricket"

"Beauty is truth, truth beauty"—that is all
Ye know on earth, and all ye need to know.
    **John Keats,** "Ode on a Grecian Urn"

# The Literature of 1798–1832

When you read literature, it is important to place it in its historical context. Doing so will help you to see how it reflects the dominant ideas of its time and appreciate the techniques the writer used in conveying these ideas.

## Historical Context

During the years from 1798 to 1832, English life was dramatically influenced by the aftereffects of the French Revolution and the realities of industrialization. While many English intellectuals supported the democratic ideals upon which the French Revolution was grounded, the English ruling class took measures to ensure that a similar revolution could not occur in England. At the same time, the industrial revolution was having a profound social and economic impact on the nation. English cities grew rapidly and became the nation's economic centers. Factory workers labored long hours for extremely low wages, and young children often had to work to help support their families. It became increasingly clear that new governmental policies were needed to accommodate these changes. Yet few political changes occurred until 1832, when the First Reform Bill was passed.

## Literary Movements

Toward the end of the eighteenth century, an artistic movement known as Romanticism developed as a reaction against the dominant ideas and standards of Rationalism. Unlike the Rationalists, who stressed logic and reason, the Romantics emphasized emotions and the imagination. The Romantics also possessed a strong belief in democracy, an interest in mystery and the supernatural, a belief in excess and spontaneity, a concern for common people, and a love of nature.

## Writers' Techniques

The Romantic period was an age in which poetry flourished. Using the language of common people, the Romantics wrote lyric poems that generally focused on ordinary situations and ordinary people. Although poetry was the major form of literary expression during the period, a number of significant novels and essays were also produced. Like Romantic poetry, these works reflect the dominant ideas and attitudes of the age.

On the following pages is a poem by William Wordsworth, a major Romantic poet. The annotations in the side column should help you to place the selection in its historical context.

# The Solitary Reaper

## William Wordsworth

*This poem was inspired by a passage from Thomas Willkinson's* Tour of Scotland *(1824): "Passed a female who was reaping alone; she sung in Erse (Scottish Gaelic) as she bended over her sickle; the sweetest human voice I ever heard: her strains were tenderly melancholy, and felt delicious long after they were heard no more."*

Behold her, single in the field,
Yon solitary Highland lass!
Reaping and singing by herself;
Stop here, or gently pass!
5  Alone she cuts and binds the grain,
And sings a melancholy strain;
O listen! for the vale profound
Is overflowing with the sound.

**Literary Movement:** Wordsworth uses his imagination to transform a passage from Wilkinson's book into a poem. The poem's subject reflects the Romantic interest in common people and rural life.

No nightingale did ever chaunt
10  More welcome notes to weary bands
Of travelers in some shady haunt,
Among Arabian sands;
A voice so thrilling ne'er was heard
In springtime from the cuckoo-bird,
15  Breaking the silence of the seas
Among the farthest Hebrides.

**Literary Movement:** Wordsworth's references to the songs of birds reflect the Romantic love of nature.

Will no one tell me what she sings?—
Perhaps the plaintive numbers flow
For old, unhappy, far-off things,
20  And battles long ago;
Or is it some more humble lay,
Familiar matter of today?
Some natural sorrow, loss, or pain,
That has been, and may be again?

**Writer's Technique:** The poem is a lyric written in octaves, or eight-line stanzas, using an *ababccdd* rhyme scheme.

**Writer's Technique:** The poem is written in common, everyday language.

25  Whate'er the theme, the maiden sang
As if her song could have no ending;

I saw her singing at her work,
And o'er the sickle bending;
I listened, motionless and still;
30   And, as I mounted up the hill,
The music in my heart I bore,
Long after it was heard no more.

## THINKING ABOUT THE SELECTION

### Recalling

1. What is the "solitary Highland lass" doing when the speaker sees her?
2. To what does the speaker compare the woman's singing in the second stanza?
3. What possible subjects of the woman's song does the speaker imagine?
4. What does the speaker bear in his heart as he continues his walk?

### Interpreting

5. What do the comparisons in the second stanza suggest about the woman's song?
6. What does the final stanza reveal about the impact of the experience on the speaker?

### Applying

7. In what ways does the type of life portrayed in the poem contrast with the type of life you would imagine the nineteenth-century factory workers must have led?

## ANALYZING LITERATURE

### Appreciating a Writer's Diction

Diction refers to a writer's choice of words. When writing a literary work, a writer uses language that is appropriate for the subject and characters.

1. In this poem Wordsworth uses simple, direct language. Why is this type of language appropriate?

2. Why would the poem be less effective if it were written using elegant, ornate language?

## CRITICAL THINKING AND READING

### Understanding Sound Devices

In "The Solitary Reaper," Wordsworth uses a number of sound devices to give the poem a musical quality. For example, he uses alliteration—the repetition of similar sounds, usually consonants, at the beginnings of words and accented syllables—in line 9, repeating the *n* sound: "*No nightingale* did ever chant." Wordsworth also uses assonance, or the repetition of similar vowel sounds. Notice the repetition of the *i* sound in line 1: "Behold her, *single in* the field."

1. Find two more examples of alliteration.
2. Find two more examples of assonance.
3. How does the poem's musical quality reflect its meaning?

## THINKING AND WRITING

### Writing a Poem

Write a poem in which the Highland lass describes the experience that Wordsworth's speaker observes. Use your imagination to develop her character. When writing your poem, make sure it conveys the character you have developed. In your poem, reveal the subject of her song and present her impressions of the speaker of Wordsworth's poem. When you revise, make sure you have used concrete images, or word pictures.

# Poetry

**SALISBURY CATHEDRAL**
*John Constable*
Museu de Arte, Sao Paulo,
Art Resource

# WILLIAM WORDSWORTH

## 1770–1850

William Wordsworth is among the small group of writers and poets who truly deserve the title "pioneer." His name is almost synonymous with the movement known as *Romanticism*. Wordsworth demonstrated that poetry was a free—a *living*—form of artistic expression, a view that contrasted sharply with that held by the generation writing before him. Whereas the Neoclassicists, as these earlier poets were called, insisted that poetry address a narrow range of topics and be rigidly structured, Wordsworth's poems were written for the common people—and in a common language.

Born in the beautiful Lake District of England, Wordsworth loved to roam the hills and sit and meditate by the streams. He was well-suited to country living and in later years found nature to be the source of his poetic inspiration and internal peace. Though his parents died when he was young—his mother when he was eight, his father when he was thirteen—Wordsworth's education was seen to, and in 1787 he entered Cambridge. After graduation he traveled through Europe, spending considerable time in France. Here he became caught up in the popular side of the French Revolution, with its emphasis on the rights of the individual. He also found time to fall in love with a young woman named Annette Vallon.

Wordsworth's involvement in the Revolution and his affair with Annette ended abruptly, however, when England declared war on France in 1793 and he was forced to return to his homeland. A year later, the Revolution was halted altogether with the execution of its leader, Robespierre. Wordsworth, seeing his ideals dashed, lapsed into a deep depression. Two people who came to his spiritual rescue were his sister Dorothy and his good friend Samuel Taylor Coleridge.

With Coleridge, Wordsworth composed *Lyrical Ballads* (1798), a collection of poems that reflected his "revolutionary" approach to poetry. In the preface to the collection, Wordsworth put forth his view that poetry should deal with common people and ordinary experiences—that its style and form should reflect "a spontaneous overflow of emotion." Though the book was not received favorably at first, it eventually gained recognition as a major poetic work and is seen today as one of the most influential works on poetic theory ever written in the English language.

# GUIDE FOR INTERPRETING

## Lines Composed a Few Miles Above Tintern Abbey; My Heart Leaps Up When I Behold

**Writer's Technique**

**Romanticism.** Romanticism was a literary movement in Europe in the late eighteenth century. It grew out of a negative reaction to the rigid, formal guidelines and forced subject matter that typified the poetry and art of the previous age. Whereas rationalism and a reliance on scientific doctrine were highly valued by the earlier Neoclassicists, Romanticists believed in the virtues of the imagination and fantasy. The Romantic writer was not only permitted, but encouraged, to give vent to his or her emotions—to write spontaneously, from the heart. Love of nature and an idealization of rural life were naturals for the Romantic poet. Many of these aspects of the Romantic credo figure in the poems of William Wordsworth. Subjectivity in particular is clearly visible in his "Lines Composed a Few Miles Above Tintern Abbey."

**Writing**

Think about a place you have been that made a vivid impression on you. You might choose a place you visited on vacation or one where you lived. Close your eyes and try to visualize this locale, concentrating on details. Then, freewrite, describing everything you "see."

**Primary Source**

To offset the cost of a hike to the Valley of Stones, Wordsworth and Coleridge planned to collaborate on a ballad for publication in *The New Monthly Magazine*. They began to compose "The Ancient Mariner" as they walked but soon realized that their styles were too different. Instead, they decided to collaborate on a book of poems. Twenty years later, in 1817, Coleridge described the division of labor:

> The thought suggested itself (to which of us I do not recollect) that a series of poems might be composed of two sorts. In the one, the incidents and agents were to be, in part at least, supernatural. . . . For the second class, subjects were to be chosen from ordinary life; the characters and incidents were to be such as will be found in every village and vicinity. . . .

# Lines Composed a Few Miles Above Tintern Abbey

William Wordsworth

*This poem was written in 1798 during Wordsworth's second visit to the valley of the River Wye and the ruins of Tintern Abbey, once a great medieval church, in Wales. Having passed through the region alone five years earlier, Wordsworth brought his sister with him to share the experience this time. Of this experience and the poem it inspired, Wordworth wrote, "No poem of mine was composed under circumstances more pleasant for one to remember than this."*

Five years have past; five summers, with the length
Of five long winters! and again I hear
These waters, rolling from their mountain springs
With a soft inland murmur. Once again
5    Do I behold these steep and lofty cliffs,
That on a wild secluded scene impress
Thoughts of more deep seclusion; and connect
The landscape with the quiet of the sky.
The day is come when I again repose
10   Here, under this dark sycamore, and view
These plots of cottage ground, these orchard tufts,
Which at this season, with their unripe fruits,
Are clad in one green hue, and lose themselves
'Mid groves and copses. Once again I see
15   These hedgerows, hardly hedgerows, little lines
Of sportive wood run wild: these pastoral farms,
Green to the very door; and wreaths of smoke
Sent up, in silence, from among the trees!
With some uncertain notice, as might seem
20   Of vagrant dwellers in the houseless woods,
Or of some hermit's cave, where by his fire
The hermit sits alone.

                These beauteous forms,
Through a long absence, have not been to me
As is a landscape to a blind man's eye:
25   But oft, in lonely rooms, and 'mid the din
Of towns and cities, I have owed to them

**TINTERN ABBEY**
*J. M. W. Turner*
British Museum

*Lines Composed a Few Miles Above Tintern Abbey*   645

In hours of weariness, sensations sweet,
Felt in the blood, and felt along the heart;
And passing even into my purer mind,
30 With tranquil restoration—feelings too
Of unremembered pleasure: such, perhaps,
As have no slight or trivial influence
On that best portion of a good man's life.
His little, nameless, unremembered, acts
35 Of kindness and of love. Nor less, I trust,
To them I may have owed another gift,
Of aspect more sublime; that blessed mood,
In which the burthen[1] of the mystery,
In which the heavy and the weary weight
40 Of all this unintelligible world,
Is lightened—that serene and blessed mood,
In which the affections gently lead us on—
Until, the breath of this corporeal frame[2]
And even the motion of our human blood
45 Almost suspended, we are laid asleep
In body, and become a living soul;
While with an eye made quiet by the power
Of harmony, and the deep power of joy,
We see into the life of things.

                              If this
50 Be but a vain belief, yet, oh! how oft—
In darkness and amid the many shapes
Of joyless daylight; when the fretful stir
Unprofitable, and the fever of the world,
Have hung upon the beatings of my heart—
55 How oft, in spirit, have I turned to thee,
O sylvan[3] Wye! thou wanderer through the woods,
How often has my spirit turned to thee!

        And now, with gleams of half-extinguished thought,
With many recognitions dim and faint,
60 And somewhat of a sad perplexity,
The picture of the mind revives again;
While here I stand, not only with the sense
Of present pleasure, but with pleasing thoughts
That in this moment there is life and food
65 For future years. And so I dare to hope,
Though changed, no doubt, from what I was when first
I came among these hills; when like a roe[4]

---

1. **burthen:** Burden.
2. **corporeal** (kôr pôr′ ē əl) **frame:** Body.
3. **sylvan** (sil′ vən): Wooded.
4. **roe:** A type of deer.

I bounded o'er the mountains, by the sides
Of the deep rivers, and the lonely streams,
70    Wherever nature led: more like a man
Flying from something that he dreads, than one
Who sought the thing he loved. For nature then
(The coarser pleasures of my boyish days,
And their glad animal movements all gone by)
75    To me was all in all—I cannot paint
What then I was. The sounding cataract
Haunted me like a passion; the tall rock,
The mountain, and the deep and gloomy wood,
Their colors and their forms, were then to me
80    An appetite; a feeling and a love,
That had no need of a remoter charm,
By thought supplied, nor any interest
Unborrowed from the eye. That time is past,
And all its aching joys are now no more,
85    And all its dizzy raptures. Not for this
Faint[5] I, nor mourn nor murmur; other gifts
Have followed; for such loss, I would believe,
Abundant recompense. For I have learned
To look on nature, not as in the hour
90    Of thoughtless youth; but hearing oftentimes
The still, sad music of humanity,
Nor harsh nor grating, though of ample power
To chasten and subdue. And I have felt
A presence that disturbs me with the joy
95    Of elevated thoughts; a sense sublime
Of something far more deeply interfused,
Whose dwelling is the light of setting suns,
And the round ocean and the living air,
And the blue sky, and in the mind of man;
100    A motion and a spirit, that impels
All thinking things, all objects of all thought,
And rolls through all things. Therefore am I still
A lover of the meadows and the woods
And mountains; and of all that we behold
105    From this green earth; of all the mighty world
Of eye, and ear—both what they half create,
And what perceive; well pleased to recognize
In nature and the language of the sense,
The anchor of my purest thoughts, the nurse,
110    The guide, the guardian of my heart, and soul
Of all my moral being.

               Nor perchance.
If I were not thus taught, should I the more

---

**5. faint:** Lose heart.

Suffer[6] my genial spirits[7] to decay;
For thou art with me here upon the banks
115 Of this fair river; thou my dearest Friend,[8]
My dear, dear Friend, and in thy voice I catch
The language of my former heart, and read
My former pleasures in the shoooting lights
Of thy wild eyes. Oh! yet a little while
120 May I behold in thee what I was once,
My dear, dear Sister! and this prayer I make,
Knowing that Nature never did betray
The heart that loved her; 'tis her privilege,
Through all the years of this our life, to lead
125 From joy to joy; for she can so inform
The mind that is within us, so impress
With quietness and beauty, and so feed
With lofty thoughts, that neither evil tongues,
Rash judgments, nor the sneers of selfish men,
130 Nor greetings where no kindness is, nor all
The dreary intercourse of daily life,
Shall e'er prevail against us, or disturb
Our cheerful faith, that all which we behold
Is full of blessings. Therefore let the moon
135 Shine on thee in thy solitary walk;
And let the misty mountain winds be free
To blow against thee: and, in after years,
When these wild ecstasies shall be matured
Into a sober pleasure; when thy mind
140 Shall be a mansion for all lovely forms,
Thy memory be as a dwelling place
For all sweet sounds and harmonies; oh! then,
If solitude, or fear, or pain, or grief,
Should be thy portion, with what healing thoughts
145 Of tender joy wilt thou remember me,
And these my exhortations! Nor, perchance—
If I should be where I no more can hear
Thy voice, nor catch from thy wild eyes these gleams
Of past existence—wilt thou then forget
150 That on the banks of this delightful stream
We stood together; and that I, so long
A worshipper of Nature, hither came
Unwearied in that service: rather say
With warmer love—oh! with far deeper zeal
155 Of holier love. Nor wilt thou then forget,
That after many wanderings, many years

---

**6. suffer:** Allow.
**7. genial spirits:** Creative powers.
**8. Friend:** His sister Dorothy.

Of absence, these steep woods and lofty cliffs,
And this green pastoral landscape, were to me
More dear, both for themselves and for thy sake!

---

## THINKING ABOUT THE SELECTION
### Recalling

1. In "Lines Composed a Few Miles Above Tintern Abbey," how have the poet's memories
   of his first visit to the Wye valley altered him?
2. (a) Apart from his pleasure at the moment,
   what does the poet hope to gain from his
   second visit to the valley? (b) What does he
   hope his sister will gain?

### Interpreting

3. (a) At what time of year does the poet make
   his second visit to the area near Tintern
   Abbey? (b) Find evidence in the poem that
   supports your answer.
4. In line 35 of the poem, the poet mentions
   "another gift" which his contact with this rural
   scene has bestowed upon him. Briefly describe this gift.
5. To what is the poet referring in line 109 as the
   "anchor of my purest thoughts?"

### Applying

6. Do you think it was Wordsworth's wish that
   everyone attempt to share his experience with
   and attitudes toward nature? Do you think he
   believed everyone was capable? Explain.

## ANALYZING LITERATURE
### Understanding Romanticism

**Romanticism** stressed the importance of
emotion and imagination as tools of the artist. To
Wordsworth, one of the movement's foremost
practitioners, Romanticism also meant a return to
nature and an escape from the contamination of
modern civilization. Wordsworth urged the poet
to explore his or her innermost feelings—to be-

come attuned to the stirrings of the soul. For this
reason, much of Romantic art and poetry has a
spiritual, at times almost mystical, quality about
it.

Look again at "Lines Composed a Few Miles
Above Tintern Abbey," and as you read be on
the lookout for the words *soul, heart,* and *spirit.*
Paraphrase (state in your own words) each of the
poet's thoughts that contains one or more of
these words. Explain how each thought relates to
the ideals of the Romantic movement.

## CRITICAL THINKING AND READING
### Comparing and Contrasting Experiences

A careful reading of "Tintern Abbey" reveals
that even as a young man Wordsworth was a
sensitive and perceptive person. And yet the
poem details certain differences between his
first and second trips to the Wye valley. Skim the
poem for details and then describe:
1. the differences in the poet's behavior.
2. the differences and similarities in his thoughts
   and attitudes.

## THINKING AND WRITING
### Writing About Romanticism

The twentieth-century American writer
Thomas Wolfe defined the true Romantic feeling
as "not the desire to escape life, but to prevent
life from escaping you." Freewrite, exploring the
meaning of this quotation. Then write an essay
explaining how "Tintern Abbey" typifies the true
Romantic feeling as defined by Wolfe. When you
revise make sure you have supported your opinion with details from the poem.

# My Heart Leaps Up When I Behold

## William Wordsworth

My heart leaps up when I behold
    A rainbow in the sky:
So was it when my life began;
So is it now I am a man;
So be it when I shall grow old,
    Or let me die!
The child is father of the Man;
And I could wish my days to be
Bound each to each by natural piety.[1]

---

**1. natural piety:** Devotion to nature.

**LANDSCAPE WITH RAINBOW**
*Joseph Wright of Derby*
Derby Art Gallery

## THINKING ABOUT THE SELECTION

### Recalling

1. What is the poet's hope in the poem "My Heart Leaps Up"?

### Interpreting

2. What general statement might the poet have used in place of the first two lines?
3. What do you think the poet means when he speaks of "natural piety"?

### Applying

4. (a) What interest of yours would you like to share with other people? (b) How best might you communicate this to them?

## CRITICAL THINKING AND READING

### Interpreting a Paradox

A **paradox** is a statement that makes sense in spite of an apparent contradiction. "Youth is wasted on the young," for example, is paradoxical. However, it makes perfect sense when we consider that hindsight, or the experience of age, can help us better appreciate the value of what we have when we are young.

1. The statement, "The child is Father of the Man" is one of the most famous paradoxes in literature. Explain how this seeming contradiction can be true.
2. Explain what belief of the Romantic movement this paradox illustrates.

## THINKING AND WRITING

### Writing a Nature Poem

Write a short poem about the joy you find in some aspect of nature. The poem need not rhyme but should contain ample description of the source of your pleasure, as well as an account of precisely how this aspect of nature makes you feel.

When you revise, make sure you have used sensory details to make your description of nature vivid. Have you chosen words that carry the appropriate connotations?

---

**Primary Source**

In his memoirs, Christopher Wordsworth, William's youngest brother, describes the countryside that inspired his brother's lyrical verse. What elements in the following scene do you think would make your heart "leap up"?

"The weather being fine, Wordsworth agreed to go with us into Easedale . . . he trudging before, with his green gauze shade over his eyes, and in his plaid jacket and waistcoat. First, he turned aside at a little farmhouse, and took us into a swelling field, to look down on the tumbling stream which bounded it, and which we saw precipitated at a distance, in a broad white sheet, from the mountain. . . . Oh, what a scene! The day one of the softest and brightest in autumn; the lights various; the mountains in the richest coloring, fern covering them with reddish gold in great part; here and there, trees in every variety of autumn foliage; and the rock itself of a kind of lilac tint; the outlines of the mountains very fine; the Tarn, which might almost be called a lake for size and abundance of water, with no culture, trees, or habitation around it, here and there a great rock stretching into it like a promontory, and high mountains surrounding it on three sides, on two of them almost precipitate; on the fourth side, it is more open, and on this the stream, crossed by four great steppingstones, runs out of it, and descends into Grasmere vale and lake."

# GUIDE FOR INTERPRETING

## Literary Forms

### Composed Upon Westminster Bridge, September 3, 1802; It Is a Beauteous Evening, Calm and Free; London, 1802; The World Is Too Much with Us

**The Sonnet.** A sonnet is a fourteen-line poem in which each line contains five strong beats and five weak beats. While most sonnets follow one of two general rhyme schemes—the Shakespearean (or English) and the Petrarchan (or Italian)—many poets adapt the rhyme to fit their own needs. The sonnet occupies a particular place of distinction among the poems of Wordsworth. Though a champion of freedom and spontaneity in poetry, Wordsworth nevertheless recognized the importance of order and discipline. The sonnet, as a relatively short and decisive poetic statement, was the logical vehicle for treating such subjects as the human condition and the importance of nature to the human spirit. "Scarcely one of my poems," Wordsworth wrote, "does not aim to direct attention to some moral sentiment." His purpose, as he saw it, was "to console the afflicted" and "to add sunshine to daylight by making the happy happier." These and related other goals could best be served, he felt, through the sonnet.

## Writing

Think of a topic that holds importance for you. The topic could range from such social issues as finding shelter for the homeless of our country to such personal ones as the love between a pet and a person. Write down specific details of your topic that might be covered in a poem.

## Primary Source

The journal that Wordsworth's younger sister Dorothy kept from 1895, when she was twenty-four, until her death five years after her brother's, provides an invaluable clue to the life of a great poet. Wordsworth and his sister enjoyed a close relationship; in his own journals, the poet wrote that Dorothy "preserved me still a Poet" through times of personal crisis. In her journal for September 3, 1802, Dorothy records the following entry:

> It was a beautiful morning. The city, St. Paul's, with the river and a multitude of little boats, made a most beautiful sight as we crossed Westminster Bridge. The houses were not overhung by their cloud of smoke, and they were spread out endlessly, yet the sun shone so brightly, with such a fierce light, that there was even something like the purity of one of nature's own grand spectacles.

# Composed Upon Westminster Bridge

# September 3, 1802

William Wordsworth

Earth has not anything to show more fair:
Dull would he be of soul who could pass by
A sight so touching in its majesty;
This City now doth, like a garment, wear
5   The beauty of the morning; silent, bare,
Ships, towers, domes, theaters, and temples, lie
Open unto the fields, and to the sky;
All bright and glittering in the smokeless air,
Never did sun more beautifully steep
10  In his first splendor, valley, rock, or hill;
Ne'er saw I, never felt, a calm so deep!
The river glideth at his own sweet will:
Dear God! the very houses seem asleep:
And all that mighty heart is lying still!

---

## THINKING ABOUT THE SELECTION

### Recalling

1. At what time of day is the poem "Composed Upon Westminster Bridge" set?
2. What sights does the poet see around him?

### Interpreting

3. In lines 9–10, the poet sums up his reaction to his own description of the first eight lines.

State this reaction in your own words.
4. Paraphrase the last four lines of this poem.

### Applying

5. In what way is this poem contrary to some of the ideas expressed by Wordsworth in "My Heart Leaps Up"? How can you account for these differences? With which attitude are you more in sympathy? Explain your answer.

# It Is a Beauteous Evening, Calm and Free

William Wordsworth

It is a beauteous evening, calm and free,
The holy time is quiet as a Nun
Breathless with adoration; the broad sun
Is sinking down in its tranquility;
5   The gentleness of heaven broods o'er the Sea:
Listen! the mighty Being is awake,
And doth with his eternal motion make
A sound like thunder—everlastingly.
Dear Child! dear Girl! that walkest with me here,
10   If thou appear untouched by solemn thought,
Thy nature is not therefore less divine:
Thou liest in Abraham's bosom[1] all the year;
And worship'st at the Temple's inner shrine,
God being with thee when we know it not.

_____

**1. Abraham's bosom:** Heaven (Luke 16:22).

---

## THINKING ABOUT THE SELECTION

### Recalling

1. Describe the setting of "It Is a Beauteous Evening."
2. Who is the poet's companion?

### Interpreting

3. What is meant by "eternal motion" and "thunder"?

4. How does the poet's response to the scene differ from that of the child?
5. (a) How would you summarize the poet's advice to the child? (b) to the reader?

### Applying

6. What differences in the last six lines of the poem might you expect if they were addressed to another adult? Explain.

**CORNFIELD BY MOONLIGHT**
*Samuel Palmer*
*British Museum*

## ANALYZING LITERATURE

### Recognizing a Sonnet

A **sonnet** is a poem with fourteen lines, each with five strong and five weak beats. Sonnets are generally divided into two main types, Shakespearean or Petrarchan, on the basis of rhyme scheme and stanza division. The Shakespearean sonnet is divided into three *quatrains* (or stanzas of four lines) and a closing *couplet* (pair of lines). Its rhyme scheme is most often *abab cdcd efef gg.* The Petrarchan sonnet, by con-trast, is composed of a group of eight lines (called an *octet*), followed by a group of six (the *sestet*). The rhyme scheme is usually *abbaabba cdecde,* though variations exist in the sestet.

1. Which kind of sonnet is "It Is a Beauteous Evening, Calm and Free"?
2. What is its rhyme scheme?
3. (a) What is the subject matter of the first eight lines? (b) What is the subject matter of the last six lines? (c) Explain how both parts comple-ment each other.

# London, 1802

## William Wordsworth

Milton! thou shouldst be living in this hour:
England hath need of thee: she is a fen[1]
Of stagnant waters: altar, sword, and pen,
Fireside, the heroic wealth of hall and bower,
5  Have forfeited their ancient English dower
Of inward happiness. We are selfish men;
Oh! raise us up, return to us again;
And give us manners, virtue, freedom, power.
Thy soul was like a Star, and dwelt apart,
10  Thou hadst a voice whose sound was like the sea:
Pure as the naked heavens, majestic, free,
So didst thou travel on life's common way,
In cheerful godliness; and yet thy heart
The lowliest duties on herself did lay.

---

**1. fen:** Bog.

## THINKING ABOUT THE SELECTION

### Recalling

1. (a) What other poet does Wordsworth address in "London, 1802"? (b) What does he ask that poet to do?

### Interpreting

2. According to the poet, in what way is England like a "fen/Of stagnant waters"?

3. Which classes do you think are represented by the terms "altar," "sword," "pen," and "fireside"?

### Applying

4. (a) In what ways does the poet's image of London differ with that expressed in "Composed Upon Westminster Bridge," written in the same year? (b) How might Wordsworth explain these differences?

# The World Is Too Much with Us

## William Wordsworth

The world is too much with us; late and soon,
Getting and spending, we lay waste our powers:
Little we see in Nature that is ours;
We have given our hearts away, a sordid boon![1]
5   This sea that bares her bosom to the moon;
The winds that will be howling at all hours,
And are upgathered now like sleeping flowers;
For this, for everything, we are out of tune;
It moves us not.—Great God! I'd rather be
10  A Pagan suckled in a creed outworn;
So might I, standing on this pleasant lea,[2]
Have glimpses that would make me less forlorn;
Have sight of Proteus[3] rising from the sea;
Or hear old Triton[4] blow his wreathèd horn.

---

**1. boon:** Favor.
**2. lea:** Meadow.
**3. Proteus** (prō′ tyo͞os): In Greek mythology, a sea god who could change his appearance at will.
**4. Triton:** In Greek mythology, a sea god with the head and upper body of a man and the tail of a fish.

---

## THINKING ABOUT THE SELECTION

### Recalling

1. In "The World Is Too Much with Us," what does the poet say "we" have given away?

### Interpreting

2. Explain what the poet means by the words *world* and *Nature*.
3. (a) Why would the poet rather be "A Pagan suckled in a creed outworn"? (b) How would even a "creed outworn" be preferable to the materialistic faith Wordsworth observed?

### Applying

4. In 1955 in the United States, Erich Fromm wrote, "We live in a world of things, and our only connection with them is that we know how to manipulate or to consume them." How do you think Wordsworth would respond to this contemporary viewpoint?

# SAMUEL TAYLOR COLERIDGE

## 1772–1834

Samuel Taylor Coleridge is the classic case of the gifted writer whose genius was hampered by lifelong problems, among them self-doubt and poor health. Coleridge was born in Ottery St. Mary on the Devon coast of England, the last of fourteen children, only four of whom survived. Spoiled by his father, Coleridge withdrew into a world of books and fantasy. At age nine, after his father died, Coleridge was sent to school in London. There the boy excelled and began developing an ability to speak on such matters as philosophy in a way that left his fellow students spellbound.

In 1791 Coleridge entered Cambridge University on a scholarship, but left before he graduated. He discussed plans with several other thinkers of the age to start up a colony in America whose members would live on a high intellectual plane. It was agreed that each member would have a wife. Though the plans for the community fell through, Coleridge's marriage plans did not, and in 1795 he married Sara Fricker.

With his wife, Coleridge moved in 1797 to Somerset, where he developed a close friendship with William Wordsworth, an important poet of the period. In 1798 the two turned out *Lyrical Ballads,* a joint collection of their work. The four poems that make up Coleridge's contribution to the volume deal with matters of the spiritual world and include his masterpiece, "The Rime of the Ancient Mariner." Though at first public response to this collection of poems was lukewarm, the book slowly gained critical attention, ultimately causing a revolution in poetic style and thought and firmly establishing the movement known as Romanticism.

As Coleridge's fame grew, his marriage, his health, and his friendship with Wordsworth all gradually failed. He suffered increasingly from asthma and rheumatism, and he began to rely heavily on painkillers, which dulled his creative powers. Still, Coleridge managed to turn out a good deal of work in the years left him, and in a variety of areas. He worked variously as a journalist, as a lecturer on Shakespeare and Milton, as an essayist, and as a playwright, earning a tidy sum of money in 1812 with his tragedy *Remorse.* And all the time, despite his personal hardships, Coleridge continued to make himself available to visitors, which ultimately proved to have a great impact on the young crop of Romanticists writing at that time.

Perhaps Coleridge's greatest legacy was the insight he affords his reader on the role of imagination in literature. His belief that literature is a magical blend of thought and emotion is at the very heart of his greatest works, in which the unreal is often made to seem real.

# GUIDE FOR INTERPRETING

## The Rime of the Ancient Mariner

**Sound Devices.** The relationship between poetry and music has often been noted. Just as music achieves its effect through rhythms and harmonies, so poetry achieves its effect through sound devices, or techniques that enhance the meter and rhyme of a poem.

Chief among the sound devices available to the poet is *alliteration,* the repetition of a given consonant sound at the beginning of words or accented syllables that occur close together. Notice, for example, the repeated *f* sound in these lines from "The Rime of the Ancient Mariner": "The *f*air breeze blew, the white *f*oam *f*lew,/ The *f*urrow *f*ollowed *f*ree. . . ."

*Consonance,* a device related to alliteration, is the repetition of a given consonant sound at the end of words or accented syllables appearing close by. Consider another line from Coleridge, this one capitalizing on the *v* sound: "When the i*v*y tod is hea*v*y with snow . . ."

In the sound device known as *assonance,* it is a vowel sound that is repeated in nearby words or syllables. In the following passage, the long *a* sound is so treated: "Th*e* western w*a*ve was all a*f*lame./ The d*a*y was well-nigh done!"

*Internal rhyme,* a fourth sound device, features rhyming words within the space of a single line. As an example, note the following line: "With heavy *thump,* a lifeless *lump* . . ."

**Commentary**

Coleridge once opened an essay by asking his readers to "sit down to a book . . . as a well-behaved visitor does to a banquet." But he knew that good readers need more than manners. To make his point, he discussed what he saw as the four kinds of readers:

1. Sponges, who absorb all they read and return it nearly in the same state, only a little dirtied.
2. Sand-glasses, who retain nothing and are content to get through a book for the sake of getting through the time.
3. Strain-bags, who retain merely the dregs of what they read.
4. Mogul diamonds, equally rare and valuable, who profit from what they read and enable others to profit by it also.
   What type of reader are you?

**Writing**

Imagine a contest: A friend has dreamed of a skeleton ship manned by spectral figures. You and a group of friends decide to flesh out the dream. The best narrative will win the contest. Write your tale of this skeleton ship.

# The Rime of the Ancient Mariner

Samuel Taylor Coleridge

*The Rime of the Ancient Mariner, based on a dream of Coleridge's friend, John Cruikshank, was originally planned as a collaboration between Coleridge and Wordsworth. Eventually Wordsworth dropped out of the project, but not before making a number of valuable suggestions, including the shooting of the albatross and the navigation of the ship by the dead men. Several years after the poem was first published in* Lyrical Ballads *(1798), Coleridge added the prose explanations in the margins to aid the reader in understanding the poem's meaning.*

### Argument

How a Ship having passed the Line[1] was driven by storms to the cold Country towards the South Pole: and how from thence she made her course to the tropical Latitude of the Great Pacific Ocean; and of the strange things that befell: and in what manner the Ancyent Marinere came back to his own Country.

### Part I

*An ancient Mariner meeteth three Gallants bidden to a wedding feast and detaineth one.*

It is an ancient Mariner,
And he stoppeth one of three.
"By thy long gray beard and glittering eye,
Now wherefore stopp'st thou me?

"The Bridegroom's doors are opened wide,     5
And I am next of kin;
The guests are met, the feast is set:
May'st hear the merry din."

---

**1. Line:** Equator.

He holds him with his skinny hand,
"There was a ship," quoth he.                    10
"Hold off! unhand me, graybeard loon!"
Eftsoons[2] his hand dropped he.

He holds him with his glittering eye—
The Wedding Guest stood still,
And listens like a three years' child:            15
The Mariner hath his will.

The Wedding Guest sat on a stone:
He cannot choose but hear;
And thus spake on that ancient man,
The bright-eyed Mariner.                          20

"The ship was cheered, the harbor cleared,
Merrily did we drop

Below the kirk,[3] below the hill,
Below the lighthouse top.

"The Sun came up upon the left,             25
Out of the sea came he!
And he shone bright, and on the right
Went down into the sea.

"Higher and higher every day,
Till over the mast at noon[4]—"
The Wedding Guest here beat his breast,    30
For he heard the loud bassoon.

The bride hath paced into the hall.
Red as a rose is she;
Nodding their heads before her goes         35
The merry minstrelsy.

The Wedding Guest he beat his breast,
Yet he cannot choose but hear;
And thus spake on that ancient man
The bright-eyed Mariner.                          40

"And now the Storm blast came, and he
Was tyrannous and strong:
He struck with his o'ertaking wings,
And chased us south along.

---

**2. eftsoons:** Immediately.
**3. kirk:** Church.
**4. over . . . noon:** The ship has reached the equator.

"With sloping masts and dipping prow,     45
As who pursued with yell and blow
Still treads the shadow of his foe,
And forward bends his head,
The ship drove fast, loud roared the blast,
And southward aye[5] we fled.     50

"And now there came both mist and snow.
And it grew wondrous cold;
And ice, mast-high, came floating by,
As green as emerald.

"And through the drifts the snowy clifts[6]     55
Did send a dismal sheen;
Nor shapes of men nor beasts we ken[7]—
The ice was all between.

"The ice was here, the ice was there,
The ice was all around;     60
It cracked and growled, and roared and howled,
Like noises in a swound![8]

"At length did cross an Albatross,
Thorough[9] the fog it came;
As if it had been a Christian soul,     65
We hailed it in God's name.

"It ate the food it ne'er had eat,[10]
And round and round it flew.
The ice did split with a thunder-fit;
The helmsman steered us through!     70

"And a good south wind sprung up behind;
The Albatross did follow,
And every day, for food or play,
Came to the mariner's hollo!

"In mist or cloud, on mast or shroud,[11]     75
It perched for vespers[12] nine;
Whiles all the night, through fog-smoke white,
Glimmered the white Moonshine."

---

**5. aye:** Ever.
**6. cliffs:** Icebergs.
**7. ken:** knew.
**8. swound:** swoon.
**9. thorough:** Through.
**10. eat** (et): Old form of *eaten.*
**11. shroud** *n.*: Ropes stretching from the ship's side to the masthead.
**12. vespers:** Evenings.

**ENGRAVING BY GUSTAVE DORÉ FOR THE RIME OF THE ANCIENT MARINE**
*by Samuel Taylor Coleridge*

*The ancient Mariner in-hospitably killeth the pious bird of good omen.*

"God save thee, ancient Mariner!
From the fiends, that plague thee thus!—
Why look'st thou so?"[13] "With my crossbow
I shot the Albatross."

80

## Part II

"The Sun now rose upon the right:[14]
Out of the sea came he,
Still hid in mist, and on the left
Went down into the sea.

85

"And the good south wind still blew behind,
But no sweet bird did follow,
Nor any day for food or play
Came to the mariners' hollo!

90

*His shipmates cry out against the ancient Mari-ner for killing the bird of good luck.*

"And I had done a hellish thing,
And it would work 'em woe:
For all averred, I had killed the bird
That made the breeze to blow.
Ah wretch! said they, the bird to slay,
That made the breeze to blow!

95

*But when the fog cleared off, they justify the same, and thus make them-selves accomplices in the crime.*

"Nor dim nor red, like God's own head,
The glorious Sun uprist;[15]
Then all averred, I had killed the bird
That brought the fog and mist.
'Twas right, said they, such birds to slay,
That bring the fog and mist.

100

*The fair breeze continues; the ship enters the Pacific Ocean, and sails north-ward, even till it reaches the Line.*

"The fair breeze blew, the white foam flew,
The furrow[16] followed free;
We were the first that ever burst
Into that silent sea.

105

*The ship hath been sud-denly becalmed.*

"Down dropped the breeze, the sails dropped
     down,
'Twas sad as sad could be;
And we did speak only to break
The silence of the sea!

110

---

**13. God . . . so:** Spoken by the Wedding Guest.
**14. The Sun . . . right:** The ship is now headed north.
**15. uprist:** Arose.
**16. furrow:** Ship's wake.

**ENGRAVING BY GUSTAVE DORÉ FOR THE RIME OF THE ANCIENT MARINER**
*by Samuel Taylor Coleridge*

**ENGRAVING BY GUSTAVE DORÉ FOR THE RIME OF THE ANCIENT MARINER**
by Samuel Taylor Coleridge

"All in a hot and copper sky,
The bloody Sun, at noon,
Right up above the mast did stand,
No bigger than the Moon.

"Day after day, day after day,                                    115
We stuck, nor breath nor motion;
As idle as a painted ship
Upon a painted ocean.

*And the Albatross begins*
*to be avenged.*

"Water, water, everywhere,
And all the boards did shrink;                                    120
Water, water, everywhere,
Nor any drop to drink.

"The very deep did rot: O Christ!
That ever this should be!
Yea, slimy things did crawl with legs                             125
Upon the slimy sea.

"About, about, in reel and rout[17]
The death fires[18] danced at night;
The water, like a witch's oils,
Burned green, and blue and white.                                130

*A Spirit had followed*
*them; one of the invisible*
*inhabitants of this planet,*
*neither departed souls*
*nor angels. They are very*
*numerous, and there is*
*no climate or element*
*without one or more.*

"And some in dreams assurèd were
Of the Spirit that plagued us so;
Nine fathom deep he had followed us
From the land of mist and snow.

"And every tongue, through utter drought,    135
Was withered at the root;
We could not speak, no more than if
We had been choked with soot.

*The shipmates, in their*
*sore distress, would fain*
*throw the whole guilt on*
*the ancient Mariner: in*
*sign whereof they hang*
*the dead sea bird round*
*his neck.*

"Ah! well a-day! what evil looks
Had I from old and young!                                        140
Instead of the cross, the Albatross
About my neck was hung.

---

**17. rout:** Disorderly crowd.
**18. death fires:** St. Elmo's fire, a visible electrical discharge from a
ship's mast, believed by sailors to be an omen of disaster.

## Part III

"There passed a weary time. Each throat
Was parched, and glazed each eye.
A weary time! a weary time!                                      145
How glazed each weary eye,
When looking westward, I beheld
A somthling in the sky.

"At first it seemed a little speck,
And then it seemed a mist;                                       150
It moved and moved, and took at last
A certain shape, I wist.[19]

"A speck, a mist, a shape, I wist!
And still it neared and neared:
As if it dodged a water sprite,                                  155
It plunged and tacked and veered.

"With throats unslaked, with black lips baked,
We could nor laugh nor wail;
Through utter drought all dumb we stood!
I bit my arm, I sucked the blood,                               160
And cried, A sail! a sail!

"With throats unslaked, with black lips
   baked,
Agape they heard me call:
Gramercy![20] they for joy did grin,
And all at once their breath drew in,                           165
As they were drinking all.

"See! see! (I cried) she tacks no more!
Hither to work us weal;[21]
Without a breeze, without a tide,
She steadies with upright keel!                                 170

"The western wave was all aflame.
The day was well nigh done!
Almost upon the western wave
Rested the broad bright Sun;
When that strange shape drove suddenly                          175
Betwixt us and the Sun.

---

**19. wist:** Knew.
**20. Gramercy** (grə mur′ sē): Great thanks.
**21. work us weal:** Assist us.

"And straight the Sun was flecked with bars,
(Heaven's Mother send us grace!)
As if through a dungeon grate he peered
With broad and burning face.                    180

*And its ribs are seen as bars on the face of the setting Sun. The Specter Woman and her Death-mate, and no other on board the skeleton ship.*

"Alas! (thought I, and my heart beat loud)
How fast she nears and nears!
Are those *her* sails that glance in the Sun,
Like restless gossameres?[22]

"Are those *her* ribs through which the
    Sun                                          185
Did peer, as through a grate?
And is that Woman all her crew?
Is that a Death? and are there two?
Is Death that woman's mate?

*Like vessel, like crew!*

*Death and Life-in-Death have diced for the ship's crew, and she (the latter) winneth the ancient Mariner.*

"*Her* lips, were red, *her* looks were free,     190
Her locks were yellow as gold;
Her skin was as white as leprosy,
The Nightmare Life-in-Death was she,
Who thicks man's blood with cold.

"The naked hulk alongside came,               195
And the twain were casting dice;
'The game is done! I've won! I've won!'
Quoth she, and whistles thrice.

*No twilight within the courts of the Sun.*

"The Sun's rim dips; the stars rush out:
At one stride comes the dark;                  200
With far-heard whisper, o'er the sea,
Off shot the specter bark.

*At the rising of the Moon,*

"We listened and looked sideways up!
Fear at my heart, as at a cup,
My lifeblood seemed to sip!                     205
The stars were dim, and thick the night,
The steersman's face by his lamp gleamed
    white;
From the sails the dew did drip—
Till clomb[23] above the eastern bar
The hornèd[24] Moon, with one bright star       210
Within the nether tip.

---

**22. gossameres:** Floating cobwebs.
**23. clomb:** Climbed.
**24. hornèd:** Crescent.

"One after one, by the star-dogged Moon,[25]
Too quick for groan or sigh,
Each turned his face with a ghastly pang,
And cursed me with his eye.                          215

*His shipmates drop down
dead.*

"Four times fifty living men,
(And I heard nor sigh nor groan)
With heavy thump, a lifeless lump,
They dropped down one by one.

*But Life-in-Death begins
her work on the ancient
Mariner.*

"The souls did from their bodies fly—        220
They fled to bliss or woe!
And every soul, it passed me by,
Like the whizz of my crossbow!"

## Part IV

*The Wedding Guest fear-
eth that a Spirit is talking
to him;*

"I fear thee, ancient Mariner!
I fear thy skinny hand!                              225
And thou art long, and lank, and brown,
As is the ribbed sea sand.

*But the ancient Mariner
assureth him of his bodily
life, and proceedeth to relate his horrible penance.*

"I fear thee and thy glittering eye,
And thy skinny hand, so brown."
"Fear not, fear not, thou Wedding Guest!       230
This body dropped not down.

"Alone, alone, all, all alone,
Alone on a wide wide sea!
And never a saint took pity on
My soul in agony.                                   235

*He despiseth the crea-
tures of the calm,*

"The many men, so beautiful!
And they all dead did lie:
And a thousand thousand slimy things
Lived on; and so did I.

*And envieth that they
should live, and so many
lie dead.*

"I looked upon the rotting sea,               240
And drew my eyes away;
I looked upon the rotting deck,
And there the dead men lay.

"I looked to heaven, and tried to pray;
But or[26] ever a prayer had gushed,         245
A wicked whisper came, and made
My heart as dry as dust.

---

**25. star-dogged Moon:** An omen of impending evil to sailors.
**26. or:** Before.

"I closed my lids, and kept them close,
And the balls like pulses beat;
For the sky and the sea and the sea and the
    sky                                    250
Lay like a load on my weary eye,
And the dead were at my feet.

"The cold sweat melted from their limbs,
Nor rot nor reek did they;
The look with which they looked on me      255
Had never passed away.

"An orphan's curse would drag to hell
A spirit from on high;
But oh! more horrible than that
Is the curse in a dead man's eye!       260
Seven days, seven nights, I saw that curse,
And yet l could not die.

"The moving Moon went up the sky,
And nowhere did abide:
Softly she was going up,          265
And a star or two beside—

"Her beams bemocked the sultry main,[27]
Like April hoarfrost spread;
But where the ship's huge shadow lay,
The charmèd water burned alway    270
A still and awful red.

"Beyond the shadow of the ship,
I watched the water snakes:
They moved in tracks of shining white,
And when they reared, the elfish light    275
Fell off in hoary flakes.

"Within the shadow of the ship
I watched their rich attire:
Blue, glossy green, and velvet black,
They coiled and swam; and every track    280
Was a flash of golden fire.

"O happy living things! no tongue
Their beauty might declare:
A spring of love gushed from my heart,
And I blessed them unaware;    285
Sure my kind saint took pity on me,
And I blessed them unaware.

---

**27. main:** Open sea.

*The spell begins to break.*

"The selfsame moment I could pray;
And from my neck so free
The Albatross fell off, and sank                    290
Like lead into the sea.

**Part V**

"Oh sleep! it is a gentle thing,
Beloved from pole to pole!
To Mary Queen the praise be given!
She sent the gentle sleep from Heaven,          295
That slid into my soul.

*By grace of the holy Mother, the ancient Mariner is refreshed with rain.*

"The silly[28] buckets on the deck.
That had so long remained,
I dreamed that they were filled with dew;
And when I awoke, it rained.                         300

"My lips were wet, my throat was cold,
My garments all were dank;
Sure I had drunken in my dreams,
And still my body drank.

"I moved, and could not feel my limbs:            305
I was so light—almost
I thought that I had died in sleep,
And was a blessèd ghost.

*He heareth sounds and seeth strange sights and commotions in the sky and the element.*

"And soon I heard a roaring wind:
It did not come anear;                               310
But with its sound it shook the sails,
That were so thin and sere.[29]

"The upper air burst into life!
And a hundred fire flags sheen,[30]
To and fro they were hurried about!              315
And to and fro, and in and out,
The wan stars danced between.

"And the coming wind did roar more loud,
And the sails did sigh like sedge;[31]
And the rain poured down from one black
    cloud;                                           320
The Moon was at its edge.

---

**28. silly:** Empty.
**29. sere:** Dried up.
**30. fire flags sheen:** The aurora australis, or southern lights, shone.
**31. sedge** *n.*: A rushlike plant that grows in wet soil.

**ENGRAVING BY GUSTAVE DORÉ FOR THE RIME OF THE ANCIENT MARINER**
*by Samuel Taylor Coleridge*

"The thick black cloud was cleft, and still
The Moon was at its side:
Like waters shot from some high crag,
The lightning fell with never a jag,                325
A river steep and wide.

*The bodies of the ship's crew are inspired[32] and the ship moves on;*

"The loud wind never reached the ship,
Yet now the ship moved on!
Beneath the lightning and the Moon
The dead men gave a groan.                          330

"They groaned, they stirred, they all uprose,
Nor spake, nor moved their eyes;
It had been strange, even in a dream,
To have seen those dead men rise.

"The helmsman steered, the ship moved
    on:                                             335
Yet never a breeze up-blew;
The mariners all 'gan work the ropes,
Where they were wont[33] to do;
They raised their limbs like lifeless tools—
We were a ghastly crew.                             340

"The body of my brother's son
Stood by me, knee to knee;
The body and I pulled at one rope,
But he said nought to me.

"I fear thee, ancient Mariner!"                     345
"Be calm, thou Wedding Guest!
'Twas not those souls that fled in pain,
Which to their corses[34] came again,
But a troop of spirits blessed:

*But not by the souls of the men, nor by demons of earth or middle air, but by a blessed troop of angelic spirits, sent down by the invocation of the guardian saint.*

"For when it dawned—they dropped their
    arms,                                           350
And clustered round the mast;
Sweet sounds rose slowly through their
    mouths,
And from their bodies passed.

---

**32. inspired:** Inspirited.
**33. wont:** Accustomed.
**34. corses:** Corpses.

"Around, around, flew each sweet sound,
Then darted to the Sun;                                    355
Slowly the sounds came back again,
Now mixed, now one by one.

"Sometimes a-dropping from the sky
I heard the skylark sing;
Sometimes all little birds that are,                       360
How they seemed to fill the sea and air
With their sweet jargoning![35]

"And now 'twas like all instruments,
Now like a lonely flute;
And now it is an angel's song,                             365
That makes the heavens be mute.

"It ceased; yet still the sails made on
A pleasant noise till noon,
A noise like of a hidden brook
In the leafy month of June,                                370
That to the sleeping woods all night
Singeth a quiet tune.

"Till noon we quietly sailed on,
Yet never a breeze did breathe;
Slowly and smoothly went the ship,                         375
Moved onward from beneath.

*The lonesome Spirit from the South Pole carries on the ship as far as the Line, in obedience to the angelic troop, but still requireth vengeance.*

"Under the keel nine fathom deep,
From the land of mist and snow,
The spirit slid; and it was he
That made the ship to go.                                  380
The sails at noon left off their tune,
And the ship stood still also.

"The Sun, right up above the mast,
Had fixed her to the ocean:
But in a minute she 'gan stir,                             385
With a short uneasy motion—
Backwards and forwards half her length
With a short uneasy motion.

"Then like a pawing horse let go,
She made a sudden bound:                                   390
It flung the blood into my head,
And I fell down in a swound.

———————

**35. jargoning:** Singing.

"How long in that same fit I lay,
I have not to declare;
But ere my living life returned,                    395
I heard and in my soul discerned
Two voices in the air.

" 'Is it he?' quoth one, 'Is this the man?
By him who died on cross,
With his cruel bow he laid full low              400
The harmless Albatross.

" 'The spirit who bideth by himself
In the land of mist and snow,
He loved the bird that loved the man
Who shot him with his bow.'                      405

"The other was a softer voice,
As soft as honeydew:
Quoth he, 'The man hath penance done,
And penance more will do.'

## Part VI

FIRST VOICE

" 'But tell me, tell me! speak again,            410
Thy soft response renewing—
What makes that ship drive on so fast?
What is the ocean doing?'

SECOND VOICE

" 'Still as a slave before his lord,
The ocean hath no blast;                         415
His great bright eye most silently
Up to the Moon is cast—

"If he may know which way to go;
For she guides him smooth or grim.
See, brother, see! how graciously               420
She looketh down on him.'

FIRST VOICE

" 'But why drives on that ship so fast,
Without or wave or wind?'

*The Mariner hath been cast into a trance; for the angelic power causeth the vessel to drive northward faster than human life could endure.*

" 'The air is cut away before,
And closes from behind.         425

"Fly, brother, fly! more high, more high!
Or we shall be belated;
For slow and slow that ship will go,
When the Mariner's trance is abated.'

*The super-natural motion is retarded; the Mariner awakes, and his penance begins anew.*

"I woke, and we were sailing on         430
As in a gentle weather;
'Twas night, calm night, the moon was high;
The dead men stood together.

"All stood together on the deck,
For a charnel dungeon[36] litter;         435
All fixed on me their stony eyes,
That in the Moon did glitter.

"The pang, the curse, with which they died,
Had never passed away;
I could not draw my eyes from theirs,         440
Nor turn them up to pray.

*The curse is finally expiated.*

"And now this spell was snapped; once more
I viewed the ocean green,
And looked far forth, yet little saw
Of what had else been seen—         445

"Like one, that on a lonesome road
Doth walk in fear and dread,
And having once turned round walks on,
And turns no more his head;
Because he knows, a frightful fiend         450
Doth close behind him tread.

"But soon there breathed a wind on me,
Nor sound nor motion made:
Its path was not upon the sea,
In ripple or in shade.         455

"It raised my hair, it fanned my cheek
Like a meadow-gale of spring—
It mingled strangely with my fears,
Yet it felt like a welcoming.

---

**36. charnel dungeon:** Vault where corpses or bones are deposited.

"Swiftly, swiftly flew the ship,                              460
Yet she sailed softly too:
Sweetly, sweetly blew the breeze—
On me alone it blew.

*And the ancient Mariner beholdeth his native country.*

"Oh! dream of joy! is this indeed
The lighthouse top I see?                                     465
Is this the hill? is this the kirk?
Is this mine own countree?

"We drifted o'er the harbor bar,
And I with sobs did pray—
O let me be awake, my God!                                    470
Or let me sleep alway.

"The harbor bay was clear as glass,
So smoothly it was strewn!³⁷
And on the bay the moonlight lay,
And the shadow of the Moon.                                   475

"The rock shone bright, the kirk no less,
That stands above the rock;
The moonlight steeped in silentness
The steady weathercock.

"And the bay was white with silent light,      480
Till rising from the same,

*The angelic spirits leave the dead bodies,*

Full many shapes, that shadows were,
In crimson colors came.

*And appear in their own forms of light.*

"A little distance from the prow
Those crimson shadows were;                                   485
I turned my eyes upon the deck—
Oh, Christ! what saw I there!

"Each corse lay flat, lifeless and flat,
And, by the holy rood!³⁸
A man all light, a seraph³⁹ man,                              490
On every corse there stood.

"This seraph band, each waved his hand:
It was a heavenly sight!
They stood as signals to the land,
Each one a lovely light;                                      495

---

**37. strewn:** spread.
**38. rood:** Cross.
**39. seraph:** Angel.

"This seraph band, each waved his hand,
No voice did they impart—
No voice; but oh! the silence sank
Like music on my heart.

"But soon I heard the dash of oars,            500
I heard the Pilot's cheer;
My head was turned perforce away
And I saw a boat appear.

"The Pilot and the Pilot's boy,
I heard them coming fast:                        505
Dear Lord in Heaven! it was a joy
The dead men could not blast.

"I saw a third—I heard his voice:
It is the Hermit good!
He singeth loud his godly hymns                  510
That he makes in the wood.
He'll shrieve[40] my soul, he'll wash away
The Albatross's blood.

**Part VII**

*The Hermit of the Wood,*

"This Hermit good lives in that wood
Which slopes down to the sea.                     515
How loudly his sweet voice he rears!
He loves to talk with mariners
That come from a far countree.

"He kneels at morn, and noon, and eve—
He hath a cushion plump:                          520
It is the moss that wholly hides
The rotted old oak-stump.

"The skiff boat neared; I heard them talk.
'Why, this is strange, I trow![41]
Where are those lights so many and fair,         525
That signal made but now?'

*Approacheth the ship
with wonder.*

"'Strange, by my faith!' the Hermit said—
'And they answered not our cheer!
The planks looked warped! and see those
      sails,
How thin they are and sere!                      530
I never saw aught like to them,
Unless perchance it were

---

**40. shrieve** (shrēv): Absolve from sin.
**41. trow:** Believe.

"'Brown skeletons of leaves that lag
My forest brook along;
When the ivy tod[42] is heavy with snow,                          535
And the owlet whoops to the wolf below,
That eats the she-wolf's young.'

"'Dear Lord! it hath a fiendish look'
(The Pilot made reply)
'I am a-feared'—'Push on, push on!'                              540
Said the Hermit cheerily.

"The boat came closer to the ship,
But I nor spake nor stirred;
The boat came close beneath the ship,
And straight[43] a sound was heard.                              545

*The ship suddenly sink-
eth.*

"Under the water it rumbled on,
Still louder and more dread;
It reached the ship, it split the bay;
The ship went down like lead.

*The ancient Mariner is
saved in the Pilot's boat.*

"Stunned by that loud and dreadful sound,              550
Which sky and ocean smote,
Like one that hath been seven days drowned
My body lay afloat;
But swift as dreams, myself I found
Within the Pilot's boat.                                        555

"Upon the whirl, where sank the ship,
The boat spun round and round;
And all was still, save that the hill
Was telling of the sound.

"I moved my lips—the Pilot shrieked                    560
And fell down in a fit;
The holy Hermit raised his eyes,
And prayed where he did sit.

"I took the oars; the Pilot's boy,
Who now doth crazy go,                                          565
Laughed loud and long, and all the while
His eyes went to and fro.
'Ha! ha!' quoth he, 'full plain I see,
The Devil knows how to row.'

---

**42. tod:** Bush.
**43. straight:** Immediately.

"And now, all in my own countree,                    570
I stood on the firm land!
The Hermit stepped forth from the boat,
And scarcely he could stand.

"'O shrieve me, shrieve me, holy man!'
The Hermit crossed his brow.[44]                      575
'Say, quick,' quoth he, 'I bid thee say—
What manner of man art thou?'

"Forthwith this frame of mine was wrenched
With a woful agony,
Which forced me to begin my tale;                     580
And then it left me free.

"Since then, at an uncertain hour,
That agony returns;
And till my ghastly tale is told,
This heart within me burns.                           585

"I pass, like night, from land to land;
I have strange power of speech;
That moment that his face I see,
I know the man that must hear me:
To him my tale I teach.                               590

"What loud uproar bursts from that door!
The wedding guests are there;
But in the garden bower the bride
And bridemaids singing are;
And hark the little vesper bell,                      595
Which biddeth me to prayer!

"O Wedding Guest! this soul hath been
Alone on a wide wide sea:
So lonely 'twas, that God himself
Scarce seemed there to be.                            600

"O sweeter than the marriage feast,
'Tis sweeter far to me,
To walk together to the kirk
With a goodly company!—

---

**44. crossed his brow:** Made the sign of the cross on his forehead.

"To walk together to the kirk,                605
And all together pray,
While each to his great Father bends,
Old men, and babes, and loving friends
And youths and maidens gay!

"Farewell, farewell! but this I tell         610
To thee, thou Wedding Guest!
He prayeth well, who loveth well
Both man and bird and beast.

"He prayeth best, who loveth best
All things both great and small;             615
For the dear God who loveth us,
He made and loveth all."

The Mariner, whose eye is bright,
Whose beard with age is hoar,
Is gone; and now the Wedding Guest          620
Turned from the bridegroom's door.

He went like one that hath been stunned
And is of sense forlorn;
A sadder and a wiser man,
He rose the morrow morn.                     625

---

## THINKING ABOUT THE SELECTION

### Recalling

1. (a) What happens to the ship as a result of the storm? (b) What change occurs when the Albatross appears?
2. (a) What "hellish thing" does the Mariner do? (b) How do the other sailors at first react to this deed? (c) What changes their minds?
3. (a) Who is the crew of the strange ship that appears in Part III? (b) What happens to the Mariner's shipmates soon after the appearance of this ship?
4. (a) What changes take place in the Mariner in Part IV? (b) What burden is he freed of as a result of these changes?

5. (a) According to the margin notes in Part V, what force causes the ship to move? (b) Who serves as the crew of the ship on this leg of its journey? (c) What force takes control of the ship at the equator?
6. What does the Mariner hope the Hermit will do for him?
7. What is the Mariner's lifelong penance?

### Interpreting

8. What do you think the Albatross symbolizes, or stands for? Find evidence to support your answer.
9. In what ways might the journey of the Mariner be seen as spiritual as well as actual?
10. Some of the events Coleridge describes are

real and some are supernatural. Why do you think he includes both kinds in this poem?

## Applying

11. Reread lines 614–617. How might this advice be useful for today's world?
12. What do we mean when we say that some past action stays with a person "like an albatross around his or her neck"?

## ANALYZING LITERATURE
### Understanding Sound Devices

Alliteration, consonance, assonance, and internal rhyme are four sound devices used to enhance the meaning and create the mood of a poem. **Alliteration** is the repetition of a first consonant sound in words or accented syllables ("the owlet *whoops* to the *wolf*"). **Consonance** is the repetition of a final consonant sound in words or accented syllables ("thy ski*nny* ha*nd*, so brow*n*"). **Assonance** is the repetition of a vowel sound ("the Sun's *rim* *dips*"). **Internal rhyme** is a rhyme within a line ("on the *bay* the moonlight *lay*").

Identify the sound device or devices in each of the following lines from "The Rime of the Ancient Mariner."

1. lines 7–8
2. lines 31–32
3. lines 121–122
4. lines 236–237
5. lines 452–453
6. lines 478–479

## CRITICAL THINKING AND READING
### Analyzing the Effects of Sound Devices

Sound devices in poetry please the ear and also reinforce meaning and create moods. In lines 41–44, for example, the repetition of the *s* sound, through both alliteration and consonance, enables us almost to hear the hissing of the sea foam as the ship is tossed about.

1. Reread lines 331–340. Identify the sound devices used and explain how they add to the eerie mood of the scene.
2. Reread lines 472–483. State the feeling you think Coleridge was trying to establish in his reader. Tell whether, in your opinion, his use of sound devices helps, and give your reasons.

## UNDERSTANDING LANGUAGE
### Using Archaic Words and Meanings

To give his poem the feeling of something written long ago, Coleridge used archaic, or outdated, language in "The Rime of the Ancient Mariner." Old verb forms such as *stoppeth* (line 2), Middle English words such as *eftsoons* (line 12), and earlier meanings of familiar words, such as *silly* to mean "empty" (line 297) all sounded as odd to Coleridge's original audience as they do to us today.

Find at least one other example each of old verb forms, Middle English words, and former word meanings in the poem. State whether you feel they help achieve the feeling Coleridge was striving after.

## THINKING AND WRITING
### Responding to a Statement

Coleridge wrote that successful poetry is poetry that will arouse "the sympathy of the reader by a faithful adherence to the truth of nature" while, at the same time, "giving the interest of novelty by the modifying colors of imagination." In an essay, argue whether or not you feel Coleridge met these standards in "The Rime of the Ancient Mariner." Begin by defining *sympathy* and *interest* as you believe he has used the words here. Support your claims by quoting passages from the poem. When you revise make sure you have included details from the poem to support your judgment. Proofread your essay and prepare a final draft.

# GUIDE FOR INTERPRETING

## Kubla Khan

**Romanticism.** Romanticism was a literary and artistic movement that began in Europe toward the end of the eighteenth century. A rebellion against the cold rationalism and strict adherence to form that typified the earlier Neoclassical movement, Romanticism stressed imagination and subjectivity as key literary virtues. The Romantic writer was free to express his or her personal views in a spontaneous and nonlogical fashion. The goal of the Romantics thus was to bring people to an awareness of their "oneness" with all other living things. It was in the spirit of this movement and its goal that Coleridge gave his poem "Kubla Khan" the subtitle "A Vision in a Dream." The word *vision* here reminds us that the Romantics were fond of mysticism and fantasy—the stuff of visions. The word *dream* calls to mind a freedom from the rules and logical order of the day-to-day world—traits that were at the very heart of Romanticism.

**Writing**

Recall as best you can a dream you had in which you made a trip to a strange place. Write a vivid description. Use as many details of sight, sound, touch, taste, and smell as you are able.

**Primary Source**

From his memories of childhood, it is apparent that Romanticism exerted a tug at Coleridge's nature from the very start. He was especially taken with mystery and fantasy:

> My father's sister kept an *every-thing* shop at Crediton," he recalled, "and there I read through all the gilt-covered little books that could be had at that time, and likewise all the uncovered tales of *Tom Hickathrift, Jack the Giant-Killer,* etc. and . . . I used to lie by the wall, and mope—and my spirits used to come upon me suddenly, and in a flood —and then I was accustomed to run up and down the church-yard, and act over all I had been reading on the docks, the nettles, and the rank-grass. At six years old . . . I found the Arabian Nights entertainments—one tale of which . . . made so deep an impression on me (I had read it in the evening while my mother was mending stockings) that I was haunted by specters whenever I was in the dark—and I distinctly remember the anxious and fearful eagerness with which I used to watch the window in which the books lay—and whenever the sun lay upon them, I would seize it, carry it by the wall, and bask, and read. My father found out the effect which these books had produced —and burnt them. So I became a dreamer. . . .

# Kubla Khan

## Samuel Taylor Coleridge

*This poem was inspired by a passage about Kubla Khan (kōō' ble kän'), the founder of the Mongol dynasty in China in the thirteenth century, in Samuel Purchas's* Purchas His Pilgrimage *(1613): "Here the Khan Kubla commanded a palace to be built, and a stately garden thereunto. And thus ten miles of fertile ground were inclosed with a wall." Coleridge claims to have fallen asleep while reading this passage due to the effects of medication he was taking for an illness at the time (1797). Three hours later, he awoke from a dream, finding his mind was filled with two to three hundred lines of poetry, which were an elaboration of the description he had read immediately before drifting off to sleep. Coleridge immediately began to write down the lines that filled his head, but when he was interrupted by a visitor, he forgot the lines that he had not yet transcribed. As a result, he was unable to complete the poem.*

In Xanadu[1] did Kubla Khan
A stately pleasure dome decree:
Where Alph,[2] the sacred river, ran
Through caverns measureless to man
5      Down to a sunless sea.
So twice five miles of fertile ground
With walls and towers were girdled round;
And there were gardens bright with sinuous rills,[3]
Where blossomed many an incense-bearing tree;
10  And here were forests ancient as the hills,
Enfolding sunny spots of greenery.

But oh! that deep romantic chasm which slanted
Down the green hill athwart[4] a cedarn cover![5]
A savage place! as holy and enchanted
15  As e'er beneath a waning moon was haunted
By woman wailing for her demon lover!
And from this chasm, with ceaseless turmoil seething,
As if this earth in fast thick pants were breathing.

---

**1. Xanadu** (zan' ə dōō): An indefinite area in China.
**2. Alph:** Probably derived from the Greek river Alpheus, the waters of which, it was believed in Greek mythology, joined with a stream to form a fountain in Sicily.
**3. rills:** Brooks.
**4. athwart:** Across.
**5. cedarn cover:** Covering of cedar trees.

A mighty fountain momently was forced;
20 Amid whose swift half-intermitted burst
Huge fragments vaulted like rebounding hail,
Or chaffy grain beneath the thresher's flail;
And 'mid these dancing rocks at once and ever
It flung up momently the sacred river.
25 Five miles meandering with a mazy motion
Through wood and dale the sacred river ran,
Then reached the caverns measureless to man,
And sank in tumult to a lifeless ocean:
And 'mid this tumult Kubla heard from far
30 Ancestral voices prophesying war!
  The shadow of the dome of pleasure
  Floated midway on the waves;
  Where was heard the mingled measure
  From the fountain and the caves.
35 It was a miracle of rare device,[6]
A sunny pleasure dome with caves of ice!

  A damsel with a dulcimer[7]
  In a vision once I saw:
  It was an Abyssinian[8] maid,
40   And on her dulcimer she played,
  Singing of Mount Abora.[9]
  Could I revive within me
  Her symphony and song,
  To such a deep delight 'twould win me,
45 That with music loud and long,
I would build that dome in air,
That sunny dome! those caves of ice!
And all who heard should see them there,
And all should cry, Beware! Beware!
50 His flashing eyes, his floating hair!
Weave a circle round him thrice,
And close your eyes with holy dread,
For he on honeydew hath fed,
And drunk the milk of Paradise.

---

**6. device:** Design.
**7. dulcimer:** (dul′ sə mər) n.: A musical instrument with metal strings which produce sounds when struck by two small hammers.
**8. Abyssinian** (ab ə sin′ ē ən): Ethiopian.
**9. Mount Abora:** Probably Mount Amara in Abyssinia.

**KUBLAI KHAN**
*Chinese Silk Album Leaf, Yuan Dynasty*
The Granger Collection

## THINKING ABOUT THE SELECTION

### Recalling

1. What was the size of the palatial estate that Kubla Khan ordered built?
2. What, according to the second stanza, was forced up through "that deep romantic chasm"?
3. What did Kubla Khan hear in the noise made by the river emptying into the ocean?
4. (a) According to the last stanza, what did the speaker once see in a vision? (b) What part of that vision does the speaker wish he could revive?

### Interpreting

5. Using your own words, what does the speaker say would happen to him and "all who heard" if he were able to revive his vision?

6. What statement do you think Coleridge is making here about the power of imagination?
7. (a) Find one example each of Coleridge's use of alliteration and assonance. (b) Explain how each example enhances the meaning or mood of the words.
8. (a) Do you feel that Coleridge's imagination and "music" combine to make his vision seem real for the reader? (b) Support your answer with quotations from the poem.

### Applying

9. Do you think people should be governed more by their emotions or their reason? Do you think there should be a balance between the two? Explain your answer.

# GEORGE GORDON, LORD BYRON

## 1788–1824

In his life as well as in his work, George Gordon, Lord Byron, typified the Romanticist's zest for life. As much a public figure as a literary genius, Byron lived life "in the fast lane"—a point that was looked on with disapproval by his contemporaries.

Whether distasteful behavior is purely a matter of example is open to debate. Nevertheless, it is significant to note that Byron was born in London to a father whose good looks—which his son inherited—made him irresistible to women. The father, John Byron, died when his son was three. When the young Byron was ten, the death of a great-uncle brought him the title of Baron, along with an estate at Newstead. Here the boy and his mother went to live until, at seventeen, Byron left home to attend Trinity College at Cambridge. At college, Byron made many friends, played many sports, and spent much money. He also published his first book of poems, *Hours of Idleness* (1807), which received harsh criticism from the *Edinburgh Review*. He was hurt but not crushed by this attack on his work, and two years later he came out with *English Bards and Scotch Reviewers,* a poem poking fun at the magazine.

That same year, Byron journeyed to the Near East, and spent the next two years traveling. When he returned home, he brought with him two sections of a book-length poem titled *Childe Harold,* which depicted a young hero not unlike himself—moody, reckless, sensitive, and adventuresome. The work was received with great enthusiasm, and Byron became a very popular figure in important English circles. So great was his popularity, in fact, that his next published work, *The Corsair,* sold 10,000 copies in one day.

During this period Byron saw a great many women. In 1815 he married Ann Isabella Milbanke, with whom he had a daughter. The couple seemed mismatched from the start and, after about a year, separated. Hurt by nasty gossip, Byron left England, never to return. It was in Italy that he began work on his most ambitious opus, *Don Juan* (pronounced "JOO-en"), a mock epic of the Romantic hero.

It was also at this point that tragedy struck, and then struck again—first with the death of his daughter, later with that of his friend, the poet Shelley. In 1823 Byron joined a group of revolutionaries seeking to free Greece from Turkish rule. Before the revolt got underway, however, Byron died of rheumatic fever, at the age of thirty-six.

Although Byron openly spurned the works of other Romantics, including Wordsworth and Coleridge, his independence was a hallmark of the Romantic movement.

# GUIDE FOR INTERPRETING

## She Walks in Beauty;
## So We'll Go No More A-Roving;
## Apostrophe to the Ocean

**Writer's Technique**

**Figurative Language.** Figurative language is the name given to a class of literary conventions that purposely distort language to make ideas more interesting and memorable. As opposed to literal language, or language "by the rules," figurative language is not to be taken at face value. When a poet writes, for instance, of trees "standing by the side of the road like sentinels," he or she is attempting to get the reader to picture trees that are very upright, much like soldiers.

**Writing**

Develop a list of about twenty adjectives and descriptive phrases, such as *blue, filled with holes, slippery,* and so on. Randomly choose three entries from your list, and write them at the top of a sheet of paper. Then try to think of two objects that share each of the three traits. Write a sentence that compares one of the objects to the other. Try this with at least four pairs of objects.

**Primary Source**

Lady Caroline Lamb, wildly in love with Byron, confided in her diary that he was "Mad, bad, and dangerous to know." Whether we completely believe the lovesick, we cannot deny that Byron had an astonishing effect on those he met. Critic Gilbert Highet has an intriguing theory to explain Byron's remarkable personality.

Highet claims that Byron was "not naturally a slender, elegant, athletic, grave young man at all. Naturally, he was a plump, pleasant, pot-bellied person, and he spent tremendous, almost unremitting efforts on keeping down his natural fat. He was about five feet eight. When he was nineteen years old, he weighed 202 pounds. . . . He resolved to get it off, and keep it off. He did so by painful exercises and the most Spartan regime of dieting, which may well have wrecked his liver. He took exercise wearing seven waistcoats and a heavy topcoat; then he took hot baths; he ate hardly anything. By the time he was twenty, he had got down to 147 pounds. . . . He was starving.

"He was a thin man, and inside him was a fat man roaring to be set free. . . . Byron had several vultures with their beaks buried deep into his vitals; but the one which he felt most constantly, if not most painfully, was that haggard-eyed, sharp-clawed, tireless monster, a starvation diet."

# She Walks in Beauty

## George Gordon, Lord Byron

*This poem, written to be set to music, was inspired by Byron's first meeting with Lady Wilmot Horton, his cousin by marriage, who wore a black mourning gown with spangles.*

She walks in beauty, like the night
    Of cloudless climes and starry skies;
And all that's best of dark and bright
    Meet in her aspect and her eyes:
5  Thus mellowed to that tender light
    Which heaven to gaudy day denies.

One shade the more, one ray the less,
    Had half impaired the nameless grace
Which waves in every raven tress,
10    Or softly lightens o'er her face;
Where thoughts serenely sweet express
    How pure, how dear their dwelling place.

And on that cheek, and o'er that brow,
    So soft, so calm, yet eloquent,
15  The smiles that win, the tints that glow,
    But tell of days in goodness spent,
A mind at peace with all below,
    A heart whose love is innocent!

---

## THINKING ABOUT THE SELECTION

### Recalling

1. In "She Walks in Beauty," to what does the speaker of the poem compare the lady's beauty?
2. What color is the lady's hair?

### Interpreting

3. What do you think is the meaning of "that tender light" in line 5?
4. What does the speaker believe the woman's appearance reveals about her character?

### Applying

5. (a) Why was nature a logical choice for Byron as something with which to compare a lady's beauty? (b) Why would it be a logical choice for any comparison by Byron?

# So We'll Go No More A-Roving

George Gordon, Lord Byron

*This poem was included in a letter to Thomas Moore, written from Venice on February 28, 1817. Carnival season had just passed and Byron, at the age of twenty-nine, found himself in a prolonged period of reflection. The poem is based on the refrain of the Scottish song, "The Jolly Beggar."*

So we'll go no more a-roving
    So late into the night,
Though the heart be still as loving,
    And the moon be still as bright.

5   For the sword outwears its sheath,
    And the soul wears out the breast,
And the heart must pause to breathe,
    And Love itself have rest.

Though the night was made for loving,
10    And the day returns too soon,
Yet we'll go no more a-roving
    By the light of the moon.

---

## THINKING ABOUT THE SELECTION

### Recalling

1. What does the speaker say that "Love itself" must have?

### Interpreting

2. (a) What do you think is meant by the line "And the soul wears out the breast"? (b) Why must the heart "pause to breathe"?

3. (a) Why will the speaker "go no more a-roving"? (b) How might you summarize in one sentence the speaker's message?

### Applying

4. Which properties of the Romantic spirit are evident in this poem?

# from Childe Harold's Pilgrimage

## Apostrophe to the Ocean

George Gordon, Lord Byron

There is a pleasure in the pathless woods,
There is a rapture on the lonely shore,
There is society, where none intrudes,
By the deep sea, and music in its roar;
5    I love not man the less, but nature more,
From these our interviews, in which I steal
From all I may be, or have been before,
To mingle with the universe, and feel
What I can ne'er express, yet cannot all conceal.

10    Roll on, thou deep and dark blue ocean—roll!
Ten thousand fleets sweep over thee in vain;
Man marks the earth with ruin—his control
Stops with the shore; upon the watery plain
The wrecks are all thy deed, nor doth remain
15    A shadow of man's ravage, save[1] his own,
When, for a moment, like a drop of rain,
He sinks into thy depths with bubbling groan,
Without a grave, unknelled, uncoffined, and unknown.

His steps are not upon thy paths—thy fields
20    Are not a spoil for him—thou dost arise
And shake him from thee; the vile strength he wields
For earth's destruction thou dost all despise,
Spurning him from thy bosom to the skies,
And send'st him, shivering in thy playful spray
25    And howling, to his gods, where haply[2] lies
His petty hope in some near port or bay,
And dashest him again to earth—there let him lay.[3]

---

**1. save:** Except.
**2. haply:** Perhaps.
**3. lay:** A note on Byron's proof suggests that he intentionally made this grammatical error for the sake of the rhyme.

SHIPWRECK
J.C.C. Dahl
Munich Neue Pinakothek/Kavaler

The armaments which thunderstrike the walls
Of rock-built cities, bidding nations quake,
30    And monarchs tremble in their capitals,
The oak leviathans,[4] whose huge ribs make
Their clay creator[5] the vain title take
Of lord of thee, and arbiter of war—
These are thy toys, and, as the snowy flake,
35    They melt into thy yeast of waves, which mar
Alike the Armada's[6] pride or spoils of Trafalgar.[7]

Thy shores are empires, changed in all save thee—
Assyria, Greece, Rome, Carthage, what are they?
Thy waters washed them power while they were free,
40    And many a tyrant since; their shores obey

**4. leviathans** (lə vī′ ə thənz): Monstrous sea creatures, described in
the Old Testament. Here the word means giant ships.
**5. clay creator:** Human beings.
**6. Armada's:** Refers to the Spanish Armada, defeated by the English
in 1588.
**7. Trafalgar:** The battle in 1805 during which the French and
Spanish fleets were defeated by the British fleet led by Lord Nelson.

The stranger, slave, or savage; their decay
Has dried up realms to deserts—not so thou,
Unchangeable, save to thy wild waves' play.
Time writes no wrinkle on thine azure brow;
45    Such as creation's dawn beheld, thou rollest now.

Thou glorious mirror, where the Almighty's form
Glasses[8] itself in tempests; in all time,
Calm or convulsed—in breeze, or gale, or storm,
Icing the pole, or in the torrid clime
50    Dark-heaving—boundless, endless, and sublime;
The image of eternity, the throne
Of the Invisible; even from out thy slime
The monsters of the deep are made; each zone
Obeys thee; thou goest forth, dread, fathomless, alone.

55    And I have loved thee, ocean! and my joy
Of youthful sports was on thy breast to be
Borne, like thy bubbles, onward; from a boy
I wantoned with thy breakers—they to me
Were a delight; and if the freshening sea
60    Made them a terror—'twas a pleasing fear,
For I was as it were a child of thee,
And trusted to thy billows far and near,
And laid my hand upon thy mane—as I do here.

---

**8. glasses:** Mirrors.

**Primary Source**

How do poets evaluate their own works? How did Byron feel about his much-celebrated "Childe Harold's Pilgrimage"? In a letter to his printer, Byron offered his opinion.

Dear Sir,

I enclose a sheet for correction, if you ever get to another edition. You will observe the blunder in printing makes it appear as if the Château was over St. Gingo, instead of being on the opposite shore of the Lake, over Clarens. So, separate the paragraphs, otherwise my topography will be seen as inaccurate as your typography on this occasion.

The other day I wrote to convey my proposition with regard to the 4th and concluding canto [of "Childe Harold's Pilgrimage"]. I have gone over and extended it to one hundred and fifty stanzas. . . . I look upon Childe Harold as my best; and as I begun, I think of concluding with it. But I make no resolutions on that head, as I broke my former intention with regard to "The Corsair." However, I fear that I shall never do better; and yet, not being thirty years of age, for some moons to come, one ought to be progressive as far as Intellect goes for many a good year. But I have had a devilish deal of wear and tear of mind and body in my time, besides having published too often and much already.

## THINKING ABOUT THE SELECTION

### Recalling

1. How does the speaker of the poem say the ocean makes him feel?
2. How does he say the ocean treats such things as warships and sea monsters?
3. What childhood memories of the ocean does the speaker have?

### Interpreting

4. In line 10, the speaker describes the movement of ships over the ocean as "in vain." What might he mean by this?
5. What property of the ocean does the speaker admire in the fifth stanza?
6. What double meaning might the speaker have intended in his reference to the ocean as a glorious mirror in line 46?

### Applying

7. Do you believe it is still true today that humans control of the planet "stops with the shore," as Byron puts it in "Apostrophe to the Ocean"? Explain.

## ANALYZING LITERATURE

### Understanding Figurative Language

**Figurative language** is language that links, in one way or another, things or ideas that are generally unrelated. Also known as figures of speech, figurative language is actually a category heading for a number of literary devices. Simile, among the best known of these, is a comparison using a word such as *like* or *as*. The line "the sheen of their spears was like stars on the sea" contains a simile.

Metaphor, often thought of as a companion to the simile, compares two objects without making use of a linking word. The line "The moon was a ghostly galleon tossed upon cloudy seas" contains a metaphor.

A third device, personification, gives human characteristics to nonhuman subjects. The line "The moon peeked out from behind a cloud" contains an example of personification.

Identify the type of figurative language in each quotation, and express in your own words what it adds to the poem.

1. "She walks in beauty, like the night . . ." (p. 690)
2. ". . . the heart must pause to breathe . . ." (p. 691)
3. ". . . like a drop of rain,/He sinks into thy depths . . ." (p. 692)
4. "These are thy toys, and, as the snowy flake,/ They melt into the yeast of waves . . ." (p. 693)
5. "Thou glorious mirror, where the Almighty's form/Glasses itself . . ." (p. 694)

## THINKING AND WRITING

### Evaluating a Poem

When you read a review of a film or book in a newspaper, you are reading an evaluation. Write an evaluation of one of the three poems by Byron. First jot down ideas about this poem. Then write your first draft. Mention such things as language, style, and subject matter, and conclude with your personal reactions to the piece, giving conclusive reasons for why you feel as you do. When you revise make sure that your arguments are sound. Proofread your essay and prepare a final draft.

# GUIDE FOR INTERPRETING

## *from* Don Juan

**Literary Forms**

**Mock Epic.** A mock epic is a long poem that mocks, or pokes fun at, a trivial subject by treating it in the grand style of epic poetry. The epic poem, which found its loftiest expression in such timeless works as the *Iliad,* the *Odyssey,* and *Paradise Lost,* was defined not only by its style but also by certain regular features. The poem usually began, for example, with an *invocation,* or request for inspiration and guidance from a muse or deity, and it was usually divided into long sections called *cantos* or books. In addition, the epic generally contained lengthy and carefully worded speeches by heroes and included descriptions of battles fought by noble warriors. In a mock epic, this combination of ingredients—a lofty style and a base subject—leads to humorous results. When, for example, the romantic adventures of a beautiful young man are narrated in a grand fashion, as is the case in *Don Juan,* the end product is hilarious.

**Writing**

Think of an activity that is especially trival or commonplace, such as walking a dog or going to the supermarket for groceries. Now think of several adjectives that might be used—or *misused*—to describe this activity in a heroic manner. Finally, write a "mini-mock epic" that paints a lofty picture of this routine task.

**Commentary**

Despite a great enthusiasm for reading, public taste became increasing conservative during the Romantic Age. Groups such as the Society for the Suppression of Vice were remarkably effective in controlling public taste. The fear of prosecution made many book-sellers unwilling to print works that were either risqué or immoral. Byron's publisher, for example, was reluctant to print the first two cantos of *Don Juan* because he feared he might be prosecuted. When *Don Juan* did appear, although the vice society took no action against it, many reviewers denounced it as indecent and immoral. The *Eclectic Review,* for example, warned that Byron wrote poetry "such as no brother could read aloud to his sister, no husband to his wife—poetry in which the deliberate purpose of the author is to corrupt by inflaming the mind." One woman was horrified when a clergyman told her he had bought an edition of Byron's poems, though he "boasted that he had burned *Don Juan*."

What do you see in this excerpt from *Don Juan* that might inflame readers in Byron's day?

# *from* Don Juan

## George Gordon, Lord Byron

*Though it is unfinished, Don Juan is generally regarded as Byron's finest work. The long poem, a mock epic that was described by Shelley as being "something wholly new and relative to the age," satirizes the political and social problems of Byron's time.*

*Traditionally the character of Don Juan, the poem's hero, had been portrayed as being a wicked and immoral man driven solely by his obsession with beautiful women. In Byron's work Don Juan is depicted as an innocent young man whose physical beauty, charm, and spirit prove to be extremely alluring for ladies, leading him into many difficult situations.*

*Many people feel that what makes Don Juan such a great poem is the lapses in the story, during which the speaker drifts away from the subject. During these lapses the speaker comments on the issues of the time and on life in general. In this excerpt the speaker abandons his hero to reflect on old age and death.*

But now at thirty years my hair is gray
    (I wonder what it will be like at forty?
I thought of a peruke[1] the other day)—
    My heart is not much greener; and, in short, I
5  Have squandered my whole summer while 'twas May,
    And feel no more the spirit to retort; I
Have spent my life, both interest and principal,
And deem not, what I deemed, my soul invincible.

No more—no more—Oh! never more on me
10      The freshness of the heart can fall like dew,
Which out of all the lovely things we see
    Extracts emotions beautiful and new,
Hived in our bosoms like the bag o' the bee:
    Think'st thou the honey with those objects grew?
15  Alas! 'twas not in them, but in thy power
To double even the sweetness of a flower.

No more—no more—Oh! never more, my heart,
    Canst thou be my sole world, my universe!

---

**1. peruke** (pə rōok'): Wig.

Once all in all, but now a thing apart,
20      Thou canst not be my blessing or my curse:
The illusion's gone forever, and thou art
      Insensible, I trust, but none the worse,
And in thy stead I've got a deal of judgment,
Though heaven knows how it ever found a lodgment.

25   My days of love are over; me no more
      The charms of maid, wife, and still less of widow
Can make the fool of which they made before—
      In short, I must not lead the life I did do;
The credulous hope of mutual minds is o'er,
30      The copious use of claret is forbid too,
So for a good old-gentlemanly vice,
I think I must take up with avarice.

Ambition was my idol, which was broken
      Before the shrines of Sorrow and of Pleasure;
35   And the two last have left me many a token
      O'er which reflection may be made at leisure:
Now, like Friar Bacon's brazen head, I've spoken,
      "Time is, Time was, Time's past,"[2] a chymic[3] treasure
Is glittering youth, which I have spent betimes—
40   My heart in passion, and my head on rhymes.

What is the end of fame? 'tis but to fill
      A certain portion of uncertain paper:
Some liken it to climbing up a hill,
      Whose summit, like all hills, is lost in vapor;
45   For this men write, speak, preach, and heroes kill,
      And bards burn what they call their "midnight taper,"
To have, when the original is dust,
A name, a wretched picture, and worse bust.

What are the hopes of man? Old Egypt's King
50      Cheops erected the first pyramid
And largest, thinking it was just the thing
      To keep his memory whole, and mummy hid:
But somebody or other rummaging
      Burglariously broke his coffin's lid:
55   Let not a monument give you or me hopes,
Since not a pinch of dust remains of Cheops.

---

**2. Friar Bacon . . . Time's past":** In Robert Greene's comedy *Friar Bacon and Friar Burgandy* (1594), these words are spoken by a bronze bust, made by Friar Bacon.
**3. chymic** (kim′ ik): Alchemic; counterfeit.

But I, being fond of true philosophy,
　　Say very often to myself, "Alas!
All things that have been born were born to die,
60　　　And flesh (which Death mows down to hay) is grass;
You've passed your youth not so unpleasantly,
　　And if you had it o'er again—'twould pass—
So thank your stars that matters are no worse,
And read your Bible, sir, and mind your purse."

65　But for the present, gentle reader! and
　　　Still gentler purchaser! the bard—that's I—
Must, with permission, shake you by the hand,
　　And so your humble servant, and good-bye!
We meet again, if we should understand
70　　　Each other; and if not, I shall not try
Your patience further than by this short sample—
'Twere well if others followed my example.

"Go, little book, from this my solitude!
　　　I cast thee on the waters—go thy ways!
75　And if, as I believe, thy vein be good,
　　The world will find thee after many days."[4]
When Southey's read, and Wordsworth understood,
　　I can't help putting in my claim to praise—
The four first rhymes are Southey's, every line:
80　For God's sake, reader! take them not for mine!

_____

**4. "Go . . . days":** The lines are from the last stanza of Robert Southey's (1774–1843) *Epilogue to the Lay of the Laureate.*

## THINKING ABOUT THE SELECTION
### Recalling

1. What causes the speaker to think of a peruke, or wig?
2. (a) What, according to lines 17 and 18 does the speaker say has been his "sole world" and "universe" up until now? (b) According to the fourth stanza, with what "old-gentlemanly vice" will he replace it?

### Interpreting

3. In the fifth stanza, the speaker notes that "glittering youth" is a "chymic," or counterfeit, "treasure." In what way do you think he means this?
In what way do you think he means this?

4. Summarize in your own words the point the speaker is making in his mention of Cheops.

### Applying

5. What do you think is meant by the remark "flesh . . . is grass" in line 60?

## THINKING AND WRITING
### Writing About the Byronic Hero

Byron saw himself as melancholy, sensitive, rebellious, fearless, moody, and adventurous. These traits, characterize the "Byronic hero." Choose a fictional character that comes close to fitting this description. In an essay, explain in what ways this character is, and is not, a Byronic hero. When you revise be sure you have supported your main idea.

# PERCY BYSSHE SHELLEY

## 1792–1822

When he died in a boating accident at age thirty, Percy Bysshe Shelley was eulogized by his friend Byron as "without exception the best and least selfish man I ever knew." This seems strange praise indeed, considering it was directed at a man whose disenchantment with the world was at least as great as his appreciation of its beauties. At once modest and intense, Shelley was a poet of rare gift. He was also a self-appointed reformer who believed that humankind was capable of attaining a more perfect society.

Shelley was born in Sussex and raised on a fine country estate where he spent a quiet childhood. He was sent to excellent schools—first Eton, a prestigious boarding school, and later Oxford —but was never able to settle into the routine of a student. Instead he preferred to wander over the countryside or perform private scientific experiments. At Oxford Shelley became friends with a young man named Thomas Jefferson Hogg, whose political views were as strong as his own. The friendship further fueled Shelley's rebellious nature, and when with Hogg's support he wrote a pamphlet titled *The Necessity of Atheism;* both were expelled.

The incident led to trouble between Shelley and his father, and instead of going home Shelley headed for London. There he met sixteen-year-old Harriet Westbrook, who played on his sympathy for the underdog by describing her miserable situation at home and at school. The two married and went to Ireland, where Shelley tried unsuccessfully to "deliver the Irish people from tyranny."

In 1813 he completed his first important poem, "Queen Mab," a philosophical work that explored some of the ideas he had read about in Godwin's *Political Justice.* The view that Shelley put forth—that government and institutions should be reshaped to better conform to the will of the people—was evident in much of his poetry, even in his nature poems.

Shelley's marriage, meanwhile, was in trouble. Harriet felt she could not keep up with her husband, whose political ideals, in any case, she had come to question. Shelley was unhappy too, and after divorcing Harriet in 1814 he married Mary Wollstonecraft Godwin.

Shelley spent the last four years of his life in Italy, where he became close friends with Byron. Here Shelley wrote some of his best poetry, including "Ode to the West Wind" and *Prometheus Unbound,* the second of these a long poem predicting that some-day humanity would be free of tyranny.

Shelley has been called the perfect poet of the Romantic era. One need only consider his emotional response to life and his belief in personal freedom to appreciate how fitting that title is.

# GUIDE FOR INTERPRETING

## Literary Forms

### Ozymandias; Ode to the West Wind; To a Skylark; To—; A Dirge

**The Ode.** Poetic structure is the framework or blueprint on which a poem is built. The structure takes into account the number of stanzas, the rhyme scheme, and the rhythmic patterns to be used.

An *ode* is a lyrical poem that pays homage to a person, a quality, or a thing. The first odes were written in Classical times by the Greek poet Pindar (552?–443? B.C.) and the Latin poet Horace (65–8 B.C.) The Pindaric ode, which is the more often imitated of the two types, consists mainly of three-line stanzas called *triads*. Shelley's "Ode to the West Wind" is a Pindaric ode.

## Writing

Think of several individuals, objects, and qualities which you hold in high regard. To get yourself started, you might think of people who do important work in your community, and who have such character traits as honesty and reliability. Write each at the top of a sheet of paper and under it jot down some of your thoughts.

## Commentary

The following story is told about Shelley's death. Notice how it illuminates the men. On July 8, 1822, Shelley and Edward Williams boarded their small boat to return to their summer home on the Gulf of Spezia, but their friend E. J. Trelawny was denied port clearance. As he stood sullenly on the dock watching his friends sail off, a sailor pointed to the water and said, "Look at the smoke on the water; the devil is brewing mischief." Oppressed by the heat, Trelawny dozed off. When he awoke around dinner time, a fierce storm had blown in. Although Trelawny anxiously scanned every dot on the horizon, he could see no sign of Shelley's small boat. Three days passed in terrible anxiety as he spoke with the crews of all returning boats.

On the morning of the third day, Trelawny rode to Pisa where he summoned Byron and dispatched a number of searchers. A water-keg and some bottles from Shelley's boat had washed up on the sand. Over a week later the two bodies were found on the shore. Although the bodies were badly mutilated, Trelawny recognized his friend by the volume of Sophocles in one pocket and a copy of Keats's poems in the other. In a similar fashion he identified Williams's body. Shortly thereafter he arranged to have both bodies cremated. Despite the fierce blaze, the poet's heart did not burn. Trelawny snatched it out of the fire, badly burning his hand. He gave the relic to Mary Shelley. He took the remains to a Protestant cemetery near Rome, where they were buried. When he died in 1881, his ashes were buried in a tomb beside that of his friend.

# Ozymandias[1]

## Percy Bysshe Shelley

I met a traveler from an antique land
Who said: Two vast and trunkless legs of stone
Stand in the desert. Near them, on the sand,
Half sunk, a shattered visage lies, whose frown,
5   And wrinkled lip, and sneer of cold command,
Tell that its sculptor well those passions read
Which yet survive, stamped on these lifeless things,
The hand that mocked them and the heart that fed:
And on the pedestal these words appear:
10   "My name is Ozymandias, king of kings:
Look on my works, ye Mighty, and despair!"
Nothing beside remains. Round the decay
Of that colossal wreck, boundless and bare,
The lone and level sands stretch far away.

---

**1. Ozymandias** (ŏz ĭ män′ dē əs): The Greek name for Ramses.
Ramses II, the king referred to in the poem, was a pharoah who ruled
Egypt during the thirteenth century B.C. and built many great palaces
and statues. One statue was inscribed with the words: "I am
Ozymandias, king of kings, if anyone wishes to know what I am and
where I lie, let him surpass me in some of my exploits."

## THINKING ABOUT THE SELECTION

### Recalling

1. (a) Whom has the speaker met? (b) What sight does this person describe?

### Interpreting

2. What sort of person is suggested by the visage that is described?
3. Think of the words on the pedestal. (a) Why is it ironic that the statue has crumbled? (b) Why is it ironic that it is surrounded by desert?
4. What is the theme of this poem?

### Applying

5. (a) What is your definition of power? (b) What is your definition of pride? (c) In what way do the two complement each other?

## ANALYZING LITERATURE

### Understanding Poetic Structure

The poetic structure of a poem is the plan on which it is built. Poetic structure includes such elements as rhyme, rhythm, and number of stanzas. Analyze the poetic structure of "Ozymandias." State whether or not you feel this structure enhances the poem's message. When you revise make sure you have provided adequate support for your main idea.

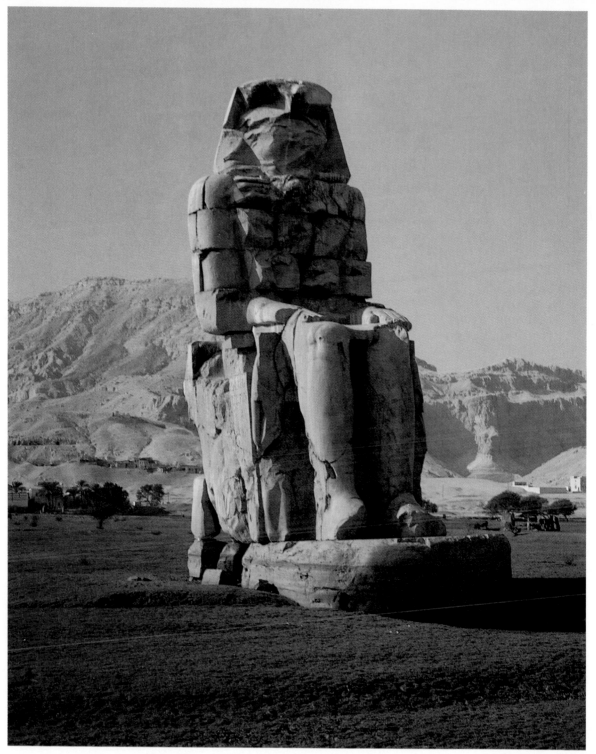

THE COLOSSI OF MEMNON

# Ode to the West Wind

**Percy Bysshe Shelley**

*Shelley composed this poem in the woods near Florence, Italy. He described the day of its composition as one "when that tempestuous wind, whose temperature is at once mild and animating, was collecting the vapors which pour down the autumnal rains."*

## I

O wild West Wind, thou breath of Autumn's being,
Thou, from whose unseen presence the leaves dead
Are driven, like ghosts from an enchanter fleeing,

Yellow, and black, and pale, and hectic red,
5  Pestilence-stricken multitudes: O thou,
Who chariotest to their dark and wintry bed

The wingèd seeds, where they lie cold and low,
Each like a corpse within its grave, until
Thine azure sister of the Spring[1] shall blow

10  Her clarion[2] o'er the dreaming earth, and fill
(Driving sweet buds like flocks to feed in air)
With loving hues and odors plain and hill:

Wild Spirit, which art moving everywhere;
Destroyer and preserver; hear, oh, hear!

## II

15  Thou on whose stream, 'mid the steep sky's commotion,
Loose clouds like earth's decaying leaves are shed,
Shook from the tangled boughs of Heaven and Ocean,

Angels[3] of rain and lightning: there are spread
On the blue surface of thine aery surge,
20  Like the bright hair uplifted from the head

---

**1. sister of Spring:** The south wind.
**2. clarion:** *n.:* A trumpet producing clear, sharp, shrill tones.
**3. angels:** Messengers.

Of some fierce Maenad,[4] even from the dim verge
Of the horizon to the zenith's height,
The locks of the approaching storm. Thou dirge

Of the dying year, to which this closing night
25  Will be the dome of a vast sepulcher,
Vaulted with all thy congregated might

Of vapors, from whose solid atmosphere
Black rain, and fire, and hail will burst: oh, hear!

### III

Thou who didst waken from his summer dreams
30  The blue Mediterranean, where he lay,
Lulled by the coil of his crystalline streams,

---

**4. Maenad** (mē' nad): A priestess of Bacchus, the Greek and Roman
god of wine and revelry.

Beside a pumice[5] aisle in Baiae's bay,[6]
And saw in sleep old palaces and towers
Quivering within the wave's intenser day,

35  All overgrown with azure moss and flowers
So sweet, the sense faints picturing them! Thou
For whose path the Atlantic's level powers

Cleave themselves into chasms, while far below
The sea-blooms and the oozy woods which wear
40  The sapless foliage of the ocean, know

Thy voice, and suddenly grow gray with fear,
And tremble and despoil themselves: oh, hear!

### IV

If I were a dead leaf thou mightest bear;
If I were a swift cloud to fly with thee;
45  A wave to pant beneath thy power, and share

The impulse of thy strength, only less free
Than thou, O uncontrollable! If even
I were as in my boyhood, and could be

The comrade of thy wanderings over Heaven,
50  As then, when to outstrip thy skyey speed
Scarce seemed a vision; I would ne'er have striven

As thus with thee in prayer in my sore need.
Oh, lift me as a wave, a leaf, a cloud!
I fall upon the thorns of life! I bleed!

55  A heavy weight of hours has chained and bowed
One too like thee: tameless, and swift, and proud.

### V

Make me thy lyre,[7] even as the forest is:
What if my leaves are falling like its own!
The tumult of thy mighty harmonies

---

**5. pumice** (pum′ is) *n.*: Volcanic rock.
**6. Baiae's** (bā′ yēz) **bay:** An ancient Roman resort near Naples.
**7. lyre:** Aeolian (ē o′ lē ən) lute, or wind harp, a stringed instrument
which produces musical sounds when the wind passes over it.

60  Will take from both a deep, autumnal tone,
    Sweet though in sadness. Be thou, Spirit fierce,
    My spirit! Be thou me, impetuous one!

    Drive my dead thought over the universe
    Like withered leaves to quicken a new birth!
65  And, by the incantation of this verse,

    Scatter, as from an extinguished hearth
    Ashes and sparks, my words among mankind!
    Be through my lips to unawakened earth

    The trumpet of a prophecy! O Wind,
70  If Winter comes, can Spring be far behind?

---

## THINKING ABOUT THE SELECTION

### Recalling

1. According to the poem, with what season is the west wind associated?
2. (a) What does the wind do to dead leaves? (b) What does it do to the ocean?
3. What does the speaker ask of the wind in section V of the poem?

### Interpreting

4. In what sense is the wind a "destroyer and preserver"?
5. (a) How, according to section IV, has the speaker changed? (b) What caused this change?
6. Whose "new birth" (line 65) do you think the speaker wishes to bring about?
7. (a) Interpret the last line of this poem. (b) How does this famous last line tie the poem together?

### Applying

8. In what way is the message in this poem related to Shelley's lifelong mission?

## ANALYZING LITERATURE

### Understanding the Ode

An ode is a poem that honors an individual, a thing, or a trait. The form dates back to classical times, when it was written to be sung at a festival or as part of a play. Many features of the classical ode are to be found in "Ode to the West Wind." Find evidence in Shelley's poem of each of the following properties.

1. Direct form of address to the individual, trait, or thing being honored
2. An almost fearful reverence for the thing or person being honored
3. Dignified and lofty language and examples

# To a Skylark

Percy Bysshe Shelley

Hail to thee, blithe spirit!
   Bird thou never wert,
That from heaven, or near it,
   Pourest thy full heart
5  In profuse strains of unpremeditated art.

Higher still and higher,
   From the earth thou springest
Like a cloud of fire;
   The blue deep thou wingest,
10  And singing still dost soar, and soaring ever singest.

In the golden lightning
   Of the sunken sun,
O'er which clouds are brightening,
   Thou dost float and run;
15  Like an unbodied joy whose race is just begun.

The pale purple even[1]
   Melts around thy flight;
Like a star of heaven,
   In the broad daylight
20  Thou art unseen, but yet I hear thy shrill delight,

Keen as are the arrows
   Of that silver sphere,[2]
Whose intense lamp narrows
   In the white dawn clear,
25  Until we hardly see—we feel that it is there.

All the earth and air
   With thy voice is loud,
As, when night is bare,
   From one lonely cloud
30  The moon rains out her beams, and Heaven is overflowed.

---

**1. even:** Evening.
**2. silver sphere:** The morning star.

What thou art we know not;
    What is most like thee?
From rainbow clouds there flow not
    Drops so bright to see,
35 As from thy presence showers a rain of melody.

Like a poet hidden
    In the light of thought,
Singing hymns unbidden,
    Till the world is wrought
40 To sympathy with hopes and fears it heeded not:

Like a highborn maiden
    In a palace tower,
Soothing her love-laden
    Soul in secret hour
45 With music sweet as love, which overflows her bower:

Like a glowworm golden
    In a dell of dew,
Scattering unbeholden
    Its aerial hue
50 Among the flowers and grass, which screen it from the
    view!

Like a rose embowered
      In its own green leaves,
By warm winds deflowered,[3]
      Till the scent it gives
55  Makes faint with too much sweet those heavy-wingèd
            thieves.[4]

Sound of vernal showers
      On the twinkling grass,
Rain-awakened flowers,
      All that ever was
60  Joyous, and clear, and fresh, thy music doth surpass:

Teach us, sprite or bird,
      What sweet thoughts are thine:
I have never heard
      Praise of love or wine
65  That panted forth a flood of rapture so divine.

Chorus Hymeneal,[5]
      Or triumphal chant,
Matched with thine would be all
      But an empty vaunt,
70  A thing wherein we feel there is some hidden want.

What objects are the fountains[6]
      Of thy happy strain?
What fields, or waves, or mountains?
      What shapes of sky or plain?
75  What love of thine own kind? what ignorance of pain?

With thy clear keen joyance
      Languor cannot be;
Shadow of annoyance
      Never came near thee;
80  Thou lovest—but ne'er knew love's sad satiety.

Waking or asleep,
      Thou of death must deem[7]
Things more true and deep
      Than we mortals dream,
85  Or how could thy notes flow in such a crystal stream?

---

**3. deflowered:** Fully open.
**4. thieves:** The "warm winds."
**5. Chorus Hymeneal** (hī′ mə nē′ əl): Marriage song, named after Hymen, the Greek god of marriage.
**6. fountains:** Sources, inspiration.
**7. deem:** Know.

We look before and after,
　　And pine for what is not;
Our sincerest laughter
　　With some pain is fraught;
90　Our sweetest songs are those that tell of saddest thought.

　　Yet if[8] we could scorn
　　　Hate, and pride, and fear;
　　If we were things born
　　　Not to shed a tear,
95　I know not how thy joy we ever should come near.

　　Better than all measures
　　　Of delightful sound,
　　Better than all treasures
　　　That in books are found,
100　Thy skill to poet were,[9] thou scorner of the ground!

　　Teach me half the gladness
　　　That thy brain must know,
　　Such harmonious madness
　　　From my lips would flow,
105　The world should listen then, as I am listening now.

---

**8. if:** Even if.
**9. were:** Would be.

---

## THINKING ABOUT THE SELECTION
### Recalling

1. At what time of day does the "blithe spirit" fly?
2. (a) To what four things does the speaker compare the bird in lines 36–55? (b) In what ways does he say the bird is like these things?

### Interpreting

3. Why does the poet say of the bird, "Bird thou never wert"?
4. What do you suppose the speaker means in line 80 by "love's sad satiety"?
5. (a) How is the poet's song different from the bird's song? (b) Why can the bird's song "flow in such a crystal stream"?
6. (a) What does the speaker ask the skylark to teach him? (b) What effect does he think this would have on the world? (c) Why does he feel this way?

### Applying

7. The twentieth-century poet W. H. Auden wrote, "A verbal art like poetry is reflective; it stops to think. Music is immediate; it goes on to become." Discuss the meaning of this quotation.

# To ————

## Percy Bysshe Shelley

Music, when soft voices die,
Vibrates in the memory—
Odors, when sweet violets sicken,
Live within the sense they quicken.

5   Rose leaves, when the rose is dead,
Are heaped for the belovèd's bed;
And so thy thoughts,[1] when thou art gone,
Love itself shall slumber on.

---

**1. thy thoughts:** Thoughts of thee.

---

## THINKING ABOUT THE SELECTION

### Recalling

1. What does the speaker of the poem say will happen to "thy thoughts, when thou art gone"?

### Interpreting

2. Explain how music, odors, and roses will live on.
3. What idea about love is the speaker communicating?

### Applying

4. How differently would this idea come across if it were presented in simple prose rather than as a poem? Explain.

## CRITICAL THINKING AND READING

### Recognizing an Author's Style

Style is the way an author chooses and arranges words to express ideas. Just as no two personalities are identical, no two writing styles are identical. Sentence length, variation in sentence patterns, and word usage are among the features that define a writer's style. Carefully reread "To ————" and any other poem of your choice by Shelley, noting stylistic similarities in the areas mentioned above. Briefly describe this style, and tell whether or not you like it, and why. When you revise make sure you have included details from the poems to support your thesis.

## THINKING AND WRITING

### Writing an Ode

Select one of the objects about which you jotted down some thoughts before you read these poems by Shelley. Examine the observations you made regarding that person, thing, or trait, and decide whether you want to change, add, or remove any of these observations. Then write an ode to that person, quality, or thing. When you revise make sure you have created a vivid description.

# A Dirge

## Percy Bysshe Shelley

Rough wind, that moanest loud
    Grief too sad for song;
Wild wind, when sullen cloud
    Knells all the night long;
5  Sad storm, whose tears are vain,
Bare woods, whose branches strain,
Deep caves and dreary main,—
    Wail, for the world's wrong!

---

## THINKING ABOUT THE SELECTION

### Recalling

1. What does the speaker of the poem ask the wind, a storm, and bare branches to do?

### Interpreting

2. What do you think the speaker means by "the world's wrong"?

3. What effect is created by calling upon the natural elements to bemoan the world's wrong? How does this device help portray the poet's sense of moral indignation?

### Applying

4. If Shelley were living in the contemporary world, what aspects of life might he bemoan?

## THINKING AND WRITING

### Comparing and Contrasting Nature Views

Select a poem by one of the other Romantic poets you have read so far, and compare that poet's view of nature with Shelley's. Start by jotting down notes about each poem. Use quotes from each of the poems to illustrate similarities and differences. When you revise make sure you have presented your information in a logical order.

# JOHN KEATS

## 1795–1821

Despite his early death and the fact that the most important of his works were composed in the space of two years, John Keats remains one of the major influences on English poetry. Known as a pure artist, Keats saw the appreciation of beauty as an end in itself and made the pursuit of beauty the goal of his poetry. As Keats himself so eloquently put it, "Beauty is truth, truth beauty."

Born in London of working-class parents, Keats was unusually handsome and active as a child. He developed a reputation for fighting, not so much out of rowdiness as from a readiness to take sides in a worthy cause. It was not until he became a close friend of his schoolmaster's son, Charles Cowden Clarke, that Keats developed an interest in poetry and became an avid reader.

In 1815 Keats began the study of medicine at a London hospital. By this time he had already begun writing poetry, and though his studies earned him a pharmacist's license, he ultimately abandoned medicine for a career as a poet. His first major effort, *Endymion,* published in the spring of 1818, was severely attacked by the journals of the day. Part of the reason for the harsh criticism was Keats's association with Leigh Hunt, a radical poet, but much of it had to do with the verse itself. Far from being crushed by the assault, Keats began the second of his long poems, *Hyperion,* which was never completed.

The end of the year found Keats mourning the loss of his brother Tom to tuberculosis. It also found the poet deliriously happy over his engagement to Fanny Brawne, a lively 18-year-old who was a light in Keats's life. The following year, 1819, was when Keats turned out his finest work, including "The Eve of St. Agnes," "The Eve of St. Mark," and his famous odes. This might have been only the beginning, but Keats's health took a turn for the worse. He moved to Italy, which promised a warmer climate, but to no avail. After a long battle with tuberculosis, the disease that had claimed his brother, he died at 25.

Though Keats and Shelley knew each other, their visions of what the poet should be could not have been more different. Keats did not share Shelley's rebellious spirit, nor did he feel that poetry was the proper vehicle for political statements. Rather, Keats sought to refine his idea of beauty, and in so doing, refined ours. His extraordinary sensitivity enabled him to see beauty in the most ordinary of circumstances, while his mastery of verse enabled him to unveil that beauty to the world.

# GUIDE FOR INTERPRETING

## On First Looking into Chapman's Homer; Bright Star! Would I Were Steadfast as Thou Art; When I Have Fears That I May Cease to Be

**Literary Forms**

**The Sonnet.** The sonnet is a poem of fourteen lines arranged according to a specific rhyme scheme, with five strong beats and five weak beats per line. In each of the two basic types of sonnet, Petrarchan and Shakespearean, a portion of the poem is used to present a problem or ask a question, and another portion to resolve it. Despite the demands of its form, the successful sonnet is one that flows smoothly, creates powerful impressions, and delivers an important message without sounding forced. These features are hallmarks of the sonnets written by Keats.

**Writing**

Think about a book you have read or a film or work of art you have seen that in some way has changed your life. Consider what particular features of the work led to this change. Then freewrite, comparing this experience to other moving experiences people have.

**Primary Source**

We now know that ill health, aggravated by severe financial and family problems, is the true cause of Keats's premature death. However, for many years his early death was blamed on the effects of two vicious articles in leading literary journals of his day.

Both attacks were anonymous. One article assaulted Keats as a member of fellow-author Leigh Hunt's radical literary circle in London. The other piece ripped into his poem "Endymion." Although Keats himself had the common sense to see that the attacks were brought about by political and social snobbery, many of his contemporaries supported the myth of the cause of his death. One in particular was Lord Byron, who penned the following epitaph:

> John Keats, who was really killed off by one critique
>> Just as he really promised something great,
> If not intelligible, without Greek
>> Contrived to talk about the gods of late
> Much as they might have been supposed to speak.
>> Poor fellow! His was an untoward fate;
>>> 'Tis strange the mind, that very fiery particle,
>>> Should let itself be snuffed out by an article.

# On First Looking into Chapman's Homer

John Keats

*When Keats was twenty-one, his former teacher, Charles Cowden Clarke, introduced him to a translation of Homer by Elizabethan poet George Chapman. The two men spent the evening reading this book, and early the next morning Keats presented this sonnet to Clarke.*

Much have I traveled in the realms of gold,
    And many goodly states and kingdoms seen;
    Round many western islands have I been
Which bards in fealty to Apollo[1] hold.
5  Oft of one wide expanse had I been told
    That deep-browed Homer ruled as his demesne;[2]
    Yet did I never breathe its pure serene[3]
Till I heard Chapman speak out loud and bold:
Then felt I like some watcher of the skies
10     When a new planet swims into his ken;
Or like stout Cortez[4] when with eagle eyes
    He stared at the Pacific—and all his men
Looked at each other with a wild surmise—
    Silent, upon a peak in Darien.[5]

---

**1. Apollo:** In Greek and Roman mythology, the god of music, poetry, and medicine.
**2. demesne** (di mān'): Realm.
**3. serene:** Clear air.
**4. Cortez:** Here, Keats was mistaken. The Pacific was discovered in 1513 by Balboa, not Cortez.
**5. Darien** (der' ē ən): The Isthmus of Panama.

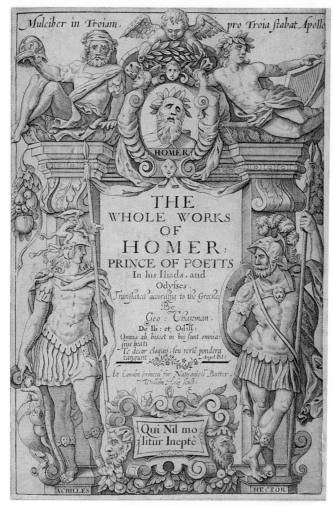

**FRONTISPIECE, HOMER'S ILIAD AND ODYSSEY, 1612**
*William Hole*
The British Library

## THINKING ABOUT THE SELECTION

### Recalling

1. What does the speaker of the poem claim he missed before reading Chapman?

### Interpreting

2. (a) What transportation did the speaker use in his "travels"? (b) To what does he compare his new-found wonderment?

3. Dante Gabriel Rossetti, a poet of the nineteenth century, wrote that "A Sonnet is a coin: its face reveals/The soul—it converse, to what Power tis due." (a) How would you describe Keats's "soul," as it is revealed in "On First Looking into Chapman's Homer"? (b) What is the "power" to which that soul owes its due?

### Applying

4. Do you think books can change people's lives? Explain your answer.

# Bright Star, Would I Were Steadfast as Thou Art

## John Keats

Bright star, would I were steadfast as thou art—
    Not in lone splendor hung aloft the night
And watching, with eternal lids apart,
    Like nature's patient, sleepless Eremite,[1]
5  The moving waters at their priestlike task
    Of pure ablution round earth's human shores,
Or gazing on the new soft-fallen mask
    Of snow upon the mountains and the moors—
No—yet still steadfast, still unchangeable,
10    Pillowed upon my fair love's ripening breast,
To feel forever its soft fall and swell,
    Awake forever in a sweet unrest,
Still, still to hear her tender-taken breath,
And so live ever—or else swoon to death.

---

**1. Eremite** (ĕr′ ə mīt′): Hermit.

---

## THINKING ABOUT THE SELECTION

### Recalling

1. What two things does the speaker say the star watches from its position in the sky?

### Interpreting

2. (a) In what ways does the speaker wish to be like the star? (b) In what ways does he wish to be different?
3. What do do think is meant by "sweet unrest" in line 12?
4. In a Petrarchan, or Italian, sonnet, the first eight lines pose a question or problem, while the last six lines offer a solution or comment on or extend the issue. (a) What question or problem is presented in the octave, or first eight lines? (b) What response is given in the sestet, or next six lines? (c) What word signals this response?

### Applying

5. Based on this poem, describe Keats's attitudes toward nature and emotion. Explain how these attitudes are typical of the Romantic movement.

# When I Have Fears That I May Cease to Be

**John Keats**

When I have fears that I may cease to be
    Before my pen has gleaned my teeming brain,
Before high-piled books, in charactery,[1]
    Hold like rich garners[2] the full ripened grain;
5  When I behold, upon the night's starred face,
    Huge cloudy symbols of a high romance,
And think that I may never live to trace
    Their shadows, with the magic hand of chance;[3]
And when I feel, fair creature of an hour,
10    That I shall never look upon thee more,
Never have relish in the fairy power
    Of unreflecting love—then on the shore
Of the wide world I stand alone, and think
Till love and fame to nothingness do sink.

---

**1. charactery:** Written or printed letters of the alphabet.
**2. garners:** Storehouses for grain.
**3. chance:** Inspiration.

**JOHN KEATS, 1821**
*Joseph Severn*
*By Courtesy of the National Portrait Gallery, London*

---

## THINKING ABOUT THE SELECTION

### Recalling

1. (a) What does the speaker say he fears missing in lines 1–8? (b) In lines 9–12?

### Interpreting

2. What do you think is meant by "cloudy symbols of a high romance" in line 6?
3. Whom is the speaker addressing in line 10?
4. How does the speaker resolve his fears?

### Applying

5. What does this poem suggest about Keats's views on death? Do you feel these views would be held by the other Romantic poets you have read? Why or why not?

## THINKING AND WRITING

### Comparing and Contrasting Sonnets

Choose one of the sonnets by William Wordsworth (pages 653–657). On a sheet of paper take notes on how this sonnet is similar to and different from the sonnets of Keats in form, subject matter, word usage, and theme. In an essay of one page or more write about your findings. When you revise make sure you have included details from the poems as support.

# GUIDE FOR INTERPRETING

## Ode to a Nightingale; Ode on a Grecian Urn; To Autumn

**Imagery.** Imagery is language that helps a reader form a mental picture of an object or idea by appealing to one or more of the five senses. Taken by itself the word *bread,* for example, is nothing more than just that—a word. When, however, the word is part of the image "warm loaf of freshly baked bread," our sense of sight and especially our sense of smell are both called into play. In his odes Keats used imagery with a degree of skill that few poets before or since have achieved.

We all have different methods of writing, depending on our audience, topic, and purpose as well as our personalities and moods. Sometimes we need a great deal of time to gather and arrange our thoughts; other times we can write with feverish haste, inspired perhaps by a vivid image or idea.

It's not easy to describe the writing process. At times, too, we may want to recount our creative experiences somewhat differently from how they actually occurred. Perhaps we want to make the story more impressive, or try to conform to prevailing ideas of creativity.

After Charles Brown found the scraps of paper containing Keats's ode to the nightingale, he continued his search for more of Keats's work. With his friend's help, Brown found other short poems, which otherwise might have vanished. "From that day on he gave me permission to copy any verses he might write," Brown recounts. "He cared so little for them himself when once, as it appeared to me, his imagination was released from their influence, that it required a friend at hand to preserve them."

We have no reason to doubt Brown's account, yet perhaps his version is colored by the Romantic notion of creativity. What do you see in Brown's account and Keats's poetry that supports the Romantic idea that poetry is "the spontaneous overflow of powerful feelings"? What other Romantic ideas do you find here?

Picture a setting in nature with which you are very familiar—a park, a wooded area, or the like. On a sheet of paper jot down as many physical features of the scene as you can. You might, for instance, mention trees, grass, rocks, and sky. Lastly, think up an image for each feature you mentioned that would enable a reader to develop a strong mental picture.

# Ode to a Nightingale

## John Keats

*Keats composed the following ode in 1819, while living in Hampstead with his friend Charles Brown. Brown wrote the following description about how the ode was composed: "In the spring of 1819 a nightingale had built her nest near my house. Keats felt a tranquil and continued joy in her song; and one morning he took his chair from the breakfast table to the grass plot under the plum tree, where he sat for two or three hours. When he came into the house, I perceived he had some scraps of paper in his hand, and these he was quietly thrusting behind the books. On inquiry, I found those scraps, four or five in number, contained his poetic feeling on the song of our nightingale."*

### I

My heart aches, and a drowsy numbness pains
    My sense, as though of hemlock[1] I had drunk,
Or emptied some dull opiate to the drains
    One minute past, and Lethe-wards[2] had sunk:
5  'Tis not through envy of thy happy lot,
    But being too happy in thine happiness,—
      That thou, light-winged Dryad[3] of the trees,
        In some melodious plot
    Of beechen green, and shadows numberless,
10      Singest of summer in full-throated ease.

### II

O, for a draft[4] of vintage! that hath been
    Cooled a long age in the deep-delved earth,
Tasting of Flora[5] and the country green,
    Dance, and Provençal[6] song, and sunburnt mirth!

---

**1. hemlock:** A poisonous herb.
**2. Lethe-wards:** Toward Lethe, the river of forgetfulness in Hades, the underworld, in classical mythology.
**3. Dryad** (drī′ əd): In classical mythology, a wood nymph.
**4. draft:** Drink.
**5. Flora:** In classical mythology, the goddess of flowers, or the flowers themselves.
**6. Provençal** (prō′ vən säl′): Pertaining to Provence, a region in southern France, renowned in the late Middle Ages for its troubadours, who composed and sang love songs.

**SMALL BIRD ON A FLOWERING PLUM BRANCH**
*Attributed to Ma Lin*
The Gotoh Museum

15  O for a beaker full of the warm South,
    Full of the true, the blushful Hippocrene,[7]
       With beaded bubbles winking at the brim,
          And purple-stained mouth;
       That I might drink, and leave the world unseen,
20       And with thee fade away into the forest dim:

---

**7. Hippocrene** (hĭp′ ə krēn′): In classical mythology, the fountain of the Muses on Mt. Helicon. From this fountain flowed the waters of inspiration.

# III

Fade far away, dissolve, and quite forget
    What thou among the leaves hast never known,
The weariness, the fever, and the fret
    Here, where men sit and hear each other groan;
25 Where palsy shakes a few, sad, last gray hairs,
    Where youth grows pale, and specter-thin, and dies;[8]
        Where but to think is to be full of sorrow
          And leaden-eyed despairs,
        Where Beauty cannot keep her lustrous eyes,
30         Or new Love pine at them beyond tomorrow.

# IV

Away! away! for I will fly to thee,
    Not charioted by Bacchus[9] and his pards,
But on the viewless[10] wings of Poesy,[11]
    Though the dull brain perplexes and retards:
35 Already with thee! tender is the night,
    And haply[12] the Queen-Moon is on her throne,
        Clustered around by all her starry Fays;[13]
          But here there is no light,
        Save what from heaven is with the breezes blown
40         Through verdurous[14] glooms and winding mossy
        ways.

# V

I cannot see what flowers are at my feet,
    Nor what soft incense hangs upon the boughs,
But, in embalmed[15] darkness, guess each sweet
    Wherewith the seasonable month endows
45 The grass, the thicket, and the fruit-tree wild;
    White hawthorn, and the pastoral eglantine;[16]
        Fast fading violets covered up in leaves;
          And mid-May's eldest child,
        The coming musk-rose, full of dewy wine,
50         The murmurous haunt of flies on summer eves.

---

**8. youth . . . dies:** Keats is referring to his brother, Tom, who had died from tuberculosis the previous winter.
**9. Bacchus** (băk′ əs): In classical mythology, the god of wine, who was often represented in a chariot drawn by leopards ("pards").
**10. viewless:** Invisible.
**11. Poesy:** Poetic fancy.
**12. haply:** Perhaps.
**13. Fays:** Fairies.
**14. verdurous:** Green-foliaged.
**15. embalmed:** Perfumed.
**16. eglantine** (eg′ lən tīn′): Sweetbrier or honeysuckle.

## VI

Darkling[17] I listen; and, for many a time
    I have been half in love with easeful Death,
Called him soft names in many a mused[18] rhyme,
    To take into the air my quiet breath;
55  Now more than ever seems it rich to die,
    To cease upon the midnight with no pain,
      While thou art pouring forth thy soul abroad
        In such an ecstasy!
    Still wouldst thou sing, and I have ears in vain—
60      To thy high requiem become a sod.

## VII

Thou wast not born for death, immortal Bird!
    No hungry generations tread thee down;
The voice I hear this passing night was heard
    In ancient days by emperor and clown:
65  Perhaps the selfsame song that found a path
    Through the sad heart of Ruth,[19] when, sick for home,
      She stood in tears amid the alien corn;
        The same that ofttimes hath
    Charmed magic casements, opening on the foam
70      Of perilous seas, in fairylands forlorn.

## VIII

Forlorn! the very word is like a bell
    To toll me back from thee to my sole self!
Adieu! the fancy cannot cheat so well
    As she is famed[20] to do, deceiving elf.
75  Adieu! adieu! thy plaintive anthem[21] fades
    Past the near meadows, over the still stream,
      Up the hillside; and now 'tis buried deep
        In the next valley-glades:
    Was it a vision, or a waking dream?
80      Fled is that music:—Do I wake or sleep?

---

**17. darkling:** In the dark.
**18. mused:** Meditated.
**19. Ruth:** In the Bible (Ruth 2:1–23), a widow who left her home and went to Judah to work in the corn (wheat) fields.
**20. famed:** Reported.
**21. anthem:** Hymn.

## THINKING ABOUT THE SELECTION

### Recalling

1. What is the speaker's mood in stanza I?
2. (a) What wish does the speaker express at the end of stanza II and at the beginning of stanza III? (b) According to stanza IV, how will he accomplish this wish?
3. What effect does the word "forlorn" have on the speaker in stanza VIII?

### Interpreting

4. (a) What is the "draught of vintage" the speaker craves in stanza II? (b) What would it help him to escape?
5. (a) What differences between the speaker's world and the bird's are described in stanza IV? (b) What is meant in line 38 by "here there is no light"?
6. (a) What does the speaker find tempting in stanza VI? (b) What changes his mind in stanza VII?

### Applying

7. The poem ends with a question. What is its relevance, both to the poem and to the spirit of the Romantic movement?

8. The twentieth-century American novelist F. Scott Fitzgerald took the title of one of his novels from line 35: "Already with thee! Tender is the night." (a) In what way can the night be tender? (b) Why are the words "tender is the night" especially appropriate for one who has been "half in love with easeful Death"?

## ANALYZING LITERATURE

### Using Imagery

**Imagery** is language that appeals to the senses and, by so doing, creates a vivid picture in the reader's mind. The phrase "blustery, wind-swept day" provides the reader with a strong impression that the simple phrase "cold day" does not. Such is the impact of imagery. Find an everyday equivalent for each of the following images from "Ode to a Nightingale." Then state which of Keats's words are central to his image.

1. "With beaded bubbles winking at the brim,/ And purple-stained mouth;" (lines 17–18)
2. "Where palsy shakes a few, sad, last gray hairs,/Where youth grows pale, and specter-thin, and dies;" (lines 25–26)
3. The coming musk-rose, full of dewy wine,/The murmurous haunt of flies on summer eves." (lines 49–50)

# Ode on a Grecian Urn

John Keats

## I

Thou still unravished bride of quietness,
    Thou foster child of silence and slow time,
Sylvan[1] historian, who canst thus express
    A flowery tale more sweetly than our rhyme:
5       What leaf-fringed legend haunts about thy shape
        Of deities or mortals, or of both,
          In Tempe[2] or the dales of Arcady?[3]
    What men or gods are these? What maidens loath?[4]
What mad pursuit? What struggle to escape?
10       What pipes and timbrels?[5] What wild ecstasy?

## II

Heard melodies are sweet, but those unheard
    Are sweeter; therefore, ye soft pipes, play on;
Not to the sensual[6] ear, but, more endeared,
    Pipe to the spirit ditties of no tone:
15 Fair youth, beneath the trees, thou canst not leave
    Thy song, nor ever can those trees be bare;
      Bold Lover, never, never canst thou kiss,
Though winning near the goal—yet, do not grieve;
    She cannot fade, though thou hast not thy bliss,
20       Forever wilt thou love, and she be fair!

## III

Ah, happy, happy boughs! that cannot shed
    Your leaves, nor ever bid the Spring adieu;
And, happy melodist, unwearied,
    Forever piping songs forever new;

---

**1. sylvan:** Rustic, representing the woods or forest.
**2. Tempe** (tem′ pē): A beautiful valley in Greece that has become a symbol of supreme rural beauty.
**3. Arcady** (är′ kə dē): A region in Greece that has come to represent supreme pastoral contentment.
**4. loath:** Unwilling.
**5. timbrels:** Tambourines.
**6. sensual:** Involving the physical sense of hearing.

25　More happy love! more happy, happy love!
　　　　Forever warm and still to be enjoyed,
　　　　　Forever panting, and forever young;
　　All breathing human passion far above,
　　　　That leaves a heart high-sorrowful and cloyed,
30　　　　　A burning forehead, and a parching tongue.


### IV

　　Who are these coming to the sacrifice?
　　　　To what green altar, O mysterious priest,
　　Lead'st thou that heifer lowing at the skies,
　　　　And all her silken flanks with garlands dressed?
35　What little town by river or seashore,
　　　　Or mountain-built with peaceful citadel,
　　　　　Is emptied of this folk, this pious morn?
　　And, little town, thy streets forevermore
　　　　Will silent be; and not a soul to tell
40　　　　　Why thou art desolate, can e'er return.

COLUMN KRATER (CALLED THE "ORCHARD VASE"),
SIDE A: WOMEN GATHERING APPLES
*The Metropolitan Museum of Art*

*Ode on a Grecian Urn*　727

## V

O Attic[7] shape! Fair attitude! with brede[8]
    Of marble men and maidens overwrought,[9]
With forest branches and the trodden weed;
    Thou, silent form, dost tease us out of thought
45 As doth eternity: Cold[10] Pastoral!
    When old age shall this generation waste,
    Thou shalt remain, in midst of other woe
Than ours, a friend to man, to whom thou say'st,
    "Beauty is truth, truth beauty,"—that is all
50     Ye know on earth, and all ye need to know.

---

**7. Attic:** Attica was the region of Greece in which Athens was located;
a region characterized by grace and simplicity.
**8. brede:** An interwoven pattern.
**9. overwrought:** All over.
**10. cold:** Unchanging.

## THINKING ABOUT THE SELECTION

### Recalling

1. As the speaker studies the scene on a Grecian urn, it takes hold of his imagination. (a) Whom does the speaker address in stanza II of the poem? (b) Whom does he address in stanza III?
2. What ritual is described in the first four lines of stanza IV?

### Interpreting

3. (a) In what way is the urn a "Sylvan historian"? (b) How can it tell its "flowery tale more sweetly than our rhyme"?
4. (a) Interpret lines 11–12: "Heard melodies are sweet, but those unheard/Are sweeter . . ." (b) What do these lines indicate about the power of the imagination?

5. (a) Why might the lover in stanza II grieve? (b) Why does the speaker advise him not to grieve?
6. (a) What is the "Cold Pastoral" mentioned in line 45? (b) With what does the speaker contrast it?

### Applying

7. (a) Explain the meaning of the last two lines of the poem. (b) In what ways might this finish have been appropriate to "Ode to a Nightingale"?
8. In *Endymion*, John Keats wrote, "A thing of beauty is a joy forever;/Its loveliness increases; it will never/Pass into nothingness." Compare and contrast the idea of beauty expressed in these lines with that expressed in lines 49–50 of "Ode on a Grecian Urn".

# To Autumn

**John Keats**

## I

Season of mists and mellow fruitfulness,
    Close bosom-friend of the maturing sun;
Conspiring with him how to load and bless
    With fruit the vines that round the thatch-eves run;
5  To bend with apples the mossed cottage-trees,
    And fill all fruit with ripeness to the core;
      To swell the gourd, and plump the hazel shells
    With a sweet kernel; to set budding more,
And still more, later flowers for the bees,
10  Until they think warm days will never cease,
    For Summer has o'er-brimmed their clammy cells.

## II

Who hath not seen thee oft amid thy store?
    Sometimes whoever seeks abroad may find
Thee sitting careless on a granary floor,
15    Thy hair soft-lifted by the winnowing[1] wind;
Or on a half-reaped furrow sound asleep,
    Drowsed with the fume of poppies, while thy hook[2]
      Spares the next swath and all its twined flowers:
And sometimes like a gleaner thou dost keep
20    Steady thy laden head across a brook;
    Or by a cider-press, with patient look,
      Thou watchest the last oozings hours by hours.

## III

Where are the songs of Spring? Ay, where are they?
    Think not of them, thou hast thy music too—
25  While barred clouds bloom the soft-dying day,
    And touch the stubble-plains with rosy hue;
Then in a wailful choir the small gnats mourn
    Among the river sallows,[3] borne aloft
      Or sinking as the light wind lives or dies;

---

**1. winnowing:** Fanning; winnowing is a process in which the chaff is
fanned from the grain.
**2. hook:** Scythe.
**3. sallows:** Willow trees.

30  And full-grown lambs loud bleat from hilly bourn;[4]
        Hedge-crickets sing; and now with treble soft
        The red-breast whistles from a garden croft;[5]
        And gathering swallows twitter in the skies.

---

**4. bourn:** Region.
**5. croft:** An enclosed plot of farm land.

---

## THINKING ABOUT THE SELECTION
### Recalling

1. (a) In stanza I of the poem, what is the season described as "doing"? (b) With whom is the season "conspiring"?
2. What are some of the songs of autumn?

### Interpreting

3. In what way can Autumn be described as a "close bosom-friend of the maturing sun"?
4. (a) What activities frequently associated with the season are described in the second stanza? (b) What impression of Autumn is created by mentioning these activities?
5. Why do you think the speaker mentions the songs of Spring in stanza III?

### Applying

6. What do you suppose was Keats's attitude toward winter? Explain your answer in terms of the three odes you have just read.

## SPEAKING AND LISTENING
### Selecting Music to Accompany a Poem

In "To Autumn," Keats mentions the songs of Spring and of Autumn. Many of the images he presents in the poem, in fact, suggest music. Find a piece of music that you feel would provide good background to Keats's poem about autumn. Try reading the poem aloud as the music plays. If possible, bring a recording of the music you select to class.

## THINKING AND WRITING
### Comparing and Contrasting Odes

Choose one of the odes by Shelley that you read. Reread it, noting such features as word choice, stanza structure, and overall message. In a one-page composition, discuss the ways in which the three odes by Keats are similar to and different from that of Shelley. Include mention of whose work you like better and state your reasons.

# Prose

**FISHERMAN UPON A LEE SHORE**
*J. M. W. Turner*
The Iveagh Bequest, Kenwood,
Bridgeman/Art Resource

# MARY SHELLEY

## 1797–1851

Even the most serious and dedicated of writers have their lighter moments. It is interesting to note that had it not been for such a moment involving two of English literature's most gifted writers, one of the most celebrated Gothic novels of all time might never have seen the light of day. More interesting still, the novel in question, *Frankenstein,* was penned by neither of the aforementioned greats —the poets Percy Bysshe Shelley and Lord Byron—but by the wife of the former, Mary Shelley.

Born in London, Mary Wollstonecraft Godwin was the daughter of William Godwin, a political thinker and writer given to radical ideas. One of her father's books, *Political Justice,* managed to attract the attention of the young and equally radically minded Percy Shelley, who became one of Godwin's disciples. Mary Godwin in turn became a great admirer of the young poet, and the two of them eloped to Switzerland when she was seventeen.

Mary Shelley's first piece of writing, *Journal of a Six Weeks' Tour* (1817), was a collaborative effort with her husband. Her first solo work—the novel with which her name is most often associated today—grew, quite innocently, out of idle conversation between Byron and another friend during a visit to the Shelleys' home on Lake Geneva in 1816. As a result of the conversation, it was suggested as a means of passing the time that each of the four friends attempt to write a ghost story. Though the results of the contest were largely unremarkable, Mary Shelley's horrific tale of the creation of a monster so impressed the gathering that her husband later urged her to develop it into a full-length novel. Thus was born *Frankenstein* (1818), and the creature that has thrilled countless readers and fueled the imaginations of generations of film makers.

After *Frankenstein,* Mary Shelley produced five more novels: *Valperga* (1823) and *Perkin Warbeck* (1830), which are historical works; the autobiographical *Lodore* (1835); *Falkner* (1837), a complicated mystery tale; and *The Last Man* (1826).

If *Frankenstein* is, as scholars have noted, structurally weak, it is nevertheless a "good read." More important from a historical perspective, the novel was the first in a long line of works to explore the potential dangers of technology that falls into the wrong hands.

# GUIDE FOR INTERPRETING

## Introduction to *Frankenstein*

**Gothic Tradition.** The Gothic novel was a late eighteenth-century revival of the tale of terror, which has its roots in antiquity. Gothic fiction, or *Gothicism,* is formally defined by two elements—the historical and the "wonderful," or supernatural. One of the earliest and best-known Gothic novels was Horace Walpole's *The Castle of Otranto* (1765), a hair-raising account of a castle terrorized by a giant. Within the pages of Walpole's thriller, paintings and statues come to life for the first time in fiction. The next important contributor to the "renaissance of wonder" was Clara Reeve, a critic, whose *The Old English Baron* (1777) was, in her own humble opinion, an improvement on Walpole's haunted castle story. The Gothic tradition was refined considerably in the hands of Matthew Gregory Lewis, who, at the age of twenty, published *The Monk* (1796), a cleverly conceived and simply told tale of a Spanish friar who enters into a contract with the devil. The first novel to depict its horrors in graphic terms, *The Monk* paved the way for Mary Shelley's *Frankenstein* (1818), whose main character breathes life into one of the best-known and most terrifying monsters of all time.

Mary Shelley's mother, Mary Wollstonecraft, was as radical a thinker as her father, William Godwin. Her 1792 book, *A Vindication of the Rights of Women,* was the first great work devoted to equality for women.

For centuries, she said, women had willingly served men. To escape from slavery, women must cultivate their minds, find new occupations, and refuse to accept an inferior role. Equality for women could help all people fulfill their potential, she wrote.

If her book had appeared earlier, it might merely have provoked amusement, but it fell upon a frightened world. Educators vetoed the freedom for which Wollstonecraft had pleaded. Female writers urged that women accept their subordinate position and use their "feminine wiles"—acting delicate and helpless, for example—to get their way with men.

Wollstonecraft died ten days after Mary's birth, but her ideas permeate her daughter's work. Where in the *Introduction to Frankenstein* do you see the influence of her writing and beliefs?

Give some thought to ideas that might be incorporated into a tale of terror. Well-used but always-dependable possibilities include graveyards at night, dark winding staircases, and ghosts. Sketch a rough outline to a story that contains some of these ideas.

# Introduction to *Frankenstein*

## Mary Wollstonecraft Shelley

*In this introduction to the third edition of* Frankenstein, *published in 1831, Mary Shelley recalls the circumstances that led her to write the novel during the summer of 1816.*

The Publishers of the Standard Novels, in selecting *Frankenstein* for one of their series, expressed a wish that I should furnish them with some account of the origin of the story. I am the more willing to comply, because I shall thus give a general answer to the question, so very frequently asked me: "How I, then a young girl, came to think of, and to dilate upon, so very hideous an idea?" It is true that I am very averse to bringing myself forward in print; but as my account will only appear as an appendage to a former production, and as it will be confined to such topics as have connection with my authorship alone, I can scarcely accuse myself of a personal intrusion. . . .

In the summer of 1816, we[1] visited Switzerland, and became the neighbors of Lord Byron. At first we spent our pleasant hours on the lake or wandering on its shores; and Lord Byron, who was writing the third canto of *Childe Harold*, was the only one among us who put his thoughts upon paper. These, as he brought them successively to us, clothed in all the light and harmony of poetry, seemed to stamp as divine the glories of heaven and earth, whose influences we partook with him.

But it proved a wet, ungenial summer, and incessant rain often confined us for days to the house. Some volumes of ghost stories, translated from the German into French,[2] fell into our hands. There was "The History of the Inconstant Lover,"[3] who, when he thought to clasp the bride to whom he had pledged his vows, found himself in the arms of the pale ghost of her whom he had deserted. There was the tale of the sinful founder of his race,[4] whose miserable doom it was to bestow the kiss of death on all the younger sons of his fated house, just when they reached the age of promise. His gigantic, shadowy form, clothed like the ghost in Hamlet, in complete armor but with the beaver[5] up, was seen at midnight, by the moon's fitful beams, to advance slowly along the gloomy avenue. The shape was lost beneath the shadow of the castle walls; but soon a gate swung back, a step was heard, the door of the chamber opened, and he advanced to the couch of the blooming youths, cradled in healthy sleep. Eternal sorrow sat upon his face as he bent down and kissed the foreheads of the boys, who from that hour withered like flowers snap-

---

**1. we:** Mary Shelley, her husband Percy Bysshe Shelley, and their two children.

**2. volumes . . . French:** *Fantasmagoriana,* or *Collected Stories of Apparitions of Specters, Ghosts, Phantoms, Etc.,* published anonymously in 1812.
**3. "The History . . . Lover":** The true name of the story is "The Dead Fiancée."
**4. the tale . . . race:** "Family Portraits."
**5. beaver:** The hinged piece of armor that covers the face.

**A VIEW OF CHAMONIX AND MT. BLANC**
*Julius Schnon von Carolsfeld*
Austrian Gallery, Vienna

ped upon the stalk. I have not seen these stories since then, but their incidents are as fresh in my mind as if I had read them yesterday.

"We will each write a ghost story," said Lord Byron; and his proposition was acceded to. There were four of us.[6] The noble author began a tale, a fragment of which he printed at the end of his poem of Mazeppa. Shelley, more apt to embody ideas and sentiments in the radiance of brilliant imagery, and in the music of the most melodious verse that adorns our language, than to invent the machinery of a story, commenced one founded on the experiences of his early life. Poor Polidori had some terrible idea about a skull-headed lady, who was so punished for peeping through a keyhole —what to see I forget—something very shocking and wrong of course; but when she

was reduced to a worse condition than the renowned Tom of Coventry,[7] he did not know what to do with her, and was obliged to despatch her to the tomb of the Capulets,[8] the only place for which she was fitted. The illustrious poets also, annoyed by the platitude of prose, speedily relinquished their uncongenial task.

I busied myself *to think of a story*— a story to rival those which had excited us to this task. One which would speak to the mysterious fears of our nature and awaken thrilling horror—one to make the reader dread to look round, to curdle the blood, and quicken the beatings of the heart. If I did not accomplish these things, my ghost story would be unworthy of its name. I thought and pondered—vainly. I felt that blank in-

---

**6. four of us:** Byron, the two Shelleys, and John William Polidori, Byron's physician.

---

**7. Tom of Coventry:** "Peeping Tom" who, according to legend, was struck blind for looking at Lady Godiva as she rode naked through Coventry.
**8. tomb of the Capulets:** Where Romeo and Juliet died.

capability of invention which is the greatest misery of authorship, when dull Nothing replies to our anxious invocations. *Have you thought of a story?* I was asked each morning, and each morning I was forced to reply with a mortifying negative. . . .

Many and long were the conversations between Lord Byron and Shelley, to which I was a devout but nearly silent listener. During one of these, various philosophical doctrines were discussed, and among others the nature of the principle of life and whether there was any probability of its ever being discovered and communicated. They talked of the experiments of Dr. Darwin[9] (I speak not of what the Doctor really did or said that he did, but, as more to my purpose, of what was then spoken of as having been done by him), who preserved a piece of vermicelli in a glass case till by some extraordinary means it began to move with voluntary motion. Not thus, after all, would life be given. Perhaps a corpse would be reanimated: galvanism[10] had given token of such things. Perhaps the component parts of a creature might be manufactured, brought together, and endued with vital warmth.

Night waned upon this talk, and even the witching hour had gone by, before we retired to rest. When I placed my head on my pillow, I did not sleep, nor could I be said to think. My imagination, unbidden, possessed and guided me, gifting the successive images that arose in my mind with a vividness far beyond the usual bounds of reverie. I saw—with shut eyes but acute mental vision—I saw the pale student of unhallowed arts kneeling beside the thing he had put together. I saw the hideous phantasm of a man stretched out, and then, on the working of some powerful engine, show signs of life and stir with an uneasy, half vital motion. Frightful must it be, for supremely frightful would be the effect of any human endeavor to mock the stupendous mechanism of the Creator of the world. His success would terrify the artist; he would rush away from his odious handiwork, horror-stricken. He would hope that, left to itself, the slight spark of life which he had communicated would fade; that this thing, which had received such imperfect animation, would subside into dead matter; and he might sleep in the belief that the silence of the grave would quench forever the transient existence of the hideous corpse which he had looked upon as the cradle of life. He sleeps; but he is awakened; he opens his eyes; behold the horrid thing stands at his bedside, opening his curtains, and looking on him with yellow, watery, but speculative eyes.

I opened mine in terror. The idea so possessed my mind, that a thrill of fear ran through me, and I wished to exchange the ghastly image of my fancy for the realities around. I see them still: the very room, the dark parquet,[11] the closed shutters, with the moonlight struggling through, and the sense I had that the glassy lake and white high Alps were beyond. I could not so easily get rid of my hideous phantom: still it haunted me. I must try to think of something else. I recurred to my ghost story—my tiresome unlucky ghost story! O! if I could only contrive one which would frighten my reader as I myself had been frightened that night!

Swift as light and as cheering was the idea that broke in upon me. "I have found it! What terrified me will terrify others, and I need only describe the specter which had haunted my midnight pillow." On the morrow I announced that I had *thought of a story.* I began that day with the words, *It was on a dreary night of November,* making only a transcript of the grim terrors of my waking dream.

At first I thought but of a few pages—of

---

**9. Dr. Darwin:** Erasmus Darwin (1731–1802), physician, natural scientist, and poet.
**10. galvanism:** The use of electric current to induce twitching in dead muscles.

**11. parquet** (pär kā´): Flooring made of wooden pieces arranged in a pattern.

a short tale—but Shelley urged me to develop the idea at greater length. I certainly did not owe the suggestion of one incident, nor scarcely of one train of feeling, to my husband, and yet but for his incitement, it would never have taken the form in which it was presented to the world. From this declaration I must except the preface. As far as I can recollect, it was entirely written by him.

And now, once again, I bid my hideous progeny go forth and prosper. I have an affection for it, for it was the offspring of happy days, when death and grief were but words, which found no true echo in my heart. Its several pages speak of many a walk, many a drive, and many a conversation, when I was not alone; and my companion was one who, in this world, I shall never see more. But this is for myself: my readers have nothing to do with these associations.

---

## THINKING ABOUT THE SELECTION

### Recalling

1. What question does the author say people frequently ask her?
2. (a) What forced the author, her husband, and their friends to stay indoors? (b) What did they do to pass the time?
3. What was Byron's proposition?
4. (a) What provided the author with inspiration for her story? (b) What "vision" came to the author after she retired for the night?

### Interpreting

5. What do the goals the author sets for herself in writing her ghost story suggest about her as a person?
6. Based on her description of her "vision," what seems to be the author's attitude toward work of the sort carried out by Dr. Darwin?

### Applying

7. Many areas of scientific investigation carry both potential benefits and potential dangers for humankind. (a) What such areas in our own age can you name? (b) Which areas do you believe human beings should never have become involved in? Give reasons for your answer.

## ANALYZING LITERATURE

### Recognizing Gothic Tradition

The Gothic tradition of the horror story, which began in the eighteenth century, traces back to ancient times. In *The Spirit of the Public Journals,* a 1797 pamphlet, a "recipe" for the Gothic novel is given. Among the "ingredients" listed are: an old castle, a long gallery with secret doors, three freshly murdered bodies, assorted skeletons, and "noises, whispers, and groans." In *Frankenstein,* Mary Shelley endeavored to improve slightly on that formula.

1. Based on your reading of her introduction, what most likely is the theme of *Frankenstein?*
2. Based on the French translations of ghost stories Shelley mentions, what other "ingredients" might be added to the above list?

### THINKING AND WRITING

### Writing in the Gothic Tradition

Review the ideas and outline you developed for the assignment under Writing on page 733. Then write an original story or episode that follows the Gothic tradition. You may add as many of the elements mentioned. If you can, build a theme into your horror story. When you revise make sure you have told your tale in chronological order.

# CROSS CURRENTS

## Goethe's *Faust*

The play opens in a narrow, high-vaulted Gothic room. Faust, a deeply learned scholar, speaks restlessly from his armchair by the desk:

> I have pursued, alas, philosophy,
> Jurisprudence, and medicine,
> And, help me God, theology,
> With fervent zeal through thick and
>     thin.
> And here, poor fool, I stand once
>     more,
> No wiser than I was before.

His life is dull, dusty, and empty; he has neither fame and fortune nor contentment. In despair he tries a less legitimate road to knowledge and satisfaction:

> So I resorted to Magic's art,
> To see if by spirit mouth and might
> Many a secret might come to light;
> So I need toil no longer so,
> Propounding what I do not know.

Mephistopheles, the Devil, appears from the mist. Faust gladly signs a pact with him—in blood!—exchanging his soul for knowledge, "all treasures of the human mind." The Devil promises Faust that

> I shall be at your service by this
>     bond
> Without relief or respite here on
>     earth;

but makes the scholar swear

> And if or when we meet again
>     beyond,
> You are to give me equal worth.

With this, a great change comes over the life of the learned doctor. He tastes experience through a great many wondrous adventures but does not find the happiness he is seeking until the very last act. And this is what Goethe is asking: What is happiness? Is it living within your abilities? Or is it daring to be more than human? Faust—and the audience—learn the answer as the curtain drops.

### A LIFETIME OF WORK

The legend of Doctor Faustus, the famous magician who sells his soul to the devil in return for knowledge of mystical secrets, is a thrilling horror story with a moral. It was first published in 1587, and different versions were sold year after year at country fairs. In Christopher Marlowe's hands, the legend became a play for the Elizabethan stage. The theme was taken up by troupes of traveling puppeteers and soon became a favorite around the country.

Young Goethe, familiar with the Faust legend through the early books and the puppet shows, sensed that the wild tale would allow him to explore the exciting new aspirations of the human soul. In the early 1770's, he began to jot down the first scenes for a projected Faust play. When he moved to Weimar in the autumn of 1775—where he would settle for the rest of his life—he brought these sketches with him. He worked on the manuscript on and off for more than a decade. Fearing that he would never complete it, he issued an unfinished version in 1790. Encouraged by his friend Schiller, he finally published *Faust, Part One* in 1808. Meanwhile he had begun work on the second part, very different from the first in time, place, and style. Although he released portions of *Part Two* during his life, he worked on the manuscript right up until his death. The complete play was published in 1832, more than sixty years after he had first begun it. The lifetime of work yielded the masterpiece of Germany's finest poet.

## FAUST AND ROMANTICISM

Although Romanticism didn't cause a political upheaval in Germany, it did spark the imagination of German writers. Like their English and French counterparts, young German writers began to rebel against the restraints of Neoclassicism.

The Romantic movement exploded on the German scene during the *Sturm und Drang* (storm and stress) movement of the 1770's. As the name suggests, the era saw the rise of highly emotional writing. Goethe, as with many writers of the time, was inspired by the movement to explore the new values of imagination and emotion.

To previous generations Faust was a symbol of humanity gone astray, and his story was taken as a warning. To the Romantics, in contrast, Faust represented human freedom from authority. Whether his decision would lead to salvation or not, his courage in venturing into the world of the forbidden makes him heroic. As he struggles between the real and the ideal, we see Goethe's deep love of humanity.

Goethe's *Faust* is the greatest and most famous version of the Faust legend, the one upon which all subsequent retellings are based. Fascinating, provocative, and compelling, *Faust* probes deeply into the human soul in its search for answers to the timeless quest for the meaning of human existence.

**FAUST: HENRY IRVING AS MEPHISTOPHELES**
*Theatre Museum/E. T. Archive*

# CHARLES LAMB

## 1775–1834

A personal friend of most of the great English writers of his day, Charles Lamb was considered one of the foremost prose writers of the Romantic Era—a distinction he has retained through the present time.

The son of a clerk and the grandson of a housekeeper, Lamb was born in London. He was educated at Christ's Hospital, a school for poor children, where he met and became lifelong friends with a fellow student, Samuel Taylor Coleridge, who later became a well-known poet and critic. At seventeen Lamb left school and took a job with the South Sea House, a large London trading company. He soon received a better position as an accountant at a rival firm, the East India House, where he remained employed for thirty-three years.

In 1796 an event occurred that shadowed the rest of Lamb's life. His sister Mary, given to brief fits of insanity, killed their mother. After this, Lamb, always a loving brother, devoted himself to Mary's care and protection. Upon his retirement from East India House, he was granted a comfortable pension and after his sister's confinement to an asylum, took her to live in the country.

Throughout most of his life, Lamb wrote to supplement his regular income. Although he composed a number of poems and plays, it was with his essays and literary criticism that he made his mark as a writer. In 1808 he published a book on Elizabethan dramatic poets that established his reputation as a critic. Thereafter, he began to contribute essays to periodicals such as the *Examiner,* the *Quarterly Review,* the *London Magazine,* and the *Reflector,* a magazine published by the poet Leigh Hunt.

It was in the *London Magazine* that Lamb's series of personal essays written under the name Elia first appeared in printed form. Later these essays were collected and published in the volumes *Essays of Elia* (1832) and *Last Essays of Elia* (1833). Lamb also collaborated with his sister Mary on a number of works, including the ever-popular *Tales from Shakespeare* (1807), a collection designed to introduce young readers to Shakespeare's plays.

Many of Lamb's essays are autobiographical, with characters modeled on his father, his grandmother, his brother John, and other relatives. Though they are known for their gentle humor, the essays often display an undercurrent of great sadness, the result of the tragedies that Lamb experienced in his life.

## Writer's Technique

### Dream Children: A Reverie

**Familiar Essay.** An essay is a short prose composition that focuses on a single subject. A familiar or informal essay is a loosely constructed essay that uses conversational English to communicate a writer's thoughts in a manner that will interest or entertain the reader. Since familiar essays frequently include details from the author's own life, they are sometimes referred to as "personal" essays.

The familiar essay has its origins in the writings of Michel de Montaigne, a French author of the sixteenth century. It was Montaigne who first used the term *essai*—French for "attempt"—to describe the somewhat rambling, often amusing compositions in which he communicated highly personal thoughts to his readers.

## Commentary

In their tone and style, Lamb's familiar essays no doubt drew on his frequent conversations with friends, a distinguished circle of great writers. Many anecdotes survive of their witty conversations. For example, the host of a party attended by Lamb, Wordsworth, and Keats, among others, remarked that Lamb's wit "so speeded the stream of conversation, that in my life I never passed a more delightful time." The following story describes an encounter between Lamb and Coleridge.

Coleridge had been especially talkative that evening. He had covered every topic imaginable, from Moses on downward. Finally his monologue came to his own concerns. He turned to Lamb and continued: "At this place, at Shrewsbury (which is not only remarkable for its celebrated cakes, and for having been the point of rendezvous for Falstaff's regiment of foot, but also, if I may presume to speak of it, for the first development of the imaginative faculty in myself, by which faculty I would be understood to mean, etc. etc.)—at Shrewsbury I was accustomed to preach. I believe, Charles Lamb, that you have heard me preach?" His exhausted friend quickly replied, "I—I—never heard you do anything else."

What characteristics of daily conversation do you see in the following familiar essay?

## Writing

Choose a fairly light topic that allows some room for opinion, such as whether the school week should be shortened or lengthened. Freewrite, expressing your opinion on this topic, defending your position with abundant examples from your own life and experience.

# Dream Children: A Reverie

## Charles Lamb

Children love to listen to stories about their elders when *they* were children; to stretch their imagination to the conception of a traditionary great-uncle, or grandame whom they never saw. It was in this spirit that my little ones crept about me the other evening to hear about their great-grandmother Field,[1] who lived in a great house in Norfolk (a hundred times bigger than that in which they and papa lived) which had been the scene—so at least it was generally believed in that part of the country—of the tragic incidents which they had lately become familiar with from the ballad of "The Children in the Wood."[2] Certain it is that the whole story of the children and their cruel uncle was to be seen fairly carved out in wood upon the chimney piece of the great hall, the whole story down to the Robin Redbreasts;[3] till a foolish rich person pulled it down to set up a marble one of modern invention in its stead, with no story upon it. Here Alice put out one of her dear mother's looks, too tender to be called up-braiding.

Then I went on to say, how religious and how good their great-grandmother Field was, how beloved and respected by everybody, though she was not indeed the mistress of this great house, but had only the charge of it (and yet in some respects she might be said to be the mistress of it too) committed to her by the owner, who preferred living in a newer and more fashionable mansion which he had purchased somewhere in the adjoining county; but still she lived in it in a manner as if it had been her own, and kept up the dignity of the great house in a sort while she lived, which afterwards came to decay, and was nearly pulled down, and all its old ornaments stripped and carried away to the owner's other house, where they were set up, and looked as awkward as if someone were to carry away the old tombs they had seen lately at the Abbey, and stick them up in Lady C.'s tawdry gilt drawing room. Here John smiled, as much as to say, "that would be foolish indeed."

And then I told how, when she came to die, her funeral was attended by a concourse of all the poor, and some of the gentry too, of the neighborhood for many miles round, to show their respect for her memory, because she had been such a good and religious woman; so good indeed that she knew all the Psaltery[4] by heart, ay, and a great part of the Testament besides. Here little Alice spread her hands.

Then I told what a tall, upright, graceful person their great-grandmother Field once was; and how in her youth she was esteemed the best dancer—here Alice's little right foot played an involuntary movement, till, upon my looking grave, it desisted—the

---

**1. great-grandmother Field:** Mary Field, Lamb's grandmother.

**2. "The Children in the Wood":** A popular ballad of the time about the mysterious disappearance of two children.

**3. Robin Redbreasts:** At the end of the story, the robin buries the bodies of the children with leaves.

---

**4. Psaltery** (sôl' tə rē): The Psalms of David.

best dancer, I was saying, in the county, till a cruel disease, called a cancer, came, and bowed her down with pain; but it could never bend her good spirits, or make them stoop, but they were still upright, because she was so good and religious.

Then I told how she was used to sleep by herself in a lone chamber of the great lone house; and how she believed that an apparition of two infants was to be seen at midnight gliding up and down the great staircase near where she slept, but she said "those innocents would do her no harm"; and how frightened I used to be, though in those days I had my maid to sleep with me, because I was never half so good or religious as she—and yet I never saw the infants. Here John expanded all his eyebrows and tried to look courageous.

Then I told how good she was to all her grandchildren, having us to the great house in the holidays, where I in particular used to spend many hours by myself, in gazing upon the old busts of the Twelve Caesars that had been Emperors of Rome, till the old marble heads would seem to live again, or I to be turned into marble with them; how I never could be tired with roaming about that huge mansion, with its vast empty rooms, with their worn-out hangings, fluttering tapestry, and carved oaken panels, with the gilding almost rubbed out—sometimes in the spacious old-fashioned gardens, which I had almost to myself, unless when now and then a solitary gardening man would cross me—and how the nectarines and peaches hung upon the walls, without my ever offering to pluck them, because they were forbidden fruit, unless now and then—and because I had more pleasure in strolling about among the old melancholy-looking yew trees, or the firs, and picking up the red berries, and the fir apples,[5] which were good for nothing but to look at—or in lying about upon the fresh grass, with all the fine garden smells around me—or basking in the orangery, till I could almost fancy myself ripening too along with the oranges and the limes in that grateful warmth—or in watching the dace that darted to and fro in the fishpond, at the bottom of the garden, with here and there a great sulky pike hanging midway down the water in silent state, as if it mocked at their impertinent friskings—I had more pleasure in these busy-idle diversions than in all the sweet flavors of peaches, nectarines, oranges, and such like common baits of children. Here John slyly deposited back upon the plate a bunch of grapes, which, not unobserved by Alice, he had meditated dividing with her, and both seemed willing to relinquish them for the present as irrelevant.

Then in somewhat a more heightened tone, I told how, though their great-grandmother Field loved all her grandchildren, yet in an especial manner she might be said to love their uncle, John L—,[6] because he was so handsome and spirited a youth, and a king to the rest of us; and, instead of moping about in solitary corners, like some of us, he would mount the most mettlesome horse he could get, when but an imp no bigger than themselves, and make it carry him half over the county in a morning, and join the hunters when there were any out—and yet he loved the old great house and gardens too, but had too much spirit to be always pent up within their boundaries—and how their uncle grew up to man's estate as brave as he was handsome, to the admiration of everybody, but of their great-grandmother Field most especially; and how he used to carry me upon his back when I was a lame-footed boy—for he was a good bit older than me—many a mile when I could not walk for pain; and how in after life he became lame-footed too, and I did not always (I fear) make allowances enough for him when he was impatient, and in pain, nor remember sufficiently how considerate he had been to me when I was lame-footed;

---

**5. fir apples:** Fir cones.

**6. John L—:** John Lamb, Charles's brother.

and how when he died, though he had not been dead an hour, it seemed as if he had died a great while ago, such a distance there is betwixt life and death; and how I bore his death as I thought pretty well at first, but afterwards it haunted and haunted me; and though I did not cry or take it to heart as some do, and as I think he would have done if I had died, yet I missed him all day long, and knew not till then how much I had loved him. I missed his kindness, and I missed his crossness, and wished him to be alive again, to be quarreling with him (for we quarreled sometimes) rather than not have him again, and was as uneasy without him, as he their poor uncle must have been when the doctor took off his limb. Here the children fell a-crying, and asked if their little mourning which they had on was not for uncle John, and they looked up, and prayed me not to go on about their uncle, but to tell them some stories about their pretty dead mother.

Then I told how for seven long years, in hope sometimes, sometimes in despair, yet persisting ever, I courted the fair Alice W—n;[7] and, as much as children could understand, I explained to them what coyness, and difficulty, and denial meant in maidens—when suddenly, turning to Alice, the soul of the first Alice looked out at her eyes with such a reality of representment, that I became in doubt which of them stood there before me, or whose that bright hair was; and while I stood gazing, both the children gradually grew fainter to my view, receding, and still receding till nothing at last but two mournful features were seen in the uttermost distance, which, without speech, strangely impressed upon me the effects of speech: "We are not of Alice, nor of thee, nor are we children at all. The children of Alice called Bartrum father. We are nothing; less than nothing, and dreams. We are only what might have been, and must wait upon the tedious shores of Lethe[8] millions of ages before we have existence, and a name"—and immediately awaking, I found myself quietly seated in my bachelor armchair, where I had fallen asleep, with the faithful Bridget[9] unchanged by my side—but John L. (or James Elia) was gone forever.

---

**7. Alice W—n:** Alice Winterton, name given to Ann Simmons, whom Lamb loved in his earlier years.

**8. Lethe** (lē′ thē): In classical mythology, the river of forgetfulness, flowing through Hades, the land of the dead.
**9. Bridget:** Name given to Lamb's sister, Mary.

## THINKING ABOUT THE SELECTION

### Recalling

1. (a) According to the opening paragraph, who is listening to the narrator's story? (b) Why are these listeners interested in hearing about great-grandmother Field?
2. (a) Besides his grandmother, which relative does the narrator speak of with deep affection? (b) What has happened to this relative?
3. (a) Who was Alice W—n? (b) According to the final paragraph, who closely resembles her?
4. (a) What is revealed about the narrator's audience in the final paragraph? (b) What is revealed about Alice W—n?

### Interpreting

5. Why do you suppose the narrator's listeners are named John and Alice?
6. Identify three details in the essay that make the young John and Alice seem real.

7. In what ways does the apparition seen by great-grandmother Field foreshadow—that is, give the reader an advance glimpse of—the events at the end of the essay?
8. (a) What does this essay reveal about Charles Lamb's feelings toward his being unmarried and childless? (b) Why might such feelings be prompted by thoughts of his own childhood and especially of his brother John?

## Applying

9. Do you think it is always important to know details of an author's life to fully appreciate the author's work? Explain.

## ANALYZING LITERATURE
### Understanding the Familiar Essay

A **familiar,** or informal, **essay** is a loosely constructed piece of prose that deals with a single topic and uses conversational English. Although a familiar essay may contain some short story elements, such as plot and character, it is nevertheless considered to be nonfiction, since its chief purpose is to communicate its author's thoughts and feelings, and not those of imaginary characters.

1. Which characters in Lamb's essay are real? Which are imaginary?
2. Which elements in the essay make it seem like a short story? Give several examples.
3. In what ways is the author's style characteristic of a familiar essay?

## CRITICAL THINKING AND READING
### Inferring Tone

The **tone** of a story, poem, or essay is the attitude the writer takes with respect to the audience, a character, or a situation. In much the way a person's tone of voice will affect how his or her words are understood, so the tone of a literary selection helps shape the reader's reaction toward it. Determine the tone Lamb takes

with respect to each of the following, and describe its effect on you.
1. Great-grandmother Field.
2. Young Alice and John.
3. The great house.
4. Alice W—n.

## UNDERSTANDING LANGUAGE
### Using Multiple Meaning of Words

While good authors as a rule use words precisely, they occasionally use words with second and even third meanings to enrich a thought or sentiment. A writer might, for instance, describe a character's state of mind as "cloudy," with the intention of conveying both the meanings "confused" and "bleak or unhappy." In "Dream Children: A Reverie," Charles Lamb uses several words in this fashion. For each sentence, give two meanings for the italicized word, and describe its impact.
1. "Then I told what a tall, *upright,* graceful person their great-grandmother . . . was." (page 742)
2. ". . . upon my looking *grave,* it desisted . . ." (page 742)
3. ". . . two mournful features . . . without speech, *strangely* impressed upon me the effects of speech. . . ." (page 744)

## THINKING AND WRITING
### Analyzing a Writer's Attitudes

Lamb's attitude toward his personal fantasy world and his attitude toward reality, as expressed in the essay, appear to be different. Discuss this difference in terms of his blend of factual and fictional details. Ask: What, exactly, is Lamb escaping from? What is he escaping to? What is his view of himself in the fantasy role of father? What relationship does this view bear to his real role as brother? Organize your thoughts and write the first draft of a brief essay. When you revise make sure you have included adequate details to support your main idea.

# WILLIAM HAZLITT

## 1778–1830

Second only to Coleridge as a critic of the Romantic era, William Hazlitt was known in his day and is remembered in ours for his brisk and direct writing style. In addition Hazlitt was a true Romantic who lived life as he wrote about it—with gusto.

The son of a Unitarian minister who sympathized with the colonists during the American Revolution, Hazlitt sailed with his family to America when he was five and remained there for three years. He planned, like his father, to enter the clergy and was admitted to Hackney Theological Seminary in London. A difficulty in expressing himself both orally and on paper, however, forced him to abandon his goal and he returned to his family in Shropshire.

It was there in 1798 that Hazlitt met the poet Samuel Taylor Coleridge, who at the time was a house guest of Hazlitt's father. Recognizing Hazlitt's brilliance, Coleridge introduced the young man to his friends Wordsworth and Charles Lamb, who also found Hazlitt impressive.

Hazlitt, meanwhile, was still frustrated by his inability to communicate his ideas in writing, and at twenty-one he journeyed again to London, this time to study painting with his brother. Finding that his talents in this area were limited as well, he tried his hand once more at writing, and in 1805 published his first book, *An Essay on the Principles of Human Action.* In the six years that followed, he married, wrote two more books, and delivered a series of lectures on philosophy.

The year 1812 found Hazlitt penniless and his spirit broken. He took a paying job as a parliamentary reporter for a London newspaper and—much to his surprise and delight—he developed a following as a writer on a variety of subjects. In 1817 he published *Characters in Shakespeare's Plays,* which he followed up a year later with *A View of the English Stage,* a collection of drama criticism. At last, fame and respect had arrived!

Long an eccentric who judged everyone and everything according to his own rigid system of values, Hazlitt became more bitter and opinionated with age. He turned his talented pen to angry attacks on less liberal journalists than himself, as well as on poets and politicians, and in so doing made many enemies. Only the younger Romantic poets like Shelley and Keats admired Hazlitt's work of this period, and then only because of its intensity and dedication to the philosophy of Rousseau.

While to the modern mind Hazlitt's criticism tends to be overly subjective, scholars nevertheless respect him as one of the leading critics of Elizabethan and Romantic literature. Above all else Hazlitt is remembered for his ability to cut to the heart of an issue and to state his views firmly and honestly.

# GUIDE FOR INTERPRETING

**Literary Forms**

## Macbeth

**Critical Essay.** A critical essay is an essay that evaluates the merits of a given topic, usually artistic. While such an essay expresses the personal views and observations of its author, the essay will, if it is fair and honest, also appeal to some universal standard. Literary criticism, an area that gives rise to one of the best-known forms of critical essay, the literary essay, began with the Greek philosopher Plato and was later refined by Aristotle. From the fall of Rome through the Renaissance in the late fourteenth century, literary criticism was neglected in favor of church-related issues. With the Romantic movement came the first modern examples of the critical literary essay, as typified by the writings of Samuel Taylor Coleridge, Charles Lamb, and William Hazlitt.

**Commentary**

Drama criticism was a growing literary genre in the Romantic period because the theater had become an increasingly important feature of English life. By the 1820's, Romanticism dominated the plays presented throughout most of Europe. These plays were not characterized by one definite style, as in previous eras. Rather, they were generally strongly emotional, and their experimentation with form laid the groundwork for the later rejection of Neoclassicism.

The most important theaters in London were the Opera House, Drury Lane, and Covent Garden. Covent Garden, its wide rows packed with a stylish crowd, provided a strong contrast to the small, badly lit, makeshift theaters in which the finest plays of the Restoration period had been performed. Between acts in Restoration theaters, women walked around the theater selling apples and oranges, and it was possible to buy more filling food as well.

In the countryside, where any large building or barn had been considered appropriate for the staging of a play during the Restoration, a new group of theaters arose. Many were very well designed and built. Often, these rural theaters supported a permanent band of players.

What elements of Romanticism do you see in Hazlitt's criticism of *Macbeth*?

**Writing**

Imagine that you have been asked to review a play for your school newspaper. Make a list of the details of which you would need to take notice. Keep in mind that, in addition to such literary matters as character and theme, you would need to pay attention to how well the actors projected their voices, how effective the lighting was, and so on.

# Macbeth

### William Hazlitt

*"The poet's eye in a fine*
  *frenzy rolling*
*Doth glance from heaven to*
  *earth, from earth to heaven;*
*And as imagination bodies forth*
*The forms of things*
  *unknown, the poet's pen*
*Turns them to shape, and*
  *gives to airy nothing*
*A local habitation and a name."*[1]

*Macbeth* and *Lear*, *Othello* and *Hamlet*, are usually reckoned Shakespeare's four principal tragedies. *Lear* stands first for the profound intensity of the passion; *Macbeth* for the wildness of the imagination and the rapidity of the action; *Othello* for the progressive interest and powerful alternations of feeling; *Hamlet* for the refined development of thought and sentiment. If the force of genius shown in each of these works is astonishing, their variety is not less so. They are like different creations of the same mind, not one of which has the slightest reference to the rest. This distinctness and originality is indeed the necessary consequence of truth and nature. Shakespeare's genius alone appeared to possess the resources of nature. He is "your only *tragedy maker*." His plays have the force of things upon the mind. What he represents is brought home to the bosom as a part of our experience, implanted in the memory as if we had known the places, persons, and things of which he treats. *Macbeth* is like a record of a preternatural and tragical event. It has the rugged severity of an old chronicle with all that the imagination of the poet can engraft upon traditional belief. The castle of Macbeth, round which "the air smells wooingly," and where "the temple-haunting martlet builds," has a real subsistence in the mind; the Weird Sisters meet us in person on "the blasted heath"; the "air-drawn dagger" moves slowly before our eyes; the "gracious Duncan," the "blood-boltered Banquo" stand before us; all that passed through the mind of Macbeth passes, without the loss of a tittle,[2] through ours. All that could actually take place, and all that is only possible to be conceived, what was said and what was done, the workings of passion, the spells of magic, are brought before us with the same absolute truth and vividness.

Shakespeare excelled in the openings of his plays: that of *Macbeth* is the most striking of any. The wildness of the scenery, the sudden shifting of the situations and characters, the bustle, the expectations excited, are equally extraordinary. From the first entrance of the Witches and the description of them when they meet Macbeth:

> *What are these*
> *So wither'd and so wild*
>   *in their attire,*
> *That look not like the*
>   *inhabitants of th' earth*
> *And yet are on't?*

the mind is prepared for all that follows.

This tragedy is alike distinguished for the lofty imagination it displays, and for the

---

**1. "The poet's eye . . . name":** From Shakespeare's *A Midsummer Night's Dream*, Act V, Scene i.

**2. tittle** *n.*: A very small particle.

tumultuous vehemence of the action; and the one is made the moving principle of the other. The overwhelming pressure of preternatural agency urges on the tide of human passion with redoubled force. Macbeth himself appears driven along by the violence of his fate like a vessel drifting before a storm: he reels to and fro like a drunken man; he staggers under the weight of his own purposes and the suggestions of others; he stands at bay with his situation; and from the superstitious awe and breathless suspense into which the communications of the Weird Sisters throw him is hurried on with daring impatience to verify their predictions, and with impious and bloody hand to tear aside the veil which hides the uncertainty of the future. He is not equal to the struggle with fate and conscience. He now "bends up each corporal instrument to the terrible feat"; at other times his heart misgives him, and he is cowed and abashed by his success. "The deed, no less than the attempt, confounds him." His mind is assailed by the stings of remorse, and full of "preternatural solicitings." His speeches and soliloquies are dark riddles on human life, baffling solution, and entangling him in their labyrinths. In thought he is absent and perplexed, sudden and desperate in act, from a distrust of his own resolution. His energy springs from the anxiety and agitation of his mind. His blindly rushing forward on the objects of his ambition and revenge, or his recoiling from them, equally betrays the harassed state of his feelings. This part of his character is admirably set off by being brought in connection with that of Lady Macbeth, whose obdurate strength of will and masculine firmness give her the ascendancy over her husband's faltering virtue. She at once seizes on the opportunity that offers for the accomplishment of all their wished-for greatness, and never flinches from her object till all is over. The magnitude of her resolution almost covers the magnitude of her guilt. She is a great bad woman, whom we hate, but whom we fear more than we hate. She does not excite our loathing and abhorrence like Regan and Goneril.[3] She is only wicked to gain a great end and is perhaps more distinguished by her commanding presence of mind and inexorable self-will, which do not suffer her to be diverted from a bad purpose, when once formed, by weak and womanly regrets, than by the hardness of her heart or want of natural affections. The impression which her lofty determination of character makes on the mind of Macbeth is well described where he exclaims:

> *Bring forth men children only;*
> *For thy undaunted mettle should*
>   *compose*
> *Nothing but males!*

Nor do the pains she is at to "screw his courage to the sticking-place," the reproach to him, not to be "lost so poorly in himself," the assurance that "a little water clears them of this deed," show anything but her greater consistency in depravity. Her strong-nerved ambition furnishes ribs of steel to "the sides of his intent"; and she is herself wound up to the execution of her baneful project with the same unshrinking fortitude in crime, that in other circumstances she would probably have shown patience in suffering. The deliberate sacrifice of all other considerations to the gaining "for their future days and nights sole sovereign sway and masterdom," by the murder of Duncan, is gorgeously expressed in her invocation on hearing of "his fatal entrance under her battlements":

>   *Come all you spirits*
> *That tend on mortal*
>   *thoughts, unsex me here:*
> *And fill me, from the*
>   *crown to th' toe, top-full*
> *Of direst cruelty; make*
>   *thick my blood,*
> *Stop up the access and*
>   *passage to remorse,*

---

**3. Regan and Goneril:** King Lear's evil daughters in Shakespeare's *King Lear*.

*That no compunctious
    visitings of nature
Shake my fell purpose,
    nor keep peace between
The effect and it. Come to
    my woman's breasts,
And take my milk for gall,
    you murthering ministers,
Wherever in your
    sightless substances
You wait on nature's
    mischief. Come, thick
    night!
And pall thee in the
    dunnest smoke of hell,
That my keen knife see
    not the wound it makes,
Nor heav'n peep through
    the blanket of the dark,
To cry, hold, hold!*

When she first hears that "Duncan comes there to sleep" she is so overcome by the news, which is beyond her utmost expectations, that she answers the messenger, "Thou 'rt mad to say it"; and on receiving her husband's account of the predictions of the Witches, conscious of his instability of purpose, and that her presence is necessary to goad him on to the consummation of his promised greatness, she exclaims:

*Hie thee hither,
That I may pour my
    spirits in thine ear,
And chastise with the
    valor of my tongue
All that impedes thee
    from the golden round,
Which fate and
    metaphysical aid doth seem
To have thee crowned withal.*

This swelling exultation and keen spirit of triumph, this uncontrollable eagerness of anticipation, which seems to dilate her form and take possession of all her faculties, this solid, substantial flesh and blood display of passion, exhibit a striking contrast to the cold, abstracted, gratuitous, servile malignity of the Witches, who are equally instrumental in urging Macbeth to his fate for the mere love of mischief, and from a disinterested delight in deformity and cruelty. They are hags of mischief, obscene panders to iniquity, malicious from their impotence of enjoyment, enamored of destruction, because they are themselves unreal, abortive, half-existences, who become sublime from their exemption from all human sympathies and contempt for all human affairs, as Lady Macbeth does by the force of passion! Her fault seems to have been an excess of that strong principle of self-interest and family aggrandizement, not amenable to the common feelings of compassion and justice, which is so marked a feature in barbarous nations and times. A passing reflection of this kind, on the resemblance of the sleeping king to her father, alone prevents her from slaying Duncan with her own hand. . . .

*Macbeth* (generally speaking) is done upon a stronger and more systematic principle of contrast than any other of Shakespeare's plays. It moves upon the verge of an abyss, and is a constant struggle between life and death. The action is desperate and the reaction is dreadful. It is a huddling together of fierce extremes, a war of opposite natures which of them shall destroy the other. There is nothing but what has a violent end or violent beginnings. The lights and shades are laid on with a determined hand; the transitions from triumph to despair, from the height of terror to the repose of death, are sudden and startling; every passion brings in its fellow-contrary, and the thoughts pitch and jostle against each other as in the dark. The whole play is an unruly chaos of strange and forbidden things, where the ground rocks under our feet. Shakespeare's genius here took its full swing, and trod upon the farthest bounds of nature and passion.

## THINKING ABOUT THE SELECTION

### Recalling

1. According to Hazlitt, what does each of Shakespeare's "four principal tragedies" embody?
2. Which of these plays does Hazlitt say has the best dramatic opening? Why?
3. On pages 749–750, Hazlitt quotes a long passage spoken by Lady Macbeth that begins with the words, "Come all you spirits." What aspect of her character does he say this passage reveals?
4. In Hazlitt's opinion, what "systematic principle" sets *Macbeth* apart from Shakespeare's other plays?

### Interpreting

5. On page 748, Hazlitt states that Shakespeare is "your only *tragedy maker*." (a) What do you think he means by this? (b) What do you think is the significance of the quotation marks around this phrase?
6. What two qualities does Hazlitt claim advance the action in the play, and what effect do they have on the characters of Macbeth and Lady Macbeth?
7. Hazlitt concludes his essay with the observation that in *Macbeth* Shakespeare's genius "took its full swing, and trod upon the farthest bounds of nature and passion." What evidence does he offer in support of this view?

### Applying

8. How does Hazlitt's writing style compare with modern editorial style? Tell which you prefer and why.

## ANALYZING LITERATURE

### Understanding a Critical Essay

A **critical essay** is a prose piece that reviews or critiques a work of art or literature. In the present day, standards for objective criticism have been established by experts. In the eighteenth century, by contrast, these standards varied pretty much from critic to critic. The essays of William Hazlitt, in particular, are marked by a tendency toward subjective, highly personal observations, although these observations are often supported with examples and quotations from the work. Reread Hazlitt's essay on *Macbeth,* and locate the following:

1. Three opinions that are supported by examples or quotes from the play.
2. Three opinions that are not supported.
3. Three phrases that demonstrate Hazlitt's enthusiasm for Shakespeare's writing in general and for *Macbeth* in particular.

## CRITICAL THINKING AND READING

### Finding Main Ideas

The **main idea** in a paragraph is the key point the author wishes to get across to the reader. Each main idea is backed up by one or more **supporting details.** Read the following quotations from Hazlitt's essay on *Macbeth.* Each is a supporting detail. Find the paragraph from which it was taken, and state the main idea of that paragraph.

1. "The wildness of the scenery, the sudden shifting of the situations and characters . . . are equally extraordinary." (page 748)
2. "The action is desperate and the reaction is dreadful." (page 750)
3. "The whole play is an unruly chaos of strange and forbidden things, where the ground rocks under our feet." (page 750)

## THINKING AND WRITING

### Evaluating Literary Criticism

In a magazine or newspaper, find a review of a book you have read or a play you have seen. As you read the review, ask yourself the following questions: What facts does the critic present? Which statements are opinions? What details does the critic offer in support of his or her opinions? Does the critic convey any strong feeling for the work? How interesting is the review?

After you have organized your thoughts regarding these and other questions that might occur to you, write an essay evaluating the review. When you revise make sure you have included adequate supporting details.

# GREAT WORKS

## PRIDE AND PREJUDICE
## by Jane Austen

It is a truth universally acknowledged, that a single man in possession of a good fortune must be in want of a wife.

**Illustration from PRIDE AND PREJUDICE**
*Hugh Thomson*
*The Granger Collection*

*"She is tolerable," Darcy said of Elizabeth.*

So begins Jane Austen's *Pride and Prejudice,* a highly amusing examination of "the business of getting married" in early nineteenth-century England. Marriages are not based on the mutual pitter-patter of hearts in this society: It's money, social standing, and family connections that make the match. Marriage is like a shop where people drive a hard bargain to conserve or improve their status in life.

As the novel opens, Mrs. Bennet, the mother of five marriageable daughters, is eagerly questioning her husband as to the identity of the "the young man of large fortune" who has just rented a mansion not far from the Bennet home. Since the girls have no inheritance and society affords almost no opportunity for employment, Mrs. Bennet has set as her life's work the successful marriage of her daughters. Frantic that Mrs. Lucas, who also has daughters to marry, may beat her to the punch, she insists that her husband visit the young man at once. Mr. Bennet refuses to take her seriously. Referring to his daughter, he says:

"They have none of them much to recommend them," replied he; "they are silly and ignorant, like other girls: but Lizzy has something more of quickness than her sisters."

"Mr. Bennet, how can you abuse your own children in such a way! You take delight in vexing me. You have no compassion for my poor nerves."

"You mistake me, my dear. I have a high respect for your nerves. They are my old friends. I have heard you mention them with consideration these twenty years at least."

It is clear from his comments that Mr. Bennet favors Lizzy—and with good reason. Her quick wit, common sense, and high moral standards reveal an intelligent person superior to the nonsense that swirls around her. To Austen herself, Elizabeth was "as delightful a creature as ever appeared in print, and how I shall be able to tolerate those who do not like her at least, I do not know."

## The Plot Unfolds

Despite his protests, Mr. Bennet does call on Mr. Bingley, their new neighbor, who is pleasant and unpretentious despite his wealth. Bingley's friend Mr. Darcy, however, is as arrogant as Bingley is humble. Darcy's pride quickly becomes apparent when he refuses to dance with Elizabeth. "She is tolerable, but not handsome enough to tempt me," he huffs. Although offended, the slight appeals to her sense of humor, and Elizabeth takes great delight in relating the story to her friends. And so we have "pride" and "prejudice," as Darcy's pride—his sense of his own superior status—sparks Elizabeth's prejudice against him.

## Pride and Prejudice

In many ways, the novel is the story of Elizabeth's education, as the twenty-year-old young woman learns about pride and prejudice in the world. Through her honesty, courage, and flexibility, we see action at last guided by reason.

In Chapter 19, for example, Elizabeth is cornered by a young man too proud to understand that she has no intention of accepting his astonishingly unromantic pro-

*She wanted to compose her own feelings and to make herself agreeable to all.*

**Illustration from PRIDE AND PREJUDICE**
*Hugh Thomson*
The Granger Collection

The outcome? Her mother won't speak to her if she refuses; her father won't speak to her if she accepts! Elizabeth stands her ground, and the situation blows over . . . until Darcy's speech.

Soon, he is so taken with her that were it not for the "inferiority of her connections, he should be in some danger." She, however, feels no attraction to him at all. As the other characters begin to pair off in relationships, Elizabeth and Darcy are unable to judge each other accurately because of his pride and her prejudice.

Imagine, then, Elizabeth's shock when Darcy comes to visit her one day and says, "In vain have I struggled. It will not do. My feelings for you will not be repressed. You must allow me to tell you how ardently I admire and love you." What does she do?

After more than a century and a half, we return to *Pride and Prejudice* because it helps us retain our moral balance amid the temptation of pride, prejudice, and greed— and because it's highly entertaining!

## Jane Austen

Who was the woman who wrote with such sensibility of pride and prejudice? If nothing else, the life and work of Jane Austen explode the myth that it is impossible to produce a great novel without having first sampled a broad range of life experiences. Her social comedies are considered by critics today to be masterpieces of character portrayal and dialogue.

Born at Steventon in southwestern England to loving parents of modest means, Jane Austen (1775–1817) was the seventh of eight children. From an early age she enjoyed writing, and entertained her family with parodies, or humorous sendups, of the syrupy, sentimental fiction and drama that were fashionable at the time. When she was in her late teens, she began her first novel, *Sense and Sensibility,* which is the story of two sisters. Prior to its completion, however,

posal of marriage. Here, Mr. Collins outlines his plan to Elizabeth:

> "Almost as soon as I entered the house, I singled you out as the companion of my future life. But before I run away with my feelings on this subject, perhaps it would be advisable for me to state my reasons for marrying . . .

The idea of Mr. Collins, with all his solemn composure, being "run away with" by his feelings, made Elizabeth so near laughing that she could not use the short pause he allowed in any attempt to stop his going farther, and he continued:—

> "My reasons for marrying are, first, that I think it a right thing for every clergyman in easy circumstances (like myself) to set an example of matrimony in his parish; secondly, that I am convinced it will add very greatly to my happiness . . ."

she put it aside to concentrate on another novel, *First Impressions.* Written as a series of letters, the work that would eventually be reshaped into her highly acclaimed *Pride and Prejudice* rapidly became the family favorite. So certain, in fact, was her father of its merits that he offered the work to a book publisher, who rejected it. Not easily discouraged, Austen plunged into a third novel, *Northanger Abbey,* a mock horror tale, which she finished in 1797.

In 1801 the family relocated to Bath, near the sea, where Austen for the first time in her life experienced unhappiness. In letters she described herself as an "exile" from the rural surroundings that she loved so much. When her father died in 1806, the family, or what remained of it—by now all the male children had married—left Bath for a cottage on an estate outside London. On the death of his wife, Austen's brother Edward and his eleven children came to live on the estate, and once again Austen found herself surrounded by relatives in a bustling household. The writer's block that had plagued her during her period of sadness vanished, and she eagerly returned to work, revising her early novels and completing three new ones.

*Sense and Sensibility,* the first to be published, appeared in 1811. It was followed two years later by *Pride and Prejudice,* and a year after that by *Mansfield Park.* In 1816 Austen became ill but continued to write, completing two more novels, *Persuasion* and *Northanger Abbey,* before her death. Her brother Henry saw to the publication of both works, including a biographical sketch of his sister, who during her life had insisted on anonymity.

Because in her writing Austen places intellect above emotion, she is seen by some as more neoclassical than Romantic. What all critics seem to be in agreement on, however, is that Jane Austen ranks as one of the greatest English novelists and *Pride and Prejudice* as one of the greatest literary works of any period.

**Illustration from PRIDE AND PREJUDICE**
*Hugh Thomson*
*The Granger Collection*

*Before she could reply to the entreaties of several that she would sing again, she was eagerly succeeded at the instrument by her sister Mary.*

# THE CHANGING ENGLISH LANGUAGE

## The Romantic Age 1798–1832

### BRITANNIA RULES THE WAVES

During the Romantic Age, Britannia ruled the waves and English ruled much of the land. Great Britain's smashing conquests in the course of the Napoleonic Wars in the beginning of the century—culminating in Nelson's famous victory at Trafalgar in 1805—had left her in a position of undisputed naval supremacy. This, in turn, gave her control over most of the world's commerce. As English ships traveled throughout the world, they left the language of the mother country in their wake.

New inventions and improvements affected the spread of English within the mother country as well. The establishment of the first affordable newspaper in 1816 and the creation of inexpensive postage in 1840 served to more closely unite the different parts of England and spread the influence of standard speech. Improved means of travel and communication brought about by the railroad, the steamboat, and the telegraph also served to unify the country and blanket the language across the land.

### COLONIES ASSERT THEMSELVES

Not everyone accepted the dominance of British English quite so placidly, however. As England's larger colonies became increasingly independent, their citizens felt entitled to speak English in their fashion. Feisty Americans, for example, flushed with the acquisition of great tracts of land, asserted their right to speak American English, complete with such Native-American words as *caribou*, *hickory*, *moccasin*, *moose*, *opossum*, *raccoon*, *skunk*, *squaw*, *toboggan*, *tomahawk*, *totem*, and *wigwam*.

American English was also marked by borrowings from other peoples. From the Mexicans we took *chili*, *chocolate*, *tomato*; from Cuba and the West Indies came *barbecue*, *canoe*, and *hurricane*.

### NEW PLACES, NEW VOCABULARY

The most obvious results of English expansion can be seen in growth of the vocabulary. The acquisition of new lands meant new experiences, new products, and new occupations to name. From India, English acquired such varied and important words as *bandanna*, *bangle*, *Bengal*, *Brahman*, *bungalow*, *calico*, *cashmere*, *china*, *chintz*, *coolie*, *cot*, *curry*, *dinghy*, *juggernaut*, *jungle*, *jute*, *loot*, *mandarin*, *nirvana*, *pariah*, *polo*, *punch* (beverage), *rajah*, *rupee*, *thug*, *toddy*, *tom-tom*, and *verandah*. From even farther East, the language welcomed terms that have today become commonplace: *gingham*, *indigo*, and *mango*. One of the most interesting new words was *seersucker*, an Indian corruption of a Persian expression meaning "milk and sugar" that came to be linked to a thin, striped cotton fabric. Many words entered English from Africa as well, either directly or from contact with Dutch and Portuguese traders. These include *banana*, *Boer*, *boorish*, *chimpanzee*, *gorilla*, *gumbo*, *voodoo*, and *zebra*. Although Australia has not given us many words, two have become extremely common: *boomerang* and *kangaroo*.

### GRAMMAR REFORMS TAKE SHAPE

The language reforms begun in the Restoration and eighteenth century continued into the Romantic era. There was an especially strong movement to reorganize grammar, now that spelling improvements were well underway. Those seeking to mend grammar wanted to create rules, settle disputed points, and isolate errors to improve the language. As one writer commented in the preface to his grammar book:

> It is not the Language, but the Practice that is at fault. The Truth is, Grammar is very much neglected among us; and it is not the difficulty of the Language, but on the contrast the simplicity and the facility of it, that occasions this neglect. Were the Language less easy and simple, we should find ourselves under a necessity of studying it with more care and attention.

Many of the grammar rules we follow were first established during this period. The distinction between "lie" and "lay" was set out in the late eighteenth century; the preference for "different from" (rather than "different than") and the condemnation of "between you and I" and "it is me," in the early nineteenth. "Between" came to be used for groups of two; "among" came to be used for groups of three or more. It was decided that the comparative rather than the superlative should be used when only two things are involved ("the bigger," not "biggest," of two). Finally, we can note that the double negative was abolished in the late eighteenth century. One grammarian stated

the rule that now binds us: "Two Negatives in English destroy one another, or are equivalent to an Affirmative." Here, as elsewhere, grammar reformers were setting down what was apparently a frequent but not absolute tendency in the written language.

Although the rules many seem arbitrary and annoying, the results were noteworthy. English was no longer a language without rules. We now had guidelines to help us integrate the new words acquired through exploration and conquest.

*Like people in the colonies, Scottish and Irish writers asserted their national identity. Sir Walter Scott is credited with reviving interest in the Scots tongue.*

**SIR WALTER SCOTT**
*Sir Edwin Landseer*
National Portrait Gallery, London,

# YOU THE WRITER

**Assignment**

**1.** If there was one poetic form that permitted the Romantic poet to pour out his or her heart, it was the ode, a poem that pays tribute to an individual, quality, or place. Of course, the particular subject a poet chose for an ode was to an extent limited by circumstances of the times. Had Shelley and Keats lived in our present era of high technology, they might well have dedicated odes to the vastness of our universe.

**Prewriting.** Brainstorm to come up with an inspirational topic related to the current age, perhaps organ implants or high-speed electronic computers.

**Writing.** Write an original ode of at least three stanzas that expresses your awe for this modern wonder.

**Revising.** Review what you have written, making sure you have used vivid words. Check troublesome spellings.

**Assignment**

**2.** The Romantic movement grew out of an opposition to the tightly structured view of art and the reliance on scientific doctrine that typified writers of the previous age. The Romantic poet was concerned with emotions and concentrated on natural topics. Imagine you are the editor of a literary magazine and you have just received a poem by an unknown poet named Wordsworth or Coleridge (or any Romantic you have read).

**Prewriting.** List the tasks you think a magazine editor might be responsible for. Make notes for a response letter to this new poet.

**Writing.** Write a one-page letter explaining your feelings. State why you like or dislike this new submission.

**Revising.** Reread your letter for coherence and punctuation. Make sure you have maintained a single tone throughout.

**Assignment**

**3.** Essays, whether formal or personal, present the views of their authors in a well-organized and readable manner, sometimes using casual language to enhance a point. Imagine you are living during the Romantic Age. You are invited to write a guest column of approximately 500 words for a local newspaper.

**Prewriting.** Get your mind spinning to come up with a topic that is both timely and of general interest to the inhabitants of your city or community. Jot down notes to test your knowledge.

**Writing.** Do at least two drafts of your essay—one to develop the general structure and a second to iron out rough spots.

**Revising.** Check your essay for continuity. Be sure that any casual language you have used is general enough to be understood by your audience.

# YOU THE CRITIC

**Assignment**

**1.** In the preface to the second edition of his *Lyrical Ballads,* William Wordsworth stated that his goal was "to choose incidents . . . from common life" and make them "interesting by tracing in them . . . the primary laws of our nature." It might be argued that this statement fairly summarized the goal of all Romantics. Write an essay demonstrating that the work of a Romantic poet of your choosing fits the above description.

**Prewriting.** Before you begin to write, make sure you understand all parts of the Wordsworth statement. Decide in particular what you believe the phrase "primary laws of our nature" means.

**Writing.** Write the first draft of your essay. Quote specific poems that illustrate your claim.

**Revising.** Check to see that main subpoints of your essay support the thesis statement. Correct any run-on sentences or fragments.

**Assignment**

**2.** A writer's style is like a personal stamp that uniquely identifies his or her work. Style is determined by such features as word choice and sentence length. Evaluate the prose styles of two of the Romantic writers you have read and, in a comparative essay, tell which of the works you find more enjoyable.

**Prewriting.** Plan your essay by comparing and contrasting the features mentioned above, along with such considerations as fit of style to subject matter. Organize your presentation of similarities and differences.

**Writing.** Quote freely from the two writers' works. Devote one paragraph to a clear statement of preference, including reasons for your feelings.

**Revising.** Reread your essay for internal consistency. Be sure you have anticipated and addressed any opposing views.

**Assignment**

**3.** Most of the major literary figures of the Romantic movement were supporters of the rebel cause in the French Revolution. Coleridge, for instance, while still in school, composed an ode celebrating the storming of the Bastille, the prison where "enemies" of the French state had been sent. In an expository paper, discuss what aspects of the Romantic temperament would logically lead to such a political stance.

**Prewriting.** Divide a sheet of paper into two columns. In one, list traits of the liberal mind; in the other, list aspects of the Romantic world view. Draw lines connecting corresponding traits.

**Writing.** Write your first draft. In the first paragraph include a definitive statement of your purpose in writing.

**Revising.** Make sure you have adequately supported your main idea. Proofread your paper for possible errors and omissions.

**QUEEN VICTORIA'S VISIT TO CHERBOURG**
*Jules Achille Noel*
Royal Academy, London

# THE VICTORIAN AGE

## (1833–1901)

The year's at the spring
And the day's at the morn;
Morning's at seven;
The hillside's dew-pearled;
The lark's on the wing;
The snail's on the thorn;
God's in his heaven—
All's right with the world!
　　From "Pippa Passes"
　　**Robert Browning**

Queen Victoria reigned for sixty-four years, from 1837 to 1901 —the longest reign of any British monarch. With occasional exceptions, those were years of prosperity for Britain. Robert Browning's lines on the preceding page echo the ringing optimism and self-assurance that marked the Victorian Age. The Victorians recognized that, in fact, all was not really "right with the world," and they worked hard to make improvements. Yet they firmly believed that theirs was the best nation in the best era history had yet produced.

## LIVING IN THE VICTORIAN AGE

Britain's booming economy and rapid expansion encouraged great optimism. Profiting from its early industrial revolution, Britain became the world leader in manufacturing. Factories dotted the land. Factory towns grew into large cities. Banks, retail shops, and other businesses expanded. These changes in turn spurred the growth of two important classes—an industrial working class and a modern middle class, able to live a better life because of the low cost and large variety of mass-produced factory goods.

As its industry and commerce prospered, Britain expanded its merchant fleet and its powerful navy. Economic and military power helped Britain to acquire new colonies in far-flung parts of the globe. Victorians could quite literally boast that "the sun never sets on the British empire."

Yet, for all its self-satisfaction, the Victorian Age was also a time of social concern. Victorian writers exposed a dark underside of the industrial age—brutal factory conditions and stinking slums that bred poverty and disease. Goaded by reformers and radicals of many sorts, Victorian leaders took steps to expand democracy and better the lot of the poor. By the time Victoria died in 1901, Britain had shed some of its complacency and was grappling with the social and economic problems industrialization had caused.

**LONDON'S CRYSTAL PALACE**
*The British Museum*

# Victoria and Albert

Victoria became queen at the age of eighteen. She impressed the members of Parliament with her grace and self-assurance, but she could also be very stubborn. In 1840 she insisted on marrying a first cousin, a minor German princeling named Albert of Saxe-Coburg-Gotha. Many Britons disliked the marriage: What if Prince Albert filled the queen's head with "European" notions of absolute rule? As it turned out, Albert understood the limited powers of British royalty. His wisdom and impartial advice did much to soften the personality of the queen. (It was she who reigned; Albert was not king but *prince consort*—the monarch's husband.)

Victoria and Albert produced a large family and restored to the monarchy a sense of decorum, sadly lacking since the madness of George III and the scandalous behavior of his sons. The twentieth century would tend to look back on Victoria as prim to the point of prudishness. However, we must remember that her restrained behavior came in reaction to those earlier royal excesses.

When Albert died of typhoid fever in 1861, Victoria went into deep mourning. For a time she was almost a recluse, leaving day-to-day government in the hands of her prime ministers. Victoria's limited involvement in political affairs helped to turn Britain into the modern constitutional monarchy it is today, in which the duties of the sovereign are largely ceremonial.

# Victorian Politics

The prime ministers who govern Britain serve at the sufferance of Parliament, and can be dismissed at any time by a vote of no confidence. Such a system produces a more rapid turnover of leadership than does our own presidential system.

The years of Victoria's reign brought a change in the policies and even the names of the two parties that had dominated eighteenth-century politics. The Whig party formerly had championed Britain's commercial dominance and colonial empire. Gradually, the Whigs adopted new attitudes and became known as the Liberal party. Liberals often attacked colonial expansion and, under the leadership of William Gladstone, pressed for reforms at home and in Ireland. Meanwhile, the Tory party began to abandon its old stance of isolationism in foreign affairs and stubborn resistance to social change. The Tories (or Conservatives, as they came to be called) now supported imperialism—the expansion of empire. Under leaders like Benjamin Disraeli, the Conservatives also supported electoral reform. It was Disraeli who helped push through the Second Reform Bill of 1867, doubling the electorate by granting voting rights to tenant farmers and to better-paid male workers.

The Liberals and Conservatives alternated in power. Each party had its die-hard followers, but each had to compete for the same middle-of-the-road "swing" voters. As a result, Victorian politics emphasized compromise and slow reform.

1833    Slavery abolished in British empire.

1837    Victoria becomes queen.

          **Charles Dickens** writes *The Pickwick Papers* and *Oliver Twist*.

          Thomas Carlyle writes *The French Revolution*.

1840    Michael Faraday experiments with electric currents.

1843    **William Wordsworth** becomes poet laureate.

1844    George Williams founds YMCA.

1845    Irish Potato Famine begins.

1847    Factory Act passed.

          **Charlotte Brontë** publishes *Jane Eyre*.

          **Emily Brontë** publishes *Wuthering Heights*.

1848    First Public Health Act.

          Women begin attending University of London.

1850    Public Libraries Act.

          **Elizabeth Barrett Browning** publishes *Sonnets from the Portuguese*.

1854    Britain enters Crimean War.

          Parliament abolishes religious restrictions for university attendance.

1856    Henry Bessemer introduces steelmaking process.

1859    Charles Darwin publishes *On the Origin of Species*.

1860    Florence Nightingale founds school for nurses.

          Food and Drugs Act passed.

Queen Victoria

Charles Darwin

Charlotte Brontë

Battle from

Charles Dickens

Karl Marx

the Crimean War

Samuel Morse

Sepoy Mutiny

Richard Wagner

| | |
|---|---|
| 1836 | United States: Ralph Waldo Emerson publishes *Nature*. |
| 1841 | South Pacific: New Zealand becomes a British colony. |
| | United States: Edgar Allan Poe publishes "The Murders in the Rue Morgue." |
| 1842 | Asia: Hong Kong becomes a British colony. |
| | France: Honoré de Balzac publishes *The Human Comedy*. |
| 1844 | America: Samuel F. B. Morse patents telegraph. |
| 1846 | America: Elias Howe patents sewing machine. |
| | France: Pierre Joseph Proudhon publishes *The Philosophy of Poverty*. |
| 1848 | France: Revolution establishes new republic under Louis Napoleon. |
| | Belgium: Marx and Engels publish *Communist Manifesto*. |
| 1850 | France: Life insurance introduced. |
| | Germany: Wagner's opera *Lohengrin* first performed. |
| 1851 | Australia: Gold discovered in New South Wales. |
| 1853 | Eastern Europe: Beginning of Crimean War. |
| 1854 | Japan: Trade with West reopened. |
| | United States: Henry David Thoreau publishes *Walden*. |
| 1856 | France: Gustave Flaubert publishes *Madame Bovary*. |
| 1857 | India: Sepoy Mutiny against British. |
| 1858 | India: Political power of East India Company abolished. |

# BRITISH EVENTS

**Illustration from** *Treasure Island*

1863  Construction of London Underground begins.

1864  **Robert Browning** publishes *The Ring and the Book*.

1865  Joseph Lister initiates antiseptic surgery.

London Fire Department established.

Lewis Carroll publishes *Alice's Adventures in Wonderland*.

1867  **Matthew Arnold** publishes "Dover Beach."

1869  Debtors' prisons abolished.

1878  Salvation Army established.

1879  **George Meredith** publishes *The Egoist*.

1880  Joseph Swan installs first electric lighting.

1883  **Robert Louis Stevenson** publishes *Treasure Island*.

1884  First edition of *Oxford English Dictionary* published.

1886  English Lawn Tennis Association founded at Wimbledon.

1887  First Sherlock Holmes tale published.

1888  Jack the Ripper stalks London's East End.

1891  **Thomas Hardy** publishes *Tess of the d'Urbervilles*.

1892  **Rudyard Kipling** publishes *Barrack-room Ballads*.

1895  Oscar Wilde publishes *The Importance of Being Earnest*.

1896  **A. E. Housman** publishes *A Shropshire Lad*.

1901  Queen Victoria dies.

Robert Browning

*Alice's Adventures*

Suez Canal

Alexander Graham Bell

Civil War Begins

in Wonderland

Anton Chekhov

Boxer Rebellion

# WORLD EVENTS

**1861**   United States: Civil War begins.

**1865**   Russia: Leo Tolstoy publishes *War and Peace*.

Austria: Gregor Mendel proposes laws of heredity.

**1866**   Europe: Seven Weeks' War leads to unification of modern Germany.

**1869**   Egypt: Suez Canal completed.

**1873**   France: Jules Verne publishes *Around the World in Eighty Days*.

**1876**   United States: Alexander Graham Bell patents telephone.

**1877**   United States: Thomas Edison patents phonograph.

**1878**   Afghanistan: British troops fight Second Afghan War.

**1879**   South Africa: Zulu War against British.

**1880**   Russia: Feodor Dostoevsky publishes *The Brothers Karamazov*.

**1882**   Egypt: Britain invades and conquers nation.

**1884**   United States: Mark Twain publishes *The Adventures of Huckleberry Finn*.

**1885**   Belgium: van Gogh paints *The Potato Eaters*.

**1894**   Asia: Sino-Japanese War begins.

**1896**   Greece: First modern Olympics held.

**1898**   China: Boxer Rebellion against foreign influence.

France: Marie and Pierre Curie discover radium.

**1899**   Russia: Anton Chekhov publishes *Uncle Vanya*.

**WARRINGTON HIGH STREET**
*T. Hesketh*
*Warrington Museum and Art Gallery*

## Domestic Problems and Reforms

Two key issues—trade policy and electoral reform—dominated domestic politics during the first half of the Victorian era. Trade debate centered on the Corn Laws, which had long slapped high tariffs on "corn" (grain). This discouraged food imports and helped British landlords and farmers. However, it also tended to keep food prices high, which angered consumers and the poorer classes. At stake was not just money but life itself, as became evident in 1845, when a failure of Ireland's potato crop caused a massive famine in which as many as one million Irish people died.

Seeking to increase the supply of food, Parliament repealed the Corn Laws in 1846. Over the following decade, Parliament changed other trade laws, putting an end to the policy of protectionism (restriction of imports to protect domestic producers). Instead, Britain now adopted a policy of free trade (allowing imports and exports with few or no restrictions). The new policy reflected the interests of rising British industries, which prospered by importing raw materials and exporting finished goods. Times had changed, and Britain was fast becoming an industrial rather than an agricultural nation.

Many Britons thought that the second issue—electoral reform—had been settled in 1832, when the Reform Law gave the vote to middle-class males. They were wrong; working-class people wanted further reform. In 1837, a group of radicals drew up a "People's Charter" demanding, among other things, universal suffrage for males. This so-called Chartist movement fizzled out after a decade or so, but new demands for electoral change led to the Second Reform Bill of 1867 and to almost complete male suffrage in 1885.

The urge for reform also affected many other areas. Women, although still not eligible to vote, began to attend universities. Parliament passed laws to reduce the working day for women and children, to establish a system of free grammar schools, and to legalize trade unions. It voted to improve public sanitation and to regulate factories and housing. Still, such measures did not go far enough to suit everyone, and agitation continued for further reform.

One of the most important issues left unresolved in the Victorian Age was the future of Ireland, where widespread poverty had bred bitter opposition to British control. In the 1880's and 1890's the Liberal leader William Gladstone supported Irish demands for home rule (self-government). However, a hard-line faction of Liberals joined Conservatives to block action on Gladstone's proposals.

## EMPIRE AND FOREIGN POLICY

Britain was not alone in its drive to form a world empire in the Victorian Age. Other European powers were grabbing colonies too. British diplomats tried to protect and expand the British empire while promoting a balance of power within Europe.

## The Imperialist Urge

Victorian Britons who supported a policy of imperialism could cite a long list of arguments: Colonies would provide raw materials and markets for British industry. They would offer a home for British settlers. Britain had no choice; if it didn't seize a territory, one of its European rivals would do so. Perhaps the clinching argument was the writer Rudyard Kipling's notion of "the white man's burden." Victorians tended to believe that Western civilization—commonly perceived as white, Christian, and progressive—was superior to all other cultures. This attitude led many Victorians to look condescendingly on non-Westerners as people in need of assistance. What could be more noble than to help those "natives" by offering them the protection of the British empire? While such an argument seems faintly ridiculous by today's lights, many Victorians sincerely believed it.

Britain's empire had two sorts of land—"settled" territories, where whites made up a large part of the population, and outright colonies, in which few whites lived. During the Victorian Age Britain granted considerable self-government to "settled" territories such as Canada, Australia, and New Zealand. On the other hand, it exercised strict rule over places such as Hong Kong (acquired from China in 1841). After a rebellion in 1856 by sepoys (Indian troops under British command), Britain shouldered aside the British East India Company and took direct control of India. Victoria would thus add "Empress of India" to her formal titles.

## The Crimean War

The Victorian years were generally peaceful. Britain fought only one major European war—the Crimean War (1854–56), so called because it took place on the Crimean peninsula in southern Russia. Britain, France, and Turkey teamed up to thwart Russian expansion, but the battles were largely inconclusive. Today we remember the war mainly for the brave but disastrous charge of Britain's Light Brigade. This was commemorated in a famous poem by Alfred, Lord Tennyson, including these lines:

> Theirs not to make reply,
> Theirs not to reason why,
> Theirs but to do and die.

## Britain as a World Power

In the last three decades of Victoria's rule, Britain reached new heights of wealth and power. It gained control of the new Suez Canal in Egypt. It acquired Cyprus, an island in the eastern Mediterranean. It joined other European powers in a scramble to carve up Africa, acquiring such territories as Kenya, Uganda, Nigeria, and Rhodesia (Zimbabwe). Also, Britain expanded its control over what is now South Africa, defeating Dutch settlers there in the Boer War of 1899–1902.

**THE TRIUMPHS OF THE BRITISH ARMY AND NAVY, 1897 COMMEMORATING THE DIAMOND JUBILEE OF QUEEN VICTORIA**
*English Lithograph, 1897*
The Granger Collection

Even in those years of expansion, however, Britons could not help worrying about the future. Other nations, especially the United States and Germany, were rapidly building up industry and competing with Britain in world markets. How long could Britain maintain its economic superiority? How would economic changes affect the balance of power? For how long would Britain's navy "rule the waves"? By the end of Victoria's reign in 1901, British leaders had many disturbing questions to ponder.

## VICTORIAN THOUGHT

Victorian thinkers often disagreed on the crucial issues of their times, but they shared a deep confidence in humanity's ability to better itself. "Man is not the creature of circumstances," said Benjamin Disraeli. "Circumstances are the creatures of man." This spirit of optimism prevailed up to the closing years of the Victorian era.

### Responses to Industrialization

The changes brought about by the industrial revolution stirred conflicting feelings among Victorian thinkers. On the one hand, they admired the material benefits industrialization had brought. On the other, they deplored the brutality of factory life and of industrial slums.

We can divide into three groups the political and economic theories Victorians employed for dealing with the changed conditions of the industrial age:

---

**Theories**

- **Laissez-faire theory.** This theory holds that government should avoid meddling in the affairs of business—should "let it be" (the meaning of the French term). When allowed full freedom, the theory goes, industry will use the most efficient techniques and reach the highest possible level of prosperity.
- **Reformist liberalism.** Those who held this theory believed that rapid change brings problems that *laissez-faire* policies cannot solve. They argued that government intervention and regulation were sometimes necessary to protect the rights of the weak against the strong.
- **Socialism.** Some thinkers and activists favored a more far-reaching policy, ending private ownership of major industries and substituting public ownership. Supporters of socialism also called for sweeping government measures to promote equality and help the poor.

---

## Religion and Science

At the same time they were debating the political problems posed by industrialization, the Victorians were grappling with the religious and philosophical implications of modern life. A religious movement called evangelicalism influenced many Victorians. The movement linked strict personal morality with a strong commitment to social reform, leading to the founding of such institutions as the Young Men's Christian Association (YMCA) and the Salvation Army. The Liberal leader William Gladstone was among those inspired by evangelicalism to devote his life to public service and social reform. The Oxford Movement expressed a second strain of religious thought, seeking a return to more traditional church ritual.

Other Victorians turned to science for answers. The theory of evolution proposed by Charles Darwin (1809–82) in *On the Origin of Species* (1859) stirred bitter controversy. Some Victorian thinkers saw Darwin's theory as a direct challenge to Biblical truth and traditional religious faith. Some accepted both Darwin's theory and religion, striving to reconcile scientific and religious insights.

Darwin believed that a process called natural selection guides evolution. By this process, some organisms survive (because they can adapt to changing conditions) and some die out (because they cannot adapt). A social scientist named Herbert Spencer (1820 –1903) applied Darwin's idea—which Spencer called "the survival of the fittest"—to social life. In Spencer's harsh philosophy, called Social Darwinism, the "fittest" humans achieve social and economic success while the "unfit" fail. Neither government nor private charities should attempt to interfere with this "natural" process, said the Social Darwinists—applying *laissez-faire* theory to social as well as economic life.

# VICTORIAN LITERATURE

The ideas of the Victorian Age—political and moral, scientific and religious—helped to shape the works you will read in this unit. Indeed, they helped to define the Victorians themselves. Education was spreading in the Victorian Age, and as literacy increased, so did the impact of the written word. Probably at no other time before or since did books enjoy such enormous popularity and influence.

## Romanticism, Realism, and Naturalism

The Romantic movement continued to influence writers of the Victorian Age, but new styles of writing came into vogue. Romanticism had begun as a radical departure from literary practice; now it was part of mainstream culture, safe but slightly stale. A new generation of writers, coming of age in a time of rapid technological change, began to examine the social effects of that change. The heroes of the new generation's literature would be ordinary people

**DUDLEY STREET, SEVEN DIALS, LONDON, 1872**
*Gustave Doré*
*The Granger Collection*

facing the day-to-day problems of life. Life would be presented as it is, rather than as it might be. We call this new literary movement realism, because it sought to portray human life realistically, as it is actually lived, without sugar coating.

Romantic thinking had lent itself to poetic language, and we study the Romantic Age chiefly for its poetry. Realism, on the other hand, focused on more down-to-earth or prosaic events especially suited to prose. The shift in style helped to make the Victorian Age the great age of the British novel.

By focusing on ordinary people, realist literature reflected the nineteenth-century trend to democracy and appealed to a growing middle-class audience. Realist writing often dealt with family relationships, religion and morality, social change, and social reform —topics of special interest to middle-class readers.

New ideas in science also made their mark on Victorian literature. A movement known as naturalism—an outgrowth of realism—sought to apply the techniques of scientific observation to writing about life in the industrial age. Naturalists crammed their novels with details—the sour smells of poverty, the harsh sounds of factory life—often with the aim of promoting social reform. Naturalist writers directly contradicted the romantic view of nature as kindly and benevolent. To naturalists, the idea that nature mirrored human feelings was false—a "pathetic fallacy." Instead, naturalist writers portrayed nature as harsh and indifferent to the human suffering it often caused.

It would be a mistake to assume that Victorian writers abandoned romanticism altogether. Some writers blended romanticism with realism or naturalism; others sought to revive romanticism as the radical force it once had been. Two Victorian literary movements deserve special mention here. One is a group of painters and poets known as the Pre-Raphaelite Brotherhood. Formed about 1850, this short-lived group sought to ignore the ugliness of industrial life by portraying nature with the fidelity found in medieval Italian art before the Renaissance painter Raphael (1483–1520). The leading Pre-Raphaelite was Dante Gabriel Rossetti (1828–82), who excelled both as a painter and as a poet. The second group, known as the aesthetic movement, appeared toward the end of the Victorian Age. Aesthetes like the writer Oscar Wilde (1854–1900) turned away from the everyday world and sought to create "art for art's sake"—works whose sole reason for being was their perfection or beauty.

## Victorian Poetry

The Victorian Age produced a large and diverse body of poetry. The Romantic style predominated at first, but realism and naturalism gained force as time went on.

The most popular poet of the era, however, was a romantic —Alfred, Lord Tennyson (1809–92). Influenced by earlier romantic poets, especially Walter Scott, Tennyson wrote many long narrative poems on ancient and medieval themes like the King Arthur legend. His verse displays a keen sense of the music of language, and some of his more sentimental lyrics reappeared in popular songs. Yet Tennyson also revealed a deeper, more thoughtful side in such powerful poems as "Ulysses" (1842) and *In Memoriam* (1850). Tennyson became poet laureate after Wordsworth died in 1850.

Robert Browning (1812–89) produced a body of poetry as diverse as Tennyson's, although in his lifetime he never achieved equal public acclaim. Many of Browning's poems display Romantic attitudes. Others, however, show the influence of realism in seeking to portray individuals with un-Romantic authenticity. Critics have especially admired Browning's use of the dramatic monologue—a long speech by an imaginary character—to expose pretense and

**BEATA BEATRIX, c. 1863**
*Dante Gabriel Rossetti*
The Granger Collection

**ALFRED, LORD TENNYSON, CARICATURE, 1871**
*Carlo Pellegrini*
The Granger Collection

reveal a character's inner self. In 1846, Browning plunged into one of literature's most famous romances when he eloped with the poet Elizabeth Barrett, whose father had forbidden the marriage. At the time, Elizabeth was a more famous poet than Robert. History has since reversed that verdict, but Elizabeth Barrett Browning (1806 –61) is still remembered for the beautiful love poems she wrote her husband.

A number of other Victorian poets also worked in the Romantic vein. You have already read of the Pre-Raphaelites, who include Dante Gabriel Rossetti; his sister, Christina Rossetti (1830–94); and George Meredith (1828–1909). Another poet with a Romantic style was Emily Brontë (1818–48), who often described characters and settings from the imaginative world of her own childhood.

Matthew Arnold (1822–88) was probably the first Victorian poet to focus on "the bewildering confusion" of the industrial age. Many of Arnold's poems deal with alienation: separation from nature, isolation from other human beings. In his most famous poem, "Dover Beach" (1867), he breaks with poetic tradition and employs free verse—poetry with no fixed rhythm—to portray the confusion and loss of faith of his times. Arnold was a forerunner of the more pessimistic naturalist writers.

Late Victorian naturalism found its strongest voice in Thomas Hardy (1840–1928), whose poetry, like his prose, focuses on workers and farmers overwhelmed by the forces of nature and society. Life's disappointments were also a frequent subject of A. E. Housman (1859–1936), whose quiet lyrics speak of personal loss and rural change.

Rudyard Kipling (1865–1936), who wrote fiction and children's stories as well as poetry, gained great popularity in the 1890's. Kipling created action-packed narrative poems such as "Gunga Din" (1892) and many short lyric poems that became popular songs. He employs the dialect of working-class soldiers in realist poems such as "Tommy" (1892):

> For it's Tommy this, an' Tommy that, an' "Chuck 'im out, the brute!"
> But it's "Savior of 'is Country" when the guns begin to shoot.

One final Victorian poet, Gerard Manley Hopkins (1844–89), remained unpublished during his own century but would later inspire twentieth-century poets. Hopkins, a Catholic priest, wrote deeply religious verse influenced by the earlier Romantic poets and the philosopher Duns Scotus. He was also an innovative craftsman, introducing a rhythmic pattern called sprung rhythm that abandoned traditional metric feet.

## Victorian Drama

Compared to poetry, drama in the Victorian Age seemed pale and uninspired. Playhouses were few in number and hemmed in by government restrictions. Only toward the end of the century did the theater begin to show some sparkle, with serious dramas like Sir Arthur Wing Pinero's *The Second Mrs. Tanqueray* (1893) and satirical ones like Oscar Wilde's *The Importance of Being Earnest* (1895).

## Victorian Fiction

If one form of literature can be seen as quintessentially Victorian, it is the novel. Members of the new middle class were avid readers, and they loved novels—especially novels that reflected the main social issues of the day. Responding to the demand, weekly and monthly magazines published novels chapter by chapter, in serial form. Curious readers had to keep buying the magazine to learn what happened next. Most of the best novelists of the day wrote, at one time or another, for the magazines.

Romanticism heavily influenced early Victorian novels, especially those written by three sisters—Emily Brontë (1818–48), Charlotte Brontë (1816–55), and the lesser-known Anne Brontë (1820–49). Emily's classic *Wuthering Heights* (1847) tells the poetic tale of the doomed passions of Catherine Earnshaw and of Heathcliff, one of English fiction's outstanding Byronic heroes. Charlotte's famous *Jane Eyre* (1847) recounts the adventures of a governess who falls in love with her mysterious employer, Mr. Rochester. Nevertheless, both works also contain elements of the new realism—as in *Jane Eyre*'s vivid portrait of the heroine's harsh childhood.

The realistic elements of *Jane Eyre* probably owe much to the influence of Charles Dickens (1812–70), who surpassed all other Victorian novelists in popularity. Dickens never forgot his impoverished childhood, filling his novels with poignant details that dramatized the problems of a grimy industrial England. Although Dickens treated social problems realistically and became an outspoken voice for social reform, he tempered his criticism with humor. Many of his characters are comic caricatures in which a particular human foible or vice is exaggerated. Dickens also showed a sentimental

**BAYSWATER OMNIBUS**
*G. W. Joy*
*Museum of London*

**HYDE PARK NEAR GROSVENOR GATE, 1842**
*Thomas Shotter Boys*
Guildhall Art Gallery

side, providing happy endings for many of his plucky heroes and heroines.

Other Victorian realists were less sentimental in their portraits of people and society. George Meredith, already mentioned as a romantic poet, produced careful psychological studies of characters and their motives in novels such as *The Egoist* (1879). Mary Ann Evans, writing under the pen name George Eliot (1819–80), examined moral issues and personal relationships in novels such as *Adam Bede* (1859). Also choosing realistic themes were William Makepeace Thackeray (1811–63), Anthony Trollope (1815–82), Elizabeth Gaskell (1810–65), and Samuel Butler (1835–1902).

As the century drew to a close, British novelists leaned more and more to naturalism. Thomas Hardy was the most highly regarded of late Victorian naturalists. Hardy set his fiction in western England, which he called by its old Saxon name, Wessex. His pessimistic novels often portray rural characters who have been disappointed in life and love.

Such downbeat themes did not attract the enthusiastic reception for naturalist novels that earlier realist novels had won. Late Victorian readers tended to prefer the action-packed adventure stories of writers like Robert Louis Stevenson (1850–94) and Rudyard Kipling or the Sherlock Holmes mysteries of Sir Arthur Conan Doyle (1859–1930).

## Nonfiction Prose

Novels, of course, were only one of the many types of prose available to Victorian readers. British writers poured out a steady stream of histories, biographies, essays, and criticism.

Greatest of the historians were Thomas Carlyle (1795–1881) and Thomas Babington Macaulay (1800–59). Carlyle also wrote historical biographies. Perhaps the outstanding literary biography of the era was Elizabeth Gaskell's *Life of Charlotte Brontë* (1857), still a primary source of information on the Brontë family.

All the great Victorian thinkers produced influential prose works. Matthew Arnold, for example, made a sharp attack on the British class system in *Culture and Anarchy* (1869), his most famous work of social criticism. Other influential works included *Modern Painters* (1843) by John Ruskin (1819–1900), *On Liberty* (1859) by John Stuart Mill (1806–73), *The Idea of a University Defined* (1873) by John Henry Newman (1801–90), and *Studies in the History of the Renaissance* (1873) by Walter Pater (1839–94).

All in all, the Victorian Age produced a diverse body of literature—entertaining, scholarly, humorous, profound. Because the era is so close to our own times—and because in it we see the beginnings of our own problems, many of them still unresolved —Victorian literature has a special relevance to readers in the twentieth century. In addition, the Victorian writers were brilliant storytellers, and we read their works not only for literary appreciation and historical understanding but for pure reading pleasure.

# ENGLISH VOICES
## Quotations by Prominent Figures of the Period

Man is a tool-making animal.
   **Thomas Carlyle,** *Sartor Resartus*

Youth is a blunder; manhood a struggle; old age a regret.
   **Benjamin Disraeli,** *Coningsby*

If thou must love me, let it be for naught
Except for love's sake only.
   **Elizabeth Barrett Browning,** *Sonnets from the Portuguese*

The only purpose for which power can be rightfully exercised
over any member of a civilized community, against his will, is
to prevent harm to others.
   **John Stuart Mill,** *On Liberty*

You cannot fight against the future. Time is on our side.
   **William E. Gladstone,** Speech on the Second Reform Bill

It's them as take advantage
that get advantage i'
this world.
   **George Eliot,** *Adam Bede*

'Tis better to have loved and lost
Than never to have loved at all.
   **Alfred, Lord Tennyson,** *In Memoriam, A.H.H.*

A man's reach should exceed his grasp,
Or what's a heaven for?
   **Robert Browning,** "Andrea del Sarto"

He had used the word in its Pickwickian sense.
   **Charles Dickens,** *The Pickwick Papers*

# The Literature of 1832–1901

When you read literature it is important to place it in its historical context. Doing so will help you to see how the writer was influenced by the dominant ideas and attitudes of the time and how the work fits into a particular literary movement.

## Historical Context

The Victorian Age was a period marked by industrial and scientific advances, social progress, political stability, and economic prosperity. When the period began, England was the world's wealthiest and most powerful nation, and the British Empire spanned the globe. As the age progressed, the nation continued to flourish, as industrial growth and development strengthened its economy and its empire reached its peak. With the expansion of industry, the middle class became a dominant force in British society, whose belief in hard work and strict morality came to represent the age. The middle class also possessed a sense of social responsibility that helped to bring about reforms that gradually improved the living and working conditions of the lower classes.

## Literary Movements

The dominant attitudes and beliefs of the Victorian period are reflected in the literature of the time. While some writers embodied the Victorian ideals, others reacted against them. Many Victorian works conveyed the optimism and conservatism that characterized the age. Other works explored the problems that arose from industrialization and confronted the materialism, hypocrisy, and social pretense that accompanied the nation's prosperity. Because of the contrasting approaches of writers of the time, Victorian literature is extremely varied and diverse.

## Writers' Techniques

The English novel came of age during the Victorian period. Often published in serial form, Victorian novels are generally characterized by their episodic plots and their realistic portrayal of nineteenth-century life. In poetry, writers displayed a wide array of voices and styles. However, Victorian poets were generally more detached and objective than their predecessors from the Romantic Age.

On the following pages is a poem by Alfred, Lord Tennyson, a major Victorian poet. The notes in the side column should help you to place the selection in its historical context.

# Ulysses

## Alfred, Lord Tennyson

*In Homer's epic poem, the* Odyssey, *Ulysses (yoo lis'
ēz), the hero of the poem, sets out for his home in Ithaca
after ten years of fighting in the Trojan War. The journey
is long and filled with adventure. Another decade passes
before Ulysses finally reaches his destination. The story
of Ulysses is continued in Tennyson's poem, as Ulysses
finds himself growing restless years after his return to
Ithaca, and he contemplates making a final voyage.*

It little profits that an idle king,
By this still hearth, among these barren crags,
Matched with an aged wife, I mete and dole[1]
Unequal[2] laws unto a savage race,
5   That hoard, and sleep, and feed, and know not me.
I cannot rest from travel; I will drink
Life to the lees.[3] All times I have enjoyed
Greatly, have suffered greatly, both with those
That loved me, and alone; on shore, and when
10   Through scudding drifts the rainy Hyades[4]
Vexed the dim sea. I am become a name;
For always roaming with a hungry heart
Much have I seen and known—cities of men
And manners, climates, councils, governments,
15   Myself not least, but honored of them all—
And drunk delight of battle with my peers,
Far on the ringing plains of windy Troy.
I am a part of all that I have met;
Yet all experience is an arch wherethrough
20   Gleams that untraveled world, whose margin fades
Forever and forever when I move.

**Writer's Technique:**
Tennyson's poem is a
dramatic monologue, a
poem in which the
speaker addresses one or
more listeners whose
replies are not given. The
dramatic monologue was
a popular poetic form
during the Victorian age.

**Writer's Technique:** The
poem is written in blank
verse, or unrhymed lines
of iambic pentameter.

**Writer's Technique:**
Tennyson's imagery
recalls Ulysses's
adventures in Homer's
*Iliad* and *Odyssey*.

---

**1. mete and dole:** Measure and give out.
**2. unequal:** Unfair.
**3. lees:** Sediment.
**4. Hyades** (hī' ə dez): A group of stars whose rising
was assumed to be followed by rain.

**ULYSSES**
*Jean-Auguste-Dominique Ingres*
National Gallery of Art, Washington

How dull it is to pause, to make an end,
To rust unburnished, not to shine in use!
As though to breathe were life. Life piled on life
25    Were all too little, and of one to me
Little remains; but every hour is saved
From that eternal silence, something more,
A bringer of new things; and vile it were
For some three suns to store and hoard myself,
30    And this gray spirit yearning in desire
To follow knowledge like a sinking star,
Beyond the utmost bound of human thought.

This is my son, mine own Telemachus,
To whom I leave the scepter and the isle[5]
35 Well-loved of me, discerning to fulfill
This labor, by slow prudence to make mild
A rugged people, and through soft degrees
Subdue them to the useful and the good.
Most blameless is he, centered in the sphere
40 Of common duties, decent not to fail
In offices of tenderness, and pay
Meet[6] adoration to my household gods,
When I am gone. He works his work, I mine.
  There lies the port; the vessel puffs her sail;
45 There gloom the dark broad seas. My mariners,
Souls that have toiled and wrought, and thought with
    me—
That ever with a frolic welcome took
The thunder and the sunshine, and opposed
Free hearts, free foreheads—you and I are old;
50 Old age hath yet his honor and his toil;
Death closes all; but something ere the end,
Some work of noble note, may yet be done,
Not unbecoming men that strove with Gods.
The lights begin to twinkle from the rocks;
55 The long day wanes; the slow moon climbs; the deep
Moans round with many voices. Come, my friends,
'Tis not too late to seek a newer world.
Push off, and sitting well in order smite
The sounding furrows; for my purpose holds
60 To sail beyond the sunset, and the baths
Of all the western stars, until I die.
It may be that the gulfs will wash us down;
It may be we shall touch the Happy Isles,[7]
And see the great Achilles,[8] whom we knew.
65 Though much is taken, much abides; and though
We are not now that strength which in old days
Moved earth and heaven, that which we are, we are—
One equal temper of heroic hearts,
Made weak by time and fate, but strong in will
70 To strive, to seek, to find, and not to yield.

**Historical Context:** Ulysses's efforts to "subdue" the people of Ithaca parallels the efforts of the British Empire to "civilize" the natives of many of its colonies.

**Literary Movement:** Ulysses's desires reflect the Victorian work ethic.

**Writer's Technique:** The sunset symbolizes Ulysses's advancing age and the approach of his death.

**Literary Movement:** Ulysses's assertion reflects the sense of optimism and self-assurance that characterizes Victorian life.

---

**5. isle:** Ithaca, an island off the coast of Greece.
**6. meet:** Appropriate.
**7. Happy Isles:** Elysium, or the Islands of the Blessed; in classical mythology, the place where heroes went after death.
**8. Achilles** (ə′ kil′ ēz): The Greek hero of the Trojan War.

## THINKING ABOUT THE SELECTION
### Recalling

1. (a) How does Ulysses describe his current situation? (b) What past experiences does he describe?
2. What work is Ulysses leaving to Telemachus?
3. According to lines 58–61, what is Ulysses's purpose?
4. What comments does Ulysses make about his present condition in the final six lines?

### Interpreting

5. How does Ulysses's current situation contrast with his previous experiences?
6. (a) What is Ulysses's attitude toward his experiences and accomplishments? (b) What are his feelings about aging? (c) What is his attitude toward life in general?
7. How is Telemachus different from his father?
8. What is the poem's theme?

### Applying

9. Do you think that most people share Ulysses's feelings about aging? Why or why not?


## ANALYZING LITERATURE
### Understanding Dramatic Monologues

A dramatic monologue is a poem in which one character speaks to one or more silent listeners at a critical point in the speaker's life. The speaker's comments reveal the circumstances surrounding the conversation and offer insights into his or her personality. For example, in Tennyson's poem Ulysses reveals his attitudes concerning old age and death.

1. Why is the occasion of this poem a critical point in Ulysses's life?
2. What do Ulysses's comments reveal about his view concerning his purpose in life?
3. What are the dominant traits of Ulysses's personality?


## CRITICAL THINKING AND READING
### Understanding a Character's Motivation

In portraying any type of character, a writer must provide a motivation, or a stated or implied reason for the character's behavior, to make the character's actions believable. The motivation is the cause for the action. The ensuing action is the effect, or result. For example, in "Ulysses" Tennyson makes it clear that Ulysses's desire to make a final voyage is partly the result of his disenchantment with his current situation.

1. Name one other motivation for Ulysses's desire to make a final voyage.
2. How is this motivation conveyed in the poem?


## THINKING AND WRITING
### Writing a Continuation of the Poem

Write a dramatic monologue in which Ulysses describes the final voyage that he contemplates in Tennyson's poem. Brainstorm about the details and outcome of the journey. Arrange the details in chronological order. Then write your poem, using formal, dignified language similar to the language Tennyson uses in "Ulysses." When you revise, make sure you have used concrete details in describing the voyage. After you have finished revising, proofread your poem and share it with your classmates.

# Major Victorian Poets

**FAIR, QUIET AND SWEET REST**
*Luke Fildes*
*Warrington Museum and Art Gallery*

# ALFRED, LORD TENNYSON

## 1809–1892

When Alfred Tennyson was named baron by Queen Victoria in 1883, he was doubly honored—first by the title *Lord,* second by being the first English writer so titled. The honor seemed fitting for one whom most Victorians regarded as the poetic voice of their age. His commitment to responsible action and his belief in the inherent goodness of people were just two of many traits that made Tennyson the object of his contemporaries' admiration and affection. Yet, beyond these qualities was the man himself, forever struggling to overcome shyness and self-doubt, his mind keenly attuned to the problems of his century. Tennyson's best poems reflect both the inner and outer being, expressing through a clear and richly haunting music those certainties that sustain the human spirit.

Tennyson was born in the rural town of Somersby in Lincolnshire, the fourth of twelve children. His father, a rector, had a large library and personally supervised his son's early education. In 1827 Tennyson entered Trinity College, Cambridge, where he became close friends with Arthur Henry Hallam, the son of a noted historian and a great fan of Tennyson's early efforts at poetry. In 1830, with Hallam's encouragement, Tennyson published *Poems, Chiefly Lyrical,* which he followed up two years later with the simply titled *Poems.* When Hallam died suddenly in Vienna in 1833, the loss left a void in Tennyson's life that nearly destroyed him.

Grief, however, was ultimately to prove to be the inspiration behind some of the poet's greatest work. Relatively soon after Hallam's death, Tennyson began work on a collection of memorial poems dedicated to his friend. When the lengthy tribute, titled *In Memoriam,* finally appeared in 1850, the Queen's husband, Prince Albert, was so impressed that he encouraged the Queen to appoint Tennyson next Poet Laureate of England. For the next forty years Tennyson continued to publish regularly. Among his most celebrated works was *Idylls of the King,* a series of poems based on the legend of King Arthur, which began appearing in 1859 and was completed in 1885.

Modern scholars are in general agreement that there is much of lasting value in Tennyson's works. Certainly, there is no denying what the twentieth-century poet and critic T. S. Eliot has called the "abundance, variety, and complete competence" in Tennyson's poetry. Nor can one ignore the number of quotable lines Tennyson has added to the language, among them "'Tis better to have loved and lost, than never to have loved at all." These aspects of his verse and others have earned Tennyson yet another honor—that of being one of the best-known poets of any age.

# GUIDE FOR INTERPRETING

## The Lady of Shalott; Tears, Idle Tears; The Splendor Falls

**Writer's Technique**

**Meter and Stanza Structure.** Meter is the regular pattern of stressed and unstressed syllables in poetry. Stanza structure is a term that takes into account the meter, rhyme scheme, line length, and number of lines within each stanza of a poem. Through the structure of the stanza, the poet establishes unity, of both form and thought, within a poem.

For "The Lady of Shalott," a poem inspired by Arthurian legend, Tennyson appropriately chose a meter and stanza structure that recalled medieval romances—tales in verse that described the deeds of knights and ladies. The stanza of these romances, known as a "tail-rhyme stanza," was traditionally six lines long and composed of two pairs of rhyming lines, each followed by a short third line, or "tail." The rhyming lines, moreover, customarily contained four stressed syllables, or beats, while the tail contained three. Tennyson, as will be seen, altered this traditional pattern somewhat in "The Lady of Shalott," and in so doing, lent his poem a magical, almost dreamlike quality.

**Commentary**

"Modern fame is nothing," Tennyson remarked to a friend. "I'd rather have an acre of land. I shall go down, down! I'm up now. Action and reaction."

At the time of Tennyson's death, he was indeed immensely popular. But shortly thereafter, just as he had predicted, a reaction against his work set in, and as with a pebble thrown into a pond, rippled ever wider. It became fashionable in the 1920's and 1930's to belittle his work; critic Harold Nicholson, for example, called him "a morbid and unhappy mystic" who "should be read carelessly or not at all."

By the 1940's, however, the ripples had begun to die down, and critic Arthur J. Carr could write, "At some crucial points Tennyson is a modern poet, and there are compelling reasons why we should try to comprehend him."

Do you think such a swing in opinion is inevitable? Why do you think that Tennyson's poetry might appeal to us today?

**Writing**

Imagine that the only view of the world you had was a reflection of it, as through a mirror. Freewrite, describing what sensations you would miss in not experiencing life firsthand, and tell how this would make you feel.

# The Lady of Shalott

Alfred, Lord Tennyson

**Part I**

On either side the river lie
Long fields of barley and of rye,
That clothe the wold[1] and meet the sky;
And through the field the road runs by
5     To many-towered Camelot,[2]
And up and down the people go,
Gazing where the lilies blow[3]
Round an island there below,
      The island of Shalott.

10   Willows whiten, aspens quiver,
Little breezes dusk and shiver
Through the wave that runs forever
By the island in the river
      Flowing down to Camelot.
15   Four gray walls, and four gray towers,
Overlook a space of flowers,
And the silent isle imbowers
      The Lady of Shalott.

By the margin, willow-veiled.
20   Slide the heavy barges trailed
By slow horses; and unhailed
The shallop[4] flitteth silken-sailed
      Skimming down to Camelot:
But who hath seen her wave her hand?
25   Or at the casement seen her stand?
Or is she known in all the land,
      The Lady of Shalott?

Only reapers, reaping early
In among the bearded barley,
30   Hear a song that echoes cheerly,

---

**1. wold:** Rolling plains.
**2. Camelot:** A legendary English town where King Arthur had his court and Round Table.
**3. blow:** Bloom.
**4. shallop:** A light open boat.

From the river winding clearly,
    Down to towered Camelot:
And by the moon the reaper weary,
Piling sheaves in uplands airy,
35    Listening, whispers, '' 'Tis the fairy
    Lady of Shalott.''

## Part II

There she weaves by night and day
A magic web with colors gay.
She has heard a whisper say,
40    A curse is on her if she stay
    To look down to Camelot.
She knows not what the curse may be,
And so she weaveth steadily,
And little other care hath she,
45    The Lady of Shalott.

**THE LADY OF SHALOTT**
*John Waterhouse*
The Tate Gallery, London

And moving through a mirror[5] clear
That hangs before her all the year,
Shadows of the world appear.
There she sees the highway near
50     Winding down to Camelot:
There the river eddy whirls,
And there the surly village churls,
And the red cloaks of market girls,
     Pass onward from Shalott.

55  Sometimes a troop of damsels glad,
An abbot on an ambling pad,[6]
Sometimes a curly shepherd lad,
Or long-haired page in crimson clad,
     Goes by to towered Camelot;
60  And sometimes through the mirror blue
The knights come riding two and two:
She hath no loyal knight and true,
     The Lady of Shalott.

But in her web she still delights
65  To weave the mirror's magic sights,
For often through the silent nights
A funeral, with plumes and lights
     And music, went to Camelot:
Or when the moon was overhead,
70  Came two young lovers lately wed;
"I am half sick of shadows," said
     The Lady of Shalott.

**Part III**

A bow-shot from her bower eaves,
He rode between the barley sheaves,
75  The sun came dazzling through the leaves,
And flamed upon the brazen greaves[7]
     Of bold Sir Lancelot.
A red-cross knight[8] forever kneeled
To a lady in his shield,
80  That sparkled on the yellow field,
     Beside remote Shalott.

---

**5. mirror:** Weavers placed mirrors in front of their looms, so that they could view the progress of their work.
**6. pad:** An easy-paced horse.
**7. greaves:** Armor that protects the legs below the kneecaps.
**8. red-cross knight:** Refers to the Redcrosse Knight from *The Faerie Queene* by Edmund Spenser. In Spenser's work, the knight represents St. George, the patron saint of England, in addition to being a symbol of holiness.

The gemmy[9] bridle glittered free,
Like to some branch of stars we see
Hung in the golden Galaxy.[10]
85   The bridle bells rang merrily
     As he rode down to Camelot:
And from his blazoned baldric[11] slung
A mighty silver bugle hung,
And as he rode his armor rung,
90     Beside remote Shalott.

All in the blue unclouded weather
Thick-jeweled shone the saddle leather,
The helmet and the helmet feather
Burned like one burning flame together,
95     As he rode down to Camelot.
As often through the purple night,
Below the starry clusters bright,
Some bearded meteor, trailing light,
     Moves over still Shalott.

100   His broad clear brow in sunlight glowed;
On burnish'd hooves his war horse trode;
From underneath his helmet flowed
His coal-black curls as on he rode,
     As he rode down to Camelot.
105   From the bank and from the river
He flashed into the crystal mirror,
"Tirra lirra," by the river
     Sang Sir Lancelot.

She left the web, she left the loom,
110   She made three paces through the room,
She saw the waterlily bloom,
She saw the helmet and the plume,
     She looked down to Camelot.
Out flew the web and floated wide;
115   The mirror cracked from side to side;
"The curse is come upon me," cried
     The Lady of Shalott.

## Part IV

In the stormy east wind straining,
The pale yellow woods were waning,

---

**9. gemmy:** Jeweled.
**10. Galaxy:** The Milky Way.
**11. blazoned baldric:** A decorated sash worn diagonally across the chest.

120    The broad stream in his banks complaining,
Heavily the low sky raining
      Over towered Camelot;
Down she came and found a boat
Beneath a willow left afloat,
125   And round about the prow she wrote
      *The Lady of Shalott.*

And down the river's dim expanse
Like some bold seër in a trance,
Seeing all his own mischance—
130   With a glassy countenance
      Did she look to Camelot.
And at the closing of the day
She loosed the chain, and down she lay;
The broad stream bore her far away,
135      The Lady of Shalott.

Lying, robed in snowy white
That loosely flew to left and right—
The leaves upon her falling light—
Through the noises of the night
140      She floated down to Camelot:
And as the boathead wound along
The willowy hills and fields among,
They heard her singing her last song,
      The Lady of Shalott.

145   Heard a carol, mournful, holy,
Chanted loudly, chanted lowly,
Till her blood was frozen slowly,
And her eyes were darkened wholly,
      Turned to towered Camelot.
150   For ere she reached upon the tide
The first house by the waterside,
Singing in her song she died,
      The Lady of Shalott.

Under tower and balcony,
155   By garden wall and gallery,
A gleaming shape she floated by,
Dead-pale between the houses high,
      Silent into Camelot.
Out upon the wharfs they came,
160   Knight and burgher, lord and dame,
And round the prow they read her name,
      *The Lady of Shalott.*

Who is this? and what is here?
And in the lighted palace near
165 Died the sound of royal cheer;
And they crossed themselves for fear,
    All the knights at Camelot:
But Lancelot mused a little space;
He said, "She has a lovely face;
170 God in his mercy lend her grace,
    The Lady of Shalott."

## THINKING ABOUT THE SELECTION

### Recalling

1. (a) According to the poem, where does the Lady live? (b) How do the people of Camelot know of her existence?
2. What does the Lady spend all of her time doing, and why?
3. Where does she glimpse "shadows of the world"?
4. (a) What action does the Lady take when she sees Sir Lancelot in the mirror? (b) What happens to her as a result?

### Interpreting

5. In line 42, the speaker says the Lady "knows not what the curse may be." Explain the curse in your own words?
6. Critics have seen this poem as a commentary on the plight of the artist. In the light of this interpretation, what is meant by the Lady's complaint in lines 71–72?
7. (a) Why do you think the author devotes so much space to his description of Sir Lancelot? (b) How does it relate to the Lady's action and to the overall meaning of the poem?

### Applying

8. Why do you find the legend of King Arthur an especially effective—or especially poor—vehicle for the author's commentary on art and the artist in "The Lady of Shalott"?

## ANALYZING LITERATURE

### Recognizing Meter and Stanza Structure

**Meter** is a pattern of stressed and unstressed syllables that creates a predictable rhythm in a poem. Meter is expressed in terms of units called *feet*, each consisting of one stressed syllable and one or more unstressed syllables. Meter is but one ingredient in a poem's **stanza structure,** which also takes into account such matters as variation in line length, overall number of lines, and rhyme scheme. In "The Lady of Shalott," Tennyson adapted—or altered to suit his needs—an ancient stanza form that had the following structure: 1. six lines per stanza; 2. four feet in lines 1, 2, 4, and 5; 3. three feet in lines 3 and 6; 4. the rhyme scheme *aabccb*.

Examine several stanzas of "The Lady of Shalott." Note the ways in which the stanza structure differs from the one above. Tell how the changes add to the poem's chantlike effect.

## CRITICAL THINKING AND READING

### Understanding the Author's Purpose

It has been suggested that Tennyson's purpose in writing "The Lady of Shalott" was to show how the past reflects the problems of the present day.
1. Which events or statements in the poem point to a possible problem?
2. What is the nature of that problem?
3. What specific instances of this problem are evident in modern society?

# from The Princess

**Alfred, Lord Tennyson**

*The Princess (1847) is a long narrative poem that contains a number of songs. Some of these songs, including the two that follow, are considered to be among the finest of Tennyson's lyrics.*

## Tears, Idle Tears

Tears, idle tears, I know not what they mean,
Tears from the depth of some divine despair
Rise in the heart, and gather to the eyes,
In looking on the happy autumn fields,
5   And thinking of the days that are no more.

Fresh as the first beam glittering on a sail,
That brings our friends up from the underworld,
Sad as the last which reddens over one
That sinks with all we love below the verge;
10   So sad, so fresh, the days that are no more.

Ah, sad and strange as in dark summer dawns
The earliest pipe of half-awakened birds
To dying ears, when unto dying eyes
The casement slowly grows a glimmering square;
15   So sad, so strange, the days that are no more.

Dear as remembered kisses after death,
And sweet as those by hopeless fancy feigned
On lips that are for others; deep as love,
Deep as first love, and wild with all regret;
20   O Death in Life, the days that are no more.

## THINKING ABOUT THE SELECTION

### Recalling

1. According to the first stanza, what causes the tears to rise?
2. In what three ways does the speaker describe "the days that are no more."

### Interpreting

3. Why are the tears described as "idle"?
4. What do you think is meant in line 2 by "some divine despair"?
5. What comment is Tennyson making about our ability to remember things past?
6. A refrain is a repeated line or phrase in a poem or song. Identify the refrain in this poem, and explain how you think it was intended to make the reader feel.

### Applying

7. (a) Why do you think people feel nostalgia for "days that are no more"? (b) In what way is nostalgia bittersweet?

## UNDERSTANDING LANGUAGE

### Fitting the Context

Words have great versatility. Often they can be used as more than one part of speech and have several different meanings. For example, consider the word *fancy* in line 17: "And sweet as those by hopeless fancy feigned." In this line, *fancy* is a noun that means "imagination." However, one dictionary provides twenty different meanings for the word *fancy* and shows it used as four parts of speech.

For each sentence below, find the meaning of *fancy* that fits the context and tell as what part of speech the word is being used.

1. She refused to wear clothing with fancy trimming.
2. He didn't fancy the way the painting captured his likeness.
3. The young people took a fancy to each other.
4. "Well, fancy that!" exclaimed elderly Mrs. Kane.

## THINKING AND WRITING

### Describing the Poet's Style

A poet's **style** is the way he or she strings together words and ideas to communicate a particular image or message. In "Tears, Idle Tears," Tennyson's style includes the abundant use of repetition and the contrast between positive and negative impressions (such as "sad" and "fresh" in the second stanza). Write an essay explaining how Tennyson's style relates to his theme. Begin by stating the theme of the poem. Use quotations freely to illustrate the points you cover. When you revise, make sure you have quoted exactly and punctuated your quotations accurately.

# The Splendor Falls

## Alfred, Lord Tennyson

The splendor falls on castle walls
And snowy summits old in story;
The long light shakes across the lakes,
And the wild cataract leaps in glory.
5  Blow, bugle, blow, set the wild echoes flying,
Blow, bugle; answer, echoes, dying, dying, dying.

O hark, O hear! how thin and clear,
And thinner, clearer, farther going!
O sweet and far from cliff and scar[1]
10      The horns of Elfland faintly blowing!
Blow, let us hear the purple glens replying;
Blow, bugle; answer, echoes, dying, dying, dying.

O love, they die in yon rich sky,
They faint on hill or field or river:
15  Our echoes roll from soul to soul,
And grow forever and forever.
Blow, bugle, blow, set the wild echoes flying,
And answer, echoes, answer, dying, dying, dying.

---

**1. scar:** Mountainside.

---

## THINKING ABOUT THE SELECTION

### Recalling

1. Where exactly, according to the poem, does the splendor fall?
2. What do the bugles "set flying"?

### Interpreting

3. (a) What do you think is the meaning of the phrase "horns of Elfland" in line 10? (b) Of "wild echoes" in lines 5 and 17?

### Applying

4. (a) This poem was published in 1847. What "splendor" do you suppose Tennyson had in mind that he felt was "dying" from the world around him? (b) What "splendor" might a contemporary poet have in mind in writing about today's world?

**THE BARD**
*John Martin*
Yale Center for British Art

# GUIDE FOR INTERPRETING

## *from* In Memoriam A. H. H.;
## The Lotos Eaters; Crossing the Bar

**Literary Forms**

**Elegy.** An *elegy* is any poem that mourns the passing of an individual. The writing of elegies traces back to ancient times and, since the Renaissance, has been an enduring tradition among English poets. Tennyson's *In Memoriam* is widely acknowledged as one of the finest elegies ever written. The poem not only laments the death of Tennyson's closest friend, Arthur Henry Hallam, but also provides a ''chronicle'' of the poet/speaker's emotions as he moves gradually away from sheer grief and doubt, and ultimately toward understanding, acceptance, and faith. In this sense *In Memoriam* is more about life, love, and hope than it is about death, anger, and despair.

**Writer's Technique**

**Symbol.** A *symbol* is a person, place, object, or action that represents an abstract idea. For example, a parent might be a symbol of authority and a spring flower might be a symbol of rebirth. Poets often use symbols to fill images with a deeper significance. In ''The Lady of Shalott,'' for instance, Tennyson uses the web and mirror as symbols for, respectively, art and the artist's tendency to experience life secondhand.

**Writing**

The sudden death of a friend or relative, especially a young one, can stir up a wide range of emotions in the survivors, including despair, anger, and doubt. Describe what in particular might lead to these feelings about such a loss.

**Primary Source**

Critics have written enthusiastically about *In Memoriam*. Paul F. Baum, for instance, sees the *elegy* form as well matched to both its subject and to Tennyson's genius. *''In Memoriam,''* he writes, ''is not only a monument to Arthur Hallam and a record of Tennyson's personal suffering at Hallam's early death, it is also 'the way of the soul' . . . his representation of everyman's pain when confronted with death, the struggle with doubt, and the triumphant assertion of God's love.''

Few scholars, however, have matched T. S. Eliot's impassioned response to the poem: ''It is, in my opinion, in *In Memoriam* that Tennyson finds full expression. Its technical merit alone is enough to ensure its perpetuity. While Tennyson's technical competence is everywhere masterly and satisfying, *In Memoriam* is the most unapproachable of all his poems. Here are one hundred and thirty-two passages, each of several quatrains in the same form, and never monotony or repetition. . . . It is unique.''

# *from* In Memoriam, A. H. H.

## Alfred, Lord Tennyson

*In Memoriam, A.H.H. is an elegiac poem that conveys Tennyson's feelings and reflections about the death of his close friend Arthur Hallam, a talented young man who died suddenly at the age of twenty-two. Though Milton's* Lycidas *and Shelley's* Adonais *also lamented the deaths of promising young men, the structure of Tennyson's poem is quite different from these earlier elegies. Unlike the earlier elegies,* In Memoriam, A.H.H. *is made up of 131 seemingly self-sustaining lyrics that were composed over a period of seventeen years, as the poet struggled to come to terms with the feelings of doubt and despair that stemmed from his friend's early death.*

### 1

I held it truth, with him who sings
    To one clear harp in divers tones,
    That men may rise on stepping stones
Of their dead selves to higher things.

5  But who shall so forecast the years
    And find in loss a gain to match?
    Or reach a hand through time to catch
The far-off interest of tears?

Let Love clasp Grief lest both be drowned,
10    Let darkness keep her raven gloss.
    Ah, sweeter to be drunk with loss,
To dance with death, to beat the ground,

Than that the victor Hours should scorn
    The long result of love, and boast,
15    "Behold the man that loved and lost,
But all he was is overworn."

### 7

Dark house, by which once more I stand
    Here in the long unlovely street,
    Doors, where my heart was used to beat
20  So quickly, waiting for a hand,

**NOCTURNE: GREY AND GOLD—CHELSEA SNOW**
*James McNeill Whistler*
The Fogg Art Museum, Cambridge, Mass.

A hand that can be clasped no more—
    Behold me, for I cannot sleep,
    And like a guilty thing I creep
At earliest morning to the door.

25 He is not here; but far away
    The noise of life begins again,
    And ghastly through the drizzling rain
On the bald street breaks the blank day.

## 82

I wage not any feud with Death
30     For changes wrought on form and face;
    No lower life that earth's embrace
May breed with him, can fright my faith.

Eternal process moving on,
    From state to state the spirit walks;
35     And these are but the shattered stalks,
Or ruined chrysalis of one.

Nor blame I Death, because he bare
    The use of virtue out of earth;
    I know transplanted human worth
40 Will bloom to profit, otherwhere.

For this alone on Death I wreak
    The wrath that garners in my heart;
    He put our lives so far apart
We cannot hear each other speak.

## 130

45 Thy voice is on the rolling air;
    I hear thee where the waters run;
    Thou standest in the rising sun,
And in the setting thou art fair.

What art thou then? I cannot guess;
50     But though I seem in star and flower
    To feel thee some diffusive power,
I do not therefore love thee less.

My love involves the love before;
    My love is vaster passion now;
55     Though mixed with God and Nature thou,
I seem to love thee more and more.

Far off thou art, but ever nigh;
    I have thee still, and I rejoice;
    I prosper, circled with thy voice;
60 I shall not lose thee though I die.

from *In Memoriam A.H.H.*   799

## THINKING ABOUT THE SELECTION

### Recalling

1. In Part 1, what truth does the speaker say he once held but now doubts?
2. Where is the speaker standing in Part 7?
3. For what one thing, in Part 82, does the speaker "wreak the wrath" in his heart on death?
4. In Part 130, what does the speaker say has happened to his love for his friend?

### Interpreting

5. (a) According to the excerpts, what part of his friend does the poet finally accept is lost forever? (b) What part does he come to recognize will live forever?
6. Explain the paradox in line 57: "Far off thou art, but ever nigh."
7. Compare the first two excerpts with the last two. How have the poet's emotions changed?

### Applying

8. (a) If you had to console someone who had lost a loved one, what advice might you give to help that person cope? (b) How close would your ideas be to those implied in the last excerpt of *In Memoriam*?
9. The English novelist Samuel Butler has written, "To die completely, a person must not only forget but be forgotten, and he who is not forgotten is not dead." (a) Discuss the meaning of this quotation. (b) How does it relate to *In Memoriam*?

## ANALYZING LITERATURE

### Understanding an Elegy

An **elegy** is a poem or song that laments a death, usually recent. *In Memoriam* is an especially strong elegy since, as Tennyson himself put it, the poem is "rather the cry of the whole human race than mine. In the poem altogether private grief swells out into thought of, and hope for, the whole world."

1. Which details in the four excerpts seem particularly "private"? .
2. Which seem to apply to "the whole human race"?
3. What hope for future generations is implied in the final excerpt.

## CRITICAL THINKING AND READING

### Making Inferences About the Subject

In *In Memoriam* Tennyson never actually describes his friend directly but rather drops clues as to the man's personality. The reader must thus **infer,** or piece together from these clues, a picture of the man. What personality traits can you infer from the following?

1. Tennyson's reminiscence in Part 7 of his friend's hand clasp.
2. His comparing of his friend's remains to a "ruined crysalis."
3. His sensing in Part 130 of his friend's "diffusive power" in a star and flower.

# The Lotos-Eaters

Alfred, Lord Tennyson

*During their long voyage homeward in Homer's Odyssey, the Greek veterans of the Trojan War come to the land of the Lotos-Eaters, where, upon consuming the lotos's honeyed fruit, they are tempted by the desire to abandon their journey. Instead, the men wanted to forget about going home and stay in the land of the Lotos-Eaters forever.*

*In "The Lotos-Eaters," Tennyson expands upon Homer's brief account of the men's stay in the land of the Lotos-Eaters, delving into the men's desire for rest and the feelings of guilt that grew out of this desire.*

"Courage!" he[1] said, and pointed toward the land,
"This mounting wave will roll us shoreward soon."
In the afternoon they came unto a land
In which it seemed always afternoon.
5   All round the coast the languid air did swoon,
Breathing like one that hath a weary dream.
Full-faced above the valley stood the moon;
And like a downward smoke, the slender stream
Along the cliff to fall and pause and fall did seem.

10  A land of streams! some, like a downward smoke,
Slow-dropping veils of thinnest lawn[2] did go;
And some through wavering lights and shadows broke,
Rolling a slumbrous sheet of foam below.
They saw the gleaming river seaward flow
15  From the inner land: far off, three mountaintops,
Three silent pinnacles of aged snow,
Stood sunset-flushed; and, dewed with showery drops,
Up clomb the shadowy pine above the woven copse.

The charmed sunset lingered low adown
20  In the red West: through mountain clefts the dale
Was seen far inland, and the yellow down[3]
Bordered with palm, and many a winding vale
And meadow, set with slender galingale;[4]
A land where all things always seemed the same!

---

**1. he:** Odysseus (ō dis′ ē əs) (or Ulysses), the hero of the *Odyssey*.
**2. lawn** *n.*: A fine, thin linen.
**3. down** *n.*: An expanse of open, high, grassy land.
**4. galingale** *n.*: A plant similar in appearance to tall grass.

25   And round about the keel with faces pale,
      Dark faces pale against that rosy flame,
      The mild-eyed melancholy Lotos-eaters came.

      Branches they bore of that enchanted stem,
      Laden with flower and fruit, whereof they gave
30   To each, but whoso did receive of them,
      And taste, to him, the gushing of the wave
      Far far away did seem to mourn and rave
      On alien shores; and if his fellow spake,
      His voice was thin, as voices from the grave;
35   And deep asleep he seemed, yet all awake,
      And music in his ears his beating heart did make.

      They sat them down upon the yellow sand,
      Between the sun and moon upon the shore;
      And sweet it was to dream of Fatherland,
40   Of child, and wife, and slave; but evermore
      Most weary seemed the sea, weary the oar,
      Weary the wandering fields of barren foam.
      Then someone said, "We will return no more";
      And all at once they sang, "Our island home[5]
45   Is far beyond the wave; we will no longer roam."

### *Choric Song*[6]

#### I

      There is sweet music here that softer falls
      Than petals from blown roses on the grass,
      Or night dews on still waters between walls
      Of shadowy granite, in a gleaming pass;
50   Music that gentler on the spirit lies,
      Than tired eyelids upon tired eyes;
      Music that brings sweet sleep down from the blissful skies.
      Here are cool mosses deep.
      And through the moss the ivies creep,
      And in the stream the long-leaved flowers weep,
55   And from the craggy ledge the poppy hangs in sleep.

#### II

      Why are we weighed upon with heaviness
      And utterly consumed with sharp distress,
      While all things else have rest from weariness?
      All things have rest: why should we toil alone,
60   We only toil, who are the first of things,

---

**5. home:** Ithaca, an island off the coast of Greece.
**6. Choric Song:** Sung by the Greek travelers in chorus.

And make perpetual moan,
Still from one sorrow to another thrown;
Nor ever fold our wings,
And cease from wanderings,
65   Nor steep our brows in slumber's holy balm;
Nor harken what the inner spirit sings,
"There is no joy but calm!"
Why should we only toil, the roof and crown of things?[7]

### III

Lo! in the middle of the wood,
70   The folded leaf is wooed from out the bud
With winds upon the branch, and there
Grows green and broad, and takes no care,
Sun-steeped at noon, and in the moon
Nightly dew-fed; and turning yellow
75   Falls, and floats adown the air.
Lo! sweetened with the summer light,
The full-juiced apple, waxing over-mellow,
Drops in a silent autumn night.
All its allotted length of days,
80   The flower ripens in its place,
Ripens and fades, and falls, and hath no toil,
Fast-rooted in the fruitful soil.

### IV

Hateful is the dark-blue sky,
Vaulted o'er the dark-blue sea.
85   Death is the end of life; ah, why
Should life all labor be?
Let us alone. Time driveth onward fast,
And in a little while our lips are dumb.
Let us alone. What is it that will last?
90   All things are taken from us, and become
Portions and parcels of the dreadful Past.
Let us alone. What pleasure can we have
To war with evil? Is there any peace
In ever climbing up the climbing wave?
95   All things have rest, and ripen toward the grave
In silence; ripen, fall and cease:
Give us long rest or death, dark death, or dreamful ease.[8]

---

**7. Why . . . things?:** This line echoes the following passage from
Edmund Spenser's *Faerie Queene*: "Why then dost thou, O man, that
of them all/Art Lord, and eke of nature Soveraine/willfully . . . waste
thy joyous hours in needless pain . . . ?"
**8. All . . . ease:** This passage echoes the following lines in Spenser's
*Faerie Queene*: "Sleep after toyle, port after stormie seas/Ease after
war, death after life does greatly please."

## V

How sweet it were, hearing the downward stream,
With half-shut eyes ever to seem
100  Falling asleep in a half dream!
To dream and dream, like yonder amber light,
Which will not leave the myrrh[9] bush on the height;
To hear each other's whispered speech;
Eating the Lotos day by day,
105  To watch the crisping[10] ripples on the beach,
And tender curving lines of creamy spray;
To lend our hearts and spirits wholly
To the influence of mild-minded melancholy;
To muse and brood and live again in memory,
110  With those old faces of our infancy
Heaped over with a mound of grass,
Two handfuls of white dust, shut in an urn of brass!

## VI

Dear is the memory of our wedded lives,
And dear the last embraces of our wives
115  And their warm tears; but all hath suffered change;
For surely now our household hearths are cold,
Our sons inherit us, our looks are strange,
And we should come like ghosts to trouble joy.
Or else the island princes[11] over-bold
120  Have eat our substance, and the minstrel sings
Before them of the ten years' war in Troy,
And our great deeds, as half-forgotten things.
Is there confusion in the little isle?
Let what is broken so remain.
125  The Gods are hard to reconcile;
'Tis hard to settle order once again.
There *is* confusion worse than death,
Trouble on trouble, pain on pain,
Long labor unto aged breath,
130  Sore task to hearts worn out by many wars
And eyes grown dim with gazing on the pilot stars.

---

**9. myrrh** (mŭr) *n.*: A plant that produces a fragrant gum resin used in making incense and perfume.
**10. crisping** *adj.*: Curling.
**11. princes**: Suitors who were courting Ulysses' wife, Penelope.

## VII

But, propped on beds of amaranth[12] and moly,[13]
How sweet (while warm airs lull us, blowing lowly)
With half-dropped eyelid still,

135     Beneath a heaven dark and holy,
To watch the long bright river drawing slowly
His waters from the purple hill—
To hear the dewy echoes calling
From cave to cave through the thick-twined vine—

140     To watch the emerald-colored water falling
Through many a woven acanthus[14] wreath divine!
Only to hear and see the far-off sparkling brine,
Only to hear were sweet, stretched out beneath the pine.

---

**12. amaranth** (am′ ə ranth′) *n.*: An imaginary flower that never fades or dies.

**13. moly** (mō′ lē) *n.*: In classical mythology, an herb of magic powers. In the Odyssey, Ulysses uses moly to protect himself from the incantation of Circe (sər′ sē), an enchantress who turned men into swine.

**14. acanthus** (ə kan′ thəs) *n.*: A thistlelike plant.

**ULYSSES MOURNING FOR HOME**
*Carved Gem of Light Brown Sardonyx*
*Roman 3rd to 2nd Century B.C.*
Staatliche Museen zu Berlin

## VIII

The Lotos blooms below the barren peak,
145 The Lotos blows by every winding creek;
All day the wind breathes low with mellower tone;
Through every hollow cave and alley lone
Round and round the spicy downs the yellow Lotos dust is
      blown.
We have had enough of action, and of motion we,
150 Rolled to starboard, rolled to larboard, when the surge was
      seething free,
Where the wallowing monster spouted his foam fountains
   in the sea.
Let us swear an oath, and keep it with an equal mind,
In the hollow Lotos land to live and lie reclined
On the hills like Gods together, careless of mankind.
155 For they lie beside their nectar, and the bolts[15] are hurled
Far below them in the valleys, and the clouds are lightly
      curled
Round their golden houses, girdled with the gleaming
      world;
Where they smile in secret, looking over wasted lands,
Blight and famine, plague and earthquake, roaring deeps
      and fiery sands,
160 Clanging fights, and flaming towns, and sinking ships, and
      praying hands.
But they smile, they find a music centered in a doleful song.
Steaming up, a lamentation and an ancient tale of wrong,
Like a tale of little meaning though the words are strong;
Chanted from an ill-used race of men that cleave the soil,
165 Sow the seed, and reap the harvest with enduring toil,
Storing yearly little dues of wheat, and wine and oil;
Till they perish and they suffer—some, 'tis
      whispered—down in hell
Suffer endless anguish, others in Elysian valleys[16] dwell,
Resting weary limbs at last on beds of asphodel.[17]
170 Surely, surely, slumber is more sweet than toil, the shore
Than labor in the deep mid-ocean, wind and wave and oar;
Oh rest ye, brother mariners, we will not wander more.

---

**15. bolts:** Thunderbolts.
**16. Elysian** (i lizh′ ən) **valleys:** In Greek mythology, heroes went to
Elysia after death.
**17. asphodel** (as′ fə del′): A plant with yellow or white lilylike
flowers.

## THINKING ABOUT THE SELECTION

### Recalling

1. What strange property of the land is mentioned in lines 4 and 24 of the poem?
2. (a) How do the men describe this new land in the poem's "choric song"? (b) How do they describe the lives they had led up till now? (c) What reasons do they give for wanting to remain?

### Interpreting

3. (a) What do the men find so appealing about the land of the lotos-eaters? (b) What nagging concerns haunt them in spite of the effect of the lotos plants?
4. (a) What differences can you find between the odd-numbered and even-numbered stanzas of the poem's "choric song"? (b) What do these differences suggest about the decision the men have made?

### Applying

5. To what extent do you think Tennyson is "prescribing" the sailors' decision in "The Lotos-Eaters" as a solution for problems of life in his time? Explain your answer.

## CRITICAL THINKING AND READING

### Recognizing Allusions

An **allusion** is a reference to a person, place, statement, or event in another work of art or cultural work. Writers use allusions to help the reader grasp a greater truth. Suppose that Tennyson had written "The Lotos-Eaters" without any of its allusions to classical mythology.

1. What general truth might have been missed?
2. What qualities of the poem would have been lost?
3. What other qualities might have been more evident?

## UNDERSTANDING LANGUAGE

### Finding Antonyms

Antonyms are words that have opposite or nearly opposite meanings. For example, in line 154 Tennyson writes, "On the hills like Gods together, careless of mankind." An antonym for the word *careless* is *concerned*.

Choose an antonym for each of the italicized words below.

1. "This *mounting* wave will roll us shoreward soon."
   a. swelling  b. climbing  c. falling  d. dramatic
2. "And some through *wavering* lights and shadows broke . . ."
   a. uncertain  b. trembling  c. bright  d. steady
3. "The charmed sunset *lingered* low adown . . ."
   a. faltered      b. departed
   c. operated      d. remained
4. "The mild-eyed *melancholy* Lotus-eaters came."
   a. sad     b. lonely     c. beautiful     d. joyful
5. "The folded leaf is *wooed* from out the bud . . ."
   a. coaxed      b. wed
   c. shunned      d. humored

# Crossing the Bar

Alfred, Lord Tennyson

*Tennyson requested that this poem, written three years before his death, be printed at the end of all editions of his poetry.*

Sunset and evening star,
    And one clear call for me!
And may there be no moaning of the bar,[1]
    When I put out to sea,

5   But such a tide as moving seems asleep,
    Too full for sound and foam,
When that[2] which drew from out the boundless deep
    Turns again home.

Twilight and evening bell,
10  And after that the dark!
And may there be no sadness of farewell,
    When I embark;

For though from out our bourne[3] of Time and Place
    The flood may bear me far,
15  I hope to see my Pilot face to face
    When I have crossed the bar.

---

**1. bar:** Sandbar.
**2. that:** The soul.
**3. bourne:** Boundary.

**THE ANGRY SEA**
*James McNeill Whistler*
*Freer Gallery of Art, Smithsonian Institution*

## THINKING ABOUT THE SELECTION

### Recalling

1. What does the speaker of the poem request in lines 3–4 and again in lines 11–12?

### Interpreting

2. What do you think is actually meant by the phrase "crossing the bar"?
3. Who do you think the "Pilot" is?

### Applying

4. Which excerpt from *In Memoriam* do you think is most in keeping with the attitude Tennyson expresses in "Crossing the Bar"? Explain why you feel as you do.

## ANALYZING LITERATURE

### Recognizing Symbols

A **symbol** is a thing, person, place, or idea whose meaning transcends, or goes beyond, its usual literal definition. When the reader of "Crossing the Bar" recognizes that the sea journey described in the poem is in actuality the passage into death, the symbolic meaning of many of the ideas and images becomes obvious. State the meaning symbolized by each of the following:

1. moaning of the bar.
2. putting out to sea.
3. twilight.
4. the dark.
5. the flood bearing one far.

## CRITICAL THINKING AND READING

### Comparing Attitudes

Writers may write about the same subject but take quite different positions. Read each statement below about death. Explain which one you feel comes closest to the attitude Tennyson expresses in "Crossing the Bar."

1. Oliver Wendell Holmes: "Death tugs at my ear and says: 'Live, I am coming.'"
2. John Dryden: "To die is landing on some distant shore."
3. Genesis 3:19: "Dust thou art, and unto dust shalt thou return."
4. Ralph Waldo Emerson: "Our fear of death is like our fear that summer will be short, but when we will have had our swing of pleasure, our fill of fruit, and our swelter of heat, we say we have had our day."
5. William Hazlitt: "Our repugnance to death increases in proportion to our consciousness of having lived in vain."

## THINKING AND WRITING

### Writing About Symbols

In "Crossing the Bar" Tennyson uses a series of interrelated symbols to deliver his thoughts on the issues of serenity at life's end and faith in an afterlife. He might, of course, have selected a different set of symbols to express these thoughts. Choose a symbolic vehicle other than a boat trip that could stand for the journey at life's end. Some possibilities are a walk up a hill, or the writing of the last chapter of a book. Make notes on the various details that might be used in such a symbolic representation. Then express Tennyson's ideas, in either a poem or brief story that uses this set of symbols.

# ROBERT BROWNING

## 1812–1889

In Victorian England, clubs to promote the works of the masters of English literature were fairly common. In 1881, a group of amateur scholars banded together to found another such club, the Browning Society. What made this literary club unique was that the poet it paid tribute to was *living.* Yet if honor in this form came unusually early to Robert Browning, then fame came unusually late, for it was not until nearly a half century after the publication of his first book that the public came to recognize his genius.

Robert Browning was born in London and spent the first twenty-eight years of his life there. Like Tennyson, he was educated mainly at home, spending much of his time during his early years in his father's large library. Here he immersed himself in art, history, literature, philosophy, religion, music, medicine, and zoology. At twenty-one, Browning published his first book, *Pauline,* a highly personal record of his religious skepticism, no doubt influenced by the writings of Shelley. Discouraged by the book's poor critical reception, Browning tried his hand next at something less personal, publishing *Paracelsus,* a long dramatic poem, in 1835. Failing again to please the critics, he turned to drama and two years later produced *Strafford,* which closed after five performances.

Despite his inability to establish himself in the public eye as a writer to be reckoned with, Browning was all the while shaping the distinctive dramatic voice that would ensure his eventual fame. In *Dramatic Lyrics* (1842), *Dramatic Romances and Lyrics* (1845), and *Men and Women* (1855) he reveals a rich and varied talent in both the short lyrical poem and the dramatic monologue.

In 1846 he married Elizabeth Barrett, a poet whose fame greatly exceeded his own. They established a home in Florence, Italy, a setting that figured in many of Browning's works. The marriage was an extremely happy one, and when his wife died in 1861, Browning, unable to face constant reminders of her in Florence, returned to London. Here, he soon became a popular figure, especially among university students, who were attracted to his next book, *Dramatis Personnae* (1864). This was followed by his masterpiece, *The Ring and the Book* (1868), which was hailed as the most "profound spiritual treasure that England had produced since the days of Shakespeare." Based on an actual seventeenth-century Italian murder trial, this long poem comprises ten dramatic monologues.

Browning's dramatic monologues have greatly influenced many twentieth-century poets. Today, he is admired not only for these complex psychological portraits, but also for his masterly blending of natural speech rhythms with strict poetic forms.

# GUIDE FOR INTERPRETING

## My Last Duchess; Home-Thoughts, from Abroad; Love Among the Ruins; Prospice

**Dramatic Monologue.** A dramatic monologue is a dramatic poem by a single speaker, much like a speech from a play. Unlike a play, however, where each speech is preceded by the name of its speaker, the dramatic monologue contains no such outward label. Rather, the identity of the speaker is revealed through his or her words. In "My Last Duchess," we learn, strictly through the speaker's conversation with an unnamed companion, the setting of the poem and—more importantly—the inner conflict that prompts the character's speech.

**Writing**

Write a brief fictional account of *your* life in the Oval Office titled "I, The President." Focus not on affairs of state but on the day-to-day routine in your household—your relationship with your family and friends, the stress that your job places on those relationships, and so on. Be sure to answer, somewhere in your account, the question "How has power changed me?"

**Primary Source**

In contemporary life, we often live by the dictum that less is more. Alfred, Lord Tennyson once told Robert Browning that "if he got rid of two-thirds, the remaining third would be much finer." After Browning had left the room, Tennyson expanded on his comments.

> "It is necessary to respect the limits," he explained. "An artist is one who recognizes bounds to his work as a necessity, and does not overflow illimitably [boundlessly] to all extent about a matter. I soon found that if I meant to make any mark at all, it must be done by shortness, for all the men before me had been so diffuse, and all the big things had been done. To get workmanship as nearly perfect as possible is the best chance for going down the stream of time. A small vessel on fine lines is likely to float further than a great raft."

Do you agree with Tennyson's definition of an artist? What do you think he meant by the "big things," "a small vessel on fine lines," and "a great raft"? Would Browning's poems be better if he had followed Tennyson's advice?

# My Last Duchess

## Robert Browning

*This poem, set in the sixteenth century in a castle in
northern Italy, is based on events from the life of the Duke of
Ferrara, an Italian nobleman, whose first wife died after
only three years of marriage. Following his wife's death, the
Duke began making arrangements to remarry. In Browning's poem, the Duke is showing a painting of his first wife to
an agent who represents the father of the woman he hopes
to marry.*

That's my last Duchess painted on the wall,
Looking as if she were alive. I call
That piece a wonder, now: Frà Pandolf's[1] hands
Worked busily a day, and there she stands.
5  Will 't please you sit and look at her? I said
"Frà Pandolf" by design, for never read
Strangers like you that pictured countenance,
The depth and passion of its earnest glance,
But to myself they turned (since none puts by
10  The curtain I have drawn for you, but I)
And seemed as they would ask me, if they durst,[2]
How such a glance came there; so, not the first
Are you to turn and ask thus. Sir, 'twas not
Her husband's presence only, called that spot
15  Of joy into the Duchess' cheek: perhaps
Frà Pandolf chanced to say "Her mantle laps
Over my lady's wrist too much," or "Paint
Must never hope to reproduce the faint
Half-flush that dies along her throat"; such stuff
20  Was courtesy, she thought, and cause enough
For calling up that spot of joy. She had
A heart—how shall I say?—too soon made glad,
Too easily impressed; she liked whate'er
She looked on, and her looks went everywhere.
25  Sir, 'twas all one! My favor at her breast,
The dropping of the daylight in the West,
The bough of cherries some officious fool
Broke in the orchard for her, the white mule
She rode with round the terrace—all and each

---

**1. Frà Pandolf's:** The work of Brother Pandolf, an imaginary
painter.
**2. durst:** Dared.

30    Would draw from her alike the approving speech,
Or blush, at least. She thanked men—good! but thanked
Somehow—I know not how—as if she ranked
My gift of a nine-hundred-years-old name
With anybody's gift. Who'd stoop to blame

35    This sort of trifling? Even had you skill
In speech—(which I have not)—to make your will
Quite clear to such an one, and say, "Just this
Or that in you disgusts me; here you miss,
Or there exceed the mark"—and if she let

40    Herself be lessoned so, nor plainly set
Her wits to yours, forsooth,[3] and made excuse,
—E'en then would be some stooping; and I choose
Never to stoop. Oh sir, she smiled, no doubt,
Whene'er I passed her; but who passed without

45    Much the same smile? This grew; I gave commands;
Then all smiles stopped together. There she stands
As if alive. Will 't please you rise? We'll meet
The company below, then. I repeat,
The Count your master's known munificence

50    Is ample warrant that no one just pretense
Of mine for dowry will be disallowed;
Though his fair daughter's self, as I avowed
At starting, is my object. Nay, we'll go
Together down, sir! Notice Neptune,[4] though,

55    Taming a sea horse, thought a rarity,
Which Claus of Innsbruck[5] cast in bronze for me!

---

**3. forsooth:** In truth.
**4. Neptune:** In Roman mythology, the god of the sea.
**5. Claus of Innsbruck:** An imaginary Austrian sculptor.

---

## THINKING ABOUT THE SELECTION

### Recalling

1. (a) Where are the speaker and his companion? (b) What are they looking at?
2. What was the Duke's "gift" to his wife?

### Interpreting

3. (a) What question are we to understand the speaker's companion to have asked. (b) What is the speaker's reply?

4. (a) What aspects of the Duke's personality are revealed in his keeping the painting behind a curtain? (b) What aspects are revealed in his being the only one allowed to draw the curtain?
5. (a) What has happened to the "last" Duchess? (b) Where in the poem is this revealed?
6. (a) How would you state the sentiment expressed in lines 21–22? (b) What examples does the speaker give as an illustration of this trait? (c) What feelings did it stir up in him?

## Applying

7. The eighteenth century English stateman and writer Edmund Burke has written, "The greater the power, the more dangerous the abuse." What are your reactions to this statement?

## ANALYZING LITERATURE

### Dramatic Monologue

A **dramatic monologue** is a poem that reveals a character's personality through what he or she says in a dramatic situation. In most dramatic monologues, the character addresses another character who is merely a silent listener. By drawing conclusions based on the character's words, the reader can piece together the poem's setting, the situation that prompts the character to speak, and the character's motives and actions.

1. Imagine that this dramatic monologue is part of a play or movie that you are directing. Describe the setting and the situation that prompts the Duke's speech.
2. What tone of voice do you think the Duke uses? Explain your answer.
3. What motives do you suppose the Duke has for showing the Count's agent the portrait of his dead wife?
4. The Count's agent never speaks. How do you imagine he acts when he learns of the Duke's displeasure with his wife?
5. (a) What makes this kind of poem an especially strong vehicle for conveying information about a character? (b) How differently would you see the Duke if Browning had written "My Last Duchess" as a short story?

## CRITICAL THINKING AND READING

### Making Inferences About the Speaker

An **inference** is a conclusion arrived at through known facts or evidence. In "My Last Duchess," Browning never directly describes the Duke's personality. Rather, he relies upon the reader to make inferences, from selected information, about the sort of man the Duke is. Find evidence in the poem that the Duke is: (1) jealous, (2) overly proud, (3) determined to have things his way, (4) preoccupied with possessions, (5) a stern boss.

## UNDERSTANDING LANGUAGE

### Revealing Diction

The **diction,** or choice of words, in "My Last Duchess" is an important ingredient of the Duke's character. To show that the man is a member of the nobility and, therefore, schooled in the social graces, Browning has the Duke use such formal constructions as "Will't please you sit and look at her?" Yet, there are clues in his speech habits that suggest the Duke's good manners are only skin-deep. Locate examples of language in the poem that demonstrate:

1. that the Duke is rude and insulting to his staff
2. that he wants to appear humble
3. that he thinks of himself as reasonable

## THINKING AND WRITING

### Writing a Dramatic Monologue

Assume for the moment that the Duke has presented an accurate description of his last Duchess. List as many of her personality traits as you can. Then write an original dramatic monologue in which the Duchess reveals her impressions of her husband. In planning your monologue, consider the setting you want to convey and the occasion that prompts the speech. When you revise, make sure you have created a consistent picture of the Duchess.

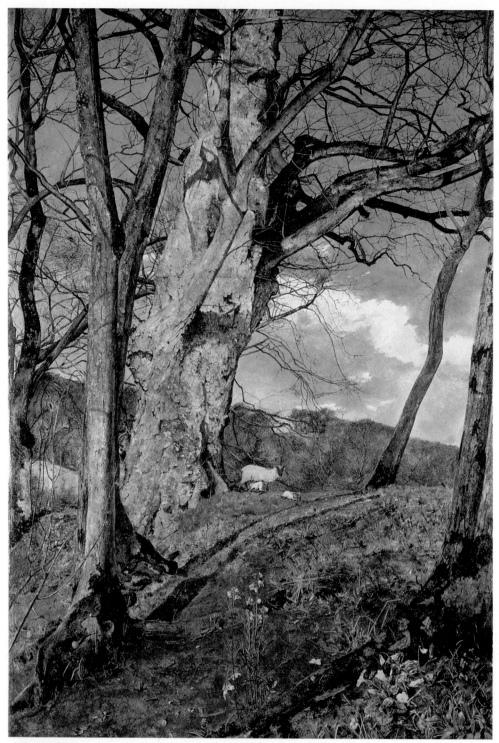

**IN EARLY SPRING**
*John William Inchbold*
Ashmolean Museum, Oxford

# Home-Thoughts, from Abroad

## Robert Browning

Oh, to be in England
Now that April's there,
And whoever wakes in England
Sees, some morning, unaware,
5   That the lowest boughs and the brushwood sheaf
Round the elm-tree bole are in tiny leaf,
While the chaffinch[1] sings on the orchard bough
In England—now!

And after April, when May follows,
10  And the whitethroat[2] builds, and all the swallows!
Hark, where my blossomed pear tree in the hedge
Leans to the field and scatters on the clover
Blossoms and dewdrops—at the bent spray's edge—
That's the wise thrush; he sings each song twice over..
15  Lest you should think he never could recapture
The first fine careless rapture!
And though the fields look rough with hoary dew,
All will be gay when noontide wakes anew
The buttercups, the little children's dower
20  —Far brighter than this gaudy melon flower![3]

---

**1. chaffinch** (chaf′ finch′) *n.*: A small European songbird.
**2. whitethroat** *n.*: Bird having white around the throat.
**3. melon flower:** The large, yellow flower of melon plants, native to a warm climate.

---

## THINKING ABOUT THE SELECTION

### Recalling

1. What time and place does the poem celebrate?
2. List four birds and six plants that the speaker says "whoever wakes in England" sees.

### Interpreting

3. (a) Where do you suppose the speaker of the poem is? (b) What details of the poem provide clues?

4. How do you think the speaker is using the phrase "the little children's dower" in line 19?
5. Browning wrote this poem in England, following a trip to Italy. Why do you think he chose to write the poem as though he were far away at the time?

### Applying

6. Think of a time when you were homesick, or try to imagine what it would be like. What details of home do you think would come to mind for you?

# Love Among the Ruins

Robert Browning

*This poem presents the contrast between past and present through the eyes of a shepherd, anxious to return to his waiting wife. The ruins that the shepherd and his wife live among may be the remains of ancient Babylon or Nineveh or one of the Etruscan cities of Italy.*

Where the quiet-colored end of evening smiles,
    Miles and miles
On the solitary pastures where our sheep
    Halt asleep
5  Tinkle homeward through the twilight, stray or stop
    As they crop—
Was the site once of a city great and gay
    (So they say),
Of our country's very capital, its prince
10    Ages since
Held his court in, gathered councils, wielding far
    Peace or war.

Now—the country does not even boast a tree,
    As you see,
15  To distinguish slopes of verdure, certain rills
    From the hills
Intersect and give a name to (else they run
    Into one),
Where the domed and daring palace shot its spires
20    Up like fires
O'er the hundred-gated circuit of a wall
    Bounding all,
Made of marble, men might march on nor be pressed,
    Twelve abreast.

25  And such plenty and perfection, see, of grass
    Never was!
Such a carpet as, this summertime, o'erspreads
    And embeds
Every vestige of the city, guessed alone,[1]
30    Stock or stone—

---

**1. guessed alone:** Because the site of the city is now covered with grass, one can only guess where it was.

Where a multitude of men breathed joy and woe
    Long ago;
Lust of glory pricked their hearts up, dread of shame
    Struck them tame;
35  And that glory and that shame alike, the gold
    Bought and sold.

Now—the single little turret that remains
    On the plains,
By the caper[2] overrooted, by the gourd
40    Overscored,
While the patching houseleek's[3] head of blossom winks
    Through the chinks—
Marks the basement whence a tower in ancient time
    Sprang sublime,
45  And a burning ring, all round, the chariots traced
    As they raced,
And the monarch and his minions and his dames
    Viewed the games.

---

**2. caper** *n.*: A prickly, trailing Mediterranean bush.
**3. houseleek** *n.*: A plant with yellow, pink, or red flowers and
compact rosettes of thick, fleshy leaves.

50 And I know, while thus the quiet-colored eve
      Smiles to leave
To their folding, all our many-tinkling fleece
      In such peace,
And the slopes and rills, in undistinguished gray
      Melt away—
55 That a girl with eager eyes and yellow hair
      Waits me there
In the turret whence the charioteers caught soul
      For the goal,
When the king looked, where she looks now, breathless,
  dumb
60       Till I come.

But he looked upon the city, every side,
      Far and wide,
All the mountains topped with temples, all the glades'
      Colonnades,[4]
65 All the causeys,[5] bridges, aqueducts—and then,
      All the men!
When I do come, she will speak not, she will stand,
      Either hand
On my shoulder, give her eyes the first embrace
70       Of my face,
Ere we rush, ere we extinguish sight and speech
      Each on each.

In one year they sent a million fighters forth
      South and North,
75 And they built their gods a brazen pillar[6] high
      As the sky,
Yet reserved a thousand chariots in full force—
      Gold, of course.
Oh heart! oh blood that freezes, blood that burns!
80       Earth's returns
For whole centuries of folly, noise and sin!
      Shut them in,
With their triumphs and their glories and the rest!
      Love is best.

---

**4. Colonnades** (käl′ ə nädz′) *n.*: Series of columns set at regular
intervals; here, groups of trees surrounding an open area.
**5. causeys** *n.*: Causeways or raised roads.
**6. brazen pillar:** Built from the brass of captured chariots.

## THINKING ABOUT THE SELECTION

### Recalling

1. (a) What does the speaker say once stood where sheep pastures now stand? (b) What single trace remains?
2. What does the speaker say awaits him on the pastures at twilight?

### Interpreting

3. What do you suppose is the identity of the speaker?
4. (a) How would you summarize the speaker's comments on the civilization mentioned in lines 33–36? (b) How would you describe his feelings toward this civilization?
5. (a) What do you think is the purpose of the speaker's noting in line 67 that his companion "will not speak" when he arrives? (b) What might he expect his companion to say?
6. (a) What do you think is the meaning of the speaker's lament in lines 81–82? (b) To what "folly" might he be referring?
7. Explain why "Love Among the Ruins" is or is not an appropriate title for the poem.

### Applying

8. Reread "Ozymandias" by Shelley on page 702. (a) What similarities do you see between the messages in the two poems? (b) What differences do you see in the conclusions reached by the two poets?

## CRITICAL THINKING AND READING

### Interpreting Tone

**Tone** is the author's attitude toward his or her subject or audience. A work may have a tone that is lighthearted or serious, ironic or sincere, or any of numerous other possibilities. Just as a person's tone of voice can affect the way a remark is interpreted by others, so the tone of a literary work affects how the reader perceives the author's purpose.

1. (a) How would you describe the tone of the speaker of "Love Among the Ruins" with respect to the ruined splendor? (b) With respect to the civilzation? (c) With respect to his companion?
2. Consider what other tone Browning might have used to make the point he makes here. Would another tone strengthen or weaken the poem's impact? Explain your answer.

## THINKING AND WRITING

### Comparing and Contrasting Two Places

Think about how your town or city might have appeared 100 years ago. Write a description of the "two faces" of your city. Begin by listing ways in which the locale has undoubtedly changed, as well as ways in which it has probably remained the same, over the century. In writing your description, use vivid details so that your audience will be able to picture both the "old" city and the "new" one.

# Prospice

## Robert Browning

*This poem, the title of which means "look forward,"
was written by Browning after the death of his wife. It
is the classic expression of Browning's feelings about
death.*

Fear death?—to feel the fog in my throat,
    The mist in my face,
When the snow begins, and the blasts denote
    I am nearing the place,
5  The power of the night, the press of the storm,
    The post of the foe;
Where he stands, the Arch Fear in a visible form,
    Yet the strong man must go.
For the journey is done and the summit attained,
10    And the barriers fall,
Though a battle's to fight ere the guerdon be gained,
    The reward of it all.
I was ever a fighter, so—one fight more,
    The best and the last!
15  I would hate that death bandaged my eyes, and forbore,
    And bade me creep past.
No! let me taste the whole of it, fare like my peers,
    The heroes of old,
Bear the brunt, in a minute pay glad life's arrears
20    Of pain, darkness, and cold.
For sudden the worst turns the best to the brave,
    The black minute's at end,
And the elements' rage, the fiend-voices that rave,
    Shall dwindle, shall blend,
25  Shall change, shall become first a peace out of pain,
    Then a light, then thy breast,
Oh thou soul of my soul![1] I shall clasp thee again,
    And with God be the rest!

---

**1. soul of my soul:** Browning's wife.

## THINKING ABOUT THE SELECTION

### Recalling

1. (a) With what question does the speaker open the poem? (b) What is his answer in line 17?
2. (a) To what, in lines 1–14, does the speaker compare the process of dying? (b) Who, in lines 17–18, does the speaker say are his peers?

### Interpreting

3. (a) What opposing forces does the speaker suggest are fighting at the moment of death? (b) What, according to line 21, is ironic about the nature of this battle?
4. (a) Whom do you think Browning is addressing in line 27 as "thou soul of my soul"? (b) What does this suggest about his belief in an afterlife?
5. In what way is this poem a look forward?

### Applying

6. Browning has sometimes been criticized for being overly optimistic about situations in which others would be more skeptical. (a) Do you think this is true of his views in "Prospice?" Why or why not? (b) What other poets have you read who seem to share his attitudes?

## CRITICAL THINKING AND READING

### Making Inferences About Attitudes

Students of literature are warned repeatedly of the dangers of misidentifying the first-person narrator of a work with the work's author. Yet, in dealing with "Prospice," scholars generally assume that the attitudes reflected in the poem are precisely those of its author.

1. Based on what you have read about Robert Browning and his attitudes, how justified do you think scholars are in making this assumption?
2. What subjects besides death might an author choose to address without the use of a fictitious narrator?

## THINKING AND WRITING

### Comparing and Contrasting Two Poems

Both Tennyson's "Crossing the Bar" and Browning's "Prospice" express the poet's deepest feelings about dying. Reread the two poems, and think about the similarities and differences between them. Consider especially the following questions as you plan an essay comparing and contrasting the poems: What do Tennyson's image of the tide and Browning's image of the battle reveal about each poet's attitudes toward dying? How do the poets' notions of the afterlife differ? Which poem seems more effective to you? Begin your essay by summarizing your conclusions. Support your opinions by quoting freely from the poems. When you revise, make sure you have quoted precisely and have punctuated your sentences accurately.

# MATTHEW ARNOLD

## 1822–1888

Of all the great Victorian poets, Matthew Arnold strikes twentieth-century readers as the most modern. The persistent theme of his poems—people's isolation and alienation from nature and from one another—has been echoed by many writers and thinkers of our own age. His pessimistic outlook too—that "there is everything to be endured, nothing to be done"—coincides with the view of many today that we are a generation of lost souls.

Matthew Arnold was born in Laleham, Middlesex, and educated at Rugby School, where his father, a believer in the good of social change, was headmaster. After entering Oxford in 1841, Arnold startled his contemporaries by dressing and behaving like an aristocratic dandy. Yet, behind this Byronic mask was developing the serious and sensitive social conscience that was to guide Arnold's career as a public servant, poet, and literary critic.

In 1851 Arnold accepted the post of Inspector of Schools, which he held until two years before his death. In this job he traveled through England and the Continent, and published reports that did much to improve public education in Great Britain. All the while, he remained a poet at heart, though his first two books, published in 1849 and 1851, met with little success.

His fortunes changed in 1853, with the publication of *Poems: A New Edition,* which included a long preface that established Arnold as a writer of clear critical prose as well as of quality poetry. With *New Poems* (1867), which contained his celebrated "Dover Beach," Arnold felt that he had expressed everything he had to say through poetry. From that point forward, he thus focused his creative energies on literary criticism.

The melancholy outlook of his poems, Arnold himself noted, was unrelieved by hope. Nevertheless, it was his belief that the role of literature was to "inspirit and rejoice the reader: that it shall convey a charm and infuse delight." In such critical works as *Culture and Anarchy* (1869), Arnold argued also that literature should train us to open our minds to what is true and valuable in life. For Arnold, then, literature's truth and cultural value lay in its ability to enlarge and develop humanity's "moral and social passion for doing good." Even his critical examinations of the classics and of Dante and Shakespeare were in part attempts to help readers of his day find permanent values in an industrialized society that Arnold viewed as increasingly materialistic and self-serving.

Despite his own opinions regarding the shortcomings of his poetic vision, Arnold's "dark" poems are a mirror of his critical beliefs: They charm and delight audiences, as well as point out enduring truths.

# GUIDE FOR INTERPRETING

## To Marguerite—Continued; Self-Dependence; Dover Beach

**Writer's Technique**

**Imagery and Mood.** Imagery is language that appeals to one or more of the senses. Poets rely on imagery to help establish *mood,* the overall feeling that a poem awakens in the reader. For example, if a poet wishes to create a mood of frustration, he or she may rely on imagery associated with a summer traffic jam—the sight of countless cars gleaming in the sunshine, the sound of motors humming, the feel of the heat rising from the pavement, the smell and perhaps even the taste of exhaust fumes. The same imagery, however, can be used to convey a mood of excitement and energy when the focus of the poem becomes a raceway, where roaring cars zoom past cheering spectators.

**Figurative Language.** Figurative language is the name applied to a group of literary devices that use words and phrases in an unorthodox way to create interesting effects. Figurative language is not to be taken literally. Among the many figures of speech used by poets are *apostrophe,* in which the poet directly addresses an absent person or some object or idea, and *personification,* the assigning of human qualities to nonhuman things. Both of these devices are used by Matthew Arnold in "Self-Dependence."

**Commentary**

Critics assume that Arnold wrote "Dover Beach" with his wife in mind. The lines ". . . the world, which seems/To lie before us like a land of dreams,/So various, so beautiful, so new," and the image of Dover Beach in the moonlight perhaps represent the stop that the poet and his wife made at Dover on their wedding journey in June of 1851. The wild beauty of the famed "white cliffs of Dover" continues to attract scores of people yearly.

The Straits of Dover, about twenty-one miles across, connect the English Channel and the Atlantic Ocean with the North Sea. It is a strikingly beautiful spot, for both the French and English shores are lined by high chalk cliffs. The outcropping of the stark white cliffs is the result of the swift erosion of the soft chalk. The lashing of the waves, wind, and rain and the seeping of groundwater combine to create striking shore-front sculpture.

Why do you think Arnold picked Dover Beach as the setting for his poem? How does the imagery help create the poem's mood?

**Writing**

Imagine yourself on a beach, watching the ebb and flow of the ocean. Freewrite, exploring the thoughts that spring to mind.

# To Marguerite—Continued

## Matthew Arnold

Yes! in the sea of life enisled,
With echoing straits between us thrown,
Dotting the shoreless watery wild,
We mortal millions live *alone*.
5    The islands feel the enclasping flow,
And then their endless bounds they know.

But when the moon their hollows lights,
And they are swept by balms of spring,
And in their glens, on starry nights,
10   The nightingales divinely sing;
And lovely notes, from shore to shore,
Across the sounds and channels pour—

Oh! then a longing like despair
Is to their farthest caverns sent;
15   For surely once, they feel, we were
Parts of a single continent!
Now round us spreads the watery plain—
Oh might our marges meet again!

Who ordered, that their longing's fire
20   Should be, as soon as kindled, cooled?
Who renders vain their deep desire?
A God, a God their severance ruled!
And bade betwixt their shores to be
The unplumbed, salt, estranging sea.

---

**1. enisled** (in īld') *adj.*: Isolated, as if placed on an
island.

## THINKING ABOUT THE SELECTION

### Recalling

1. Where and how, according to lines 1–4, do "we mortal millions live"?
2. (a) According to lines 7–14, what sights and sounds seem to trigger "a longing like despair"? (b) What true cause for this longing is explained in lines 15–18?
3. According to the last stanza, who ordered that this longing's "fire" be "cooled"?

### Interpreting

4. To what or whom do you think Arnold is comparing the islands?
5. What human condition is Arnold lamenting in this poem?
6. (a) Who do you suppose the "god" mentioned in line 22 might be? (b) What evidence do you have that this is not a "good" god?

### Applying

7. John Donne wrote, "No man is an island entire of itself; every man is a piece of the continent, a part of the main." Arnold's "Yes!" at the beginning of this poem seems to be a flat contradiction of Donne's view. Which poet's view do you agree with more? Why?

## ANALYZING LITERATURE

### Creating Imagery and Mood

An **image** is a word or phrase that appeals to one or more of the five senses. Poets string together images to create a particular **mood,** or emotional response in the reader. In "To Marguerite—Continued," the dominant imagery is intended to help the reader form a mental picture of islands in a vast ocean. Arnold contrasts this imagery, however, with images of springtime in the second stanza.

1. What mood does Arnold establish with the island imagery in the first stanza? How do the sounds of the words themselves contribute to this mood?
2. What mood is suggested by the springtime images in the second stanza? How does the third stanza destroy this mood? How does this intentional undermining of a positive mood fit in with the theme of the poem?

## THINKING AND WRITING

### Writing About Imagery and Mood

The image of an island is an almost perfect vehicle for suggesting a mood of loneliness and, in the case of Arnold's poem, for a commentary on human isolation. Consider other images Arnold might have chosen that would have created a similar mood and been equally well suited to his theme. Make notes on one such image and on the senses to which it would appeal. Then write a brief poem or prose narrative that carries the message of "To Marguerite—Continued." When you revise, make sure you have used as many descriptive words as you can to enhance the vividness of your imagery and to sharpen the focus of the piece's mood.

# Self-Dependence

Matthew Arnold

Weary of myself, and sick of asking
What I am, and what I ought to be,
At this vessel's prow I stand, which bears me
Forwards, forwards, o'er the starlit sea.

5   And a look of passionate desire
O'er the sea and to the stars I send:
"Ye who from my childhood up have calmed me,
Calm me, ah, compose me to the end!

"Ah, once more," I cried, "ye stars, ye waters,
10  On my heart your mighty charm renew;
Still, still let me, as I gaze upon you,
Feel my soul becoming vast like you!"

From the intense, clear, star-sown vault of heaven,
Over the lit sea's unquiet way,
15  In the rustling night air came the answer:
"Wouldst thou *be* as these are? *Live* as they.

"Unaffrighted by the silence round them,
Undistracted by the sights they see,
These demand not that the things without them
20  Yield them love, amusement, sympathy.

"And with joy the stars perform their shining,
And the sea its long moon-silvered roll;
For self-poised they live, nor pine with noting
All the fever of some differing soul.

25  "Bounded by themselves, and unregardful
In what state God's other works may be,
In their own tasks all their powers pouring,
These attain the mighty life you see."

O air-born voice! long since, severely clear,
30  A cry like thine in mine own heart I hear:
"Resolve to be thyself; and know that he,
Who finds himself, loses his misery!"

## THINKING ABOUT THE SELECTION

### Recalling

1. (a) What emotional state do we find the speaker in at the poem's beginning? (b) Where does the speaker say he is standing and going?
2. (a) What does the poet ask of the sea and the stars? (b) What answer does he receive in line 16?
3. What characteristics of the sea and stars enable them to "attain the mighty life" the speaker so admires?
4. What cry does the speaker finally hear in his own heart?
5. Why do you think the poet calls this poem "Self-Dependence," not "Independence"?

### Interpreting

6. (a) In your own words, identify the problem that Arnold presents in the first two lines of the poem. (b) Identify the solution offered in the last two lines.
7. Lines 7–12 mention the speaker's childhood. What does the passage imply that the speaker has lost?
8. What do you suppose is the source of the "air-born voice" in the poem?
9. What is meant by "the fever of some differing soul" in line 24?

### Applying

10. According to lines 19–20, nature is self-dependent because it does not require love, amusement, or sympathy. Do you think it is possible for human beings to attain such self-dependence? Explain your answer.

## ANALYZING LITERATURE

### Using Figurative Language

**Figurative language** is language not to be taken at face value. Many devices used by poets fall into the category of figurative language. In one such device, apostrophe, the poet directly addresses an absent human being or some object or idea. In personification, another device, human qualities are assigned to a nonhuman object. Both of these devices, or figures of speech, are used by Arnold in "Self-Dependence."

1. In which lines does Arnold use apostrophe? What or whom is he addressing?
2. What does Arnold personify in the poem? What human characteristics does he assign to these nonhuman things?
3. What reason might Arnold have had for using apostrophe and personification in this poem? How would the poem have been different had he not chosen to use these devices?

---

**Primary Source**

In "A Definition of Poetry," an essay that appeared in a volume entitled *Essays in Criticism: First Series,* Matthew Arnold explained poetry's appeal:

"The grand power of poetry is its interpretative power; by which I mean, not a power of drawing out in black and white an explanation of the mystery of the universe, but the power of so dealing with things as to awaken in us a wonderfully full, new, and intimate sense of them, and of our relations with them. When this sense is awakened in us, as to objects without us, we feel ourselves to be in contact with the essential nature of these objects, to be no longer bewildered and oppressed by them, but to have their secret, and to be in harmony with them; and this feeling calms and satisfies us as no other can . . . it illuminates man; it gives him a satisfying sense of reality; it reconciles him with himself and the universe."

# Dover Beach

## Matthew Arnold

The sea is calm tonight.
The tide is full, the moon lies fair
Upon the straits:[1] on the French coast the light
Gleams and is gone; the cliffs of England stand,
5   Glimmering and vast, out in the tranquil bay.
Come to the window, sweet is the night air!
Only, from the long line of spray

Where the sea meets the moon-blanched land,
Listen! you hear the grating roar
10  Of pebbles which the waves draw back, and fling,
At their return, up the high strand,[2]
Begin, and cease, and then again begin,
With tremulous cadence slow, and bring
The eternal note of sadness in.

15  Sophocles[3] long ago
Heard it on the Aegaean,[4] and it brought
Into his mind the turbid ebb and flow
Of human misery; we
Find also in the sound a thought,
20  Hearing it by this distant northern sea.

The Sea of Faith
Was once, too, at the full, and round earth's shore
Lay like the folds of a bright girdle furled.
But now I only hear
25  Its melancholy, long, withdrawing roar,
Retreating, to the breath
Of the night wind, down the vast edges drear
And naked shingles[5] of the world.

---

**1. straits:** Strait of Dover, between England and France.
**2. strand:** Shore.
**3. Sophocles** (säf′ ə klēz′): A Greek tragic dramatist (496?–406 B.C.)
**4. Aegaean** (ē jē′ ən): The arm of the Mediterranean Sea between Greece and Turkey.
**5. shingles** *n.*: Beaches covered with large, coarse, waterworn gravel.

Ah, love, let us be true
30 To one another! for the world, which seems
To lie before us like a land of dreams,
So various, so beautiful, so new,
Hath really neither joy, nor love, nor light,
Nor certitude, nor peace, nor help for pain;
35 And we are here as on a darkling[6] plain
Swept with confused alarms of struggle and flight,
Where ignorant armies clash by night.

---

**6. darkling** *adj.*: In the dark.

---

## THINKING ABOUT THE SELECTION

### Recalling

1. (a) According to the first stanza, what does the speaker see and hear from his window? (b) What does the "tremulous cadence" of the pebbles against the beach "bring in"? (c) Who else does the speaker say "long ago" heard this same sound?
2. What, according to lines 21–28, has happened to the "Sea of Faith?"
3. What sad reality does the speaker describe for his companion in lines 30–34?

### Interpreting

4. A symbol is a thing, person, or place that stands for something beyond itself. (a) What might the "cliffs of England" symbolize in line 4? (b) The "naked shingles of the world" in line 28? (c) "Night" in line 37?
5. (a) What effect do you think Arnold aimed to achieve by varying the length of lines and using an irregular rhyme scheme? (b) How do these poetic devices relate to the theme?
6. (a) How is the battle image in the last three lines a fitting conclusion to this poem? (b) How would you state the message of these lines in your own words?

### Applying

7. (a) To what extent does Arnold's plea to "be true to one another" in lines 29–30 provide a satisfactory solution to the "ebb and flow of human misery" he sees in the world? (b) Where does this solution break down?
8. (a) State the similarities in theme and imagery you find between this poem and "To Marguerite—Continued" on page 826. (b) State the differences.

## THINKING AND WRITING

### Writing About a Victorian Poet

From what you know of Victorian society and of Arnold's career, which attitudes of the Victorian Age do you think his poem's reflect? Consider, among other things, the effects that industrialization and science had on nineteenth-century England—both positive and negative. Comment on the effects of such forces in an essay that identifies Arnold's place as a poet of his time. When you revise, make sure you have mentioned mood and theme in your treatment of the topic.

# THOMAS HARDY

## 1840–1928

Both a novelist and a poet, Thomas Hardy is sometimes called "the last of the great Victorians." Like Matthew Arnold, Hardy held a pessimistic view of the world. In his great novels he depicted people striving against overwhelming odds within a society and universe that were uncaring. Unlike Arnold, however, who sought to improve society, Hardy remained a passive observer of the ills of his century; if he offered comfort at all, it was in the uncertain hope that the future would be at least different, if not better.

Thomas Hardy was born in Dorset, a region in southwest England noted for its agriculture and, perhaps more importantly, for its ruins which date to Anglo–Saxon and Roman times. This "Wessex," as Hardy fictionalized the region in his poems and novels, is the setting for the works that established Hardy's reputation as a writer. In *Far from the Madding Crowd* (1874), *The Return of the Native* (1878), *The Mayor of Casterbridge* (1886), *Tess of the D'Urbervilles* (1891), and his masterpiece, *Jude the Obscure* (1895), Hardy's characters move against a haunting landscape that is at once ancient and modern, starkly beautiful yet indifferent to the tragic lives of its inhabitants.

Despite the undeniable greatness of Hardy's novels, the bleak view they presented was distressing to a public who much preferred the life-affirming optimism of Tennyson and Browning. So intense, in fact, was the angry response to *Jude the Obscure* upon its publication that Hardy thought it wise to abandon the novel in favor of his first literary love, poetry. An epic verse drama about the Napoleonic Wars, *The Dynasts* (1904–1908), earned Hardy immense public acclaim. With each book of verse that he produced over the next two decades, his reputation as a man of letters grew. When he died, the world honored him by burying his ashes in the Poet's Corner of Westminster Abbey, though, as a token to the region that he loved, his heart was buried in Dorset.

Hardy's poetry marks a bridge between the Victorian Age and the Modernist movement of the twentieth century. In his use of strict meters and stanza structure, Hardy was unmistakably Victorian. One contemporary critic called him "the most fertile inventor of stanza-forms in all English literature." Another critic, however, Leonard Woolf, viewed Hardy as one of the spiritual parents of the modern generation. Hardy's use of "nonpoetic" language and odd rhymes, coupled with his fatalistic outlook, were both source and inspiration to numerous twentieth-century writers, among them such important figures as Virginia Woolf, Siegfried Sassoon, and Robert Graves.

## The Darkling Thrush; The Man He Killed; "Ah, Are You Digging on My Grave?"

**Writer's Technique**

**Simile and Metaphor.** A simile is a figure of speech that compares two unlike things, using an explicit word such as *like* or *as*. In "Love Among the Ruins," Robert Browning uses a simile to compare the towers on a castle to flames: ". . . the doomed and daring palace shot its spires/Up *like* fires. . . ." A metaphor is a figure of speech that compares two unlike things directly, without the use of an intervening word. In "London, 1802," William Wordsworth laments the sorrowful state of affairs in the England of his day by comparing the country metaphorically to a swamp: "England hath need of thee: she is a fen/Of stagnant waters. . . ." Poets use similes and metaphors to broaden the meanings of their images by making surprising connections between generally unrelated things and ideas.

**Writer's Technique**

**Irony.** Irony is the intentional difference between expectation and reality in a poem or story. In *situational irony* the outcome of an event or situation is different from what the author has led the reader to predict. By using situational irony in "'Ah, Are You Digging on My Grave?'" Hardy communicates an especially strong message to the reader.

**Writing**

Write an account of an occasion when something relatively unimportant managed to change your mood entirely. Consider possibilities such as a beautiful flower growing through a crack in the pavement of a city sidewalk. Give details of how you felt before and after the mood-changing experience.

**Primary Source**

Although Hardy had written many poems in his late twenties, his first book of poetry was not published until he was fifty-eight years old. In the thirty years remaining to him, he published nearly one thousand poems. Why would a highly successful novelist abandon prose for poetry? We know that writing novels caused him great stress, and the uproar over *Jude the Obscure* sickened him. But there was more to it. Looking back in 1918, he wrote: "A sense of the truth of poetry, of its supreme place in literature, had awakened itself in me. At the risk of ruining all my wordly prospects I dabbled in it. . . . was forced out of it. . . . It came back upon me. . . . All was of the nature of being led by a mood, without foresight, or regard to whither it led."

# The Darkling[1] Thrush

## Thomas Hardy

I leant upon a coppice gate[2]
    When Frost was specter-gray,
And Winter's dregs made desolate
    The weakening eye of day.
5  The tangled bine-stems[3] scored the sky
    Like strings of broken lyres,
And all mankind that haunted nigh
    Had sought their household fires.

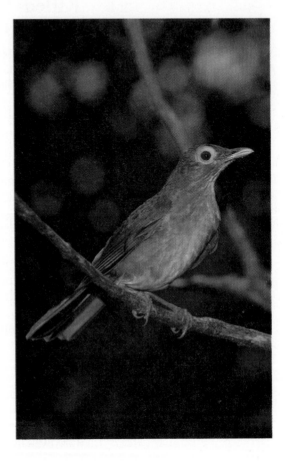

The land's sharp features seemed to be
10    The Century's corpse[4] outleant,
His crypt the cloudy canopy,
    The wind his death-lament.
The ancient pulse of germ[5] and birth
    Was shrunken hard and dry,
15  And every spirit upon earth
    Seemed fervorless as I.

At once a voice arose among
    The bleak twigs overhead
In a full-hearted evensong
20    Of joy illimited;
An aged thrush, frail, gaunt, and small,
    In blast-beruffled plume,
Had chosen thus to fling his soul
    Upon the growing gloom.

25  So little cause for carolings
    Of such ecstatic sound
Was written on terrestrial things
    Afar or nigh around,
That I could think there trembled through
30    His happy good-night air
Some blessed Hope, whereof he knew
    And I was unaware.

---

**1. darkling** *adj.*: In the dark.
**2. coppice** (kop' is) **gate:** Gate leading to a thicket, or small wood.
**3. bine-stems:** Twining stems.
**4. Century's corpse:** This poem was written on December 31, 1900,
the last day of the nineteenth century.
**5. germ:** Seed or bud.

## THINKING ABOUT THE SELECTION

### Recalling

1. In what season of the year and at what time of day is the poem set?
2. What do the "land's sharp features" suggest to the speaker?
3. (a) What does the speaker suddenly hear in the third stanza? (b) What does the speaker think about as a result of this experience?

### Interpreting

4. (a) What mood does the poet establish in the first two stanzas? (b) What images contribute to this mood? (c) With what does the poet contrast these images in the last two stanzas?
5. (a) Why do you think the poet characterizes the thrush as he does in lines 21–22? (b) What might the thrush symbolize?

### Applying

6. Depressed people react in different ways to others who display "joys illimited." The poem describes one possible reaction. What are some other possibilities?
7. Reread "To a Skylark" by Shelley on page 708. (a) What similarities are evident in the speaker's response to the thrush in this poem? (b) What differences do you detect?

## ANALYZING LITERATURE

### Using Simile and Metaphor

A **simile** is a figure of speech that compares basically dissimilar things, using such connective words as *like* or *as*. Consider the following simile from Tennyson's "The Lotos-Eaters," which makes use of the connective word *than:* "There is sweet music here that softer falls/Than petals from blown roses on the grass. . . ." A **metaphor** compares basically dissimilar things as well, but without the use of a connective word.

When, again in "The Lotos-Eaters," Tennyson refers to the ocean as "fields of barren foam," he is speaking in metaphorical terms. Similes and metaphors are used by poets to heighten the meanings of their images.

1. Identify each of the following italicized images from "The Darkling Thrush" as either a simile or a metaphor. Tell what two objects are being compared in each case.
   a. Winter's *dregs* made desolate/The *weakening eye of day*. (Lines 3–4)
   b. The tangled bine-stems *scored* the sky/Like *strings of broken lyres*. . . . (Lines 5–6)
   c. An aged thrush . . . /Had chosen thus to *fling his soul*/Upon the *growing gloom*. (Lines 21–24)
2. To what are the land's sharp features compared in lines 9–11? Explain why this metaphor is especially appropriate for the time and place in which the poem is set.

## SPEAKING AND LISTENING

### Preparing an Oral Report on Wessex

Hardy's novels and many of his poems are set in "Wessex," his fictional name for the Dorset countryside that he loved. Using reference books, biographies of Hardy, histories of the Victorian Age, and Hardy's own works, prepare a five-to-ten-minute oral report on some aspect of Hardy's Wessex. You might consider one of the following topics:
   a. the geography of Wessex (Dorset)
   b. the history of the region (prehistoric, Roman, Anglo–Saxon)
   c. Wessex life in Victorian times
   d. Wessex as depicted in Hardy's works

# The Man He Killed

Thomas Hardy

"Had he and I but met
 By some old ancient inn,
We should have sat us down to wet
 Right many a nipperkin![1]

5   "But ranged as infantry,
 And staring face to face,
I shot at him as he at me,
 And killed him in his place.

"I shot him dead because—
10  Because he was my foe,
Just so: my foe of course he was;
 That's clear enough; although

"He thought he'd 'list,[2] perhaps,
 Off-hand like—just as I—
15 Was out of work—had sold his traps—
 No other reason why.

"Yes; quaint and curious war is!
 You shoot a fellow down
You'd treat if met where any bar is,
20  Or help to half-a-crown."[3]

---

**1. nipperkin** *n.*: A small glass for beer or wine.
**2. 'list:** Enlist.
**3. half-a-crown:** A British coin.

## THINKING ABOUT THE SELECTION

### Recalling

1. (a) What does the speaker suggest might have happened had he and the other man met "by some old ancient inn"? (b) Where did they meet instead? (c) What happened?
2. What similarities between himself and the other man does the speaker note in lines 13–16?

### Interpreting

3. (a) What do you think is the significance of the quotation marks in each stanza? (b) Who do you suppose the speaker is? (c) To whom do you think the poem is addressed?
4. Why do you think the speaker hesitates at the end of line 9?
5. (a) What point about the nature of war is Hardy making in this poem? (b) In what way is war "quaint and curious," as his speaker notes in line 17?
6. Do you think Hardy is writing about a specific war or about war in general? Explain your answer.

### Applying

7. Why is it easier for an enemy to be faceless than to have a face?

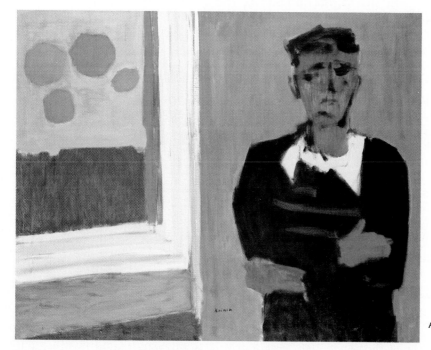

AT THE WINDOW, 1960
*Jacob Kainen*

*The Man He Killed* 837

# "Ah, Are You Digging on My Grave?"

Thomas Hardy

"Ah, are you digging on my grave
    My loved one?—planting rue?"
—"No: yesterday he went to wed
One of the brightest wealth has bred.
5  'It cannot hurt her now,' he said,
    'That I should not be true.'"

"Then who is digging on my grave?
    My nearest dearest kin?"
—"Ah, no: they sit and think, 'What use!
10  What good will planting flowers produce?
No tendance of her mound can loose
    Her spirit from Death's gin.'"[1]

"But some one digs upon my grave?
    My enemy?—prodding sly?"
15  —"Nay: when she heard you had passed the Gate
That shuts on all flesh soon or late,
She thought you no more worth her hate,
    And cares not where you lie."

"Then, who is digging on my grave?
20    Say—since I have not guessed!"
—"O it is I, my mistress dear,
Your little dog, who still lives near,
And much I hope my movements here
    Have not disturbed your rest?"

25    "Ah, yes! *You* dig upon my grave . . .
    Why flashed it not on me
That one true heart was left behind!
What feeling do we ever find
To equal among human kind
30    A dog's fidelity!"

---

**1. gin** *n.*: Trap.

"Mistress, I dug upon your grave
    To bury a bone, in case
I should be hungry near this spot
When passing on my daily trot.
35  I am sorry, but I quite forgot
    It was your resting-place."

---

## THINKING ABOUT THE SELECTION

### Recalling

1. (a) In the first stanza, who does the dead woman suspect is digging on her grave? (b) In the second stanza? (c) In the third stanza? (d) What response does she receive?
2. (a) Who in fact is doing the digging? (b) How does the woman react when she learns the answer to this question? (c) What reason does the digger give for disturbing the grave?

### Interpreting

3. (a) At what point do you begin to suspect the identity of the voice responding to the woman's questions? (b) What effect does Hardy achieve by withholding this information?
4. (a) What mood does Hardy create by having a dead person speak? (b) How does this mood change once the digger is identified?
5. What point about human vanity and self-esteem is Hardy making in this poem?

### Applying

6. (a) Of "The Darkling Thrush," "The Man He Killed," and this poem, which strikes you as the most pessimistic? (b) The least pessimistic? (c) Why?

## ANALYZING LITERATURE

### Understanding Irony

**Irony** is a purposeful contrast between expectation and reality. In "'Ah, Are You Digging on My Grave?'" Hardy uses situational irony. That is, he leads the reader to expect one kind of outcome but instead delivers another.

1. What is ironic about the voice in the last four lines of each of the first three stanzas?
2. What emotions does the dead woman express when she learns the identity of the digger? How do the digger's final words ironically alter the woman's emotional expectations?
3. Irony is often related to tone—the author's attitude toward the subject or audience. Explain how the irony in this poem is related to Hardy's pessimism and lack of sentimentality.

## THINKING AND WRITING

### Writing a Response to a Poem

In "'Ah, Are You Digging on My Grave?'" Hardy delivers pessimistic pronouncements on two different but related topics—human self-worth and human apathy. Consider your reaction to Hardy's views on these subjects by asking yourself questions such as the following. To what extent are Hardy's attitudes typical only of the era in which he lived? To what degree are tributes to the dead really tributes to the living? How thoroughly do we know the feelings others have toward us? How well do we understand our own feelings toward others? In an essay, sum up your response to the views Hardy presents. When you revise, make sure you have provided adequate support for your opinion.

# GERARD MANLEY HOPKINS

## 1844–1889

Though Gerard Manley Hopkins saw none of his work published during his lifetime, he was nevertheless the most innovative poet of the Victorian Age. Born in Essex, just outside London, Hopkins was the oldest of nine children in a well-educated and prosperous family. While still in grammar school, Hopkins began writing poetry, a practice that he maintained throughout his years at Oxford, where he also studied the classics.

It was during his third year at Oxford that Hopkins decided to become a Catholic, much to the dismay of his parents, who were devout Anglicans. Upon being accepted into the Society of Jesus in 1868, he symbolically burned his early poems, resolving "to write no more." Though he remained true to his word for the next seven years, Hopkins continued to keep detailed notebooks—as he had done ever since childhood—that recorded his fascination with words and his love of nature.

In 1874, as part of his preparation for the priesthood, Hopkins went to St. Bueno's College in Wales to study theology. There he learned to speak Welsh. He also began again to write poetry, though of a sort that was different not only from his earlier verse but from anything ever before done in English. Encouraged by a Jesuit superior, Hopkins wrote a long poem about a tragic shipwreck in which five nuns had drowned. "The Wreck of the Deutschland," apart from the great emotional power packed into it, was the first poem in which Hopkins used what he called "sprung rhythm." This is a system of versification in which accented syllables are grouped in emphatic patterns somewhat like those of Anglo-Saxon alliterative verse. The resulting meter is quite different from conventional English meter, in which accented and unaccented syllables alternate in regular patterns.

In 1877, the year he was ordained a priest, Hopkins wrote some of his best and best-known poems, including "God's Grandeur," "Pied Beauty," and "Hurrahing in Harvest." Like most of Hopkins's poems, the goal of these was to reveal and glorify the individual essence—or "inscape," as he called it—of everything in nature.

Hopkins served as a parish priest and missionary preacher among the poor in London, Liverpool, and Glasgow. Despite his total dedication to his calling, long hours and a tendency toward perfectionism left him depressed and in poor health. He died of typhoid fever one month before his forty-fifth birthday.

# GUIDE FOR INTERPRETING

## God's Grandeur; Hurrahing in Harvest; Pied Beauty; Spring and Fall

**Rhythm and Rhyme.** *Rhythm* is the pattern of stressed and unstressed syllables in a line of poetry. Every poem has rhythm, but not every poem has meter, a regular, predictable rhythmic pattern made up of units called "feet." Each foot consists of one stressed syllable and a fixed number of unstressed syllables. In the 1870's, Gerard Manley Hopkins created a new kind of rhythm that resembled natural speech. In *sprung rhythm,* as Hopkins termed his creation, the number of unstressed syllables varies from foot to foot. Precisely which syllables receive stress, moreover, is not accidental but carefully planned to help convey meaning and emotion. Finally, sprung rhythm calls for the innovative use of language, for the combining of existing words, the extending of word meanings, the invention of new words, and the elimination of words that do not add to the desired effect.

*Rhyme* is the repetition of the same or similar sounds in two or more words. When rhyme occurs at the ends of lines in a poem it is called *end rhyme.* When rhyme occurs within a single line it is called *internal rhyme.* Again breaking with tradition, Hopkins used both types of rhyme, as well as *approximate rhyme,* or rhyme that relates words similar in function or meaning.

Write the name of a prized possession, much-loved pastime, or favorite season at the top of a sheet of paper. Write whatever words and phrases come to mind. Read over what you have written. Note phrases and words whose *sounds* seem to relate to your topic.

In his work among the poor, Hopkins no doubt encountered scenes such as this one described by a fellow worker:

> I attended a family of thirteen—twelve of whom had typhus fever, without a bed in the *cellar,* without straw or timber shavings—frequent substitutes. They lay on the floor, and so crowded that I could scarcely pass between them . . . there is only one supply of water for all its inhabitants and it occupies a good deal of time to procure it and carry it back to the different rooms, where it soon becomes covered with black scum . . . One woman informed me that her husband lay dead, and that she could not obtain water without the greatest difficulty to wash his "rags" . . . the deaths . . . were for that year 36, or 1 death to 14.6 persons.

# God's Grandeur

## Gerard Manley Hopkins

The world is charged with the grandeur of God.
    It will flame out, like shining from shook foil;[1]
    It gathers to a greatness, like the ooze of oil
Crushed.[2] Why do men then now not reck his rod?[3]
Generations have trod, have trod, have trod;
    And all is seared with trade; bleared, smeared with toil;
    And wears man's smudge and shares man's smell: the
        soil
Is bare now, nor can foot feel, being shod.

And for all this, nature is never spent;
10    There lives the dearest freshness deep down things;
And though the last lights off the black West went
    Oh, morning, at the brown brink eastward, springs—
Because the Holy Ghost over the bent
    World broods with warm breast and with ah! bright
        wings.

---

**1. foil** *n*.: Tinsel.
**2. crushed:** Squeezed from olives.
**3. reck his rod:** Heed God's authority.

---

## THINKING ABOUT THE SELECTION

1. According to this poem, with what is the world charged?

### Recalling

2. (a) According to lines 5–8, what has human-kind done to God's grandeur? (b) According to line 9, what difference has man's behavior made? Explain.

3. (a) What is the Holy Ghost compared to in the last two lines? (b) What verb describes what it does? (c) What two adjectives describe it?

## Interpreting

4. What kind of emotional response do you suppose Hopkins hoped to awaken in the reader of lines 1–4? Do you think he succeeds?

5. What do you think is the meaning of the question raised in line 4?

6. (a) What effect do you think the poet hoped to achieve by the repetition in line 5? (b) By the alliteration, or consonant repetition, of *sm* in lines 6–7?

**BIRD'S NEST**
*Ros. W. Jenkins*
Warrington Museum and Art Gallery

7. "God's Grandeur" is a sonnet, a poetic form with very specific rhyme requirements. Note, for instance, the number of words rhyming with *God* and *foil* in the first eight lines.
(a) Why do you suppose Hopkins chose so rigid a poetic form for this poem? In what way does the form reinforce his message? (b) What effect do you think Hopkins wanted to achieve by the sounds of the words *ooze, oil,* and *crushed* in lines 3 and 4? By the repetition of *d* sounds in line 10? Of *b* sounds in the last two lines?

## Applying

8. (a) Although Hopkins notes many abuses in this poem, do you think his overall outlook is optimistic or pessimistic? Explain. (b) How would you define the diiference between an optimist and a pessimist?

## THINKING ABOUT THE SELECTION

### Recalling

1. (a) In line 4, what does the speaker see on the ground? (b) In the sky? (c) How are these two things alike for the speaker?
2. (a) What does the speaker do in line 5? (b)

What does he see?
3. According to the last stanza, what happens to someone who beholds nature's beauties?

### Interpreting

4. How would you describe the speaker's emotional state in the poem? Support your answer

# Hurrahing in Harvest

## Gerard Manley Hopkins

Summer ends now; now, barbarous in beauty, the stooks[1]
  arise
    Around; up above, what wind-walks! what lovely
      behavior
    Of silk-sack clouds! has wilder, wilful-wavier
Meal-drift molded ever and melted across skies?

5  I walk, I lift up, I lift up heart, eyes,
    Down all that glory in the heavens to glean our Savior;
    And, éyes, héart, what looks, what lips yet gave you a
Rapturous love's greeting of realer, of rounder replies?

And the azurous hung hills are his world-wielding shoulder
10    Majestic—as a stallion stalwart, very-violet-sweet!—
These things, these things were here and but the beholder
    Wanting; which two when they once meet,
The heart rears wings bold and bolder
    And hurls for him, O half hurls earth for him off under
      his feet.

---

**1. stooks** *n.*: Sheaves of corn stacked together on end to dry.

**HARVEST FIELD WITH GLEANERS, HAYWOOD, HEREFORDSHIRE**
*George Robert Lewis*
*The Tate Gallery, London*

with quotations.
5. In your own words, what question does the speaker ask in lines 7–8?
6. (a) Who is "him" in line 14? (b) What does the speaker say is happening to "him?"

## Applying

7. (a) In what ways is this poem more typical of the Romantic than the Victorian period? (b) In what ways is it typical of neither?

# Pied Beauty

## Gerard Manley Hopkins

Glory be to God for dappled things—
    For skies of couple-color as a brinded[1] cow;
      For rose-moles all in stipple[2] upon trout that swim;
Fresh-firecoal chestnut-falls;[3] finches' wings;
5      Landscape plotted and pieced—fold, fallow, and plow;
      And áll trádes, their gear and tackle and trim.

All things counter,[4] original, spare, strange;
    Whatever is fickle, freckled (who knows how?)
    With swift, slow; sweet, sour; adazzle, dim;
10  He fathers-forth whose beauty is past change:
      Praise him.

---

**1. brinded** *adj.*: Having a gray or tawny coat streaked with a darker color.
**2. stipple** *n.*: Dots or small spots.
**3. fresh-firecoal chestnut-falls:** Roasted chestnuts.
**4. counter:** Contrary.

## THINKING ABOUT THE SELECTION

### Recalling

1. What five "dappled things" does the speaker name in the first five lines?
2. What does the speaker ask the reader to do in line 11?

### Interpreting

3. (a) What do you think is the meaning of "couple-color" in line 2? (b) Why do you think Hopkins chose this, rather than a more conventional way, of expressing the thought?
4. What difference can you see between the "dappled things" of the first stanza and the sorts of things hinted at in the second?
5. What significance do you attach to the words in parentheses in line 8?
6. What do you think is meant by the phrase "whose beauty is past change" in line 10?

### Applying

7. Compare "Pied Beauty" with "God's Grandeur." (a) In what ways are the two poems similar? (b) How are they different in their outlook on the world as altered by humans? (c) How might Hopkins have explained this apparent paradox, or self-contradiction.

# Spring and Fall
## To a Young Child

Gerard Manley Hopkins

A MOTHER AND CHILD ON THE ISLE OF WIGHT
*James Collinson*
*Yale Center for British Art*

Márgarét, are you grieving
Over Goldengrove unleaving?
Leáves, like the things of man, you
With your fresh thoughts care for, can you?
5   Ah! ás the heart grows older
It will come to such sights colder
By and by, nor spare a sigh
Though worlds of wanwood[1] leafmeal[2] lie;
And yet you will weep and know why.
10  Now no matter, child, the name:
Sórrow's spríngs áre the same.
Nor mouth had, no nor mind, expressed
What heart heard of, ghost[3] guessed:
15  It ís the blight man was born for,
It is Margaret you mourn for.

---

1. **wanwood** (wän′ wŏŏd): Pale wood.
2. **leafmeal:** Ground-up decomposed leaves.
3. **ghost:** Spirit.

---

## THINKING ABOUT THE SELECTION

### Recalling

1. According to the speaker, in what way will Margaret change as she grows older?

### Interpreting

2. What do you think is meant by "fresh thoughts" in line 4? By "worlds of wanwood leafmeal" in line 8?
3. What is the theme?

### Applying

4. (a) What is the relevance of the title "Spring and Fall?" (b) What might "spring" stand for?

(c) What second meaning of "fall" might be relevant to the speaker's advice to the child?

## THINKING AND WRITING

### Writing Margaret's Reply

Imagine that you are Margaret. Try to put yourself in the position of a child who has just suffered a grave disappointment over something an adult would find trivial. Now write a response to the adult speaker of "Spring and Fall" that gives the child's view of the world and defends the child's right to his or her feelings, however inappropriate they might seem to an adult. Your response may take the form of either a poem or prose piece, but it should offer some insight on how children view the world of grownups.

# A. E. HOUSMAN

## 1859–1936

A leading classical scholar of his age, Alfred Edward Housman devoted his life to teaching and translating the great Latin poets. Yet, most modern readers who know Housman know him as the author of three slender volumes of poetry that are as romantic and melancholy as any ever written.

Housman was born in Worcestershire, the oldest of seven children in a middle-class family. His childhood came to an end when his mother died, following a long illness, on his twelfth birthday. Money became a problem for the family, but Housman, a bright and resourceful young man, won a scholarship to Oxford, where he studied classical literature and philosophy. Though he was a brilliant student, his intolerance of any error by himself or others left him with few friends.

While at Oxford, Housman fell secretly in love with a person who was interested only in his friendship. His despair over this relationship combined with his unhappy teen years seems to have darkened the rest of Housman's life and to have given his poetry its bitter undertones.

Upon leaving Oxford, Housman went to work in the Patent Office. Determined to prove himself in the classics, he studied Greek and Latin at night and wrote scholarly articles for academic journals. In 1892, his hard-earned reputation as an expert in his field led to his appointment as professor of Latin at University College in London.

Though Housman spent the balance of his life engaged in scholarly pursuits, he found time to write poetry. His first and most famous collection of verse, *A Shropshire Lad* (1896), has as its fictitious narrator a homesick farmboy living in the city. In simple, precise language and brisk, regular rhythms, Housman focuses on the grim realities and fleeting joys of life. Housman paid for the first publication of *A Shropshire Lad* out of his own pocket, but it soon became highly popular. More than twenty-five years later, *Last Poems* (1922) was an instant best seller. After Housman's death, his brother Laurence edited and published *More Poems* (1936).

In a famous lecture that he delivered in 1933, Housman, who worked at projecting a public image as an emotionless intellectual, stated that the goal of poetry is to "transfuse emotion," not to transmit thought. A well-written poem, he maintained, makes a physical impact on the reader, like a shiver down the spine or a punch in the stomach. It is because of this impact in much of his own work that the best of A. E. Housman's poems have been marked for immortality.

# GUIDE FOR INTERPRETING

## To an Athlete Dying Young; Loveliest of Trees; When I Was One-and-Twenty; With Rue My Heart Is Laden

**Writer's Technique**

**Theme.** The theme in a literary work is the insight into life that it communicates to the reader. One of several recurring themes in Housman's verse is the bittersweet notion that youth is beautiful but that, like beauty itself, it passes too quickly. Even in those upbeat instances where Housman is describing happiness and glory, the reader senses an undercurrent of doom and a concern with the courage and endurance that will be required to face it. The charming, easy rhymes in his poems contrast sharply with his melancholy themes, which reflect both the pessimism of the late Victorian Age and the sadness in his own life.

**Commentary**

Housman led a life of harsh self-discipline and solitary habits: By the age of twenty-seven, he had fully embraced the monk-like seclusion that would characterize the rest of his life. Although a thorough teacher, he was distant and humorless. Much respected for his keen intelligence and devotion to his duties, neither his students nor colleagues were comfortable with him, and he had few close friends. By the time he was in his mid-forties, A *Shropshire Lad* had become a best seller. But despite his fame and affluence, he still spent his evenings working on his studies or reading detective stories, especially those of Conan Doyle, which were then very popular. His scholarly excellence was rewarded in 1911 when he was made Kennedy Professor of Latin at Cambridge University and a Fellow at Trinity College. He soon established the same reputation in his new positions as he had in his old: meticulous with his work, sour and surly with people. His rooms at Trinity were as grim as the man: The only decoration was a large tortoise shell; there was not even a comfortable chair. He refused the many honors and awards he was offered, including the royal Order of Merit; he would be condescended to by no one, not even the king. How do you see the man in his work?

**Writing**

Reflect on a topic to which you have a strong response—both positive and negative. Possibilities might include the promise of the future mixed with its uncertainties, or bittersweet memories of a favorite afterschool gathering spot that no longer exists. Freewrite, attempting to capture—using vivid details—the happy and sad sides of your topic.

# To an Athlete Dying Young

A. E. Housman

The time you won your town the race
We chaired you through the marketplace;
Man and boy stood cheering by,
And home we brought you shoulder-high.

5    Today, the road all runners come,
Shoulder-high we bring you home,
And set you at your threshold down,
Townsman of a stiller town.

Smart lad, to slip betimes away
10   From fields where glory does not stay
And early though the laurel[1] grows
It withers quicker than the rose.

Eyes the shady night has shut
Cannot see the record cut,
15   And silence sounds no worse than cheers
After earth has stopped the ears:

Now you will not swell the rout
Of lads that wore their honors out,
Runners whom renown outran
20   And the name died before the man.

So set, before its echoes fade,
The fleet foot on the sill of shade.
And hold to the low lintel up
The still-defended challenge cup.

25   And round that early-laureled head
Will flock to gaze the strengthless dead,
And find unwithered on its curls
The garland briefer than a girl's.

---

**1. laurel:** A symbol of victory.

## THINKING ABOUT THE SELECTION
### Recalling

1. (a) In what sport did the athlete excel? (b) What did the townspeople do to show their admiration for the athlete following the contest mentioned in the first stanza?
2. (a) Where is the athlete "today"? (b) What does the speaker say the athlete will not have to be concerned about "now"?

### Interpreting

3. (a) What visual image presented in the first stanza is repeated in the second stanza? (b) How is the meaning of the image different in the second stanza. (c) How does this difference affect the mood, or reader's emotional reaction?
4. (a) How would you summarize the speaker's comments in lines 9–20? (b) What is meant by "the name died before the man"?
5. (a) In what way is the challenge cup mentioned in line 24 "still-defended"? (b) What double meaning might the poet have intended for the word "still"?

### Applying

6. Tell whether you agree or disagree with the speaker in this poem. Give reasons for your answer.
7. What advice would you give an athlete who is concerned about growing old and losing his or her "glory"?

## ANALYZING LITERATURE
### Finding the Theme

The **theme** in a poem is its insight into life. A poem's theme should not be confused with its subject, which can usually be described in a single word, such as "love" or "war." Rather, the theme reflects the author's thoughts on that subject—for instance, "love is blind," "love is a battlefield." Since poets seldom state the theme directly, the reader must *infer,* or figure out, the theme from the events and descriptions in the poem. One effective way of doing this is by constructing a series of meaningful questions that take into account the facts of the poem, as well as such features as its setting, tone, and mood. Answer the following questions on "To an Athlete Dying Young." Then state the poem's theme.

1. (a) Who is the "main character" in the poem? (b) What is the character's main accomplishment?
2. (a) What has happened to this character that is the occasion for this poem? (b) What details in the second stanza alert you to this happening? (c) What is the speaker's tone—that is, what seems to be his true feelings toward this happening?
3. (a) What does the speaker assume in lines 9–20 might have happened to the main character in later years? (b) On what evidence does the speaker most likely base this assumption?
4. (a) What generalization might be made about the relationship between accomplishment and praise? (b) To what other areas of life might this generalization apply?
5. What is the speaker's attitude toward life and death?
6. What is the theme of the poem?

# Loveliest of Trees

A. E. Housman

Loveliest of trees, the cherry now
Is hung with bloom along the bough,
And stands about the woodland ride
Wearing white for Eastertide.

5  Now, of my threescore years and ten,
Twenty will not come again,
And take from seventy springs a score,
It only leaves me fifty more.

And since to look at things in bloom
10  Fifty springs are little room,
About the woodlands I will go
To see the cherry hung with snow.

## THINKING ABOUT THE SELECTION

### Recalling

1. (a) During what season of the year is the poem set? (b) How can you tell?
2. What is the speaker of the poem doing?
3. (a) How old is the speaker? (b) To what age does he expect to live?

### Interpreting

4. What realization does the speaker come to in the second stanza?
5. In the third stanza the speaker makes a resolution for himself. Do you think this resolution has to do only with trees? Explain.

### Applying

6. (a) What is the theme of the poem? (b) Judging from this theme, what would you guess is the speaker/poet's attitude toward an afterlife?

# When I Was One-and-Twenty

A. E. Housman

When I was one-and-twenty
    I heard a wise man say,
"Give crowns and pounds and guineas[1]
    But not your heart away;
5 Give pearls away and rubies
    But keep your fancy free."
But I was one-and-twenty,
    No use to talk to me.

When I was one-and-twenty
10     I heard him say again,
"The heart out of the bosom
    Was never given in vain;
'Tis paid with sighs a plenty
    And sold for endless rue."
15 And I am two-and-twenty,
    And oh, 'tis true, 'tis true.

---

**1. crowns . . . guineas:** Denominations of money.

## THINKING ABOUT THE SELECTION

### Recalling

1. (a) What does the speaker say he "heard a wise man say" when he was "one-and-twenty?" (b) What, according to lines 7–8, was the speaker's reaction to this advice?
2. What is the speaker's comment in the last line on the wise man's second piece of advice?

### Interpreting

3. With what is the speaker/poet equating the age of one-and-twenty in this poem? Explain your answer.
4. (a) What is significant about the fact that the speaker has twice received advice? (b) How is this relevant in light of the poem's theme?
5. What do you suppose happened to the speaker that changed his mind?

### Applying

6. What event in Housman's life may have prompted the writing of this poem?

# With Rue My Heart Is Laden

A. E. Housman

With rue my heart is laden
    For golden friends I had,
For many a rose-lipped maiden
    And many a lightfoot lad.

5  By brooks too broad for leaping
    The lightfoot boys are laid;
The rose-lipped girls are sleeping
    In fields where roses fade.

---

## THINKING ABOUT THE SELECTION

### Recalling

1. What has happened to the speaker's friends?

### Interpreting

2. What is meant by "golden" in line 2?
3. What do the adjectives "rose-lipped" and "lightfoot" suggest about the speaker's memories of his friends?
4. (a) What do you suppose is the meaning of the phrase "too broad for leaping" in line 5? (b) By the phrase "where roses fade" in line 8?
5. The subjects of this poem are youth and beauty. What statement is the poet making about those subjects?

### Applying

6. In what ways do you think young people and adults view the passage of time differently?

## THINKING AND WRITING

### Responding to Criticism

William Archer, a critic and contemporary of Housman, wrote in a review of *A Shropshire Lad* that "there is nothing whining about Mr. Housman's melancholy" in his verse. "Rather," the critic continued, "it is bracing, invigorating . . ." In an essay, state whether you agree or disagree with this assessment. Quote freely from the poems to support your view and to defend against the opposing view. In either case, respond to Archer's criticism as, itself, a product of the Victorian Age. Ask yourself what difference there might have been in his statements had they not been made at a time when the public was up in arms about the writings of such pessimists as Thomas Hardy. When you revise, make sure you have provided adequate support for your opinions.

# Other Victorian Poets

## Elizabeth Barrett Browning (1806–1861)

One of the best-known woman poets of her own or any time, Elizabeth Barrett was the oldest of twelve children in an upper middle class family. She received no formal education, but a zest for knowledge enabled her to learn eight languages on her own.

Barrett began writing poetry as a child and, by the time she reached adulthood, had published four immensely popular volumes of verse. Though she met many of the leading writers of the day, a longtime illness made her something of a recluse.

Then, in 1845, she began to receive letters from the poet Robert Browning, who, after five months of correspondence, paid her a visit. Her doctors suggested that she spend the winter of 1846 in Italy, which offered a warmer climate. When her stern father refused to allow her to leave, she and Browning eloped there.

In 1849 their son was born, whom they nicknamed "Pen." A year later, Mrs. Browning revised and published *Sonnets from the Portuguese,* a sequence of 44 love poems written to her husband. *Aurora Leigh* (1857), a love story in blank verse, was completed during the second of two trips she made back to London.

## Dante Gabriel Rossetti (1828–1882)

A successful painter as well as a poet, Dante Gabriel Rossetti was the son of an Italian patriot who had been exiled from his homeland. Growing up in a bilingual household under the watchful eye of parents who, themselves, were devoted to literature and the arts, Rossetti began writing plays and poetry at the age of five.

In 1837 he was sent to King's College School, but when money became a problem for the family, the young Rossetti was encouraged to pursue a more lucrative career as a painter. He was admitted to the Royal Academy, a prestigious art school, but could not adjust to a structured education and left after two years to study privately.

At twenty Rossetti founded the Pre-Raphaelite Brotherhood, a group of painters and writers who favored a return to the styles of artists who had lived before the time of the Italian Renaissance artist Raphael. In 1860 he married Elizabeth Siddal, a model who had posed for him. She became the subject of many of the poems in *The House of Life* (1870), a sequence of sonnets reflecting different aspects of love. When his wife died, he buried his poems with her, but later had them retrieved.

Rossetti's poems, like his paintings, are filled—sometimes to the point of crowding—with color and pictorial detail. The despair in his later poems anticipated the pessimism of many modern writers.

# GUIDE FOR INTERPRETING

## Sonnet 43; Silent Noon

**The Sonnet.** A sonnet is a lyric poem that has fourteen lines and a fixed rhyme scheme. Of the two most common forms of sonnet, the Italian and English, the Italian is the older, dating back to the thirteenth century. The form, also known as the Petrarchan sonnet, reached its height in the hands of Francesco Petrarch (1304–1374), who wrote over three hundred sonnets to a woman named Laura. The Italian sonnet has two parts—the *octave,* consisting of eight lines, which asks a question or raises a problem; and the *sestet,* consisting of six lines, which answers the question or resolves the problem. Though the rhyme scheme of the sestet varies, the octave always has the rhyme scheme *abbaabba.*

Despite occasional lapses in its popularity, the sonnet has surfaced again and again throughout the ages as the poetic form of choice among poets. In the nineteenth century, Elizabeth Barrett Browning and Dante Gabriel Rossetti, writing independently, revived the *sonnet cycle,* a series of sonnets loosely connected by subject or theme. Both of these cycles treat, in their own fashion, the subject of love.

## Writing

Write the word *love* at the top of a sheet of paper. Then write ten complete sentences that explore your thoughts and feelings on the subject. Avoid mentioning specific names of individuals. When you have finished writing, read over your work and decide which of your impressions might be unique to you and could, therefore, be expanded into a poem or series of personal reflections.

## Primary Source

Although the numerous reviews for Elizabeth Barrett Browning's 1844 *Poems* were complimentary, perhaps she would have been most pleased, had she been aware of it, by the praise of two teenage brothers, Dante Gabriel and William Michael Rossetti. Michael later recalled that "the poems of Miss Elizabeth Barrett Browning first caught the attention of my brother and myself. We revelled in them with profuse delight. Our perceptions of poetry were not then of the totally uncritical order, and we found some things which we thought faulty, both in excess and in defect; but in the main our pleasure was unalloyed. 'The Drama of Exile,' 'The Rhyme of the Duchess May,' 'The Lost Bower,' 'Lady Geraldine's Courtship,' 'A Vision of Poets,' and numerous other pieces, held us spellbound. In the course of two or three years we must have read some of these more than half-a-hundred times over; and either of us . . . could repeat them with great exactness."

# Sonnet 43

## Elizabeth Barrett Browning

How do I love thee? Let me count the ways.
I love thee to the depth and breadth and height
My soul can reach, when feeling out of sight
For the ends of Being and ideal Grace.
5  I love thee to the level of every day's
Most quiet need, by sun and candlelight.
I love thee freely, as men strive for Right;
I love thee purely, as they turn from Praise.
I love thee with the passion put to use
10  In my old griefs, and with my childhood's faith.
I love thee with a love I seemed to lose
With my lost saints—I love thee with the breath,
Smiles, tears, of all my life!—and, if God choose,
I shall but love thee better after death.

---

## THINKING ABOUT THE SELECTION

### Recalling

1. (a) What question does the speaker ask? (b) How many answers to this question does she give?
2. What does the speaker say she will do "if God choose"?

### Interpreting

3. (a) What do you think the speaker means in lines 9–10 by "with the passion put to use/In my old griefs"? (b) By "with a love I seemed to lose/With my lost saints" in lines 11–12?
4. What effect is created by the repetition of the words "I love thee" throughout the poem?

### Applying

5. Consult the list of ten sentences you wrote for the Writing assignment on page 857. What thoughts and feelings of your own might you add to those expressed by Elizabeth Barrett Browning in this poem?

## ANALYZING LITERATURE

### Understanding a Sonnet

A **sonnet** is a fourteen-line lyric poem with a fixed pattern of rhyme. The Italian sonnet has two parts. The first part, the octave, poses a question or presents a problem in eight lines. The second part, the sestet, answers that question or problem in six lines.

1. What line in the octet (first eight lines) ends with an irregular rhyming word? How might this irregularity be explained?
2. What is the rhyme scheme of the sestet?
3. Based on what you have learned about the Italian sonnet, tell in what critical way Sonnet 43 violates the rules. How does this violation help the poem to deliver its message?

# Silent Noon

## Dante Gabriel Rossetti

Your hands lie open in the long fresh grass—
    The finger-points look through like rosy blooms:
    Your eyes smile peace. The pasture gleams and glooms
'Neath billowing skies that scatter and amass.
5  All round our nest, far as the eye can pass,
    Are golden kingcup fields with silver edge
    Where the cow-parsley skirts the hawthorn hedge.
'Tis visible silence, still as the hourglass.

    Deep in the sun-searched growths the dragonfly
10  Hangs like a blue thread loosened from the sky—
    So this winged hour is dropped to us from above.
Oh! clasp we to our hearts, for deathless dower,
This close-companioned inarticulate hour
    When twofold silence was the song of love.

"WEY" CHINTZ
*William Morris*
*The Granger Collection*

## THINKING ABOUT THE SELECTION

### Recalling

1. (a) Where are the speaker and his companion? (b) What time of day is it? (c) What time of year? (d) How can you tell?

### Interpreting

2. (a) What do you think the speaker means when he says the "pasture gleams and glooms"? (b) How might this detail be related to his training as an artist?
3. Is it possible for silence to be "visible," as the speaker states in line 8? Explain.
4. How do you explain the paradox in the last line?

### Applying

5. Under what circumstances does silence have an effect opposite to the one described? What details might the poet have used to "paint" an impression of that kind of silence?

# BIOGRAPHIES

## George Meredith (1828–1909)

Meredith was born in the coastal city of Portsmouth. When his first volume of verse, *Poems* (1851), failed to sell, he turned to fiction but, again, enjoyed little success. It was not until the publication of *The Egoist* in 1879 that Meredith received the public recognition he had been seeking. Though Meredith is known primarily as a novelist, he always thought of himself first and foremost as a poet. Indeed, his best poems evoke the power of nature and the joy of humanity's relationship to it.

## Christina Rossetti (1830–1894)

The younger sister of the poet Dante Gabriel Rossetti, Christina Rossetti is considered by some critics to be the greatest woman poet in all of English literature. In 1871 Rossetti fell victim to a disease that disfigured her and left her an invalid. In spite of this, she continued to write, turning out in the space of her lifetime five collections of verse, a book of poems for children, a book of prayers, and a book of religious meditations. Her simple lyrical poems exhibit a grace and precision that are rare.

## Rudyard Kipling (1865–1936)

Rudyard Kipling was equally skillful as a poet and writer of prose. Born in Bombay, India, to English parents, Kipling was placed, when he was five, in a foster home in England. Kipling returned to India in 1882 to work as a journalist. During the next seven years, he published a number of witty poems and stories, and by the time he visited London in 1890, he was a celebrity. Kipling wrote several books that have since become children's classics: *The Jungle Books* (1895), *Captains Courageous* (1897), and *Kim* (1905).

## Robert Louis Stevenson (1850–1894)

Robert Louis Stevenson was born in Edinburgh, Scotland. An essayist, poet, dramatist, and novelist, he is perhaps best remembered for such thrilling tales of suspense and adventure as *The Strange Case of Dr. Jekyll and Mr. Hyde, The Master of Ballantrae, Kidnapped,* and *Treasure Island.* Traveling constantly for his health, Stevenson died in Samoa, where he was buried "under the wide and starry sky."

# GUIDE FOR INTERPRETING

## Lucifer in Starlight; A Birthday; Recessional; Requiem

**Imagery.** Imagery is language, often in the form of poetic details, that appeals to one or more of the five senses. Poets use imagery to communicate experience vividly, to make you see, feel, hear, smell, and taste the ideas they present to you in words. Since imagery is often visual, images are often thought of as "word pictures." The Pre-Raphaelite poets included images in their poems that would ordinarily go unnoticed, such as shadows on a wall or the scraping sound of chairs pushed across a floor. The poems of George Meredith and Christina Rossetti show influences of the Pre-Rapaelite movement. The sense-related details and elaborate word pictures in their verse provide a sharp contrast to the more stately images of Kipling's "Recessional."

The Victorian tendency toward self-congratulation was especially evident at the Great Exhibition of 1851, the first international public display of commercial products. The Exhibition was hugely successful: Queen Victoria, for example, visited it forty-four times that summer. Addressing a dinner at the Exhibition, Albert, the Prince Consort, voiced the nation's optimism when he said:

> Nobody who has paid any attention to the peculiar features of our present era will doubt for a moment that we are living at a period of the most wonderful transition which tends rapidly to accomplish that Great End, to which, indeed, all history points—the realization of the unity of mankind . . .
>
> The distances which separated the different nations and parts of the globe are rapidly vanishing before the achievements of modern invention . . . thought is communicated with the rapidity, and even by the power of lightning. On the other hand, the great principle of the division of labor—which may be called the moving power of civilization, is being extended to all branches of science, industry and art.

How might the tone and content of Albert's speech move Kipling to write a poem such as "Recessional"?

Try to recall an experience you had that created vivid sense impressions, such as weathering a violent storm, or attempting to sleep on a blisteringly hot night without the aid of a fan or air conditioner. Freewrite about your experience.

# Lucifer in Starlight

## George Meredith

On a starred night Prince Lucifer uprose.
Tired of his dark dominion swung the fiend
Above the rolling ball in cloud part screened,
Where sinners hugged their specter of repose.
5   Poor prey to his hot fit of pride were those.
And now upon his western wing he leaned,
Now his huge bulk o'er Afric's sands careened,
Now the black planet shadowed Arctic snows.
Soaring through wider zones that pricked his scars
10  With memory of the old revolt from Awe,
He reached a middle height, and at the stars,
Which are the brain of heaven, he looked, and sank.
Around the ancient track marched, rank on rank,
The army of unalterable law.

## THINKING ABOUT THE SELECTIONS

### Recalling

1. (a) Why does Prince Lucifer rise up? (b) Where does he go?
2. (a) What does he look at when he reaches "the middle height?" (b) What is his reaction to what he sees?

### Interpreting

3. What do you understand "the rolling ball in cloud part screened" in line 3 to signify?
4. What are you able to gather about the appearance of "the fiend" from lines 6–9?
5. What do you think has caused Lucifer's scars, mentioned in line 9?
6. (a) Who or what makes up "the army of unalterable law"? (b) What situation is unalterable?
7. "Lucifer in Starlight" is a sonnet. (a) What question or problem is raised in the octet? (b) What answer or resolution is provided in the sestet?

8. In Milton's *Paradise Lost*, Satan (also known as Lucifer) is an angel who has fallen from grace and has, thus, been cast out of Heaven. How might this allusion explain Lucifer's feelings and "mission" in "Lucifer in Starlight?" What might be the meaning of "old revolt from Awe" in line 10?
9. In classical mythology, Lucifer (which means "lightbearer") was the morning star —that is, the planet Venus at dawn. The rising of Prince Lucifer, thus, also refers to the appearance of Venus on the horizon. How does knowing this enhance your appreciation of the poem?

### Applying

10. Meredith may have come upon the idea for this poem while gazing up at a nighttime sky. What thoughts come to you when you gaze up at the stars? What themes might the vastness of the sky suggest?

# A Birthday

## Christina Rossetti

My heart is like a singing bird
    Whose nest is in a watered shoot:
My heart is like an apple tree
    Whose boughs are bent with thickset fruit;
5  My heart is like a rainbow shell
    That paddles in a halcyon sea;
My heart is gladder than all these
    Because my love is come to me.

Raise me a dais of silk and down;
10    Hang it with vair[1] and purple dyes;
Carve it in doves and pomegranates,
    And peacocks with a hundred eyes;
Work it in gold and silver grapes,
    In leaves and silver fleurs-de-lys;[2]
15  Because the birthday of my life
    Is come, my love is come to me.

---

**1. vair** *n.*: Squirrel fur.
**2. fleurs-de-lys** (flŭr′ də lēz′) *n*: Emblems resembling lilies or irises.

---

## THINKING ABOUT THE SELECTION

### Recalling

1. (a) To what three things does the speaker compare her heart in the first stanza? (b) Why does she feel as she does?
2. (a) What does the speaker ask for in the second stanza? (b) What does she say has come?

### Interpreting

3. (a) What feeling does the poem convey? (b) Find three images that contribute to that feeling.

4. The poet makes abundant use of repetition, especially in the first stanza. How does this affect the mood of the poem?
5. What possible meanings might you attach to the phrase "the birthday of my life"?

### Applying

6. The second stanza of "A Birthday" has been called a "fully Pre-Raphaelite word-picture." Using what you have learned about the Pre-Raphaelite movement along with evidence from the poem explain why you think this is so.

# Recessional[1]

## Rudyard Kipling

*In 1897 a national celebration called the "Diamond Jubilee" was held in honor of the sixtieth anniversary of Queen Victoria's reign. The occasion prompted a great deal of boasting about the strength and greatness of the empire. Kipling responded to the celebration by writing this poem, reminding the people of England that the British empire might not last forever.*

God of our fathers, known of old—
    Lord of our far-flung battle-line—
Beneath whose awful Hand we hold
    Dominion over palm and pine—
5   Lord God of Hosts, be with us yet
Lest we forget—lest we forget!

The tumult and the shouting dies—
    The Captains and the Kings depart—
Still stands Thine ancient Sacrifice,
10     An humble and a contrite heart.[2]
Lord God of Hosts, be with us yet,
Lest we forget—lest we forget!

Far-called, our navies melt away—
    On dune and headland sinks the fire[3]—
15  Lo, all our pomp of yesterday
    Is one with Nineveh[4] and Tyre![5]
Judge of the Nations, spare us yet,
Lest we forget—lest we forget!

---

**1. recessional** *n.*: A hymn sung at the end of a religious service.
**2. An . . . heart:** An allusion to the Bible (Psalms 51:17): "The sacrifices of God are a broken spirit: a broken and contrite heart, O God, thou wilt not despise."
**3. On . . . fire:** Bonfires were lit on high ground all over Britain as part of the opening ceremonies of the Jubilee celebration.
**4. Nineveh** (nĭn' ə və): The ancient capital of the Assyrian Empire, the ruins of which were discovered buried in desert sands in the 1850's.
**5. Tyre** (tīr): Once a great port and the center of ancient Phoenician culture, now a small town in Lebanon.

If, drunk with sight of power, we loose
20      Wild tongues that have not Thee in awe—
Such boasting as the Gentiles use
        Or lesser breeds without the Law[6]—
Lord God of Hosts, be with us yet,
Lest we forget—lest we forget!

25   For heathen heart that puts her trust
        In reeking tube[7] and iron shard[8]—
All valiant dust that builds on dust,
        And guarding calls not Thee to guard—
For frantic boast and foolish word,
30   Thy mercy on Thy People, Lord!

---

**6. Such boasting . . . Law:** An allusion to the Bible (Romans 2:14):
"For when the Gentiles, which have not the law, do by nature things
contained in the law, these, having not the law, are a law unto
themselves."
**7. tube:** The barrel of a gun.
**8. shard:** Fragment of a bombshell.

## THINKING ABOUT THE SELECTION

### Recalling

1. (a) To whom is this poem addressed? (b) To
   whom is Kipling really speaking?
2. What does the speaker suggest, in lines
   15–16, happens to "our pomp of yesterday?"
3. What does the speaker beg in the last line?

### Interpreting

4. What qualities and actions does the poem
   condemn? Support your answer.
5. What is the poem's theme?

### Applying

6. What differences do you detect in the images
   used by Kipling in "Recessional" and those
   used by George Meredith in "Lucifer in Starlight"? Which poet's imagery do you find more
   effective? Explain.

## THINKING AND WRITING

### Writing About Historical Context

Kipling's "Recessional" may be seen as a
rejection of some of the values of the England in
which he lived. Supplement what you have
learned about Victorian England by consulting
an encyclopedia or other historical reference.
Note, in addition to the economic, political, and
religious climates of the period, specific events
that may have shaped the thoughts of the citi-
zenry. Weigh all possible influences on Kipling at
the time during which he composed this poem in
1897 and discard those that are irrelevant. Then
write an explanatory paper in which you identify
"Recessional" as a product of its period. Refer to
specific lines of the poem to strengthen your
thesis. When you revise, make sure your essay is
organized in a logical order.

# Requiem

## Robert Louis Stevenson

Under the wide and starry sky
Dig the grave and let me lie.
Glad did I live and gladly die.
    And I laid me down with a will.

5    This be the verse you grave for me:
*Here he lies where he longed to be;*
*Home is the sailor, home from sea,*
    *And the hunter home from the hill.*

---

## THINKING ABOUT THE SELECTION

### Recalling

1. Where does the speaker wish to be buried?
2. How does the speaker approach his death?

### Interpreting

3. Explain why the speaker's epitaph is appropriate.

### Applying

4. Explain why you think people like to write their own epitaphs.
5. What epitaph would you create for yourself? Explain the reason for your choice.

# Prose

**A SUMMER DAY IN HYDE PARK**
*John Ritchie*
*Museum of London*

# CHARLES DICKENS

## (1812–1870)

No other writer since Shakespeare has occupied a more important place in popular culture than Charles Dickens. From his own time on, his works, with their unforgettable characters, have held special appeal for both scholars and the reading public at large, and have been transformed time and again into plays and films.

Dickens was born in Portsmouth on England's southern coast. Except for a few happy years at Chatham, east of London, his childhood was darkened by his father's wavering economic status. After years of eluding creditors, his father was finally sent to debtor's prison. Dickens in the meantime was sent to a "prison" of his own—to a factory where he worked long hours pasting labels. These experiences and other ills of the newly industrialized society figure prominently in his novels.

After becoming a law clerk at the age of fifteen, Dickens taught himself shorthand and became a court reporter. At twenty-one he began applying his keen powers of observation to humorous literary sketches of everyday life in London while reporting on the Parliamentary debates. A collection of these, *Sketches by Boz* (1835–36), earned him a small following, which he built up considerably with his first novel *The Pickwick Papers,* published in 1837.

Next came such favorites as *Oliver Twist* (1837), *Nicholas Nickleby* (1839), and, after a trip to America where his fame had already spread, *A Christmas Carol* (1843). In these early novels, which paint a sweeping satiric picture of Victorian England, Dickens displayed both a passion for social reform and a unique ability to combine humor with horror—themes and techniques that became the hallmark of all his fiction. He also developed his lifelong practice of writing for serial publications. Paid by the word, he wove elaborate plots with vast numbers of characters.

A turn toward more serious planning and characterization of greater psychological depth are evident in *Dombey and Son* (1848) and *David Copperfield* (1850), which also contain social criticism that is more direct and less optimistic. In the later novels Dickens blended these elements together most successfully, and the results were his masterpieces: *Bleak House* (1853), *Hard Times* (1854), and *Great Expectations* (1861). "The Signalman" was published in 1866 in a collection including several other railway stories.

Dickens never gave up journalism as a second outlet for his social conscience. In later life, the work load imposed by his many writing responsibilities coupled with his exhausting public reading tours took its toll on his health. In 1870, while at work on a novel, *The Mystery of Edwin Drood,* he died of a stroke.

# GUIDE FOR INTERPRETING

## The Signalman

**Plot in a Ghost Story.** Plot is the ordered arrangement of happenings that make up a story or novel. Plot can be structured in a straight *chronological* progression, from the earliest event in time to the latest, or it can jump backwards and forward in time. In either case, plot generally builds on some *conflict,* or struggle between characters or forces, until it reaches a *climax,* or height of tension. The portion of the story from this point to the end, during which all remaining problems are solved, is called the *resolution.*

In a ghost story, the plot is built around *supernatural* elements —events beyond the normal order of things. The conflict is often between these supernatural forces and the human beings whose world they have invaded. At times, however, the conflict takes the form of a difference of opinion between two characters as to the explanation of certain mysterious events. In "The Signalman," for example, the first-person narrator attempts to explain away in rational terms the "ghost" that is plaguing a railroad employee.

Prepare the groundwork for an original ghost story. Consider the story's setting and characters by asking yourself questions such as the following: Is the story to take place in the here and now? What form will the "ghost" take? Who will be the person haunted by the ghost, and what will be the ghost's purpose? Jot down your answers to these and related questions.

Ghost stories are a special—and particularly enjoyable—type of fantastic literature. Alberto Manguel describes fantastic literature in the following manner:

> . . . fantastic literature deals with what can be best defined as the impossible seeping into the possible, what Wallace Stevens calls "black water breaking into reality." Fantastic literature never really explains everything. Like the ghost train at the fair, it takes us through the darkness of a real world, from terror to laughable terror, diving into walls that swing away at the very last minute, racing under eerie nothings that touch us with cobweb fingers, suddenly slowing down and lengthening that last encounter (with what? with what?), using our expectancy of horror more effectively than horror itself.

# The Signalman

## Charles Dickens

"Halloa! Below there!"

When he heard a voice thus calling to him, he was standing at the door of his box, with a flag in his hand, furled round its short pole. One would have thought, considering the nature of the ground, that he could not have doubted from what quarter the voice came; but instead of looking up to where I stood on the top of the steep cutting nearly over his head, he turned himself about, and looked down the Line. There was something remarkable in his manner of doing so, though I could not have said for my life what. But I know it was remarkable enough to attract my notice, even though his figure was foreshortened and shadowed, down in the deep trench, and mine was high above him, so steeped in the glow of an angry sunset, that I had shaded my eyes with my hand before I saw him at all.

"Halloa! Below!"

From looking down the Line, he turned himself about again, and, raising his eyes, saw my figure high above him.

"Is there any path by which I can come down and speak to you?"

He looked up at me without replying, and I looked down at him without pressing him too soon with a repetition of my idle question. Just then there came a vague vibration in the earth and air, quickly changing into a violent pulsation, and an oncoming rush that caused me to start back, as though it had force to draw me down. When such vapor as rose to my height from this rapid train had passed me and was skimming away over the landscape, I looked down again, and saw him refurling the flag he had shown while the train went by.

I repeated my inquiry. After a pause, during which he seemed to regard me with fixed attention, he motioned with his rolled-up flag towards a point on my level, some two or three hundred yards distant. I called down to him, "All right!" and made for that point. There, by dint of looking closely about me, I found a rough zigzag descending path notched out, which I followed.

The cutting was extremely deep, and unusually precipitate. It was made through a clammy stone, that became oozier and wetter as I went down. For these reasons, I found the way long enough to give me time to recall a singular air of reluctance or compulsion with which he had pointed out the path.

When I came down low enough upon the zigzag descent to see him again, I saw that he was standing between the rails on the way by which the train had lately passed, in an attitude as if he were waiting for me to appear. He had his left hand at his chin, and that left elbow rested on his right hand, crossed over his breast. His attitude was one of such expectation and watchfulness, that I stopped a moment, wondering at it.

I resumed my downward way, and stepping out upon the level of the railroad, and drawing nearer to him, saw that he was a dark sallow man, with a dark beard and rather heavy eyebrows. His post was in as solitary and dismal a place as ever I saw. On either side, a dripping-wet wall of jagged stone, excluding all view but a strip of sky; the perspective one way only a crooked prolongation of this great dungeon; the shorter perspective in the other direction terminating in a gloomy red light, and the gloomier entrance to a black tunnel, in whose massive architecture there was a barbarous, depressing, and forbidding air. So little sunlight ever found its way to this spot, that it had an earthy, deadly smell; and so much cold wind rushed through it, that it struck chill to me, as if I had left the natural world.

Before he stirred, I was near enough to him to have touched him. Not even then removing his eyes from mine, he stepped back one step, and lifted his hand.

This was a lonesome post to occupy (I said), and it had riveted my attention when I looked down from up yonder. A visitor was a rarity, I should suppose; not an unwelcome rarity, I hoped? In me, he merely saw a man who had been shut up within narrow limits all his life, and who, being at last set free, had a newly awakened interest in these great works. To such purpose I spoke to him; but I am far from sure of the terms I used; for, besides that I am not happy in opening any conversation, there was something in the man that daunted me.

He directed a most curious look towards the red light near the tunnel's mouth, and looked all about it, as if something were missing from it, and then looked at me.

That light was part of his charge? Was it not?

He answered in a low voice, "Don't you know it is?"

The monstrous thought came into my mind, as I perused the fixed eyes and the saturnine face, that this was a spirit, not a man. I have speculated since, whether there may have been infection in his mind.

In my turn, I stepped back. But in making the action, I detected in his eyes some latent fear of me. This put the monstrous thought to flight.

"You look at me," I said, forcing a smile, "as if you had a dread of me."

"I was doubtful," he returned, "whether I had seen you before."

"Where?"

He pointed to the red light he had looked at.

"There?" I said.

Intently watchful of me, he replied (but without sound), "Yes."

"My good fellow, what should I do there? However, be that as it may, I never was there, you may swear."

"I think I may," he rejoined. "Yes, I am sure I may."

His manner cleared, like my own. He replied to my remarks with readiness, and in well-chosen words. Had he much to do there? Yes; that was to say, he had enough responsibility to bear; but exactness and watchfulness were what was required of him, and of actual work—manual labor —he had next to none. To change that signal, to trim those lights, and to turn this iron handle now and then, was all he had to do under that head. Regarding those many long and lonely hours of which I seemed to make so much, he could only say that the routine of his life had shaped itself into that form, and he had grown used to it. He had taught himself a language down here—if only to know it by sight, and to have formed his own crude ideas of its pronunciation, could be called learning it. He had also worked at fractions and decimals, and tried a little algebra; but he was, and had been as a boy, a poor hand at figures. Was it necessary for him when on duty always to remain in that channel of damp air, and could he never rise into the sunshine from between those high stone walls? Why, that depended upon times and circumstances. Under some conditions there would be less upon the Line than under others, and the same held good as to certain hours of the day and night. In bright weather, he did choose occasions for getting a little above these lower shadows; but, being at all times liable to be called by his electric bell, and at such times listening for it with redoubled anxiety, the relief was less than I would suppose.

He took me into his box, where there was a fire, a desk for an official book in which he had to make certain entries, a telegraphic instrument with its dial, face, and needles, and the little bell of which he had spoken. On my trusting that he would excuse the

**TWO TUNNELS, 1975**
*Guy Worsdell*

remark that he had been well educated, and
(I hoped I might say without offense) perhaps
educated above that station, he observed
that instances of slight incongruity in such
wise would rarely be found wanting among
large bodies of men; that he had heard it was
so in workhouses, in the police force, even in
that last desperate resource, the army; and
that he knew it was so, more or less, in any
great railway staff. He had been, when
young (if I could believe it, sitting in that
hut—he scarcely could), a student of natural philosophy, and had attended lectures;
but he had run wild, misused his opportunities, gone down, and never risen again. He

had no complaint to offer about that. He had
made his bed, and he lay upon it. It was far
too late to make another.

All that I have here condensed, he said
in a quiet manner, with his grave dark regards divided between me and the fire. He
threw in the word, "Sir," from time to time,
and especially when he referred to his
youth, as though to request me to understand that he claimed to be nothing but
what I found him. He was several times
interrupted by the little bell, and had to read
off messages, and send replies. Once he had
to stand without the door, and display a flag
as a train passed, and make some verbal

communication to the driver. In the discharge of his duties, I observed him to be remarkably exact and vigilant, breaking off his discourse at a syllable, and remaining silent until what he had to do was done.

In a word, I should have set this man down as one of the safest of men to be employed in that capacity, but for the circumstance that while he was speaking to me he twice broke off with a fallen color, turned his face towards the little bell when it did NOT ring, opened the door of the hut (which was kept shut to exclude the unhealthy damp), and looked out towards the red light near the mouth of the tunnel. On both of those occasions, he came back to the fire with the inexplicable air upon him which I had remarked, without being able to define, when we were so far asunder.

Said I, when I rose to leave him, "You almost make me think that I have met with a contented man."

(I am afraid I must acknowledge that I said it to lead him on.)

"I believe I used to be so," he rejoined, in the low voice in which he had first spoken; "but I am troubled, sir, I am troubled."

He would have recalled the words if he could. He had said them, however, and I took them up quickly.

"With what? What is your trouble?"

"It is very difficult to impart, sir. It is very, very difficult to speak of. If ever you make me another visit, I will try to tell you."

"But I expressly intend to make you another visit. Say, when shall it be?"

"I go off early in the morning, and I shall be on again at ten tomorrow night, sir."

"I will come at eleven."

He thanked me, and went out at the door with me. "I'll show my white light, sir," he said, in his peculiar low voice, "till you have found the way up. When you have found it, don't call out! And when you are at the top, don't call out!"

His manner seemed to make the place strike colder to me, but I said no more than, "Very well."

"And when you come down tomorrow night, don't call out! Let me ask you a parting question. What made you cry, 'Halloa! Below there!' tonight?"

"Heaven knows," said I. "I cried something to that effect——"

"Not to that effect, sir. Those were the very words. I know them well."

"Admit those were the very words. I said them, no doubt, because I saw you below."

"For no other reason?"

"What other reason could I possibly have?"

"You had no feeling that they were conveyed to you in any supernatural way?"

"No."

He wished me good night, and held up his light. I walked by the side of the down Line of rails (with a very disagreeable sensation of a train coming behind me) until I found the path. It was easier to mount than to descend, and I got back to my inn without any adventure.

Punctual to my appointment, I placed my foot on the first notch of the zigzag next night, as the distant clocks were striking eleven. He was waiting for me at the bottom, with his white light on. "I have not called out," I said, when we came close together; "may I speak now?" "By all means, sir." "Good night, then, and here's my hand." "Good night, sir, and here's mine." With that we walked side by side to his box, entered it, closed the door, and sat down by the fire.

"I have made up my mind, sir," he began, bending forward as soon as we were seated, and speaking in a tone but a little above a whisper, "that you shall not have to ask me twice what troubles me. I took you for someone else yesterday evening. That troubles me."

"That mistake?"

"No. That someone else."

"Who is it?"

"I don't know."

"Like me?"

"I don't know. I never saw the face. The

left arm is across the face, and the right arm is waved—violently waved. This way."

I followed his action with my eyes, and it was the action of an arm gesticulating, with the utmost passion and vehemence, "For God's sake, clear the way!"

"One moonlight night," said the man, "I was sitting here, when I heard a voice cry, 'Halloa! Below there!' I started up, looked from that door, and saw this Someone else standing by the red light near the tunnel, waving as I just now showed you. The voice seemed hoarse with shouting, and it cried, 'Look out! Look out!' And then again, 'Halloa! Below there! Look out!' I caught up my lamp, turned it on red, and ran towards the figure, calling, 'What's wrong? What has happened? Where?' It stood just outside the blackness of the tunnel. I advanced so close upon it that I wondered at its keeping the sleeve across its eyes. I ran right up at it, and had my hand stretched out to pull the sleeve away, when it was gone."

"Into the tunnel," said I.

"No. I ran on into the tunnel, five hundred yards. I stopped, and held my lamp above my head, and saw the figures of the measured distance, and saw the wet stains stealing down the walls and trickling through the arch. I ran out again faster than I had run in (for I had a mortal abhorrence of the place upon me), and I looked all round the red light with my own red light, and I went up the iron ladder to the gallery top of it, and I came down again, and ran back here. I telegraphed both ways, 'An alarm has been given. Is anything wrong?' The answer came back, both ways, 'All well.'"

Resisting the slow touch of a frozen finger tracing out my spine, I showed him how that this figure must be a deception of his sense of sight; and how that figures, originating in disease of the delicate nerves that minister to the functions of the eye, were known to have often troubled patients, some of whom had become conscious of the nature of their affliction, and had even proved it by experiments upon themselves. "As to

an imaginary cry," said I, "do but listen for a moment to the wind in this unnatural valley while we speak so low, and to the wild harp it makes of the telegraph wires!"

That was all very well, he returned, after we had sat listening for a while, and he ought to know something of the wind and the wires—he who so often passed long winter nights there, alone and watching. But he would beg to remark that he had not finished.

I asked his pardon, and he slowly added these words, touching my arm:

"Within six hours after the Appearance, the memorable accident on this Line happened, and within ten hours the dead and wounded were brought along through the tunnel over the spot where the figure had stood."

A disagreeable shudder crept over me, but I did my best against it. It was not to be denied, I rejoined, that this was a remarkable coincidence, calculated deeply to impress his mind. But it was unquestionable that remarkable coincidences did continually occur, and they must be taken into account in dealing with such a subject. Though to be sure I must admit, I added (for I thought I saw that he was going to bring the objection to bear upon me), men of common sense did not allow much for coincidences in making the ordinary calculations of life.

He again begged to remark that he had not finished.

I again begged his pardon for being betrayed into interruptions.

"This," he said, again laying his hand upon my arm, and glancing over his shoulder with hollow eyes, "was just a year ago. Six or seven months passed, and I had recovered from the surprise and shock, when one morning, as the day was breaking, I, standing at the door, looked towards the red light, and saw the specter again." He stopped, with a fixed look at me.

"Did it cry out?"

"No. It was silent."

"Did it wave its arm?"

"No. It leaned against the shaft of the light, with both hands before the face. Like this."

Once more I followed his action with my eyes. It was an action of mourning. I have seen such an attitude in stone figures on tombs.

"Did you go up to it?"

"I came in and sat down, partly to collect my thoughts, partly because it had turned me faint. When I went to the door again, daylight was above me, and the ghost was gone."

"But nothing followed? Nothing came of this?"

He touched me on the arm with his forefinger twice or thrice, giving a ghastly nod each time:

"That very day, as a train came out of the tunnel, I noticed, at a carriage window on my side, what looked like a confusion of hands and heads, and something waved. I saw it just in time to signal the driver, Stop! He shut off, and put his brake on, but the train drifted past here a hundred and fifty yards or more. I ran after it, and, as I went along, heard terrible screams and cries. A beautiful young lady had died instantaneously in one of the compartments, and was brought in here, and laid on this floor between us."

Involuntarily I pushed my chair back, as I looked from the boards at which he pointed to himself.

"True, sir. True. Precisely as it happened, so I tell it you."

I could think of nothing to say, to any purpose, and my mouth was very dry. The wind and the wires took up the story with a long lamenting wail.

He resumed. "Now, sir, mark this, and judge how my mind is troubled. The specter came back a week ago. Ever since, it has been there, now and again, by fits and starts."

"At the light?"

"At the Danger light."

"What does it seem to do?"

He repeated, if possible with increased passion and vehemence, that former gesticulation of, "For God's sake, clear the way!"

Then he went on. "I have no peace or rest for it. It calls to me, for many minutes together, in an agonized manner, 'Below there! Look out! Look out!' It stands waving to me. It rings my little bell—"

I caught at that. "Did it ring your bell yesterday evening when I was here, and you went to the door?"

"Twice."

"Why, see," said I, "how your imagination misleads you. My eyes were on the bell, and my ears were open to the bell, and if I am a living man, it did NOT ring at those times. No, nor at any other time, except when it was rung in the natural course of physical things by the station communicating with you."

He shook his head. "I have never made a mistake as to that yet, sir. I have never confused the specter's ring with the man's. The ghost's ring is a strange vibration in the bell that it derives from nothing else, and I have not asserted that the bell stirs to the eye. I don't wonder that you failed to hear it. But *I* heard it."

"And did the specter seem to be there, when you looked out?"

"It WAS there."

"Both times?"

He repeated firmly: "Both times."

"Will you come to the door with me, and look for it now?"

He bit his under lip as though he were somewhat unwilling, but arose. I opened the door, and stood on the step, while he stood in the doorway. There was the Danger light. There was the dismal mouth of the tunnel. There were the high, wet stone walls of the cutting. There were the stars above them.

"Do you see it?" I asked him, taking particular note of his face. His eyes were prominent and strained, but not very much more so, perhaps, than my own had been when I had directed them earnestly towards the same spot.

"No," he answered. "It is not there."

"Agreed," said I.

We went in again, shut the door, and resumed our seats. I was thinking how best to improve this advantage, if it might be called one, when he took up the conversation in such a matter-of-course way, so assuming that there could be no serious question of fact between us, that I felt myself placed in the weakest of positions.

"By this time you will fully understand, sir," he said, "that what troubles me so dreadfully is the question, What does the specter mean?"

I was not sure, I told him, that I did fully understand.

"What is its warning against?" he said, ruminating, with his eyes on the fire, and only by times turning them on me. "What is the danger? Where is the danger? There is danger overhanging somewhere on the Line. Some dreadful calamity will happen. It is not to be doubted this third time, after what has gone before. But surely this is a cruel haunting of *me*. What can *I* do?"

He pulled out his handkerchief, and wiped the drops from his heated forehead.

"If I telegraph Danger, on either side of me, or on both, I can give no reason for it," he went on, wiping the palms of his hands. "I should get into trouble, and do no good. They would think I was mad. This is the way it would work: Message: "Danger! Take care!" Answer: "What Danger? Where?" Message: "Don't know. But for God's sake, take care!" They would displace me. What else could they do?"

His pain of mind was most pitiable to see. It was the mental torture of a conscientious man, oppressed beyond endurance by an unintelligible responsibility involving life.

"When it first stood under the Danger light," he went on, putting his dark hair back from his head, and drawing his hands outward across and across his temples in an extremity of feverish distress, "why not tell me where that accident was to happen—if it must happen? Why not tell me how it could be averted—if it could have been averted? When on its second coming it hid its face, why not tell me, instead, "She is going to die. Let them keep her at home"? If it came, on those two occasions, only to show me that its warnings were true, and so to prepare me for the third, why not warn me plainly now? And I, Lord help me! A mere poor signalman on this solitary station! Why not go to somebody with credit to be believed, and power to act?"

When I saw him in this state, I saw that for the poor man's sake, as well as for the public safety, what I had to do for the time was to compose his mind. Therefore, setting aside all question of reality or unreality between us, I represented to him that whoever thoroughly discharged his duty must do well, and that at least it was his comfort that he understood his duty, though he did not understand these confounding Appearances. In this effort I succeeded far better than in the attempt to reason him out of his conviction. He became calm; the occupations incidental to his post as the night advanced began to make larger demands on his attention: and I left him at two in the morning. I had offered to stay through the night, but he would not hear of it.

That I more than once looked back at the red light as I ascended the pathway, that I did not like the red light, and that I should have slept but poorly if my bed had been under it, I see no reason to conceal. Nor did I like the two sequences of the accident and the dead girl. I see no reason to conceal that either.

But what ran most in my thoughts was the consideration how ought I to act, having become the recipient of this disclosure? I had proved the man to be intelligent, vigilant, painstaking, and exact; but how long might he remain so, in his state of mind? Though in a subordinate position, still he held a most important trust, and would I (for instance) like to stake my own life on the chances of his continuing to execute it with precision?

Unable to overcome a feeling that there would be something treacherous in my communicating what he had told me to his superiors in the Company, without first being plain with himself and proposing a middle course to him, I ultimately resolved to offer to accompany him (otherwise keeping his secret for the present) to the wisest medical practitioner we could hear of in those parts, and to take his opinion. A change in his time of duty would come round next night, he had apprised me, and he would be off an hour or two after sunrise, and on again soon after sunset. I had appointed to return accordingly.

Next evening was a lovely evening, and I walked out early to enjoy it. The sun was not yet quite down when I traversed the field-path near the top of the deep cutting. I would extend my walk for an hour, I said to myself, half an hour on and half an hour back, and it would then be time to go to my signal-man's box.

Before pursuing my stroll, I stepped to the brink, and mechanically looked down, from the point from which I had first seen him. I cannot describe the thrill that seized upon me, when, close at the mouth of the tunnel, I saw the appearance of a man, with his left sleeve across his eyes, passionately waving his right arm.

The nameless horror that oppressed me passed in a moment, for in a moment I saw that this appearance of a man was a man indeed, and that there was a little group of other men, standing at a short distance, to whom he seemed to be rehearsing the gesture he made. The Danger light was not yet lighted. Against its shaft, a little low hut, entirely new to me, had been made of some wooden supports and tarpaulin. It looked no bigger than a bed.

With an irresistible sense that something was wrong—with a flashing self-reproachful fear that fatal mischief had come of my leaving the man there, and causing no one to be sent to overlook or correct what he did—I descended the notched path with all the speed I could make.

"What is the matter?" I asked the men.

"Signalman killed this morning, sir."

"Not the man belonging to that box?"

"Yes, sir."

"Not the man I know?"

"You will recognize him, sir, if you knew him," said the man who spoke for the others, solemnly uncovering his own head, and raising an end of the tarpaulin, "for his face is quite composed."

"O, how did this happen, how did this happen?" I asked, turning from one to another as the hut closed in again.

"He was cut down by an engine, sir. No man in England knew his work better. But somehow he was not clear of the outer rail. It was just at broad day. He had struck the light, and had the lamp in his hand. As the engine came out of the tunnel, his back was towards her, and she cut him down. That man drove her, and was showing how it happened. Show the gentleman, Tom."

The man, who wore a rough dark dress, stepped back to his former place at the mouth of the tunnel.

"Coming round the curve in the tunnel, sir," he said, "I saw him at the end, like as if I saw him down a perspective-glass. There was no time to check speed, and I knew him to be very careful. As he didn't seem to take heed of the whistle, I shut it off when we were running down upon him, and called to him as loud as I could call."

"What did you say?"

"I said, 'Below there! Look out! Look out! For God's sake, clear the way!'"

I started.

"Ah! it was a dreadful time, sir. I never left off calling to him. I put this arm before my eyes not to see, and I waved this arm to the last; but it was no use."

Without prolonging the narrative to dwell on any one of its curious circumstances more than on any other, I may, in closing it, point out the coincidence that the warning of the Engine Driver included, not only the words which the unfortunate Signalman had repeated to me as haunting him, but also the words which I myself—not he—had attached and that only in my own mind, to the gesticulation he had imitated.

# THINKING ABOUT THE SELECTION

## Recalling

1. (a) How does the signalman behave during his first meeting with the narrator? (b) What explanation for this behavior is given in the second meeting?
2. (a) What tragedy followed the specter's first appearance? (b) Its second appearance? (c) How has it been warning the signalman lately?
3. What happens to the signalman?

## Interpreting

4. Do you think the narrator is totally convinced of his own explanations of the events on the railroad line? Explain.
5. (a) What do you think is the narrator's view of the supernatural? (b) What evidence are you given that the events he narrates have changed his views?

## Applying

6. In light of his description of the signalman's job, how does this story serve Dickens's goal of promoting social change in England?

# ANALYZING LITERATURE

## Following the Plot in a Ghost Story

The **plot** is the series of events in a story or novel that answers the question "What happens?" Plot usually involves a conflict, or clash between characters or opposing forces, that builds to a high point called the climax. In a ghost story, the plot revolves around supernatural—or "otherworldly"—elements.

1. What supernatural elements are featured in "The Signalman"? How do these elements tie in directly to the story's plot?
2. The story features several different conflicts. Identify:
   a. The conflict between the narrator and the signalman.
   b. The signalman's inner conflict.
   c. The narrator's inner conflict.

# CRITICAL THINKING AND READING

## Separating Details

Like any good ghost story, "The Signalman" is filled with details that lend themselves to both realistic and supernatural interpretation. What the signalman, for example, identifies as the specter's cry, the narrator "writes off" as the sound of the wind whistling through the telegraph wires. Yet not all details in the story can be explained away so simply. Identify the realistic and supernatural significance of each of the following details.

1. The ringing of the bell.
2. The words "For God's sake, clear the way!"
3. A figure with its left sleeve across its face and its right arm waving frantically.

# UNDERSTANDING LANGUAGE

## Fitting the Context

Occasionally writers use words that, in a given context, are *ambiguous,* or open to more than one interpretation. In each case below, give the intended meaning of the italicized word, and identify a second possible reading.

1. ". . . an oncoming rush . . . caused me to *start* back . . . " (page 870)
2. ". . . in [the tunnel's] architecture there was a . . . forbidding *air*. . . ." (page 871)
3. "That light was part of his *charge*?" (page 871)
4. "I have seen such an *attitude* in stone figures on tombs." (page 875)

# THINKING AND WRITING

## Writing a Ghost Story

Using the notes you developed earlier, write an original ghost story. Before you proceed, map out your story's plot. Ask: What will happen in the story, and in what order will you report the events? What is the conflict, and who does it involve? How will the conflict be resolved? When you have answered these questions, you may begin your first draft.

# THOMAS HARDY

## 1840–1928

In addition to being a highly regarded poet, Thomas Hardy was one of the most important fiction writers of the Victorian Age. Set in the imaginary region of Wessex, Hardy's novels and stories focused on the plight of the underdog in an unfeeling society.

Hardy was born in the Dorset countryside in southwestern England, the area upon which his fictional setting of Wessex is based. After leaving school at the age of fifteen, Hardy was trained to be an architect. He developed a strong interest in fiction and poetry, however, and eventually decided to focus his energy on writing. His first novel, *Desperate Remedies,* was published anonymously in 1871. The following year he achieved success as a novelist with the publication of *Under the Greenwood Tree.* Hardy went on to produce several more novels, but when his book *Jude the Obscure* (1896) prompted a hostile reaction, he turned to writing poetry.

In his novels and stories, Hardy often depicted characters whose destinies were shaped by forces beyond their control. Many of his works, including "The Three Strangers," also contain an element of mystery, resulting in part from the rough, unforgiving landscape that serves as their setting. (For additional information on Hardy, see page 832.)

# GUIDE FOR INTERPRETING

**Writer's Technique**

**Setting and Mood.** Setting is the time when and place where the events in a story occur. This information is sometimes vital to a story's *mood,* or the feelings it stirs in the reader. If, for example, the story is set in a crowded, bustling city, the mood will be tense and hectic. If, on the other hand, the story is set on a lush tropical island, the mood will be calm and tranquil.

**Writing**

Imagine that a stranger appeared at the front door of your home one evening. Letting your imagination run free, describe this person's appearance, as well as yours and your family's initial reaction to him or her. Finally, state the reason for the stranger's visit.

**Primary Source**

One afternoon, Robert Graves, his wife, and T. E. Lawrence found themselves near Hardy's home in Dorchester. Since they had met Hardy not long before, when he had traveled to Oxford to receive an honorary degree from the university, they decided to stop in and visit him.

Graves, himself a well-known poet, novelist, and critic, wrote out a record of their conversation. It clearly shows the influence of setting and mood on Hardy's word choice and writing style.

> He said that he regarded professional critics as parasites no less noxious than autograph-hunters, and wished the world rid of them. He also wished that he had not listened to them when he was a young man; on their advice he had cut out dialect-words from his early poems, though they had no exact synonyms to fit the context. And still the critics were plaguing him. One of them recently complained of a poem of his where he had written "his shape *smalled* in the distance." Now what in the world else could he have written? Hardy then laughed a little and said that once or twice recently he had looked up a word in the dictionary for fear of being again accused of coining, and had found it there right enough—only to read on and find that the sole authority quoted was himself in a half-forgotten novel! He talked of early literary influences, and said that he had none at all, for he did not come of literary stock. Then he corrected himself and said that a friend, a fellow-apprentice in the architect's office where he had worked as a young man, used to lend him books.

How do you think the language of "The Three Strangers" might have differed if Hardy had used another setting and mood?

# The Three Strangers

## Thomas Hardy

Among the few features of agricultural England which retain an appearance but little modified by the lapse of centuries, may be reckoned the long, grassy and furzy downs, coombs,[1] or ewe-leases, as they are called according to their kind, that fill a large area of certain counties in the south and southwest. If any mark of human occupation is met with hereon, it usually takes the form of the solitary cottage of some shepherd.

Fifty years ago such a lonely cottage stood on such a down, and may possibly be standing there now. In spite of its loneliness, however, the spot, by actual measurement, was not three miles from a county town. Yet that affected it little. Three miles of irregular upland, during the long inimical seasons, with their sleets, snows, rains, and mists, afford withdrawing space enough to isolate a Timon[2] or a Nebuchadnezzar;[3] much less, in fair weather, to please that less repellent tribe, the poets, philosophers, artists, and others who "conceive and meditate of pleasant things."

Some old earthen camp or barrow,[4] some clump of trees, at least some starved fragment of ancient hedge is usually taken advantage of in the erection of these forlorn dwellings. But, in the present case, such a kind of shelter had been disregarded. Higher Crowstairs, as the house was called, stood quite detached and undefended. The only reason for its precise situation seemed to be the crossing of two footpaths at right angles hard by, which may have crossed there and thus for a good five hundred years. Hence the house was exposed to the elements on all sides. But, though the wind up here blew unmistakably when it did blow, and the rain hit hard whenever it fell, the various weathers of the winter season were not quite so formidable on the down as they were imagined to be by dwellers on low ground. The raw rimes[5] were not so pernicious as in the hollows, and the frosts were scarcely so severe. When the shepherd and his family who tenanted the house were pitied for their sufferings from the exposure, they said that upon the whole they were less inconvenienced by "wuzzes and flames" (hoarses and phlegms) than when they had lived by the stream of a snug neighboring valley.

The night of March 28, 182– was precisely one of the nights that were wont to call forth these expressions of commiseration. The level rainstorm smote walls, slopes, and hedges like the clothyard shafts of Senlac and Crecy.[6] Such sheep and outdoor animals as had no shelter stood with their buttocks to the winds; while the tails of little birds trying to roost on some scraggy thorn were blown inside out like umbrellas. The gable-end of the cottage was stained with wet, and the eavesdroppings flapped against the wall. Yet never was commiseration for the shepherd more misplaced. For that cheerful rustic was entertaining a large

---

**1. coombs** (ko͞oms) *n*: Deep, narrow valleys.
**2. Timon** (tī′mən): A fifth-century Greek hermit who lived in a cave.
**3. Nebuchadnezzar** (neb′ yə kəd nez′ ər): A Babylonian king who isolated himself in the fields after becoming insane.
**4. barrow** *n*.: A heap of earth or rocks marking a grave.

**5. rimes** (rīmz) *n*: White frost.
**6. clothyard . . . Crecy** (krā sē′): Yard-long arrows used in battles fought in England (at Senlac) and France (at Crecy).

party in glorification of the christening of his second girl.

The guests had arrived before the rain began to fall, and they were all now assembled in the chief or living room of the dwelling. A glance into the apartment at eight o'clock on this eventful evening would have resulted in the opinion that it was as cozy and comfortable a nook as could be wished for in boisterous weather. The calling of its inhabitant was proclaimed by a number of highly polished sheep crooks without stems that were hung ornamentally over the fireplace, the curl of each shining crook varying from the antiquated type engraved in the patriarchal pictures of old family Bibles to the most approved fashion of the last local sheep fair. The room was lighted by half a dozen candles, having wicks only a trifle smaller than the grease which enveloped them, in candlesticks that were never used but at high days, holy days, and family feasts. The lights were scattered about the room, two of them standing on the chimney piece. This position of candles was in itself significant. Candles on the chimney piece always meant a party.

On the hearth, in front of a backbrand to give substance, blazed a fire of thorns, that crackled "like the laughter of the fool."

Nineteen persons were gathered here. Of these, five women, wearing gowns of various bright hues, sat in chairs along the wall; girls shy and not shy filled the window bench; four men, including Charley Jake the hedge carpenter, Elijah New the parish clerk, and John Pitcher, a neighboring dairyman, the shepherd's father-in-law, lolled in the settle; a young man and maid, who were blushing over tentative *pourparlers*[7] on a life companionship, sat beneath the corner cupboard; and an elderly engaged man of fifty or upward moved restlessly about from spots where his betrothed was not to the spot where she was. Enjoyment was pretty general, and so much the more prevailed in being unhampered by conventional restrictions. Absolute confidence in each other's good opinion begat perfect ease, while the finishing stroke of manner, amounting to a truly princely serenity, was lent to the majority by the absence of any expression or trait denoting that they wished to get on in the world, enlarge their minds, or do any eclipsing thing whatever —which nowadays so generally nips the bloom and *bonhomie*[8] of all except the two extremes of the social scale.

Shepherd Fennel had married well, his wife being a dairyman's daughter from a vale at a distance, who brought fifty guineas in her pocket—and kept them there, till they should be required for ministering to the needs of a coming family. This frugal woman had been somewhat exercised as to the character that should be given to the gathering. A sit-still party had its advantages; but an undisturbed position of ease in chairs and settles was apt to lead on the men to such an unconscionable deal of toping[9] that they would sometimes fairly drink the house dry. A dancing party was the alternative; but this, while avoiding the foregoing objection on the score of good drink, had a counterbalancing disadvantage in the matter of good victuals, the ravenous appetites engendered by the exercise causing immense havoc in the buttery. Shepherdess Fennel fell back upon the intermediate plan of mingling short dances with short periods of talk and singing, so as to hinder any ungovernable rage in either. But this scheme was entirely confined to her own gentle mind: the shepherd himself was in the mood to exhibit the most reckless phases of hospitality.

The fiddler was a boy of those parts, about twelve years of age, who had a wonderful dexterity in jigs and reels, though his fingers were so small and short as to necessitate a constant shifting for the high notes, from which he scrambled back to the first

---

**7. pourparlers** (po͞or′ pär lä′): Informal discussions (French).

**8. bonhomie** (bän′ ə mē′): Good nature (French).
**9. toping:** Drinking.

**SUMMER, AFTERNOON AFTER A SHOWER**
*John Constable*
The Tate Gallery, London

position with sounds not of unmixed purity of tone. At seven the shrill tweedle-dee of this youngster had begun, accompanied by a booming ground bass from Elijah New, the parish clerk, who had thoughtfully brought with him his favorite musical instrument, the serpent.[10] Dancing was instantaneous, Mrs. Fennel privately enjoining the players on no account to let the dance exceed the length of a quarter of an hour.

But Elijah and the boy in the excitement of their position quite forgot the injunction. Moreover, Oliver Giles, a man of seventeen, one of the dancers, who was enamored of his partner, a fair girl of thirty-three rolling years, had recklessly handed a new crown-piece to the musicians, as a bribe to keep going as long as they had muscle and wind. Mrs. Fennel seeing the steam begin to generate on the countenances of her guests, crossed over and touched the fiddler's elbow and put her hand on the serpent's mouth. But they took no notice, and fearing she might lose her character of genial hostess if

she were to interfere too markedly, she retired and sat down helpless. And so the dance whizzed on with cumulative fury, the performers moving in their planet-like courses, direct and retrograde,[11] from apogee to perigee,[12] till the hand of the well-kicked clock at the bottom of the room had traveled over the circumference of an hour.

While these cheerful events were in course of enactment within Fennel's pastoral dwelling an incident having considerable bearing on the party had occurred in the gloomy night without. Mrs. Fennel's concern about the growing fierceness of the dance corresponded in point of time with the ascent of a human figure to the solitary hill of Higher Crowstairs from the direction of the distant town. This personage strode on through the rain without a pause, following the little-worn path which, further on in its course, skirted the shepherd's cottage.

It was nearly the time of full moon, and on this account, though the sky was lined with a uniform sheet of dripping cloud, ordi-

---

**10. serpent** *n.*: An obsolete, coiled bass wind instrument.

**11. direct and retrograde:** Orbital directions.
**12. from apogee to perigee:** From the points in orbit farthest from and nearest to the earth.

nary objects out of doors were readily visible. The sad wan light revealed the lonely pedestrian to be a man of supple frame; his gait suggested that he had somewhat passed the period of perfect and instinctive agility, though not so far as to be otherwise than rapid of motion when occasion required. At a rough guess, he might have been about forty years of age. He appeared tall, but a recruiting sergeant, or other person accustomed to the judging of men's heights by the eye, would have discerned that this was chiefly owing to his gauntness, and that he was not more than five-feet-eight or nine.

Notwithstanding the regularity of his tread there was caution in it, as in that of one who mentally feels his way; and despite the fact that it was not a black coat nor a dark garment of any sort that he wore, there was something about him which suggested that he naturally belonged to the black-coated tribes[13] of men. His clothes were of fustian,[14] and his boots hobnailed, yet in his progress he showed not the mud-accustomed bearing of hobnailed and fustianed peasantry.

By the time that he had arrived abreast of the shepherd's premises the rain came down, or rather came along, with yet more determined violence. The outskirts of the little settlement partially broke the force of wind and rain, and this induced him to stand still. The most salient of the shepherd's domestic erections was an empty sty at the forward corner of his hedgeless garden, for in these latitudes the principle of masking the homelier features of your establishment by a conventional frontage was unknown. The traveler's eye was attracted to this small building by the pallid shine of the wet slates that covered it. He turned aside, and, finding it empty, stood under the pent roof for shelter.

While he stood the boom of the serpent within the adjacent house, and the lesser strains of the fiddler, reached the spot as an accompaniment to the surging hiss of the flying rain on the sod, its louder beating on the cabbage leaves of the garden, on the straw hackles of eight or ten beehives just discernible by the path, and its dripping from the eaves into a row of buckets and pans that had been placed under the walls of the cottage. For at Higher Crowstairs, as at all such elevated domiciles, the grand difficulty of housekeeping was an insufficiency of water; and a casual rainfall was utilized by turning out, as catchers, every utensil that the house contained. Some queer stories might be told of the contrivances for economy in suds and dishwaters that are absolutely necessitated in upland habitations during the droughts of summer. But at this season there were no such exigencies; a mere acceptance of what the skies bestowed was sufficient for an abundant store.

At last the notes of the serpent ceased and the house was silent. This cessation of activity aroused the solitary pedestrian from the reverie into which he had lapsed, and, emerging from the shed, with an apparently new intention, he walked up the path to the house door. Arrived here, his first act was to kneel down on a large stone beside the row of vessels, and to drink a copious draft from one of them. Having quenched his thirst he rose and lifted his hand to knock, but paused with his eye upon the panel. Since the dark surface of the wood revealed absolutely nothing, it was evident that he must be mentally looking through the door, as if he wished to measure thereby all the possibilities that a house of this sort might include, and how they might bear upon the question of his entry.

In his indecision he turned and surveyed the scene around. Not a soul was anywhere visible. The garden path stretched downward from his feet, gleaming like the track of a snail; the roof of the little well (mostly dry), the well cover, the top rail of the garden gate, were varnished with the same dull liquid glaze; while, far away in the vale, a faint whiteness of more than usual extent

---

**13. black-coated tribes:** Middle class.
**14. fustian** (fus′chən) n.: A coarse cotton cloth.

showed that the rivers were high in the meads. Beyond all this winked a few bleared lamplights through the beating drops —lights that denoted the situation of the county town from which he had appeared to come. The absence of all notes of life in that direction seemed to clinch his intentions, and he knocked at the door.

Within, a desultory chat had taken the place of movement and musical sound. The hedge carpenter was suggesting a song to the company, which nobody just then was inclined to undertake, so that the knock afforded a not unwelcome diversion.

"Walk in!" said the shepherd promptly.

The latch clicked upward, and out of the night our pedestrian appeared upon the doormat. The shepherd arose, snuffed two of the nearest candles, and turned to look at him.

Their light disclosed that the stranger was dark in complexion and not unprepossessing as to feature. His hat, which for a moment he did not remove, hung low over his eyes, without concealing that they were large, open, and determined, moving with a flash rather than a glance around the room. He seemed pleased with his survey, and, baring his shaggy head, said, in a rich deep voice, "The rain is so heavy, friends, that I ask leave to come in and rest awhile."

"To be sure, stranger," said the shepherd. "And faith, you've been lucky in choosing your time, for we are having a bit of a fling for a glad cause—though, to be sure, a man could hardly wish that glad cause to happen more than once a year."

"Nor less," spoke up a woman. "For 'tis best to get your family over and done with, as soon as you can, so as to be all the earlier out of the fag o't."[15]

"And what may be this glad cause?" asked the stranger.

"A birth and christening," said the shepherd.

The stranger hoped his host might not be made unhappy either by too many or too few of such episodes, and being invited by a gesture to a pull at the mug, he readily acquiesced. His manner, which, before entering, had been so dubious, was now altogether that of a careless and candid man.

"Late to be traipsing athwart this coomb—hey?" said the engaged man of fifty.

"Late it is, master, as you say.—I'll take a seat in the chimney corner, if you have nothing to urge against it, ma'am; for I am a little moist on the side that was next the rain."

Mrs. Shepherd Fennel assented, and made room for the self-invited comer, who, having got completely inside the chimney corner, stretched out his legs and his arms with the expansiveness of a person quite at home.

"Yes, I am rather cracked in the vamp,"[16] he said freely, seeing that the eyes of the shepherd's wife fell upon his boots, "and I am not well fitted either. I have had some rough times lately, and have been forced to pick up what I can get in the way of wearing, but I must find a suit better fit for working days when I reach home."

"One of hereabouts?" she inquired.

"Not quite that—farther up the country."

"I thought so. And so be I; and by your tongue you come from my neighborhood."

"But you would hardly have heard of me," he said quickly. "My time would be long before yours, ma'am, you see."

This testimony to the youthfulness of his hostess had the effect of stopping her cross-examination.

"There is only one thing more wanted to make me happy," continued the newcomer. "And that is a little baccy,[17] which I am sorry to say I am out of."

"I'll fill your pipe," said the shepherd.

"I must ask you to lend me a pipe likewise."

"A smoker, and no pipe about 'ee?"

---

**15. fag o't:** Fatigue of it.

**16. vamp** n.: The part of a shoe or boot covering the instep.
**17. baccy:** Tobacco.

"I have dropped it somewhere on the road."

The shepherd filled and handed him a new clay pipe, saying, as he did so, "Hand me your baccy box—I'll fill that too, now I am about it."

The man went through the movement of searching his pockets.

"Lost that too?" said his entertainer, with some surprise.

"I am afraid so," said the man with some confusion. "Give it to me in a screw of paper." Lighting his pipe at the candle with a suction that drew the whole flame into the bowl, he resettled himself in the corner and bent his looks upon the faint steam from his damp legs, as if he wished to say no more.

Meanwhile the general body of guests had been taking little notice of this visitor by reason of an absorbing discussion in which they were engaged with the band about a tune for the next dance. The matter being settled, they were about to stand up when an interruption came in the shape of another knock at the door.

At sound of the same the man in the chimney corner took up the poker and began stirring the brands as if doing it thoroughly were the one aim of his existence; and a second time the shepherd said, "Walk in!" In a moment another man stood upon the straw-woven doormat. He too was a stranger.

This individual was one of a type radically different from the first. There was more of the commonplace in his manner, and a certain jovial cosmopolitanism sat upon his features. He was several years older than the first arrival, his hair being slightly frosted, his eyebrows bristly, and his whiskers cut back from his cheeks. His face was rather full and flabby, and yet it was not altogether a face without power. A few grog blossoms marked the neighborhood of his nose. He flung back his long drab greatcoat, revealing that beneath it he wore a suit of cinder-gray shade throughout, large heavy seals, of some metal or other that would take a polish, dangling from his fob as his only personal ornament. Shaking the water drops from his low-crowned glazed hat, he said, "I must ask for a few minutes' shelter, comrades, or I shall be wetted to my skin before I get to Casterbridge."

"Make yourself at home, master," said the shepherd, perhaps a trifle less heartily than on the first occasion. Not that Fennel had the least tinge of niggardliness in his composition; but the room was far from large, spare chairs were not numerous, and damp companions were not altogether desirable at close quarters for the women and girls in their bright-colored gowns.

However, the second comer, after taking off his greatcoat, and hanging his hat on a nail in one of the ceiling beams as if he had been specially invited to put it there, advanced and sat down on the table. This had been pushed so closely into the chimney corner, to give all available room to the dancers, that its inner edge grazed the elbow of the man who had ensconced himself by the fire; and thus the two strangers were brought into close companionship. They nodded to each other by way of breaking the ice of unacquaintance, and the first stranger handed his neighbor the family mug—a huge vessel of brown ware, having its upper edge worn away like a threshold by the rub of whole generations of thirsty lips that had gone the way of all flesh, and bearing the following inscription burnt upon its rotund side in yellow letters:

THERE IS NO FUN

UNTiLL i CUM

The other man, nothing loth,[18] raised the mug to his lips, and drank on, and on, and on—till a curious blueness overspread the countenance of the shepherd's wife, who had regarded with no little surprise the first stranger's free offer to the second of what did not belong to him to dispense.

"I knew it!" said the toper to the shepherd with much satisfaction. "When I walked up your garden before coming in, and saw the hives all of a row, I said to myself, 'Where there's bees there's honey, and where there's honey there's mead.' But mead of such a truly comfortable sort as this I really didn't expect to meet in my older days." He took yet another pull at the mug, till it assumed an ominous elevation.

"Glad you enjoy it!" said the shepherd warmly.

"It is goodish mead," assented Mrs. Fennel, with an absence of enthusiasm which seemed to say that it was possible to buy praise for one's cellar at too heavy a price. "It is trouble enough to make—and really I hardly think we shall make any more. For honey sells well, and we ourselves can make shift with a drop o' small mead and metheglin[19] for common use from the comb-washings."

"O, but you'll never have the heart!" reproachfully cried the stranger in cinder gray, after taking up the mug a third time and setting it down empty. "I love mead, when 'tis old like this, as I love to go to church o' Sundays, or to relieve the needy any day of the week."

"Ha, ha, ha!" said the man in the chimney corner, who, in spite of the taciturnity induced by the pipe of tobacco, could not or would not refrain from this slight testimony to his comrade's humor.

Now the old mead of those days, brewed of the purest first-year or maiden honey, four pounds to the gallon—with its due complement of white of eggs, cinnamon, ginger, cloves, mace, rosemary, yeast, and processes of working, bottling, and cellaring —tasted remarkably strong; but it did not taste so strong as it actually was. Hence,

---

**18. nothing loth:** Not reluctant.

**19. small mead and metheglin:** Weaker types of mead.

presently, the stranger in cinder gray at the table, moved by its creeping influence, unbuttoned his waistcoat, threw himself back in his chair, spread his legs, and made his presence felt in various ways.

"Well, well, as I say," he resumed, "I am going to Casterbridge, and to Casterbridge I must go. I should have been almost there by this time; but the rain drove me into your dwelling, and I'm not sorry for it."

"You don't live in Casterbridge?" said the shepherd.

"Not as yet; though I shortly mean to move there."

"Going to set up in trade, perhaps?"

"No, no," said the shepherd's wife. "It is easy to see that the gentleman is rich, and don't want to work at anything."

The cinder-gray stranger paused, as if to consider whether he would accept that definition of himself. He presently rejected it by answering, "Rich is not quite the word for me, dame. I do work, and I must work. And even if I only get to Casterbridge by midnight I must begin work there at eight tomorrow morning. Yes, het or wet, blow or snow, famine or sword, my day's work tomorrow must be done."

"Poor man! Then, in spite o' seeming, you be worse off than we?" replied the shepherd's wife.

"'Tis the nature of my trade, men and maidens. 'Tis the nature of my trade more than my poverty. . . . But really and truly I must up and off, or I shan't get a lodging in the town." However, the speaker did not move, and directly added, "There's time for one more draft of friendship before I go; and I'd perform it at once if the mug were not dry."

"Here's a mug o' small," said Mrs. Fennel. "Small, we call it, though to be sure 'tis only the first wash o' the combs."

"No," said the stranger disdainfully. "I won't spoil your first kindness by partaking o' your second."

"Certainly not," broke in Fennel. "We don't increase and multiply every day, and I'll fill the mug again." He went away to the dark place under the stairs where the barrel stood. The shepherdess followed him.

"Why should you do this?" she said reproachfully, as soon as they were alone. "He's emptied it once, though it held enough for ten people; and now he's not contented wi' the small, but must needs call for more o' the strong! And a stranger unbeknown to any of us. For my part, I don't like the look o' the man at all."

"But he's in the house, my honey; and 'tis a wet night, and a christening. Daze it, what's a cup of mead more or less? There'll be plenty more next bee-burning."

"Very well—this time, then," she answered, looking wistfully at the barrel. "But what is the man's calling, and where is he one of, that he should come in and join us like this?"

"I don't know. I'll ask him again."

The catastrophe of having the mug drained dry at one pull by the stranger in cinder gray was effectually guarded against this time by Mrs. Fennel. She poured out his allowance in a small cup, keeping the large one at a discreet distance from him. When he had tossed off his portion, the shepherd renewed his inquiry about the stranger's occupation.

The latter did not immediately reply, and the man in the chimney corner, with sudden demonstrativeness, said, "Anybody may know my trade—I'm a wheelwright."

"A very good trade for these parts," said the shepherd.

"And anybody may know mine—if they've the sense to find it out," said the stranger in cinder gray.

"You may generally tell what a man is by his claws," observed the hedge carpenter, looking at his own hands. "My fingers be as full of thorns as an old pincushion is of pins."

The hands of the man in the chimney corner instinctively sought the shade, and he gazed into the fire as he resumed his pipe. The man at the table took up the hedge carpenter's remark, and added smartly, "True; but the oddity of my trade is that, instead of setting a mark upon me, it sets a mark upon my customers.''

No observation being offered by anybody in elucidation of this enigma the shepherd's wife once more called for a song. The same obstacles presented themselves as at the former time—one had no voice, another had forgotten the first verse. The stranger at the table, whose soul had now risen to a good working temperature, relieved the difficulty by exclaiming that, to start the company, he would sing himself. Thrusting one thumb into the armhole of his waistcoat, he waved the other hand in the air, and, with an extemporizing gaze at the shining sheep crooks above the mantelpiece, began:

> *"O my trade it is the rarest one,*
> *Simple shepherds all—*
> *My trade is a sight to see;*
> *For my customers I tie, and*
>   *take them up on high,*
> *And waft 'em to a far countree!"*

The room was silent when he had finished the verse—with one exception, that of the man in the chimney corner, who, at the singer's word, "Chorus!" joined him in a deep bass voice of musical relish—

> *"And waft 'em to a far countree!"*

Oliver Giles, John Pitcher the dairyman, the parish clerk, the engaged man of fifty, the row of young women against the wall, seemed lost in thought not of the gayest kind. The shepherd looked meditatively on the ground, the shepherdess gazed keenly at the singer, and with some suspicion; she was doubting whether this stranger were merely singing an old song from recollection, or was composing one there and then for the occasion. All were as perplexed at the obscure revelation as the guests at Belshazzar's Feast,[20] except the man in the chimney

---

**20. as the . . . Belshazzar's** (bel shaz'ərz) **Feast:** In the Old Testament, writing appeared on the wall during a feast held by the king of Babylon warning him of defeat (Ezekiel 5:1).

corner, who quietly said, "Second verse, stranger," and smoked on.

The singer thoroughly moistened himself from his lips inwards, and went on with the next stanza as requested:

> *"My tools are but common ones,*
> *Simple shepherds all—*
> *My tools are no sight to see:*
> *A little hempen string, and a post*
>   *whereon to swing,*
> *Are implements enough for me!"*

Shepherd Fennel glanced round. There was no longer any doubt that the stranger was answering his question rhythmically. The guests one and all started back with suppressed exclamations. The young woman engaged to the man of fifty fainted halfway, and would have proceeded, but finding him wanting in alacrity for catching her she sat down trembling.

"Oh, he's the—!" whispered the people in the background, mentioning the name of an ominous public officer. "He's come to do it! 'Tis to be at Casterbridge jail tomorrow —the man for sheep-stealing—the poor clockmaker we heard of, who used to live away at Shottsford and had no work to do —Timothy Summers, whose family were a-starving, and so he went out of Shottsford by the high road, and took a sheep in open daylight, defying the farmer and the farmer's wife and the farmer's lad, and every man jack among 'em. He' (and they nodded towards the stranger of the deadly trade) 'is come from up the country to do it because there's not enough to do in his own county town, and he's got the place here now our own county man's dead; he's going to live in the same cottage under the prison wall."

The stranger in cinder gray took no notice of this whispered string of observations, but again wetted his lips. Seeing that his friend in the chimney corner was the only one who reciprocated his joviality in any way, he held out his cup towards that appreciative comrade, who also held out his own. They clinked together, the eyes of the rest of the room hanging upon the singer's actions. He parted his lips for the third verse; but at that moment another knock was audible upon the door. This time the knock was faint and hesitating.

The company seemed scared; the shepherd looked with consternation towards the entrance, and it was with some effort that he resisted his alarmed wife's deprecatory glance, and uttered for the third time the welcoming words, "Walk in!"

The door was gently opened, and another man stood upon the mat. He, like those who had preceded him, was a stranger. This time it was a short, small personage, of fair complexion, and dressed in a decent suit of dark clothes.

"Can you tell me the way to—?" he began; when, gazing round the room to observe the nature of the company amongst whom he had fallen, his eyes lighted on the stranger in cinder gray. It was just at the instant when the latter, who had thrown his mind into his song with such a will that he scarcely heeded the interruption, silenced all whispers and inquiries by bursting into his third verse:

*"Tomorrow is my working day,*
*Simple shepherds all—*
*Tomorrow is a working day for me:*
*For the farmer's sheep is slain,*
*  and the lad who did it ta'en,*
*And on his soul may God ha' merc-y!"*

The stranger in the chimney corner, waving cups with the singer so heartily that his mead splashed over on the hearth, repeated in his bass voice as before:—

*"And on his soul may God ha' merc-y!"*

All this time the third stranger had been standing in the doorway. Finding now that he did not come forward or go on speaking, the guests particularly regarded him. They noticed to their surprise that he stood before them the picture of abject terror—his knees trembling, his hand shaking so violently

that the door latch by which he supported himself rattled audibly; his white lips were parted, and his eyes fixed on the merry officer of justice in the middle of the room. A moment more and he had turned, closed the door, and fled.

"What a man can it be?" said the shepherd.

The rest, between the awfulness of their late discovery and the odd conduct of this third visitor, looked as if they knew not what to think, and said nothing. Instinctively they withdrew farther and farther from the grim gentleman in their midst, whom some of them seemed to take for the Prince of Darkness himself, till they formed a remote circle, an empty space of floor being left between them and him—. . . *circulus, cujus centrum diabolus.*[21] The room was so silent—though there were more than twenty people in it—that nothing could be heard but the patter of the rain against the window shutters, accompanied by the occasional hiss of a stray drop that fell down the chimney into the fire, and the steady puffing of the man in the corner, who had now resumed his pipe of long clay.

The stillness was unexpectedly broken. The distant sound of a gun reverberated through the air—apparently from the direction of the county town.

"Be jiggered!" cried the stranger who had sung the song, jumping up.

"What does that mean?" asked several.

"A prisoner escaped from the jail —that's what it means."

All listened. The sound was repeated, and none of them spoke but the man in the chimney corner, who said quietly, "I've often been told that in this county they fire a gun at such times; but I never heard it till now."

"I wonder if it is *my* man?" murmured the personage in cinder gray.

"Surely it is!" said the shepherd invol-

---

**21. *circulus . . . diabolus:*** A circle with the devil at its center.

untarily. "And surely we've zeed him! That little man who looked in at the door by now, and quivered like a leaf when he zeed ye and heard your song!"

"His teeth chattered, and the breath went out of his body," said the dairyman.

"And his heart seemed to sink within him like a stone," said Oliver Giles.

"And he bolted as if he'd been shot at," said the hedge carpenter.

"True—his teeth chattered, and his heart seemed to sink; and he bolted as if he'd been shot at," slowly summed up the man in the chimney corner.

"I didn't notice it," remarked the hangman.

"We were all a-wondering what made him run off in such a fright," faltered one of the women against the wall, "and now 'tis explained!"

The firing of the alarm gun went on at intervals, low and sullenly, and their suspicions became a certainty. The sinister gentleman in cinder gray roused himself. "Is there a constable here?" he asked, in thick tones. "If so, let him step forward."

The engaged man of fifty stepped quavering out from the wall, his betrothed beginning to sob on the back of the chair.

"You are a sworn constable?"

"I be, sir."

"Then pursue the criminal at once, with assistance, and bring him back here. He can't have gone far."

"I will, sir, I will—when I've got my staff. I'll go home and get it, and come sharp here, and start in a body."

"Staff!—never mind your staff; the man'll be gone!"

"But I can't do nothing without my staff—can I, William, and John, and Charles Jake? No; for there's the king's royal crown a painted on en in yaller and gold, and the lion and the unicorn, so as when I raise en up and hit my prisoner, 'tis made a lawful blow thereby. I wouldn't 'tempt to take up a man without my staff—no, not I. If I hadn't the law to gie me courage, why, instead o' my taking up him he might take up me!"

"Now, I'm a king's man myself, and can give you authority enough for this," said the formidable officer in gray. "Now then, all of ye, be ready. Have ye any lanterns?"

"Yes—have ye any lanterns?—I demand it!" said the constable.

"And the rest of you able-bodied—"

"Able-bodied men—yes—the rest of ye!" said the constable.

"Have you some good stout staves and pitchforks—"

"Staves and pitchforks—in the name o' the law! And take 'em in yer hands and go in quest, and do as we in authority tell ye!"

Thus aroused, the men prepared to give chase. The evidence was, indeed, though circumstantial, so convincing, that but little argument was needed to show the shepherd's guests that after what they had seen it would look very much like connivance if they did not instantly pursue the unhappy third stranger, who could not as yet have gone more than a few hundred yards over such uneven country.

A shepherd is always well provided with lanterns; and, lighting these hastily, and with hurdle staves in their hands, they poured out of the door, taking a direction along the crest of the hill, away from the town, the rain having fortunately a little abated.

Disturbed by the noise, or possibly by unpleasant dreams of her baptism, the child who had been christened began to cry heartbrokenly in the room overhead. These notes of grief came down through the chinks of the floor to the ears of the women below, who jumped up one by one, and seemed glad of the excuse to ascend and comfort the baby, for the incidents of the last half-hour greatly oppressed them. Thus in the space of two or three minutes the room on the ground floor was deserted quite.

But it was not for long. Hardly had the sound of footsteps died away when a man returned round the corner of the house from the direction the pursuers had taken. Peeping in at the door, and seeing nobody there, he entered leisurely. It was the stranger of the chimney corner, who had gone out with the rest. The motive of his return was shown by his helping himself to a cut piece of skimmer cake that lay on a ledge beside where he had sat, and which he had apparently forgotten to take with him. He also poured out half a cup more mead from the quantity that remained, ravenously eating and drinking these as he stood. He had not finished when another figure came in just as quietly—his friend in cinder gray.

"O—you here?" said the latter, smiling. "I thought you had gone to help in the capture." And this speaker also revealed the object of his return by looking solicitously round for the fascinating mug of old mead.

"And I thought you had gone," said the other, continuing his skimmer cake with some effort.

"Well, on second thoughts, I felt there were enough without me," said the first confidentially, "and such a night as it is, too. Besides, 'tis the business o' the government to take care of its criminals—not mine."

"True; so it is. And I felt as you did, that there were enough without me."

"I don't want to break my limbs running over the humps and hollows of this wild country."

"Nor I neither, between you and me."

"These shepherd people are used to it —simple-minded souls, you know, stirred up to anything in a moment. They'll have him ready for me before the morning, and no trouble to me at all."

"They'll have him, and we shall have saved ourselves all labor in the matter."

"True, true. Well, my way is to Casterbridge; and 'tis as much as my legs will do to take me that far. Going the same way?"

"No, I am sorry to say! I have to get home over there" (he nodded indefinitely to the right), "and I feel as you do, that it is quite enough for my legs to do before bedtime."

The other had by this time finished the mead in the mug, after which, shaking hands heartily at the door, and wishing each other well, they went their several ways.

In the meantime the company of pursuers had reached the end of the hog's-back elevation which dominated this part of the down. They had decided on no particular plan of action; and, finding that the man of the baleful trade was no longer in their company, they seemed quite unable to form any such plan now. They descended in all directions down the hill, and straightway several of the party fell into the snare set by Nature for all misguided midnight ramblers over this part of the cretaceous formation. The 'lanchets,' or flint slopes, which belted the escarpment at intervals of a dozen yards, took the less cautious ones unawares, and losing their footing on the rubbly steep they slid sharply downwards, the lanterns rolling from their hands to the bottom, and there lying on their sides till the horn was scorched through.

When they had again gathered themselves together the shepherd, as the man who knew the country best, took the lead, and guided them round these treacherous inclines. The lanterns, which seemed rather to dazzle their eyes and warn the fugitive than to assist them in the exploration, were extinguished, due silence was observed; and in this more rational order they plunged into the vale. It was a grassy, briery, moist defile, affording some shelter to any person who had sought it; but the party perambulated it in vain, and ascended on the other side. Here they wandered apart, and after an interval closed together again to report progress. At the second time of closing in they found themselves near a lonely ash, the single tree on this part of the coomb, probably sown there by a passing bird some fifty years before. And here, standing a little to one side of the trunk, as motionless as the trunk itself, appeared the man they were in quest of, his outline being well defined against the sky beyond. The band noiselessly drew up and faced him.

"Your money or your life!" said the constable sternly to the still figure.

"No, no," whispered John Pitcher. "'Tisn't our side ought to say that. That's the doctrine of vagabonds like him, and we be on the side of the law."

"Well, well," replied the constable impatiently; "I must say something, mustn't I? and if you had all the weight o' this undertaking upon your mind, perhaps you'd say the wrong thing too! Prisoner at the bar, surrender, in the name of the Father—the Crown, I mane!"

The man under the tree seemed now to notice them for the first time, and, giving them no opportunity whatever for exhibiting their courage, he strolled slowly towards them. He was, indeed, the little man, the third stranger; but his trepidation had in a great measure gone.

"Well, travelers," he said, "did I hear ye speak to me?"

"You did; you've got to come and be our prisoner at once!" said the constable. "We arrest 'ee on the charge of not biding in Casterbridge jail in a decent proper manner to be hung tomorrow morning. Neighbors, do your duty, and seize the culpet!"

On hearing the charge the man seemed enlightened, and, saying not another word, resigned himself with preternatural civility to the search party, who, with their staves in their hands, surrounded him on all sides, and marched him back towards the shepherd's cottage.

It was eleven o'clock by the time they arrived. The light shining from the open door, a sound of men's voices within, proclaimed to them as they approached the house that some new events had arisen in their absence. On entering they discovered the shepherd's living room to be invaded by two officers from Casterbridge jail, and a well-known magistrate who lived at the nearest county seat, intelligence of the escape having become generally circulated.

"Gentlemen," said the constable, "I have brought back your man—not without risk and danger; but everyone must do his duty! He is inside this circle of able-bodied persons, who have lent me useful aid, considering their ignorance of Crown work. Men, bring forward your prisoner!" And the third stranger was led to the light.

"Who is this?" said one of the officials.

"The man," said the constable.

"Certainly not," said the turnkey; and the first corroborated his statement.

"But how can it be otherwise?" asked the constable. "Or why was he so terrified at sight o' the singing instrument of the law who sat there?" Here he related the strange behavior of the third stranger on entering the house during the hangman's song.

"Can't understand it," said the officer coolly. "All I know is that it is not the condemned man. He's quite a different character from this one; a gauntish fellow, with dark hair and eyes, rather good-looking, and with a musical bass voice that if you heard it once you'd never mistake as long as you lived."

"Why, souls—'twas the man in the chimney corner!"

"Hey—what?" said the magistrate, coming forward after inquiring particulars from the shepherd in the background. "Haven't you got the man after all?"

"Well, sir," said the constable, "he's the man we were in search of, that's true; and yet he's not the man we were in search of. For the man we were in search of was not the man we wanted, sir, if you understand my everyday way; for 'twas the man in the chimney corner!"

"A pretty kettle of fish altogether!" said the magistrate. "You had better start for the other man at once."

The prisoner now spoke for the first time. The mention of the man in the chimney corner seemed to have moved him as nothing else could do. "Sir," he said, stepping forward to the magistrate, "take no more trouble about me. The time is come when I may as well speak. I have done nothing; my crime is that the condemned man is my brother. Early this afternoon I left home at Shottsford to tramp it all the way to Casterbridge jail to bid him farewell. I was benighted, and called here to rest and ask the way. When I opened the door I saw before me the very man, my brother, that I thought to see in the condemned cell at Casterbridge. He was in this chimney corner; and jammed close to him, so that he could not have got out if he had tried, was the executioner who'd come to take his life, singing a song about it and not knowing that it was his victim who was close by, joining in to save appearances. My brother threw a glance of agony at me, and I knew he meant, 'Don't reveal what you see; my life depends on it.' I was so terror-struck that I could hardly stand, and, not knowing what I did, I turned and hurried away.''

The narrator's manner and tone had the stamp of truth, and his story made a great impression on all around. "And do you know where your brother is at the present time?'' asked the magistrate.

"I do not. I have never seen him since I closed this door.''

"I can testify to that, for we've been between ye ever since,'' said the constable.

"Where does he think to fly to? What is his occupation?''

"He's a watch-and-clock-maker, sir.''

"'A said 'a was a wheelwright—a wicked rogue,'' said the constable.

"The wheels of clocks and watches he meant, no doubt,'' said Shepherd Fennel. "I thought his hands were palish for's trade.''

"Well, it appears to me that nothing can be gained by retaining this poor man in custody,'' said the magistrate; "your business lies with the other, unquestionably.''

And so the little man was released offhand; but he looked nothing the less sad on that account, it being beyond the power of magistrate or constable to raze out the written troubles in his brain, for they concerned another whom he regarded with more solicitude than himself. When this was done, and the man had gone his way, the night was found to be so far advanced that it was deemed useless to renew the search before the next morning.

Next day, accordingly, the quest for the clever sheep stealer became general and keen, to all appearance at least. But the intended punishment was cruelly disproportioned to the transgression, and the sympathy of a great many country folk in that district was strongly on the side of the fugitive. Moreover, his marvelous coolness and daring in hob-and-nobbing with the hangman, under the unprecedented circumstances of the shepherd's party, won their admiration. So that it may be questioned if all those who ostensibly made themselves so busy in exploring woods and fields and lanes were quite so thorough when it came to the private examination of their own lofts and outhouses. Stories were afloat of a mysterious figure being occasionally seen in some old overgrown trackway or other, remote from turnpike roads; but when a search was instituted in any of these suspected quarters nobody was found. Thus the days and weeks passed without tidings.

In brief, the bass-voiced man of the chimney corner was never recaptured. Some said that he went across the sea, others that he did not, but buried himself in the depths of a populous city. At any rate, the gentleman in cinder gray never did his morning's work at Casterbridge, nor met anywhere at all, for business purposes, the genial comrade with whom he had passed an hour of relaxation in the lonely house on the slope of the coomb.

The grass has long been green on the graves of Shepherd Fennel and his frugal wife; the guests who made up the christening party have mainly followed their entertainers to the tomb; the baby in whose honor they all had met is a matron in the sere and yellow leaf. But the arrival of the three strangers at the shepherd's that night, and the details connected therewith, is a story as well known as ever in the country about Higher Crowstairs.

## THINKING ABOUT THE SELECTION
### Recalling

1. (a) Where and when does the story take place? (b) What event is being celebrated?
2. (a) Describe the appearance of the first stranger. (b) Of the second stranger.
3. (a) What is the second stranger's occupation? (b) How is this revealed?
4. (a) Whom does Shepherd Fennel assume the third stranger to be? (b) Why?

### Interpreting

5. What do the speech habits of the Fennels and their guests reveal about them?
6. (a) How early on did you guess the identity of the first stranger? (b) The second? (c) The third? (d) What clues did you use?

### Applying

7. What does this story suggest about its author's respect for institutions such as the law in nineteenth-century England? Explain.

## ANALYZING LITERATURE
### Setting and Mood

The setting of a story is when and where the action occurs. In addition to such "factual" details as place names and historical references, setting also accounts for time of day, season, weather conditions, and the like. Aspects of setting, especially of the latter type help determine a story's mood—the emotional response it excites in its readers. Read the following details of setting from "The Three Strangers." Tell the mood suggested by each detail and by all of them taken together. Explain why each detail creates the mood it does.

1. Fifty years ago such a lonely cottage stood.
2. The level rainstorm smote walls, slopes, and hedges . . . ; the tails of little birds trying to roost on some scraggy thorn were blown inside out like umbrellas. The gable-end of the cottage was stained wet.
3. The room was lighted by half a dozen candles. . . . On the hearth . . . blazed a fire of thorns that crackled.

## CRITICAL THINKING AND READING
### Inferring the Author's Attitude

In "The Three Strangers" fate plays an important—and sometimes fickle—role. Had fate, for instance, not decreed a rainstorm, the sheep-stealer might never have come face-to-face with his executioner. And it is the same fateful rainstorm that enables the guilty man to escape capture by his pursuers. From these and other events in the story, attempt to **infer,** or arrive at an understanding of, Hardy's attitude toward the role of fate. Ask yourself: Does he seem to feel that fate governs our lives? To what extent does he believe that we can and should alter fate by exercising our own free will?

## UNDERSTANDING LANGUAGE
### Reading Dialect

Most of the characters in the story speak in a particular **dialect,** or manner of speech that typifies a particular region or group. The use of dialect in a story adds to both its realism and its local flavor. Restate each of the following quotations in standard English.

1. "Late to be traipsing athwart this coomb —hey?" (page 886)
2. "A smoker, and no pipe about 'ee?" (page 886)
3. ". . . That little man . . . quivered . . . when he zeed ye . . . !" (page 892)
4. "'A said 'a was a wheelwright . . ." (page 895)

## THINKING AND WRITING
### Describing a Place

Choose a place that you know well —perhaps the neighborhood you live in or a city that you have visited often. On a sheet of paper jot down as many details of the place as you can think of. Try to include in your list features that make the location unique, or at least easy to visualize. Then convert your notes into a description that would enable a stranger to picture it with little difficulty. Be prepared to share your description with your class.

# MASTERS OF THE VICTORIAN NOVEL

### The Victorian Novel

From the sprawling canvas of Dickens's London to the compelling atmosphere of Emily Brontë's wild moors, the Victorian novel has made a lasting impression on literature and readers. Most of the novels written during this era are concerned with manners, morals, and money. Frequently the plot centers around the struggles of a main character to find self-knowledge with regard to others, in love or marriage, with family or neighbors, or within the working world. Sometimes the quest for self has spiritual overtones, as in the later novels of Thomas Hardy, although the major Victorian novelists in the main were more concerned with people's relationships to society than to religion.

The novels were frequently published in inexpensive monthly installments. To hold their readers' interest between parts, the writers built a minor climax into each installment. This led to a loose, episodic treatment with a vast, intricate plot, numerous characters, and much repetition to jog the reader's memory. Modern novelist Henry James called Victorian novels "large loose baggy monsters," but readers delighted in the suspenseful form.

### Giants of the Victorian Novel

In such novels as *Ivanhoe* (1820), Sir Walter Scott, the first major historical novelist, created vivid portraits of Scotland, England, and the Continent from medieval times to the eighteenth century. William Makepeace Thackeray's foray into the historical novel, *Henry Esmond* (1852), was very successful, but *Vanity Fair* (1847) remains his masterpiece. Because of its narrative skill and vivid characterization, the satire immediately established his reputation as one of the major literary figures of the time. Many heroines were modeled on the main character, Becky Sharp. Charlotte Brontë's fictionalized autobiography of a young orphan, *Jane Eyre* (1847), sparked a series of novels on governesses, which became a popular genre through which to explore women's role in society. Her sister Emily's unique tale of love, revenge, and redemption, *Wuthering Heights*, comments on the tensions of nineteenth-century life in a different fashion. The most popular writer of the age, Charles Dickens, combined vivid storytelling, humor, pathos, and irony with sharp social criticism and acute observations of people and places, both real and imagined. His fame was based on an astonishing stream of novels, including *Nicholas Nickleby* (1837–1838), *Bleak House* (1852–1853), and *Great Expectations* (1860–1861).

"The art of novels," wrote Thackeray, "*is* to represent nature: to convey as strongly as possible the sentiment of reality." The continued appeal of Victorian novels comes in large part from their realistic portrayal of Victorian life.

# GREAT WORKS

## WUTHERING HEIGHTS
### by Emily Brontë

## A Tale of Love

If all else perished, and he remained I should continue to be; and if all else remained, and he were annihilated, the universe would turn to a mighty stranger: I should not seem a part of it. My love for Linton is like the foliage in the woods: time will change it, I'm well aware, as winter changes the trees. My love for Heathcliff resembles the eternal rocks beneath: a source of little visible delight, but necessary. Nelly, I am Heathcliff. He's always, always in my mind: not as a pleasure, any more than I am always a pleasure to myself, but as my own being.

Who could inspire such devotion in the heart of the willful, passionate Catherine Earnshaw? Only wild, fierce Heathcliff, more villain than hero, a man whose soul is torn between love and hate.

## Heathcliff

Emily Brontë's *Wuthering Heights* opens in 1801 with the arrival of Mr. Lockwood at Thrushcross Grange, a house that he has rented on the windswept Yorkshire moor. He crosses the moor to meet his landlord, Heathcliff. His curiosity is sparked by gloomy, crumbling Wuthering Heights, Heathcliff's home. The savagely handsome Heathcliff is initially unfriendly but unbends enough to offer Lockwood some small social courtesy.

Lockwood's next visit goes far less smoothly. He is repulsed by the hatred among those gathered: Heathcliff, sullen young Hareton Earnshaw, and Heathcliff's beautiful, defiant daughter-in-law. Trapped by a raging snowstorm, he is reluctantly allowed to spend the night. During a violent nightmare, he imagines himself smashing the window, grabbing an icy cold hand, and hearing a voice sobbing, "I'm Catherine Linton, I'm home!" His scream awakens Heathcliff, who reacts violently to Lockwood's tale, wrenching open the window and crying, "Come in! come in! Cathy, do come. Oh do—*once* more! Oh! my heart's darling, hear me *this* time—Catherine, at last!" Lockwood makes his way home as soon as he can, soaked and chilled to the bone. What are we to make of all this?

## Mrs. Dean's Tale

Lockwood questions his housekeeper, Nelly Dean, about the strange people he has met. We learn that Heathcliff was married to Isabella, sister of Mr. Linton, the previous owner of Wuthering Heights. Hareton Earnshaw is Heathcliff's nephew. The rest of the wild story unfolds through Nelly's eyes.

Many years ago, Mr. Earnshaw, the former master, had returned from a trip with a "dirty, ragged, black-haired" waif he had picked up on the streets of Liverpool. Although both of Earnshaw's children—Hindley and Catherine—hated the boy on sight, Nelly named him "Heathcliff," and he remained. Catherine grew passionately attached to him, but with Mr. Earnshaw's death two years later, Hindley was freed to enact his resentment and mistreat Heathcliff fiercely. The outcast becomes even more brutal and morose. Catherine and Heathcliff, now closer than ever, seize any opportunity to escape, running wildly across the desolate moors. Hindley's wife gives birth to Hareton and dies; Hindley becomes a drunken brute.

One evening Catherine and Heathcliff end up at the Grange, and peer in the window at the spoiled Linton children, Edgar and Isabella. Catherine is injured and recuperates with the Lintons. A closeness grows between the families, and despite the love she feels for Heathcliff, she marries Edgar Linton. Tender, constant, and loving, he has all the qualities of the hero of conventional Victorian novels—and is no match for headstrong, selfish Catherine. Heathcliff bolts from Wuthering Heights.

When he returns six months later, he is rich and well-groomed. Torn between her love for Heathcliff and her husband's jealousy, she weakens. After giving birth to Edgar's child, Cathy, she dies. For the next seventeen years, Heathcliff is bent on revenge. He marries Edgar's sister, Isabella, and turns Hindley into a drunken gambler, obtaining all his property. Isabella has a son, Linton, whom Heathcliff marries off to Cathy. His plans fall apart, however, when Linton dies and Cathy falls in love with and marries Hareton. Heathcliff's end is the most astonishing of all, however . . .

## Emily Brontë

The daughter of an Irish clergyman, Emily Brontë (1818–1848) whose efforts gave the world *Wuthering Heights* in 1847, was one of three novel-writing sisters. Charlotte wrote *Jane Eyre* and Anne wrote *Agnes Grey.*

Born in the Yorkshire town of Hartshead-cum-Clifton, Brontë was raised, along with her brother and four sisters, by an aunt, following the early death of their mother. As children, the Brontës were often left to themselves. For recreation they walked the bleak moors near Haworth, where the family had moved from Hartshead, and invented imaginary "histories" for toy soldiers, a pastime they continued to pursue up through their teen years. In 1842 Emily went to Brussels with her sister Charlotte, to study at the Pensionnat Heger, in the hopes of starting their own school. The death of their aunt, however, brought the sisters prematurely back to Yorkshire.

In 1845 Charlotte accidentally discovered some poems that Emily had composed. The discovery led in turn to the revelation that Charlotte and Anne had secretly been writing poetry as well, and in 1846 the three talented Brontës published at their own expense a book of verses by "Currer, Ellis, and Acton Bell," the pen names that kept the sisters' initials but hid their real names. The book sold only two copies, but the venture had stoked the sisters' creative fires, and each began work on a novel.

For her project Emily chose to write about the Yorkshire countryside she knew so well. And she chose to write about it with the same poetic voice that typified the romantic tales she had produced as a child.

The result, *Wuthering Heights,* is a tale of love, revenge, and redemption that comments on the tensions of nineteenth-century society. Unlike Charlotte's *Jane Eyre,* which became an instant success, *Wuthering Heights* failed in its day to gain the recognition it deserved.

Emily, meanwhile, was in poor health, having long suffered from a respiratory condition. She died at the age of thirty.

That Emily Brontë may have intended her masterpiece as a visionary work is suggested by a study of her poetry, which expresses her impatience with social order and her yearning for a "dazzling sea" of infinity. As some contemporary critics have suggested, *Wuthering Heights* clouds rather than explains the mysteries of Brontë's brief life, yet there is no denying the enormous imaginative power behind the words.

## An Unnoticed Masterpiece

*Wuthering Heights* went unnoticed when it was published in 1847. The handful of people who did read it were repulsed by the brutal violence of the characters and by its differences from the conventional romantic novels of the day. Critics today consider *Wuthering Heights* as the "one perfect work of art amid all the vast varied canvases of Victorian fiction." Brontë died on December 19, 1848, knowing nothing at all of the overwhelming success that would finally be accorded to her book. "*Wuthering Heights* is a strange sort of book," said a critic the year after her death, "baffling all regular criticism; yet, it is impossible to begin and not finish it; and quite impossible to lay it aside afterwards and say nothing about it. . . . We strongly recommend all our readers who love novelty to get this story, for we can promise them that they will never have read anything like it before."

## THE IMPORTANCE OF BEING EARNEST
by Oscar Wilde

### Oscar Wilde

Oscar Wilde (1854–1900) was born in Dublin, Ireland, the son of a famous surgeon and a Dublin poet. He was educated at Trinity college, Dublin, and later at Magdalen College, Oxford where he excelled in his studies and received the prestigious Newdigate prize for poetry. Wilde's full name was as extravagant as he was. The unconventional Oscar Fingal O'Flahertie Wills Wilde delighted in shocking his audiences. In plays like *Lady Windermere's Fan*, *A Woman of No Importance*, and *An Ideal Husband*, he turned the correct and proper on its head, poking fun at the conventions of Victorian behavior. As an advocate of the school of Aestheticism, Wilde championed the cause of "art for art's sake."

### The Celebrated Mr. Wilde

The celebrated Oscar Wilde was known for his witty barbs and word play. On January 1882, he arrived in New York City by ocean liner to begin a lecture tour. The reporters who clustered around him were disappointed in the ordinary appearance of such a celebrated writer. He, too, was dissatisfied. Expecting inquiries about his planned lectures, he was instead bombarded with questions on how he liked his eggs fried, how he trimmed his fingernails, and what temperature he liked his bath to be. When his answers lacked the wit the reporters had come to expect, they buttonholed passengers for livelier responses. The passengers responded, recounting that they had heard him complain that the trip was dull and that the ocean did not roar.

The reporters gleefully printed that Wilde was "disappointed with the Atlantic Ocean," a phrase that got him far more publicity that any statement on his literary views could have done. Realizing that he had not done himself justice, Wilde made amends the moment he stepped ashore. "Have you anything to declare?" asked the customs official. "No, I have nothing to de-

**LITHOGRAPH OF OSCAR WILDE FROM VANITY FAIR, MAY 24, 1884**
*Ape (also known as "Singe")*
*The Mansell Collection*

clare," he replied. After a perfectly timed pause, he added "except my genius." Few remarks in history have circulated as widely and quickly as that one.

## "The Importance of Being Earnest"

As the title proclaims, Wilde's 1895 farce is about earnestness, that is, Victorian solemnity. It's subtitle, *A Trivial Comedy for Serious People*, sets its tone, The play attacks the kind of false seriousness that means priggishness, hypocrisy, and lack of irony, all the qualities Wilde detested in nineteenth-century England. Now widely recognized as one of the finest comedies in English, *The Importance of Being Earnest* challenges almost everything we are likely to take seriously: death, money, marriage, status, economics, beauty and truth, morality, and the class system.

The play opens in the London apartment of Algernon Moncrieff, a young man about town. He is being visited by a friend whom he knows by the name of Ernest Worthing but whose real name is Jack. Jack lives in the country, where he is the guardian of Miss Cecily Cardew, a task he is anxious to escape. To do so, he invents a ne'er-do-well brother whom he must frequently visit in London to rescue from various scrapes. For no apparent reason, he uses the name "Ernest" in town and "Jack" in the country. As you can imagine, the confusion over names sets the plot spinning.

## An Earnest by Any Other Name

Jack falls in love with Algernon's first cousin, Gwendolen Fairfax, and soon proposes:

JACK: [nervously] Miss Fairfax, ever since I met you I have admired you more than any girl . . . I have ever met since . . . I met you.

GWENDOLYN: Yes, I am quite aware of the fact. . . . For me you have always had an irresistible fascination. . . . my ideal has always been to love someone of the name of Ernest. There is something in that name that inspires absolute confidence. The moment that Algernon first mentioned to me that he had a friend called Ernest, I knew I was destined to love you.

Jack anxiously inquires whether Gwendolyn could love him if his name were different; say, "Jack." "No," she protests, "The only really safe name is Ernest."

In sails Gwendolyn's impossibly snobbish mother, Lady Bracknell, anxious to make sure that Jack is an acceptable candidate for her daughter's hand. In the absurd dialogue that follows, Wilde attacks all the values most dear to Victorians:

LADY BRACKNELL: I have always been of the opinion that a man who desires to get married should either know everything or nothing. Which do you know?

JACK: [after some hesitation] I know nothing, Lady Bracknell.

LADY BRACKNELL: I am pleased to hear it. I do not approve of anything that tampers with natural ignorance. . . . The whole theory of modern education is radically unsound. Fortunately in England, at any rate, education produces no effect whatsoever. . . .

She next inquires after his assets:

JACK: Well, I own a house in Belgrave Square. . . .

LADY BRACKNELL: What number in Belgrave Square?

JACK: 149.

LADY BRACKNELL: [shaking her head] The unfashionable side. I thought there was something. However, that could easily be altered.

JACK: Do you mean the fashion, or the side?

LADY BRACKNELL: [sternly] Both, if necessary, I presume. . . .

LADY BRACKNELL: Now to minor matters. Are your parents living?

JACK: I have lost both my parents.

LADY BRACKNELL: Both? To lose one parent may be regarded as a misfortune—to lose both seems like carelessness. . . .

Weaving ridiculous characters and sparkling wit together in a delightfully unbelievable plot, Wilde challenges us to reexamine the values we take most seriously. The result is an hilarious look at a totally absurd world—ours! No wonder the play was an immediate hit and has since become a theater classic.

## A Tragic Ending

Unfortunately, Oscar Wilde's life ended tragically with little time for him to enjoy his success. His friendship with the son of the Marquess of Queensberry led to his eventual imprisonment for immoral conduct. During the two years he spent in prison, his health was ruined. He died, poor and alone—having seen during his lifetime the peaks of success and the abyss of failure.

## Changing Views of Women

### SEVENTEENTH-CENTURY VIEWS

Times were tough for women in seventeenth-century England. Although womanhood was idealized in the courtly love poetry of the day, the more common view held that women were conniving and inconstant. A popular writer expressed the general attitude against women in 1615:

Eagles eat not men till they are
dead but women devour them alive,
for a woman will pick thy pocket
and empty thy purse, laugh in thy
face and cut thy throat, they are
ungrateful, perjured, full of fraud,
flouting and deceit, unconstant,
waspish, toyish, light, sullen,
proud, discourteous, and cruel.

Things were hardly better across the ocean. Although women in New England enjoyed relative equality battling side-by-side with their men to survive in a hostile land, there were limits to their rights. Mental, not physical, strength was at issue here, for women's minds were thought too frail to absorb excessive learning. Puritan culture reinforced the power of the father as the head of the family, and the penalty for trespassing the accepted order was dire indeed. Governor John Winthrop reported the following sad case in his diary entry for April 13, 1645:

Mr. Hopkins, the governor of
Hartford upon Connecticut, came to
Boston, and brought his wife with
him who was fallen into a sad
infirmity, the loss of her
understanding and reason, which
had been growing upon her divers
years, by occasion of her giving
herself wholly to reading and

writing, and had written many
books. Her husband, being very
loving and tender with her, was
loath to grieve her; but he saw his
error, when it was too late. For if
she had attended her household
affairs, and such things as belong
to women, and not gone out of her
way and calling to meddle in such
things as are proper for men, whose
minds are stronger, etc., she had
kept her wits, and might have
improved them usefully and
honorably in the place God had
sent her.

### RESTORATION VIEWS

Society's view of women had not changed drastically by the Restoration and early eighteenth century, although growing urbanization paved the way for the entrance of women into areas previously closed to them. After Charles II granted licenses to theaters, women dramatists such as Aphra Behn began publishing their own plays. With the end of the patronage system for the support of authors, women freely entered the ranks of novelists, wisely realizing that writing was one of the few careers open to them. Despite these inroads, women were still scorned. Many agreed with Alexander Pope's famous judgment—"Most women have no character at all." By the nineteenth century, satire gave way to sentiment, and views of women changed.

### VICTORIAN VIEWS

Women in Victorian England were considered incapable of governing themselves. A wife separated from her husband for whatever reason had no right to see her children. Married women could not own property; Charlotte Brontë was astonished to learn upon her marriage in 1854 that the copyrights of her novels and any royalties paid had passed from her hands to her husband's.

But the Victorian Age saw the start of women's emancipation. The first important step came in 1857, when the Divorce Act moved matrimonial cases from the religious to a nonreligious court. A woman could divorce her husband if he had been unfaithful and cruel, but divorce still carried a sizable social stigma. The greatest change came in 1881 with the Married Women's Property Act, granting women rights to their own possessions.

Despite these strides, many men—as well as women—still felt that women were best suited for hearth and home. A woman writing in 1837 stressed:

**SUFFRAGETTES EXPELLED AFTER DEMONSTRATING AT WESTMINSTER**
*A. Beltrame*

"In everything that women attempt,
they should show their
consciousness of dependence.
There is something so unpleasant
in female self-sufficiency. . . . Their
sex should ever teach them to be
subordinate; and they should
remember that, by them, influence
is to be obtained, not by
assumption, but by a delicate
appeal to affection or principle.
Women, in this respect, are
something like children: the more
they show their need of support,
the more engaging they are."

Curiously, these rules held only for affluent women, who were thought too delicate for anything but the mildest pastimes. Their delicate nerves had to be cared for as carefully as their bodies. Although remarkably productive, Elizabeth Barrett Browning, for example, spent six years in bed following her brother's death.

Someone had to pick up the slack—hence, a different view of working-class women. They were thought to be healthy and strong, although in truth they suffered far more from contagious diseases and complications from childbirth than their wealthy counterparts. A visitor to a cotton mill in 1897 reported on working conditions, "The place was full of women, young, all of them, some large with child, and obliged to stand twelve hours each day. . . . The heat was excessive in some of the rooms; the stink pestiferous, and in all an atmosphere of cotton flue. I nearly fainted."

By the twentieth century, the position of women and views toward them had changed dramatically, as men and women made strides toward equalizing all areas of life.

## The Victorian Age 1833–1901

### LANGUAGE CONTINUES TO GROW

The swift progress in every field of intellectual activity in the Victorian period was marked by a corresponding increase in new words. Great advances in industry, science, and modes of living all added new words to the vocabulary. In the field of electricity, for example, words like *dynamo, alternating current,* and *arc light* entered the language about 1870. The explosive number of words contributed by the field of science is especially dramatic.

Although some new words are technical terms used only by specialists, the vast numbers of new scientific words contributed to English during the Victorian age have since passed into general use. We now have names for medical conditions such as *anemia, appendicitis, bronchitis,* and *diphtheria,* to mention just a few.

*Bacteriology* and *immunology* were also coined during this age. Although the study of bacteria began with Dutch naturalist van Leeuwenhoek in 1683, the science of bacteriology was not firmly established until the nineteenth century. In 1860 Louis Pasteur established that bacteria come only from other similar organisms; in 1880 scientists began discovering immunity against specific bacteria. The bacteria for typhoid fever was isolated in 1880; tetanus, 1885; tuberculosis, 1890; and plague, 1894.

Thanks to Victorian scientists, we run *clinics* to help the ill, can *vaccinate* against many diseases, and use *anesthesia* to relieve pain. British chemist Sir Humphry Davis discovered nitrous oxide about 1800; it was first used by an American dentist, Horace Wells, in 1844. In 1847 British physician Sir James Simpson found chloroform to be an effective anesthesia.

We have efficient remedies such as *iodine* and *aspirin,* too. Although a crude aspirin compound found in the bark of the willow tree was used by the ancient Greeks and American Indians, it is bitter and irritates the stomach. German chemist Felix Hoffman first synthesized a purer form of aspirin in 1893 in response to the urging of his father, who suffered painfully from rheumatism.

And the movies! William Talbot in England and Louis Daguerre in France perfected the first practical photographic process in 1839; by 1861 American inventor Coleman Sellers had patented the Kinematoscope, the

**DISRAELI AND QUEEN VICTORIA (cartoon)**
*John Tenniel*
The Granger Collection

"NEW CROWNS FOR OLD ONES!"
(ALADDIN ADAPTED.)

first *moving picture*. Thomas Edison patented a refined version in 1891; by 1895 coin operated machines projecting fifty feet of film appeared in London, Berlin, and Paris. Edison's assistant produced a rudimentary talking picture in 1889, and the term *cinema* was coined.

## ENGLISH BECOMES FORMAL

Despite the onslaught of new terms, the Victorians were extremely cautious about their language. Language was formal, polite—and a sure sign of social class. *Etiquette for the Ladies: Eighty Maxims on Dress, Manners and Accomplishments,* published in 1837, includes these guidelines on language:

> It is not only absurd, it is in bad taste, for people of inadequate means to ape the manners of the great. . . . Scarcely anything is so repulsive in a lady, so utterly plebeian, as speaking in a loud, harsh voice. . . . In speaking to her husband, a lady may address him by his Christian name. In speaking of him to others, it is more proper to style him Mr —. To degrade him to a mere initial, to call him *Mr. A.* or *Mr. B.,* is worse than vulgar, it is heathenish.

Not everyone was pleased by the stuffy formality English had acquired under Victoria's reign. Noted Victorian humorist Edward Lear, writing in 1844, remarked, "The uniform apathetic tone assumed by lofty society irks me *dreadfully*: nothing I long for half so much as to giggle heartily and to hop on one leg down the great gallery—but I dare not."

## DIALECTS

Language was strictly conventional among the upper classes—and those who aspired to join their "betters"—but such was not the case among the common folk, as this excerpt from the Cockney Song "Wot Cher! O, Knocked 'em in the Old Kent Road" shows:

> Last week down our alley came a toff,
> Nice old geezer with a nasty cough,
> Sees my Missus, takes 'is topper off
>     In a very gentlemanly way!
>
> 'Ma'am,' says 'e, 'I'ave some news to tell,
> Your rich Uncle Tom of Camberwell
> Popped off recent, which it ain't a sell,
>     Leaving' you 'is little Donkey Shay.'
> 'Wot cher!' all the neighbors cried,
>     'Who're yer going' to meet, Bill?
>     Have yer bought the street, Bill?'
> Laugh! I thought I should 'ave died,
> Knocked 'em in the Old Kent Road!

A story is told that Tennyson stood looking at his grand home just after its completion, turned to his friend, and said, "You will live longer than I shall. That house will last five hundred years." His friend answered, "I think the English language will last longer."

By all indications, his friend was right.

# YOU THE WRITER

### Assignment

**1.** Suppose you had traveled back in time to Victorian England and met one of the poets whose works you have read. Record an imaginary conversation between you and that poet in which you asked and received answers to three good questions about his or her poetry or about life in the Victorian era.

**Prewriting.** Brainstorm to develop questions that will provide some insight into the art of the poet or into the social climate as reflected by the works and background material you have read.

**Writing.** Include in your composition details about the appearance of the poet and the setting of your conversation. Attempt to word the poet's responses in a manner consistent with his or her writing style.

**Revising.** Read your composition to see whether your description and dialogue are lifelike and interesting. Replace dull words with vivid ones.

### Assignment

**2.** Choose one of the fiction selections you read and enjoyed in this unit, and write either a brief chapter that extends the action of the original or an entirely new episode in the life of one of the characters. Tell your story as you think the author of the original might have done.

**Prewriting.** Before you begin to write, make a study of the characters, paying particular attention to such details as physical appearance and speech habits. Familiarize yourself also with the author's style of narration.

**Writing.** Add new characters and settings, if you like, but make sure your additions are reasonable in terms of the original story. Strive for consistency in your characters' words and actions.

**Revising.** Compare the punctuation of your dialogue with that of the original, and correct any errors. Look for inconsistencies.

### Assignment

**3.** Although every literary period has its outstanding poets, none rivals the Victorian era in the individuality of its poetic voices. This was the age when Browning was experimenting with his dramatic monologues, Hopkins with his sprung rhythm, Tennyson with his elaborate stanza forms. Write an original poem that imitates the style of one of the poets from this unit.

**Prewriting.** Get your creative juices flowing by considering possible subjects for a poem. Bear in mind that the majority of Victorian poets were quite pessimistic in their outlook on life.

**Writing.** As you write, be mindful of such details as line length, rhyme scheme, word choice, types of images used, and meter.

**Revising.** Adjust any weaknesses in structure and rhyme. Check the spellings of any words of which you are unsure.

**Assignment**

**1.** Vivian de Sola Pinto, a scholar of Victorian literature, wrote that Thomas Hardy, unlike most other Victorian poets, was out "to produce a dramatic, rather than a pictorial or musical effect." Write an essay that either addresses this commentary on Hardy or explores the goals of another Victorian poet you have read.

**Prewriting.** Consider the possible meanings of the word *dramatic* as it is used in this sense. Scan the works by the poet you intend to focus on, and jot down words or phrases.

**Writing.** Open your essay with a clear thesis statement. Support each point you make with quotations from the poems or the background material on your poet.

**Revising.** Assess the first draft of your essay for clarity and coherence. Look out for any unwanted shifts in tense in the course of your discussion.

**Assignment**

**2.** A writer in the *Edinburgh Review* for July 1858 described the nineteenth century as an "age of transition—a period when changes, deeply and permanently affecting the whole condition of mankind, are occurring more rapidly . . . than at any prior time in human history." Extending the statement to include our own time, write a paper that agrees or disagrees.

**Prewriting.** On a sheet of paper note what you have learned about the history of the Victorian era, with specific regard to technological advances. On a second sheet make notes about similar advances in our own time.

**Writing.** Convert your notes into an essay. Back up each change with examples of the effects it has had on the human race, explaining in what way these effects are irreversible.

**Revising.** Examine your paper for evidence of faulty logic or grammar.

**Assignment**

**3.** The Victorian period is often regarded as one of pessimism. One need only recall the poetry of Arnold or Hardy to understand why. Yet at least two of the Victorians you read, Browning and Hopkins, were quite positive, or at least hopeful, most of the time. Select one pessimistic Victorian and one nonpessimistic one, and write an essay that compares and contrasts the two.

**Prewriting.** Begin by rereading the poetry of each of the poets you choose. As you read, jot down on separate sheets of paper thoughts and feelings the poem awakens in you.

**Writing.** State the purpose of your essay in your first paragraph. Quote specific lines and images from the poems to support the claims you make.

**Revising.** Proofread your paper to ensure that all your sentences make sense.

**BIG BEN, 1905–1906**
*André Derain*
Art Resource

# THE MODERN PERIOD
## 1901–1945

Turning and turning in the widening gyre
The falcon cannot hear the falconer;
Things fall apart; the center cannot hold;
Mere anarchy is loosed upon the world,
The blood-dimmed tide is loosed, and everywhere
The ceremony of innocence is drowned.

from "The Second Coming,"
**William Butler Yeats**

A complacent world floated into the twentieth century on a mood of hope and anticipation. Science and technology were off and soaring. *Progress* was the word on everyone's lips. What could possibly go wrong?

Plenty, as it turned out. While advances in communications and transportation drew the world closer together, modern warfare —William Butler Yeats's "blood-dimmed tide"—nearly destroyed it. World War I (1914–18) killed more than eight million people. World War II (1939–45) took an even higher toll. The wars, and the economic and moral upheaval they caused, shattered countless illusions.

British literature of the modern period (1901–1945) reflects these historical events, riding a swinging pendulum of hope and despair. First, the new century spurred a spirit of innovation in all the arts. Then World War I caused a backswing of disillusionment. Those two spirits, innovation and disillusionment, prompted modern writers to reject many of the traditions of nineteenth-century literature. It was time to experiment with fresh themes, fresh literary styles. "Make it new," exhorted American poet Ezra Pound, the London representative of Chicago's *Poetry* magazine. Pound's advice became the rallying cry of a generation of writers on both sides of the Atlantic.

## THE EDWARDIAN AGE

When Queen Victoria died in 1901, her eldest son succeeded her as Edward VII. We call the years from 1901 to 1914 the Edwardian Age (although Edward died in 1910).

The rigid class distinctions and moral certainties of Victorian times lingered on into the Edwardian Age. We can read about the English country manors of this era in the novels of the American-born Henry James (1843–1916). James vividly portrays the opulence, the pampered gentry, the armies of servants. At the beginning of the century, one Briton in every six worked as a servant.

The rapid pace of change doomed this outdated way of life. Electricity became the "silent servant." It powered household appliances and made many of the jobs of servants obsolete. Telephones (and later radios) brought news from distant places. Automobiles (and later airplanes) opened new possibilities for travel.

As people gained new knowledge and greater sophistication, they began to question Victorian values and ideas. Women marched for the right to vote. A new Labor party, demanding greater rights for the working class, challenged the dominance of the existing Liberal and Conservative parties. In Ireland and in Britain's colonies, nationalists agitated for home rule or independence. By the time George V came to the throne in 1910, the nineteenth-century way of life was fading into memory.

AN ENGLISH ROSE
*Joseph Clark*
Gallerie George, London

**A STAR SHELL, c. 1916**
*Christopher Richard Wynne Nevinson*
Tate Gallery

## THE FIRST WORLD WAR AND ITS CONSEQUENCES

World War I erupted suddenly, but pressure had been building since the nineteenth century. Then, Britain and France had grabbed colonial empires, while Germany lagged behind. When the Germans later sought colonies of their own, their desires clashed with established British and French interests. The nations of Europe chose sides. Tensions grew. All it took was a spark to ignite the war—and the assassination in 1914 of Austria-Hungary's Archduke Ferdinand provided the spark.

Britain went to war in a light-hearted and confident spirit. Many had the romantic notion that the war would offer "good sport" and end in a few weeks. Sir Edward Grey, the foreign minister, saw more clearly. Gazing out on a London street at dusk, he said: "The lamps are going out all over Europe. We shall not see them lit again in our lifetime."

Poisonous gas, massive artillery barrages, and machine guns turned the fields of France and Belgium into a killing ground. Heroic cavalry charges and chivalrous hand-to-hand combat had little place in this first modern war. For four grim years of stalemate, the opposing armies slugged it out. The slaughter decimated a generation of young men and shredded the very fabric of British society. Poets perished by the scores. Many posthumously published poems tell the horrors of trench warfare and mourn the loss of heroic ideals.

# BRITISH EVENTS

**1901**   Edward VII becomes king.

**1902**   **Joseph Conrad** publishes *Heart of Darkness*.

**1903**   Emmeline Pankhurst founds women's suffrage organization.

**1904**   **Saki** publishes his first stories.

**1905**   First London motor buses appear.

**1908**   Boy Scouts founded.

   London hosts Olympic games.

**1910**   George V becomes king.

King Edward VII          Joseph Conrad

**1912**   **George Bernard Shaw** publishes *Pygmalion*.

**1913**   **D.H. Lawrence** publishes *Sons and Lovers*.

**1914**   Britain enters World War I.

**1916**   Easter Rebellion in Ireland.

**1917**   **Siegfried Sassoon** publishes *Counter-Attack and Other Poems*.

**1918**   Women achieve right to vote.

   **Rupert Brooke's** *Collected Poems* published.

**1919**   Britain joins League of Nations.

   Lady Astor becomes first female member of Parliament.

**1920**   **Katherine Mansfield** publishes *Bliss and Other Stories*.

**1921**   Irish free state formed.

   BBC begins regular radio broadcasts.

King George V and His Family

1908 Olympic Games

Battle Scene from World War I

Flight of the Wright Brothers at Kitty Hawk

Albert Einstein          Mohandas Gandhi

STARS AND STRIPES NAILED TO THE NORTH POLE

DR. FREDERICK A. COOK          COMMANDER ROBERT E. PEARY
APRIL 21 1908          APRIL 6 1909

O DAUNTLESS AMERICANS WHO REACHED THE GOAL OF A
USAND YEARS AND PLANTED THE STARS AND STRIPES
N THE AXIS OF THE WORLD.

Postcard Commemorating Discovery of North Pole

# WORLD EVENTS

**1901**  United States: Ragtime music develops.

Germany: Thomas Mann publishes *Buddenbrooks*.

**1903**  United States: Orville and Wilbur Wright build first successful airplane.

**1904**  Asia: Russo-Japanese War begins.

**1905**  Germany: Albert Einstein proposes theory of relativity.

**1909**  Arctic: Explorers reach North Pole.

**1911**  China: Republic established under Sun Yat-sen.

Antarctic: Explorers reach South Pole.

Atlantic: *R.M.S. Titanic* sinks.

**1913**  Africa: Albert Schweitzer opens hospital in Congo.

France: Marcel Proust publishes *Remembrance of Things Past*.

**1914**  Europe: Archduke Ferdinand assassinated; World War I begins.

Central America: Panama Canal opens.

**1917**  Russia: Tsar overthrown; Bolsheviks seize power.

Austria: Sigmund Freud publishes *Introduction to Psychoanalysis*.

**1920**  Switzerland: League of Nations holds first meeting.

India: Gandhi leads nonviolent protests.

**1921**  Italy: Luigi Pirandello publishes *Six Characters in Search of an Author*.

# BRITISH EVENTS

**1922**    **T.S. Eliot** publishes *The Waste Land*.

**1924**    First British airline begins regular operations.

         **E.M. Forster** publishes *A Passage to India*.

**1925**    John L. Baird transmits first television pictures.

**1927**    **Virginia Woolf** publishes *To the Lighthouse*.

**1928**    Shakespeare Theatre opens in Stratford-upon-Avon.

         **W.B. Yeats** writes "Sailing to Byzantium."

**1930**    **W.H. Auden** publishes *Poems*.

**1934**    **Dylan Thomas** writes "The Force That Through the Green Fuse…."

**1935**    Radar developed by British physicists.

**1936**    First BBC television broadcast.

**1937**    **Louis MacNeice** writes "The Sunlight on the Garden."

**1938**    **Graham Greene** publishes *Brighton Rock*.

**1939**    Britain enters World War II.

**1940**    Winston Churchill becomes prime minister.

         Bombing of Britain begins.

**1945**    **George Orwell** publishes *Animal Farm*.

         **Elizabeth Bowen** writes "The Demon Lover."

London After Bombing by Germans

Winston Churchill

Charles Lindbergh

George VI and His Family

*Mandolin and Guitar*

T.S. Eliot

Dylan Thomas

Persistence of Memory

Adolf Hitler

| 1922 | Italy: Mussolini forms fascist government. |
| | France: James Joyce publishes *Ulysses*. |
| 1923 | France: Le Corbusier publishes *Towards a New Architecture*. |
| 1924 | Soviet Union: Lenin dies; Stalin comes to power. |
| 1925 | Germany: Adolf Hitler publishes *Mein Kampf*, part I. |
| | Austria: Franz Kafka's *The Trial* published. |
| 1927 | Charles Lindbergh crosses the Atlantic. |
| 1928 | France: Sixty-five nations sign Kellogg-Briand pact outlawing war. |
| 1929 | Beginning of worldwide depression. |
| 1931 | China: Japanese invade Manchuria. |
| | France: Salvador Dali paints *Persistence of Memory*. |
| 1932 | Soviet Union: Famine kills 5 million. |
| 1933 | Germany: Hitler comes to power. |
| | United States: Franklin D. Roosevelt becomes President. |
| 1935 | Africa: Mussolini invades Ethiopia. |
| 1936 | Spain: Civil War begins. |
| 1937 | France: Spanish artist Pablo Picasso creates *Guernica* mural. |
| 1938 | Europe: Hitler annexes Austria. |
| 1939 | Europe: Hitler invades Poland; World War II begins. |
| 1941 | Pacific: Pearl Harbor bombed; America enters war. |
| 1945 | Japan: Atomic bombs dropped on Hiroshima and Nagasaki. |

## The Russian Revolution

Meanwhile, the war was toppling empires and convulsing whole societies. Russia's tottering monarchy collapsed in the spring of 1917. A democratic government took over and kept Russia in the war as an ally of Britain and France. Overwhelmed by the miserable conditions at the front, however, many Russian soldiers simply refused to fight on. Later in 1917, in a second spasm of revolution, Lenin's Bolsheviks ousted Russia's democratic leadership and set up the world's first Communist state. Russia's was the first of many European monarchies that the war would sweep away. Within a short time, the German and Austro-Hungarian monarchies vanished as well.

## The Irish Rebellion

Meanwhile, unrest festered in Ireland. The Irish, predominantly Roman Catholic, had long resented British rule. At Easter of 1916 Irish nationalists in Dublin launched a rebellion that British troops quickly smashed. However, by executing the rebel leaders, Britain turned them into martyrs. Irish men and women who had previously held back—including major literary figures like William Butler Yeats (1865–1939)—now rallied to the cause of Irish independence.

The surge of Irish nationalism led to a hard-fought guerrilla war. In 1921 Britain capitulated. It granted independence to the Irish Free State. The new nation included all of Ireland except six mainly Protestant counties of the province of Ulster, in the north, which gained home rule but remained part of the United Kingdom. Violent disputes continue to this day over the future of the six counties of Northern Ireland.

OVER THE TOP (AT MARCOING, DECEMBER 1917)
*John Nash*

## The Peace

In 1917 the United States entered the war on the side of Britain and France. World War I finally ground to a halt as Germany, starved and wracked by internal disputes, sued for peace. On armistice day—November 11, 1918—the guns fell silent. A year later, negotiators signed the Treaty of Versailles, calling for Germany to disarm and to pay huge reparations for war damages. "This is not peace," prophesied France's Marshal Ferdinand Foch. "This is an armistice for twenty years." The world would have to bear the legacy of bitterness spawned by the Great War and the Petty Peace, as writer H. G. Wells (1866–1946) called them.

## BETWEEN THE WARS

European civilization struggled to recover from the war as hunger and hardship persisted into the 1920's. In Britain, strikes and unrest kept industry in turmoil. Although Britain's overseas empire remained intact, stirrings of discontent began to trouble the tranquility of colonies like India and Burma. More and more angry voices questioned the right of European powers to rule distant lands.

## The Lost Generation

For years, "progress" had been undermining old traditions and values. World War I had added to the damage, exposing the sham of heroic myths and fostering an attitude of cynicism and despair. What modern values or rituals could fill the emptiness? In his poem *The Waste Land* (1922), T. S. Eliot expressed a widely felt disillusionment with twentieth-century life:

> You know only
> A heap of broken images, where the sun beats,
> And the dead tree gives no shelter, the cricket no relief,
> And the dry stone no sound of water. . . .
> I think we are in rats' alley
> Where the dead men lost their bones.

People spoke of the disillusioned youth of postwar Europe as a "lost generation." Some drowned their cares in the pursuit of pleasure. They drove fast cars, danced to wild new jazz tunes, and experimented with many passing fads. Having won the right to vote in 1918, British women displayed a startling sense of independence. "Flappers" bobbed their hair short and wore low-waisted and daringly brief dresses. This postwar decade of extravagant behavior came to a shuddering halt when the New York Stock Market crash of 1929 began the worldwide Great Depression.

## The Rise of Fascism

Hungry Europeans—people without jobs or future prospects—pinned their hopes on political extremes. Some embraced communism. Others, more numerous, leaned toward fascism—first in Italy under dictator Benito Mussolini, then in Germany under another dictator, Adolf Hitler.

As the 1930's wore on, the menace of fascism grew. Hitler built up Germany's military strength. Italy invaded Ethiopia. The two fascist dictators aided the rightist side in Spain's civil war, allied themselves with Japan, and threatened their neighbors.

A crucial moment came in 1938, when Hitler demanded territory from Czechoslovakia. Czechoslovakia's allies, Britain and France, agreed to the transfer of territory after Hitler promised he would make no more demands. "I believe it is peace for our time . . . peace with honor," British Prime Minister Neville Chamberlain proclaimed on returning from a meeting with Hitler in Munich, Germany, that September.

However, appeasement failed. In March 1939, Hitler seized what was left of Czechoslovakia. His invasion of Poland in September 1939 touched off World War II. Marshal Foch had been right: The armistice lasted barely twenty years.

# THE SECOND WORLD WAR

The Second World War was, if anything, more destructive than the First. Hitler's "final solution" to "the Jewish problem" brought death to six million Jews. A German invasion of Russia killed soldiers and civilians by the millions. Battles raged all the way from Europe to North Africa, from the mountains of Burma and China to Hawaii. Massive bombing campaigns turned cities like London, Dresden, and Tokyo into raging infernos. Finally, in the waning days of the war in 1945, American atomic bombs blasted two Japanese cities, Hiroshima and Nagasaki, into cinder and ash. The war's death toll has been estimated at 35 million—not counting the millions who died in German concentration camps.

Somehow, Britain muddled through. The darkest days came in 1940, when France had fallen and Britain alone bore the brunt of German attacks. Inspired by Prime Minister Winston Churchill's ringing oratory, and joined in 1941 by two allies, the United States and Russia, Britain fought on to victory. However, it was a bitter, draining victory, ousting Britain from the ranks of first-rate powers and marking an end to Britain's long age of imperial glory.

# MODERNISM AND THE INTERNATIONAL ARTISTIC COMMUNITY

Against this backdrop of chaos and violence, writers and other artists put forth a burst of creative energy. Often they left their own countries to work abroad—some as refugees from war, some by choice. Cultural centers like London, Paris, New York, and Berlin developed communities of painters, composers, architects, and writers—people who had come from many different lands. More than ever before, a truly international artistic community took shape.

This community of artistic people responded to the spirit of the times with a frenzy of innovation. How many ways were there to "make it new"? The ways seemed endless—and often puzzling. Controversy raged over radical new techniques in painting, music, architecture, and literature. What did the odd shapes and figures of cubist painters like Pablo Picasso of Spain and Georges Braque of France actually mean? Why did the Russian composer Igor Stravinsky put so much discordance into his *Rite of Spring* (1913)? Could people actually live and work in the modernistic buildings of architects such as France's Le Corbusier or Spain's Antonio Gaudí or in the glass-and-steel structures of Germany's Bauhaus school? Why did modern writers focus so much attention on human weakness and social decay?

In all fields of artistic life, innovators sought to create new art forms appropriate for the twentieth century. They all seemed to have one motto: "Out with the old, in with the new." Today we group the various schools and movements of this generation under the heading of modernism.

# THE IDEAS OF MODERNISM

Although the specific movements that composed modernism were frequently short-lived, they shared a number of characteristics. First, all sought to be new and different, to experiment with new forms, to innovate, to startle, even to shock. In his poem "L'Art 1910," the American Ezra Pound (1885–1972) described a modernist painting:

> Green arsenic smeared on an egg-white cloth,
> Crushed strawberries! Come, let us feast our eyes.

Pound's poem illustrates some of the principles of a technique called imagism, which Pound helped introduce to British and American poetry. It uses *images*—details that can be perceived by the senses—to communicate its message. It employs *precise language.* It abandons nineteenth-century "poetic" diction for the vocabulary of *everyday speech.* It uses *free verse* instead of the fixed rhythm, or meter, of most nineteenth-century poetry. Finally, it *suggests* its message instead of stating it directly. Nowhere does Pound tell us that art in 1910 was startling. He merely implies it through words like "smeared" and through the juxtaposition of clashing images like "arsenic" and "strawberries."

One of the chief influences on modernism was the symbolist movement of the late nineteenth century. Symbolism originated with French poets like Charles Baudelaire (1821–67) and Stéphane Mallarmé (1842–98), whose methods then influenced such late Victorian writers as Oscar Wilde (1854–1900) and Algernon Swinburne (1837–1909). The symbolists rejected naturalism. Their poetry was deeply emotional and personal, like earlier romantic poetry, but it was at times far more subtle. It presented an array of imaginative symbols, seeking to evoke emotions in readers' minds.

**EZRA POUND, 1938–39**
*Wyndham Lewis*
The Granger Collection

The use of images as subtle symbols would become characteristic of modernist poetry by Yeats and Eliot as well as the imagists.

A second characteristic of modernist art and literature was a tendency to present human experiences in fragments that viewers or readers had to piece together in their own minds. For example, Picasso's cubist paintings broke things into component parts. They showed the angles and planes that made up an object, an action, or a human form. The dadaists, who came after the cubists, saw the world as a meaningless jumble. One method of dadaist composition was simply to cut up words, dump them in a hat, and remove them in haphazard order to form a "poem." The message was not in the poem but in the method.

A third characteristic was the use of the techniques of realism and naturalism. Often this meant taking up subjects previously considered too trivial or too unpleasant for art and literature. Realism focused on the details of everyday life. Naturalism examined social and economic problems of the working class.

A fourth characteristic was attention to the new psychological insights of Austria's Sigmund Freud, Switzerland's Carl Jung, and other pioneer psychologists. Psychological realism—called expressionism in drama—sought to duplicate the inner workings of characters' minds, rather than merely to capture outer actions and experiences as earlier realism had done. Psychologist William James, brother of the American author Henry James, observed that the human mind works not in chronological order but in a series of associations. The mind leaps from thought to thought in what William James called the stream of consciousness.

## LITERATURE OF THE MODERN PERIOD

British writing of the period 1900–45 does not fall into clear-cut categories or movements. However, we can divide the period into three broad stages: before 1910, from 1910 to 1930, and from 1930 to 1945. In the first, or Edwardian, stage, writers used the techniques of realism and naturalism to examine the social problems caused by rapid change. The most radical and characteristic works of modernism appeared during the second stage—especially in the years of disillusionment at the end of World War I. After 1930, writers tried to cope with the enormous problems posed by the Great Depression, the rise of fascism, and World War II. During this third stage a more direct, even somewhat didactic literature of conscience came into prominence.

Cutting across these three stages was an Irish Literary Revival, spurred by the explosion of nationalism in Ireland. The Revival—also called the Irish Literary Renaissance or Celtic Renaissance—began in late Victorian times. It sought to revive the dying Gaelic language, to explore early Celtic history and literature, and to express the Irish spirit.

**THE ARTIST'S GARDEN AT DURBINS.** *c.* **1915**
*Roger Fry*
*Yale Center for British Art, Paul Mellon Fund*

## Achievements in Poetry

The stages of the modern period appear clearly in poetry, and even within the evolving styles of individual poets. William Butler Yeats, a leading light of the Irish Literary Revival, provides an example. Yeats's early poetry (he was born in 1865) blends a Romantic love of nature with an interest in the myths and mysticism of Celtic antiquity. It uses traditional rhyme and verse patterns. In later years, Yeats abandoned Romanticism and relaxed the strictness of his form, often adopting the direct, more colloquial diction of the modernists. He employed symbolic images to delve into troubling questions of history and modern life. By the time of Yeats's death in 1939, many considered him the finest English-language poet of the twentieth century.

A Romantic strain also persisted in other British poetry of the early twentieth century. Even some of the brutally realistic poems that developed from World War I reflected romantic longings—to flee battle for the peace and beauty of the English countryside, for example. Among the best-known poets to die in the Great War was Rupert Brooke (1887–1915). The many other poets of World War I included Siegfried Sassoon (1886–1967), Ivor Gurney (1890–1937), Wilfred Owen (1893–1918), and Robert Graves (1895–1985).

Many of the poets who survived the war went on to express the attitudes of the "lost generation" in the modernist poetry of the 1920's. An important influence on these poets was the Victorian writer Gerard Manley Hopkins (1844–89), whose verse appeared posthumously in 1918. Hopkins used what he called sprung rhythm instead of more traditional metric patterns. Hopkins prepared the way for the modernists' experiments with new verse forms.

Preeminent among modernist poets of the 1920's was T. S. Eliot, whose verse reflects the influence of Freud and modern psychology. His "Love Song of J. Alfred Prufrock" (1917), for example, takes the form of a dramatic monologue. It offers the fragmentary interior thoughts of a character's stream of consciousness. Eliot's long poem *The Waste Land* (1922) stands as a monument to the despair and bitterness of the "lost generation." Only later did Eliot shed some of his skepticism and find solace within the Anglican church.

In the 1930's and 1940's, poets showed greater interest in political and social topics. W. H. Auden (1907–73), Louis MacNeice (1907–63), Stephen Spender (born 1909), and Henry Reed (born 1914) continued to employ subtle symbolism and imagery. However, they also made direct statements of social protest. Consider these lines from Auden's famous "September 1, 1939," meditating on the eruption of World War II:

> I and the public know
> What all schoolchildren learn;
> Those to whom evil is done
> Do evil in return.

Romanticism did not die out completely, even in the latter years of the modern period. It flared into a wild brilliance in the verses of Dylan Thomas (1914–53), a Welsh poet who often focused on themes of life and death, as in "When, Like a Running Grave" (1934).

## Achievements in Drama

The towering figure of late Victorian and modern drama is Irish-born George Bernard Shaw (1856–1960). Shaw was delving into the problems of a changing society even before the Edwardian Age. Blending realism with witty satire, he evoked laughter while prodding theatergoers to think about social issues such as class prejudice, the role of women, education, poverty, and war.

The Edwardian Age produced other important dramatists as well. James Matthew Barrie (1860–1937) wrote the classic children's fantasy *Peter Pan* (1904). John Galsworthy (1867–1933) wrote plays that each focus on a timely social problem. *Strife* (1909), for example, deals with labor-management relations. *Justice* (1910) looks at the prison system.

In the Depression years of the 1930's, Noel Coward (1899–1973) won attention for a series of smartly sophisticated dramas and musicals. The poet T. S. Eliot revived verse drama with works like *Murder in the Cathedral* (1935), a play about Thomas Becket, an archbishop of twelfth-century England.

The Irish Literary Revival led to the founding in 1904 of an Irish national theater (the Abbey Theater of Dublin) and produced some of the modern period's finest plays. John Millington Synge (1871–1909) vividly captures Irish rural life in plays like *Riders to the Sea* (1904). Sean O'Casey (1884–1964) turned to urban themes. He depicts the life of the poor in violence-torn Dublin in tragicomedies like *The Shadow of a Gunman* (1925).

# Achievements in Fiction

We cannot fit the fiction of the modern period into neat, clear categories. The fiction swings between romanticism and realism, between misty fantasy and cynical disillusionment. Sometimes it probes the human mind, dwelling on the neuroses and longings of isolated individuals. Sometimes it sweeps across the vastness of history, pondering the mystery of human achievement and human suffering.

Arnold Bennett (1867–1931) was among several fiction writers of the Edwardian Age who produced brilliant works of realism and naturalism. In books such as *The Old Wives' Tale* (1901), Bennett depicted the working-class life of industrial England. He avoided authorial intrusion—the nineteenth-century practice of inserting the author's asides and opinions into a tale. Like Bennett, other modernist fiction writers want readers to draw their own conclusions about characters and events.

A second Edwardian novelist, Joseph Conrad (1857–1924), pioneered in the use of psychological realism. The Polish-born Conrad settled in London after learning English as a sailor on a British ship. He explored the individual's struggle with nature in tales of the sea such as *Lord Jim* (1900) and depicted colonialism in the brooding short novel *Heart of Darkness* (1902). Conrad's tales helped to popularize the short novel, or novella.

The British short story, earlier overshadowed by the Russian, the French, and the American short story, gained new attention in the modern period. Among the first masters of modern British short stories was the humorist H. H. Munro (1870–1916), who wrote under the pen name Saki. Another talented short-story writer was New Zealand-born Katherine Mansfield (1888–1923), who crafted sensitive tales of middle-class life.

The class system and the plight of the industrial worker emerged as key themes in the short stories and novels of D. H. Lawrence (1885–1930). Lawrence was a naturalist, but he had a Romantic abhorrence for the march of factories across the rural landscape. His savage hatred of conventional British manners and morals gives bite to novels like *Sons and Lovers* (1913) and the notorious *Lady Chatterley's Lover* (1928–29).

Perhaps the greatest pioneer of modernist fiction was the Irish writer James Joyce (1882–1941). Joyce revolutionized the form and structure of both the short story and the novel. In *The Dubliners* (1914), he presents a group of realistic short tales about working-class life in Dublin. Joyce tried to have each story achieve what he called an epiphany—a flash of awareness in which all the story elements come together to illuminate the story's meaning. Joyce's brilliant novel *Ulysses* (1922) was one of the first works of fiction to employ stream of consciousness. Joyce labored for years on this book, using an immense variety of techniques and symbols to pair an ancient Greek myth with a tale of twentieth-century Dublin.

**STUDLAND BEACH (detail)**
*Vanessa Bell*
*The Tate Gallery*

**THE MUD BATH**
*David Bomberg*
The Tate Gallery

Another writer famous for capturing the stream of consciousness in fiction is Virginia Woolf (1882–1941). Woolf's major works include *Mrs. Dalloway* (1922) and *To the Lighthouse* (1927). She was the most distinguished member of a group of modernists known as the Bloomsbury set, named for the London neighborhood in which they congregated. E. M. Forster (1879–1970) also formed part of the Bloomsbury set. Forster portrayed the tragic clash of British and Indian cultures in his most famous novel, *A Passage to India* (1924).

As we have seen, social and political issues gained new attention in the 1930's and 1940's. In his futuristic novel *Brave New World* (1932), Aldous Huxley (1894–1963) used biting satire to criticize the misuse of science in totalitarian states. George Orwell (1903–50) ridiculed communism in his modern fable *Animal Farm* (1945) and in *1984* (1949). Like other dystopian novels, *1984* depicts a frightening future society, seeking to warn readers of the horror that may result from current trends. Other noteworthy British fiction writers of the era include Graham Greene (born 1904), Evelyn Waugh (1903–66), Nancy Mitford (1904–73), C. P. Snow (1905–80), and the Irish writer Elizabeth Bowen (1899–1973).

It is probably too soon to evaluate fully the achievements of the modern period, but clearly the writers of the era had an enormous influence on those who would follow them. Writers such as Joyce and Woolf revolutionized the novel by developing new techniques suited to the chaotic confusions and groping skepticisms of modern times. Writers such as Yeats, Eliot, and Auden crafted new poetic tools and prepared a firm foundation for all subsequent twentieth-century verse. Moreover, the plays of Shaw and of the Irish Literary Revival became classics of the British theater, opening up new subject matter that would serve as a starting point for further innovation in later generations. The literature of the years 1900 –1945 remains profoundly relevant in our contemporary period, in a world still chaotic, still torn by doubts, where people of talent are still eager to "make it new."

# ENGLISH VOICES
## Quotations by Prominent Figures of the Period

The greatest of evils and the worst of crimes is poverty.
**George Bernard Shaw,** *Major Barbara*

Vanity plays lurid tricks with our memory.
**Joseph Conrad,** *Lord Jim*

And what rough beast, its hour come round at last,
Slouches towards Bethlehem to be born?
**William Butler Yeats,** "The Second Coming"

Nothing could have been more obvious to the peoples of the early twentieth century than the rapidity with which war was becoming impossible. And as certainly they did not see it. They did not see it until the atomic bombs burst in their fumbling hands.
**H. G. Wells,** *The World Set Free*

Only two classes of books are of universal appeal: the very best and the very worst.
**Joseph Conrad,** *No More Parades*

I cannot forecast to you the actions of Russia. It is a riddle wrapped in a mystery inside an enigma.
**Sir Winston Churchill,** Radio broadcast

I have nothing to offer but blood, toil, tears, and sweat. . . .
**Winston Churchill,** First speech as Prime Minister

Impropriety is the soul of wit.
**William Somerset Maugham,** *The Moon and Sixpence*

Ireland is the old sow that eats her farrow.
**James Joyce,** *A Portrait of the Artist as a Young Man*

It is a symbol of Irish art. The cracked looking glass of a servant.
**James Joyce,** *Ulysses*

Women have served all these centuries as looking glasses possessing the magic and delicious power of reflecting the figure of man at twice its natural size.
**Virginia Woolf,** *A Room of One's Own*

# READING CRITICALLY

# The Literature of 1901–1945

When you read literature it is important to place it in its historical context. Doing so will help you to see how it was shaped by the events and attitudes of the time.

## Historical Context

The Modern Age was one of the most turbulent and traumatic periods in British history. Numerous British colonies were granted their independence, and the British Empire was gradually transformed into the British Commonwealth, an association of self-governing countries. The country suffered through two tragic wars that caused the deaths of thousands of its citizens and experienced an economic depression that resulted in a startlingly high unemployment rate. At the same time, technological advances occurred that significantly changed the nature of people's lives. As a result of these events, there was a dramatic shift in the dominant attitudes and sentiments of the English people, as the sense of optimism and self-assurance that characterized the Victorian Age was replaced by a sense of uncertainty, disjointedness, and disillusionment.

## Literary Movements

As the nation's attitude shifted, a new literary movement developed called Modernism. Rejecting previous literary traditions, the Modernists sought to capture the essence of modern life in both the form and content of their work. Delving into the minds of their characters, writers explored the sense of isolation, uncertainty, and disillusionment that had come to characterize modern life. The disjointedness of modern life was also reflected in the form of typical Modernist works, which often lack the expositions, resolutions, transitions, and explanations used in traditional works.

## Writers' Techniques

During the Modern Age, writers explored a number of new literary techniques. Poets created works using free verse; fiction writers used shifting points of view; and both poets and fiction writers experimented with the stream-of-consciousness technique, attempting to recreate the natural flow of their characters' thoughts. At the same time, modern writers relied heavily on such traditional devices as symbols and allusions, often using these devices in conveying the themes of their works.

On the following pages is a short story by Katherine Mansfield, a prominent modern fiction writer. The notes in the side column should help you to place the selection in its historical context.

# A Dill Pickle

## Katherine Mansfield

And then, after six years, she saw him again. He was seated at one of those little bamboo tables decorated with a Japanese vase of paper daffodils. There was a tall plate of fruit in front of him, and very carefully, in a way she recognized immediately as his "special" way, he was peeling an orange.

He must have felt that shock of recognition in her for he looked up and met her eyes. Incredible! He didn't know her! She smiled; he frowned. She came toward him. He closed his eyes an instant, but opening them his face lit up as though he had struck a match in a dark room. He laid down the orange and pushed back his chair, and she took her little warm hand out of her muff and gave it to him.

"Vera!" he exclaimed. "How strange. Really, for a moment I didn't know you. Won't you sit down? You've had lunch? Won't you have some coffee?"

She hesitated, but of course she meant to.

"Yes, I'd like some coffee." And she sat down opposite him.

"You've changed. You've changed very much," he said, staring at her with that eager, lighted look. "You look so well. I've never seen you look so well before."

"Really?" She raised her veil and unbuttoned her high fur collar. "I don't feel very well. I can't bear this weather, you know."

"Ah, no. You hate the cold. . . ."

"Loathe it." She shuddered. "And the worst of it is that the older one grows . . ."

He interrupted her. "Excuse me," and tapped on the table for the waitress. "Please bring some coffee and cream." To her: "You are sure you won't eat anything? Some fruit, perhaps. The fruit here is very good."

"No, thanks. Nothing."

"Then that's settled." And smiling just a hint too broadly he took up the orange again. "You were saying—the older one grows—"

"The colder," she laughed. But she was thinking how well she remembered that trick of his—the trick of interrupting her—and of how it used to exasperate her six years ago. She used to feel then as though he, quite suddenly, in the middle of what she was saying, put his hand over her lips, turned from her, attended to something different, and then took his hand away, and with just the same slightly too broad smile, gave her his attention again. . . . Now we are ready. That is settled.

"The colder!" He echoed her words, laughing too. "Ah, ah. You still say the same things. And there is another thing about you that is not changed at all—your beautiful voice —your beautiful way of speaking." Now he was very grave; he leaned toward her, and she smelled the warm, stinging scent of the orange peel. "You have only to say one word and I would know your voice among all other voices. I don't know what it is—I've often wondered—that makes your voice such a— haunting memory. . . . Do you remember that first afternoon we spent together at Kew Gardens? You were so surprised because I did not know the names of any flowers. I am still just as ignorant for all your telling me. But whenever it is very fine and warm, and I see some bright colors—it's awfully strange—I hear your voice saying: 'Geranium, marigold and verbena.' And I feel those three words are all I recall of some forgotten, heavenly language. . . . You remember that afternoon?"

**Writer's Technique:**
Mansfield interrupts the sequence of events in the story by presenting flashbacks in which Vera reminisces about previous events. The use of this technique reflects the Modernist perception of life as fragmented and disjointed.

"Oh, yes, very well." She drew a long, soft breath, as though the paper daffodils between them were almost too sweet to bear. Yet, what had remained in her mind of that particular afternoon was an absurd scene over the tea table. A great many people taking tea in a Chinese pagoda, and he behaving like a maniac about the wasps—waving them away, flapping at them with his straw hat, serious and infuriated out of all proportion to the occasion. How delighted the sniggering tea drinkers had been. And how she had suffered.

But now, as he spoke, that memory faded. His was the truer. Yes, it had been a wonderful afternoon, full of geranium and marigold and verbena, and—warm sunshine. Her thoughts lingered over the last two words as though she sang them.

In the warmth, as it were, another memory unfolded. She saw herself sitting on a lawn. He lay beside her, and suddenly, after a long silence, he rolled over and put his head in her lap.

"I wish," he said, in a low, troubled voice, "I wish that I had taken poison and were about to die—here now!"

At that moment a little girl in a white dress, holding a long, dripping water lily, dodged from behind a bush, stared at them, and dodged back again. But he did not see. She leaned over him.

"Ah, why do you say that? I could not say that."

But he gave a kind of soft moan, and taking her hand he held it to his cheek.

"Because I know I am going to love you too much—far too much. And I shall suffer so terribly, Vera, because you never, never will love me."

He was certainly far better looking now than he had been then. He had lost all that dreamy vagueness and indecision. Now he had the air of a man who has found his place in life, and fills it with a confidence and an assurance which was, to say the least, impressive. He must have made money, too. His clothes were admirable, and at that moment he pulled a Russian cigarette case out of his pocket.

> **Writer's Technique:** The man's personality is revealed through Vera's impressions of his appearance.

"Won't you smoke?"

"Yes, I will." She hovered over them. "They look very good."

"I think they are. I get them made for me by a little man in St. James's Street. I don't smoke very much. I'm not like you—but when I do, they must be delicious, very fresh cigarettes. Smoking isn't a habit with me; it's a luxury—like perfume. Are you still so fond of perfumes? Ah, when I was in Russia . . ."

She broke in: "You've really been to Russia?"

"Oh, yes. I was there for over a year. Have you forgotten how we used to talk of going there?"

"No, I've not forgotten."

He gave a strange half laugh and leaned back in his chair. "Isn't it curious. I have really carried out all those journeys that we planned. Yes, I have been to all those places that we talked of, and stayed in them long enough to—as you used to say, 'air oneself' in them. In fact, I have spent the last three years of my life traveling all the time. Spain, Corsica, Siberia, Russia, Egypt. The only country left is China, and I mean to go there, too, when the war is over."

As he spoke, so lightly, tapping the end of his cigarette against the ashtray, she felt the strange beast that had slumbered so long within her bosom stir, stretch itself, yawn, prick up its ears, and suddenly bound to its feet, and fix its longing, hungry stare upon those faraway places. But all she said was, smiling gently: "How I envy you."

> **Writer's Technique:** Mansfield uses a third-person limited point of view, focusing on Vera's thoughts and feelings. The use of a limited point of view reflects the Modernist belief that reality is shaped by people's perceptions.

He accepted that. "It has been," he said, "very wonderful

—especially Russia. Russia was all that we had imagined, and far, far more. I even spent some days on a river boat on the Volga. Do you remember that boatman's song that you used to play?"

"Yes." It began to play in her mind as she spoke.

"Do you ever play it now?"

"No, I've no piano."

He was amazed at that. "But what has become of your beautiful piano?"

She made a little grimace. "Sold. Ages ago."

"But you were so fond of music," he wondered.

"I've no time for it now," said she.

He let it go at that. "That river life," he went on, "is something quite special. After a day or two you cannot realize that you have ever known another. And it is not necessary to know the language—the life of the boat creates a bond between you and the people that's more than sufficient. You eat with them, pass the day with them, and in the evening there is that endless singing."

She shivered, hearing the boatman's song break out again loud and tragic, and seeing the boat floating on the darkening river with melancholy trees on either side. . . . "Yes, I should like that," said she, stroking her muff.

"You'd like almost everything about Russian life," he said warmly. "It's so informal, so impulsive, so free without question. And then the peasants are so splendid. They are such human beings—yes, that is it. Even the man who drives your carriage has—has some real part in what is happening. I remember the evening a party of us, two friends of mine and the wife of one of them, went for a picnic by the Black Sea. We took supper and champagne and ate and drank on the grass. And while we were eating the coachman came up. 'Have a dill pickle,' he said. He wanted to share with us. That seemed to me so right, so—you know what I mean?"

And she seemed at that moment to be sitting on the grass beside the mysteriously Black Sea, black as velvet and rippling against the banks in silent, velvet waves. She saw the carriage drawn up to one side of the road, and the little group on the grass, their faces and hands white in the moonlight. She saw the pale dress of the woman outspread and her folded parasol, lying on the grass like a huge pearl crochet hook. Apart from them, with his supper in a cloth on his knees, sat the coachman. "Have a dill pickle," said he, and although she was not certain what a dill pickle was, she saw the greenish glass jar with a red chili like a parrot's beak glimmering through. She sucked in her cheeks; the dill pickle was terribly sour. . . .

"Yes, I know perfectly what you mean," she said.

In the pause that followed they looked at each other. In the past when they had looked at each other like that they had felt such a boundless understanding between them that their souls had, as it were, put their arms round each other and dropped into the same sea, content to be drowned, like mournful lovers. But now, the surprising thing was that it was he who held back. He who said:

**Literary Movement:** Modernist writers often explore the difficulty of establishing successful relationships in the modern world.

"What a marvelous listener you are. When you look at me with those wild eyes I feel that I could tell you things that I would never breathe to another human being."

Was there just a hint of mockery in his voice or was it her fancy? She could not be sure.

"Before I met you," he said, "I had never spoken of myself to anybody. How well I remember one night, the night that I brought you the little Christmas tree, telling you all about my childhood. And of how I was so miserable that I ran away and lived under a cart in our yard for two days without being discovered. And you listened, and your eyes shone, and I felt that you had even made the little Christmas tree listen too, as in a fairy story."

But of that evening she had remembered a little pot of caviar. It had cost seven and sixpence. He could not get over it. Think of it—a tiny jar like that costing seven and six-pence. While she ate it he watched her, delighted and shocked.

**Literary Movement:** The contrast in their recollections of the evening reflects the Modernist belief in the subjectivity of human experience.

"No, really, that is eating money. You could not get seven shillings into a little pot that size. Only think of the profit they must make. . . ." And he had begun some immensely compli-cated calculations. . . . But now good-bye to the caviar. The Christmas tree was on the table, and the little boy lay under the cart with his head pillowed on the yard dog.

**Writer's Technique:** The man's character is revealed through his comments.

"The dog was called Bosun," she cried delightedly.

But he did not follow. "Which dog? Had you a dog? I don't remember a dog at all."

"No, no. I mean the yard dog when you were a little boy." He laughed and snapped the cigarette case to.

"Was he? Do you know I had forgotten that. It seems such ages ago. I cannot believe that it is only six years. After I had recognized you today—I had to take such a leap—I had to take a leap over my whole life to get back to that time. I was such a kid then." He drummed on the table. "I've often thought how I must have bored you. And now I understand so perfectly why you wrote to me as you did—although at the time that letter nearly finished my life. I found it again the other day, and I couldn't help laughing as I read it. It was so clever—such a true picture of me." He glanced up. "You're not going?"

She had buttoned her collar again and drawn down her veil.

"Yes, I am afraid I must," she said, and managed a smile. Now she knew that he had been mocking.

"Ah, no, please," he pleaded. "Don't go just for a moment," and he caught up one of her gloves from the table and clutched at it as if that would hold her. "I see so few people to talk to nowadays, that I have turned into a sort of barbarian," he said. "Have I said something to hurt you?"

**Writer's Techniques:** Vera refuses to admit that his comments have hurt her, though it is clear from her actions that they have.

"Not a bit," she lied. But as she watched him draw her glove through his fingers, gently, gently, her anger really did die down, and besides, at the moment he looked more like himself of six years ago. . . .

"What I really wanted then," he said softly, "was to be a sort of carpet—to make myself into a sort of carpet for you to walk on so that you need not be hurt by the sharp stones and the mud that you hated so. It was nothing more positive than that—nothing more selfish. Only I did desire, eventually, to turn into a magic carpet and carry you away to all those lands you longed to see."

As he spoke she lifted her head as though she drank something; the strange beast in her bosom began to purr. . . .

**Literary Movement:** The man's comment reflects the sense of pessimism that often characterizes modern life.

"I felt that you were more lonely than anybody else in the world," he went on, "and yet, perhaps, that you were the only person in the world who was really, truly alive. Born out of your time," he murmured, stroking the glove, "fated."

What had she done! How had she dared to throw away her happiness like this. This was the only man who had ever understood her. Was it too late? Could it be too late? *She* was that glove that he held in his fingers. . . .

"And then the fact that you had no friends and never had made friends with people. How I understood that, for neither had I. Is it just the same now?"

"Yes," she breathed. "Just the same. I am as alone as ever."

"So am I," he laughed gently, "just the same."

Suddenly with a quick gesture he handed her back the glove and scraped his chair on the floor. "But what seemed to me so mysterious then is perfectly plain to me now. And to you, too, of course. . . . It simply was that we were such egoists, so self-engrossed, so wrapped up in ourselves that we hadn't a corner in our hearts for anybody else. Do you know," he cried, naive and hearty, and dreadfully like another side of that old self again, "I began studying a Mind System when I was in Russia, and I found that we were not peculiar at all. It's quite a well known form of . . ."

She had gone. He sat there, thunderstruck, astounded beyond words. . . . And then he asked the waitress for his bill.

"But the cream has not been touched," he said. "Please do not charge me for it."

**Historical Context:** Psychology was a common interest in the Modernist period.

**Literary Movement:** Like most Modernist stories, the story ends abruptly, without a resolution.

---

**Katherine Mansfield** (1888-1923) was born Kathleen Mansfield Beauchamp in Wellington, New Zealand. At the age of fifteen she headed to London where she studied for three years at Queens College. In London she became acquainted with a number of literary figures, the most significant of whom were D. H. Lawrence and Virginia Woolf. It was the latter who, along with her husband, published Mansfield's first book of short stories, *Preludes,* in 1917. The overall bittersweet tone of the volume anticipated her second and more ambitious collection, *The Garden Party and Other Stories* (1922), in which she successfully combined her angry and sentimental impulses in portraits of impoverished single women.

Her writing brought her into contact with the literary critic J. Middleton Murray, whom she married. The two lived a nomadic and at times penniless life, moving back and forth between the Continent and London. Increasingly ill with tuberculosis, Mansfield spent the last few years of her life in and out of clinics and hospitals before the disease finally claimed her in 1923.

Critics credit Mansfield with having greatly refined the art of the short story. Her works have often been compared to those of Joyce and the Russian writer Chekhov, whom she greatly admired. When called upon to describe her motivation as a writer, Katherine Mansfield replied that she wrote out of both a sense of joy and a sense of doom. Indeed, her short stories—which alternately express cynicism toward the corruption of modern English society and recall fond memories of a blissful childhood—reflect this dual outlook.

---

## THINKING ABOUT THE SELECTION

### Recalling

1. (a) How does Vera's friend react when he first sees her? (b) How does this make Vera feel?
2. (a) What does the man remember about the first afternoon they spent together? (b) What does Vera remember?
3. Where has the man been for the past six years?
4. (a) What does Vera begin to feel toward the end of the story, as her friend explains their mutual loneliness? (b) What changes her mind?

## Interpreting

5. (a) What difference between Vera and her friend is revealed in the first two paragraphs of the story? (b) What difference is revealed through their attitudes toward the pot of caviar?
6. Vera decides that her friend's recollections of the afternoon at Kew Gardens are "truer" than hers. What does this reveal about her?
7. What action do you think is symbolized by Vera's unbuttoning and buttoning her collar?
8. Do you think Vera's and the man's behavior reveal the truth of his statement about their being egoists? Support your answer with details from the story.
9. (a) What do you think is the significance of the story's title? (b) Do you think the title is an appropriate one? Explain.

## Applying

10. The man claims that Vera and he were so wrapped up in themselves that they didn't have room in their hearts for anyone else. What qualities do you think are necessary for a person to be open to love?

## ANALYZING LITERATURE
### Understanding Dialogue

**Dialogue** is conversation that takes place between two or more characters in a literary work. One key purpose of dialogue is to present information about the characters in a direct and interesting manner. Knowing precisely when to let a character speak for himself or herself through dialogue and when to speak *for* that character requires great skill on the part of a writer.

Locate the following passages from the story, and read the paragraphs that precede and follow each. In each case explain what effect you feel the author achieves through dialogue that would be lost through direct narration.
1. "Loathe it." She shuddered. "And the worst of it is that the older one grows . . ." (page 929)
2. "The colder!" He echoed her words, laughing too. "Ah, ah. You still say the same things." (page 930)
3. "And while we were eating, the coachman came up. 'Have a dill pickle,' he said. He wanted to share with us. That seemed to me so right, so—you know what I mean?" (page 932)
4. "What a marvelous listener you are . . ." (page 933)

## CRITICAL THINKING AND READING
### Making Inferences Based on Dialogue

It has been said that language is "a window on the mind." If we accept this observation as true, then we can use dialogue to learn a great deal about the workings of a character's mind. Notice, for instance, Vera's tendency to speak in very short, almost clipped sentences—a habit that might lead us to infer that she is a guarded, cautious person, which, in fact, as the narrator assures us, she is. Her friend, too, reveals much about his thoughts, feelings, and ideas through his dialogue, though in this instance we receive no additional clues from the narrator.

What impression do you form of the narrator from what he says? Find lines of dialogue to back up your answer.

# Prose

**GARDENS IN THE POUND, COOKHAM, 1936**
*Stanley Spencer*
*Leeds City Art Galleries*

# JOSEPH CONRAD

## 1857–1924

To become one of the most distinguished novelists of one's age would be accomplishment enough for most writers. To do so in a language other than one's own native tongue, as Joseph Conrad did, is an achievement almost without parallel.

Born in Poland to a scholarly father, Josef Teodor Konrad Nalecz Korzeniowski was orphaned at the age of ten. He fled his Russian-occupied homeland to France and England when he was sixteen, and spent the next dozen years as an apprentice seaman. The voyages that he made to exotic corners of the globe—Asia, Africa, and South America—were later put to use as the vivid settings for much of his fiction. In 1886, he became a ship's captain and an English citizen.

It was not until he was thirty-eight that Conrad published his first novel, *Almayer's Folly.* That year, 1895, also marked his marriage and his retirement from the sea. In the next few years, Conrad so far overcame the difficulties of writing in an adopted tongue (English was actually his third language; Polish and Russian were his first and second) that he became one of the masters of Modernist prose. In 1897 he published his first important novel, *The Nigger of The Narcissus,* and within the next seven years produced three master-pieces: *Lord Jim* (1900), *Youth,* a collection of shorter pieces that includes his well-known "Heart of Darkness" (1902), and the ambitious *Nostromo* (1904).

After a brief collaboration with novelist Ford Maddox Ford, Conrad came out with two novels about revolutionaries, *The Secret Agent* (1907) and *Under Western Eyes* (1911). Remaining active through the end of his life, he was at work on *Suspense,* an ambitious historical novel in the classic tradition, when he died in 1924.

Conrad often used the tradition of the sea yarn to create what, on the surface, were thrilling adventure tales. His serious thematic concerns, however, are readily apparent. Almost invariably the notion of "voyage" in a Conrad novel translates to a voyage of self-discovery. The menacing jungles and vast oceans that confront his characters become metaphors for the hidden depths of the self; the requirement for loyalty among crew members of a ship, often unmet, symbolizes the frailty of human relationships in a world filled with deception, corruption, and betrayal.

If Conrad's themes were Modernist, his technical treatments of those themes were even more so. Often, and memorably, as in "The Lagoon," he shifts the point of view from which the story is told.

# GUIDE FOR INTERPRETING

**Writer's Technique**

## The Lagoon

**Shifting Point of View and Theme.** Point of view is the vantage point from which an author elects to narrate a story. Traditionally, writers have narrated stories from either the first-person point of view, in which the speaker is also a character, or the third-person point of view, in which the speaker is not specifically identified by name. With the arrival of the Modernist movement in the early twentieth century, a third option was available—that of using both points of view within the space of a single narrative. By so doing, the writer was able to "move" the narrator from the foreground to the background as the action dictated. In "The Lagoon" Joseph Conrad shifts between a third- and first-person narrator with the additional purpose of emphasizing the story's theme, or central idea, that the line between reality and illusion is often blurred.

**Commentary**

"The Lagoon" is one of Conrad's most admired tales. Although it was only the fourth story he published, it nonetheless shows many elements that would become characteristic of his later work: exotic setting, intriguing ending, and unique narrative style. "The Lagoon" has the distinction of being the first tale in which Conrad borrowed from himself. When his editors requested a piece more characteristic of his exotic style, Conrad tried to reproduce the tangled landscape of his Malayan novels, complete with "forests rivers—stars—wind sunrise." Perhaps part of the story's enduring appeal stems from its eerie atmosphere, for "The Lagoon" is more of a mood piece than any of his other tales. Conrad was fond of the story himself: In 1897, thanking an acquaintance for a note of praise, he called it his favorite short story, written to please himself. Although the context of the letter and other information from his life suggest that his remark may have been voiced more out of politeness than genuine conviction, it nonetheless suggests that the mysterious tale exerted a story hold even over its author.

**Writing**

Try to recall, or invent, an occasion when a friend took you into his or her confidence and shared a problem with you. In a paragraph, describe the emotions you experienced as you listened to your friend. Note in particular whether you were sympathetic to your friend's dilemma, whether you were able to offer any useful advice, and whether there were implications of the problem that applied to yourself and others.

# The Lagoon

## Joseph Conrad

The white man, leaning with both arms over the roof of the little house in the stern of the boat, said to the steersman—

"We will pass the night in Arsat's clearing. It is late."

The Malay[1] only grunted, and went on looking fixedly at the river. The white man rested his chin on his crossed arms and gazed at the wake of the boat. At the end of the straight avenue of forests cut by the intense glitter of the river, the sun appeared unclouded and dazzling, poised low over the water that shone smoothly like a band of metal. The forests, somber and dull, stood motionless and silent on each side of the broad stream. At the foot of big, towering trees, trunkless nipa palms rose from the mud of the bank, in bunches of leaves enormous and heavy, that hung unstirring over the brown swirl of eddies. In the stillness of the air every tree, every leaf, every bough, every tendril of creeper and every petal of minute blossoms seemed to have been bewitched into an immobility perfect and final. Nothing moved on the river but the eight paddles that rose flashing regularly, dipped together with a single splash; while the steersman swept right and left with a periodic and sudden flourish of his blade describing a glinting semicircle above his head. The churned-up water frothed alongside with a confused murmur. And the

white man's canoe, advancing up stream in the short-lived disturbance of its own making, seemed to enter the portals of a land from which the very memory of motion had forever departed.

The white man, turning his back upon the setting sun, looked along the empty and broad expanse of the sea-reach. For the last three miles of its course the wandering, hesitating river, as if enticed irresistibly by the freedom of an open horizon, flows straight into the sea, flows straight to the east—to the east that harbors both light and darkness. Astern of the boat the repeated call of some bird, a cry discordant and feeble, skipped along over the smooth water and lost itself, before it could reach the other shore, in the breathless silence of the world.

The steersman dug his paddle into the stream, and held hard with stiffened arms, his body thrown forward. The water gurgled aloud; and suddenly the long straight reach seemed to pivot on its center, the forests swung in a semicircle, and the slanting beams of sunset touched the broadside of the canoe with a fiery glow, throwing the slender and distorted shadows of its crew upon the streaked glitter of the river. The white man turned to look ahead. The course of the boat had been altered at right-angles to the stream, and the carved dragonhead of its prow was pointing now at a gap in the fringing bushes of the bank. It glided through, brushing the overhanging twigs, and disappeared from the river like some

---

1. **Malay** (mā′ lā): A native of the Malay peninsula in Southeast Asia.

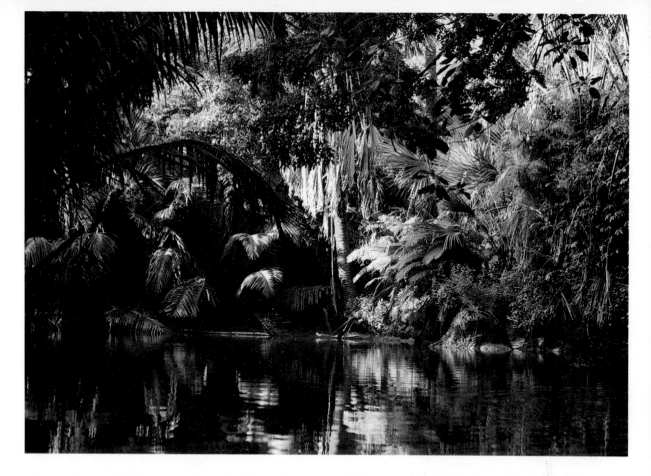

slim and amphibious creature leaving the water for its lair in the forests.

The narrow creek was like a ditch: tortuous, fabulously deep; filled with gloom under the thin strip of pure and shining blue of the heaven. Immense trees soared up, invisible behind the festooned draperies of creepers. Here and there, near the glistening blackness of the water, a twisted root of some tall tree showed amongst the tracery of small ferns, black and dull, writhing and motionless, like an arrested snake. The short words of the paddlers reverberated loudly between the thick and somber walls of vegetation. Darkness oozed out from between the trees, through the tangled maze of the creepers, from behind the great fantastic and unstirring leaves; the darkness, mysterious and invincible; the darkness scented and poisonous of impenetrable forests.

The men poled in the shoaling[2] water. The creek broadened, opening out into a wide sweep of a stagnant lagoon. The forests receded from the marshy bank, leaving a level strip of bright green, reedy grass to frame the reflected blueness of the sky. A fleecy pink cloud drifted high above, trailing the delicate coloring of its image under the floating leaves and the silvery blossoms of the lotus. A little house, perched on high piles, appeared black in the distance. Near it, two tall nibong palms, that seemed to have come out of the forests in the background, leaned slightly over the ragged roof, with a suggestion of sad tenderness and care in the droop of their leafy and soaring heads.

---

**2. shoaling:** Shallow.

The steersman, pointing with his paddle, said, "Arsat is there. I see his canoe fast between the piles."

The polers ran along the sides of the boat glancing over their shoulders at the end of the day's journey. They would have preferred to spend the night somewhere else than on this lagoon of weird aspect and ghostly reputation. Moreover, they disliked Arsat, first as a stranger, and also because he who repairs a ruined house, and dwells in it, proclaims that he is not afraid to live amongst the spirits that haunt the places abandoned by mankind. Such a man can disturb the course of fate by glances or words; while his familiar ghosts are not easy to propitiate by casual wayfarers upon whom they long to wreak the malice of their human master. White men care not for such things, being unbelievers and in league with the Father of Evil, who leads them unharmed through the invisible dangers of this world. To the warnings of the righteous they oppose an offensive pretense of disbelief. What is there to be done?

So they thought, throwing their weight on the end of their long poles. The big canoe glided on swiftly, noiselessly, and smoothly, toward Arsat's clearing, till, in a great rattling of poles thrown down, and the loud murmurs of "Allah[3] be praised!" it came with a gentle knock against the crooked piles below the house.

The boatmen with uplifted faces shouted discordantly, "Arsat! O Arsat!" Nobody came. The white man began to climb the rude ladder giving access to the bamboo platform before the house. The juragan[4] of the boat said sulkily, "We will cook in the sampan,[5] and sleep on the water."

"Pass my blankets and the basket," said the white man curtly.

He knelt on the edge of the platform to receive the bundle. Then the boat shoved off, and the white man, standing up, confronted Arsat, who had come out through the low door of his hut. He was a man young, powerful, with a broad chest and muscular arms. He had nothing on but his sarong.[6] His head was bare. His big, soft eyes stared eagerly at the white man, but his voice and demeanor were composed as he asked, without any words of greeting—

"Have you medicine, Tuan?"[7]

"No," said the visitor in a startled tone. "No. Why? Is there sickness in the house?"

"Enter and see," replied Arsat, in the same calm manner, and turning short round, passed again through the small doorway. The white man, dropping his bundles, followed.

In the dim light of the dwelling he made out on a couch of bamboos a woman stretched on her back under a broad sheet of red cotton cloth. She lay still, as if dead; but her big eyes, wide open, glittered in the gloom, staring upward at the slender rafters, motionless and unseeing. She was in a high fever, and evidently unconscious. Her cheeks were sunk slightly, her lips were partly open, and on the young face there was the ominous and fixed expression—the absorbed, contemplating expression of the unconscious who are going to die. The two men stood looking down at her in silence.

"Has she been long ill?" asked the traveler.

"I have not slept for five nights," answered the Malay, in a deliberate tone. "At first she heard voices calling her from the water and struggled against me who held her. But since the sun of today rose she hears nothing—she hears not me. She sees nothing. She sees not me—me!"

He remained silent for a minute, then asked softly—

---

**3. Allah** (al′ ə): The Moslem name for God.
**4. juragan** (jōō rä′ gän): Captain or master.
**5. sampan:** A small flat-bottomed boat with a cabin formed by mats.

**6. sarong:** A long, brightly colored strip of cloth worn like a skirt.
**7. Tuan** (twan): Malayan for "sir."

"Tuan, will she die?"

"I fear so," said the white man sorrowfully. He had known Arsat years ago, in a far country in times of trouble and danger, when no friendship is to be despised. And since his Malay friend had come unexpectedly to dwell in the hut on the lagoon with a strange woman, he had slept many times there, in his journeys up and down the river. He liked the man who knew how to keep faith in council and how to fight without fear by the side of his white friend. He liked him—not so much perhaps as a man likes his favorite dog—but still he liked him well enough to help and ask no questions, to think sometimes vaguely and hazily in the midst of his own pursuits, about the lonely man and the long-haired woman with audacious face and triumphant eyes, who lived together hidden by the forests—alone and feared.

The white man came out of the hut in time to see the enormous conflagration of sunset put out by the swift and stealthy shadows that, rising like a black and impalpable vapor above the treetops, spread over the heaven, extinguishing the crimson glow of floating clouds and the red brilliance of departing daylight. In a few moments all the stars came out above the intense blackness of the earth, and the great lagoon gleaming suddenly with reflected lights resembled an oval patch of night sky flung down into the hopeless and abysmal night of the wilderness. The white man had some supper out of the basket, then collecting a few sticks that lay about the platform, made up a small fire, not for warmth, but for the sake of the smoke, which would keep off the mosquitos. He wrapped himself in his blankets and sat with his back against the reed wall of the house, smoking thoughtfully.

Arsat came through the doorway with noiseless steps and squatted down by the fire. The white man moved his outstretched legs a little.

"She breathes," said Arsat in a low voice, anticipating the expected question.

"She breathes and burns as if with a great fire. She speaks not; she hears not—and burns!"

He paused for a moment, then asked in a quiet, incurious tone—

"Tuan . . . will she die?"

The white man moved his shoulders uneasily, and muttered in a hesitating manner—

"If such is her fate."

"No, Tuan," said Arsat calmly. "If such is my fate. I hear, I see, I wait. I remember . . . Tuan, do you remember the old days? Do you remember my brother?"

"Yes," said the white man. The Malay rose suddenly and went in. The other, sitting still outside, could hear the voice in the hut. Arsat said: "Hear me! Speak!" His words were succeeded by a complete silence. "O Diamelen!" he cried suddenly. After that cry there was a deep sigh. Arsat came out and sank down again in his old place.

They sat in silence before the fire. There was no sound within the house, there was no sound near them; but far away on the lagoon they could hear the voices of the boatmen ringing fitful and distinct on the calm water. The fire in the bows of the sampan shone faintly in the distance with a hazy red glow. Then it died out. The voices ceased. The land and the water slept invisible, unstirring and mute. It was as though there had been nothing left in the world but the glitter of stars streaming, ceaseless and vain, through the black stillness of the night.

The white man gazed straight before him into the darkness with wide-open eyes. The fear and fascination, the inspiration and the wonder of death—of death near, unavoidable, and unseen, soothed the unrest of his race and stirred the most indistinct, the most intimate of his thoughts. The ever-ready suspicion of evil, the gnawing suspicion that lurks in our hearts, flowed out into the stillness round him—into the stillness profound and dumb, and made it appear untrustworthy and infamous, like the placid and impenetrable mask of an unjustifiable violence. In that fleeting and powerful disturbance of his being the earth enfolded in the starlight peace became a shadowy country of inhuman strife, a battlefield of phantoms terrible and charming, august or ignoble, struggling ardently for the possession of our helpless hearts. An unquiet and mysterious country of inextinguishable desires and fears.

A plaintive murmur rose in the night; a murmur saddening and startling, as if the great solitudes of surrounding woods had tried to whisper into his ear the wisdom of their immense and lofty indifference. Sounds hesitating and vague floated in the air round him, shaped themselves slowly into words; and at last flowed on gently in a murmuring stream of soft and monotonous sentences. He stirred like a man waking up and changed his position slightly. Arsat, motionless and shadowy, sitting with bowed head under the stars, was speaking in a low and dreamy tone—

". . . for where can we lay down the heaviness of our trouble but in a friend's heart? A man must speak of war and of love. You, Tuan, know what war is, and you have seen me in time of danger seek death as other men seek life! A writing may be lost; a lie may be written; but what the eye has seen is truth and remains in the mind!"

"I remember," said the white man quietly. Arsat went on with mournful composure—

"Therefore I shall speak to you of love. Speak in the night. Speak before both night and love are gone—and the eye of day looks upon my sorrow and my shame; upon my blackened face; upon my burnt-up heart."

A sigh, short and faint, marked an almost imperceptible pause, and then his words flowed on, without a stir, without a gesture.

"After the time of trouble and war was over and you went away from my country in the pursuit of your desires, which we, men of the islands, cannot understand, I and my brother became again, as we had been before, the sword bearers of the Ruler. You know we were men of family, belonging to a ruling race, and more fit than any to carry on our right shoulder the emblem of power. And in the time of prosperity Si Dendring showed us favor, as we, in time of sorrow, had showed to him the faithfulness of our courage. It was a time of peace. A time of deer hunts and cock fights; of idle talks and foolish squabbles between men whose bellies are full and weapons are rusty. But the sower watched the young rice shoots grow up without fear, and the traders came and went, departed lean and returned fat into the river of peace. They brought news too. Brought lies and truth mixed together, so that no man knew when to rejoice and when to be sorry. We heard from them about you also. They had seen you here and had seen you there. And I was glad to hear, for I remembered the stirring times, and I always remembered you, Tuan, till the time came when my eyes could see nothing in the past, because they had looked upon the one who is dying there—in the house."

He stopped to exclaim in an intense whisper, "O Mara bahia! O Calamity!" then went on speaking a little louder.

"There's no worse enemy and no better friend than a brother, Tuan, for one brother knows another, and in perfect knowledge is strength for good or evil. I loved my brother. I went to him and told him that I could see nothing but one face, hear nothing but one voice. He told me: 'Open your heart so that she can see what is in it—and wait. Patience is wisdom. Inchi Midah may die or our Ruler may throw off his fear of a woman!' . . . I waited! . . . You remember the lady with the veiled face, Tuan, and the fear of our Ruler before her cunning and temper. And if she wanted her servant, what could I do? But I fed the hunger of my heart on short glances and stealthy words. I loitered on the path to the bath houses in the daytime, and when the sun had fallen behind the forest I crept along the jasmine hedges of the women's courtyard. Unseeing, we spoke to one another through the scent of flowers, through the veil of leaves, through the blades of long grass that stood still before our lips; so great was our prudence, so faint was the murmur of our great longing. The time passed swiftly . . . and there were whispers amongst women—and our enemies watched—my brother was gloomy, and I began to think of killing and of a fierce death. . . . We are of a people who take what they want—like you whites. There is a time when a man should forget loyalty and respect. Might and authority are given to rulers, but to all men is given love and strength and courage. My brother said, 'You shall take her from their midst. We are two who are like one.' And I answered, 'Let it be soon, for I find no warmth in sunlight that does not shine upon her.' Our time came when the Ruler and all the great people went to the mouth of the river to fish by torchlight. There were hundreds of boats, and on the white sand, between the water and the forests, dwellings of leaves were built for the households of the Rajahs.[8] The smoke of cooking fires was like a blue mist of the evening, and many voices rang in it joyfully. While they were making the boats ready to beat up the fish, my brother came to me and said, 'Tonight!' I looked to my weapons, and when the time came our canoe took its place in the circle of boats carrying the torches. The lights blazed on the water, but behind the boats there was darkness. When the shouting began and the excitement made them like mad we dropped out. The water swallowed our fire, and we floated back to the shore that was dark with only here and there the glimmer of embers. We could hear the talk of slave girls amongst the sheds. Then we found a place deserted and silent. We waited there. She came. She came running along the shore, rapid and leaving no trace, like a leaf driven by the wind into the sea. My brother said gloomily, 'Go and take

---

**8. Rajahs** (rä′ jəz): Malayan chiefs.

her; carry her into our boat.' I lifted her in my arms. She panted. Her heart was beating against my breast. I said, 'I take you from those people. You came to the cry of my heart, but my arms take you into my boat against the will of the great!' 'It is right,' said my brother. 'We are men who take what we want and can hold it against many. We should have taken her in daylight.' I said, 'Let us be off'; for since she was in my boat I began to think of our Ruler's many men. 'Yes. Let us be off,' said my brother. 'We are cast out and this boat is our country now —and the sea is our refuge.' He lingered with his foot on the shore, and I entreated him to hasten, for I remembered the strokes of her heart against my breast and thought that two men cannot withstand a hundred. We left, paddling downstream close to the bank; and as we passed by the creek where they were fishing, the great shouting had ceased, but the murmur of voices was loud like the humming of insects flying at noonday. The boats floated, clustered together, in the red light of torches, under a black roof of smoke; and men talked of their sport. Men that boasted, and praised, and jeered—men that would have been our friends in the morning, but on that night were already our enemies. We paddled swiftly past. We had no more friends in the country of our birth. She sat in the middle of the canoe with covered face; silent as she is now; unseeing as she is now—and I had no regret at what I was leaving because I could hear her breathing close to me—as I can hear her now.''

He paused, listened with his ear turned to the doorway, then shook his head and went on.

''My brother wanted to shout the cry of challenge—one cry only—to let the people know we were freeborn robbers who trusted our arms and the great sea. And again I begged him in the name of our love to be silent. Could I not hear her breathing close to me? I knew the pursuit would come quick enough. My brother loved me. He dipped his paddle without a splash. He only said,

'There is half a man in you now—the other half is in that woman. I can wait. When you are a whole man again, you will come back with me here to shout defiance. We are sons of the same mother.' I made no answer. All my strength and all my spirit were in my hands that held the paddle—for I longed to be with her in a safe place beyond the reach of men's anger and of women's spite. My love was so great, that I thought it could guide me to a country where death was unknown, if I could only escape from Inchi Midah's fury and from our Ruler's sword. We paddled with haste, breathing through our teeth. The blades bit deep into the smooth water. We passed out of the river; we flew in clear channels amongst the shallows. We skirted the black coast; we skirted the sand beaches where the sea speaks in whispers to the land; and the gleam of white sand flashed back past our boat, so swiftly she ran upon the water. We spoke not. Only once I said, 'Sleep, Diamelen, for soon you may want all your strength.' I heard the sweetness of her voice, but I never turned my head. The sun rose and still we went on. Water fell from my face like rain from a cloud. We flew in the light and heat. I never looked back, but I knew that my brother's eyes, behind me, were looking steadily ahead, for the boat went as straight as a bushman's dart, when it leaves the end of the sumpitan.[9] There was no better paddler, no better steersman than my brother. Many times, together, we had won races in that canoe. But we never had put out our strength as we did then—then, when for the last time we paddled together! There was no braver or stronger man in our country than my brother. I could not spare the strength to turn my head and look at him, but every moment I heard the hiss of his breath getting louder behind me. Still he did not speak. The sun was high. The heat clung to my back like a flame of fire. My ribs were ready to burst, but I could no longer get enough air into my chest. And then I felt I must cry out with my last breath. 'Let us rest!' . . . 'Good!' he answered; and his voice was firm. He was strong. He was brave. He knew not fear and no fatigue . . . My brother!''

A murmur powerful and gentle, a murmur vast and faint; the murmur of trembling leaves, of stirring boughs, ran through the tangled depths of the forests, ran over the starry smoothness of the lagoon, and the water between the piles lapped the slimy timber once with a sudden splash. A breath of warm air touched the two men's faces and passed on with a mournful sound—a breath loud and short like an uneasy sigh of the dreaming earth.

Arsat went on in an even, low voice:

''We ran our canoe on the white beach of a little bay close to a long tongue of land that seemed to bar our road; a long wooded cape going far into the sea. My brother knew that place. Beyond the cape a river has its entrance, and through the jungle of that land there is a narrow path. We made a fire and cooked rice. Then we lay down to sleep on the soft sand in the shade of our canoe, while she watched. No sooner had I closed my eyes than I heard her cry of alarm. We leaped up. The sun was halfway down the sky already, and coming in sight in the opening of the bay we saw a prau[10] manned by many paddlers. We knew it at once; it was one of our Rajah's praus. They were watching the shore, and saw us. They beat the gong, and turned the head of the prau into the bay. I felt my heart become weak within my breast. Diamelen sat on the sand and covered her face. There was no escape by sea. My brother laughed. He had the gun you had given him, Tuan, before you went away, but there was only a handful of powder. He spoke to me quickly: 'Run with her along the path. I shall keep them back, for they have

---

**9. sumpitan** (sump' ə tän): A Malayan blowgun which discharges poisonous darts.

**10. prau** (prou) *n.*: A swift Malayan boat with a large sail.

no firearms, and landing in the face of a man with a gun is certain death for some. Run with her. On the other side of that wood there is a fisherman's house—and a canoe. When I have fired all the shots I will follow. I am a great runner, and before they can come up we shall be gone. I will hold out as long as I can, for she is but a woman—that can neither run nor fight, but she has your heart in her weak hands.' He dropped behind the canoe. The prau was coming. She and I ran, and as we rushed along the path I heard shots. My brother fired—once—twice—and the booming of the gong ceased. There was silence behind us. That neck of land is narrow. Before I heard my brother fire the third shot I saw the shelving shore, and I saw the water again: the mouth of a broad river. We crossed a grassy glade. We ran down to the water. I saw a low hut above the black mud, and a small canoe hauled up. I heard another shot behind me. I thought, 'That is his last charge.' We rushed down to the canoe; a man came running from the hut, but I leaped on him, and we rolled together in the mud. Then I got up, and he lay still at my feet. I don't know whether I had killed him or not. I and Diamelen pushed the canoe afloat. I heard yells behind me, and I saw my brother run across the glade. Many men were bounding after him. I took her in my arms and threw her into the boat, then leaped in myself. When I looked back I saw that my brother had fallen. He fell and was up again, but the men were closing round him. He shouted, 'I am coming!' The men were close to him. I looked. Many men. Then I looked at her. Tuan, I pushed the canoe! I pushed it into deep water. She was kneeling forward looking at me, and I said, 'Take your paddle,' while I struck the water with mine. Tuan, I heard him cry. I heard him cry my name twice; and I heard voices shouting, 'Kill! Strike!' I never turned back. I heard him calling my name again with a great shriek, as when life is going out together with the voice—and I never turned my head. My own

name! . . . My brother! Three times he called—but I was not afraid of life. Was she not there in that canoe? And could I not with her find a country where death is forgotten—where death is unknown!''

The white man sat up. Arsat rose and stood, an indistinct and silent figure above the dying embers of the fire. Over the lagoon a mist drifting and low had crept, erasing slowly the glittering images of the stars. And now a great expanse of white vapor covered the land; it flowed cold and gray in the darkness, eddied in noiseless whirls round the tree-trunks and about the platform of the house, which seemed to float upon a restless and impalpable illusion of a sea. Only far away the tops of the trees stood outlined on the twinkle of heaven, like a somber and forbidding shore—a coast deceptive, pitiless and black.

Arsat's voice vibrated loudly in the profound peace.

"I had her there! I had her! To get her I would have faced all mankind. But I had her—and—"

His words went out ringing into the empty distances. He paused, and seemed to listen to them dying away very far—beyond help and beyond recall. Then he said quietly—

"Tuan, I loved my brother."

A breath of wind made him shiver. High above his head, high above the silent sea of mist the drooping leaves of the palms rattled together with a mournful and expiring sound. The white man stretched his legs. His chin rested on his chest, and he murmured sadly without lifting his head—

"We all love our brothers."

Arsat burst out with an intense whispering violence—

"What did I care who died? I wanted peace in my own heart."

He seemed to hear a stir in the house—listened—then stepped in noiselessly. The white man stood up. A breeze was coming in fitful puffs. The stars shone paler as if they had retreated into the frozen depths of immense space. After a chill gust of wind there were a few seconds of perfect calm and absolute silence. Then from behind the black and wavy line of the forests a column of golden light shot up into the heavens and spread over the semicircle of the eastern horizon. The sun had risen. The mist lifted, broke into drifting patches, vanished into thin flying wreaths; and the unveiled lagoon lay, polished and black, in the heavy shadows at the foot of the wall of trees. A white eagle rose over it with a slanting and ponderous flight, reached the clear sunshine and appeared dazzlingly brilliant for a moment, then soaring higher, became a dark and motionless speck before it vanished into the blue as if it had left the earth forever. The white man, standing gazing upward before the doorway, heard in the hut a confused and broken murmur of distracted words ending with a loud groan. Suddenly Arsat stumbled out with outstretched hands, shivered, and stood still for some time with fixed eyes. Then he said—

"She burns no more."

Before his face the sun showed its edge above the treetops, rising steadily. The breeze freshened; a great brilliance burst upon the lagoon, sparkled on the rippling water. The forests came out of the clear shadows of the morning, became distinct, as if they had rushed nearer—to stop short in a great stir of leaves, of nodding boughs, of swaying branches. In the merciless sunshine the whisper of unconscious life grew louder, speaking in an incomprehensible voice round the dumb darkness of that human sorrow. Arsat's eyes wandered slowly, then stared at the rising sun.

"I can see nothing," he said half aloud to himself.

"There is nothing," said the white man, moving to the edge of the platform and waving his hand to his boat. A shout came faintly over the lagoon and the sampan began to glide toward the abode of the friend of ghosts.

"If you want to come with me, I will wait all the morning," said the white man, looking away upon the water.

"No, Tuan," said Arsat softly. "I shall not eat or sleep in this house, but I must first see my road. Now I can see nothing—see nothing! There is no light and no peace in the world; but there is death—death for many. We were sons of the same mother —and I left him in the midst of enemies; but I am going back now."

He drew a long breath and went on in a dreamy tone:

"In a little while I shall see clear enough to strike—to strike. But she has died, and . . . now . . . darkness."

He flung his arms wide open, let them fall along his body, then stood still with unmoved face and stony eyes, staring at the sun. The white man got down into his canoe. The polers ran smartly along the sides of the boat, looking over their shoulders at the beginning of a weary journey. High in the stern, his head muffled up in white rags, the juragan sat moody, letting his paddle trail in the water. The white man, leaning with both arms over the grass roof of the little cabin, looked back at the shining ripple of the boat's wake. Before the sampan passed out of the lagoon into the creek he lifted his eyes. Arsat had not moved. He stood lonely in the searching sunshine; and he looked beyond the great light of a cloudless day into the darkness of a world of illusions.

## THINKING ABOUT THE SELECTION

### Recalling

1. Why do the members of the white man's crew want nothing to do with Arsat?
2. What does the white man discover when he reaches Arsat's clearing?
3. What happened to Arsat's brother?
4. At the end of the story, what does Arsat say he will do?

### Interpreting

5. Compare and contrast the white man and Arsat?
6. Conrad devotes a good deal of space to descriptions of the sky and air. What events in the story are paralleled by the "conflagration of sunset" (page 943) and the rattling of the palm trees (page 947)?
7. When, following Diamelen's death, Arsat says "I can see nothing," the white man replies, "There is nothing" (page 948). (a) What do you think is meant by this remark? (b) How might it relate to the final line of the story?

### Applying

8. (a) What might have been Conrad's purpose in not naming the white man in this story? (b) How does this decision reinforce the theme?

## ANALYZING LITERATURE

### Shifting Point of View and Theme

**Point of view** in a story is the vantage point from which the events are narrated. In a first-person narrative, the speaker is either a participant or observer in the story; whereas in a third-person narrative, the speaker is not directly identified. In "The Lagoon" Joseph Conrad narrates most of the story from the third-person point of view, though the "story within a story" —Arsat's tale—is narrated by Arsat himself.

1. What would have been lost if the entire story had been narrated by Arsat?
2. Why do you think Conrad chose to have Arsat narrate his own story?
3. How is the story's theme reinforced by the shift between points of view?

## CRITICAL THINKING AND READING

### Making Inferences About a Moral Code

When, for the second time in the story, Arsat says "I loved my brother" (page 947), the white man observes that "We all love our brothers." Though the remark might be taken at face value, the theme of the story suggests that its author is stating a larger truth about the "brotherhood" between all human beings and about the rules by which we should, but perhaps do not always, conduct our lives. Tell, based on Arsat's narrative, what you believe to be Conrad's views on the following moral issues:

1. The division of a society into classes.
2. The crossing of class lines in such a society.
3. The defiance of law in any society.
4. The degree to which we should feel free to pursue a goal at any cost.

## SPEAKING AND LISTENING

### Setting Up a Reader's Theater

Arrange a theatrical reading of "The Lagoon" in class. After assigning the parts of the narrator, the white man, and Arsat (you may wish to have several readers do the longer parts), consider what sound effects you will need and how they might be achieved. The sound of the natives in pursuit might be undertaken by the class as a whole. When you have finished planning and rehearsing, perform your reading.

## THINKING AND WRITING

### Responding to Theme

A lagoon is a pool of brackish water separated from the sea by sand bars and reefs. Knowing this, write an essay explaining the relevance of the story's title to its theme. Begin by stating the theme. Then develop your essay around the following questions. In Conrad's view of things, what does the lagoon represent? What is represented by the sea beyond? What does a voyage to and from the lagoon represent? Feel free to add and answer questions of your own that you feel clarify the relationship between theme and title.

# SAKI (H. H. MUNRO)

## 1870–1916

The creation of an individualistic style and the adaptation of form to fit one's material are major challenges for every writer. Few can be said to have met these challenges as skillfully and elegantly as the satirist Saki (H. H. Munro).

Born in Burma, Hector Hugh Munro was raised by two aunts in the English county of Devon. He seems to have spent his childhood under a strict, authoritarian regime, if one is to judge by the satirical portraits of aunts in many of his later short stories. As a young adult, Munro returned to Burma to serve in that colony's military police force. After a couple of years, however, recurrent bouts of ill health forced his return to England where he remained for good. Determined to earn a living as a writer, he settled in London.

The turn of the century found Munro writing a regular column for the *Westminster Gazette.* After a year of writing political satire, he became a foreign news correspondent for the *Morning Post,* taking posts in Poland, Russia, and France. It was not until 1904 that Munro capitalized on his true calling, when he published a collection of short stories titled *Reginald,* writing under the pen name Saki (possibly borrowed from the name of the cupbearer in Edward Fitzgerald's popular poem *The Rubaiyat of Omar Khayyam*). The stories in *Reginald,* seldom over a few pages in length, were comically satirical glimpses of upper-class British society during the Edwardian period. With remarkable economy of language, Saki was able to re-create precisely the manners and costumes, not to mention the snobbery and boorishness, that typified the group.

The success of *Reginald* secured Saki's reputation as a master of the comedy of manners, and in his later collections—*Reginald in Russia* (1910) and *The Chronicles of Clovis* (1911)—he revived some of the zany characters from his original cast. The tone of many of these stories, which might be described as playful yet bitingly ironic, was similar to that used by Alexander Pope in *The Rape of the Lock.* Saki's refraining from serious treatments of his subject matter was probably rooted at least partly in the fact that he was a member of the very social class that he mocked.

With the outbreak of World War I in 1914, Saki enlisted for duty in the British army. Two years later he was killed in action in France. Among the collections of his stories published after his death are *The Toys of Peace* (1919) and *The Square Egg* (1924). Although some readers regard his stories as an acquired taste, Saki remains one of the present century's foremost "cupbearers" in the long tradition of English social satire.

# GUIDE FOR INTERPRETING

## The Schartz-Metterklume Method

**Literary Forms**

**Satire.** Satire is a mode of writing that exposes faults in human beings or institutions and holds those faults up to ridicule. Although virtually any literary form can be cast in the satiric mode, satire has its roots in the plays of ancient Greece and Rome. In the time between then and now, satire flourished especially in the eighteenth century and especially in such lengthy poems as Alexander Pope's mock-epic *The Rape of the Lock* and Samuel Johnson's intensely bitter "The Vanity of Human Wishes."

Despite the lack of any formal guidelines in the writing of satire, modern satirists make free use of irony, a discrepancy between what is said and what is actually intended or between appearances and reality. In his satirical "The Schartz-Metterklume Method," Saki uses irony, along with a companion device, understatement, to poke innocent fun at the pretentious manners of the English "upper crust" of the early twentieth century.

**Commentary**

What do critics think of Saki's work? While celebrated in his day chiefly for his short stories, critics now think that Saki's abilities were even more suited to drama and the novel. Playwright Noel Coward represents the critics of Saki's day when he isolates Saki's short stories for admiration. Believing that "high comedy was undoubtedly his greatest gift," he praises "The Schartz-Metterklume Method" as one of Saki's "masterpieces." But as Saki's career advanced, he turned to writing novels and plays as well. He was seeking a larger literary form in which to more fully develop characters and explore social issues, especially the question of Britain's survival on the eve of World War I. As with much of his drama, *The Watched Pot,* a comedy of manners completed just before he enlisted, shows his sparkling dialogue, complex plot and brisk pace. Wherever his fullest talents lay, critics agree that Saki died before his writing attained its potential. "Let those who come after see to it that his name not be forgotten," concludes the scroll the king issued to honor Saki's memory. It seems certain that his work will continue to command a loyal following.

**Writing**

Imagine that on your way to school one day you were mistaken for someone famous. Suppose, moreover, that despite your assurances to the contrary, the person who mistook your identity refused to be dissuaded. Freewrite, telling whom you were mistaken for, and describing the funny sequence of events that followed this initial mistake.

# The Schartz-Metterklume Method

### Saki

Lady Carlotta stepped out onto the platform of the small wayside station and took a turn or two up and down its uninteresting length, to kill time till the train should be pleased to proceed on its way. Then, in the roadway beyond, she saw a horse struggling with a more than ample load, and a carter of the sort that seems to bear a sullen hatred against the animal that helps him to earn a living. Lady Carlotta promptly betook her to the roadway, and put rather a different complexion on the struggle. Certain of her acquaintances were wont to give her plentiful admonition as to the undesirability of interfering on behalf of a distressed animal, such interference being "none of her business." Only once had she put the doctrine of noninterference into practice, when one of its most eloquent exponents had been besieged for nearly three hours in a small and extremely uncomfortable may tree by an angry boar-pig, while Lady Carlotta, on the other side of the fence, had proceeded with the water-color sketch she was engaged on, and refused to interfere between the boar and his prisoner. It is to be feared that she lost the friendship of the ultimately rescued lady. On this occasion she merely lost the train, which gave way to the first sign of impatience it had shown throughout the journey, and steamed off without her. She bore the desertion with philosophical indifference; her friends and relations were thoroughly well used to the fact of her luggage arriving without her. She wired a vague noncommittal message to her destination to say that she was coming on "by another train." Before she had time to think what her next move might be she was confronted by an imposingly attired lady, who seemed to be taking a prolonged mental inventory of her clothes and looks.

"You must be Miss Hope, the governess I've come to meet," said the apparition, in a tone that admitted of very little argument.

"Very well, if I must I must," said Lady Carlotta to herself with dangerous meekness.

"I am Mrs. Quabarl," continued the lady; "and where, pray, is your luggage?"

"It's gone astray," said the alleged governess, falling in with the excellent rule of life that the absent are always to blame; the luggage had, in point of fact, behaved with perfect correctitude. "I've just telegraphed about it," she added, with a nearer approach to truth.

"How provoking," said Mrs. Quabarl; "these railway companies are so careless. However, my maid can lend you things for the night," and she led the way to her car.

During the drive to the Quabarl mansion Lady Carlotta was impressively introduced to the nature of the charge that had been thrust upon her; she learned that Claude and Wilfrid were delicate, sensitive young people, that Irene had the artistic temperament highly developed, and that Viola was something or other else of a mold equally commonplace among children of that class and type in the twentieth century.

"I wish them not only to be *taught*," said

Mrs. Quabarl, "but *interested* in what they learn. In their history lessons, for instance, you must try to make them feel that they are being introduced to the life stories of men and women who really lived, not merely committing a mass of names and dates to memory. French, of course, I shall expect you to talk at mealtimes several days in the week."

"I shall talk French four days of the week and Russian in the remaining three."

"Russian? My dear Miss Hope, no one in the house speaks or understands Russian."

"That will not embarrass me in the least," said Lady Carlotta coldly.

Mrs. Quabarl, to use a colloquial expression, was knocked off her perch. She was one of those imperfectly self-assured individuals who are magnificent and autocratic as long as they are not seriously opposed. The least show of unexpected resistance goes a long way toward rendering them cowed and apologetic. When the new governess failed to express wondering admiration of the large newly purchased and expensive car, and lightly alluded to the superior advantages of one or two makes which had just been put on the market, the discomfiture of her patroness became almost abject. Her feelings were those which might have animated a general of ancient warfaring days, on beholding his heaviest battle-elephant ignominiously driven off the field by slingers and javelin throwers.

At dinner that evening, although reinforced by her husband, who usually duplicated her opinions and lent her moral support generally, Mrs. Quabarl regained none of her lost ground. The governess not only helped herself well and truly to wine, but held forth with considerable show of critical knowledge on various vintage matters, concerning which the Quabarls were in no wise able to pose as authorities. Previous governesses had limited their conversation on the wine topic to a respectful and doubtless sincere expression of a preference for water. When this one went as far as to recommend a wine firm in whose hands you could not go

very far wrong Mrs. Quabarl thought it time to turn the conversation into more usual channels.

"We got very satisfactory references about you from Canon Teep," she observed; "a very estimable man, I should think."

"Drinks like a fish and beats his wife, otherwise a very lovable character," said the governess imperturbably.

"My *dear* Miss Hope! I trust you are exaggerating," exclaimed the Quabarls in unison.

"One must in justice admit that there is some provocation," continued the romancer. "Mrs. Teep is quite the most irritating bridge player that I have ever sat down with; her leads and declarations would condone a certain amount of brutality in her partner, but to souse her with the contents of the only soda-water siphon in the house on a Sunday afternoon, when one couldn't get another, argues an indifference to the comfort of others which I cannot altogether overlook. You may think me hasty in my judgments, but it was practically on account of the siphon incident that I left."

"We will talk of this some other time," said Mrs. Quabarl hastily.

"I shall never allude to it again," said the governess with decision.

Mr. Quabarl made a welcome diversion by asking what studies the new instructress proposed to inaugurate on the morrow.

"History to begin with," she informed him.

"Ah, history," he observed sagely; "now in teaching them history you must take care to interest them in what they learn. You must make them feel that they are being introduced to the life stories of men and women who really lived—"

"I've told her all that," interposed Mrs. Quabarl.

"I teach history on the Schartz-Metterklume method," said the governess loftily.

"Ah, yes," said her listeners, thinking it expedient to assume an acquaintance at least with the name.

"What are you children doing out here?" demanded Mrs. Quabarl the next morning, on finding Irene sitting rather glumly at the head of the stairs, while her sister was perched in an attitude of depressed discomfort on the window seat behind her, with a wolfskin rug almost covering her.

"We are having a history lesson," came the unexpected reply. "I am supposed to be Rome, and Viola up there is the she-wolf; not a real wolf, but the figure of one that the Romans used to set store by—I forget why. Claude and Wilfrid have gone to fetch the shabby women."

"The shabby women?"

"Yes, they've got to carry them off. They didn't want to, but Miss Hope got one of father's fives bats[1] and said she'd give them a number nine spanking if they didn't, so they've gone to do it."

A loud, angry screaming from the direction of the lawn drew Mrs. Quabarl thither in hot haste, fearful lest the threatened castigation might even now be in process of infliction. The outcry, however, came principally from the two small daughters of the lodge-keeper, who were being hauled and pushed toward the house by the panting and disheveled Claude and Wilfrid, whose task was rendered even more arduous by the incessant, if not very effectual, attacks of the captured maidens' small brother. The governess, fives bat in hand, sat negligently on the stone balustrade, presiding over the scene with the cold impartiality of a goddess of battles. A furious and repeated chorus of "I'll tell muvver" rose from the lodge children, but the lodge mother, who was hard of hearing, was for the moment immersed in the preoccupation of her washtub. After an apprehensive glance in the direction of the lodge (the good woman was gifted with the highly militant temper which is sometimes the privilege of deafness) Mrs. Quabarl flew indignantly to the rescue of the struggling captives.

"Wilfrid! Claude! Let those children go at once. Miss Hope, what on earth is the meaning of this scene?"

"Early Roman history; the Sabine women, don't you know? It's the Schartz-Metterklume method to make children understand history by acting it themselves; fixes it in their memory, you know. Of course, if, thanks to your interference, your boys go through life thinking that the Sabine women ultimately escaped, I really cannot be held responsible."

"You may be very clever and modern, Miss Hope," said Mrs. Quabarl firmly, "but I should like you to leave here by the next train. Your luggage will be sent after you as soon as it arrives."

"I'm not certain exactly where I shall be for the next few days," said the dismissed instructress of youth; "you might keep my luggage till I wire my address. There are only a couple of trunks and some golf clubs and a leopard cub."

"A leopard cub!" gasped Mrs. Quabarl. Even in her departure this extraordinary person seemed destined to leave a trail of embarrassment behind her.

"Well, it's rather left off being a cub; it's more than half grown, you know. A fowl every day and a rabbit on Sundays is what it usually gets. Raw beef makes it too excitable. Don't trouble about getting the car for me, I'm rather inclined for a walk."

And Lady Carlotta strode out of the Quabarl horizon.

The advent of the genuine Miss Hope, who had made a mistake as to the day on which she was due to arrive, caused a turmoil which that good lady was quite unused to inspiring. Obviously the Quabarl family had been woefully befooled, but a certain amount of relief came with the knowledge.

"How tiresome for you, dear Carlotta," said her hostess, when the overdue guest ultimately arrived; "how very tiresome losing your train and having to stop overnight in a strange place."

"Oh dear, no," said Lady Carlotta; "not at all tiresome—for me."

---

**1. fives bats:** Wooden bats used in playing a variation of *fives*, a kind of handball played in England.

## THINKING ABOUT THE SELECTION
### Recalling

1. What causes Lady Carlotta to miss her train?
2. (a) What mistake does Mrs. Quabarl make when she sees Lady Carlotta on the platform? (b) How does Lady Carlotta react to this mistake?
3. What is the Schartz-Metterklume Method?
4. (a) Why do the Quabarls dismiss Lady Carlotta? (b) What is her reaction? (c) What request does she make as she is about to leave?
5. How do the Quabarls learn that they have been fooled?

### Interpreting

6. (a) How would you describe the Quabarls? (b) How would you describe Lady Carlotta?
7. In your opinion do the characters' names enhance the story's humorous tone? Explain.

### Applying

8. A contemporary of Saki, the critic Max Beerbohm remarked that laughter "rejoices in bonds [meaning chains]," if only to break them. Comment on whether you think Saki's humor in this story illustrates the remark.

## ANALYZING LITERATURE
### Understanding Satire

**Satire** is writing in which irony, humor, ridicule, or some combination of the three is used to make the reader aware of some evil or folly. In "The Schartz-Metterklume Method" Saki takes satiric aim at customs and attitudes of the English upper-class of his day.

1. Find at least two examples of irony in the story.
2. (a) How is the last sentence of the story an example of understatement? (b) How does the use of understatement bring home the satiric point of the story?
3. Do you think Saki's satire is characterized by biting wit or by more subtle methods? Support your answer.

## CRITICAL THINKING AND READING
### Making Inferences About Tone

**Tone** is the attitude taken by the author toward a particular character or subject. Although Saki never directly expresses his feelings about the Quabarls, and particularly Lady Quabarl, the reader has no trouble inferring his tone. Identify the character trait represented by each of the following details. Then, based on the sum of these traits, state Saki's tone.

1. Mrs. Quabarl's taking a "prolonged mental inventory" of Lady Carlotta on the platform
2. Mrs. Quabarl's assuming "in a tone that admitted of very little argument" that Lady Carlotta was the governess
3. Mr. Quabarl's duplicating his wife's opinions
4. The Quabarls' not admitting to never having heard of the Schartz-Metterklume Method

## UNDERSTANDING LANGUAGE
### Understanding Words with Latin Roots

The following words, which appear in "The Schartz-Metterklume Method," are each based on a Latin root. Look the words up in a good dictionary, noting the precise meaning of the root in each case. Find at least three words that share the root.

1. admonition      4. militant
2. eloquent        5. arduous
3. abject

## THINKING AND WRITING
### Comparing and Contrasting Approaches

Reread the introduction to and a portion of either *Gulliver's Travels* on page 520 or the excerpts from *The Rape of the Lock* on page 548. When you feel you have regained the flavor of the eighteenth-century work, write an essay in which you highlight the differences and similarities between this early satiric effort and the Saki story. Pay particular attention to language, tone, and theme. Conclude your essay by stating which satire you enjoyed more, giving your reasons. When you revise, make sure you have used details from the selections.

# E. M. FORSTER

## 1879–1970

To understand who E. M. Forster was, it is perhaps best to start with what he was not. He was staunchly opposed to imperialism, to capitalism, to ecclesiasticism, and to just about any other *ism* except for humanism. Forster's ideal, in short, was a civilization in which the rights of the individual are held supreme over those of any collective or organization. It is precisely this message that serves as a theme in most of his novels.

Having lost his father at the age of one, Edward Morgan Forster was raised by his mother and a wealthy aunt. It was the latter's money that made it possible for him to attend the finest schools, beginning with Tonbridge School in Kent, which Forster later attacked as typifying what he called the "materialism of the English school system." In 1897 he entered King's College at Cambridge, which he considered his "spiritual home." After receiving his degree he traveled to Greece and then lived for some time in Italy.

While abroad he penned his first three novels. *Where Angels Fear to Tread* (1905) and *A Room with a View* (1908), set in Italy, examine the conflict between culture and falseness on the one hand, and passion and truth on the other. *The Longest Journey* (1907) recalls Forster's days at his beloved Cambridge, where he returned in 1910 to complete work on an advanced degree. It was in this same year that Forster published *Howard's End,* a carefully drawn portrait of pre-war society in England.

In 1912 Forster visited India. After serving in the International Red Cross during World War I, he returned there in 1921. His experiences and observations provided the inspiration for his most celebrated work, *A Passage to India* (1924). The novel, which treats the difficulties that arise in attempting to establish personal relationships, also delivered a prophetic glimpse of England's relations with India.

Dabbling in criticism and in shorter fiction as well, Forster turned out *Aspects of the Novel* in 1927 and *The External Moment,* a collection of short stories, the following year. He also produced several collections of essays, including *Abinger Harvest* (1936) and *Two Cheers for Democracy* (1951). In 1969 he was named to the Order of Merit.

Although some critics have suggested that Forster's novels deal ultimately with the age-old struggle between good and evil, the situation is more complicated than that. Invariably his villains value possessions over people and appearances over realities. And invariably, as in "The Helping Hand," those villains are made, in the end, to pay for their shallowness.

# GUIDE FOR INTERPRETING

## The Helping Hand

**Characterization.** Characterization is the technique whereby a writer makes known the personality of the characters in a work of fiction. Characterization can be accomplished in one of two ways —directly or indirectly. In direct characterization the writer comments openly on the character's personality, using descriptive phrases and adjectives to telegraph impressions straight to the reader. In indirect characterization the writer permits the reader to make up his or her own mind as to what kind of person the character is. To equip the reader to do this, the writer provides information in the form of one or more of the following: (1) the character's words, including speech habits; (2) the character's actions; (3) the character's appearance; (4) the character's thoughts and feelings; and (5) the views of that character held by other characters in the story. Because it mimics the process we use in life to form impressions and opinions of the people we meet, indirect characterization has the effect of making the characters in a story seem real and lifelike.

Write a rough draft of a short poem or story titled "The Borrower." You may, if you wish, base it on a real-life occurrence, but avoid using the real names of individuals. The poem or story should tell about an individual who borrows habitually without ever returning the items borrowed. Include descriptions of the personalities of both the borrower and the lender.

Forster's work is unified by a concern with shared humanity and the importance of personal relationships, as the title of "The Helping Hand" suggests. The epigraph of his 1910 novel *Howards End* —"Only connect!"—introduces this theme, picked up later when one of the characters cries: "Only connect the prose and the passion, and both will be exalted, and human love will soon be at its height." But Forster's experience had taught him that this is far more easily said than done. *A Passage to India,* his last novel, represents the climax of this theme in his fiction. Some have seen the haunting image in the novel's end as representing the impossibility of forging true connections between people and cultures. The Englishman Fielding, debating the role of the British in India, asks the Indian Aziz, "Why can't we be friends now?" The novel ends with the narrator's answer: "But the horses didn't want it—they swerved apart; the earth didn't want it, sending up rocks through which riders must pass single file. . . ."

Do you think people can ever truly "connect" with each other?

# The Helping Hand

## E. M. Forster

When Lady Anstey's book on Giovanni da Empoli[1] was published, Mr. Henderson found in it much that needed forgiveness. His friend did not write as charmingly as she talked: a horrid slime of culture oozed over her style, her criticisms were affected, her enthusiasms abominable. This he could have forgiven; but how could he forgive the subject matter? The dear lady had appropriated, without acknowledgement, facts and theories for which he, and he alone, was responsible. He had studied Giovanni da Empoli for years, and the premature fruit of his labors now lay upon the breakfast table —a little apple-green book, four shillings net, being one of Messrs. Angerstein's series of Pocket Painters.

Mrs. Henderson, a devoted wife, was turning over the leaves with a smile upon her face, for she was pleased that the words of Lady Anstey had been printed on such heavy paper. She knew nothing of the shameful plagiarism, her interest in art being sympathetic rather than intelligent: she was always glad when her friends and her husband got on in it, just as she was glad when her son got on at school.

"What a long list of books she has read to write it!" she observed. "Did you know she could read German? And when did she go to Italy? Wasn't Empoli[2] the place you made us go to—the dirty hotel where you made us go to—the dirty hotel where you

had to hunt the chickens out of the bedroom window?"

"Yes," replied Mr. Henderson, remembering with anguish the nights at Empoli which he had spent and Lady Anstey had not.

"Why did we go there? I've forgotten."

"I had things to look up in the archives." He held up the newspaper as a screen.

"I think you look up too much. Here's Lady Anstey who a little time back knew no more about Italian art than I do, and yet look! I wish you'd write a little book like this. I'm sure you could do it."

"I haven't the knack of putting things brightly." He never said all he thought about the Pocket Painters and similar editions, believing that anything which induces people to look at pictures has its value.

"Yes: I dare say it's all superficial and wrong."

He answered with some animation, "What makes you think so?"

"Because I mistrust new theories—not that I should have known there was a theory. But she says there is one in the preface."

"Giovanni da Empoli," said Mr. Henderson eagerly, "is one of the great puzzles of the Quattrocento.[3] It is highly probable from internal and external evidence that many pictures attributed to other painters should be given to him."

---

**1. Giovanni** (jō van' ē) **da Empoli** (em' pō lē): A fictional painter.
**2. Empoli:** Town in central Italy.

**3. Quattrocento** (kwät' trō chen' tō): The fifteenth century.

"Cut your bread and butter, dear, do not bite it," said Mrs. Henderson to their son.

"If we take one of the Pieros[4] in the National Gallery, the portrait in the Poldi-Pezzoli at Milan, the so-called Baldovinetti[5] at Naples, and the *cassoni* attributed to Pesellino,[6] we notice in all a certain—"

"'Empoli is a quaint old town not untinged with the modern spirit,'" interrupted their son, who was reading out of Lady Anstey's book in the nasal twang that is considered humorous by the young. "'Here in 1409'—then a long note saying why not in 1429—"

---

4. **Pieros** (pye′ rōz): Paintings by Italian painter Piero della Francesca (1410 or 1420–1492).
5. **Baldovinetti** (bäl′ dō vē net′ tē): Painting by Florentine painter Alessio Baldovinetti (1425–1499).
6. **Pesellino** (pes ə lē′ nō): Francesco Pesellino, an Italian Renaissance painter (1422–1457).

"Exactly," said his father.

"'—in 1409 young Giovanni was born, here, when not on his travels, he lived, and here he died in 1473. Our painter never married. Of his six children four—'"

"Don't read at meals, dear," said his mother, taking the book. "This is a great surprise to me and a great pleasure. I never thought Lady Anstey had it in her."

No more she had. The book was the work of Mr. Henderson. He had no one to blame but himself. Lady Anstey had said, "I want to write a book about Giovanni da Empoli: tell me everything you know," and he had told her, cautiously at first in barren statements, then, as he grew warm, infusing the facts with life, till at last the whole theory stood up before her delighted eyes. "Tell it me again," she said, for she was not quick at following, and he had told it her again and she had made notes of it, and he had placed his own notes at her disposal.

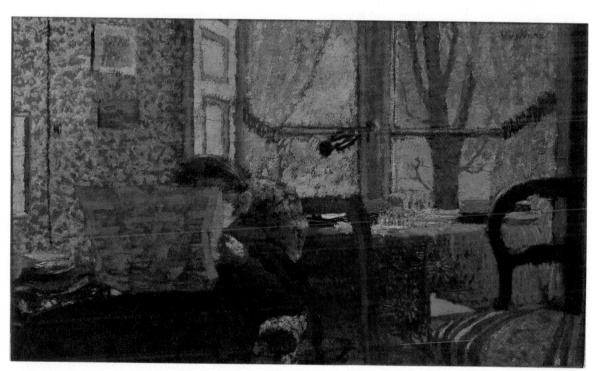

**THE NEWSPAPER**
*Edouard Vuillard*
*The Phillips Collection*

*The Helping Hand* 959

He reminded himself that facts are universal property, and it is no matter who gives them to the world. But ideas—should there not be some copyright in ideas? He had only meant to stimulate Lady Anstey, not to equip her. However, she had Virgil[7] on her side, and Molière[8] and Shakespeare, and all the ancient Greeks who had taken everything and said nothing to anybody, and splendid fellows they were.

She was perfectly open when they next met, greeting him with "And here is someone else to whom I owe more than I can say." For her book was a success, and Messrs. Angerstein had asked her to do one on Botticelli.[9]

"I'm so glad he's been of use," said Mrs. Henderson, imagining herself to be engaged in conventional civilities. "I never knew he had studied the man." For Mr. Henderson had decided to bear his burden in silence, and neither to his wife nor to anyone else did he give one hint of his mortification. He had in him something of the saint, and knew it would be wrong as well as undignified to repine.

"And now tell me all about Botticelli," said Lady Anstey. But Mr. Henderson told very little about Botticelli. He regarded Lady Anstey with frozen admiration, almost with terror, as a being devoid of conscience and consciousness. They continued great friends, but he saw her as seldom as possible.

Her book, in spite of its popular form, made a considerable impression in artistic circles, and she was soon drawn into the congenial and lucrative atmosphere of controversy. In a fortunate hour Sir William Magnus disagreed with her, and a duel ensued, conducted with courtesy on his side and spirit on hers. Wisely refraining from venturing into new fields, she contented herself with repeating the statements she had made in her book. Mrs. Henderson, who always followed anything personal, was able to write her a hearty letter of congratulation on her victory.

Mr. Henderson did not write. The triumph of his theory gave him no pleasure, for it had triumphed in a mangled form. Lady Anstey had wielded it fairly well, but she had missed all the subtleties, she had spoiled the purity of its outline. Yet she had not spoiled it enough to justify his publishing it anew, under his own name.

He suffered a good deal, though he trained himself to laugh at the irony of the situation. He would like to have found someone to laugh with, but all his friends were embroiled on one side or the other, and he could not trust them to keep silent. As for his wife, she did not believe in irony. Meanwhile the book ran through several editions, and there was a rumor that the powers that be in the National Gallery were troubled, and meditated changing the label on the Piero della Francesca.

By the time Professor Rinaldi came to England, Mr. Henderson was tired of laughing and needed sympathy. Rinaldi, whom Mrs. Henderson called the Italian, was a man of great learning and artistic insight, who had become so disgusted with controversies over beauty that he had left Rome and retired to the curatorship of a small provincial gallery. There he lived, or as others said rotted, studying continually because he could not help it, but avowing his intention of never publishing again.

Here was a man to whom Mr. Henderson could speak freely. They were old friends, and he determined to pay him a visit in London.

"Do," said Mrs. Henderson, "and I will finish off the spring cleaning."

Mr. Henderson left on the Thursday, and Mrs. Henderson turned out the dining room. On Friday she did the drawing room. On Saturday she began at her husband's study, and came across a pasteboard box labeled Giovanni da Empoli.

---

**7. Virgil:** Classical Roman poet (70–19 B.C.).
**8. Molière** (mōl yer'): French dramatist (1622–1673).
**9. Botticelli** (bät' ə chel' ē): Italian Renaissance painter (1445?–1510).

Recognizing the name, she opened it and read on the top sheet inside: "Reasons for believing G. to be born in 1409." A strange impulse moved her, and she went for Lady Anstey's book. It gave identical reasons.

Then in one moment the loving wife became a student of art. All Saturday she sat with the book and the papers before her, and discovered that they coincided, not here and there but everywhere. The last paper in the box was a letter from Lady Anstey saying "Many thanks for loan of notes, which have been most acceptable."

All Sunday she thought over the revelation, all Monday and all Tuesday she acted on it. Mr. Henderson returned on the Wednesday.

He was looking more cheerful than she had seen him for weeks. "The world is ruled by irony," he observed, and smiled, as if he found the rule easy to bear.

"And how is the Italian?" she asked, rather ill at ease.

"As fine as ever. 'A little less imagination in archaeology and a little more in art' was his advice to Sir William yesterday."

The word "art" gave her an opening, and she exclaimed, "Yes indeed! Yes indeed! Yes indeed!"

"Why this enthusiasm?"

"You dear thing!" she cried, embracing him; "you're too good to be alive!"

"What have I done?" he asked, looking grave.

"I've found you out—that you wrote Lady Anstey's book—that she took all your facts and ideas and never said a word. And all these months you've let her talk and become famous and make money. I do admire and love you for it—but do be glad I'm different!"

"What have you been doing?" he said sternly.

"Nothing rude—don't be cross. I only let it out in the course of conversation, or put it in a letter if I was writing one."

"And to whom have you written?"

"Oh, not to Lady Anstey: to Lady Magnus about the vacuum cleaner, and one or two more. And yesterday I met the editor of the *Dudley* and he was horrified. Don't be angry—no, I don't mind if you are angry; it's simple justice I want; she shall *not* pick your brains and no one know; you *shall* have the credit for your own theory."

"Unfortunate," said Mr. Henderson. "Professor Rinaldi has just proved to me that the theory in question is wrong, that the facts are wrong, that the book is wrong, that I am wrong. Unfortunate."

## THINKING ABOUT THE SELECTION
### Recalling

1. (a) How does Mr. Henderson feel when Lady Anstey's book appears? Why? (b) How does his wife feel? Why?
2. (a) What do Lady Anstey's publishers ask her to do following the success of her book? (b) What does she, in turn, ask of Mr. Henderson?
3. (a) What does Mrs. Henderson come across during her cleaning? (b) What does she do as a result of this discovery? (c) What is her husband's response to her actions?

### Interpreting

4. What is ironic about Lady Anstey's having the title "lady?"
5. Why do you suppose Mr. Henderson decides to "bear his burden in silence?"
6. (a) What does Mrs. Henderson's behavior at the breakfast table reveal about her? (b) What does Lady Anstey's request for information on Botticelli reveal about her?
7. Do you find the title of the story appropriate? Why or why not?

### Applying

8. (a) How did you feel at the end of the story? (b) How would you have behaved if you had been Mr. Henderson?

## ANALYZING LITERATURE
### Understanding Characterization

**Characterization** is the method a writer uses to reveal the personalities of characters in a story. In direct characterization, the writer tells us directly what sort of person the character is. In indirect characterization, the writer allows us to arrive at our own judgments based on what the character says, does, thinks, and looks like, as well as on how the character is regarded by other characters in the story. In "The Helping Hand," Forster uses a mixture of the two types of characterization. Identify the following characterizations as direct or indirect. For each example of indirect characterization, find the quoted words in the story. Then tell what trait each of the indirect characterizations reveals and to which character each refers.

1. Mrs. Henderson, a devoted wife, was turning over the leaves with a smile . . . (page 958)
2. "I think you look up too much. . . ." (page 958)
3. He held up the newspaper as a screen. (page 958)
4. "I haven't the knack of putting things brightly." (page 958)
5. . . . he had told her, cautiously at first . . . , then, as he grew warm, infusing the facts with life. . . . (page 959)
6. Wisely refraining from venturing into new fields, she contented herself with repeating the statements she had made in her book. (page 960)
7. "Nothing rude—don't be cross. I only let it out in the course of a conversation, or put it in a letter if I was writing one." (page 962)
8. "Unfortunate," said Mr. Henderson. "Professor Rinaldi has just proved to me that the theory in question is wrong, that the facts are wrong, that the book is wrong, that I am wrong. Unfortunate." (page 962)

## CRITICAL THINKING AND READING
### Making Inferences About Character

When a writer uses indirect characterization, that writer is leaving it up to the reader to **infer,** or piece together from presented facts, a profile of the character. Read the following profiles of the three main characters in the story. State which of the traits you think are applicable and which are not, backing up your opinions with evidence from the story.

*Mr. Henderson:* defensive, overly cautious, meek, given to rationalization

*Mrs. Henderson:* simplistic, shallow, dishonest, a good friend

*Lady Anstey:* intelligent, poised, treacherous, self-centered

## UNDERSTANDING LANGUAGE
### Understanding Word Origins

As a rule, the meanings of words change over time. Some word meanings change so much, however, that they leave no trace of the word's original intent. One of the words in the story, *plagiarism*—the passing off of another's writing as one's own—has its roots in a Latin word meaning "kidnap." With the aid of a good dictionary, match up the ancient definitions in the second column with the words from the story.

1. abominable    a. fill with breath, soul
2. theory        b. beginning, first place
3. archives      c. shun as a bad omen
4. animation     d. observe, a viewing

## THINKING AND WRITING
### Writing About a Character

Choose one of the undeveloped characters in the story—the Hendersons' son, Sir William Magnus, or Professor Rinaldi—and, using the little information provided, create a personality for that character. You may describe the person's appearance and likes and dislikes, but focus the main part of your description on what the person is like. To begin, ask yourself in what ways this person is different from and similar to the other characters in the story. Strive for originality. Then write the first draft of your character sketch. When you revise make sure you have fleshed out your character with vivid details. Proofread your sketch and prepare a final draft.

# VIRGINIA WOOLF

## 1882–1941

One can scarcely think of twentieth-century trends in fiction without thinking of "stream of consciousness," the technique whereby a character's innermost thoughts, emotions, and memories are woven together into a complex psychological fabric. And one can scarcely think of stream of consciousness without thinking of Virginia Woolf, the brilliant literary pioneer whose novels and short stories introduced this technique to the world.

Ironically for a writer who would become one of the leading lights of Modernism, Virginia Woolf was born into a family of prim and proper Victorians. Her father, Leslie Stephen, who served as the first editor of the renowned *Dictionary of National Biography,* saw to it that his daughter grew up surrounded by books, and at the age of twenty-three Virginia began contributing reviews to the Literary Supplement of *The Times of London.* In 1912 she married Leonard Woolf, an author and social reformer, with whom she founded the Hogarth Press. Their house in the Bloomsbury section of London became an informal meeting place for some of the more important thinkers of the era, attracting such figures as the writers E. M. Forster and Lytton Strachey, the art critic Roger Fry, and the economist John Maynard Keynes.

Woolf's first two novels, *The Voyage Out* (1915) and *Night and Day* (1919) were more or less conventional works. Her third was anything but. *Jacob's Room* (1922), which shattered the conventions of modern fiction-writing, tells the story of a young man's life entirely through an examination of his room and its cluttered contents. Although we never actually meet the title character, we come to know a great deal about him through an artful arrangement of photographs.

In the years between the wars, Woolf continued to refine her fluid, inward-looking style with three more stream-of-consciousness novels—*Mrs. Dalloway* (1925), *To the Lighthouse* (1927), and *The Waves* (1931)—and with four slightly less experimental ones. In her more revolutionary works, she virtually abolished the traditional concept of plot, preferring instead to concentrate on what she called "an ordinary mind on an ordinary day."

For much of her adult life Woolf suffered from painful bouts of depression brought on by poor health and a consuming hatred of war. In 1941, two years after the outbreak of World War II, she ended her life. Today Woolf is recognized, along with James Joyce, whose life span almost exactly paralleled her own, as one of the most influential shapers of contemporary modern fiction.

# GUIDE FOR INTERPRETING

## The Lady in the Looking Glass

Writer's Technique

**Stream of Consciousness.** Stream of consciousness is a narrative technique that relies on a character's feelings, memories, and thoughts, as well as associations between the three, to tell a story. Pioneered in the early 1920's by Virginia Woolf, James Joyce, and the American novelist William Faulkner, stream of consciousness marks an attempt to tune in directly to the workings of the character's mind—to capture the random flow of insights and thoughts much as they would naturally occur, moment by moment.

The stream-of-consciousness narrative dispenses with such conventions of traditional fiction as chronological ordering of events and the use of formal transitions. The responsibility for organizing the fragments into a meaningful whole often falls to the reader, who thus becomes more actively involved in the work than is the case with fiction of a more conventional design. The reader must piece together—from memories, unconnected thoughts, and glimpses of the subconscious mind—a meaningful whole. Though its demands on the reader are great, the result of the technique is often an intensely revealing, psychologically complete portrait of a human being.

### Writing

Make a list of the contents of a person's room, using your own room at home, the room of someone you know, or one that you have invented for a fictional character. After each item on the list, jot down some notes as to its origin, its physical appearance, and its significance to the occupant.

### Primary Source

Woolf's most famous explanation of her stream-of-consciousness technique appears in her essay "Modern Fiction." Focusing on an "ordinary mind on an ordinary day," Woolf notes: "The mind receives a myriad of impressions—trivial, fantastic, evanescent, or engraved with the sharpness of steel. From all sides they come, an incessant shower of innumerable atoms; and as they fall, as they shape themselves into the life of Monday or Tuesday, the accent falls differently from of old; the moment of importance came not here but there; so that, if a writer were a free man and not a slave, if he could write what he chose, not what he must, if he could base his work upon his own feeling and not upon convention, there would be no plot, no comedy, no tragedy, no love interest or catastrophe in the accepted style, and perhaps not a button sewn on as the Bond Street tailors would have it. . . . Life is a luminous halo, a semi-transparent envelope surrounding us from the beginning of consciousness to the end."

# The Lady in the Looking Glass

## A Reflection

### Virginia Woolf

People should not leave looking glasses hanging in their rooms any more than they should leave open checkbooks or letters confessing some hideous crime. One could not help looking, that summer afternoon, in the long glass that hung outside in the hall. Chance had so arranged it. From the depths of the sofa in the drawing room one could see reflected in the Italian glass not only the marble-topped table opposite, but a stretch of the garden beyond. One could see a long grass path leading between banks of tall flowers until, slicing off an angle, the gold rim cut it off.

The house was empty, and one felt, since one was the only person in the drawing room, like one of those naturalists who, covered with grass and leaves, lie watching the shyest animals—badgers, otters, kingfishers—moving about freely, themselves unseen. The room that afternoon was full of such shy creatures, lights and shadows, curtains blowing, petals falling—things that never happen, so it seems, if someone is looking. The quiet old country room with its rugs and stone chimney pieces, its sunken bookcases and red and gold lacquer cabinets, was full of such nocturnal creatures. They came pirouetting across the floor, stepping delicately with high-lifted feet and spread tails and pecking allusive beaks as if

they had been cranes or flocks of elegant flamingoes whose pink was faded, or peacocks whose trains were veiled with silver. And there were obscure flushes and darkening too, as if a cuttlefish had suddenly suffused the air with purple; and the room had its passions and rages and envies and sorrows coming over it and clouding it, like a human being. Nothing stayed the same for two seconds together.

But, outside, the looking glass reflected the hall table, the sunflowers, the garden path so accurately and so fixedly that they seemed held there in their reality unescapably. It was a strange contrast—all changing here, all stillness there. One could not help looking from one to the other. Meanwhile, since all the doors and windows were open in the heat, there was a perpetual sighing and ceasing sound, the voice of the transient and the perishing, it seemed, coming and going like human breath, while in the looking glass things had ceased to breathe and lay still in the trance of immortality.

Half an hour ago the mistress of the house, Isabella Tyson, had gone down the grass path in her thin summer dress, carrying a basket, and had vanished, sliced off by the gilt rim of the looking glass. She had gone presumably into the lower garden to pick flowers; or as it seemed more natural to

*The Lady in the Looking-Glass: A Reflection*   967

suppose, to pick something light and fantastic and leafy and trailing, traveler's-joy, or one of those elegant sprays of convolvulus that twine round ugly walls and burst here and there into white and violet blossoms. She suggested the fantastic and the tremulous convolvulus rather than the upright aster, the starched zinnia, or her own burning roses alight like lamps on the straight posts of their rose trees. The comparison showed how very little, after all these years, one knew about her; for it is impossible that any woman of flesh and blood of fifty-five or sixty should be really a wreath or a tendril. Such comparisons are worse than idle and superficial—they are cruel even, for they come like the convolvulus itself trembling between one's eyes and the truth. There must be truth; there must be a wall. Yet it was strange that after knowing her all these years one could not say what the truth about Isabella was; one still made up phrases like this about convolvulus and traveler's joy. As for facts, it was a fact that she was a spinster; that she was rich; that she had bought this house and collected with her own hands—often in the most obscure corners of the world and at great risk from poisonous stings and Oriental diseases—the rugs, the chairs, the cabinets which now lived their nocturnal life before one's eyes. Sometimes it seemed as if they knew more about her than we, who sat on them, wrote at them, and trod on them so carefully, were allowed to know. In each of these cabinets were many little drawers, and each almost certainly held letters, tied with bows of ribbon, sprinkled with sticks of lavender or rose leaves. For it was another fact—if facts were what one wanted—that Isabella had known many people, had had many friends; and thus if one had the audacity to open a drawer and read her letters, one would find the traces of many agitations, of appointments to meet, of upbraidings for not having met, long letters of intimacy and affection, violent letters of jealousy and reproach, terrible final words of parting—for all those interviews and assignations had led to nothing —that is, she had never married, and yet, judging from the masklike indifference of her face, she had gone through twenty times more of passion and experience than those whose loves are trumpeted forth for all the world to hear. Under the stress of thinking about Isabella, her room became more shadowy and symbolic; the corners seemed darker, the legs of chairs and tables more spindly and hieroglyphic.

Suddenly these reflections were ended violently and yet without a sound. A large black form loomed into the looking glass; blotted out everything, strewed the table with a packet of marble tablets veined with pink and gray, and was gone. But the picture was entirely altered. For the moment it was unrecognizable and irrational and entirely out of focus. One could not relate these tablets to any human purpose. And then by degrees some logical process set to work on them and began ordering and arranging them and bringing them into the fold of common experience. One realized at last that they were merely letters. The man had brought the post.

There they lay on the marble-topped table, all dripping with light and color at first and crude and unabsorbed. And then it was strange to see how they were drawn in and arranged and composed and made part of the picture and granted that stillness and immortality which the looking glass conferred. They lay there invested with a new reality and significance and with a greater heaviness, too, as if it would have needed a chisel to dislodge them from the table. And, whether it was fancy or not, they seemed to have become not merely a handful of casual letters but to be tablets graven with eternal truth—if one could read them, one would know everything there was to be known about Isabella, yes, and about life, too. The pages inside those marble-looking envelopes must be cut deep and scored thick with meaning. Isabella would come in, and take them, one by one, very slowly, and open them, and read them carefully word by word, and then with a profound sigh of comprehension, as if she had seen to the bottom of everything, she would tear the envelopes to little bits and tie the letters together and lock the cabinet drawer in her determination to conceal what she did not wish to be known.

The thought served as a challenge. Isabella did not wish to be known—but she should no longer escape. It was absurd, it was monstrous. If she concealed so much and knew so much one must prize her open with the first tool that came to hand—the imagination. One must fix one's mind upon her at that very moment. One must fasten her down there. One must refuse to be put off any longer with sayings and doings such as the moment brought forth—with dinners and visits and polite conversations. One must put oneself in her shoes. If one took the phrase literally, it was easy to see the shoes in which she stood, down in the lower garden, at this moment. They were very narrow and long and fashionable —they were made of the softest and most flexible leather. Like everything she wore, they were exquisite. And she would be standing under the high hedge in the lower part of the garden, raising the scissors that were tied to her waist to cut some dead flower, some overgrown branch. The sun would beat down on her face, into her eyes; but no, at the critical moment a veil of cloud covered the sun, making the expression of her eyes doubtful—was it mocking or tender, brilliant or dull? One could only see the indeterminate outline of her rather faded, fine face looking at the sky. She was thinking, perhaps, that she must order a new net for the strawberries; that she must send flowers to Johnson's widow; that it was time she drove over to see the Hippesleys in their new house. Those were the things she talked about at dinner certainly. But one was tired of the things that she talked about at dinner. It was her profounder state of being that one wanted to catch and turn to words, the state that is to the mind what breathing is to the body, what one calls happiness or unhappiness. At the mention of those words it became obvious, surely, that she must be happy. She was rich; she was distinguished; she had many friends; she traveled—she bought rugs in Turkey and blue pots in Persia. Avenues of pleasure radiated this way and that from where she stood with her scissors raised to cut the trembling branches while the lacy clouds veiled her face.

Here with a quick movement of her scissors she snipped the spray of traveler's joy and it fell to the ground. As it fell, surely some light came in too, surely one could penetrate a little farther into her being. Her mind then was filled with tenderness and regret. . . . To cut an overgrown branch saddened her because it had once lived, and life was dear to her. Yes, and at the same time the fall of the branch would suggest to her how she must die herself and all the futility and evanescence of things. And then again quickly catching this thought up, with her instant good sense, she thought life had treated her well; even if fall she must, it was to lie on the earth and molder sweetly into the roots of violets. So she stood thinking. Without making any thought precise—for she was one of those reticent people whose minds hold their thoughts enmeshed in clouds of silence—she was filled with thoughts. Her mind was like her room, in which lights advanced and retreated, came pirouetting and stepping delicately, spread their tails, pecked their way; and then her whole being was suffused, like the room again, with a cloud of some profound knowledge, some unspoken regret, and then she was full of locked drawers, stuffed with letters, like her cabinets. To talk of "prizing her open" as if she were an oyster, to use any but the finest and subtlest and most pliable tools upon her was impious and absurd. One must imagine— here was she in the looking glass. It made one start.

She was so far off at first that one could not see her clearly. She came lingering and pausing, here straightening a rose, there lifting a pink to smell it, but she never stopped; and all the time she became larger and larger in the looking glass, more and more completely the person into whose mind one had been trying to penetrate. One verified her by degrees—fitted the qualities one had discovered into this visible body. There were her gray-green dress, and her long shoes, her basket, and something sparkling at her throat. She came so gradually that she did not seem to derange the pattern in the glass, but only to bring in some new element which gently moved and altered the other objects as if asking them, courteously, to make room for her. And the letters and the table and the grass walk and the sunflowers which had been waiting in the looking glass separated and opened out so that she might be received among them. At last there she was, in the hall. She stopped dead. She stood by the table. She stood perfectly still. At once the looking glass began to pour over her a light that seemed to fix her; that seemed like some acid to bite off the unessential and superficial and to leave only the truth. It was an enthralling spectacle. Everything dropped from her—clouds, dress, basket, diamond—all that one had called the creeper and convolvulus. Here was the hard wall beneath. Here was the woman herself. She stood naked in that pitiless light. And there was nothing. Isabella was perfectly empty. She had no thoughts. She had no friends. She cared for nobody. As for her letters, they were all bills. Look, as she stood there, old and angular, veined and lined, with her high nose and her wrinkled neck, she did not even trouble to open them.

People should not leave looking glasses hanging in their rooms.

---

## THINKING ABOUT THE SELECTION

### Recalling

1. Where does the story take place?
2. (a) What has Isabella Tyson gone to do? (b) What arrives while she is out?
3. How does Isabella feel about cutting the flower?
4. What do the letters turn out to be?

### Interpreting

5. Who do you think is the narrator of the story? Explain your answer.
6. (a) Based on the information provided, how would you describe Isabella? (b) How would you summarize what the narrator wishes to "prize" from her?
7. The last sentence of the story repeats the first sentence. What is the effect of this repetition, if you consider it together with the story's title and subtitle?
8. What, in your view, is the theme of the story?

### Applying

9. Have you ever sought to know what made another person, perhaps a celebrity, "tick" and been disappointed by what you discovered? Give details of your experience and discuss the general truth it suggests.

## ANALYZING LITERATURE

### Recognizing Stream of Consciousness

**Stream of consciousness** is a literary technique that attempts to reproduce a character's thought processes as they might naturally occur within the human mind. Often fragmented and seemingly unconnected, the thoughts, emotions, and memories that make up a stream-of-consciousness narrative paint a telling portrait of the character when seen from a larger perspective.

Reread carefully the paragraph of the story that begins, "Here with a quick movement of her scissors . . ." (page 969). Then answer the following questions.

1. If one traces her thought patterns from the cutting of the flower through the mention of the "locked drawers" of her mind, how many stages of thought can Isabella be seen to go through? What details of her personality are revealed in this paragraph?
2. What comment on her own technique of stream of consciousness does the author seem to be making in this paragraph?
3. What conclusion about Isabella does the narrator draw from this imaginative examination of Isabella's thoughts?

## CRITICAL THINKING AND READING
### Evaluating an Author's Purpose

Usually, behind a work of literature is a **purpose,** or intention, that was uppermost in the author's mind when he or she sat down to write. The purpose of some stories, for example, is to impart an understanding about people or life in general, while the purpose of others is merely to

entertain. For Virginia Woolf, one ever-present purpose in her writing was to get beyond what she termed "the tyranny of plot"—that is, the requirement of "stylizing" a character's words and actions in accordance with the rules of traditional storytelling.

Give a short synopsis, or summary, of the "plot" implied in "The Lady in the Looking Glass." Then find evidence of the following aspects of Woolf's stream-of-consciousness technique in the story, and tell how they helped her achieve her purpose.

1. The use of random details to develop a character
2. The repetition of details of setting
3. The repetition of specific images, words, and phrases

## THINKING AND WRITING
### Using Stream of Consciousness

Use the list of possessions you developed earlier to tell a story about the occupant of the room. Use a stream-of-consciousness approach, modeling your story on Woolf's. Before you begin to write, map out what happens to the main character, using the time and manner in which the various objects were acquired as a guideline. When you revise make sure you capture the intermingling of conscious thought and memory. Be prepared to share your story with your class.

---

### Commentary

In her fiction Virginia Woolf tried to find a way to convey the interplay of thought, emotion, and insight that lies below the surface of reality. In this attempt she boldly experimented with radical ways of telling her stories. Stream of consciousness, new structure, and innovative experiments with time were the result. She was influential in her own day for her brilliant personality as well as for her work; however, her reputation has fallen somewhat in the postwar years. The violence of World War II made her subtleties of technique seem mild and old-fashioned. The revolution in technique she furthered is taken for granted where it has not been eclipsed by the political and social concerns of more recent works. Yet one critic believes that in the final analysis "she did supremely well what no one else has attempted to do. She mapped the world of the mind . . . under certain precise conditions of character and environment."

# D. H. LAWRENCE

## 1885–1930

D. H. Lawrence occupies a unique position among the leading Modernist writers of the generation that came of age before the outbreak of the First World War. The originality of his literary achievements was partly clouded by the explosive controversy attached to his name during his lifetime and for some years after. As with Shelley and Byron before him, the controversy that swirled around Lawrence touched on several points, not the least of which were his unorthodox opinions on politics, society, and morality.

David Herbert Lawrence was born near Nottingham in the English Midlands, the son of a miner. His childhood was marked by poverty, illness, constant bickering between his parents, and his mother's driving ambition to make something of her son. After attending local schools, the young Lawrence spent several years as a teacher before turning to writing as a livelihood.

As a writer Lawrence was deeply influenced by the pioneering psychological theories of Sigmund Freud and by the philosophy of Friedrich Nietzsche. He restlessly searched and researched their writings, seeking confirmation of the underlying moral rightness of his strongest convictions—that the industrial social order was unjust, that open expression of sexuality was healthy, and that human beings could find true fulfillment only by living in harmony with nature.

In 1913, shortly before eloping to Germany with a woman several years older than himself, Lawrence published his first major novel, *Sons and Lovers*—a thinly disguised autobiographical account of his childhood and adolescent years. During World War I, he returned with his wife to England where he published his next major work, *The Rainbow* (1915). His frank treatment of sexuality in the book caused it to be declared obscene.

At the end of the war, the Lawrences left England for extended travels in Italy, Ceylon, Australia, Mexico, and the United States. Lawrence used many of these locales in his fiction: *Kangaroo* (1923), for example, is set in Australia; and *The Plumed Serpent* (1926) is steeped in the mythology of ancient Mexico. It was during his prolonged absence from England that Lawrence found a publisher for one of his greatest novels, *Women in Love* (1921). Ill from tuberculosis, Lawrence completed his last novel, *Lady Chatterley's Lover* (1928), while living in Italy.

In the half century since his death, society's views on Lawrence's writings have changed profoundly. Today, his fiction is almost universally admired for its vivid settings, fine craftsmanship, and psychological insight.

# GUIDE FOR INTERPRETING

## The Rocking-Horse Winner

**Omniscient Narration.** Omniscient narration means an all-knowing third-person point of view. Unlike the first-person narrator, who doubles as a character, the third-person narrator is strictly an observer who reports the events of the story from a position beyond or outside them. Because of this remote vantage point, the third-person narrator is said to be omniscient, or all-knowing, privileged with the ability to see into the minds of the characters and to know what fate holds in store for them. While such a narrator is bound by literary convention to remain neutral—is prohibited, that is, from meddling in the affairs of the characters—the particular style of the narration often adds another, and sometimes colorful, dimension to the story. In "The Rocking-Horse Winner," for example, D. H. Lawrence adopts a third-person narrative style reminiscent of that used in fairy tales—a choice that is especially well-suited to the curious proceedings in the story.

"The Rocking-Horse Winner," as with much of Lawrence's work, has sparked a staggering outpouring of critical commentary. There's even a film version! Nevertheless, the story's richness still leaves room for inquiry. In an article entitled "A Rocking-Horse: The Symbol, the Pattern, the Way to Live," critic W. D. Snodgrass scrutinizes the various meanings the rocking horse might have in the story. In one of his most intriguing points, Snodgrass examines the names of the horses upon which Paul, his uncle Oscar, and Bassett the gardener gamble. Snodgrass notes that Paul's first winner, Singhalese, and his last, Malabar, have names which refer to former British colonial regions in India. He sees in a third name, Mirza, the suggestion of still another colony, "Mirzapur." Did Lawrence deliberately select the names of former British colonies to make a point in his story? Snodgrass would have us think so. He notes that for years these colonies were winners for the British Empire. As with any colonial power or large corporation, the British tried to control peoples and materials with which they had little direct contact. He sees a clear parallel between the actions and fate of the British empire and Paul. Read the story and see what you think. Do you agree with Snodgrass's conclusion?

Think about people who believe in such things as superstitions, fortunetellers, and the like. List the qualities that these people have in common. Then attempt to develop a profile of the believer in what many others regard as coincidence or chance.

# The Rocking-Horse Winner

## D. H. Lawrence

There was a woman who was beautiful, who started with all the advantages, yet she had no luck. She married for love, and the love turned to dust. She had bonny children, yet she felt they had been thrust upon her, and she could not love them. They looked at her coldly, as if they were finding fault with her. And hurriedly she felt she must cover up some fault in herself. Yet what it was that she must cover up she never knew. Nevertheless, when her children were present, she always felt the center of her heart go hard. This troubled her, and in her manner she was all the more gentle and anxious for her children, as if she loved them very much. Only she herself knew that at the center of her heart was a hard little place that could not feel love, no, not for anybody. Everybody else said of her: "She is such a good mother. She adores her children." Only she herself, and her children themselves, knew it was not so. They read it in each other's eyes.

There were a boy and two little girls. They lived in a pleasant house, with a garden, and they had discreet servants, and felt themselves superior to anyone in the neighborhood.

Although they lived in style, they felt always an anxiety in the house. There was never enough money. The mother had a small income, and the father had a small income, but not nearly enough for the social position which they had to keep up. The father went into town to some office. But though he had good prospects, these prospects never materialized. There was always the grinding sense of the shortage of money, though the style was always kept up.

At last the mother said, "I will see if *I* can't make something." But she did not know where to begin. She racked her brains, and tried this thing and the other, but could not find anything successful. The failure made deep lines come into her face. Her children were growing up, they would have to go to school. There must be more money, there must be more money. The father, who was always very handsome and expensive in his tastes, seemed as if he never *would* be able to do anything worth doing. And the mother, who had a great belief in herself, did not succeed any better, and her tastes were just as expensive.

And so the house came to be haunted by the unspoken phrase: *There must be more money! There must be more money!* The children could hear it all the time, though nobody said it aloud. They heard it at Christmas, when the expensive and splendid toys filled the nursery. Behind the shining modern rocking horse, behind the smart doll's house, a voice would start whispering: "There *must* be more money! There *must* be more money!" And the children would stop playing, to listen for a moment. They would look into each other's eyes to see if they had all heard. And each one saw in the eyes of the other two that they too had heard. "There *must* be more money! There *must* be more money!"

It came whispering from the springs of

the still-swaying rocking horse, and even the horse, bending his wooden, champing head, heard it. The big doll, sitting so pink and smirking in her new pram,[1] could hear it quite plainly, and seemed to be smirking all the more self-consciously because of it. The foolish puppy, too, that took the place of the teddy bear, he was looking so extraordinarily foolish for no other reason but that he heard the secret whisper all over the house: "There *must* be more money."

Yet nobody ever said it aloud. The whisper was everywhere, and therefore no one spoke it. Just as no one ever says: "We are breathing!" in spite of the fact that breath is coming and going all the time.

"Mother!" said the boy Paul one day. "Why don't we keep a car of our own? Why do we always use uncle's, or else a taxi?"

"Because we're the poor members of the family," said the mother.

"But why *are* we, mother?"

"Well—I suppose," she said slowly and bitterly, "it's because your father has no luck."

The boy was silent for some time.

"Is luck money, mother?" he asked, rather timidly.

"No, Paul! Not quite. It's what causes you to have money."

"Oh!" said Paul vaguely. "I thought when Uncle Oscar said *filthy lucker,* it meant money."

"*Filthy lucre* does mean money," said the mother. "But it's lucre, not luck."

"Oh!" said the boy. "Then what *is* luck, mother?"

"It's what causes you to have money. If you're lucky you have money. That's why it's better to be born lucky than rich. If you're rich, you may lose your money. But if you're lucky, you will always get more money."

"Oh! Will you! And is father not lucky?"

"Very unlucky, I should say," she said bitterly.

The boy watched her with unsure eyes.

"Why?" he asked.

"I don't know. Nobody ever knows why one person is lucky and another unlucky."

"Don't they? Nobody at all? Does *nobody* know?"

"Perhaps God! But He never tells."

"He ought to, then. And aren't you lucky either, mother?"

"I can't be, if I married an unlucky husband."

"But by yourself, aren't you?"

"I used to think I was, before I married. Now I think I am very unlucky indeed."

"Why?"

"Well—never mind! Perhaps I'm not really," she said.

The child looked at her, to see if she meant it. But he saw, by the lines of her mouth, that she was only trying to hide something from him.

"Well, anyhow," he said stoutly, "I'm a lucky person."

"Why?" said his mother, with a sudden laugh.

He stared at her. He didn't even know why he had said it.

"God told me," he asserted, brazening it out.

"I hope He did, dear!" she said, again with a laugh, but rather bitter.

"He did, mother!"

"Excellent!" said the mother, using one of her husband's exclamations.

The boy saw she did not believe him; or rather, that she paid no attention to his assertion. This angered him somewhere, and made him want to compel her attention.

He went off by himself, vaguely, in a childish way, seeking for the clue to "luck." Absorbed, taking no heed of other people, he went about with a sort of stealth, seeking inwardly for luck. He wanted luck, he wanted it, he wanted it. When the two girls were playing dolls, in the nursery, he would sit on his big rocking horse, charging madly into space, with a frenzy that made the little girls peer at him uneasily. Wildly the horse ca-

---

**1. pram:** Baby carriage.

reered, the waving dark hair of the boy tossed, his eyes had a strange glare in them. The little girls dared not speak to him.

When he had ridden to the end of his mad little journey, he climbed down and stood in front of his rocking horse, staring fixedly into its lowered face. Its red mouth was slightly open, its big eye was wide and glassy bright.

"Now!" he would silently command the snorting steed. "Now take me to where there is luck! Now take me!"

And he would slash the horse on the neck with the little whip he had asked Uncle Oscar for. He *knew* the horse could take him to where there was luck, if only he forced it. So he would mount again, and start on his furious ride, hoping at last to get there. He knew he could get there.

"You'll break your horse, Paul!" said the nurse.

"He's always riding like that! I wish he'd leave off!" said his elder sister Joan.

But he only glared down on them in silence. Nurse gave him up. She could make nothing of him. Anyhow he was growing beyond her.

One day his mother and his Uncle Oscar came in when he was on one of his furious rides. He did not speak to them.

"Hallo! you young jockey! Riding a winner?" said his uncle.

"Aren't you growing too big for a rocking horse? You're not a very little boy any longer, you know," said his mother.

But Paul only gave a blue glare from his big, rather close-set eyes. He would speak to nobody when he was in full tilt. His mother watched him with an anxious expression on her face.

At last he suddenly stopped forcing his horse into the mechanical gallop, and slid down.

"Well, I got there!" he announced fiercely, his blue eyes still flaring, and his sturdy long legs straddling apart.

"Where did you get to?" asked his mother.

"Where I wanted to go to," he flared back at her.

"That's right, son!" said Uncle Oscar. "Don't you stop till you get there. What's the horse's name?"

"He doesn't have a name," said the boy.

"Gets on without all right?" asked the uncle.

"Well, he has different names. He was called Sansovino last week."

"Sansovino, eh? Won the Ascot.[2] How did you know his name?"

"He always talks about horse races with Bassett," said Joan.

The uncle was delighted to find that his small nephew was posted with all the racing news. Bassett, the young gardener who had been wounded in the left foot in the war, and had got his present job through Oscar Cresswell, whose batman[3] he had been, was a perfect blade of the "turf."[4] He lived in the racing events, and the small boy lived with him.

Oscar Cresswell got it all from Bassett.

"Master Paul comes and asks me, so I can't do more than tell him, sir," said Bassett, his face terribly serious, as if he were speaking of religious matters.

"And does he ever put anything on a horse he fancies?"

"Well—I don't want to give him away—he's a young sport, a fine sport, sir. Would you mind asking him yourself? He sort of takes a pleasure in it, and perhaps he'd feel I was giving him away, sir, if you don't mind."

Bassett was serious as a church.

The uncle went back to his nephew, and took him off for a ride in the car.

"Say, Paul, old man, do you ever put anything on a horse?" the uncle asked.

The boy watched the handsome man closely.

"Why, do you think I oughtn't to?" he parried.

---

2. **Ascot:** A major English horse race.
3. **batman:** A British military officer's orderly.
4. **blade . . . "turf":** Horse-racing fan.

"Not a bit of it! I thought perhaps you might give me a tip for the Lincoln."[5]

The car sped on into the country, going down to Uncle Oscar's place in Hampshire.

"Honor bright?" said the nephew.

"Honor bright, son!" said the uncle.

"Well, then, Daffodil."

"Daffodil! I doubt it, sonny. What about Mirza?"

"I only know the winner," said the boy. "That's Daffodil!"

"Daffodil, eh?"

There was a pause. Daffodil was an obscure horse comparatively.

"Uncle!"

"Yes, son?"

"You won't let it go any further, will you? I promised Bassett."

"Bassett be hanged, old man! What's he got to do with it?"

"We're partners! We've been partners from the first! Uncle, he lent me my first five shillings, which I lost. I promised him, honor bright, it was only between me and him: only you gave me that ten-shilling note I started winning with, so I thought you were lucky. You won't let it go any further, will you?"

The boy gazed at his uncle from those big, hot, blue eyes, set rather close together. The uncle stirred and laughed uneasily.

"Right you are, son! I'll keep your tip private. Daffodil, eh! How much are you putting on him?"

"All except twenty pounds," said the boy. "I keep that in reserve."

The uncle thought it a good joke.

"You keep twenty pounds in reserve, do you, you young romancer? What are you betting, then?"

"I'm betting three hundred," said the boy gravely. "But it's between you and me, Uncle Oscar! Honor bright?"

The uncle burst into a roar of laughter.

"It's between you and me all right, you young Nat Gould,"[6] he said, laughing. "But where's your three hundred?"

"Bassett keeps it for me. We're partners."

"You are, are you! And what is Bassett putting on Daffodil?"

"He won't go quite as high as I do, I expect. Perhaps he'll go a hundred and fifty."

"What, pennies?" laughed the uncle.

"Pounds," said the child, with a surprised look at his uncle. "Bassett keeps a bigger reserve than I do."

Between wonder and amusement, Uncle Oscar was silent. He pursued the matter no further, but he determined to take his nephew with him to the Lincoln races.

"Now, son," he said, "I'm putting twenty on Mirza, and I'll put five for you on any horse you fancy. What's your pick?"

"Daffodil, uncle!"

"No, not the fiver on Daffodil!"

"I should if it was my own fiver," said the child.

"Good! Good! Right you are! A fiver for me and a fiver for you on Daffodil."

The child had never been to a race meeting before, and his eyes were blue fire. He pursed his mouth tight, and watched. A Frenchman just in front had put his money on Lancelot. Wild with excitement, he flayed his arms up and down, yelling *Lancelot! Lancelot!* in his French accent.

Daffodil came in first, Lancelot second, Mirza third. The child, flushed and with eyes blazing, was curiously serene. His uncle brought him five five-pound notes: four to one.

"What am I to do with these?" he cried, waving them before the boy's eyes.

"I suppose we'll talk to Bassett," said the boy. "I expect I have fifteen hundred now; and twenty in reserve; and this twenty."

---

**5. Lincoln:** A major English horse race.

**6. Nat Gould:** A famous English sportswriter and authority on horse racing.

His uncle studied him for some moments.

"Look here, son!" he said. "You're not serious about Bassett and that fifteen hundred, are you?"

"Yes, I am. But it's between you and me, uncle! Honor bright!"

"Honor bright all right, son! But I must talk to Bassett."

"If you'd like to be a partner, uncle, with Bassett and me, we could all be partners. Only you'd have to promise, honor bright, uncle, not to let it go beyond us three. Bassett and I are lucky, and you must be lucky, because it was your ten shillings I started winning with. . . ."

Uncle Oscar took both Bassett and Paul into Richmond Park for an afternoon, and there they talked.

"It's like this, you see, sir," Bassett said. "Master Paul would get me talking about racing events, spinning yarns, you know, sir. And he was always keen on knowing if I'd made or if I'd lost. It's about a year since, now, that I put five shillings on Blush of Dawn for him—and we lost. Then the luck turned, with that ten shillings he had from you, that we put on Singhalese. And since that time, it's been pretty steady, all things considering. What do you say, Master Paul?"

"We're all right when we're *sure*," said Paul. "It's when we're not quite sure that we go down."

"Oh, but we're careful then," said Bassett.

"But when are you *sure?*" smiled Uncle Oscar.

"It's Master Paul, sir," said Bassett, in a secret, religious voice. "It's as if he had it from heaven. Like Daffodil now, for the Lincoln. That was as sure as eggs."

"Did you put anything on Daffodil?" asked Oscar Cresswell.

"Yes, sir. I made my bit."

"And my nephew?"

Bassett was obstinately silent, looking at Paul.

"I made twelve hundred, didn't I,

Bassett? I told uncle I was putting three hundred on Daffodil."

"That's right," said Bassett, nodding.

"But where's the money?" asked the uncle.

"I keep it safe locked up, sir. Master Paul, he can have it any minute he likes to ask for it."

"What, fifteen hundred pounds?"

"And twenty! And *forty*, that is, with the twenty he made on the course."

"It's amazing!" said the uncle.

"If Master Paul offers you to be partners, sir, I would, if I were you; if you'll excuse me," said Bassett.

Oscar Cresswell thought about it.

"I'll see the money," he said.

They drove home again, and sure enough, Bassett came round to the garden house with fifteen hundred pounds in notes. The twenty pounds reserve was left with Joe Glee, in the Turf Commission deposit.

"You see, it's all right, uncle, when I'm *sure!* Then we go strong, for all we're worth. Don't we, Bassett?"

"We do that, Master Paul."

"And when are you sure?" said the uncle, laughing.

"Oh, well, sometimes I'm *absolutely* sure, like about Daffodil," said the boy, "and sometimes I have an idea; and sometimes I haven't even an idea, have I, Bassett? Then we're careful, because we mostly go down."

"You do, do you! And when you're sure, like about Daffodil, what makes you sure, sonny?"

"Oh, well, I don't know," said the boy uneasily. "I'm sure, you know, uncle; that's all."

"It's as if he had it from heaven, sir," Bassett reiterated.

"I should say so!" said the uncle.

But he became a partner. And when the Leger was coming on, Paul was "sure" about Lively Spark, which was a quite inconsiderable horse. The boy insisted on putting a thousand on the horse, Bassett went for five hundred, and Oscar Cresswell two hundred. Lively Spark came in first, and the betting had been ten to one against him. Paul had made ten thousand.

"You see," he said. "I was absolutely sure of him."

Even Oscar Cresswell had cleared two thousand.

"Look here, son," he said, "this sort of thing makes me nervous."

"It needn't, uncle! Perhaps I shan't be sure again for a long time."

"But what are you going to do with your money?" asked the uncle.

"Of course," said the boy, "I started it for mother. She said she had no luck, because father is unlucky, so I thought if *I* was lucky, it might stop whispering."

"What might stop whispering?"

"Our house! I *hate* our house for whispering."

"What does it whisper?"

"Why—why"—the boy fidgeted—"why, I don't know! But it's always short of money, you know, uncle."

"I know it, son, I know it."

"You know people send mother writs, don't you, uncle?"

"I'm afraid I do," said the uncle.

"And then the house whispers like people laughing at you behind your back. It's awful, that is! I thought if I was lucky . . ."

"You might stop it," added the uncle.

The boy watched him with big blue eyes, that had an uncanny cold fire in them, and he said never a word.

"Well then!" said the uncle. "What are we doing?"

"I shouldn't like mother to know I was lucky," said the boy.

"Why not, son?"

"She'd stop me."

"I don't think she would."

"Oh!"—and the boy writhed in an odd way— "I *don't* want her to know, uncle."

"All right, son! We'll manage it without her knowing."

They managed it very easily. Paul, at the other's suggestion, handed over five thousand pounds to his uncle, who deposited it with the family lawyer, who was then to inform Paul's mother that a relative had put five thousand pounds into his hands, which sum was to be paid out a thousand pounds at a time, on the mother's birthday, for the next five years.

"So she'll have a birthday present of a thousand pounds for five successive years," said Uncle Oscar. "I hope it won't make it all the harder for her later."

Paul's mother had her birthday in November. The house had been "whispering" worse than ever lately, and even in spite of his luck, Paul could not bear up against it. He was very anxious to see the effect of the birthday letter, telling his mother about the thousand pounds.

When there were no visitors, Paul now took his meals with his parents, as he was beyond the nursery control. His mother went into town nearly every day. She had discovered that she had an odd knack of sketching furs and dress materials, so she worked secretly in the studio of a friend who was the chief "artist" for the leading drapers. She drew the figures of ladies in furs and ladies in silk and sequins for the newspaper advertisements. This young woman artist earned several thousand pounds a year, but Paul's mother only made several hundreds, and she was again dissatisfied. She so wanted to be first in something, and she did not succeed, even in making sketches for drapery advertisements.

She was down to breakfast on the morning of her birthday. Paul watched her face as she read her letters. He knew the lawyer's letter. As his mother read it, her face hardened and became more expressionless. Then a cold, determined look came on her mouth. She hid the letter under the pile of others, and said not a word about it.

"Didn't you have anything nice in the post for your birthday, mother?" said Paul.

"Quite moderately nice," she said, her voice cold and absent.

She went away to town without saying more.

But in the afternoon Uncle Oscar appeared. He said Paul's mother had had a long interview with the lawyer, asking if the whole five thousand could not be advanced at once, as she was in debt.

"What do you think, uncle?" said the boy.

"I leave it to you, son."

"Oh, let her have it, then! We can get some more with the other," said the boy.

"A bird in the hand is worth two in the bush, laddie!" said Uncle Oscar.

"But I'm sure to *know* for the Grand National; or the Lincolnshire; or else the Derby.[7] I'm sure to know for *one* of them," said Paul.

So Uncle Oscar signed the agreement, and Paul's mother touched the whole five thousand. Then something very curious happened. The voices in the house suddenly went mad, like a chorus of frogs on a spring evening. There were certain new furnishings, and Paul had a tutor. He was *really* going to Eton,[8] his father's school, in the following autumn. There were flowers in the winter, and a blossoming of the luxury Paul's mother had been used to. And yet the voices in the house, behind the sprays of mimosa and almond blossom, and from under the piles of iridescent cushions, simply trilled and screamed in a sort of ecstasy: "There *must* be more money! Oh-h-h! There *must* be more money! Oh, now, now-w! now-w-w—there *must* be more money!—more than ever! More than ever!"

It frightened Paul terribly. He studied away at his Latin and Greek with his tutors. But his intense hours were spent with Bassett. The Grand National had gone by: he had not "known," and had lost a hundred pounds. Summer was at hand. He was in agony for the Lincoln. But even for the Lincoln he didn't "know," and he lost fifty pounds. He became wild-eyed and strange,

as if something were going to explode in him.

"Let it alone, son! Don't you bother about it!" urged Uncle Oscar. But it was as if the boy couldn't really hear what his uncle was saying.

"I've got to know for the Derby! I've *got* to know for the Derby!" the child reiterated, his big blue eyes blazing with a sort of madness.

His mother noticed how overwrought he was.

"You'd better go to the seaside. Wouldn't you like to go now to the seaside, instead of waiting? I think you'd better," she said, looking down at him anxiously, her heart curiously heavy because of him.

But the child lifted his uncanny blue eyes.

"I couldn't possibly go before the Derby, mother!" he said. "I couldn't possibly!"

"Why not?" she said, her voice becoming heavy when she was opposed. "Why not? You can still go from the seaside to see the Derby with your Uncle Oscar, if that's what you wish. No need for you to wait here. Besides, I think you care too much about these races. It's a bad sign. My family has been a gambling family, and you won't know till you grow up how much damage it has done. But it has done damage. I shall have to send Bassett away, and ask Uncle Oscar not to talk racing to you, unless you promise to be reasonable about it; go away to the seaside and forget it. You're all nerves!"

"I'll do what you like, mother, so long as you don't send me away till after the Derby," the boy said.

"Send you away from where? Just from this house?"

"Yes," he said, gazing at her.

"Why, you curious child, what makes you care about this house so much, suddenly? I never knew you loved it!"

He gazed at her without speaking. He had a secret within a secret, something he had not divulged, even to Bassett or to his Uncle Oscar.

---

**7. Grand National . . . Derby:** Major English horse races.

**8. Eton:** A prestigious private school in England.

But his mother, after standing undecided and a little bit sullen for some moments, said:

"Very well, then! Don't go to the seaside till after the Derby, if you don't wish it. But promise me you won't let your nerves go to pieces! Promise you won't think so much about horse racing and *events,* as you call them!"

"Oh, no!" said the boy, casually. "I won't think much about them, mother. You needn't worry. I wouldn't worry, mother, if I were you."

"If you were me and I were you," said his mother, "I wonder what we *should* do!"

"But you know you needn't worry, mother, don't you?" the boy repeated.

"I should be awfully glad to know it," she said wearily.

"Oh, well, you *can,* you know. I mean you *ought* to know you needn't worry!" he insisted.

"Ought I? Then I'll see about it," she said.

Paul's secret of secrets was his wooden horse, that which had no name. Since he was emancipated from a nurse and a nursery governess, he had had his rocking horse removed to his own bedroom at the top of the house.

"Surely you're too big for a rocking horse!" his mother had remonstrated.

"Well, you see, mother, till I can have a *real* horse, I like to have *some* sort of animal about," had been his quaint answer.

"Do you feel he keeps you company?" she laughed.

"Oh, yes! He's very good, he always keeps me company, when I'm there," said Paul.

So the horse, rather shabby, stood in an arrested prance in the boy's bedroom.

The Derby was drawing near, and the boy grew more and more tense. He hardly heard what was spoken to him, he was very frail, and his eyes were really uncanny. His mother had sudden strange seizures of uneasiness about him. Sometimes, for half an hour, she would feel a sudden anxiety about him that was almost anguish. She wanted to rush to him at once, and know he was safe.

Two nights before the Derby, she was at a big party in town, when one of her rushes of anxiety about her boy, her firstborn, gripped her heart till she could hardly speak. She fought with the feeling, might and main, for she believed in common sense. But it was too strong. She had to leave the dance and go downstairs to telephone to the country. The children's nursery governess was terribly surprised and startled at being rung up in the night.

"Are the children all right, Miss Wilmot?"

"Oh yes, they are quite all right."

"Master Paul? Is he all right?"

"He went to bed as right as a trivet.[9] Shall I run up and look at him?"

"No!" said Paul's mother reluctantly. "No! Don't trouble. It's all right. Don't sit up. We shall be home fairly soon." She did not want her son's privacy intruded upon.

"Very good," said the governess.

It was about one o'clock when Paul's mother and father drove up to their house. All was still. Paul's mother went to her room and slipped off her white fur cloak. She had told her maid not to wait up for her. She heard her husband downstairs, mixing a whisky-and-soda.

And then, because of the strange anxiety at her heart, she stole upstairs to her son's room. Noiselessly she went along the upper corridor. Was there a faint noise? What was it?

She stood, with arrested muscles, outside his door, listening. There was a strange, heavy, and yet not loud noise. Her heart stood still. It was a soundless noise, yet rushing and powerful. Something huge, in violent, hushed motion. What was it? What in God's name was it? She ought to know. She felt that she *knew* the noise. She knew what it was.

---

**9. right as a trivet:** Perfectly right.

Yet she could not place it. She couldn't say what it was. And on and on it went, like a madness.

Softly, frozen with anxiety and fear, she turned the door handle.

The room was dark. Yet in the space near the window, she heard and saw something plunging to and fro. She gazed in fear and amazement.

Then suddenly she switched on the light, and saw her son, in his green pajamas, madly surging on his rocking horse. The blaze of light suddenly lit him up, as he urged the wooden horse, and lit her up, as she stood, blond, in her dress of pale green and crystal, in the doorway.

"Paul!" she cried. "Whatever are you doing?"

"It's Malabar!" he screamed, in a powerful, strange voice. "It's Malabar!"

His eyes blazed at her for one strange and senseless second, as he ceased urging his wooden horse. Then he fell with a crash to the ground, and she, all her tormented motherhood flooding upon her, rushed to gather him up.

But he was unconscious, and unconscious he remained, with some brain fever. He talked and tossed, and his mother sat stonily by his side.

"Malabar! It's Malabar! Bassett, Bassett, I *know* it's Malabar!"

So the child cried, trying to get up and urge the rocking horse that gave him his inspiration.

"What does he mean by Malabar?" asked the heart-frozen mother.

"I don't know," said the father, stonily.

"What does he mean by Malabar?" she asked her brother Oscar.

"It's one of the horses running for the Derby," was the answer.

And, in spite of himself, Oscar Cresswell spoke to Bassett, and himself put a thousand on Malabar: at fourteen to one.

The third day of the illness was critical: they were watching for a change. The boy, with his rather long, curly hair, was tossing ceaselessly on the pillow. He neither slept nor regained consciousness, and his eyes were like blue stones. His mother sat, feeling her heart had gone, turned actually into a stone.

In the evening, Oscar Cresswell did not come, but Bassett sent a message, saying could he come up for one moment, just one moment? Paul's mother was very angry at the intrusion, but on second thoughts she agreed. The boy was the same. Perhaps Bassett might bring him to consciousness.

The gardener, a shortish fellow with a little brown moustache and sharp little brown eyes, tiptoed into the room, touched his imaginary cap to Paul's mother, and stole to the bedside, staring with glittering, smallish eyes at the tossing, dying child.

"Master Paul!" he whispered. "Master Paul! Malabar came in first all right, a clean win. I did as you told me. You've made over seventy thousand pounds, you have; you've got over eighty thousand. Malabar came in all right, Master Paul."

"Malabar! Malabar! Did I say Malabar, mother? Did I say Malabar? Do you think I'm lucky, mother? I knew Malabar, didn't I? Over eighty thousand pounds! I call that lucky, don't you, mother? Over eighty thousand pounds! I knew, didn't I know I knew? Malabar came in all right. If I ride my horse till I'm sure, then I tell you, Bassett, you can go as high as you like. Did you go for all you were worth, Bassett?"

"I went a thousand on it, Master Paul."

"I never told you, mother, that if I can ride my horse, and *get there*, then I'm absolutely sure—oh, absolutely! Mother, did I ever tell you? I *am* lucky!"

"No, you never did," said the mother.

But the boy died in the night.

And even as he lay dead, his mother heard her brother's voice saying to her: "My God, Hester, you're eighty-odd thousand to the good, and a poor devil of a son to the bad. But, poor devil, poor devil, he's best gone out of a life where he rides his rocking horse to find a winner."

# THINKING ABOUT THE SELECTION

## Recalling

1. Why is the family in the story always short of money?
2. How does Paul try to change the family's luck?
3. (a) What birthday present does Paul give his mother? (b) What is her reaction to it?
4. What does Paul's mother discover upon returning from the big party?

## Interpreting

5. What comment does Lawrence seem to be making about the concerns of Paul's parents?
6. On page 975 Paul's mother describes her husband as unlucky? (a) What do you think she means by this? (b) What does the remark reveal about her as a person?
7. What comment about life do you think the author is suggesting in Uncle Oscar's statement on Paul's death at the story's close?
8. Identify Lawrence's theme in this story.

## Applying

9. Tell to what extent the problems he addresses are problems primarily of this century.

# ANALYZING LITERATURE

## Understanding Omniscient Narration

**Omniscient narration** is narration by a third-person speaker who, knowing all, is able to "read" the characters' minds and see into their futures. In "The Rocking-Horse Winner," D. H. Lawrence uses a narrative style of the sort ordinarily found in fairy tales. The opening line of the story, for example, has some of the ring of the familiar "Once upon a time" beginning.

1. Identify at least two other features of the story that give it the flavor of a fairy tale. Describe what you feel these features add to the impact of the ending.

2. (a) How different might your overall impression of the story be if Lawrence had used the mother as the narrator? (b) If he had used Uncle Oscar?

# UNDERSTANDING LANGUAGE

## Understanding Synonyms

**Synonyms** are words that share a common meaning. The word *luck,* for instance, which appears in one form or another throughout the story has synonyms in the words *fate, fortune,* and *chance,* to name a few. Yet, not all of these words mean the same thing, which suggests that *luck* has several related, but very different, meanings. Reread the section on page 975 where Paul's mother explains luck. Then turn to Paul's final words on page 982. Tell which synonyms apply to the mother's use of the word. Then tell which apply to Paul's use, and explain why that use is ironic.

# THINKING AND WRITING

## Telling the Story

Imagine that Paul, and not an omniscient narrator, were telling the story. Try to imagine, based on examples Lawrence provides of the child's language, what words Paul might use to express events. More important, try to envision what takes place inside Paul's mind when he is astride his horse and galloping toward another "victory." Then retell a portion of the story from Paul's point of view. You may wish to concentrate on the section that immediately precedes Paul's lapse into unconsciousness. When you revise make sure you have maintained a consistent point of view. Have you included information Paul would not know? Does your narrator sound like Paul? Proofread your story and prepare a final draft. Read it aloud to your classmates.

# JAMES JOYCE

## 1882–1941

Although James Joyce left Ireland early in his career and associated with the radical literary experimentalists on the Continent, he never lost the respect for tradition that he had learned from his Jesuit teachers. All of his works are set in his native Dublin, and all have firm roots in the literature of the past. If Joyce's innovativeness in the areas of plot, character, and language are undeniable, so then is the notion that part of his greatness was his ability to reinterpret and transform familiar literary forms.

James Joyce was born and educated in Dublin. Choosing, much to the disappointment of his family and teachers, not to enter the priesthood, he briefly considered careers in medicine and singing. His true calling, however, was as a writer, and in 1907 he published *Chamber Music,* a collection of poems. At the time of the book's publication, Joyce was living in Trieste, Italy, where he remained until the outbreak of the First World War.

The year he relocated to Zurich, 1914, also marks the appearance of his landmark volume of short stories *Dubliners.* This collection of deceptively simple tales focuses on people who, on the surface, are quite ordinary but whose minds are filled with raging psychological and emotional conflicts. Each of the main characters in *Dubliners* experiences in some way a growth of self-awareness that leads to a climactic peak in the story.

This process is developed still more fully in *A Portrait of the Artist as a Young Man,* a fictionalized account of Joyce's own life from infancy through age twenty. Like Joyce, Stephen Dedalus, the novel's main character, finds himself in conflict with his family, the Roman Catholic Church, and the nationalistic fervor of his countrymen. The book also reveals a heightened awareness of the power of language and a deeper immersion into the mind of the character. Both these traits are carried forward into *Ulysses* (1922), whose ultimate banning in England and the United States, made Joyce famous, if not wealthy. This novel, which roughly parallels Homer's *Odyssey,* presents a single day in the life of three Dubliners. The world Joyce depicts, while as solidly three-dimensional as any conjured up by nineteenth-century realists, is nevertheless one in which language can be seen to provide keys to the exploration of truth.

Joyce's last novel, *Finnegan's Wake* (1939), was in many ways the most challenging. Written in what one scholar terms "a dream language of Joyce's own invention," this highly experimental work presents its author's view of human existence as moving through various cycles.

# GUIDE FOR INTERPRETING

## Araby

**Writer's Technique**

**Epiphany.** Epiphany (i pif′ ə nē) is a profound mental or spiritual revelation experienced by the hero of a literary work. The term is derived from Greek mythology, where it was used to describe the occasion when a god or goddess, wearing a disguise or concealed in a cloud, would suddenly reveal his or her true divine identity to a mortal. In modern fiction epiphany generally occurs in stories that operate on a mental, or "cerebral," level, rather than on a purely physical level. In such stories the major events are so constructed as to lead up to this dawning, or sudden awareness of an important truth, on the part of a character. What the character *thinks* under circumstances of this sort is more important than what he or she *does*. In his collection of stories *Dubliners,* James Joyce frequently depicts characters who experience epiphany.

**Writing**

Logan Pearsall Smith wrote, "All mirrors are magical mirrors; never can we see our faces in them." Freewrite, exploring the meaning of the quotation and your reactions to it.

**Primary Source**

The reactions people have to others may shed light on their own character. What was Joyce's reaction to William Butler Yeats, an older and more established writer? By 1905, when he was forty years old, Yeats was a famous man in Ireland: A greatly admired poet and playwright, he was also a leader in both the Irish Literary Revival and the Irish National Movement. In 1905 James Joyce was only twenty-three. In contrast to Yeats, he had yet to publish anything; his first work, a collection of poems called *Chamber Music,* was still two years off. One would think, then, that Joyce would be very much in awe of Yeats's accomplishments in light of his own youth and inexperience. Just the opposite was true, as revealed in the famous story his friend Oliver St. John Gogarty recounts: "We both lived on the north side of the city, and we were going up Rutland Square, I think it was a horse-drawn tram in those days. I happened to mention that thing that the newspapers were full of—that it was Yeats's fortieth birthday and that Lady Gregory had collected from his friends forty pounds with which she bought a Kelmscott edition of Chaucer by William Morris. Everybody knew that it was Yeats's birthday. But when I made an epiphany, so to speak, and told Joyce this, at the first tram stop he got out. Yeats was lodging in the Cavendish Hotel, in Rutland Square, and he solemnly walked in and knocked at Yeats's door. When Yeats opened the door of the sitting-room he said, 'What age are you, sir?' and Yeats said, 'I'm 40.'—'You are too old for me to help. I bid you goodbye.' And Yeats was greatly impressed at the impertinence of the thing."

**ST. PATRICK'S CLOSE**
*Walter Osborne*
National Gallery of Ireland

# Araby

## James Joyce

North Richmond Street, being blind,[1] was a quiet street except at the hour when the Christian Brothers' School set the boys free. An uninhabited house of two stories stood at the blind end, detached from its neighbors in a square ground. The other houses of the street, conscious of decent lives within them, gazed at one another with brown imperturbable faces.

The former tenant of our house, a priest, had died in the back drawing room. Air, musty from having been long enclosed, hung in all the rooms, and the waste room behind the kitchen was littered with old useless papers. Among these I found a few paper-covered books, the pages of which were curled and damp: *The Abbot,* by Walter Scott, *The Devout Communicant* and *The Memoirs of Vidocq.*[2] I liked the last best because its leaves were yellow. The wild garden behind the house contained a central apple tree and a few straggling bushes under one of which I found the late tenant's rusty bicycle pump. He had been a very charitable priest; in his will he had left all his money to institutions and the furniture of his house to his sister.

When the short days of winter came dusk fell before we had well eaten our dinners. When we met in the street the houses had grown somber. The space of sky above us was the color of ever-changing violet and toward it the lamps of the street lifted their feeble lanterns. The cold air stung us and we played till our bodies glowed. Our shouts echoed in the silent street. The career of our play brought us through the dark muddy lanes behind the houses where we ran the gantlet of the rough tribes from the cottages, to the back doors of the dark dripping gardens where odors arose from the ashpits, to the dark odorous stables where a coachman smoothed and combed the horse or shook music from the buckled harness. When we returned to the street, light from the kitchen windows had filled the areas. If my uncle was seen turning the corner we hid in the shadow until we had seen him safely housed. Or if Mangan's sister came out on the doorstep to call her brother in to his tea we watched her from our shadow peer up and down the street. We waited to see whether she would remain or go in and, if she remained, we left our shadow and walked up to Mangan's steps resignedly. She was waiting for us, her figure defined by the light from the half-opened door. Her brother always teased her before he obeyed and I stood by the railings looking at her. Her dress swung as she moved her body and the soft rope of her hair tossed from side to side.

Every morning I lay on the floor in the front parlor watching her door. The blind was pulled down to within an inch of the sash so that I could not be seen. When she came out on the doorstep my heart leaped. I

---

1. **blind:** Dead end.
2. **The Abbot . . . Vidocq:** A historical tale, a religious manual, and the remembrances of a French adventurer, respectively.

ran to the hall, seized my books and followed her. I kept her brown figure always in my eye and, when we came near the point at which our ways diverged, I quickened my pace and passed her. This happened morning after morning. I had never spoken to her, except for a few casual words, and yet her name was like a summons to all my foolish blood.

Her image accompanied me even in places the most hostile to romance. On Saturday evenings when my aunt went marketing I had to go to carry some of the parcels. We walked through the flaring streets, jostled by drunken men and bargaining women, amid the curses of laborers, the shrill litanies of shopboys who stood on guard by the barrels of pigs' cheeks, the nasal chanting of street singers, who sang a *come-all-you* about O'Donovan Rossa,[3] or a ballad about the troubles in our native land. These noises converged in a single sensation of life for me: I imagined that I bore my chalice safely through a throng of foes. Her name sprang to my lips at moments in strange prayers and praises which I myself did not understand. My eyes were often full of tears (I could not tell why) and at times a flood from my heart seemed to pour itself out into my bosom. I thought little of the future. I did not know whether I would ever speak to her or not or, if I spoke to her, how I could tell her of my confused adoration. But my body was like a harp and her words and gestures were like fingers running upon the wires.

One evening I went into the back drawing room in which the priest had died. It was a dark rainy evening and there was no sound in the house. Through one of the broken panes I heard the rain impinge upon the earth, the fine incessant needles of water playing in the sodden beds. Some distant lamp or lighted window gleamed below me. I was thankful that I could see so little. All my senses seemed to desire to veil themselves and, feeling that I was about to

slip from them, I pressed the palms of my hands together until they trembled, murmuring: *"O love! O love!"* many times.

At last she spoke to me. When she addressed the first words to me I was so confused that I did not know what to answer. She asked me was I going to *Araby.* I forget whether I answered yes or no. It would be a splendid bazaar, she said; she would love to go.

"And why can't you?" I asked.

While she spoke she turned a silver bracelet round and round her wrist. She could not go, she said, because there would be a retreat[4] that week in her convent.[5] Her brother and two other boys were fighting for their caps and I was alone at the railings. She held one of the spikes, bowing her head towards me. The light from the lamp opposite our door caught the white curve of her neck, lit up her hair that rested there and, falling, lit up the hand upon the railing. It fell over one side of her dress and caught the white border of a petticoat, just visible as she stood at ease.

"It's well for you," she said.

"If I go," I said, "I will bring you something."

What innumerable follies laid waste my waking and sleeping thoughts after that evening! I wished to annihilate the tedious intervening days. I chafed against the work of school. At night in my bedroom and by day in the classroom her image came between me and the page I strove to read. The syllables of the word *Araby* were called to me through the silence in which my soul luxuriated and cast an Eastern enchantment over me. I asked for leave to go to the bazaar on Saturday night. My aunt was surprised and hoped it was not some Freemason[6] affair. I answered few questions in

---

**3. *come-all-you* . . . Rossa:** The opening of a ballad about an Irish hero.

**4. retreat** *n.*: A period of retirement or seclusion for prayer, religious study, and meditation.
**5. convent** *n.*: A school run by an order of nuns.
**6. Freemason:** The Free and Accepted Masons, an international secret society.

class. I watched my master's face pass from amiability to sternness; he hoped I was not beginning to idle. I could not call my wandering thoughts together. I had hardly any patience with the serious work of life which, now that it stood between me and my desire, seemed to me child's play, ugly monotonous child's play.

On Saturday morning I reminded my uncle that I wished to go to the bazaar in the evening. He was fussing at the hallstand, looking for the hat brush, and answered me curtly:

"Yes, boy, I know."

As he was in the hall I could not go into the front parlor and lie at the window. I left the house in bad humor and walked slowly toward the school. The air was pitilessly raw and already my heart misgave me.

When I came home to dinner my uncle had not yet been home. Still it was early. I sat staring at the clock for some time and, when its ticking began to irritate me, I left the room. I mounted the staircase and gained the upper part of the house. The high cold empty gloomy rooms liberated me and I went from room to room singing. From the front window I saw my companions playing below in the street. Their cries reached me weakened and indistinct and, leaning my forehead against the cool glass, I looked over at the dark house where she lived. I may have stood there for an hour, seeing nothing but the brown-clad figure cast by my imagination, touched discreetly by the lamplight at the curved neck, at the hand upon the railings and at the border below the dress.

When I came downstairs again I found Mrs. Mercer sitting at the fire. She was an old garrulous woman, a pawnbroker's widow, who collected used stamps for some pious purpose. I had to endure the gossip of the tea table. The meal was prolonged beyond an hour and still my uncle did not come. Mrs. Mercer stood up to go: she was sorry she couldn't wait any longer, but it was after eight o'clock and she did not like to be out late, as the night air was bad for her. When she had gone I began to walk up and down the room, clenching my fists. My aunt said:

"I'm afraid you may put off your bazaar for this night of Our Lord."

At nine o'clock I heard my uncle's latch-key in the hall door. I heard him talking to himself and heard the hallstand rocking when it had received the weight of his overcoat. I could interpret these signs. When he was midway through his dinner I asked him to give me the money to go to the bazaar. He had forgotten.

"The people are in bed and after their first sleep now," he said.

I did not smile. My aunt said to him energetically:

"Can't you give him the money and let him go? You've kept him late enough as it is."

My uncle said he was very sorry he had forgotten. He said he believed in the old saying: *All work and no play makes Jack a dull boy.* He asked me where I was going and, when I had told him a second time he asked me did I know *The Arab's Farewell to His Steed.*[7] When I left the kitchen he was about to recite the opening lines of the piece to my aunt.

I held a florin[8] tightly in my hand as I strode down Buckingham Street toward the station. The sight of the streets thronged with buyers and glaring with gas recalled to me the purpose of my journey. I took my seat in a third-class carriage of a deserted train. After an intolerable delay the train moved out of the station slowly. It crept onward among ruinous houses and over the twinkling river. At Westland Row Station a crowd of people pressed to the carriage doors; but the porters moved them back, saying that it was a special train for the bazaar. I remained alone in the bare car-

---

**7. The Arab's . . . His Steed:** A popular nineteenth-century poem.
**8. florin** *n.*: A former two-shilling coin.

riage. In a few minutes the train drew up beside an improvised wooden platform. I passed out onto the road and saw by the lighted dial of a clock that it was ten minutes to ten. In front of me was a large building which displayed the magical name.

I could not find any sixpenny entrance and, fearing that the bazaar would be closed, I passed in quickly through a turnstile, handing a shilling to a weary-looking man. I found myself in a big hall girdled at half its height by a gallery. Nearly all the stalls were closed and the greater part of the hall was in darkness. I recognized a silence like that which pervades a church after a service. I walked into the center of the bazaar timidly. A few people were gathered about the stalls which were still open. Before a curtain, over which the words *Café Chantant*[9] were written in colored lamps, two men were counting money on a salver.[10] I listened to the fall of the coins.

Remembering with difficulty why I had come I went over to one of the stalls and examined porcelain vases and flowered tea sets. At the door of the stall a young lady was talking and laughing with two young gentlemen. I remarked their English accents and listened vaguely to their conversation.

---

**9. Café Chantant:** A café with musical entertainment.
**10. salver** *n.*: A tray usually used for the presentation of letters or visiting cards.

"O, I never said such a thing!"
"O, but you did!"
"O, but I didn't!"
"Didn't she say that?"
"Yes. I heard her."
"O, there's a . . .fib!"

Observing me the young lady came over and asked me did I wish to buy anything. The tone of her voice was not encouraging; she seemed to have spoken to me out of a sense of duty. I looked humbly at the great jars that stood like Eastern guards at either side of the dark entrance to the stall and murmured:

"No, thank you."

The young lady changed the position of one of the vases and went back to the two young men. They began to talk of the same subject. Once or twice the young lady glanced at me over her shoulder.

I lingered before her stall, though I knew my stay was useless, to make my interest in her wares seem the more real. Then I turned away slowly and walked down the middle of the bazaar. I allowed the two pennies to fall against the sixpence in my pocket. I heard a voice call from one end of the gallery that the light was out. The upper part of the hall was now completely dark.

Gazing up into the darkness I saw myself as a creature driven and derided by vanity; and my eyes burned with anguish and anger.

---

## THINKING ABOUT THE SELECTION

### Recalling

1. (a) What does the narrator feel toward Mangan's sister? (b) What are her first words to him?
2. (a) Why is going to the bazaar so important to the narrator? (b) Why is he late getting there?

(c) What does he buy?
3. How does the narrator feel at the end of the story?

### Interpreting

4. How would you describe the mood, or feeling, established in the opening paragraphs?
5. What might have been the author's reason for

not giving Mangan's sister a name?

6. What makes the narrator feel as he does at the end of the story?

7. (a) Why do you think the author chose "Araby" as a name for the bazaar? (b) As a title for the story? (c) How does it relate to the narrator's experiences?

### Applying

8. (a) Look up the meaning of the word *vanity*. Which meaning is intended in the last paragraph of this story? (b) Do you agree with the narrator that he is a "creature driven and derided by vanity"? Support your answer. (c) Do you think vanity is or is not necessary to some degree for survival in today's world? Explain your answer.

## ANALYZING LITERATURE
### Understanding Epiphany

**Epiphany** is the sudden recognition of an important truth by a character in a work of fiction. Tracing back to Greek mythology where it referred to the sudden disclosure to one character of a deity's identity, epiphany in contemporary fiction is the unmasking of a truth that was present all along in a character's mind. In the short stories of James Joyce, this truth usually relates to the essential nature of something commonplace—a person, situation, or object—that the character now sees in a new light.

1. Where in "Araby" does the epiphany occur?
2. What does the hero suddenly realize?
3. What suddenly causes him to feel this way?

## CRITICAL THINKING AND READING
### Analyzing Joyce's Attitude

It is important to keep in mind that, as with many stories told from the first-person point of view, the narrator of "Araby" is not the author. Yet as with any such story, the author expresses his attitude toward the character of the narrator through the character's words, thoughts, and actions. Read the following quotes from "Araby." Tell what they reveal, as a whole, about Joyce's attitude toward his narrator's romantic goals.

1. "Every morning I lay on the floor in the parlor watching her door." (page 987)
2. "Her image accompanied me even in places the most hostile to romance." (page 988)
3. "Her name sprang to my lips at moments in strange prayers. . . ." (page 988)
4. "'If I go,' I said, 'I will bring you something.'" (page 988)

## UNDERSTANDING LANGUAGE
### Appreciating Image-Making Words

An **image** is a word that appeals to the senses. Joyce is widely recognized as a master of imagery, and "Araby" amply demonstrates why. Identify which words help make each of the following images so vivid, and name the sense or senses to which the image appeals.

1. "The cold air stung us and we played till our bodies glowed." (page 987)
2. ". . . we ran . . . [to] the dark dripping gardens where odors rose from ashpits, to the dark odorous stables where a coachman smoothed and combed the horse or shook music from the buckled harness." (page 987)
3. "Her dress swung as she moved her body and the soft rope of her hair tossed from side to side." (page 987)
4. "The . . . streets thronged with buyers and glaring with gas recalled to me the purpose of my journey." (page 989)

## THINKING AND WRITING
### Writing an Extended Conversation

Choose an episode from the story involving the narrator and Mangan's sister—perhaps when he passes her going to school or when they talk about the bazaar. Imagine an extended conversation between them, giving particular emphasis to what they might say and the way in which they would most likely say it. Record this bit of dialogue, permitting yourself ample time to revise any sections that do not ring true.

# ELIZABETH BOWEN

## 1899–1973

The fiction of Elizabeth Bowen is distinguished by the author's subtle observation of landscape, by her innovative and believable use of the supernatural, and by her haunting portrayal of England during one of the darkest eras of that country's history—the years between 1939 and 1945.

Bowen was born in Dublin and raised in County Cork, Ireland. She published her first novel, *The Hotel,* in 1927. During the 1930's she perfected her craft and in 1938, on the eve of the Second World War, completed one of her best-known works, *The Death of the Heart.* This novel traces the intertwining loves and fortunes of a group of sophisticated but vulnerable Londoners in the 1930's.

During the war Bowen observed England's hardships keenly and with compassion. The brutal realities of the conflict—air raids, blackouts, and espionage—were incorporated into some of her best short stories. Typically she played on the heightening of emotions and perceptions in wartime to probe the inner workings of her characters' minds. Shortly after the end of the war Bowen published another novel, *The Heat of the Day* (1949), which was received with much acclaim. Set in wartime London, the work movingly juxtaposes a tragic love affair with the larger national dilemma of a country's fight for its survival.

After the war, Bowen widened her literary activities to include literary criticism and book reviews for such journals as the *Tatler,* as well as scripts for the British Broadcasting Company. She was honored by her own country in 1948, when she received a prestigious award, the C.B.E. (Commander, Order of the British Empire). During the 1950's she spent a great deal of time in the United States, writing and lecturing.

After the death of her husband in 1952, Bowen returned to Ireland to live. Although her earlier work was influenced by the psychological realism of Henry James, her later novels—*A World of Love* (1955), *The Little Girls* (1964), and *Eva Trout* (1969)—exhibit a more symbolic, more poetic style. Bowen never fully adopted the stream-of-consciousness technique practiced by her contemporaries, Virginia Woolf and James Joyce. Yet readers may easily sense more than a trace of this technique in Bowen's novels and stories —such is her sensitivity to fine shades of emotion and her eye for small but important detail.

Bowen defined the novel as the "non-poetic statement of poetic truth," and in her straightforward, deceptively simple writing style and exploration of complex human relationships, she achieved this literary integrity and verisimilitude.

# GUIDE FOR INTERPRETING

## The Demon Lover

**Historical Context**

**War and the Ghost Story.** Despite the number of times humans have waged warfare on one another throughout history, war has never, happily, become a natural state of affairs for the species. The unnaturalness of a civilization in wartime is especially evident off the battlefield, in the streets of a city. Here the horrors that attend war—loss of life, destruction of property, suffering, fear, and despair—seem ever so much like the work of a band of demonic spirits. The Second World War, in particular, struck individuals living in the war-ravaged cities of Europe as akin to a nightmare. Warning sirens and blackouts were a part of everyday life; whole communities were sometimes evacuated against the danger of an enemy attack, leaving street after street of deserted buildings. These "ghost towns" within metropolises like London impressed some writers as ideal backdrops for stories that deal in events of the supernatural, or ghost stories. One such writer was Elizabeth Bowen, who sought in "The Demon Lover" to pit the horrifying landscape of the battlefield against the still more horrifying landscape closer to home.

**Commentary**

"The Demon Lover" is, in part, a subtle reworking of an English ballad of the same name. In the ballad a faithless, fickle woman betrays her absent lover and marries another man. When the lover returns years later—now supposedly very wealthy—the woman is quick to abandon her husband and children to run off with him. Too late, she discovers that the lover is, in fact, not at all what she imagined. On a superficial level, Bowen's story resembles the ballad, and one critic, Douglas A. Hughes, has remarked that the author even relies on the poem to suggest how the story's main character, Mrs. Drover, views herself. But Bowen's genius in this story lies partly in the way she refashions the ballad's basic plot and terrifying atmosphere to suggest important things about the effect of war's devastation on the human psyche. In a recent study of Elizabeth Bowen, critic Allan E. Austin wrote that "'The Demon Lover' is a ghost story that builds up and then culminates like an Alfred Hitchcock movie."

**Writing**

Imagine that a mysterious letter or other piece of mail is delivered to your home. In a brief narrative, describe the specific contents of the letter, as well as your and your family's reaction to it. Conclude your account with an explanation of how the mystery was resolved.

# The Demon Lover

## Elizabeth Bowen

Toward the end of her day in London Mrs. Drover went round to her shut-up house to look for several things she wanted to take away. Some belonged to herself, some to her family, who were by now used to their country life. It was late August; it had been a steamy, showery day: at the moment the trees down the pavement glittered in an escape of humid yellow afternoon sun. Against the next batch of clouds, already piling up ink-dark, broken chimneys and parapets stood out. In her once familiar street, as in any unused channel, an unfamiliar queerness had silted up; a cat wove itself in and out of railings, but no human eye watched Mrs. Drover's return. Shifting some parcels under her arm, she slowly forced round her latchkey in an unwilling lock, then gave the door, which had warped, a push with her knee. Dead air came out to meet her as she went in.

The staircase window having been boarded up, no light came down into the hall. But one door, she could just see, stood ajar, so she went quickly through into the room and unshuttered the big window in there. Now the prosaic woman, looking about her, was more perplexed than she knew by everything that she saw, by traces of her long former habit of life—the yellow smoke stain up the white marble mantelpiece, the ring left by a vase on the top of the escritoire;[1] the bruise in the wallpaper where, on the door being thrown open widely, the china handle had always hit the wall. The piano, having gone away to be stored, had left what looked like claw marks on its part of the parquet.[2] Though not much dust had seeped in, each object wore a film of another kind; and, the only ventilation being the chimney, the whole drawing room smelled of the cold hearth. Mrs. Drover put down her parcels on the escritoire and left the room to proceed upstairs; the things she wanted were in a bedroom chest.

She had been anxious to see how the house was—the part-time caretaker she shared with some neighbors was away this week on his holiday, known to be not yet back. At the best of times he did not look in often, and she was never sure that she trusted him. There were some cracks in the structure, left by the last bombing, on which she was anxious to keep an eye. Not that one could do anything—

A shaft of refracted daylight now lay across the hall. She stopped dead and stared at the hall table—on this lay a letter addressed to her.

She thought first—then the caretaker *must* be back. All the same, who, seeing the house shuttered, would have dropped a letter in at the box? It was not a circular, it was not a bill. And the post office redirected, to the address in the country, everything for her that came through the post. The care-

---

1. **escritoire** (es′ krə twär′) *n.*: A writing desk or table.

2. **parquet** (pär kā′) *n.*: A flooring of inlaid woodwork in geometric forms.

taker (even if he *were* back) did not know she was due in London today—her call here had been planned to be a surprise—so his negligence in the manner of this letter, leaving it to wait in the dusk and the dust, annoyed her. Annoyed, she picked up the letter, which bore no stamp. But it cannot be important, or they would know . . . She took the letter rapidly upstairs with her, without a stop to look at the writing till she reached what had been her bedroom, where she let in light. The room looked over the garden and other gardens: the sun had gone in; as the clouds sharpened and lowered, the trees and rank lawns seemed already to smoke with dark. Her reluctance to look again at the letter came from the fact that she felt intruded upon—and by someone contemptuous of her ways. However, in the tenseness preceding the fall of rain she read it: it was a few lines.

DEAR KATHLEEN,

You will not have forgotten that today is our anniversary, and the day we said. The years have gone by at once slowly and fast. In view of the fact that nothing has changed, I shall rely upon you to keep your promise. I was sorry to see you leave London, but was satisfied that you would be back in time. You may expect me, therefore, at the hour arranged.

Until then . . . K.

Mrs. Drover looked for the date: it was today's. She dropped the letter onto the bedsprings, then picked it up to see the writing again—her lips, beneath the remains of lipstick, beginning to go white. She felt so much the change in her own face that

**HOLY BUSH HILL, HAMPSTEAD, 1921**
*Ethelbert White*

she went to the mirror, polished a clear patch in it and looked at once urgently and stealthily in. She was confronted by a woman of forty-four, with eyes starting out under a hatbrim that had been rather carelessly pulled down. She had not put on any more powder since she left the shop where she ate her solitary tea. The pearls her husband had given her on their marriage hung loose round her now rather thinner throat, slipping into the V of the pink wool jumper her sister knitted last autumn as they sat round the fire. Mrs. Drover's most normal expression was one of controlled worry, but of assent. Since the birth of the third of her little boys, attended by a quite serious illness, she had had an intermittent muscular flicker to the left of her mouth, but in spite of this she could always sustain a manner that was at once energetic and calm.

Turning from her own face as precipitately as she had gone to meet it, she went to the chest where the things were, unlocked it, threw up the lid and knelt to search. But as rain began to come crashing down she could not keep from looking over her shoulder at the stripped bed on which the letter lay. Behind the blanket of rain the clock of the church that still stood struck six— with rapidly heightening apprehension she counted each of the slow strokes. "The hour arranged . . . My God," she said, "*What* hour? How should I . . . ? After twenty-five years. . . ."

The young girl talking to the soldier in the garden had not ever completely seen his face. It was dark; they were saying goodbye under a tree. Now and then—for it felt, from not seeing him at this intense moment, as though she had never seen him at all—she verified his presence for these few moments longer by putting out a hand, which he each time pressed, without very much kindness, and painfully, on to one of the breast buttons of his uniform. That cut of the button on the palm of her hand was, principally, what she was to carry away. This was so near the end of a leave from France that she could only wish him already gone. It was August 1916. Being not kissed, being drawn away from and looked at intimidated Kathleen till she imagined spectral glitters in the place of his eyes. Turning away and looking back up the lawn she saw, through branches of trees, the drawing-room window alight; she caught a breath for the moment when she could go running back there into the safe arms of her mother and sister, and cry: "What shall I do, what shall I do? He has gone."

Hearing her catch her breath, her fiancé said, without feeling: "Cold?"

"You're going away such a long way."

"Not so far as you think."

"I don't understand?"

"You don't have to," he said. "You will. You know what we said."

"But that was—suppose you—I mean, suppose."

"I shall be with you," he said, "sooner or later. You won't forget that. You need do nothing but wait."

Only a little more than a minute later she was free to run up the silent lawn. Looking in through the window at her mother and sister, who did not for the moment perceive her, she already felt that unnatural promise drive down between her and the rest of all humankind. No other way of having given herself could have made her feel so apart, lost and foresworn. She could not have plighted a more sinister troth.

Kathleen behaved well when, some months later, her fiancé was reported missing, presumed killed. Her family not only supported her but were able to praise her courage without stint because they could not regret, as a husband for her, the man they knew almost nothing about. They hoped she would, in a year or two, console herself—and had it been only a question of consolation things might have gone much straighter ahead. But her trouble, behind just a little grief, was a complete dislocation from everything. She did not reject other lovers, for these failed to appear: for years she failed to attract men—and with the approach of her thirties she became natural enough to share her family's anxiousness on this score. She began to put herself out, to wonder; and at thirty-two she was very greatly relieved to find herself being courted by William Drover. She married him, and the two of them settled down in this quiet, arboreal part of Kensington; in this house the years piled up, her children were born and they all lived till they were driven out by the bombs of the next war. Her movements as Mrs. Drover were circumscribed, and she dismissed any idea that they were still watched.

As things were—dead or living the letter writer sent her only a threat. Unable, for some minutes, to go on kneeling with her back exposed to the empty room, Mrs. Drover rose from the chest to sit on an upright chair whose back was firmly against the wall. The desuetude of her former bedroom, her married London home's whole air of being a cracked cup from which memory, with its reassuring power, had either evaporated or leaked away, made a crisis—and at just this crisis the letter writer had, knowledgeably, struck. The hollowness of the house this evening canceled years on years of voices, habits and steps. Through the shut windows she only heard rain fall on the roofs around. To rally herself, she said she was in a mood—and, for two or three seconds shutting her eyes, told herself that she had imagined the letter. But she opened them—there it lay on the bed.

On the supernatural side of the letter's entrance she was not permitting her mind to dwell. Who, in London, knew she meant to call at the house today? Evidently, however, this had been known. The caretaker, *had* he come back, had had no cause to expect her: he would have taken the letter in his pocket, to forward it, at his own time, through the post. There was no other sign that the caretaker had been in—but, if not?

OX HOUSE, SHAFTESBURY, 1932
*John R. Biggs*

Letters dropped in at doors of deserted houses do not fly or walk to tables in halls. They do not sit on the dust of empty tables with the air of certainty that they will be found. There is needed some human hand—but nobody but the caretaker had a key. Under circumstances she did not care to consider, a house can be entered without a key. It was possible that she was not alone now. She might be being waited for, downstairs. Waited for—until when? Until "the hour arranged." At least that was not six o'clock; six has struck.

She rose from the chair and went over and locked the door.

The thing was, to get out. To fly? No, not that: she had to catch her train. As a woman whose utter dependability was the keystone of her family life she was not willing to return to the country, to her husband, her little boys and her sister, without the objects she had come up to fetch. Resuming work at the chest she set about making up a number of parcels in a rapid, fumbling-decisive way. These, with her shopping parcels, would be too much to carry; these meant a taxi—at the thought of the taxi her heart went up and her normal breathing resumed. I will ring up the taxi now; the taxi cannot come too soon; I shall hear the taxi out there running its engine, till I walk calmly down to it through the hall. I'll ring up—But no: the telephone is cut off . . . She tugged at a knot she had tied wrong.

The idea of flight . . . He was never kind to me, not really. I don't remember him kind at all. Mother said he never considered me. He was set on me, that was what it was —not love. Not love, not meaning a person well. What did he do, to make me promise like that? I can't remember—But she found that she could.

She remembered with such dreadful acuteness that the twenty-five years since then dissolved like smoke and she instinctively looked for the weal left by the button on the palm of her hand. She remembered not only all that he said and did but the complete suspension of *her* existence during that August week. I was not myself —they all told me so at the time. She remembered—but with one white burning blank as where acid has dropped on a photograph: *under no conditions* could she remember his face.

So wherever he may be waiting, I shall not know him. You have no time to run from a face you do not expect.

The thing was to get to the taxi before any clock struck what could be the hour. She would slip down the street and round the side of the square to where the square gave on the main road. She would return in the taxi, safe, to her own door, and bring the solid driver into the house with her to pick up the parcels from room to room. The idea

of the taxi driver made her decisive, bold; she unlocked her door, went to the top of the staircase and listened down.

She heard nothing—but while she was hearing nothing the *passé*[3] air of the staircase was disturbed by a draft that traveled up to her face. It emanated from the basement: down there a door or window was being opened by someone who chose this moment to leave the house.

The rain had stopped; the pavements steamily shone as Mrs. Drover let herself out by inches from her own front door into the empty street. The unoccupied houses opposite continued to meet her look with their damaged stare. Making toward the thoroughfare and the taxi, she tried not to keep looking behind. Indeed, the silence was so intense—one of those creeks of London silence exaggerated this summer by the damage of war—that no tread could have gained on hers unheard. Where her street debouched on the square where people went on living, she grew conscious of, and checked, her unnatural pace. Across the open end of the square two buses impassively passed each other; women, a perambulator,[4] cyclists, a man wheeling a barrow signalized, once again, the ordinary flow of life. At the square's most populous corner should be—and was—the short taxi rank. This evening, only one taxi—but this, although it presented its blank rump, appeared already to be alertly waiting for her. Indeed, without looking round the driver started his engine as she panted up from behind and put her hand on the door. As she did so, the clock struck seven. The taxi faced the main road. To make the trip back to her house it would have to turn—she had settled back on the seat and the taxi *had* turned before she, surprised by its knowing movement, recollected that she had not "said where." She leaned forward to scratch

---

3. *passé* (pa sā´) *adj.*: Stale.
4. **perambulator:** A baby carriage.

at the glass panel that divided the driver's head from her own.

The driver braked to what was almost a stop, turned round and slid the glass panel back. The jolt of this flung Mrs. Drover forward till her face was almost into the glass. Through the aperture driver and passenger, not six inches between them, remained for an eternity eye to eye. Mrs. Drover's mouth hung open for some seconds before she could issue her first scream. After that she continued to scream freely and to beat with her gloved hands on the glass all round as the taxi, accelerating without mercy, made off with her into the hinterland of deserted streets.

---

## THINKING ABOUT THE SELECTION

### Recalling

1. (a) Where and when does the story take place? (b) Why does Mrs. Drover visit her house in London?
2. (a) Who has written the letter Mrs. Drover discovers? (b) Why is she so upset by it?
3. (a) How does Mrs. Drover plan to escape from the house? (b) Does she succeed in her plan? Explain.

### Interpreting

4. In the first paragraph the narrator remarks that "no human eye watched Mrs. Drover's return" to her house? In what way is this remark ironic?
5. (a) What words does the author use to describe Mrs. Drover's reaction to the letter? (b) What feelings do you think the author hoped this description would prompt in the reader?
6. One of the strengths of this short story is its ambiguity. Provide both a supernatural and a rational explanation for (a) the letter, and (b) the cab driver's knowing in which direction to take his passenger before she has spoken up.
7. Why do you think the author devotes so much space to Mrs. Drover's thought processes following the flashback?
8. What do you think is Mrs. Drover's ultimate fate? Explain the basis for your answer.

### Applying

9. The story seems to be suggesting that one of the most damaging effects of war is the psychological vulnerability it produces in human beings? Do you agree? Defend your opinion.

## ANALYZING LITERATURE

### Considering War and the Ghost Story

The devastation that was war-torn London —shells of bombed-out dwellings facing empty streets, periods of blackout, the roar of airplane engines in the sky—provides a choice setting for a story involving the presence of a ghostlike figure. In fact, for the people who lived during that era, the specter was very real, lurking in every darkened doorway and known variously by the names of fear, desperation, and grief. Consider the following war-related details in "The Demon Lover," and explain how each in its own turn adds to the terror the reader feels on the part of Mrs. Drover.

1. The empty house in which the Drovers had lived
2. The break in the routine of mail delivery
3. The prospect of never knowing the fate of a loved one reported "missing in action"
4. The blocks of deserted streets in an evacuated neighborhood

# GRAHAM GREENE

## 1904–1991

The search for a source of inner peace, launched earlier in the century by such poets as William Butler Yeats and T. S. Eliot, continues up through our own time in the novels and short stories of Graham Greene. A religious convert like Eliot, Greene wrote—like Eliot—of pain, fear, despair, and alienation. His conclusion, which again mirrors the poet's, was that the ultimate key to salvation is a belief in God.

Greene was born in the town of Berkhamstead in Hertfordshire and educated at Berkhamstead School, where his father was headmaster. Though his grades were good enough to earn him admission to Oxford, he disliked school, describing it later as his "first impression of hell."

Much of Greene's early working life was spent as a journalist and travel writer. His training in these areas helped him develop the powers of keen observation, sensitivity to atmosphere, and simplicity of language that have become hallmarks of his fictional style. His journey to Mexico in 1938 provided the setting for his best-known novel, *The Power and the Glory* (1940). His trips to Africa resulted in travelogues as well as two novels, *The Heart of the Matter* (1944) and *A Burnt-Out Case* (1961).

Greene was also an author of books for children, an essayist, and an editor, and enjoyed considerable success writing films and adapting his own stories for the screen. His cinematic work is tied to yet another outlet for his creativity, which Greene called his "entertainments." These are adventure stories and spy thrillers, often dealing with the secret service and with pursuit. Among these are *Our Man in Havana* (1958) and *The Human Factor* (1978).

Greene's more serious work focuses more on the psychology of human character than on plot. Many of his protagonists are people without roots or beliefs—people in pain. They come across as real and believable individuals in whom good and evil, weakness and strength are intermingled. Though the characters in a Greene story often provide the reader with little reason for finding them likable, they almost always excite the reader's curiosity and pity—and, almost always, their author treats them with compassion.

The settings for Greene's fiction are usually hot, decaying, and poorly governed places, like the border town in "Across the Bridge." These parched, crumbling landscapes, presented to us in vivid detail, represent the distressed condition of a key character's troubled soul.

# GUIDE FOR INTERPRETING

## Across the Bridge

**Theme and Point of View.** Theme is the central idea of a work of literature. The theme of a work should not be confused with its subject, which can often be summed up in a single word or phrase, such as *love of money.* Rather, the theme is a commentary on the subject and is presented in the form of a statement: for example, *The love of money is the root of all evil.* Of the many fiction elements that bear on a work's theme, one of the most critical is point of view, or vantage point from which the events of the story are related. By choosing a first-person point of view—telling the story, that is, from the vantage point of "I" or "we"—an author creates an illusion of immediacy, which adds emphasis to certain themes. The theme suggested by the events described in "Across the Bridge," for example, comes home to the reader with special force, partly because those events are related by a firsthand observer of them.

**Commentary**

Graham Greene was among the most private of writers and always discouraged speculation about his personality. His autobiographical writings discuss his publications, not his personal life, as if the man was created by his work and not the other way around. While he shared a number of characteristics with other writers of his generation—he came from the English professional classes, his father was the headmaster of a private school, and he was aware of World War I but was too young to fight in it—his playful sense of humor set him apart. He was an active practical joker all of his life, a trait reflected in his writing. A surprising number of the characters in his works are named "Greene, as well as "Henry," the name he was christened. The tragic hero in *The Heart of the Matter* is named Henry Scobie; the narrator in *Travels with My Aunt* is Henry Pulling. *Yes and No* includes a character named Henry Privet, "privett" being an evergreen shrub. As with the illustrator Al Hirschfeld who often includes his daughter Nina's name in his cartoons, Greene frequently mentioned the color green in his work. Can you find the reference to green in "Across the Bridge"?

**Writing**

After obtaining the person's permission, observe a friend or family member for an entire day, perhaps over the course of a weekend. Keep a detailed journal on where this person goes and what he or she does. Note any patterns of behavior in which the person engages, as well as any strange moves he or she might make.

# Across the Bridge

## Graham Greene

"They say he's worth a million," Lucia said. He sat there in the little hot damp Mexican square, a dog at his feet, with an air of immense and forlorn patience. The dog attracted your attention at once; for it was very nearly an English setter, only something had gone wrong with the tail and the feathering. Palms wilted over his head, it was all shade and stuffiness round the bandstand, radios talked loudly in Spanish from the little wooden sheds where they changed your pesos into dollars at a loss. I could tell he didn't understand a word from the way he read his newspaper—as I did myself picking out the words which were like English ones. "He's been here a month," Lucia said. "They turned him out of Guatemala and Honduras."

You couldn't keep any secrets for five hours in this border town. Lucia had only been twenty-four hours in the place, but she knew all about Mr. Joseph Calloway. The only reason I didn't know about him (and I'd been in the place two weeks) was because I couldn't talk the language any more than Mr. Calloway could. There wasn't another soul in the place who didn't know the story —the whole story of the Halling Investment Trust and the proceedings for extradition. Any man doing dusty business in any of the wooden booths in the town is better fitted by long observation to tell Mr. Calloway's tale than I am, except that I was in—literally —at the finish. They all watched the drama proceed with immense interest, sympathy and respect. For, after all, he had a million.

Every once in a while through the long steamy day, a boy came and cleaned Mr. Calloway's shoes: he hadn't the right words to resist them—they pretended not to know his English. He must have had his shoes cleaned the day Lucia and I watched him at least half a dozen times. At midday he took a stroll across the square to the Antonio Bar and had a bottle of beer, the setter sticking to heel as if they were out for a country walk in England (he had, you may remember, one of the biggest estates in Norfolk). After his bottle of beer, he would walk down between the money changers' huts to the Rio Grande[1] and look across the bridge into the United States: people came and went constantly in cars. Then back to the square till lunchtime. He was staying in the best hotel, but you don't get good hotels in this border town: nobody stays in them more than a night. The good hotels were on the other side of the bridge: you could see their electric signs twenty stories high from the little square at night, like lighthouses marking the United States.

You may ask what I'd been doing in so drab a spot for a fortnight. There was no interest in the place for anyone; it was just damp and dust and poverty, a kind of shabby replica of the town across the river: both had squares in the same spots; both had the same number of cinemas. One was cleaner than the other, that was all, and more ex-

---

**1. Rio Grande** (rē' ō grand'): River that flows between Mexico and Texas.

pensive, much more expensive. I'd stayed across there a couple of nights waiting for a man a tourist bureau said was driving down from Detroit to Yucatan and would sell a place in his car for some fantastically small figure—twenty dollars, I think it was. I don't know if he existed or was invented by the optimistic half-caste in the agency; anyway, he never turned up and so I waited, not much caring, on the cheap side of the river. It didn't much matter; I was living. One day I meant to give up the man from Detroit and go home or go south, but it was easier not to decide anything in a hurry. Lucia was just waiting for a car going the other way, but she didn't have to wait so long. We waited together and watched Mr. Calloway waiting —for God knows what.

I don't know how to treat this story—it was a tragedy for Mr. Calloway, it was poetic retribution, I suppose, in the eyes of the shareholders he'd ruined with his bogus transactions, and to Lucia and me, at this stage, it was pure comedy—except when he kicked the dog. I'm not a sentimentalist about dogs, I prefer people to be cruel to animals rather than to human beings, but I couldn't help being revolted at the way he'd kick that animal—with a hint of cold-blooded venom, not in anger but as if he were getting even for some trick it had played him a long while ago. That generally happened when he returned from the bridge: it was the only sign of anything resembling emotion he showed. Otherwise he looked a small, set, gentle creature with silver hair and a silver moustache, and gold-rimmed glasses, and one gold tooth like a flaw in character.

Lucia hadn't been accurate when she said he'd been turned out of Guatemala and Honduras; he'd left voluntarily when the extradition proceedings seemed likely to go through and moved north. Mexico is still not a very centralized state, and it is possible to get round governors as you can't get round cabinet ministers or judges. And so he waited there on the border for the next move. That earlier part of the story is, I suppose, dramatic, but I didn't watch it and I can't invent what I haven't seen—the long waiting in anterooms, the bribes taken and refused, the growing fear of arrest, and then the flight—in gold-rimmed glasses —covering his tracks as well as he could, but this wasn't finance and he was an amateur at escape. And so he'd washed up here, under my eyes and Lucia's eyes, sitting all day under the bandstand, nothing to read but a Mexican paper, nothing to do but look across the river at the United States, quite unaware, I suppose, that everyone knew everything about him, once a day kicking his dog. Perhaps in its semi-setter way it reminded him too much of the Norfolk estate —though that, too, I suppose, was the reason he kept it.

And the next act again was pure comedy. I hesitate to think what this man worth a million was costing his country as they edged him out from this land and that. Perhaps somebody was getting tired of the business, and careless; anyway, they sent across two detectives, with an old photograph. He'd grown his silvery moustache since that had been taken, and he'd aged a lot, and they couldn't catch sight of him. They hadn't been across the bridge two hours when everybody knew that there were two foreign detectives in town looking for Mr. Calloway—everybody knew, that is to say, except Mr. Calloway, who couldn't talk Spanish. There were plenty of people who could have told him in English, but they didn't. It wasn't cruelty, it was a sort of awe and respect: like a bull, he was on show, sitting there mournfully in the plaza with his dog, a magnificent spectacle for which we all had ringside seats.

I ran into one of the policemen in the Bar Antonio. He was disgusted; he had had some idea that when he crossed the bridge life was going to be different, so much more color and sun, and—I suspect—love, and all he found were wide mud streets where the nocturnal rain lay in pools, and mangy dogs, smells and cockroaches in his bedroom, and the nearest to love, the open door of the Academia Comercial, where pretty mestizo[2] girls sat all the morning learning to typewrite. Tip-tap-tip-tap-tip—perhaps they had a dream, too—jobs on the other side of the bridge, where life was going to be so much more luxurious, refined and amusing.

We got into conversation; he seemed surprised that I knew who they both were and what they wanted. He said: "We've got information this man Calloway's in town."

"He's knocking around somewhere," I said.

"Could you point him out?"

"Oh, I don't know him by sight," I said.

He drank his beer and thought a while. "I'll go out and sit in the plaza. He's sure to pass sometime."

I finished my beer and went quickly off and found Lucia. I said, "Hurry, we're going to see an arrest." We didn't care a thing about Mr. Calloway, he was just an elderly man who kicked his dog and swindled the poor, and who deserved anything he got. So we made for the plaza; we knew Calloway would be there, but it had never occurred to either of us that the detectives wouldn't recognize him. There was quite a surge of people round the place; all the fruit-sellers and bootblacks in town seemed to have arrived together; we had to force our way through, and there in the little green stuffy

---

**2. mestizo** (mes tē′ zō) *adj.*: Of Spanish and Indian parentage.

center of the place, sitting on adjoining seats, were the two plainclothesmen and Mr. Calloway. I've never known the place so silent; everybody was on tiptoe, and the plainclothesmen were staring at the crowd looking for Mr. Calloway, and Mr. Calloway sat on his usual seat staring out over the money-changing booths at the United States.

"It can't go on. It just can't," Lucia said. But it did. It got more fantastic still. Somebody ought to write a play about it. We sat as close as we dared. We were afraid all the time we were going to laugh. The semi-setter scratched for fleas and Mr. Calloway watched the U.S.A. The two detectives watched the crowd, and the crowd watched the show with solemn satisfaction. Then one of the detectives got up and went over to Mr. Calloway. That's the end, I thought. But it wasn't, it was the beginning. For some reason they had eliminated him from their list of suspects. I shall never know why. The man said:

"You speak English?"

"I *am* English," Mr. Calloway said.

Even that didn't tear it, and the strangest thing of all was the way Mr. Calloway came alive. I don't think anybody had spoken to him like that for weeks. The Mexicans were too respectful—he was a man with a million—and it had never occurred to Lucia and me to treat him casually like a human being; even in our eyes he had been magnified by the colossal theft and the worldwide pursuit.

He said: "This is rather a dreadful place, don't you think?"

"It is," the policeman said.

"I can't think what brings anybody across the bridge."

"Duty," the policeman said gloomily. "I suppose you are passing through."

"Yes," Mr. Calloway said.

"I'd have expected over here there'd have been—you know what I mean—life. You read things about Mexico."

"Oh, life," Mr. Calloway said. He spoke firmly and precisely, as if to a committee of shareholders. "That begins on the other side."

"You don't appreciate your own country until you leave it."

"That's very true," Mr. Calloway said. "Very true."

At first it was difficult not to laugh, and then after a while there didn't seem to be much to laugh at; an old man imagining all the fine things going on beyond the international bridge. I think he thought of the town opposite as a combination of London and Norfolk—theaters and cocktail bars, a little shooting and a walk round the field at evening with the dog—that miserable imitation of a setter—poking the ditches. He'd never been across, he couldn't know that it was just the same thing over again—even the same layout; only the streets were paved and the hotels had ten more stories, and life was more expensive, and everything was a little bit cleaner. There wasn't anything Mr. Calloway would have called living—no galleries, no bookshops, just *Film Fun* and the local paper, and *Click* and *Focus* and the tabloids.

"Well," said Mr. Calloway, "I think I'll take a stroll before lunch. You need an appetite to swallow the food here. I generally go down and look at the bridge about now. Care to come, too?"

The detective shook his head. "No," he said, "I'm on duty. I'm looking for a fellow." And that, of course, gave *him* away. As far as Mr. Calloway could understand, there was only one "fellow" in the world anyone was looking for—his brain had eliminated friends who were seeking their friends, husbands who might be waiting for their wives, all objectives of any search but just the one. The power of elimination was what had made him a financier—he could forget the people behind the shares.

That was the last we saw of him for a while. We didn't see him going into the Botica Paris to get his aspirin, or walking back from the bridge with his dog. He simply disappeared, and when he disappeared, people began to talk, and the detectives heard the talk. They looked silly enough, and they got busy after the very man they'd been sitting next to in the garden. Then they, too, disappeared. They, as well as Mr. Calloway, had gone to the state capital to see the Governor and the Chief of Police, and it must have been an amusing sight there, too, as they bumped into Mr. Calloway and sat with him in the waiting rooms. I suspect Mr. Calloway was generally shown in first, for everyone knew he was worth a million. Only in Europe is it possible for a man to be a criminal as well as a rich man.

Anyway, after about a week the whole pack of them returned by the same train. Mr. Calloway traveled Pullman,[3] and the two policemen traveled in the day coach. It was evident that they hadn't got their extradition order.

Lucia had left by that time. The car came and went across the bridge. I stood in Mexico and watched her get out at the United States Customs. She wasn't anything in particular but she looked beautiful at a distance as she gave me a wave out of the United States and got back into the car. And I suddenly felt sympathy for Mr. Calloway, as if there were something over there which you couldn't find here, and turning round I saw him back on his old beat, with the dog at his heels.

I said "Good afternoon," as if it had been all along our habit to greet each other. He looked tired and ill and dusty, and I felt sorry for him—to think of the kind of victory he'd been winning, with so much expenditure of cash and care—the prize this dirty and dreary town, the booths of the money changers, the awful little beauty parlors with their wicker chairs and sofas looking like the reception rooms of brothels, that hot and stuffy garden by the bandstand.

He replied gloomily, "Good morning,"

and the dog started to sniff at some ordure and he turned and kicked it with fury, with depression, with despair.

And at that moment a taxi with the two policemen in it passed us on its way to the bridge. They must have seen that kick; perhaps they were cleverer than I had given them credit for, perhaps they were just sentimental about animals, and thought they'd do a good deed, and the rest happened by accident. But the fact remains—those two pillars of the law set about the stealing of Mr. Calloway's dog.

He watched them go by. Then he said, "Why don't you go across?"

"It's cheaper here," I said.

"I mean just for an evening. Have a meal at that place we can see at night in the sky. Go to the theater."

"There isn't a chance."

He said angrily, sucking his gold tooth, "Well, anyway, get away from here." He stared down the hill and up the other side. He couldn't see that that street climbing up from the bridge, contained only the same money-changers' booths as this one.

I said, "Why don't *you* go?"

He said evasively. "Oh—business."

I said, "It's only a question of money. You don't *have* to pass by the bridge."

He said with faint interest, "I don't talk Spanish."

"There isn't a soul here," I said, "who doesn't talk English."

He looked at me with surprise. "Is that so?" he said. "Is that so?"

It's as I have said; he'd never tried to talk to anyone, and they respected him too much to talk to him—he was worth a million. I don't know whether I'm glad or sorry that I told him that. If I hadn't he might be there now, sitting by the bandstand having his shoes cleaned—alive and suffering.

Three days later his dog disappeared. I found him looking for it, calling it softly and shamefacedly between the palms of the garden. He looked embarrassed. He said in a low angry voice, "I *hate* that dog. The beast-

---

**3. Pullman:** A railroad car with private compartments of seats that can be made into berths for sleeping.

ly mongrel,'' and called "Rover, Rover" in a voice which didn't carry five yards. He said, "I bred setters once. I'd have shot a dog like that." It reminded him, I *was* right, of Norfolk, and he lived in the memory, and he hated it for its imperfection. He was a man without a family and without friends, and his only enemy was that dog. You couldn't call the law an enemy; you have to be intimate with an enemy.

Late that afternoon someone told him they'd seen the dog walking across the bridge. It wasn't true, of course, but we didn't know that then—they'd paid a Mexican five pesos to smuggle it across. So all that afternoon and the next Mr. Calloway sat in the garden having his shoes cleaned over and over again, and thinking how a dog could just walk across like that, and a human being, an immortal soul, was bound here in the awful routine of the little walk and the unspeakable meals and the aspirin at the botica. That dog was seeing things he couldn't see—that hateful dog. It made him mad—I think literally mad. You must remember the man had been going on for months. He had a million and he was living on two pounds a week, with nothing to spend his money on. He sat there and brooded on the hideous injustice of it. I think he'd have crossed over one day in any case, but the dog was the last straw.

Next day when he wasn't to be seen, I guessed he'd gone across and I went too. The American town is as small as the Mexican. I knew I couldn't miss him if he was there, and I was still curious. A little sorry for him, but not much.

I caught sight of him first in the only drugstore, having a Coca-Cola, and then once outside a cinema looking at the posters; he had dressed with extreme neatness, as if for a party, but there was no party. On my third time round, I came on the detectives—they were having Coca-Colas in the drugstore, and they must have missed Mr. Calloway by inches. I went in and sat down at the bar.

"Hello," I said, "you still about." I suddenly felt anxious for Mr. Calloway, I didn't want them to meet.

One of them said, "Where's Calloway?"

"Oh," I said, "he's hanging on."

"But not his dog," he said, and laughed. The other looked a little shocked, he didn't like anyone to *talk* cynically about a dog. Then they got up—they had a car outside.

"Have another?" I said.

"No thanks. We've got to keep moving."

The man bent close and confided to me: "Calloway's on this side."

"No!" I said.

"And his dog."

"He's looking for it," the other said.

"I'm damned if he is," I said, and again one of them looked a little shocked, as if I'd insulted the dog.

I don't think Mr. Calloway was looking for his dog, but his dog certainly found him. There was a sudden hilarious yapping from the car and out plunged the semi-setter and gamboled furiously down the street. One of the detectives—the sentimental one—was into the car before we got to the door and was off after the dog. Near the bottom of the long road to the bridge was Mr. Calloway—I do believe he'd come down to look at the Mexican side when he found there was nothing but the drugstore and the cinemas and the paper shops on the American. He saw the dog coming and yelled at it to go home—"home, home, home," as if they were in Norfolk—it took no notice at all, pelting towards him. Then he saw the police car coming, and ran. After that, everything happened too quickly, but I think the order of events was this—the dog started across the road right in front of the car, and Mr. Calloway yelled, at the dog or the car, I don't know which. Anyway, the detective swerved—he said later, weakly, at the inquiry, that he couldn't run over a dog, and down went Mr. Calloway, in a mess of broken glass and gold rims and silver hair, and blood. The dog was on to him before any of us could reach him, licking and whimpering and licking. I saw Mr. Calloway put up his hand, and down it went across the dog's neck and the whimper rose to a stupid bark of triumph, but Mr. Calloway was dead—shock and a weak heart.

"Poor old geezer," the detective said, "I bet he really loved that dog," and it's true that the attitude in which he lay looked more like a caress than a blow. I thought it was meant to be a blow, but the detective may have been right. It all seemed to me a little too touching to be true as the old crook lay there with his arm over the dog's neck, dead with his million between the money-changers' huts, but it's as well to be humble in the face of human nature. He had come across the river for something, and it may, after all, have been the dog he was looking for. It sat there, baying its stupid and mongrel triumph across his body, like a piece of sentimental statuary. The nearest he could get to the fields, the ditches, the horizon of his home. It was comic and it was pitiable; but it wasn't less comic because the man was dead. Death doesn't change comedy to tragedy, and if that last gesture was one of affection, I suppose it was only one more indication of a human being's capacity for self-deception, our baseless optimism that is so much more appalling than our despair.

---

## THINKING ABOUT THE SELECTION

### Recalling

1. (a) Where does the story take place? (b) What is Mr. Calloway's reason for being there? (c) What is the narrator's reason?
2. (a) Who is Mr. Calloway's constant "companion"? (b) How does he treat this companion?
3. Why do the two detectives not arrest Mr. Calloway at first?
4. (a) What finally brings Mr. Calloway across the bridge? (b) What happens to him?

### Interpreting

5. What effect does the repetition of the sentence "He was worth a million" have on you?
6. What trait of Mr. Calloway's personality is revealed by his not knowing that the inhabitants of the town speak English?

7. Both Mr. Calloway and the detectives are disappointed by what they find on the "other side" of the bridge. (a) What proverb does this call to mind? (b) How does this disappointment reflect the story's theme?
8. Consider the role of justice in the story. (a) In what ways is justice served by Mr. Calloway's death? (b) In what way is Mr. Calloway "saved"?

### Applying

9. At the end of the story, the narrator says, " . . . I suppose it was only one more indication of a human being's capacity for self-deception, our baseless optimism that is so much more appalling than our despair." Explain your reactions to this statement.

## ANALYZING LITERATURE

### Understanding Theme and Point of View

**Theme** is the insight into life revealed through a literary work. Often misidentified with a story's subject, the theme is a statement about the subject. **Point of view**—the angle from which the story is told—can affect the reader's grasp of the theme. When a story is told, for instance, by a first-person narrator, the reader is made to feel almost a part of the events. This in turn brings the theme, or "moral," into sharp focus. Consider the theme of "Across the Bridge." Evaluate the impact that the following facts of narration have on the reader's awareness of the theme.

1. The narrator, in the fourth paragraph, gives us his firsthand impressions of the town on the American side.
2. The description of Mr. Calloway's relationship with the dog comes from one who is by his own admission not a lover of dogs.
3. The narrator begins to feel sympathy toward Mr. Calloway.

## CRITICAL THINKING AND READING

### Understanding Comedy and Tragedy

On page 1003 of the story, the narrator states, "I don't know how to treat this story—it was a tragedy for Mr. Calloway . . . [while to] me, at this stage, it was pure comedy. . . ." Again, at the end, after Mr. Calloway has died, he observes, "It was comic and it was pitiable; but it wasn't less comic because the man was dead. Death doesn't change comedy to tragedy. . . ."

1. In what sense might the death of Mr. Calloway have struck the narrator as comical?
2. Do you agree that death doesn't change comedy to tragedy? Why or why not?
3. The ancient Greeks defined comedy as a play in which the main character triumphs over opposing forces. According to this definition,

would you consider "Across the Bridge" more comedy than tragedy, or vice versa? Explain your answer.

## UNDERSTANDING LANGUAGE

### Learning About Word Completions

Suffixes, the meaning-bearing fragments added to the end of word roots to form new words, fall into two basic types. Derivational suffixes change the part of speech of the word root. The suffix -al, which converts the verb *arrive* to the noun *arrival,* is an example of a derivational suffix. Inflectional suffixes affect such matters as number and verb tense without changing the part of speech of the root. The suffix -es, which forms the plural noun *churches* from the singular noun *church,* is an example of an inflectional suffix. Identify the italicized part of each of the following words from the story as either a derivational or inflectional suffix. Use each in an original word.

1. pretend*ed*
2. stuff*iness*
3. invest*ment*
4. piti*able*
5. kick*ing*
6. expens*ive*

## THINKING AND WRITING

### Analyzing the Effects of Point of View

Choose another story that you read in this book, and identify its theme and its narrative point of view. In an essay explain how the point of view affects the theme. Structure your essay on the following questions: Would the impact of the theme have been different had the author used a first-person (or third-person) narrator? What details of narration helped make the theme apparent? What facets of the narrator's character were relevant to the theme? Make sure your essay opens with a clear thesis statement. When you revise make sure you have provided adequate support for your thesis. Proofread your essay and prepare a final draft.

# GEORGE ORWELL

## 1903–1950

Although George Orwell's popular fame is most directly linked to his two novels of political satire, *Animal Farm* and *1984,* many discerning readers insist that his genius is most readily apparent in his essays and nonfiction. Orwell's prose style, precise yet informal, contributed to making his essays some of the most eloquent short pieces in English writing of the twentieth century.

George Orwell was the pen name chosen by Eric Blair, born in colonial Bengal, an eastern region of India. Schooled in England at Eton, Orwell returned to the East—like H. H. Munro (Saki)—to serve in the Imperial Police in Burma. His experiences in that post, which span the years 1922 to 1927, form the basis of his first novel *Burmese Days* (1934). Disillusioned by his country's policy in the Orient, Orwell left military service to pursue jobs in journalism, publishing, and bookselling in England and France. This period of his life was marked by struggles with poverty, as he recalls in his autobiographical *Down and Out in Paris and London* (1933).

During the 1930's Orwell became deeply involved in social and international causes. *The Road to Wigan Pier* (1937) movingly chronicles the miseries of the English working class during the later phases of the Depression. The coming of the Spanish Civil War (1936–1939) found Orwell firmly committed to the Republican cause. Deploring what he saw as the totalitarianism of the Nationalist victors of the conflict, Orwell paid tribute to the victims in *Homage to Catalonia* (1939).

During World War II Orwell served as literary editor of the *Tribune* from 1943 to 1945 and also contributed political columns to a number of newspapers and journals. In 1945 he published *Animal Farm,* a savage fable that indirectly denounces the evils of both Fascism and Communism. Suffering acutely from the tuberculosis that would ultimately end his life, he completed *1984* (1948), a grim vision of a future in which language and thought would be everywhere manipulated to serve totalitarian ends.

Orwell's passionate concern for the preservation of political freedom was allied with his efforts to save the English language from "double speak," jargon, and bureaucratic vagueness. In "Politics and the English Language" he dramatically demonstrates how language can be used subtly to conceal political corruption, thereby blinding members of a society to the necessity of moral choice. Although 1984 has come and gone without the fulfillment of Orwell's grim prophecies, his lifelong commitment to political freedom and to the integrity of language remain as relevant today as ever.

# GUIDE FOR INTERPRETING

## Shooting an Elephant

**Tone.** Tone is the attitude the writer of a work of fiction takes toward his or her subject, his or her audience, or a character. Just as a speaker's tone of voice can affect the way in which a remark is taken, so the tone of a literary work will help shape the reader's response to it. Tone in a piece of literature is conveyed through the particular words the writer chooses as well as through details of description. For example, a writer who adopts a lighthearted and carefree tone toward the subject of sunshine might refer to the "kiss of warm rays," while the same writer, in approaching the subject with a bitter tone, might make reference to the sun's "cruel, harsh glare." In his essay, "Shooting an Elephant," George Orwell's diction, or word choice, reveals unambiguously his attitude toward the task that has fallen to him as a military police officer in Burma, as well as toward the people to whom he must account for his actions.

Considerable family sacrifice and reduced tuition enabled Orwell's parents to send their only son to a fashionable preparatory school on the south coast of England while they remained in India. But the boy was intimidated by the wealth and position of the others at school: "I had no money, I was weak, I was ugly, I was unpopular, I had a chronic cough, I smelt," he later wrote. Despite his later academic success—at age thirteen he was awarded not one but two scholarships to England's most prestigious private high schools —he never lost his ability to identify with society's downtrodden. As he remarked: "The conviction that it was not possible for me to be a success went deep enough to influence my actions till far into adult life." Out of personal escape rather than any political conviction, therefore, he took a position with the Indian Imperial police in Burma rather than continuing his education at Cambridge University as expected. His ability to see life through the eyes of the underdog forms the basis of "Shooting an Elephant," and partly explains why the essay was ranked as a classic within his own lifetime. The essay relfects Orwell's own early humiliations and frustrations as a poor boy among wealthier classmates, recalled now in the difficult and hurtful official relationships between the British and Burmese.

What is power? Freewrite about the meaning of the word, exploring its effects on both the person who exerts power and the people on whom power is brought to bear.

# Shooting an Elephant

### George Orwell

In Moulmein, in lower Burma, I was hated by large numbers of people—the only time in my life that I have been important enough for this to happen to me. I was subdivisional police officer of the town, and in an aimless, petty kind of way anti-European feeling was very bitter. No one had the guts to raise a riot, but if a European woman went through the bazaars alone somebody would probably spit betel juice over her dress. As a police officer I was an obvious target and was baited whenever it seemed safe to do so. When a nimble Burman tripped me up on the football field and the referee (another Burman) looked the other way, the crowd yelled with hideous laughter. This happened more than once. In the end the sneering yellow faces of young men that met me everywhere, the insults hooted after me when I was at a safe distance, got badly on my nerves. The young Buddhist priests were the worst of all. There were several thousands of them in the town and none of them seemed to have anything to do except stand on street corners and jeer at Europeans.

All this was perplexing and upsetting. For at that time I had already made up my mind that imperialism was an evil thing and the sooner I chucked up my job and got out of it the better. Theoretically—and secretly, of course—I was all for the Burmese and all against their oppressors, the British. As for the job I was doing, I hated it more bitterly than I can perhaps make clear. In a job like that you see the dirty work of Empire at close quarters. The wretched prisoners huddling in the stinking cages of the lockups, the gray, cowed faces of the long-term convicts, the scarred buttocks of the men who had been flogged with bamboos—all these oppressed me with an intolerable sense of guilt. But I could get nothing into perspective. I was young and ill educated and I had had to think out my problems in the utter silence that is imposed on every Englishman in the East. I did not even know that the British Empire is dying, still less did I know that it is a great deal better than the younger empires that are going to supplant it. All I knew was that I was stuck between my hatred of the empire I served and my rage against the evil-spirited little beasts who tried to make my job impossible. With one part of my mind I thought of the British Raj[1] as an unbreakable tyranny, as something clamped down, *in saecula saeculorum*,[2] upon the will of prostrate peoples; with another part I thought that the greatest joy in the world would be to drive a bayonet into a Buddhist priest's guts. Feelings like these are the normal byproducts of imperialism; ask any Anglo-Indian official, if you can catch him off duty.

One day something happened which in a roundabout way was enlightening. It was a tiny incident in itself, but it gave me a better glimpse than I had had before of the real

---

**1. Raj** (räj): Rule.
**2. *in saecula saeculorum*** (sē′ kōō lə sē′ kōō lôr′ əm): Forever and ever.

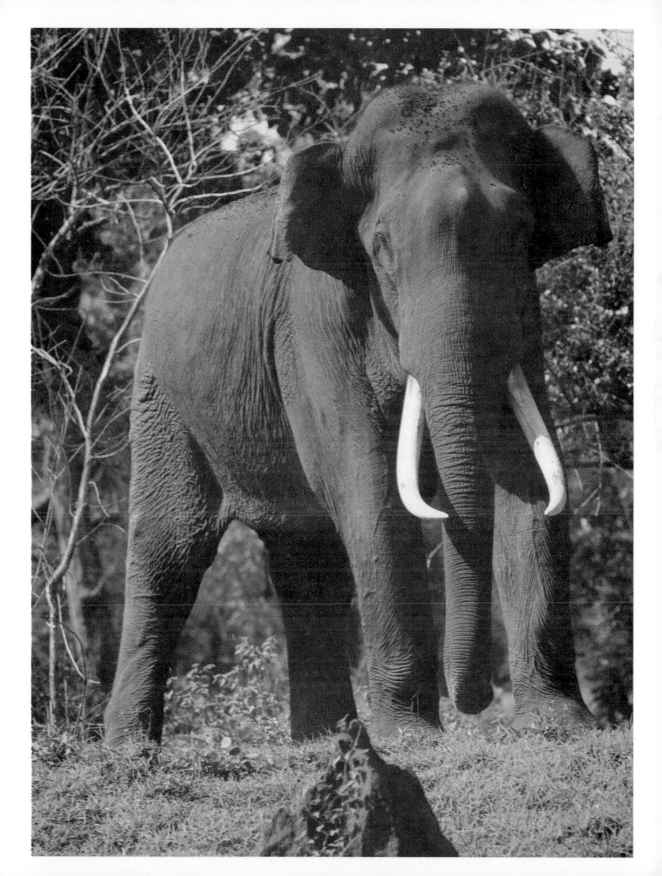

nature of imperialism—the real motives for which despotic governments act. Early one morning the subinspector at a police station the other end of the town rang me up on the phone and said that an elephant was ravaging the bazaar. Would I please come and do something about it? I did not know what I could do, but I wanted to see what was happening and I got onto a pony and started out. I took my rifle, an old .44 Winchester and much too small to kill an elephant, but I thought the noise might be useful *in terrorem*.[3] Various Burmans stopped me on the way and told me about the elephant's doings. It was not, of course, a wild elephant, but a tame one which had gone "must."[4] It had been chained up, as tame elephants always are when their attack of "must" is due, but on the previous night it had broken its chain and escaped. Its mahout,[5] the only person who could manage it when it was in that state, had set out in pursuit, but had taken the wrong direction and was now twelve hours' journey away, and in the morning the elephant had suddenly reappeared in the town. The Burmese population had no weapons and were quite helpless against it. It had already destroyed somebody's bamboo hut, killed a cow and raided some fruit stalls and devoured the stock; also it had met the municipal rubbish van and, when the driver jumped out and took to his heels, had turned the van over and inflicted violences upon it.

The Burmese subinspector and some Indian constables were waiting for me in the quarter where the elephant had been seen. It was a very poor quarter, a labyrinth of squalid bamboo huts, thatched with palm leaf, winding all over a steep hillside. I remember that it was a cloudy, stuffy morning at the beginning of the rains. We began questioning the people as to where the elephant had gone and, as usual, failed to get any definite information. That is invariably the case in the East; a story always sounds clear enough at a distance, but the nearer you get to the scene of events the vaguer it becomes. Some of the people said that the elephant had gone in one direction, some said that he had gone in another, some professed not even to have heard of any elephant. I had almost made up my mind that the whole story was a pack of lies, when we heard yells a little distance away. There was a loud, scandalized cry of "Go away, child! Go away this instant!" and an old woman with a switch in her hand came round the corner of a hut, violently shooing away a crowd of naked children. Some more women followed, clicking their tongues and exclaiming; evidently there was something that the children ought not to have seen. I rounded the hut and saw a man's dead body sprawling in the mud. He was an Indian, a black Dravidian[6] coolie,[7] almost naked, and he could not have been dead many minutes. The people said that the elephant had come suddenly upon him round the corner of the hut, caught him with its trunk, put its foot on his back and ground him into the earth. This was the rainy season and the ground was soft, and his face had scored a trench a foot deep and a couple of yards long. He was lying on his belly with arms crucified and head sharply twisted to one side. His face was coated with mud, the eyes wide open, the teeth bared and grinning with an expression of unendurable agony. (Never tell me, by the way, that the dead look peaceful. Most of the corpses I have seen looked devilish.) The friction of the great beast's foot had stripped the skin from his back as neatly as one skins a rabbit. As soon as I saw the dead man I sent an orderly to a friend's house nearby to borrow an elephant rifle. I had already sent back the pony, not wanting it to

**3. *in terrorem*:** For terror.
**4. must:** Into a dangerous, frenzied state.
**5. mahout** (mə hōōt′): An elephant keeper and rider.

**6. Dravidian** (drə vid′ ē ən): Belonging to the race of people inhabiting southern India.
**7. coolie:** Laborer.

go mad with fright and throw me if it smelled the elephant.

The orderly came back in a few minutes with a rifle and five cartridges, and meanwhile some Burmans had arrived and told us that the elephant was in the paddy fields[8] below, only a few hundred yards away. As I started forward practically the whole population of the quarter flocked out of the houses and followed me. They had seen the rifle and were all shouting excitedly that I was going to shoot the elephant. They had not shown much interest in the elephant when he was merely ravaging their homes, but it was different now that he was going to be shot. It was a bit of fun to them, as it would be to an English crowd; besides they wanted the meat. It made me vaguely uneasy. I had no intention of shooting the elephant—I had merely sent for the rifle to defend myself if necessary—and it is always unnerving to have a crowd following you. I marched down the hill, looking and feeling a fool, with the rifle over my shoulder and an ever-growing army of people jostling at my heels. At the bottom, when you got away from the huts, there was a metaled road[9] and beyond that a miry waste of paddy fields a thousand yards across, not yet plowed but soggy from the first rains and dotted with coarse grass. The elephant was standing eight yards from the road, his left side toward us. He took not the slightest notice of the crowd's approach. He was tearing up bunches of grass, beating them against his knees to clean them, and stuffing them into his mouth.

I had halted on the road. As soon as I saw the elephant I knew with perfect certainty that I ought not to shoot him. It is a serious matter to shoot a working elephant—it is comparable to destroying a huge and costly piece of machinery—and obviously one ought not to do it if it can possibly be avoided. And at that distance, peacefully eating, the elephant looked no more dangerous than a cow. I thought then and I think now that his attack of "must" was already passing off; in which case he would merely wander harmlessly about until the mahout came back and caught him. Moreover, I did not in the least want to shoot him. I decided that I would watch him for a little while to make sure that he did not turn savage again, and then go home.

But at that moment I glanced round at the crowd that had followed me. It was an immense crowd, two thousand at the least and growing every minute. It blocked the road for a long distance on either side. I looked at the sea of yellow faces above the garish clothes—faces all happy and excited over this bit of fun, all certain that the elephant was going to be shot. They were watching me as they would watch a conjurer about to perform a trick. They did not like me, but with the magical rifle in my hands I was momentarily worth watching. And suddenly I realized that I should have to shoot the elephant after all. The people expected it of me and I had got to do it; I could feel their two thousand wills pressing me forward, irresistibly. And it was at this moment, as I stood there with the rifle in my hands, that I first grasped the hollowness, the futility of the white man's dominion in the East. Here was I, the white man with his gun, standing in front of the unarmed native crowd —seemingly the leading actor of the piece; but in reality I was only an absurd puppet pushed to and fro by the will of those yellow faces behind. I perceived in this moment that when the white man turns tyrant it is his own freedom that he destroys. He becomes a sort of hollow, posing dummy, the conventionalized figure of a sahib.[10] For it is the condition of his rule that he shall spend his life in trying to impress the "natives," and so in every crisis he has got to do what

---

**8. paddy fields:** Rice fields.
**9. metaled road:** A road in which the pavement is reinforced with metal strips.

**10. sahib** (sä′ ib): Indian word for European gentleman.

the "natives" expect of him. He wears a mask, and his face grows to fit it. I had got to shoot the elephant. I had committed myself to doing it when I sent for the rifle. A sahib has got to act like a sahib; he has got to appear resolute, to know his own mind and do definite things. To come all that way, rifle in hand, with two thousand people marching at my heels, and then to trail feebly away, having done nothing—no, that was impossible. The crowd would laugh at me. And my whole life, every white man's life in the East, was one long struggle not to be laughed at.

But I did not want to shoot the elephant. I watched him beating his bunch of grass against his knees with that preoccupied grandmotherly air that elephants have. It seemed to me that it would be murder to shoot him. At that age I was not squeamish about killing animals, but I had never shot an elephant and never wanted to. (Somehow it always seems worse to kill a *large* animal.) Besides, there was the beast's owner to be considered. Alive, the elephant was worth at least a hundred pounds, dead, he would only be worth the value of his tusks, five pounds, possibly. But I had got to act quickly. I turned to some experienced-looking Burmans who had been there when we arrived, and asked them how the elephant had been behaving. They all said the same thing: he took no notice of you if you left him alone, but he might charge if you went too close to him.

It was perfectly clear to me what I ought to do. I ought to walk up to within, say, twenty-five yards of the elephant and test his behavior. If he charged, I could shoot; if he took no notice of me, it would be safe to leave him until the mahout came back. But also I knew that I was going to do no such thing. I was a poor shot with a rifle and the ground was soft mud into which one would sink at every step. If the elephant charged and I missed him. I should have about as much chance as a toad under a steam-roller. But even then I was not thinking particular-

ly of my own skin, only of the watchful yellow faces behind. For at that moment, with the crowd watching me, I was not afraid in the ordinary sense, as I would have been if I had been alone. A white man mustn't be frightened in front of "natives"; and so, in general, he isn't frightened. The sole thought in my mind was that if anything went wrong those two thousand Burmans would see me pursued, caught, trampled on, and reduced to a grinning corpse like that Indian up the hill. And if that happened it was quite probable that some of them would laugh. That would never do. There was only one alternative. I shoved the cartridges into the magazine and lay down on the road to get a better aim.

The crowd grew very still, and a deep, low, happy sigh, as of people who see the theater curtain go up at last, breathed from innumerable throats. They were going to have their bit of fun, after all. The rifle was a beautiful German thing with cross-hair sights. I did not then know that in shooting an elephant one would shoot to cut an imaginary bar running from ear hole to ear hole. I ought, therefore, as the elephant was sideways on, to have aimed straight at his ear-hole; actually I aimed several inches in front of this, thinking the brain would be further forward.

When I pulled the trigger I did not hear the bang or feel the kick—one never does when a shot goes home—but I heard the devilish roar of glee that went up from the crowd. In that instant, in too short a time, one would have thought, even for the bullet to get there, a mysterious, terrible change had come over the elephant. He neither stirred nor fell, but every line of his body had altered. He looked suddenly stricken, shrunken, immensely old, as though the frightful impact of the bullet had paralyzed him without knocking him down. At last, after what seemed a long time—it might have been five seconds, I dare say—he sagged flabbily to his knees. His mouth slobbered. An enormous senility seemed to have settled upon him. One could have imagined him thousands of years old. I fired again into the same spot. At the second shot he did not collapse but climbed with desperate slowness to his feet and stood weakly upright, with legs sagging and head drooping. I fired a third time. That was the shot that did for him. You could see the agony of it jolt his whole body and knock the last remnant of strength from his legs. But in falling he seemed for a moment to rise, for as his hind legs collapsed beneath him he seemed to tower upward like a huge rock toppling, his trunk reaching skyward like a tree. He trumpeted, for the first and only time. And then down he came, his belly toward me, with a crash that seemed to shake the ground even where I lay.

I got up. The Burmans were already racing past me across the mud. It was obvious that the elephant would never rise again, but he was not dead. He was breathing very rhythmically with long rattling gasps, his great mound of a side painfully rising and falling. His mouth was wide open—I could see far down into caverns of pale pink throat. I waited a long time for him to die, but his breathing did not weaken. Finally I fired my two remaining shots into the spot where I thought his heart must be. The thick blood welled out of him like red velvet, but still he did not die. His body did not even jerk when the shots hit him, the tortured breathing continued without a pause. He was dying, very slowly and in great agony, but in some world remote from me where not even a bullet could damage him further. I felt that I had got to put an end to that dreadful noise. It seemed dreadful to see the great beast lying there, powerless to move and yet powerless to die, and not even to be able to finish him. I sent back for my small rifle and poured shot after shot into his heart and down his throat. They seemed to make no impression. The tortured gasps continued as steadily as the ticking of a clock.

In the end I could not stand it any longer and went away. I heard later that it took him half an hour to die. Burmans were bringing dahs[11] and baskets even before I left, and I was told they had stripped his body almost to the bones by the afternoon.

Afterward, of course, there were endless discussions about the shooting of the elephant. The owner was furious, but he was only an Indian and could do nothing. Besides, legally I had done the right thing, for a mad elephant has to be killed, like a mad dog, if its owner fails to control it. Among the Europeans opinion was divided. The older man said I was right, the younger men said it was a shame to shoot an elephant for killing a coolie, because an elephant was worth more than any Coringhee[12] coolie. And afterward I was very glad that the coolie had been killed; it put me legally in the right and it gave me a sufficient pretext for shooting the elephant. I often wondered whether any of the others grasped that I had done it solely to avoid looking a fool.

---

**11. dahs** (däz): Knives.
**12. Coringhee** (cor in′ gē): Southern Indian.

# THINKING ABOUT THE SELECTION

## Recalling

1. (a) Why was the narrator hated in Burma? (b) Why were his reactions to this hatred mixed?
2. What grisly sight does the narrator encounter when he arrives in the quarter where the elephant has been seen?
3. (a) What reasons does the narrator give for not wanting to shoot the elephant? (b) Why does he shoot it in spite of these reasons?
4. How many shots does it take to bring the elephant down?
5. What do the Burmans do once the elephant is dead?

## Interpreting

6. How would you summarize the sentiments the narrator expresses in the first two paragraphs?
7. What do you think the narrator means when he states at the beginning of the third paragraph that this incident was "enlightening" in "a roundabout way"?
8. What do you think was the narrator's reason for providing his lengthy and detailed description of the elephant's death?
9. (a) What evidence is there in this essay that the narrator was divided in his sympathies? (b) How might the narrator's complex feelings be related to the essay's theme?

## Applying

10. If you had been in the narrator's place do you think you would have shot the elephant? Why or why not?

## ANALYZING LITERATURE

### Identifying Tone

**Tone** is a writer's attitude toward his or her subject, audience, or a character. In a literary work, tone is communicated through details and the author's choice of words. As a recollection of an incident from a period of George Orwell's life that was "perplexing and upsetting," "Shooting an Elephant" sums up the author's attitude toward several separate but related subjects. In your own words, identify the author's tone toward each of the following subjects, and locate specific words and passages that support your assumption.

1. The Burmans         3. Killing and death
2. The British Empire

## CRITICAL THINKING AND READING

### Understanding Stereotypes

A **stereotype** is a generalization about a whole group of people that does not apply to all individuals belonging to a certain group. The acceptance and use of stereotypes are forms of prejudice. In "Shooting an Elephant" Orwell explains that he was disliked by Burmans not because of any specific limitation of his own character but because he was European. The Burmans, thus, had a preconceived notion, or stereotype, of the European. What do you think is Orwell's reaction to stereotypes? Explain your answer.

## UNDERSTANDING LANGUAGE

### Understanding Word Origins

Several words used by Orwell in this selection are "Anglicizations," that is, words from another language which have been given English spellings and pronunciations that imitate the original. In a good dictionary, find each of the following Anglicized words, and trace their origins as far back as you can.

1. raj          4. sahib
2. mahout       5. dahs
3. coolie

## THINKING AND WRITING

### Supporting an Opinion

In an opinion paper, argue your belief that Orwell was justified, or not justified, in shooting the elephant. Your essay should not only support your own position but should pinpoint and refute arguments that might be raised by the opposition. Draw, if you can, from outside sources to drive home your point. When you revise make sure you have provided adequate support for your opinion.

# GREAT WORKS

## 1984
## by George Orwell

### A Terrifying Warning

WAR IS PEACE
FREEDOM IS SLAVERY
IGNORANCE IS STRENGTH

Behind these seemingly contradictory phrases is the most terrifying warning that a writer has ever uttered—George Orwell's masterpiece, *1984*. Centering on the abuse of power, the novel portrays people in the not-so-distant future brutally crushed by the iron fist of repression. As the three slogans illustrate, in the world of *1984* language is manipulated to create a new—and utterly false—reality in which any lie can become a truth.

Orwell's horrifying vision of the future has become famous the world over. For instance, many terms Orwell coined to describe the perversion of language and personal freedom have entered daily speech. These include "Doublespeak," "Newspeak," and "Big Brother," to name just a few. Indeed, Orwell's very name has become synonymous with totalitarianism. The adjective "Orwellian" is used to describe the fear and horror of repressive governments. Just what did Orwell say in *1984* that has had such a lasting impression?

**"WHO CONTROLS THE PAST CONTROLS THE FUTURE"**
*Quote from George Orwell*
*Illustration by Richard*

## The Near Future

The novel is set sometime in the near future—the date is never specified. As a matter of fact, Orwell decided on the title by simply transposing the last two digits of the book's intended publication date, 1948. Unfortunately, illness prevented him from completing the novel until 1949, and he lived less than a year after its publication before succumbing to the ravages of tuberculosis. Despite the title Orwell did not intend the reader to assume that the action was definitely set in 1984. Time, like truth, is fluid in the novel.

It is a world of new alliances. Countries as we presently know them have been re-formed into three large nations: Oceania, Eurasia, and East Asia. Oceania is made up of the Americas, the Atlantic islands including the British Isles, Australia, and the southern portion of Africa. Eurasia includes the whole of the northern part of Europe and Asia from Portugal to the Bering Strait. Eastasia, smaller than the others and with a less definite western frontier, comprises China and the country to the south of it, the Japanese islands, and a large but fluctuating portion of Manchuria, Mongolia, and Tibet. The immediate action takes place in the part of Oceania called Air-Strip One (England), in a city still called London.

These three countries are constantly at war with one another, furiously shifting allegiances. When the novel opens, Oceania is at war with Eurasia, allied with Eastasia. Four years before, Oceania had been at war with Eastasia and allied with Eurasia; by the end of the book, the battlefield has shifted once again. It is against this background of never-ending war, uncertainty, and fear that the novel unfolds.

## "A Bright Cold Day"

This is how the novel begins: "It was a bright cold day in April, and the clocks were striking thirteen. Winston Smith, his chin nuzzled into his breast in an effort to escape the vile wind, slipped quickly through the glass doors of Victory Mansions, though not quickly enough to prevent a swirl of gritty dust from entering along with him . . . On each landing, opposite the lift shaft, the poster with the enormous face gazed from the wall. It was one of those pictures which are so contrived that the eyes follow you about when you move. BIG BROTHER IS WATCHING YOU, the caption beneath it ran."

In most literary works, spring is a time of rebirth and love, happiness and promise. Instead, Orwell immediately plunges us here into a dirty, bitter world of "vile wind" and "gritty dust." It is very different from the shining future we often imagine. The clock tolls thirteen, a symbol of bad luck. The poster with Big Brother's ever-present eyes suggests that privacy, dignity, and peace have been swept away. Later in the opening chapter we see that bombs explode constantly; buildings are shabby and depressing. The name "Victory Mansions" is far more wish than reality, as the run-down state of Winston's small apartment shows. Because of the constant wars, all goods are in short supply, including necessities such as food, clothing, and housing. Since the kinds of consumer goods that we take for granted in our world—razor blades, tobacco, and chocolate—are nearly impossible to obtain, they are carefully hoarded. Telescreens, microphones, and networks of spies ("Thought Police") keep people under constant surveillance; children are taught to spy on their parents. The commanding face of the semi-mythical leader Big Brother gazes from every street corner. It is a world of pain, deprivation, and terror.

## The Novel's Structure

The structure of the novel is somewhat unusual. The narrative is told in three sections, followed by a brief Appendix that is an important part of the story. Part One introduces us to Winston Smith and his bitterly lonely and fearful life in Oceania. Part Two describes his attempt to find hope by falling in love and rebelling against the ruling political party. Part Three shows what happens to his quest for a better life. The Appendix clarifies the structure and purpose of "Newspeak," the language Orwell created for *1984.*

In Part One we are introduced to the main character, Winston Smith. Although as a member of the Outer Party he is on the fringes of the ruling Inner Party, he nonetheless has no special privileges. As a result, he is frail and seems far older than his thirty-nine years. Decades of poor nourishment have taken their toll on his health and spirit.

Winston begins a diary, an act not strictly forbidden by law (for there are no written laws) but understood by the all-inclusive offense of "Thoughtcrime" to be punishable by death. Because of the unusual placement of the telescreen in his living room, he is able to scrape a crumb of privacy by huddling in an alcove, where he fearfully scribbles his thoughts. His thoughts drift to O'Brien, a member of the elite Inner Party. O'Brien is so important—and the Inner Party held in such fear—that a hush falls over the workers when he enters a room. We also learn that Winston works at the "Ministry of Truth," where he rewrites past documents —in effect forging history—to make the past conform to current Party doctrine. Winston wonders why a bold-looking dark-haired girl had caught his eye during the "Two Minutes Hate." Is she an agent of the Thought Police? Could she be spying on him? Will he mysteriously disappear as so many others have?

Part Two opens with the dark-haired girl's astonishing action: Risking death, she slips Winston a note declaring her love. After elaborate precautions they are able to meet and soon fall in love. Wanting a place in which to be alone, Winston and Julia risk everything by renting a room above an antique store and setting up housekeeping. Amazingly, the room has no telescreen and the couple freely discuss rebellion against the Party and its symbol, Big Brother. Something almost as amazing happens one day at work: O'Brien, the Inner Party member, approaches Winston and invites him and Julia to his luxurious apartment. There he reveals that he is secretly involved in the resistance movement, The Brotherhood. Under his guidance Winston learns how the Party works—that its main goal is the exercise of power for its own sake. Part Two ends with a shattering climax.

In Part Three Winston learns the full truth about the Party—and himself. Under O'Brien's hand he sees what lies behind the resistance movement. This wrenching section lays bare the true effects of loss of freedom on the human soul. It contains some of the most unforgettable scenes you will ever read.

The Appendix explores how Newspeak, the official language of Oceania, provides a means of expression for the Party members while simultaneously making it impossible to express any unorthodox thought. In so doing it provides a detailed exploration of how language can be twisted to abolish free thinking.

## Power Abused

The central question of life, Orwell once remarked, is "how to prevent power from being abused." O'Brien explains the Party's exercise of power to Winston's incredulous ears: "Power is inflicting pain and humiliation. Power is in tearing human minds to pieces and putting them together again in new shapes of your own choosing. Do you begin to see, then, what kind of world we are creating? It is the exact opposite of the stupid hedonistic Utopias that the old reformers imagined. A world of fear and treachery and torment, a world of trampling and being trampled upon, a world which will grow not less but more merciless as it refines itself. Progress in our world will be towards more pain . . . triumph after triumph: an endless pressing, pressing, pressing upon the nerve of power."

In part the novel's bleak despair emerged from the deep hopelessness of the 1930's and 1940's. It appeared for a time that most of the world would be ground under the heel of totalitarian dictatorships. Fascism, for example, required unquestioning loyalty to its leader. People were totally subordinated to the service of the state. As in *1984*, military supremacy was achieved at the expense of civilian standards of living. Orwell drew aspects of Big Brother, the Party, and the constant warfare from the Fascist oppression he saw burning through Europe. Fascism flowered in Italy, Spain, Japan, and Germany; even liberal democracies such as France and England had vocal Fascist movements. At the same time, terror and oppression were evident in Russia with the rise of Communism.

People have especially noted the similarities between "Big Brother" and the events of Orwell's day. Much has been written on the parallels between Big Brother and the Russian dictator Joseph Stalin, who consolidated his power in the mid-thirties through a major campaign of political terror. The purges, arrests, and deportations he ordered left few Russian families untouched. Much of his terror was exercised through a system of secret police. In their abuse of power, they greatly resemble the fictional "Thought Police" in *1984*. There are elements of the Nazi demagogue Adolph Hitler and the Spanish dictator Francisco Franco in Big Brother as well.

Orwell had raised his pen against dictatorships before. In his lucid essays and piercing satires, he had championed the cause of the downtrodden and oppressed. His 1945 fable *Animal Farm*, for example, grimly attacked the evils of both Fascism and Communism. Orwell felt so strongly about the threat of Fascism that he laid his life on the line to try to halt its encroachment. From 1936 to 1939, he fought in the Spanish Civil War against the Fascist forces of General Francisco Franco. He regarded the actions of the Fascists in Spain as a betrayal of the popular revolution, which might otherwise have given the working classes real freedom and status. He was badly wounded in the throat.

But Orwell did not write *1984* to comment on life in the thirties and forties nor to predict the state of world leadership and society in the future. He exaggerates what life could be like in the future if totalitarian regimes seized control of governments to warn people to struggle to prevent the loss of decency and dignity in life. Recognizing that political freedom is solidly linked to linguistic freedom, he sought to warn readers that corrupting language corrupts life.

# Poetry

**HOUSES OF PARLIAMENT, 1903**
*Claude Monét*
The Granger Collection

# WILLIAM BUTLER YEATS

## 1865–1939

Winner of the Nobel Prize for Literature in 1923, William Butler Yeats (yāts) is generally regarded as one of the finest poets of this century. Born near Dublin, Ireland, Yeats was educated there and in London, but his heart lay to the west, in County Sligo, Ireland, where he spent childhood vacations with his grandparents. In the shadow of Sligo's barren mountains, he became immersed in the mythology and legends of Ireland.

After three years of studying painting in Dublin, Yeats moved to London to pursue a literary career. He became friends with the poet Arthur Symons, who awakened his interest in the symbolic poetry of William Blake and the French Symbolists. Yeats's early poetry shows the Symbolist influence as well as that of the Pre-Raphaelites, a group who believed that art needs a moral center which they felt it had lost nearly three centuries earlier. Symbolism, Pre-Raphaelism, and Irish myth combined in Yeats's first important collection, *The Wanderings of Oisin,* published in 1889.

Yeats led the Irish Literary Revival, helping to establish the Irish Literary Society in London in 1892 and the Irish National Literary Society in Dublin. He was also active in the Irish National Movement, whose members sought Ireland's independence from England. In this, he was spurred by his unrequited love for the beautiful actress and revolutionary, Maud Gonne. To his sorrow—after many refusals of his proposals—she chose a soldier, and Yeats, years later, married another woman.

Near the end of the century, Yeats joined with his friend Lady Augusta Gregory in founding the Irish National Theatre Society. He turned his attention to writing plays, among them *The Shadowy Waters* (1900) and *Deirdre* (1907). When he returned to poetry, it was with a new voice, subtler but more powerful than the one he had used before that time. The poems in *The Tower,* published in 1928, show Yeats at the height of his abilities.

In 1922 Yeats was appointed a senator of the new Irish Free State, and on his seventieth birthday he was hailed by his nation as the greatest living Irishman. He continued to write poems until a day or two before his death at Roquebrune, France. One of his last poems contains his famous epitaph: Cast a cold eye / On life, on death. / Horseman, pass by!

# GUIDE FOR INTERPRETING

## When You Are Old; The Lake Isle of Innisfree; The Wild Swans at Coole; An Irish Airman Foresees His Death

**Writer's Technique**

**Speaker and Lyric Voice.** A lyric poem expresses personal thoughts and feelings on a specific subject. Among the most common subjects are love, death, nature, and war. Sometimes the speaker in a lyric poem—the one whose voice comes through—is, or appears to be, the poet. In Milton's "When I Consider How My Light Is Spent," for example, the speaker seems clearly to be the poet. In Christopher Marlowe's "The Passionate Shepherd to His Love," on the other hand, the speaker is almost certainly not the poet. In many lyric poems, such as William Blake's "The Tiger," you cannot tell for sure whether the speaker is or is not the poet.

**Writing**

Think of a subject about which you have strong feelings, either positive or negative, such as education, friendship, or marriage. Jot down some brief notes that express your feelings on the subject. Then think of a fictional character based either on your reading or your imagination. Write at least three sentences, or three lines of poetry, in which the fictional character expresses your feelings on the subject you have chosen.

**Primary Source**

Sean O'Faolain tried to explain the extraordinary influence William Butler Yeats exerted on all phases of Irish life. Elected a member of the Irish Academy of Letters founded the year before by Yeats and Shaw, O'Faolain worked with Yeats on several projects as Yeats's remarkable career drew to its close. "He had been our inspiration and our justification in the sense that all the rest of us younger men and women could not, between us, represent literature with anything like his achievement and authority in the eyes of the public. When he retired to Rapallo to die, and most of his generation had passed away or gone into exile one by one . . . there was nothing to do but wait until Time, if it ever did, created new reputations of equal authority. Time did not and could not. It was not a matter alone of literary achievement. Had, for example, Joyce returned to live in Dublin his presence would have made no difference. For the source of Yeats's authority, like the source of his poetry, was the extraordinary union in his nature of a powerful imagination, the will to enforce it, and a persistent dramatic self-image of himself as a seer and leader. . . . It was the blend that at once bestowed greatness on him and condemned him to loneliness. . . . It was his need of his nature, as poet and man, to live a foot off the ground, a foot or two, or more, away from common life."

# When You Are Old

## William Butler Yeats

When you are old and gray and full of sleep,
And nodding by the fire, take down this book,
And slowly read, and dream of the soft look
Your eyes had once, and of their shadows deep;

5   How many loved your moments of glad grace,
And loved your beauty with love false or true,
But one man loved the pilgrim soul in you,
And loved the sorrows of your changing face;

And bending down beside the glowing bars,
10  Murmur, a little sadly, how Love fled
And paced upon the mountains overhead
And hid his face amid a crowd of stars.

---

## THINKING ABOUT THE SELECTION

### Recalling

1. What does the speaker ask the person being addressed to do?
2. What happened to Love?

### Interpreting

3. Who do you think the "one man" in the second stanza is?
4. What does the phrase "pilgrim soul" suggest about the person being addressed?
5. Why is the word *Love* capitalized in line 10?

### Applying

6. When love is not reciprocated, it may be withdrawn, as it apparently was in this poem. Under what circumstances do you think it is right to withdraw love that is not being returned?

## ANALYZING LITERATURE

### Understanding Speaker and Lyric Voice

The speaker in a lyric poem may or may not be the poet. Sometimes the identity of the speaker is obvious, but often it is hard to be sure. Knowing about the poet's life, while not essential to your enjoyment of a poem, may provide clues to the identity of the speaker.

1. Look back at the biography of Yeats. What event in his life might have prompted him to write this poem?
2. In line 2 the speaker advises the person being addressed to "take down this book." In what way might that advice furnish a clue to the identity of the speaker?

# The Lake Isle of Innisfree

## William Butler Yeats

I will arise and go now, and go to Innisfree,
And a small cabin build there, of clay and wattles[1] made:
Nine bean-rows will I have there, a hive for the honeybee,
And live alone in the bee-loud glade.

5  And I shall have some peace there, for peace comes
     dropping slow,
  Dropping from the veils of the morning to where the cricket
     sings;
  There midnight's all a glimmer, and noon a purple glow,
  And evening full of the linnet's wings.[2]

  I will arise and go now, for always night and day
10  I hear lake water lapping with low sounds by the shore;
  While I stand on the roadway, or on the pavements gray,
  I hear it in the deep heart's core.

OLD HOUSE (IVY COTTAGE),
SHOREHAM, 1831–32
*Samuel Palmer*
*Ashmolean Museum, Oxford*

———————
**1. wattles** *n.*: Stakes interwoven with twigs or branches.
**2. linnet's wings:** The wings of a European singing bird.

---

## THINKING ABOUT THE SELECTION

### Recalling

1. (a) What does the speaker want most to find at Innisfree? (b) How will each of the four times of day he mentions contribute to his goal?

2. According to line 11, where is the speaker when he hears the call of Innisfree?

### Interpreting

3. Why do you think Innisfree, as the speaker describes it, has so much more appeal for him than where he is now?

4. (a) Do you think the speaker is expressing a wish or a genuine intent to go to Innisfree? (b) What evidence in the poem is there to support your answer?

5. What techniques or devices in the poem help to create a vivid picture of Innisfree?

### Applying

6. Popular music sometimes deals with the theme of leaving one place and going to a more desirable place. What song or songs can you think of that have that theme?

# The Wild Swans at Coole

### William Butler Yeats

The trees are in their autumn beauty,
The woodland paths are dry,
Under the October twilight the water
Mirrors a still sky;
5  Upon the brimming water among
    the stones
Are nine-and-fifty swans.

The nineteenth autumn has come
    upon me
Since I first made my count;
I saw, before I had well finished,
10  All suddenly mount
And scatter wheeling in great broken
    rings
Upon their clamorous wings.

I have looked upon those brilliant
    creatures,
And now my heart is sore.
15  All's changed since I, hearing at twilight,
The first time on this shore,
The bell-beat of their wings above
    my head,
Trod with a lighter tread.

Unwearied still, lover by lover,
20  They paddle in the cold
Companionable streams or climb the air;
Their hearts have not grown old;
Passion or conquest, wander where
    they will,
Attend upon them still.

25  But now they drift on the still water,
Mysterious, beautiful;
Among what rushes will they build,
By what lake's edge or pool
Delight men's eyes when I awake
    some day
30  To find they have flown away?

## THINKING ABOUT THE SELECTION
### Recalling

1. (a) When did the speaker first begin counting the swans? (b) What did the swans do before he had finished counting?
2. (a) What was the speaker's reaction when he first heard "the bell-beat of their wings"? (b) Why is his reaction different now from what it was then?
3. What will the swans inevitably do?

### Interpreting

4. For what thematic purpose does the speaker emphasize the setting in the first two stanzas?
5. In the fourth stanza, how does the speaker suggest that he and the swans are not alike?

6. What do you think the swans symbolize to the speaker?

## Applying

7. Although the wild swans in their natural setting are beautiful, the speaker feels a sense of sadness and loss. Why does great beauty sometimes arouse those feelings?

## CRITICAL THINKING AND READING
### Evaluating the Use of Imagery

**Imagery** in literature is created through the writer's use of words, singly or in combination, to produce a picture in the reader's mind. Images may appeal to any of the five senses. Sometimes they appeal to several senses at once. A writer who refers to "a crisp, shiny, sweet apple" is simultaneously appealing to hearing, sight, and taste. If imagery is to work effectively, readers must be familiar with the key words and their meanings. For example, a reader who has never heard the word *clamorous* will probably not appreciate the imagery of "clamorous wings." The following images are from "The Wild Swans of Coole." Locate each one in the poem and identify the sense or senses to which it appeals.

1. . . . the water/Mirrors a still sky
2. All suddenly mount/And scatter wheeling in great broken rings/Upon their clamorous wings
3. The bell-beat of their wings
4. They paddle in the cold/Companionable streams

# An Irish Airman Foresees His Death

**William Butler Yeats**

*Major Robert Gregory, a young Irish artist who was the son of Yeats's friend Lady Augusta Gregory, was killed during World War I while flying over Italy as a member of England's Royal Flying Corps. Gregory's death inspired Yeats to write this poem.*

I know that I shall meet my fate
Somewhere among the clouds above;
Those that I fight I do not hate,
Those that I guard I do not love;[1]
5  My country is Kiltartan[2] Cross,
My countrymen Kiltartan's poor,
No likely end could bring them loss
Or leave them happier than before.
Nor law, nor duty bade me fight,
10  Nor public men, nor cheering crowds,
A lonely impulse of delight
Drove to this tumult in the clouds;
I balanced all, brought all to mind,
The years to come seemed waste of breath,
15  A waste of breath the years behind
In balance with this life, this death.

---

**1. Those . . . love:** Because Ireland was under English rule during
World War I, many Irish fought as members of the English forces
during the war. However, because of their desire for independence
many of the Irish felt a great deal of resentment toward the English.
**2. Kiltartan:** A village near Lady Gregory's estate.

**BURNING AIRPLANE**
*Photri*

## THINKING ABOUT THE SELECTION

### Recalling

1. What does the Irish airman believe will happen to him?
2. (a) How does he feel about those he is fighting against? (b) Why is he fighting them?
3. How does he view (a) his past? (b) his future?

### Interpreting

4. The airman does not love those he guards —the English. (a) Do you think his lack of love extends to those he calls his countrymen —Kiltartan's poor? (b) What lines in the poem support your answer?
5. (a) To what extent does the airman seem worried about his fate? (b) How would you describe the airman's character?

### Applying

6. Suppose the airman were to survive the war.

What do you think he might do with the rest of his life? Explain your answer.

## THINKING AND WRITING

### Writing About the Use of a Speaker

In writing "An Irish Airman Foresees His Death," Yeats had in mind Major Robert Gregory, the son of Yeats's close friend Lady Augusta Gregory. A volunteer in England's Royal Flying Corps, Major Gregory was killed during World War I while flying over Italy. Think about why Yeats may have chosen to write his poem with Major Gregory as the first-person speaker. Write a brief essay in which you explain why the poem, as written, allows Yeats to express his thoughts about the frailty of life, the futility of war, and the problems of Ireland more powerfully than a third-person point of view would have permitted. When you revise, make sure you have included details from the poem to support your opinion.

*An Irish Airman Foresees His Death* 1031

# GUIDE FOR INTERPRETING

## The Second Coming; After Long Silence; Sailing to Byzantium

**Writer's Technique**

**Symbols.** In its broadest, most basic sense, a symbol is something that stands for something else. The word *horse* is a symbol for an actual, recognizable animal. In our culture an olive branch is a symbol for peace. A symbol in literature is a word, person, object, or action that stands for something beyond itself. For example, the white whale in Herman Melville's *Moby-Dick* is often said to stand for evil. In the art and literature of the late nineteenth century, the word *symbolism* took on special significance. A group of French artists and poets, reacting against realism, promoted the use of symbols to achieve intensity and complexity in their work, a technique that sometimes approached mysticism. Yeats, an adherent of this type of symbolism in his early poetry, abandoned it later. However, in the last decade of his life, he created an elaborate symbolic system of his own, a system that is largely a curiosity for modern readers. His later poems abound in symbols, but Yeats remains first and foremost a poet, not a system-maker or a philosopher. In his best poems, the symbols do not require mastery of his system, but only the practiced eye of a careful reader.

As you read the poems by William Butler Yeats, look for his use of symbols and be alert to the possible meanings attached to them.

**Writing**

If you wished to picture Canada symbolically, you might draw a maple leaf; for Great Britain you might draw a lion and for New York City, an apple. Countries, states, cities, companies, high schools, professional athletic teams—all sometimes develop symbols for easy and perhaps emotional identification. Think about such symbols. Jot down a number of them, identifying what each one symbolizes.

**Primary Source**

It's tempting to think that famous writers are free from the doubts that the rest of us sometimes feel. That Eliot and Yeats both received great praise in their day does not mean that they were immune to a touch of professional jealousy. Writer Richard Ellmann noted their long incompatibility in this encounter:

"Among their various mild collisions none was more defined than the dinner at Wellesley College when Yeats, seated next to Eliot but oblivious of him, conversed with the guest on the other side until late in the meal. Then he turned and said, 'My friend here and I have been discussing the defects of T. S. Eliot's poetry. What do you think of that poetry?'

"Eliot held up his place card to excuse himself from the jury."

# The Second Coming

William Butler Yeats

*"The Second Coming" was inspired by Yeats's belief that history occurs in two-thousand-year cycles, with one civilization passing through stages of development, growth, and decay, before crumbling and giving way to a new civilization that stands in direct opposition to the preceding civilization. The birth of Christ had brought about the end of one civilization and the birth of another, and Yeats believed that the society of the early twentieth century was in a state of decay that would lead to a similar sort of rebirth.*

Turning and turning in the widening gyre
The falcon cannot hear the falconer;
Things fall apart; the center cannot hold;
Mere anarchy is loosed upon the world,
5    The blood-dimmed tide is loosed, and everywhere
The ceremony of innocence is drowned;
The best lack all conviction, while the worst
Are full of passionate intensity.[1]

Surely some revelation is at hand;
10   Surely the Second Coming is at hand.
The Second Coming! Hardly are those words out
When a vast image out of *Spiritus Mundi*[2]
Troubles my sight: somewhere in sands of the desert
A shape with lion body and the head of a man,[3]
15   A gaze blank and pitiless as the sun,
Is moving its slow thighs, while all about it
Reel shadows of the indignant desert birds.
The darkness drops again; but now I know
That twenty centuries[4] of stony sleep
20   Were vexed to nightmare by a rocking cradle,[5]
And what rough beast, its hour come round at last,
Slouches towards Bethlehem to be born?

---

**1. Mere . . . intensity** (lines 4-8): Refers to the Russian Revolution of 1917.
**2. *Spiritus Mundi*** (spir′i təs mōōn′dē): The Universal Spirit or soul, the Universal Subconscious in which the memories of the entire human race are forever preserved.
**3. A . . . man:** A sphinx.
**4. twenty centuries:** The historical cycle preceding the birth of Christ.
**5. rocking cradle:** The cradle of Jesus Christ.

## THINKING ABOUT THE SELECTION

### Recalling

1. Why does the falcon not return to the falconer, as it ordinarily would in falconry (the hunting of game with falcons)?
2. In the first stanza, what is happening to government and innocence?
3. What does the speaker believe is at hand?
4. (a) What has begun to stir in the desert? (b) How long has it been dormant?
5. What does the speaker say is about to be born?

### Interpreting

6. How does Yeats use the unhearing falcon as a symbol of what is happening in the world?
7. What is the imagery in lines 5-6?
8. When did the previous "twenty centuries of stony sleep" occur (that is, before the twentieth century)?
9. (a) What would you expect to appear at the Second Coming? (b) How does that differ from what the speaker suggests will appear?

### Applying

10. What historical forces do you think prompt people, including poets, to predict vast upheavals, new civilizations, and even the end of the world?

## ANALYZING LITERATURE

### Understanding Symbols

A literary **symbol** is a word, person, object, or action that stands for something beyond itself. In "The Second Coming," for instance, the falcon flying in ever-widening circles is more than just a trained hunting bird that has lost its way. It represents something—it symbolizes something. A symbol always requires interpretation. With the falcon, it would help you to know Yeats's theories about "gyres," or cycles, which were a part of his symbolic system, although such knowledge is not really essential to an understanding of the poem.

1. Yeats does not merely talk about twenty centuries of silence. He symbolizes them. (a) What symbol does he use? (b) Why do you think he presents it through a description of its features rather than by naming it outright?
2. (a) What symbolism, if any, do you find in line 6: "The ceremony of innocence is drowned"? (b) What might the "indignant desert birds" in line 17 represent?
3. (a) What symbol does Yeats use to represent the coming era? (b) What characteristics do you associate with this symbol?

# After Long Silence

## William Butler Yeats

Speech after long silence; it is right,
All other lovers being estranged or dead,
Unfriendly lamplight hid under its shade,
The curtains drawn upon unfriendly night,
5   That we descant and yet again descant
Upon the supreme theme of Art and Song:
Bodily decrepitude is wisdom; young
We loved each other and were ignorant.

---

## THINKING ABOUT THE SELECTION
### Recalling

1. What does the speaker say should follow long silence?
2. The speaker describes two things as unfriendly. What are they?
3. What is the "supreme theme" that should be talked about after long silence?
4. Why does the speaker believe the old have more reason than the young to "descant and yet again descant"?

### Interpreting

5. (a) What relationship exists between the people who are being urged to speak? (b) How can you tell?
6. What do you suppose was taking place during the period of long silence?
7. The speaker seems to have mixed feelings about old age. How would you describe his feelings?

### Applying

8. How fully do you accept the idea that the young cannot talk meaningfully about "Art and Song"? Explain.

## THINKING AND WRITING
### Writing a Poem About Silence

"After Long Silence" treats the idea of silence symbolically. Silence, according to Yeats, is the time when human beings have little of intellectual importance to communicate to one another. That is one interpretation of silence, but only one. Choose another approach to the subject of silence. Think about it. Write some notes. Then write a poem that expresses your own view of silence. Remember that a poem requires revision just as much as an essay does —perhaps more.

# Sailing to Byzantium[1]

## W. B. Yeats

### I

That is no country for old men. The young
In one another's arms, birds in the trees
—Those dying generations—at their song,
The salmon-falls, the mackerel-crowded seas,
5   Fish, flesh, or fowl, commend all summer long
Whatever is begotten, born, and dies.
Caught in that sensual music all neglect
Monuments of unaging intellect.

### II

An aged man is but a paltry thing,
10  A tattered coat upon a stick, unless
Soul clap its hands and sing, and louder sing
For every tatter in its mortal dress,
Nor is there singing school but studying
Monuments of its own magnificence;
15  And therefore I have sailed the seas and come
To the holy city of Byzantium.

### III

O sages standing in God's holy fire
As in the gold mosaic of a wall,[2]
Come from the holy fire, perne in a gyre,[3]
20  And be the singing-masters of my soul.
Consume my heart away; sick with desire
And fastened to a dying animal
It knows not what it is; and gather me
Into the artifice of eternity.

---

**1. Byzantium** (bi zan′ s·hē əm): The ancient capital of the Eastern
Roman (or Byzantine) Empire and the seat of the Greek Orthodox
Church; today, Istanbul, Turkey. For Yeats, it symbolized the sensual
and artistic world as opposed to the natural and biological world.
**2. sages . . . wall:** Wise old men and saints portrayed in gold mosaic
on the walls of Byzantine churches.
**3. perne . . . gyre:** Spin in a spiraling motion.

# IV

25  Once out of nature I shall never take
    My bodily form from any natural thing,
    But such a form as Grecian goldsmiths make
    Of hammered gold and gold enameling
    To keep a drowsy Emperor awake;
30  Or set upon a golden bough to sing[4]
    To lords and ladies of Byzantium
    Of what is past, or passing, or to come.

---

**4. To . . . sing:** Yeats wrote, "I have read somewhere that in the Emperor's palace at Byzantium was a tree made of gold and silver, and artificial birds that sang."

---

## THINKING ABOUT THE SELECTION

### Recalling

1. (a) What do the people of the country referred to in the first stanza "commend"? (b) What do they neglect?
2. How is "an aged man" described in lines 9-10?
3. What does the speaker do in lines 15-16?
4. What does the speaker ask of the sages in the third stanza?
5. What bodily form does the speaker wish to take when he is "out of nature"?

### Interpreting

6. How does Byzantium contrast with the country described in the first two stanzas?
7. (a) What do the desires which the speaker expresses in stanzas 3 and 4 reveal about his attitude toward aging and death? (b) How does he hope to immortalize himself?
8. What does this poem suggest about the motives of artists and the purpose of art?

### Applying

9. Do you think that most people hope to immortalize themselves in some way? Why or why not?

# D. H. LAWRENCE

## 1885–1930

Although D. H. Lawrence is best known for his novels and short stories, he was also a fine poet. His poetry, like his prose, concentrates on the life-giving force of nature, exalting the physical and instinctual over the purely intellectual. Writing in free verse, Lawrence produced a number of powerful and original poems that evoke the "blood consciousness" and "dark gods" he sought. His "belief in the blood" was not merely his philosophy but was the dynamic force, the energy, that fueled his poetic imagination. For a fuller biography of D. H. Lawrence, see page 972.

## Snake

**Writer's Technique**

**Free Verse.** Free verse is poetry that has no clearly defined rhyme scheme or rhythmic pattern. Lines are based on the natural phrasing of the language, and the rhythm follows normal voice cadences. Although no less a poet than Robert Frost has defined the writing of free verse as akin to "playing tennis with the net down," the issue is not that simple. Free verse poems are not merely works of prose laid out to resemble poetry. They *are* poetry, with a long and honored history going back to the Psalms in the bible. Free verse, never so "free" as prose, has its own rhythmic integrity and commonly makes use of the traditional devices of poetry, such as alliteration (repetition of consonant sounds), assonance (repetition of vowel sounds), and onomatopoeia (words or phrases that imitate the sound being described).

**Writing**

Try to recall the most startling sight you have ever come upon. Write a short account of this event. Describe in detail what you were doing when you first became aware of the sight. Explain your feelings at the time. Tell what happened after you began to watch. Describe how the event ended and what your thoughts and feelings were when it was over.

**Primary Source**

Imagine giving a book you have written to your folks. Lawrence describes his mother's reaction: "The very first copy of *The White Peacock* that was ever sent out, I put into my mother's hands when she was dying. She looked at the outside, and then at the title-page, and then at me, with darkening eyes. And though she loved me so much, I think she doubted whether it could be much of a book, since no one more important than I had written it. Somewhere, in the helpless privacies of her being, she had wistful respect for me. But for me in the face of the world, not much."

# Snake

## D. H. Lawrence

A snake came to my water-trough
On a hot, hot day, and I in pajamas for the heat,
To drink there.

In the deep, strange-scented shade of the great dark
    carob tree
5  I came down the steps with my pitcher
And must wait, must stand and wait, for there he was at
    the trough before me.

He reached down from a fissure in the earth-wall in the
    gloom
And trailed his yellow-brown slackness soft-bellied down,
    over the edge of the stone trough
And rested his throat upon the stone bottom,
10  And where the water had dripped from the tap, in a small
    clearness,
He sipped with his straight mouth,
Softly drank through his straight gums, into his slack long
    body,
Silently.

Someone was before me at my water-trough,
15  And I, like a second comer, waiting.

He lifted his head from his drinking, as cattle do,
And looked at me vaguely, as drinking cattle do,
And flickered his two-forked tongue from his lips, and
    mused a moment,
And stooped and drank a little more,
20  Being earth-brown, earth-golden from the burning bowels
    of the earth
On the day of Sicilian July, with Etna[1] smoking.

The voice of my education said to me
He must be killed,
For in Sicily the black, black snakes are innocent, the gold
    are venomous.

---

**1. Etna:** A volcanic mountain in eastern Sicily.

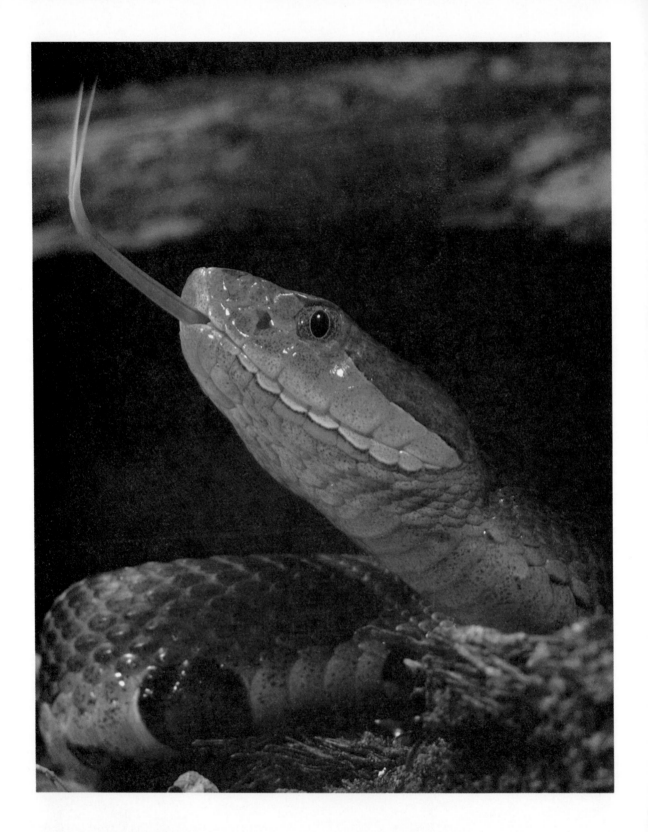

25  And voices in me said, If you were a man
    You would take a stick and break him now, and finish him
        off.

    But must I confess how I liked him,
    How glad I was he had come like a guest in quiet, to drink
        at my water-trough
    And depart peaceful, pacified, and thankless,
30  Into the burning bowels of this earth?

    Was it cowardice, that I dared not kill him?
    Was it perversity, that I longed to talk to him?
    Was it humility, to feel so honored?
    I felt so honored.

35  And yet those voices:
    *If you were not afraid, you would kill him!*

    And truly I was afraid, I was most afraid,
    But even so, honored still more
    That he should seek my hospitality
40  From out the dark door of the secret earth.

    He drank enough
    And lifted his head, dreamily, as one who has drunken,
    And flickered his tongue like a forked night on the air, so
        black;
    Seeming to lick his lips,
45  And looked around like a god, unseeing, into the air,
    And slowly turned his head,
    And slowly, very slowly, as if thrice adream,
    Proceeded to draw his slow length curving round
    And climb again the broken bank of my wall-face.

50  And as he put his head into that dreadful hole,
    And as he slowly drew up, snake-easing his shoulders, and
        entered farther,
    A sort of horror, a sort of protest against his withdrawing
        into that horrid black hole,
    Deliberately going into the blackness, and slowly drawing
        himself after,
    Overcame me now his back was turned.

55  I looked round, I put down my pitcher,
    I picked up a clumsy log
    And threw it at the water-trough with a clatter.

I think it did not hit him,
But suddenly that part of him that was left behind
 convulsed in undignified haste,
60  Writhed like lightning, and was gone
Into the black hole, the earth-lipped fissure in the
 wall-front,
At which, in the intense still noon, I stared with
 fascination.

And immediately I regretted it.
I thought how paltry, how vulgar, what a mean act!
65  I despised myself and the voices of my accursed human
 education.

And I thought of the albatross,[2]
And I wished he would come back, my snake.

For he seemed to me again like a king,
70  Like a king in exile, uncrowned in the underworld,
Now due to be crowned again.

And so, I missed my chance with one of the lords
Of life.
And I have something to expiate;
75  A pettiness.

---

**2. albatross:** In Samuel Taylor Coleridge's "The Rime of the
Ancient Mariner," the mariner shoots an albatross, a traditional
symbol of good luck.

## THINKING ABOUT THE SELECTION

### Recalling

1. (a) What is the speaker on his way to do when he first becomes aware of the snake? (b) What is the snake doing?
2. (a) What does the "voice of [his] education" tell the speaker he should do? (b) How does he actually feel about the snake when the "voices" tell him he should kill it?
3. (a) What causes the speaker's horror toward the snake? (b) What does the speaker do? (c) How does he feel about having done it? (d) What three adjectives does he use to characterize his act?

### Interpreting

4. In line 65 the speaker mentions "the voices of my accursed education." (a) What are these voices? (b) Why are they accursed?
5. Why does the speaker call the snake "a king in exile" and "one of the lords of life"?
6. The last two lines suggest that the speaker has committed a sin. (a) What is his sin? (b) Why does he call it a "pettiness"?

## Applying

7. Do you agree with the speaker that he has missed his chance? Explain your answer.


## ANALYZING LITERATURE
### Understanding Free Verse

Poetry with no clearly defined metric pattern or rhyme scheme is called **free verse.** Although inexperienced writers sometimes call their non-poetry "free verse," the truth is that free verse makes use of subtle, varying, but real rhythm as well as other traditional devices of poetry: repetition, alliteration, assonance, and onomatopoeia. It also has, in many cases, a high concentration of symbolism, figurative language, and imagery.

1. Notice how many lines of "Snake" begin with the word *And*. Notice also the repetition of words and phrases in the poem ("hot, hot" in line 2; "as cattle do" . . . "as drinking cattle do" in lines 16–17; and more). What effect do you think Lawrence intends to produce through this insistent repetition?
2. What devices—alliteration, assonance, ono-matopoeia, repetition—do you find in each of the following excerpts. Some of them contain more than one device.

a. In the deep, strange-scented shade of the great dark carobtree
b. He sipped with his straight mouth,/Softly drank through his straight gums, into his slack long body,/Silently.
c. And flickered his two-forked tongue from his lips
d. Was it humility to feel so honored?/I felt so honored.


## CRITICAL THINKING AND READING
### Making Inferences About Purpose

On the surface "Snake" is a simple poem about Lawrence's (the speaker's/author's) unexpected encounter with a snake at a water-trough on a hot day in Sicily. If you look beneath the surface, however, you will see that his purpose in describing the incident transcends the basic narrative appeal of the poem. Lawrence makes his intent clear—although not his specific message—from his continuing, almost clinical analysis of his reactions to the snake. What underlying statement do you think he is making in "Snake" about human beings in general and himself in particular? Support your answer with quotations from the poem.

# SIEGFRIED SASSOON

## 1886–1967

A decorated, twice-wounded soldier in World War I, Siegfried Sassoon witnessed first-hand the horrors of trench warfare in France. Like a number of other English writers and poets who saw action in the war, he resolved to portray for his own and future generations the grim reality of war, to show graphically its carnage and despair. No one did it better than he. Although Sassoon wrote for almost fifty years after the Armistice, he produced little to match his searing wartime verses that honor and mourn the "citizens of death's gray land."

Sassoon, born into a wealthy Jewish family in London, was something of a dilettante before the war. While attending Marlborough and Clare College, Cambridge, he found that he preferred hunting, cricket, golf, and ballet to more academic pursuits. Poetry aroused his interest also, and he published a number of pastoral poems and parodies while in his early twenties. In 1913, on the eve of World War I, his long poem, *The Daffodil Murderer,* gave evidence of his ability to combine parody with serious self-expression.

When war broke out in 1914, Sassoon joined the army the same day and showed such reckless courage in battle that he earned the nickname "Mad Jack" along with a medal for gallantry. But by the time he was wounded at Arras in April 1917, his attitude toward the supposed glory of war had changed. By then he was writing what he called "trench poems," the starkly realistic, agonized, sometimes horrifying verses on which his reputation rests. *The Old Huntsman* (1917) and *Counter-Attack* (1918) contain most of his memorable poems.

When Sassoon returned to the front in 1918, a British sentry shot him in the head by mistake, and Sassoon spent the rest of the war in a hospital.

After the Armistice, he continued to write, publishing his first prose work, *Memoirs of a Fox-Hunting Man,* in 1928. Billed as a novel, the book is essentially an autobiography, the first of several autobiographical works. Sassoon married at the age of forty-seven and settled down in rural Wiltshire. The literary innovations between the two World Wars passed him by. His niche in English literature had already been secured by a few dozen jarring, outraged, unforgettable poems from the trenches.

# GUIDE FOR INTERPRETING

## Wirers

**Historical Context.** Many poems deal with subjects unrelated to a particular time or place. A poem about love, for instance, deals with an emotion that is as old as the human race. But sometimes a historical event will create such an impact that poets feel impelled to comment on, and perhaps to explain, what happened. World War I was such an event. The war's devastation and slaughter, unprecedented at the time, gave rise to millions of words—patriotic, indignant, disillusioned, depending on the views of the writer. Those words were then, and are today, tied to their times. "Black Jack Pershing" was a household name in 1918. Soldiers were *dough-boys,* and "Mademoiselle from Armentières" was a song familiar to everyone. Those names and facts are part of the history of World War I. A Siegfried Sassoon poem about World War I is likely to contain words and references unique to the war. As a reader, you must put such words and references into historical context—a perspective required by your distance in time from the events described. Ideally, you would be able to put all of World War I into historical context, but as a practical matter, you know enough about war in general to understand and appreciate a poem about World War I, even if you lack a thorough historical knowledge of the event.

**Writing**

Think of an abstract concept such as anger, betrayal, or loss and relate it to an experience that has affected you deeply. Freewrite about this experience, showing the feelings it caused.

**Primary Source**

By 1917 Sassoon was so strongly opposed to the war that he sent a formal protest to the House of Commons and threw his Military Cross into the River Mersey. In part his declaration read: "I believe that this war, on which I entered as a war of defense and liberation, has now become a war of aggression and conquest. . . . I can no longer be a party to prolong these sufferings for ends which I believe to be evil and unjust. I am not protesting against the conduct of the war, but against the political errors and insincerities for which the fighting men are being sacrificed." He was spared a formal court-martial through the intercession of fellow poet Robert Graves, who successfully pleaded that Sassoon was suffering from shellshock. As a result, in July 1917 Sassoon entered a war hospital in Edinburgh. There he befriended fellow patient and poet Wilfred Owen. When Owen was killed in battle during Armistice week, Sassoon collected and edited Owen's poems for publication.

# Wirers[1]

## Siegfried Sassoon

"Pass it along, the wiring party's going out"—
And yawning sentries mumble, "Wirers going out."
Unraveling; twisting; hammering stakes with muffled thud,
They toil with stealthy haste and anger in their blood.

5  The Boche[2] sends up a flare. Black forms stand rigid there,
Stock-still like posts; then darkness, and the clumsy ghosts
Stride hither and thither, whispering, tripped by clutching
    snare
Of snags and tangles.
            Ghastly dawn with vaporous coasts
10 Gleams desolate along the sky, night's misery ended.

Young Hughes was badly hit; I heard him carried away,
Moaning at every lurch; no doubt he'll die today.
But *we* can say the front-line wire's been safely mended.

---

**1. wirers:** Soldiers who were responsible for repairing the
barbed-wire fences that protected the trenches in World War I.
**2. Boche** (bôsh): German soldier.

---

## THINKING ABOUT THE SELECTION

### Recalling

1. What are the wirers getting ready to do at the beginning of the poem?
2. What happens when an enemy flare lights the scene?
3. What does the speaker say will probably be the fate of the soldier named Hughes?

### Interpreting

4. How do you think the wirers feel about the job they have to do?
5. (a) What is the speaker's attitude toward what has happened to young Hughes? (b) How do you explain that attitude?

### Applying

6. (a) What kinds of nonmilitary jobs may lead to a routine acceptance of the daily presence of danger? (b) What is the difference between those jobs and a soldier's job?

## ANALYZING LITERATURE

### Historical Context

Actual events provide the historical context of "Wirers." If you knew no history at all, the

**DRAWING OF TANKS, WORLD WAR I**
*Photo Research Int.*

poem—without some kind of textual explanation —would be virtually meaningless to you. However, you know something about the trenches of World War I and about barbed-wire entanglements. You therefore have clues to the historical context of the poem.

1. How can you tell from the poem that its historical context is World War I (1914–18) and not (a) the American Civil War (1861 –65)? (b) World War II (1939–45)?

2. A historian has said that in World War I "cavalry was useless" and "artillery was absolutely indispensable." How does the content of the poem support the historian's statement?

# RUPERT BROOKE

## 1887–1915

Although Rupert Brooke had established himself as a poet before World War I, it was the war and Brooke's early death that fostered his almost legendary fame. A handsome, privileged youth, an accomplished athlete and an intellectual, he attracted a host of influential friends who mourned his loss and celebrated his achievements. Brooke's best poems, filled with striking phrases, are exuberant with delight in the simple pleasures of living.

Brooke first wrote poetry as a child and by his teens was writing seriously. As an adolescent he remarked, "There are three good things in this world. One is to read poetry, another is to write poetry, and the best of all is to *live* poetry." His efforts to "live poetry" resulted in a man Churchill celebrated as "joyous, fearless, versatile . . . ruled by high, undoubting purpose . . . all that one could wish England's noblest sons to be."

Rupert Brooke was born in Rugby, Warwickshire, and educated at the famous public school there, where his father was an assistant master. He graduated from King's College, Cambridge, and studied for a time in Munich, Germany. A long love affair ended unhappily for Brooke, after which he traveled in the United States, Canada, and the South Pacific, making a pilgrimage to the home of Robert Louis Stevenson in Samoa. His poetry at the time echoes that of John Donne and occasionally A. E. Housman.

When war broke out in 1914, Brooke obtained a commission in the Hood Battalion of the Royal Naval Division. "Well, if Armageddon's *on,*" he said at the time, "I suppose one should be there." After participating in the disastrous British expedition to Antwerp, he was ordered to the Dardanelles, where the British hoped to strike a blow against the Turks. He contracted blood poisoning on the way and entered a French military hospital on the Greek island of Skiros in the Aegean Sea. He died there on April 23, St. George's Day.

Brooke's war sonnets, which had appeared a few weeks before his death, gained extraordinary notice in the aftermath. Winston Churchill praised them in the London *Times*. The sonnets, traditional and idealistic, were among the last from the soldier-poets of World War I that expressed an unalloyed patriotism. Brooke had seen little of the trench warfare that so altered the vision of Siegfried Sassoon, Wilfred Owen, and other poets who served in the army.

Impressive as Brooke's poetry is, some of it lacks consistent vision. Contradictions abound. "Impulse was his god," wrote one critic, and it is impossible to speculate on the direction his work might have taken had he survived the war.

# GUIDE FOR INTERPRETING

## The Soldier; The Great Lover

**Writer's Technique**

**The Theme of Patriotism.** Patriotism, the love and loyal support of one's own country, has been a persistent theme in English literature. Shakespeare's lines in *King Richard II* are a stirring patriotic statement: "This royal throne of kings, this sceptered isle . . . This other Eden, demi-paradise . . . This precious stone set in the silver sea . . . This blessed plot, this earth, this realm, this England. . . ." Two centuries later, Sir Walter Scott sounded an equally patriotic note in *The Lay of the Last Minstrel:* "Breathes there the man with soul so dead,/Who never to himself hath said,/This is my own, my native land!" By the time of World War I, Great Britain had reached the height of its power, and Scott's proud boast, "The sun never sets on the immense empire," was the literal truth. At the outbreak of the war, the English were in a buoyantly patriotic mood, and Rupert Brooke's "The Soldier" catches that mood perfectly.

**Writing**

Freewrite about an occasion when you felt extreme pride in your country. The occasion might have been a flag-raising ceremony, the celebration of a national holiday, or a time of international crisis. Describe your feelings of patriotism, explaining what life in the United States meant to you at that moment.

**Primary Source**

In her diary young Vera Brittain recorded the enormous impact of Brooke's poems. One evening a friend "read us, at my request, five sonnets by Rupert Brooke, the most promising poet of the younger generation, who enlisted in the Navy when the war broke out & died at Lemnos a week or two ago—to the great loss & mourning of all modern writers & literature. The sonnets were all sad & moving, in spite of their spirit of courage & hope, & through them all ran a strangely prophetic note, a premonition of early death. I should not have asked her to read them if I had known, they were all so sad that I could scarcely keep back tears from my eyes." Mrs. Leighton, the mother of Vera's fiancé Roland, felt as strongly about Brooke's poems. Writing to her son in battle, Mrs. Leighton said, "I sent you a slip from a paper with a few quotations from the poems of Rupert Brooke. Will you let me have them back when you have read them? Because I cannot do without them, until I get the book. For they are Roland all over. . . . The last line in particular—they were from 'The Soldier,' If I should die, think only this of me'—cut through me with so many knife-stabs with their truth in the matter of likeness to him." Roland was later killed in battle.

# The Soldier

## Rupert Brooke

If I should die, think only this of me:
    That there's some corner of a foreign field
That is forever England. There shall be
    In that rich earth a richer dust concealed;
5  A dust whom England bore, shaped, made aware,
    Gave, once, her flowers to love, her ways to roam,
A body of England's, breathing English air,
    Washed by the rivers, blest by suns of home.

And think, this heart, all evil shed away,
10    A pulse in the eternal mind, no less
      Gives somewhere back the thoughts by England
        given;
Her sights and sounds; dreams happy as her day;
    And laughter, learnt of friends; and gentleness,
      In hearts at peace, under an English heaven.

---

## THINKING ABOUT THE SELECTION

### Recalling

1. How does the speaker ask his readers to remember him if he should die?
2. What are three things that England gave to the speaker?
3. What will the speaker's heart give "somewhere back"?

### Interpreting

4. (a) How does the speaker feel toward England? (b) How idealistic, or realistic, do you think his recollections are?
5. What is the "richer dust" that will be found in a foreign field?
6. The speaker says his heart will become a "pulse in the eternal mind." In your own words, what does he mean?

### Applying

7. How would you define patriotism?

## ANALYZING LITERATURE

### Feeling Patriotism

    **Patriotism** is a deep and abiding love for one's country.

1. Why do you think Brooke's war poems, including "The Soldier," are strongly patriotic while many other poems from World War I, such as "Wirers," avoid patriotic sentiments?
2. A number of young English poets died in World War I. One of them, Charles Sorley, said of Rupert Brooke, "He has clothed his attitude in fine words; but he has taken the sentimental attitude." What is your opinion of this remark?

# The Great Lover

## Rupert Brooke

I have been so great a lover: filled my days
So proudly with the splendor of Love's praise,
The pain, the calm, and the astonishment,
Desire illimitable, and still content,
5   And all dear names men use, to cheat despair,
For the perplexed and viewless streams that bear
Our hearts at random down the dark of life.
Now, ere the unthinking silence on that strife
Steals down, I would cheat drowsy Death so far,
10   My night shall be remembered for a star
That outshone all the suns of all men's days.
Shall I not crown them with immortal praise
Whom I have loved, who have given me, dared with me
High secrets, and in darkness knelt to see
15   The inenarrable godhead of delight?
Love is a flame:—we have beaconed the world's night.
A city:—and we have built it, these and I.
An emperor:—we have taught the world to die.
So, for their sakes I loved, ere I go hence,
20   And the high cause of Love's magnificence,
And to keep loyalties young, I'll write those names
Golden forever, eagles, crying flames,
And set them as a banner, that men may know,
To dare the generations, burn, and blow
25   Out on the wind of Time, shining and streaming. . . .
These I have loved:

            White plates and cups, clean-gleaming,
Ringed with blue lines; and feathery, fairy dust;
Wet roofs, beneath the lamp-light; the strong crust
Of friendly bread; and many-tasting food;

**WHITE CUP AND SAUCER, NO 1016**
*Fantin-Latour*
*Fitzwilliam Museum, Cambridge*

30    Rainbows; and the blue bitter smoke of wood;
      And radiant raindrops couching in cool flowers;
      And flowers themselves, that sway through sunny hours,
      Dreaming of moths that drink them under the moon;
      Then, the cool kindliness of sheets, that soon
35    Smooth away trouble; and the rough male kiss
      Of blankets; grainy wood; live hair that is
      Shining and free; blue-massing clouds; the keen
      Unpassioned beauty of a great machine;
      The benison of hot water; furs to touch;
40    The good smell of old clothes; and others such—
      The comfortable smell of friendly fingers,
      Hair's fragrance, and the musty reek that lingers
      About dead leaves and last year's ferns. . . .
                             Dear names,
      And thousand others throng to me! Royal flames;
45    Sweet water's dimpling laugh from tap or spring;
      Holes in the ground; and voices that do sing;
      Voices in laughter, too; and body's pain,
      Soon turned to peace; and the deep-panting train;
      Firm sands; the little dulling edge of foam
50    That browns and dwindles as the wave goes home;
      And washen stones, gay for an hour; the cold
      Graveness of iron; moist black earthen mold;
      Sleep; and high places; footprints in the dew;
      And oaks; and brown horse-chestnuts, glossy-new;
55    And new-peeled sticks; and shining pools on grass;—
      All these have been my loves. And these shall pass,
      Whatever passes not, in the great hour,
      Nor all my passion, all my prayers, have power
      To hold them with me through the gate of Death.
60    They'll play deserter, turn with the traitor breath,
      Break the high bond we made, and sell Love's trust
      And sacramented covenant to the dust.
      —Oh, never a doubt but, somewhere, I shall wake,
      And give what's left of love again, and make
      New friends, now strangers. . . .
65                    But the best I've known
      Stays here, and changes, breaks, grows old, is blown
      About the winds of the world, and fades from brains
      Of living men, and dies.
                    Nothing remains.

      O dear my loves, O faithless, once again
70    This one last gift I give: that after men
      Shall know, and later lovers, far-removed,
      Praise you, "All these were lovely"; say, "He loved."

## Recalling

1. What does the speaker say he will "crown . . . with immortal praise"?
2. What are the first three items in the speaker's list of things he has loved?
3. What does the speaker say will happen to the things he loves after he is gone?
4. The speaker asks one last favor. What is it?

## Interpreting

5. The title of this poem, "The Great Lover," might lead you to expect a different kind of poem. (a) In what sense is this not a traditional love poem? (b) In what sense is it a love poem?
6. In line 72 the speaker says, "O faithless." Whom or what is he addressing?
7. Who is being quoted in line 75, "All these were lovely"?
8. Walter de la Mare, the poet, said that Rupert Brooke delighted "in things for themselves." (a) How does this poem support that observation? (b) What properties are shared by (or missing from) all the items on Brooke's list?

## Applying

9. If you were compiling a personal list of loves similar to those on Brooke's list, what five items might you add to the ones he includes? Suggest descriptive, image-making words to go with the items—not just "wood smoke," for example, but "the blue bitter smoke of wood."

# CRITICAL THINKING AND READING

## Identifying The Georgian Poets

Rupert Brooke, Siegfried Sassoon, and D. H. Lawrence, despite their artistic differences, are commonly identified with a group called the Georgian poets. The name stems from the fact that the poets were writing early in the reign of King George V of England. The group's anthology, *Georgian Poetry,* first appeared in 1912. Four more volumes, all featuring contemporary poets, were published biennially through 1922.

1. Georgian poetry has been accused of being "pleasant and almost nonpolitical." T. S. Eliot, a contemporary, said that the poets "insist upon the English countryside and are even positively patriotic." How closely do Brooke's two poems fit those two descriptions?
2. The Georgian poets appeared to be a vital new force in 1912. By 1922 they were clinging to "a tender and prettified Nature, to the false solace of dreams." Knowing something of Rupert Brooke's life and times, what do you think caused this rapid decline of Georgian poetry?

# UNDERSTANDING LANGUAGE

## Appreciating Specific Words

Rupert Brooke's choice of words in "The Great Lover" is extraordinarily effective. His words give the reader a vivid mental picture of what he is describing. Rather than merely writing "sheets," for instance (as on a scrawled shopping list), Brooke creates "the cool kindliness of sheets." Those two words—*cool* and *kindliness*—make all the difference. Find ten other specific words in "The Great Lover" that create striking images. (Include entire phrases in your answer, underlining the descriptive word or words. For example: *drowsy* Death.)

# T. S. ELIOT

## 1888–1965

Thomas Stearns Eliot is one of the dominant figures in twentieth-century English literature. A poet, playwright, critic, thinker, and cultural pioneer who changed the consciousness of an entire generation of writers, he emerged in the 1920's as the acknowledged leader of what is now called the Modernist movement. Eliot's work is often difficult to understand, drawing as it does upon a broad range of myth, history, religion, allusion, and symbol. His poems and plays raise fundamental questions about human aspirations and the nature of civilized society.

Eliot has ties to both the United States and Great Britain. Born in St. Louis, Missouri, he was educated at Smith and Milton Academies, Harvard University, the Sorbonne, and Oxford. The outbreak of World War I found Eliot in England, where he remained throughout most of his adult life, eventually acquiring British citizenship. In 1915 he married the sensitive, witty, but highly neurotic Vivienne Haigh-Wood. While writing poetry and critical reviews, Eliot taught school, worked for the banking firm of Lloyd's, and in 1925 took an editorial position with the publishing company that became Faber and Faber.

His earliest work, owing to its unconventional style, was greeted with less than universal acclaim, although the poet Ezra Pound was a vocal supporter from the beginning. Pound saw, as many did not, that Eliot spoke in an authentic new voice and offered an original, if bleak, vision. In *Prufrock and Other Observations* (1917) through *The Waste Land* (1922) and "The Hollow Men" (1925), Eliot pictured the disturbed, fragmented western world wrought by World War I and its aftermath. Then, gradually, came renewed hope through religion, his faith leading him to join the Church of England in 1927. "Journey of the Magi" (1927) and "Ash Wednesday" (1930) mark the new religious phase of his life and writing, capped by his poetic masterpiece, *Four Quartets,* published in 1943, during the dark days of World War II.

As he grew older, Eliot turned his attention increasingly to poetic drama and criticism. Although *Murder in the Cathedral* (1935) and *The Cocktail Party* (1950) are often performed, none of his plays have gained the widespread critical admiration accorded his poetry. As a literary critic, Eliot's influence on his contemporaries was profound. His *Notes Towards the Definition of Culture,* one of many noteworthy critical works, appeared in 1948, the same year in which he received the Nobel Prize for Literature. In 1967, on the second anniversary of Eliot's death, a memorial was unveiled in Poet's Corner, Westminster Abbey.

# GUIDE FOR INTERPRETING

## Writer's Technique

### Preludes; Journey of the Magi

**Synecdoche.** Synecdoche (si nĕk′ də kē) is a figure of speech in which a part stands for the whole, an individual for a class, a material for the thing—or the reverse of any of these. For example, in the sentence, "Give us this day our daily bread," the word *bread* (part) stands for *food* (whole). In the sentence "The thief knew that a loud noise would bring the law," the word *law* (whole) stands for *police officer* (part). As a poetic device, synecdoche can some-times make thought-provoking connections that startle and enlight-en the reader.

**Mood.** Mood is the dominant emotion created by a piece of writing. If the mood of a poem is serious and reflective, the reader, upon finishing it, will in all likelihood be somber and pensive. If, on the other hand, the mood of a poem is light and whimsical, the reader, upon completing it, should be in high spirits and perhaps smiling. Mood must not be confused with either theme or subject matter. For instance, "The Cremation of Sam McGee," a ballad by Robert Service, deals with the death and cremation of a man in the Yukon, but the mood of the ballad is anything but melancholy.

## Writing

Look through a newspaper or magazine for examples of synec-doche. When you have collected ten or more examples, write a brief analysis of the device. In your analysis indicate (a) which kind of synecdoche occurs most often, and (b) why you think the device came into such common use in English.

## Primary Source

Eliot's distinctive style and theme lend themselves very easily to parody; fortunately, he had a sense of humor where such imitations were concerned. "Most parodies of one's own work strike one as very poor," Mr. Eliot writes, "but there is one which deserves the success it has had, Henry Reed's 'Chard Whitlow.'" Judge for yourself from the following excerpt:

Chard Whitlow

(Mr. Eliot's Sunday Evening Postscript)
AS WE GET OLDER we do not get any younger.
Seasons return, and today I am fifty-five,
And this time last year I was fifty-four,
And this time next year I shall be sixty-two.
And I cannot say I should like (to speak for myself)
To see my time over again—if you can call it time:
Fidgeting uneasily under a draughty stair,
Or counting sleepless nights in the crowded tube . . .

# Preludes

## T. S. Eliot

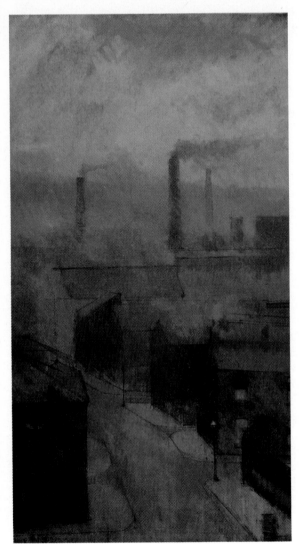

### I

The winter evening settles down
With smell of steaks[1] in passageways.
Six o'clock.
The burnt-out ends of smoky days.
5   And now a gusty shower wraps
The grimy scraps
Of withered leaves about your feet
And newspapers from vacant lots;
The showers beat
10   On broken blinds and chimney-pots,
And at the corner of the street
A lonely cab-horse steams and stamps.
And then the lighting of the lamps.

### II

The morning comes to consciousness
15   Of faint stale smells of beer
From the sawdust-trampled street
With all its muddy feet that press
To early coffee-stands.
With the other masquerades
20   That time resumes,
One thinks of all the hands
That are raising dingy shades
In a thousand furnished rooms.

### III

You tossed a blanket from the bed,
25   You lay upon your back, and waited;
You dozed, and watched the night revealing
The thousand sordid images
Of which your soul was constituted;
They flickered against the ceiling.

---

**1. steaks:** In 1910, when this poem was composed, steaks were inexpensive and were commonly eaten by members of the lower class.

30 And when all the world came back
And the light crept up between the shutters
And you heard the sparrows in the gutters,
You had such a vision of the street
As the street hardly understands;
35 Sitting along the bed's edge, where
You curled the papers from your hair,
Or clasped the yellow soles of feet
In the palms of both soiled hands.

### IV

His soul stretched tight across the skies
40 That fade behind a city block,
Or trampled by insistent feet
At four and five and six o'clock;
And short square fingers stuffing pipes,
And evening newspapers, and eyes
45 Assured of certain certainties,
The conscience of a blackened street
Impatient to assume the world.

I am moved by fancies that are curled
Around these images, and cling:
50 The notion of some infinitely gentle
Infinitely suffering thing.

Wipe your hands across your mouth, and laugh;
The worlds revolve like ancient women
Gathering fuel in vacant lots.

## THINKING ABOUT THE SELECTION

### Recalling

1. In Prelude I what is (a) the time of year? (b) The time of day?
2. In Prelude II what is taking place "in a thousand furnished rooms"?
3. What did "you" hear in Prelude III "when all the world came back"?
4. What are the "ancient women" in the simile doing in Prelude IV?

### Interpreting

5. (a) To what social class do the people in "Preludes" belong? (b) How can you tell?
6. The symbol of cycles, or cyclic progression, says one critic, "is almost Mr. Eliot's trademark." What cycle do you find in "Preludes"?
7. A musical prelude can introduce a longer work or can stand alone. Each of Eliot's four preludes stands alone, but they all project a similar mood. How would you describe that mood?

### Applying

8. "Preludes," written in 1910–11, reflects Eliot's views before the renewal of his religious faith. How might this poem be different if Eliot had written it twenty years later?

## ANALYZING LITERATURE

### Using Synecdoche

**Synecdoche** is a figure of speech in which a part stands for the whole ("Five thousand tongues applauded") or the whole for one of its parts ("Wall Street believes that . . ."). In literature, a synecdoche can enable readers to see an idea or an object in a new light. Sometimes, especially in Eliot's poetry, a synecdoche functions as a symbol. In Prelude II Eliot pictures the crowds of people that hurry to get their morning coffee before going to work. Rather than making such a prosaic statement, however, he uses the synecdoche "muddy feet" (line 17), providing the reader with a more visual and revealing image of the faceless morning bustle in a large city. For each of the following lines from "Preludes," (a) identify the synecdoche; (b) tell what the key word stands for; and (c) comment on how it adds to the mood of the poem.

1. The morning comes to consciousness (l. 14)
2. One thinks of all the hands (l. 21)
3. . . . all the world came back (l. 30)
4. You had such a vision of the street/As the street hardly understands (l. 33–34)
5. . . . and eyes/Assured of certain certainties (l. 44–45)

## SPEAKING AND LISTENING

### Selecting Music That Evokes the Poem

Like much of Eliot's early poetry, "Preludes" implies disenchantment with the twentieth century and reflects a bleak outlook on life. In this respect his poetry has much in common with the music composed in the early twentieth century. Do some library research on modern composers and their music, finding examples of music that expresses a similar disillusionment and seems to complement Eliot's poem. If possible, obtain a tape or tapes of this music to bring to class for listening and discussion.

## THINKING AND WRITING

### Writing a Poem Using Synecdoche

Choose a theme that interests you and write an original poem on it. You may choose any rhyme scheme and any metric pattern you like, and the poem may be of any reasonable length. Think carefully about how you can work two synecdoches into your poem—one using the part for the whole, the other using the whole for the part. Write the poem, using the synecdoches. Even with good planning, you will find that thoughtful revision is essential to a well-written poem.

# Journey of the Magi

## T. S. Eliot

*In this poem, the speaker, one of the three wise men who traveled to Bethlehem to pay homage to the baby Jesus, reflects upon the meaning of his journey.*

"A cold coming we had of it,
Just the worst time of the year
For a journey, and such a long journey:
The ways deep and the weather sharp,
5    The very dead of winter."[1]
And the camels galled, sore-footed, refractory,
Lying down in the melting snow.
There were times we regretted
The summer palaces on slopes, the terraces,
10    And the silken girls bringing sherbet.
Then the camel men cursing and grumbling
And running away, and wanting their liquor and women,
And the night-fires going out, and the lack of shelters,
And the cities hostile and the towns unfriendly
15    And the villages dirty and charging high prices:
A hard time we had of it.
At the end we preferred to travel all night,
Sleeping in snatches,
With the voices singing in our ears, saying
20    That this was all folly.

Then at dawn we came down to a temperate valley,
Wet, below the snow line, smelling of vegetation;
With a running stream and a water-mill beating the
    darkness,
And three trees on the low sky,
25    And an old white horse galloped away in the meadow.
Then we came to a tavern with vine-leaves over the lintel,
Six hands at an open door dicing for pieces of silver,
And feet kicking the empty wine-skins.

---

**1. "A . . . winter.":** Adapted from a part of a sermon delivered by 17th-century Bishop Lancelot Andrews: "A cold coming they had of it at this time of year, just the worst time of the year to take a journey, and specially a long journey in. The ways deep, the weather sharp, the days short, the sun farthest off . . . the very dead of winter."

But there was no information, and so we continued
30 And arrived at evening, not a moment too soon
Finding the place; it was (you may say) satisfactory.

All this was a long time ago, I remember,
And I would do it again, but set down
This set down
35 This: were we led all that way for
Birth or Death? There was a Birth, certainly,
We had evidence and no doubt. I had seen birth and death,
But had thought they were different; this Birth was
Hard and bitter agony for us, like Death, our death.
40 We returned to our places, these Kingdoms,
But no longer at ease here, in the old dispensation,
With an alien people clutching their gods.
I should be glad of another death.

## THINKING ABOUT THE SELECTION

### Recalling

1. What kind of weather did the speaker and his companions have on their journey?
2. What are three other problems they encountered?
3. (a) What did they find when they arrived at the tavern? (b) What did they not find?
4. How had circumstances changed for the speaker and his companions when they returned home?

### Interpreting

5. Why did others, and perhaps the wise men themselves, think that "this was all folly"?
6. Why do you think the speaker uses understatement, including the parenthetical "you may say," in line 31?
7. In lines 33–35 the speaker says, and then repeats, the words "set down this." What do you think is the purpose of the repetition?
8. The last line of the poem is ambiguous; there is no single, agreed-upon meaning for it. What do you think it means?

### Applying

9. In "Journey of the Magi" Eliot retells the story of the wise men traveling to Bethlehem to visit the newborn Jesus. He adds something of his own to the story. What other Biblical stories do you know that Eliot might have treated in a similar way?

## ANALYZING LITERATURE

### Conveying a Mood

The main feeling or atmosphere a piece of writing conveys is its **mood.** Mood is independent of content and theme, since the same story can be presented in various moods. Indeed, Eliot's "Journey of the Magi" has a different mood from the biblical story on which it is based. Read the original story (Matthew 2: 1–12).

1. How does the mood of Eliot's poem differ from the mood of the biblical story?
2. "Journey of the Magi" was published in 1927. How is the ending of the poem consistent with Eliot's views following his renewal of religious faith in the late 1920's?

# THINKING AND WRITING

## Analyzing Eliot's Use of Ambiguity

Although Eliot's poetry was viewed by his contemporaries as a break from tradition, Eliot maintained, as do critics today, that it is steeped in tradition. The continuing challenge of his poems lies in their many layers of meaning and their seeming lack of connectedness. This intentional complexity grows out of Eliot's deep learning, his conscious use of the literature of the past, and a belief that serious themes demand the "logic of the imagination."

**Ambiguity** means having the potential for being understood in two or more ways. Once when a magazine editor wished to find out movie actor Cary Grant's age, he sent Grant's agent a telegram: "How old Cary Grant?" The telegraphic response came back: "Old Cary Grant fine." Poets often use ambiguity intentionally and quite seriously, as Eliot does in the last line of "Journey of the Magi." If your class has discussed question 8, you already have some idea of the different possible interpretations of that line. If not, think about them now. There are at least three reasonable and entirely different interpretations. Jot them down—and any others you can think of—before beginning to write. Then write a brief analytical essay in which you state these interpretations and comment on them. Indicate which one or more you think Eliot intended. Give your reasons. Before handing in the final draft of your paper, read it over carefully for logic. Refer to the poem, making sure that what you say is defensible in the context of what Eliot has written.

---

## Primary Source

In Eliot's time as now, it was hard to make an adequate living as a writer, especially of poetry. Many influential poets toiled in unrelated jobs, writing in their free time. Eliot wrote what is likely the representative poem of the first half of the century, "The Waste-Land" (1921), while handling foreign exchanges for Lloyd's Bank. But then as now, society's expectations often clash with literature's calling, and many found it difficult to see why Eliot would prefer writing poetry to advancing in the bank. Critic I. A. Richards had this conversation with just such a man, one of Eliot's superiors in the bank:

*Mr. W.:* "You know him, I suppose, as a literary man, as a writer and . . . er . . . and . . . er . . . as a poet? Tell me, if you will—you won't mind my asking, will you? Tell me, is he, in your judgment, would you say, would you call him a good poet?"

*Richards:* "Well, in my judgment—not everyone would agree, of course, far from it—he *is* a good poet."

*Mr. W:* "Many of my colleagues . . . think a banker has no business whatever to be a poet. . . . But I believe that anything a man does, whatever his *hobby* may be, it's all the better if he is really keen on it and does it well. I think it helps him with his work. If you see our young friend, you might tell him that we think he's doing quite well at the bank. In fact, if he goes on as he has been doing, I don't see why—in time, of course, in time—he mightn't even become a bank manager."

# GUIDE FOR INTERPRETING

## The Hollow Men

**Writer's Technique**

**Tone.** A speaker uses a certain tone in communicating a message to his or her audience. A writer does much the same thing, but a writer—lacking pitch, stress, and other features of spoken language—must rely on the choice of details, words, and syntax to convey tone. In poetry, tone reveals a great deal about the writer's attitude toward the subject. In fact, identifying the tone of a poem is vital to a full understanding of the poem's meaning.

**Writing**

Find a short letter to the editor in your local newspaper that is written in a tone that is easy to recognize and describe. Ordinarily you can describe tone with a single word—*outraged,* perhaps, or *reasonable,* or *amused.* Then rewrite the letter in an entirely different tone. If the tone is outraged, make it sweet and pleasant. If the tone is amused, make it bitter and angry.

**Primary Source**

The tone of a poem such as "The Hollow Men" makes T. S. Eliot seem very stern and removed from the concerns and cares of daily life. His wide learning and brilliant publications—combined with his deep religious faith—made him seem even more unapproachable and intimidating. But Dylan Thomas's friend Roy Campbell recalls an encounter with Eliot (whom they had nicknamed the "Archbishop") that shows a very different side to his character:

> Dylan Thomas had failed his medical test for the army, and he and Caitlin [Thomas's wife] were broke. My three pounds a week did not carry far: so one day Dylan and I decided to go on a borrowing raid. "But you must stay outside, Roy," he said. "We'll never raise a penny if they see you with me, except in the case of so-and-so and so-and-so." Dylan proposed to make a vast tour . . . of all the newly rich poets in their new offices in the Central Office of Information and the Ministry of Information. . . . But we raised no cash. Dylan said that it had been the same in every office where he had been without me. We stood outside the M.O.I. scratching our heads. "What about His Grace?" I asked, "He lives around there." "You mean the Archbishop?" gasped Dylan, "I wouldn't dare."—"Come on, you'll see. He's not only a saint in his poems, he's a bloody saint in his life too." We went to see Eliot, and the great man helped us so lavishly that it lasted till by some curious coincidence we both got our first considerable radio jobs, almost simultaneously, and were able to pay Elliot back. (Dylan never forgot his kindness. Neither do I.)

# The Hollow Men

'T. S. Eliot

*Mistah Kurtz*[1]*—he dead.*

*A penny for the Old Guy*[2]

### I

We are the hollow men
We are the stuffed men
Leaning together
Headpiece filled with straw. Alas!
5  Our dried voices, when
We whisper together
Are quiet and meaningless
As wind in dry grass
Or rats' feet over broken glass
10  In our dry cellar

Shape without form, shade without color,
Paralyzed force, gesture without motion;

Those who have crossed
With direct eyes, to death's other Kingdom[3]
15  Remember us—if at all—not as lost
Violent souls, but only
As the hollow men
The stuffed men.

---

**1. Mistah Kurtz:** A character in Joseph Conrad's *Heart of Darkness*
who travels to Africa hoping to improve the lives of the natives, but
finds that, instead, he is corrupted by the worst elements of native life.
Horrified by what he had become, Kurtz dies in the jungle.

**2. A . . . Guy:** A traditional cry used by children on Guy Fawkes Day.
Guy Fawkes (1570–1606) was executed for participating in a plot to
blow up the king and both Houses of Parliament in 1605. Each year
on November 5, children beg for pennies to buy firecrackers which
they use to destroy stuffed dummies representing Fawkes.

**3. Those . . . Kingdom:** An allusion to Dante's *Paradiso*, in which
those "with direct eyes" are blessed by God in Heaven.

## II

Eyes I dare not meet in dreams
20  In death's dream kingdom
These do not appear:
There, the eyes are
Sunlight on a broken column
There, is a tree swinging
25  And voices are
In the wind's singing
More distant and more solemn
Than a fading star.

Let me be no nearer
30  In death's dream kingdom
Let me also wear
Such deliberate disguises
Rat's coat, crowskin, crossed staves
In a field[4]
35  Behaving as the wind behaves
No nearer—

Not that final meeting
In the twilight kingdom

## III

This is the dead land
40  This is cactus land
Here the stone images
Are raised, here they receive
The supplication of a dead man's hand
Under the twinkle of a fading star.

45  Is it like this
In death's other kingdom
Waking alone
At the hour when we are
Trembling with tenderness
50  Lips that would kiss
Form prayers to broken stone.

---

**4. crossed . . . field:** Scarecrows.

**IV**

The eyes are not here
There are no eyes here
In this valley of dying stars
55   In this hollow valley
This broken jaw of our lost kingdoms

In this last of meeting places
We grope together
And avoid speech
60   Gathered on this beach of the tumid river[5]

Sightless, unless
The eyes reappear
As the perpetual star[6]
Multifoliate rose[7]
65   Of death's twilight kingdom
The hope only
Of empty men.

**V**

*Here we go round the prickly pear*
*Prickly pear prickly pear*
70   *Here we go round the prickly pear*
*At five o'clock in the morning.*[8]

Between the idea
And the reality
Between the motion
75   And the act[9]
Falls the Shadow

*For Thine is the Kingdom*[10]

---

  **5. river:** From Dante's *Inferno*, the river Archeron, the river which
the dead cross over as they pass into Hell.
  **6. star:** A traditional symbol for Christ.
  **7. Multifoliate rose:** In Dante's *Paradiso*, Paradise was described as
a "multifoliate rose," or a rose with many leaves. Also, the rose is a
traditional symbol for the Virgin Mary.
  **8. Here . . . morning:** Adaptation of a common nursery rhyme. A
prickly pear is a cactus.
  **9. Between . . . act:** A reference to *Julius Caesar*, Act II, Scene i,
63–65: "Between the acting of a dreadful thing/And the first motion,
all the interim is/Like a phantasma or hideous dream."
  **10. For . . . Kingdom:** From the ending of the Lord's Prayer.

Between the conception
And the creation
80 Between the emotion
And the response
Falls the Shadow

*Life is very long*[11]

Between the desire
85 And the spasm
Between the potency
And the existence
Between the essence
And the descent
90 Falls the Shadow

*For Thine is the Kingdom*

For Thine is
Life is
For Thine is the

95 *This is the way the world ends*
*This is the way the world ends*
*This is the way the world ends*
*Not with a bang but a whimper.*

---

**11. Life . . . long:** Quotation from Joseph Conrad's *An Outcast of the Islands.*

## THINKING ABOUT THE SELECTION

### Recalling

1. How does the speaker say that he and others like him are remembered by those "with direct eyes"?
2. In "death's dream kingdom" what disguise will the speaker wear?
3. What do the hollow men do in the "hollow valley . . . this last of meeting places"?
4. What is it that forever falls between idea and achievement, preventing the hollow men from accomplishing anything?
5. According to the speaker, how does the world end?

### Interpreting

6. Although Kurtz was a "hollow sham" and Guy Fawkes was a traitor, the speaker suggests that they were superior to the hollow men. Why were they superior?
7. What aspects of modern life might the "stone images" in part III represent?
8. Both part III and part V suggest a particular kind of landscape in which the hollow men exist. What kind of landscape is it?
9. What do you think "the Shadow" is in part V?

### Applying

10. In "The Hollow Men," published in 1925, Eliot presents a bleak picture of his generation. To what extent, if at all, do you think his implied criticism applies to the people of today?

## ANALYZING LITERATURE

### Conveying Tone

The **tone** of a poem reveals the writer's attitude toward the subject or theme. Tone is conveyed through details and images—hollow men stuffed with straw, a cactus land, a twilight kingdom. It is also carried by words and their connotations—*hollow, meaningless, fading, death, Shadow, whimper*. Syntax, the way in which words are put together, plays a part, too—"Shape without form, shade without color"

(parallelism); "The hope only/Of empty men" (ambiguity). How would you describe the tone of "The Hollow Men"? (One adjective can usually describe tone, but since Eliot's poem is more complex than most, you may find it necessary to go into greater detail.)

## CRITICAL THINKING AND READING

### Interpreting Allusions

An **allusion** in literature is a brief, often indirect reference to a person, a place, an event, or another literary work. "The Hollow Men" is a poem rich in allusions. Choose any three of the following allusions from "The Hollow Men." Explain each one. Tell how the allusion adds meaning to the poem by introducing, as a kind of literary shorthand, a number of associations through the use of only a few words. Try to go somewhat beyond the footnote text.

1. *Mistah Kurtz—he dead.*
2. Those who have crossed/With direct eyes, to death's other Kingdom
3. As the perpetual star/Multifoliate rose
4. Between the motion/And the act
5. *For Thine is the Kingdom*

## THINKING AND WRITING

### Writing About Tone

Write an essay in which you analyze the tone of T. S. Eliot's poetry. Describe the tone of each of the three Eliot poems in this unit and explain how the tone adds to the meaning of each one. Use quotations from the poems to illustrate and support your points. Follow the three basic steps in the writing process. In prewriting, take notes and make a rough outline. Then write your first draft, using appropriate quotations. In revising, make any major changes that are needed —structural, logical, organizational—as well as checking your grammar and usage. Finally, make any needed proofreading corrections.

# ROBERT GRAVES

## 1895–1985

Robert Graves has written successfully in almost every literary form, but he is perhaps best known as the author of the best-selling novel *I, Claudius* (1934), which was made into an outstanding BBC television series a few years ago. Graves achieved his first fame in 1929 with a classic memoir of World War I, *Good-bye to All That.* Despite his prose efforts, however, Graves's true calling is poetry, as he has said. Ever since his first two volumes appeared in 1916, he has been recognized as a major British poet.

The son of a prominent poet, Robert Graves grew up in a London household with an extensive private library, which provided much of his early education. World War I began while he was attending the Charterhouse School and producing his earliest poems. Graves enlisted in the Royal Welsh Fusiliers, the same outfit to which Siegfried Sassoon belonged. Fighting in the trenches, he was severely wounded and reported dead. He later suffered shell shock and received a medical discharge. Graves, like Sassoon, lost all illusions about the glory of war, as shown by his two wartime poetry collections, *Over the Brazier* (1916) and *Fairies and Fusiliers* (1917).

Graves studied at Oxford, received his degree, and in 1927 took a teaching position at the Royal Egyptian University in Cairo. For a number of years he collaborated with the American poet Laura Riding on many writing and publishing projects. In 1929 he and Riding settled in Majorca, an island off the coast of Spain, where he remained except for intervals during the Spanish Civil War, World War II, and a teaching stint at Oxford in the 1960's.

A respected scholar and critic, Graves aroused controversy in 1948 with the publication of *The White Goddess,* a critical study of the origin, value, and history of poetry, whose main thesis—the dominance of a mythic female Muse—is impressively argued but widely questioned. Its influence on Graves's poetry, however, has been substantial and beneficial. His poems, a blend of traditional and modern, sometimes exhibit a deceptive simplicity. According to the American poet Richard Wilbur, they "have the air of being spontaneous answers to actual experience."

Graves refused to seek praise, for fame would make him hostage to public opinion. A poet who writes for others has forsaken his honor, which "consists in his not forming ties that can impair critical independence, or prevent him from telling the whole truth about anything, or force him to do anything out of character." Yet in his independence Graves achieved immortality.

# GUIDE FOR INTERPRETING

## Interruption; One Hard Look; She Tells Her Love While Half Asleep

**Period Trends**

**The Modernist Movement.** The Modernist movement, or Modernism, followed World War I. Art, architecture, dance, and literature —all were in revolt against the rigid traditional forms of earlier periods. Disillusioned by the war and unhappy with the postwar world, artists sought new forms, new techniques, new subjects. It was a time of ferment. The Modernist writers, like the Georgian poets, demanded a break with the past, but the Modernists were much more radical than the Georgians. The aftermath of war, which doomed the pastoral-minded Georgians, spurred the Modernists to action. Many poets who began as Georgians—D. H. Lawrence, Siegfried Sassoon, Robert Graves—changed and grew. In the 1920's T. S. Eliot in England, James Joyce in Ireland, and E. E. Cummings in the United States experimented in ways that earlier generations would have found incomprehensible.

**Commentary**

What is the difference between "major" and "minor" achievements —especially in a field as personal as literature? George Stade judges Graves to be "a minor poet of major proportions." Stade claims that Graves has deliberately chosen to be a minor poet, citing as support Graves's remark: "Minor poetry, so called to differentiate it from major, is the real stuff." But a great many others claim that he is indeed a major poet. Stade, for one, declares that Graves is "the most important poet writing in English and the best model for young poets seeking to establish a new tradition or recover the native one." To Stade, Graves's steadfast refusal to be "major" establishes much of what is unique and valuable about his career. As another critic, Daniel Hoffman, has remarked, "In prose as well as poetry, Graves was an original."

**Writing**

Choose an everyday object to write about. Set an alarm to go off at the end of five minutes. Then, on a sheet of paper, begin writing nonstop, putting down any thoughts or associations that come to mind in regard to your subject. You need not write full sentences, but try to keep your pen or pencil in motion until the alarm sounds. When your time is up, read over your random jottings. Select the most interesting of them and share them with your classmates.

# Interruption

**Robert Graves**

If ever against this easy blue and silver
Hazed-over countryside of thoughtfulness,
Far behind in the mind and above,
Boots from before and below approach trampling,
5   Watch how their premonition will display
A forward countryside, low in the distance—
A picture-postcard square of June grass;
Will warm a summer season, trim the hedges,
Cast the river about on either flank,
10  Start the late cuckoo emptily calling,
Invent a rambling tale of moles and voles,
Furnish a path with stiles.
Watch how the field will broaden, the feet nearing,
Sprout with great dandelions and buttercups,
15  Widen and heighten. The blue and silver
Fogs at the border of this all-grass.
Interruption looms gigantified,
Lurches against, treads thundering through,
Blots the landscape, scatters all,
20  Roars and rumbles like a dark tunnel,
Is gone.
       The picture-postcard grass and trees
Swim back to central: it is a large patch,
It is a modest, failing patch of green,
25  The postage stamp of its departure,
Clouded with blue and silver, closing in now
To a plain countryside of less and less,
Unpeopled and unfeatured blue and silver,
Before, behind, above.

**SUN, WIND, AND RAIN**
*David Cox*
The City Museum and Art Gallery, Birmingham

## THINKING ABOUT THE SELECTION

### Recalling

1. (a) Where does the interruption occur? (b) What time of year is it?
2. With what does the field sprout when the feet near it?
3. What is the sound of the interruption at its height?
4. When the interruption is over, how is the "blue and silver" countryside described?

### Interpreting

5. (a) What is the interruption? (b) What is the first indication of the nature of the interruption?

6. Why do you think the interruption is described as being "all-grass"?
7. Why do you think the poet chose to break line 21 abruptly?
8. The meaning of "Interruption" is not expressed in a series of logically ordered sentences. How is it expressed?

### Applying

9. Short stories sometimes have an interruption as their main plot device. (a) What short story do you know that uses this device? (b) What is the nature of the interruption? (c) What precedes and follows the interruption?

# One Hard Look

## Robert Graves

Small gnats that fly
In hot July
And lodge in sleeping ears,
Can rouse therein
5  A trumpet's din
With Day of Judgment fears.

Small mice at night
Can wake more fright
Than lions at midday;
10  A straw will crack
The camel's back—
There is no easier way.

One smile relieves
A heart that grieves
15  Though deadly sad it be,
And one hard look
Can close the book
That lovers love to see.

---

## THINKING ABOUT THE SELECTION

### Recalling

1. What does the buzz of a gnat sound like in the ear of a sleeper?
2. What can one hard look do?

### Interpreting

3. What is the common characteristic of gnats, mice, and straw that contribute to the meaning of the poem?
4. What main observation does the poem make?

### Applying

5. (a) Do you agree with Graves's observation? (b) What experience have you had that supports or casts doubt on what he says?

# She Tells Her Love While Half Asleep

Robert Graves

She tells her love while half asleep,
   In the dark hours,
     With half-words whispered low:
As Earth stirs in her winter sleep
5      And puts out grass and flowers
      Despite the snow,
      Despite the falling snow.

---

## THINKING ABOUT THE SELECTION

### Recalling

1. What is the time of day in the poem?
2. "Despite the falling snow," what does the earth do?

### Interpreting

3. To what in nature are the "half-words whispered low" compared?
4. What might falling snow represent metaphorically in the relationship between the speaker and the one who "tells her love"?

### Applying

5. The flowers of spring are probably the most widely used symbol of rebirth. Why do you think this is so?

## THINKING AND WRITING

### Writing About the Modernist Movement

The modernist movement began and peaked in the 1920's. To understand the movement, you need a general understanding of that tumultuous decade. You also should know the works of a few of the major writers—T. S. Eliot, Robert Graves, James Joyce, and Virginia Woolf. Do some library research on the modernism of the Twenties. Take notes, particularly on the changes in style that modernism introduced.

Write an essay in which you explain why writers and other artists in that decade felt compelled to strike out in new directions. Include quotations from the sources you have used. When you revise your first draft, check to make sure you have introduced and punctuated the quotations properly.

# W. H. AUDEN

## 1907–1977

Much as T. S. Eliot became established as the poetic voice of the 1920's, so W. H. Auden emerged as the poetic voice of the 1930's. Born in York, England, Auden moved to the United States at the age of thirty-two and took out citizenship papers, reversing the odyssey of Eliot, who was born in St. Louis, Missouri, and became a British subject. The youthful Auden was greatly influenced by Eliot's *The Waste Land,* but in later life both men replaced their anger and despair with a staunch Christian faith. Versatility, wit, and dazzling technique characterize Auden's poetry.

Wystan Hugh Auden, the son of a doctor, was interested in science as a child and planned to become an engineer. He received his education at St. Edmund's School and Gresham's School, and later attended Oxford University. His first appearance in print was in *Oxford Poetry,* a series of annual collections of verse by the university's undergraduates. The volumes in which his poems appear—1926, 1927, and 1928—also contain poems by Stephen Spender, C. Day Lewis, and Louis MacNeice, all of whom became important poets.

Auden's first published collection, entitled simply *Poems,* appeared in 1930. These poems, innovative and eloquent, struck many readers of the day as strange, even impenetrable. His second volume, *On This Island,* published in 1937, is more down-to-earth and generated greater enthusiasm. He was awarded the King's Poetry Medal that year. In 1939 Auden left England for the United States, where he taught in a number of universities while continuing to write. He became an American citizen in 1946, and his poetry collection, *The Age of Anxiety,* won a Pulitzer Prize in 1948. In 1956, having been elected Professor of Poetry at Oxford University, he returned to England where he remained through 1961.

Auden was a more prolific poet than Eliot, and his output is remarkable for its variety, originality, and craftsmanship. He writes equally well in the current idiom of the street or in the archaic measures of *Beowulf,* in the sing-song manner of a traditional ballad or in the formal cadences of an elegy. He has been called "the most provocative as well as the most unpredictable poet of his generation." With Yeats and Eliot, he shares honors as the most significant British poet of the first half of the twentieth century.

# GUIDE FOR INTERPRETING

## In Memory of W. B. Yeats; Musée des Beaux Arts

**Writer's Technique**

**Elegy and Figurative Language.** An elegy is a poem of mourning for the dead. The great Greek and Latin elegies, forerunners of elegies in English, were written in distichs. A *distich* is a pair of rhyming lines considered as a unit. The third part of W. H. Auden's "In Memory of W. B. Yeats" is composed of distichs, or couplets, similar to those in a classical elegy. Elegies sum up, often in heroic terms, the lifetime accomplishments of an individual, or, as in Gray's "Elegy Written in a Country Churchyard," a group of people. Elegies frequently make use of figurative language; that is, language rich in figures of speech such as simile, metaphor, and personification. An elegy may also contain literary devices such as paradox and allusion.

**Commentary**

One of Auden's friends has remarked that Auden thinks of himself as "a giant personal enterprise—Auden, Auden, Auden, and Company." The remark is fitting, for it suggests that the poet is made up of many different sides, bounded by contrast and intricacy. Early poems such as "Musée des Beaus Arts" (1938) and "In Memory of W. B. Yeats" (1939) are deeply serious explorations of the nature and function of poetry and the artist's special role in society. Later poems, in contrast, are lighter in tone. They often use surprising, comic touches to probe the place of art in the world and eternity. Auden's discussion of the role of art and the artist in *Secondary Worlds*, a series of lectures he delivered in 1967, serves to reaffirm what he created thirty years earlier in "Musée des Beaux Arts," and "In Memory of W. B. Yeats," as well as in much of his later work. "To believe in the value of art," he wrote, "is to believe that it is possible to make an object, be it an epic or a two-line epigram, which will remain permanently on hand in the world." This function of art, Auden emphasizes, is the opposite of much of the work of the world, which is to make things designed to be obsolete. To Auden, then, a work of art can give us the moral and intellectual nourishment we need to survive. What role do you think art serves in today's world?

**Writing**

Think of a person, living or dead, whom you greatly admire. This person can be either someone you know (or knew) firsthand or someone famous. Write a few memorial lines for the person, using a figure of speech in each of the lines. Try to use at least one simile, one metaphor, and one personification.

# In Memory of W. B. Yeats

W. H. Auden

**1**

He disappeared in the dead of winter:
The brooks were frozen, the airports almost deserted,
And snow disfigured the public statues;
The mercury sank in the mouth of the dying day.
5   O all the instruments agree
The day of his death was a dark cold day.

Far from his illness
The wolves ran on through the evergreen forests,
The peasant river was untempted by fashionable quays;[1]
10   By mourning tongues
The death of the poet was kept from his poems.

But for him it was his last afternoon as himself,
An afternoon of nurses and rumors;
The provinces of his body revolted,
15   The squares of his mind were empty,
Silence invaded the suburbs,
The current of his feeling failed: he became his admirers.

Now he is scattered among a hundred cities
And wholly given over to unfamiliar affections;
20   To find his happiness in another kind of wood
And be punished by another code of conscience.
The words of a dead man
Are modified in the guts of the living.

But in the importance and noise of tomorrow
25   When the brokers are roaring like beasts on the floor of the
        Bourse,[2]
And the poor have the sufferings to which they are fairly
        accustomed,

---

1. **quays** (kēz): Wharfs with facilities for loading or unloading ships.
2. **Bourse** (bo͞ ors): The Paris Stock Exchange.

And each in the cell of himself is almost convinced of his
    freedom;
A few thousand will think of this day
As one thinks of a day when one did something slightly
    unusual.

30    O all the instruments agree
    The day of his death was a dark cold day.

## 2

You were silly like us: your gift survived it all;
The parish of rich women, physical decay,
Yourself; mad Ireland hurt you into poetry.
35    Now Ireland has her madness and her weather still,
For poetry makes nothing happen: it survives
In the valley of its saying where executives
Would never want to tamper; it flows south
From ranches of isolation and the busy griefs,
40    Raw towns that we believe and die in; it survives,
A way of happening, a mouth.

## 3

Earth, receive an honored guest;
William Yeats is laid to rest:
Let the Irish vessel lie
45    Emptied of its poetry.

Time that is intolerant
Of the brave and innocent,
And indifferent in a week
To a beautiful physique,

50    Worships language and forgives
Everyone by whom it lives;
Pardons cowardice, conceit
Lays its honors at their feet.

Time with this strange excuse
55    Pardoned Kipling and his views,[3]

---

**3. Kipling . . . views:** English writer Rudyard Kipling (1865–1936)
was a supporter of imperialism.

And will pardon Paul Claudel,[4]
Pardons him for writing well.

In the nightmare of the dark
All the dogs of Europe bark,
60  And the living nations wait,
Each sequestered in its hate;

Intellectual disgrace
Stares from every human face,
And the seas of pity lie
65  Locked and frozen in each eye.

Follow, poet, follow right
To the bottom of the night,
With your unconstraining voice
Still persuade us to rejoice;

70  With the farming of a verse
Make a vineyard of the curse,
Sing of human unsuccess
In a rapture of distress;

In the deserts of the heart
75  Let the healing fountain start,
In the prison of his days
Teach the free man how to praise.

---

**4. pardon Paul Claudel** (klō del'): French poet, dramatist, and
diplomat. Paul Claudel (1868–1955) had antidemocratic political
views, which Yeats at times shared.

---

## THINKING ABOUT THE SELECTION

### Recalling

1. What two things were present on Yeats's last afternoon "as himself"?
2. How many people are likely to remember Yeats's death the next day?
3. What was it that "hurt" Yeats into writing poetry?
4. According to the third section of the poem, to whom is time (a) intolerant? (b) indifferent?
5. What does the speaker ask the poet to teach free men?

### Interpreting

6. Twice in the first section, the speaker uses the words "all the instruments agree." What instruments might he mean (a) in a literal

sense? (b) in a metaphorical sense?

7. What do you think the poet means by stating in line 18 that Yeats is now "scattered among a hundred cities"?

8. Whom is the speaker addressing in (a) the second section? (b) the third section?

9. (a) How favorably or unfavorably does the speaker view the situation in Europe? (b) How does he think the poet should react to it? Find evidence to support your answer.

## Applying

10. This poem is an elegy to William Butler Yeats. Yet, in a sense, it could be addressed to any poet, for Auden sets down the responsibilities and rewards he thinks belong to the poet. What are these responsibilities and rewards?

## ANALYZING LITERATURE
### Understanding Elegy

An **elegy** is a poem that pays tribute to a person (or, less commonly, more than one person) who has died. Throughout history elegies have been written to immortalize people who, at least in the eyes of the poet, have achieved greatness. Most elegies contain imaginative comparisons—figures of speech such as simile, metaphor, and personification. W. H. Auden uses all three of these kinds of figurative language in "In Memory of W. B. Yeats." Write the line or lines of the poem in which each of the following occurs.

1. Personification in which a day coming to an end is said to display a facial feature,
2. Personification of a body of water as being susceptible to temptation,
3. Metaphor that compares body and mind to geographic areas,
4. Simile in which certain professional people are compared to wild animals,
5. Simile that compares thinking about the death of a great man with thinking about doing something unusual,

6. Personification where something inanimate and abstract has the power to worship and pardon,
7. Metaphor that relates something bad to a place where grapes are grown.

## CRITICAL THINKING AND READING
### Understanding the Legacy of an Artist

"In Memory of W. B. Yeats" is a poet's tribute not to a lost friend but to a fellow poet. Auden never knew Yeats personally, but he knew of him by reading his poetry. Most poets, as you might suppose, read poetry as well as write it. They are aware of the classics and trends. Poetry —indeed, all literature—is part of an ever-expanding archive, one in which, as in the National Archives, "the past is prologue." Auden, in his elegy, is responding to the loss he believes the world should feel at the loss of a great artist. Yet he is also aware, as the poem makes clear, that while Yeats himself is gone, the poetry of Yeats lives on.

1. What does Auden mean in line 11, "The death of the poet was kept from his poems"?
2. In the third section of the poem, what evidence is there that Auden is mourning the passing of an artist more than the passing of Yeats the man?

## THINKING AND WRITING
### Writing About a Paradox

In line 36 Auden observes that "poetry makes nothing happen." But in the next section of the poem he beseeches the poet (any poet) to use his or her gift to lead the human race out of the darkness of hatred. How, you may ask, is it possible for a poet to accomplish this monumental task if "poetry makes nothing happen"? In an essay explain how you might get around this apparent contradiction—this paradox—by drawing upon other insights from the poem. When you revise make sure your essay is well organized and that you have provided adequate support for your thesis.

# Musée des Beaux Arts[1]

W. H. Auden

About suffering they were never wrong,
The Old Masters: how well they understood
Its human position; how it takes place
While someone else is eating or opening a window or just
    walking dully along;
5  How, when the aged are reverently, passionately waiting
For the miraculous birth, there always must be
Children who did not specially want it to happen, skating
On a pond at the edge of the wood:
They never forgot
10  That even the dreadful martyrdom must run its course
Anyhow in a corner, some untidy spot
Where the dogs go on with their doggy life and the
    torturer's horse
Scratches its innocent behind on a tree.

In Brueghel's *Icarus*,[2] for instance: how everything turns
    away
15  Quite leisurely from the disaster; the ploughman may
Have heard the splash, the forsaken cry,
But for him it was not an important failure; the sun shone
As it had to on the white legs disappearing into the green
Water; and the expensive delicate ship that must have seen
20  Something amazing, a boy falling out of the sky,
Had somewhere to get to and sailed calmly on.

--------

**1. Musée des Beaux Arts:** The Museum of Fine Arts in Brussels,
Belgium.
**2. Brueghel's** (brōo′ gəlz) ***Icarus*** (ik′ ə rəs): *The Fall of Icarus*, a
painting by Flemish painter Pieter Brueghel (1522?–1599).

**THE FALL OF ICARUS**
*Pieter Bruegel*
*Musées Royaux des Beaux-Arts de Belgique*

## THINKING ABOUT THE SELECTION

### Recalling

1. (a) What do the Old Masters show "someone else" doing while suffering occurs? (b) According to the speaker, what do the Old Masters understand about martyrdom?
2. (a) How does the ploughman react to the disaster in the Brueghel painting, *Icarus*? (b) How does the ship respond?

### Interpreting

3. What do you think Auden intends the activities in line 4 to represent?
4. What is your understanding of the "miracu-lous birth" the aged are awaiting?

5. Icarus is a figure in Greek mythology who flies with artificial wings. Coming too close to the sun, the wax of his wings melts, and he falls into the sea and drowns. (a) What does Brueghel mean to imply by calling his painting *Icarus* but showing only Icarus's disappearing legs in the corner of the picture? (b) How closely does Auden's poem adhere to the same theme?

### Applying

6. The poem describes an age-old irony. (a) In your own words, what is this irony? (b) What are some examples of it that exist today?

# LOUIS MACNEICE

## 1907–1963

Four members of the "Auden group" at Oxford went on to achieve an honored place in English literature: Auden himself, C. Day Lewis, Stephen Spender, and Louis MacNeice. Of these, MacNeice was generally regarded as the junior member, not because of age but rather because he lacked the artistic certainty and political commitments of the others. A lyric and reflective poet of distinction, he was always modest about the aims of poetry, doubting that poetry could truly change the world. MacNeice's reputation has risen steadily over the years, and today many consider him second only to Auden among the poets of his generation.

MacNeice, the son of a Protestant clergyman, was born in Belfast, Northern Ireland. Surrounded by books as a child, he began to write poetry at the age of seven. By the time he went to Merton College, Oxford, he was familiar with the works of T. S. Eliot and other modern poets. MacNeice's first collection of poems, *Blind Fireworks,* appeared in 1929, while he was still an undergraduate. *Poems,* the collection that established his reputation, came out six years later.

A teacher during the 1930's, MacNeice lectured in Classics at the University of Birmingham from 1930 to 1936 and in Greek at Bedford College for Women from 1936 to 1940. As a writer, he tried his hand at various genres, including drama, but his lasting achievements are in poetry. One of his notable books from the late 1930's, *Letters from Iceland* (1937), co-authored by W. H. Auden, is an unusual travel book in which the poetry outweighs the prose.

In 1941 MacNeice joined the British Broadcasting Company as a feature writer and producer. Among his radio credits are two powerful BBC plays, *Christopher Columbus* (1944) and *The Dark Tower* (1947). He wrote *The Poetry of W. B. Yeats* (1941), a critical summary of that author's work, and produced a number of excellent translations, including Aeschylus' *Agamemnon* and Goethe's *Faust.* MacNeice died in London in 1963 while he was working on his autobiography.

MacNeice's poetry, usually dealing with contemporary life, is restrained and precise, with overtones of melancholy. It is the poetry of a man who, as the poet Edwin Muir put it, "is never swept off his feet."

# GUIDE FOR INTERPRETING

## The Sunlight on the Garden;
## Sunday Morning

**Scansion.** Scansion is the analysis of lines of poetry according to their patterns of rhythm. The key to scansion is meter. Meter is a recurring pattern of stressed and unstressed syllables in poetry. Meter is to poetry approximately what beat is to music. In scansion, stressed syllables are marked with a /; unstressed syllables are marked with a ∪. Each group of syllables makes up a foot. Feet are marked off with a |. In scansion, do not expect to find perfectly regular patterns repeated over and over. After you have identified a metrical foot, look for and expect to find irregularities or breaks from the pattern.

Choose four lines from any poem that appears earlier in this book. First, mark all the syllables in the lines as either stressed or unstressed. To do this, say the lines aloud. Next, find the pattern of stress that predominates. There are four common patterns:

1. Unstressed/stressed (iambic)
2. Stressed/unstressed (trochaic)
3. Stressed/unstressed/unstressed (dactylic)
4. Unstressed/unstressed/stressed (anapaestic)

Finally, put in the vertical bars that show the end of one foot and the beginning of another. Notice that a vertical bar may divide a word rather than going between two words, as in the line below from a poem by William Wordsworth.

```
 ∪   /  ∪ /  ∪  /  ∪  / ∪   /
With sac|rifice|before|the ris|ing morn
```

MacNeice's 1938 book *Modern Poetry* is primarily a defense of modern verse, especially the work of Auden, Spender, Day-Lewis, and MacNeice himself. It also offers an intriguing glimpse into MacNeice's own poetic theories. Mainly, he tried to bridge the gap between the poet and the ordinary person. He felt that the poet should communicate and, to best accomplish this goal, be "a blend of the entertainer and the critic or informer." In fact, the poet is a great deal like MacNeice himself: "I would have a poet able-bodied, fond of talking, a reader of newspapers, capable of pity and laughter, informed in economics, appreciative of women, involved in personal relationships, actively interested in politics, susceptible to physical impressions."

# The Sunlight on the Garden

Louis MacNeice

The sunlight on the garden
Hardens and grows cold,
We cannot cage the minute
Within its nets of gold,
5  When all is told
We cannot beg for pardon.

Our freedom as free lances
Advances towards its end;
The earth compels, upon it
10  Sonnets and birds descend;
And soon, my friend,
We shall have no time for dances.

The sky was good for flying
Defying the church bells
15  And every evil iron
Siren and what it tells:
The earth compels,
We are dying, Egypt, dying[1]

And not expecting pardon,
20  Hardened in heart anew,
But glad to have sat under
Thunder and rain with you,
And grateful too
For sunlight on the garden.

---

**1. We . . . dying:** An allusion to a line
spoken by Antony to Cleopatra after he
has been mortally wounded in Shakespeare's
*Antony and Cleopatra*: "I am dying, Egypt,
dying."

**OLD THATCHED SUMMER HOUSE**
*Lilian Stannard*
Christopher Wood Gallery, London

## THINKING ABOUT THE SELECTION

### Recalling

1. What does the speaker say we shall soon have no time for?
2. What two things does the speaker say he is happy to have experienced?

### Interpreting

3. In line 6 and again in line 19 the speaker uses the word *pardon.* From what do you think he is implying there is no pardon?
4. There is an apparent reference to wartime in this poem. What is it?
5. What or whom do you think is dying in this poem—the speaker, a generation, a nation, or something or someone else? Explain your answer.

### Applying

6. Death is a familiar theme in poetry. (a) What other poem have you read that conveys an attitude similar to the one expressed here? (b) How does that poem differ from MacNeice's?

## ANALYZING LITERATURE

### Understanding Scansion

Most poems contain regular rhythmic patterns of stressed and unstressed syllables. The identification of these patterns is called **scansion,** and the act of reading a poem to identify its patterns is called **scanning.**

1. On a sheet of paper, copy "The Sunlight on the Garden." Scan the poem, analyzing it for unstressed and stressed syllables and for feet. Your analysis will show both the recurring patterns and any deviations from them.
2. The poem has an unusual rhyme scheme. Look carefully at the rhyming words Mac-Neice uses. What makes his rhyme scheme different from that in most poems?

# Sunday Morning

Louis MacNeice

Down the road someone is practicing scales,
The notes like little fishes vanish with a wink of tails,
Man's heart expands to tinker with his car
For this is Sunday morning, Fate's great bazaar;
5  Regard these means as ends, concentrate on this Now,
And you may grow to music or drive beyond Hindhead[1]
    anyhow,
Take corners on two wheels until you go so fast
That you can clutch a fringe or two of the windy past,
That you can abstract this day and make it to the week of
    time
10  A small eternity, a sonnet self-contained in rhyme.

But listen, up the road, something gulps, the church spire
Opens its eight bells out, skulls' mouths which will not tire
To tell how there is no music or movement which secures
Escape from the weekday time. Which deadens and
    endures.

---

**1. Hindhead:** A district in the county of Surrey, England.

# THINKING ABOUT THE SELECTION

## Recalling

1. What are two Sunday-morning activities the speaker mentions?
2. What will "skulls' mouths" never tire of telling?

## Interpreting

3. Why do you think the speaker refers to Sunday morning as "Fate's great bazaar"?
4. What does the speaker suggest is required to make the most of a Sunday?
5. The last four lines contrast rather sadly with the first ten. What is the point of the contrast?

## Applying

6. "The Sunlight on the Garden" and "Sunday Morning" express a similar futile wish. In your own words, what is that wish?

# THINKING AND WRITING

## Writing About Rhyme and Rhythm

Modern poets differ in their use of rhyme and rhythm. In "Sunday Morning," MacNeice uses a basic *aabb* rhyme scheme. Scan the poem to determine its metric pattern. Then, in a brief essay, explain what effects the rhyme and rhythm of the poem have on your appreciation of it. Also, try to answer these broader questions: (a) Do you generally prefer rhyming poems to free verse? (b) What effect, if any, does rhyme have on meaning? (c) Do you think subject matter helps to determine the appropriate rhyme and rhythm for a poem?)

Before you start to write, make at least a sketchy outline of the main points you will cover. Your first draft may follow this outline closely or may deviate from it as necessary. When you revise the paper for your final draft, pay special attention to organization. See that your points appear in logical and persuasive order.

---

### Primary Source

As with T. S. Eliot and W. H. Auden, Louis MacNeice believed that one function of poetry should be to convey important, difficult ideas about the modern experience. But everyday language proved insufficient to express the complexity of today's dilemmas. Instead, he and others explored the poetic use of wit and symbols to make their ideas known. Thus, the old ways of looking at a poem no longer work. Critics Wright Thomas and Stuart Gerry Brown explain how MacNeice used wit in "The Sunlight on the Garden" to convey his theme. While we can see "the sunlight on the garden" clearly enough, we cannot see it "hardening," they begin. Similarly, we can see "nets of gold" but we cannot visualize a "minute" being "caged." When we look more closely, we see that in spite of what we feel about being unable to understand, we have in fact made the comparisons and been able to imagine the experience that he describes. As Thomas and Brown conclude: "We do in fact know what he means by the sunlight hardening and by caging a minute within golden nets. But we have not understood him by means of impossible sensory reactions; we have got beyond or beside or perhaps through sensory experience into intellectual experience. We have understood what we could not imagine. . . . It is the impossibility of the thing which makes the poem, paradoxical as that may be. . . . The trick by which this is managed is called 'wit.'"

In this way MacNeice uses language to explore the dilemmas of modern life.

## Stephen Spender (1909–    )

No poet of the 1930's has provided posterity with a more detailed and honest picture of the era between the wars than has Stephen Spender. Much of his early poetry deals with the world of the Thirties, that "low dishonest decade" that saw the world lurch from depression to fascism to war. Yet Spender, never a pessimist in the manner of T. S. Eliot, celebrates technology at the same time he confronts the problems of industrial civilization.

The son of a political journalist, Spender was born in London and educated at University College, Oxford, where he met and fell under the spell of W. H. Auden. In 1928, while at Oxford, he hand-printed a limited edition of Auden's *Poems*. Spender contributed his own early poems to *Oxford Poetry*. He lived in Germany in the early 1930's and published his first important book, *Poems,* in 1933, the year Hitler became chancellor of the Third Reich.

Spender, a political activist, traveled to Spain to promote antifascist propaganda during the Spanish Civil War. From 1939 to 1941, he coedited the literary magazine *Horizon* and later coedited the political, cultural, and literary review *Encounter.* In his autobiography *World Within World* (1951), Spender is candid and perceptive about people, politics, and himself, as he explores and attempts to integrate his lyrical and idealistic vision with the realities of society.

## Henry Reed (1914–    )

Although Henry Reed is well-known in England for his many radio plays, his reputation as a poet rests mainly on one slim volume, *A Map of Verona,* published in 1946. In fact, it rests principally on thirty lines in that collection—"Naming of Parts," which is a satirical section of a longer poem, "Lessons of War." Reed's few poems, always precise and assured, vary widely in subject matter, mood, and theme. So do his highly regarded radio plays, among which are an adaptation of *Moby-Dick,* the partly autobiographical *Return to Naples,* and a dramatic prose poem, *The Streets of Pompeii.*

Henry Reed was born in Birmingham, England, and educated at King Edward VI School and the University of Birmingham. After graduation he worked for several years on a biography of Thomas Hardy, then taught school for a year before being drafted into the army in 1941. He received a transfer to the Foreign Office, where he worked in Naval Intelligence. Most of Reed's career since the end of World War II has involved radio drama for the British Broadcasting Corporation (BBC), with some time out for translating and for teaching at the University of Washington in Seattle. His poetic output, though limited, is of high quality.

# GUIDE FOR INTERPRETING

## Writer's Technique

## What I Expected; Naming of Parts

**Speaker.** The speaker in a poem is the poem's narrator. Narration can occur either in the first person *(I, we)* or in the third person *(he, she, it, they)*. Often a first-person speaker is a persona created by the poet. Consider, for instance, the first-person speakers who are already dead, as, for example, in Edgar Lee Masters's *Spoon River Anthology*. But even if the speaker is represented as being alive, he or she may not be the poet. In Robert Browning's "My Last Duchess," for example, no one would mistake the speaker (the cruel Duke of Ferrara) for the likable Browning. Sometimes a poet uses a first-person speaker to lend immediacy to the poem's content.

**Satire.** Satire is writing that uses wit and humor to attack human follies, stupidities, and abuses. It can be directed at a single person or at an entire society. Satire can be written in any genre—novels, short stories, poems, or plays. Always a mixture of humor and criticism, it is intended to persuade the reader, without the use of formal argument, to accept the author's viewpoint. Among the most famous satires in English are Jonathan Swift's *Gulliver's Travels* and George Orwell's *Animal Farm*.

## Commentary

Henry Reed and Louis MacNeice led an astonishing array of brilliant talent onto the airwaves during the twenty years after the war. With such poets as Dylan Thomas, Sylvia Plath, Ted Hughes, and Stevie Smith, Reed and MacNeice created a series of masterpieces for the British Broadcasting System. Office hours were largely ignored, and a generation of talent was nurtured in the BBC studios and two adjacent pubs. Reed was closely involved with the exceptional groups of writers, composers, actors, and technical staff that essentially constituted a permanent company. Consequently he wrote many of his radio scripts with particular players in mind, and their individual ability often sparked his imagination. *The Complete Lessons of War*, broadcast in 1960, for example, was written with actor Frank Duncan in the role of the drill sergeant; Reed spoke the descriptive passages himself.

## Writing

Choose an event in history that happened long before you were born. Possibilities include the signing of the Declaration of Independence, the defense of the Alamo, and the assassination of Abraham Lincoln. Put yourself in the place of a participant in the event. Jot down notes in the first person, just as if you had observed what happened. Include as many details as you can that, prior to your account, were unknown to the general public.

# What I Expected

## Stephen Spender

What I expected, was
Thunder, fighting,
Long struggles with men
And climbing.
5   After continual straining
I should grow strong;
Then the rocks would shake
And I rest long.

What I had not foreseen
10   Was the gradual day
Weakening the will
Leaking the brightness away,
The lack of good to touch,
The fading of body and soul
15   Smoke before wind,
Corrupt, unsubstantial.

The wearing of Time,
And the watching of cripples pass
With limbs shaped like questions
20   In their odd twist,
The pulverous grief
Melting the bones with pity,
The sick falling from earth—
These, I could not foresee.

25   Expecting always
Some brightness to hold in trust
Some final innocence
Exempt from dust,
That, hanging solid,
30   Would dangle through all
Like the created poem,
Or the faceted crystal.

# THINKING ABOUT THE SELECTION

## Recalling

1. What are four things the speaker says he expected?
2. What are six things he had not foreseen?
3. Besides "Some brightness to hold in trust," what was the speaker always expecting?

## Interpreting

4. (a) What do you think is the setting of this poem? (b) What lines in the poem support your answer?
5. In line 12 and again in line 26 the speaker uses the word *brightness*. What do you think this brightness represents?
6. In line 22 the speaker mentions the melting of bones. To whose bones is he referring?

## Applying

7. The speaker seems to have been deeply disappointed when reality did not match his expectations. In the eighteenth century, the poet Alexander Pope wrote, "Blessed is he who expects nothing, for he shall never be disappointed." How do you think the speaker would react to this statement? Support your answer.

# ANALYZING LITERATURE

## Determining the Speaker

The speaker in a poem is the individual who does the telling, the narrator. Speakers fall into two main categories, (1) first person *(I, we)*, in which the speaker is in essence a character in the poem; (2) third-person *(he, she, it, they)*, in which the speaker is an outsider. Sometimes a first-person speaker is the poet, but more often he or she is not. Rather, the speaker is assuming a particular role to create a desired effect. In determining whether a first-person speaker is probably the poet, it may help you to know something of the poet's life. For instance, you know that Rupert Brooke and the soldier-speaker in "The Soldier" might be one and the same. On the other hand, if you know that Stephen Spender was not a front-line soldier in World War II, you would know he could not have written a first-person battlefield scene except through an assumed identity.

1. Identify the kind of speaker in Stephen Spender's "What I Expected."
2. In view of the subject matter of the poem, why is this kind of speaker a logical one?
3. The speaker and the poet are not one and the same in "What I Expected." How do you know?

# THINKING AND WRITING

## Comparing and Contrasting Two Poems

Reread Louis MacNeice's "The Sunlight on the Garden," noting in particular the references to flying and to sirens in the third stanza. Some critics have called this a war poem, pointing to "flying" as a reference to fighter planes and to the "evil iron siren" as an air-raid siren. Assuming that this interpretation is correct, write an essay in which you compare and contrast MacNeice's "The Sunlight on the Garden" with Spender's "What I Expected." Concentrate not only on the subject matter of the two poems, but also on their structure—speakers, metric patterns, line lengths, and rhyme schemes. Begin by making notes on both poems. When you write your first draft, quote lines from the poems where appropriate. In revising, be sure you have made your comparisons and contrast clear.

# Naming of Parts

Henry Reed

Today we have naming of parts. Yesterday,
We had daily cleaning. And tomorrow morning,
We shall have what to do after firing. But today,
Today we have naming of parts. Japonica[1]
5    Glistens like coral in all of the neighboring gardens,
      And today we have naming of parts.

This is the lower sling swivel. And this
Is the upper sling swivel, whose use you will see,
When you are given your slings. And this is the piling
  swivel,
10   Which in your case you have not got. The branches
Hold in the gardens their silent, eloquent gestures,
      Which in our case we have not got.

This is the safety-catch, which is always released
With an easy flick of the thumb. And please do not let me
15   See anyone using his finger. You can do it quite easy
If you have any strength in your thumb. The blossoms
Are fragile and motionless, never letting anyone see
      Any of them using their finger.

And this you can see is the bolt. The purpose of this
20   Is to open the breech, as you see. We can slide it
Rapidly backwards and forwards: we call this
Easing the spring. And rapidly backwards and forwards
The early bees are assaulting and fumbling the flowers:
      They call it easing the Spring.

25   They call it easing the Spring: it is perfectly easy
If you have any strength in your thumb; like the bolt,
And the breech, and the cocking-piece, and the point of
  balance,
Which in our case we have not got; and the almond-blossom
Silent in all of the gardens and the bees going backwards
  and forwards,
30      For today we have naming of parts.

---

**1. japonica** (jə păn′ i kə): A spiny plant with pink or red flowers.

## THINKING ABOUT THE SELECTION

### Recalling

1. (a) What does the speaker say the members of his group ("we") had yesterday? (b) What will they have tomorrow?
2. What part of the rifle does the speaker not have?
3. What is the purpose of the bolt?
4. What is silent in the gardens?

### Interpreting

5. (a) Who are the members of the group identified as "we" in the poem? (b) Why are they having "naming of parts"?
6. (a) In the fourth stanza, what are the two meanings of "easing the Spring"? (b) In the fifth stanza, what are two possible meanings of "the point of balance"?

### Applying

7. Suppose you were the instructor giving the "naming of parts" lesson, and you became aware of what is on the mind of the speaker (or second voice). (a) How would you react? (b) How would you rate the chances of the recruit becoming a good soldier?

## ANALYZING LITERATURE

### Using Satire

**Satire** is writing that shows the folly or evil of something through the use of wit and humor. In "Naming of Parts," the poet is not directly attacking war or the military, despite the sharp contrast he draws between instruction in rifle parts and the wonders of spring.

1. What specifically is Reed satirizing in the poem?
2. How does he use the repetition of words and phrases to make his point? Give at least two examples.

## CRITICAL THINKING AND READING

### Comparing and Contrasting Speakers

There may be two speakers in this poem, one the instructor-speaker, the other the trainee-speaker. Or there may be only one speaker who first parrots the dull, mechanical words of the instructor, then gives his own personal thoughts on the attractions of nature in springtime. Whichever way you interpret Reed's method (two different speakers or two opposing voices within the same speaker), the satiric message is the same.

1. (a) Which lines, or parts of lines, in each stanza are the instructor's words or mechanical repetitions of them? (b) Which express the personal feelings of the trainee?
2. Which stanza deviates from this pattern?
3. Describe the similarities and differences between the language of the two voices (or speakers).

## THINKING AND WRITING

### Writing About Satire

A number of newspaper and magazine columnists write satire. Erma Bombeck's satiric columns on domestic life and Art Buchwald's on politics, among others, have been reprinted in many books. Find a modern satirical column, either original or reprinted, and write an essay analyzing it. Before you start to write, read the column carefully, making a list of devices the writer uses—exaggeration, understatement, analogy, figurative language, and so on. Jot down an example of each device. When you begin to write, first identify the author, topic, and source of the column you are analyzing. Then write the first draft of your essay. Stick to the point; avoid clever but irrelevant comments. When you revise, pay special attention to unity. Every sentence in your essay should relate to the main point you want to make.

# DYLAN THOMAS

## 1914–1953

When Dylan Thomas burst upon the literary scene in 1933, he was barely twenty years old. His poems, romantic, effusive, and melodic, spoke to readers then, as now, in a voice that could be mistaken for no one else's. Despite some critical bewilderment at first, Thomas gained remarkable popularity in his lifetime, probably greater than that of any poet since Byron. The rich, glowing magic of his language propels the reader onward in spite of its often complex imagery, visionary landscapes, and puzzling ambiguities. Stephen Spender called Thomas "a linguistic genius." The critic Louis Untermeyer says that his lines "leap and shout and all but leave the printed page. . . ."

Dylan Thomas was born in Swansea, an industrial city on the southern coast of Wales. His father was a school teacher, and young Dylan, surrounded by his father's books, seems to have spent his childhood in training to be a poet. He attended Swansea Grammar School until 1931, after which he worked intermittently as a newspaper reporter, radio broadcaster, and film scriptwriter. In 1941 he published a collection of stories about his childhood and youth, *Portrait of the Artist as a Young Dog.* He recorded a number of his poems, as well as his "play for voices," *Under Milk Wood,* which premiered in May 1953 at the Fogg Theater of Harvard University, with Thomas reading all the parts.

Thomas did his best work while living in Wales, far from the temptations of London and New York. At work, he was a meticulous craftsman, shy when sober, exercising strict formal control over what on paper seems so spontaneous. But in London, and on his four speaking tours to the United States, he was a different man, flamboyant, childish, hard-drinking, dissolute, an "outlaw defiant." His marriage to the Irish beauty Caitlin Macnamara was stormy but enduring. She was at his side when he died of the effects of alcoholism at St. Vincent's Hospital in New York City.

Poetry, to Thomas, was "the rhythmic, inevitably narrative, movement from an overclothed blindness to a naked vision." That vision is almost always free of the political themes and overtones found in the works of such contemporaries as Auden and Spender. On Thomas's place in literary history, the verdict is mixed. The poet Conrad Aiken sums him up as a "language-lover and language-juggler." The critic David Daiches says that "he was growing in poetic stature to the last" but, more important, "he wrote some poems that the world will not willingly let die."

# GUIDE FOR INTERPRETING

## The Force That Through the Green Fuse Drives the Flower; Fern Hill; Do Not Go Gentle into That Good Night

**Writer's Technique**

**Parallelism.** Parallelism is the matching or contrasting of two or more ideas through the use of similar phrasing. Sometimes parallelism can produce almost a list or catalog, as in *Ecclesiastes* 3:4: "A time to weep, and a time to laugh; a time to mourn, and a time to dance." Another well-known example of this kind of parallelism, also featuring contrasts, is the beginning of Charles Dickens's *A Tale of Two Cities:* "It was the best of times; it was the worst of times. . . ." In poetry, parallelism can appear within a single line, as in Coleridge's "Without a breeze, without a tide." Or it can be within a stanza, as in Shelley's "The seed ye sow, another reaps/The wealth ye find, another keeps." Or it can be from stanza to stanza, as in Byron's "And there lay the steed with his nostril all wide" [stanza four]; "And there lay the rider distorted and pale" [stanza five].

**Villanelle.** A villanelle is a nineteen-line poem with specific and rather complicated requirements. The first fifteen lines are arranged in three-line stanzas. The first and third lines of the opening stanza are repeated alternately as the closing line of each of the remaining three-line stanzas. They then appear together as a concluding couplet. Only two rhymes are permitted throughout the poem, the rhyme scheme being this: *aba aba aba aba aba abaa.* The villanelle originated in fifteenth-century France, where its aim was to lend a surface simplicity to pastoral poems. Following its revival in the nineteenth century, the villanelle has been used for a broad range of subjects.

**Commentary**

What image do you get when you think of a "poet"? According to critic David Daiches, Dylan Thomas was "the most poetical poet of our time. He talked and dressed and behaved like a poet; he was reckless, flamboyant, irreverent, innocent. . . . His verse, too, had a romantic wildness about it that even a reader who could make nothing of it recognized as 'poetic.'"

**Writing**

Describe a chain of events in your life, beginning each link of the chain with the words, "If it were not for . . ." You might write, for example, "If it were not for my family moving to this city two years ago, I would not have attended this school. If it were not for my attending this school, I would not have met my best friend. If it were not for having met my best friend . . ." and so on. See how far you can take your chain by the end of one page.

# The Force That Through the Green Fuse Drives the Flower

Dylan Thomas

The force that through the green fuse drives the flower
Drives my green age; that blasts the roots of trees
Is my destroyer.
And I am dumb to tell[1] the crooked rose
5   My youth is bent by the same wintry fever.

The force that drives the water through the rocks
Drives my red blood; that dries the mouthing streams
Turns mine to wax.
And I am dumb to mouth unto my veins
10  How at the mountain spring the same mouth sucks.

The hand that whirls the water in the pool
Stirs the quicksand; that ropes the blowing wind
Hauls my shroud sail.
And I am dumb to tell the hanging man
15  How of my clay is made the hangman's lime.[2]

The lips of time leech to the fountain head;
Love drips and gathers, but the fallen blood
Shall calm her sores.
And I am dumb to tell a weather's wind
20  How time has ticked a heaven round the stars.

And I am dumb to tell the lover's tomb
How at my sheet goes the same crooked worm.

---

**1. dumb to tell:** Unable to tell.
**2. hangman's lime:** Quicklime used to bury those who had been hanged.

## THINKING ABOUT THE SELECTION

### Recalling

1. (a) What does the speaker say he is unable to tell the hangman? (b) What is he unable to tell the lover's tomb?

### Interpreting

2. What do you think the speaker means by the phrase (a) "green fuse"? (b) "green age"?
3. (a) What force do you think the speaker has in mind in the first two stanzas? (b) What word does he use in the third stanza to refer to this force?
4. The force in the poem brings about two very different outcomes. In general terms what are they?

### Applying

5. To what extent would you describe this poem as one about faith? Explain.

## ANALYZING LITERATURE

### Using Parallelism

**Parallelism,** which is a form of repetition, matches or contrasts ideas through the use of similar phrasing or grammatic structures. In "The Force That Through the Green Fuse Drives the Flower," Dylan Thomas uses a complex, interlocking parallelism within stanzas:

```
The force  that  drives the green fuse
                 drives the flower
                 Drives my green age
           that  blasts the roots of trees
```

He also uses parallelism from stanza to stanza.

1. In what way are the second lines of the first three stanzas parallel?
2. In what way are the fourth lines of the first four stanzas parallel?
3. What parallel element exists in the last lines of the last four stanzas?

---

### Primary Source

Like Joyce, Yeats, and Hopkins, Thomas was in love with words. According to critic William York Tindall, "words were Thomas's matter, his tool, and his refuge; but so great his delight in them and in what Rimbaud [a French symbolist poet] called their 'alchemy' that, as Thomas complains, they sometimes got between him and the object. Sometimes they became the object." People are often bothered by the ambiguity of Thomas's language, but he celebrated the different meanings that words held and the ways in which they could be manipulated to suggest layers of meaning. He fiddled with the sound and shape of words to create his poetic images. In an often-quoted letter, he remarks, "A poem by myself needs a host of images, because its center is a host of images. I make one image . . . let it breed another, let that image contradict the first, make of the third image bred out of the two together, a fourth contradictory image, and let them all, within my formal imposed limits, conflict." Once in New York, not long before he died, he was talking to a friend about writing. "When I experience anything," he said, "I experience it as a thing and a word at the same time, both equally amazing." Writing the "Ballad of the Long Legged Bait," he said, had been like carrying a huge armful of words to a table he thought was upstairs, and wondering if he could reach it in time, or if it would still be there.

# Fern Hill

## Dylan Thomas


Now as I was young and easy under the apple boughs
About the lilting house and happy as the grass was green,
    The night above the dingle starry,
      Time let me hail and climb
5      Golden in the heydays of his eyes,
And honored among wagons I was prince of the apple
    towns
And once below a time I lordly had the trees and leaves
      Trail with daisies and barley
    Down the rivers of the windfall light.

10  And as I was green and carefree, famous among the barns
About the happy yard and singing as the farm was home,
    In the sun that is young once only,
      Time let me play and be
    Golden in the mercy of his means,
15  And green and golden I was huntsman and herdsman, the
    calves
Sang to my horn, the foxes on the hills barked clear and
    cold,
      And the sabbath rang slowly
    In the pebbles of the holy streams.

All the sun long it was running, it was lovely, the hay
20  Fields high as the house, the tunes from the chimneys, it
    was air
    And playing, lovely and watery
      And fire green as grass.
    And nightly under the simple stars
As I rode to sleep the owls were bearing the farm away,
25  All the moon long I heard, blessed among stables, the
    nightjars[1]
      Flying with the ricks,[2] and the horses
      Flashing into the dark.

And then to awake, and the farm, like a wanderer white
With the dew, come back, the cock on his shoulder; it was
    all

---

**1. nightjars** *n.*: Common nocturnal birds, named for the whirring
sound which the male makes.
**2. ricks** *n.*: Haystacks.

**THE MAGIC APPLE TREE, c. 1830**
*Samuel Palmer*
Fitzwilliam Museum, Cambridge

*Fern Hill* 1099

30      Shining, it was Adam and maiden,
            The sky gathered again
            And the sun grew round that very day.
    So it must have been after the birth of the simple light
    In the first, spinning place, the spellbound horses walking
            warm
35          Out of the whinnying green stable
            On to the fields of praise.

    And honored among foxes and pheasants by the gay house
    Under the new made clouds and happy as the heart was
            long,
            In the sun born over and over,
40              I ran my heedless ways,
            My wishes raced through the house-high hay
    And nothing I cared, at my sky blue trades, that time allows
    In all his tuneful turning so few and such morning songs
            Before the children green and golden
45              Follow him out of grace,

    Nothing I cared, in the lamb white days, that time would
            take me
    Up to the swallow thronged loft by the shadow of my hand,
            In the moon that is always rising,
                Nor that riding to sleep
50          I should hear him fly with the high fields
    And wake to the farm forever fled from the childless land.
    Oh as I was young and easy in the mercy of his means,
        Time held me green and dying
    Though I sang in my chains like the sea.

## THINKING ABOUT THE SELECTION

### Recalling

1. What two colors does the speaker use repeatedly to describe himself as a youth?
2. What descriptive words about the hayfields suggest that the speaker was a youngster when observing them?
3. What does the speaker say happened each night as he "rode to sleep"?
4. In the last stanza, where does the speaker suggest that time has taken him?

### Interpreting

5. (a) How would you describe the speaker's feelings about his childhood? (b) What are some of the words and phrases that convey this feeling?
6. What do you think is meant in lines 33–34 by "the birth of the simple light/In the first, spinning place"?
7. The mood in the last stanza changes from that in the preceding stanzas. (a) What is the change? (b) What are two lines or phrases earlier in the poem that foreshadow this change?
8. Line 53, "Time held me green and dying," expresses the basic idea of the poem. In your own words, what does the line mean?

### Applying

9. Passing from the innocence of childhood to the reality and responsibility of adulthood is the subject of many rituals, proverbs, and literary works. What are a few of these?

## CRITICAL READING AND THINKING

### Interpreting Connotative Meaning

The **connotation** of a word is the meaning the word has beyond its dictionary definition. For example, *lilting,* in line 2, means "metrical, rhythmic," but, beyond that meaning—or *denotation* —the word has favorable connotations of melodic singing and cheerfulness. By contrast, the word *eurhythmic* has a denotation similar to that of *lilting,* but its connotations, if not actually unfavorable, are rather stuffy and academic.

Poets take great care with the connotations of the words they use. (Dylan Thomas is said to have been unhappy with the word *heedless* in line 40, but could not find a word he considered more appropriate for his meaning.)

Find the following words and phrases in "Fern Hill." Explain what connotations you believe the poet intends:

(1) apple towns (l. 6); (2) sun (l. 18); (3) moon (l. 25); (4) sky blue trades (l. 42); (5) lamb white (l. 46); (6) swallow thronged loft (l. 47); (7) in my chains (l. 54); (8) like the sea (l. 54).

## UNDERSTANDING LANGUAGE

### Using Words from Middle English

Middle English, the English language as it existed from about 1150 to 1500, included many words that are in widespread use today. It also included some that are less familiar—for example, *dingle* (l. 3) and *ricks* (l. 26). "Fern Hill" contains a high percentage of words from Middle English.

1. Using a good dictionary, check the etymologies of *young, easy, green, sabbath, sun, house.*
2. Explain why many of the etymologies show ME (Middle English) being directly preceded by OF (Old French) rather than by OE (Old English) or something else.

## THINKING AND WRITING

### Writing a Poem About Childhood

The farm in "Fern Hill" belonged to Ann Jones, Dylan Thomas's aunt. As a child, Thomas spent many vacations and holidays there. As an adult, he remembered it as a happy world, an innocent Eden, forever lost. Write a poem about the place where you spent some or all of your childhood. You may have pleasant recollections, like Thomas, or ones that are less pleasant. Write in whatever poetic form you wish. Include as many images as you can to help a reader visualize both the setting and your experiences. Remember that a poem requires prewriting and revision, just as other forms of composition do.

# Do Not Go Gentle into That Good Night

Dylan Thomas

Do not go gentle into that good night,
Old age should burn and rave at close of day;
Rage, rage against the dying of the light.

Though wise men at their end know dark is right,
5  Because their words had forked no lightning they
Do not go gentle into that good night.

Good men, the last wave by, crying how bright
Their frail deeds might have danced in a green bay,
Rage, rage against the dying of the light.

10  Wild men who caught and sang the sun in flight,
And learn, too late, they grieved it on its way,
Do not go gentle into that good night.

Grave men, near death, who see with blinding sight
Blind eyes could blaze like meteors and be gay,
15  Rage, rage against the dying of the light.

And you, my father, there on the sad height,
Curse, bless, me now with your fierce tears, I pray.
Do not go gentle into that good night.
Rage, rage against the dying of the light.

---

## THINKING ABOUT THE SELECTION
### Recalling

1. Starting with the second stanza of this villa-nelle, what four kinds of men does the speak-er describe as they go "into that good night"?

### Interpreting

2. (a) In this poem, what does *night* seem to represent? (b) What does *light* represent?
3. Considering the speaker's advice to "rage" against the "dying of the light," why do you think he regards night as "good"?
4. What double meaning does the word *grave* have in line 13?
5. How would you paraphrase the speaker's advice in the final couplet?

### Applying

6. Do you think "Do Not Go Gentle into That Good Night" might have been a better poem if Thomas had chosen to work with a less restrictive poetic form than the villanelle? Ex-plain your reasoning.

# Drama

**SET DESIGN OF COVENT GARDEN FOR PYGMALION**
*Donald Oenslager*
*Harvard Theater Collection*

# GEORGE BERNARD SHAW

## 1856–1950

During his ninety-four years, George Bernard Shaw was a novelist, a critic on many subjects, a champion of all sorts of reform, and, finally, a playwright. Original, witty, and opinionated, he often managed to offend people when he was not busy charming them.

Born in Ireland to a family with musical talent but little money, Shaw saw to his own education. At the age of twenty he arrived in London, where he remained for the rest of his life. After trying, and essentially failing, as a writer of fiction, he turned to reviewing—first books, then paintings, and finally music.

Shaw was a restless man, however, with boundless tastes and interests. In 1884 he joined the Fabian Society, an organization whose aim was the peaceful reform of social, economic, and political systems. His personal ambition, as he put it, was "to force the public to reconsider its morals," and toward this end he invested every ounce of his energies. In the process he established himself as a debater and public speaker of some stature.

The enjoyment he derived from crafting lines for his public addresses coupled with his earlier enthusiasm for writing criticism naturally led him in the direction of drama criticism. From there it was a short jump to playwriting itself. Shaw's first play, *Widower's House* (1892), was a rather heavy-handed and ironical exposure of the slum landlord practices and municipal graft that were common ills of the day. His next effort, *Mrs. Warren's Profession* (1894), ran into trouble with official censorship due to its serious treatment of prostitution and the inequities of industrialism. In the same year, *Arms and the Man* enjoyed a limited success.

If people would not attend productions of his plays, Shaw reasoned, they might at least read them. In 1898 he published his first collection, *Plays Pleasant and Unpleasant,* adding the prefaces and epilogues that came to be his trademark.

Shaw's plays, forty-seven in all, continued to challenge the "spiritual sleep" of England's "middle-class morality." When *Pygmalion* was completed in 1913, it was produced in German in Vienna, as a means of avoiding the usual bad press. Its success there led it to London, where, in April of 1914, it opened to immediate acclaim. Like his professor of phonetics, Henry Higgins, Shaw believed in the power of language to break down class barriers. In his will he left a sizable bequest to furthering a system of phonetic spelling. In the interests of spelling simplification, he left out the apostrophe in some contractions, as in this text.

# GUIDE FOR INTERPRETING

## Preface to Pygmalion and Pygmalion, Act I

**Historical Context**

**The Play.** Historical context refers both to the backdrop of historical events against which a work is set and to attitudes and events of the time during which the author lived. The first of these two aspects relates to such matters as when and where the work takes place, to whether the author has used real places and people, and to the degree to which the events have been fictionalized. The second aspect of historical context—the relevance of "current events" and attitudes of the author's day—takes into account any social conditions and values that may have impacted on the subject matter of the work or its execution.

**Writing**

To demonstrate the irregularities of English spelling, George Bernard Shaw once suggested that the word *fish* be written *ghoti*. (The *gh,* he explained, was to be pronounced as it is in *rough,* the *o* as in *women,* and the *ti* as in *station.)* Play with English spellings until you have devised three or four "outrageous" words of your own. Show these to your classmates on paper, and see if anyone can read them correctly.

**Primary Source**

More than any of Shaw's other plays, *Pygmalion* shows how seemingly minor events simmered in his mind, emerging years later transformed in his work. According to Shaw, the play's opening scene was suggested by the following incident:

> Some time ago, happening to be caught in a pelting shower in St. Martin's Lane on a gloomy evening, I took refuge in the entry to a narrow court, where I was presently joined by three men of prosaic appearance, apparently respectable artisans. To my surprise, instead of beginning to talk about horses, they began to talk about music— . . . illustrating their conversation by singing passages in which certain pet singers of theirs had come out wonderfully. This led to a discussion as to whether they could remember some work which had been an old favorite of theirs. Finally, one of them pulled out a pitch pipe; the three sang a chord; and away they went, *sotto voce,* but very prettily, into a three-part song, raising their voices a little when they found that the passers-by were too preoccupied by the deluge to notice them. They were wholly untroubled by a consciousness of the distinguished critic lurking in the shadow a few feet off, greatly pleased with the performance but withal sufficiently master of his business not to be surprised at this survival.

# Preface to *Pygmalion*

## George Bernard Shaw

### A Professor of Phonetics

The English have no respect for their language, and will not teach their children to speak it. They cannot spell it because they have nothing to spell it with but an old foreign alphabet of which only the consonants—and not all of them—have any agreed speech value. Consequently no man can teach himself what it should sound like from reading it; and it is impossible for an Englishman to open his mouth without making some other Englishman despise him. Most European languages are now accessible in black and white to foreigners: English and French are not thus accessible even to Englishmen and Frenchmen. The reformer we need most today is an energetic phonetic enthusiast: that is why I have made such a one the hero of a popular play.

There have been heroes of that kind crying in the wilderness for many years past. When I became interested in the subject towards the end of the eighteen-seventies, the illustrious Alexander Melville Bell, the inventor of Visible Speech, had emigrated to Canada, where his son invented the telephone; but Alexander J. Ellis[1] was still a London Patriarch, with an impressive head always covered by a velvet skull cap, for which he would apologize to public meetings in a very courtly manner. He and Tito Pagliardini, another phonetic veteran, were men whom it was impossible to dislike.

Henry Sweet,[2] then a young man, lacked their sweetness of character: he was about as conciliatory to conventional mortals as Ibsen[3] or Samuel Butler.[4] His great ability as a phonetician (he was, I think the best of them all at his job) would have entitled him to high official recognition, and perhaps enabled him to popularize his subject, but for his Satanic contempt for all academic dignitaries and persons in general who thought more of Greek than of phonetics. Once, in the days when the Imperial Institute rose in South Kensington, and Joseph Chamberlain[5] was booming the Empire, I induced the editor of a leading monthly review to commission an article from Sweet on the imperial importance of his subject. When it arrived, it contained nothing but a savagely derisive attack on a professor of language and literature whose chair Sweet regarded as proper to a phonetic expert only. The article, being libellous, had to be returned as impossible; and I had to renounce my dream of dragging its author into the limelight. When I met him afterwards, for the first time for many years, I found to my astonishment that he, who had been a quite tolerably presentable young man, had actually managed by sheer scorn to alter his personal appearance until he had become a sort of

---

**1. Alexander J. Ellis:** English phonetician and mathematician (1814–1890).

**2. Henry Sweet:** English phonetician (1845–1912).
**3. Ibsen:** Norwegian playwright Henrik Ibsen (1828–1906).
**4. Samuel Butler:** English novelist (1835–1902).
**5. Joseph Chamberlain:** British statesman (1836–1914).

walking repudiation of Oxford and all its traditions. It must have been largely in his own despite that he was squeezed into something called a Readership[6] of phonetics there. The future of phonetics rests probably with his pupils, who all swore by him; but nothing could bring the man himself into any sort of compliance with the university to which he nevertheless clung by divine right in an intensely Oxonian[7] way. I daresay his papers, if he has left any, include some satires that may be published without too destructive results fifty years hence. He was, I believe, not in the least an ill-natured man: very much the opposite, I should say; but he would not suffer fools gladly; and to him all scholars who were not rabid phoneticians were fools.

Those who knew him will recognize in my third act the allusion to the Current Shorthand in which he used to write postcards. It may be acquired from a four and sixpenny manual published by the Clarendon Press. The postcards which Mrs Higgins describes are such as I have received from Sweet. I would decipher a sound which a cockney would represent by *zerr*, and a Frenchman by *seu*, and then write demanding with some heat what on earth it meant. Sweet, with boundless contempt for my stupidity, would reply that it not only meant but obviously was the word Result, as no other word containing that sound, and capable of making sense with the context, existed in any language spoken on earth. That less expert mortals should require fuller indications was beyond Sweet's patience. Therefore, though the whole point of his Current Shorthand is that it can express every sound in the language perfectly, vowels as well as consonants, and that your hand has to make no stroke except the easy and current ones with which you write m, n, and u, l, p, and q, scribbling them at whatev-

er angle comes easiest to you, his unfortunate determination to make this remarkable and quite legible script serve also as a shorthand reduced it in his own practice to the most inscrutable of cryptograms. His true objective was the provision of a full, accurate, legible script for our language; but he was led past that by his contempt for the popular Pitman system of shorthand, which he called the Pitfall system. The triumph of Pitman was a triumph of business organization: there was a weekly paper to persuade you to learn Pitman: there were cheap textbooks and exercise books and transcripts of speeches for you to copy, and schools where experienced teachers coached you up to the necessary proficiency. Sweet could not organize his market in that fashion. He might as well have been the Sybil[8] who tore up the leaves of prophecy that nobody would attend to. The four and sixpenny manual, mostly in his lithographed handwriting, that was never vulgarly advertized, may perhaps some day be taken up by a syndicate and pushed upon the public as The Times[9] pushed the Encyclopoedia Britannica; but until then it will certainly not prevail against Pitman. I have bought three copies of it during my lifetime; and I am informed by the publishers that its cloistered existence is still a steady and healthy one. I actually learned the system two several times; and yet the shorthand in which I am writing these lines is Pitman's. And the reason is, that my secretary cannot transcribe Sweet, having been perforce taught in the schools of Pitman. In America I could use the commercially organized Gregg shorthand, which has taken a hint from Sweet by making its letters writable (current, Sweet would have called them) instead of having to be geometrically drawn like Pitman's; but all these systems, including

----

**6. Readership** *n.*: A position as a lecturer or instructor.
**7. Oxonian** *adj.*: Pertaining to Oxford University.

**8. Sybil:** One of the women consulted as prophetesses by the ancient Greeks or Romans.
**9. The Times:** The *London Times*, a British newspaper.

Sweet's, are spoilt by making them available for verbatim reporting, in which complete and exact spelling and word division are impossible. A complete and exact phonetic script is neither practicable nor necessary for ordinary use; but if we enlarge our alphabet to the Russian size, and make our spelling as phonetic as Spanish, the advance will be prodigious.

Pygmalion Higgins is not a portrait of Sweet, to whom the adventure of Eliza Doolittle would have been impossible; still, as will be seen, there are touches of Sweet in the play. With Higgins's physique and temperament Sweet might have set the Thames on fire. As it was, he impressed himself professionally on Europe to an extent that made his comparative personal obscurity, and the failure of Oxford to do justice to his eminence, a puzzle to foreign specialists in his subject. I do not blame Oxford, because I think Oxford is quite right in demanding a certain social amenity from its nurslings (heavens knows it is not exorbitant in its requirement!); for although I well know how hard it is for a man of genius with a seriously underrated subject to maintain serene and kindly relations with the men who underrate it, and who keep all the best places for less important subjects which they profess without originality and sometimes without much capacity for them, still, if he overwhelms them with wrath and disdain, he cannot expect them to heap honors on him.

Of the later generations of phoneticians I know little. Among them towered Robert Bridges, to whom perhaps Higgins may owe his Miltonic sympathies, though here again I must disclaim all portraiture. But if the play makes the public aware that there are such people as phoneticians, and that they are among the most important people in England at present, it will serve its turn.

I wish to boast that Pygmalion has been an extremely successful play, both on stage and screen, all over Europe and North America as well as at home. It is so intensely and deliberately didactic, and its subject is esteemed so dry, that I delight in throwing it at the heads of the wiseacres who repeat the parrot cry that art should never be didactic. It goes to prove my contention that great art can never be anything else.

Finally, and for the encouragement of people troubled with accents that cut them off from all high employment, I may add that the change wrought by Professor Higgins in the flower-girl is neither impossible nor uncommon. The modern concierge's daughter who fulfills her ambition by playing the Queen of Spain in Ruy Blas[10] at the Théâtre Français is only one of many thousands of men and women who have sloughed off their native dialects and acquired a new tongue. Our West End shop assistants and domestic servants are bilingual. But the thing has to be done scientifically, or the last state of the aspirant may be worse than the first. An honest slum dialect is more tolerable than the attempts of phonetically untaught persons to imitate the plutocracy. Ambitious flower-girls who read this play must not imagine that they can pass themselves off as fine ladies by untutored imitation. They must learn their alphabet over again, and different, from a phonetic expert. Imitation will only make them ridiculous.

_____

**10. Ruy Blas** (rōō ē' blas'): A play by French writer Victor Hugo (1802–1885).

NOTE FOR TECHNICIANS. A complete representation of the play as printed in this edition is technically possible only on the cinema screen or on stages furnished with exceptionally elaborate machinery. For ordinary theatrical use the scenes separated by rows of asterisks are to be omitted.

In the dialogue an e upside down indicates the indefinite vowel, sometimes called obscure or neutral, for which, though it is one of the commonest sounds in English speech, our wretched alphabet has no letter.

# Pygmalion

## CHARACTERS

| | | |
|---|---|---|
| Henry Higgins | Eliza Doolittle | Taximen |
| Colonel Pickering | Mrs Eynsford Hill | Count Nepommuck |
| Freddy Eynsford Hill | Miss Eynsford Hill | Host |
| Alfred Doolittle | Mrs Higgins | Hostess |
| Bystanders | Mrs Pearce | Footmen |
| | Parlormaid | Constables |

## ACT I

*London at* 11.15 P.M. *Torrents of heavy summer rain. Cab whistles blowing frantically in all directions. Pedestrians running for shelter into the portico of St Paul's church (not Wren's cathedral but Inigo Jones's church in Covent Garden vegetable market), among them a lady and her daughter in evening dress. All are peering out gloomily at the rain, except one man with his back turned to the rest, wholly preoccupied with a notebook in which he is writing.*

*The church clock strikes the first quarter.*[1]

THE DAUGHTER [*in the space between the central pillars, close to the one on her left*] I'm getting chilled to the bone. What can Freddy be doing all this time? He's been gone twenty minutes.

THE MOTHER [*on her daughter's right*] Not so long. But he ought to have got us a cab by this.

A BYSTANDER [*on the lady's right*] He wont get no cab not until half-past eleven, missus, when they come back after dropping their theatre fares.

THE MOTHER. But we must have a cab. We cant stand here until half-past eleven. It's too bad.

THE BYSTANDER. Well, it ain't my fault, missus.

THE DAUGHTER. If Freddy had a bit of gumption, he would have got one at the theatre door.

THE MOTHER. What could he have done, poor boy?

THE DAUGHTER. Other people got cabs. Why couldn't he?

FREDDY *rushes in out of the rain from the Southampton Street side, and comes between them closing a dripping umbrella.*

*He is a young man of twenty, in evening dress, very wet round the ankles.*

THE DAUGHTER. Well, havnt you got a cab?

FREDDY. Theres not one to be had for love or money.

THE MOTHER. Oh, Freddy, there must be one. You cant have tried.

THE DAUGHTER. It's too tiresome. Do you expect us to go and get one ourselves?

FREDDY. I tell you theyre all engaged. The rain was so sudden: nobody was prepared; and everybody had to take a cab. Ive been to Charing Cross one way and nearly to Ludgate Circus the other; and they were all engaged.

THE MOTHER. Did you try Trafalgar Square?

FREDDY. There wasn't one at Trafalgar Square.

THE DAUGHTER. Did you try?

FREDDY. I tried as far as Charing Cross Station. Did you expect me to walk to Hammersmith?

THE DAUGHTER. You havnt tried at all.

THE MOTHER. You really are very helpless, Freddy. Go again; and dont come back until you have found a cab.

FREDDY. I shall simply get soaked for nothing.

THE DAUGHTER. And what about us? Are we to stay here all night in this draught,[2] with next to nothing on? You selfish pig—

FREDDY. Oh, very well: I'll go, I'll go. [*He opens his umbrella and dashes off Strandwards, but comes into collision with a flower girl who is hurrying in for shelter, knocking her basket out of her hands. A blinding flash of lightning, followed instantly by a rattling peal of thunder, orchestrates the incident*].

THE FLOWER GIRL. Nah then, Freddy: look wh' y' gowin, deah.

---

**1. first quarter:** Fifteen minutes past the hour.

**2. draught** (draft): Draft.

FREDDY. Sorry [*he rushes off*].

THE FLOWER GIRL [*picking up her scattered flowers and replacing them in the basket*] Theres menners f' yer! Tə-oo banches o voylets trod into the mad. [*She sits down on the plinth[3] of the column sorting her flowers, on the lady's right. She is not at all a romantic figure. She is perhaps eighteen, perhaps twenty, hardly older. She wears a little sailor hat of black straw that has long been exposed to the dust and soot of London and has seldom if ever been brushed. Her hair needs washing rather badly: its mousy color can hardly be natural. She wears a shoddy black coat that reaches nearly to her knees and is shaped to her waist. She has a brown skirt with a coarse apron. Her boots are much the worse for wear. She is no doubt as clean as she can afford to be; but compared to the ladies she is very dirty. Her features are no worse than theirs; but their condition leaves something to be desired; and she needs the services of a dentist*].

THE MOTHER. How do you know that my son's name is Freddy, pray?

THE FLOWER GIRL. Ow, eez yə-ooa, san, is e? Wal, fewd dan y' də-ooty bawmz a mather should, eed now bettern to spawl a pore gel's flahrzn than ran awy athaht pyin. Will ye-oo py me f'them? [*Here, with apologies, this desperate attempt to represent her dialect without a phonetic alphabet must be abandoned as unintelligible outside London*].

THE DAUGHTER. Do nothing of the sort, mother. The idea!

THE MOTHER. Please allow me, Clara. Have you any pennies?

THE DAUGHTER. No. Ive nothing smaller than sixpence.

THE FLOWER GIRL [*hopefully*] I can give you change for a tanner,[4] kind lady.

_____
3. **plinth:** The block at the base of a column.
4. **tanner:** Slang for a sixpence.

THE MOTHER [*to* CLARA] Give it to me. [CLARA *parts reluctantly*]. Now [*to the* GIRL] This is for your flowers.

THE FLOWER GIRL. Thank you kindly, lady.

THE DAUGHTER. Make her give you the change. These things are only a penny a bunch.

THE MOTHER. Do hold your tongue, Clara. [*To the* GIRL] You can keep the change.

THE FLOWER GIRL. Oh, thank you, lady.

THE MOTHER. Now tell me how you know that young gentleman's name.

THE FLOWER GIRL. I didnt.

THE MOTHER. I heard you call him by it. Dont try to deceive me.

THE FLOWER GIRL [*protesting*] Who's trying to deceive you? I called him Freddy or Charlie same as you might yourself if you was talking to a stranger and wished to be pleasant.

THE DAUGHTER. Sixpence thrown away! Really, mamma, you might have spared Freddy that. [*She retreats in disgust behind the pillar*].

*An elderly gentleman of the amiable military type rushes into the shelter, and closes a dripping umbrella. He is in the same plight as* FREDDY, *very wet above the ankles. He is in evening dress, with a light overcoat. He takes the place left vacant by* THE DAUGHTER.

THE GENTLEMAN. Phew!

THE MOTHER. [*to the* GENTLEMAN] Oh, sir, is there any sign of its stopping?

THE GENTLEMAN. I'm afraid not. It started worse than ever about two minutes ago [*he goes to the plinth beside the* FLOWER GIRL; *puts up his foot on it; and stoops to turn down his trouser ends*].

THE MOTHER. Oh dear! [*She retires sadly and joins her daughter*].

THE FLOWER GIRL [*taking advantage of the military gentleman's proximity to establish friendly relations with him*] If it's worse, it's a sign it's nearly over. So cheer up, Captain; and buy a flower off a poor girl.

THE GENTLEMAN. I'm sorry. I havnt any change.

THE FLOWER GIRL. I can give you change, Captain.

THE GENTLEMAN. For a sovereign? Ive nothing less.

THE FLOWER GIRL. Garn! Oh do buy a flower off me, Captain. I can change half-a-crown. Take this for tuppence.

THE GENTLEMAN. Now dont be troublesome: theres a good girl. [*Trying his pockets*] I really havnt any change—Stop: heres three hapence, if thats any use to you [*he retreats to the other pillar*].

THE FLOWER GIRL [*disappointed, but thinking three half-pence better than nothing*] Thank you, sir.

THE BYSTANDER [*to the* GIRL] You be careful: give him a flower for it. Theres a bloke here behind taking down every blessed word youre saying. [*All turn to the man who is taking notes*].

THE FLOWER GIRL [*springing up terrified*] I aint done nothing wrong by speaking to the gentleman. Ive a right to sell flowers if I keep off the kerb. [*Hysterically*] I'm a respectable girl: so help me, I never spoke to him except to ask him to buy a flower off me.

*General hubbub, mostly sympathetic to the* FLOWER GIRL, *but deprecating her excessive sensibility. Cries of* Dont start hollerin. Who's hurting you? Nobody's going to touch you. Whats the good of fussing? Steady on. Easy, easy, etc., *come from the elderly staid spectators, who pat her comfortingly. Less patient ones bid her shut her head, or ask her roughly what is wrong with her. A remoter group, not knowing what the matter is, crowd in and increase the noise with* question and answer: What's the row? What-she do? Where is he? A tec[5] taking her down. What! him? Yes: him over there: Took money off the gentleman, etc.

THE FLOWER GIRL [*breaking through them to the* GENTLEMAN, *crying wildly*] Oh, sir, dont let him charge me. You dunno what it means to me. Theyll take away my character and drive me on the streets for speaking to gentlemen. They—

THE NOTE TAKER [*coming forward on her right, the rest crowding after him*] There! there! there! there! who's hurting you, you silly girl? What do you take me for?

THE BYSTANDER. It's aw rawt: e's a genleman: look at his bə-oots. [*Explaining to the* NOTE TAKER] She thought you was a copper's nark, sir.

THE NOTE TAKER [*with quick interest*] Whats a copper's nark?

THE BYSTANDER [*inapt at definition*] It's a—well, it's a copper's nark, as you might say. What else would you call it? A sort of informer.

THE FLOWER GIRL [*still hysterical*] I take my Bible oath I never said a word—

THE NOTE TAKER [*overbearing but good-humored*] Oh, shut up, shut up. Do I look like a policeman?

THE FLOWER GIRL [*far from reassured*] Then what did you take down my words for? How do I know whether you took me down right? You just shew me what youve wrote about me. [*The* NOTE TAKER *opens his book and holds it steadily under her nose, though the pressure of the mob trying to read it over his shoulders would upset a weaker man*]. Whats that? That aint proper writing. I cant read that.

THE NOTE TAKER. I can. [*Reads, reproducing her pronunciation exactly*] "Cheer ap, Keptin; n' baw ya flahr orf a pore gel."

5. tec: A slang abbreviation for detective.

THE FLOWER GIRL [*much distressed*] It's because I called him Captain. I meant no harm. [*To the* GENTLEMAN] Oh, sir, dont let him lay a charge agen me for a word like that. You—

THE GENTLEMAN. Charge! I make no charge. [*To the* NOTE TAKER] Really, sir, if you are a detective, you need not begin protecting me against molestation by young women until I ask you. Anybody could see that the girl meant no harm.

THE BYSTANDERS GENERALLY [*demonstrating against police espionage*] Course they could. What business is it of yours? You mind your own affairs. He wants promotion, he does. Taking down people's words! Girl never said a word to him. What harm if she did? Nice thing a girl cant shelter from the rain without being insulted, etc., etc., etc. [*She is conducted by the more sympathetic demonstrators back to her plinth, where she resumes her seat and struggles with her emotion*].

THE BYSTANDER. He aint a tec. He's a blooming busybody: thats what he is. I tell you, look at his bɔ-oots.

THE NOTE TAKER [*turning on him genially*] And how are all your people down at Selsey?

THE BYSTANDER [*suspiciously*] Who told you my people come from Selsey?

THE NOTE TAKER. Never you mind. They did. [*To the* GIRL] How do you come to be up so far east? You were born in Lisson Grove.

THE FLOWER GIRL [*appalled*] Oh, what harm is there in my leaving Lisson Grove? It wasnt fit for a pig to live in; and I had to pay four-and-six a week. [*In tears*] Oh, boo—hoo—oo—

THE NOTE TAKER. Live where you like; but stop that noise.

THE GENTLEMAN [*to the* GIRL] Come, come! he cant touch you: you have a right to live where you please.

A SARCASTIC BYSTANDER [*thrusting himself between the* NOTE TAKER *and the* GENTLEMAN] Park Lane, for instance. I'd like to go into the Housing Question with you, I would.

THE FLOWER GIRL [*subsiding into a brooding melancholy over her basket, and talking very low-spiritedly to herself*] I'm a good girl, I am.

THE SARCASTIC BYSTANDER [*not attending to her*] Do you know where I come from?

THE NOTE TAKER [*promptly*] Hoxton.

*Titterings. Popular interest in the* NOTE TAK-ER*'s performance increases.*

THE SARCASTIC ONE [*amazed*] Well, who said I didnt? Bly me! you know everything, you do.

THE FLOWER GIRL [*still nursing her sense of injury*] Aint no call to meddle with me, he aint.

THE BYSTANDER [*to her*] Of course he aint. Dont you stand it from him. [*To the* NOTE TAKER] See here: what call have you to know about people what never offered to meddle with you?

THE FLOWER GIRL. Let him say what he likes. I dont want to have no truck with him.

THE BYSTANDER. You take us for dirt under your feet, dont you? Catch you taking liberties with a gentleman!

THE SARCASTIC BYSTANDER. Yes: tell him where he come from if you want to go fortune-telling.

THE NOTE TAKER. Cheltenham, Harrow, Cambridge, and India.

THE GENTLEMAN. Quite right.

*Great laughter. Reaction in the* NOTE TAKER*'s favor. Exclamations of* He knows all about it. Told him proper. Hear him tell the toff[6] where he come from? *etc.*

---

**6. toff:** English slang for a fashionable person.

THE GENTLEMAN. May I ask, sir, do you do this for your living at a music hall?

THE NOTE TAKER. I've thought of that. Perhaps I shall some day.

*The rain has stopped; and the persons on the outside of the crowd begin to drop off.*

THE FLOWER GIRL [*resenting the reaction*] He's no gentleman, he aint, to interfere with a poor girl.

THE DAUGHTER [*out of patience, pushing her way rudely to the front and displacing the* GENTLEMAN, *who politely retires to the other side of the pillar*] What on earth is Freddy doing? I shall get pneumownia if I stay in this draught any longer.

THE NOTE TAKER [*to himself, hastily making a note of her pronunciation of "monia"*] Earlscourt.

THE DAUGHTER [*violently*] Will you please keep your impertinent remarks to yourself.

THE NOTE TAKER. Did I say that out loud? I didn't mean to. I beg your pardon. Your mother's Epsom, unmistakeably.

THE MOTHER [*advancing between the* DAUGHTER *and the* NOTE TAKER] How very curious! I was brought up in Largelady Park, near Epsom.

THE NOTE TAKER [*uproariously amused*] Ha! ha! What a devil of a name! Excuse me. [*To the* DAUGHTER] You want a cab, do you?

THE DAUGHTER. Dont dare speak to me.

THE MOTHER. Oh please, please, Clara. [*Her daughter repudiates her with an angry shrug and retires haughtily*] We should be so grateful to you, sir, if you found us a cab. [*The* NOTE TAKER *produces a whistle*] Oh, thank you. [*She joins her daughter*].
*The* NOTE TAKER *blows a piercing blast.*

THE SARCASTIC BYSTANDER. There! I knowed he was a plainclothes copper.

THE BYSTANDER. That aint a police whistle: thats a sporting whistle.

THE FLOWER GIRL [*still preoccupied with her wounded feelings*] He's no right to take away my character. My character is the same to me as any lady's.

THE NOTE TAKER. I dont know whether youve noticed it; but the rain stopped about two minutes ago.

THE BYSTANDER. So it has. Why didn't you say so before? and us losing our time listening to your silliness! [*He walks off towards the Strand*].

THE SARCASTIC BYSTANDER. I can tell where you come from. You come from Anwell. Go back there.

THE NOTE TAKER [*helpfully*] Hanwell.

THE SARCASTIC BYSTANDER [*affecting great distinction of speech*] Thenk you, teacher. Haw haw! So long [*he touches his hat with mock respect and strolls off*].

THE FLOWER GIRL. Frightening people like that! How would he like it himself?

THE MOTHER. It's quite fine now, Clara. We can walk to a motor bus. Come. [*She gathers her skirts above her ankles and hurries off towards the Strand*].

THE DAUGHTER. But the cab—[*her mother is out of hearing*]. Oh, how tiresome! [*She follows angrily*].

*All the rest have gone except the* NOTE TAKER, *the* GENTLEMAN, *and the* FLOWER GIRL, *who sits arranging her basket, and still pitying herself in murmurs.*

THE FLOWER GIRL. Poor girl! Hard enough for her to live without being worrited and chivied.[7]

THE GENTLEMAN [*returning to his former place on the* NOTE TAKER'*s left*] How do you do it, if I may ask?

THE NOTE TAKER. Simple phonetics. The science of speech. Thats my profession: also

---

**7. worrited and chivied:** Worried and tormented.

my hobby. Happy is the man who can make a living by his hobby! You can spot an Irishman or a Yorkshireman by his brogue. *I* can place any man within six miles. I can place him within two miles in London. Sometimes within two streets.

**THE FLOWER GIRL.** Ought to be ashamed of himself, unmanly coward.

**THE GENTLEMAN.** But is there a living in that?

**THE NOTE TAKER.** Oh yes. Quite a fat one. This is an age of upstarts. Men begin in Kentish Town with £80 a year, and end in Park Lane with a hundred thousand. They want to drop Kentish Town; but they give themselves away every time they open their mouths. Now I can teach them—

**THE FLOWER GIRL.** Let him mind his own business and leave a poor girl—

**THE NOTE TAKER** [*explosively*] Woman: cease this detestable boohooing instantly; or else seek the shelter of some other place of worship.

**THE FLOWER GIRL** [*with feeble defiance*] Ive a right to be here if I like, same as you.

**THE NOTE TAKER.** A woman who utters such depressing and disgusting sounds has no right to be anywhere—no right to live. Remember that you are a human being with a soul and the divine gift of articulate speech: that your native language is the language of Shakespear and Milton and The Bible; and dont sit there crooning like a bilious pigeon.

**THE FLOWER GIRL** [*quite overwhelmed, looking up at him in mingled wonder and deprecation without daring to raise her head*] Ah-ah-ah-ow-ow-ow-oo!

**THE NOTE TAKER** [*whipping out his book*] Heavens! what a sound! [*He writes; then holds out the book and reads, reproducing her vowels exactly*] Ah-ah-ah-ow-ow-ow-oo!

**THE FLOWER GIRL** [*tickled by the performance, and laughing in spite of herself*] Garn!

**THE NOTE TAKER.** You see this creature with her kerbstone English: the English that will keep her in the gutter to the end of her days. Well, sir, in three months I could pass that girl off as a duchess at an ambassador's garden party. I could even get her a place as lady's maid or shop assistant, which requires better English.

**THE FLOWER GIRL.** What's that you say?

**THE NOTE TAKER.** Yes, you squashed cabbage leaf, you disgrace to the noble architecture of these columns, you incarnate insult to the English language: I could pass you off as the Queen of Sheba. [*To the* GENTLEMAN] Can you believe that?

**THE GENTLEMAN.** Of course I can. I am myself a student of Indian dialects; and—

**THE NOTE TAKER** [*eagerly*] Are you? Do you know Colonel Pickering, the author of Spoken Sanscrit?

**THE GENTLEMAN.** I am Colonel Pickering. Who are you?

**THE NOTE TAKER.** Henry Higgins, author of Higgins's Universal Alphabet.

**PICKERING** [*with enthusiasm*] I came from India to meet you.

**HIGGINS.** I was going to India to meet you.

**PICKERING.** Where do you live?

**HIGGINS.** 27A Wimpole Street. Come and see me tomorrow.

**PICKERING.** I'm at the Carlton. Come with me now and lets have a jaw over some supper.

**HIGGINS.** Right you are.

**THE FLOWER GIRL** [*to* PICKERING, *as he passes her*] Buy a flower, kind gentleman. I'm short for my lodging.

**PICKERING.** I really havnt any change. I'm sorry [*he goes away*].

**HIGGINS** [*shocked at the* GIRL'*s mendacity*] Liar. You said you could change half-a-crown.

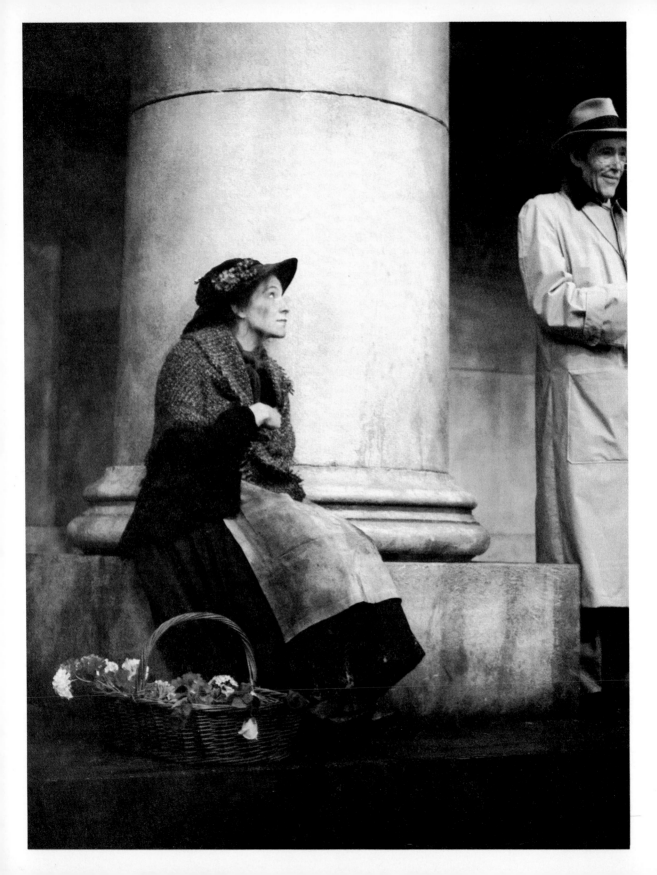

**THE FLOWER GIRL** [*rising in desperation*] You ought to be stuffed with nails, you ought. [*Flinging the basket at his feet*] Take the whole blooming basket for sixpence.

*The church clock strikes the second quarter.*

**HIGGINS** [*hearing in it the voice of God, rebuking him for his Pharisaic[8] want of charity to the poor girl*] A reminder. [*He raises his hat solemnly; then throws a handful of money into the basket and follows* PICKERING].

**THE FLOWER GIRL** [*picking up a half-crown*] Ah-ow-ooh! [*Picking up a couple of florins*] Aaah-ow-ooh! [*Picking up several coins*] Aaaaah-ow-ooh! [*Picking up a half-sovereign*] Aaaaaaaaaaaaah-ow-ooh!!!

**FREDDY** [*springing out of a taxicab*] Got one at last. Hello! [*To the* GIRL] Where are the two ladies that were here?

**THE FLOWER GIRL.** They walked to the bus when the rain stopped.

**FREDDY.** And left me with a cab on my hands! Damnation!

**THE FLOWER GIRL** [*with grandeur*] Never mind, young man. *I'm* going home in a taxi. [*She sails off to the cab. The driver puts his hand behind him and holds the door firmly shut against her. Quite understanding his mistrust, she shews him her handful of money*]. A taxi fare aint no object to me, Charlie. [*He grins and opens the door*]. Here. What about the basket?

**THE TAXIMAN.** Give it here. Tuppence extra.

**LIZA.** No: I dont want nobody to see it. [*She crushes it into the cab and gets in, continuing the conversation through the window*] Good-bye, Freddy.

**FREDDY** [*dazedly raising his hat*] Goodbye.

**TAXIMAN.** Where to?

---

**8. Pharisaic** (far′ ə sā′ ik) *adj.*: Referring to the Pharisees, an ancient Jewish party or fellowship that carefully observed the written law; hypocritically self-righteous.

**LIZA.** Bucknam Pellis [Buckingham Palace].

**TAXIMAN.** What d'ye mean—Bucknam Pellis?

**LIZA.** Dont you know where it is? In the Green Park, where the King lives. Goodbye, Freddy. Dont let me keep you standing there. Goodbye.

**FREDDY.** Goodbye [*He goes*].

**TAXIMAN.** Here? Whats this about Bucknam Pellis? What business have you at Bucknam Pellis?

**LIZA.** Of course I havnt none. But I wasn't going to let him know that. You drive me home.

**TAXIMAN.** And wheres home?

**LIZA.** Angel Court, Drury Lane, next Meiklejohn's oil shop.

**TAXIMAN.** That sounds more like it, Judy. [*He drives off*].

    ★    ★    ★    ★    ★    ★

Let us follow the taxi to the entrance to Angel Court, a narrow little archway between two shops, one of them Meiklejohn's oil shop. When it stops there, Eliza gets out, dragging her basket with her.

**LIZA.** How much?

**TAXIMAN** [*indicating the taximeter*] Cant you read? A shilling.

**LIZA.** A shilling for two minutes!!

**TAXIMAN.** Two minutes or ten: it's all the same.

**LIZA.** Well, I dont call it right.

**TAXIMAN.** Ever been in a taxi before?

**LIZA** [*with dignity*] Hundreds and thousands of times, young man.

**TAXIMAN** [*laughing at her*] Good for you, Judy. Keep the shilling, darling, with best love from all at home. Good luck! [*He drives off*].

**LIZA** [*humiliated*] Impidence!

*She picks up the basket and trudges up the alley with it to her lodging: a small room with very old wall paper hanging loose in the damp places. A broken pane in the window is mended with paper. A portrait of a popular actor and a fashion plate of ladies' dresses, all wildly beyond poor* ELIZA'*s means, both torn from newspapers, are pinned up on the wall. A birdcage hangs in the window; but its tenant died long ago: it remains as a memorial only.*

*These are the only visible luxuries: the rest is the irreducible minimum of poverty's needs: a wretched bed heaped with all sorts of coverings that have any warmth in them, a draped packing case with a basin and jug on it and a little looking glass over it, a chair and table, the refuse of some suburban kitchen, and an American alar-*um clock on the shelf above the unused fireplace: the whole lighted with a gas lamp with a penny in the slot meter. Rent: four shillings a week.*

Here Eliza, chronically weary, but too excited to go to bed, sits, counting her new riches and dreaming and planning what to do with them, until the gas goes out, when she enjoys for the first time the sensation of being able to put in another penny without grudging it. This prodigal mood does not extinguish her gnawing sense of the need for economy sufficiently to prevent her from calculating that she can dream and plan in bed more cheaply and warmly than sitting up without a fire. So she takes off her shawl and skirt and adds them to the miscellaneous bedclothes. Then she kicks off her shoes and gets into bed without any further change.*

---

## THINKING ABOUT THE SELECTION

### Recalling

1. What kind of reformer does Shaw claim, in the Preface, that "we need most today"?
2. (a) What is the point of Current Shorthand? (b) Why does Shaw find it superior to previous systems?
3. (a) Where and when does the play open? (b) What are the mother and daughter doing?
4. How does The Note Taker amaze the crowd?
5. What feat does The Note Taker say he could accomplish in three months?

### Interpreting

6. Based on Shaw's description of Henry Sweet in the Preface, what traits might you say the two men shared?
7. (a) What effect does Shaw achieve by spelling out words according to the speaker's pronunciation? (b) by identifying characters by labels at first?

### Applying

8. In the seventh century, Ali ibn-abi-Talib, who was fourth caliph of the Moslems, wrote, "A man is hid under his tongue." (a) Explain the meaning of this quotation. (b) Under what circumstances do you feel that a person's speech habits are important?

## ANALYZING LITERATURE

### Understanding Historical Context

**Historical context** refers both to a play's historical validity (if it depicts events at a time other than that at which it was written) and to events and attitudes of the author's day that may have been influential. *Pygmalion* provides us with a glimpse of English city life shortly after the turn of the century. Tell what the following details from Act I reveal about that lifestyle, and describe any differences you might expect today in your own city.

1. Freddy's searching for a cab while his mother and sister remain sheltered.
2. The crowd's suspicions about The Note Taker.
3. (a) The verbal exchanges between The Note Taker and The Flower Girl. (b) between The Flower Girl and the Taximan.

## CRITICAL THINKING AND READING
### Generalizing About People

The Note Taker in Act I bases his assumptions about the speech habits of Eliza and the others on well-founded **generalizations,** or observations that apply to classes of people. While such observations, when based on scientific principles as they are here, can be valid, generalizing as a rule is a dangerous practice. Tell what generalizations underlie the following acts, and judge their validity.

1. Shaw's remarking in the Preface that "it is impossible for an Englishman to open his mouth without making some other Englishman despise him."
2. Eliza's assuming that Higgins is a "tec."
3. The crowd's sizing up Pickering as a "toff."
4. The Taximan's holding the door shut against Eliza when she first approaches.

## SPEAKING AND LISTENING
### Understanding Dialect

A **dialect** is a collection of speech habits that typifies a particular social class or region. A dialect may vary from the standard form of a language in pronunciation, in grammar, and in the use of certain expressions. Whatever its defining features may be, every dialect is *systematic*—or governed by rules. The Cockney accent used by Eliza is used to this day by lower-class inhabitants of London's East End. Arrange for members of the class to read aloud Eliza's speeches on pages 1130 and 1135. After "translating" them into standard English, develop as many rules of pronunciation and grammar as you can for the Cockney dialect.

## THINKING AND WRITING
### Writing About Historical Context

Reread Shaw's Preface to the play. Then write a short essay evaluating the Preface's contribution to the play's historical context. Begin by asking yourself the following questions. How relevant are Shaw's attitudes about language to the events of Act I? How important is the background information on Henry Sweet? On systems of shorthand? When you revise, make sure you have provided details from the Preface and from Act I to support your thesis. Proofread your essay and prepare a final draft.

# GUIDE FOR INTERPRETING

## Writer's Technique

### Pygmalion, Act II

**Character Development.** Character development is the fleshing out of a character in a work of fiction through confrontations with other characters or forces. Depending upon the extent to which a character changes as a result of these confrontations, he or she is said to be either static or dynamic. A *static character* is one who remains relatively unchanged by events. A *dynamic character,* by contrast, is one who changes considerably, sometimes shedding altogether character traits which he or she possessed earlier in the work. In Shakespeare's *The Taming of the Shrew,* for example, the character Kate begins as a feisty, hot-tempered individual who, through the course of the play, is transformed into a mellow, even-tempered person.

## Commentary

Shaw's own character, as with the ones he created, was developed through encounters with different forces. These forces must have been powerful, for at twenty-four Shaw did not seem destined for greatness. He was considered a total failure, ignored by his mother, despised by his sister, passed over by relatives and family friends. St. John Ervine describes him as "tall, over six feet in height, and pale with the pallor of people with red hair, although his was not notably red. . . . It was worn flat on his head, divided in the middle, and was matched on his chin by a thin, scrubby beard which was slow in its growth. . . . His eyes were his most notable feature, far more notable than the long, slightly twisted nose which seemed at first sight to prevail over the whole face, or the tightly-drawn lips or the large projecting ears. The eyebrows . . . revealed already the strange dissimilarity between the two sides of his face. . . . One side was genial, almost benign and full of fun and laughter; the other side had a brooding look that was to become almost torment-ed in his old age. . . . He wears the features of a sober young man, over-earnest, perhaps about the state of the world and eager to deliver messages, though unable yet to find an audience which will listen for more than a minute or two; but he shows in his laughing eye as well as in the eye that is somber, and in the resolute lips, that he will one day make the casual and disinterested passers-by stand and look and listen."

## Writing

What motivates people to change? Why do people decide to alter the way they look, behave, or even speak? Freewrite, exploring your thoughts on these questions.

## ACT II

*Next day at* 11 A.M. HIGGINS'S *laboratory in Wimpole Street. It is a room on the first floor, looking on the street, and was meant for the drawing room. The double doors are in the middle of the back wall; and persons entering find in the corner to their right two tall file cabinets at right angles to one another against the walls. In this corner stands a flat writing-table, on which are a phonograph, a laryngoscope,*[1] *a row of tiny organ pipes with a bellows, a set of lamp chimneys for singing flames with burners attached to a gas plug in the wall by an indiarubber tube, several tuning-forks of different sizes, a life-size image of half a human head, shewing in section the vocal organs, and a box containing a supply of wax cylinders for the phonograph.*

*Further down the room, on the same side, is a fireplace, with a comfortable leather-covered easy-chair at the side of the hearth nearest the door, and a coal-scuttle. There is a clock on the mantlepiece. Between the fireplace and the phonograph table is a stand for newspapers.*

*On the other side of the central door, to the left of the visitor, is a cabinet of shallow drawers. On it is a telephone and the telephone directory. The corner beyond, and most of the side wall, is occupied by a grand piano, with the keyboard at the end furthest from the door, and a bench for the players extending the full length of the keyboard. On the piano is a dessert dish heaped with fruit and sweets, mostly chocolates.*

*The middle of the room is clear. Besides the easy-chair, the piano bench, and two chairs at the phonograph table, there is one stray chair. It stands near the fireplace. On the walls, engravings: mostly Piranesis*[2] *and mezzotint*[3] *portraits. No paintings.*

---

**1. laryngoscope** (lə riŋ′ gō skōp′) *n.*: An instrument for examining the throat.
**2. Piranesis** (pēr′ ə nā′ zēz): Works of Italian artist Giambattista Piranesi (1720–1778).
**3. mezzotint:** An engraving made from a copper or steel plate.

PICKERING *is seated at the table, putting down some cards and a tuning-fork which he has been using.* HIGGINS *is standing up near him, closing two or three file drawers which are hanging out. He appears in the morning light as a robust, vital, appetizing sort of man of forty or thereabouts, dressed in a professional-looking black frock-coat with a white linen collar and black silk tie. He is of energetic, scientific type, heartily, even violently interested in everything that can be studied as a scientific subject, and careless about himself and other people, including their feelings. He is, in fact, but for his years and size, rather like a very impetuous baby "taking notice" eagerly and loudly, and requiring almost as much watching to keep him out of unintended mischief. His manner varies from genial bullying when he is in a good humor to stormy petulance when anything goes wrong; but he is so entirely frank and void of malice that he remains likeable even in his least reasonable moments.*

**HIGGINS** [*as he shuts the last drawer*] Well, I think thats the whole show.

**PICKERING.** It's really amazing. I havnt taken half of it in, you know.

**HIGGINS.** Would you like to go over any of it again?

**PICKERING** [*rising and coming to the fireplace, where he plants himself with his back to the fire*] No, thank you: not now. I'm quite done up for this morning.

**HIGGINS** [*following him, and standing beside him on his left*] Tired of listening to sounds?

**PICKERING.** Yes. It's a fearful strain. I rather fancied myself because I can pronounce twenty-four distinct vowel sounds; but your hundred and thirty beat me. I cant hear a bit of difference between most of them.

**HIGGINS** [*chuckling, and going over to the piano to eat sweets*] Oh, that comes with practice. You hear no difference at first; but you keep on listening, and presently you find theyre all as different as A from B. [MRS PEARCE *looks in; she is* HIGGINS's *housekeeper*]. Whats the matter?

**MRS PEARCE** [*hesitating, evidently perplexed*] A young woman asks to see you, sir.

**HIGGINS.** A young woman! What does she want?

**MRS PEARCE.** Well, sir, she says youll be glad to see her when you know what she's come about. She's quite a common girl, sir. Very common indeed. I should have sent her away, only I thought perhaps you wanted her to talk into your machines. I hope Ive not done wrong; but really you see such queer people sometimes—youll excuse me, I'm sure, sir—

**HIGGINS.** Oh, thats all right, Mrs Pearce. Has she an interesting accent?

**MRS PEARCE.** Oh, something dreadful, sir, really. I dont know how you can take an interest in it.

**HIGGINS** [*to* PICKERING] Lets have her up. Shew her up, Mrs Pearce [*he rushes across to his working table and picks out a cylinder to use on the phonograph*].

**MRS PEARCE** [*only half resigned to it*] Very well, sir. It's for you to say. [*She goes downstairs*].

**HIGGINS.** This is rather a bit of luck. I'll shew you how I make records. We'll set her talking; and I'll take it down first in Bell's Visible Speech; then in broad Romic; and then we'll get her on the phonograph so that you can turn her on as often as you like with the written transcript before you.

**MRS PEARCE** [*returning*] This is the young woman, sir.

*The* FLOWER GIRL *enters in state. She has a hat with three ostrich feathers, orange, sky-blue, and red. She has a nearly clean apron, and the shoddy coat has been tidied a little. The pathos of this deplorable figure, with its innocent vanity and consequential*

*air, touches* PICKERING, *who has already straightened himself in the presence of* MRS PEARCE. *But as to* HIGGINS, *the only distinction he makes between men and women is that when he is neither bullying nor exclaiming to the heavens against some feather-weight cross,*[4] *he coaxes women as a child coaxes its nurse when it wants to get anything out of her.*

**HIGGINS** [*brusquely, recognizing her with unconcealed disappointment, and at once, babylike, making an intolerable grievance of it*] Why, this is the girl I jotted down last night. She's no use: I've got all the records I want of the Lisson Grove lingo; and I'm not going to waste another cylinder on it. [*To the* GIRL] Be off with you: I dont want you.

**THE FLOWER GIRL.** Dont you be so saucy. You aint heard what I come for yet. [*To* MRS PEARCE, *who is waiting at the door for further instructions*] Did you tell him I come in a taxi?

**MRS PEARCE.** Nonsense, girl! What do you think a gentleman like Mr Higgins cares what you came in?

**THE FLOWER GIRL.** Oh, we are proud! He aint above giving lessons, not him: I heard him say so. Well, I aint come here to ask for any compliment; and if my money's not good enough I can go elsewhere.

**HIGGINS.** Good enough for what?

**THE FLOWER GIRL.** Good enough for yǝ-oo. Now you know, dont you? I've come to have lessons, I am. And to pay for em tǝ-oo: make no mistake.

**HIGGINS** [*stupent*[5]] Well!!! [*Recovering his breath with a gasp*] What do you expect me to say to you?

**THE FLOWER GIRL.** Well, if you was a gentleman, you might ask me to sit down, I think. Dont I tell you I'm bringing you business?

---

**4. feather-weight cross:** A very minor inconvenience.
**5. stupent:** Astonished.

HIGGINS. Pickering: shall we ask this baggage to sit down, or shall we throw her out of the window?

THE FLOWER GIRL [*running away in terror to the piano, where she turns at bay*] Ah-ah-oh-ow-ow-ow-oo! [*Wounded and whimpering*] I wont be called a baggage when Ive offered to pay like any lady.

*Motionless, the two men stare at her from the other side of the room, amazed.*

PICKERING [*gently*] But what is it you want?

THE FLOWER GIRL. I want to be a lady in a flower shop stead of sellin at the corner of Tottenham Court Road. But they wont take me unless I can talk more genteel. He said he could teach me. Well, here I am ready to pay him—not asking any favor—and he treats me zif I was dirt.

MRS PEARCE. How can you be such a foolish ignorant girl as to think you could afford to pay Mr Higgins?

THE FLOWER GIRL. Why shouldnt I? I know what lessons cost as well as you do; and I'm ready to pay.

HIGGINS. How much?

THE FLOWER GIRL [*coming back to him, triumphant*] Now youre talking! I thought youd come off it when you saw a chance of getting back a bit of what you chucked at me last night. [*Confidentially*] Youd had a drop in,[6] hadn't you?

HIGGINS [*peremptorily*] Sit down.

THE FLOWER GIRL. Oh, if youre going to make a compliment of it—

HIGGINS [*thundering at her*] Sit down.

MRS PEARCE [*severely*] Sit down, girl. Do as youre told.

THE FLOWER GIRL. Ah-ah-ah-ow-ow-oo! [*She stands, half rebellious, half bewildered*].

––––––––––

6. **had a drop in:** Been drinking.

PICKERING [*very courteous*] Wont you sit down? [*He places the stray chair near the hearthrug between himself and* HIGGINS].

LIZA [*coyly*] Dont mind if I do. [*She sits down.* PICKERING *returns to the hearthrug*].

HIGGINS. Whats your name?

THE FLOWER GIRL. Liza Doolittle.

HIGGINS [*declaiming gravely*]
　　Eliza, Elizabeth, Betsy and Bess,
　　They went to the woods to get a bird's
　　　　nes':

PICKERING. They found a nest with four eggs in it:

HIGGINS. They took one apiece, and left three in it.
*They laugh heartily at their own fun.*
LIZA. Oh, dont be silly.

MRS PEARCE [*placing herself behind* ELIZA'*s chair*] You mustnt speak to the gentleman like that.

LIZA. Well, why wont he speak sensible to me?

HIGGINS. Come back to business. How much do you propose to pay me for the lessons?

LIZA. Oh, I know whats right. A lady friend of mine gets French lessons for eighteenpence an hour from a real French gentleman. Well, you wouldnt have the face to ask me the same for teaching me my own language as you would for French; so I wont give more than a shilling. Take it or leave it.

HIGGINS [*walking up and down the room, rattling his keys and his cash in his pockets*] You know, Pickering, if you consider a shilling, not as a simple shilling, but as a percentage of this girl's income, it works out as fully equivalent to sixty or seventy guineas from a millionaire.

PICKERING. How so?

HIGGINS. Figure it out. A millionaire has about £150 a day. She earns about half-a-crown.

LIZA [*haughtily*] Who told you I only—

HIGGINS [*continuing*] She offers me two-fifths of her day's income for a lesson. Two-fifths of a millionaire's income for a day would be somewhere about £60. It's handsome. By George, it's enormous! it's the biggest offer I ever had.

LIZA [*rising, terrified*] Sixty pounds! What are you talking? I never offered you sixty pounds. Where would I get—

HIGGINS. Hold your tongue.

LIZA [*weeping*] But I aint got sixty pounds. Oh—

MRS PEARCE. Dont cry, you silly girl. Sit down. Nobody is going to touch your money.

HIGGINS. Somebody is going to touch you, with a broomstick, if you dont stop snivelling. Sit down.

LIZA [*obeying slowly*] Ah-ah-ah-ow-oo-o! One would think you was my father.

HIGGINS. If I decide to teach you, I'll be worse than two fathers to you. Here [*he offers her his silk handkerchief*]!

LIZA. Whats this for?

HIGGINS. To wipe your eyes. To wipe any part of your face that feels moist. Remember: thats your handkerchief; and thats your sleeve. Dont mistake the one for the other if you wish to become a lady in a shop.
LIZA, *utterly bewildered, stares helplessly at him.*

MRS PEARCE. It's no use talking to her like that, Mr Higgins: she doesnt understand you. Besides, youre quite wrong: she doesnt do it that way at all [*she takes the handkerchief*].

LIZA [*snatching it*] Here! You give me that handkerchief. He gev it to me, not to you.

PICKERING [*laughing*] He did. I think it must be regarded as her property, Mrs Pearce.

MRS PEARCE [*resigning herself*] Serve you right, Mr Higgins.

PICKERING. Higgins: I'm interested. What about the ambassador's garden party? I'll say youre the greatest teacher alive if you make that good. I'll bet you all the expenses of the experiment you cant do it. And I'll pay for the lessons.

LIZA. Oh, you are real good. Thank you, Captain.

HIGGINS [*tempted, looking at her*] It's almost irresistible. She's so deliciously low—so horribly dirty—

LIZA [*protesting extremely*] Ah-ah-ah-ah-ow-ow-oo-oo!!! I aint dirty: I washed my face and hands afore I come, I did.

PICKERING. Youre certainly not going to turn her head with flattery, Higgins.

MRS PEARCE [*uneasy*] Oh, dont say that, sir: theres more ways than one of turning a girl's head; and nobody can do it better than Mr Higgins, though he may not always mean it. I do hope, sir, you wont encourage him to do anything foolish.

HIGGINS [*becoming excited as the idea grows on him*] What is life but a series of inspired follies? The difficulty is to find them to do. Never lose a chance: it doesnt come every day. I shall make a duchess of this draggle-tailed guttersnipe.

LIZA [*strongly deprecating this view of her*] Ah-ah-ah-ow-ow-oo!

HIGGINS [*carried away*] Yes: in six months —in three if she has a good ear and a quick tongue—I'll take her anywhere and pass her off as anything. We'll start today: now! this moment! Take her away and clean her, Mrs Pearce. Monkey Brand,[7] if it wont come off any other way. Is there a good fire in the kitchen?

MRS PEARCE [*protesting*] Yes; but—

HIGGINS [*storming on*] Take all her clothes off and burn them. Ring up Whitely or some-

---

**7. Monkey Brand:** A strong cleaning agent.

body for new ones. Wrap her up in brown paper til they come.

**LIZA.** Youre no gentleman, youre not, to talk of such things. I'm a good girl, I am; and I know what the like of you are, I do.

**HIGGINS.** We want none of your Lisson Grove prudery here, young woman. Youve got to learn to behave like a duchess. Take her away, Mrs Pearce. If she gives you any trouble, wallop her.

**LIZA** [*springing up and running between* PICKERING *and* MRS PEARCE *for protection*] No! I'll call the police, I will.

**MRS PEARCE.** But Ive no place to put her.

**HIGGINS.** Put her in the dustbin.

**LIZA.** Ah-ah-ah-ow-ow-oo!

**PICKERING.** O come, Higgins! be reasonable.

**MRS PEARCE** [*resolutely*] You must be reasonable, Mr Higgins: really you must. You cant walk over everybody like this.

HIGGINS, *thus scolded, subsides. The hurricane is succeeded by a zephyr of amiable surprise.*

**HIGGINS** [*with professional exquisiteness of modulation*] I walk over everybody! My dear Mrs Pearce, my dear Pickering, I never had the slightest intention of walking over anyone. All I propose is that we should be kind to this poor girl. We must help her to prepare and fit herself for her new station in life. If I did not express myself clearly it was because I did not wish to hurt her delicacy, or yours.

LIZA, *reassured, steals back to her chair.*

**MRS PEARCE** [*to* PICKERING] Well, did you ever hear anything like that, sir?

**PICKERING** [*laughing heartily*] Never, Mrs Pearce: never.

**HIGGINS** [*patiently*] Whats the matter?

**MRS PEARCE.** Well, the matter is, sir, that you cant take a girl up like that as if you were picking up a pebble on the beach.

**HIGGINS.** Why not?

**MRS PEARCE.** Why not! But you dont know anything about her. What about her parents? She may be married.

**LIZA.** Garn!

**HIGGINS.** There! As the girl very properly says, Garn! Married indeed! Dont you know that a woman of that class looks a worn out drudge of fifty a year after she's married?

**LIZA.** Whood marry me?

**HIGGINS** [*suddenly resorting to the most thrillingly beautiful low tones in his best elocutionary style*] By George, Eliza, the streets will be strewn with the bodies of men shooting themselves for your sake before Ive done with you.

**MRS PEARCE.** Nonsense, sir. You mustnt talk like that to her.

**LIZA** [*rising and squaring herself determinedly*] I'm going away. He's off his chump, he is. I dont want no balmies teaching me.

**HIGGINS** [*wounded in his tenderest point by her insensibility to his elocution*] Oh, indeed! I'm mad, am I? Very well, Mrs Pearce: you neednt order the new clothes for her. Throw her out.

**LIZA** [*whimpering*] Nah-ow. You got no right to touch me.

**MRS PEARCE.** You see now what comes of being saucy. [*Indicating the door*] This way, please.

**LIZA** [*almost in tears*] I didnt want no clothes. I wouldnt have taken them [*she throws away the handkerchief*]. I can buy my own clothes.

**HIGGINS** [*deftly retrieving the handkerchief and intercepting her on her reluctant way to the door*] Youre an ungrateful wicked girl. This is my return for offering to take you out of the gutter and dress you beautifully and make a lady of you.

MRS PEARCE. Stop, Mr Higgins. I wont allow it. It's you that are wicked. Go home to your parents, girl; and tell them to take better care of you.

LIZA. I aint got no parents. They told me I was big enough to earn my own living and turned me out.

MRS PEARCE. Wheres your mother?

LIZA. I aint got no mother. Her that turned me out was my sixth stepmother. But I done without them. And I'm a good girl, I am.

HIGGINS. Very well, then, what on earth is all this fuss about? The girl doesnt belong to anybody—is no use to anybody but me. [*He goes to* MRS PEARCE *and begins coaxing*]. You can adopt her, Mrs Pearce: I'm sure a daughter would be a great amusement to you. Now don't make any more fuss. Take her downstairs; and—

MRS PEARCE. But whats to become of her? Is she to be paid anything? Do be sensible, sir.

HIGGINS. Oh, pay her whatever is necessary: put it down in the housekeeping book. [*Impatiently*] What on earth will she want with money? She'll have her food and her clothes. She'll only drink if you give her money.

LIZA [*turning on him*] Oh you are a brute. It's a lie: nobody ever saw the sign of liquor on me. [*To* PICKERING] Oh, sir: youre a gentleman: dont let him speak to me like that.

PICKERING [*in good-humored remonstrance*] Does it occur to you, Higgins, that the girl has some feelings?

HIGGINS [*looking critically at her*] Oh no, I dont think so. Not any feelings that we need bother about. [*Cheerily*] Have you, Eliza?

LIZA. I got my feelings same as anyone else.

HIGGINS [*to* PICKERING, *reflectively*] You see the difficulty?

PICKERING. Eh? What difficulty?

HIGGINS. To get her to talk grammar. The mere pronunciation is easy enough.

LIZA. I dont want to talk grammar. I want to talk like a lady in a flower-shop.

MRS PEARCE. Will you please keep to the point, Mr Higgins. I want to know on what terms the girl is to be here. Is she to have any wages? And what is to become of her when youve finished your teaching? You must look ahead a little.

HIGGINS [*impatiently*] Whats to become of her if I leave her in the gutter? Tell me that, Mrs Pearce.

MRS PEARCE. Thats her own business, not yours, Mr Higgins.

HIGGINS. Well, when Ive done with her, we can throw her back into the gutter; and then it will be her own business again; so thats all right.

LIZA. Oh, youve no feeling heart in you: you dont care for nothing but yourself. [*She rises and takes the floor resolutely*]. Here! Ive had enough of this. I'm going [*making for the door*]. You ought to be ashamed of yourself, you ought.

HIGGINS [*snatching a chocolate cream from the piano, his eyes suddenly beginning to twinkle with mischief*] Have some chocolates, Eliza.

LIZA [*halting, tempted*] How do I know what might be in them? Ive heard of girls being drugged by the like of you.

HIGGINS *whips out his penknife; cuts a chocolate in two; puts one half into his mouth and bolts it; and offers her the other half.*

HIGGINS. Pledge of good faith, Eliza. I eat one half: you eat the other. [LIZA *opens her mouth to retort: he pops the half chocolate into it*]. You shall have boxes of them, barrels of them, every day. You shall live on them. Eh?

LIZA [*who has disposed of the chocolate after being nearly choked by it*] I wouldnt have ate it, only I'm too ladylike to take it out of my mouth.

**HIGGINS.** Listen, Eliza. I think you said you came in a taxi.

**LIZA.** Well, what if I did? Ive as good a right to take a taxi as anyone else.

**HIGGINS.** You have, Eliza; and in future you shall have as many taxis as you want. You shall go up and down and round the town in a taxi every day. Think of that, Eliza.

**MRS PEARCE.** Mr Higgins: youre tempting the girl. It's not right. She should think of the future.

**HIGGINS.** At her age! Nonsense! Time enough to think of the future when you havnt any future to think of. No, Eliza: do as this lady does: think of other people's futures; but never think of your own. Think of chocolates, and taxis, and gold, and diamonds.

**LIZA.** No: I dont want no gold and no diamonds. I'm a good girl, I am. [*She sits down again, with an attempt at dignity*].

**HIGGINS.** You shall remain so, Eliza, under the care of Mrs Pearce. And you shall marry an officer in the Guards, with a beautiful moustache: the son of a marquis, who will disinherit him for marrying you, but will relent when he sees your beauty and goodness—

**PICKERING.** Excuse me, Higgins; but I really must interfere. Mrs Pearce is quite right. If this girl is to put herself in your hands for six months for an experiment in teaching, she must understand thoroughly what she's doing.

**HIGGINS.** How can she? She's incapable of understanding anything. Besides, do any of us understand what we are doing? If we did, would we ever do it?

**PICKERING.** Very clever, Higgins; but not to the present point. [*To* ELIZA] Miss Doolittle—

**LIZA** [*overwhelmed*] Ah-ah-ow-oo!

**HIGGINS.** There! Thats all youll get out of Eliza. Ah-ah-ow-oo! No use explaining. As a military man you ought to know that. Give her her orders: thats enough for her. Eliza: you are to live here for the next six months, learning how to speak beautifully, like a lady in a florist's shop. If youre good and do whatever youre told, you shall sleep in a proper bedroom, and have lots to eat, and money to buy chocolates and take rides in taxis. If youre naughty and idle you will sleep in the back kitchen among the black beetles, and be walloped by Mrs Pearce with a broomstick. At the end of six months you shall go to Buckingham Palace in a carriage, beautifully dressed. If the King finds out youre not a lady, you will be taken by the police to the Tower of London, where your head will be cut off as a warning to other presumptuous flower girls. If you are not found out, you shall have a present of seven-and-sixpence to start life with as a lady in a shop. If you refuse this offer you will be a most ungrateful wicked girl; and the angels will weep for you. [*To* PICKERING] Now are you satisfied, Pickering? [*To* MRS PEARCE] Can I put it more plainly and fairly, Mrs Pearce?

**MRS PEARCE** [*patiently*] I think youd better let me speak to the girl properly in private. I dont know that I can take charge of her or consent to the arrangement at all. Of course I know you dont mean her any harm; but when you get what you call interested in people's accents, you never think or care what may happen to them or you. Come with me, Eliza.

**HIGGINS.** Thats all right. Thank you, Mrs Pearce. Bundle her off to the bath-room.

**LIZA** [*rising reluctantly and suspiciously*] Youre a great bully, you are. I wont stay here if I dont like. I wont let nobody wallop me. I never asked to go to Bucknam Palace, I didnt. I was never in trouble with the police, not me. I'm a good girl—

**MRS PEARCE.** Dont answer back, girl. You dont understand the gentleman. Come with me. [*She leads the way to the door, and holds it open for* ELIZA].

**LIZA** [*as she goes out*] Well, what I say is right. I wont go near the King, not if I'm going to have my head cut off. If I'd known what I was letting myself in for, I wouldnt have come here. I always been a good girl; and I never offered to say a word to him; and I dont owe him nothing; and I dont care; and I wont be put upon; and I have my feelings the same as anyone else—
MRS PEARCE *shuts the door; and* ELIZA*'s plaints are no longer audible.*

★     ★     ★     ★     ★     ★

Eliza is taken upstairs to the third floor greatly to her surprise; for she expected to be taken down to the scullery.[8] There Mrs Pearce opens a door and takes her into a spare bedroom.

**MRS PEARCE.** I will have to put you here. This will be your bedroom.

**LIZA.** O-h, I couldn't sleep here, missus. It's too good for the likes of me. I should be afraid to touch anything. I aint a duchess yet, you know.

**MRS PEARCE.** You have got to make yourself as clean as the room: then you wont be afraid of it. And you must call me Mrs Pearce, not missus. [*She throws open the door of the dressingroom, now modernized as a bathroom*].

**LIZA.** Gawd! whats this? Is this where you wash clothes? Funny sort of copper[9] I call it.

---

**8. scullery** *n.*: A room adjoining the kitchen, where pots and pans are cleaned and stored.
**9. copper** *n.*: A large metal container or boiler used for washing clothes.

**MRS PEARCE.** It is not a copper. This is where we wash ourselves, Eliza, and where I am going to wash you.

**LIZA.** You expect me to get into that and wet myself all over! Not me. I should catch my death. I knew a woman did it every Saturday night; and she died of it.

**MRS PEARCE.** Mr Higgins has the gentlemen's bathroom downstairs; and he has a bath every morning, in cold water.

**LIZA.** Ugh! He's made of iron, that man.

**MRS PEARCE.** If you are to sit with him and the Colonel and be taught you will have to do the same. They wont like the smell of you if you don't. But you can have the water as hot as you like. There are two taps: hot and cold.

**LIZA** [*weeping*] I couldnt. I dursnt. Its not natural: it would kill me. I've never had a bath in my life: not what youd call a proper one.

**MRS PEARCE.** Well, dont you want to be clean and sweet and decent, like a lady? You know you cant be a nice girl inside if youre a dirty slut outside.

**LIZA.** Boohoo!!!!

**MRS PEARCE.** Now stop crying and go back into your room and take off all your clothes. Then wrap yourself in this [*Taking down a gown from its peg and handing it to her*] and come back to me. I will get the bath ready.

**LIZA** [*all tears*] I cant. I wont. I'm not used to it. Ive never took off all my clothes before. It's not right: it's not decent.

**MRS PEARCE.** Nonsense, child. Dont you take off all your clothes every night when you go to bed?

**LIZA** [*amazed*] No. Why should I? I should catch my death. Of course I take off my skirt.

**MRS PEARCE.** Do you mean that you sleep in the underclothes you wear in the daytime?

**LIZA.** What else have I to sleep in?

**MRS PEARCE.** You will never do that again as long as you live here. I will get you a proper nightdress.

**LIZA.** Do you mean change into cold things and lie awake shivering half the night? You want to kill me, you do.

**MRS PEARCE.** I want to change you from a frowzy slut to a clean respectable girl fit to sit with the gentlemen in the study. Are you going to trust me and do what I tell you or be thrown out and sent back to your flower basket?

**LIZA.** But you dont know what the cold is to me. You dont know how I dread it.

**MRS PEARCE.** Your bed won't be cold here: I will put a hot water bottle in it. [*Pushing her into the bedroom*] Off with you and undress.

**LIZA.** Oh, if only I'd known what a dreadful thing it is to be clean I'd never have come. I didnt know when I was well off. I—[MRS PEARCE *pushes her through the door, but leaves it partly open lest her prisoner should take to flight*].

MRS PEARCE *puts on a pair of white rubber sleeves, and fills the bath, mixing hot and cold, and testing the result with the bath thermometer. She perfumes it with a handful of bath salts and adds a palmful of mustard. She then takes a formidable looking long handled scrubbing brush and soaps it profusely with a ball of scented soap.*

ELIZA *comes back with nothing on but the bath gown huddled tightly round her, a piteous spectacle of abject terror.*

**MRS PEARCE.** Now come along. Take that thing off.

**LIZA.** Oh I couldnt, Mrs Pearce: I reely couldnt. I never done such a thing.

**MRS PEARCE.** Nonsense. Here: step in and tell me whether its hot enough for you.

**LIZA.** Ah-oo! Ah-oo! It's too hot.

MRS PEARCE [*deftly snatching the gown away and throwing* ELIZA *down on her back*]. It wont hurt you. [*She sets to work with the scrubbing brush*].

ELIZA's *screams are heartrending.*

\*　　\*　　\*　　\*　　\*　　\*

Meanwhile the Colonel has been having it out with Higgins about Eliza. Pickering has come from the hearth to the chair and seated himself astride of it with his arms on the back to cross-examine him.

PICKERING. Excuse the straight question, Higgins. Are you a man of good character where women are concerned?

HIGGINS [*moodily*] Have you ever met a man of good character where women are concerned?

PICKERING. Yes: very frequently.

HIGGINS [*dogmatically, lifting himself on his hands to the level of the piano, and sitting on it with a bounce*] Well, I havnt. I find that the moment I let a woman make friends with me, she becomes jealous, exacting, suspicious, and a damned nuisance. I find that the moment I let myself make friends with a woman, I become selfish and tyrannical. Women upset everything. When you let them into your life, you find that the woman is driving at one thing and youre driving at another.

PICKERING. At what, for example?

HIGGINS [*coming off the piano restlessly*] Oh, Lord knows! I suppose the woman wants to live her own life; and the man wants to live his; and each tries to drag the other on to the wrong track. One wants to go north and the other south; and the result is that both have to go east, though they both hate the east wind. [*He sits down on the bench at the keyboard*]. So here I am, a confirmed old bachelor, and likely to remain so.

PICKERING [*rising and standing over him gravely*] Come, Higgins! You know what I mean. If I'm to be in this business I shall feel responsible for that girl. I hope it's understood that no advantage is to be taken of her position.

HIGGINS. What! That thing! Sacred, I assure you. [*Rising to explain*] You see, she'll be a pupil; and teaching would be impossible unless pupils were sacred. Ive taught scores of American millionairesses how to speak English: the best looking women in the world. I'm seasoned. They might as well be blocks of wood. *I* might as well be a block of wood. It's—

MRS PEARCE *opens the door. She has* ELIZA's *hat in her hand.* PICKERING *retires to the easy-chair at the hearth and sits down.*

HIGGINS [*eagerly*] Well, Mrs Pearce is it all right?

MRS PEARCE [*at the door*] I just wish to trouble you with a word, if I may, Mr. Higgins.

HIGGINS. Yes, certainly. Come in. [*She comes forward*]. Dont burn that, Mrs Pearce. I'll keep it as a curiosity. [*He takes the hat*].

MRS PEARCE. Handle it carefully, sir, please. I had to promise her not to burn it; but I had better put it in the oven for a while.

HIGGINS [*putting it down hastily on the piano*] Oh! thank you. Well, what have you to say to me?

PICKERING. Am I in the way?

MRS PEARCE. Not in the least, sir. Mr Higgins: will you please be very particular what you say before the girl?

HIGGINS [*sternly*] Of course. I'm always particular about what I say. Why do you say this to me?

MRS PEARCE [*unmoved*] No, sir: youre not at all particular when youve mislaid anything or when you get a little impatient. Now it doesnt matter before me: I'm used to it. But you really must not swear before the girl.

HIGGINS [*indignantly*] I swear! [*Most emphatically*] I never swear. I detest the habit. What the devil do you mean?

**MRS PEARCE** [*stolidly*] Thats what I mean, sir. You swear a great deal too much. I dont mind your damning and blasting, and what the devil and where the devil and who the devil—

**HIGGINS.** Mrs Pearce: this language from your lips! Really!

**MRS PEARCE** [*not to be put off*]—but there is a certain word I must ask you not to use. The girl used it herself when she began to enjoy the bath. It begins with the same letter as bath. She knows no better: she learnt it at her mother's knee. But she must not hear it from your lips.

**HIGGINS** [*loftily*] I cannot charge myself with having ever uttered it, Mrs Pearce. [*She looks at him steadfastly. He adds, hiding an uneasy conscience with a judicial air*] Except perhaps in a moment of extreme and justifiable excitement.

**MRS PEARCE.** Only this morning, sir, you applied it to your boots, to the butter, and to the brown bread.

**HIGGINS.** Oh, that! Mere alliteration, Mrs Pearce, natural to a poet.

**MRS PEARCE.** Well, sir, whatever you choose to call it, I beg you not to let the girl hear you repeat it.

**HIGGINS.** Oh, very well, very well. Is that all?

**MRS PEARCE.** No, sir. We shall have to be very particular with this girl as to personal cleanliness.

**HIGGINS.** Certainly. Quite right. Most important.

**MRS PEARCE.** I mean not to be slovenly about her dress or untidy in leaving things about.

**HIGGINS** [*going to her solemnly*] Just so. I intended to call your attention to that. [*He passes on to* PICKERING, *who is enjoying the conversation immensely*]. It is these little things that matter, Pickering. Take care of the pence and the pounds will take care of themselves is as true of personal habits as of money. [*He comes to anchor on the hearth-rug, with the air of a man in an unassailable position*].

**MRS PEARCE.** Yes, sir. Then might I ask you not to come down to breakfast in your dressing-gown, or at any rate not to use it as a napkin to the extent you do, sir. And if you would be so good as not to eat everything off the same plate, and to remember not to put the porridge saucepan out of your hand on the clean tablecloth, it would be a better example to the girl. You know you nearly choked yourself with a fishbone in a jam only last week.

**HIGGINS** [*routed from the hearthrug and drifting back to the piano*] I may do these things sometimes in absence of mind; but surely I dont do them habitually. [*Angrily*] By the way: my dressing-gown smells most damnably of benzine.

**MRS PEARCE.** No doubt it does, Mr Higgins. But if you will wipe your fingers—

**HIGGINS** [*yelling*] Oh very well, very well: I'll wipe them in my hair in future.

**MRS PEARCE.** I hope youre not offended, Mr Higgins.

**HIGGINS** [*shocked at finding himself thought capable of an unamiable sentiment*] Not at all, not at all. Youre quite right, Mrs Pearce: I shall be particularly careful before the girl. Is that all?

**MRS PEARCE.** No, sir. Might she use some of those Japanese dresses you brought from abroad? I really cant put her back into her old things.

**HIGGINS.** Certainly. Anything you like. Is that all?

**MRS PEARCE.** Thank you, sir. Thats all. [*She goes out*].

**HIGGINS.** You know, Pickering, that woman has the most extraordinary ideas about me. Here I am, a shy, diffident sort of man. I've never been able to feel really grown-up and tremendous, like other chaps. And yet she's firmly persuaded that I'm an arbitrary overbearing bossing kind of person. I cant account for it.

MRS PEARCE *returns.*

**MRS PEARCE.** If you please, sir, the trouble's beginning already. Theres a dustman[10] downstairs, Alfred Doolittle, wants to see you. He says you have his daughter here.

**PICKERING** [*rising*] Phew! I say!

**HIGGINS** [*promptly*] Send the blackguard[11] up.

**MRS PEARCE.** Oh, very well, sir. [*She goes out*].

**PICKERING.** He may not be a blackguard, Higgins.

**HIGGINS.** Nonsense. Of course he's a blackguard.

**PICKERING.** Whether he is or not, I'm afraid we shall have some trouble with him.

**HIGGINS** [*confidently*] Oh no: I think not. If theres any trouble he shall have it with me, not I with him. And we are sure to get something interesting out of him.

**PICKERING.** About the girl?

**HIGGINS.** No. I mean his dialect.

**PICKERING.** Oh!

**MRS PEARCE** [*at the door*] Doolittle, sir. [*She admits* DOOLITTLE *and retires*].

ALFRED *is an elderly but vigorous dustman, clad in the costume of his profession, including a hat with a back brim covering his neck and shoulders. He has well marked and rather interesting features, and seems equally free from fear and conscience. He has a remarkably expressive voice, the result of a habit of giving vent to his feelings without reserve. His present pose is that of wounded honor and stern resolution.*

---

**10. dustman** *n.*: A garbage collector.
**11. blackguard** (blag′ ərd) *n.*: Scoundrel.

**DOOLITTLE** [*at the door, uncertain which of the two gentlemen is his man*] Professor Iggins?

**HIGGINS.** Here. Good morning. Sit down.

**DOOLITTLE.** Morning, Governor. [*He sits down magisterially*]. I come about a very serious matter, Governor.

**HIGGINS** [*to* PICKERING] Brought up in Hounslow. Mother Welsh, I should think. [DOOLITTLE *opens his mouth, amazed.* HIGGINS *continues*] What do you want, Doolittle?

**DOOLITTLE** [*menacingly*] I want my daughter: thats what I want. See?

**HIGGINS.** Of course you do. Youre her father, arnt you? You dont suppose anyone else wants her, do you? I'm glad to see you have some spark of family feeling left. She's upstairs. Take her away at once.

**DOOLITTLE** [*rising, fearfully taken aback*] What!

**HIGGINS.** Take her away. Do you suppose I'm going to keep your daughter for you?

**DOOLITTLE** [*remonstrating*] Now, now, look here, Governor. Is it reasonable? Is it fairity to take advantage of a man like this? The girl belongs to me. You got her. Where do I come in? [*He sits down again*].

**HIGGINS.** Your daughter had the audacity to come to my house and ask me to teach her how to speak properly so that she could get a place in a flower-shop. This gentleman and my housekeeper have been here all the time. [*Bullying him*] How dare you come here and attempt to blackmail me? You sent her here on purpose.

**DOOLITTLE** [*protesting*] No, Governor.

**HIGGINS.** You must have. How else could you possibly know that she is here?

**DOOLITTLE.** Don't take a man up like that, Governor.

**HIGGINS.** The police shall take you up. This is a plant—a plot to extort money by threats. I

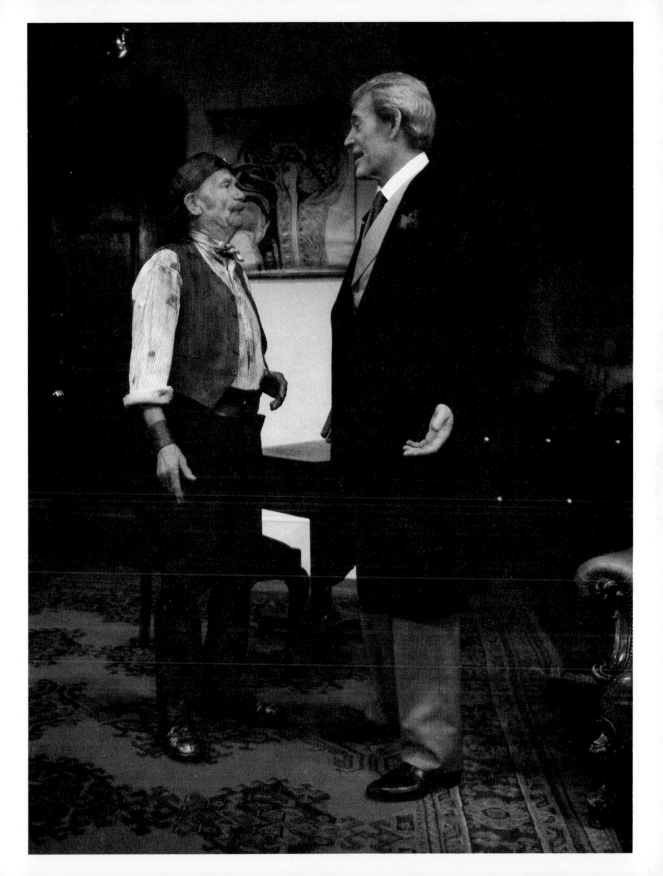

shall telephone for the police [*he goes reso-lutely to the telephone and opens the directory*]

**DOOLITTLE.** Have I asked you for a brass farthing? I leave it to the gentleman here: have I said a word about money?

**HIGGINS** [*throwing the book aside and marching down on* DOOLITTLE *with a poser*] What else did you come for?

**DOOLITTLE** [*sweetly*] Well, what would a man come for? Be human, Governor.

**HIGGINS** [*disarmed*] Alfred: did you put her up to it?

**DOOLITTLE.** So help me, Governor. I never did. I take my Bible oath I aint seen the girl these two months past.

**HIGGINS.** Then how did you know she was here?

**DOOLITTLE** [*"most musical, most melancholy"*] I'll tell you, Governor, if youll only let me get a word in. I'm willing to tell you. I'm wanting to tell you. I'm waiting to tell you.

**HIGGINS.** Pickering: this chap has a certain natural gift of rhetoric. Observe the rhythm of his native woodnotes wild. "I'm willing to tell you: I'm wanting to tell you: I'm waiting to tell you." Sentimental rhetoric! thats the Welsh strain in him. It also accounts for his mendacity and dishonesty.

**PICKERING.** Oh, please, Higgins: I'm west country myself. [*To* DOOLITTLE] How did you know the girl was here if you didnt send her?

**DOOLITTLE.** It was like this, Governor. The girl took a boy in the taxi to give him a jaunt. Son of her landlady, he is. He hung about on the chance of her giving him another ride home. Well, she sent him back for her luggage when she heard you was willing for her to stop here. I met the boy at the corner of Long Acre and Endell Street.

**HIGGINS.** Public house. Yes?

**DOOLITTLE.** The poor man's club, Governor: why shouldnt I?

**PICKERING.** Do let him tell his story, Higgins.

**DOOLITTLE.** He told me what was up. And I ask you, what was my feelings and my duty as a father? I says to the boy, "You bring me the luggage," I says—

**PICKERING.** Why didnt you go for it yourself?

**DOOLITTLE.** Landlady wouldnt have trusted me with it, Governor. She's that kind of woman: you know. I had to give the boy a penny afore he trusted me with it, the little swine. I brought it to her just to oblige you like, and make myself agreeable. Thats all.

**HIGGINS.** How much luggage?

**DOOLITTLE.** Musical instrument, Governor. A few pictures, a trifle of jewelry, and a bird-cage. She said she didn't want no clothes. What was I to think from that, Governor? I ask you as a parent what was I to think?

**HIGGINS.** So you came to rescue her from worse than death, eh?

**DOOLITTLE** [*appreciatively: relieved at being so well understood*] Just so, Governor. That's right.

**PICKERING.** But why did you bring her luggage if you intended to take her away?

**DOOLITTLE.** Have I said a word about taking her away? Have I now?

**HIGGINS** [*determinedly*] Youre going to take her away, double quick. [*He crosses to the hearth and rings the bell*].

**DOOLITTLE** [*rising*] No, Governor. Dont say that. I'm not the man to stand in my girl's light. Heres a career opening for her, as you might say; and—

MRS PEARCE *opens the door and awaits orders.*

**HIGGINS.** Mrs Pearce: this is Eliza's father. He has come to take her away. Give her to him. [*He goes back to the piano, with an air of* *washing his hands of the whole affair*].

**DOOLITTLE.** No. This is a misunderstanding. Listen here—

**MRS PEARCE.** He cant take her away. Mr Higgins: how can he? You told me to burn her clothes.

**DOOLITTLE.** Thats right. I cant carry the girl through the streets like a blooming monkey, can I? I put it to you.

**HIGGINS.** You have put it to me that you want your daughter. Take your daughter. If she has no clothes go out and buy her some.

**DOOLITTLE** [*desperate*] Wheres the clothes she come in? Did I burn them or did your missus here?

**MRS PEARCE.** I am the housekeeper, if you please. I have sent for some clothes for your girl. When they come you can take her away. You can wait in the kitchen. This way, please.

DOOLITTLE, *much troubled, accompanies her to the door; then hesitates; finally turns confidentially to* HIGGINS.

**DOOLITTLE.** Listen here, Governor. You and me is men of the world, aint we?

**HIGGINS.** Oh! Men of the world, are we? Youd better go, Mrs Pearce.

**MRS PEARCE.** I think so, indeed, sir. [*She goes, with dignity*].

**PICKERING.** The floor is yours, Mr Doolittle.

**DOOLITTLE** [*to* PICKERING] I thank you, Governor. [*To* HIGGINS, *who takes refuge on the piano bench, a little overwhelmed by the proximity of his visitor; for* DOOLITTLE *has a professional flavour of dust about him*]. Well, the truth is, I've taken a sort of fancy to you, Governor; and if you want the girl, I'm not so set on having her back home again but what I might be open to an arrangement. Regarded in the light of a young woman, she's a fine handsome girl. As a daughter she's not worth her keep; and so I tell you straight. All I ask is my rights as a father; and youre the last man alive to expect me to let her go for nothing; for I can see youre one of the straight sort, Governor. Well, whats a five-pound note to you? and whats Eliza to me? [*He turns to his chair and sits down judicially*].

**PICKERING.** I think you ought to know, Doolittle, that Mr Higgins's intentions are entirely honorable.

**DOOLITTLE.** Course they are, Governor. If I thought they wasnt, I'd ask fifty.

**HIGGINS** [*revolted*] Do you mean to say that you would sell your daughter for £50?

**DOOLITTLE.** Not in a general way I would; but to oblige a gentleman like you I'd do a good deal, I do assure you.

**PICKERING.** Have you no morals, man?

**DOOLITTLE** [*unabashed*] Cant afford them, Governor. Neither could you if you was as poor as me. Not that I mean any harm, you know. But if Liza is going to have a bit out of this, why not me too?

**HIGGINS** [*troubled*] I dont know what to do, Pickering. There can be no question that as a matter of morals it's a positive crime to give this chap a farthing. And yet I feel a sort of rough justice in his claim.

**DOOLITTLE.** Thats it, Governor. Thats all I say. A father's heart, as it were.

**PICKERING.** Well, I know the feeling; but really it seems hardly right—

**DOOLITTLE.** Dont say that, Governor. Dont look at it that way. What am I, Governors both? I ask you, what am I? I'm one of the undeserving poor: thats what I am. Think of what that means to a man. It means that he's up agen middle class morality all the time. If theres anything going, and I put in for a bit of it, it's always the same story: "Youre undeserving; so you cant have it." But my needs is as great as the most deserving widows' that ever got money out of six different charities in one week for the death of the same husband. I dont need less than a deserving man: I need more. I dont eat less hearty than him; and I drink a lot more. I want a bit of amusement, cause I'm a thinking man. I want cheerfulness and a song and a band when I feel low. Well, they charge me just the same for everything as they charge the deserving. What is middle class morality? Just an excuse for never giving me anything. Therefore, I ask you, as two gentlemen, not to play that game on me. I'm playing straight with you. I aint pretending to be deserving. I'm undeserving; and I mean to go on being undeserving. I like it; and thats the truth. Will you take advantage of a man's nature to do him out of the price of his own daughter what he's brought up and fed and clothed by the sweat of his brow until she's growed big enough to be interesting to you two gentlemen? Is five pounds unreasonable? I put it to you; and I leave it to you.

HIGGINS [*rising, and going over to* PICKERING] Pickering: if we were to take this man in hand for three months, he could choose between a seat in the Cabinet and a popular pulpit in Wales.

PICKERING. What do you say to that, Doolittle?

DOOLITTLE. Not me, Governor, thank you kindly. Ive heard all the preachers and all the prime ministers—for I'm a thinking man and game for politics or religion or social reform same as all the other amusements—and I tell you it's a dog's life any way you look at it. Undeserving poverty is my line. Taking one station in society with another, it's—it's—well, it's the only one that has any ginger in it, to my taste.

HIGGINS. I suppose we must give him a fiver.

PICKERING. He'll make a bad use of it, I'm afraid.

DOOLITTLE. Not me, Governor, so help me I wont. Dont you be afraid that I'll save it and

spare it and live idle on it. There wont be a penny of it left by Monday: I'll have to go to work same as if I'd never had it. It wont pauperize me, you bet. Just one good spree for myself and the missus, giving pleasure to ourselves and employment to others, and satisfaction to you to think it's not been throwed away. You couldn't spend it better.

HIGGINS [*taking out his pocket book and coming between* DOOLITTLE *and the piano*] This is irresistible. Lets give him ten. [*He offers two notes to the* DUSTMAN]

DOOLITTLE. No, Governor. She wouldnt have the heart to spend ten; and perhaps I shouldnt neither. Ten pounds is a lot of money: it makes a man feel prudent like; and then good-bye to happiness. You give me what I ask you, Governor: not a penny more, and not a penny less.

PICKERING. Why dont you marry that missus of yours? I rather draw the line at encouraging that sort of immorality.

DOOLITTLE. Tell her so, Governor: tell her so. I'm willing. It's me that suffers by it. Ive no hold on her. I got to be agreeable to her. I got to give her presents. I got to buy her clothes something sinful. I'm a slave to that woman, Governor, just because I'm not her lawful husband. And she knows it too. Catch her marrying me! Take my advice, Governor: marry Eliza while she's young and dont know no better. If you dont youll be sorry for it after. If you do, she'll be sorry for it after; but better her than you, because youre a man, and she's only a woman and dont know how to be happy anyhow.

HIGGINS. Pickering: if we listen to this man another minute, we shall have no convictions left. [*To* DOOLITTLE] Five pounds I think you said.

DOOLITTLE. Thank you kindly, Governor.

HIGGINS. Youre sure you wont take ten?

DOOLITTLE. Not now. Another time, Governor.

HIGGINS [*handing him a five-pound note*] Here you are.

DOOLITTLE. Thank you, Governor. Good morning. [*He hurries to the door, anxious to get away with his booty. When he opens it he is confronted with a dainty and exquisitely clean young Japanese lady in a simple blue cotton kimono printed cunningly with small white jasmine blossoms.* MRS PEARCE *is with her. He gets out of her way deferentially and apologizes*]. Beg pardon, miss.

THE JAPANESE LADY. Garn! Dont you know your own daughter?

| DOOLITTLE | { *exclaiming* | { Bly me! it's Eliza! |
| HIGGINS | *simul-* | Whats that? This! |
| PICKERING | *taneously* | By Jove! |

LIZA. Dont I look silly?

HIGGINS. Silly?

MRS PEARCE [*at the door*] Now, Mr Higgins, please dont say anything to make the girl conceited about herself.

HIGGINS [*conscientiously*] Oh! Quite right, Mrs Pearce. [*To* ELIZA] Yes: damned silly.

MRS PEARCE. Please, sir.

HIGGINS [*correcting himself*] I mean extremely silly.

LIZA. I should look all right with my hat on. [*She takes up her hat; puts it on; and walks across the room to the fireplace with a fashionable air*].

HIGGINS. A new fashion, by George! And it ought to look horrible!

DOOLITTLE [*with fatherly pride*] Well, I never thought she'd clean up as good looking as that, Governor. She's a credit to me, aint she?

LIZA. I tell you, it's easy to clean up here. Hot and cold water on tap, just as much as you like, there is. Woolly towels, there is; and a towel horse[12] so hot, it burns your fingers. Soft brushes to scrub yourself, and a wooden bowl of soap smelling like primroses. Now I know why ladies is so clean. Washing's a treat for them. Wish they could see what it is for the like of me!

HIGGINS. I'm glad the bathroom met with your approval.

LIZA. It didnt: not all of it; and I dont care who hears me say it. Mrs Pearce knows.

HIGGINS. What was wrong, Mrs Pearce?

MRS PEARCE [*blandly*] Oh, nothing, sir. It doesnt matter.

LIZA. I had a good mind to break it. I didnt know which way to look. But I hung a towel over it, I did.

HIGGINS. Over what?

MRS PEARCE. Over the looking-glass, sir.

HIGGINS. Doolittle: you have brought your daughter up too strictly.

DOOLITTLE. Me! I never brought her up at all, except to give her a lick of a strap now and again. Dont put it on me, Governor. She aint accustomed to it, you see: thats all. But she'll soon pick up your free-and-easy ways.

LIZA. I'm a good girl, I am; and I wont pick up no free-and-easy ways.

HIGGINS. Eliza: if you say again that youre a good girl, your father shall take you home.

LIZA. Not him. You dont know my father. All he come here for was to touch you for some money to get drunk on.

DOOLITTLE. Well, what else would I want money for? To put into the plate in church, I suppose. [*She puts out her tongue at him. He is so incensed by this that* PICKERING *presently finds it necessary to step between*

---

**12. towel horse:** Towel rack; in this case the rack is heated to dry the towels.

them]. Dont you give me none of your lip; and dont let me hear you giving this gentleman any of it neither, or youll hear from me about it. See?

HIGGINS. Have you any further advice to give her before you go, Doolittle? Your blessing, for instance.

DOOLITTLE. No, Governor: I aint such a mug as to put up my children to all I know myself. Hard enough to hold them in without that. If you want Eliza's mind improved, Governor, you do it yourself with a strap. So long, gentlemen. [He turns to go].

HIGGINS [impressively] Stop. Youll come regularly to see your daughter. It's your duty, you know. My brother is a clergyman; and he could help you in your talks with her.

DOOLITTLE [evasively] Certainly, I'll come, Governor. Not just this week, because I have a job at a distance. But later on you may depend on me. Afternoon, gentlemen. Afternoon, maam. [He touches his hat to MRS PEARCE, who disdains the salutation and goes out. He winks at HIGGINS, thinking him probably a fellow-sufferer from MRS PEARCE's difficult disposition, and follows her].

**LIZA.** Dont you believe the old liar. He'd as soon you set a bulldog on him as a clergyman. You wont see him again in a hurry.

**HIGGINS.** I dont want to, Eliza. Do you?

**LIZA.** Not me. I dont want never to see him again, I dont. He's a disgrace to me, he is, collecting dust,[13] instead of working at his trade.

**PICKERING.** What is his trade, Eliza?

**LIZA.** Talking money out of other people's pockets into his own. His proper trade's a navvy;[14] and he works at it sometimes too —for exercise—and earns good money at it. Aint you going to call me Miss Doolittle any more?

**PICKERING.** I beg your pardon, Miss Doolittle. It was a slip of the tongue.

**LIZA.** Oh, I dont mind; only it sounded so genteel. I should just like to take a taxi to the corner of Tottenham Court Road and get out there and tell it to wait for me, just to put the girls in their place a bit. I wouldnt speak to them, you know.

**PICKERING.** Better wait til we get you something really fashionable.

**HIGGINS.** Besides, you shouldnt cut your old friends now that you have risen in the world. Thats what we call snobbery.

**LIZA.** You dont call the like of them my friends now, I should hope. Theyve took it out of me often enough with their ridicule when they had the chance; and now I mean to get a bit of my own back. But if I'm to have fashionable clothes, I'll wait. I should like to have some. Mrs Pearce says youre going to give me some to wear in bed at night different to what I wear in the daytime; but it do seem a waste of money when you could get something to shew. Besides, I never could fancy changing into cold things on a winter night.

---

13. **collecting dust:** Picking up garbage.
14. **navvy** (nav′ ē) *n*.: An unskilled laborer.

**MRS PEARCE** [*coming back*] Now, Eliza. The new things have come for you to try on.

**LIZA.** Ah-ow-oo-ooh! [*She rushes out*].

**MRS PEARCE** [*following her*] Oh, dont rush about like that, girl. [*She shuts the door behind her*].

**HIGGINS.** Pickering: we have taken on a stiff job.

**PICKERING** [*with conviction*] Higgins: we have.

★    ★    ★    ★    ★    ★

There seems to be some curiosity as to what Higgins's lessons to Eliza were like. Well, here is a sample: the first one.

Picture Eliza, in her new clothes, and feeling her inside put out of step by a lunch, dinner, and breakfast of a kind to which it is unaccustomed, seated with Higgins and the Colonel in the study, feeling like a hospital out-patient at a first encounter with the doctors.

Higgins, constitutionally unable to sit still, discomposes her still more by striding restlessly about. But for the reassuring presence and quietude of her friend the Colonel she would run for her life, even back to Drury Lane.

**HIGGINS.** Say your alphabet.

**LIZA.** I know my alphabet. Do you think I know nothing? I dont need to be taught like a child.

**HIGGINS** [*thundering*] Say your alphabet.

**PICKERING.** Say it, Miss Doolittle. You will understand presently. Do what he tells you; and let him teach you in his own way.

**LIZA.** Oh well, if you put it like that—Ahyee, bəyee, cəyee, dəyee—

**HIGGINS** [*with the roar of a wounded lion*] Stop. Listen to this, Pickering. This is what we pay for as elementary education. This unfortunate animal has been locked up for nine years in school at our expense to teach her to speak and read the language of

Shakespear and Milton. And the result is Ahyee, Bə-yee, Cə-yee, Dəyee. [*To* ELIZA] Say A, B, C, D.

LIZA [*almost in tears*] But I'm sayin it. Ahyee, Bəyee, Cəyee—

HIGGINS. Stop. Say a cup of tea.

LIZA. A cappətə-ee.

HIGGINS. Put your tongue forward until it squeezes against the top of your lower teeth. Now say cup.

LIZA. C-c-c—I cant. C-Cup.

PICKERING. Good. Splendid, Miss Doolittle.

HIGGINS. By Jupiter, she's done it the first shot. Pickering: we shall make a duchess of her. [*To* ELIZA] Now do you think you could possibly say tea? Not tə-yee, mind: if you ever say bə-yee cə-yee də-yee again you shall be dragged round the room three times by the hair of your head. [*Fortissimo*] T, T, T, T.

LIZA [*weeping*] I cant hear no difference cep that it sounds more genteel-like when you say it.

HIGGINS. Well, if you can hear the difference, what the devil are you crying for? Pickering: give her a chocolate.

PICKERING. No, no. Never mind crying a little, Miss Doolittle: you are doing very well; and the lessons wont hurt. I promise you I wont let him drag you round the room by your hair.

HIGGINS. Be off with you to Mrs Pearce and tell her about it. Think about it. Try to do it by yourself: and keep your tongue well forward in your mouth instead of trying to roll it up and swallow it. Another lesson at half-past four this afternoon. Away with you.

ELIZA, *still sobbing, rushes from the room.*

And that is the sort of ordeal Eliza has to go through for months before we meet her again on her first appearance in London society of the professional class.

---

## THINKING ABOUT THE SELECTION

### Recalling

1. (a) Why has Eliza come to see Higgins? (b) With what does she offer to pay him?
2. What are the terms of the bet Pickering proposes?
3. (a) What are Mrs. Pearce's concerns with regard to the arrangement? (b) What are Pickering's?
4. (a) What is the purpose of Alfred Doolittle's visit? (b) How does Higgins respond to his demands?

### Interpreting

5. What differences between Higgins and Pickering are pointed out in Act II?

6. (a) What is revealed about the role of women of this era? (b) About middle-class and lower-class ideals?

### Applying

7. (a) How does Higgins's treatment of Eliza strike you? (b) Do you think this was Shaw's intention? Explain.

## ANALYZING LITERATURE

### Understanding Character Development

**Character development** is the technique of adding depth to characters by causing them to grow by reacting to other characters and events. A static character is essentially unaltered by involvements of plot, whereas a dynamic character is affected, sometimes radically. In order to observe changes in a character, we must have a clear idea of what qualities that character possesses in the first place.

Using at least five adjectives or descriptive phrases, profile each of the five characters appearing in Act II. Then tell which of the characters is static and which is dynamic, giving your reasons for your classifications.

## CRITICAL THINKING AND READING
### Making Inferences About Characters

Occasionally, in a literary work, we receive conflicting reports on a character's ambitions, motives, and thoughts. This is because, as in real life, a character's self-image often differs drastically from the image other characters hold of her or him. It is the responsibility of the alert reader to consider all information and then to *infer,* or assemble, from it an accurate picture of the character in question. Tell what impression the speaker of each of the following lines hopes to convey, and what impression he or she succeeds in conveying.

1. THE FLOWER GIRL. Did you tell him I come in a taxi? (page 1122)
2. HIGGINS. *I* walk over everybody! My dear Mrs Pearce, my dear Pickering, I never had the slightest intention of walking over anyone. (page 1125)
3. DOOLITTLE. I come about a very serious matter, Governor. (page 1132)

## SPEAKING AND LISTENING
### Reading Dialogue Aloud

**Dialogue** consists of lines that represent the actual speech utterances or conversations of the characters in a literary work. In a play, dialogue is everything. Ideally, dialogue should give the impression of actual conversation, not separate speeches. Shaw orchestrated his dialogue like music, varying tempo and intonation to emphasize the ideas and attitudes being expressed. Choose sections of Act II, assign roles, and stage an in-class reading. To make the dialogue as natural and lifelike as possible, readers should consider what they know about each character, including his or her speech habits.

## THINKING AND WRITING
### Comparing and Contrasting Characters

Using information you have accumulated about the characters thus far, write an essay that explores similarities and differences between any two of the characters in Act II. First select the characters and jot down notes about them. Then write your first draft, remembering to pay attention to underlying motives and stage directions in arriving at an understanding of each character. When you revise, make sure your essay is ordered logically and that you have supported your thesis with details from the play. Proofread your essay and prepare a final draft.

# GUIDE FOR INTERPRETING

## Pygmalion, Act III

**Satire.** Satire is a technique that combines humor with criticism to expose flaws and shortcomings in institutions or human beings. Shaw, as an advocate of reform, saw in this brand of "serious comedy" an effective tool. "After all," he wrote, "the salvation of the world depends on the men who will not take evil good-humoredly, and whose laughter destroys the fool instead of encouraging him." The targets, methods, and styles of satire are many and varied. Unfair or outdated laws, pointless rules and regulations, prejudices and mindless conventions, illogical political policies, fads and styles—all have been held up to ridicule in poems, novels, essays, and plays. Today satire flourishes in such diverse media as film, television, cartoons, comic strips, and comedy acts, not to mention, of course, literature. Novels such as George Orwell's *Nineteen Eighty-four,* Evelyn Waugh's *The Loved One,* and Joseph Heller's *Catch-22* satirize many aspects of twentieth-century life.

Brainstorm in small groups in an effort to come up with a list of styles and habits that you find especially laughable. Attempt to pinpoint the features of your subject that seem silly, unreasonable, or unfair.

One of the literary weapons that Shaw used in *Pygmalion* to right society's wrongs was satire. In his criticism as well he pointed out society's faults through whatever means might be effective—and he never hesitated to voice his opinion. Answering complaints that his criticism was full of personal feeling, he said,

> It is the capacity for making good or bad art a personal matter that makes a man a critic. When people do less than their best, and do that less at once badly and self-complacently, I hate them, loathe them, detest them, long to tear them limb from limb. . . . In the same way, really fine artists inspire me with the warmest personal regard, which I gratify in writing my notices without the smallest reference to . . . justice, impartiality, and the rest of the ideals. When my critical mood is at its height, personal feeling is not the word: it is passion: the passion for artistic perfection—for the noblest beauty of sound, sight, and action—that rages in me. Let all young artists look to it, and pay no heed to the idiots who declare that criticism should be free from personal feeling. The true critic, I repeat, is the man who becomes your personal enemy on the sole provocation of a bad performance and will only be appeased by a good performance.

## ACT III

*It is* MRS HIGGINS'*s at-home day.*[1] *Nobody has yet arrived. Her drawing room, in a flat on Chelsea Embankment, has three windows looking on the river; and the ceiling is not so lofty as it would be in an older house of the same pretension. The windows are open, giving access to a balcony with flowers in pots. If you stand with your face to the windows, you have the fireplace on your left and the door in the right-hand wall close to the corner nearest the windows.*

MRS HIGGINS *was brought up on Morris*[2] *and Burne Jones;*[3] *and her room, which is very unlike her son's room in Wimpole Street, is not crowded with furniture and little tables and nicknacks. In the middle of the room there is a big ottoman; and this, with the carpet, the Morris wall-papers, and the Morris chintz window curtains and brocade covers of the ottoman and its cushions, supply all the ornament, and are much too handsome to be hidden by odds and ends of useless things. A few good oil-paintings from the exhibitions in the Grosvenor Gallery thirty years ago (the Burne Jones, not the Whistler*[4] *side of them) are on the walls. The only landscape is a Cecil Lawson*[5] *on the scale of a Rubens.*[6] *There is a portrait of* MRS HIGGINS *as she was when she defied the fashion in her youth in one of the beautiful Rossettian*[7] *costumes which, when caricatured by peo-ple who did not understand, led to the absurdities of popular estheticism in the eighteen-seventies.*

*In the corner diagonally opposite the door* MRS HIGGINS, *now over sixty and long past taking the trouble to dress out of the fashion, sits writing at an elegantly simple writing-table with a bell button within reach of her hand. There is a Chippendale chair further back in the room between her and the window nearest her side. At the other side of the room, further forward, is an Elizabethan chair roughly carved in the taste of Inigo Jones.*[8] *On the same side a piano in a decorated case. The corner between the fireplace and the window is occupied by a divan cushioned in Morris chintz.*

*It is between four and five in the afternoon.*

*The door is opened violently; and* HIGGINS *enters with his hat on.*

**MRS HIGGINS** [*dismayed*] Henry! [*Scolding him*] What are you doing here today? It is my at-home day: you promised not to come. [*As he bends to kiss her, she takes his hat off, and presents it to him*].

**HIGGINS.** Oh bother! [*He throws the hat down on the table*].

**MRS HIGGINS.** Go home at once.

**HIGGINS** [*kissing her*] I know, mother. I came on purpose.

**MRS HIGGINS.** But you mustnt. I'm serious, Henry. You offend all my friends: they stop coming whenever they meet you.

**HIGGINS.** Nonsense! I know I have no small talk; but people dont mind. [*He sits on the settee*].

**MRS HIGGINS.** Oh! dont they? Small talk indeed! What about your large talk? Really, dear, you mustnt stay.

---

**1. at-home day:** The day of the week when a lady regularly receives visitors.
**2. Morris:** William Morris (1834–1896), English poet, artist, and craftsman.
**3. Burne Jones:** Sir Edward Corley Burne-Jones (1833–1898), English painter and designer.
**4. Whistler:** James Abbott McNeill Whistler (1834–1903), an American painter who lived in England.
**5. Cecil Lawson:** Cecil Gordon Lawson (1851–1882), English landscape painter.
**6. Rubens:** Peter Paul Rubens (1577–1640), a Flemish painter famous for his large paintings.
**7. Rossettian:** Referring to Dante Gabriel Rossetti (1828–1882), English poet and painter.

**8. Inigo Jones:** English architect and stage designer (1573–1652).

**HIGGINS.** I must. Ive a job for you. A phonetic job.

**MRS HIGGINS.** No use, dear. I'm sorry; but I cant get round your vowels; and though I like to get pretty postcards in your patent shorthand, I always have to read the copies in ordinary writing you so thoughtfully send me.

**HIGGINS.** Well, this isn't a phonetic job.

**MRS HIGGINS.** You said it was.

**HIGGINS.** Not your part of it. Ive picked up a girl.

**MRS HIGGINS.** Does that mean that some girl has picked you up?

**HIGGINS.** Not at all. I dont mean a love affair.

**MRS HIGGINS.** What a pity!

**HIGGINS.** Why?

**MRS HIGGINS.** Well, you never fall in love with anyone under forty-five. When will you discover that there are some rather nice-looking young women about?

**HIGGINS.** Oh, I cant be bothered with young women. My idea of a lovable woman is somebody as like you as possible. I shall never get into the way of seriously liking young women: some habits lie too deep to be changed. [*Rising abruptly and walking about, jingling his money and his keys in his trouser pockets*] Besides, theyre all idiots.

**MRS HIGGINS.** Do you know what you would do if you really loved me, Henry?

**HIGGINS.** Oh bother! What? Marry, I suppose.

**MRS HIGGINS.** No. Stop fidgeting and take your hands out of your pockets. [*With a gesture of despair, he obeys and sits down again*]. Thats a good boy. Now tell me about the girl.

**HIGGINS.** She's coming to see you.

**MRS HIGGINS.** I dont remember asking her.

**HIGGINS.** You didn't. *I* asked her. If youd known her you wouldnt have asked her.

**MRS HIGGINS.** Indeed! Why?

**HIGGINS.** Well, it's like this. She's a common flower girl. I picked her off the kerbstone.

**MRS HIGGINS.** And invited her to my at-home!

**HIGGINS** [*rising and coming to her to coax her*] Oh, thatll be all right. Ive taught her to speak properly; and she has strict orders as to her behavior. She's to keep to two subjects: the weather and everybody's health —Fine day and How do you do, you know —and not to let herself go on things in general. That will be safe.

**MRS HIGGINS.** Safe! To talk about our health! about our insides! perhaps about our outsides! How could you be so silly, Henry?

**HIGGINS** [*impatiently*] Well, she must talk about something. [*He controls himself and sits down again*]. Oh, she'll be all right: dont you fuss. Pickering is in it with me. Ive a sort of bet on that I'll pass her off as a duchess in six months. I started on her some months ago; and she's getting on like a house on fire. I shall win my bet. She has a quick ear; and she's easier to teach than my middle-class pupils because she's had to learn a complete new language. She talks English almost as you talk French.

**MRS HIGGINS.** Thats satisfactory, at all events.

**HIGGINS.** Well, it is and it isnt.

**MRS HIGGINS.** What does that mean?

**HIGGINS.** You see, Ive got her pronunciation all right; but you have to consider not only how a girl pronounces, but what she pronounces; and that's where—

*They are interrupted by the* PARLORMAID, *announcing guests.*

**THE PARLORMAID.** Mrs and Miss Eynsford Hill. [*She withdraws*].

**HIGGINS.** Oh Lord! [*He rises; snatches his hat from the table; and makes for the door; but before he reaches it his mother introduces him*].

*Mrs and Miss Eynsford Hill are the mother and daughter who sheltered from the rain in Covent Garden. The mother is well bred, quiet, and has the habitual anxiety of straitened means. The daughter has acquired a gay air of being very much at home in society: the bravado of genteel poverty.*

**MRS EYNSFORD HILL** [*to* MRS HIGGINS] How do you do? [*They shake hands*].

**MISS EYNSFORD HILL.** How d'you do? [*She shakes*].

**MRS HIGGINS** [*introducing*] My son Henry.

**MRS EYNSFORD HILL.** Your celebrated son! I have so longed to meet you, Professor Higgins.

**HIGGINS** [*glumly, making no movement in her direction*] Delighted. [*He backs against the piano and bows brusquely*].

**MISS EYNSFORD HILL** [*going to him with confident familiarity*] How do you do?

**HIGGINS** [*staring at her*] Ive seen you before somewhere. I havnt the ghost of a notion where; but Ive heard your voice. [*Drearily*] It doesnt matter. Youd better sit down.

**MRS HIGGINS.** I'm sorry to say that my celebrated son has no manners. You mustnt mind him.

**MISS EYNSFORD HILL** [*gaily*] I dont. [*She sits in the Elizabethan chair*].

**MRS EYNSFORD HILL** [*a little bewildered*] Not at all. [*She sits on the ottoman between her daughter and* MRS HIGGINS, *who has turned her chair away from the writing-table*].

**HIGGINS.** Oh, have I been rude? I didnt mean to be.

*He goes to the central window, through which, with his back to the company, he contemplates the river and the flowers in Battersea Park on the opposite bank as if they were a frozen desert.*

*The* PARLORMAID *returns, ushering in* PICKERING.

**THE PARLORMAID.** Colonel Pickering. [*She withdraws*].

**PICKERING.** How do you do, Mrs Higgins?

**MRS HIGGINS.** So glad youve come. Do you know Mrs Eynsford Hill—Miss Eynsford Hill? [*Exchange of bows. The* COLONEL *brings the Chippendale chair a little forward between* MRS HILL *and* MRS HIGGINS, *and sits down*].

**PICKERING.** Has Henry told you what weve come for?

**HIGGINS.** [*over his shoulder*] We were interrupted: damn it!

**MRS HIGGINS.** Oh, Henry, Henry, really!

**MRS EYNSFORD HILL** [*half rising*] Are we in the way?

**MRS HIGGINS** [*rising and making her sit down again*] No, no. You couldnt have come more fortunately: we want you to meet a friend of ours.

**HIGGINS** [*turning hopefully*] Yes, by George! We want two or three people. You'll do as well as anybody else.

*The* PARLORMAID *returns, ushering* FREDDY.

**THE PARLORMAID.** Mr Eynsford Hill.

**HIGGINS** [*almost audibly, past endurance*] God of Heaven! another of them.

**FREDDY** [*shaking hands with* MRS HIGGINS] Ahdedo?

**MRS HIGGINS.** Very good of you to come. [*Introducing*] Colonel Pickering.

**FREDDY** [*bowing*] Ahdedo?

**MRS HIGGINS.** I don't think you know my son, Professor Higgins.

**FREDDY** [*going to* HIGGINS] Ahdedo?

**HIGGINS** [*looking at him much as if he were a pickpocket*] I'll take my oath Ive met you before somewhere. Where was it?

**FREDDY.** I dont think so.

**HIGGINS** [*resignedly*] It dont matter, anyhow. Sit down.

*He shakes* FREDDY*'s hand, and almost slings him on to the ottoman with his face to the window; then comes round to the other side of it.*

**HIGGINS.** Well, here we are, anyhow! [*He sits down on the ottoman next* MRS EYNSFORD HILL, *on her left*] And now, what the devil are we going to talk about until Eliza comes?

**MRS HIGGINS.** Henry: you are the life and soul of the Royal Society's soirées;[9] but really youre rather trying on more commonplace occasions.

**HIGGINS.** Am I? Very sorry. [*Beaming suddenly*] I suppose I am, you know. [*Uproariously*] Ha, ha!

**MISS EYNSFORD HILL** [*who considers* HIGGINS *quite eligible matrimonially*] I sympathize. I havnt any small talk. If people would only be frank and say what they really think!

**HIGGINS** [*relapsing into gloom*] Lord forbid!

**MRS EYNSFORD HILL** [*taking up her daughter's cue*] But why?

**HIGGINS.** What they think they ought to think is bad enough, Lord knows; but what they really think would break up the whole show. Do you suppose it would be really agreeable if I were to come out now with what *I* really think?

**MISS EYNSFORD HILL** [*gaily*] Is it so very cynical?

**HIGGINS.** Cynical! Who the dickens said it was cynical? I mean it wouldnt be decent.

**MRS EYNSFORD HILL** [*seriously*] Oh! I'm sure you dont mean that, Mr Higgins.

**HIGGINS.** You see, we're all savages, more or less. We're supposed to be civilized and

---

**9. soirées** (swä räz′) *n*.: Parties held in the evening.

cultured—to know all about poetry and philosophy and art and science, and so on; but how many of us know even the meanings of these names? [*To* MISS HILL] What do you know of poetry? [*To* MRS HILL] What do you know of science? [*Indicating* FREDDY] What does he know of art or science or anything else? What the devil do you imagine I know of philosophy?

**MRS HIGGINS** [*warningly*] Or of manners, Henry?

**THE PARLORMAID** [*opening the door*] Miss Doolittle. [*She withdraws*].

**HIGGINS** [*rising hastily and running to* MRS HIGGINS] Here she is, mother. [*He stands on tiptoe and makes signs over his mother's head to* ELIZA *to indicate to her which lady is her hostess*].

ELIZA, *who is exquisitely dressed, produces an impression of such remarkable distinction and beauty as she enters that they all rise, quite fluttered. Guided by* HIGGINS*'s signals, she comes to* MRS HIGGINS *with studied grace.*

**LIZA** [*speaking with pedantic correctness of pronunciation and great beauty of tone*] How do you do, Mrs Higgins? [*She gasps slightly in making sure of the H in Higgins, but is quite successful*]. Mr Higgins told me I might come.

**MRS HIGGINS** [*cordially*] Quite right: I'm very glad indeed to see you.

**PICKERING.** How do you do, Miss Doolittle?

**LIZA** [*shaking hands with him*] Colonel Pickering, is it not?

**MRS EYNSFORD HILL.** I feel sure we have met before, Miss Doolittle. I remember your eyes.

**LIZA.** How do you do? [*She sits down on the ottoman gracefully in the place just left vacant by* HIGGINS].

**MRS EYNSFORD HILL** [*introducing*] My daughter Clara.

LIZA. How do you do?

CLARA [*impulsively*] How do you do? [*She sits down on the ottoman beside* ELIZA, *devouring her with her eyes*].

FREDDY [*coming to their side of the ottoman*] Ive certainly had the pleasure.

MRS EYNSFORD HILL [*introducing*] My son Freddy.

LIZA. How do you do?

FREDDY *bows and sits down in the Elizabethan chair, infatuated.*

HIGGINS [*suddenly*] By George, yes: it all comes back to me! [*They stare at him*]. Covent Garden! [*Lamentably*] What a damned thing!

MRS HIGGINS. Henry, please! [*He is about to sit on the edge of the table*] Dont sit on my writing-table: youll break it.

HIGGINS [*sulkily*] Sorry.

*He goes to the divan, stumbling into the fender and over the fire-irons on his way; extricating himself with muttered imprecations; and finishing his disastrous journey by throwing himself so impatiently on the divan that he almost breaks it.* MRS HIGGINS *looks at him, but controls herself and says nothing.*

*A long and painful pause ensues.*

MRS HIGGINS [*at last, conversationally*] Will it rain, do you think?

LIZA. The shallow depression in the west of these islands is likely to move slowly in an easterly direction. There are no indications of any great change in the barometrical situation.

FREDDY. Ha! ha! how awfully funny!

LIZA. What is wrong with that, young man? I bet I got it right.

FREDDY. Killing!

MRS EYNSFORD HILL. I'm sure I hope it wont turn cold. Theres so much influenza about. It runs right through our whole family regularly every spring.

LIZA [*darkly*] My aunt died of influenza: so they said.

MRS EYNSFORD HILL [*clicks her tongue sympathetically*]!!!

LIZA [*in the same tragic tone*] But it's my belief they done the old woman in.

MRS HIGGINS [*puzzled*] Done her in?

LIZA. Y-e-e-e-es, Lord love you! Why should she die of influenza? She come through diphtheria right enough the year before. I saw her with my own eyes. Fairly blue with it, she was. They all thought she was dead; but my father he kept ladling gin down her throat til she came to so sudden that she bit the bowl off the spoon.

MRS EYNSFORD HILL [*startled*] Dear me!

LIZA [*piling up the indictment*] What call would a woman with that strength in her have to die of influenza? What become of her new straw hat that should have come to me? Somebody pinched it; and what I say is, them as pinched it done her in.

MRS EYNSFORD HILL. What does doing her in mean?

HIGGINS [*hastily*] Oh, thats the new small talk. To do a person in means to kill them.

MRS EYNSFORD HILL [*to* ELIZA, *horrified*] You surely dont believe that your aunt was killed?

LIZA. Do I not! Them she lived with would have killed her for a hat-pin, let alone a hat.

MRS EYNSFORD HILL. But it cant have been right for your father to pour spirits down her throat like that. It might have killed her.

LIZA. Not her. Gin was mother's milk to her. Besides, he'd poured so much down his own throat that he knew the good of it.

MRS EYNSFORD HILL. Do you mean that he drank?

LIZA. Drank! My word! Something chronic.

MRS EYNSFORD HILL. How dreadful for you!

LIZA. Not a bit. It never did him no harm what I could see. But then he did not keep it up regular. [*Cheerfully*] On the burst, as you might say, from time to time. And always more agreeable when he had a drop in. When he was out of work, my mother used to give him fourpence and tell him to go out and not come back until he'd drunk himself cheerful and loving-like. Theres lots of women has to make their husbands drunk to make them fit to live with. [*Now quite at her ease*] You see, it's like this. If a man has a bit of conscience, it always takes him when he's sober; and then it makes him low-spirited. A drop of booze just takes that off and makes him happy. [*To* FREDDY, *who is in convulsions of suppressed laughter*] Here! what are you sniggering at?

FREDDY. The new small talk. You do it so awfully well.

LIZA. If I was doing it proper, what was you laughing at? [*To* HIGGINS] Have I said anything I oughtnt?

MRS HIGGINS [*interposing*] Not at all, Miss Doolittle.

LIZA. Well, thats a mercy, anyhow. [*Expansively*] What I always say is—

HIGGINS [*rising and looking at his watch*] Ahem!

LIZA [*looking round at him; taking the hint; and rising*] Well: I must go. [*They all rise.* FREDDY *goes to the door*]. So pleased to have met you. Goodbye. [*She shakes hands with* MRS HIGGINS].

MRS HIGGINS. Goodbye.

LIZA. Goodbye, Colonel Pickering.

PICKERING. Goodbye, Miss Doolittle. [*They shake hands*].

LIZA [*nodding to the others*] Goodbye, all.

FREDDY [*opening the door for her*] Are you walking across the Park, Miss Doolittle? If so—

LIZA [*with perfectly elegant diction*] Walk! Not bloody likely. [*Sensation*]. I am going in a taxi. [*She goes out*].

PICKERING *gasps and sits down.* FREDDY *goes out on the balcony to catch another glimpse of* ELIZA.

MRS EYNSFORD HILL [*suffering from shock*] Well, I really cant get used to the new ways.

CLARA [*throwing herself discontentedly into the Elizabethan chair*] Oh, it's all right, mamma, quite right. People will think we never go anywhere or see anybody if you are so old-fashioned.

MRS EYNSFORD HILL. I daresay I am very old-fashioned; but I do hope you wont begin using that expression, Clara. I have got accustomed to hear you talking about men as rotters, and calling everything filthy and beastly; though I do think it horrible and unladylike. But this last is really too much. Dont you think so, Colonel Pickering?

PICKERING. Dont ask me. Ive been away in India for several years; and manners have changed so much that I sometimes dont know whether I'm at a respectable dinner-table or in a ship's forecastle.

CLARA. It's all a matter of habit. Theres no right or wrong in it. Nobody means anything by it. And it's so quaint, and gives such a smart emphasis to things that are not in themselves very witty. I find the new small talk delightful and quite innocent.

MRS EYNSFORD HILL [*rising*] Well, after that, I think it's time for us to go.

PICKERING *and* HIGGINS *rise.*

CLARA [*rising*] Oh yes: we have three at-homes to go to still. Goodbye, Mrs Higgins. Goodbye, Colonel Pickering. Goodbye, Professor Higgins.

**HIGGINS** [*coming grimly at her from the divan, and accompanying her to the door*] Goodbye. Be sure you try on that small talk at the three at-homes. Dont be nervous about it. Pitch it in strong.

**CLARA** [*all smiles*] I will. Goodbye. Such nonsense, all this early Victorian prudery!

**HIGGINS** [*tempting her*] Such damned nonsense!

**CLARA.** Such bloody nonsense!

**MRS EYNSFORD HILL** [*convulsively*] Clara!

**CLARA.** Ha! Ha! [*She goes out radiant, conscious of being thoroughly up to date, and is heard descending the stairs in a stream of silvery laughter*].

**FREDDY** [*to the heavens at large*] Well, I ask you— [*He gives it up, and comes to* MRS HIGGINS]. Goodbye.

**MRS HIGGINS** [*shaking hands*] Goodbye. Would you like to meet Miss Doolittle again?

**FREDDY** [*eagerly*] Yes, I should, most awfully.

**MRS HIGGINS.** Well, you know my days.

**FREDDY.** Yes. Thanks awfully. Goodbye. [*He goes out*].

**MRS EYNSFORD HILL.** Goodbye, Mr Higgins.

**HIGGINS.** Goodbye. Goodbye.

**MRS EYNSFORD HILL** [*to* PICKERING] It's no use. I shall never be able to bring myself to use that word.

**PICKERING.** Dont. It's not compulsory, you know. Youll get on quite well without it.

**MRS EYNSFORD HILL.** Only, Clara is so down on me if I am not positively reeking with the latest slang. Goodbye.

**PICKERING.** Goodbye [*They shake hands*].

**MRS EYNSFORD HILL.** [*to* MRS HIGGINS] You mustnt mind Clara. [PICKERING, *catching from her lowered tone that this is not meant for him to hear, discreetly joins* HIGGINS *at the window*]. We're so poor! and she gets so few parties, poor child! She doesn't quite know. [MRS HIGGINS, *seeing that her eyes are moist, takes her hand sympathetically and goes with her to the door*]. But the boy is nice. Dont you think so?

**MRS HIGGINS.** Oh, quite nice. I shall always be delighted to see him.

**MRS EYNSFORD HILL.** Thank you, dear. Goodbye. [*She goes out*].

**HIGGINS** [*eagerly*] Well? Is Eliza presentable [*he swoops on his mother and drags her to the ottoman, where she sits down in* ELIZA's *place with her son on her left*]?

PICKERING *returns to his chair on her right.*

**MRS HIGGINS.** You silly boy, of course she's not presentable. She's a triumph of your art and of her dressmaker's; but if you suppose for a moment that she doesn't give herself away in every sentence she utters, you must be perfectly cracked about her.

**PICKERING.** But dont you think something might be done? I mean something to eliminate the sanguinary[10] element from her conversation.

**MRS HIGGINS.** Not as long as she is in Henry's hands.

**HIGGINS** [*aggrieved*] Do you mean that my language is improper?

**MRS HIGGINS.** No, dearest: it would be quite proper—say on a canal barge; but it would not be proper for her at a garden party.

**HIGGINS** [*deeply injured*] Well I must say—

**PICKERING** [*interrupting him*] Come, Higgins: you must learn to know yourself. I havnt heard such language as yours since we used to review the volunteers in Hyde Park twenty years ago.

**HIGGINS** [*sulkily*] Oh, well, if you say so, I suppose I dont always talk like a bishop.

---

**10. sanguinary** (saŋ′ gwi ner′ ē) *adj.*: Bloody.

**MRS HIGGINS** [*quieting* HENRY *with a touch*] Colonel Pickering: will you tell me what is the exact state of things in Wimpole Street?

**PICKERING** [*cheerfully: as if this completely changed the subject*] Well, I have come to live there with Henry. We work together at my Indian Dialects; and we think it more convenient—

**MRS HIGGINS.** Quite so. I know all about that: it's an excellent arrangement. But where does this girl live?

**HIGGINS.** With us, of course. Where should she live?

**MRS HIGGINS.** But on what terms? Is she a servant? If not, what is she?

**PICKERING** [*slowly*] I think I know what you mean, Mrs Higgins.

**HIGGINS.** Well, dash me if *I* do! Ive had to work at the girl every day for months to get her to her present pitch. Besides, she's useful. She knows where my things are, and remembers my appointments and so forth.

**MRS HIGGINS.** How does your housekeeper get on with her?

**HIGGINS.** Mrs Pearce? Oh, she's jolly glad to get so much taken off her hands; for before Eliza came, she used to have to find things and remind me of my appointments. But she's got some silly bee in her bonnet about Eliza. She keeps saying "You dont think, sir": doesn't she, Pick?

**PICKERING.** Yes: thats the formula. "You dont think, sir." Thats the end of every conversation about Eliza.

**HIGGINS.** As if I ever stop thinking about the girl and her confounded vowels and consonants. I'm worn out, thinking about her, and watching her lips and her teeth and her tongue, not to mention her soul, which is the quaintest of the lot.

**MRS HIGGINS.** You certainly are a pretty pair of babies, playing with your live doll.

**HIGGINS.** Playing! The hardest job I ever tackled: make no mistake about that, mother. But you have no idea how frightfully interesting it is to take a human being and change her into a quite different human being by creating a new speech for her. It's filling up the deepest gulf that separates class from class and soul from soul.

**PICKERING** [*drawing his chair closer to* MRS HIGGINS *and bending over to her eagerly*] Yes: it's enormously interesting. I assure you, Mrs Higgins, we take Eliza very seriously. Every week—every day almost—there is some new change. [*Closer again*] We keep records of every stage—dozens of gramophone disks and photographs—

**HIGGINS** [*assailing her at the other ear*] Yes, by George: it's the most absorbing experiment I ever tackled. She regularly fills our lives up: doesn't she, Pick?

**PICKERING.** We're always talking Eliza.

**HIGGINS.** Teaching Eliza.

**PICKERING.** Dressing Eliza.

**MRS HIGGINS.** What!

**HIGGINS.** Inventing new Elizas.

| | | |
|---|---|---|
| **HIGGINS.** | *(speaking together)* | You know, she has the most extraordinary quickness of ear: |
| **PICKERING.** | | I assure you, my dear Mrs Higgins, that girl |
| **HIGGINS.** | | just like a parrot. Ive tried her with every |
| **PICKERING.** | | is a genius. She can play the piano quite beautifully. |
| **HIGGINS.** | | possible sort of sound that a human being can make— |
| **PICKERING.** | | We have taken her to classical concerts and to music |
| **HIGGINS.** | | Continental dialects, African dialects, Hottentot |

PICKERING. (speaking) halls; and it's all the same to her: she plays everything

HIGGINS. clicks, things it took me years to get hold of; and

PICKERING. she hears right off when she comes home, whether it's

HIGGINS. she picks them up like a shot, right away, as if she had Beethoven and Brahms or Lehar, and Lionel Monckton;

HIGGINS. / PICKERING. been at it all her life. though six months ago, she'd never as much as touched a piano—

MRS HIGGINS [putting her fingers in her ears, as they are by this time shouting one another down with an intolerable noise] Sh-sh-sh—sh! [They stop].

PICKERING. I beg your pardon. [He draws his chair back apologetically].

HIGGINS. Sorry. When Pickering starts shouting nobody can get a word in edgeways.

MRS HIGGINS. Be quiet, Henry. Colonel Pickering: dont you realize that when Eliza walked in Wimpole Street, something walked in with her?

PICKERING. Her father did. But Henry soon got rid of him.

MRS HIGGINS. It would have been more to the point if her mother had. But as her mother didnt something else did.

PICKERING. But what?

MRS HIGGINS. (unconsciously dating herself by the word) A problem.

PICKERING. Oh, I see. The problem of how to pass her off as a lady.

HIGGINS. I'll solve that problem. Ive half solved it already.

MRS HIGGINS. No, you two infinitely stupid male creatures: the problem of what is to be done with her afterwards.

HIGGINS. I dont see anything in that. She can go her own way, with all the advantages I have given her.

MRS HIGGINS. The advantages of that poor woman who was here just now! The manners and habits that disqualify a fine lady from earning her own living without giving her a fine lady's income! Is that what you mean?

PICKERING. [Indulgently, being rather bored] Oh, that will be all right, Mrs Higgins. [He rises to go].

HIGGINS. [Rising also] We'll find her some light employment.

PICKERING. She's happy enough. Dont you worry about her. Goodbye. [He shakes hands as if he were consoling a frightened child, and makes for the door].

HIGGINS. Anyhow, theres no good bothering now. The thing's done. Goodbye, mother. [He kisses her, and follows PICKERING].

PICKERING [turning for a final consolation] There are plenty of openings. We'll do whats right. Goodbye.

HIGGINS [to Pickering as they go out together] Lets take her to the Shakespear exhibition at Earls Court.

PICKERING. Yes: lets. Her remarks will be delicious.

HIGGINS. She'll mimic all the people for us when we get home.

PICKERING. Ripping. [Both are heard laughing as they go downstairs].

MRS HIGGINS [rises with an impatient bounce, and returns to her work at the writing-table. She sweeps a litter of disarranged papers out of the way; snatches a *sheet of paper from her stationery case; and tries resolutely to write. At the third time she gives it up; flings down her pen; grips the table angrily and exclaims]* Oh, men! men!! men!!!

★    ★    ★    ★    ★    ★

Clearly Eliza will not pass as a duchess yet; and Higgins's bet remains unwon. But the six months are not yet exhausted and just in time Eliza does actually pass as a princess. For a glimpse of how she did it imagine an Embassy in London one summer evening after dark. The hall door has an awning and a carpet across the sidewalk to the kerb, because a grand reception is in progress. A small crowd is lined up to see the guests arrive.

A Rolls-Royce car drives up. Pickering in evening dress, with medals and orders, alights, and hands out Eliza, in opera cloak, evening dress, diamonds, fan, flowers and all accessories. Higgins follows. The car drives off; and the three go up the steps and into the house, the door opening for them as they approach.

Inside the house they find themselves in a spacious hall from which the grand staircase rises. On the left are the arrangements for the gentlemen's cloaks. The male guests are depositing their hats and wraps there.

On the right is a door leading to the ladies' cloakroom. Ladies are going in cloaked and coming out in splendor. Pickering whispers to Eliza and points out the ladies' room. She goes into it. Higgins and Pickering take off their overcoats and take tickets for them from the attendant.

One of the guests, occupied in the same way, has his back turned. Having taken his ticket, he turns round and reveals himself as an important looking young man with an astonishingly hairy face. He has an enormous moustache, flowing out into luxuriant whiskers. Waves of hair cluster on his brow. His hair is cropped closely at the back, and glows with oil. Otherwise he is very smart. He wears several worthless orders. He is evidently a foreigner, guessable as a whis-

kered Pandour[11] from Hungary; but in spite of the ferocity of his moustache he is amiable and genially voluble.

Recognizing Higgins, he flings his arms wide apart and approaches him enthusiastically.

**WHISKERS.** Maestro, maestro. [*He embraces* HIGGINS *and kisses him on both cheeks*]. You remember me?

**HIGGINS.** No I dont. Who the devil are you?

**WHISKERS.** I am your pupil: your first pupil, your best and greatest pupil. I am little Nepommuck, the marvellous boy. I have made your name famous throughout Europe. You teach me phonetic. You cannot forget ME.

**HIGGINS.** Why dont you shave?

**NEPOMMUCK.** I have not your imposing appearrance, your chin, your brow. Nobody notice me when I shave. Now I am famous: they call me Hairy Faced Dick.

**HIGGINS.** And what are you doing here among all these swells?

**NEPOMMUCK.** I am interpreter. I speak 32 languages. I am indispensable at these international parties. You are great cockney specialist: you place a man anywhere in London the moment he open his mouth. I place any man in Europe.

*A* FOOTMAN *hurries down the grand staircase and comes to* NEPOMMUCK.

**FOOTMAN.** You are wanted upstairs. Her Excellency cannot understand the Greek gentleman.

**NEPOMMUCK.** Thank you, yes, immediately.

*The* FOOTMAN *goes and is lost in the crowd.*

**NEPOMMUCK** [*to* HIGGINS] This Greek diplomatist pretends he cannot speak nor understand English. He cannot deceive me. He is the son of a Clerkenwell watchmaker. He

---

**11. Pandour:** A bodyguard or servant of Hungarian nobles.

speaks English so villainously that he dare not utter a word of it without betraying his origin. I help him to pretend; but I make him pay through the nose. I make them all pay. Ha ha! [*He hurries upstairs*].

PICKERING. Is this fellow really an expert? Can he find out Eliza and blackmail her?

HIGGINS. We shall see. If he finds her out I lose my bet.

ELIZA *comes from the cloakroom and joins them.*

PICKERING. Well, Eliza, now for it. Are you ready?

LIZA. Are you nervous, Colonel?

PICKERING. Frightfully. I feel exactly as I felt before my first battle. It's the first time that frightens.

LIZA. It is not the first time for me, Colonel. I have done this fifty times—hundreds of times—in my little piggery in Angel Court in my day-dreams. I am in a dream now. Promise me not to let Professor Higgins wake me; for if he does I shall forget everything and talk as I used to in Drury Lane.

PICKERING. Not a word, Higgins. [*To* ELIZA] Now, ready?

LIZA. Ready.

PICKERING. Go.

*They mount the stairs,* HIGGINS *last.* PICKERING *whispers to the* FOOTMAN *on the first landing.*

FIRST LANDING FOOTMAN. Miss Doolittle, Colonel Pickering, Professor Higgins.

SECOND LANDING FOOTMAN. Miss Doolittle, Colonel Pickering, Professor Higgins.

*At the top of the staircase the* AMBASSADOR *and his* WIFE, *with* NEPOMMUCK *at her elbow, are receiving.*

HOSTESS [*taking* ELIZA*'s hand*] How d'ye do?

HOST [*same play*] How d'ye do? How d'ye do, Pickering?

LIZA [*with a beautiful gravity that awes her hostess*] How do you do? [*She passes on to the drawingroom*].

HOSTESS. Is that your adopted daughter, Colonel Pickering? She will make a sensation.

PICKERING. Most kind of you to invite her for me. [*He passes on*].

HOSTESS [*to* NEPOMMUCK] Find out all about her.

NEPOMMUCK [*bowing*] Excellency—[*he goes into the crowd*].

HOST. How d'ye do, Higgins? You have a rival here tonight. He introduced himself as your pupil. Is he any good?

HIGGINS. He can learn a language in a fortnight—knows dozens of them. A sure mark of a fool. As a phonetician, no good whatever.

HOSTESS. How d'ye do, Professor?

HIGGINS. How do you do? Fearful bore for you this sort of thing. Forgive my part in it. [*He passes on*].

In the drawing room and its suite of salons the reception is in full swing. Eliza passes through. She is so intent on her ordeal that she walks like a somnambulist in a desert instead of a débutante in a fashionable crowd. They stop talking to look at her, admiring her dress, her jewels, and her strangely attractive self. Some of the younger ones at the back stand on their chairs to see.

The Host and Hostess come in from the staircase and mingle with their guests. Higgins, gloomy and contemptuous of the whole business, comes into the group where they are chatting.

HOSTESS. Ah, here is Professor Higgins: he will tell us. Tell us all about the wonderful young lady, Professor.

HIGGINS [*almost morosely*] What wonderful young lady?

HOSTESS. You know very well. They tell me there has been nothing like her in London since people stood on their chairs to look at

Mrs Langtry.[12]

NEPOMMUCK *joins the group, full of news.*

**HOSTESS.** Ah, here you are at last, Nepommuck. Have you found out all about the Doolittle lady?

**NEPOMMUCK.** I have found out all about her. She is a fraud.

**HOSTESS.** A fraud! Oh no.

**NEPOMMUCK.** YES, yes. She cannot deceive me. Her name cannot be Doolittle.

**HIGGINS.** Why?

**NEPOMMUCK.** Because Doolittle is an English name. And she is not English.

**HOSTESS.** Oh, nonsense! She speaks English perfectly.

**NEPOMMUCK.** Too perfectly. Can you shew me any English woman who speaks English as it should be spoken? Only foreigners who have been taught to speak it speak it well.

**HOSTESS.** Certainly she terrified me by the way she said How d'ye do. I had a schoolmistress who talked like that; and I was mortally afraid of her. But if she is not English what is she?

**NEPOMMUCK.** Hungarian.

**ALL THE REST.** Hungarian!

**NEPOMMUCK.** Hungarian. And of royal blood. I am Hungarian. My blood is royal.

**HIGGINS.** Did you speak to her in Hungarian?

**NEPOMMUCK.** I did. She was very clever. She said "Please speak to me in English: I do not understand French." French! She pretend not to know the difference between Hungarian and French. Impossible: she knows both.

**HIGGINS.** And the blood royal? How did you find that out?

**NEPOMMUCK.** Instinct, maestro, instinct. Only the Magyar races can produce that air of the divine right, those resolute eyes. She is a princess.

**HOST.** What do you say, Professor?

**HIGGINS.** I say an ordinary London girl out of the gutter and taught to speak by an expert. I place her in Drury Lane.

**NEPOMMUCK.** Ha ha ha! Oh, maestro, maestro, you are mad on the subject of cockney dialects. The London gutter is the whole world for you.

**HIGGINS** [*to the* HOSTESS] What does your Excellency say?

**HOSTESS.** Oh, of course I agree with Nepommuck. She must be a princess at least.

**HOST.** Not necessarily legitimate, of course. Morganatic[13] perhaps. But that is undoubtedly her class.

**HIGGINS.** I stick to my opinion.

**HOSTESS.** Oh, you are incorrigible.
*The group breaks up, leaving* HIGGINS *isolated.* PICKERING *joins him.*

**PICKERING.** Where is Eliza? We must keep an eye on her.

ELIZA *joins them.*

**LIZA.** I don't think I can bear much more. The people all stare so at me. An old lady has just told me that I speak exactly like Queen Victoria. I am sorry if I have lost your bet. I have done my best; but nothing can make me the same as these people.

**PICKERING.** You have not lost it, my dear. You have won it ten times over.

**HIGGINS.** Let us get out of this. I have had enough of chattering to these fools.

**PICKERING.** Eliza is tired; and I am hungry. Let us clear out and have supper somewhere.

---

**12. Mrs. Langtry:** Lily Langtry (1852–1929), a beautiful English actress.

**13. Morganatic** (môr′ gə nat′ ik) *adj.*: Referring to a form of marriage in which a person of royalty or nobility marries a spouse of inferior social status. While such a marriage is considered valid, children produced by it do not inherit titles.

# THINKING ABOUT THE SELECTION

## Recalling

1. Why is Mrs. Higgins upset when her son arrives at her house?
2. To what two "safe" topics is Eliza limited?
3. How does Higgins explain Eliza's language to the Eynsford Hills?
4. Who does Nepommuck declare Eliza to be?
5. Explain the outcome of Pickering's bet with Higgins.

## Interpreting

6. (a) What humor arises out of Higgins's telling Eliza to limit her conversation to two topics? (b) Out of Nepommuck's "investigation" of Eliza?
7. At the end of the embassy ball Eliza comments that "nothing can make me the same as these people." (a) What do you suppose to be her state of mind as she utters this comment? Why? (b) What is Shaw suggesting about Eliza through this comment?

## Applying

8. What parallels to an "at-home day," if any, can you find in modern American social customs? Explain the similarities and point out any differences.

# ANALYZING LITERATURE

## Using Satire

**Satire** is a technique that unites comedy and criticism to ridicule an offensive behavior or institution. The targets of satire, since its origins in ancient Greek and Roman drama, have included unjust or overly harsh laws, mindless social customs, and shallow trends. In Act III of *Pygmalion,* Shaw aims his satiric arrows at several customs and foibles of his day that continue to exist in our own. These include

1. the need (of some) to make small talk,
2. proper social etiquette,
3. the effort to pass oneself off as someone one is not.

Locate and describe the places in the act where Shaw pokes fun at each of these human failings.

# CRITICAL THINKING AND READING

## Comparing and Contrasting Attitudes

In Act III of *Pygmalion,* the characters express a variety of attitudes on a number of topics. Compare and contrast the following characters' views on the topics mentioned, and tell how you believe each of the characters came by those views.

1. Good manners: Higgins, Mrs. Higgins.
2. Love: Higgins, Mrs. Higgins, Freddy.
3. Slang: Mrs. Eynsford Hill, her daughter.
4. The fate of Eliza: Mrs. Higgins, Higgins, Pickering.
5. Formal dress affairs: Eliza, Higgins, Pickering.

# UNDERSTANDING LANGUAGE

## Understanding Slang

**Slang** is language used and understood by members of a particular group or culture. Unlike words from the standard language, which change very slowly over long periods of time, slang terms are literally "in" one year, "out" the next. Give the meaning of the following slang terms from Act III. Note any slang used by your own culture—modern-day high school students—to convey the same idea.

1. *Done her in?* (page 1149)
2. Somebody *pinched* it. (page 1149)
3. *On the burst,* as you might say. (page 1150)
4. [And always more agreeable] when he *had a drop in.* (page 1150)

# THINKING AND WRITING

## Evaluating the Effectiveness of Satire

Satire is a difficult form of comedy to write. A well-conceived satire will neither be so light as to lack punch nor so biting as to lack humor. In a short essay, explain whether or not you find the humor and criticism of Shaw's satire in Act III well-balanced. To get yourself started, answer questions such as the following. What is funny and why? What is being criticized? How clear are Shaw's intentions? When you revise, make sure you have included examples from Act III to back up your theses.

# GUIDE FOR INTERPRETING

## Pygmalion, Act IV

**Crisis.** Crisis is a highpoint of emotion or action that occurs near the end of a work of fiction. Also known as *climax,* the crisis is one key point in the carefully arranged sequence of elements in a story known as *plot.* Historically the plot contains five such elements, the first of which, the *exposition,* is a playbill of sorts. The exposition tells us who the characters are and what sort of *conflict,* or struggle, they face. Often this conflict is between the characters themselves, although at times an outside force like nature or society is involved. In any event *complications* arise in one form or another, causing the action or emotional intensity to build. Once the crisis has been reached, the work begins to wind down. In this final stage, known as the *resolution* or *denouement,* all problems are solved and any loose ends are tied up. This pattern of elements has been abandoned in whole or in part by a number of modern writers. Shaw, in an effort to create a more lifelike drama, deviated somewhat from this formula, especially in his comedies.

Imagine you are sitting in a theater watching this play. The curtain has come down on Act III. During intermission, you turn to the person sitting next to you and discuss the play. Create a conversation in which both of you provide ideas on what will happen next.

Shaw broke away from the traditional arrangement of plot elements, such as crisis, in a drama. He explained his reasoning this way:

> You will understand that my plays are not constructed plays: they grow naturally. If you "construct" a play: that is, if you plan your play beforehand, and then carry out your plan, you will find yourself in the position of a person putting together a jig-saw puzzle . . . which, to a spectator, is unbearably dull. The scenes must be born alive. If they are not new to you as you write, and sometimes quite contrary to the expectations with which you have begun them, they are dead wood. A live play constructs itself with a subtlety, and often with a mechanical ingenuity, that often deludes critics into holding the author up as the most crafty of artificers when he has never, in writing his play, known what one of his characters would say until another gave the clue. . . . Now what the drama can do, and what it actually does, is to take this unmeaning, haphazard show of life . . . and arrange it in such a way as to make you think very much more deeply about it than you ever dreamed of thinking about actual incidents that came to your knowledge.

## ACT IV

*The Wimpole Street laboratory. Midnight. Nobody in the room. The clock on the mantelpiece strikes twelve. The fire is not alight: it is a summer night.*

*Presently* HIGGINS *and* PICKERING *are heard on the stairs.*

**HIGGINS** [*calling down to* PICKERING] I say, Pick: lock up, will you? I shant be going out again.

**PICKERING.** Right. Can Mrs Pearce go to bed? We dont want anything more, do we?

**HIGGINS.** Lord, no!

ELIZA *opens the door and is seen on the lighted landing in all the finery in which she has just won* HIGGINS's *bet for him. She comes to the hearth, and switches on the electric lights there. She is tired: her pallor contrasts strongly with her dark eyes and hair; and her expression is almost tragic. She takes off her cloak; puts her fan and gloves on the piano; and sits down on the bench, brooding and silent.* HIGGINS, *in evening dress, with overcoat and hat, comes in, carrying a smoking jacket which he has picked up downstairs. He takes off the hat and overcoat; throws them carelessly on the newspaper stand; disposes of his coat in the same way; puts on the smoking jacket; and throws himself wearily into the easy-chair at the hearth.* PICKERING, *similarly attired, comes in. He also takes off his hat and overcoat, and is about to throw them on* HIGGINS's *when he hesitates.*

**PICKERING.** I say: Mrs Pearce will row if we leave these things lying about in the drawing room.

**HIGGINS.** Oh, chuck them over the bannisters into the hall. She'll find them there in the morning and put them away all right. She'll think we were drunk.

**PICKERING.** We are, slightly. Are there any letters?

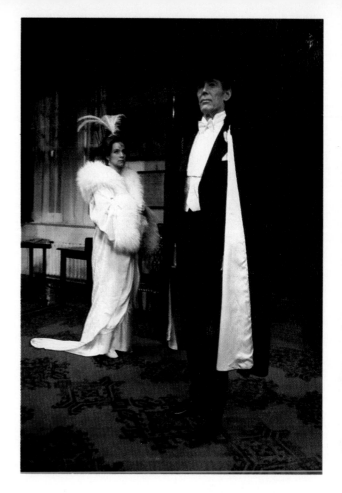

**HIGGINS.** I didnt look. [PICKERING *takes the overcoats and hats and goes downstairs.* HIGGINS *begins half singing half yawning an air from* La Fanciulla Del Golden West.[1] *Suddenly he stops and exclaims*] I wonder where the devil my slippers are!

ELIZA *looks at him darkly; then rises suddenly and leaves the room.*

HIGGINS *yawns again, and resumes his song.*

PICKERING *returns, with the contents of the letter-box in his hand.*

---

**1. La Fanciulla** (fan chōō′ la) **del Golden West:** *The Girl of the Golden West,* an opera by Italian composer Giacomo Puccini (1858–1924).

**PICKERING.** Only circulars, and this coroneted billet-doux[2] for you. [*He throws the circulars into the fender, and posts himself on the hearthrug, with his back to the grate*].

**HIGGINS** [*glancing at the billet-doux*] Moneylender. [*He throws the letter after the circulars*].

ELIZA *returns with a pair of large down-at-heel slippers. She places them on the carpet before* HIGGINS, *and sits as before without a word.*

**HIGGINS** [*yawning again*] Oh Lord! What an evening! What a crew! What a silly tomfoolery! [*He raises his shoe to unlace it, and catches sight of the slippers. He stops unlacing and looks at them as if they had appeared there of their own accord*]. Oh! theyre there, are they?

**PICKERING** [*stretching himself*]. Well, I feel a bit tired. It's been a long day. The garden party, a dinner party, and the reception! Rather too much of a good thing. But youve won your bet, Higgins. Eliza did the trick, and something to spare, eh?

**HIGGINS** [*fervently*] Thank God it's over!

ELIZA *flinches violently; but they take no notice of her; and she recovers herself and sits stonily as before.*

**PICKERING.** Were you nervous at the garden party? *I* was. Eliza didnt seem a bit nervous.

**HIGGINS.** Oh, she wasnt nervous. I knew she'd be all right. No: it's the strain of putting the job through all these months that has told on me. It was interesting enough at first, while we were at the phonetics; but after that I got deadly sick of it. If I hadnt backed myself to do it I should have chucked the whole thing up two months ago. It was a silly notion: the whole thing has been a bore.

**PICKERING.** Oh come! the garden party was frightfully exciting. My heart began beating like anything.

**HIGGINS.** Yes, for the first three minutes. But when I saw we were going to win hands down, I felt like a bear in a cage, hanging about doing nothing. The dinner was worse: sitting gorging there for over an hour, with nobody but a damned fool of a fashionable woman to talk to! I tell you, Pickering, never again for me. No more artificial duchesses. The whole thing has been simple purgatory.

**PICKERING.** Youve never been broken in properly to the social routine. [*Strolling over to the piano*] I rather enjoy dipping into it occasionally myself: it makes me feel young again. Anyhow, it was a great success: an immense success. I was quite frightened once or twice because Eliza was doing it so well. You see, lots of the real people cant do it at all: theyre such fools that they think style comes by nature to people in their position; and so they never learn. Theres always something professional about doing a thing superlatively well.

**HIGGINS.** Yes: thats what drives me mad: the silly people dont know their own silly business. [*Rising*] However, it's over and done with; and now I can go to bed at last without dreading tomorrow.

ELIZA'*s beauty becomes murderous.*

**PICKERING.** I think I shall turn in too. Still, it's been a great occasion: a triumph for you. Goodnight. [*He goes*].

**HIGGINS** [*following him*] Goodnight. [*Over his shoulder, at the door*] Put out the lights, Eliza; and tell Mrs Pearce not to make coffee for me in the morning: I'll take tea. [*He goes out*].

ELIZA *tries to control herself and feel indifferent as she rises and walks across to the hearth to switch off the lights. By the time she gets there she is on the point of screaming. She sits down in* HIGGINS's *chair and holds on hard to the arms. Finally she gives way and flings herself furiously on the floor, raging.*

---

**2. billet-doux** (bil' ā dōō'): Love letter.

**HIGGINS** [*in despairing wrath outside*] What the devil have I done with my slippers? [*He appears at the door*].

**LIZA** [*snatching up the slippers, and hurling them at him one after the other with all her force*] There are your slippers. And there. Take your slippers; and may you never have a day's luck with them!

**HIGGINS** [*astounded*] What on earth—! [*He comes to her*]. Whats the matter? Get up. [*He pulls her up*] Anything wrong?

**LIZA** [*(breathless*] Nothing wrong—with you. Ive won your bet for you, havnt I? Thats enough for you. *I* dont matter, I suppose.

**HIGGINS.** You won my bet! You! Presumptuous insect! *I* won it. What did you throw those slippers at me for?

**LIZA.** Because I wanted to smash your face. I'd like to kill you, you selfish brute. Why didnt you leave me where you picked me out of—in the gutter? You thank God it's all over, and that now you can throw me back again there, do you? [*She crisps her fingers[3] frantically*].

**HIGGINS** [*looking at her in cool wonder*] The creature is nervous, after all.

**LIZA** [*gives a suffocated scream of fury, and instinctively darts her nails at his face*]!!

**HIGGINS** [*catching her wrists*] Ah! would you? Claws in, you cat. How dare you shew your temper to me? Sit down and be quiet. [*He throws her roughly into the easy-chair*].

**LIZA** [*crushed by superior strength and weight*] Whats to become of me? Whats to become of me?

**HIGGINS.** How the devil do I know whats to become of you? What does it matter what becomes of you?

**LIZA.** You dont care. I know you dont care. You wouldnt care if I was dead. I'm nothing

---

3. **crisps her fingers:** Clenches her fingers into fists.

to you—not so much as them slippers.

**HIGGINS** [*thundering*] Those slippers.

**LIZA** [*with bitter submission*]. Those slippers. I didnt think it made any difference now.

*A pause.* ELIZA *hopeless and crushed.* HIGGINS *a little uneasy.*

**HIGGINS** [*in his loftiest manner*] Why have you begun going on like this? May I ask whether you complain of your treatment here?

**LIZA.** No.

**HIGGINS.** Has anybody behaved badly to you? Colonel Pickering? Mrs Pearce? Any of the servants?

**LIZA.** No.

**HIGGINS.** I presume you dont pretend that *I* have treated you badly?

**LIZA.** No.

**HIGGINS.** I am glad to hear it. [*He moderates his tone*]. Perhaps youre tired after the strain of the day. Will you have a glass of champagne? [*He moves towards the door*].

**LIZA.** No. [*Recollecting her manners*] Thank you.

**HIGGINS** [*good-humored again*] This has been coming on you for some days. I suppose it was natural for you to be anxious about the garden party. But thats all over now. [*He pats her kindly on the shoulder. She writhes*]. Theres nothing more to worry about.

**LIZA.** No. Nothing more for you to worry about. [*She suddenly rises and gets away from him by going to the piano bench, where she sits and hides her face*]. Oh God! I wish I was dead.

**HIGGINS** [*staring after her in sincere surprise*] Why? In heaven's name, why? [*Reasonably, going to her*] Listen to me, Eliza. All this irritation is purely subjective.

**LIZA.** I dont understand. I'm too ignorant.

**HIGGINS.** It's only imagination. Low spirits and nothing else. Nobody's hurting you. Nothing's wrong. You go to bed like a good girl and sleep it off. Have a little cry and say your prayers: that will make you comfortable.

**LIZA.** I heard your prayers. "Thank God it's all over!"

**HIGGINS** [*impatiently*] Well, dont you thank God it's all over? Now you are free and can do what you like.

**LIZA** [*pulling herself together in desperation*] What am I fit for? What have you left me fit for? Where am I to go? What am I to do? Whats to become of me?

**HIGGINS** [*enlightened, but not at all impressed*] Oh, thats whats worrying you, is it? [*He thrusts his hands into his pockets, and walks about in his usual manner, rattling the contents of his pockets, as if condescending to a trivial subject out of pure kindness*]. I shouldnt bother about it if I were you. I should imagine you wont have much difficulty in settling yourself somewhere or other, though I hadnt quite realized that you were going away. [*She looks quickly at him: he does not look at her, but examines the dessert stand on the piano and decides that he will eat an apple*]. You might marry, you know. [*He bites a large piece out of the apple and munches it noisily*]. You see, Eliza, all men are not confirmed old bachelors like me and the Colonel. Most men are the marrying sort [poor devils!]; and youre not bad-looking: it's quite a pleasure to look at you sometimes—not now, of course, because youre crying and looking as ugly as the very devil; but when youre all right and quite yourself, youre what I should call attractive. That is, to the people in the marrying line, you understand. You go to bed and have a good nice rest; and then get up and look at yourself in the glass; and you wont feel so cheap.

ELIZA *again looks at him, speechless, and does not stir.*

The look is quite lost on him: he eats his apple with a dreamy expression of happiness, as it is quite a good one.

**HIGGINS** [*a genial afterthought occurring to him*] I daresay my mother could find some chap or other who would do very well.

**LIZA.** We were above that at the corner of Tottenham Court Road.

**HIGGINS** [*waking up*] What do you mean?

**LIZA.** I sold flowers. I didnt sell myself. Now youve made a lady of me I'm not fit to sell anything else. I wish youd left me where you found me.

HIGGINS [*slinging the core of the apple decisively into the grate*] Tosh, Eliza. Dont you insult human relations by dragging all this cant about buying and selling into it. You neednt marry the fellow if you dont like him.

LIZA. What else am I to do?

HIGGINS. Oh, lots of things. What about your old idea of a florist's shop? Pickering could set you up in one: he has lots of money. [*Chuckling*] He'll have to pay for all those togs you have been wearing today; and that, with the hire of the jewellery, will make a big hole in two hundred pounds. Why, six months ago you would have thought it the millennium to have a flower shop of your own. Come! youll be all right. I must clear off to bed: I'm devilish sleepy. By the way, I came down for something: I forgot what it was.

LIZA. Your slippers.

HIGGINS. Oh yes, of course. You shied them at me. [*He picks them up, and is going out when she rises and speaks to him*].

LIZA. Before you go, sir—

HIGGINS [*dropping the slippers in his surprise at her calling him Sir*] Eh?

LIZA. Do my clothes belong to me or to Colonel Pickering?

HIGGINS [*coming back into the room as if her question were the very climax of unreason*] What the devil use would they be to Pickering?

LIZA. He might want them for the next girl you pick up to experiment on.

HIGGINS [*shocked and hurt*] Is that the way you feel towards us?

LIZA. I dont want to hear anything more about that. All I want to know is whether anything belongs to me. My own clothes were burnt.

HIGGINS. But what does it matter? Why need you start bothering about that in the middle of the night?

LIZA. I want to know what I may take away with me. I dont want to be accused of stealing.

HIGGINS [*now deeply wounded*] Stealing! You shouldnt have said that, Eliza. That shews a want of feeling.

LIZA. I'm sorry. I'm only a common ignorant girl; and in my station I have to be careful. There cant be any feelings between the like of you and the like of me. Please will you tell me what belongs to me and what doesnt?

HIGGINS [*very sulky*] You may take the whole damned houseful if you like. Except the jewels. Theyre hired. Will that satisfy you? [*He turns on his heel and is about to go in extreme dudgeon*].

LIZA [*drinking in his emotion like nectar, and nagging him to provoke a further supply*] Stop, please. [*She takes off her jewels*]. Will you take these to your room and keep them safe? I don't want to run the risk of their being missing.

HIGGINS [*furious*] Hand them over. [*She puts them into his hands*]. If these belonged to me instead of to the jeweller, I'd ram them down your ungrateful throat. [*He perfunctorily thrusts them into his pockets, unconsciously decorating himself with the protruding ends of the chains*].

LIZA [*taking a ring off*]. This ring isnt the jeweller's: it's the one you bought me in Brighton. I dont want it now. [HIGGINS *dashes the ring violently into the fireplace, and turns on her so threateningly that she crouches over the piano with her hands over her face, and exclaims*] Dont you hit me.

HIGGINS. Hit you! You infamous creature, how dare you accuse me of such a thing? It is you who have hit me. You have wounded me to the heart.

LIZA [*thrilling with hidden joy*] I'm glad. Ive got a little of my own back, anyhow.

HIGGINS [*with dignity, in his finest professional style*] You have caused me to lose my temper: a thing that has hardly ever happened to me before. I prefer to say nothing more tonight. I am going to bed.

LIZA [*pertly*] Youd better leave a note for Mrs Pearce about the coffee; for she wont be told by me.

HIGGINS [*formally*] Damn Mrs Pearce; and damn the coffee; and damn you; and [*wildly*] damn my own folly in having lavished my hard-earned knowledge and the treasure of my regard and intimacy on a heartless guttersnipe. [*He goes out with impressive decorum, and spoils it by slamming the door savagely*].

ELIZA *goes down on her knees on the hearthrug to look for the ring. When she finds it she considers for a moment what to do with it. Finally she flings it down on the dessert stand and goes upstairs in a tearing rage.*

     *    *    *    *    *    *

The furniture of Eliza's room has been increased by a big wardrobe and a sumptuous dressing-table. She comes in and switches on the electric light. She goes to the wardrobe; opens it; and pulls out a walking dress, a hat, and a pair of shoes, which she throws on the bed. She takes off her evening dress and shoes; then takes a padded hanger from the wardrobe; adjusts it carefully in the evening dress; and hangs it in the wardrobe, which she shuts with a slam. She puts on her walking shoes, her walking dress, and hat. She takes her wrist watch from the dressing-table and fastens it on. She pulls on her gloves; takes her vanity bag; and looks into it to see that her purse is there before hanging it on her wrist. She makes for the door. Every movement expresses her furious resolution.

She takes a last look at herself in the glass.

She suddenly puts out her tongue at herself; then leaves the room, switching off the electric light at the door.

Meanwhile, in the street outside, Freddy Eynsford Hill, lovelorn, is gazing up at the second floor, in which one of the windows is still lighted.

The light goes out.

FREDDY. Goodnight, darling, darling, darling.

ELIZA *comes out, giving the door a considerable bang behind her.*

LIZA. Whatever are you doing here?

FREDDY. Nothing. I spend most of my nights here. It's the only place where I'm happy. Dont laugh at me, Miss Doolittle.

LIZA. Dont you call me Miss Doolittle, do you hear? Liza's good enough for me. [*She breaks down and grabs him by the shoulders*] Freddy: you dont think I'm a heartless guttersnipe, do you?

FREDDY. Oh no, no, darling: how can you imagine such a thing? You are the loveliest, dearest—

*He loses all self-control and smothers her with kisses. She, hungry for comfort, responds. They stand there in one another's arms.*

*An elderly police constable arrives.*

CONSTABLE [*scandalized*] Now then! Now then!! Now then!!!

*They release one another hastily.*

FREDDY. Sorry, constable. Weve only just become engaged.

*They run away.*

The constable shakes his head, reflecting on his own courtship and on the vanity of human hopes. He moves off in the opposite direction with slow professional steps.

The flight of the lovers takes them to Cavendish Square. There they halt to consider their next move.

LIZA [*out of breath*] He didnt half give me a fright, that copper. But you answered him proper.

FREDDY. I hope I havnt taken you out of your way. Where were you going?

**LIZA.** To the river.

**FREDDY.** What for?

**LIZA.** To make a hole in it.

**FREDDY** [*horrified*] Eliza, darling. What do you mean? What's the matter?

**LIZA.** Never mind. It doesnt matter now. There's nobody in the world now but you and me, is there?

**FREDDY.** Not a soul.

*They indulge in another embrace, and are again surprised by a much younger constable.*

**SECOND CONSTABLE.** Now then, you two! What's this? Where do you think you are? Move along here, double quick.

**FREDDY.** As you say, sir, double quick.

They run away again, and are in Hanover Square before they stop for another conference.

**FREDDY.** I had no idea the police were so devilishly prudish.

**LIZA.** It's their business to hunt girls off the street.

**FREDDY.** We must go somewhere. We cant wander about the streets all night.

**LIZA.** Cant we? I think it'd be lovely to wander about for ever.

**FREDDY.** Oh, darling.

*They embrace again, oblivious of the arrival of a crawling taxi. It stops.*

**TAXIMAN.** Can I drive you and the lady anywhere, sir?

*They start asunder.*

**LIZA.** Oh, Freddy, a taxi. The very thing.

**FREDDY.** But, damn it, I've no money.

**LIZA.** I have plenty. The Colonel thinks you should never go out without ten pounds in your pocket. Listen. We'll drive about all night; and in the morning I'll call on old Mrs Higgins and ask her what I ought to do. I'll tell you all about it in the cab. And the police wont touch us there.

**FREDDY.** Righto! Ripping. [*To the* TAXIMAN] Wimbledon Common. [*They drive off*].

---

## THINKING ABOUT THE SELECTION
### Recalling

1. (a) How are Higgins and Pickering feeling as the act opens? (b) How does Eliza feel?
2. What does Higgins suggest when Eliza asks what will become of her?
3. (a) What does Eliza do after Higgins goes to bed? (b) Whom does she run into?

### Interpreting

4. (a) What two characters earlier in the play anticipated the concern Eliza expresses here? (b) What was Higgins's response to them?

5. (a) In what ways does Higgins act differently from how he behaved earlier in the play? (b) In what ways is his behavior predictable? (c) What does his behavior reveal about him?

### Applying

6. What aspects of being a woman of this era compound Eliza's problems?

## ANALYZING LITERATURE
### Explaining Crisis

The **crisis** in a work of fiction is the turning point—that moment when the conflict presented earlier in the work comes to a head. Also referred to as the *climax,* this highpoint, which occurs close to the end of the work, is followed by a resolution of all problems. The crisis in Act IV of *Pygmalion* is quite obviously the outgrowth of a conflict between Higgins and Eliza.

1. What is the nature of that conflict; that is, what has each of the two characters been trying to achieve from the start?
2. What problems mentioned (or raised) in Act IV remain to be resolved? How do you think they will be resolved? Explain why you feel as you do.

## CRITICAL THINKING AND READING
### Understanding Cause and Effect

Events, both in real life and in fiction, seldom happen in a vacuum. More commonly put, one thing "usually leads to another." Your ride to school does not show up and, therefore, you are late to your first-period class. Because of your lateness, you miss getting down an important assignment due the following day. And so on. An event that leads to a particular result is called a **cause.** The result of the cause is called an **effect.** Most works of fiction are chains of causes and effects.

For each of the following events, supply one cause and one effect.

1. Eliza pays Professor Higgins a visit.
2. Pickering proposes a bet with Higgins.

3. Higgins appears at his mother's "at-home."
4. Eliza throws Higgins's slippers at him.

## UNDERSTANDING LANGUAGE
### Finding Synonyms and Antonyms

Two words with the same or similar meanings are **synonyms.** *Boy* and *lad* are examples of synonyms. Two words opposite in meaning are **antonyms.** *Light* and *dark* are examples of antonyms. The word in italics to the left of each list appears in Act IV. From each list, select the one synonym and the one antonym. Consult a dictionary if necessary.

1. *resumes:* desists, incites, continues, inures
2. *genial:* reclusive, mystical, cordial, glacial
3. *infamous:* disgraceful, attractive, adorable, obscure
4. *intimacy:* estrangement, confidence, befuddlement, familiarity
5. *oblivious:* apparent, unmindful, self-effacing, self-conscious

## THINKING AND WRITING
### Writing a Letter of Advice

What do you think about the engagement of Eliza and Freddy? Is she making the right choice? Does she have other options? List any suggestions you would offer Eliza. Then write a letter to her offering advice. When you revise your letter, make sure your advice is practical. Have you presented it in a persuasive manner? Proofread your letter and prepare a final draft.

# GUIDE FOR INTERPRETING

## Pygmalion, Act V

**The Complete Play.** A play consists of many elements. The first of these is plot, the sequence of events. Will the plot be structured *chronologically,* moving ever forward in time? Or will it contain flashbacks? Next comes setting, the *when* and *where* of the play. How will time and location be conveyed to the audience? Through speakers' words? Through stage sets? Another element is characters, the people in the action. How many characters will be *round,* that is, complex and true-to-life? How many will be *flat,* one-dimensional figures included purely to advance the plot? Then comes tone, the playwright's attitude toward his or her subject or audience. Will the tone be lighthearted? Serious? A mixture? There is the issue of symbols—people, places, and events that stand for something beyond themselves. Last but not least is theme, the central idea of the play. What central idea or insight into life does the play communicate to the audience?

How will the play end? Based on the first four acts, draft your own ending. What will become of Eliza? Of Higgins? Of Freddy? Compare your hunches with those of your classmates.

Much of *Pygmalion* was radically different from what theatergoers were accustomed to seeing. In "An Aside" in *To Myself and My Friends,* Shaw explained the radical changes he introduced into modern English theater. He began:

> In a generation which knew nothing of any sort of acting but drawing-room acting, and which considered a speech of more than twenty words impossibly long, I went back to the classical style and write long rhetorical speeches like operatic solos, regarding my plays as musical perfomances precisely as Shakespeare did. As a producer I went back to the forgotten heroic stage business and the exciting or impressive declamation I had learnt from oldtimers like Risotori, Salvini, and Barry Sullivan. Yet so novel was my post-Marx post-Ibsen outlook on life that nobody suspected that my methods were as old as the stage itself. They would have seemed the merest routine to Kemble or Mrs. Siddons; but to the Victorian leading ladies they seemed to be unleadingladylike barnstorming. . . . I was continually struggling with the conscientious efforts of our players to underdo their parts lest they should be considered stagey. . . . It took a European war to cure them of wanting to be ladies and gentlemen first and actresses and actors later.

**Writer's Technique**

**Writing**

**Primary Source**

# ACT V

MRS HIGGINS's *drawing room. She is at her writing-table as before. The* PARLORMAID *comes in.*

**THE PARLORMAID** [*at the door*] Mr Henry, maam, is downstairs with Colonel Pickering.

**MRS HIGGINS.** Well, shew them up.

**THE PARLORMAID.** Theyre using the telephone, maam. Telephoning to the police, I think.

**MRS HIGGINS.** What!

**THE PARLORMAID** [*coming further in and lowering her voice*] Mr Henry is in a state, maam. I thought I'd better tell you.

**MRS HIGGINS.** If you had told me that Mr Henry was not in a state it would have been more surprising. Tell them to come up when theyve finished with the police. I suppose he's lost something.

**THE PARLORMAID.** Yes, maam [*going*].

**MRS HIGGINS.** Go upstairs and tell Miss Doolittle that Mr Henry and the Colonel are here. Ask her not to come down til I send for her.

**THE PARLORMAID.** Yes, maam.

HIGGINS *bursts in. He is, as the* PARLORMAID *has said, in a state.*

**HIGGINS.** Look here, mother: heres a confounded thing!

**MRS HIGGINS.** Yes, dear. Good morning. [*He checks his impatience and kisses her, whilst the* PARLORMAID *goes out*]. What is it?

**HIGGINS.** Eliza's bolted.

**MRS HIGGINS** [*calmly continuing her writing*] You must have frightened her.

**HIGGINS.** Frightened her! nonsense! She was left last night, as usual, to turn out the lights and all that; and instead of going to bed she changed her clothes and went right off: her bed wasnt slept in. She came in a cab for her things before seven this morning; and that fool Mrs Pearce let her have them without telling me a word about it. What am I to do?

**MRS HIGGINS.** Do without, I'm afraid, Henry. The girl has a perfect right to leave if she chooses.

**HIGGINS** [*wandering distractedly across the room*] But I cant find anything. I dont know what appointments Ive got. I'm—[PICKERING *comes in.* MRS HIGGINS *puts down her pen and turns away from the writing-table*].

**PICKERING** [*shaking hands*] Good morning, Mrs Higgins. Has Henry told you? [*He sits down on the ottoman*].

**HIGGINS.** What does that ass of an inspector say? Have you offered a reward?

**MRS HIGGINS** [*rising in indignant amazement*] You dont mean to say you have set the police after Eliza.

**HIGGINS.** Of course. What are the police for? What else could we do? [*He sits in the Elizabethan chair*].

**PICKERING.** The inspector made a lot of difficulties. I really think he suspected us of some improper purpose.

**MRS HIGGINS.** Well, of course, he did. What right have you to go to the police and give the girl's name as if she were a thief, or a lost umbrella, or something? Really! [*She sits down again, deeply vexed*].

**HIGGINS.** But we want to find her.

**PICKERING.** We cant let her go like this, you know, Mrs Higgins. What were we to do?

**MRS HIGGINS.** You have no more sense, either of you, than two children. Why—

*The* PARLORMAID *comes in and breaks off the conversation.*

**THE PARLORMAID.** Mr Henry: a gentleman wants to see you very particular. He's been sent on from Wimpole Street.

**HIGGINS.** Oh, bother! I cant see anyone now. Who is it?

THE PARLORMAID. A Mr Doolittle, sir.

PICKERING. Doolittle! Do you mean the dustman?

THE PARLORMAID. Dustman! Oh no, sir: a gentleman.

HIGGINS [*springing up excitedly*] By George, Pick, it's some relative of hers that she's gone to. Somebody we know nothing about. [*To the* PARLORMAID] Send him up, quick.

THE PARLORMAID. Yes, sir. [*She goes*].

HIGGINS [*eagerly, going to his mother*] Genteel relatives! now we shall hear something. [*He sits down in the Chippendale chair*].

MRS HIGGINS. Do you know any of her people?

PICKERING. Only her father: the fellow we told you about.

THE PARLORMAID [*announcing*] Mr Doolittle. [*She withdraws*].

DOOLITTLE *enters. He is resplendently dressed as for a fashionable wedding, and might, in fact, be the bridegroom. A flower in his buttonhole, a dazzling silk hat, and patent leather shoes complete the effect. He is too concerned with the business he has come on to notice* MRS HIGGINS. *He walks straight to* HIGGINS, *and accosts him with vehement reproach.*

DOOLITTLE [*indicating his own person*] See here! Do you see this? You done this.

HIGGINS. Done what, man?

DOOLITTLE. This, I tell you. Look at it. Look at this hat. Look at this coat.

PICKERING. Has Eliza been buying you clothes?

DOOLITTLE. Eliza! not she. Why would she buy me clothes?

MRS HIGGINS. Good morning, Mr Doolittle. Wont you sit down?

DOOLITTLE [*taken aback as he becomes conscious that he has forgotten his hostess*]
Asking your pardon, maam. [*He approaches her and shakes her proffered hand*]. Thank you. [*He sits down on the ottoman, on* PICKERING*'s right*]. I am that full of what has happened to me that I cant think of anything else.

HIGGINS. What the dickens has happened to you?

DOOLITTLE. I shouldn't mind if it had only happened to me: anything might happen to anybody and nobody to blame but Providence, as you might say. But this is something that you done to me: yes, you, Enry Iggins.

HIGGINS. Have you found Eliza?

DOOLITTLE. Have you lost her?

HIGGINS. Yes.

DOOLITTLE. You have all the luck, you have. I aint found her; but she'll find me quick enough now after what you done to me.

MRS HIGGINS. But what has my son done to you, Mr Doolittle?

DOOLITTLE. Done to me! Ruined me. Destroyed my happiness. Tied me up and delivered me into the hands of middle class morality.

HIGGINS [*rising intolerantly and standing over* DOOLITTLE] Youre raving. Youre drunk. Youre mad. I gave you five pounds. After that I had two conversations with you, at half-a-crown an hour. Ive never seen you since.

DOOLITTLE. Oh! Drunk am I? Mad am I? Tell me this. Did you or did you not write a letter to an old blighter in America that was giving five millions to found Moral Reform Societies all over the world, and that wanted you to invent a universal language for him?

HIGGINS. What! Ezra D. Wannafeller! He's dead. [*He sits down again carelessly*].

DOOLITTLE. Yes: he's dead; and I'm done for. Now did you or did you not write a letter to him to say that the most original moralist at

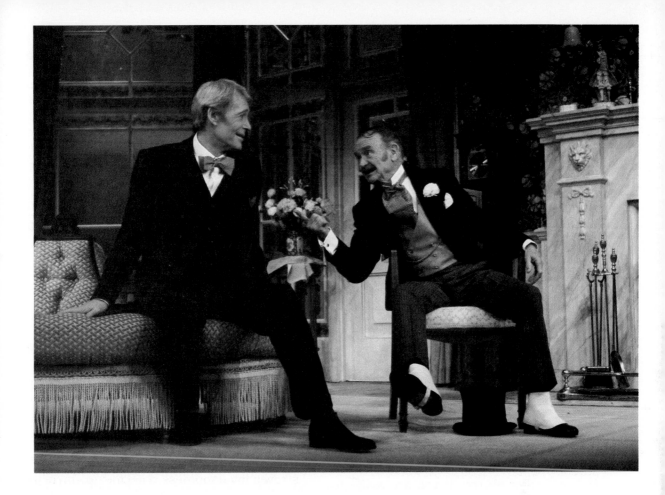

present in England, to the best of your knowledge, was Alfred Doolittle, a common dustman?

**HIGGINS.** Oh, after your first visit I remember making some silly joke of the kind.

**DOOLITTLE.** Ah! You may well call it a silly joke. It put the lid on me right enough. Just give him the chance he wanted to shew that Americans is not like us: that they reckonize and respect merit in every class of life, however humble. Them words is in his blooming will, in which, Henry Higgins, thanks to your silly joking, he leaves me a share in his Predigested Cheese Trust worth [three] thousand a year on condition that I lecture for his Wannafeller Moral Reform World League as often as they ask me up to six times a year.

**HIGGINS.** The devil he does! Whew! [*Brightening suddenly*] What a lark!

**PICKERING.** A safe thing for you, Doolittle. They wont ask you twice.

**DOOLITTLE.** It aint the lecturing I mind. I'll lecture them blue in the face, I will, and not turn a hair. It's making a gentleman of me that I object to. Who asked him to make a gentleman of me? I was happy. I was free. I touched pretty nigh everybody for money when I wanted it, same as I touched you, Enry Iggins. Now I am worrited; tied neck and heels; and everybody touches me for money. It's a fine thing for you, says my solicitor.[1] Is it? says I. You mean it's a good

---

**1. solicitor** *n.*: A member of the legal profession who is not allowed to plead cases in superior court.

thing for you, I says. When I was a poor man and had a solicitor once when they found a pram[2] in the dust cart, he got me off, and got shut of me and got me shut of him as quick as he could. Same with the doctors: used to shove me out of the hospital before I could hardly stand on my legs, and nothing to pay. Now they finds out that I'm not a healthy man and cant live unless they looks after me twice a day. In the house I'm not let do a hand's turn for myself: somebody else must do it and touch me for it. A year ago I hadnt a relative in the world except two or three that wouldn't speak to me. Now Ive fifty, and not a decent week's wages among the lot of them. I have to live for others and not for myself: that middle class morality. You talk of losing Eliza. Dont you be anxious: I bet she's on my doorstep by this: she that could support herself easy by selling flowers if I wasnt respectable. And the next one to touch me will be you, Enry Iggins. I'll have to learn to speak middle class language from you, instead of speaking proper English. Thats where youll come in; and I daresay thats what you done it for.

**MRS HIGGINS.** But, my dear Mr Doolittle, you need not suffer all this if you are really in earnest. Nobody can force you to accept this bequest. You can repudiate it. Isnt that so, Colonel Pickering?

**PICKERING.** I believe so.

**DOOLITTLE** [*softening his manner in deference to her sex*] Thats the tragedy of it, maam. It's easy to say chuck it; but I havnt the nerve. Which of us has? We're all intimidated. Intimidated, maam: thats what we are. What is there for me if I chuck it but the workhouse in my old age? I have to dye my hair already to keep my job as a dustman. If I was one of the deserving poor, and had put by a bit, I could chuck it; but then why should I, acause the deserving poor might as well be millionaires for all the happiness they ever has. They dont know what happi-

ness is. But I, as one of the undeserving poor, have nothing between me and the pauper's uniform but this here blasted three thousand a year that shoves me into the middle class. (Excuse the expression, maam; youd use it yourself if you had my provocation). Theyve got you every way you turn: it's a choice between the Skilly of the workhouse and the Char Bydis[3] of the middle class; and I havnt the nerve for the workhouse. Intimidated: thats what I am. Broke. Bought up. Happier men than me will call for my dust, and touch me for their tip; and I'll look on helpless, and envy them. And thats what your son has brought me to. [*He is overcome by emotion*].

**MRS HIGGINS.** Well, I'm very glad youre not going to do anything foolish, Mr Doolittle. For this solves the problem of Eliza's future. You can provide for her now.

**DOOLITTLE** [*with melancholy resignation*] Yes, maam: I'm expected to provide for everyone now, out of [three] thousand a year.

**HIGGINS** [*jumping up*] Nonsense! he cant provide for her. He shant provide for her. She doesnt belong to him. I paid him five pounds for her. Doolittle: either youre an honest man or a rogue.

**DOOLITTLE** [*tolerantly*] A little of both, Henry, like the rest of us: a little of both.

**HIGGINS.** Well, you took that money for the girl; and you have no right to take her as well.

**MRS HIGGINS.** Henry: dont be absurd. If you want to know where Eliza is, she is upstairs.

**HIGGINS** [*amazed*] Upstairs!!! Then I shall

---

2. **pram** *n.*: Baby carriage.

3. **Skilly . . . Char Bydis:** Doolittle means Scylla (sil′ ə) and Charybdis (kə rib′ dis), a dangerous rock and whirlpool on either side of the narrow passage between Italy and Sicily. Scylla and Charybdis, personified by the ancient Greeks as two monsters, have come to stand for any two dangers neither of which can be evaded without risking the other.

jolly soon fetch her downstairs. [*He makes resolutely for the door*].

**MRS HIGGINS** [*rising and following him*] Be quiet, Henry. Sit down.

**HIGGINS.** I—

**MRS HIGGINS.** Sit down, dear; and listen to me.

**HIGGINS.** Oh very well, very well, very well. [*He throws himself ungraciously on the ottoman, with his face towards the windows*]. But I think you might have told us this half an hour ago.

**MRS HIGGINS.** Eliza came to me this morning. She told me of the brutal way you two treated her.

**HIGGINS** [*bounding up again*] What!

**PICKERING** [*rising also*] My dear Mrs Higgins, she's been telling you stories. We didnt treat her brutally. We hardly said a word to her; and we parted on particularly good terms. [*Turning on* Higgins] Higgins: did you bully her after I went to bed?

**HIGGINS.** Just the other way about. She threw my slippers in my face. She behaved in the most outrageous way. I never gave her the slightest provocation. The slippers came bang into my face the moment I entered the room—before I had uttered a word. And used perfectly awful language.

**PICKERING** [*astonished*] But why? What did we do to her?

**MRS HIGGINS.** I think I know pretty well what you did. The girl is naturally rather affectionate, I think. Isnt she, Mr Doolittle?

**DOOLITTLE.** Very tender-hearted, maam. Takes after me.

**MRS HIGGINS.** Just so. She had become attached to you both. She worked very hard for you, Henry. I don't think you quite realize what anything in the nature of brain work means to a girl of her class. Well, it seems that when the great day of trial came, and she did this wonderful thing for you without

making a single mistake, you two sat there and never said a word to her, but talked together of how glad you were that it was all over and how you had been bored with the whole thing. And then you were surprised because she threw your slippers at you! *I* should have thrown the fire-irons at you.

**HIGGINS.** We said nothing except that we were tired and wanted to go to bed. Did we, Pick?

**PICKERING** [*shrugging his shoulders*] That was all.

**MRS HIGGINS** [*ironically*] Quite sure?

**PICKERING.** Absolutely. Really, that was all.

**MRS HIGGINS.** You didnt thank her, or pet her, or admire her, or tell her how splendid she'd been.

**HIGGINS** [*impatiently*] But she knew all about that. We didnt make speeches to her, if thats what you mean.

**PICKERING** [*conscience stricken*] Perhaps we were a little inconsiderate. Is she very angry?

**MRS HIGGINS** [*returning to her place at the writing-table*] Well, I'm afraid she wont go back to Wimpole Street, especially now that Mr Doolittle is able to keep up the position you have thrust on her; but she says she is quite willing to meet you on friendly terms and to let bygones be bygones.

**HIGGINS** [*furious*] Is she, by George? Ho!

**MRS HIGGINS.** If you promise to behave yourself, Henry, I'll ask her to come down. If not, go home; for you have taken up quite enough of my time.

**HIGGINS.** Oh, all right. Very well. Pick: you behave yourself. Let us put on our best Sunday manners for this creature that we picked out of the mud. [*He flings himself sulkily into the Elizabethan chair*].

**DOOLITTLE** [*remonstrating*] Now, now, Enry Iggins! Have some consideration for my feelings as a middle class man.

MRS HIGGINS. Remember your promise, Henry. [*She presses the bell-button on the writing-table*]. Mr Doolittle: will you be so good as to step out on the balcony for a moment. I dont want Eliza to have the shock of your news until she has made it up with these two gentlemen. Would you mind?

DOOLITTLE. As you wish, lady. Anything to help Henry to keep her off my hands. [*He disappears through the window*].

*The* PARLORMAID *answers the bell.* PICKERING *sits down in* DOOLITTLE'S *place.*

MRS HIGGINS. Ask Miss Doolittle to come down, please.

THE PARLORMAID. Yes, maam. [*She goes out*].

MRS HIGGINS. Now, Henry: be good.

HIGGINS. I am behaving myself perfectly.

PICKERING. He is doing his best, Mrs Higgins.

*A pause.* HIGGINS *throws back his head; stretches out his legs; and begins to whistle.*

MRS HIGGINS. Henry, dearest, you dont look at all nice in that attitude.

HIGGINS [*pulling himself together*] I was not trying to look nice, mother.

MRS HIGGINS. It doesnt matter, dear. I only wanted to make you speak.

HIGGINS. Why?

MRS HIGGINS. Because you cant speak and whistle at the same time.

HIGGINS *groans. Another very trying pause.*

HIGGINS [*springing up, out of patience*] Where the devil is that girl? Are we to wait here all day?

ELIZA *enters, sunny, self-possessed, and giving a staggeringly convincing exhibition of ease of manner. She carries a little work-basket, and is very much at home.* PICKERING *is too much taken aback to rise.*

LIZA. How do you do, Professor Higgins? Are you quite well?

HIGGINS [*choking*] Am I— [*He can say no more*].

LIZA. But of course you are: you are never ill. So glad to see you again, Colonel Pickering. [*He rises hastily; and they shake hands*]. Quite chilly this morning, isn't it? [*She sits down on his left. He sits beside her*].

HIGGINS. Dont you dare try this game on me. I taught it to you; and it doesnt take me in. Get up and come home; and dont be a fool.

ELIZA *takes a piece of needlework from her basket, and begins to stitch at it, without taking the least notice of this outburst.*

MRS HIGGINS. Very nicely put, indeed, Henry. No woman could resist such an invitation.

HIGGINS. You let her alone, mother. Let her speak for herself. You will jolly soon see whether she has an idea that I havnt put into her head or a word that I havnt put into her mouth. I tell you I have created this thing out of the squashed cabbage leaves of Covent Garden; and now she pretends to play the fine lady with me.

MRS HIGGINS [*placidly*] Yes, dear; but youll sit down, wont you?

HIGGINS *sits down again, savagely.*

LIZA [*to* PICKERING, *taking no apparent notice of* HIGGINS, *and working away deftly*] Will you drop me altogether now that the experiment is over, Colonel Pickering?

PICKERING. Oh dont. You mustnt think of it as an experiment. It shocks me, somehow.

LIZA. Oh, I'm only a squashed cabbage leaf—

PICKERING [*impulsively*] No.

LIZA [*continuing quietly*]—but I owe so much to you that I should be very unhappy if you forgot me.

PICKERING. It's very kind of you to say so, Miss Doolittle.

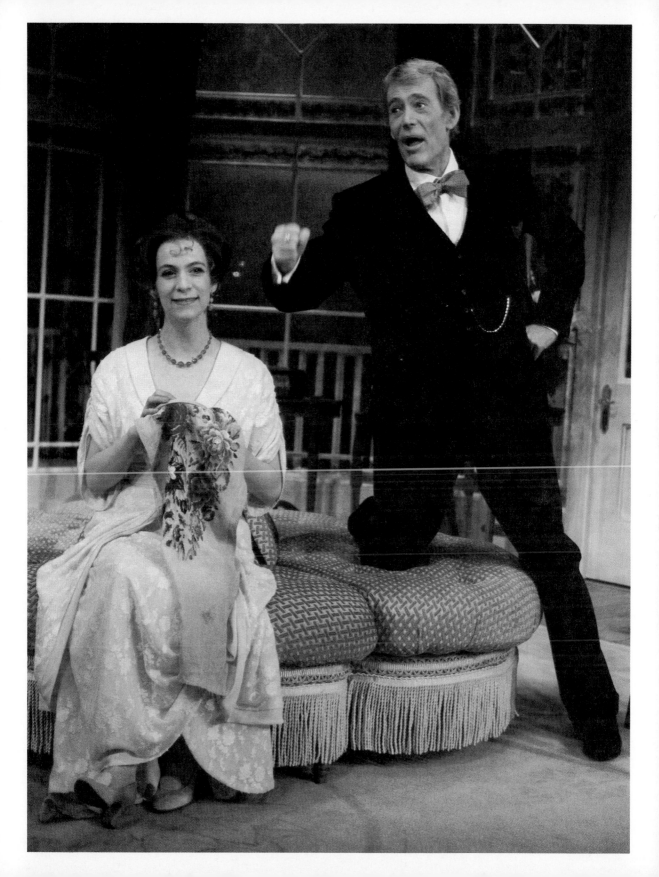

LIZA. It's not because you paid for my dresses. I know you are generous to everybody with money. But it was from you that I learnt really nice manners; and that is what makes one a lady, isnt it? You see it was so very difficult for me with the example of Professor Higgins always before me. I was brought up to be just like him, unable to control myself, and using bad language on the slightest provocation. And I should never have known that ladies and gentlemen didnt behave like that if you hadnt been there.

HIGGINS. Well!!

PICKERING. Oh, thats only his way, you know. He doesnt mean it.

LIZA. Oh, *I* didnt mean it either, when I was a flower girl. It was only my way. But you see I did it; and thats what makes the difference after all.

PICKERING. No doubt. Still, he taught you to speak; and I couldn't have done that, you know.

LIZA [*trivially*] Of course: that is his profession.

HIGGINS. Damnation!

LIZA [*continuing*] It was just like learning to dance in the fashionable way: there was nothing more than that in it. But do you know what began my real education?

PICKERING. What?

LIZA [*stopping her work for a moment*] Your calling me Miss Doolittle that day when I first came to Wimpole Street. That was the beginning of self-respect for me. [*She resumes her stitching*] And there were a hundred little things you never noticed, because they came naturally to you. Things about standing up and taking off your hat and opening doors——

PICKERING. Oh, that was nothing.

LIZA. Yes: things that shewed you thought and felt about me as if I were something better than a scullery-maid; though of course I know you would have been just the same to a scullery-maid if she had been let into the drawing room. You never took off your boots in the dining room when I was there.

PICKERING. You mustnt mind that. Higgins takes off his boots all over the place.

LIZA. I know. I am not blaming him. It is his way, isn't it? But it made such a difference to me that you didnt do it. You see, really and truly, apart from the things anyone can pick up (the dressing and the proper way of speaking, and so on), the difference between a lady and a flower girl is not how she behaves, but how she's treated. I shall always be a flower girl to Professor Higgins, because he always treats me as a flower girl, and always will; but I know I can be a lady to you, because you always treat me as a lady, and always will.

MRS HIGGINS. Please dont grind your teeth, Henry.

PICKERING. Well, this is really very nice of you, Miss Doolittle.

LIZA. I should like you to call me Eliza, now, if you would.

PICKERING. Thank you. Eliza, of course.

LIZA. And I should like Professor Higgins to call me Miss Doolittle.

HIGGINS. I'll see you damned first.

MRS HIGGINS. Henry! Henry!

PICKERING [*laughing*] Why dont you slang back at him? Dont stand it. It would do him a lot of good.

LIZA. I cant. I could have done it once; but now I cant go back to it. You told me, you know, that when a child is brought to a foreign country, it picks up the language in a few weeks, and forgets its own. Well, I am a child in your country. I have forgotten my own language, and can speak nothing but yours. Thats the real break-off with the corner of Tottenham Court Road. Leaving Wimpole Street finishes it.

PICKERING [*much alarmed*] Oh! but youre coming back to Wimpole Street, arnt you? Youll forgive Higgins?

HIGGINS [*rising*] Forgive! Will she, by George! Let her go. Let her find out how she can get on without us. She will relapse into the gutter in three weeks without me at her elbow.

DOOLITTLE *appears at the centre window. With a look of dignified reproach at* HIGGINS, *he comes slowly and silently to his daughter, who, with her back to the window, is unconscious of his approach.*

PICKERING. He's incorrigible, Eliza. You wont relapse, will you?

LIZA. No: not now. Never again. I have learnt my lesson. I dont believe I could utter one of the old sounds if I tried. [DOOLITTLE *touches her on the left shoulder. She drops her work, losing her self-possession utterly at the spectacle of her father's splendor*] A-a-a-a-a-ah-ow-ooh!

HIGGINS [*With a crow of triumph*] Aha! Just so. A-a-a-a-ahowooh! A-a-a-a-ahowooh! A-a-a-a-ahowooh! Victory! Victory! [*He throws himself on the divan, folding his arms, and spraddling arrogantly*].

DOOLITTLE. Can you blame the girl? Dont look at me like that, Eliza. It aint my fault. Ive come into some money.

LIZA. You must have touched a millionaire this time, dad.

DOOLITTLE. I have. But I'm dressed something special today. I'm going to St George's, Hanover Square. Your stepmother is going to marry me.

LIZA [*angrily*] Youre going to let yourself down to marry that low common woman!

PICKERING [*quietly*] He ought to, Eliza. [*To* DOOLITTLE] Why has she changed her mind?

DOOLITTLE [*sadly*] Intimidated, Governor. Intimidated. Middle class morality claims its victim. Wont you put on your hat, Liza, and come and see me turned off?

LIZA. If the Colonel says I must, I—I'll [*almost sobbing*] I'll demean myself. And get insulted for my pains, like enough.

DOOLITTLE. Dont be afraid: she never comes to words with anyone now, poor woman! respectability has broke all the spirit out of her.

PICKERING [*squeezing* ELIZA'S *elbow gently*] Be kind to them, Eliza. Make the best of it.

LIZA [*forcing a little smile for him through her vexation*] Oh well, just to shew theres no ill feeling. I'll be back in a moment. [*She goes out*].

DOOLITTLE [*sitting down beside* PICKERING] I feel uncommon nervous about the ceremony, Colonel. I wish youd come and see me through it.

PICKERING. But youve been through it before, man. You were married to Eliza's mother.

DOOLITTLE. Who told you that, Colonel?

PICKERING. Well, nobody told me. But I concluded—naturally——

DOOLITTLE. No: that aint the natural way, Colonel: it's only the middle class way. My way was always the undeserving way. But dont say nothing to Eliza. She dont know: I always had a delicacy about telling her.

PICKERING. Quite right. We'll leave it so, if you dont mind.

DOOLITTLE. And youll come to the church, Colonel, and put me through straight?

PICKERING. With pleasure. As far as a bachelor can.

MRS HIGGINS. May I come, Mr Doolittle? I should be very sorry to miss your wedding.

DOOLITTLE. I should indeed be honored by your condescension, maam; and my poor old woman would take it as a tremenjous compliment. She's been very low, thinking of the happy days that are no more.

**MRS HIGGINS** [*rising*] I'll order the carriage and get ready. [*The men rise, except* HIGGINS]. I shant be more than fifteen minutes. [*As she goes to the door* ELIZA *comes in, hatted and buttoning her gloves*]. I'm going to the church to see your father married, Eliza. You had better come in the brougham[4] with me. Colonel Pickering can go on with the bridegroom.

MRS HIGGINS *goes out.* ELIZA *comes to the middle of the room between the centre window and the ottoman.* PICKERING *joins her.*

**DOOLITTLE.** Bridegroom. What a word! It makes a man realize his position, somehow. [*He takes up his hat and goes towards the door*].

**PICKERING.** Before I go, Eliza, do forgive Higgins and come back to us.

**LIZA.** I dont think dad would allow me. Would you, dad?

**DOOLITTLE** [*sad but magnanimous*] They played you off very cunning, Eliza, them two sportsmen. If it had been only one of them, you could have nailed him. But you see, there was two; and one of them chaperoned the other, as you might say. [*To* PICKERING] It was artful of you, Colonel; but I bear no malice: I should have done the same myself. I been the victim of one woman after another all my life, and I dont grudge you two getting the better of Liza. I shant interfere. It's time for us to go, Colonel. So long, Henry. See you in St George's, Eliza. [*He goes out*].

**PICKERING.** [*coaxing*] Do stay with us, Eliza. [*He follows Doolittle*].

ELIZA *goes out on the balcony to avoid being alone with* HIGGINS. *He rises and joins her there. She immediately comes back into the room and makes for the door; but he*

_____

4. **brougham** (brō͞om) *n.*: A type of carriage.

goes along the balcony and gets his back to the door before she reaches it.

**HIGGINS.** Well, Eliza, you've had a bit of your own back, as you call it. Have you had enough? and are you going to be reasonable? Or do you want any more?

**LIZA.** You want me back only to pick up your slippers and put up with your tempers and fetch and carry for you.

**HIGGINS.** I havnt said I wanted you back at all.

**LIZA.** Oh, indeed. Then what are we talking about?

**HIGGINS.** About you, not about me. If you come back I shall treat you just as I have always treated you. I cant change my nature; and I dont intend to change my manners. My manners are exactly the same as Colonel Pickering's.

**LIZA.** That's not true. He treats a flower girl as if she was a duchess.

**HIGGINS.** And I treat a duchess as if she was a flower girl.

**LIZA.** I see [*She turns away composedly, and sits on the ottoman, facing the window*]. The same to everybody.

**HIGGINS.** Just so.

**LIZA.** Like father.

**HIGGINS** [*grinning, a little taken down*] Without accepting the comparison at all points, Eliza, it's quite true that your father is not a snob, and that he will be quite at home in any station of life to which his eccentric destiny may call him. [*Seriously*] The great secret, Eliza, is not having bad manners or good manners or any other particular sort of manners, but having the same manner for all human souls: in short, behaving as if you were in Heaven, where there are no third-class carriages, and one soul is as good as another.

**LIZA.** Amen. You are a born preacher.

HIGGINS [*irritated*] The question is not whether I treat you rudely, but whether you ever heard me treat anyone else better.

LIZA [*with sudden sincerity*] I dont care how you treat me. I dont mind you swearing at me. I shouldnt mind a black eye: Ive had one before this. But [*standing up and facing him*] I wont be passed over.

HIGGINS. Then get out of my way; for I wont stop for you. You talk about me as if I were a motor bus.

LIZA. So you are a motor bus: all bounce and go, and no consideration for anyone. But I can do without you: dont think I cant.

HIGGINS. I know you can. I told you you could.

LIZA [*wounded, getting away from him to the other side of the ottoman with her face to the hearth*] I know you did, you brute. You wanted to get rid of me.

HIGGINS. Liar.

LIZA. Thank you. [*She sits down with dignity*]

HIGGINS. You never asked yourself, I suppose, whether I could do without you.

LIZA . [*earnestly*] Don't you try to get round me. You'll have to do without me.

HIGGINS [*arrogant*] I can do without anybody. I have my own soul: my own spark of divine fire. But [*with sudden humility*] I shall miss you, Eliza. [*He sits down near her on the ottoman*] I have learnt something from your idiotic notions: I confess that humbly and gratefully. And I have grown accustomed to your voice and appearance. I like them, rather.

LIZA. Well, you have both of them on your gramophone and in your book of photographs. When you feel lonely without me, you can turn the machine on. It's got no feelings to hurt.

HIGGINS. I cant turn your soul on. Leave me those feelings; and you can take away the voice and the face. They are not you.

LIZA. Oh, you are a devil. You can twist the heart in a girl as easy as some could twist her arms to hurt her. Mrs Pearce warned me. Time and again she has wanted to leave you; and you always got round her at the last minute. And you dont care a bit for her. And you dont care a bit for me.

HIGGINS. I care for life, for humanity; and you are a part of it that has come my way and been built into my house. What more can you or anyone ask?

LIZA. I wont care for anybody that doesnt care for me.

HIGGINS. Commercial principles, Eliza. Like [*reproducing her Covent Garden pronunciation with professional exactness*] s'yollin voylets [selling violets], isnt it?

LIZA. Dont sneer at me. It's mean to sneer at me.

HIGGINS. I have never sneered in my life. Sneering doesnt become either the human face or the human soul. I am expressing my righteous contempt for Commercialism. I dont and wont trade in affection. You call me a brute because you couldnt buy a claim on me by fetching my slippers and finding my spectacles. You were a fool: I think a woman fetching a man's slippers is a disgusting sight: did I ever fetch your slippers? I think a good deal more of you for throwing them in my face. No use slaving for me and then saying you want to be cared for: who cares for a slave? If you come back, come back for the sake of good fellowship; for youll get nothing else. Youve had a thousand times as much out of me as I have out of you; and if you dare to set up your little dog's tricks of fetching and carrying slippers against my creation of a Duchess Eliza, I'll slam the door in your silly face.

LIZA. What did you do it for if you didnt care for me?

HIGGINS [*heartily*] Why, because it was my job.

**LIZA.** You never thought of the trouble it would make for me.

**HIGGINS.** Would the world ever have been made if its maker had been afraid of making trouble? Making life means making trouble. Theres only one way of escaping trouble; and thats killing things. Cowards, you notice, are always shrieking to have troublesome people killed.

**LIZA.** I'm no preacher: I dont notice things like that. I notice that you dont notice me.

**HIGGINS** [*jumping up and walking about intolerantly*] Eliza: youre an idiot. I waste the treasures of my Miltonic mind by spreading them before you. Once for all, understand that I go my way and do my work without caring twopence what happens to either of us. I am not intimidated, like your father and your stepmother. So you can come back or go to the devil: which you please.

**LIZA.** What am I to come back for?

**HIGGINS** [*bouncing up on his knees on the ottoman and leaning over it to her*] For the fun of it. Thats why I took you on.

**LIZA** [*with averted face*] And you may throw me out tomorrow if I dont do everything you want me to?

**HIGGINS.** Yes; and you may walk out tomorrow if I dont do everything you want me to.

**LIZA.** And live with my stepmother?

**HIGGINS.** Yes, or sell flowers.

**LIZA.** Oh, if I only could go back to my flower basket! I should be independent of both you and father and all the world! Why did you take my independence from me? Why did I give it up? I'm a slave now, for all my fine clothes.

**HIGGINS.** Not a bit. I'll adopt you as my daughter and settle money on you if you like. Or would you rather marry Pickering?

**LIZA** [*looking fiercely round at him*] I wouldnt marry you if you asked me; and youre nearer my age than what he is.

**HIGGINS** [*gently*] Than he is: not "than what he is."

**LIZA** [*losing her temper and rising*] I'll talk as I like. Youre not my teacher now.

**HIGGINS** [*reflectively*] I dont suppose Pickering would, though. He's as confirmed an old bachelor as I am.

**LIZA.** Thats not what I want; and dont you think it. I've always had chaps enough wanting me that way. Freddy Hill writes to me twice and three times a day, sheets and sheets.

**HIGGINS** [*disagreeably surprised*] Damn his impudence! [*He recoils and finds himself sitting on his heels*].

**LIZA.** He has a right to if he likes, poor lad. And he does love me.

**HIGGINS** [*getting off the ottoman*] You have no right to encourage him.

**LIZA.** Every girl has a right to be loved.

**HIGGINS.** What! By fools like that?

**LIZA.** Freddy's not a fool. And if he's weak and poor and wants me, may be he'd make me happier than my betters that bully me and dont want me.

**HIGGINS.** Can he make anything of you? Thats the point.

**LIZA.** Perhaps I could make something of him. But I never thought of us making anything of one another; and you never think of anything else. I only want to be natural.

**HIGGINS.** In short, you want me to be as infatuated about you as Freddy? Is that it?

**LIZA.** No I dont. Thats not the sort of feeling I want from you. And dont you be too sure of yourself or of me. I could have been a bad girl if I'd liked. Ive seen more of some things than you, for all your learning. Girls like me can drag gentlemen down to make love to them easy enough. And they wish each other dead the next minute.

**HIGGINS.** Of course they do. Then what in thunder are we quarrelling about?

**LIZA** [*much troubled*] I want a little kindness. I know I'm a common ignorant girl, and you a book-learned gentleman; but I'm not dirt under your feet. What I done [*correcting herself*] what I did was not for the dresses and the taxis: I did it because we were pleasant together and I come—came—to care for you; not to want you to make love to me, and not forgetting the difference between us, but more friendly like.

**HIGGINS.** Well, of course. Thats just how I feel. And how Pickering feels. Eliza: youre a fool.

**LIZA.** Thats not a proper answer to give me [*she sinks on the chair at the writing-table in tears*].

**HIGGINS.** It's all youll get until you stop being a common idiot. If youre going to be a lady, youll have to give up feeling neglected if the men you know dont spend half their time snivelling over you and the other half giving you black eyes. If you cant stand the coldness of my sort of life, and the strain of it, go back to the gutter. Work til youre more a brute than a human being; and then cuddle and squabble and drink til you fall asleep. Oh, it's a fine life, the life of the gutter. It's real: it's warm: it's violent: you can feel it through the thickest skin: you can taste it and smell it without any training or any work. Not like Science and Literature and Classical Music and Philosophy and Art. You find me cold, unfeeling, selfish, dont you? Very well: be off with you to the sort of people you like. Marry some sentimental hog or other with lots of money, and a thick pair of lips to kiss you with and a thick pair of boots to kick you with. If you cant appreciate what youve got, youd better get what you can appreciate.

**LIZA.** [*Desperate*] Oh, you are a cruel tyrant. I cant talk to you: you turn everything against me: I'm always in the wrong. But you know very well all the time that youre nothing but a bully. You know I cant go back to the gutter, as you call it, and that I have no real friends in the world but you and the Colonel. You know well I couldnt bear to live with a low common man after you two; and it's wicked and cruel of you to insult me by pretending I could. You think I must go back to Wimpole Street because I have nowhere else to go but father's. But dont you be too sure that you have me under your feet to be trampled on and talked down. I'll marry Freddy, I will, as soon as I'm able to support him.

**HIGGINS** [*thunderstruck*] Freddy!!! that young fool! That poor devil who couldnt get a job as an errand boy even if he had the guts to try for it! Woman: do you not understand that I have made you a consort for a king?

**LIZA.** Freddy loves me: that makes him king enough for me. I dont want him to work: he wasnt brought up to it as I was. I'll go and be a teacher.

**HIGGINS.** Whatll you teach, in heaven's name?

**LIZA.** What you taught me. I'll teach phonetics.

**HIGGINS.** Ha! ha! ha!

**LIZA.** I'll offer myself as an assistant to that hairyfaced Hungarian.

**HIGGINS** [*rising in a fury*] What! That imposter! that humbug! that toadying ingoramus! Teach him my methods! my discoveries! You take one step in his direction and I'll wring your neck. [*He lays hands on her*]. Do you hear?

**LIZA** [*defiantly non-resistant*] Wring away. What do I care? I knew youd strike me some day. [*He lets her go, stamping with rage at having forgotten himself, and recoils so hastily that he stumbles back into his seat on the ottoman*]. Aha! Now I know how to deal with you. What a fool I was not to think of it before! You cant take away the knowledge you gave me. You said I had a finer ear than you. And I can be civil and kind to people, which is more than you can. Aha!

[*Purposely dropping her aitches to annoy him*] Thats done you, Enry Iggins, it az. Now I dont care that [*snapping her fingers*] for your bullying and your big talk. I'll advertize it in the papers that your duchess is only a flower girl that you taught, and that she'll teach anybody to be a duchess just the same in six months for a thousand guineas. Oh, when I think of myself crawling under your feet and being trampled on and called names, when all the time I had only to lift up my finger to be as good as you, I could just kick myself.

**HIGGINS** [*wondering at her*] You damned impudent slut, you! But it's better than snivelling; better than fetching slippers and finding spectacles, isnt it? [*Rising*] By George, Eliza. I said I'd make a woman of you; and I have. I like you like this.

**LIZA.** Yes: you turn round and make up to me now that I'm not afraid of you, and can do without you.

**HIGGINS.** Of course I do, you little fool. Five minutes ago you were like a millstone round my neck. Now youre a tower of strength: a consort battleship. You and I and Pickering will be three old bachelors instead of only two men and a silly girl.

MRS HIGGINS *returns, dressed for the wedding.* ELIZA *instantly becomes cool and elegant.*

**MRS HIGGINS.** The carriage is waiting, Eliza. Are you ready?

**LIZA.** Quite. Is the Professor coming?

**MRS HIGGINS.** Certainly not. He cant behave himself in church. He makes remarks out loud all the time on the clergyman's pronunciation.

**LIZA.** Then I shall not see you again, Professor. Goodbye. [*She goes to the door*].

**MRS HIGGINS** [*coming to* HIGGINS] Goodbye, dear.

**HIGGINS.** Goodbye, mother. [*He is about to kiss her, when he recollects something*]. Oh, by the way, Eliza, order a ham and a Stilton cheese, will you? And buy me a pair of reindeer gloves, number eights, and a tie to match that new suit of mine. You can choose the color. [*His cheerful, careless, vigorous voice shews that he is incorrigible*].

**LIZA** [*disdainfully*] Number eights are too small for you if you want them lined with lamb's wool. You have three new ties that you have forgotten in the drawer of your washstand. Colonel Pickering prefers double Gloucester to Stilton; and you dont notice the difference. I telephoned Mrs Pearce this morning not to forget the ham. What you are to do without me I cannot imagine. [*She sweeps out*].

**MRS HIGGINS.** I'm afraid youve spoilt that girl, Henry. I should be uneasy about you and her if she were less fond of Colonel Pickering.

**HIGGINS.** Pickering! Nonsense: she's going to marry Freddy. Ha ha! Freddy! Freddy!! Ha ha ha ha ha!!!!! [*He roars with laughter as the play ends*].

# Epilogue

The rest of the story need not be shewn in action, and indeed, would hardly need telling if our imaginations were not so enfeebled by their lazy dependence on the ready-mades and reach-me-downs of the ragshop in which Romance keeps its stock of "happy endings" to misfit all stories. Now, the history of Eliza Doolittle, though called a romance because the transfiguration it records seems exceedingly improbable, is common enough. Such transfigurations have been achieved by hundreds of resolutely ambitious young women since Nell Gwynne[1] set them the example by playing queens and fascinating kings in the theatre in which she began by selling oranges. Nevertheless, people in all directions have assumed, for no other reason than that she became the heroine of a romance, that she must have married the hero of it. This is unbearable, not only because her little drama, if acted on such a thoughtless assumption, must be spoiled, but because the true sequel is patent to anyone with a sense of human nature in general, and of feminine instinct in particular.

Eliza, in telling Higgins she would not marry him if he asked her, was not coquetting: she was announcing a well-considered decision. When a bachelor interests, and dominates, and teaches, and becomes important to a spinster, as Higgins with Eliza, she always, if she has character enough to be capable of it, considers very seriously indeed whether she will play for becoming that bachelor's wife, especially if he is so little interested in marriage that a determined and devoted woman might capture him if she set herself resolutely to do it. Her decision will depend a good deal on whether she is really free to choose; and that, again, will depend on her age and income. If she is at the end of her youth, and has no security for her livelihood, she will marry him because she must marry anybody who will provide for her. But at Eliza's age a good-looking girl does not feel that pressure: she feels free to pick and choose. She is therefore guided by her instinct in the matter. Eliza's instinct tells her not to marry Higgins. It does not tell her to give him up. It is not in the slightest doubt as to his remaining one of the strongest personal interests in her life. It would be very sorely strained if there was another woman likely to supplant her with him. But as she feels sure of him on that last point, she has no doubt at all as to her course, and would not have any, even if the difference of twenty years in age, which seems so great to youth, did not exist between them.

As our own instincts are not appealed to by her conclusion, let us see whether we

---

**1. Nell Gwynne:** Eleanor Gwynne (1650–1687), an English actress and favorite of Charles II.

cannot discover some reason in it. When Higgins excused his indifference to young women on the ground that they had an irresistible rival in his mother, he gave the clue to his inveterate old-bachelordom. The case is uncommon only to the extent that remarkable mothers are uncommon. If an imaginative boy has a sufficiently rich mother who has intelligence, personal grace, dignity of character without harshness, and a cultivated sense of the best art of her time to enable her to make her house beautiful, she sets a standard for him against which very few women can struggle, besides effecting for him a disengagement of his affections, his sense of beauty, and his idealism from his specifically sexual impulses. This makes him a standing puzzle to the huge number of uncultivated people who have been brought up in tasteless homes by commonplace or disagreeable parents, and to whom, consequently, literature, painting, sculpture, music, and affectionate personal relations come as modes of sex if they come at all. The word passion means nothing else to them; and that Higgins could have a passion for phonetics and idealize his mother instead of Eliza, would seem to them absurd and unnatural. Nevertheless, when we look round and see that hardly anyone is too ugly or disagreeable to find a wife or a husband if he or she wants one, whilst many old maids and bachelors are above the average in quality and culture, we cannot help suspecting that the disentanglement of sex from the associations with which it is so commonly confused, a disentanglement which persons of genius achieve by sheer intellectual analysis, is sometimes produced or aided by parental fascination.

Now, though Eliza was incapable of thus explaining to herself Higgins's formidable powers of resistance to the charm that prostrated Freddy at the first glance, she was instinctively aware that she could never obtain a complete grip of him, or come between him and his mother (the first necessity of the married woman). To put it shortly, she knew that for some mysterious reason he had not the makings of a married man in him, according to her conception of a husband as one to whom she would be his nearest and fondest and warmest interest. Even had there been no mother-rival, she would still have refused to accept an interest in herself that was secondary to philosophic interests. Had Mrs Higgins died, there would still have been Milton and the Universal Alphabet. Landor's[2] remark that to those who have the greatest power of loving, love is a secondary affair, would not have recommended Landor to Eliza. Put that along with her resentment of Higgins's domineering superiority, and her mistrust of his coaxing cleverness in getting round her and evading her wrath when he had gone too far with his impetuous bullying, and you will see that Eliza's instinct had good grounds for warning her not to marry her Pygmalion.

And now, whom did Eliza marry? For if Higgins was a predestinate old bachelor, she was most certainly not a predestinate old maid. Well, that can be told very shortly to those who have not guessed it from the indications she has herself given them.

Almost immediately after Eliza is stung into proclaiming her considered determination not to marry Higgins, she mentions the fact that young Mr Frederick Eynsford Hill is pouring out his love for her daily through the post. Now Freddy is young, practically twenty years younger than Higgins: he is a gentleman [or, as Eliza would qualify him, a toff], and speaks like one. He is nicely dressed, is treated by the Colonel as an equal, loves her unaffectedly, and is not her master, nor ever likely to dominate her in spite of his advantage of social standing. Eliza has no use for the foolish romantic tradition that all women love to be mastered, if not actually bullied and beaten. "When

---

**2. Landor's:** Referring to Walter Savage Landor (1775–1864), an English writer.

you go to women'' says Nietzsche[3] "take your whip with you.'' Sensible despots have never confined that precaution to women: they have taken their whips with them when they have dealt with men, and been slavishly idealized by the men over whom they have flourished the whip much more than by women. No doubt there are slavish women as well as slavish men; and women, like men, admire those that are stronger than themselves. But to admire a strong person and to live under that strong per-

son's thumb are two different things. The weak may not be admired and hero-worshipped; but they are by no means disliked or shunned; and they never seem to have the least difficulty in marrying people who are too good for them. They may fail in emergencies; but life is not one long emergency: it is mostly a string of situations for which no exceptional strength is needed, and with which even rather weak people can cope if they have a stronger partner to help them out. Accordingly, it is a truth everywhere in evidence that strong people, masculine or feminine, not only do not marry stronger people, but do not shew any preference for them in selecting their

---

**3. Nietzsche** (nē′ chə): German philosopher Friedrich Wilhelm Nietzsche (1844–1900).

friends. When a lion meets another with a louder roar "the first lion thinks the last a bore." The man or woman who feels strong enough for two, seeks for every other quality in a partner than strength.

The converse is also true. Weak people want to marry strong people who do not frighten them too much; and this often leads them to make the mistake we describe metaphorically as "biting off more than they can chew." They want too much for too little; and when the bargain is unreasonable beyond all bearing, the union becomes impossible: it ends in the weaker party being either discarded or borne as a cross, which is worse. People who are not only weak, but silly or obtuse as well, are often in these difficulties.

This being the state of human affairs, what is Eliza fairly sure to do when she is placed between Freddy and Higgins? Will she look forward to a lifetime of fetching Higgins's slippers or to a lifetime of Freddy fetching hers? There can be no doubt about the answer. Unless Freddy is biologically repulsive to her, and Higgins biologically attractive to a degree that overwhelms all her other instincts, she will, if she marries either of them, marry Freddy.

And that is just what Eliza did.

Complications ensued; but they were economic, not romantic. Freddy had no money and no occupation. His mother's jointure,[4] a last relic of the opulence of Largelady Park, had enabled her to struggle along in Earlscourt with an air of gentility, but not to procure any serious secondary education for her children, much less give the boy a profession. A clerkship at thirty shillings a week was beneath Freddy's dignity, and extremely distasteful to him besides. His prospects consisted of a hope that if he kept up appearances somebody would do something for him. The something appeared vaguely to his imagination as a pri-

vate secretaryship or a sinecure[5] of some sort. To his mother it perhaps appeared as a marriage to some lady of means who could not resist her boy's niceness. Fancy her feelings when he married a flower girl who had become disclassed under extraordinary circumstances which were now notorious!

It is true that Eliza's situation did not seem wholly ineligible. Her father, though formerly a dustman, and now fantastically disclassed, had become extremely popular in the smartest society by a social talent which triumphed over every prejudice and every disadvantage. Rejected by the middle class, which he loathed, he had shot up at once into the highest circles by his wit, his dustmanship (which he carried like a banner), and his Nietzschean transcendence of good and evil. At intimate ducal dinners he sat on the right hand of the Duchess; and in country houses he smoked in the pantry and was made much of by the butler when he was not feeding in the dining room and being consulted by cabinet ministers. But he found it almost as hard to do all this on [three] thousand a year as Mrs Eynsford Hill to live in Earlscourt on an income so pitiably smaller that I have not the heart to disclose its exact figure. He absolutely refused to add the last straw to his burden by contributing to Eliza's support.

Thus Freddy and Eliza, now Mr and Mrs Eynsford Hill, would have spent a penniless honeymoon but for a wedding present of £500 from the Colonel to Eliza. It lasted a long time because Freddy did not know how to spend money, never having had any to spend, and Eliza, socially trained by a pair of old bachelors, wore her clothes as long as they held together and looked pretty, without the least regard to their being many months out of fashion. Still, £500 will not last two young people for ever; and they both knew, and Eliza felt as well, that they must

---

**4. jointure** *n.*: Widow's inheritance.

**5. sinecure** (sī′ nə kyo͞or′) *n.*: Any office or position that brings advantage but involves little or no work.

shift for themselves in the end. She could quarter herself on Wimpole Street because it had come to be her home; but she was quite aware that she ought not to quarter Freddy there, and that it would not be good for his character if she did.

Not that the Wimpole Street bachelors objected. When she consulted them, Higgins declined to be bothered about her housing problem when that solution was so simple. Eliza's desire to have Freddy in the house with her seemed of no more importance than if she had wanted an extra piece of bedroom furniture. Pleas as to Freddy's character, and the moral obligation on him to earn his own living, were lost on Higgins. He denied that Freddy had any character, and declared that if he tried to do any useful work some competent person would have the trouble of undoing it: a procedure involving a net loss to the community, and great unhappiness to Freddy himself, who was obviously intended by Nature for such light work as amusing Eliza, which, Higgins declared, was a much more useful and honorable occupation than working in the city. When Eliza referred again to her project of teaching phonetics, Higgins abated not a jot of his violent opposition to it. He said she was not within ten years of being qualified to meddle with his pet subject; and as it was evident that the Colonel agreed with him, she felt she could not go against them in this grave matter, and that she had no right, without Higgins's consent, to exploit the knowledge he had given her; for his knowledge seemed to her as much his private property as his watch: Eliza was no communist. Besides, she was superstitiously devoted to them both, more entirely and frankly after her marriage than before it.

It was the Colonel who finally solved the problem, which had cost him much perplexed cogitation. He one day asked Eliza, rather shyly, whether she had quite given up her notion of keeping a flower shop. She replied that she had thought of it, but had put it out of her head, because the Colonel had said, that day at Mrs Higgins's, that it would never do. The Colonel confessed that when he said that, he had not quite recovered from the dazzling impression of the day before. They broke the matter to Higgins that evening. The sole comment vouchsafed by him very nearly led to a serious quarrel with Eliza. It was to the effect that she would have in Freddy an ideal errand boy.

Freddy himself was next sounded on the subject. He said he had been thinking of a shop himself; though it had presented itself to his pennilessness as a small place in which Eliza should sell tobacco at one counter whilst he sold newspapers at the opposite one. But he agreed that it would be extraordinarily jolly to go early every morning with Eliza to Covent Garden and buy flowers on the scene of their first meeting: a sentiment which earned him many kisses from his wife. He added that he had always been afraid to propose anything of the sort, because Clara would make an awful row about a step that must damage her matrimonial chances, and his mother could not be expected to like it after clinging for so many years to that step of the social ladder on which retail trade is impossible.

This difficulty was removed by an event highly unexpected by Freddy's mother. Clara, in the course of her incursions into those artistic circles which were the highest within her reach, discovered that her conversational qualifications were expected to include a grounding in the novels of Mr H. G. Wells.[6] She borrowed them in various directions so energetically that she swallowed them all within two months. The result was a conversion of a kind quite common today. A modern Acts of the Apostles would fill fifty whole Bibles if anyone were capable of writing it.

Poor Clara, who appeared to Higgins and

---

**6. H. G. Wells:** Herbert George Wells (1866–1946), English novelist and historian.

his mother as a disagreeable and ridiculous person, and to her own mother as in some inexplicable way a social failure, had never seen herself in either light; for, though to some extent ridiculed and mimicked in West Kensington like everybody else there, she was accepted as a rational and normal—or shall we say inevitable?—sort of human being. At worst they called her The Pusher; but to them no more than to herself had it ever occurred that she was pushing the air, and pushing it in a wrong direction. Still, she was not happy. She was growing desperate. Her one asset, the fact that her mother was what the Epsom greengrocer called a carriage lady, had no exchange value, apparently. It had prevented her from getting educated, because the only education she could have afforded was education with the Earlscourt greengrocer's daughter. It had led her to seek the society of her mother's class; and that class simply would not have her, because she was much poorer than the greengrocer, and, far from being able to afford a maid, could not afford even a housemaid, and had to scrape along at home with an illiberally treated general servant. Under such circumstances nothing could give her an air of being a genuine product of Largelady Park. And yet its tradition made her regard a marriage with anyone within her reach as an unbearable humiliation. Commercial people and professional people in a small way were odious to her. She ran after painters and novelists; but she did not charm them; and her bold attempts to pick up and practise artistic and literary talk irritated them. She was, in short, an utter failure, an ignorant, incompetent, pretentious, unwelcome, penniless, useless little snob; and though she did not admit these disqualifications (for nobody ever faces unpleasant truths of this kind until the possibility of a way out dawns on them) she felt their effects too keenly to be satisfied with her position.

Clara had a startling eyeopener when,
on being suddenly wakened to enthusiasm by a girl of her own age who dazzled her and produced in her a gushing desire to take her for a model, and gain her friendship, she discovered that this exquisite apparition had graduated from the gutter in a few months time. It shook her so violently, that when Mr H. G. Wells lifted her on the point of his puissant[7] pen, and placed her at the angle of view from which the life she was leading and the society to which she clung appeared in its true relation to real human needs and worthy social structure, he effected a conversion and a conviction of sin comparable to the most sensational feats of General Booth[8] or Gypsy Smith.[9] Clara's snobbery went bang. Life suddenly began to move with her. Without knowing how or why, she began to make friends and enemies. Some of the acquaintances to whom she had been a tedious or indifferent or ridiculous affliction, dropped her: others became cordial. To her amazement she found that some "quite nice" people were saturated with Wells, and that this accessibility to ideas was the secret of their niceness. People she had thought deeply religious, and had tried to conciliate on that tack with disastrous results, suddenly took an interest in her, and revealed a hostility to conventional religion which she had never conceived possible except among the most desperate characters. They made her read Galsworthy; and Galsworthy exposed the vanity of Largelady Park and finished her. It exasperated her to think that the dungeon in which she had languished for so many unhappy years had been unlocked all the time, and that the impulses she had so carefully struggled with and stifled for the sake of keeping well with society, were pre-

---

**7. puissant** (pyo͞o′ i sənt) *adj.*: Powerful.
**8. General Booth:** William Booth (1829–1912), the founder of the Salvation Army.
**9. Gypsy Smith:** Gipsy Rodney Smith (1860–1947), an English evangelist.

cisely those by which alone she could have come into any sort of sincere human contact. In the radiance of these discoveries, and the tumult of their reaction, she made a fool of herself as freely and conspicuously as when she so rashly adopted Eliza's expletive in Mrs Higgins's drawing room; for the new-born Wellsian had to find her bearings almost as ridiculously as a baby; but nobody hates a baby for its ineptitudes, or thinks the worse of it for trying to eat the matches; and Clara lost no friends by her follies. They laughed at her to her face this time; and she had to defend herself and fight it out as best she could.

When Freddy paid a visit to Earlscourt (which he never did when he could possibly help it) to make the desolating announcement that he and his Eliza were thinking of blackening the Largelady scutcheon[10] by opening a shop, he found the little household already convulsed by a prior announcement from Clara that she also was going to work in an old furniture shop in Dover Street, which had been started by a fellow Wellsian. This appointment Clara owed, after all, to her old social accomplishment of Push. She had made up her mind that, cost what it might, she would see Mr Wells in the flesh; and she had achieved her end at a garden party. She had better luck than so rash an enterprise deserved. Mr Wells came up to her expectations. Age had not withered him, nor could custom stale his infinite variety in half an hour. His pleasant neatness and compactness, his small hands and feet, his teeming ready brain, his unaffected accessibility, and a certain fine apprehensiveness which stamped him as susceptible from his topmost hair to his tipmost toe, proved irresistible. Clara talked of nothing else for weeks and weeks afterwards. And as she happened to talk to the lady of the furniture shop, and that lady also desir-

ed above all things to know Mr Wells and sell pretty things to him, she offered Clara a job on the chance of achieving that end through her.

And so it came about that Eliza's luck held, and the expected opposition to the flower shop melted away. The shop is in the arcade of a railway station not very far from the Victoria and Albert Museum; and if you live in that neighbourhood you may go there any day and buy a buttonhole from Eliza.

Now here is a last opportunity for romance. Would you not like to be assured that the shop was an immense success, thanks to Eliza's charms and her early business experience in Covent Garden? Alas! the truth is the truth: the shop did not pay for a long time, simply because Eliza and her Freddy did not know how to keep it. True, Eliza had not to begin at the very beginning: she knew the names and prices of the cheaper flowers; and her elation was unbounded when she found that Freddy, like all youths educated at cheap, pretentious, and thoroughly inefficient schools, knew a little Latin. It was very little, but enough to make him appear to her a Porson or Bentley,[11] and to put him at his ease with botanical nomenclature. Unfortunately he knew nothing else; and Eliza, though she could count money up to eighteen shillings or so, and had acquired a certain familiarity with the language of Milton from her struggles to qualify herself for winning Higgins's bet, could not write out a bill without utterly disgracing the establishment. Freddy's power of stating in Latin that Balbus built a wall and that Gaul was divided into three parts[12] did not carry with it the slightest knowledge of accounts or business: Colonel

---

**10. scutcheon** (skuch′ ən) *n.*: Coat of arms.

**11. Porson, Bentley:** Richard Porson (1759–1808) and Richard Bentley (1662–1742), English classical scholars.
**12. Balbus . . . parts:** Referring to elementary Latin exercises.

Pickering had to explain to him what a cheque book and a bank account meant. And the pair were by no means easily teachable. Freddy backed up Eliza in her obstinate refusal to believe that they could save money by engaging a bookkeeper with some knowledge of the business. How, they argued, could you possible save money by going to extra expense when you already could not make both ends meet? But the Colonel, after making the ends meet over and over again, at last gently insisted; and Eliza, humbled to the dust by having to beg from him so often, and stung by the uproarious derision of Higgins, to whom the notion of Freddy succeeding at anything was a joke that never palled, grasped the fact that business, like phonetics, has to be learned.

On the piteous spectacle of the pair spending their evenings in shorthand schools and polytechnic classes, learning bookkeeping and typewriting with incipient junior clerks, male and female, from the elementary schools, let me not dwell. There were even classes at the London School of Economics, and a humble personal appeal to the director of that institution to recommend a course bearing on the flower business. He, being a humorist, explained to them the method of the celebrated Dickensian essay on Chinese Metaphysics by the gentleman who read an article on China and an article on Metaphysics and combined the information. He suggested that they should combine the London School with Kew Gardens. Eliza, to whom the procedure of the Dickensian gentleman seemed perfectly correct (as in fact it was) and not in the least funny (which was only her ignorance), took the advice with entire gravity. But the effort that cost her the deepest humiliation was a request to Higgins, whose pet artistic fancy, next to Milton's verse, was calligraphy, and who himself wrote a most beautiful Italian hand, that he would teach her to write. He declared that she was congenitally incapable of forming a single letter worthy of the least of Milton's words; but she persisted; and again he suddenly threw himself into the task of teaching her with a combination of stormy intensity, concentrated patience, and occasional bursts of interesting disquisition on the beauty and nobility, the august mission and destiny, of human handwriting. Eliza ended by acquiring an extremely uncommercial script which was a positive extension of her personal beauty, and spending three times as much on stationery as anyone else because certain qualities and shapes on paper became indispensable to her. She could not even address an envelope in the usual way because it made the margins all wrong.

Their commercial schooldays were a period of disgrace and despair for the young couple. They seemed to be learning nothing about flower shops. At last they gave it up as hopeless, and shook the dust of the shorthand schools, and the polytechnics, and the London School of Economics from their feet for ever. Besides, the business was in some mysterious way beginning to take care of itself. They had somehow forgotten their objections to employing other people. They came to the conclusion that their own way was the best, and that they had really a remarkable talent for business. The Colonel, who had been compelled for some years to keep a sufficient sum on current account at his bankers to make up their deficits, found that the provision was unnecessary: the young people were prospering. It is true that there was not quite fair play between them and their competitors in trade. Their week-ends in the country cost them nothing, and saved them the price of their Sunday dinners; for the motor car was the Colonel's; and he and Higgins paid the hotel bills. Mr F. Hill, florist and greengrocer (they soon discovered that there was money in asparagus; and asparagus led to other vegetables), had an air which stamped the business as classy; and in private life he was still Frederick Eynsford Hill, Esquire. Not that there was any swank[13] about him: nobody but Eliza knew that he had been christened Frederick Chaloner. Eliza herself swanked like anything.

That is all. That is how it has turned out. It is astonishing how much Eliza still manages to meddle in the housekeeping at Wimpole Street in spite of the shop and her own family. And it is notable that though she never nags her husband, and frankly loves the Colonel as if she were his favorite daughter, she has never got out of the habit of nagging Higgins that was established on the fatal night when she won his bet for him. She snaps his head off on the faintest provocation, or on none. He no longer dares to tease her by assuming an abysmal inferiority of Freddy's mind to his own. He storms and bullies and derides; but she stands up to him so ruthlessly that the Colonel has to ask her from time to time to be kinder to Higgins; and it is the only request of his that brings a mulish expression into her face. Nothing but some emergency or calamity great enough to break down all likes and dislikes, and throw them both back on their common humanity—and may they be spared any such trial!—will ever alter this. She knows that Higgins does not need her, just as her father did not need her. The very

scrupulousness with which he told her that day that he had become used to having her there, and dependent on her for all sorts of little services, and that he should miss her if she went away (it would never have occurred to Freddy or the Colonel to say anything of the sort) deepens her inner certainty that she is "no more to him than them slippers"; yet she has a sense, too, that his indifference is deeper than the infatuation of commoner souls. She is immensely interested in him. She has even secret mischievous moments in which she wishes she could get him alone, on a desert island, away from all ties and with nobody else in the world to consider, and just drag him off his pedestal and see him making love like any common man. We all have private imaginations of that sort. But when it comes to business, to the life that she really leads as distinguished from the life of dreams and fancies, she likes Freddy and she likes the Colonel; and she does not like Higgins and Mr Doolittle. Galatea never does quite like Pygmalion:[14] his relation to her is too godlike to be altogether agreeable.

---

**13. swank** *n.*: Ostentatious behavior.

**14. Galatea** (gal′ə tē′ə) **. . . Pygmalion:** Pygmalion was a mythological king of Cyprus who carved a statue of a woman so beautiful that he fell in love with her. The king prayed to the gods to bring the statue, Galatea, to life, and his prayers were answered by Aphrodite, the goddess of love.

## THINKING ABOUT THE SELECTION

### Recalling

1. Who has Pickering been talking with on the phone at the beginning of Act V? Why?
2. (a) What has happened to Alfred Doolittle? (b) How has this change affected his life?
3. Why is Eliza grateful to Pickering?
4. (a) In their conversation together what does Eliza tell Higgins she wants from him? (b) What does he want from her?
5. (a) What, according to the Epilogue, becomes of Eliza? (b) Of Clara Eynsford Hill?

### Interpreting

6. Explain what the changes in Alfred Doolittle suggest is Shaw's attitude toward "middle-class morality."
7. Do you think the outcome of Higgins's last discussion with Eliza was inevitable? Why or why not?

### Applying

8. The Epilogue describes developments in Eliza's life after the action of the play. Would you have preferred to see these developments played out? Explain your reasons.

## ANALYZING LITERATURE

### Understanding the Complete Play

The paradoxical saying that "the whole is greater than the sum of its parts" is true of works of art. A play is a weaving-together of many elements, among them: the plot (or story line), the setting (time and place of the action), the characters (roles), the tone (playwright's attitude toward the subject or audience), the symbols (representative values attached to events, people, or things), and the theme (main idea). When these separate elements come together, a "chemical reaction" results. Create a checklist similar to the following for *Pygmalion*.

| plot | setting | character | tone | symbol | theme |
|------|---------|-----------|------|--------|-------|
|      |         |           |      |        |       |

Write a brief description for each of the play's elements, entering "NA" when the element is not applicable. Then discuss how the various elements interact in Shaw's play. (Consider, for example, how setting affects theme.)

## CRITICAL THINKING AND READING

### Summarizing a Play

When a newspaper or magazine critic writes a review of a play, he or she includes a **summary,** or brief description of the action. A good summary captures a sense of the play as a whole, focusing not only on what is said and done but on such details as setting. The amount of information that a summary provides depends, of course, on its overall length. List the details you find important to include in a one-page summary of *Pygmalion*. Decide how you would handle such matters as Shaw's Preface and Epilogue.

## THINKING AND WRITING

### Writing About the Title

At the end of the Epilogue, Shaw mentions Pygmalion and Galatea, who are figures from Greek mythology. The sculptor Pygmalion created a statue of a beautiful woman. After he fell in love with his creation, the goddess Aphrodite brought her to life. Write an essay and discuss the effectiveness of the title Shaw chose for his play. Proceed by addressing the following questions: How godlike do you think Eliza finds Higgins? To what extent has Higgins "created" a new person? Might Higgins's feelings toward Eliza at any point in the play be fairly described as "love?" How much impact will the title have on a person who views, rather than reads, the play and who is, therefore, unfamiliar with the Epilogue? When you revise, make sure you have included adequate support for your theses.

## Pygmalion Becomes My Fair Lady

It was the undisputed smash musical of 1956. From the moment the first hints drifted north from Philadelphia—where the musical was having its tryout run—tickets were eagerly snatched up. By March 15, when the show officially opened in New York City, only a few tickets were still available. By March 16 tickets were sold out for months ahead. Critics raved: "One of the best musicals of the century!" Writer James Thurber proclaimed it to be "the finest union of comedy and music" in his experience. Its male lead made the cover of the July 23 issue of *Time* magazine. Although it was one of those rare musicals that did not have a title song—it took its name from an old poem about London Bridge falling down—within weeks an astonishing number of its songs were famous. People were humming "The Rain in Spain," "I Could Have Danced All Night," and "Get Me to the Church on Time." By 1962, when it completed its run of 2,717 performances, its 1912 period costumes had even influenced American fashion. What play had taken America by such storm? Why, *My Fair Lady,* of course!

### LERNER AND LOEWE

What could account for the play's outrageous success and impact on American culture? Obviously much of its success was due to Lerner and Loewe, the brilliant duo responsible for such classic hits as *Brigadoon* (1947) and *Camelot* (1960). Except for the play's girl-gets-boy ending that Shaw would not have tolerated, Lerner had the sense not to tamper with a good thing—almost all of *My Fair Lady* comes directly from Shaw's *Pygmalion.*

Recall that Shaw declared in the Epilogue to *Pygmalion* that to assume that the heroine of a romance "must have married the hero of it" is "unbearable." But perhaps in his adaptation Lerner was only doing what so many had wanted to do before him. Take, for instance, the case of the first actor to play Henry Higgins, Beerbohm Tree. Handpicked by Shaw for the role, the actor nonetheless chose to ignore Shaw's directions and play the role his own way. Accounts have it that Shaw was absolutely livid with Tree who, when the curtain fell in the last act, threw a flower to Eliza—indicating his affections for her and holding out the hope that they would indeed be united. Aside from the ending, Lerner was much more respectful of Shaw's writing and made almost no changes in the original.

In at least one spot, Lerner changed a scene's location, though the plot remains the same. In *Pygmalion* Henry Higgins first presents Eliza to society at his mother's house. In *My Fair Lady* her presentation is at the Ascot races, where there are many more chances for Eliza to slip back into her Tottenham Court Road lingo. He has also eliminated or added minor characters to point up situations. In the main, however, he has faithfully followed Shaw's lead. Stage directions are, for the most part, word for word from Shaw. As the critic for *Time* magazine remarked, "At bottom, *My Fair Lady* is nothing more than George Bernard Shaw's play *Pygmalion* with music added."

## A GLITTERING CAST

Credit is also due to the glittering cast. Theatergoers and fellow actors alike were stunned by Harrison's brilliant performance as Henry Higgins. Famed actor Charles Laughton rushed backstage to offer his congratulations to his friend Harrison: "In all my theater experience," he raved, "I've only seen a handful of performances to match Rex's. He makes every man in the audience laugh at himself, and every woman laugh at the man beside her." Interestingly, Harrison had met Shaw in person in the course of performing in Shaw's play *Major Barbara* in 1934. *My Fair Lady* marked the debut of twenty-year-old English actress Julie Andrews, who was described as playing the role of the flower-girl Eliza with "heart-lifting simplicity."

## THE MOVIE VERSION

If possible, the 1964 movie version was as splendid as the stage play. Studio head Jack Warner originally wanted Cary Grant or Rock Hudson to play Higgins and James Cagney to be Doolittle. Cary Grant refused Warner's offer by saying that if the studio mogul chose anyone but Rex Harrison for the role of Higgins he would not even bother to see the film. Without a bankable leading man, Warner was worried: After all, he had put up more than five million for the rights to the musical, set aside nearly twenty million for production costs, and promised the authors and producers of the stage show almost fifty percent of the net. As it turned out, his fears were groundless. The screen version proved a stunning hit, earning Oscars for Best Picture, Best Actor, Best Director, Best Color Cinematography, Best Costume Design, Best Musical Score, Best Sound, and Best Art Direction. The only major award it did not win was Best Actress. In one of life's little twists of fate, Julie Andrews won Best Actress that year for her role in Mary Poppins—and Audrey Hepburn did not even receive a nomination as Eliza Doolittle.

In the long run, however, we must go back to Shaw and present our laurels to him, for without him there would be no *Pygmalion;* and without *Pygmalion* there would be no *My Fair Lady.*

**Assignment**

**1.** A character sketch is like a painting in words. Unlike a visual portrait, however, a character sketch delves into the mind of the subject, revealing his or her innermost thoughts and attitudes. Choose one of the characters you read about in this unit and write a character sketch.

**Prewriting.** In selecting a character, make sure there is ample material to develop. Divide a sheet of paper into several sections, labeling one "Physical Details," another "Habits and Behaviors," and a third "Beliefs."

**Writing.** Begin your sketch by describing the relevance of your character to the story in which he or she appears. Use the author's terms, along with vivid terms of your own, to describe the character's appearance and mental makeup.

**Revising.** Make sure you have arranged your information in an orderly way.

**Assignment**

**2.** Robert Frost, the prominent twentieth-century poet, described the writing of free verse as "like playing tennis with the net down." As the careful reader of this unit will have observed, free verse is more structured than Frost's glib dismissal suggests. Write an original poem in free verse. Model your effort on the work of one of the poets you read and admired.

**Prewriting.** Get your wheels spinning to come up with a topic. When you have selected one, write it at the center of a sheet of paper and cluster ideas around it.

**Writing.** Write your first draft. Attempt to use vivid images and figures of speech.

**Revising.** Put your poem aside for several hours. Then reread it. Look for areas that are weak or in need of clarification.

**Assignment**

**3.** The stream-of-consciousness technique perfected by Virginia Woolf and others was one of the significant literary breakthroughs of the Modernist period. Write a short fictional account in which a character enters a room and sees an object—either familiar or new—that triggers a string of mental associations.

**Prewriting.** Brainstorm for details about your character, including his or her appearance, habits, attitudes, and so on. Create in outline form a past for your character.

**Writing.** In your first draft, mention the object the character sees and then let your mind lead you. Freewrite without regard to correctness of form, spelling, or sentence structure.

**Revising.** Check doubtful spellings and polish any rough edges.

**Assignment**

**1.** Several of the writers in this unit—Shaw, Saki, and the poet Henry Reed among them—use satire or irony to put across their ideas to the reader. Select a satirical work and a work that expresses its theme in a totally straightforward manner. In an essay, compare and contrast the two approaches. Tell which you believe to be more effective, and give reasons.

**Prewriting.** Review the concept of satire and the manner in which the author of your satirical selection uses it. In a single sentence, identify the theme of each of the selections.

**Writing.** In an opening paragraph, discuss the relationship between theme and satire. Devote some space to speculation on how the impact of the two works would have been altered had the authors opted for a different approach.

**Revising.** Check your essay for coherence and economy of language.

**Assignment**

**2.** T. S. Eliot wrote that William Butler Yeats "was one of those few [poets] whose history is the history of their own times, who are part of the consciousness of an age which cannot be understood without them." In an essay, evaluate this statement as it applies to Yeats, to Eliot himself, or to some other poet of the Modernist period.

**Prewriting.** Prepare for your composition by reviewing the background material on your poet and on the history of the period. Jot down notes on this interrelation.

**Writing.** Write your first draft. Spend at least a paragraph describing the uniqueness of your poet's contribution to his or her age. Quote the poems where relevant.

**Revising.** Examine your essay for unity and logic. Substitute strong, specific words for any that strike you as vague or weak.

**Assignment**

**3.** Perhaps the two events that most profoundly shaped the literature of the Modernist period were World Wars I and II. Select any three writers of the period and describe the differences and similarities the impact of the wars had on their lives and works.

**Prewriting.** After you have selected your three writers, develop a profile for each in which you identify the relevance of the wars. Note whether the individual saw action on the battlefield, whether he or she used the notion of war literally or figuratively in stories or poems, and so on.

**Writing.** Begin your composition with a brief biographical sketch of each writer. Quote liberally from the literary works in your discussion.

**Revising.** Review your composition to be sure you have covered all points raised in your outline.

**PAPAGENA**
*Gillian Ayres*
Photograph Courtesy of The South Bank Center

# CONTEMPORARY WRITERS
## 1945–present

We are living at one of the great turning points
of history. . . . Yesterday, we split the atom.
We assaulted that colossal citadel of power, the
tiny unit of the substance of the universe. And
because of this, the great dream and the great
nightmare of centuries of human thought have taken
flesh and walk beside us all, day and night.*

from "The Small Personal Voice,"
**Doris Lessing**

A new world dawned in 1945—a world of great promise and yet of great danger. First the United States, then the Soviet Union, then Britain, France, and a number of other nations gained the ability to build massively destructive atomic weapons. Henceforth all humanity would dwell in the shadow of the bomb. That fact made a deep impression on writers like Doris Lessing, whose words are quoted on the preceding page.

The postwar period has not been kind to Britain. Its Empire has crumbled, its military rank has declined, and its traditional industries have rusted away. However, Britain has struggled gamely to resolve its problems while taking pride in a still-vibrant literary and artistic life.

## THE AFTERMATH OF WAR

World War II shook British society to its very core. The months after the fighting stopped were a time of privation and misery, as people made do with meager food rations and walked through streets lined with bombed-out ruins. Faced with the urgent need for reconstruction, Britons sought to shape a new social and political climate. Out went the wartime coalition government of Winston Churchill. In came a peacetime Labor government, bubbling with optimism. The Labor party's goals were sweeping: nationalize major industries, improve social services, attack the system of class privileges. Parliament set to work to transform class-bound Britain into a twentieth-century welfare state. The Age of the Common Man had dawned.

### An End to Empire

Meanwhile, shadows descended on the British Empire. Nationalists in Asia and Africa were demanding their freedom—by force if necessary, by negotiation if possible. British leaders hesitated. They sent troops to put down rebellions, but they also sent diplomats to negotiate an orderly transfer of power.

The dismantling of empire did not always go smoothly. In South Asia, seeking to avert conflict between Hindus and Moslems, Britain split the Indian subcontinent into two nations, India and Pakistan. Partition and independence came in 1947. Almost immediately, bloody communal fighting swept the subcontinent. In the Middle East, unable to mediate the bitter Arab-Jewish feud over Palestine, Britain withdrew from its Palestine mandate. Israel's birth in 1948 touched off the first of many Arab-Israeli wars. In Malaya, Kenya, Rhodesia, and other territories too, bloodshed accompanied the process of withdrawal.

Slowly, the British Empire passed into history. In its place emerged a new Commonwealth of Nations, its members bound together not by force and the myth of empire but by common loyalties and common needs.

## Evolving Europe

On the Continent, too, British power declined sharply after the war. By 1947 disputes and quarrels had ended the wartime alliance that linked Britain, the United States, and the Soviet Union. An Iron Curtain (Churchill's term) divided Europe. East of the Iron Curtain, the Soviet Union dominated a string of dependent or "satellite" nations with Socialist governments. West of the Iron Curtain, Britain and many other nations huddled under the umbrella of United States power. In 1949 they joined together in a military alliance called the North Atlantic Treaty Organization (NATO). Later Britain would join the European Economic Community, or Common Market, a group of nations (now numbering twelve) that are trying to merge their economic systems into a "united Europe."

## RECOVERY AND CONTEMPORARY PROBLEMS

War memories faded, Britons cleared away the rubble, and life got better. By the 1960's Britain was once again a center of cultural excitement. The dazzling popularity of the Beatles carried British rock music to the far corners of the world. Trendy young people on

**BERLIN WALL**
*P. Zachmann/Magnum*

# BRITISH EVENTS

1945    Churchill resigns.

1946    United Nations meets in London.

1947    Coal mines nationalized.

1949    Britain joins NATO.

       Irish Free State becomes Republic of Ireland.

1950    London dock strike.

1952    Elizabeth II becomes queen.

1953    Winston Churchill knighted, wins Nobel Prize for Literature.

1954    Track star Roger Bannister breaks four-minute mile.

       William Golding publishes *Lord of the Flies*.

       Philip Larkin publishes *The Less Deceived*.

1956    British troops sent to Egypt in Suez Crisis.

1957    P.G. Wodehouse publishes *The World of Jeeves*.

1959    First televised election coverage.

1960    Alan Sillitoe publishes *The Loneliness of the Long Distance Runner*.

1962    Doris Lessing publishes *The Golden Notebook*.

1964    Stevie Smith publishes *Selected Poems*.

1966    Seamus Heaney publishes *Death of a Naturalist*.

1967    New Scotland Yard opens.

Albert Camus

Sir Winston Churchill

Hungarian Uprising

World War II Ends

Mao Tse-tung

Martin Luther King, Jr.

Fidel Castro

Doris Lessing

# WORLD EVENTS

1945    World War II ends.

1947    India and Pakistan gain independence from Britain.

France: Albert Camus publishes *The Plague*.

1948    Mideast: Palestine partitioned; nation of Israel established.

South Africa: Alan Paton publishes *Cry, the Beloved Country*.

1949    China: Mao Tse-tung establishes People's Republic.

1950    Asia: Korean War begins.

South Africa: Riots against apartheid crushed.

1952    United States: Ernest Hemingway publishes *The Old Man and the Sea*.

1953    Tibet: Edmund Hillary climbs Mount Everest.

1954    United States: Jonas Salk begins inoculations against polio.

Algeria: War of independence from France begins.

1955    Eastern Europe: Communist nations sign Warsaw Pact.

United States: Martin Luther King, Jr. leads black boycott of Montgomery buses.

Australia: Patrick White publishes *The Tree of Life*.

1956    Hungary: Revolt against Russian influence crushed.

1957    Russia: Sputnik I, first spaceship, launched.

1959    Cuba: Fidel Castro seizes power.

Canada: St. Lawrence Seaway opens.

# BRITISH EVENTS

1972    Britain imposes direct rule on Northern Ireland.

1973    Britain and Ireland join Common Market.

1975    North Sea oil production begins.

1976    First supersonic passenger flight leaves London.

1977    John Fowles publishes *Daniel Martin.*

1979    Margaret Thatcher becomes first female prime minister.

1980    V.S. Naipaul publishes *A Bend in the River.*

Britain suffers worst recession since 1930s.

Strikes in government-run steel and mining industries.

1981    Unemployment and racial tensions lead to Brixton riots.

Royal wedding of Prince Charles and Princess Diana.

1982    Britain defeats Argentina in Falklands war.

1983    William Golding wins Nobel Prize for Literature.

1984    Ted Hughes named poet laureate.

1985    Hillsborough Agreement gives Republic of Ireland voice in governing Northern Ireland.

1986    First American football game played in England.

1987    Poetry recitations given in London's Waterloo Station.

1990    Violent protests arise in response to proposed poll tax.

Direct Rule Imposed on Northern Ireland

Margaret Thatcher        Labor Strike

Famine in Ethiopia

V. S. Naipaul

Jean Anouilh

Gabriel Garcia Marquez

North Sea Oil Platforms

Corazon Aquino

Ayatollah Khomeini

# WORLD EVENTS

| | |
|---|---|
| 1960 | Russia: Yuri Gagarin becomes first person in space. |
| | Germany: Berlin Wall built. |
| 1961 | France: Jean Anouilh publishes *Becket.* |
| 1962 | Caribbean: Cuban Missile Crisis. |
| 1963 | United States: President John F. Kennedy assassinated. |
| | Germany: Günther Grass publishes *Dog Years.* |
| 1964 | Vietnam: American troops begin fighting. |
| 1966 | India: Indira Gandhi becomes prime minister. |
| 1967 | South Africa: Christiaan Bernard performs first heart transplant. |
| 1968 | Colombia: Gabriel García Márquez publishes *One Hundred Years of Solitude.* |
| 1969 | America's *Apollo 11* lands on moon. |
| 1971 | Switzerland: Women gain right to vote. |
| 1973 | Worldwide energy crisis. |
| 1974 | France: Russia's Alexander Solzhenitsyn publishes *The Gulag Archipelago.* |
| 1977 | Africa: Djibouti, last remaining European colony, granted independence. |
| 1979 | Iran: Ayatollah Khomeini overthrows Shah. |
| | Nicaragua: Sandinistas oust Somoza government. |
| 1980 | Poland: Lech Walesa leads Solidarity movement. |
| 1985 | Ethiopia: Warfare and drought result in great famine. |
| 1986 | Russia: Accident at Chernobyl nuclear plant. |
| | Philippines: Democratic government established under Corazon Aquino. |
| 1989 | Germany: Closed border, symbolized by Berlin Wall, opens between East and West Germany. |

the Continent and in America looked to London for inspiration. They wore their hair long like the Beatles, and they bought "mod" fashions from London's Carnaby Street.

## A Series of Shocks

Unfortunately, rock bands and boutiques did not suffice to restore Britain's economic vitality. The industries that had hauled Britain and the world into the industrial revolution of the eighteenth century—textiles, steelmaking, shipbuilding—had lost their old magic. Now British industries were lagging behind. First in America, then in Japan and other Asian countries, new factories sprang up that could turn out goods more cheaply than could Britain's aging factories. By the score, British factories closed their gates. By the thousands, laid-off British workers "went on the dole" (signed up for welfare benefits).

For Britons, economic troubles were not the only shocks of the postwar period. British society was changing rapidly. The many changes included the following:

- *Large-scale immigration.* Indians, Africans, West Indians, and others poured in from Britain's former colonies and Britain was transformed into a multiracial, "melting-pot" society.
- *Greater equality.* The barriers that had long divided Britons by social class began to break down, as changes in the system of education opened new opportunities to working-class people.
- *New roles for women.* Despite Britain's long history of ruling queens, women had held few other prominent positions. In 1979

INDUSTRIAL LANDSCAPE
*L. S. Lowry*
*Tate Gallery, London*

the nation elected its first female prime minister, Margaret Thatcher. At the same time, more and more women began rising to prominence in politics, science, business, education, and the arts.

## The Thatcher Era

Thatcher was a woman with a mission. She prescribed a stiff dose of free enterprise as the cure for Britain's troubles. Her Conservative-party government set about selling off state-owned industries and imposing cost-cutting measures on Britain's welfare agencies. Her government also encouraged the growth of new-style industries based on computer technology.

Thatcher's task would not be an easy one. Britain's economy remained shaky, despite the discovery and exploitation of oil deposits in the North Sea. The country also faced a number of challenges. In 1982 it fought a war with Argentina over Britain's tiny South Atlantic possession, the Falkland Islands. Britain won the war, but paid a high price in blood and money. Meanwhile, the violence in Ulster (Northern Ireland) dragged on. A 1985 agreement gave the Republic of Ireland a consultative role in Ulster's affairs. But hard-line Ulster Catholics continued to fight for union with Ireland, and hard-line Ulster Protestants rejected any cooperation with that Catholic country.

Today, Britain seeks to adapt to a much-changed postwar world. In some ways the most modern of nations, Britain is in other ways among the most traditional. The ancient institutions of monarchy still play a central role in British life, inspiring awe and reverence in many

**MARGARET THATCHER, 1983**
*Stuart Franklin-Sygma*

**ARCHBISHOP OF CANTERBURY LEADING PRINCE AND PRINCESS TO HIGH ALTAR OF ST. PAUL'S, JULY 29, 1981**
*The Granger Collection*

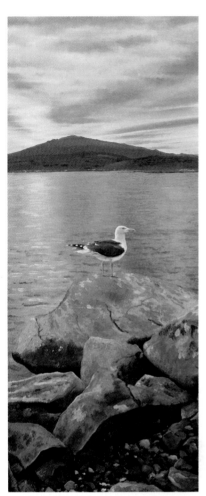

**GREAT BLACK-BACKED GULL**
*Douglas Anderson*
Oscar and Peter Johnson Ltd., London

Britons. Huge, happy crowds celebrated the marriages of the heir to the throne—Charles, Prince of Wales—in 1981 and of his brother Andrew in 1986. For each occasion, the pomp and splendor of honored traditions blended with the glitz and glamor of the media age. Like the poet T. S. Eliot, Britons seem to have turned to the past as a source of comfort while moving ahead into the swirl and bustle of contemporary life.

## CONTEMPORARY BRITISH LITERATURE

Both in subject matter and in style, British literature since World War II has displayed enormous diversity. Faced with an ever-shrinking world, many British writers have turned outward. They have addressed such global concerns as the destruction of the environment and the threat of nuclear war. Other writers have turned inward, exploring personal relationships and the individual's attempts to cope with modern urban and suburban life. Many recent works have examined Britain's past or its new role as a secondary power. Other works have addressed the specific problems and concerns of the British working class, whose problems and attitudes they address in their writings. Finally, with the decline of empire has come a blossoming of "post-colonial" literature. Writers in Ireland and in many former British colonies often use the English language to explore the legacy of empire.

### Achievements in Drama

Britain has continued to enjoy preeminence in the world of drama. In New York City, America's theater capital, for example, Broadway's most successful new dramas are often British imports. Many British plays go on to become films seen the world over. British television, too, has produced a string of noteworthy original dramas and a number of fine adaptations of classic novels and plays.

Many contemporary British dramatists use the techniques of realism. For example, Shelagh Delaney (born 1939) specializes in slice-of-life dramas like *A Taste of Honey* (1958). Her works are acutely realistic in depicting the lives of ordinary people. A group of dramatists known as Britain's "angry young men" also used realistic techniques in plays of the 1950's and 1960's attacking the injustices of Britain's class system. Typical of their work is John Osborne's *Look Back in Anger,* which focuses on a working-class youth rebelling against the establishment.

A second strain of contemporary British drama is represented by the so-called theater of the absurd. Plays of this school often feature dialogue and actions that seem disconnected and senseless—as if to say that life itself is an absurd series of tribulations. The Irish-born Samuel Beckett (born 1906), author of *Waiting for Godot* (1952), is foremost among the playwrights who use such techniques. The early plays of Harold Pinter (born 1930) also show the influence of the theater of the absurd.

A third type of contemporary British play is the historical drama that explores figures, events, and attitudes from times gone by. One such play is *A Man for All Seasons* (1960) by Robert Bolt (born 1924), which tells the story of Thomas More, the sixteenth-century scholar and Catholic martyr. Employing powerful, almost Shakespearean language, the play captures the grandeur of times past. Yet Bolt also creates a narrator called the Common Man, through whose eyes More's life unfolds—a strikingly contemporary touch. Tom Stoppard employs a similar device in *Rosencrantz and Guildenstern Are Dead* (1967).

## Achievements in Poetry

Contemporary British poets are less widely known than British playwrights. Still, many poets have come to teach at American universities and have won international reputations. During the 1950's and 1960's, a number of outstanding British poets associated themselves with what is called simply the Movement—the poetic equivalent of drama's angry young men. These poets rejected the style of Romantic poets such as Dylan Thomas, aiming to capture everyday experiences in the language of "the common man." Philip Larkin (1922–85), among the finest poets in the Movement, brought

**KING'S COOKHAM RISE, 1947**
*Stanley Spencer*
*The Metropolitan Museum of Art*

to his well-crafted verse a background as a music critic. Also part of the Movement were Thom Gunn (born 1929) and Donald Davie (born 1922), both of whom went on to teach and write in America.

The British have plucked poets out of musty libraries and thrust them before live audiences. Colorful festivals keep alive the Anglo-Saxon and Celtic traditions of oral poetry recitation. Poets have even recited their verse for rush-hour commuters at London's Waterloo Station. One of the first contemporary poets to stress oral performance was Stevie Smith, born Florence Margaret Smith (1902–71). Influenced by traditional English lyrics and early church music, Smith often recited her verse aloud in the singsong manner of traditional British bards.

British poets of recent years have exhibited a great deal of diversity in the form and content of their work. Ted Hughes (born 1930), named Britain's poet laureate in 1984, writes frequently of the beauty and violence of nature. His best-known volumes include *Hawk in the Rain* (1957) and *Crow* (1971). Nature is also a common subject in the work of Irish poet Seamus Heaney (born 1939). In his poetry Heaney also frequently explores the terror and hope of Ireland's stormy history. Another well-known contemporary poet, Elaine Feinstein (born 1930) writes a lyric poetry that balances an awareness of human limitations against a deep faith in human endurance. Other significant contemporary poets include William Empson (1906–84), Molly Holden (1927–81), Geoffrey Hill (born 1932), and the Irish poets Patrick Kavanagh (1905–67) and Thomas Kinsella (born 1928).

## Achievements in Prose

The English novel has continued to flourish in the contemporary period. With the introduction of the inexpensive paperback, books have become more accessible to the general public, and people have been able to to build larger personal libraries than ever before.

Several writers who began their careers in the modern period continued to prosper in contemporary times. On such writer was Graham Greene who produced a string of best sellers which often dealt with Cold War politics. Another was P. G. Wodehouse (1881–1975), who began his series of charming novels about dimwitted Bertie Wooster and his clever butler, Jeeves, in 1939. As late as the 1960's, Wodehouse was delighting readers with new Jeeves books.

Many new novelists also came on the scene. Four of the most successful have been William Golding (born 1911 and winner of the 1983 Nobel Prize for Literature), Anthony Burgess (born 1917), Kingsley Amis (born 1922), and John Fowles (born 1926). Golding's *Lord of the Flies* (1954) tells of a group of British schoolboys who revert to savage behavior after being stranded on a tropical island. Burgess has carried on in the tradition of George Orwell's *1984,* imagining a brutal future in the dystopian novel *A Clockwork Orange* (1962). Amis gives a comic touch to novels like *Lucky Jim* (1953) and *Stanley and the Women* (1984). Fowles often experiments with novel forms, as in *The Collector* (1963), which tells the same story twice—from two characters' different points of view.

In literature as in other realms of British life, women have risen to the forefront since 1945. Margaret Drabble (born 1939) has produced such well-received novels as *The Summer Birdcage* (1963) and *The Needle's Eye* (1972). The Irish-born Iris Murdoch (born 1919) has written many intricate novels exploring human relationships. Doris Lessing (born 1919), who grew up in Rhodesia (Zimbabwe), gained fame for a series of novels set in Africa about a character named Martha Guest. Later she wrote *The Golden Notebook* (1962) and a string of novels with futuristic settings. Another important female author is Nadine Gordimer (born 1923), who writes well-crafted novels and short stories that examine the moral and political dilemmas of racially divided South Africa, where she lives.

Many British fiction writers in addition to Gordimer have excelled at writing short stories. Sean O'Faolain (born 1900) creates stories that capture the flavor of rural life in his native Ireland. Michael McLaverty (born 1907), another Irishman, usually deals with plots and themes relating to nature. Among the finest of England's native short-story writers is Alan Sillitoe (born 1928), whose lyrical tales often focus on the painful predicaments of working-class people.

Meanwhile, a number of talented writers from what used to be called "the colonies" have added to the richness of contemporary British literature. These authors include Mordecai Richler (born 1931) of Canada, Wilson Harris (born 1921) of Guyana, V. S. Naipaul (born 1932) of Trinidad, Frank Sargeson (1903–82) of New Zealand, and Patrick White (born 1912) of Australia.

Nonfiction has also prospered in contemporary times. The Irish writer Lawrence Durrell (born 1912), who is also a skilled novelist and poet, has earned praise for his travel writing and humorous sketches. Antonia Fraser (born 1932), wife of the playwright Harold Pinter, is a widely read popular historian. Bertrand Russell (1872 –1970), the controversial philosopher, mathematician, and political activist, produced one of the best British autobiographies of recent decades. Several writers have also earned widespread recognition as literary critics. These writers include V. S. Pritchett (born 1900) and David Daiches (born 1912), as well as the poets Donald Davie and Thom Gunn, and the novelists Anthony Burgess and Margaret Drabble.

# ENGLISH VOICES
## Quotations by Prominent Figures of the Period

So always look for the silver lining
And try to find the sunny side of life.
**P. G. Wodehouse,** *Sally*

Why does my Muse only speak when she is unhappy?
She does not, I only listen when I am unhappy.
**Stevie (Florence Margaret) Smith,** "My Muse"

So winter closed its fist
And got it stuck in the pump.
**Seamus Heaney,** "Rite of Spring" (from *Door Into the Dark*)

The point is, . . . the point is, that as far as I can see, everything's cracking up.
**Doris Lessing,** Anne in *The Golden Notebook*

Columbus' huckstering breath
Blew inland through North America

Killing the last of the mammoths.
**Ted Hughes,** "Fourth of July" (from *Lupercal*)

Duty largely consists of pretending that the trivial is critical.
**John Fowles,** *The Magus*

Life should be a humane
undertaking. I know. I
undertook it. Yet have found
that in every move
I prevent someone
from stepping where I step.
**Thom Gunn,** "Positives"

While we can, for as long as we can, oh let us believe.
**Isabel Colegate,** *The Shooting Party*

Eternity is a terrible thought. I mean, where's it going to end?
**Tom Stoppard,** *Rosencrantz and Guildenstern Are Dead*

*Source: Doris Lessing, *A Small Personal Voice: Essays, Reviews,
Interviews* (New York: Vintage Books, 1975) p. 7. Essay "The Small
Personal Voice" first appeared 1957.

# READING CRITICALLY

# The Literature of 1945–Present

Because writers tend to be influenced by literary movements and historical trends, placing a literary work in its historical context can help you to fully understand and appreciate it.

## Historical Context

The period from 1945 to the present has been a time of transition for the English nation and people. During World War II London and other English towns and cities were severely damaged by German air raids, and in the aftermath of the war the British people struggled to rebuild their nation. At the same time, as the transformation of the British Empire into the British Commonwealth was completed, the nation was forced to accept a sharp decline in its economic and political status. Despite the decline in its status, however, the government has taken strong measures to insure adequate health care, housing, education, and pensions for the entire British population.

## Literary Movements

Contemporary British literature is extremely diverse in content. Like their predecessors from the modern period, many contemporary writers have delved into the human mind, focusing on people's inner thoughts and feelings. Responding to the changing complexion of British life, some writers have explored the effects of change on the British traditions, institutions, and people. Others have confronted additional problems and issues facing today's British society, and still others have presented shocking visions of futuristic societies in which personal freedoms are denied.

## Writer's Techniques

Although contemporary British writers have used a wide variety of literary forms and devices, few new techniques have been developed. While many contemporary poets have relied on traditional poetic forms, others have used the unconventional forms that became popular during the Modern Age. In fiction, writers have generally modeled their stories and novels after typical modern works, omitting expositions, transitions, and resolutions, and using the stream-of-consciousness technique.

On the following pages is a story by William Trevor, a highly regarded contemporary fiction writer. The notes in the side column should help you to place the selection in its historical context.

# The Distant Past

## William Trevor

In the town and beyond it they were regarded as harmlessly peculiar. Odd, people said, and in time this reference took on a burnish of affection.

They had always been thin, silent with one another, and similar in appearance: a brother and sister who shared a family face. It was a bony countenance, with pale blue eyes and a sharp, well-shaped nose and high cheekbones. Their father had had it too, but unlike them their father had been an irresponsible and careless man, with red flecks in his cheeks that they didn't have at all. The Middletons of Carraveagh the family had once been known as, but now the brother and sister were just the Middletons, for Carraveagh didn't count any more, except to them.

They owned four Herefords,[1] a number of hens, and the house itself, three miles outside the town. It was a large house, built in the reign of George II,[2] a monument that reflected in its glory and later decay the fortunes of a family. As the brother and sister aged, its roof increasingly ceased to afford protection, rust ate at its gutters, grass thrived in two thick channels all along its avenue. Their father had mortgaged his inherited estate, so local rumor claimed, in order to keep a Catholic Dublin woman in brandy and jewels. When he died, in 1924, his two children discovered that they possessed only a dozen acres. It was locally said also that this adversity hardened their will and that because of it they came to love the remains of Carraveagh more than they could ever have loved a husband or a wife. They blamed for their ill-fortune the Catholic Dublin woman whom they'd never met and they blamed as well the new national regime, contriving in their eccentric way to relate the two. In the days of the union jack[3] such women would have known their place—wasn't it all part and parcel?

**Writer's Technique:** Unlike most contemporary stories, the story begins with an exposition, in which background information is provided.

**Literary Movements:** The decay of the Middleton estate parallels the decline of the British Empire.

**Historical Context:** The story is set in southern Ireland. After being ruled by the English for hundreds of years, the Irish people rebelled against British rule in 1920. Following a period of bloody conflict, the British granted southern Ireland its independence in 1921, and the Irish Free State was established.

---

1. **Herefords** *n.*: A breed of cattle.
2. **reign of George II:** 1727-1760.
3. **union jack:** The British flag; the symbol of British rule.

**Literary Movement:** Like Trevor's characters, many British people have had difficulty accepting the dramatic changes that have occurred during the twentieth century and have tried to cling to the institutions and traditions of the past.

Twice a week, on Fridays and Sundays, the Middletons journeyed into the town, first of all in a trap[4] and later in a Ford Anglia car. In the shops and elsewhere they made, quite gently, no secret of their continuing loyalty to the past. They attended on Sundays St. Patrick's Protestant Church, a place that matched their mood, for prayers were still said there for the King whose sovereignty their country had denied. The revolutionary regime would not last, they quietly informed the Reverend Packham—what sense was there in green-painted pillar boxes[5] and a language that nobody understood?

---

**4. trap** *n.*: A two-wheeled horse-drawn carriage.
**5. pillar boxes:** Mail collection boxes.

On Fridays, when they took seven or eight dozen eggs to the town, they dressed in pressed tweeds and were accompanied over the years by a series of red setters, the breed there had always been at Carraveagh. They sold the eggs in Keogh's grocery and then had a drink with Mrs. Keogh in the part of her shop that was devoted to the consumption of refreshment. They enjoyed the occasion, for they liked Mrs. Keogh and were liked by her in return. Afterwards they shopped, chatting to the shopkeepers about whatever news there was, and then they went to Healy's Hotel for a few more drinks before driving home.

In spite of their loyalty to the past, they built up convivial relationships with the people of the town. Fat Driscoll, who kept the butcher's shop, used even to joke about the past when he stood with them in Healy's Hotel or stood behind his own counter cutting their slender chops or thinly slicing their liver. "Will you ever forget it, Mr. Middleton? I'd ha' run like a rabbit if you'd lifted a finger at me." Fat Driscoll would laugh then, rocking back on his heels with a glass of stout in his hand or banging their meat on to his weighing-scales. Mr. Middleton would smile. "There was alarm in your eyes, Mr. Driscoll,' Miss Middleton would murmur, smiling also at the memory of the distant occasion.

Fat Driscoll, with a farmer called Maguire and another called Breen, had stood in the hall of Carraveagh, each of them in charge of a shotgun. The Middletons, children then, had been locked with their mother and father and an aunt into an upstairs room. Nothing else had happened: the expected British soldiers had not, after all, arrived and the men in the hall had eventually relaxed their vigil. "A massacre they wanted," the Middletons' father said after they'd gone. "Bloody ruffians."

The Second World War took place. Two Germans, a man and his wife called Winkelmann who ran a glove factory in the town, were suspected by the Middletons of being spies for the Third Reich.[6] People laughed, for they knew the Winkelmanns well and could lend no credence to the Middletons' latest fantasy—typical of them, they explained to the Winkelmanns, who had been worried. Soon after the War the Reverend Packham died and was replaced by the Reverend Bradshaw, a younger man who laughed also and regarded the Middletons as an anachronism. They protested when prayers

**Literary Movement:** The changes in the church reflect the ongoing changes in society as a whole. The Irish Free State had become increasingly detached from Great Britain, and in 1949 severed all ties with Great Britain and renamed itself the Republic of Ireland.

---

**6. Third Reich** (rīk): The German government under the Nazis (1933–1945).

were no longer said for the Royal Family in St. Patrick's, but the Reverend Bradshaw considered that their protests were as absurd as the prayers themselves had been. Why pray for the monarchy of a neighboring island when their own island had its chosen President now? The Middletons didn't reply to that argument. In the Reverend Bradshaw's presence they rose to their feet when the BBC played "God Save the King," and on the day of the coronation of Queen Elizabeth II they drove into the town with a small union jack propped up in the back window of their Ford Anglia. "Bedad, you're a holy terror, Mr. Middleton!" Fat Driscoll laughingly exclaimed, noticing the flag as he lifted a tray of pork steaks from his display shelf. The Middletons smiled. It was a great day for the Commonwealth of Nations, they replied, a remark which further amused Fat Driscoll and which he later repeated in Phelan's public house. "Her Britannic Majesty," guffawed his friend Mr. Breen.

Situated in a valley that was noted for its beauty and with convenient access to rich rivers and bogs over which game-birds flew, the town benefited from post-war tourism. Healy's Hotel changed its title and became, overnight, the New Or-monde. Shopkeepers had their shopfronts painted and Mr. Healy organized an annual Salmon Festival. Even Canon Kelly, who had at first commented severely on the habits of the tourists, and in particular on the summertime dress of the women, was in the end obliged to confess that the morals of his flock remained unaffected. "God and good sense," he proclaimed, meaning God and his own teaching. In time he even derived pride from the fact that people with other values came briefly to the town and that the values esteemed by his parishioners were in no way diminished.

From the windows of their convent the Loretto nuns observed the long, sleek cars with G.B. plates; English and American accents drifted on the breeze to them. Mothers cleaned up their children and sent them to the Golf Club to seek employment as caddies. Sweet shops sold holiday me-mentoes. The brown, soda and currant breads of Murphy-Flood's bakery were declared to be delicious. Mr. Healy dou-bled the number of local girls who served as waitresses in his dining room, and in the winter of 1961 he had the builders in again, working on an extension for which the Munster and Leinster Bank had lent him twenty-two thousand pounds.

But as the town increased its prosperity Carraveagh continued its decline. The Middletons were in their middle sixties now and were reconciled to a life that became more

**Historical Context:**
Queen Elizabeth II was crowned in 1952, three years after Ireland officially severed its ties with Great Britain.

**Writer's Technique:**
Trevor provides important details of the setting.

uncomfortable with every passing year. Together they roved the vast lofts of their house, placing old paint tins and flowerpot saucers beneath the drips from the roof. At night they sat over their thin chops in a dining room that had once been gracious and which in a way was gracious still, except for the faded appearance of furniture that was dry from lack of polish and of a wallpaper that time had rendered colorless. In the hall their father gazed down at them, framed in ebony and gilt, in the uniform of the Irish Guards. He had conversed with Queen Victoria, and even in their middle sixties they could still hear him saying that God and Empire and Queen formed a trinity unique in any worthy soldier's heart. In the hall hung the family crest, and on ancient Irish linen the Cross of St. George.[7]

**Historical Context:** Their father's portrait reminds them of the Victorian age, an era in which British life was characterized by a sense of optimism and patriotism.

The dog that accompanied the Middletons now was called Turloch, an animal whose death they dreaded for they felt they couldn't manage the antics of another pup. Turloch, being thirteen, moved slowly and was blind and a little deaf. He was a reminder to them of their own advancing years and of the effort it had become to tend the Herefords and collect the weekly eggs. More and more they looked forward to Fridays, to the warm companionship of Mrs. Keogh and Mr. Healy's chatter in the hotel. They stayed longer now with Mrs. Keogh and in the hotel, and idled longer in the shops, and drove home more slowly. Dimly, but with no less loyalty, they still recalled the distant past and were listened to without ill-feeling when they spoke of it and of Carraveagh as it had been, and of the Queen whose company their careless father had known.

The visitors who came to the town heard about the Middletons and were impressed. It was a pleasant wonder, more than one of them remarked, that old wounds could heal so completely, that the Middletons continued in their loyalty to the past and that, in spite of it, they were respected in the town. When Miss Middleton had been ill with a form of pneumonia in 1958 Canon Kelly had driven out to Carraveagh twice a week with pullets and young ducks that his housekeeper had dressed. "An upright couple," was the Canon's public opinion of the Middletons, and he had been known to add that eccentric views would hurt you less than malice. "We can disagree without guns in this town," Mr. Healy pronounced in his cocktail room, and his visitors usually replied that as far as they could see that was the

---

**7. St. George:** The patron saint of England.

result of living in a Christian country. That the Middletons bought their meat from a man who had once locked them into an upstairs room and had then waited to shoot soldiers in their hall was a fact that amazed the seasonal visitors. You lived and learned, they remarked to Mr. Healy.

The Middletons, privately, often considered that they led a strange life. Alone in their two beds at night they now and again wondered why they hadn't just sold Carraveagh forty-eight years ago when their father had died—why had the tie been so strong and why had they in perversity encouraged it? They didn't fully know, nor did they attempt to discuss the matter in any way. Instinctively they had remained at Carraveagh, instinctively feeling that it would have been cowardly to go. Yet often it seemed to them now to be no more than a game they played, this worship of the distant past. And at other times it seemed as real and as important as the remaining acres of land, and the house itself.

"Isn't that shocking?" Mr. Healy said one day in 1967. "Did you hear about that, Mr. Middleton, blowing up them post offices in Belfast?"

Mr. Healy, red-faced and short-haired, spoke casually in his Cocktail Room, making midday conversation. He had commented in much the same way at breakfast-time, looking up from the *Irish Independent*. Everyone in the town had said it too: that the blowing up of sub-post offices in Belfast was a shocking matter.

"A bad business," Fat Driscoll remarked, wrapping the Middletons' meat. "We don't want that old stuff all over again."

"We didn't want it in the first place," Miss Middleton reminded him. He laughed, and she laughed, and so did her brother. Yes, it was a game, she thought—how could any of it be as real or as important as the afflictions and problems of the old butcher himself, his rheumatism and his reluctance to retire? Did her brother, she wondered, privately think so too?

"Come on, old Turloch," he said, stroking the flank of the red setter with the point of his shoe, and she reflected that you could never tell what he was thinking. Certainly it wasn't the kind of thing you wanted to talk about.

"I've put him in a bit of mince," Fat Driscoll said, which was something he often did these days, pretending the mince would otherwise be thrown away. There'd been a red setter about the place that night when he waited in the hall for the soldiers; Breen and Maguire had pushed it down into a cellar, frightened of it.

**Writer's Technique:** The Middletons' personalities are revealed through the descriptions of their thoughts and actions.

**Historical Context:** The bombing was carried out by Catholics in Northern Ireland who believed that the Protestant majority in that country was discriminating against them. This was the beginning of a violent conflict between Catholics and Protestants in Northern Ireland.

"There's a heart of gold in you, Mr. Driscoll," Miss Middleton murmured, nodding and smiling at him. He was the same age as she was, sixty-six—he should have shut up shop years ago. He would have, he'd once told them, if there'd been a son to leave the business to. As it was, he'd have to sell it and when it came to the point he found it hard to make the necessary arrangements. "Like us and Carraveagh," she'd said, even though on the face of it it didn't seem the same at all.

Every evening they sat in the big old kitchen, hearing the news. It was only in Belfast and Derry, the wireless said; outside Belfast and Derry you wouldn't know anything was happening at all. On Fridays they listened to the talk in Mrs. Keogh's bar and in the hotel. "Well, thank God it has nothing to do with the South," Mr. Healy said often, usually repeating the statement.

The first British soldiers landed in the North of Ireland, and soon people didn't so often say that outside Belfast and Derry you wouldn't know anything was happening. There were incidents in Fermanagh and Armagh, in border villages and towns. One Prime Minister resigned and then another one. The troops were unpopular, the newspapers said; internment became part of the machinery of government. In the town, in St. Patrick's Protestant Church and in the Church of the Holy Assumption, prayers for peace were offered, but no peace came.

**Historical Context:** In 1969, following bloody riots in the cities of Belfast and Londonderry, British troops were sent into Northern Ireland. In 1972, as the violence continued, the British government took over direct control of the country.

"We're hit, Mr. Middleton," Mr. Healy said one Friday morning. "If there's a dozen visitors this summer it'll be God's own stroke of luck for us."

"Luck?"

"Sure, who wants to come to a country with all that malarkey in it?"

"But it's only in the North."

"Tell that to your tourists, Mr. Middleton."

The town's prosperity ebbed. The border was more than sixty miles away, but over that distance had spread some wisps of the fog of war. As anger rose in the town at the loss of fortune so there rose also the kind of talk there had been in the distant past. There was talk of atrocities and counteratrocities, and of guns and gelignite[8] and the rights of people. There was bitterness suddenly in Mrs. Keogh's bar because of the lack of trade, and in the empty hotel there was bitterness also.

**Writer's Techniques:** Trevor implies that the townspeople's resentment of the British has resurfaced as a result of the violence in Northern Ireland and the implications of the violence.

---

**8. gelegnite** *n.*: An explosive.

On Fridays, only sometimes at first, there was a silence when the Middletons appeared. It was as though, going back nearly twenty years, people remembered the union jack in the window of their car and saw it now in a different light. It wasn't something to laugh at any more, nor were certain words that the Middletons had gently spoken, nor were they themselves just an old, peculiar couple. Slowly the change crept about, all around them in the town, until Fat Driscoll didn't wish it to be remembered that he had ever given them mince for their dog. He had stood with a gun in the enemy's house, waiting for soldiers so that soldiers might be killed—it was better that people should remember that.

One day Canon Kelly looked the other way when he saw the Middletons' car coming and they noticed this movement of his head, although he hadn't wished them to. And on another day Mrs. O'Brien, who had always been keen to talk to them in the hotel, didn't reply when they addressed her.

The Middletons naturally didn't discuss these rebuffs but they each of them privately knew that there was no conversation they could have at this time with the people of the town. The stand they had taken and kept to for so many years no longer seemed ridiculous in the town. Had they driven with a union jack now they would, astoundingly, have been shot.

"It will never cease." He spoke disconsolately one night, standing by the dresser where the wireless was.

She washed the dishes they'd eaten from, and the cutlery. "Not in our time," she said.

"It is worse than before."

"Yes, it is worse than before."

They took from the walls of the hall the portrait of their father in the uniform of the Irish Guards because it seemed wrong to them that at this time it should hang there. They took down also the crest of their family and the Cross of St. George, and from a vase on the drawing-room mantelpiece they removed the small union jack that had been there since the coronation of Queen Elizabeth II. They did not remove these articles in fear but in mourning for the *modus vivendi*[9] that had existed for so long between them and the people of the town. They had given their custom to a butcher who had planned to shoot down soldiers in their hall and he, in turn, had given them mince for their dog. For fifty years they had experienced, after suspicion had seeped away, a tolerance

---

**9. modus vivendi** (vi ven′ dī): Manner of getting along.

that never again in the years that were left to them would they know.

One November night their dog died and he said to her after he had buried it that they must not be depressed by all that was happening. They would die themselves and the house would become a ruin because there was no one to inherit it, and the distant past would be set to rest. But she disagreed: the *modus vivendi* had been easy for them, she pointed out, because they hadn't really minded the dwindling of their fortunes while the town prospered. It had given them a life, and a kind of dignity: you could take a pride out of living in peace.

**Literary Movement:** The fate of the Middleton family and estate reflects the disappearance of a glorious age in British history

He did not say anything and then, because of the emotion that both of them felt over the death of their dog, he said in a rushing way that they could no longer at their age hope to make a living out of the remains of Carraveagh. They must sell the hens and the four Herefords. As he spoke, he watched her nodding, agreeing with the sense of it. Now and again, he thought, he would drive slowly into the town, to buy groceries and meat with the money they had saved, and to face the silence that would sourly thicken as their own two deaths came closer and death increased in another part of their island. She felt him thinking that and she knew that he was right. Because of the distant past they would die friendless. It was worse than being murdered in their beds.

**William Trevor** (1928–    ) was born and educated in Ireland, but he moved to England after beginning his writing career. Set in both Ireland and England, his stories explore a wide variety of subjects and themes. Displaying a deep understanding of human nature, Trevor often portrays the seemingly pointless misunderstandings that develop between people and groups of people. Perhaps Trevor's deep understanding of people comes from his unusual education. The son of a bank manager, he was enrolled in thirteen different schools. For long periods, however, he simply roamed the countryside, occasionally tutored by neighboring farmers or failed clergymen. Interestingly, he completed his education formally, graduating from Trinity College in 1950. Initially a history teacher and sculptor, he turned to writing, he said, to express a humanity he could not find in his art. Trevor has published numerous collections of short stories, including *The Collected Stories of William Trevor.*

## THINKING ABOUT THE SELECTION

### Recalling

1. Whom do the Middletons blame for the decay of their estate?
2. What event do Fat Driscoll and the Middletons recall when they visit Driscoll's butcher shop?
3. (a) What do the Middletons do on the day of Queen Elizabeth II's coronation? (b) How do the townspeople respond to this action?
4. Why does the town prosper in the years after World War II?
5. (a) What type of relationship do the Middletons have with the townspeople? (b) How does the relationship change after the town's prosperity fades?

### Interpreting

6. How does the decline of the Middletons' fortunes parallel the decline of the British Empire?
7. What is ironic, or surprising, about the fact that throughout most of the story the townspeople respected the Middletons?
8. What does the change in the townspeople's attitude toward the Middletons reveal about human nature?

### Applying

9. Why do you think that many Irish people feel a sense of resentment toward the British?

## ANALYZING LITERATURE

### Recognizing Character

A variety of different types of characters are used in literary works. When a character is well-developed and posseses a variety of traits, he or she is referred to as a round character. A character who embodies a single trait, ideal, or quality is referred to as a flat character. Static characters are characters who do not change during the course of a literary work. Dynamic characters are characters who do change.

1. Are the Middletons flat characters or round characters? Support your answer.
2. Are the Middletons static characters or dynamic characters? Support your answer.
3. Are the townspeople static characters or dynamic characters? Support your answer.

## CRITICAL THINKING AND READING

### Understanding a Character's Motivation

In portraying any type of character, a writer must provide a motivation, or a stated or implied reason for the character's behavior, to make the character's actions believable. For example, in "The Distant Past" it is clear that the Middletons' actions on the day of Queen Elizabeth II's coronation are motivated by their loyalty to Great Britain.

1. What motivates the townspeople to change their behavior toward the Middletons?
2. How does Trevor reveal this motivation?

## THINKING AND WRITING

### Writing a Dialogue

Write a dialogue in which the Middletons discuss the decline in their fortunes and the change in the townspeoples' attitude toward them. Reread the story, trying to put yourself in the Middletons' place. Then write your dialogue, having the Middletons discuss the reasons for and feelings about their present situation. When you finish writing, revise your dialogue and share it with your classmates.

# Prose

THE IDENTI-KIT MAN, 1974
*Derek Boshier*
*Tate Gallery Publications Department*

# SEAN O'FAOLAIN

## 1900–1991

Although the Irish writer Sean O'Faolain is best known for his short stories, he wrote widely in many genres—novels, plays, biographies, travel books, literary criticism. His works, which draw upon a powerful sense of tradition, deal with Ireland and its people with a universality that transcends their locale. Over fifty years, his writings promoted liberal, humane values in a state that he, as a revolutionary, helped to bring into existence.

Sean O'Faolain, originally named John Whelan, was born in the city of Cork in southern Ireland, the son of a policeman and a theatrical landlady. Schooled by priests and later at University College, Cork, he "became one with the emotion of Ireland" in the aftermath of the Easter Rebellion of 1916. He joined the Irish volunteers, learned Gaelic, and changed his name to its Gaelic variant. During the Irish revolution, 1918–1921, he served as director of publicity for the Irish Republican Army. An idealist, he found himself disillusioned by the struggle and its consequences and drifted away from war and politics.

After a year of graduate study at Harvard, O'Faolain sent for Eileen Gould, whom he had met during the revolution. He married her, and for their honeymoon they took a camping trip across the United States. Although both he and Eileen loved America, they returned to Ireland "where every field, every path, every ruin had its memories, where every last corner had its story."

The war, which made O'Faolain a bitter young man, furnished the material for his first short stories, collected in *Midsummer Night Madness* (1932). His later collections, such as *A Purse of Coppers* (1937) and *The Man Who Invented Sin* (1948), showed increasing maturity. They depict everyday Irish life in a lyrical yet unsentimental manner.

O'Faolain wrote that "the longing . . . not merely to describe chaos but to bring it, before God, to imaginative form" led him to become a writer. He concluded: "Being a writer I had to—as the spider must spin, and the clouds must drift and fall, and the trees grow and shed and grow again—go on writing, waiting and watching for the appearance, within me, of the theme . . . to say: 'This is what you dreamed as a boy. There is no break, no chasm, just a larger shape, a more human, a more complex form.' "

O'Faolain, who said his aim in writing was a "blend of reason and sensibility," founded *The Bell,* an Irish literary journal, in 1940, and edited it for a number of years. A reformer, deeply concerned with Irish culture, he was not always popular with conservatives in Ireland. Nevertheless, his compassion and humor never left him, and his portraits of Irish life are sympathetic and compelling.

# GUIDE FOR INTERPRETING

## A Touch of Autumn in the Air

**First-person Narration.** The purpose of narration is to tell a story. Narration may be either factual (as is history and biography) or fictional (as in novels and short stories). In fictional narration, the story may be told from various perspectives, depending on the narrator's point of view. The narrator—the person who tells the story—may be someone within the story or someone outside it. A first-person narrator is a character within the story. He or she uses the word *I* in telling it. A third-person narrator stands outside the story and uses *he, she, they,* or *it.*

First-person narration, or point of view, falls into two main types. A first-person narrator, using the pronoun *I,* may be a main character in a story—a first-person participant—like the narrator in Mary Wollstonecraft Shelley's *Frankenstein.* Or the narrator, using *I,* may be a first-person observer, like Dr. Watson in the Sherlock Holmes stories.

In either kind of role, the narrator serves as a persona, or mask, through which the writer tells the story. He or she relates events in accordance with the writer's artistic purpose. The narrator, being a fictional creation, does *not* necessarily reflect the writer's own attitudes or beliefs.

Writers whose careers span a long period of time face a particular problem: Should they go back and revise earlier works to reflect their changed style? For example, if like O'Faolain they wrote their early works in a romantic style that is not characteristic of their later work, should they rewrite these early works to make the style consistent with their later writing?

Critics have noted that the realistic style of "A Touch of Autumn" is characteristic of much of O'Faolain's work from the fifties on. However, it contrasts with that of his earlier short stories, which are far more heavily poetical, "full of romantic words, such as *dawn, dew, onwards, youth, world, adamant,* and *dusk,*" as O'Faolain himself remarked. However, this romantic mood passed out of fashion, replaced by the harder edge found in his later stories.

O'Faolain resisted the impulse to rewrite his stories once they were published. Explaining his decision not to rewrite, O'Faolain said, "You can rewrite while you are the same man. To rewrite years after is a form of forgery."

What is memory? Why do we remember some things and not others? Why do some events spring to mind after lying dormant in memory for many years? Freewrite, exploring your answers.

# A Touch of Autumn in the Air

Sean O'Faolain

It was, of all people, Daniel Cashen of Roscommon who first made me realize that the fragments of any experience that remain in a man's memory, like bits and scraps of a ruined temple, are preserved from time not at random but by the inmost desires of his personality.

Cashen was neither sensitive nor intelligent. He was a caricature of the self-made, self-educated, nineteenth-century businessman. Some seventy years ago he had set up a small woollen factory in County Roscommon which, by hard work from early morning to late at night, and by making everybody around him work at the same pace, he developed into a thriving industry which he personally owned. His Swansdown Blankets, for example, were the only kind of blankets my mother ever bought. Though old when I made his acquaintance, he was still a powerful horse of a man, always dressed in well-pressed Irish tweeds, heavy countryman's boots, and a fawn, flat-topped bowler hat set squat above a big, red, square face, heavy handlebar moustaches and pale blue, staring eyes of which one always saw the complete circle of the iris, challenging, concentrated, slightly mad.

One would not expect such a man to say anything very profound about the workings of the memory, and he did not. All he did was to indulge in a brief burst of reminiscence in a hotel foyer, induced by my casual remark that it was a lovely, sunny day outside but that there was a touch of autumn in the air. The illuminating thing was the bewildered look that came into those pale, staring eyes as he talked. It revealed that he was much more touched and troubled by the Why of memory than by the Fact of memory. He was saying, in effect: Why do I remember that? Why do I not remember the other thing? For the first time in his life something within him had gone out of control.

What he started to talk about was a holiday he spent when just under fifteen, in what was at that time called the Queen's County. It had lasted two months, September and October. "Lovely, sunny weather, just like today." What had begun to bother him was not so much that the days had merged and melted together in his memory —after so many years that was only natural —but that here and there, from a few days of no more evident importance than any other days, a few trivial things stuck up above the tides of forgetfulness. And as he mentioned them I could see that he was fumbling, a little fearfully, towards the notion that there might be some meaning in the pattern of those indestructible bits of the jigsaw of his youth, perhaps even some sort of revelation in their obstinacy after so much else had dropped down the crevices of time.

He did not come directly to the major memory that had set his mind working in this way. He mentioned a few lesser memories first, staring out through the revolving glass doors at the sunny street. There was the afternoon when, by idle chance, he leaned over a small stone bridge near his Uncle Bartle's farm and became held for an hour by the mesmerism of the stream flickering through the chickweed. As could happen likewise to a great number of busy men, who normally never think at all about the subjective side of themselves, and are overwhelmed by the mystery of it if once they do advert to it, he attached an almost magical import to the discovery that he had never forgotten the bright pleasure of that casual hour.

"No, John! Although it must be near sixty years ago. And I don't believe I ever will forget it. Why is that?"

Of course, he admitted modestly, he had a phenomenal memory, and to prove it he invited me to ask him the telephone numbers of any half-dozen shops in town. But, yet, there was that red hay barn where he and his cousin, Kitty Bergin, played and tumbled a score of times—it was a blur.

"I can't even remember whether the thing was made of timber or corrugated iron!"

Or there was the sunken river, away back on the level leas, a stream rather than a river, where one warm September Sunday after Mass he saw, with distasteful pleasure, the men splashing around naked, roughly ducking a boy who had joined them, laughing at his screams. But, whereas he also still possessed the soft, surrounding fields, the imperceptibly moving clouds, the crunch of a jolting cart far away, the silence so deep that you could have heard an apple falling, he had lost every detail of the walk to and from the river, and every hour before and after it. A less arrogant man might have accepted the simple explanation that the mind wavers in and out of alertness, is bright at one moment, dim at the next. Those mad, round irises glared at the suggestion that his mind could at any time be dim.

He pointed out that he knew the country for miles around, intimately, walking it and cycling it day after day: what clung to him of it all, like burrs, were mere spots—a rusty iron gate falling apart, a crossroads tree with a black patch burnt at its base, an uneventful turn off the main road, a few undistinguished yards of the three miles of wall around the local demesne. He laughed scornfully at my idea that his mind became bright only for those few yards of wall.

"Well, perhaps it became dim then? You were thinking hard about other things up to that point in your walk?"

Here he allowed his real trouble to expose itself. He had not only remembered pointless scraps, but, I found, those scraps had been coming back to him repeatedly during the last few days with a tormenting joy, so that here he was, an old man, fondling nothings as lovingly as if he were fondling a lock of a dead woman's hair. It was plain, at last, that he was thinking of all those fragments of his boyhood as the fish scales of some wonderful fish, never-to-be-seen, sinuous and shining, that had escaped from his net into the ocean.

What had started him off was simple. (I reconstruct it as well as I can, intuiting and enlarging from his own brief, blunt words.) A few mornings before our meeting, fine and sunny also, he had happened to go into a toyshop where they also sold sweets. He was suddenly transfixed by the smell peculiar to these shops—scented soaps, the paint on the tin toys and the sprayed wooden trucks, the smell of the children's gift books, the sweetness of the sweets. At once he was back in that holiday, with his cousin Kitty Bergin, on the leas behind her father's farmhouse (his Uncle Bartle's), one sunny, mistified October morning, driving in a donkey cart down to where his uncle and his cousin Jack were ditching a small meadow that they had retrieved from the rushes and the bog water.

As Kitty and he slowly jolted along the rutted track deeper and deeper into this

**THE SOOTHSAYER FROM THE GREEN ISLAND, 1946**
*John Petts*

wide, flat river basin of the Barrow, whose hundreds of streams and dikes feed into what, by a gradual addition, becomes a river some twenty miles away, the two men whom they were approaching looked so minute on the level bog, under the vast sky, that Dan got a queer feeling of his own smallness in observing theirs. As he looked back, the white, thatched farmhouse nestling into the earth had never seemed so homely, cozy and comforting.

Ferns crackled at the hub. When he clutched one its fronds were warm but wet. It was the season when webs are flung with a wild energy across chasms. He wiped his face several times. He saw dew drops in a row in midair, invisibly supported between frond and frond. A lean swath of mist, or was it low cloud, floated beneath far hills. Presently they saw behind the two men a pond with a fringe of reeds. Against an outcrop of delicately decayed limestone was a bent hawthorn in a cloud of ruby berries. Or could it have been a rowan tree? The sky was a pale green. The little shaven meadow was as lemon-bright as fallen ash leaves before the dew dries on their drifts, so that it would have been hard to say whether the liquid lemon of the meadow was evaporating into the sky or the sky melting down into the field.

They were on a happy mission. Mulvaney the postman had brought two letters to the farmhouse from two other sons: Owen, who was a pit manager in the mines at Castlecomer, and Christopher (who, out of respect, was never referred to as Christy), then studying for the priesthood in a Dublin seminary. Aunt Molly had sent them off with the letters, a jug of hot tea and thick rounds of fresh, homemade bread and homemade apple jam smelling of cloves, a great favorite of Uncle Bartle's. They duly reached the two men, relieved the donkey of bridle, bit and winkers so that he could graze in the meadow, spread sacks to sit on, and while Kitty poured the tea into mugs Bartle reverently wiped his clayey hands on

the sides of his trousers and took the letters. As he read them aloud in a slow, singsong voice, like a man intoning his prayers, it was clear that those two sons had gone so far outside his own experience of the big world that he stood a little in awe of them both. It was a picture to be remembered for years: the meadow, the old man, the smoke of the distant farmhouse, partriarchal, sheltered, simple.

When he laid down the letter from the priest-to-be he said:

"He's doing well. A steady lad."

When he had read the letter from the mines he said:

"He's doing fine. If he escapes the danger he will go far."

While Jack was reading the letters Kitty whispered to Danny, thumbing the moon's faint crescent:

"Look! It says D for Danny."

"Or," he murmured to her boldly, 'it could be D for Dear?"

Her warning glare towards her father was an admission.

"I see here," Jack commented, while his father sucked at the tea, "that Christopher is after visiting Fanny Emphie. Her name in religion is Sister Fidelia."

Dan had seen this girl at the Curragh Races during the first week of his holidays, a neighbor's daughter who, a few weeks later, entered the convent. He had heard them joking one night about how she and Christopher had at one time been "great" with one another. He remembered a slight, skinny girl with a cocked nose, laughing moist lips and shining white teeth.

"Read me out that bit," Bartle ordered. "I didn't note that."

" 'I got special leave from the President to visit Sister Fidelia, last week, at Saint Joachim's. She is well and happy but looked pale. She asked after you all. Saint Joachim's has nice grounds, but the trams pass outside the wall and she said that for the first couple of weeks she could hardly sleep at all.' "

The two men went on drinking their tea. It occurred to Dan that they did not care much for Fanny Emphie. He saw her now in her black robes walking along a graveled path under the high walls of the convent, outside which the trams at night drew their glow in the air overhead. It also occurred to him, for no reason, that Kitty Bergin might one day think of becoming a nun, and he looked at her with a pang of premonitory loss. Why should any of them leave this quiet place?

"Ha!" said old Bartle suddenly, and winked at Danny, and rubbed his dusty hands and drew out his pipe. This meant that they must all get back to work.

Kitty gathered up the utensils, Danny tackled the donkey, the others went back to their ditching and she and Danny drove back to where the fern was plentiful for bedding. Taking two sickles, they began to rasp through the stalks. After a while she straightened up, so did he, and they regarded one another, waist-deep in the fern.

"Do you think," she asked him pertly, "would I make a nice nun?"

"You!" he said, startled that the same thought had entered their heads at the same time.

She came across to him, slipped from his pocket the big blue handkerchief in which the bread had been wrapped, cast it in an arc about her fair head, drew it tightly under her chin with her left hand, and then with a deft peck of her right finger and thumb cowled it forward over her forehead and her up-looking blue eyes.

"Sister Fidelia, sir," she curtsied, provokingly.

He grappled with her as awkwardly as any country boy, paying the sort of homage he expected was expected of him, and she, laughing, wrestled strongly with him. They swayed in one another's arms, aware of each other's bodies, until she cried, "Here's Daddy," and when he let her go mocked him from a safe distance for his innocence. But as they cut the fern again her sidelong glances made him happy.

They piled the cut fern into the cart, climbed on top of it, and lay face down on it, feeling the wind so cold that they instinctively pressed closer together. They jolted out to the main road, and as they ambled along they talked, and it seemed to him that it was very serious talk, but he forgot every word of it. When they came near the crossroads with its little sweetshop, they decided to buy a half-penny-worth of their favorite sweets, those flat, odd-shaped sweets —diamonds, hearts, hexagonals—called Conversation Lozenges because each sweet bore on its coarse surface a ring posy[1] in colored ink, such as Mizpah, Truth Tries Troth, Do You Care? or All for Love. Some bore girls' names, such as Gladys or Alice. His first sweet said, Yours in Heart. He handed it to her with a smile; she at once popped it into her mouth, laughing at his folly. As they ambled along so, slowly, chatting and chewing, the donkey's hooves whispering through the fallen beech leaves, they heard high above the bare arches of the trees the faint honking of the wild geese called down from the north by the October moon.

It was to those two or three hours of that October morning many years ago that he was whirled back as he stood transfixed by the smells of the sweets-and-toys shop. Forgetting what he had come there to buy, he asked them if they sold Conversation Lozenges. They had never heard of them. As he turned to go he saw a nun leafing through the children's gift books. He went near her and, pretending to look at a book, peered under her cowl. To his surprise she was a very old nun. On the pavement he glanced up at the sky and was startled to see there the faint crescent moon. He was startled because he remembered that he had seen it earlier in the morning, and had quite forgotten the fact.

---

**1. ring posy:** A verse or motto inscribed in a circle.

He at once distrusted the message of his memory. Perhaps it was not that the smells had reminded him of little Kitty Bergin eating Yours in Heart, or pretending to be a nun, or wrestling with him in the fern? Perhaps what had called him back was the indifference of those two men to the fate of the nun? Or was there some special meaning for him in those arrowing geese? Or in the cozy, sheltered farmhouse? Maybe the important thing that day had been the old man humbly reading the letters? Why had the two men looked so small under the open sky of the bogland? D, she had said, for Danny . . .

As he stared at me there in the hotel foyer, my heart softened towards him. The pain in his eyes was the pain of a man who has begun to lose one of the great pleasures of life in the discovery that we can never truly remember anything at all, that we are for a great part of our lives at the mercy of uncharted currents of the heart. It would have been futile to try to comfort him by

**KNOCKALLA HILLS, DONEGAL**
*Dan O'Neill*
Ulster Museum, Belfast

saying that those currents may be charted elsewhere, that even when those revolving glass doors in front of us flashed in the October sun the whole movement of the universe since time began was involved in that coincidence of light. Daniel Cashen of Roscommon would get small comfort out of thinking of himself as a little blob of phosphorescence running along the curl of a wave at night.

And then, by chance, I did say something that comforted him, because as he shook hands with me and said he must be off, I said, without thinking:

"I hope the blankets are doing well?"

"Aha!" he cried triumphantly. "Better than ever."

And tapped his flat-topped hat more firmly on his head and whirled the doors before him out into the sunny street as imperiously as any man accustomed to ordering everything that comes his way.

Through the slowing doors I watched him halt on the pavement. He looked slowly to the right, and then he looked towards his left, and then, slowly, he looked up around the sky until he found what he was looking for. After a few moments he shivered up his shoulders around his neck, looked at the ground at his feet, put his two hands into his pockets, and moved very slowly away, still down-looking, out of sight.

Poor man, I thought when he was gone; rash, blunt, undevious; yet, in his own crude way, more true to life than his famous French contemporary[2] who recaptured lost time only by dilating, inventing, suppressing, merging such of its realities as he could recall, and inventing whatever he could not. Cashen was playing archaeology with his boyhood, trying to deduce a whole self out of a few dusty shards.[3] It was, of course, far too late. My guess was that of the few scraps that he now held in his hands the clue lay not so much in the offer of love and the images of retirement, the girl's courtship, the white farmhouse snuggling down cozily into the earth under the vast dome of the sky, and the old man left behind by his sons, as in the challenging sight of his own littleness on that aqueous plain whose streams barely trickled to the open sea. He said he hadn't thought of it for sixty years. Perhaps not? But he was thinking of it now, when the adventure was pretty well over. As it was. A week later a friend rang me up and said, "Did you hear who's died?" I knew at once, but I asked the question.

He left nearly a hundred and fifty thousand pounds—a lot of money in our country—and, since he never married, he divided it all up among his relatives by birth, most of them comparatively poor people and most of them living in what used to be called, in his boyhood, the Queen's County.

---

**2. famous French contemporary:** French novelist Marcel Proust (1871-1922).
**3. shards** *n.*: Fragments or broken pieces.

---

## THINKING ABOUT THE SELECTION

### Recalling

1. (a) What prompts Daniel Cashen to start talking about the holiday he spent long ago? (b) Where does he engage in this "brief burst of reminiscence"?
2. (a) Who is Kitty Bergin? (b) Why did Aunt Molly send her and Dan to the meadow?
3. (a) Whom did Kitty pretend to be? (b) How did Dan respond to her play-acting? (c) Why?
4. What does the narrator ask that brings Cashen back from his reminiscence?
5. What does the narrator think affected Cashen most about his boyhood recollection?

## Interpreting

6. Why does the narrator think Cashen is troubled by his memories?
7. Why do you think Cashen, as an old man, asks for Conversation Lozenges in the candy shop?
8. Near the end of the story, why does the narrator's heart soften toward Cashen?
9. What is the significance of the story's title?
10. What is your own interpretation of Daniel Cashen's story and his motives for telling it?

## Applying

11. Do you agree with the narrator that we can never truly remember anything at all? Explain your answer.

## ANALYZING LITERATURE
### First-person Narration

A first-person observer may be a fully developed character, with a name, a life history, and a personality, as is Dr. Watson in the Sherlock Holmes stories. On the other hand, a first-person observer, as in Sean O'Faolain's "A Touch of Autumn in the Air," may exist mostly in the background of the story.

1. In "A Touch of Autumn in the Air," the narrator introduces the story of Daniel Cashen and then lets the story take over. (a) What does the narrator say the story made him realize? (b) If this is true, what does the story reveal about the "inmost desires" of Cashen's personality?
2. What inferences do you make about the narrator, based on the story he tells?

## CRITICAL THINKING AND READING
### Identifying Subjective Information

A narrator will often provide you with subjective information—that is, information based on the narrator's own personal thoughts, feelings, and judgments. The reader has to judge the reliability of information about characters, taking into consideration not only the source of the information but also its nature. Purely factual information—for instance, that Cashen was just under fifteen at the time of the incident—seems objective enough. But that Cashen "looked at her [Kitty] with a pang of premonitory loss" is subjective regardless of who is doing the narrating.

Reread "A Touch of Autumn in the Air," identifying at least *five* apparently objective statements about Daniel Cashen and at least *five* subjective statements about him.

## UNDERSTANDING LANGUAGE
### Learning What a Caricature Is

When the narrator says that Daniel Cashen is "a caricature of the self-made, self-educated, nineteenth-century businessman," he means that Cashen is an exaggerated or distorted example of that type of person. In using the word *caricature*, he is ridiculing Cashen. The word *caricature* comes from the Italian noun *caricatura*, meaning "an overloading," which in turn comes from the verb *caricare*, "to load, exaggerate." One type of caricature is a picture or cartoon in which a person's features are exaggerated or distorted to produce an absurd effect. Political cartoonists produce caricatures.

Taking the whole story into account, how accurate do you think the narrator's statement about Cashen being a caricature of the self-made businessman is? Support your answer.

## THINKING AND WRITING
### Responding to a Thematic Statement

Very few short stories begin with an explicit statement of the story's theme. This story does. Write a brief composition in which you explain how "A Touch of Autumn in the Air" develops the theme stated in the opening sentence. First, restate the opening sentence in your own words. Then reread the story, making notes for your composition. Write your first draft, telling how the events in the story demonstrate the truth of the opening sentence. Revise your paper before handing it in. Proofread carefully to eliminate misspellings and mistakes in grammar, usage, and punctuation.

# P. G. WODEHOUSE

## 1881–1975

P(elham) G(renville) Wodehouse (pronounced wood-house) wrote for eighty years, indifferent to fame, fortune, and age. He did so, he once said, for the "pleasure of turning out the stuff." A prolific writer of humorous short stories, plays, novels, and essays, P. G. Wodehouse, known to his friends as "Plum," insisted that he had no message for humanity in his delightfully zany works. Nevertheless, his spoofs of the British gentry of a bygone era, often involving the befuddled Bertie Wooster and his unflappable valet Jeeves, are a unique contribution to modern English literature.

Wodehouse, born to a well-to-do family in Surrey, England, was educated in English boarding schools and at Dulwich College, near London. Even at an early age, Wodehouse seemed destined for greatness: In *A Portrait of a Master,* David A. Jasen quotes one of Wodehouse's classmates: "Plum's talk was exhilarating. I had never known such talk. Even at . . . seventeen he could discuss lucidly writers of whom I had never heard . . . But it was impossible to say who were his favorite authors. He liked so many and all kinds. And from the first time I met him, he had decided to write. He never swerved." As a trainee in banking, he began writing humorous fiction, articles, and verse for publication. He joined the staff of the London *Globe* in 1901 as a humor columnist, and in 1908 published his first adult novel, *Love Among the Chickens.*

He first visited the United States, "the land of romance," in 1904, and within a few years became a transatlantic commuter. After a two-month courtship, he married Ethel Rowley, a young English widow whom he had met in New York. His popularity and his income rose rapidly when his stories began appearing in *The Saturday Evening Post,* which at that time was the leading publisher of short fiction in the United States.

Wodehouse had a long and distinguished career in the theater, writing parts of more than forty plays and screenplays. His theatrical experience affected his books, for he began to think of episodes as scenes and characters as actors, and he wrote a number of stories set in Hollywood. His reputation, however, rests primarily on his novels, of which he wrote nearly a hundred, and on his more than three hundred short stories. Among his many notable books are *Carry On, Jeeves* (1934), *The Code of the Woosters* (1938), *Spring Fever* (1948), and *Plum Pie* (1966).

An international commuter for much of his life, Wodehouse lived in Paris after World War II, then moved to Long Island in 1952. Four Wodehouse novels appeared at about the time he was celebrating his ninetieth birthday. He was knighted in 1975, shortly before his death.

# GUIDE FOR INTERPRETING

## The Truth About George

**Writer's Techniques**

**Humor.** Humor is the quality that makes something seem amusing, funny, or comic. It emphasizes the ludicrous aspects of life. Yet the elements that make up humor—those characteristics that can be listed as making something humorous—are not easy to identify. What one person finds funny, another may not. The word *humor* (the British spell it *humour)* was originally a physiological term describing the fluids, or humors, in the human body, especially the four "cardinal humors" that were thought to be responsible for one's health and disposition. As time went on, the word came to mean "a mood or state of mind," then "a whim or fancy," and finally "the quality that makes something seem amusing, funny, or comic." Humor, in the modern sense, often relies upon exaggeration, misunderstandings, odd juxtapositions, repetition, wordplay, stock characters, and so on. But such explanations of humor, like similar explanations of music or art, add very little to one's understanding or enjoyment. It is the experience that counts.

**Writing**

Think about something that has made you laugh recently. Jot down a few notes about the incident, including your opinion of the source of the humor. What was it that made you laugh?

**Primary Source**

Interviewed on his eightieth birthday, Wodehouse said:

> From my earliest years I had always wanted to be a writer. It was not that I had any particular message for humanity. I am still plugging away and not the ghost of one so far, so it begins to look as though, unless I suddenly hit mid-season form in my eighties, humanity will remain a message short. The curious thing about those early days is that, in spite of the blizzard of rejection slips, I had the most complete confidence in myself. . . . It was only later that doubts on this point began to creep in. . . . Today I am a mass of diffidence and I-wonder-if-this-is-going-to-be-all-right-ness, and I envy those tough authors, square-jawed and spitting out of the side of their mouths, who are perfectly sure, every time they start a new book, that it will be a masterpiece. But with each new book of mine I have always the feeling that this time I have picked a lemon in the garden of literature. A good thing . . . keeps one up on one's toes and makes one write every sentence ten times. . . . When in due course Charon ferries me across the Styx and everyone is telling eveyone else what a rotten writer I was, I hope at least one voice will be heard piping up: "But he did take trouble."

# The Truth About George

## P. G. Wodehouse

Two men were sitting in the bar parlor of the Anglers' Rest as I entered it; and one of them, I gathered from his low, excited voice and wide gestures, was telling the other a story. I could hear nothing but an occasional "Biggest I ever saw in my life!" and "Fully as large as that!" but in such a place it was not difficult to imagine the rest; and when the second man, catching my eye, winked at me with a sort of humorous misery, I smiled sympathetically back at him.

The action had the effect of establishing a bond between us; and when the storyteller finished his tale and left, he came over to my table as if answering a formal invitation.

"Dreadful liars some men are," he said genially.

"Fishermen," I suggested, "are traditionally careless of the truth."

"He wasn't a fisherman," said my companion. "That was our local doctor. He was telling me about his latest case of dropsy. Besides"—he tapped me earnestly on the knee—"you must not fall into the popular error about fishermen. Tradition has maligned them. I am a fisherman myself, and I have never told a lie in my life."

I could well believe it. He was a short, stout, comfortable man of middle age, and the thing that struck me first about him was the extraordinary childlike candor of his eyes. They were large and round and honest. I would have bought oil stock from him without a tremor.

The door leading into the white dusty road opened, and a small man with rimless pince-nez[1] and an anxious expression shot in like a rabbit. He stood looking at us, seemingly ill at ease.

"N-n-n-n-n-n—" he said.

We looked at him inquiringly.

"N-n-n-n-n-ice d-d-d-d—"

His nerve appeared to fail him, and he vanished as abruptly as he had come.

"I think he was leading up to telling us that it was a nice day," hazarded my companion.

"It must be very embarrassing," I said, "for a man with such a painful impediment in his speech to open conversation with strangers."

"Probably trying to cure himself. Like my nephew George. Have I ever told you about my nephew George?"

I reminded him that we had only just met, and that this was the first time I had learned that he had a nephew George.

"Young George Mulliner. My name is Mulliner. I will tell you about George's case —in many ways a rather remarkable one."

My nephew George (said Mr. Mulliner) was as nice a young fellow as you would ever wish to meet, but from childhood up he had been cursed with a terrible stammer. If he had had to earn his living, he would undoubtedly have found this affliction a great handicap, but fortunately his father had left

---

**1. pince-nez** (pans′ nā′): Eyeglasses without sidepieces, held in place by springs gripping the bridge of the nose.

him a comfortable income; and George spent a not unhappy life, residing in the village where he had been born and passing his days in the usual country sports and his evenings in doing crossword puzzles. By the time he was thirty he knew more about Eli,[2] the prophet, Ra,[3] the sun god, and the bird Emu than anybody else in the county except Susan Blake, the vicar's daughter, who had also taken up the solving of crossword puzzles and was the first girl in Worcestershire to find out the meaning of "stearine" and "crepuscular."

It was his association with Miss Blake that first turned George's thoughts to a serious endeavor to cure himself of his stammer. Naturally, with this hobby in common, the young people saw a great deal of one another; for George was always looking in at the vicarage to ask her if she knew a word of seven letters meaning "appertaining to the profession of plumbing," and Susan was just as constant a caller at George's cozy little cottage—being frequently stumped, as girls will be, by words of eight letters signifying "largely used in the manufacture of poppet valves." The consequence was that one evening, just after she had helped him out of a tight place with the word "disestablishmentarianism," the boy suddenly awoke to the truth and realized that she was all the world to him—or, as he put it to himself from force of habit, precious, beloved, darling, much-loved, highly esteemed or valued.

And yet, every time he tried to tell her so, he could get no farther than a sibilant gurgle which was no more practical use than a hiccup.

Something obviously had to be done, and George went to London to see a specialist.

"I-I-I-I-I-I—" said George.

"You were saying—?"

"Woo-woo-woo-woo-woo-woo—"

**2. Eli:** From the Bible, a high priest of Israel.
**3. Ra:** The sun god and principal deity of the ancient Egyptians.

"Sing it," said the specialist.

"S-s-s-s-s-s-s-s—?" said George, puzzled.

The specialist explained. He was a kindly man with moth-eaten whiskers and an eye like a meditative codfish.

"Many people," he said, "who are unable to articulate clearly in ordinary speech find themselves lucid and bell-like when they burst into song."

It seemed a good idea to George. He thought for a moment; then threw his head back, shut his eyes, and let it go in a musical baritone.

"I love a lassie, a bonny, bonny lassie," sang George. "She's as pure as the lily in the dell."

"No doubt," said the specialist, wincing a little.

"She's as sweet as the heather, the bonny purple heather—Susan, my Worcestershire bluebell."

"Ah!" said the specialist. "Sounds a nice girl, Is this she?" he asked, adjusting his glasses and peering at the photograph which George had extracted from the interior of the left side of his undervest.

George nodded and drew in breath.

"Yes, sir," he caroled, "that's my baby. No, sir, don't mean maybe. Yes, sir, that's my baby now. And, by the way, by the way, when I meet that preacher I shall say: 'Yes, sir, that's my . . .'"

"Quite," said the specialist hurriedly. He had a sensitive ear. "Quite, quite."

"If you knew Susie like I know Susie," George was beginning, but the other stopped him.

"Quite. Exactly. I shouldn't wonder. And now," said the specialist, "what precisely is the trouble? No " he added hastily, as George inflated his lungs, "don't sing it. Write the particulars on this piece of paper."

George did so.

"H'm!" said the specialist, examining the screed. "You wish to woo, court, and become betrothed, engaged, affianced to this girl, but you find yourself unable, incapable, incompetent, impotent, and powerless. Every time you attempt it, your vocal cords fail, fall short, are insufficient, wanting, deficient, and go blooey.''

George nodded.

"A not unusual case. I have had to deal with this sort of thing before. The effect of love on the vocal cords of even a normally eloquent subject is frequently deleterious. As regards the habitual stammerer, tests have shown that in ninety-seven point five six nine recurring of cases the divine passion reduces him to a condition where he sounds like a soda-water siphon trying to recite 'Gunga Din.' There is only one cure."

"W-w-w-w-w—?" asked George.

"I will tell you. Stammering," proceeded the specialist, putting the tips of his fingers together and eyeing George benevolently, "is mainly mental and is caused by shyness, which is caused by the inferiority complex, which in its turn is caused by suppressed desires or introverted inhibitions or something. The advice I give to all young men who come in here behaving like soda-water siphons is to go out and make a point of speaking to at least three perfect strangers every day. Engage these strangers in conversation, persevering no matter how priceless a chump you may feel, and before many weeks are out you will find that the little daily dose has had its effect. Shyness will wear off, and with it the stammer."

And, having requested the young man—in a voice of the clearest timbre, free from all trace of impediment—to hand over a fee of five guineas, the specialist sent George out into the world.

The more George thought about the advice he had been given, the less he liked it. He shivered in the cab that took him to the station to catch the train back to East Wobsley. Like all shy young men, he had never hitherto looked upon himself as shy —preferring to attribute his distaste for the society of his fellows to some subtle rareness of soul. But now that the thing had been put

squarely up to him, he was compelled to realize that in all essentials he was a perfect rabbit. The thought of accosting perfect strangers and forcing his conversation upon them sickened him.

But no Mulliner has ever shirked an unpleasant duty. As he reached the platform and strode along it to the train, his teeth were set, his eyes shone with an almost fanatical light of determination, and he intended before his journey was over to conduct three heart-to-heart chats if he had to sing every bar of them.

The compartment into which he had made his way was empty at the moment, but just before the train started a very large, fierce-looking man got in. George would have preferred somebody a little less formidable for his first subject, but he braced himself and bent forward, And, as he did so, the man spoke.

"The wur-wur-wur-wur-weather," he said, "sus-sus-seems to be ter-ter-taking a tur-tur-turn for the ber-ber-better, der-doesn't it?"

George sank back as if he had been hit between the eyes. The train had moved out of the dimness of the station by now, and the sun was shining brightly on the speaker, illuminating his knobbly shoulders, his craggy jaw, and, above all, the shockingly choleric look in his eyes. To reply "Y-y-y-y-y-y-y-yes" to such a man would obviously be madness.

But to abstain from speech did not seem to be much better as a policy. George's silence appeared to arouse this man's worst passions. His face had turned purple and he glared painfully.

"I uk-uk-asked you a sus-sus-civil quk-quk-quk," he said irascibly. "Are you d-d-d-d-deaf?"

All we Mulliners have been noted for our presence of mind. To open his mouth, point to his tonsils, and utter a strangled gurgle was with George the work of a moment.

The tension relaxed. The man's annoyance abated.

"D-d-d-dumb?" he said commiserat-ingly. "I beg your p-p-p-p-pup. I t-t-trust I have not caused you p-p-p-p-pup. It m-must be tut-tut-tut-tut-tut not to be able to to sus-sus-speak fuf-fuf-fuf-fuf-fluently."

He then buried himself in his paper, and George sank back in his corner, quivering in every limb.

To get to East Wobsley, as you doubtless know, you have to change at Ippleton and take the branch line. By the time the train reached this junction, George's composure was somewhat restored. He deposited his belongings in a compartment of the East Wobsley train, which was waiting in a glued manner on the other side of the platform, and, finding that it would not start for some ten minutes, decided to pass the time by strolling up and down in the pleasant air.

It was a lovely afternoon. The sun was gilding the platform with its rays, and a gentle breeze blew from the west. A little brook ran tinkling at the side of the road; birds were singing in the hedgerows; and through the trees could be discerned dimly

the noble façade of the County Lunatic Asy-lum. Soothed by his surroundings, George began to feel so refreshed that he regretted that in this wayside station there was no one present whom he could engage in talk.

It was at this moment that the distinguished-looking stranger entered the platform.

The newcomer was a man of imposing physique, simply dressed in pajamas, brown boots, and a mackintosh. In his hand he carried a top hat, and into this he was dipping his fingers, taking them out, and then waving them in a curious manner to right and left. He nodded so affably to George that the latter, though a little surprised at the other's costume, decided to speak. After all, he reflected, clothes do not make the man, and, judging from the other's smile, a warm heart appeared to beat beneath that orange-and-mauve striped pajama jacket.

"N-n-n-n-nice weather," he said.

"Glad you like it," said the stranger. "I ordered it specially."

George was a little puzzled by this remark, but he persevered.

"M-might I ask wur-wur-what you are dud-doing?"

"Doing?"

"With that her-her-her-her-hat?"

"Oh, with this hat? I see what you mean. Just scattering largess to the multitude," replied the stranger, dipping his fingers once more and waving them with a generous gesture. "Devil of a bore, but it's expected of a man in my position. The fact is," he said, linking his arm in George's and speaking in a confidential undertone, "I'm the Emperor of Abyssinia. That's my palace over there," he said, pointing through the trees. "Don't let it go any farther. It's not supposed to be generally known."

It was with a rather sickly smile that George now endeavored to withdraw his arm from that of his companion, but the other would have none of this aloofness. He seemed to be in complete agreement with Shakespeare's dictum that a friend, when found, should be grappled to you with hoops of steel. He held George in a viselike grip and drew him into a recess of the platform. He looked about him and seemed satisfied.

"We are alone at last," he said.

This fact had already impressed itself with sickening clearness on the young man. There are few spots in the civilized world more deserted than the platform of a small country station. The sun shone on the smooth asphalt, on the gleaming rails, and on the machine which, in exchange for a penny placed in the slot marked "Matches," would supply a package of wholesome butterscotch—but on nothing else.

What George could have done with at the moment was a posse of police armed with stout clubs, and there was not even a dog in sight.

"I've been wanting to talk to you for a long time," said the stranger genially.

"Huh-huh-have you?" said George.

"Yes. I want your opinion of human sacrifices."

George said he didn't like them.

"Why not?" asked the other, surprised.

George said it was hard to explain. He just didn't.

"Well, I think you're wrong," said the Emperor. "I know there's a school of thought growing up that holds your views, but I disapprove of it. I hate all this modern advanced thought. Human sacrifices have always been good enough for the Emperors of Abyssinia, and they're good enough for me. Kindly step in here, if you please."

He indicated the lamp-and-mop room, at which they had now arrived. It was a dark and sinister apartment, smelling strongly of oil and porters, and was probably the last place on earth in which George would have wished to be closeted with a man of such peculiar views. He shrank back.

"You go in first," he said.

"No larks," said the other suspiciously.

"L-l-l-l-larks?"

"Yes. No pushing a fellow in and locking the door and squirting water at him through the window. I've had that happen to me before."

"Sus-certainly not."

"Right!" said the Emperor. "You're a gentleman and I'm a gentleman. Both gentlemen. Have you a knife, by the way? We shall need a knife."

"No. No knife."

"Ah, well," said the Emperor, "then we'll have to look about for something else. No doubt we shall manage somehow."

And with the debonair manner which so became him, he scattered another handful of largess and walked into the lamp room.

It was not the fact that he had given his word as a gentleman that kept George from locking the door. There is probably no family on earth more nicely scrupulous as regards keeping its promises than the Mulliners, but I am compelled to admit that, had George been able to find the key, he would have locked the door without hesitation. Not being able to find the key, he had to be satisfied with banging it. This done, he leaped back and raced away down the platform. A confused noise within seemed to indicate that the Emperor had become involved with some lamps.

George made the best of the respite. Covering the ground at a high rate of speed, he flung himself into the train and took refuge under the seat.

There he remained, quaking. At one time he thought that his uncongenial acquaintance had got upon his track, for the door of the compartment opened and a cool wind blew in upon him. Then, glancing along the floor, he perceived feminine ankles. The relief was enormous, but even in his relief George, who was the soul of modesty, did not forget his manners. He closed his eyes.

A voice spoke.

"Porter!"

"Yes, ma'am?"

"What was all that disturbance as I came into the station?"

"Patient escaped from the asylum, ma'am."

"Good gracious!"

The voice would undoubtedly have spoken further, but at this moment the train began to move. There came the sound of a body descending upon a cushioned seat, and some little time later the rustling of a paper.

George had never before traveled under the seat of a railway carriage; and, though he belonged to the younger generation, which is supposed to be so avid of new experiences, he had no desire to do so now. He decided to emerge, and, if possible, to emerge with the minimum of ostentation. Little as he knew of women, he was aware that as a sex they are apt to be startled by the sight of men crawling out from under the seats of compartments. He began his maneuvers by poking out his head and surveying the terrain.

All was well. The woman, in her seat across the way, was engrossed in her paper. Moving in a series of noiseless wriggles, George extricated himself from his hiding place and, with a twist which would have been impossible to a man not in the habit of doing Swedish exercises daily before breakfast, heaved himself into the corner seat. The woman continued reading her paper.

The events of the past quarter of an hour had tended rather to drive from George's mind the mission which he had undertaken on leaving the specialist's office. But now, having leisure for reflection, he realized that, if he meant to complete his first day of the cure, he was allowing himself to run sadly behind schedule. Speak to three strangers, the specialist had told him, and up to the present he had spoken to only one. True, this one had been a pretty considerable stranger, and a less conscientious young man than George Mulliner might have considered himself justified in chalking him up on the scoreboard as one and a half or even two. But George had the dogged, honest Mulliner streak in him, and he refused to quibble.

He nerved himself for action and cleared his throat.

"Ah-h'rm!" said George.

And, having opened the ball, he smiled a winning smile and waited for his companion to make the next move.

The move which his companion made was in an upwards direction, and measured from six to eight inches. She dropped her paper and regarded George with a pale-eyed horror. One pictures her a little in the position of Robinson Crusoe[4] when he saw the footprint in the sand. She had been convinced that she was completely alone, and lo! out of space a voice had spoken to her. Her face worked, but she made no remark.

George, on his side, was also feeling a little ill at ease. Women always increased his

___

4. **Robinson Crusoe:** The hero of Daniel Defoe's novel *Robinson Crusoe* (1719), a sailor who is shipwrecked on a tropical island.

natural shyness. He never knew what to say to them.

Then a happy thought struck him. He had just glanced at his watch and found the hour to be nearly four-thirty. Women, he knew, loved a drop of tea at about this time, and fortunately there was in his suitcase a full thermos flask.

"Pardon me, but I wonder if you would care for a cup of tea?" was what he wanted to say, but, as so often happened with him when in the presence of the opposite sex, he could get no farther than a sort of sizzling sound like a cockroach calling to its young.

The woman continued to stare at him. Her eyes were now about the size of regulation standard golf balls, and her breathing suggested the last stages of asthma. And it was at this point that George, struggling for speech, had one of those inspirations which frequently came to Mulliners. There flashed into his mind what the specialist had told him about singing. Say it with music—that was the thing to do.

He delayed no longer.

"Tea for two and two for tea and me for you and you for me—"

He was shocked to observe his companion turning Nile green. He decided to make his meaning clearer.

"I have a nice thermos. I have a full thermos. Won't you share my thermos, too? When skies are gray and you feel you are blue, tea sends the sun smiling through. I have a nice thermos. I have a full thermos. May I pour out some for you?"

You will agree with me, I think, that no invitation could have been more happily put, but his companion was not responsive. With one last agonized look at him, she closed her eyes and sank back in her seat. Her lips had now turned a curious gray-blue color, and they were moving feebly. She reminded George, who, like myself, was a keen fisherman, of a newly gaffed salmon.

George sat back in his corner, brooding. Rack his brain as he might, he could think

of no topic which could be guaranteed to interest, elevate, and amuse. He looked out of the window with a sigh.

The train was now approaching the dear old familiar East Wobsley country. He began to recognize landmarks. A wave of sentiment poured over George as he thought of Susan, and he reached for the bag of buns which he had bought at the refreshment room at Ippleton. Sentiment always made him hungry.

He took his thermos out of the suitcase, and, unscrewing the top, poured himself out a cup of tea. Then, placing the thermos on the seat, he drank.

He looked across at his companion. Her eyes were still closed, and she uttered little sighing noises. George was half inclined to renew his offer of tea, but the only tune he could remember was "Hard-Hearted Hannah, the Vamp from Savannah," and it was difficult to fit suitable words to it. He ate his bun and gazed out at the familiar scenery.

Now, as you approach East Wobsley, the train, I must mention, has to pass over some points; and so violent is the sudden jerking that strong men have been known to spill their beer. George, forgetting this in his preoccupation, had placed the thermos only a few inches from the edge of the seat. The result was that, as the train reached the points, the flask leaped like a live thing, dived to the floor, and exploded.

Even George was distinctly upset by the sudden sharpness of the report. His bun sprang from his hand and was dashed to fragments. He blinked thrice in rapid succession. His heart tried to jump out of his mouth and loosened a front tooth.

But on the woman opposite the effect of the untoward occurrence was still more marked. With a single piercing shriek, she rose from her seat straight into the air like a rocketing pheasant; and, having clutched the communication cord, fell back again. Impressive as her previous leap had been, she excelled it now by several inches. I do not know what the existing record for the sitting high jump is, but she undoubtedly lowered it; and if George had been a member of the Olympic Games Selection Committee, he would have signed this woman up immediately.

It is a curious thing that, in spite of the railway companies' sporting willingness to let their patrons have a tug at the extremely moderate price of five pounds a go, very few people have ever either pulled a communication cord or seen one pulled. There is, thus, a widespread ignorance as to what precisely happens on such occasions.

The procedure, George tells me, is as follows: First there comes a grinding noise, as the brakes are applied. Then the train stops. And finally, from every point of the compass, a seething mob of interested onlookers begins to appear.

It was about a mile and a half from East Wobsley that the affair had taken place, and as far as the eye could reach the countryside was totally devoid of humanity. A moment before nothing had been visible but smiling cornfields and broad pasturelands; but now from east, west, north, and south running figures began to appear. We must remember that George at the time was in a somewhat overwrought frame of mind, and his statements should therefore be accepted with caution; but he tells me that out of the middle of a single empty meadow, entirely devoid of cover, no fewer than twenty-seven distinct rustics suddenly appeared, having undoubtedly shot up through the ground.

The rails, which had been completely unoccupied, were now thronged with so dense a crowd of navvies[5] that it seemed to George absurd to pretend that there was any unemployment in England. Every member of the laboring classes throughout the country was so palpably present. Moreover, the train, which at Ippleton had seemed sparsely occupied, was disgorging passengers from every door. It was the sort of mob scene which would have made David W. Griffith[6] scream with delight; and it looked, George says, like Guest Night at the Royal Automobile Club. But, as I say, we must remember that he was overwrought.

It is difficult to say what precisely would have been the correct behavior of your polished man of the world in such a situation. I think myself that a great deal of sang-froid[7] and address would be required even by the most self-possessed in order to pass off such a contretemps. To George, I may say at once, the crisis revealed itself immediately as one which he was totally incapable of handling. The one clear thought that stood out from the welter of his emotions was the reflection that it was advisable to remove himself, and to do so without delay. Drawing a deep breath, he shot swiftly off the mark.

All we Mulliners have been athletes; and George, when at the University, had been noted for his speed of foot. He ran now as he had never run before. His statement, however, that as he sprinted across the first field he distinctly saw a rabbit shoot an envious glance at him as he passed and shrug its shoulders hopelessly, I am inclined to discount. George, as I have said before, was a little overexcited.

Nevertheless, it is not to be questioned that he made good going. And he had need to, for after the first instant of surprise, which had enabled him to secure a lead, the whole mob was pouring across country after him; and dimly, as he ran, he could hear voices in the throng informally discussing the advisability of lynching him. Moreover, the field through which he was running, a moment before a bare expanse of green, was now black with figures, headed by a man with a beard who carried a pitchfork. George swerved sharply to the right,

---

5. **navvies** (nav′ ēz): Laborers.

6. **David W. Griffith:** American motion-picture director and producer (1875–1948).

7. **sang-froid** (säŋ′ frwä′): Composure.

casting a swift glance over his shoulder at his pursuers. He disliked them all, but especially the man with the pitchfork.

It is impossible for one who was not an eyewitness to say how long the chase continued and how much ground was covered by the interested parties. I know the East Wobsley country well, and I have checked George's statements; and, if it is true that he traveled east as far as Little-Wigmarsh-in-the-Dell and as far west as Higgleford-cum-Wortlebury-beneath-the-Hill, he must undoubtedly have done a lot of running.

But a point which must not be forgotten is that, to a man not in a condition to observe closely, the village of Higgleford-cum-Wortlebury-beneath-the-Hill might easily not have been Higgleford-cum-Wortlebury-beneath-the-Hill at all, but another hamlet which in many respects closely resembles it. I need scarcely say that I allude to Lesser-Snodsbury-in-the-Vale.

Let us assume, therefore, that George, having touched Little-Wigmarsh-in-the-Dell, shot off at a tangent and reached Lesser-Snodsbury-in-the-Vale. This would be a considerable run. And, as he remembers flitting past Farmer Higgins's pigsty and the Dog and Duck at Pondlebury Parva and splashing through the brook Wipple at the point where it joins the River Wopple, we can safely assume that, wherever else he went, he got plenty of exercise.

But the pleasantest of functions must end, and, just as the setting sun was gilding the spire of the ivy-covered church of St. Barnabas the Resilient, where George as a child had sat so often, enlivening the tedium of the sermon by making faces at the choirboys, a damp and bedraggled figure might have been observed crawling painfully along the High Street of East Wobsley in the direction of the cozy little cottage known to its builder as Chatsworth and to the village tradesmen as "Mulliner's."

It was George, home from the hunting field.

Slowly George Mulliner made his way to the familiar door, and, passing through it, flung himself into his favorite chair. But a moment later a more imperious need than the desire to rest forced itself upon his attention. Rising stiffly, he tottered to the kitchen and mixed himself a revivifying drink. Then, refilling his glass, he returned to the sitting room, to find that it was no longer empty. A slim, fair girl, tastefully attired in tailor-made tweeds, was leaning over the desk on which he kept his Dictionary of English Synonyms.

She looked up as he entered, startled.

"Why, Mr. Mulliner!" she exclaimed. "What has been happening? Your clothes are torn, rent, ragged, tattered, and your hair is all disheveled, untrimmed, hanging loose or negligently, at loose ends!"

George smiled a wan smile.

"You are right," he said. "And, what is more, I am suffering from extreme fatigue, weariness, lassitude, exhaustion, prostration, and languor."

The girl gazed at him, a divine pity in her soft eyes.

"I'm so sorry," she murmured. "So very sorry, grieved, distressed, afflicted, pained, mortified, dejected, and upset."

George took her hand. Her sweet sympathy had effected the cure for which he had been seeking so long. Coming on top of the violent emotions through which he had been passing all day, it seemed to work on him like some healing spell, charm, or incantation. Suddenly, in a flash, he realized that he was no longer a stammerer. Had he wished at that moment to say, "Peter Piper picked a peck of pickled peppers," he could have done it without a second thought.

But he had better things to say than that.

"Miss Blake—Susan—Susie." He took her other hand in his. His voice rang out clear and unimpeded. It seemed to him incredible that he had ever yammered at this girl like an overheated steam radiator. "It cannot have escaped your notice that I have long entertained toward you sentiments warmer and deeper than those of ordinary friendship. It is love, Susan, that has been animating my bosom. Love, first a tiny seed, has burgeoned in my heart till, blazing into flame, it has swept away on the crest of its wave my diffidence, my doubt, my fears, and my foreboding, and now, like the topmost topaz of some ancient tower, it cries to all the world in a voice of thunder: 'You are mine!· My mate! Predestined to me since Time first began!' As the star guides the mariner when, battered by boiling billows, he hies him home to the haven of hope and happiness, so do you gleam upon me along life's rough road and seem to say, 'Have courage, George! I am here!' Susan, I am not an eloquent man—I cannot speak fluently as I could wish—but these simple words which you have just heard come from the heart, from the unspotted heart of an English gentleman. Susan, I love you. Will you be my wife, married woman, matron, spouse, helpmeet, consort, partner or better half?"

"Oh, George!" said Susan. "Yes, yea, ay, aye! Decidedly, unquestionably, indubitably, incontrovertibly, and past all dispute!"

He folded her in his arms. And, as he did so, there came from the street outside —faintly, as from a distance—the sound of feet and voices. George leaped to the window. Rounding the corner, just by the Cow and Wheelbarrow public house, licensed to sell ales, wines, and spirits, was the man with the pitchfork, and behind him followed a vast crowd.

"My darling," said George. "For purely personal and private reasons, into which I need not enter, I must now leave you. Will you join me later?"

"I will follow you to the ends of the earth," replied Susan passionately.

"It will not be necessary," said George. "I am only going down to the coal cellar. I shall spend the next half hour or so there. If anybody calls and asks for me, perhaps you would not mind telling them that I am out."

"I will, I will," said Susan. "And, George, by the way. What I really came here for was to ask you if you knew a word of nine letters, ending in k and signifying an implement employed in the pursuit of agriculture."

"Pitchfork, sweetheart," said George. "But you may take it from me, as one who knows, that agriculture isn't the only thing it is used in pursuit of."


And since that day (concluded Mr. Mulliner) George, believe me or believe me not, has not had the slightest trace of an impediment in his speech. He is now the chosen orator at all political rallies for miles around; and so offensively self-confident has his manner become that only last Friday he had his eye blacked by a hay-corn-and-feed merchant of the name of Stubbs. It just shows you, doesn't it?

---

## THINKING ABOUT THE SELECTION
### Recalling

1. What incident prompts Mulliner to tell the story of his nephew George?
2. (a) Why does George decide to seek a cure? (b) What action does he take? (c) What two pieces of advice does he receive?
3. What happens when George tries to speak to (a) the first stranger? (b) the second stranger?
4. How does the woman on the train react when George begins singing "Tea for Two"?
5. (a) What cures George's stammering? (b) To what does he credit the cure?

### Interpreting

6. (a) Why does George think it would be

madness to reply to the stutterer on the train? (b) Why does his response placate the stutterer?

7. (a) Who does the woman in the train compartment think George is? (b) What effect do you think George's "sizzling . . . like a cockroach" has on the woman?

8. What is humorous about the explanation of the amount of ground George must have covered while being chased?

9. Why do George and Susan both use long strings of synonyms in their speech?

## Applying

10. George is a timid soul who becomes "offensively self-confident." (a) What conditions make a person timid? (b) What conditions can make the same person self-confident?

## ANALYZING LITERATURE

### Understanding Humor

**Humor,** the quality that makes something seem amusing, funny, or comic, is easier to recognize than it is to explain. Exaggeration is often a part of humor, as when the doctor in "The Truth About George" says of the habitual stammerer that "tests have shown that in ninety-seven point five six nine" percent of cases, love "reduces him to a condition where he sounds like a soda-water siphon trying to recite 'Gunga Din.'" Misunderstandings often figure in humor, as when George tries to communicate with the woman in the train compartment by singing, and she takes it as proof of his being a lunatic. Look through "The Truth About George" and find what you consider to be the five most amusing incidents, situations, or statements. Try to explain what it is about each one that makes it humorous.

## CRITICAL THINKING AND READING

### Recognizing Caricature

When P. G. Wodehouse describes the antics of George and other characters in this story, you know that real people do not behave or talk that way. Yet there is a core of truth, greatly exaggerated and distorted, in what the characters do and say. Wodehouse is creating caricatures, just as a cartoonist creates caricatures by drawing people with recognizable but grotesque features. George is a caricature of a person who stutters. Point out three other caricatures in this story and explain why each fits that category.

## UNDERSTANDING LANGUAGE

### Using Synonyms

A **synonym** is a word that means almost the same thing as another word. Since one word seldom has exactly the same meaning as another, you cannot arbitrarily substitute synonyms for each other in speaking and writing. In "The Truth About George," both George and Susan use a series of synonyms for comic effect. George says, "Will you be my wife, married woman, matron, spouse, helpmeet, consort, partner or better half?" Those words are all synonyms, but they do not all have precisely the same meaning. A *spouse,* for instance, may be either a husband or a wife; a *matron* is usually an older woman; a *consort* is often a royal partner.

The following groups of synonyms appear in the story. Using a good dictionary, define each word, distinguishing it from the synonyms included with it.

1. incapable, incompetent, powerless
2. torn, rent, ragged
3. fatigue, lassitude, prostration
4. pained, mortified, dejected

## THINKING AND WRITING

### Writing About Humor

Does "The Truth About George" make you laugh, chuckle, snicker, giggle, guffaw? What do you find funny in it? Why do you find it funny? Look back at your answers in Analyzing Literature. Use the five examples of humor that you chose in that assignment as the basis for a composition on the topic, "What Is Humor?" Make further notes, if necessary. In your first draft, be as precise and specific as you can. When you revise the material for your final draft, check to make sure that your sentences are clear and to the point, not simply abstract thoughts or unsupported generalizations.

# DORIS LESSING

## 1919–

Doris Lessing is one of the most powerful of contemporary authors. Her novels and short stories explore the evils of racism, the role of women in modern life, the importance of intuition, and the limits of idealism in solving the problems facing society. Her books, profound and highly personal, confront a host of post-World War II issues, supplying almost a history of the times, with special emphasis on Africa and feminism.

The focus on Africa in Doris Lessing's work is not surprising. Born in Persia of British parents, she grew up on a three-thousand-acre farm in Southern Rhodesia (now Zimbabwe), where her parents raised maize with the help of native labor. She remained in Africa through two unsuccessful marriages, living principally in the Rhodesian capital of Salisbury, until she was thirty.

Explaining how her career began, Lessing said: "I've always been a writer . . . but not until I was quite old—twenty-six or -seven—did I realize that I'd better . . . get down to business. I was working in a lawyer's office at the time, and I remember walking in and saying to my boss, 'I'm giving up my job because I'm going to write a novel.' He very properly laughed, and I indignantly walked home and wrote *The Grass Is Singing*."

She moved to London in 1949 and published her first novel, *The Grass Is Singing,* the next year, having brought the manuscript with her from Rhodesia. Her African experiences provided the material for this deeply moving, highly acclaimed work. In an interview in 1962, Lessing commented, "I feel the best thing that ever happened to me was that I was brought up out of England. I took for granted kinds of experiences that would be impossible to a middle-class girl here."

*The Golden Notebook,* published in 1962, is her most renowned and technically sophisticated work. It represents a junction between the two main paths her fiction has taken—her realistic, sometimes reportorial early style, and her visionary, at times apocalyptic, "inner space fiction" that came later. The dominant theme in *The Golden Notebook* is that of the free woman who struggles for individuality and equality despite her social and psychological conditioning.

A self-described "architect of the soul," Lessing is one of the most serious and intelligent of today's writers. Hers is a uniquely twentieth-century odyssey. Writing in what she calls a "straight, broad, direct" manner, she has produced a remarkable body of novels and short stories, works that are distinguished not only for their breadth of subject matter but also for their breadth of vision.

# GUIDE FOR INTERPRETING

## Writer's Techniques

## A Mild Attack of Locusts

**Conflict.** One of the ingredients of an effective story or play is conflict, the struggle between a main character and another person or force. Often the conflict involves two main characters—protagonist and antagonist—as in many of Shakespeare's tragedies. Sometimes the conflict is between a main character and society as a whole, or between a main character and nature. These conflicts are external. An external conflict is one between a main character and another person or between a character and an outside force. There may also be internal conflict, or psychological conflict. Internal conflict occurs within the mind of a main character. Many plots contain both external and internal conflicts. Fictional conflicts, like real-life conflicts, are often complex, and you may occasionally find them puzzling to sort out.

## Writing

Human beings are often pitted against nature in both real life and in fiction. For example, a family may struggle against a fast-flowing river, or fire fighters may battle a forest fire. Make a list of natural forces against which human beings must battle—and win—to survive.

## Primary Source

Lessing describes life on an isolated South African farm.

> Our neighbors were four, five, seven miles off. . . . The seasons were bad, prices bad, crops failed. This was the sort of thing that made it impossible for him [her father] ever to "get off the farm," which, he agreed with my mother, was what he most wanted to do. . . . But it was my mother who suffered. After a period of neurotic illness, which was a protest against her situation, she became brave and resourceful. But she never saw that her husband was not living in a real world, that he had made a captive of her common sense. We were always about to "get off the farm." A miracle would do it—a sweepstake, a goldmine, a legacy. And then? What a question! We would go to England where life would be normal with people coming in for musical evenings and nice supper parties at the Trocadero after a show. Poor woman, for the twenty years we were on the farm, she waited for when life would begin for her and for her children, for she never understood that what was a calamity for her was for them a blessing.

> As you read "A Mild Attack of Locusts," see how Margaret's conflicts parallel those Lessing's mother faced.

# A Mild Attack of Locusts

Doris Lessing

The rains that year were good; they were coming nicely just as the crops needed them —or so Margaret gathered when the men said they were not too bad. She never had an opinion of her own on matters like the weather, because even to know about what seems a simple thing like the weather needs experience. Which Margaret had not got. The men were Richard her husband, and old Stephen, Richard's father, a farmer from way back; and these two might argue for hours whether the rains were ruinous or just ordinarily exasperating. Margaret had been on the farm three years. She still did not understand how they did not go bankrupt altogether, when the men never had a good word for the weather, or the soil, or the Government. But she was getting to learn the language. Farmers' language. And they neither went bankrupt nor got very rich. They jogged along doing comfortably.

Their crop was maize.[1] Their farm was three thousand acres on the ridges that rise up toward the Zambesi escarpment[2]—high, dry windswept country, cold and dusty in winter, but now, in the wet season, steamy with the heat rising in wet soft waves off miles of green foliage. Beautiful it was, with the sky blue and brilliant halls of air, and the bright green folds and hollows of country beneath, and the mountains lying sharp and bare twenty miles off across the rivers.

The sky made her eyes ache; she was not used to it. One does not look so much at the sky in the city she came from. So that evening when Richard said: "The Government is sending out warnings that locusts are expected, coming down from the breeding grounds up North," her instinct was to look about her at the trees. Insects —swarms of them—horrible! But Richard and the old man had raised their eyes and were looking up over the mountain. "We haven't had locusts in seven years," they said. "They go in cycles, locusts do." And then: "There goes our crop for this season!"

But they went on with the work of the farm just as usual until one day they were coming up the road to the homestead for the midday break, when old Stephen stopped, raised his finger and pointed: "Look, look, there they are!"

Out ran Margaret to join them, looking at the hills. Out came the servants from the kitchen. They all stood and gazed. Over the rocky levels of the mountain was a streak of rust-colored air. Locusts. There they came.

At once Richard shouted at the cookboy. Old Stephen yelled at the houseboy. The cookboy ran to beat the old plowshare[3] hanging from a tree branch, which was used to summon the laborers at moments of crisis. The houseboy ran off to the store to collect tin cans, any old bit of metal. The farm was ringing with the clamor of the gong; and they could see the laborers come

---

**1. maize** (māz) *n.*: Corn.
**2. Zambesi** (zam bē′ zē) **escarpment:** Steep cliffs along the Zambesi River in southern Africa.

**3. plowshare** *n.*: The cutting blade of a plow.

pouring out of the compound, pointing at the hills and shouting excitedly. Soon they had all come up to the house, and Richard and old Stephen were giving them orders —Hurry, hurry, hurry.

And off they ran again, the two white men with them, and in a few minutes Margaret could see the smoke of fires rising from all around the farmlands. Piles of wood and grass had been prepared there. There were seven patches of bared soil, yellow and ox-blood color and pink, where the new meal-ies[4] were just showing, making a film of bright green; and around each drifted up thick clouds of smoke. They were throwing wet leaves on to the fires now, to make it acrid and black. Margaret was watching the hills. Now there was a long, low cloud advancing, rust-color still, swelling forward and out as she looked. The telephone was ringing. Neighbors—quick, quick, there come the locusts. Old Smith had had his crop eaten to the ground. Quick, get your fires started. For of course, while every farmer hoped the locusts would overlook his farm and go on to the next, it was only fair to warn each other; one must play fair. Everywhere, fifty miles over the countryside, the smoke was rising from myriads of fires. Margaret answered the telephone calls, and between calls she stood watching the locusts. The air was darkening. A strange darkness, for the sun was blazing—it was like the darkness of a veldt fire, when the air gets thick with smoke. The sunlight comes down distorted, a thick, hot orange. Oppressive it was, too, with the heaviness of a storm. The locusts were coming fast. Now half the sky was darkened. Behind the reddish veils in front, which were the advance guards of the swarm, the main swarm showed in dense black cloud, reaching almost to the sun itself.

Margaret was wondering what she could do to help. She did not know. Then up came

---

**4. mealies** *n*.: Ears of corn.

old Stephen from the lands. "We're finished, Margaret, finished! Those beggars can eat every leaf and blade off the farm in half an hour! And it is only early afternoon—if we can make enough smoke, make enough noise till the sun goes down, they'll settle somewhere else perhaps. . . ." And then: "Get the kettle going. It's thirsty work, this."

So Margaret went to the kitchen, and stoked up the fire, and boiled the water. Now, on the tin roof of the kitchen she could hear the thuds and bangs of falling locusts, or a scratching slither as one skidded down. Here were the first of them. From down on the lands came the beating and banging and clanging of a hundred gasoline cans and bits of metal. Stephen impatiently waited while one gasoline can was filled with tea, hot, sweet and orange-colored, and the other with water. In the meantime, he told Margaret about how twenty years back he was eaten out, made bankrupt, by the locust armies. And then, still talking, he hoisted up the gasoline cans, one in each hand, by the wood pieces set cornerwise across each, and jogged off down to the road to the thirsty laborers. By now the locusts were falling like hail on to the roof of the kitchen. It sounded like a heavy storm. Margaret looked out and saw the air dark with a criss-cross of the insects, and she set her teeth and ran out into it—what the men could do, she could. Overhead the air was thick, locusts everywhere. The locusts were flopping against her, and she brushed them off, heavy red-brown creatures, looking at her with their beady old-men's eyes while they clung with hard, serrated legs. She held her breath with disgust and ran through into the house. There it was even more like being in a heavy storm. The iron roof was reverberating, and the clamor of iron from the lands was like thunder. Looking out, all the trees were queer and still, clotted with insects, their boughs weighed to the ground. The earth seemed to be moving, locusts crawling everywhere, she could not see the lands at

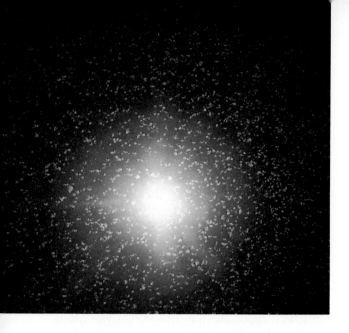

all, so thick was the swarm. Towards the mountains it was like looking into driving rain—even as she watched, the sun was blotted out with a fresh onrush of them. It was a half-night, a perverted blackness. Then came a sharp crack from the bush—a branch had snapped off. Then another. A tree down the slope leaned over and settled heavily to the ground. Through the hail of insects a man came running. More tea, more water was needed. She supplied them. She kept the fires stoked and filled cans with liquid, and then it was four in the afternoon, and the locusts had been pouring across overhead for a couple of hours. Up came old Stephen again, crunching locusts underfoot with every step, locusts clinging all over him; he was cursing and swearing, banging with his old hat at the air. At the doorway he stopped briefly, hastily pulling at the clinging insects and throwing them off, then he plunged into the locust-free living-room.

"All the crops finished. Nothing left," he said.

But the gongs were still beating, the men still shouting, and Margaret asked: "Why do you go on with it, then?"

"The main swarm isn't settling. They are heavy with eggs. They are looking for a place to settle and lay. If we can stop the main body settling on our farm, that's everything. If they get a chance to lay their eggs, we are going to have everything eaten flat with hoppers[5] later on." He picked a stray locust off his shirt and split it down with his thumbnail—it was clotted inside with eggs. "Imagine that multiplied by millions. You ever seen a hopper swarm on the march? Well, you're lucky."

Margaret thought an adult swarm was bad enough. Outside now the light on the earth was a pale, thin yellow, clotted with moving shadows; the clouds of moving insects thickened and lightened like driving rain. Old Stephen said, "They've got the wind behind them, that's something."

"Is it very bad?" asked Margaret fearfully, and the old man said emphatically: "We're finished. This swarm may pass over, but once they've started, they'll be coming down from the North now one after another. And then there are the hoppers—it might go on for two or three years."

Margaret sat down helplessly, and thought: Well, if it's the end, it's the end. What now? We'll all three have to go back to town. . . . But at this, she took a quick look at Stephen, the old man who had farmed forty years in this country, been bankrupt twice, and she knew nothing would make him go and become a clerk in the city. Yet her heart ached for him, he looked so tired, the worry lines deep from nose to mouth. Poor old man. . . . He had lifted up a locust that had got itself somehow into his pocket, holding it in the air by one leg. "You've got the strength of a steel-spring in those legs of yours," he was telling the locust, good-humoredly. Then, although he had been fighting locusts, squashing locusts, yelling at locusts, sweeping them in great mounds into the fires to burn for the last three hours, nevertheless he took this one to the door and carefully threw it out to join its fellows, as if

---

**5. hoppers** *n.*: Baby locusts.

he would rather not harm a hair of its head. This comforted Margaret; all at once she felt irrationally cheered. She remembered it was not the first time in the last three years the man had announced their final and irremediable ruin.

"Get me a drink, lass," he then said, and she set the bottle of whisky by him.

In the meantime, out in the pelting storm of insects, her husband was banging the gong, feeding the fires with leaves, the insects clinging to him all over—she shuddered. "How can you bear to let them touch you?" she asked. He looked at her, disapproving. She felt suitably humble—just as she had when he had first taken a good look at her city self, hair waved and golden, nails red and pointed. Now she was a proper farmer's wife, in sensible shoes and a solid skirt. She might even get to letting locusts settle on her—in time.

Having tossed back a whisky or two, old Stephen went back into the battle, wading now through glistening brown waves of locusts.

Five o'clock. The sun would set in an hour. Then the swarm would settle. It was as thick overhead as ever. The trees were ragged mounds of glistening brown.

Margaret began to cry. It was all so hopeless—if it wasn't a bad season, it was locusts; if it wasn't locusts, it was army worm[6] or veldt fires. Always something. The rustling of the locust armies was like a big forest in the storm; their settling on the roof was like the beating of the rain; the ground was invisible in a sleek, brown, surging tide—it was like being drowned in locusts, submerged by the loathsome brown flood. It seemed as if the roof might sink in under the weight of them, as if the door might give in under their pressure and these rooms fill with them—and it was getting so dark . . . she looked up. The air was thinner; gaps of blue showed in the dark, moving clouds. The

blue spaces were cold and thin—the sun must be setting. Through the fog of insects she saw figures approaching. First old Stephen, marching bravely along, then her husband, drawn and haggard with weariness. Behind them the servants. All were crawling all over with insects. The sound of the gongs had stopped. She could hear nothing but the ceaseless rustle of a myriad wings.

The two men slapped off the insects and came in.

"Well," said Richard, kissing her on the cheek, "the main swarm has gone over."

"For the Lord's sake," said Margaret angrily, still half-crying, "what's here is bad enough, isn't it?" For although the evening air was no longer black and thick, but a clear blue, with a pattern of insects whizzing this way and that across it, everything else—trees, buildings, bushes, earth, was gone under the moving brown masses.

"If it doesn't rain in the night and keep them here—if it doesn't rain and weight them down with water, they'll be off in the morning at sunrise."

"We're bound to have some hoppers. But not the main swarm—that's something."

Margaret roused herself, wiped her eyes, pretended she had not been crying, and fetched them some supper, for the servants were too exhausted to move. She sent them down to the compound to rest.

She served the supper and sat listening. There is not one maize plant left, she heard. Not one. The men would get the planters out the moment the locusts had gone. They must start all over again.

But what's the use of that, Margaret wondered, if the whole farm was going to be crawling with hoppers? But she listened while they discussed the new government pamphlet that said how to defeat the hoppers. You must have men out all the time, moving over the farm to watch for movement in the grass. When you find a patch of hoppers, small lively black things, like crickets, then you dig trenches around the

---

**6. army worm:** Larva of certain moths that travel in large groups, ruining crops.

patch or spray them with poison from pumps supplied by the Government. The Government wanted them to cooperate in a world plan for eliminating this plague forever. You should attack locusts at the source. Hoppers, in short. The men were talking as if they were planning a war, and Margaret listened, amazed.

In the night it was quiet; no sign of the settled armies outside, except sometimes a branch snapped, or a tree could be heard crashing down.

Margaret slept badly in the bed beside Richard, who was sleeping like the dead, exhausted with the afternoon's fight. In the morning she woke to yellow sunshine lying across the bed—clear sunshine, with an occasional blotch of shadow moving over it. She went to the window. Old Stephen was ahead of her. There he stood outside, gazing down over the bush. And she gazed, astounded—and entranced, much against her will. For it looked as if every tree, every bush, all the earth, were lit with pale flames. The locusts were fanning their wings to free them of the night dews. There was a shimmer of red-tinged gold light everywhere.

She went out to join the old man, stepping carefully among the insects. They stood and watched. Overhead the sky was blue, blue and clear.

"Pretty," said old Stephen, with satisfaction.

Well, thought Margaret, we may be ruined, we may be bankrupt, but not everyone has seen an army of locusts fanning their wings at dawn.

Over the slopes, in the distance, a faint red smear showed in the sky, thickened and spread. "There they go," said old Stephen. "There goes the main army, off south."

And now from the trees, from the earth all round them, the locusts were taking wing. They were like small aircraft, maneuvering for the take-off, trying their wings to see if they were dry enough. Off they went. A reddish-brown steam was rising off the miles of bush, off the lands, the earth. Again the sunlight darkened.

And as the clotted branches lifted, the weight on them lightening, there was nothing but the black spines of branches, trees. No green left, nothing. All morning they watched, the three of them, as the brown crust thinned and broke and dissolved, flying up to mass with the main army, now a brownish-red smear in the southern sky. The lands which had been filmed with green, the new tender mealie plants, were stark and bare. All the trees stripped. A devastated landscape. No green, no green anywhere.

By midday the reddish cloud had gone. Only an occasional locust flopped down. On the ground were the corpses and the wounded. The African laborers were sweeping these up with branches and collecting them in tins.

"Ever eaten sun-dried locust?" asked old Stephen. "That time twenty years ago, when I went broke, I lived on mealie meal and dried locusts for three months. They aren't bad at all—rather like smoked fish, if you come to think of it."

But Margaret preferred not even to think of it.

After the midday meal the men went off to the lands. Everything was to be replanted. With a bit of luck another swarm would not come traveling down just this way. But they hoped it would rain very soon, to spring some new grass, because the cattle would die otherwise—there was not a blade of grass left on the farm. As for Margaret, she was trying to get used to the idea of three or four years of locusts. Locusts were going to be like bad weather, from now on, always imminent. She felt like a survivor after war—if this devastated and mangled countryside was not ruin, well, what then was ruin?

But the men ate their supper with good appetites.

"It could have been worse," was what they said. "It could be much worse."

## THINKING ABOUT THE SELECTION

### Recalling

1. (a) How long has Margaret lived on the farm? (b) Where did she come from? (c) How has her appearance changed since coming to the farm?
2. What are the farmers' two main defenses against the locusts?
3. Why do the farmers want to prevent the main swarm of locusts from settling?
4. What three problems besides locusts do the farmers sometimes have to face?
5. (a) How much damage do the locusts do to the farm? (b) When morning comes, what do the locusts do?

### Interpreting

6. What is Margaret's attitude toward the locust attack?
7. Why does old Stephen fight on even after saying they are finished?
8. Why do you think Margaret is comforted when Stephen releases the locust that was in his pocket?
9. In what sense is the locust attack "mild," as the title of the story calls it?

### Applying

10. People react differently when faced with what seems to be a hopeless situation. (a) How does this story make that point? (b) What have you seen in your own experience that proves it?

## ANALYZING LITERATURE

### Recognizing Conflict

In a work of fiction, the opposition between a character and another force is the story's conflict. This conflict may be external, as between the farmers and the invading locusts in "A Mild Attack of Locusts." Or it may be internal, as in Margaret's love for her husband opposed to her despair for his future as a farmer on the veldt.

1. There are a number of conflicts in "A Mild Attack of Locusts." One of them concerns Margaret's struggle to define herself as a farmer's wife. What evidence is there in the story that she does not regard herself as entirely satisfied with her role in life?
2. The immediate external conflict in the story is the locust attack. But there is a long-term conflict as well, one that is unresolved by the farmers' minor victory in keeping the main swarm from settling. (a) What is the long-term, unresolved external conflict? (b) How successful do you think Richard, Stephen, and Margaret will be in resolving it?

## CRITICAL THINKING AND READING

### Understanding the Role of Style

A writer's **style** is his or her distinctive way of using language to express thoughts. Style is a broad term. It includes word choice, sentence structure, point of view, and all aspects of organization. A writer's style is influenced by the literary fashion of the times and by his or her own personality and preferences. Some writers pay close attention to their style; others do not. The style of some writers stands out in sharp relief; that of others is hardly noticeable. Doris Lessing's style in "A Mild Attack of Locusts" is plain and precise. Her use of inverted sentence structure is perhaps its most noticeable feature —"Beautiful it was, with the sky blue."

What makes Lessing's "straight, broad, direct" style effective in this story?

## THINKING AND WRITING

### Writing About a Paradox

A **paradox** is a statement or circumstance that at first seems untrue or self-contradictory but upon reflection proves to be true in some sense. In "A Mild Attack of Locusts," Margaret, after a day of feeling revulsion for the locusts, is entranced the next morning as they fan their wings, making "a shimmer of red-tinged gold light everywhere." Her feelings are paradoxical. Write a composition in which you explain the paradox of how something so destructive and even loathsome can also be beautiful. When revising your first draft, make sure you have supported your ideas with specific details.

# NADINE GORDIMER

## 1923–

The fiction of Nadine Gordimer has been shaped by her life in South Africa and by her firm opposition to the government's policy of apartheid. Initially honored for her short fiction, she says that in time she found the short story "too delicate for what I have to say." In recent years her novels, some of them banned in South Africa, have gained an international reputation.

Nadine Gordimer was born in Springs, South Africa, a small town near Johannesburg. Her mother took her out of a local private school when she was eleven, and from then until she was sixteen she "read tremendously," wrote much fiction, and published her first adult short story, "Come Again Tomorrow," when she was fifteen. She studied for a year at the University of Witwatersrand, continuing to write short stories. *The Soft Voice of the Serpent* (1952) was the first collection of her stories to be published in the United States.

Following the critical success of that book, Gordimer's stories began appearing in *The New Yorker,* the *Atlantic, Harper's,* and other well-known periodicals. In her stories she often describes the enforced entrapment of whites who have inherited political and economic power in South Africa's closed society. Frequently she builds a personal tale around a fleeting but sharply focused moment of insight.

In her short stories, and later in her novels—including the critically acclaimed *A Guest of Honor* (1970), *The Conservationist* (1974), and *Burger's Daughter* (1979)—she displays an ability to write from the perspectives of Anglo, black, and Afrikaner and to delineate a variety of economic and social settings. She writes as a compassionate observer of the human condition. In lyric tones yet without sentimentality, she pictures the South African scene with awareness and humanity, stressing the themes of understanding, adjustment, and forgiveness.

Until she was thirty, Nadine Gordimer had never been outside South Africa. Since then she has traveled widely and lectured in a number of universities, including Princeton, Columbia, and the University of Michigan. In recent years she has won many literary awards.

Since 1954, Gordimer has been married to Reinhold Cassier, the director of the Johannesburg branch of Sotheby Parke Bernet. She has two children, one by a previous marriage. Called "a luminous symbol of at least one white person's understanding of the black man's burden," there can be little doubt that she is one of the leading African novelists writing in English.

# GUIDE FOR INTERPRETING

**Writer's
Techniques**

## The Train from Rhodesia

**Theme.** Theme is the insight into life revealed by a work of literature. In fiction the writer's central idea becomes the theme of the work. Often the theme can be stated in a single sentence, such as "A small mistake in judgment can have serious consequences." Sometimes it demands a more detailed description. A work of fiction may have one theme or several. In developing a theme, the writer introduces conflict, typically a problem or problems that must be solved by the protagonist, or main character.

When the protagonist has to choose between two or more undesirable alternatives, he or she faces a dilemma. In familiar terms a dilemma is a choice between the frying pan and the fire; in mythological terms, between Scylla and Charybdis. A dilemma involves a difficult choice between actions or values, and any choice that the character makes may have unfortunate results.

**Commentary**

An author's entire literary output is frequently characterized by one overriding theme that ties together all the individual works. Each work rarely states the same theme in the same way. Rather, readers can see one general concern expressed differently in each poem, story, novel, or essay. These themes can be drawn from the writer's personal situation, or combined with some political, social, or moral concern of the day. On the surface, it would not seem possible that Nadine Gordimer's work would show one dominant theme, since she writes about such a wide range of people and places. Indeed, one critic has remarked that "the image of the bazaar comes to mind when one thinks of Miss Gordimer's variety and resourcefulness." For example, many of her stories concern wealthy, sophisticated, and frequently bored urban and suburban people in Johannesburg, South Africa. Other tales deal with people on the lowest economic rung eking out a bare living among the wretched thatched roofs and mud floors of native locations. Many of her best tales, such as "The Train from Rhodesia," intermingle these two worlds to more fully illuminate the situation in contemporary South Africa. But critic Robert F. Haugh has identified a tension between "what might be" and "what is " in a majority of her work. How do you see this theme in "The Train form Rhodesia"?

**Writing**

According to an African proverb, "The earth is a beehive; we all enter by the same door but live in different cells." Freewrite, exploring the meaning of this proverb.

# The Train from Rhodesia[1]

## Nadine Gordimer

The train came out of the red horizon and bore down toward them over the single straight track.

The stationmaster came out of his little brick station with its pointed chalet roof, feeling the creases in his serge uniform in his legs as well. A stir of preparedness rippled through the squatting native vendors waiting in the dust; the face of a carved wooden animal, eternally surprised, stuck out of a sack. The stationmaster's barefoot children wandered over. From the gray mud huts with the untidy heads that stood within a decorated mud wall, chickens, and dogs with their skin stretched like parchment over their bones, followed the piccanins[2] down to the track. The flushed and perspiring west cast a reflection, faint, without heat, upon the station, upon the tin shed marked "Goods," upon the walled kraal,[3] upon the gray tin house of the stationmaster and upon the sand, that lapped all around, from sky to sky, cast little rhythmical cups of shadow, so that the sand became the sea, and closed over the children's black feet softly and without imprint.

The stationmaster's wife sat behind the mesh of her veranda. Above her head the hunk of a sheep's carcass moved slightly, dangling in a current of air.

They waited.

The train called out, along the sky; but there was no answer; and the cry hung on: I'm coming . . . I'm coming . . .

The engine flared out now, big, whisking a dwindling body behind it; the track flared out to let it in.

Creaking, jerking, jostling, gasping, the train filled the station.

Here, let me see that one—the young woman curved her body further out of the corridor window. Missus? smiled the old boy, looking at the creatures he held in his hand. From a piece of string on his gray finger hung a tiny woven basket; he lifted it, questioning. No, no, she urged, leaning down toward him, across the height of the train, toward the man in the piece of old rug; that one, that one, her hand commanded. It was a lion, carved out of soft dry wood that looked like spongecake; heraldic, black and white, with impressionistic detail burnt in. The old man held it up to her still smiling, not from the heart, but at the customer. Between its Vandyke[4] teeth, in the mouth opened in an endless roar too terrible to be heard, it had a black tongue. Look, said the young husband, if you don't mind! And round the neck of the thing, a piece of fur (rat? rabbit? meerkat?); a real mane, majestic, telling you somehow that the artist had delight in the lion.

---

1. **Rhodesia** (rō de′ zhə): Former name of Zimbabwe (zim bä′ bwe), a country in southern Africa.
2. **piccanins** *n.*: Native children.
3. **kraal** (kräl) *n.*: A fenced-in enclosure for cattle or sheep.

4. **Vandyke** (van dīk′) *adj.*: In the style of the subjects of the portraits of Flemish painter Anthony Vandyke (1599–1641).

All up and down the length of the train in the dust the artists sprang, walking bent, like performing animals, the better to exhibit the fantasy held toward the faces on the train. Buck, startled and stiff, staring with round black and white eyes. More lions, standing erect, grappling with strange, thin, elongated warriors who clutched spears and showed no fear in their slits of eyes. How much, they asked from the train, how much?

Give me penny, said the little ones with nothing to sell. The dogs went and sat, quite still, under the dining car, where the train breathed out the smell of meat cooking with onion.

A man passed beneath the arch of reaching arms meeting gray-black and white in the exchange of money for the staring wooden eyes, the stiff wooden legs sticking up in the air; went along under the voices and the bargaining, interrogating the wheels. Past the dogs; glancing up at the dining car where he could stare at the faces, behind glass, drinking beer, two by two, on either side of a uniform railway vase with its pale dead flower. Right to the end, to the guard's van, where the stationmaster's children had just collected their mother's two loaves of bread; to the engine itself, where the stationmaster and the driver stood talking against the steaming complaint of the resting beast.

The man called out to them, something loud and joking. They turned to laugh, in a twirl of steam. The two children careered over the sand, clutching the bread, and burst through the iron gate and up the path through the garden in which nothing grew.

Passengers drew themselves in at the corridor windows and turned into compartments to fetch money, to call someone to look. Those sitting inside looked up: suddenly different, caged faces, boxed in, cut off, after the contact of outside. There was an orange a piccanin would like. . . . What about that chocolate? It wasn't very nice. . . .

A young girl had collected a handful of the hard kind, that no one liked, out of the chocolate box, and was throwing them to the dogs, over at the dining car. But the hens darted in, and swallowed the chocolates, incredibly quick and accurate, before they had even dropped in the dust, and the dogs, a little bewildered, looked up with their brown eyes, not expecting anything.

—No, leave it, said the girl, don't take it. . . .

Too expensive, too much, she shook her head and raised her voice to the old boy, giving up the lion. He held it up where she had handed it to him. No, she said, shaking her head. Three-and-six?[5] insisted her husband, loudly. Yes baas! laughed the boy. *Three-and-six?*—the young man was incredulous. Oh leave it—she said. The young man stopped. Don't you want it? he said, keeping his face closed to the boy. No, never mind, she said, leave it. The old native kept his head on one side, looking at them sideways, holding the lion. Three-and-six, he murmured, as old people repeat things to themselves.

The young woman drew her head in. She went into the coupé[6] and sat down. Out of the window, on the other side, there was nothing; sand and bush; a thorn tree. Back through the open doorway, past the figure of her husband in the corridor, there was the station, the voices, wooden animals waving, running feet. Her eye followed the funny little valance of scrolled wood that outlined the chalet roof of the station; she thought of the lion and smiled. That bit of fur round the neck. But the wooden buck, the hippos, the elephants, the baskets that already bulked out of their brown paper under the seat and on the luggage rack! How will they look at home? Where will you put them? What will they mean away from the places you found

---

**5. three-and-six:** Three shillings and sixpence.
**6. coupé** (ko͞o pā′) *n.*: A half-compartment at the end, with seats on only one side.

them? Away from the unreality of the last few weeks? The man outside. But he is not part of the unreality; he is for good now. Odd . . . somewhere there was an idea that he, that living with him, was part of the holiday, the strange places.

Outside, a bell rang. The stationmaster was leaning against the end of the train, green flag rolled in readiness. A few men who had got down to stretch their legs sprang on to the train, clinging to the observation platforms, or perhaps merely standing on the iron step, holding the rail; but on the train, safe from the one dusty platform, the one tin house, the empty sand.

There was a grunt. The train jerked. Through the glass the beer drinkers looked out, as if they could not see beyond it. Behind the flyscreen, the stationmaster's wife sat facing back at them beneath the darkening hunk of meat.

There was a shout. The flag drooped out. Joints not yet coordinated, the segmented body of the train heaved and bumped back against itself. It began to move; slowly the scrolled chalet moved past it, the yells of the natives, running alongside, jetted up into the air, fell back at different levels. Staring wooden faces waved drunkenly, there, then gone, questioning for the last time at the windows. Here, one-and-six baas!—As one automatically opens a hand to catch a thrown ball, a man fumbled wildly down his pocket, brought up the shilling and sixpence and threw them out; the old native, gasping, his skinny toes splaying the sand, flung the lion.

The piccanins were waving, the dogs stood, tails uncertain, watching the train go: past the mud huts, where a woman turned to look, up from the smoke of the fire, her hand pausing on her hip.

The stationmaster went slowly in under the chalet.

The old native stood, breath blowing out the skin between his ribs, feet tense, balanced in the sand, smiling and shaking his head. In his opened palm, held in the atti-tude of receiving, was the retrieved shilling and sixpence.

The blind end of the train was being pulled helplessly out of the station.

The young man swung in from the corridor, breathless. He was shaking his head with laughter and triumph. Here! he said. And waggled the lion at her. One-and-six!

What? she said.

He laughed. I was arguing with him for fun, bargaining—when the train had pulled out already, he came tearing after. . . . One-and-six baas! So there's your lion.

She was holding it away from her, the head with the open jaws, the pointed teeth, the black tongue, the wonderful ruff of fur facing her. She was looking at it with an expression of not seeing, of seeing something different. Her face was drawn up, wryly, like the face of a discomforted child. Her mouth lifted nervously at the corner. Very slowly, cautious, she lifted her finger and touched the mane, where it was joined to the wood.

But how could you, she said. He was shocked by the dismay of her face.

Good heavens, he said, what's the matter?

If you wanted the thing, she said, her voice rising and breaking with the shrill impotence of anger, why didn't you buy it in the first place? If you wanted it, why didn't you pay for it? Why didn't you take it decently, when he offered it? Why did you have to wait for him to run after the train with it, and give him one-and-six? One-and-six!

She was pushing it at him, trying to force him to take it. He stood astonished, his hands hanging at his sides.

But you wanted it! You liked it so much?

—It's a beautiful piece of work, she said fiercely, as if to protect it from him.

You liked it so much! You said yourself it was too expensive—

Oh *you*—she said, hopeless and furious. *You*. . . . She threw the lion onto the seat.

He stood looking at her.

She sat down again in the corner and, her face slumped in her hand, stared out of the window. Everything was turning around inside her. One-and-six. One-and-six. One-and-six for the wood and the carving and the sinews of the legs and the switch of the tail. The mouth open like that and the teeth. The black tongue, rolling, like a wave. The mane round the neck. To give one-and-six for that. The heat of shame mounted through her legs and body and sounded in her ears like the sound of sand pouring. Pouring, pouring. She sat there, sick. A weariness, a tastelessness, the discovery of a void made her hands slacken their grip, atrophy emptily, as if the hour was not worth their grasp. She was feeling like this again. She had thought it was something to do with singleness, with being alone and belonging too much to oneself.

She sat there not wanting to move or speak, or to look at anything, even; so that the mood should be associated with nothing, no object, word or sight that might recur and so recall the feeling again. . . . Smuts blew in grittily, settled on her hands. Her back remained at exactly the same angle, turned against the young man sitting with his hands drooping between his sprawled legs, and the lion, fallen on its side in the corner.

The train had cast the station like a skin. It called out to the sky, I'm coming, I'm coming; and again, there was no answer.

## THINKING ABOUT THE SELECTION

### Recalling

1. At the beginning of the story, what are three details that show the isolation of the small-town railway station?
2. (a) How much money does the vendor want for the carved lion? (b) How much does he finally accept?
3. (a) What have the young couple already bought on their holiday? (b) After the "unreality" of the vacation, what does the wife realize "is for good now"?
4. (a) At the end of the story, how is the young woman sitting in her seat? (b) Where is the lion?

### Interpreting

5. Why is the arrival of the train important to the people in the town?
6. Why do you think the young woman wants the carved lion?
7. (a) Why is the young woman angry when her husband bargains for and obtains the lion at a low price? (b) What does she mean to imply when she says, "If you wanted the thing . . . why didn't you pay for it"?
8. This story is highly symbolic. (a) What may the train symbolize? (b) The station?

### Applying

9. At the end of the story, the young wife feels isolated and alone. Her husband is confused by her unexpected reactions. (a) What has happened in this apparently trivial incident to make her feel shame, sickness, weariness, and emptiness? (b) How would you advise her husband to try to reassure her?

## ANALYZING LITERATURE

### Understanding Theme

Theme is the central idea in a literary work. Conflict, which occurs as the theme is developed, may present one or more dilemmas. A dilemma is a situation in which the main character, or protagonist, has to choose between undesirable alternatives. A short-story writer will not necessarily resolve all dilemmas, but may leave them for the reader to ponder. With a partner or in a small group, discuss two of the dilemmas —apart from isolation in marriage—that the young woman in "The Train from Rhodesia" appears to be facing. For example:

1. The dilemma of belonging to the well-to-do white minority in an impoverished black nation
2. The dilemma of trying to make connections with other people in a setting that makes it hard to do so

## CRITICAL THINKING AND READING
### Understanding Cultural Attitudes

The scene at the railway station that is described in "The Train from Rhodesia" is probably unfamiliar to you. The custom of white train passengers bargaining with native craftsmen for the purchase of their hand-carved wares reflects circumstances in southern Africa at the time the fictional incident occurs. Both the passengers on the train and the natives at the station accept the custom as normal. They see nothing to object to, although to an outside observer it might suggest inequality, racism, and exploitation.

Describe the scene at a subway, bus station, train station, or airport in your community or nearby. Your viewpoint should be that of total stranger to your community—a visitor from another country, perhaps. Point out any behavior, habits, or activities that appear unusual to you as an outsider.

## UNDERSTANDING LANGUAGE
### Using Concrete and Abstract Words

A **concrete word** is one that names a person or an object that can be directly observed through the senses. For example, you can see a pencil, hear a dog bark, taste salt. The words *pencil, bark,* and *salt* are concrete words. An **abstract word** is one that names qualities, conditions, or ideas that cannot be directly observed. Some interpretation is required. For example, while you can define *heroism, joy,* and *freedom,* you cannot point to them as objects. You must base your definition, instead, on specific examples of them.

Since a good short-story writer like Nadine Gordimer seldom moralizes, she favors concrete words in telling the story, although she may use abstract words in dialogue or to show the feelings of the main characters.

1. List and define five concrete words that contribute to the atmosphere of the story.
2. List and define five abstract words that show the thoughts or emotions of the characters.
3. The woman complains that her husband did not take the lion "decently." How do you think she would define the word *decency?* Explain your answer.

## THINKING AND WRITING
### Writing About Theme

The events in "The Train from Rhodesia" work together to reveal an insight into life. Identify the major theme in "The Train from Rhodesia." Write it in one carefully considered sentence. Then choose another short story in this book that has a similar theme. Write this theme, too, in a single sentence. Then write an essay in which you explain the similarities and differences between the two stories. Be specific. Give examples to support your main points. In revising the first draft, pay close attention to word choice. Have you chosen the right word in each place where an exact word is important—not merely a word that comes close? Careful word choice is one distinguishing mark of a good writer. Proofread your essay and share it with your classmates.

# ALAN SILLITOE

## 1928–

When Alan Sillitoe's first novel, *Saturday Night and Sunday Morning,* was published in 1958, one critic commented, "For the first time, English working-class life is treated . . . as a normal aspect of the human condition and as normal subject matter for a writer." Most of Sillitoe's heroes are rebellious members of the laboring class, "simple men caught in the cog-wheels of society."

Alan Sillitoe, the son of a tannery worker, was born and raised in Nottingham, an industrial city northwest of London. He left school at fourteen and worked in a bicycle plant and a plywood mill. From 1946 to 1949 he served in the Royal Air Force as a radio operator in Malaya.

He began to write while in Malaya, scrapping the manuscripts of nine complete novels before publishing and achieving immediate success with *Saturday Night and Sunday Morning.*

Sillitoe has been called one of the last of Britain's "angry young men," a group of writers in the 1950's and 1960's whose protagonists defy what they regard as outmoded political traditions and social norms. Like the other authors in this group, Sillitoe explores the theme of rebellion. Unlike them, he keeps his heroes firmly rooted in the working class, seeking self-discovery through a shared opposition to much of organized society.

His first collection of short stories, *The Loneliness of the Long-Distance Runner,* appeared in 1959. This collection, like his first novel, won immediate acclaim. The title story tells of a young juvenile delinquent who refuses to repent of the crimes that have landed him in an English reform school.

Sillitoe has also written poems and plays. Although his later work extends the range of his protagonists' rebellion, he remains primarily a chronicler of the English working classes. His restless energy has produced a body of work that is sometimes compared with that of D. H. Lawrence, another writer from Nottingham.

As with Lawrence, being poor left a permanent impression on Sillitoe's writing. Most of his work revolves around those scratching out a living on the lowest rungs of society's ladder. His understanding of poverty's effects is shown in this excerpt from his essay on the subject: "The very poor are too busy surviving to want to get on. To get on is something often dinned into them, handed down by the culture beneath which they exist. They are unable to take advantage of it, for to reach next week with clothes on your back, food still on the table, and enough life in your brain to face another week is the most they can do."

## The Fiddle

**Setting.** The setting in a work of fiction is the place and time in which the action occurs. In some stories the setting is of great importance; in others it is not. A writer presents setting in various ways. A playwright can use costumes and stage scenery to help establish the place and time of the events. A novelist or short-story writer, on the other hand, has to do it all with words. The most direct way is through extended description, although this tends to slow down the action. Many contemporary writers prefer to establish the setting by interspersing description with ongoing narration. If the setting is vital to the theme and action of the story, the writer is likely to give it prominence, often through detailed and memorable description.

Every time and every place provides a setting. As you read this assignment, you are in a setting of your own. You may be in a classroom. You may be in a living room, or a bedroom, or a kitchen. Think of some words and ideas that you associate with your present setting. Jot them down. Then write ten descriptive sentences that show the main features of your immediate environment.

From 1953 to 1958, Sillitoe and his wife lived as inexpensively as possible in Majorca while he tried to get his work published. He supplemented his small service pension by translating and teaching; his wife worked for a travel agency. Sillitoe sent several of his poems to Robert Graves, already famous. Graves, too, was living in Majorca, in a home he had built from the royalties from *I Claudius.* At Graves's invitation, Sillitoe visited him one Sunday, riding a borrowed bicycle. Graves autographed a copy of his book while they talked of England and the problems which writers face. Sillitoe recorded this exchange:

> "Some of your poems are good," he said, still looking at me as if waiting for some sort of recognition. "At least you end them well. So many people get off to a good start, then fizzle out half way through" . . . I said I found his remarks about my poetry encouraging, but that so far none had been published. "That doesn't matter," he replied. "As long as you keep on writing them." This wasn't the sort of truth I wanted to hear: "I'd like to see them in print." "That's no problem if you keep writing."

Graves was right; soon after, Sillitoe published his first book and has published steadily ever since.

# The Fiddle

## Alan Sillitoe

On the banks of the sinewy River Leen, where it flowed through Radford, stood a group of cottages called Harrison's Row. There must have been six to eight of them, all in a ruinous condition, but lived in nevertheless.

They had been put up for stockingers[1] during the Industrial Revolution a hundred years before, so that by now the usual small red English housebricks had become weatherstained and, in some places, almost black.

Harrison's Row had a character all of its own, both because of its situation, and the people who lived there. Each house had a space of pebbly soil rising in front, and a strip of richer garden sloping away from the kitchen door down to the diminutive River Leen at the back. The front gardens had almost merged into one piece of common ground, while those behind had in most cases retained their separate plots.

As for the name of the isolated row of cottages, nobody knew who Harrison had been, and no one was ever curious about it. Neither did they know where the Leen came from, though some had a general idea as to where it finished up.

A rent man walked down cobblestoned Leen Place every week to collect what money he could. This wasn't much, even at the best of times which, in the "thirties," were not too good—though no one in their conversa-

tion was able to hark back to times when they had been any better.

From the slight rise on which the houses stood, the back doors and windows looked across the stream into green fields, out towards the towers and pinnacles of Wollaton Hall in one direction, and the woods of Aspley Manor in the other.

After a warm summer without much rain the children were able to wade to the fields on the other side. Sometimes they could almost paddle. But after a three-day downpour when the air was still heavy with undropped water, and colored a menacing gun-metal blue, it was best not to go anywhere near the river, for one false slip and you would get sucked in, and be dragged by the powerful current along to the Trent some miles away. In that case there was no telling where you'd end up. The water seemed to flow into the River Amazon[2] itself, indicated by the fact that Frankie Buller swore blind how one day he had seen a crocodile snapping left and right downstream with a newborn baby in its mouth. You had to be careful—and that was a fact. During the persistent rain of one autumn water came up over the gardens and almost in at the back doors.

Harrison's Row was a cut-off place in that not many people knew about it unless they were familiar with the district. You went to it along St. Peter's Street, and down

---

1. **stockingers** *n.*: Stocking weavers.

2. **River Amazon:** The largest, most powerful river in South America.

**HILLSIDE IN WALES** (detail)
*L.S. Lowry*
*The Tate Gallery, London*

Leen Place. But it was delightful for the kids who lived there because out of the back gardens they could go straight into the stream of the Leen. In summer an old tin hip bath would come from one of the houses. Using it for a boat, and stripped to their white skins, the children were happy while sun and weather lasted.

The youths and older kids would eschew this fun and set out in a gang, going far beyond, to a bend of the canal near Wollaton Pit where the water was warm—almost hot —due to some outlet from the mine itself. This place was known as "'otties," and they'd stay all day with a bottle of lemonade and a piece of bread, coming back late in the evening looking pink and tired as if out of a prolonged dipping in the ritual bath. But a swim in 'otties was only for the older ones, because a boy of four had once been drowned there.

Harrison's Row was the last of Nottingham where it met the countryside. Its houses were at the very edge of the city, in the days before those numerous housing estates had been built beyond. The line of dwellings called Harrison's Row made a sort of outpost bastion before the country began.

Yet the houses in the city didn't immediately start behind, due to gardens and a piece of wasteground, which gave to Harrison's Row a feeling of isolation. It stood somewhat on its own, as if the city intended one day to leapfrog over it and obliterate the country beyond.

On the other hand, any foreign army attacking from the west, over the green fields that glistened in front, would first have to flatten Harrison's Row before getting into the innumerable streets of houses behind.

Across the Leen, horses were sometimes to be seen in the fields and, in other fields beyond, the noise of combine harvesters could be heard at work in the summer. Children living there, and adults as well, had the advantage of both town and country. On a fine evening late in August one of the unemployed husbands might be seen looking across at the noise of some machinery working in a field, his cap on but wearing no shirt, as if wondering why he was here and not over there, and why in fact he had ever left those same fields in times gone by to be forced into this bit of a suburb where he now had neither work nor purpose in life. He was not bitter, and not much puzzled perhaps, yet he couldn't help being envious of those still out there in the sunshine.

In my visions of leaving Nottingham for good—and they were frequent in those days—I never reckoned on doing so by the high road or railway. Instead I saw myself wading or swimming the Leen from Harrison's Row, and setting off west once I was on the other side.

A tale remembered with a laugh at that time told about how young Ted Griffin, who had just started work, saw two policemen one day walking down Leen Place towards Harrison's Row. Convinced they had come to arrest him for meter-breaking, he ran through the house and garden, went over the fence, jumped into the Leen—happily not much swollen—waded across to the field, then four-legged it over the railway, and made his way to Robins Wood a mile or so beyond. A perfect escape route. He stayed two days in hiding, and then crept home at night, famished and soaked, only to find that the police had not come for him, but to question Blonk next door, who was suspected of poaching. When they did get Ted Griffin he was pulled out of bed one morning even before he'd had time to open his eyes and think about a spectacular escape across the Leen.

Jeff Bignal was a young unmarried man of twenty-four. His father had been killed in the Great War,[3] and he lived with his mother at Number Six Harrison's Row, and worked down nearby Radford Pit. He was short in height, and plump, his white skin scarred back and front with livid blue patches where he had been knocked with coal at the mine face. When he went out on Saturday night he brilliantined his hair.

After tea in summer while it was still light and warm he would sit in his back garden playing the fiddle, and when he did everybody else came out to listen. Or they opened the doors and windows so that the sound of his music drifted in, while the woman stayed at the sink or wash-copper,

3. **Great War:** World War I.

or the man at his odd jobs. Anyone with a wireless would turn it down or off.

Even tall dark sallow-faced elderly Mrs. Deaffy (a kid sneaked into her kitchen one day and thieved her last penny-packet of cocoa and she went crying to tell Mrs. Atkin who, when her youngest came in, hit him so hard with her elbow that one of his teeth shot out and the blood washed away most of the cocoa-stains around his mouth)—old Mrs. Deaffy stood by her back door as if she weren't stone deaf any more and could follow each note of Jeffrey Bignal's exquisite violin. She smiled at seeing everyone occupied, fixed or entranced, and therefore no torment to herself, which was music enough to her whether she could hear it or not.

And Blonk, in the secretive dimness of the kitchen, went on mending his poaching nets before setting out with Arthur Bede next door on that night's expedition to Gunthorpe by the banks of the Trent, where the green escarpment between there and Kneeton was riddled with warrens and where, so it was said, if you stood sufficiently still the rabbits ran over your feet, and it was only necessary to make a quick grab to get one.

Jeff sat on a chair, oblivious to everybody, fed up with his day's work at the pit and only wanting to lose himself in his own music. The kids stopped splashing and shouting in the water, because if they didn't they might get hauled in and clouted with just the right amount of viciousness to suit the crime and the occasion. It had happened before, though Jeff had always been too far off to notice.

His face was long, yet generally cheerful—contrary to what one would expect—a smile settling on it whenever he met and passed anybody on the street, or on his way to the group of shared lavatories at the end of the Row. But his face was almost down and lost to the world as he sat on his chair and brought forth his first sweet notes of a summer's evening.

It was said that a neighbor in the last place they had lived had taught him to play like that. Others maintained it was an uncle who had shown him how. But nobody knew for sure because when someone asked directly he said that if he had any gift at all it must have come from God above. It was known that on some Sundays of the year, if the sun was out, he went to the Methodist chapel on St. Peter's Street.

He could play anything from "Greensleeves" to "Mademoiselle from Armentières'." He could do a beautiful heart-pulling version of Handel's *Largo*, and throw in bits from *The Messiah* as well. He would go from one piece to another with no rhyme or reason, from ridiculousness to sublimity, with almost shocking abruptness, but as the hour or so went by it all appeared easy and natural, part of a long piece coming from Jeff Bignal's fiddle while the ball of the sun went down behind his back.

To a child it seemed as if the songs lived in the hard collier's muscle at the top of his energetic arm, and that they queued one by one to get out. Once free, they rushed along his flesh from which the shirtsleeves had been rolled up, and split into his fingertips, where they were played out with ease into the warm evening air.

The grass in the fields across the stream was livid and lush, almost blue, and a piebald horse stood with bent head, eating oats out of a large old pram whose wheels had long since gone. The breeze wafted across from places farther out, from Robins Wood and the Cherry Orchard, Wollaton Roughs and Bramcote Hills and even, on a day that was not too hot, from the tops of the Pennines in Derbyshire.

Jeff played for himself, for the breeze against his arm, for the soft hiss of the flowing Leen at the end of the garden, and maybe also for the horse in the field, which took no notice of anything and which, having grown tired of its oats in the pram, bent its head over the actual grass and began to roam in search of succulent pastures.

In the middle of the winter Jeff's fiddling

was forgotten. He went into the coal mine before it was light, and came up only after it had got dark. Walking down Leen Place, he complained to Blonk that it was hard on a man not to see daylight for weeks at a time.

"That's why I wain't go anywhere near the bleddy pit," Blonk said vehemently, though he had worked there from time to time, and would do so again when harried by his wife and children. "You'd do better to come out on a bit o' poaching with me and Arthur," he suggested.

It was virtually true that Jeff saw no daylight, because even on Sunday he stayed in bed most of the day, and if it happened to be dull there was little enough sky to be seen through his front bedroom window, which looked away from the Leen and up the hill.

The upshot of his complaint was that he would do anything to change such a situation. A man was less than an animal for putting up with it.

"I'd do anything," he repeated to his mother over his tea in the single room downstairs.

"But what, though?" she asked. "What can you do, Jeff?"

"Well, how do I know?" he almost snapped at her. "But I'll do summat,[4] you can be sure of that."

He didn't do anything till the weather got better and life turned a bit sweeter. Maybe this improvement finally got him going, because it's hard to help yourself towards better things when you're too far down in the dumps.

On a fine blowy day with both sun and cloud in the sky Jeff went out in the morning, walking up Leen Place with his fiddle under his arm. The case had been wiped and polished.

In the afternoon he came back without it.

"Where's your fiddle?" Ma Jones asked.

He put an awkward smile on to his pale face, and told her: "I sold it."

---

**4. summat:** Something.

"Well I never! How much for?"

He was too shocked at her brazen question not to tell the truth: "Four quid."

"That ain't much."

"It'll be enough," he said roughly.

"Enough for what, Jeff?"

He didn't say, but the fact that he had sold his fiddle for four quid rattled up and down the line of cottages till everybody knew of it. Others swore he'd got ten pounds for it, because something that made such music must be worth more than a paltry four, and in any case Jeff would never say how much he'd really got for it, for fear that someone would go in and rob him.

They wondered why he'd done it, but had to wait for the answer, as one usually does. But there was nothing secretive about Jeff Bignal, and if he'd sold his music for a mess of pottage he saw no point in not letting them know why. They'd find out sooner or later, anyway.

All he'd had to do was make up his mind, and he'd done that lying on his side at the pit face while ripping coal out with his pick and shovel. Decisions made like that can't be undone, he knew. He'd brooded on it all winter, till the fact of having settled it seemed to have altered the permanent expression of his face, and given it a new look which caused people to wonder whether he would ever be able to play the fiddle again anyway—at least with his old spirit and dash.

With the four quid he paid the first week's rent on a butcher's shop on Denman Street, and bought a knife, a chopper, and a bit of sharpening stone, as well as a wooden block. Maybe he had a quid or two more knocking around, though if he had it couldn't have been much, but with four quid and a slice of bluff he got enough credit from a wholesaler at the meat market downtown to stock his shop with mutton and beef, and in a couple of days he was in trade. The people of Harrison's Row were amazed at how easy it was, though nobody had ever thought of doing it themselves.

Like a serious young man of business Mr. Bignal—as he was now known—parted his hair down the middle, so that he didn't look so young any more, but everyone agreed that it was better than being at Radford Pit. They'd seen how he had got fed up with selling the sweat of his brow.

No one could say that he prospered, but they couldn't deny that he made a living. And he didn't have to suffer the fact of not seeing daylight for almost the whole of the winter.

Six months after opening the shop he got married. The reception was held at the chapel on St. Peter's Street, which seemed to be a sort of halfway house between Harrison's Row on the banks of the Leen and the butcher's shop on Denman Street farther up.

Everybody from Harrison's Row was invited for a drink and something to eat; but he knew them too well to let any have either chops or chitterlings (or even black puddings) on tick[5] when they came into his shop.

The people of Harrison's Row missed the sound of his fiddle on long summer evenings, though the children could splash and shout with their tin bathtub undisturbed, floundering through shallows and scrambling up to grass on the other bank, and wondering what place they'd reach if they walked without stopping till it got dark.

Two years later the Second World War began, and not long afterwards meat as well as nearly everything else was put on the ration. Apart from which, Jeff was only twenty-six, so got called up into the army. He never had much chance to make a proper start in life, though people said that he came out all right in the end.

The houses of Harrison's Row were condemned as unfit to live in, and a bus depot stands on the site.

---

**5. tick:** Credit.

The packed mass of houses on the hill behind—forty years after Jeff Bignal sold his violin—is also vanishing, and high-rise hencoops (as the people call them) are put in their place. The demolition crew knock down ten houses a day—though the foreman told me there was still work for another two years.

Some of the houses would easily have lasted a few more decades, for the bricks were perfect, but as the foreman went on:

"You can't let them stand in the way of progress"—whatever that means.

The people have known each other for generations but, when they are moved to their new estates and blocks of flats,[6] they will know each other for generations more, because as I listen to them talking, they speak a language which, in spite of everything and everyone, never alters.

––––––––––

**6. flats:** Apartments.

## THINKING ABOUT THE SELECTION
### Recalling
1. (a) What is the time, or era, of the events in this story? (b) In what city is Harrison's Row? (c) In what section of the city is the mine in which Jeff Bignal works?
2. (a) Where do the younger children swim? (b) Why do they not swim there after a heavy rain? (c) Where do the older children swim?
3. (a) Whom does Jeff Bignal credit for his ability to play the violin? (b) Whom do his neighbors credit?
4. (a) What does Jeff finally do with his fiddle? (b) Why does he do this?

### Interpreting
5. Why is the River Leen important to the people of Harrison's Row?
6. Why is the fiddle important to Jeff Bignal?
7. (a) How does Jeff rebel against his situation in life? (b) How does Blonk rebel?
8. Why will Jeff not extend credit to the people from Harrison's Row?
9. (a) What do you think the fiddle symbolizes? (b) How does this symbol help reveal the story's theme?

### Applying
10. (a) What do you think of Jeff's decision to sell his fiddle? (b) How happy do you think Jeff's butcher shop made him? Explain.

## ANALYZING LITERATURE
### Understanding Setting

**Setting** is the time and place in which the events in a literary work occur. In "The Fiddle" Alan Sillitoe describes the physical setting of Harrison's Row and the activities that formerly went on there. The entire first section of the story establishes the setting. You learn a great deal about Harrison's Row before you learn anything at all about the protagonist, Jeff Bignal. The setting helps to define the people in the story.

1. The narrator is deeply interested in the history and geography of Harrison's Row. Nevertheless, he says that "no one knew who Harrison had been, and no one was ever curious about it. Neither did they know where the Leen came from, though some had a general idea as to where it finished up." How do those details about the setting help to characterize the people who live in Harrison's Row?
2. The brief last section of the story returns to the setting. How do you think the narrator feels about a bus depot standing on the site of Harrison's Row and the construction of "high rise hencoops"? Explain.
3. Slang is highly informal language that is appropriate among friends or in casual situations. (a) Find three examples of slang in "The Fiddle." (b) How does the use of slang add local color to the story?

# MARGARET DRABBLE

## 1939–

If Margaret Drabble had not become a novelist, she might have become a famous actress. While at Cambridge University she concentrated on the theater and at one point played opposite the noted actor Derek Jacobi. Upon graduation, she joined the Royal Shakespeare Company, understudying Vanessa Redgrave as Imogen in *Cymbeline*. She then left the theater, began writing fiction, and succeeded so well in her new career that a critic in 1980 observed, "She is becoming the novelist people will turn to a hundred years from now to find out how things were. . . ."

Born in Sheffield, Drabble came from a cultured and well-educated family. Her father was a circuit judge and her mother an English teacher. "A fiery child with a hyperactive mind," according to her mother, Margaret attended a Quaker boarding school prior to Cambridge. After college, she abandoned the theater for motherhood. While she was pregnant with the first of her three children, she began to write fiction. Her first novel, *A Summer Bird-Cage,* was published in 1962. Over the years she has continued to write novels that have gained both critical and popular success. Among her best-known works are *The Millstone* (1965), *The Waterfall* (1969), *The Realms of Gold* (1975), and *The Middle Ground* (1980). Most of Drabble's protagonists are, like their creator, well-educated professional women: scholars, poets, journalists.

Sociable, composed, and levelheaded, Drabble is in great demand for interviews and personal appearances. In the fall of 1980, she received a great honor when the Queen Mother dubbed her a Commander of the British Empire. Although she possesses enormous creative energy, Drabble does not regard herself as remarkable, but—in keeping with her themes—"ordinary" and fortunate. She is a clear and perceptive writer whose dry humor and penetrating technical skill have become the hallmarks of her style. Her work has steadily flowered; many critics and readers believe that in its maturity it will achieve greatness.

Drabble, in commenting on her own work, declares that she is firmly committed to the realistic tradition of the nineteenth century. Although sometimes called a "women's novelist," she disavows feminism as a theme, believing that equal rights and opportunity for women are part of a larger whole. She maintains that her fundamental concerns are "privilege, justice, and salvation." Working in the literary tradition of Jane Austen, Charlotte Brontë, and George Eliot, she creates brilliantly realized characters who reflect the dilemmas of women in the modern world, women who are trying to integrate the demands of family life and a career.

# GUIDE FOR INTERPRETING

## Writer's Techniques

## A Voyage to Cythera

**Flat and Round Characters.** A flat character, sometimes called a stereotype or stock character, is a one-dimensional human being in literature. For example, in "The Schartz-Metterklume Method," Saki does not portray the Quabarls family in depth. It is their very shallowness, in fact, that he wishes to satirize. He has therefore made them flat characters, or stereotypes. They do not change in the course of the story, and they contribute to the plot in a predictable way.

The fictional opposite of a flat character is a round character. A round character is a three-dimensional portrait that readers can accept as resembling an actual person. The writer may provide a detailed description of the character. More important, the writer will reveal the character's motivations, emotions, and inner conflicts. Round characters may be complex, unpredictable, and inconsistent, just like real people. In narrative fiction they are generally *dynamic*—that is, they change or grow in some way during the story. (Flat characters are *static*—they do not change or grow.) An example of a round character in a short story is Margaret in Doris Lessing's "A Mild Attack of Locusts."

## Writing

An epigraph is a quotation at the beginning of a book, chapter, or story. Read the epigraph to Margaret Drabble's story carefully. Then brainstorm for several minutes on the associations and emotions suggested by this fragment of Rilke's poetry. Jot down your impressions of what the epigraph (and the story's title) may suggest about the narrative to follow.

## Primary Source

Margaret Drabble's comments in *A Woman Writer* relate closely to the dilemma that Helen, the main character in "A Voyage to Cythera," faces. Drabble thinks that the large amount of fiction written by women recently shows that "a lot of women worry about the same things at the same time, and turned to fiction to express their anxieties—not only because . . . they still had nowhere else to turn, but also because fiction is ideally suited to such themes. . . . Many people read novels in order to find patterns or images for a possible future—to know how to behave, what to hope to be like. We do not want to resemble the women of the past, but where is our future. . . . We live in an uncharted world, as far as manners and morals are concerned, we are having to make up our own morality as we go. Our subject matter is enormous, there are whole new patterns to create."

# A Voyage to Cythera[1]

## Margaret Drabble

*Beloved, lost to begin with, never greeted,*
*I do not know what tones most please you.*
*No more when the future's wave*
*hangs poised is it you I try to discern there.*
*All the greatest images in me,*
*far-off experienced landscape,*
*towers and towns and bridges and*
*unsuspected turns of the way,*
*and the power of those lands*
*once intertwined with the life of the gods:*
*mount up within me to mean you,*
*who forever elude.*

*Oh, you are the garden. . . .*
      —*Rainer Maria Rilke*[2]

There are some people who cannot get onto a train without imagining that they are about to voyage into the significant unknown; as though the notion of movement were inseparably connected with the notion of discovery, as though each displacement of the body were a displacement of the soul. Helen was so much this way, and with so little lasting justification, that she was continually surprising herself by the intensity of her expectation; she could get excited by the prospect of any journey longer than 30 miles, and the thought of travel to the Continent was enough to reduce her to a state of feverish anticipation. The mere mention of the names of certain places would make her tremble, and she was addicted to railway stations, air terminals, ports, motorways, travel brochures, and all other points and emblems of departure. A phrase in a novel could make her feel weak with desire, and when once at the Gare de l'Est[3] in Paris she saw a train with Budapest written on it, she felt her skin tighten and her hair stand on end. Her most erotic dreams were not of men but of places; she would dream of piazzas and marble fountains, of mountains and terraces with great lumps of baroque statuary, of great buildings abandoned in green fields, and she would wake from these dreams cold with the sweat of fading passion. There was a certain angle of road that never failed to affect her, whenever she approached it: a rising angle, with a bare empty curve breasting infinity, the blue-sky space of infinity. She always felt that the sea might lie beyond such rising nothingness, and sometimes it was the sea, but more often it was the Caledonian[4] Market or a row of Hampstead houses; though whatever it was was somehow irrelevant, for it was that tense moment of expectation before revelation that she so much cherished.

Once she talked of this preoccupation of hers to a much-traveled old man, and he said that she felt this way because whenever

---

**1. Cythera** (si thir′ ə): A Greek island, near which the Greek goddess of love, Aphrodite, was supposed to have arisen full-grown from the sea.
**2. Rainer Maria Rilke:** A German poet (1875–1926). The lines are from an untitled poem by Rilke.
**3. Gare de l'Est** (gär də lest): A Paris train station.
**4. Caledonian:** Scottish.

she went to a new place she hoped to fall in love. He had been the same, he said; restless, expectant; and she knew that he was telling the truth, for his life illustrated his explanation. "When I was young," he said, "I thought there was a woman waiting for me in every railway compartment, on every airplane, in every hotel. How can one not think this? One thinks the plane will crash, and that one will die, and that one must die in the arms of the woman in the next seat. Isn't that so?"

And she had, in a way, thought that it was so, though the truth was that she herself would never fall in love in any of these temporary places, for she could not speak to strangers. Though that in itself proved nothing, for she supposed that nevertheless she might one day do so, and that it might be for this one moment of sudden communication that she so persistently sought. People spoke to her, from time to time, but always the wrong people, always the motherly and the fatherly men and the dull irrepressible youths. Her own kind did not speak to her, nor she to them. She traveled once overnight from Milan, alone in a compartment with a girl who was reading the same book she herself was reading; a book both of them might have been proud to acknowledge and not a word did they exchange. Another time, in a crowded train from Edinburgh, she sat opposite a woman who started to weep as the train left the station; she wept silently and effortlessly for hours, great tears rolling down her white cheeks into the neck of her emerald-green sweater, and at York Helen offered her a cigarette, and she declined it, and ceased weeping. On another occasion a man kissed her in a corridor as they drew into Oxford; she liked him, he was a lovely man, but he was drunk and she turned away her face and turned up the collar of her coat.

And yet despite these wasted opportunities she continued to expect. Truly, she thought to herself, as she got into the London train at Reading Station late one cold night, truly, it is a proof of madness that the prospect of this journey should not appall. It is cold, the train is half an hour late, I am hungry; this is the kind of situation about which I hear my friends most tirelessly and tiresomely complain. And yet I am looking forward to it. I shall sit here in the dark and the cold, with nothing to watch but the reflection of my own face in the cold pane, and I shall not care. As soon as the train moves, I shall sit back, and feel it move with me, and feel that I am moving, although I know quite well that all I am doing is going back home again to an empty flat.[5] There will be rain and steam on the glass of this window by my face, and I shall look at it, and that will be all. What a hardened case I am, that such dull mileage should recall those other landscapes, those snowy precipices, those sunny plains, those fields of corn, those gritty swaying breakfasts in the pale light of transient Switzerland or angel-watched Marseilles. I am a child, I like to rock and dream, I dream as if I were in a cradle.

And she shut her eyes, waiting for the whistle and the metallic connections of machinery; so with her eyes shut she did not see the man come into the compartment, and could never know for certain whether he had seen her, whether he had joined her because he had wanted to join her. All she knew was that when she opened her eyes, aware of the intrusion, aware of the draft from the opened door, he was already there, putting his overcoat up on the rack, arranging his books and papers on the seat next to him, settling himself in the empty compartment as far away from her as he could, on the corridor side, diagonally opposite, where she could not fail to watch him. She turned her fur collar up defensively against her face, and arranged her legs more tidily together, and opened her book upon her knee, disclaiming all threat of human contact, coldly repelling any acknowledgment of her

---

**5. flat** *n*.: Apartment.

**SHUNTERS 1965**
*James Dolby*

presence, and all the time she watched him discreetly through her half-shut eyes. Because the truth was that not since she was 17, more years ago than she cared to think, had she sat on a train so near to such a man. When she was 17 she had sat in a compartment with an actor, on the late night train to Brighton, and he had talked to her all the way, and amused her by imitating Laurence Olivier[6] for her and other famous men whom she did not recognize and when they had parted on the station he had kissed her soft and girlish and impressionable cheek, and murmured, "Bless you, bless you," as though he had a right to bless. She had subsequently followed his unremarkable career, catching sight of his name in the *Radio Times*, admiring him once on the television, glimpsing him as he passed on the cinema screen; she felt quietly possessive about him, quietly amused by her sense of intimacy with one who must so long ago have forgotten her, and who would hardly now recognize her from what she then had been. Sometimes she wondered idly whether her preoccupation with journeys might not date from this experience; but chronologically this was not so, for her preoccupation had long preceded it. She had been this way since childhood, when she had shrunk and trembled at the sight of the huge pistons, when she had stopped her ears in delighted terror as she heard the roar of the approaching seaside train.

This man, this night, did not look as though he wished to amuse her with imitations of Laurence Olivier. He looked preoccupied. In fact, the more she watched him, the more she realized that he was almost grotesquely preoccupied. He was restless; he could not sit still: he kept picking up one book from his pile, then another, then turning over the pages of his *New Statesman*, then staring out into the corridor and onto

___
**6. Laurence Olivier:** A famous British actor (1907–1989).

the dark platform. At first she thought that he might be waiting for someone to come, half-expecting somebody to join him, but she decided that this was not so, for she could perceive no augmenting of his anxiety as the time drew on, no sudden start when the loudspeaker apologized for the delay and said that the train would leave in two minutes; nor did his nervousness seem to be directed toward the door and the platform, as it would have been had he been waiting. She recalled that she herself had once developed a dreadful pain in the neck from sitting with her neck to the window through which she knew that she might glimpse the first sign of a long-awaited arrival. But this man's nervousness was as it were diffused, rather than directed; it attached itself to nothing and to everything. She could not take her eyes off him, and not only because of the nakedness of his condition, which in another might have appeared merely ludicrous; indeed, embarrassment would have turned away her eyes, had it not been for the extreme elegance of his gestures, and the lovely angles into which each struggle against immobility brought him. There was the way he had of clutching his eyebrows with one wide-spanned long nicotine-fingered hand that filled her with an intense delight; the hand covered the eyes, bringing to him no doubt an illusion of concealment, but she could see beneath it the anxious movement of the lips, trembling with some expression that she could not catch, with speech or smiling or perhaps with a sigh. And as he made this gesture, each time, he tossed his head slightly backward, and then again forward, so that his long hair fell tenderly over his fingers. It was the color that she had always liked, but she had never before seen it adorning such vexed, haggard, and experienced features: for it was a dark gold, the color of health and innocence. It was a dark golden yellow, and it was streaked with gray. It was soft hair, and it fell gently.

When the train moved off, he flung himself back into his corner, and shut his eyes, with an appearance of resolution, as though his own restlessness had finally begun to irritate him: as though he had decided to sit still. Helen looked out of the window by her face, into the lights and darkness of the disappearing town. In one piece of glass she could see the reflection of his face, and she watched it, quite confidently aware that he would not be able to keep his eyes shut, and after a few minutes he was leaning forward in his seat once more, his elbows on his knees, staring at the ground. Then, even as she watched, she saw a thought strike him: she saw the conception of the idea, she saw him reach into his pocket and take out a pack of cigarettes and a box of matches, and abstract a cigarette, and light it, all with the dreamy movements of a habitual smoker, and yet with a kind of surprise, for the truth was, as she could so clearly see, that he had even in his abstraction forgotten the possibility of such a trivial solace. As he drew on the cigarette she could see his relief, his gratitude toward his own recollection. The smoke consoled him, and she could feel in her the nature of the consolation: for she herself, when tormented by love, had found comfort in the repetition of small and necessary acts, in washing cups and emptying bins and fastening her stockings and remembering that it was time to have a meal. It seemed clear to her that it was love that was tormenting him: she knew those painful symptoms of disease.

And indeed, ten minutes later, when the ash of his last activity lay scattered all over the floor and all over his trousers, he stood up and got a packet of letters out of his overcoat pocket, and began to read them. He could not more clearly have indicated his malady if he had turned to her and told her what was in his mind. She watched the reflection of his face as he read, ashamed now to watch him directly, though she knew that he could not know that she so keenly watched him, that she was so expert in the intimate language of his state. She felt that she could tell everything from the way he handled those letters: he was still rapt in the first five minutes of love, that brief and indefinite breathless pause before familiarity, affection, disillusion, rot, decay. The number of letters in his hands supported her divination, as well as the quality of his attention; there were five of them, only five, and the paper of them was new, although they were crumbling wearily at the folds from overuse. She felt such pangs, in his presence, of she knew not what: of envy, of regret, of desire. At his age, with those graying strands and those profound wrinkles, he must surely know the folly of his obsession, and the inevitable tragic close before him; and she found such a willful confrontation of pain almost unbearably moving. She herself, enduring daily the painful death of such an attitude, the chilly destination of such deliberately romantic embarkations, could hardly prevent the tears from rising to her eyes; and in fact, they rose, warm in the cold skin of her lids, making her nose prick and her eyes ache, yet warm, coming from within her, and chilling only at the touch of the outside air. Absurd, she said to herself, absurd: absurd to weep. His image turned into a blur, and it was like the image of time itself, human, lovely, perishing, intent.

When he had read and reread his letters, he stood up again, and got a pen out of his coat pocket, and tore a piece of paper off a block of typing paper, and started to write. He wrote slowly, after the first three words, hesitantly, as though what he was saying was of no interest, as though all the interest lay in the way of saying it. She wondered what he was, who he was, what his woman was, and jealously whether she were worth such care. He took a quarter of an hour to write his letter, and when he had finished it he had covered only half a page. She wondered whether he would have an envelope, and saw that he had; it was a brown business envelope. He folded his letter up and put it in the envelope, and then sealed it up. She waited for him to write the address, but he did not write the address: he sat there looking down at the small brown oblong, and as he looked at it she became in some indefinable way aware that he had become aware of her own presence, that he was at last considering her, in some significant way. Later, she wondered how this shadowy and delicate intimation could ever have reached her—for reach her it did, and she was one of those who believe that no intimations are too delicate to exist—and she concluded that it could only have been a sudden stillness on his part, a sudden fading of restlessness, as he returned from whatever other place he had been in to contemplate her in her proximity. She felt his attention: she endured it, for five minutes at least, before he spoke.

She was pretending to read when he spoke to her. He said to her, "I wonder, I wonder if you would do something for me?" and she looked up and met his eyes, and found that he was smiling at her with a most peculiar mixture of diffidence and vanity: he was truly nervous at the prospect of speaking to her, and those five silent minutes were a measure of his nervousness, and yet at the same time he had taken the measure of her curiosity and helpless attraction: she knew that he knew that she would like to be addressed. And his tone enchanted her, for it was her own tone: a tone of cool, anxious, irresistible appeal. She knew that he too did not speak often to strangers.

"It depends what it is," she said, smiling back at him with his own smile.

"It's a very simple thing," he said, "not at all incriminating. Or at least, not for you."

"It would be, then, for you?" she said.

"Of course it would," he said. "That's why I'm making the effort of asking you to do it."

"What is it?" she said.

"I wondered if you would address this envelope for me," he said.

"Well, yes," she said. "I don't see any harm in that. I'd do that for you."

"I thought you would do it," he said. "If I hadn't thought that you would, I wouldn't have asked you. I wouldn't have liked it if you had said no."

"I might ask you what it was about me that made you think I would say yes," she said, "but such a question might embarrass you."

"Oh," he said, "oh, no," rising to his feet and crossing to her with the envelope, "oh, no, I don't mind answering, it was because of that book you're reading, and the kind of shoes you're wearing, and the way your hair is. I liked that book when I read it."

And then he sat down by her, and handed her the envelope, and said, "Look, I'll write it down for you and you can copy it. It's hard to hear when people dictate things, isn't it?"

And he wrote the name and address on another piece of his block of paper. He wrote:

Mrs. H. Smithson,
24 Victoria Place,
London N.W.1.

And Helen dutifully copied it out, on the brown envelope, then handed it back to him.

"I hope," she said, "that my handwriting is sufficiently unlike yours."

"I was thinking," he said, "that after all it's rather similar. But dissimilar enough."

Then he said no more, but he remained sitting by her. She would in a way have preferred him to move, because where he now was she could not really see him, either overtly or covertly. And she had nothing to say to him: for she could hardly have said, I was right about you, I guessed right. He said nothing to her, for a while: he got a wallet from his pocket, and took out a sheet of fourpenny stamps, and tore one off, licked it, and stuck it on. She liked watching his hands, and the way they moved. Then, still holding the letter, he said to her, "Where do you live?"

She must have recoiled slightly from the question, because immediately he followed it up with, "Only, I was meaning, from the point of view of postmarks."

"Oh," she said. "I see. Yes. I live in S.W.7. You want me to post it, do you?"

"Would you mind posting it?" he asked.

"No. I would post it for you," she said.

"You take my point very quickly," he said, then, with some difficulty, looking downward and away from her, hardly able to bring himself to thank her more formally.

"I've had to make such points before myself," she said.

"I thought, somehow, that you would not mind about such things," he said.

"You wouldn't have asked me if you'd thought I minded. Tell me, do you really trust me to remember to post it?"

"Of course I do," he said. "One wouldn't not post a stranger's letter."

And this was so exactly the truth that it silenced her, and they said no more to each other until the train drew into Paddington: and as they walked together off the platform, he said, "Thank you, and good-bye."

And she said, "Good-bye," and she carried the letter in her hand all the way home, and dropped it into the letterbox on her block. Then she went down the basement steps to her dark flat, and she knew that the name and the address, written there in her own writing, so strangely, were imprinted upon her memory forever.

And indeed, over the next month, she sometimes fancied that she thought of little else. She knew that this was not the truth, that it was merely a fancy, because of course she did think of other things; of her job, of her friends, of her mother, of what to buy for supper, of whether she wanted to go to the cinema on Wednesday night. But she did not think of these other things in the mad, romantic, obsessive way that she thought of Mrs. H. Smithson, and the nameless man, and the whole curious, affecting incident: in a sense she resented the incident, because it did so much to vindicate her own crazy expectancy, her foolish faith in revelation. She knew, in her better, saner self, that such faith was foolish, and she suspected that such partial hints of its validity were a delusion, a temptation, and that if she heeded them she would be disabled forever, and disqualified from real life, as Odysseus would have been by the Sirens.[7] And yet at the same time she knew, in her other self, that it was that man she was thinking about, however unreasonably. She looked for him as she walked along the streets of London, and she could not convince herself that it was not for him that she was looking. She speculated about the identity and appearance of Mrs. Smithson, and supplied her endlessly with Christian names, until she remembered that the H. might well have stood for her husband's name, not hers. She speculated about the deceived husband. Although most of her own friends were married and had children, she still found it hard to acknowledge that Mrs. Smithson might well be a woman of her own generation, for the prefix *Mrs.* invariably supplied her with a material image, the image of her own mother: and she would realize from time to time, with a start, that the women that she thought of as mothers were in fact grandmothers, and that the young girls she saw pushing prams on Saturday mornings and quarreling with vigorous toddlers on buses were not in fact elder sisters but mothers,

---

**7. Odysseus . . . Sirens:** In Homer's *Odyssey*, Odysseus, the hero, plugs his ears so that he will not be tempted by the singing of the sirens, sea nymphs whose enchanting songs lured sailors to their deaths on rocky coastlines.

Mrs. Smithson, Mrs. Smithson. She could not give form to Mrs. Smithson.

It was in the week before Christmas that she decided to go and have a look at Mrs. Smithson. The idea occurred to her at lunchtime one day, in the middle of a lunchtime business Christmas party. She stood there, drinking too much and not getting enough to eat, defeated as ever by the problems of buffet technique, and as she listened to a very nice man whom she had known and liked for several years describe to her the felicities of his new central heating, she suddenly decided to go and look at Mrs. Smithson. After all, she said to herself, what could be more harmless, what more undetectable? All I need to do is to knock on her door and ask, say, for Alice. And then I would know. I don't know what I would know, but I would know it. And she smiled at the man, and allowed her glass to be once more filled, and then told him politely all about some other friends of hers whose central heating had entirely ruined all their antique furniture, and split all the antique paneling of their rather priceless house. And as she talked, she was already in her heart on her way to Mrs. Smithson's, already surrendering to the lure of that fraught, romantic, painful world, which seemed to call her, to call her continually from the endurable sorrows of daily existence to some possible other country of the passions, a country where she felt she would recognize, though strange to it, the scenery and landmarks. She thought often of this place, as of some place perpetually existing, and yet concealed: and she could describe it to herself only in terms of myth or allegory, unsatisfactory terms, she felt, and perniciously implanted in her by her classical education. It was a place other than the real world, or what she felt to be the real world, and it was both more beautiful and more valid, though valid in itself only: and it could be entered not at will, but intermittently, by accident, and yet always

with some sense of temptation and surrender. Some people, she could see, passed most of their lives in its confines, and governed by its laws only, like that old man, himself a poet, who had first defined for her the nature of her expectations. There were enough of such people in the world to keep alive before her the possibility of a permanent, irreversible entry through those mysteriously inscribed and classic gates: a poet, a drunken Frenchman, a girl she had known who said one day: "I will go to Baghdad," and went. They crossed her path, these people, or their names came to her, garlanded with wreaths of that unfamiliar foliage: Yves was seen in Marseilles carrying a lobster, Esther was seen in a bookshop in New York wearing a fur coat and with diamonds in her hair, Esther was in Marrakesh, living in one room with an Arab. Yves had gone to Ireland and started a lobster farm. Oh, messages from a foreign country, oh, disquieting glimpses of brightness. Helen gulped down the remains of her fourth glass of wine, and looked at her watch, which said that it was five past three; and said to the central-heating man that she must go.

She walked to Victoria Place, pausing dazed at traffic lights, stumbling at each irregularity of the pavement, running her hand idly along grimy railings. It was cold, but she could not feel the cold: her face was burning. She knew her way because she had looked Victoria Place up a month ago, the day after she had posted the letter, in her *A to Z Guide to London:* she remembered the moment when she had done so, because she had pretended to herself that she was doing no such thing, and her mind had not known what her hands and eyes were doing. But her mind now remembered what it had then refused to acknowledge, and she took herself there as though entranced, the trance persisting long after the effects of walking had dispelled the effects of so much drink on so empty a stomach. I must be mad, she said to herself more than once: I must be mad. And at the very end of the journey she began, very slightly, to lose her nerve: she thought that she would not dare to knock upon the door, she thought that perhaps after all only insignificant disaffection could await her, that she could do no more than dispel what had already in its own way been perfection.

But there was no need to knock at the door. Victoria Place, when she reached it, was a short main street of tall terraced houses, either newly recovered or so smart that they had never lapsed: the number 24 was brightly illuminated, shining brightly forth into the gathering darkness. She walked slowly toward it, realizing that she would be able to see whatever there was to see without knocking: realizing that fate had connived with her curiosity by providing a bus stop directly outside the house, so that she could stand there and wait without fear of detection. She took her place at the bus stop, and stood there for a moment before she gathered her courage to turn around, and then she turned. The lights were on in the two lower floors, and she could see straight into the basement, a room which most closely resembled in shape the one where she herself lived. The room seemed at first sight to be full of people, and there was so much activity that it took some time to sort them out. There were two women, and four children; no, five children, for there was a baby sitting in a corner on a blue rug. The larger children were putting up a Christmas tree, and one of the women was laying the table for tea, while the other, her back to the window, one elbow on the mantelpiece, appeared to be reading aloud a passage from a book. It was a large, bright room, with a green carpet, and white walls, and red painted wooden furniture; even the table was painted red. A children's room. It shone, it glittered. A mobile of golden fishes hung from the ceiling, and the carpet was strewn with colored glass and tinsel decorations for the tree. The plates on the table

were blue and white, and the silver knives caught the light; on the mantelpiece stood two many-faceted cut glasses and an open bottle of wine. Two of the children had fair hair, and the other three were dark: and the woman laying the table had red hair, a huge coil of dark red hair from which whole heavy locks escaped, dragging down the back of her neck, falling against her face at each movement, and she moved endlessly, restlessly, vigorously, taking buns out of a bag, slicing bread, pouring black currant juice into beakers, turning to listen to the other woman, and suddenly laughing, throwing back her head with a kind of violence and laughing: and the other woman at the mantelpiece laughed too, her thin shoulders shaking, and the children, irritated by their mother's laughter, flung themselves at her, clinging angrily onto her knees, shouting, until the red-haired woman tried to silence them with slices of bread and butter, which were rejected and flung around the floor: so she followed them up with the iced buns, tossing them round and yet talking, all the time talking, to the other woman and not to the children, intent upon some point, some anecdote too precious to lose, and the children chewed at the buns while she scooped up the torn pieces of bread and bestowed them all, with a smile of such lovely passing affection, upon the baby, a smile so tender and amused and solicitous that Helen, overseeing it, felt her heart stand still.

And as she stood there, out there in the cold, and watched, she felt herself stiffen slowly into the breathlessness of attention: because it seemed to her that she had been given, freely, a vision of something so beautiful that its relevance could not be measured. The hints and arrows that had led her here took on the mysterious significance of fate itself: she felt that everything was joined and drawn together, that all things were part of some pattern of which she caught by sheer chance a sudden hopeful sense: and that those two women, and their children, and the man on the train, and the bright and radiant uncurtained room, an island in the surrounding darkness, were symbols to her of things too vague to name, of happiness, of hope, of brightness, warmth, and celebration. She gazed into that room, where emotion lay, like water unimaginably profound. The red-haired woman was kneeling now, on the green carpet, rubbing with a corner of the tea towel at a buttery mark on the carpet, and at the same time looking up and listening, with an expression upon her face in which vexation with the children, carelessness of her own vexation, and a kind of soft rapt delight in the other woman's company were inextricably confused; and the other woman had turned slightly, so that Helen from the window could see her face, and she was twisting in her hands a length of red-and-silver tinsel, idly pulling shreds from it as she spoke. And Helen thought of all the other dark cold rooms of London and the world, of loneliness, of the blue chilly flickerings of television sets, of sad children, silenced mothers, and unmarried girls and she wondered if so much delight were truly gathered up and concentrated into one place, or whether these windows were not windows through which she viewed the real huge spacious anterior lovely world. And it seemed possible to see them so, because she did not know that house, nor those women, nor their names, nor the name of the man who had led her there: the poetry of inspiration being to a certain extent, as she knew, the poetry of ignorance, and the connections between symbols a destructive folly to draw. She did not even know which of these women was Mrs. Smithson, whom she had come to see, for if one woman had laid the table, the other cleared it, equally at home. She knew nothing, and could therefore believe everything, drawing faith from such a vision, as she had drawn faith from unfamiliar cities: drawing faith from the passionate vision of intimacy, where intimacy itself failed her; as Wordsworth turned from his life to his keener recollec-

tions,[8] and Yeats to lions and towers and hawks.[9]

By the time that one of the children was sent to draw the curtains, she was stiff and white with cold. She turned away, as the child, a small girl with straight dark hair and a face suddenly grave with the weight of her task, began to struggle with the heavy floor-length hangings, shutting inch by inch away from her the colored angles of refracted light, the Christmas tree, the airy fishes, the verdant green, the small angelic innocent faces, the shining spheres of glass, and those two young worn women: and as she turned she felt the first snowflakes of the year settle softly on her skin, and looking up, she saw the dim blue sky full of snow. She glanced back, to see if the child had seen it, but the curtains were already drawn, and she saw nothing but her own image, pale in the glass. So she started to walk down the street, away from the house, away from the bus stop, but before she had taken ten steps a car drew up, just by her side, a slow yard from her, and there was the man from the train, sitting there and looking at her. She paused, and he opened the door, and sitting there still he said to her, "I don't know what to say to you, you look so fragile that a word might hurt you." And she smiled at him, a slow dazed smile, knowing that as he for her, so she for him was some mysterious apparition, some faintly gleaming memorable image: and she turned away, and walked down the street away from him into the snowy darkness, and he got out of his car and went into the house.

She walked carefully, because her ankles were so brittle from the cold that she feared that if she stumbled, they would snap.

---

**8. Wordsworth . . . recollections:** British poet William Wordsworth (1770–1850) delved into memories of his youth in his poetry, recollecting the emotion of childhood in the tranquility of adulthood.
**9. Yeats . . . hawks:** British poet William Butler Yeats (1865–1939) developed his own mythology.

## THINKING ABOUT THE SELECTION
### Recalling

1. (a) At the beginning of the story, what is Helen's attitude toward journeys? (b) According to "a much-traveled old man," why does she feel this way?
2. (a) What conclusion does Helen reach about the man on the train from Reading to London? (b) What does the man ask her to do?
3. (a) What does the man at the office Christmas party talk about? (b) How does Helen respond? (c) At what point does she leave?
4. (a) When Helen visits Victoria Place, what does she plan to do there? (b) What does she actually do? (c) What does she observe? (d) Who arrives as she starts to walk away?

### Interpreting

5. Why do you think Helen is so obsessed with catching a glimpse of Mrs. Smithson?
6. (a) In the last scene of the story, what meaning does the "vision" that Helen sees have for her? (b) Why does Helen think that connections between symbols are "a destructive folly to draw"?
7. (a) The title of this story is an allusion. The reader is expected to know that Cythera is a Greek island where Aphrodite, the goddess of love, arose full-grown from the sea. How are the implications of the story's title fulfilled in an unexpected way at the end? (b) How does the title relate to the theme?
8. In what way or ways has Helen changed or grown as a consequence of her experiences?

### Applying

9. What do you think the chances are that Helen will ever fall in love with a specific man?

## CRITICAL THINKING AND READING
### Identifying Kinds of Evidence

**Direct evidence** is straightforward factual information that leads to an obvious conclusion. When the narrator says that the man on the train "took out a sheet of fourpenny stamps, and tore one off, licked it, and stuck it on" the envelope, you have direct evidence of an intent to mail the letter or to have it mailed. **Indirect evidence** requires much more interpretation. For example, when the narrator says that "there was no need to knock at the door" of the house on Victoria Place, you can infer that Helen is relieved to avoid a face-to-face meeting with Mrs. Smithson. But the evidence is indirect; you have to use other information about Helen's personality to reach that conclusion.

1. Identify the kind of evidence—direct or indirect—in each of the following inferences: (a) that Helen had been to France; (b) that Helen liked the man who kissed her on a train as it drew into Oxford; (c) that Helen had received an excellent education; (d) that Helen was bored by the man's talk about central heating at the Christmas party.
2. (a) What kind of evidence does Helen use on the train to support her conclusion about the unnamed man? (b) How accurately does she seem to have interpreted the evidence?

## THINKING AND WRITING
### Writing About Characterization

Fictional characters, whether flat or round, must be believable. They may sometimes act in unexpected ways, but they should not act out of character. A flat, stock-character clown should not suddenly and for no apparent reason become a dashing hero. A round, carefully developed character like Helen in "A Voyage to Cythera" may change and grow, but she must do so within the personality given her by the writer. Helen is a complex but consistent character. Write an essay in which you discuss three of Helen's encounters with other people, explaining how in each one she acts true to the personality that the author has given her. Begin by choosing the three encounters. Make notes about them. Then write your first draft, showing Helen's consistency from one encounter to the next. In revising your first draft, make sure you have supplied clear connections.

# LORD OF THE FLIES
## by William Golding

Picture yourself on an unspoiled, isolated tropical island. Lush green palm trees wave in the soft breeze and the sun glitters like a coin pasted on the clear blue sky. The waves gently roll over the warm golden sand. Maybe you would pass endless afternoons catching the rays, watching the sparkling ocean, and listening to the monkeys chattering as they swing among the vines. How about gathering fragrant blood-red blossoms? If you were hungry, you need only reach up to the nearest tree to pluck luscious fruit still warm from the sun or drink sweet coconut milk. Now add a group of classmates your own age—no adults, please!—and paradise would certainly be complete. This is the setting for William Golding's 1954 classic story of good and evil, *Lord of the Flies.* But on Golding's fictional tropical island, things turn out very differently from what we would expect . . .

## A Futuristic Tale

The novel opens sometime in the future, in the modern age of hostile superpowers, murderous weapons, and vicious battles. The world has been plunged into a deadly atomic war. A group of English schoolboys, aged six to twelve, has been ejected from a flaming airplane onto a South Sea island in

a last-ditch effort to save their lives. Fortunately, none of the boys has been injured. The first boy we encounter is tall, blond-haired, and good-looking. Soon we learn that his name is Ralph, that he is about twelve years old, and that he is cheerful and decent. His father was a commander in the Navy, and his well-to-do home in England was a pleasant place, with "treats" before bed, books to read, and a walled garden visited by wild ponies. As he picks his way toward the lagoon, he hears a voice.

The voice belongs to a stout, nearsighted, and asthmatic boy of about the same age as Ralph. He is identified only by the unflattering nickname "Piggy." With his thin hair, soft body, and eyeglasses, it is plain to see that he would be the butt of schoolboy jokes. As they play by the lagoon, Piggy speaks of a background very different from

Ralph's. His father dead, his mother run off, Piggy was raised by his aunt, who ran a sweet shop, a decidedly working-class occupation. Although neither handsome nor charming, Piggy seems far more intelligent than Ralph: He tells Ralph what he overheard the pilot saying about the atomic attack, stresses how slim is the possibility of rescue, and questions how to determine whether they are on an island or peninsula.

Suddenly the boys spot something large and creamy-colored in the lagoon. Ralph pulls a sapling from the bank, enabling Piggy to pull the object from the water. It is a huge conch shell, fully eighteen inches across. At Piggy's direction, Ralph blows into the shell, which emits a deep, booming cry. The blast acts like a siren, summoning the other boys.

First, a number of small boys wander over to Ralph and Piggy. Ragged and dirty, their faces smeared with sticky masses of fruit, the little boys arrange themselves on the fallen palm trunks at Ralph's feet. They are joined by a pair of identical towheaded twins, who give their names as Sam and Eric. Like an outstretched black snake, a line of boys dressed incongruously in long black cloaks with silver crosses on their chests appears on the horizon. As the line of boys approaches the others, their leader vaults to the platform and confronts Ralph. This is Jack Merridew. Tall, red-haired, and ugly, he leads his black-cloaked church choir with an iron fist. Only when Simon—a small, thin boy with a pointed chin and bright eyes—faints, does he allow the others to rest in the shade. From the way the choir obeys him, it is plain that he has leadership abilities. Yet despite the choir's allegiance, Ralph is elected chief on the basis of his appearance and his possession of the already-powerful symbol of the conch. Ralph selects Jack and Simon to accompany him on an expedition to discover whether they are indeed on an island. If you were in Ralph's place, what action would you have undertaken first—exploring, building shelter, or gathering food?

Scrambling up the cliffs and through the underbrush, the three boys learn that they are indeed stranded on an island. They also see the place where they crashed and encounter wild pigs. Upon their return, Ralph and Jack ignore Piggy's advice and order a signal fire built before they erect shelter. The chilling fear lurking just below the surface emerges that evening, when the little ones wail about a monster they call the "beastie." Things turn decidedly nasty when a little one disappears in the fire . . .

## Not a Paradise After All

Slowly, we begin to see that the tropical island may not be the paradise it first appeared—and the boys' subsequent adventure will be very different from what we expect. First, take the matter of food. Although the boys have only to pluck the fruit off the trees to eat, the fruit is often green and frequently makes them ill. At times, the island is torn by fierce tropical storms that uproot whole trees. Annoying insects, sharp thorns, rot, and decay are everywhere visible. The boys are plagued by hunger, stomach upsets, insect bites, deep scratches, and sunburn. Then there is the boys' terror of isolation and their desperate attempts to signal a passing ship which can return them to the world they have lost. Will a passing ship spot their signal fire and rescue them? But by far the most important element is the struggle for power and survival. Who will be in charge? How will he rule? And how will the others react?

## Other Tales of Castaways

Now, stories about people castaway on idyllic tropical islands are nothing new. Ever since 1719, when Daniel Defoe landed Robinson Crusoe on a desert island, literature has abounded with tales of castaways. Probably the most well-known among these are Jonathan Swift's *Gulliver's Travels*, Jules Verne's *The Mysterious Island*, and J. D. Wyss's *The Swiss Family Robinson*.

## Themes in *Lord of the Flies*

We know, then, that romantic adventure tales of castaways are not unique, and that Golding even modeled *Lord of the Flies* on one of the most well-known of these novels, *The Coral Island* by R. M. Ballantyne. But Golding is using the time-honored castaway story to a very different end. His purpose is to address the main concern we have today: the nature of the human personality and the reflection of that personality on society. The message that underlies Golding's tale, however, is so startling and controversial that *Lord of the Flies* has become the most influential novel among American high school and college students since J. D. Salinger's *Catcher in the Rye*, published in 1951. Speaking of the success of *Lord of the Flies*, noted critic Lionel Trilling remarked, "First, apparently, in the colleges, then in secondary schools, it seems to have captured the imagination of a whole generation." This first novel—from the unlikely hand of a forty-three-year-old teacher and wartime commander in the British Royal Navy—established its author as one of the most "dynamic, exciting, and controversial figures in contemporary British literature."

For *Lord of the Flies* is a bloody, tragic tale about how human behavior changes when the ordinary social controls are absent. In a completely convincing and often very frightening way, the novel shows what happens when all the trappings of everyday society are slowly stripped away.

What do you think would happen in a world without social controls? Obviously your answer depends on whether you believe that people are basically good or basically evil. Do you think people are fundamentally decent and kind but have had the misfortune of being born into a very bad world? If so, you would agree with French philosopher Jean Jacques Rousseau. He wrote that people are born noble and moral, but they are systematically corrupted by an evil society. Do you think, as Rousseau did, that if society were to change, all our troubles would lessen? Steinbeck's *The Grapes of Wrath*, Salinger's *The Catcher in the Rye*, and Shakespeare's *Hamlet* all provide examples of good people whose troubles are forced on them from the society in which they live.

Or do you think that people are basically evil? In this case, society acts as a brake to hold their vicious impulses under control. If so, you would agree with Golding's point in *Lord of the Flies*. Vividly, with a brilliantly conveyed sense of mounting terror, *Lord of the Flies* exposes Golding's view of the desperate wickedness of the human heart. As the boys attempt to impose order on chaos,

they reveal the irrationality at the heart of existence. With gruesome detail, the story unfolds the end of innocence and the realization of universal evil. It is easy to see how the view Golding takes in *Lord of the Flies* has sparked a heated controversy that continues to ignite millions of readers.

The title hints of the novel's main point. The "Lord of the Flies" is the name Simon gives to the head of a wild pig that the others have slaughtered. After the kill, the pig's skull is impaled on a stick, where it is promptly infested by flies. The term "Lord of the Flies" is a translation of the Hebrew word "Baalzebub" or "Beelzebub"–the "chief of the devils." In referring to the devil, Simon is commenting on what he sees happening around him.

In its message and method, *Lord of the Flies* seems at first glance to resemble Orwell's equally grim view of the future, *1984;* however, the novels are fundamentally very different. First, Orwell is writing as a satirist in *1984*. As such, he does not want to symbolize humanity's condition or even the plight of modern man. His object is simply to record as forcefully as he can the fearful symptoms which he had observed developing in Russia, America, and England in the thirties and forties. To do this, he exaggerates what he has seen of the abuses of power. *1984* is not about eternal values or about the future of the world; it is about the present. *Lord of the Flies*, in contrast, offers no such specific portrait of the modern world. Rather, it is an attempt to trace the defects of society back to the defects of the human race. In so doing, it offers a crushing commentary on humanity's doomed attempt to build a rational society.

According to critics Ian Gregor and Mark Kinkead-Weekes, "Mr. Golding's book is valuable to us, not because it 'tells us about' the darkness of man's heart, but because it shows us, because it is a work of art which enables us to enter into the world it creates and live at the level of a deeply perceptive and intelligent man."

# Poetry

**MOUNT FUJI AND FLOWERS, 1972**
*David Hockney*
*Metropolitan Museum of Art*

# PHILIP LARKIN

## 1922–1985

Should a poem be heavily symbolic and filled with images or should it be simple and straightforward? Few poets made better use of the ordinary in both content and style than did Philip Larkin. Once connected with "the Movement," a group of poets whose work first appeared in Robert Conquest's 1956 anthology *New Lines,* Larkin then established his own unique place in contemporary literature. Writing in a poetic form that approximates conversation, he raised familiar experiences to the level of art. His poems were often wry, self-critical, and understated, "part sigh, part affirmation," as one critic stated. Poetry for Larkin was a part-time job; his full-time job was that of librarian at the University of Hull, a major seaport on the east coast of England.

Philip Larkin was born in Coventry, England. A graduate of St. John's College, Oxford, Larkin began his writing career as a novelist. He later served as jazz correspondent of the *Daily Telegraph.* His poetry, which was the source of his international fame, displays a clear-eyed honesty that captures moments of startling truth. Often it contains a narrator who observes the world around him with detachment. Larkin's poetry has frequently been compared with that of Thomas Hardy, whom he admired.

The detachment central to much of Larkin's verse was apparent during his childhood as well. He wrote that "I was not happy in school. Admittedly it was an affair of being more frightened than hurt, but it was being hurt sometimes, and being frightened was not very pleasant." Regardless, he distinguished himself early, and won numerous academic prizes. No doubt part of his achievement was due to the strong influence of his father, Sydney Larkin. The brilliant administrator of the City Treasury of Coventry, the senior Larkin could be merciless with those who fell short of his rigid standards. Noel Hughes, Philip's childhood friend, recalled Mr. Larkin's forceful personality and the cool feeling in the household. "In spite of the unfailing graciousness of Mrs. Larkin's welcome," Huges commented, "the atmosphere of Philip's home, with its intimidating tidiness, its highly waxed furniture and practice of hushed conversation, impressed me as solemn." Hughes believes that "there is in Philip much that is reminiscent of his father."

From his father Larkin absorbed his love for the writings of D. H. Lawrence, his superb mastery of languages, and his attention to appearance. He was cultured and polite in manner—almost courtly. To the poets of ensuing generations he has left a legacy of high standards, learning, and attention to detail.

# GUIDE FOR INTERPRETING

## Days; The Explosion; Coming

**Writer's Techniques**

**Tone.** In casual conversation, the words people use and the way they say them suggest an attitude and create a mood. In poetry, the writer's attitude toward his or her subject and the mood created by the language are called **tone**. Tone can be solemn, playful, cynical, angry; or it can have any of dozens of other attributes. In general, tone reflects the writer's attitude and puts the reader in the same kind of mood. Tone is created by the ideas in the poem as well as by verbal elements such as meter, sentence structure, diction, and imagery.

**Writing**

Write a short imperative sentence. (*Do the dishes,* for example; or *Mow the lawn.*) Then rewrite it, putting the same thought into *five* different sentences, each with a different tone. Your rewritten sentences will probably be longer than the original. Choose your five different tones from the following list.

| | | | | |
|---|---|---|---|---|
| angry | bored | eager | friendly | timid |
| blunt | desperate | formal | pompous | vague |

Be prepared to read your sentences in class to see if your class-mates can identify the tone of each sentence.

**Primary Source**

One day fellow writer Kingsley Amis spoke with longtime friend Philip Larkin about two of the greatest prizes writers can receive: the Nobel Prize for Literature and the Poet Laureateship of Great Britain. Amis was astonished at his friend's reaction. Anthony Thwaite records his reaction in *Larkin At Sixty*.

> In 1976 or so he and I were in a taxi on our way to a drink in London. I said into a silence, without premeditation,
> "What chance of the Nobel?"
> "Oh, that's gone," he said decisively. "I thought they might be keeping it warm for a chap like me—you know, a chap who never *writes* anything or *does* anything or *says* anything. But now I find they've just given it to a . . . [fellow] who never *writes* anything or *does* anything or *says* anything. No, that's *gone*."
> After a pause, I asked, "What about the Laureateship?"
> "I dream about that sometimes," he said in the same tone, "*and wake up screaming.* Nah, with any luck they'll pass me over."

# Days

## Philip Larkin

What are days for?
Days are where we live.
They come, they wake us
Time and time over.
5  They are to be happy in;
Where can we live but days?

Ah, solving that question
Brings the priest and the doctor
In their long coats
10  Running over the fields.

---

## THINKING ABOUT THE SELECTION

### Recalling

1. In your own words, what is the speaker's answer to the first question in the poem?

### Interpreting

2. Why does the answer to the second question bring the priest and the doctor running?

### Applying

3. What would be different about the thought in this poem if Larkin had substituted the word *life* for the word *days*?

## ANALYZING LITERATURE

### Understanding Tone

**Tone** is the attitude that a writer takes toward his or her subject, characters, or audience. In a poem, tone is conveyed to a great extent by word choice.

1. How would you describe the tone of "Days"?
2. How does the interjection *Ah* at the beginning of line 7 affect the tone of the poem?
3. How would the tone of the poem be different if lines 6–10 did not exist?

# The Explosion

Philip Larkin

On the day of the explosion
Shadows pointed towards the pithead:
In the sun the slagheap slept.

Down the lane came men in pitboots
5   Coughing oath-edged talk and pipe-smoke,
Shouldering off the freshened silence.

One chased after rabbits; lost them;
Came back with a nest of lark's eggs;
Showed them; lodged them in the grasses.

10    So they passed in beards and moleskins,
      Fathers, brothers, nicknames, laughter,
      Through the tall gates standing open.

      At noon, there came a tremor; cows
      Stopped chewing for a second; sun,
15    Scarfed as in a heat-haze, dimmed.

      *The dead go on before us, they*
      *Are sitting in God's house in comfort,*
      *We shall see them face to face—*

      Plain as lettering in the chapels
20    It was said, and for a second
      Wives saw men of the explosion

      Larger than in life they managed—
      Gold as on a coin, or walking
      Somehow from the sun towards them,

25    One showing the eggs unbroken.

---

## THINKING ABOUT THE SELECTION

### Recalling

1. Where do the events in the poem occur?
2. What immediate effect does the explosion have on life above ground?
3. (a) What do the widows of the miners see "for a second" at the funeral services? (b) What else in the poem lasts "for a second"?

### Interpreting

4. How does the first stanza foreshadow events in the poem?

5. In your own words, explain line 5.
6. (a) What is the mood of the men going to work? (b) What details show this mood?
7. Why are lines 16–18 printed in italics?
8. What is the symbolic meaning of the eggs?
9. How would you describe the tone of "The Explosion"?

### Applying

10. What relationship is there between the theme of "Days" and the theme of "The Explosion"?

# Coming

## Philip Larkin

On longer evenings,
Light, chill and yellow,
Bathes the serene
Foreheads of houses.
5  A thrush sings,
Laurel-surrounded
In the deep bare garden,
Its fresh-peeled voice
Astonishing the brickwork.
10  It will be spring soon,
It will be spring soon—
And I, whose childhood
Is a forgotten boredom,
Feel like a child
15  Who comes on a scene
Of adult reconciling,
And can understand nothing
But the unusual laughter,
And starts to be happy.

---

## THINKING ABOUT THE SELECTION

### Recalling

1. In "Coming" what are two signs of spring that the speaker notices?
2. With what kind of attitude does the speaker look back on childhood?

### Interpreting

3. The speaker draws a comparison between the coming of spring and a child witnessing the end of an adult argument. What similarities are there between the two occasions?

### Applying

4. In writing about the seasons, the nature writer Hal Borland observed, "April is a promise that May is bound to keep." Explain this statement.

## THINKING AND WRITING

### Writing About Tone

Write an essay in which you compare and contrast the tone of the three Larkin poems. Find and jot down words, phrases, or lines that support your assessment of the tone of each poem. In your first draft, be sure that the quoted lines actually make the points you say they do. When revising, eliminate vague or meaningless statements. You will find that in writing about literature, you can easily fall into the trap of writing sentences that, upon analysis, convey very little information.

# GUIDE FOR INTERPRETING

## Taylor Street

**Thom William Gunn** (1929-    ) was born in Gravesend, England and educated at Cambridge. He became, to his own surprise, one of "the Movement" poets of the 1950's. In the mid-1950's he moved to California, studied at Stanford University, and taught at the University of California, Berkeley. In 1960 Gunn decided to settle permanently in San Francisco, give up teaching, and devote himself full-time to writing. In his verse as well as in his life, he straddles the English and American traditions. Some critics say that his celebration of men of action (such as soldiers, motorcyclists, and tough boys), his fascination with violence, and his glorification of popular heroes such as Elvis Presley come from the American culture; his low-keyed, cool, informal manner, the British. This synthesis of the two cultures partly accounts for the intense critical controversy that swirls around him. An American reviewer labeled him "a fashionable, rote versifier of some skill and intelligence . . . [whose work] has not the slightest power to touch you." Yet he is very highly regarded in England, and his first book, *Fighting Terms,* was praised by noted critic A. Alvarez as "the most impressive first book of poems since Robert Lowell's." Gunn, who has published steadily since the 1950's, is well represented in anthologies and has won many literary awards.

**Writer's Techniques**

**Diction.** Diction is word choice. Choosing the best and most appropriate words is essential to effective writing. A writer—especially a poet—must select his or her words carefully to express the exact nuances intended. Diction can be as simple as that in a primer's "See Spot run" or as ornate as that in John Milton's *Paradise Lost:*

> Nor was his name unheard or unadored
> In ancient Greece, and in Ausonian land
> Men called him Mulciber; and how he fell
> From Heaven, they fabled, thrown by angry Jove
> Over the crystal battlements.

Diction can be as formal as a speech to Parliament or as informal as current Cockney slang. In choosing their words, writers take into account the subject, the theme, and the audience. Intent determines diction.

As you read Thom Gunn's "Taylor Street," pay close attention to the words he uses. Try to determine the effect of the words.

# Taylor Street

## Thom Gunn

The small porch of imitation
marble is never sunny, but
outside the front door he
sits on his kitchen chair facing
5   the street. In the bent yellowish
face, from under the brim
of a floppy brown hat,
his small eyes watch what
he is not living. But he
10  lives what he can:
watches without a smile, with
a certain strain, the warmth
of his big crumpled
body anxiously cupped
15  by himself in himself, as
he leans over himself not
over the cold railing, unmoving but carefully getting
a little strength from the sight of the
20  passers-by. He has it
all planned: he will live
here morning by morning.

## THINKING ABOUT THE SELECTION
### Recalling

1. (a) Where is the man in the poem sitting? (b) What are three details of his appearance?
2. (a) According to lines 8 and 9, what is the man watching? (b) How is this activity made more definite in lines 19 and 20?

### Interpreting

3. What two lines suggest that the man is not leading an inactive life by choice?
4. How do you think the man "is getting a little strength from the sight of the passers-by"?
5. How would you describe the tone of this poem?
6. The poem focuses on a single man, yet its title is "Taylor Street." Why?

### Applying

7. The poet provides enough information for an imaginative reader to speculate about the life of the man on the porch. What do you think the man's background is?

## ANALYZING LITERATURE
### Recognizing the Importance of Diction

The importance of **diction,** or word choice, in a brief poem cannot be overemphasized. The poet must make every word count, and Thom Gunn does.

1. Why is it significant that the porch is (a) *small*? (b) *imitation marble*? (c) *never sunny*?
2. The man is not just sitting in a chair. He is sitting in a *kitchen* chair. Why?
3. The man's body is *crumpled*. The word *crumpled*, while specific and powerful, is open to interpretation. How do you interpret it?
4. What is symbolic about the *cold railing*?
5. (a) Why does the word *planned* seem somehow inappropriate? (b) How does it add an encouraging note?

# TED HUGHES

## 1930–

A major contemporary poet, Ted Hughes has been widely praised for his portrayal of nature in all its fierceness and primitive cruelty. Hughes differs from "the Movement" poets, who, he says, "wanted it cozy." There is nothing cozy about Hughes's starkly defined animal world. His diction, in the words of one critic, is "a solid phalanx of buffeting verbs and steel-heeled nouns." Yet Hughes, despite his verbal violence, shows a masterful ability to describe nature, seeking links between its universal force and the human condition.

Nature is a dominant theme in Hughes's poetry. His first book of poems, *The Hawk in the Rain,* appeared in 1957 and brought him immediate success. *Crow* (1970), *Crow Wakes* (1971), and *Eat Crow* (1972) reveal his characteristic style. In them, an animal observes and comments upon the human condition. Because of his use of animal characters, Hughes has been compared to both Aesop and George Orwell. The British critic A. Alvarez calls Hughes "the most powerful and original poet now writing in this country."

Hughes's fascination with nature and animals can be traced back to his childhood in the Calder Valley in western Yorkshire. The valley was full of animals of all kinds, and Hughes often went hunting with his brother, a gamekeeper. This interest in nature led to his university studies in archaeology and anthropology. After graduation in 1954, he spent the next two years in a variety of jobs: He was a rose gardener, a night watchman, a zoo attendant, a schoolteacher, and a reader at a film studio.

In 1956 Hughes and his friends published a poetry magazine called *St. Botolph's Review.* Although the magazine was a failure —it lasted only one issue—at the party held to celebrate its beginning Hughes met Sylvia Plath. They married in June of that year. After teaching briefly at universities in Massachusetts, the couple returned to England in 1959 to devote their full attention to writing. Initially, both were highly productive—Hughes writing most of the poems that later appeared in a volume called *Wodwo,* Plath completing her autobiographical novel *The Bell Jar* and beginning her famous *Ariel* poems. But despite the birth of two children, the union was not happy. The couple separated in August of 1962; the marriage ended the following February with Plath's death. Hughes was unable to write again until 1966, but since then he has produced a number of major collections of poetry. He has been called the most important figure to emerge on the British poetic scene since World War II.

# GUIDE FOR INTERPRETING

## Hawk Roosting; The Horses

**Writer's Techniques**

**Personification.** Personification is a figure of speech in which a thing, a quality, or an idea is given human attributes. For example, when Edmund Spenser writes that envy "rode upon a ravenous wolf," he is using personification. Sometimes personification is extended well beyond a phrase or sentence and involves point of view. Events are observed through the eyes or mind of a nonhuman narrator. A familiar example of such extended personification is Jack London's *The Call of the Wild,* in which the story is told from the viewpoint of Buck, a dog. Like simile, metaphor, and other figures of speech, personification presents ideas and details in fresh, original ways.

**Commentary**

Ted Hughes believes that he acquired a sense of violence very early in life. In fact, he has traced this awareness back to his earliest childhood. As the son of one of only seventeen men from a regiment of several hundred to return from Gallipoli during World War I, he learned about life's tragedy from his father's experiences. As the poems "Out" and "TV Off" recount, Hughes's father was wounded and left piled with the dead for two days; although his visible wounds healed, he never recovered from the terrifying experience. It may be true, as Hughes says, that "the shrapnel that shattered my father's paybook/Gripped me," and that his poetry replays his own visions of the horror and misery of trench warfare. Regardless of its source, his work is shot through with a sense of violence. This is apparent in his style as well as in his subjects. Notice the violent phrases and explosive verbs in these two poems, for example. Critic Calvin Bedient believes that "Hughes's great talent is for a dramatic grip of language, dead cold but bleakly pungent . . . His style is emotionally dry, yet burns." Critics have often remarked that Hughes's violent nature imagery represents a descent into the unconscious, noting parallels between the poetry of Hughes and that of D. H. Lawrence. What parallels do you see between the contemporary world and the world of nature in Hughes's poems?

**Writing**

Choose at least five inanimate objects—a pencil, a painting, a computer, for instance—and write a sentence about each one, giving the object human attributes. ("My pencil stopped short at the word *goodbye,* refusing to finish the sentence.") Although animals and plants can be the subjects of personification, try to limit your examples to purely inanimate (lifeless) objects, qualities, or ideas.

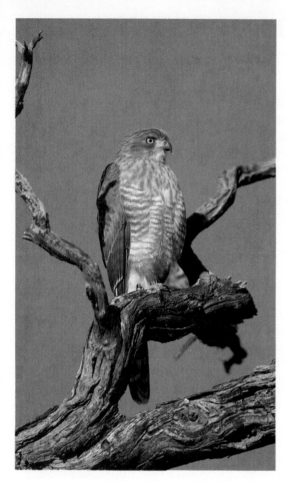

# Hawk Roosting

## Ted Hughes

I sit in the top of the wood, my eyes closed.
Inaction, no falsifying dream
Between my hooked head and hooked feet:
Or in sleep rehearse perfect kills and eat.

5   The convenience of the high trees!
The air's buoyancy and the sun's ray
Are of advantage to me;
And the earth's face upward for my inspection.

My feet are locked upon the rough bark.
10  It took the whole of Creation
To produce my foot, my each feather:
Now I hold Creation in my foot

Or fly up, and revolve it all slowly—
I kill where I please because it is all mine.
15  There is no sophistry in my body:
My manners are tearing off heads—

The allotment of death.
For the one path of my flight is direct
Through the bones of the living.
20  No arguments assert my right:

The sun is behind me.
Nothing has changed since I began.
My eye has permitted no change.
I am going to keep things like this.

## THINKING ABOUT THE SELECTION

### Recalling

1. (a) Who is the speaker in the poem? (b) Where is the speaker sitting?
2. What does the speaker do while sleeping?
3. What are three advantages that allow the speaker to "kill where I please"?

### Interpreting

4. What does stanza 3 suggest about the physical makeup and abilities of the speaker?
5. In lines 14–16, how does the speaker refute the "falsifying dream" that nature is invariably pleasant and nonviolent?
6. (a) What do you think the speaker means by "Nothing has changed since I began"? (b) How might you interpret the line in another way?
7. (a) What does the poet's (not the speaker's) view of nature seem to be? (b) How do you feel about that view?

### Applying

8. Nature can be violent. What have you seen in your own experience that shows this to be true? What other moods can you identify in nature? Provide examples that reveal these moods.

## ANALYZING LITERATURE

### Using Personification

Giving human attributes to a thing, a quality, or an idea is called **personification.** In "Hawk Roosting," Ted Hughes uses the technique to present his ideas about nature in an unusual and striking way.

1. Personification requires giving human attributes to something nonhuman. How is the hawk personified in Hughes's poem?
2. Why do you think Hughes has the hawk speak for itself in the poem rather than having a human speaker interpret what the hawk might be thinking?

## THINKING AND WRITING

### Using Personification in a Poem

Choose a bird very unlike the hawk. For example, you might choose a sparrow or a lark. Freewrite, exploring what this animal might see as it looks at the world. Then write a poem in which you personify this creature. Your poem can be short or long, rhymed or unrhymed. Have the bird speak, telling what it sees. When you revise make sure you have given your bird human characteristics.

### Commentary

In view of the striking personifications of nature's creatures and often merciless view of the world in Hughes's poetry, it is especially surprising that he is a prolific and important writer of children's books. His books for children include six books of poetry, two of fiction, and one of plays, though several of his children's plays for radio have never been collected. In addition, he has written an introduction to poetry for young readers. Originally published in England under the title *Poetry in the Making,* the American edition is called *Poetry Is.*

In part, his dedication to children's literature arises from his belief that "every new child is nature's chance to correct culture's error." To Hughes, children have the ability to reclaim the world's goodness. Their innocence and wonder can defeat evil and darkness. How does he express this idea in the following stanza?

In the little girl's angel gaze
Crow lost every feather
In the little boy's wondering eyes
Crow's bones splintered

# The Horses

## Ted Hughes

I climbed through woods in the hour-before-dawn dark.
Evil air, a frost-making stillness,

Not a leaf, not a bird—
A world cast in frost. I came out above the wood

5  Where my breath left tortuous statues in the iron light.
But the valleys were draining the darkness

Till the moorline—blackening dregs of the brightening
   gray—
Halved the sky ahead. And I saw the horses:

Huge in the dense gray—ten together—
10  Megalith-still. They breathed, making no move,

With draped manes and tilted hind-hooves,
Making no sound.

I passed: not one snorted or jerked its head.
Gray silent fragments

15  Of a gray silent world.

I listened in emptiness on the moor-ridge.
The curlew's[1] tear turned its edge on the silence.

Slowly detail leafed from the darkness. Then the sun
Orange, red, red erupted

20  Silently, and splitting to its core tore and flung cloud,
Shook the gulf open, showed blue,

And the big planets hanging—
I turned

Stumbling in the fever of a dream, down towards
25  The dark woods, from the kindling tops.

---

**1. curlew** (kʉr′ lo͞o) *n.*: A large, brownish wading bird with long legs.

And came to the horses.
                    There, still they stood,
But now steaming and glistening under the flow of light,

Their draped stone manes, their tilted hind-hooves
30  Stirring under a thaw while all around them

The frost showed its fires. But still they made no sound.
Not one snorted or stamped,

Their hung heads patient as the horizons,
High over valleys, in the red leveling rays—

35  In din of the crowded streets, going among the years, the
      faces,
May I still meet my memory in so lonely a place

Between the streams and the red clouds, hearing curlews,
Hearing the horizons endure.

---

## THINKING ABOUT THE SELECTION
### Recalling

1. What are four words in lines 1–15 that depict the atmosphere of the morning?
2. How are the horses different in the second sighting than in the first?
3. What wish does the speaker make in the last four lines of the poem?

### Interpreting

4. (a) In your own words, what does "detail leafed from the darkness" in line 18 mean? (b) What does "the sun/Orange, red, red erupted" in lines 19 and 20 mean?
5. (a) What is the figure of speech in line 33? (b) How do you explain the comparison?
6. The view of nature is different in "The Horses" from that in "Hawk Roosting." What is the basic difference?

### Applying

7. Think of a place you would like to remember later, in "the crowded streets, going among the years." (a) What kind of place is it? (b) Why would you like to remember it?

## THINKING AND WRITING
### Comparing Poems

Reread William Wordsworth's "Lines Composed a Few Miles Above Tintern Abbey." Then write an essay in which you compare Wordsworth's view of nature with that of Ted Hughes in "The Horses." Make notes before you begin to write. Jot down a few specific lines from each poem to support your comparison. In writing your first draft, be willing to speculate on the reasons for the differences between the poems. When you revise your first draft, check to be sure that your statements are supported by evidence from the poems.

# GUIDE FOR INTERPRETING

## Not Waving but Drowning; Pretty

**Stevie Smith** (1902-1971) shows intelligence, honesty, and wit in her poetry. Her poems are hard to categorize because of their variations in tone, form, and perspective. One critic calls her work "a forest of themes and attitudes." She is, the critic continues, "as surprising as she is skillful, her finesse equal to her boldness."

This independent-minded poet was born Florence Margaret Smith in Hull, Yorkshire. Small as a child, she was nicknamed "Stevie" after a famous jockey. When she was three, Smith moved with her mother and sister from the rural Yorkshire of her birth to an unfashionable London suburb. Because her mother's health was poor and her father had deserted the family to go to sea, Smith and her sister Molly were raised mainly by an aunt. The bond between "Auntie Lion" and Smith was warm and close, and the two were to live together for Smith's entire life.

Smith worked for many years in a magazine publisher's office in London, and often gave poetry readings on English radio and television. She first published her poetry and fiction when she was in her early thirties, ultimately publishing three novels and more than ten collections of poetry. Her first novel, *Novel on Yellow Paper,* appeared in 1936, and her first collection of poems, *A Good Time Was Had by All,* in 1937. "Not Waving but Drowning" was published in 1957.

**Writer's Techniques**

**Voice.** When a poet writes, the poet has a voice—a speaker's voice that can use idiom, rhythm, intonation, and other devices to achieve its effects. When you, the reader, scan a poem (even though silently), you "hear" a voice expressing the words in the poem. You notice, often without conscious thought, the pauses, the pitch, the stresses on certain words and syllables. If you are alert, you will also perceive the feelings behind the voice, such as excitement, panic, despair, or indifference. Voice, then, is an aspect of tone and can be described by an adjective or adjectives, just as tone can.

**Writing**

Freewrite for a few minutes, using your own natural voice. Make no effort to put your words into complete, grammatically correct sentences. Simply write as you think, quickly and even disjointedly. When you have finished, look back on what you have written. How would you describe your written voice? Serious? Amusing? Casual? Try to decide on the adjective that best describes it.

# Not Waving but Drowning

## Stevie Smith

Nobody heard him, the dead man,
But still he lay moaning:
I was much further out than you thought
And not waving but drowning.

5    Poor chap, he always loved larking
And now he's dead
It must have been too cold for him his heart gave way,
They said.

Oh, no no no, it was too cold always
10   (Still the dead one lay moaning)
I was much too far out all my life
And not waving but drowning.

---

## THINKING ABOUT THE SELECTION

### Recalling

1. Five lines in the poem are spoken by the dead man. Which lines are they?
2. (a) How did the spectators interpret the dead man's waving? (b) What led them to make this interpretation?
3. What caused the man's death?

### Interpreting

4. What does the *it* represent in line 9, "Oh, no no no, it was too cold always"?
5. In what sense was the dead man "too far out" all his life?
6. In line 4, the phrase "not waving but drowning" seems to be the literal truth. In line 12, the same phrase has a metaphorical meaning. What is its metaphorical meaning?

### Applying

7. What kinds of distress signals in ordinary life might be interpreted as "waving"?

## ANALYZING LITERATURE

### Understanding Voice

"Not Waving but Drowning" appears to be simple, but the appearance is deceptive. Three speakers can be identified in it: a narrator, a spectator (or spectators), and the dead man. The narrator's voice (lines 1, 2 and 10) is matter-of-fact and neutral, if a bit puzzled. The narrator's double use of the word *moaning* adds to your understanding of the dead man's distress.

1. Study lines 5–7. (a) What adjective or adjectives do you think accurately describe the voice of the spectators? (b) Explain.
2. (a) What adjective or adjectives describe the voice of the dead man? (b) Explain.

# Pretty

Stevie Smith

Why is the word pretty so underrated?
In November the leaf is pretty when it falls
The stream grows deep in the woods after rain
And in the pretty pool the pike stalks

5 He stalks his prey, and this is pretty too,
The prey escapes with an underwater flash
But not for long, the great fish has him now
The pike is a fish who always has his prey

And this is pretty. The water rat is pretty
10 His paws are not webbed, he cannot shut his nostrils
As the otter can and the beaver, he is torn between
The land and water. Not "torn," he does not mind.

The owl hunts in the evening and it is pretty
The lake water below him rustles with ice
15 There is frost coming from the ground, in the air mist
All this is pretty, it could not be prettier.

Yes, it could always be prettier, the eye abashes
It is becoming an eye that cannot see enough,
Out of the wood the eye climbs. This is prettier
20 A field in the evening, tilting up.

The field tilts to the sky. Though it is late
The sky is lighter than the hill field
All this looks easy but really it is extraordinary
Well, it is extraordinary to be so pretty.

25 And it is careless, and that is always pretty
This field, this owl, this pike, this pool are careless,
As Nature is always careless and indifferent
Who sees, who steps, means nothing, and this is pretty.

So a person can come along like a thief—pretty!—
30 Stealing a look, pinching the sound and feel,
Lick the icicle broken from the bank
And still say nothing at all, only cry pretty.

Cry pretty, pretty, pretty and you'll be able
Very soon not even to cry pretty
35 And so be delivered entirely from humanity
This is prettiest of all, it is very pretty.

## THINKING ABOUT THE SELECTION
### Recalling

1. In the first four stanzas, what are seven things that the speaker says are pretty?
2. Why does the speaker feel the need to see beyond the wood?
3. What is "prettiest of all"?

### Interpreting

4. The speaker does not define *pretty* directly but only through examples. What is the speaker's implied definition of *pretty*?
5. How does the speaker feel about the fact that nature is "careless and indifferent"?
6. (a) What do you think the speaker means by "being delivered entirely from humanity"? (b) Why might the speaker regard that as pretty?

### Applying

7. What aspect of nature—other than its prettiness—can serve as a useful example for human beings? Explain.

## CRITICAL THINKING AND READING
### Comparing and Contrasting Attitudes

Both Ted Hughes in "Hawk Roosting" and Stevie Smith in "Pretty" accept the everyday violence in nature. To Hughes, the hawk's "man-ners are tearing off heads." To Smith, the pike's stalking and capture of its prey are "pretty." Yet Hughes and Smith express themselves very differently about nature's unconcern.

1. Both the Hughes poem and the Smith poem have been described as "chilling." Which poet—or neither or both of them—do you think views nature as being essentially benign? Explain.
2. A poet's attitudes are expressed in words. List ten key words from each poem that support your answer to the preceding question.

## THINKING AND WRITING
### Evaluating a Poem

Write an essay evaluating either of Stevie Smith's poems. Begin by deciding which poem you prefer, or which poem you believe will allow you to express the most convincing opinion. Write a thesis sentence that states your opinion clearly. Use lines from the poem in writing your first draft. When you revise, make a special effort to see that the quoted lines fit smoothly and effectively into what you have written. Your final draft should be as error-free as you can make it. Prepare this draft and share it with your classmates. Compare your reaction to the poems with theirs.

## Anniversary; Out

**Elaine Feinstein** (1930-    ) is an inventive poet. Her first collection of poems, *In a Green Eye,* appeared in 1966, and her first novel, *The Circle,* four years later. In both prose and poetry, Feinstein displays a sly sense of humor coupled with a discerning fidelity to her own experience. Born in Bootle, Lancashire, Feinstein received her B.A. and M.A. from Cambridge University, then worked as an editor, teacher, translator, and journalist.

Feinstein was raised in the English Midlands, the daughter of a cabinet maker who ran his own factory until economic problems forced him to start anew. Her background was typical of the generation who profited from the 1944 Education Act, which made it possible for many to obtain a higher education. For ten years beginning in 1956, when she married biochemist Arnold Feinstein, she spent much of her time raising their three children. After the publication of her first book, she came into contact with fellow poet Donald Davie, who urged her to apply for a lectureship at Essex University, where he taught. Her application was successful, and she spent 1967–1969 collaborating with a number of fellow poets to publish their poems in a weekly mimeographed pamphlet. This experience led her to feel that her roots were not truly English. Many see her subsequent writing as a quest for those roots in European history and culture.

**Style.** Feinstein says: "I began to write poetry in the '60s very consciously influenced by American poets (Emily Dickinson and William Carlos Williams, in particular), at a time when line, and spacing, to indicate the movement of poetry was much less fashionable than it is now among young British poets."

Word associations are the uniquely personal images, experiences, or thoughts that particular words bring to mind. For example, the word *diesel* denotes a particular kind of internal-combustion engine, but its associations are not easy to predict. It might remind one person of her first close-up view of a huge locomotive in a train station. It might remind another of the distinctive smell of diesel exhaust fumes on a busy highway. Think of a common word that has unique associations for you. Jot down the random thoughts that occur to you in connection with the word.

# Anniversary

## Elaine Feinstein

Suppose I took out a slender ketch from
under the pokes of Palace pier tonight to
catch a sea going fish for you

or dressed in antique goggles and wings and
5   flew down through sycamore leaves into the park

or luminescent through some planetary strike
put one delicate flamingo leg over the sill of your lab

Could I surprise you? or would you insist on
keeping a pattern to link every transfiguration?

10  Listen, I shall have to whisper it
into your heart directly: we are all
supernatural / every day
we rise new creatures / cannot be predicted

---

## THINKING ABOUT THE SELECTION

### Recalling

1. What is the second "transfiguration" the speaker might make to surprise the *you*?
2. Where does the speaker suggest that the *you*—the person spoken to—might be found?
3. What descriptive word does the speaker say applies to all people?

### Interpreting

4. (a) What kind of person is the *you* who is being addressed? (b) How can you tell?
5. (a) What kind of person is the speaker? (b) How can you tell?
6. In what way is the speaker's meaning for *supernatural* different from the meaning that moviegoers or readers of science fiction might be inclined to give the word?
7. Why do you think the poet calls this poem "Anniversary"?
8. What makes it clear that each of the first three stanzas is complete even though none has end punctuation?
9. Why does the poet not put the second question in stanza 4 into a separate stanza?
10. What purpose do the slashes (/) serve in the last two lines of the poem?

### Applying

11. In the poem the speaker and the person spoken to seem to have quite different temperaments. How valid a perception on the poet's part do you think that is? Explain.

# Out

## Elaine Feinstein

The diesel stops. It is morning. Gray sky
is falling into the mud. At the waterside
two builders' cranes are sitting like birds

and the yellow gorse[1] pushes up
5   like camel-thorn between oil-drums and old cars.
Who shall I take for my holy poet

to lead me out of this plain? I want an
innocent spirit of invention: a Buster Keaton[2]
to sail unnaturally overhead by simple leverage and

10   fire the machinery. Then we should all spring out of our
heads, dazzled with hope, even the white-faced ticket
collector dozing over his fag,[3] at such an intervention

suddenly in this stopped engine, we should
see the white gulls rising out of the rain over
15   the fen: and know our own freedom.

---

**1. gorse** *n.*: A prickly green shrub with yellow flowers.
**2. Buster Keaton:** An American motion-picture actor (1895–1966),
who was among the most popular silent film comedians, having
created a character who, though he never smiled, was able to
overcome all obstacles.
**3. fag**: Cigarette.

# THINKING ABOUT THE SELECTION

## Recalling

1. What is the setting of this poem?
2. How does the speaker describe the kind of holy poet she is seeking?
3. What would happen if someone were to appear and "fire the machinery"?

## Interpreting

4. To what extent would the effect of the scene be different if the cranes were busily at work rather than standing idle?
5. The speaker wants to be led "out of this plain." In your own words, define *plain* as the poet is using the word.
6. Why do you think a "Buster Keaton" is needed to shake things up?
7. Explain the analogy suggested in the last stanza.

## Applying

8. Besides poetry, what is a healthful and effective way to lift oneself out of a bleak mood?

# THINKING AND WRITING

## Writing About Style

Write an essay about Elaine Feinstein's style. Consider her remarks about her own poetry (see Writer's Techniques, page 1310). Then review "Anniversary" and "Out" carefully. Think about Feinstein's subject matter and her ideas as well as about her word choice, imagery, sentence structure, usage, and punctuation. Style is a very broad concept. Make a chart comparing and contrasting the style in both. When you write your first draft, include lines from the poem to illustrate and clarify your statements. When you revise the first draft, pay close attention to your own style. A good essay should be enjoyable and thought-provoking—and your writing style largely determines if it is. Make sure you have supported your main idea with details from the poems. Have you quoted precisely and accurately? Have you punctuated quotations accurately? Proofread your essay and prepare a final draft.

---

## Commentary

In addition to writing poetry, Elaine Feinstein also writes novels, short stories, and television scripts. Talent in more than one literary genre is unusual. As a result, reviewers have encountered some difficulty characterizing her style and achievements in her nonpoetic writing. For example, she has been labeled a "poetic novelist" by one reviewer. This inability to pin a label on her writing is not limited to critics; Feinstein herself has described her first novel as a "prose poem," thereby acknowledging her interweaving of poetic techniques into prose writing. Indeed, she once remarked that she first wrote prose as "an extension of the poetic impulse."

Her first novel, *The Circle* (1970), clearly shows how she created a different style by adapting some traditional poetic devices to the form of the novel. This is especially seen in her use of spacing and pauses for emphasis and the way she fragments syntax to mirror rhythm and pacing. As with all her novels, in *The Circle* Feinstein pares down her language—as a poet would—to say what she wants in the most economical and effective manner.

Her stylistic innovations are designed, in the words of one reviewer, to enable her "to write novels which move her readers, as the great novels of the past have done, and to involve them in the fate of her characters so that they will care about what happens to them."

## Follower; Shore Woman

**Seamus Heaney** (1939-    ), born in county Derry, Northern Ireland, has devoted much of his poetry to the life, history, and conflict of his homeland. He is a gifted traditionalist whom the American poet Robert Lowell has called "the most important Irish poet since Yeats." The eldest of nine children, Heaney spent a happy childhood on the farm that had been in his family for generations. He has said that his deep regard for tradition and the past grew from his early experiences in the rich boggy land of his ancestors. After graduating from the local primary school in 1951, he left home to board in St. Columba's College in Londonderry. He first published as an undergraduate at Queen's University. Long having struggled with the role of the artist in political situations, Heaney left Northern Ireland in 1972, when a cottage on the Synge estate in County Wicklow became available. His departure was termed by some an artistic necessity; by others, a betrayal.

Despite his fame, Heaney is known to be modest and natural. A friend recalls when he met Heaney "fresh from reading at Harvard and dressed for dinner at the Princeton Club, he still managed to convey the easy intimacy of a gathering around a peat fire."

**Writer's Techniques**

**Figurative Language.** A poet, like every other writer and speaker, uses two kinds of language: literal and figurative. *Literal language* is that which means exactly what it says. "The audience applauded the candidate's speech loudly" is a literal statement. "The candidate's speech brought down the house," by contrast, is not literal. It is figurative. *Figurative language* (language containing one or more *figures of speech*) has meaning beyond its literal meaning, or apart from it.

**Writing**

The English language contains a great deal of onomatopoeia —words whose natural sound matches their meaning. Three examples are *buzz, tinkle,* and *twang.* Think about the sounds you hear every day. What words describe them? Write down at least ten examples of onomatopoeia, not including the words already given.

# Follower

**Seamus Heaney**

My father worked with a horse plow,
His shoulders globed like a full sail strung
Between the shafts and the furrow.
The horses strained at his clicking tongue.

5    An expert. He would set the wing
And fit the bright steel-pointed sock.
The sod rolled over without breaking.
At the headrig, with a single pluck

Of reins, the sweating team turned round
10   And back into the land. His eye
Narrowed and angled at the ground,
Mapping the furrow exactly.

I stumbled in his hobnailed wake,
Fell sometimes on the polished sod;
15   Sometimes he rode me on his back
Dipping and rising to his plod.

I wanted to grow up and plow,
To close one eye, stiffen my arm.
All I ever did was follow
20   In his broad shadow round the farm.

I was a nuisance, tripping, falling,
Yapping always. But today
It is my father who keeps stumbling
Behind me, and will not go away.

## THINKING ABOUT THE SELECTION

### Recalling

1. How does the speaker show that his father was an expert at plowing?
2. As the boy accompanied his father, what did he want to do?
3. (a) What three verbs does the speaker use to describe the father's actions behind the plow? (b) What parallel verb does he use in speaking of his father today?

### Interpreting

4. (a) What do you think is the approximate age of the speaker in the plowing scene he describes? (b) How can you tell?
5. Why do you think the boy wanted to close one eye and stiffen his arm?
6. The speaker says: "All I ever did was follow/In his broad shadow. . . ." What double meaning do those words suggest?
7. What is the tone of this poem? Find evidence to support your answer.

### Applying

8. (a) What does this poem suggest about the changing roles of parents and children? (b)

Do you think most young people are prepared for these changing roles? Explain your answer.

## ANALYZING LITERATURE

### Understanding Figurative Language

**Figurative language** is language that is not meant to be interpreted literally. When Heaney writes that his father's shoulders "globed like a full sail," he does not mean that they became an actual sphere or that they were as large as a ship's wind-filled sail. Yet the points of resemblance give you a clear, striking picture of his father walking behind the plow.

1. "Mapping the furrow" (line 12) is an example of figurative language. (a) Why? (b) How would you express the idea literally? (c) What does the figurative language add to the thought?
2. The line about "my father . . . stumbling" (line 23) is figurative. (a) Why? (b) How would you express the idea literally?

### Commentary

Ireland's distinctive basin-like shape—a low-lying plain ringed by mountains—results in an unusual geographic phenomenon. Since drainage is blocked by the mountains, the deep central plain retains moisture, slowing down the decay of organic matter. The ground remains wet and spongy. As a result, thick layers of dark, rich organic matter develop. Since until very recently the area was relatively untouched, astonishingly well-preserved bodies, clothing, food, tools, and artifacts have been unearthed. For centuries the peat from these bogs was cut, dried, and used as fuel; today it is also exported as peat moss after all its moisture is extracted. But the peat bogs are more than a commodity: They spark the creative imagination as well.

Heaney found in the bogs echoes of ancient Ireland. In his famous "bog" poems, Heaney sought to define and explain the present by relating it to the past. Thus, he connects the history and strife of Northern Ireland to the northern European experience. Aided by *The Bog People,* a study with fascinating photographs of the preserved bodies of Iron Age people unearthed from peat bogs, he links in *Wintering Out* and *North* the battles of long-gone Vikings to the struggles of the present-day Irish.

# Shore Woman

**Seamus Heaney**

*Man to the hills, woman to the shore.*
                    Gaelic proverb

I have crossed the dunes with their whistling bent
Where dry loose sand was riddling round the air
And I'm walking the firm margin. White pocks
Of cockle, blanched roofs of clam and oyster
5   Hoard the moonlight, woven and unwoven
Off the bay. At the far rocks
A pale sud comes and goes.

Under boards the mackerel slapped to death
Yet still we took them in at every cast,
10   Stiff flails of cold convulsed with their first breath.
My line plumbed certainly the undertow,
Loaded against me once I went to draw
And flashed and fattened up towards the light.
He was all business in the stern. I called
15   "This is so easy that it's hardly right,"
But he unhooked and coped with frantic fish
Without speaking. Then suddenly it lulled,
We'd crossed where they were running, the line rose
Like a let-down and I was conscious
20   How far we'd drifted out beyond the head.
"Count them up at your end," was all he said
Before I saw the porpoises' thick backs
Cartwheeling like the flywheels[1] of the tide,
Soapy and shining. To have seen a hill
25   Splitting the water could not have numbed me more
Than the close irruption of that school,
Tight viscous muscle, hooped from tail to snout,
Each one revealed complete as it bowled out
And under.
30            They will attack a boat.

---

**1. flywheels** *n.*: Heavy wheels for regulating the speed and uniformity
of motion of a machine.

## THINKING ABOUT THE SELECTION
### Recalling

1. Where is the speaker in the first stanza?
2. (a) What were the father and the speaker doing in the open boat? (b) How successful were they? (c) When did the speaker become aware of how far the boat had drifted?
3. (a) Why was the speaker frightened at the sight of the porpoises? (b) What was the father's reaction? (c) Who was right about the porpoises—father or speaker?
4. Where is the speaker in the last stanza?

### Interpreting

5. What basic difference is there between the father and speaker in the encounter with the porpoises? Explain your answer.
6. (a) How close does the relationship between father and speaker appear to be when the two are at sea? (b) How close is it on land? Explain.
7. What relationship is there between the Gaelic proverb and the title and theme of the poem?

### Applying

8. To what extent do you think the speaker's fear suggests weakness? Provide support for your answer.
9. What, if anything, do you think the father said to the speaker after the porpoises had left? What makes you think he said this?

I knew it and I asked him to put in
But he would not, declared it was a yarn
My people had been fooled by far too long
And he would prove it now and settle it.
35  Maybe he shrank when those sloped oily backs
Propelled towards us: I lay and screamed
Under splashed brine in an open rocking boat
Feeling each dunt and slither through the timber,
Sick at their huge pleasures in the water.

40  I sometimes walk this strand for thanksgiving
Or maybe it's to get away from him
Skittering his spit across the stove. Here
Is the taste of safety, the shelving sand
Harbors no worse than razorshell[2] or crab—
45  Though my father recalls carcasses of whales
Collapsed and gasping, right up to the dunes.
But tonight such moving sinewed dreams lie out
In darker fathoms, far beyond the head.
Astray upon a debris of scrubbed shells
50  Between parched dunes and salivating wave,
I have rights on this fallow avenue,
A membrane between moonlight and my shadow.

---

**2. razorshell** *n.*: The shell of razor clams, burrowing clams with elongated, narrow shells that resemble a straight razor.

---

## CRITICAL THINKING AND READING
### Recognizing Sound and Meaning

Poets use a number of devices to create the kinds of sounds that complement the meaning of their words. Rhyme, rhythm, repetition, harsh-or-soft consonants and vowels, and onomatopoeia all help to produce the desired effects.

1. What is one example of onomatopoeia in the first stanza?
2. What are three examples of repetition of sound in the second stanza?
3. Sound is used very effectively in line 42. What devices that make this line work so well?

## THINKING AND WRITING
### Analyzing the Use of Sound in a Poem

Write an essay in which you analyze the devices for creating sound in "Shore Woman." To appreciate the sound effects in the poem, read it aloud at least once before you begin. Jot down notes about the sound devices. What impression do they create? Then write your first draft. Remember that when you write an analysis of this kind, you have to do more than just point out the devices. You also have to explain how they work. When you revise, make sure you have provided details from the poem to support your analysis.

## Donald Davie
## 1922–

Donald Davie, one of "the Movement" poets of the 1950's, is noted today for the quiet elegance and urbane perception of his work. He is often compared to the eighteenth-century Augustan poets, whose tone, diction, and verse forms he admires and sometimes emulates. Davie, born in Yorkshire, England, has taught in England, Ireland, and the United States. A traditionalist, he believes that formal discipline in writing can free rather than restrict the poetic imagination. One of his best-known collections, *The Shires* (1974), consists of one poem for each of the forty counties of England.

Davie developed an early interest in poetry from his mother, Alice Sugden Davie, who was so fond of verse that her son was later able to remark that she knew "the greater part, perhaps the whole" of Palgrave's massive *The Golden Treasury of the Best Songs and Lyrical Poems in the English Language* (1861, 1897) by heart. Another influence in the creation of his style was what he calls the "industrially ravaged landscape" of his youth, which contributed to his favoring literature that is "spare and lean."

## Molly Holden
## 1927–1981

Born in London, Molly Holden was twelve when her family moved to the heart of Wiltshire, an area which became the geographical center of her writing. She earned her B.A. and M.A. in English at King's College, London, married, and began a family. Although her poetry was late in coming—her first creative success, *The Bright Cloud,* was published when she was thirty-seven—her verse gained in power and creativity in the 1960's and 1970's. Her work subsequently won many prizes and much critical praise.

Molly Holden wrote poetry that is subtle and sparkling. It is based on close attention to precise, telling details. Although Holden was disabled with multiple sclerosis in 1964, she did not let this progressive illness impede her writing. Her keen observation became, if anything, more acute, and her three finest collections—*To Make Me Grieve* (1968), *Air and Chill Earth* (1972), *The Country Over* (1975)—are testaments to her creative power and indomitable spirit. As she wrote, "Doubly urgent longing fills my days/to put down surely what is my obsession."

# GUIDE FOR INTERPRETING

## For Doreen: A Voice from the Garden; Some Men Create

**Writer's Techniques**

**Imagery.** When a writer's words or phrases create a picture in the reader's mind, the writer is using imagery. The mental pictures of imagery do not always involve sight; the images can also come from touch, taste, smell, or hearing. Verbal images based on the five senses are called sensory images. Imagery is important in poetry because it adds color to descriptions and helps to give concrete reality to abstract ideas.

**Writing**

Imagery is not restricted to poetry. It occurs in all forms of writing and may come up in everyday conversation. A good storyteller uses imagery to create pictures in his or her listeners' minds. For one day, keep a list of the images you hear in conversation or read in newspapers or magazines.

**Primary Source**

Do writers—especially poets—think differently from the rest of us? Is there such a thing as a "poetic mind"? If so, do poets think in mental pictures of imagery? If not, can nonpoets write poetry? Donald Davie attempted to answer these questions in a recent interview. He began with the assertion that although he wanted above all else to be a "natural poet," he has come to realize that he is not a poet by nature, only by inclination. He continued:

> Most of the poems I have written are not natural poems, in one sense not truly poems, simply because the thought in them could have been expressed—at whatever cost to terseness and point—in a nonpoetic way. This does not mean however that they are worthless, or that they are shams; for as much can be said of much of the poetry of the past that by common consent is worth reading and remembering. Nevertheless I have taken a decision to write no more poems of this kind, only poems which are, if not *naturally*, in all events *truly* poems throughout. For a true poem can be written by a mind not naturally poetic —though by the inhuman labor of thwarting at every point the natural grain and bent. This working against the grain does not damage the mind, nor is it foolish; on the contrary, only by doing this does each true poem as it is written become an authentic widening of experience—a truth won from life against all odds . . .

# For Doreen: A Voice from the Garden

## Donald Davie

We have a lawn of moss.
The next house is called The Beeches.
A towering squirrel-haunted
Trellis of trees, across
5  Our matt and trefoil, reaches
Shade where our guests have sauntered.

Cars snap by in the road.
In a famous photographed village
The High Street is our address.
10  Our guests write from abroad
Delighted to envisage
Rose arbor and wilderness.

They get them, and the lilacs.
Some frenzy in us discards
15  Lilacs and all. It will harden,
However England stacks
Her dear discolored cards
Against us, us to her garden.

Anglophobia rises
20  In Brooklyn to hysteria
At some British verses.
British, one sympathizes.
Diesel fumes cling to wistaria.[1]
One conceives of worse reverses.

25  The sough of the power brake
Makes every man an island;
But we are the island race.
We must be mad to take
Offense at our poisoned land
And the gardens that pock her face.

---

**1. wistaria** (wis tir′ ē ə) *n.*: Vines of shrubs with clusters of bluish, white, pink, or purplish flowers.

## THINKING ABOUT THE SELECTION

### Recalling

1. What are three of the natural features near the speaker's house?
2. (a) Where are the guests from? (b) What delights them about the grounds near the speaker's house?
3. How does the "frenzy in us" cause the speaker (or the English perhaps) to regard garden-like settings such as this one?
4. What does the speaker say the English "must be mad" to dislike?

### Interpreting

5. Why do you think the English ignore, or discard, the beauties that foreign guests see there?
6. How does the speaker react to Brooklyn's dislike of certain British verses?
7. If the gardens of England are in fact beautiful, why does the speaker say they "pock her face"?
8. One interpretation of this poem is that its basic theme is English literature, not the English landscape. What evidence do you find in the poem to support this interpretation?

### Applying

9. Critics have remarked on Davie's relationship with England—a somewhat antagonistic one —and on his stylistic tendency to "shut the reader out." To what extent do you think these two comments apply to this poem?

# Some Men Create

## Molly Holden

Some men create an unintended
    beauty by default,
never cut back the creeping ivy
    so its stragglers vault

5    from crumbling wall to neighboring bridge
    beside the arched lane,
to swing like hair from the parapet,
    shining with spring rain;

never gravel out the timber pile
10    nor lop the dead oak
so that the seeding traveler's joy
    smothers them like smoke.

So among orderly husbandry
    leave some plots alone
15    that the eye may reap with pleasure what
    the hand has not sown.

---

## THINKING ABOUT THE SELECTION

### Recalling

1. What does the uncut ivy do?
2. What advice does the speaker give to gardeners?

### Interpreting

3. How is the beauty described in this poem created "by default"?
4. What causes the "traveler's joy" in stanza 3?

### Applying

5. What are some examples you can point to of "beauty by default"?

6. How do you think a professional gardener or landscaper would respond to this poem?

## THINKING AND WRITING

### Writing a Poem Using Imagery

Write an original poem using imagery. The writing assignment on page 1321 should have uncovered many examples of imagery used to brighten up everyday conversation. Perhaps you can use some of these examples in your poem. Remember that your object is to choose words and phrases that will create pictures in the minds of your readers. Once you have a topic for your poem, write your first draft. When you revise, make sure your language is fresh and vivid.

## London Moves to Broadway

### THE BRITISH INVASION

Although it's commonly supposed that the British have invaded the American stage only recently, they've actually been treading our boards from the very beginning. Take musicals, for example—those entertaining productions in which a story is told by a combination of spoken dialogue and musical numbers. America claims the first musical —*The Black Crook* (1866)—but England says hers were better. Perhaps we can't settle that dispute, but no one can argue that British musicals were not exported to America from the very beginning. For example, only five years after England's first musical comedy—Osmond Carr's 1892 *In Town*—debuted in London, it was staged in New York.

The balance of trade leveled out somewhat in the next few years, as musical comedy became more firmly established. *The Belle of New York* premiered in New York in 1897, but achieved its major success a year later in London, where it became the first American musical to run for over a year. On the other hand, *Florodora* was a hit in London in 1899 but ran even longer in New York after opening there in 1900. The balance was still tipped in England's favor, however. Although the American stage prospered during the next few years, musicals imported from England (and Vienna!) continued to hold sway here in the early years of the twentieth century.

### A SUDDEN SHIFT

Things shifted suddenly with the outbreak of World War I. Swollen with anti-German feeling, Americans no longer wanted European musicals. At the same time, English playwrights suffered a dry spell, and American playwrights and composers flowered as never before. Jerome Kern, Cole Porter, and Irving Berlin set Broadway ablaze with a series of magnificent productions. Oscar Hammerstein II set toes tapping on both sides of the Atlantic with his catchy lyrics. Al Jolson crooned the smash hits from George Gershwin's musicals. Many of these productions found their way to British shores.

After a slow start in the early twenties, American musicals stormed American and British footlights. Fred Astaire and his sister Adele hoofed their way through the first musical collaboration of brothers George and Ira Gershwin; the team of Richard Rodgers and Lorenzo Hart debuted in 1925. In 1927 and 1928 more than fifty musicals opened on Broadway. Paul Robeson sang the haunting song ''Old Man River'' in the 1928 London production of the hit *Show Boat*. The heyday of the American musical continued into the thirties, with the first Pulitzer Prize awarded to a musical (*Of Thee I Sing*, 1931). The American musical continued to grow in the forties and fifties with such hits as Rodgers and Hammerstein's *South Pacific* (1949) and *The King and I* (1951), and Lerner and Loewe's *My Fair Lady* (1956).

### SIGNS OF REVIVAL

Meanwhile, the English musical had been showing signs of revival, most notably with the 1960 hit *Oliver!*, seen in New York in 1963. The heyday of the American musical was over; the stage was set for London's invasion of Broadway. Critics—and audiences—agree that England produced the only major theatrical talent of the seventies and eighties.

In an interesting reversal, a number of British musical hits debuted in America and then traveled back home. The most famous of these is the remarkable *Jesus Christ Superstar,* a musical based on the life of Christ. The smash team of lyricist Tim Rice and composer Andrew Lloyd Webber opened the play first in New York in 1971, then journeyed back with it to London a year later. But for their next success, *Evita,* the duo returned to the old pattern: This musical opened first in London in 1978, then a year later in New York. In the same decade, the American stage also imported England's *Billy,* a musical based on the play *Billy Liar; The Good Companions; Joseph and the Amazing Technicolor Dreamcoat;* and *The Moony Shapiro Songbook* as well as a number of excellent dramas. Lloyd Webber scored big again in 1981 when he brought *Cats* to the New York stage. Based on T. S. Eliot's *Old Possum's Book of Practical Cats,* this dazzling production is marked by extravagant makeup, costumes, and creative staging.

## THE 1980's

By the eighties, England had become seemingly the only source of successful musicals; of the twenty-one shows on Broadway at the beginning of 1983, more than a third came from England's theatre district, the West End. And these shows were good, too: In 1987, for example, twelve of Broadway's nineteen Tony Awards went to musicals that originated on the London stage. The musical *Me and My Girl,* for example, catapolted English actor Robert Lindsay to stardom. But the brightest light on Broadway belongs to Andrew Lloyd Webber.

Webber added to his string of commercial successes when he exported his musical wonderland *Starlight Express;* more noted for its roller skating and clever set than for its plot, it nonetheless delighted packed audiences. His astonishingly successful *Les Misérables* set the stage for the megahit *Phantom of the Opera.* Tickets are virtually unavailable for this quasi-operatic retelling of the monster-meets-girl melodrama.

Perhaps the most striking example of the way London has moved to Broadway is *Follies,* not so much an import from the West End as a complete restaging of American Stephen Sondheim's 1971 musical. Although the original version won five Tony Awards during its Broadway run, it lost nearly its entire investment. British producer Cameron Mackintosh's invitation to Sondheim to "have a wee think" about the play resulted in an entirely revamped show. The three-million-dollar London production opened to huge advance sales, and Mackintosh hopes to bring *Follies* back to Broadway, a rare reverse transfer that would be both welcome yet humbling.

As one British paper put it, "The Great White Way seems to have become an overseas colony of the West End."

# YOU THE WRITER

**Assignment**

**1.** Write an alternate ending for one of the stories in this unit. Make the ending follow logically from preceding events and from the nature of the characters.

**Prewriting.** Reread the story to see how its earlier parts prepare for the present ending. Then ask, "How might these parts lead up to a different ending?"

**Writing.** Now write your alternate ending. Start at the turning point, and, to achieve surprise, have the story move in a different direction. To make the new ending logical, link it to something presented earlier.

**Revising.** Revise with the aim of making your new ending seem as if it had been written by the author of the story.

**Assignment**

**2.** Write a letter to a friend in which you discuss a character in a story from this unit. Write as if the character were real and you had been present at the events recounted in the story.

**Prewriting.** Ask, "What is the character like? What are his or her key traits? How are they seen in the events of the story? What is the main idea I should express about the character? How can I develop and conclude my letter in an interesting and memorable way?" Freewrite exploring your answer to these questions.

**Writing.** When you have arrived at clear and definite answers to these questions, write a personal letter in conventional form.

**Revising.** Can you make your letter more interesting, more dramatic, or more startling? Have you captured the characters personality accurately? Make changes with these possibilities in view.

**Assignment**

**3.** Sometimes a poem has a central image or idea that spreads itself throughout the poem like the branches and roots of a tree. Write a poem with a central image or idea, using a poem in this unit as a model.

**Prewriting.** Find a subject you would like to write about. Then think of a central image or idea that can tie together and express your thoughts and feelings about the subject. Ask, "How might the author of my model have treated this subject?"

**Writing.** Write the first draft of your poem. Follow your model poem for rhythm, rhyme, and structure. However, make whatever modifications you feel are appropriate to what you are trying to express.

**Revising.** Make changes to improve the expressiveness of your poem. Be sure to read your verses aloud to see if their rhythm and sound can be improved.

# YOU THE CRITIC

**Assignment**

**1.** Choose two characters from two different stories in this section and write an essay discussing (1) the important actions they took, and (2) the consequences of these actions.

**Prewriting.** For each character, divide a sheet of paper into two columns. In the first column, list the major actions the characters took. In the second column, list the consequences of these actions.

**Writing.** In your opening paragraph, describe in general the actions of each character and the consequences of the actions. In the body paragraphs, treat each story separately. For both stories, discuss the characters' actions first and the consequences second.

**Revising.** Carefully review the organization of your essay to see if you can establish connections by comparison and contrast between the two characters you have discussed.

**Assignment**

**2.** Much contemporary fiction is quite different from earlier, more traditional fiction. Write an essay in which you explain why you prefer contemporary or earlier stories.

**Prewriting.** First decide on the chief differences between earlier and more recent stories. Which of these differences explain your likes and dislikes? Which specific stories would you cite to illustrate these differences?

**Writing.** Write your first draft. Begin by stating your preference. Give your reasons by discussing the qualities you like or dislike in older or contemporary fiction.

**Revising.** Revise your essay by attempting to clarify or support more strongly your reasons for your preference. See if you can use comparison and contrast to reveal more vividly the chief differences between the two periods of fiction.

**Assignment**

**3.** Some lines in a poem are memorable either because of what they say or how they say it, or both. Choose at least three poems from this unit and write an essay identifying the lines you consider most memorable, explaining why you think they are memorable.

**Prewriting.** Scan the poems in this unit for the ones you think contain the most memorable lines. Copy these lines and note why you liked them. Were you impressed by the content? Was the imagery sharp? Was the phrasing beautiful?

**Writing.** Write an introductory paragraph in which you announce your subject and indicate how you will approach it. Then discuss each of the memorable lines, quoting the line first and then explaining why you think it is memorable.

**Revising.** See if you can use transitional words and phrases to improve the unity and coherence of your essay.

# Literary Map of Great Britain

N

**Johnson and Boswell tour Hebrides, 1773**

Outer Hebrides

Isle of Skye

Inner Hebrides

SCOTTISH HIGHLANDS

*ATLANTIC OCEAN*

• King Duncan's palace (Macbeth)
• Macbeth's castle
**Dunsinane**
(Macbeth slain)

**SCOTLAND**

*NORTH SEA*

Loch Ness

Loch Lomond

Sir Patrick Spens
and Scottish lords drown:
"The Seafarer"

• **Dumferling** *"Sir Patrick Spens"*

• **Ayshire**
Burn's "Sweet Afton,"
"To a Mouse"

English-Scottish border.
Setting of many early ballads

**NORTHERN IRELAND**

**Sligo**
Yeat's
"Lake Isle
of Innisfree"

**Kelloe**
• E.B. Browning born

• **Whitby**
Caedmon's hymns

**Lake District**
Wordsworth's poetry

*IRISH SEA*

**Dublin** ✪
Birthplace of Steele,
Swift, Shaw, Wilde,
Yeats, Joyce

**Haworth Moor**
• Setting of *Jane Eyre*

• **Humberside**
Marvell lives, writes

**Wakefield**
Medieval mystery
and morality plays

**IRELAND**

Gawain vs.
Green Knight

**Lichfield**
Samuel Johnson
born

*A Shropshire Lad,*
Housman

**Kilcolman** •
Spenser composes
*Fairie Queene*

**Stratford-on-Avon**
Shakespeare

**ENGLAND**

**WALES**

**Cambridge***

**Swansea**
Dylan Thomas's poetry

Wordsworth's Tintern Abbey

**•Oxford***

✪ **London**

Thames River

Stonehenge

**Canterbury**
Destination of
Chaucer's pilgrims;
Marlowe born

**Salisbury**
Geo. Herbert's
*Temple*

Route of
Chaucer's pilgrims

**Dorset**
Hardy's Wessex
("Three Strangers")

**Dover**
Arnold's
"Dover Beach"

**Tintagel**
Legendary birthplace
of King Arthur

**Dean Prior**
Herrick a
country parson
here

**Portsmouth**
Dickens born

*ENGLISH CHANNEL*

**FRANCE**

***Oxford**
Authors who studied here include
Addison, Arnold, Donne,
T.S. Eliot, Hopkins, Housman,
Johnson, Lovelace, MacNeice,
Raleigh, Shelley, Sidney,
and Steele.

***Cambridge**
Authors who studied here include
Bacon, Brooke, Byron, Coleridge,
Dryden, Forster, Gray, Herbert,
Herrick, Marlowe, Marvell,
Pepys, Sassoon, Spenser,
Tennyson, Wordsworth,
and Wyatt.

# Rulers of England and Great Britain (including dates of reign)

This chart presents the rulers of England and Great Britain from Anglo-Saxon times to the present. The earliest English kings were rulers not of England in its entirety but of kingdoms within England. The first of an unbroken succession of kings or queens of England was William I (1066-87). In 1707, upon the passage of the Act of Union, which united England and Scotland, Queen Anne became the first monarch of Great Britain.

*[Kingdom of Kent]*
Ethelbert, 560-616

*[Kingdom of Northumbria]*
Ethelfrith, 593-617
Edwin, 617-633
Oswald, 635-642
Oswy, 642-670
Ecgfrith, 670-685

*[Kingdom of Mercia]*
Penda, 626-655
Ethelbald, 716-757
Offa II, 757-796
Cenulf, 796-821

*[Kingdom of Wessex]*
Ine, 688-726

*Saxons and Danes*
Egbert, 802-39
Æthelwulf, 839-58
Æthelbald, 858-60
Æthelbert, 860-65
Æthelred, 865-71
Alfred, 871-99
Edward 899-924
Athelstan, 924-39
Edmund, 946-55
Edred, 946-55
Edway, 955-59
Edgar, 959-78
Edward (the Martyr), 978-1016
Æthelred (the Unready), 978-1016
Edmund (Ironside), son of Æthelred 1016
Canute, by conquest, 1016-35
Harold I (Harefoot), 1037-40
Harthacunute, 1040-42
Edward (the Confessor), 1042-66
Harold II, 1066

*House of Normandy*
William I The Conquerer, 1066-87
William II, 1087-1100
Henry I, 1100-1135

*Houseof Blois*
Stephen, 1135-54

*House of Plantagenet*
Henry II, 1154-89
Richard I, (Coeur de Lion) 1189-99
John, 1199-1216
Henry III, 1216-72
Edward I, 1272-1307
Edward II, 1302-27
Edward III, 1327-77
Richard II, 1327-99

*House of Lancaster*
Henry IV, 1399-1413
Henry V, 1413-22
Henry VI, 1422-61, 1470-99

*House of York*
Edward IV, 1461-70, 1471-83
Edward V, 1483
Richard III, 1483-85

*House of Tudor*
Henry VII, 1485-1509
Henry VIII, 1509-47
Edward VI, 1547-53
Mary I, 1553-58
Elizabeth I, 1558-1603

*House of Stuart*
James I (James VI of Scotland), 1603-25
Charles I, 1625-49

*Commonwealth and Protectorate*
Council of State, 1649-53
Cromwell, Oliver, lord protector, 1653-58
Cromwell, Richard, lord protector, 1658-59

*House of Stuart (restored)*
Charles II, 1660-85
James II, 1685-88
William III, ruled jointly with Mary II, 1689-94; ruled alone, 1694-1702
Mary II, ruled jointly with William III, 1689-94
Anne, 1702-14

*House of Hanover*
George I, 1714-27
George II, 1727-60
George III, 1760-1820
George IV, 1820-30
William IV, 1830-37
Victoria, 1837-1901

*House of Saxe-Cobury*
Edward VII, 1901-10

*House of Windsor*
(family name changed during World War I)
George V, 1910-36
Edward VIII, 1936
George VI, 1936-1952
Elizabeth II, 1952

# HANDBOOK OF WRITING ABOUT LITERATURE

# SECTION 1: UNDERSTANDING THE WRITING PROCESS

## Lesson 1: Prewriting

You may wish that you could just sit down, spend a few minutes, and magically write out a polished paragraph or essay. Unfortunately, most writing is not so easy. It takes time and hard work. Nevertheless, you can write more confidently if you understand that writing is a process, not a single step. Most writers go through these stages.

1. *Prewriting:* getting and organizing ideas for writing
2. *Drafting:* writing down ideas in a rough first draft
3. *Revising:* reworking and improving the written draft
4. *Proofreading:* finding and correcting errors in spelling, punctuation, capitalization, grammar, usage, and manuscript form
5. *Publishing:* sharing the writing with other people

### STEP 1: ANALYZE THE SITUATION

Instead of just starting to write your paper, begin by thinking through what you need and want to accomplish. Ask yourself the following questions.

1. *Assignment:* To what extent does the assignment define what you should do? Does it specify a topic? Does it require a paragraph or an essay? Does the assignment contain any key words such as *explain, compare, identify, retell, discuss, contrast, describe, cite, analyze, define, develop,* or *show*?
2. *Topic:* What will you write about? How can you state your subject precisely? Is your topic exact and narrow enough? Can you sum it up

in a topic sentence or thesis statement that suggests your position or viewpoint?
3. *Purpose:* What is your goal? Will you explain, describe, tell, or argue? Do you want your reader to react by understanding, imagining, being entertained, or being persuaded?
4. *Audience:* Who will read your writing? What should you assume about the reader's background and knowledge?
5. *Voice:* How should your writing sound to a reader? Should it sound informal, formal, calm, emotional, logical, ironic, or straightforward?
6. *Content:* What information will you need to provide about the topic? Can you gather all the information you need by analyzing your reading or by thinking about the topic? Do you need to do research? If so, what resources should you draw on?
7. *Form:* How will you shape your writing? Is it to be creative—a play, a poem, or a story? Is it to be an essay, a paragraph, a report, or a term paper? What parts will the writing include? What plan will you use to arrange the parts? What will come first, second, third, and so on?

### STEP 2: MAKE A PLAN

After analyzing your writing situation, you can plan what to do next. Often you will need to find a topic or to narrow the one assigned. Then you can return to any unresolved questions that remain. For example, suppose that you are assigned an informal essay explaining to your classmates three techniques used in a poem you select. Your assignment defines your purpose (to explain), audience (classmates), and voice (informal). Your essay's topic (the poem and your point about it), content (your explanation and examples of three techniques), and form (the order of the paragraphs) will be clearer after you select and analyze a specific poem.

## STEP 3: GATHER INFORMATION

Your assignment may or may not tell you exactly what topic to work on. Either way, instead of just hoping for a brilliant idea, try one of these prewriting methods to get ideas for or about a topic.

1. *Freewriting:* Write about the topic for several minutes. Don't worry about spelling, punctuation, or logical connections between ideas. Simply get down on paper everything that comes to mind about the topic. Later you can rephrase your best ideas.
2. *Clustering:* On a blank piece of paper, write and circle your topic. Add other ideas, circling them and using lines to connect them to the topic.
3. *Questioning:* Act like a reporter and ask questions about your topic. Begin your questions with *who, what, where, when, why,* and *how.*
4. *Listing:* Make a list of events in sequence, pro and con arguments, differences, similarities, subtypes, examples, or causes.
5. *Analyzing:* Identify the parts of your topic. That is, look for subtopics and for relationships among the parts and the whole.
6. *Researching:* Look up terms, details, or whatever background you need to know.

## STEP 4: ORGANIZE YOUR NOTES

After gathering ideas, you are ready to organize your material and to work out a rough outline. Whatever order you choose should suit your topic, be logical, build from idea to idea,

and interest a reader. Try one of these patterns or the reverse of one of these patterns.

1. *Chronological order:* first to last
2. *Spatial order:* nearest to farthest, topmost to bottommost, and so on
3. *Order of complexity:* simplest to most elaborate
4. *Order of familiarity:* best to least understood
5. *Order of frequency:* most to least numerous
6. *Order of importance:* least to most significant
7. *Order of effectiveness:* least to most convincing

## CASE STUDY: PREWRITING

Brian's English teacher assigned an informal paragraph. Brian was to pick a reading that he found especially interesting and then explain briefly how and why he reacted to it as he did.

Brian decided to write about Mary Shelley's Introduction to *Frankenstein.* First he analyzed the writing situation.

- Assignment: paragraph—explain reaction
- Topic: Shelley's Introduction to *Frankenstein*—but what about it?
- Purpose: explain so reader understands
- Audience: Ms. Burton—maybe class? all have read Shelley's essay
- Voice: informal, personal reactions
- Content: why like it? why interesting?
- Form: paragraph—needs topic sentence and examples—which ones? what order?

Brian decided to try freewriting to figure out what to say about his topic.

Shelley wrote this famous story. It is also famous in movies. I thought she must of been a natural writer. Didn't expect her to have trouble writing. Byron and Shelley wrote OK stories even tho they are famous poets. But she can't get an idea. After hearing about these experiments she gets this vision. She still doesn't think she can write a story, then she sees its her story.

Brian saw two main ideas in his freewriting: Mary Shelley had written a famous story, and she had trouble writing, just as he did. He did not know how to develp the first idea but he thought he could figure out a topic sentence about the second. He made this rough outline, using details from the essay.

- Topic: I did not expect Shelley to have trouble writing.
  
  She can't get an idea—others can
  
  She gets a vision
  
  Finally she sees that it's her story
  
  conclusion?

## ACTIVITIES AND ASSIGNMENTS

A. Answer these questions about the case study:

1. Review Brian's freewriting and rough outline. Did he finally resolve all the questions about his writing situation? Revise his first chart to include his later decisions.
2. Review Brian's freewriting. What mistakes in grammar or phrasing did Brian make? Why didn't he take the time to correct these at this stage?
3. What order did Brian use to arrange the three details in his rough outline?

B. Choose a selection that interests you. Follow these prewriting steps to prepare for writing an informal paragraph about it:

1. Make notes to analyze your writing situation.
2. Decide what your next step should be. Use one of the prewriting techniques explained above to gather ideas.
3. Work out a rough outline, using your prewriting notes. Make sure that you have a specific topic and an idea about how to organize your ideas. Save all of your notes.

# Lesson 2: Drafting and Revising

## DRAFTING YOUR PAPER

*Drafting* is the process of putting ideas down on paper. The following guidelines will help you with the drafting stage of the writing process:

1. Choose a drafting method that is right for you. Some people like to make a detailed outline or prewriting plan and then to write a slow, meticulous draft based on this outline or plan. Other people like to write a very quick and very rough draft and then to revise this draft several times.

2. Whichever drafting method you choose, it is a good idea to do at least some planning before writing. In other words, you should have some idea about what you are going to say and in what order. You may wish to make a rough outline before you begin drafting.

3. Concentrate on getting your ideas down on paper. You can revise and proofread your work later.

4. Be open to new ideas that occur to you as you write. If necessary, change your writing plan to accommodate these new ideas.

## REVISING YOUR DRAFT

*Revising* is the process of reworking and refining your draft. To revise a paper, read it over carefully and ask yourself the questions in the Checklist for Revision.

If your answer to any of the questions is "no," rework your draft until you can answer "yes." You may find that you need to revise your draft several times.

## CASE STUDY: DRAFTING AND REVISING

Brian used his prewriting notes to begin writing his informal paragraph on Mary Shelley's Introduction to *Frankenstein*. After reviewing the assignment, his freewriting, and his rough out-

---

### CHECKLIST FOR REVISION

*Topic and Purpose*
☐ Is my topic clear?
☐ Does the writing have a specific purpose?
☐ Does the writing achieve its purpose?

*Audience*
☐ Will everything I have written be clear to my audience?
☐ Will my audience find the writing interesting?
☐ Will my audience respond in the way I would like?

*Voice and Word Choice*
☐ Is the impression my writing conveys the one I intended it to convey?
☐ Is my language appropriately formal or informal?
☐ Have I avoided vague, undefined terms?
☐ Have I used vivid, specific nouns, verbs, and adjectives?
☐ Have I avoided jargon that my audience will not understand?
☐ Have I avoided clichés?
☐ Have I avoided slang, odd connotations, euphemisms, and gobbledygook (except for novelty or humor)?

*Content/Development*
☐ Have I avoided including unnecessary or unrelated ideas?
☐ Have I developed my topic completely?
☐ Have I supplied examples or details that support the statements that I have made?
☐ Are my sources of information unbiased, up-to-date, and authoritative?
☐ Are my quotations verbatim, or word for word?

*Form*
☐ Have I followed a logical method of organization?
☐ Have I used transitions, or connecting words, to make the organization clear?
☐ Does the writing have a clear introduction, body, and conclusion?

line, Brian decided that he needed to work on a topic sentence. Here's how he drafted and revised that topic sentence:

- Topic idea: I did not expect Shelley to have trouble writing.

- Topic sentence: I enjoyed reading it because I found out about her trouble writing which was not what I expected.

- Revised version: I enjoyed reading Mary Shelley's Introduction to *Frankenstein* because I found out about something I didn't expect—that she had trouble coming up with ideas for writing.

Next Brian used this topic sentence to get started drafting his paragraph, shown at right.

## ACTIVITIES AND ASSIGNMENTS

A. Answer the following questions about Brian's revisions of his rough draft:

1. What transitions did Brian add to his paragraph?
2. Why did Brian delete the sentence, "She is just real terrified"?
3. Why did Brian change some of the wording in his sentence about Mary Shelley's vision?
4. Why did he add the last sentences?
5. What other changes did Brian make? Why did he make these changes?

B. Using your notes from the preceding lesson, draft and revise your own paragraph. Follow these steps:

1. Review your notes and your rough outline.
2. Work on your topic sentence, refining it so that your specific topic and your approach to or attitude toward the topic is clear.
3. If necessary, revise your rough outline. Note your subtopics (the parts of your main topic), and add any new significant details that occur to you.
4. Use your revised topic sentence to start your paragraph.
5. Write the body of your paragraph, presenting the subtopics and details from your outline.
6. Write a conclusion.
7. Revise your draft using the Checklist for Revision on page 1335. Keep all of your notes and drafts.

I enjoyed reading Mary Shelley's Introduction to Frankenstein because I found out about something I didn't expect—that she had trouble coming up with ideas for writing Since Her story has become so famous, I thought Shelley was just a natural writer. Instead, I found out, that she had trouble getting an idea for a story. Even though her husband, Shelley, Byron, and Polidori had wrote theres, she could not think of an idea. Finally she has this imaginative vision about an experiment in science. She is just real terrified. a terrifying creating life. At first, She just does not see recognise this as her story she just wishes she did write something just as creepy. frightening Then she realizes that she has this is her idea for a story. Her problem surprised me but they also reassured me. I hadn't expected to find out that a writer like her had the same writing problem I usually do.

# Lesson 3: Proofreading and Publishing

## USING EDITORIAL SYMBOLS

The last lesson discussed reorganizing, adding, cutting, and otherwise revising your writing. Once you have made these major revisions, you are ready to make more detailed changes such as adding punctuation, correcting capitalization, and refining word order. The editorial symbols on the right are especially helpful for marking such changes on your final draft.

## PROOFREADING YOUR FINAL DRAFT

*Proofreading* is your last careful review of your paper. As you proofread, look for minor errors and for rough passages that you missed earlier. If possible, let your revised draft sit for a few hours or a day before going over it. Taking a break from your manuscript should make it easier for you to see flaws. Ask yourself the questions listed on the next page as you proofread.

Use a dictionary, a style manual, or a writing textbook to check spellings and rules for punctuation, capitalization, and manuscript form. Once your paper has been proofread, make a clean final copy, if necessary. Check your final version carefully to catch any errors in copying.

## PUBLISHING, OR SHARING YOUR WORK WITH OTHERS

After proofreading your paper, you are ready to share it with readers. When you write papers for school, your teachers will be your primary readers. Nevertheless, you or your class can expand your audience in the following ways:
1. Exchange papers with a small group of students from your class.
2. Read your paper aloud to your class or to another class.
3. Share your writing with your friends and relatives.

4. Make a booklet of your writing at the end of the semester or year.
5. Make a class booklet with a paper by every student.
6. Contribute some of your writing to the school literary magazine.

| EDITORIAL SYMBOLS | | |
|---|---|---|
| Symbol | Meaning | Example |
| | move text | She never again published because of this |
| ℓ or — | delete | in this ~~this~~ book |
| ∧ | insert | the poem's scheme |
| ⌒ | no space | mono logue |
| ⊙ | add period | a line ends It |
| ⋏ | add comma | sonnets, odes and other lyric poems |
| ⋎ | add apostrophe | writers style |
| ⋎ ⋎ | add quotation marks | The Train from Rhodesia |
| ∼ | transpose | to wildly run |
| ¶ | begin paragraph | the stanza. The next image |
| / | lower case | The Poet writes |
| ≡ | capitalize | in "Shore woman" |

7. If your school does not have a literary magazine, start one.
8. Contribute your writing to your school or community newspaper.
9. Enter writing contests for student writers sponsored by community groups or by magazines.

10. Send your writing to magazines that publish student writing.

## CASE STUDY: PROOFREADING AND PUBLISHING

Brian revised his draft paragraph and made a new copy, including all his additions and changes. Then he used the Checklist for Proofreading on the left to locate any remaining problems. This is Brian's proofread draft:

---

**CHECKLIST FOR PROOFREADING**

*Grammar and Usage*
- ☐ Are all of my sentences complete? That is, have I avoided sentence fragments?
- ☐ Do all of my sentences express only one complete thought? That is, have I avoided run-on sentences?
- ☐ Do the verbs I have used agree with their subjects?
- ☐ Have all the words in my paper been used correctly? Am I sure about the meanings of all these words?
- ☐ Is the thing being referred to by each pronoun (*I, me, this, each,* etc.) clear?
- ☐ Have I used adjectives and adverbs correctly?

*Spelling*
- ☐ Am I absolutely sure that each word has been spelled correctly?

*Punctuation*
- ☐ Does every sentence end with a punctuation mark?
- ☐ Have I used commas, semicolons, colons, hyphens, dashes, parentheses, quotation marks, and apostrophes correctly?

*Capitalization*
- ☐ Have I capitalized any words that should not be capitalized?
- ☐ Should I capitalize any words that I have not capitalized?

*Manuscript Form*
- ☐ Have I indented the first line(s) of my paragraph(s)?
- ☐ Have I written my name and the page number in the top right-hand corner of each page?
- ☐ Have I double-spaced the manuscript?
- ☐ Is my manuscript neat and legible?

---

I enjoyed reading Mary Shelley's Introduction to <u>Frankenstein</u> because I found out about ~~something I didn't expect~~ —that she had trouble coming up with ideas for writing. Since her story *about Frankenstein* has become so famous, I thought Shell~~y~~ (e) was just a natural writer. Instead, I found out that she had trouble getting an idea for ~~a~~ *her* story. Even though her husband, Byron, and Polidori had *written* ~~wrote theres~~ *their stories* she could not think of an idea. Finally she *had an* ~~has this~~ imaginative vision about a terrifying experiment in creating life. At first, she *did* ~~does~~ not recognize this as her story, she just ~~wish~~ *wished* ~~es~~ she *could* ~~old~~ write something as frightening. Then she ~~realizes~~ *realized* that this ~~is~~ *was* her idea for a story. Her problems surprised me, but they also reassured me. I hadn't expected to find out that a writer like her had the same writing problem I usually do.

---

Brian recopied his paper, read it through for careless errors, and then exchanged papers with a small group in class.

## ACTIVITIES AND ASSIGNMENTS

A. Answer the following questions about Brian's proofreading in the case study.
1. Explain why Brian made each change that he did.
2. What other changes do you think Brian might have made? Explain why you would have made those changes.

B. Proofread and publish your draft from the preceding lesson on Drafting and Revising. Follow these steps:

1. Use the Checklist for Proofreading on page 1338 to review your draft. Correct any problems that the checklist helps you to identify.
2. Recopy your corrected paper. Read through this final version to make sure that you copied everything correctly.
3. Share your draft with your teacher and with the other students in class.

# SECTION 2: UNDERSTANDING THE PARTS OF A LITERARY WORK: ANALYSIS AND INTERPRETATION

## Lesson 4: Writing About Images

### WHAT IS AN IMAGE?

An *image* is a word or a phrase that presents an experience that can be sensed—a sight, sound, touch, taste, smell, or other physical sensation. For example, Stevie Smith begins "In the Park" this way:

> Walking one day in the park in winter
> I heard two silvered gentlemen talking,
> Two old friends, elderly, walking, talking
> There by the silver lake mid-pooled
>     black in winter.

These images of sight, sound, and movement create a picture, in words, of the scene in the park.

### WHY WRITERS USE IMAGES

Writers use images for several purposes:

1. To create vivid descriptions of the things they write about
2. To suggest emotions or feelings about these things
3. To create figures of speech such as metaphors, similes, and personifications

Sir Philip Sidney begins "Sonnet 31" with these lines:

> With how sad steps, O Moon, thou
>     climb'st the skies!
> How silently, and with how wan a face!

The images in these lines:

1. Describe the sight and sound of the moon moving across the sky,
2. Suggest a sad feeling, and
3. Personify the moon as a person with a wan face who can climb the sky despondently.

### CASE STUDY: WRITING ABOUT IMAGES

Jason's teacher asked each student to write a short essay about the imagery used in a favorite poem. Jason chose to write about William Butler Yeats's "The Lake Isle of Innisfree," on page 1027.

#### Prewriting

Jason first read the poem several times. Then he made the following list of the images in the poem:

- Images of sight:
   "a small cabin . . . of clay and wattles made"
   "nine bean rows"
   "a hive for the honeybee"
   "glade"
   "the veils of the morning"
   "midnight's all a glimmer"
   "noon a purple glow"
   "roadway . . . pavements gray"

- Images of sound:
   "the bee-loud glade"
   "the cricket sings"
   "the linnet's wings"
   "lake water lapping with low sounds by the shore"
   "I hear it in the deep heart's core"

Jason looked up *Innisfree, wattles, glade,* and *linnet* in a dictionary. Then he added these definitions to his notes:

- Innisfree: an island on a lake in County Sligo, Ireland

- wattles: sticks interwined with twigs and branches to make crude fences or walls

- glade: an open space in a forest

- linnet: a small songbird found in Europe, Asia, and Africa

As Jason thought about the images in the poem, he noticed that the speaker describes two scenes. The first two stanzas describe a rural setting—the island of Innisfree. The last stanza describes a city scene. Jason added these observations to his notes:

- Stanzas 1 and 2: images used to create a picture of the natural beauty on the island of Innisfree. The mood created by these images is one of peacefulness.

- Stanza 3: images used to create a picture of a street scene in a city. The mood created by these images is one of unpleasantness.

Next Jason wrote this topic sentence:

In "The Lake Isle of Innisfree," by William Butler Yeats, the speaker uses images to contrast living in an ugly city with living in a beautiful natural setting.

Finally, Jason made the following rough outline for an essay:

- Introductory paragraph: Begin by pointing out how city-dwellers often long to escape to a simpler existence in the country. End paragraph with thesis statement.

- Body paragraph 1: Discuss images used in poem to create a beautiful country scene.

- Body paragraph 2: Discuss contrast between beautiful country scene and the city in which the speaker lives.

- Conclusion: Make point that modern urban life creates many pressures and that escape often seems desirable. Point out that Yeats's beautiful imagery makes living in the country seem very desirable indeed.

**Drafting and Revising**

Jason used his notes to write a rough draft of a four-paragraph essay. Then he revised his essay, using the Checklist for Revision on page 1335.

**Proofreading and Publishing**

After revising his draft, Jason made a clean copy and proofread it carefully. Then he shared this proofread copy with his parents and with his teacher.

**ACTIVITIES AND ASSIGNMENTS**

A. Use Jason's prewriting notes to write an essay about imagery in "The Lake Isle of Innisfree," on page 1027. Revise and proofread your essay. Then share it with your classmates and with your teacher.

B. Choose a poem from your textbook and write a short essay about its imagery. Follow these steps:

1. Read the poem carefully, noting as many of the images as you can.
2. Prepare a chart of the images, arranged by type (sight, sound, taste, touch, and smell).
3. Make notes about why the writer may have used these images—what pictures they create and how they affect the reader.
4. Review your prewriting notes to decide which ideas seem most likely to produce a thoughtful and persuasive paper. Draft a thesis sentence that sums up your topic and your point about it.
5. Make a rough outline, grouping the ideas that belong together in each paragraph.
6. Write a draft of your paper, including an introductory paragraph, one or more body paragraphs, and a conclusion.
7. Revise your paper and then proofread it, using the checklists on pages 1335 and 1338.
8. Share your final copy with your family, with a friend, or with a classmate.

# Lesson 5: Writing About Sound

## DEVICES OF SOUND IN LITERATURE

Literary works, especially poems, often contain special devices of sound that are used to suggest or to reinforce meaning. Consider, for example, the use of words to imitate the sounds of musical instruments in these lines from John Dryden's "A Song for Saint Cecilia's Day":

> The soft complaining flute
> In dying notes discovers
> The woes of hopeless lovers,
> Whose dirge is whispered by the
>     warbling lute.

The list on the right describes some of the most commonly used devices of sound.

## CASE STUDY: WRITING ABOUT SOUND

Janine's English teacher asked the class to choose a passage from *The Tragedy of Macbeth* and to write about the use of devices of sound in the passage. Janine chose to write about the opening scene of the play.

### Prewriting

Janine began by reading the passage aloud several times and listening to its sounds. Then she copied the passage into her notebook and marked its devices of sound, as shown on page 1343.

Then Janine took the following notes about the devices of sound used in the passage:

- Opening sounds like a chant, very rhythmical; four-beat lines (tetrameter)

- Rhyming lines: again/rain, done/won/sun, fair/air

- Onomatopoeia: hurlyburly

- Alliteration: *f* sounds in last two lines

- Parallelism: "Fair is foul, and foul is fair"

- Break in pattern: four-beat lines continue until the Third Witch's line "There to meet with Macbeth." This change in the rhythm

---

### SOUND DEVICES

*Alliteration:* the repetition of initial consonant sounds, as in "O, my *l*uve is *l*ike a *r*ed, *r*ed rose"

*Assonance: a partial rhyme involving repetition of a stressed vowel sound but not of the surrounding consonant sounds, as in "about the house"*

*Consonance:* a partial rhyme involving repetition of similar consonant sounds but not of the intervening vowel sounds, as in "a monkey's uncle" or "dancing zebras."

*Rhyme:* the repetition of sounds at the ends of words, as in "Then look ar*ound*, and choose thy gr*ound*"

*Cacophony:* the use of harsh, unpleasant sounds, as in "hectic red,/Pestilence-stricken multitudes"

*Euphony:* the use of beautiful, pleasant sounds, as in "Much have I traveled in the realms of gold"

*Onomatopoeia:* the use of words that sound like what they refer to, as in "And full-grown lambs loud *bleat* from hilly bourn"

*Meter:* the use of a regular, recurring rhythmical pattern, as in "In Xanadu did Kubla Khan/A stately pleasure-dome decree"

*Parallelism:* the repetition of a grammatical pattern, as in "the night was dark, no father was there;/The child was wet with dew"

*Repetition:* the use, again, of a sound, word, phrase, sentence, grammatical pattern, or rhythmical pattern. Note that alliteration, assonance, consonance, rhyme, meter, and parallelism are all varieties of repetition.

---

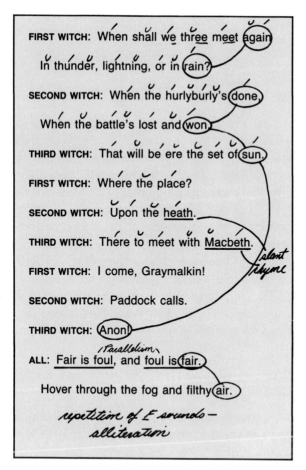

FIRST WITCH: When shall we three meet again

In thunder, lightning, or in rain?

SECOND WITCH: When the hurlyburly's done,

When the battle's lost and won.

THIRD WITCH: That will be ere the set of sun.

FIRST WITCH: Where the place?

SECOND WITCH: Upon the heath.

THIRD WITCH: There to meet with Macbeth.

*slant rhyme*

FIRST WITCH: I come, Graymalkin!

SECOND WITCH: Paddock calls.

THIRD WITCH: Anon!

*Parallelism*

ALL: Fair is foul, and foul is fair.

Hover through the fog and filthy air.

*repetition of F sounds — alliteration*

emphasizes the name "Macbeth" and is a little disconcerting.

• The parallelism of "Fair is foul and foul is fair" emphasizes the witches' desire to confuse fair things with foul things.

## Drafting and Revising

Based on these notes, Janine wrote the following rough draft:

Shakespeare's MacBeth begins with a dramatic chant. As if the withces were casting some evil spell. The chant is written in four-beat, tetrameter lines. These opening lines rhyme. As in a chant or spell. The rhyming, four beat lines continue until line 8. Which introduces Macbeth. Line 8 is peculiar because it contains only three lines and because the word *Macbeth* does not rhyme, precisely, with the word *heath,* in the preceeding line. Thus the introduction of the name of Macbeth upsets the rhythmical pattern, just as Macbeth will upset the ordered pattern of life in the kingdom of scotland. The opening scene ends with a rhyming, chantlike couplet. The parallelism of "Fair is foul, and foul is fair" emphasizes the witches desire to confuse foulness with fairness. The repeition, or alliteration, of f sounds in these last lines ties together and emphasizes the words fair, foul, fog, and filthey. Thus creating a mood, or atmosphere, of ugliness and impending horror.

After finishing her rough draft, Janine revised it carefully.

## Proofreading and Publishing

Janine proofread her revised rough draft, made a clean final copy, and handed in her paper to her English teacher.

## ACTIVITIES AND ASSIGNMENTS

A. Revise Janine's rough draft from the preceding case study. Follow these steps:

1. Correct all the sentence fragments in the draft.
2. Correct the misspellings and the improper punctuation. Italicize or underline the title of the play.
3. Make any other corrections you feel are necessary.
4. Proofread the revised draft, and then share the proofread copy with your classmates.

B. Choose a poem or a passage from a play or short story and write an analysis of the devices of sound used in it. Follow the procedure outlined in the case study. Begin by copying the passage or poem into your notebook. Then mark its devices of sound and make notes about them. Finally, write a paragraph presenting your analysis of the devices of sound, organized in order of their appearance in the poem or passage. Revise and proofread your paragraph. Then share it with your teacher and with your classmates.

# Lesson 6: Writing About Figures of Speech

## WHAT ARE FIGURES OF SPEECH?

When expressions or words are used imaginatively, rather than literally, they are called *figures of speech.* The following lines from "A Litany in Time of Plague," by Thomas Nashe, illustrate *metaphor,* a figure of speech in which one thing is described as though it were something else:

Beauty is but a flower
Which wrinkles will devour.

Besides identifying beauty with a flower that will soon wilt, Nashe implies a comparison between the flower and youthful human skin. The skin's beauty, like the flower's, soon will be gone, eaten by wrinkles as if they were hungry animals.

The following lines from "A Birthday," by Christina Rossetti, contain *similes.* A simile is a figure of speech that compares two subjects using *like* or *as:*

My heart is like a singing bird...
My heart is like an apple tree...
My heart is like a rainbow shell...

Other figures of speech are listed in the chart later in this lesson and in the Handbook of Literary Terms and Techniques.

Such figures of speech can be analyzed to figure out how they work. The literal subject in a metaphor or simile is sometimes called the *tenor.* This subject shares a certain characteristic with the *vehicle,* the figurative term to which it is compared. For example, in Rossetti's third line above, the heart is the tenor. It is compared with the vehicle, a rainbow shell. Different as a heart and a shell are, the comparison makes sense because both share the characteristic of being in a happy situation.

## WHY WRITERS USE FIGURES OF SPEECH

Writers use figurative language because its vividness and concreteness enriches what they want to say. Instead of writing the lines quoted earlier, Nashe could just have said, "Everything beautiful ends up getting old." This statement is literal and dull. It does not create lively pictures or trigger strong emotional or imaginative responses in a reader. In just two lines of figurative language, however, Nashe compares two fragile, desirable subjects—beauty and a flower—and two frightening subjects—wrinkling with age and being devoured. In this way Nashe awakens powerful feelings in his reader.

## CASE STUDY: WRITING ABOUT FIGURES OF SPEECH

Ladelle's English assignment was to write a short essay analyzing a poem's figurative language. To get the class started, the teacher listed figures of speech on the chalkboard.

### Prewriting

Ladelle started her prewriting by reviewing these terms and making a list of how each works. As she analyzed her chosen poem, "Ode to the West Wind," by Percy Bysshe Shelley, she noted figures of speech:

- Antithesis: Use of parallelism to present contrasting ideas
  Maybe "Destroyer and preserver" (first stanza)

- Apostrophe: Direct address of an object, idea, or absent person
  "O wild West Wind...Thou breath of Autumn's being Thou" (first stanza)

- Hyperbole: Exaggeration/overstatement

"azure moss and flowers/So sweet, the sense faints picturing them" (third stanza)

- Irony: Contrast between what is and what seems
    Double nature of west wind (first and fourth stanzas)—both destroyer and preserver

- Metaphor: Comparison through identification
    "I fall upon the thorns of life! I bleed!" (fourth stanza)
    "Ashes and sparks, my words among mankind!" (fifth stanza)

- Metonymy: Substitution of closely related thing
    "A heavy weight of hours" for time (fourth stanza)

- Paradox: Contradiction which is true
    "Destroyer and preserver" (first stanza)

- Personification: Use of human qualities for animal, thing, or idea
    Mediterranean Sea sleeps and dreams (third stanza)

- Simile: Comparison with *like* or *as*
    Leaves "driven, like ghosts" fleeing (first stanza)
    Seeds "Each like a corpse" in a grave (first stanza)
    Clouds shed like "decaying leaves" (second stanza)
    Clouds spread like "bright hair" (second stanza)
    "Make me thy lyre" as forest is (fifth stanza)
    "dead thought" driven like leaves (fifth stanza)

- Synecdoche: Substitution of part for the whole
    "Be through my lips," meaning through his voice and words as a poet (fifth stanza)

- Understatement: Statement of less than is meant
    can't find example in poem

Next Ladelle tried to sum up Shelley's point, or theme, so that she could see the purpose of the poem's figurative language. She turned this idea into her thesis statement and jotted it down:

- Thesis: Shelley uses figurative language to describe the west wind and to explain his ambition as a poet.

Since she had found many figures of speech but was writing only a short essay, Ladelle knew that she had to decide which figures and examples were most important. These choices resulted in her rough outline for a four-paragraph essay:

- Paragraph 1: Thesis and introduction

- Paragraph 2: Description of west wind apostrophe, paradox, and simile (transition to next paragraph)

- Paragraph 3: Explanation of Shelley's ambition as poet simile, metaphor, and synecdoche

- Paragraph 4: Conclusion and summary

**Drafting and Revising**

After drafting her first paragraph, Ladelle started on her second. Here is the rough draft of her second paragraph:

Shelley uses apostrophe, paradox, and simile to discribe the wind. The paradox, "Destroyer and preserver," tells how the wind both blows away the autum leaves and saving the seeds for next spring. The poem opens with apostrophe, as Shelly talks directly to the wind. He hails it, saying, "O wild West Wind, thou breath of Autumn's being" (line 1). Finally, the similes in the first two sections. They discribe how the wind effects the things around it. The west wind blows dead leaves "like ghosts from an enchanter fleeing." It drops the seeds on the gound where they wait "like a corpse within its grave" (line 8) for spring. It carries along clouds like leaves, like "bright hair." All these figures of speech discribe the wind.

Ladelle completed her essay and revised it.

## Proofreading and Publishing

After proofreading her final copy, Ladelle shared her paper with her best friend and then handed it in.

## ACTIVITIES AND ASSIGNMENTS

A. Answer the following questions about Ladelle's writing in the case study:
1. Why doesn't Ladelle's rough outline list every figure of speech in her chart?
2. How might Ladelle reorganize the rough draft of her second paragraph? What grammatical errors and other problems need to be corrected? Based on your answers to this question, revise and proofread Ladelle's paragraph.

B. Write a short essay about the figures of speech in a poem by Blake, Wordsworth, Byron, Keats, Hardy, Meredith, Auden, or Heaney. Follow these steps:
1. Read the poem aloud and make a handwritten copy.
2. On your copy, mark the figures of speech that you find. List them by type in a chart.
3. Decide how you want to organize your essay. Each paragraph might make a single point about the poem, using figures of speech as subtopics or examples; or each paragraph might focus on a different figure of speech, explaining how it works and what it adds to the poem. Make a rough outline and draft a thesis statement.
4. Draft your essay, following your outline. Include an introduction, several body paragraphs, and a conclusion.
5. Revise and proofread your draft using the checklists on pages 1335 and 1338.
6. Share your final copy with your teacher and with a friend.

# Lesson 7: Writing About Setting

## WHAT IS SETTING?

The *setting* of a literary work is the environment within which the action occurs. Using images and details, the writer may describe the geographical location, the historical period, the season of the year, the weather, a building or room, the furniture, the characters' clothes, their jobs or social circumstances, the local customs —whatever elements will create the sense of a particular time and place.

Often a description of the setting opens a narrative, as in Katherine Mansfield's "A Dill Pickle," on page 929.

> And then, after six years, she saw him again. He was seated at one of those little bamboo tables decorated with a Japanese vase of paper daffodils. There was a tall plate of fruit in front of him, and . . . he was peeling an orange.

This description immediately sets the scene in the restaurant, thus helping the reader imagine the two characters meeting there.

Although Mansfield uses images of sight to introduce this setting, details of sound, taste, touch, or smell may also help create a setting, as in this description of a carpenter's workshop from George Eliot's *Adam Bede:*

> The afternoon sun was warm on the five workmen there, busy upon doors and window-frames and wainscoting. A scent of pine-wood from a tent-like pile of planks outside the open door mingled itself with the scent of the elder-bushes which were spreading their summer snow close to the open window opposite. . . .

In the rest of the passage, Eliot describes the appearance of the dog lying in the workshop, the texture of its bed, and the sound of a worker singing.

## HOW WRITERS USE SETTINGS

Writers use settings for various purposes. Here are some of the ways in which setting may be used.

| USES OF SETTING |
|---|
| To make a work more believable through vivid, precise descriptions |
| To create a mood, or atmosphere |
| To create a conflict, as when a character struggles against something in his or her environment |
| To symbolize a key concept that the writer wants to express |

A setting may also reflect a character's situation, complicate the plot, highlight the theme, or otherwise add to the overall effect of the work.

## CASE STUDY: WRITING ABOUT SETTING

Anthony's class was studying Victorian prose and novels. Each student was to write a paragraph or two about the significance of the setting in one of the Victorian selections in this book.

### Prewriting

After deciding to work on the Victorian novel *Jane Eyre,* Anthony started his prewriting by listing answers to key questions about the setting:

- What is the setting?
    Place—the Reed family's house
    Time—an afternoon long ago, probably about when Brontë lived
    Season—wintry November
    Weather—cold, windy, rainy

- What details are used to create the setting?
  Description of day (paragraphs 1–2)—
  wind, clouds, and rain
  Drawing room—Mrs. Reed lying on
  sofa by fireplace with children around
  Window seat in breakfast room—
  enclosed by curtains; bookcases; out-
  side view of wintry day
  Social background—John Reed says
  Jane is a poor dependent (fight scene)

- What is significance of the setting?
  Description of day (paragraphs 1–2)—
  dreary cold; sad and "humbled" feelings from walks (mood: shows and
  reflects Jane's situation); cold outside
  like cold people inside
  Drawing room—Mrs. Reed has "her
  darlings about her" but not Jane
  (shows Jane's conflict with Reeds)
  Window seat—curtains and glass "protecting, but not separating" from the wintry day, followed by John's attack and
  throwing book (mood: shows Jane's
  feelings)

Anthony reviewed his notes. He decided that he
wanted to focus on the way the setting added to
the mood and symbolized Jane's situation at the
beginning of the novel. He worked next on a
rough outline and on a topic sentence.

## Drafting and Revising

As Anthony worked on his draft, he discovered that he was explaining Jane Eyre's situation more than the mood of the story. He then
revised his topic sentence so that it more accurately reflected the content of his paragraph. On
the right is Anthony's revised draft.

## Proofreading and Publishing

After Anthony finished revising his draft, he
let it sit overnight. Then he proofread his paragraph, made a final copy, and read it to his
discussion group during class.

---

*at the beginning of Jane Eyre*
The setting ~~adds to the mood of the novel~~

~~and~~ symbolizes Janes situation. Her story begins

~~starts~~ (on this wintrish afternoon) at the Reeds
a penny-less
home where she is dependent. The cold

wind, the 'clouds so somber,' and the 'rain so

penetrating' prevent ~~an afternoon walk on~~ ~~c~~
Jane does not mind because
~~that afternoon.~~ The walks always made ~~Jane~~ her

feel sad. ~~They also made~~ and her feel inferior.

This opening setting immediately helps to
Jane's isolated and unhappy situation.
point out ~~that Jane is very isolated and very~~

~~unhappy in this situation.~~ The indoor setting
comfortable with
also contrasts the life of the Reeds ~~up~~
cruel treatment and in the
~~against~~ Jane's isolation. The window seat breakfast room

hides and protects Jane Jane temporarily but

even their the ~~the~~ window is "protecting, but

not separating me from the drear Nov. day."
Indoors or out, isolated cold and dreary
Jane is ~~Separated~~ from others, facing a set-
with the Reed
ting that symbolizes her life.

---

## ACTIVITIES AND ASSIGNMENTS

A. Proofread Anthony's paragraph. What additional changes or corrections are needed in his
final copy?

B. Choose from this book a short story or an
excerpt from a novel. Write a paper of one or two
paragraphs analyzing the significance of the setting. Follow these steps.

1. Read your selection several times. First concentrate on the action of the story. Then read

the selection again, paying close attention to details of the setting.

2. Write out answers to these key questions about setting:

    a. What is the setting? the time? the place?

    b. What details are used to create the setting?

    c. What is the significance of the setting?

    As you do this prewriting, make notes of your answers to each question.

3. Draft a topic sentence that presents your main point. Then use your notes to prepare a rough outline.

4. Draft your paper, following your rough outline. If you want to develop two main points, you may need to write two paragraphs rather than just one.

5. Revise your paper, following the Checklist for Revision on page 1335. Make sure that your topic sentence accurately reflects the content of your paper and that it focuses on the significance of the setting.

6. Proofread your paper, using the Checklist for Proofreading on page 1338. Share your final copy with other students who have written about or are interested in the same selection.

# Lesson 8:  Writing About Plot

## WHAT IS PLOT?

A *plot* is a series of events, or occurrences, each of which is causally related to those that have preceded it. One event in a plot causes the next, which causes the next, and so on to the end of the story. Most plots involve a *central conflict,* or struggle, that is introduced, developed, and then resolved. Typically, the plot of a story, drama, or narrative poem is divided into the following parts:

1. Introduction, or exposition: presents the setting, the major characters, and the basic situation
2. Inciting incident: introduces the central conflict
3. Development: events that occur because of the central conflict
4. Climax: high point of interest or suspense that culminates the development
5. Resolution: event that ends the central conflict
6. Denouement: any events that occur after the resolution

Some critics refer to the introduction, inciting incident, development, and climax as the *rising action,* and to the resolution and denouement as the *falling action.*

Some stories do not contain all these parts in exactly this order. An author may choose, for example, to begin a story *in medias res* (literally, "in the middle part"), after the inciting incident has occurred. The inciting incident of Milton's *Paradise Lost,* for instance, is the expulsion of Satan from heaven. However, Milton begins the poem in the middle of the action, after this expulsion has taken place. In some stories the climax and the resolution are the same event. In some there is no denouement, or tying up of loose ends after the resolution.

## SPECIAL DEVICES OF PLOT

Most plots are presented in chronological order. That is, the events follow one another in time as they would in real life. However, an author may choose to vary this pattern by using flashbacks. A *flashback* is a section of a literary work that interrupts the normal sequence of events to present an event from an earlier time. The following special devices of plot are also commonly used by authors:

1. Foreshadowing: hinting about events yet to occur
2. Subplot: a series of events outside but related to the main plot; common in long works such as novels and full-length dramas
3. Suspense: the creation of a feeling of anxious uncertainty about the outcome of events
4. Surprise ending: an unexpected event occurring at the end of the story

## CASE STUDY: WRITING ABOUT PLOT

Nikki's teacher asked each student to select a short story from the text and to write a paragraph about some aspect of its plot. Nikki decided to write about Elizabeth Bowen's "The Demon Lover," on page 994.

### Prewriting

Nikki began by analyzing the plot so that she could pick one aspect to focus on in her paragraph. She worked out a list like this:

- Exposition: Mrs. Drover visits house

- Inciting incident: Mrs. Drover finds letter and feels afraid

- Development: Mrs. Drover recalls her fiancé in a flashback, remembers the promise that she made, feels afraid, wants to escape, leaves for safety of taxi

- False climax and resolution: Mrs. Drover arrives at taxi stand and thinks that she is safe

- Real climax and resolution (surprise ending): sees driver eye to eye, screams
- Denouement: taxi carries Mrs. Drover off

Nikki also noted some of Bowen's special techniques:

- Foreshadowing:
  Beginning—"dead air" in house
  Mysterious unstamped letter from K.
  "spectral glitters" in fiancé's eyes
  "suspension of her existence" during week with fiancé in August of 1916
  No memory of her fiancé's face
  Someone leaves house before she does

- Flashbacks (Mrs. Drover's memories):
  Last evening with fiancé—August, 1916
  Her life after fiancé is declared missing in action
  Why she made promise to her fiancé

- Suspense:
  Wondering who (or what) is after her
  Wondering if she will get away

- Surprise ending:
  Thinks she is safe in taxi but taxi driver carries her off screaming

Nikki wrote several possible topic sentences, as follows:

In "The Demon Lover" Elizabeth Bowen makes use of several special plot devices, including flashbacks, foreshadowing, and a surprise ending.

Elizabeth Bowen's "The Demon Lover" has a traditional plot structure consisting of an exposition, an inciting incident, a development, a climax, and a brief denouement.

In "The Demon Lover" Elizabeth Bowen builds suspense and then tricks the reader with a false resolution.

## Drafting and Revising

Nikki liked all of her topic sentences. However, she couldn't write about all of them, so she chose the third one. She wrote a quick draft of her paper, pouring all her ideas onto the page and not stopping to worry about proper spelling, grammar, and punctuation. Then she revised her paragraph several times. As she revised, she cut a lot of nonessential details, and she added direct quotations from the story to support her claims.

## Proofreading and Publishing

After her revisions were done, Nikki proofread her paper carefully to get it ready for a reader. Then she shared her final proofread paper with classmates in a small group discussion.

## ACTIVITIES AND ASSIGNMENTS

A. Read or reread "The Demon Lover," on page 994. Use Nikki's prewriting notes, plus your own ideas, to write a paragraph about an unusual or striking feature of the story's plot. Follow these steps:

1. Combine your own ideas and examples from the story with Nikki's prewriting notes. Work out a rough outline of main points and examples, using one of her narrowed topics or your own topic.
2. Begin your paragraph with a topic sentence that makes a specific point about the plot. Refine one of Nikki's topic sentences or write your own.
3. Write the body of your paragraph, following your outline. Explain the main points needed to defend your topic sentence. Quote and summarize as needed, but do not simply retell the story.
4. Write a concluding sentence.
5. Revise and proofread, using the checklists on pages 1335 and 1339.
6. Hand in your paper after sharing it with other students in your class.

B. Choose one of the following works: "The Rocking-Horse Winner," on page 974; "Araby," on page 987; "A Mild Attack of Locusts," on page 1252; *Macbeth,* on page 271; or "The Rime of the Ancient Mariner," on page 660. Then write a paragraph about some aspect of its plot. Follow these steps:

1. After reading the story twice, list the events in the story. Organize them as Nikki did in the case study. Note the parts of the plot and any special techniques used by the writer.

2. Use your prewriting notes to choose a specific focus for your paragraph. Prepare a rough outline and a statement of your topic.

3. Write a rough draft. Follow your outline, develop your topic sentence, and add a conclusion.

4. Revise and proofread your draft, using the checklists on pages 1335 and 1338.

5. Share your final paragraph with a friend in your class.

# Lesson 9: Writing About Character

## WHAT IS CHARACTERIZATION?

In a literary work, each person, or each animal or object treated like a person, is called a *character*. The *protagonist*, or *main character*, plays the central role in the work and often wins the reader's admiration or sympathy. In some works the main character is in direct conflict with another character, known as the *antagonist*. Many works contain other major and minor characters as well, each with his or her contribution to make to the work as a whole.

*Characterization* is the act of introducing and developing characters in such a way as to make them real or believable. Here is the way Jane Austen introduces the protagonist in *Emma:*

> Emma Woodhouse, handsome, clever, and rich, with a comfortable home and happy disposition, seemed to unite some of the best blessings of existence; and had lived nearly twenty-one years in the world with very little to distress or vex her.

## HOW WRITERS CREATE CHARACTERS

A writer may reveal the personality of a character directly or indirectly. When a writer uses *direct characterization*, he or she simply tells the reader what the character is like. When a writer uses *indirect characterization*, he or she presents the actions, words, and thoughts of a character as clues to the personality of that character or of another character.

A writer may decide to create a *round character*—one who is complex, just like a real person—or a *flat character*—one who has only a few distinguishing characteristics. The main character in a work is usually round, or complex. Minor characters are often flat.

In developing a character, a writer provides information about the following:

1. *Physical Appearance:* What does the character look like? What does the character wear?
2. *Background:* Where does the character come from? Who are the character's friends? Who are the character's relatives? What has the character experienced before the time of the story?
3. *Personality:* What are the character's special qualities and habits? How does the character tend to react to events or relate to others? How does the character think or feel?
4. *Actions:* How does the character behave? How does the character act toward others or cause others to act?
5. *Words:* What does the character say? What do others say about the character?
6. *Motivation:* Why does the character act or react in certain ways? What does the character want or need?
7. *Conflict:* Does the character have an external or internal conflict? How is the conflict resolved?
8. *Change:* Does the character change in the course of the story? If so, why, and in what ways?

## CASE STUDY: WRITING ABOUT CHARACTERS

Each student in Sarah's class was asked to write a paragraph about a character in a short story. Sarah decided to analyze the woman on the train in "The Train from Rhodesia," on page 1260.

### Prewriting

After rereading the story, Sarah spent five minutes writing down everything that came to mind as she thought about the character. She worked as quickly as possible, without worrying about her wording or her grammar. Here is Sarah's freewriting:

> The woman ends up feeling very sad—sort of empty and tired. She thought getting married would make her less lonesome. But her husband seems strange and unreal. Like everything else on their vacation. They have a fight because of the carved lion. He got it for her because she liked it and he liked bargaining for it. She loves the lion—it's artistic and beautiful. But she is angry and ashamed—something beautiful should not be bargained for. It should just be paid for—have its dignity. The lion and the fight make her realize how alone she still is because her husband doesn't understand. Maybe she's like the train—calling to the sky but getting no answer.

Next Sarah turned to the questions listed earlier in the lesson. She skipped those that the story did not answer and then concentrated on answering those that seemed most important.

- Motivation:
  The woman sees the lion's beauty.
  She seems afraid to take it home in case it doesn't mean anything there.
  She feels ashamed at bargaining for something beautiful.
  She wanted her husband to share her feelings—but she still feels alone.

- Conflict:
  The lion causes conflict with her husband—not resolved at the end.

- Change:
  She doesn't exactly change—she just realizes that things are the same inside her—still empty.

Now Sarah felt prepared to plan her character study. She decided that the key to the character was her loneliness at the end. Sarah worked next on listing her main ideas:

- My main points:
  woman ends up feeling very sad—
  empty

lion causes conflict—not resolved
she loved lion but he loved bargaining
she is ashamed at bargaining for
beauty
because of this conflict she realizes
that the same feelings are still inside
her—empty, tired, lonely

## Drafting and Revising

Once Sarah had an outline and a topic sentence, she was ready to write her rough draft. She wrote a paragraph, let it sit several hours, and then revised it.

## Proofreading and Publishing

Sarah proofread her paper and then took it to class. She read it aloud during the class discussion of character motivation.

## ACTIVITIES AND ASSIGNMENTS

A. Use information from the case study to complete these steps:

1. Read or reread "The Train from Rhodesia," on page 1260. Review Sarah's prewriting notes and add other notes of your own.
2. Turn Sarah's list of main points into an outline for a one-paragraph character study. Revise Sarah's notes as necessary. Then write a topic sentence for your paragraph.
3. Draft a paragraph based on your topic sentence and outline. Make sure that you include evidence from the story to support your conclusions about the character.
4. Revise and proofread your paragraph, using the checklists on pages 1335 and 1338.
5. Exchange papers with one or two other students in your class to see how your final paragraphs differ.

B. Select a short story from this book. Write a paragraph about one of the characters. Follow these steps:

1. Read the story several times, first to select a character and then to note how the character

looks, acts, speaks, thinks, and feels.

2. Freewrite for five minutes about the character as if you're trying to figure out a real person. Concentrate on getting your ideas on paper; do not worry about phrasing, spelling, punctuation, or grammar.

3. Add other notes to your freewriting, using the list of questions about character. Make sure that all your conclusions are supported by the story.

4. Decide on your main point about the charac-

ter. Write a topic sentence stating this point. Then make a rough outline that presents your main ideas and your supporting examples.

5. Begin your paragraph with a topic sentence.

6. Following your outline, draft the body of your paragraph.

7. Write a concluding sentence that sums up and re-emphasizes your point.

8. Revise and proofread your draft, using the checklists on pages 1335 and 1338. Share your final copy in class.

# Lesson 10:  Writing About Point of View

## WHAT IS POINT OF VIEW?

*Point of view* is the vantage point, or perspective, from which a story is told. If the *narrator,* or storyteller, is one of the characters in the story, then the story is written from the *first-person point of view.* If the narrator is *not* one of the characters but stands outside the action and tells about it, then the story is written from the *third-person point of view.*

In most stories written from the first-person point of view, the actions or events are reported from one person's perspective. Everything is seen through the eyes of the character/narrator. Such a point of view is said to be *limited.*

In some stories written from the third-person point of view, the narrator tells the tale from one character's limited perspective. However, in other third-person stories the narrator is all-knowing, or *omniscient,* and can present the perspectives of all or several of the characters.

To summarize, most stories are written from one of the following points of view:

1. *Limited first-person point of view:* The narrator is a character in the story and presents the action from his or her own perspective.
2. *Limited third-person point of view:* The narrator is *not* a character in the story and presents the action from the perspective of one of the characters.
3. *Omniscient third-person point of view:* The narrator is *not* a character in the story. He or she is all-knowing and can present the internal states or viewpoints of all the characters.

## DIFFERENCES BETWEEN POINTS OF VIEW

Stories told from a limited point of view tend to be highly personal and immediate in their impact. The reader usually identifies with the one character from whose perspective the story is told. However, the narrator in such a story is unable to reveal, directly, the private thoughts and feelings of all the characters.

Stories told from an omniscient point of view tend not to be as focused on a single individual. In such stories the narrator has a godlike ability to see all things and know all things. Often the narrator in such a story is able to point out or to reveal interesting or amusing contradictions between the thoughts, feelings, and perceptions of the various characters.

## OTHER QUALITIES OF NARRATORS

You have learned about two important respects in which narrators differ. Some narrators participate in the action, and some do not. Some narrators view the events from a limited perspective, and some from an omniscient perspective. Narrators also differ in the following ways:

1. *Reliability:* Some narrators can be counted on to tell the truth. Such narrators are *reliable.* Other narrators grossly distort the truth. Such narrators are *unreliable* or *ironic.*
2. *Objectivity:* Some narrators are cool, calm, and reserved. They simply report events as they occur. Such narrators are *objective.* Other narrators are highly emotional or make their attitudes toward characters and events quite clear. Such narrators are *subjective.*

## CASE STUDY: WRITING ABOUT NARRATION AND POINT OF VIEW

Travis was assigned a brief paper on point of view in a fictional narrative. He decided to analyze Emily Brontë's *Wuthering Heights,* which is introduced on page 898.

### Prewriting

Travis's class had already read the selection from *Wuthering Heights,* so Travis knew that the first-person narrator is Mr. Lockwood. Travis began his prewriting by rereading the selection and taking these notes:

- Point of view: first-person

- Narrator: Mr. Lockwood
  Tries to be reliable and give good account (even if embarrassing to him), but makes too many assumptions
  Starts out assuming that Heathcliff is like him (subjective, not objective)
  Lockwood and Healthcliff very different:
    L.'s fussy and pompous chattering vs. H.'s yelling and growling
    L. expects regular social set-up (servants, tea) and plans visits whereas H. is unsociable (dogs, barred doors, refuses guide in snowstorm).

- Effect of point of view:
  Suggests there's a hidden story since L. doesn't know what's going on
  L. guesses everybody's position in household and is totally wrong.
  Makes us curious about H. and his past because he's so different from L.
  L. seems ordinary, especially in contrast to H.; this suggests that H.'s story will be unusual.

Next Travis worked on organizing all of his material.

## Drafting and Revising

Travis planned two paragraphs: one analyzing Mr. Lockwood as the narrator, and the other discussing how Mr. Lockwood's point of view affects the reader. Here is the beginning of Travis's rough draft:

> I am writing about *Wuthering Heights.* Brontë has Mr. Lockwood tell the story. He is the narrator. He has a first-person point of view. (He is a character in the story and speaks in the first person as "I"). He tries to give an accurate account of Heathcliff. Heathcliff is his landlord. He starts out assuming that Heathcliff is like him. This is a subjective viewpoint. In fact, they are very different.

Travis finished drafting his two paragaphs.

Then he revised them several times.

## Proofreading and Publishing

Travis proofread his paragraphs and shared his final paper with his discussion group in class.

## ACTIVITIES AND ASSIGNMENTS

A. If you haven't already done so, read the Great Works feature on *Wuthering Heights,* on page 898. Revise and complete Travis's draft from the case study. Combine his short sentences to make the draft read more smoothly. Add details to the paragraph, especially at the end, to support the claims made. Rewrite and strengthen Travis's topic sentence. Then add a conclusion to the paragraph. Finally, write a paragraph about the effect of Lockwood's limited point of view on a reader.

B. Select a short story from this text. Analyze the narrator and the point of view. Then write two paragraphs discussing the narrator's point of view and its effect on the reader. Follow these steps:

1. After you have read the story once, identify the narrator and the point of view.
2. Analyze the point of view. Determine whether it is limited or omniscient, first person or third. Also determine whether the narrator is reliable or unreliable, subjective or objective.
3. Reread the story and take notes on the narrator and the point of view. Make sure that your notes address the question of the effect of the point of view on the reader.
4. Organize your ideas. First plan a rough outline. Then work on a topic sentence that states your main idea about the point of view.
5. Draft your two paragraphs. Analyze the narrator and the point of view in the first paragraph. Then discuss how the point of view influences the reader's reaction to the story.
6. Revise your paragraphs, using the Checklist for Revision on page 1335.
7. Proofread your paragraphs, using the Checklist for Proofreading on page 1338.
8. Share your writing with your classmates.

# Lesson 11:  Writing About Theme

## WHAT IS A THEME?

The central idea of a literary work is its *theme.* The theme is an insight about life or the human experience that is revealed through the details of the literary work. For example, the problems characters face and the way they resolve them may provide insight into the human condition. This insight is the theme of the work.

## HOW WRITERS EXPRESS THEMES

Occasionally, the theme of a work is stated directly. Usually, however, the theme is not stated directly. Instead, it is implied by the work as a whole. The many separate aspects of the work combine to suggest its central idea.

For instance, in the morality play *Everyman,* on page 188, the Messenger in the first scene says that the play "of our lives and ending shows/How transitory we be all day." Later in the play, the Doctor sums up the implication of Everyman's death for the playgoers:

> Ye hearers, take it of worth, old and
> young.
> And forsake Pride, for he deceiveth you
> in the end.
> And remember Beauty, Five-Wits,
> Strength, and Discretion,
> They all at the last do Everyman
> forsake.
> Save his Good Deeds there doth he
> take

This passage expresses quite directly the theme of the play: Live a good life, full of good deeds, so that you will find salvation when you die.

Many works, however, are less didactic and thus more difficult to interpret. Raleigh's "The Nymph's Reply to the Shepherd" shows how a work of literature may suggest a theme:

> If all the world and love were young,
> And truth in every shepherd's tongue,
> These pretty pleasures might me move
> To live with thee, and be thy love.

Here the nymph tells the shepherd that she would be willing to be his love under certain conditions. The last stanza echoes the same idea:

> But could youth last and love still
>   breed,
> Had joys no date nor age no need,
> Then those delights my mind might move,
> To live with thee and be thy love.

These first and last stanzas set up conditions for the nymph's agreement. She says that an idyllic love might flourish—*if* everything could stay young and *if* men always spoke the truth. Of course, she and the reader both know that the conditions in the first and last stanzas cannot be met in real life. All is not permanently young and true, and love does not always increase. Raleigh does not directly say that everything, including youth and love, changes over time. Nevertheless, careful readers will conclude that this is, in fact, the poem's theme.

## CASE STUDY: WRITING ABOUT THEME

Liz was asked to write a paragraph about the theme of a short story. She selected Doris Lessing's "A Mild Attack of Locusts," on page 1252.

### Prewriting

Liz read the story several times because she knew that finding the theme meant understanding the whole work. Then she worked on writing out a statement of the theme. When she had trouble getting started, she tried freewriting just to get something on paper.

> I am stuck. So why am I? I really do like this story. The best parts are the descriptions and the characters. Margaret keeps being amazed and feeling discouraged. Her husband and Stephen especially just keep on going. They even end up saying that it could have been worse—though everything green is eaten up. I guess Lessing is saying how amazing it is that people just keep going even when disaster strikes.

When Liz stopped freewriting, she knew that she had begun to work out the theme. After she rephrased her idea, she went back to the story to examine how Lessing actually revealed the theme.

- Theme:
  Despite disasters, human beings can show great strength and resilience.

- Expressions of theme in story:
  Opening of story—Margaret is learning "farmer's language."
  Always problems but they still manage & get along OK
  While waiting for the locusts to come and eat their crops, they keep on working as usual.
  Locusts arrive and they fight them.
  Stephen says they are finished, tells about locusts bankrupting him 20 yrs ago, and goes back out with tea.
  When crops are all eaten, they keep on fighting to prevent locusts from laying eggs (hoppers hatch later).
  Stephen tosses out locust after admiring its strength; Margaret remembers he's said they were ruined before and they've survived.
  Men are cheered because main swarm has gone by—they begin planning to fight hoppers.

Margaret admires beauty of locusts at dawn despite the damage they've done.

- Conclusion:
  Margaret feels like "a survivor after war" & men say, "It could have been worse."

### Drafting and Revising

Liz used her prewriting notes to draft her paragraph. She started with a clear topic sentence about the theme, developed the body of the paragraph, using details from the story, and then wrote a concluding sentence that summarized her analysis. Next Liz revised her paragraph, making sure that her points were clearly stated and organized.

### Proofreading and Publishing

After proofreading, Liz exchanged papers with the student sitting next to her before they both handed in their paragraphs.

### ACTIVITIES AND ASSIGNMENTS

A. Refer to the case study as you write a paragraph, following these directions:

1. Read or reread "A Mild Attack of Locusts," on page 1252. Review Liz's prewriting notes, and add other notes of your own about the theme. Use the notes to work out a rough outline of points about how the theme is revealed to the reader.
2. Write a topic sentence, identifying the story and its theme.
3. Draft the body of your paragraph, discussing how the theme is revealed or expressed in the story. Use your rough outline and Liz's and your prewriting notes to supply detailed supporting evidence from the story.
4. Write a concluding sentence that sums up your analysis of the story's theme.
5. Revise and proofread your paragraph, using the checklists on pages 1335 and 1338.

6. Share your final copy with a classmate before handing it in.

B. Write a paragraph about a literary work in this book. In your paragraph, identify the work's theme, and explain how this theme is expressed or revealed in the work. You may select any literary work or write about one of these: Shakespeare's *Macbeth*, on page 271; Orwell's "Shooting an Elephant," on page 1012; Lawrence's "The Rocking-Horse Winner," on page 974; or Blake's "A Poison Tree," on page 614. Follow these steps:

1. Read the work once or twice. Write a single sentence stating its theme. (Use freewriting if you get stuck.)
2. Refine your statement of theme. Then go through the work, taking notes on points in the work that express, reveal, or illustrate the theme.
3. Work out a rough outline of your ideas.
4. Begin your rough draft with a topic sentence identifying the work and its theme.
5. Follow your rough outline and your prewriting notes as you draft the body of your paragraph. Do not just generalize about the idea of the theme. Be sure to include details from the work to show how the writer conveys the theme.
6. Write a concluding sentence that sums up your main point.
7. Revise your paragraph, using the Checklist for Revision on page 1335.
8. Use the Checklist for Proofreading, on page 1338, to check your final version.
9. Share your paper with your classmates and with your teacher.

# SECTION 3: UNDERSTANDING THE WORK AS A WHOLE: INTERPRETATION AND SYNTHESIS

## Lesson 12: Writing About a Short Story

When you write about a short story, your task begins not with writing but with reading and understanding the story. Follow these guidelines when studying a story:

1. Read the story through to find out what happens in the plot.
2. Look up any unfamiliar words in the Glossary or in a dictionary.
3. Read the story again, this time concentrating on how the writer has created its key features.
4. Refer to the story as you analyze its main elements.

### HOW TO ANALYZE A SHORT STORY

The following list outlines the main elements of short stories (and of longer fictional works as well). Once you have made prewriting notes about these aspects of a story, you are prepared to think about how each contributes to the story's meaning.

1. *Author and title:* Who wrote the story? What is the title of the story? Does the title suggest the subject or theme of the story?
2. *Plot:* What are the story's main events? What happens during each part of the plot: the exposition, the inciting incident, the development, the climax, the resolution, and the denouement? Does the story use special plot techniques such as foreshadowing, flashbacks, suspense, or a surprise ending?
3. *Central conflict:* What is the cental conflict? Is the conflict external? Is the protagonist pitted against another character, society, or nature? Is the conflict internal? Is there a struggle between different emotions and feelings within the protagonist?
4. *Setting:* What is the place, time, and social situation of the setting? What details create the setting? What is the setting's significance? Does it contribute to the conflict or mood?
5. *Characterization:* Who is the protagonist? Is there an antagonist? If so, who is the antagonist? Who are the other major and minor characters? What roles do they play? What do readers learn about each character's appearance, background, personality, actions, words, relationships, motivations, conflicts, and changes?
6. *Point of view:* Who is the storyteller, or narrator? Is the narrator omniscient or limited, first person or third? Is the narrator subjective or objective, reliable or unreliable?
7. *Language:* Does the story contain figures of speech such as hyperbole, irony, metaphor, or simile? Does the story contain special devices of sound such as onomatopoeia or parallelism?
8. *Theme:* What is the theme—the story's insight or central idea? How is the theme expressed?
9. *Other elements:* Is the story addressed to a specific audience? if so, who? Is the story an example of a specific genre such as fantasy, science fiction, psychological fiction, mystery fiction, detective fiction, or regional fiction?

### CASE STUDY: WRITING ABOUT A SHORT STORY

Javier's English teacher assigned an essay

about the significance of a short story. Javier decided to analyze and write about James Joyce's "Araby," on page 987.

## Prewriting

Javier read the story twice and got this idea for his thesis:

> "Araby" shows how we all get ideas about how things will be and then feel disappointed with ourselves when things don't work out as expected.

Next Javier began taking prewriting notes on the story's key features, using the list found earlier in the lesson. Here are his notes about the story's setting:

- Place: boy's home with aunt and uncle, town (Ireland), train ride, and bazaar

- Details: blind street and houses
  Priest's former room with blinds where he watches Mangan's sister
  Town market full of people and shops
  Empty train going to bazaar
  Bazaar dark with stalls closed, money counting, girl flirting. Significant because reality contrasts with what he wants and imagines.
  Real market vs. knight with chalice
  Lonely train ride foreshadows bazaar
  His idea of Araby vs. real bazaar. Significant because setting suggests his state (symbolic?).
  Lives in "blind" street and watches Mangan's sister from behind blinds
  Lights are out at bazaar, leaving him in the dark but able to "see"

Javier finished his analysis, concentrating on point of view and characterization. Then he planned how to organize his essay and made a list of his main points.

## Drafting and Revising

Based on his thesis idea and on his other prewriting notes, Javier drafted a thesis state-ment and an introductory paragraph. For the body of his essay, he wrote one paragraph apiece about setting, characterization, and point of view, relating each to his thesis about the significance of the story. Then he drafted a concluding paragraph that summed up his main point about the story's theme. Finally, he revised his story, reorganizing, adding examples, and rephrasing as needed.

## Proofreading and Publishing

Next Javier proofread his paper, looking for minor errors and making a few more changes in wording. Here is his first paragraph with his proofreading changes:

> The experiences of the boy in James Joyce's "Araby" illustrates how people often expects ordinary reality more than real, true life can provide and then feel disillusioned and disappointed with themselves. The boy is infatuated with Mangan's sister, imagines that he will heroically be a big hero when he brings her something from the bazaar, and then feels very foolish when Araby is not what he expects. The story expresses its theme through the setting, where the story happens and the characterization of the boy and his point of view as the narrator.

Javier recopied his paper, read it through for copying errors, and shared it with his class discussion group.

## ACTIVITIES AND ASSIGNMENTS

A. Use the draft in the case study to answer these questions:

1. Explain why Javier made each of his proof-reading changes.
2. Why didn't Javier explain the plot in a full paragraph instead of summing it up in his second sentence?
3. Javier's first paragraph previews the next three paragraphs—one each on setting, characterization of the boy, and point of view. Read "Araby" carefully, take prewriting notes on these elements of the story, and then write the body paragraphs. Your paragraphs should support Javier's thesis and should each focus on a single element of the story. Revise and proofread your draft carefully, using the checklists on pages 1335 and 1338.

B. Write an essay interpreting a short story in this book. Follow these steps:

1. Read the story, and use the lists found earlier in this lesson to analyze it.
2. Draft a thesis statement about the significance of the story, concentrating on its theme, purpose, or overall effect.
3. Use your prewriting notes to decide which elements of the story will best support your thesis. Prepare an outline that notes the element each paragraph will discuss plus the evidence from the story that will illustrate each feature and relate it to your thesis.
4. Draft your paper, following your outline.
5. Revise and proofread your paper, using the checklists on pages 1335 and 1338.
6. Share your paper with your class.

# Lesson 13:  Writing About a Poem

Writing about a poem requires that you understand it well. Follow these general steps as you begin the process of analysis:

1. Read the poem to yourself. Look up any unfamiliar words. Identify the poem's speaker, subject, and genre (narrative, dramatic, or lyric).
2. Read the poem again, and note any images, figurative language, or allusions. Think about the functions served by these.
3. Read the poem aloud. Listen for special devices of sound such as rhythm, rhyme, alliteration, or onomatopoeia.
4. Read the poem again carefully and paraphrase it, sentence by sentence or line by line. Your paraphrase should reflect both what the poem states directly and what it implies.
5. Make notes on the genre, form, imagery, figurative language, devices of sound, theme, and other elements of the poem.

## HOW TO ANALYZE A POEM

When you take prewriting notes about a poem as a whole, look at the elements frequently used in poetry to see what features set apart this particular poem—to see what makes it different or especially meaningful. Then you will have a basis for deciding what to emphasize in your paper about the poem. The following list of elements in poetry will help you look for the key features of a poem. Once you have identified these features, you can begin to ask questions about them and to analyze how they create the poem's meaning.

1. *Author and title:* Who wrote the poem? What is the title of the poem? Does the title suggest the topic or theme of the poem?
2. *Genre:* Is the poem a lyric, such as an ode, an elegy, or a sonnet? That is, does it use musical language to express the emotions of a single speaker? If so, who is the speaker? What audience is being addressed? What is the occasion or situation? Is the poem a narrative, such as a ballad, an epic, or a metrical romance? That is, does it tell a story? If so, what plot, characters, settings, and point of view does this story have? Is it a dramatic poem, one that uses monologue, dialogue, or other dramatic techniques? What point of view, characters, setting, and situation does the poem present?
3. *Form:* Does the poem have a traditional form or pattern? If the poem is divided into stanzas, what form does each stanza take? Describe the number of lines, rhyme scheme, and metrical pattern of each stanza. Does the poem make use of couplets, quatrains, or some other standard stanza form? Does each stanza function, like a paragraph, as an independent unit of meaning? Does the poem have a unique shape or structure that adds to its meaning?
4. *Imagery:* What images of sight, sound, taste, touch, smell, and movement are used? What emotions do the images suggest?
5. *Figurative language:* What figures of speech are used in the poem? Does the poem contain examples of antithesis, apostrophe, irony, hyperbole, metaphor, metonymy, oxymoron, paradox, personification, simile, synecdoche, or understatement? Does the poem contain symbols or allusions? Is it allegorical?
6. *Devices of sound:* Does the poem contain rhyming words? Does it have a regular rhyme scheme? Does the poem contain alliteration, assonance, or consonance? Does it contain euphony, cacophony, parallel structure, or repetition? What is the poem's meter? What type and number of metrical feet does it have

in each line? If the poem is in free verse, how does it use rhythm?

7. *Other elements:* Has the poet taken liberties with spelling, mechanics, or grammar? Has the poet used words in unusual ways? If so, why has he or she done so? What tone does the speaker use? What is the mood of the poem? Does this mood change during the poem? What is the poem's theme? What overall effects do the separate parts of the poem combine to create?

## CASE STUDY: WRITING ABOUT A POEM

Jeremy's English assignment was to write an essay about a poem. He decided to write about Molly Holden's "Some Men Create," on page 1323.

### Prewriting

Jeremy began his prewriting by reading through the poem several times, studying it in detail, and making notes about its key features. here are a few of his notes:

- Author: Molly Holden

- Title: "Some Men Create"

- Form: 4 quatrains—show the situation (1), consequences (2–3), and point (4)

- Genre: lyric poem

- Imagery: sight (so that "eye may reap") ivy vaulting, swinging, and shining

- Figurative language: two similes
  Ivy will "swing like hair" (sounds like Rapunzel?)
  "seeding traveler's joy smothers" timber and oak "like smoke"

- Devices of sound:
  Rhyme scheme (*abcb*)
  Alliteration: *smothers/smoke*
  Assonance: suggests "Oh" of wonder?

*o* in so, oak/smoke, alone/sown
Repetition: word *so* used three times
Meter: variations match meaning example: 4th lines of stanzas are all the same ( ´ ˘ ´ ˘ ´ ) except in last stanza, where variation emphasizes "not sown"
Examples: line "vaults" between first two stanzas (just like ivy); line 10 (about cutting dead tree) has 5 one-syllable words—snap off like branches from dead tree

- Theme (last stanza especially):
  Even in an orderly life, people should allow some spontaneous and unanticipated things to develop.

After Jeremy read through his prewriting notes, he felt that the poem not only explains but also illustrates its theme. He outlined his paper, selecting as examples the features he thought would best support his thesis.

- Paragraph 1 Introduce poem: Name author and title; state thesis that the poem both explains & illustrates its theme

- Paragraph 2 Form is orderly (rhyme, meter): 4 quatrains follow logical pattern—show the situation, illustrate the consequences, and explain point

- Paragraph 3 Form has surprises ("not sown"):
  Meter in line 4 of last stanza
  Line that "vaults " between stanzas
  Line 10 with short words

- Paragraph 4 Language also helps reader see the point that eye likes to "reap":
  Images of sight (ivy)
  Similes (also visual)
  Assonance (suggests awe or wonder)

- Paragraph 5 Conclusion: Poem states and illustrates its point, showing us that we like order but we also like unexpected pleasures.

### Drafting and Revising

Jeremy used his outline and notes to write a rough draft. Then he revised his draft, making sure that both his interpretation and his examples were clear.

### Proofreading and Publishing

Jeremy carefully proofread his paper and then exchanged papers with a classmate.

### ACTIVITIES AND ASSIGNMENTS

A. Read or reread Molly Holden's poem, on page 1323. Then use the case study for these activities:

1. Jeremy's outline does not include alliteration and repetition. Why do you think he left them out? Could he have added them? If so, where?
2. Jeremy's outline notes the idea for his thesis.

Write this out in a sentence.
3. Add your own ideas to Jeremy's prewriting notes. Use your notes and the notes from the case study to draft, revise, and proofread your own analysis.

B. Write an interpretive essay on any poem in this text. Follow these steps:
1. Read the poem and analyze it, using the steps and key elements outlined at the beginning of this lesson.
2. Use your prewriting notes to develop a working outline and a thesis statement about the poem's overall effect, purpose, or theme.
3. Follow your outline as you write an introductory paragraph, body paragraphs, and a conclusion. Be sure to use supporting examples and quotations.
4. Revise and proofread your essay, using the checklists on pages 1335 and 1338.
5. Share the poem and your paper with your classmates.

# Lesson 14: Writing About Drama

When you analyze a play, you will find that it contains many of the literary elements found in short stories and in poetry. Like a short story, a play has a plot, a central conflict, characters, a setting, and a theme. Like poetry, a play may use poetic forms, imagery, figurative language, and devices of sound. Refer to the previous two lessons for information on analyzing and writing about these literary elements.

No matter how much a play resembles a story or a poem, it necessarily differs in one major respect. A play is written to be performed before an audience. Its action is physical and takes place on stage. Its lines are written to be spoken by actors and to be accompanied by their expressions and movements. Unlike most stories and poems, a play has dialogue for actors to speak and stage directions to explain the actors' movements, the appearance of the set, the props needed, the lighting and sound effects, and other aspects of performance and production. In addition, a play may use such *dramatic conventions* as the *aside* (a speech or comment made directly to the audience as though other characters on stage could not hear it) and the *soliloquy* (a speech delivered by a lone character on the stage, one that reveals the character's inner thoughts).

## HOW TO ANALYZE DRAMA

A play can be analyzed as a written work of literature or as a performance, as the following questions suggest.

*The drama as literature:*
1. What happens during the exposition, inciting incident, development, climax, resolution, and denouement of the plot? What happens during each act and scene?
2. What is the central conflict?

4. Who are the characters? What does each add to the play?
5. What does the audience learn about each character's background, personality, relationships, motivations, conflicts, and changes?
6. How is the theme revealed?
7. What imagery does the writer use?
8. What figurative language does the writer use?
9. What symbols does the play present?
10. What devices of sound does the language of the play include?

*The drama as performance:*
1. How is the stage set, and how does that setting affect the audience?
2. How effectively and accurately is each character portrayed in the performance?
3. How effective is the delivery of the dialogue? (Consider such factors as pacing, volume, pitch, stress, tone, and vocal quality.)
4. What is the overall effect of the performance?
5. How would you review the performance as a whole? (Consider such factors as the acting, the set, the costumes, the sound, the lighting, the direction, the properties, the makeup, and any other facts in the production.)

## CASE STUDY: WRITING ABOUT DRAMA

Michael's English teacher assigned an essay about one scene in *Macbeth*. The focus of the essay was to be how the scene contributes to the significance of the play as a whole.

### Prewriting

Michael decided to analyze Act I, Scene iii, when Macbeth first meets the three witches. He wanted to figure out how the scene moves the play forward and what significant information it gives the audience. Here is a chart Michael made to examine the play's plot, setting, characters, and themes.

Michael worked on organizing his notes into a logical outline for his essay.

| ELEMENT | SIGNIFICANCE |
|---|---|
| *Plot:* three witches on heath meet Macbeth and Banquo hail Macbeth with three titles | nature of witches<br><br><br>Macbeth is absorbed, wants to hear more from them |
| hail Banquo as father of kings | Banquo may become a threat to Macbeth's ambitions |
| Ross and Angus arrive to greet Macbeth as Thane of Cawdor | confirm witches about Cawdor raise question about crown |
| *Setting:* thunderstorm on heath "foul and fair" day | threatening, evil weather foreshadows events to come |
| *Character:* Macbeth is shaken by prophecy but wants to know more | ready to think of murdering Duncan decides not to act but leave it to chance |
| Banquo suspects betrayal from witches | contrast with Macbeth: Banquo is not ambitious and senses evil, does not react as Macbeth does warns of evil |
| *Themes:* ambition control of future— choice or destiny? | Macbeth considers how far he'll go to make prophecy true |

## Drafting and Revising

Michael began his introduction with this thesis statement:

> Through its plot, setting, and characterization, Act I, Scene iii, of *Macbeth* alerts the audience to the problem of knowing one's destiny and wanting to control the future.

Michael drafted and revised his essay, including an introductory paragraph, a concluding paragraph, and separate paragraphs on plot, setting, and character. Here is his revised version of paragraph four, on character:

> Both Macbeth and Banquo hear the prophecies and their first confirmation out on the heath. From the beginning, the two characters react differently. As Banquo points out, Macbeth acts distracted and shaken. He wants to hear more and does not want to judge the prophecy as evil or good. Still, his first thought is not of some accident to the king but of murder—of how his own action could secure the future. Finally he decides that chance may bring him the crown without any action on his part. In contrast, Banquo sees the witches as evil and warns Macbeth. Though he wants to hear their prediction he does not want anything from them. Unlike Macbeth, he has no thought of trying to control the future.

## Proofreading and Publishing

Michael proofread his paper for spelling and mechanical errors. Then he shared the paper with his older brother, who is an actor.

## ACTIVITIES AND ASSIGNMENTS

A. Use the case study to answer these questions:

1. Point out the transitional words and phrases in Michael's paragraph. Explain how Michael uses transitions to help organize his discussion of the two characters.

2. Michael does not use any quotations from the play to support his arguments. Revise his

paragraph, adding appropriate quotations. Be sure to punctuate properly and to quote the exact words of the play.

B. Choose one of these topics for an essay about a play: (1) analyze the main elements of one scene in a play from this text, and explain their contributions to the significance of the play as a whole; or (2) evaluate the ways in which Higgins and Liza change in *Pygmalion,* on page 1109. For either topic, follow these steps.

1. Read the section of the play carefully several times. Try to imagine how the scene would be presented on stage.
2. Take prewriting notes as you analyze the play.

Use the first list in this lesson for guidelines; return to the last two lessons if you need more suggestions.

3. Work out a thesis statement and an outline. Note the main point of each paragraph and the supporting evidence or details from the play. Decide whether you should organize element by element or chronologically as presented in the play.
4. Follow your outline and support your thesis statement as you draft your essay.
5. Revise and proofread your draft, using the checklists on pages 1335 and 1338.
6. Share your essay with your classmates.

# SECTION 4: JUDGING A LITERARY WORK: EVALUATION

## Lesson 15: Evaluating a Literary Work

### WHAT IS EVALUATION?

When you *evaluate* something, you judge its value. In everyday life you regularly perform this mental task—evaluating a new album, clothes that you want to buy, or the food at a new restaurant. Each evaluation states your opinion and is based on *evidence,* the facts you discover when you listen to the album, try on the clothes, or eat at the restaurant. In other words, your evaluation is based on appropriate standards or criteria—the sound and style of the music, the appearance and cost of the clothes, and the taste and price of the food.

Evaluating a literary work is just like making other judgments: You state an opinion based on certain standards or criteria. Then you support your opinion with specific evidence and details. Your opinion is your own, but it will not be accepted by anyone else unless you can marshal the facts to support it.

For example, if you argued that *The Tempest* is a juvenile play because two of the characters are a sprite and a monster, your opinion could not be supported by evidence. Since it was common for supernatural beings to appear in plays on the Elizabethan stage, their presence does not make the play juvenile. Therefore, your opinion is not sound since it cannot be supported by evidence. If, on the other hand, you argued that the overall mood of the *The Tempest* is more tragic than cheerful, some people would disagree with you, but you could provide evidence from the play to support your evaluation so that readers would understand your position.

### CRITERIA FOR EVALUATING A LITERARY WORK

Your judgment of the quality of a story, poem, play, or other work may be based on many different criteria. Here are some standards often applied to literature:

1. To what extent does the work accomplish its purpose or achieve its effect? Do you think that it succeeds in doing what it sets out to do—entertaining, amusing, scaring, surprising, persuading, teaching, or emotionally moving its reader?
2. Is its purpose or effect worth accomplishing? Do you consider its purpose more important or significant than other purposes?
3. Does the work have an ethical or moral message? Do you feel that its message is important? Do you agree with the message?
4. How original or inventive is the work? Do you find the topic or its treatment new?
5. How clear and understandable is the work? If the work is difficult, does it nonetheless reward the reader's efforts to understand it? Does the work seem indefensibly unclear or confused?
6. To what extent does the work meet other criteria important to you as a reader? Do you have personal views about its genre, subject, or style?

### CASE STUDY: EVALUATING A LITERARY WORK

Ben's teacher asked the class to suggest poems that might provoke different opinions from different people. Then each student was to write an essay stating and supporting an evaluation of the poem.

#### Prewriting

Ben decided to write about Rupert Brooke's "The Soldier," on page 1050. Ben himself had mixed feelings about the poem that depended on whether he based his judgment on realistic criteria or on the poem's success in accomplishing its purpose. He used clustering to test both ideas:

no one wants to die

no M.A.S.H. units or antibiotics during WWI

war is horrible experience

poem is unrealistic

tries to sound cheerful but just sounds naive

he won't care where he is buried if he is dead

just sentimental to like poem because poet did die young in Navy

sounds like a way of accepting fear of death when going to war

poem accomplishes its purpose

creates sense of why he loves England

traditional sonnet form

makes patriotism concrete—flowers, ways, air, rivers, suns, etc.

sonnet form suits poem on love for English traditions

shows his values—English "sights & sounds," "dreams," "laughter," "gentleness," etc.

Ben decided to write about the opinion that he could most persuasively defend with evidence from the poem. He added to and reorganized his prewriting notes until he had outlined a four-paragraph essay.

### Drafting and Revising

Ben refined his thesis statement and drafted his essay. The next day he revised his paper, carefully checking the clarity of his arguments and evidence.

### Proofreading and Publishing

After Ben proofread his paper, he shared the poem and his paper with a friend.

### ACTIVITIES AND ASSIGNMENTS

A. Read or reread Brooke's poem, on page 1050. Then review Ben's clustering notes in the case study and follow these steps:

1. Select one of Ben's criteria, and add your own notes to his; start with your own criteria for judging the poem, and use clustering or another prewriting technique to develop your ideas. Whatever your view, the prewriting notes should specify your standards or criteria for judging, your opinion about how well the poem meets those standards or criteria, and your supporting evidence (quotations, paraphrases, and analyses of the poem).
2. Write a thesis statement that states your opinion. Then outline your main points and your evidence.
3. Draft your essay, including an introduction, several body paragraphs that develop your main points, and a conclusion.
4. Revise and proofread your paper, using the checklists on pages 1335 and 1338. Check especially carefully to see that your opinions and reasons are clearly stated and that your evidence is pertinent and clear.
5. Exchange your work with someone in class who wrote a paper using a different standard for judgment. Compare your papers.

*Evaluating a Literary Work* 1371

B. Select a poem, story, or other literary work about which you have a definite opinion. Write a four- or five-paragraph essay evaluating that work. Follow these steps:

1. Use freewriting, clustering, or another prewriting technique to figure out the criterion or standard for judgment, your precise opinion, and the supporting evidence on which you will base your judgment. If you have a strong view but cannot find evidence to support it, your opinion will not be persuasive. In that case, start over with another work, or do more prewriting to develop your ideas.

2. Work out a thesis statement that presents your opinion about the work. Organize your prewriting ideas in a paragraph-by-paragraph outline. Make sure that your paper is clearly organized. You might choose to concentrate, in each paragraph, on a specific element of the work, showing how it supports your opin-ion. On the other hand, you might devote a paragraph to each reason for your opinion, drawing supporting examples of different kinds from the work.

3. Draft your essay, starting with an introduction to the literary work, your criterion for judging it, and your evaluation or opinion, based on the criterion. Next write your body paragraphs and a conclusion.

4. If possible, wait a few hours or a day so that you have more perspective about your own writing. Then revise your essay, using the checklist on page 1335. Make sure that your ideas are stated clearly and that your opinions are supported by evidence.

5. Proofread your paper, using the checklist on page 1338.

6. If possible, exchange papers with a classmate who has a different opinion about the same work.

# Lesson 16: Writing a Comparative Evaluation

## WHAT IS A COMPARATIVE EVALUATION?

A *comparative evaluation* follows the same pattern explained in the last lesson. First state your opinion about which of two works is better or worse, based on specific criteria or standards for judgment. Your basis for comparison may include one or more specific points of comparison (similarities) or contrast (differences). Then use specific evidence from both works to support your views.

## CHOOSING WORKS FOR COMPARATIVE EVALUATION

When you select two works for comparative evaluation, they should have something in common—perhaps the same theme, topic, or literary form. If the two works are totally unlike, comparison serves little purpose. You could only conclude that they are very different—that one, for example, is an Anglo-Saxon epic poem and the other, a modern short story about a fiddle.

To compare or contrast the two works effectively, you need to find comparable points in each. These points might be the elements characteristic of the type of writing. For example, you could compare and contrast the form, imagery, figurative language, and sound devices in two lyric poems with the same subject and theme. Similarly, you might look at characterization, setting, and symbolism in a short story and a play with similar plots and themes. (See the lessons in Sections 2 and 3 of this handbook for advice about how to analyze specific elements and types of literary works.)

## ORGANIZING A COMPARATIVE EVALUATION

Begin by selecting the points of comparison and contrast that seem most pertinent. Then make a chart listing each point of comparison or contrast. Allow room for an entry about each work in its own column. For each work and each point of comparison, note comments and evidence.

Next plan an outline based on the points that fit your essay. Use the organizational method that is best for the complexity and balance of your material:

| METHOD 1 | METHOD 2 |
|---|---|
| Introduction | Introduction |
| Work #1<br>—Point A<br>—Point B<br>—Point C | Point A<br>—Work #1<br>—Work #2 |
| Work # 2<br>—Point A<br>—Point B<br>—Point C | Point B<br>—Work #1<br>—Work #2 |
| Conclusion | Point C<br>—Work #1<br>—Work #2 |
| | Conclusion |

## CASE STUDY: WRITING A COMPARATIVE EVALUATION

Melissa's English teacher assigned a comparative evaluation of two poems. Melissa picked two sonnets, Shakespeare's Sonnet 29, on page 255, and Rossetti's "Silent Noon," on page 859.

### Prewriting

Melissa began the assignment by carefully rereading the two poems. She knew that she liked Shakespeare's better, but she needed to analyze why. Using elements from the lesson on writing about a poem, she worked out this chart:

| ELEMENT | SONNET 29 | "SILENT NOON" |
|---|---|---|
| Form | Shakespearean | Petrarchan |
| Imagery | sound—cries and curses, then little until thinks of beloved and lark sings | sight—lush imagery is almost too much |
| Figures of Speech | simile—he feels like a lark singing when he thinks of beloved<br><br>idea of joy bursting up fits well | simile—the dragonfly hangs like a blue thread; so this hour is dropped to lovers thread, hour, and dragonfly are less attractive<br>silence like hourglass is OK but no special fit overdone! |
| Sound Devices | repetition "like him" parallelism and trouble/ look/curse this man's/ that man's structure of lines emphasizes rut he's in | alliteration: *gl*eams/*gl*ooms *sk*ies/*sc*atter *s*un/*s*earched *d*eathless/*d*ower<br><br>lines 8 and 14 hiss instead of hush |
| Language Choices | older words "beweep" "bootless" but actually direct clear language | showy l. 13 is too dense "This close-companioned inarticulate hour" |
| Theme | love poem: remembers love when downcast and wouldn't change with a king<br>it's a bigger compliment | love poem: treasures beautiful hour together more ordinary idea than in Shakespeare sonnet |

After Melissa had enough evidence to support her opinion, she worked out an outline for her paper.

### Drafting and Revising

Melissa began her draft with this thesis statement:

> Shakespeare's Sonnet 29 is a deeper and more moving love poem than Rosetti's "Silent Noon." Although some of Shakespeare's older vocabulary is harder to understand, his sonnet's form and meaning are better matched to each other through his use of sound devices, imagery, and figurative language.

Melissa continued drafting her paper, following her outline. She then revised carefully, checking to make sure that she had included all her main points of comparison and contrast for each poem.

### Proofreading and Publishing

After proofreading, Melissa shared her paper with Ms. Thomas, her English teacher from the preceding year, who had given her extra help with comparisons and contrasts.

### ACTIVITIES AND ASSIGNMENTS

A. Use the case study to answer the following questions.
1. Which organizational plan does Melissa's thesis statement suggest that she will use? Use her prewriting notes to write out the outline that you think she has planned.
2. How else might Melissa organize her paper?

Work out a second possible outline for her paper. Write a revised thesis statement that suits this new outline.

3. Which outline better suits her material? Explain the advantages and disadvantages of each.

B. For your own comparative evaluation, select two literary works such as any of the following pairs: Marlowe's "The Passionate Shepherd to His Love," on page 230, and Raleigh's "The Nymph's Reply to the Shepherd," on page 238; Nashe's "A Litany in Time of Plague," on page 250, and the selection from Defoe's *A Journal of the Plague Year,* on page 514; Marvell's "To His Coy Mistress," on page 418, and Herrick's "To the Virgins, to Make Much of Time," on page 432; or Tennyson's "Crossing the Bar," on page 808, and Thomas's "Do Not Go Gentle into That Good Night," on page 1102. Follow these steps in writing your essay:

1. Read both works carefully.
2. Tentatively decide which you like better and for what reasons.

3. Set up a chart like the one in the case study, listing the points of comparison and contrast for both works. Begin working on the points that seem most important, but stay flexible in case other ideas occur to you.

4. Work out a rough outline and a thesis statement. Try one of the two methods of organizing outlined earlier.

5. Begin drafting your paper's introduction, including the titles and authors of the two works and your thesis statement with your evaluation. Draft the body paragraphs, following your outline and including clear supporting evidence from the works. Then write a concluding paragraph summarizing your argument.

6. Check for clear and consistent organization. Try outlining your draft itself to identify any problems or omissions.

7. Revise and proofread your essay, using the checklists on pages 1335 and 1338.

8. Share your essay with a classmate.

# Lesson 17: Evaluating Persuasion

A nonfiction work is *persuasive* if its purpose is to move readers or listeners to take some action or to adopt some view. Examples of persuasive nonfiction include editorials, advertisements, campaign speeches, and public relations materials. Often people write essays and even whole books specifically to persuade others to think or act in certain ways.

## SOUND REASONING ABOUT PERSUASION

Persuasive writing and speech present opinions—statements about which people may disagree. When evaluating persuasive language, a reader or listener must determine whether the opinions presented are sound. The following are some criteria for evaluating the soundness of opinions:

### The Consistency Principle

Is the opinion consistent with known facts? For example, the opinion that one should not take illegal drugs is consistent with the fact that illegal drugs can cause great physical and psychological harm.

### The Utility Principle

Does accepting the opinion led to consequences that are themselves acceptable? For example, the opinion that one should not drive beyond the speed limit is sound because acting on this opinion has desirable consequences. When people drive within the speed limit, there are fewer traffic accidents.

### The Principle of Appeal to Authority

Is the opinion consistent with the views of knowledgeable and reliable authorities? For example, the opinion that one should eat high-fiber, low-fat foods is consistent with the views of medical scientists and researchers. These people have found that eating such foods decreases one's risk of developing heart disease or cancer.

Each of these principles is related to the more general principle that an opinion must be supported by reasoned, logical arguments.

## UNSOUND REASONING ABOUT OPINIONS

When people write or speak persuasively, they sometimes present arguments that are unreasonable or illogical. Such arguments make use of propaganda and logical fallacies. *Propaganda* is language that is emotionally charged and intentionally misleading. A *logical fallacy* is an error in reasoning. The following propaganda devices and logical fallacies are often found in persuasive writing and speech:

*Propaganda Techniques:*
1. *Bandwagon:* urging support for an opinion simply because many other people support the opinion
2. *Loaded language:* using emotionally charged words that have little meaning beyond arousing positive or negative feelings
3. *Argument ad hominem:* (literally, "argument to the person") criticizing or attacking the opponent instead of the oponent's argument
4. *Snob appeal:* urging support for an opinion solely because an admired person or group supports it
5. *Straw man:* exaggerating or misrepresenting the opposing position so that it sounds more ridiculous than it actually it
6. *Stereotyping:* assuming, without sufficient evidence, that everyone in a particular group has certain characteristics

*Logical Fallacies:*
1. *Begging the question:* stating an opinion with-

out giving evidence to support it; simply assuming the truth of the opinion to be proved

2. *Either/or fallacy:* treating a complicated issue as if there were only two sides or two alternatives when there are actually more

3. *Post hoc, ergo propter hoc:* (literally, "after this, therefore because of this") assuming that one action or event caused another simply because it came earlier in time

4. *False analogy:* falsely treating two subjects as similar in one respect simply because they are similar in some other respect

5. *Non sequitur:* (literally, "it does not follow") stating a conclusion that is not a necessary consequence of the reasons given

6. *Overgeneralization:* making a statement that is broader in its application than the facts would warrant

When evaluating written or spoken persuasion, make sure that the opinions presented are well supported. Also make sure that the speaker or writer has avoided propaganda devices and logical fallacies.

## CASE STUDY: EVALUATING PROPAGANDA AND ARGUMENT

Carrie's English class was working on the logical evaluation of arguments. Each student brought to class an example of propaganda or faulty logic. Examples were found in editorials, in political speeches, in a letter to the editor of a newspaper, and in similar material. After the class discussion each student was asked to write a paragraph evaluating his or her example.

### Prewriting

Carrie found this letter to the editor in her local newspaper:

Dear Editor:
The recent car accident on Tunley Lane shows how irresponsible pet owners are. If that dog had not been walking along the side of the road, the car would not have run into the mailbox. People should not have pets unless they are willing to care for them. All good citizens agree that the public should not have to risk car crashes, highway mayhem, and wanton violence just because these people are nincompoops!

Sincerely,
Roger Loxley

Carrie began analyzing this letter, first noting its highly emotional vocabulary and tone as well as the lack of evidence for its assertions. She then listed some of the letter's flaws:

- Argument ad hominem and loaded language—calling people "nincompoops"

- Bandwagon appeal or snob appeal—calling on "all good citizens"

- Non sequitur—assuming that the dog by the road was not cared for and assuming that pet owners are responsible for "car crashes, highway mayhem, and wanton violence"

- Post hoc, ergo propter hoc—assuming that the dog caused the accident

- Stereotyping—characterizing all pet owners as irresponsible people

Carrie decided that the letter contained two basic flaws—lack of respect for other people, both pet owners and readers, and an illogical analysis of causes and effects.

### Drafting and Revising

Carrie used her prewriting notes to supply details for her paragraph. After drafting her paragraph, she carefully revised it, making sure that her own points were presented reasonably.

### Proofreading and Publishing

Carrie proofread her paragraph and then read it aloud to the class.

## ACTIVITIES AND ASSIGNMENTS

A. Use the case study to answer the following questions:

1. How could Carrie use her list of logical flaws to illustrate that the letter lacked respect for people and presented a faulty analysis of causes? Work out an outline for her paragraph. Feel free to add or to leave out points.
2. Do you see other logical flaws in the letter? If so, what are they?
3. What general characteristics of sound argument does the letter lack?

B. Analyze an example of faulty argument or of propaganda. Write a paragraph about it, following these steps:

1. Find an example such as a letter to the editor, an editorial, a political brochure, some campaign material, or an advertisement.
2. Analyze why your example is not a sound argument. Examine its general characteristics, its specific logical fallacies, and its propaganda techniques. List these problems. Then use the materials on your list to make an outline.
3. Begin your paragraph with a topic sentence. Then explain and illustrate your main points. Add a conclusion.
4. Revise and proofread your draft, using the checklists on pages 1335 and 1338.
5. Share your paragraph with a class discussion group.

# SECTION 5: WRITING CREATIVELY
## Lesson 18: Writing a Short Story

Writing a short story means arranging and telling about incidents, describing scenes, and developing characters in ways that will interest and entertain a reader. A short story may begin with an idea about any of the standard features of the short story—character, setting, plot, mood, or theme.

### FINDING A STORY IDEA

Here are some suggestions about how to find an idea for a short story:

1. *What happens? (plot):* Think of an incident or a conflict that could make a good story. Consider internal conflicts (choices, decisions, or other pressures) or external conflicts (struggles between people, battles with social or physical forces, contests, or other oppositions).
2. *Where does it happen? (setting):* Think of an interesting time (past, present, or future) and place (real or imaginary), perhaps someplace where you have lived or that you have visited.
3. *Who is involved? (characters):* Think of someone you know who is interesting, admirable, or unusual. Create a character based on this person.
4. *What does it mean? (theme):* Think of an insight that you would like to pass along to others.
5. *Who tells the story? (point of view):* Imagine a narrator who has a complete overview, the more limited view of an observer, or the even more limited view of a participating character.

### DEVELOPING YOUR STORY

To develop your story idea more fully, ask yourself these questions:

1. *Character:* Who will be the main character? What will be the character's name? How will he or she look and talk? What will be the character's background, personality, education, job, or status? What will be the character's motivations? Why will the character act as he or she does? What will he or she want or believe? Will the character change? If so, how and why? What will the character learn? What relationships with others will the character have? What internal or external conflicts will the character need to resolve? Who will be the minor characters? What will be their roles? What will they be like? How will they relate to the protagonist?
2. *Setting:* When will the story take place? Where will it take place? What sensory images will help you create this place for a reader?
3. *Plot:* What will happen in the story? In what order will you tell the story? Will you use flashbacks, foreshadowing, or a surprise ending? How will you build suspense? What background information will you supply at the beginning of the story? What will happen to begin the conflict? How will the conflict develop? What will be its consequences? What will be the most suspenseful moment? How will the conflict end? Will anything happen after the conflict ends? If so, what?
4. *Point of View:* Who will tell the story—an observer or a character? How much will the storyteller know—everything or what one character knows? Will the narrator speak in the first person or in the third person?
5. *Theme:* What will be your short story's central idea or insight into life? How will you express this point in the short story?

## CASE STUDY: WRITING A SHORT STORY

Erica wanted to enter a short story contest, but she did not want to write a typical romance or adventure story. She wanted to write about the future, but she needed an idea.

### Prewriting

Since the school district computers were down most of that day, Erica began to wonder what life would be like without computers. She wrote down a few notes about this idea to test whether it would make a good short story.

- Title ideas: maybe "Computers on Strike" or "The Great Computer Scam"

- What happens? (plot):
  Something damages one computer
  It breaks down; spreads to others
  All overload and stop working
  Now what? Consequences? Solution?
  Get them fixed? Live without them?

- Where does it happen? (setting):
  Future, maybe 50 years from now
  Society even more dependent on computers; people need them to work, run houses, make decisions
  Should place look cold and mechanical? or should it have deceptive surface, looking natural but depending on the computers to keep it all going?

- Who is involved? (characters):
  Probably need good person, but does he or she want to fix the computers?
  Would character rather help people become independent of them again?
  also need source of conflict: computers themselves? or evil character? (not mad scientist!) maybe the electric power-er company?

- What does it mean? (theme):
  What is my central idea?
  Should story show human ability to solve problems? or the need to stay human in an over-controlled society? or the need for people to find solutions using their intelligence?

- Who tells the story? (point of view):
  Maybe all-knowing narrator?
  —maybe the main character who feels the conflict or even the computer that causes the mess?

Erica finally had an idea. She used the list of questions in this lesson to develop her idea further.

### Drafting and Revising

Erica drafted her story in one sitting. Then she waited a day, read it through once, and began to revise section by section.

### Proofreading and Publishing

After proofreading her paper and handing it in for her teacher's reactions, Erica made a few more changes. Then she entered her work in the short story contest.

### ACTIVITIES AND ASSIGNMENTS

A. Review Erica's prewriting notes and complete them yourself, using the list of questions for developing a short story. Work out your own story outline and draft your story. After revising and proofreading your story, exchange papers with other students in your class to see how differently they developed the story.

B. Write an original story. Follow these suggestions:

1. Use the first list (the one with the *who, when, where,* and *what* questions) to come up with an idea for a story.
2. Develop your ideas by answering the questions in the second list in this lesson.
3. Make a list of the events in your story.
4. Draft your story.
5. Review your draft, checking the development

of all the elements in the second chart. Make any necessary additions, cuts, or changes so that the sequence of events, the characters' motivations, and the conflict are clear.

6. Revise your draft as you would any other paper, using the checklist on page 1335.

7. Proofread your paper using the checklist on page 1338.

8. Share your story with a reader whom you think would especially enjoy it—your parents, your English teacher, a past English teacher, a teacher in another class, or a friend.

# Lesson 19: Writing a Poem

Writing poetry can be a wonderful, rewarding experience. In this lesson you will review some common poetic forms and then try writing some poetry yourself.

## SOME COMMON VERSE FORMS

A *couplet* is a pair of rhyming lines, each with the same number of strong stresses, or beats. Long poems are often made of strings of couplets that may or may not be separated by spaces. For examples of poems written in couplets, see Marvell's "To His Coy Mistress," on page 418; the selections by Pope, on pages 548 and 561; and Hopkins's "Spring and Fall: To a Young Child," on page 847.

A *ballad* is a poem that tells a story in short, rhyming stanzas. The traditional ballad, often set to music, has four- or six-line rhyming stanzas. Most ballads have a recurring rhythmical pattern. Examples of traditional ballads appear on pages 104–112. Many traditional English and American songs are ballads, as are many popular songs.

*Free verse* is poetry that does not follow a recurring rhythmical or metrical pattern. A writer of free verse is free in the sense that he or she can ignore tha standard conventions of language and can divide up his or her lines in any way that seems appropriate to what is being said. Examples of free verse in your text include Lawrence's "Snake," on page 1039, and Smith's "Not Waving But Drowning," on page 1307.

## CASE STUDY: WRITING A POEM

Greg's class was writing poetry. He decided to write a ballad, hoping to publish it in the school newspaper.

### Prewriting

Although Greg knew roughly what a ballad was, he first read the examples of traditional ballads in the text and reviewed the definition of *ballad* in the Handbook of Literary Terms and Techniques.

Next Greg started to work on an idea. He wanted to write a ballad that would interest everybody who read the newspaper. He also thought, given his personality, that he could write a better humorous ballad than a serious or tragic one. During the next few days, he listed events at school or involving students that might be topics:

- College applications—not a story, but could be one student's trauma

- SAT scores—maybe about valiant survivors on test days

- Accident at Bell and River Road—too serious to be funny; could be done like "Sir Partick Spens," but probably not a good idea

- Cafeteria—food is always a complaint for students; maybe I could tell the story of one student braving the lunch lines, especially on a day with "mystery stew"

Greg liked his second idea and thought other students would too.

### Drafting and Revising

Greg started work on his first stanza with these lines:

> Young Bobby was a valiant lad,
> He had faced the SAT,
> He had filed his college forms
> And he . . .

Greg did not like this beginning. He decided not to specify Bobby's grade level because he wanted the poem to appeal to an audience broader than just one class. He also felt stuck after the ending with *forms.* Then Greg decided to start over with another topic. He wrote until he finished the first draft, alternating between adding new lines and rephrasing completed lines as he got new ideas. Here is the beginning of his revised ballad:

Young Bobby was a valiant lad,
~~A soccer man was he.~~
~~He had faced the SAT.~~

He never flinched from pain or grief,
'Til
~~Until~~ after period three.

Then came the line that scared the brave,

The line that scared the bold,

The line that led ~~our~~ *brave* Bobby on

~~To so meet ... wild.~~
~~To a lunch never told.~~
To a lunch never told.

### Proofreading and Publishing

After proofreading his ballad, Greg submitted his final copy to the school newspaper, where it was published two weeks later.

### ACTIVITIES AND ASSIGNMENTS

A. Answer the following questions about the case study:
1. Identify these features of traditional ballads in Greg's poem:
   a. division into four-line stanzas
   b. use of a regular rhyme scheme
   c. use of repetition
   d. use of a regular rhythmical pattern
2. Write the rest of Greg's ballad, using your imagination or adding details about your schools's cafeteria. Stick to the traditional ballad form that Greg used.

B. Try writing your own poem, following the directions below.

*Couplet (one or more)*
1. Read some of the poems written in couplets that appear in this book.
2. Choose an idea that suits the compact style of the couplet.
3. Once you have an idea, write it out. Experiment with rhymes to end the lines.
4. Rework each line until the metrical pattern is regular and the end rhyme fits.
5. Revise and proofread your poem.
6. share your poem with your class.

*Ballad*
1. Begin by thinking of an event or situation for a ballad story. Brainstorm a list of ideas until you have one you like.
2. Read the ballads in this book to review the pattern of the ballad stanza.
3. Begin writing stanza by stanza, using the traditional ballad form.
4. Add other ballad characteristics as you work. Use simple language, direct dialogue, dramatic action without extra detail, repetition, and perhaps a refrain.
5. Revise and proofread your ballad.
6. Submit it to your school newspaper or to some other student publication.

*Free verse*
1. Read a number of free-verse poems to see how they work.
2. Jot down your ideas for a subject. Use prewriting techniques such as brainstorming, clustering, freewriting, and charting.
3. Write out your poem in a prose paragraph.
4. Divide your prose into lines. Each line should be a complete grammatical unit—a phrase, a clause, or a sentence.
5. Revise and proofread your poem, paying particular attention to word choice, imagery, and special devices of sound.

Once your poem is finished, share it with friends and submit it to your school's literary magazine or to another student publication.

# Lesson 20: Writing a Short Dramatic Sketch

A full-length drama or play may last several hours and have many scenes and acts. A *dramatic sketch*, however, lasts only a few minutes and is a single short scene. A sketch uses the same form as a longer play and can be either comic or tragic, but it makes only a single point. Because of its restricted length and focus, the dramatic sketch adapts well to the pace of television and is a popular feature of comedy and variety shows.

## UNDERSTANDING THE CONVENTIONS USED IN A DRAMATIC SKETCH

Like longer dramatic works, the dramatic sketch has these features:
1. *Title*
2. *List of characters*
3. *Stage directions:* underlined or italicized in square brackets or parentheses
4. *Dialogue:* with character names in all capitals (sometimes in boldface or italic type), followed by the exact words the actors are to say

The beginning of Shaw's *Pygmalion,* on page 1109, illustrates these conventions:

Act I

*London at 11:15 P.M. Torrents of heavy summer rain. Cab whistles blowing frantically in all directions. Pedestrians running for shelter. . . .*
*The church clock strikes the first quarter.*

THE DAUGHTER *(in the space between the central pillars, close to the one on her left)* I'm getting chilled to the bone. What can Freddy be doing all this time? he's been gone twenty minutes.

THE MOTHER *(on her daughter's right)* Not so long. But he ought to have got us a cab by this.

Stage directions can explain what the set should look like and what lighting, sound, or special effects are required in production. They can explain which characters are on stage and what they are doing as a scene opens. When a character speaks, the stage directions can clarify how the actor should be positioned, how he or she should move, and what expression or tone he or she should use. The dialogue, on the other hand, supplies only the exact words the actor should speak.

## PLANNING A DRAMATIC SKETCH

Like any other creative projects, a dramatic sketch requires many decisions. As you make each decision, consider whether what you imagine can happen on stage. Ask yourself these questions as you begin your planning:
1. Will the sketch be comic or serious? How do I want the audience to react? What should be the overall effect?
2. What will be the time and place of the action? How will the set represent the setting?
3. Who will the characters be? How will they speak, move, and act? How should they look and sound to the audience? What costumes will they wear?
4. What events will occur as part of the plot? What conflict will complicate the plot? What will happen in the beginning, the middle, and the end?
5. What props, special effects, or other extras will be needed?

## CASE STUDY: WRITING A DRAMATIC SKETCH

Tamara's school service club was in charge of planning a show for the spring orientation for students who would be entering the school next fall. The show was to encourage their school spirit and to make them feel welcome.

## Prewriting

Tamara and two of her friends were in charge of drafting a script for the show. Since their English class had read *Everyman* earlier in the year, they decided to model their dramatic sketch on a morality play. Tamara wrote out their plans:

- Title: Every[fresh]man

- Characters:

  | | |
  |---|---|
  | Every[fresh]man | School Spirit |
  | Apathy | Energy |
  | Rowdy | Loyalty |
  | Foggy | Pride |
  | Lazy | Hard Work |
  | Wacky | |

- Plot summary: Every[fresh]man arrives on campus to start next year. Apathy, Rowdy, Foggy, Lazy, and Wacky try to lead Every[fresh]man astray. School Spirit, assisted by Energy, Loyalty, Pride, and Hard Work, come to the rescue. They send away the others, except Wacky, and help Every[fresh]man start the year right.

- Setting: The school—probably just a door and a walk to suggest the edge of the school building

## Drafting and Revising

Next Tamara drafted the script, and her friends helped her to revise it. Here's how their dramatic sketch began:

Every[fresh]man

*[The scene opens near Building A on the first day of school in the fall. The building door is at the back left and the front walk leads off to the right. New students are arriving, hunting for their lockers, turning their schedules and maps around, looking lost. Every[fresh]man enters from the left, drops a map, picks it up, and looks around. Every[fresh]man is printed on the character's T-shirt.]*

EVERY[FRESH]MAN. *[sounding confused and turning map upside down]* This looks like Building B, except that this walk is in the wrong place. Maybe I should try this way. . . .

ROWDY. *[runs in from right and playfully shadow boxes with Every[fresh]man]* Hiya, kiddo. What's new? Har, har.

EVERY[FRESH]MAN. Well, I'm new here, and I don't know how to find Building B.

ROWDY. *[grabbing map]* Gimme that. Har, har. Looks like an upside-down map!

APATHY. *[drifts in from right]* Oh, who cares, Rowdy?

ROWDY. *[sarcastically]* Oh, my! *[shadow boxing with Apathy, who just yawns]* You sure don't, do you, Apathy?

FOGGY. *[wandering in from right]* Now was today Wednesday or Thursday? I can't remember if I have chemistry this year. Maybe it's Algebra instead.

ROWDY. Get your station tuned in, Foggy. We've got a problem here. Definitely looks like a lost one. *[tosses map aside]*

FOGGY. *[ignores Rowdy and talks to Every[fresh]man]* Well, if you want Building B, it's here somewhere, unless it's over there now. Nope, that's definitely the gym. *[picks up map while talking and puzzling over buildings in distance]*

## Proofreading and Publishing

After proofreading, Tamara made copies of her final version for the club members in the cast and for their club advisor.

## ACTIVITIES AND ASSIGNMENTS

A. Refer to the case study as you answer these questions.

1. How does Tamara tell the audience her characters' names? Why does she describe how they act as well as what they say?

2. Add another section to Tamara's sketch. Introduce the rest of the characters, who try to lead Every[fresh]man astray. Show how they confront School Spirit, or show School Spirit and friends rescuing Every[fresh]man from the others. Follow Tamara's format for dialogue and stage directions.

B. Write your own short dramatic sketch,

following these steps:

1. Select a topic, an occasion, and an audience for your sketch.
2. Use the planning chart to work out your ideas. Write notes on your title, characters, setting, and plot.
3. Draft your sketch. Begin with the title, character list, and stage directions for the set. Then write the dialogue and the stage directions for the actors. Give only essential directions.
4. Read your draft aloud to test whether the dialogue sounds natural.
5. Revise carefully. Cut unneeded description or conversations that do not advance the plot. Add information needed for clarity, and revise your dialogue so it sounds natural.
6. Proofread your script. Share it with your classmates.

# Lesson 21: Writing an Essay

## WHAT IS AN ESSAY?

An essay allows you, the writer, to communicate directly with a reader about something that matters to you. It communicates your experiences, ideas, and feelings. This lesson explains how to adapt the steps outlined in the first section of this handbook to the personal essay.

## PLANNING AN ESSAY

In your essay, you are likely to want to sound like one thoughtful person talking with another about something that concerns or interests you. Make sure that you have some personal experience or knowledge about your topic. Even if your topic is assigned, your own viewpoint makes your essay personal.

Essays have many purposes, depending on what you write about and how you want to affect a reader. Suppose you work as a volunteer at a local nature center and care very much about its future. You might write about that topic in many ways as this list suggests:

1. *Narrative essay:* telling a story to entertain and interest a reader:

   My first trip up Waterfall Trail, at the Davis Valley Nature Center, began peacefully, giving no clue of the danger to come.

2. *Descriptive essay:* describing something so that a reader can imagine it:

   Even though the Davis Valley Nature Center is only five minutes from homes and businesses, I feel hundreds of miles from civilization when I see the sun rise there on a crisp autumn morning.

3. *Expository essay:* Explaining something so that a reader can understand it:

   The three trails at the Davis Valley Nature Center seem confusing, but they actually form a

pretzel shape, all meeting at the Education Center.

4. *Argumentative or persuasive essay:* convincing people to act or think in a certain way:

   Proposition 4 must be passed if we are to protect the plants and animals in preserves like the Davis Valley Nature Center.

For your essay, freewriting and clustering are especially helpful. They can help you to relax and to think freely about your topic. Questioning, listing, and analyzing are useful if you need to figure out how to approach or develop your idea.

Your prewriting activities also may vary with your purpose. For a narrative essay, a time line of events may help organize the key incidents in the story. A list of images, arranged by sense (sight, sound, taste, touch, and smell), can enrich a descriptive essay. For an expository essay, you may want to list examples, subtypes, or steps in a process. You may need a chart that lists causes and effects or that identifies points of comparison or contrast. Should your purpose be argumentative, you may want to list your arguments, your opponent's arguments, and reasons that support or contradict them.

## CASE STUDY: WRITING AN ESSAY

Patrick's English teacher assigned an essay. Students could select their own topics, but each essay had to have a clear thesis statement and an orderly, logical development.

### Prewriting

Patrick began prewriting by thinking about his college applications. He used clustering to pinpoint a topic, as shown on the next page.

Patrick looked over his clustering chart and decided that he wanted to explain his college choice. He reorganized his ideas in a list, identifying subtopics and details for the body of his essay:

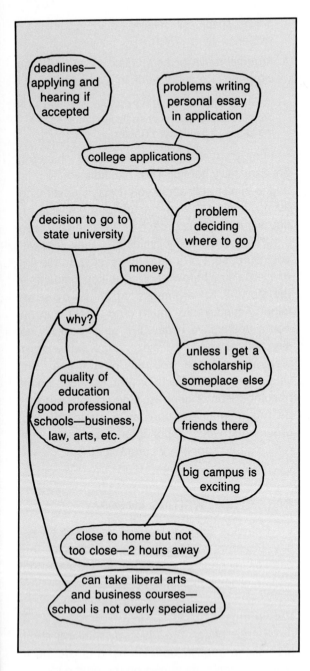

- Topic: state university is my first choice for college

- Paragraph 1   Introduction and thesis statement:
  Why state university is my first choice (add reasons to thesis)
  Qualify: unless I get a scholarship elsewhere and must take money to be fair to family

- Paragraph 2   Money:
  Most people assume money is my reason (add tuition example?)
  College is so expensive that money has to be a factor
  But it is not my main reason

- Paragraph 3   Other supposed reasons:
  Friends there
  Exciting, big campus
  Close to home but not too close (2 hours by car)
  All are factors, but all could be supplied by other schools

- Paragraph 4   Real reason is the quality of school:
  Not overly specialized, so I can take both liberal arts and business
  Good professional schools, so degree will be well regarded and faculty will be top level
  Most important is recent national honors for architecture school; architecture will be my major field

- Paragraph 5   Conclusion about reasons for choice:
  Not for economic or social reasons but for academic reasons
  Lucky to get the other benefits while getting the one that matters most about any college

**Drafting and Revising**

Because his outline was so detailed, Patrick quickly drafted a thesis statement and wrote the rest of his paper. Next he revised his essay, concentrating mainly on sentence structure and style because he felt that his organization was already clear.

**Proofreading and Publishing**

After Patrick proofread his paper, he left a copy with his guidance counselor.

## ACTIVITIES AND ASSIGNMENTS

A. Use the case study to answer the following questions:

1. Carefully review Patrick's outline. Do all of his points follow logically and support his thesis statement? What important explanation, not in his clustering, has he added to his outline?
2. Use Patrick's outline to draft a possible thesis statement for his essay. Be sure that your statement specifies the topic, states the approach or viewpoint, and prepares a reader for the content and order of the body paragraphs.
3. Given Patrick's outline, what transition would you expect to find in his essay? Point to places in his outline that suggest how he planned to link his paragraphs and sentences.

B. Write your own essay, following these steps:

1. Think of a topic that interests or concerns you. Decide whether your essay will be narrative, descriptive, expository, persuasive, or entertaining. If you have trouble thinking of a topic, try freewriting or clustering.
2. Use one of the prewriting techniques to develop ideas. Then arrange your ideas in an outline.
3. Write a thesis statement that specifies your topic and your viewpoint. If possible, also prepare a reader for the content and organization of your essay.
4. Use your thesis statement as the basis of your introductory paragraph.
5. Write body paragraphs, each developing a main point. Each should have a topic sentence that follows from your thesis plus transitions, clear explanations, and details or examples.
6. Write a concluding paragraph that sums up your essay in an interesting way.
7. Revise and proofread your essay, using the checklists on pages 1335 and 1338.
8. Share your essay with a friend.

# HANDBOOK OF LITERARY TERMS AND TECHNIQUES

**ACT**   See *Drama.*

**ALEXANDRINE**   An *alexandrine* is a line of poetry written in iambic hexameter. The line is made up of six feet, each containing one weakly stressed syllable followed by one strongly stressed syllable. The following lines from Michael Drayton's *Polyolbion,* which was written in 1613, are alexandrines:

> Mŭse, fírst | ŏf Ar|dĕn téll, | whŏse
>   foot|stĕps yet | ăre found
> Ĭn hér | rŏugh wóod|lănds, móre |thăn án|y̆
>   óth|ĕr ground

The alexandrine takes its name from the fact that the meter was often used in Old French poems about Alexander the Great. Alexandrines never became popular in England. However, Edmund Spenser did use them at the ends of stanzas in *The Faerie Queene.*
See *Meter* and *Spenserian Stanza.*

**ALLEGORY**   An *allegory* is a literary work with two or more levels of meaning—one literal level and one or more symbolic levels. The events, settings, objects, or characters in an allegory stand for ideas or qualities beyond themselves. Allegorical writing was common in the Middle Ages. Thereafter, the popularity of allegory declined, but Spenser revived the form in *The Faerie Queene,* and John Bunyan revived it yet again in *The Pilgrim's Progress.* Some modern novels, such as Joseph Conrad's *Heart of Darkness,* can be read allegorically. When reading a work allegorically, one tries to match every element at the literal level with a corresponding element at the symbolic level.

**ALLITERATION**   *Alliteration* is the repetition of initial consonant sounds. Emily Brontë used alliteration of *l* sounds in the first stanza of her poem "The Old Stoic":

> Riches I hold in *l*ight esteem,
>   And *L*ove I *l*augh to scorn;
> And *l*ust of fame was but a dream
>   That vanished with the morn

Alliteration is often used, especially in poetry, to emphasize and to link words as well as to create pleasing, musical sounds. Alliteration of stressed syllables was one of the characteristic features of Anglo-Saxon poetry.
See *Anglo-Saxon Poetry.*

**ALLUSION**   An *allusion* is a reference to a well-known person, place, event, literary work, or work of art. Writers often make allusions to tales from the Bible, classical Greek and Roman myths, plays by Shakespeare, historical or political events, and other materials with which they expect their readers to be familiar. An allusion appears in Shakespeare's *A Midsummer Night's Dream,* when Hermia swears "by Cupid's strongest bow," thus referring to the god of love in Roman mythology. Writers sometimes use allusions as a sort of shorthand to suggest ideas in a simple and concise manner.

**ANAPEST**   See *Meter.*

**ANECDOTE**   An *anecdote* is a brief story about an interesting, amusing, or strange event. In *The Life of Samuel Johnson,* an excerpt from which appears on page 576, James Boswell tells both serious and humorous anecdotes about Johnson. These anecdotes illustrate features of Johnson's temperament and character and explain why Boswell regarded Johnson as one of the most extraordinary figures in all literary history.

**ANGLO-SAXON POETRY**   *Anglo-Saxon poetry* is the rhythmic poetry composed in Old English before A.D. 1100. It generally has four accented syllables and an indefinite number of unaccented syllables in each line. Each line is divided in half by a caesura, or pause, and the halves are linked by the alliteration of two or three of the accented syllables. The following lines, translated from "Wulf and Eadwacer," show the alliteration and caesuras used in Anglo-Saxon poetry:

I *w*aited for my *W*ulf//with far-*W*andering
  yearnings,
*W*hen it was rainy *w*eather//and I sat
  weeping.

Anglo-Saxon poetry was originally composed orally and then sung or chanted to the accompaniment of a primitive harp.
See *Alliteration, Caesura,* and *Kenning.*

**ANTAGONIST**   An *antagonist* is a character or force in conflict with the main character, or protagonist, in a literary work. In many stories the plot is based on a conflict between the antagonist and the protagonist. In *Beowulf,* on page 24, the protagonist faces two antagonists—Grendel and Grendel's mother.
See *Character* and *Protagonist.*

**ANTITHESIS**   *Antithesis* is a figure of speech in which contrasting or paradoxical ideas are presented in parallel form. The following examples of antithesis come from Alexander Pope's *An Essay on Criticism:*
1. Some praise at morning what they blame at night
2. To err is human, to forgive, divine.

Antithesis was popular among the Neoclassical English poets of the eighteenth century, who often used it to make witty or satirical comments.

**APHORISM**   An *aphorism* is a general truth or observation about life, usually stated concisely and pointedly. Often witty or wise, memorable aphorisms appear in the works of Chaucer, Shakespeare, Pope, Johnson, and many other writers. An essay writer may have an *aphoristic style*—a style characterized by use of such statements—as does Francis Bacon. The following aphorisms come from Bacon's "Of Studies":
1. Crafty men condemn studies, simple men admire them, and wise men use them.
2. Reading maketh a full man, conference a ready man, and writing an exact man.

Used in an essay, an aphorism can be a memorable way to sum up or to reinforce a point or argument.

**APOSTROPHE**   An *apostrophe* is a figure of speech in which a speaker directly addresses an absent person or a personified quality, object, or idea. Shelley opens his poem "Ode to the West Wind" with an apostrophe that addresses the wind. Apostrophe is often used in poetry and in speeches to add emotional intensity.
See *Figurative Language.*

**ARGUMENTATION**   *Argumentation* is the type of writing that presents and logically supports the writer's views about an issue. Argumentation is one of the forms, or modes, of discourse. The term *argumentation* is sometimes used as though it were synonymous with *persuasion.* However, some critics and scholars distinguish between the two terms, using argumentation for works that support opinions with logical reasoning and persuasion for works that support opinions with appeals to emotion.
See *Forms of Discourse* and *Persuasion.*

**ASIDE**   An *aside* is a statement delivered by an actor to an audience in such a way that other characters on stage are presumed not to hear what is said. In an aside the character reveals his or her private thoughts, reactions, or motivations. Act III, Scene iv of *Macbeth* contains the following aside:

MURDERER. Most royal sir, Fleance is scaped.
MACBETH. [*Aside*] Then comes my fit again. I
  had else been perfect;
Whole as the marble, founded as the rock,
As broad and general as the casing air.
But now I am cabined, cribbed,

confined, bound in
To saucy doubts and fears.—but
Banquo's safe?

In this aside, Macbeth reveals his fearful reaction to the news that Fleance is still alive.

**ASSONANCE**   *Assonance* is the repetition of vowel sounds in stressed syllables containing dissimilar consonant sounds. Robert Browning used assonance in the following famous line from his poem "Andrea del Sarto":

Ah, but a man's *r*ea*ch* should ex*c*ee*d* his
grasp

The long *e* sound is repeated in the words *reach* and *exceed* in stressed syllables containing these consonants: *r–ch* and *c–d*.
See *Consonance.*

**ATMOSPHERE**   See *Mood.*

**AUTOBIOGRAPHY**   An *autobiography* is a form of nonfiction in which a person tells his or her own life story. Unlike a diary or a letter, an autobiography is written for a public audience. George Orwell's "Shooting an Elephant," on page 1014, is a fine example of the autobiographical essay.
See *Biography.*

**BALLAD**   A *ballad* is a songlike poem that tells a story, often one dealing with adventure or romance. Most ballads have the following characteristics:
1. four- or six-line stanzas
2. rhyme
3. simple language
4. dramatic action
Many ballads employ repetition of a refrain. Some make use of incremental repetition, in which a refrain is varied slightly each time it appears.
The British Isles have a rich tradition of *folk ballads*—songs that originated among illiterate peoples and were passed from singer to singer by word of mouth. Examples in your text include "Sir Patrick Spens," "The Two Corbies," and "Barbara Allan." Many English, Scottish, Welsh, and Irish writers have also created *literary ballads*—sophisticated poems in the style of folk ballads. One such literary ballad in your text is Samuel Taylor Coleridge's *The Rime of the Ancient Mariner,* on page 660.
See *Ballad Stanza, Incremental Repetition,* and *Refrain.*

**BALLAD STANZA**   A *ballad stanza* is a four- or six-line stanza form used in folk ballads and in literary imitations of folk ballads. In a typical four-line ballad stanza, the first and third lines each have four stresses; the second and fourth lines each have three stresses and also rhyme. Thus the usual rhyme scheme is *abcb,* although some ballads follow the scheme *abab.* This typical four-line ballad stanza comes from Dudley Randall's "Ballad of Birmingham":

Mother dear, may I go downtown,
Instead of out to play,
And march the streets of Birmingham
In a Freedom March today?

See *Ballad.*

**BIOGRAPHY**   A *biography* is a form of nonfiction in which a writer tells the life story of another person. A good biographer uses many sources of information, including, perhaps, the subject's letters and journals, interviews with the subject or with people who know the subject, personal knowledge about the subject, and books and other works about the subject. James Boswell's *The Life of Samuel Johnson,* an excerpt from which appears on page 576, is one of the most famous of all biographies. Boswell's work has been widely praised for its accuracy of reporting and its liveliness of style.
See *Autobiography.*

**BLANK VERSE**   *Blank verse* is poetry written in unrhymed iambic pentameter lines. Each iambic foot has one weakly stressed syllable followed by one strongly stressed syllable. A pentameter line has five of these feet. Blank verse usually contains occasional variations in rhythm—variations that are introduced to create emphasis, variety, and naturalness of sound. Because blank verse sounds much like ordinary spoken English, it is often used in drama and in poetry. Great English writers of blank verse have included Shakespeare, Wordsworth, Browning, and Auden. The following lines come from Wordsworth's blank-verse poem "Lines Composed a Few Miles Above Tintern Abbey," on page 644:

Fŏr thóu | ărt wíth | mĕ hére |ŭpón | thĕ bánks
Ŏf thís | faĭr rív|eŕ; thóu |mў déar|ĕst
friénd

See *Meter.*

**CAESURA**   A *caesura* is a natural pause, or break, in the middle of a line of poetry. The symbol // has been used to mark the caesuras in the following lines from Kathleen Raine's "In the Beck":

There is a fish,//that quivers in the
pool,
itself a shadow,//but its shadow, clear.
Catch it again and again,//it still is
there.

A poet can draw attention to a word by placing it just before or just after a caesura. In Anglo-Saxon poetry a caesura divides each four-stress line in half and thus is essential to the rhythm. See *Anglo-Saxon Poetry.*

**CANTO**   A *canto* is a section of a long poem. Both Alexander Pope's *The Rape of the Lock* and Edmund Spenser's *The Faerie Queene* were written in cantos.

**CARICATURE**   A *caricature* is a distorted or exaggerated portrayal of a person. The portrayal of Lady Bracknell, in Oscar Wilde's *The Importance of Being Earnest,* is an example. Carica-

ture is used to ridicule personal flaws and general social failings.

**CARPE DIEM**   *Carpe diem* is a Latin phrase meaning "seize the day." Many great literary works have been written with the *carpe diem* theme. All have in common the fact that they urge people to enjoy life in the present, while such enjoyment is still possible. One of the best-known poems on this theme is Robert Herrick's "To the Virgins, to Make Much of Time," on page 432, which begins with the line, "Gather ye rosebuds while ye may." Another famous work that deals with the *carpe diem* theme is Marvell's "To His Coy Mistress," on page 418.

**CATALOG**   A *catalog* is a list included in a literary work. Taking his cue from classical epics, which list warriors, ships, weapons, and other items, John Milton uses this convention in *Paradise Lost* to list the fallen angels. Alexander Pope uses the catalog in *The Rape of the Lock* to list the duties of the sylphs. Writers use catalogs to instruct readers and to convey a great deal of information concisely. The effect of a catalog is usually to overwhelm the reader with the numbers of items mentioned.
See *Epic Convention.*

**CHARACTER**   A *character* is a person or animal who takes part in the action of a literary work. Characters can be described in many different ways, as follows:

1. In terms of the importance of their roles: A character who plays an important role in a story is called a *major character.* A character who does not play an important role is called a *minor character.*
2. In terms of their roles: A character who plays the central role in a story is called the *protagonist.* A character who opposes the protagonist is called the *antagonist.*
3. In terms of their complexity: A complex character is called *round,* while a simple character is called *flat.*

4. In terms of the degree to which they change: A character who changes is called *dynamic;* a character who does not change is called *static.*

Character types that readers recognize easily, such as the hard-boiled detective or the wicked stepmother, are called *stereotypes,* or *stock charcters.*
See *Characterization* and *Motivation.*

**CHARACTERIZATION**   *Characterization* is the act of creating and developing a character. A writer uses *direct characterization* when he or she states a character's traits explicitly. *Indirect characterization* occurs when the writer reveals a character's traits by some other means. A character's traits can be revealed indirectly by means of what he or she says, thinks, or does; by means of a description of his or her appearance; or by means of the statements, thoughts, or actions of other characters. When using indirect characterization, the writer depends on the reader to infer a character's traits from the clues provided.
See *Character.*

**CLASSICISM**   *Classicism* is an approach to literature and to the other arts that stresses reason, harmony, balance, proportion, clarity, and idealism in imitation of the philosophers and artists of ancient Greece and Rome. The European Neoclassicists of the eighteenth century revived the Greek and Roman classical tradition and aspired to produce works worthy of this tradition. Classicism is often contrasted with Romanticism, which places a premium on imagination and emotion, sometimes at the expense of reason and proportion. Classicism also differs from Realism, which concentrates on the actual rather than on the ideal.
See *Neoclassicism, Realism,* and *Romanticism.*

**CLIMAX**   The *climax* is the high point of interest or suspense in a literary work. Often the climax is also the *crisis* in the plot, the point at which the protagonist changes his or her understanding or situation. Sometimes the climax coincides with the *resolution,* the point at which the central conflict is ended. In a story the climax generally occurs near the end. For example, Charles Dickens's "The Signalman," on page 870, reaches its climax with the death of the signalman. In a play the climax often falls more toward the middle and marks the end of the rising action and the beginning of the falling action. For example, in William Shakespeare's *Macbeth,* the climax is the banquet scene, in Act III. This scene begins the inevitable movement toward Macbeth's downfall.
See *Plot.*

**CLOSED COUPLET**   See *Couplet.*

**COMEDY**   A *comedy* is a work of literature, especially a play, that has a happy ending. Comedies often show ordinary characters in conflict with their societies. Their problems are resolved through laughter, reconciliation, and the correction of moral faults or social wrongs. Types of comedy include the *romantic comedy,* which involves problems among lovers, and the *comedy of manners,* which satirically challenges the social customs of a sophisticated society. George Bernard Shaw's *Pygmalion,* on page 1109, is a modern comedy of manners. Many comedies feature humorous physical action and witty dialogue. Comedy is often contrasted with tragedy, in which the central character, or protagonist, meets an unfortunate end.
See *Drama* and *Tragedy.*

**COMEDY OF MANNERS**   See *Comedy.*

**COMIC RELIEF**   *Comic relief* is the feeling created by a humorous action or speech that appears within a serious work of literature. For example, the so-called "Porter Scene" in *Macbeth,* at the beginning of Act II, Scene iii, provides comic relief after the murder of Duncan. As this scene illustrates, comic relief is often used to emphasize, by contrast, the seriousness of the main action.

**CONCEIT**   A *conceit* is an unusual and surprising comparison between two very different things. This special kind of metaphor or complicated analogy is often the basis for a whole poem. During the Elizabethan period, sonnets commonly included *Petrarchan conceits,* ones that extravagantly compared the beloved's beauty or the speaker's suffering to something else. For example, the sonnets of Sir Thomas Wyatt compare the lover's state to a storm-tossed ship, to the Alps, and to a soldier's camp. Shakespeare satirizes such overblown conceits in his Sonnet 130:

> I love to hear her speak; yet well I know
> That music hath a far more pleasing sound:
> I grant I never saw a goddess go;
> My mistress, when she walks, treads on the
>    ground.
> And yet, by heaven, I think my love as rare
> As any she belied with false compare.

The seventeenth-century metaphysical poets were especially fond of elaborate, unusual, highly intellectual conceits. For example, in "Love's Alchemy," John Donne compares the unreliability of love to the unreliability of alchemy for making gold.
See *Metaphor.*

**CONCRETE POEM**   A *concrete poem* is one with a shape that suggests its subject. An example in this text is George Herbert's "Easter Wings," on page 412.
See *Emblematic Image.*

**CONFLICT**   A *conflict* is a struggle between opposing forces. Sometimes this struggle is *internal,* or within a character. At other times the struggle is *external,* or between the character and some outside force. The outside force may be another character, nature, or some element of society such as a custom or a political institution. Often the conflict in a work is complicated and combines several of these possibilities. For example, Macbeth struggles against the better parts of his own nature, against Banquo and Fleance, against fate, and against the forces led by Malcolm, Macduff, and Siward.
See *Antagonist, Plot,* and *Protagonist.*

**CONNOTATION**   A *connotation* is an association that a word calls to mind in addition to its dictionary meaning. For example, the words *home* and *domicile* have the same dictionary meanings. However, the first has positive connotations of warmth and security while the second does not. Therefore, a writer who wants to convey a sense of warmth and security will be more likely to use the word *home* than the word *domicile,* even though the two words refer to the same thing. Because the connotations of words are so powerful, writers carefully choose words with connotations that suggest the shades of meaning they intend.
See *Denotation.*

**CONSONANCE**   *Consonance* is the repetition of consonant sounds in stressed syllables containing dissimilar vowel sounds. D.H. Lawrence uses consonance in the opening lines of "Snake":

> A snake came to my water-trough
> On a *hot, hot,* day, and I in pajamas for the
>    heat,
> To drink there.

The words *hot* and *heat* have the same consonants but different vowels. (Note also the assonance in the words *snake* and *came* and in the words *water* and *pajamas.*) When used at the ends of lines, consonance can create *approximate* or *slant rhyme.*
See *Assonance.*

**COUPLET**   A *couplet* is a pair of rhyming lines written in the same meter. The following iambic tetrameter couplets come from John Milton's "L'Allegro":

> And if I give thee honor due,
> Mirth, admit me of the crew
> To live with her, and live with thee,
> In unreproved pleasures free.

A *heroic couplet* is a rhymed pair of iambic pentameter lines. During the Neoclassical Period, the popular heroic couplet was often also a *closed couplet,* with its meaning and grammar complete within two lines. These lines from Alexander Pope's *An Essay on Criticism* illustrate the closed heroic couplet:

> True ease in writing comes from art, not
>    chance,
> As those move easiest who have learned to
>    dance.

Sonnets written in the English, or Shakespearean, style usually end with heroic couplets.
See *Sonnet.*

**CRISIS**   The *crisis* in the plot of a story or play is the turning point for the protagonist—the point at which his or her situation or understanding is changed. This point often coincides with the *climax,* or emotional high point, of the story.
See *Climax* and *Plot.*

**DACTYL**   See *Meter.*

**DEAD METAPHOR**   See *Metaphor.*

**DENOTATION**   The *denotation* of a word is its objective meaning, that to which the word refers, independent of other associations the word calls to mind. Dictionaries list the denotative meanings of words. Another term for denotative meaning is *referential meaning.*
See *Connotation.*

**DENOUEMENT**   The *denouement* in a literary work is anything that happens after the resolution of the plot. At this point the central conflict is resolved, and the consequences for the protago-

nist are already decided. Essentially, a denouement is a tying up of loose ends. In some works no denouement is needed.
See *Plot.*

**DESCRIPTION**   A *description* is a portrait, in words, of a person, place, or object. Its purpose is to provide the concrete details and lively images that make people, places, and things become clear to readers.

Descriptions use *imagery*—words and phrases that appeal to the senses of sight, sound, touch, taste, and smell. Description is one of the major forms, or modes, of discourse and is often found in conjunction with other types of writing such as narration, exposition, or persuasion.
See *Forms of Discourse* and *Imagery.*

**DEVELOPMENT**   See *Plot.*

**DIALECT**   A *dialect* is the form of a language spoken by people in a particular region or group. Dialects differ from one another in grammar, vocabulary, and pronunciation. Authors often write in regional dialects, as did Robert Burns, who used a Scots dialect in such poems as "Auld Lang Syne":

> Should auld acquaintance be forgot,
> And never brought to mind?
> Should auld acquaintance be forgot,
> And auld lang syne?

Dialect is sometimes used by writers as a part of characterization. For example, the social status of each character in George Bernard Shaw's *Pygmalion,* on page 1109, is revealed by the dialect the character speaks. In the course of Shaw's play, the central character, Eliza Doolittle, is trained to speak Received Standard English—a dialect with high social prestige—rather than her native Cockney dialect.
See *Vernacular.*

**DIALOGUE**   A *dialogue* is a conversation between characters. Writers use dialogue to reveal character, to present events, to add variety to narratives, and to interest readers. The dialogue in a story or play is usually set off by quotation marks and paragraphing. The dialogue in a play script generally follows the characters' names.

**DIARY**   A *diary* is a personal record of daily events, usually written in prose. Most diaries are not written for publication; sometimes, however, interesting diaries or diaries by influential people do find their way into print. One example of a published diary is that of Samuel Pepys, a selection from which appears on page 506. In his diary Pepys recorded anecdotes and details about his life in the 1660's.
See *Journal.*

**DICTION**   *Diction* is word choice. A writer's diction can be a major determinant of his or her style. Diction can be described as formal or informal, abstract or concrete, plain or ornate, ordinary or technical.
See *Style.*

**DIMETER**   See *Meter.*

**DIRECT CHARACTERIZATION**   See *Characterization.*

**DRAMA**   A *drama* is a story written to be performed by actors. It may consist of one or more large sections called *acts,* which are made up of any number of smaller sections called *scenes.*

Drama originated in the religious rituals and symbolic re-enactments of primitive peoples. The ancient Greeks developed drama into a sophisticated art and created such dramatic forms as tragedy and comedy.

The first dramas in England were the miracle plays and morality plays of the Middle Ages. *Miracle plays* told Biblical stories. *Morality plays,* such as *Everyman,* on page 188, dealt with personified virtues and vices. The English Re-

naissance saw a great flowering of drama in England, culminating in the works of William Shakespeare, who wrote many of the world's greatest comedies, tragedies, histories, and romances. During the Neoclassical Age, English drama turned to witty, satirical comedies of manners that probed the virtues of upper-class society. Superb examples of Neoclassical comedy include Goldsmith's *She Stoops to Conquer* and Congreve's *The Way of the World.* The Romantic and Victorian ages were not great periods for drama in England. However, a few good verse plays were written, including Percy Bysshe Shelley's *The Cenci* and *Prometheus Unbound* and Robert Browning's *Pippa Passes.* The end of the nineteenth and beginning of the twentieth centuries saw a resurgence of the drama in England and throughout the English-speaking world. Great plays of the Modern Period include George Bernard Shaw's *Pygmalion,* on page 1109, and the many plays by William Butler Yeats, John Millington Synge, Christopher Fry, T. S. Eliot, Harold Pinter, and Samuel Beckett.

**DRAMATIC IRONY**   See *Irony.*

**DRAMATIC MONOLOGUE**   A *dramatic monologue* is a poem in which an imaginary character speaks to a silent listener. During the monologue, the speaker reveals his or her personality, usually at a moment of crisis. Examples of dramatic monologues in this text are Robert Browning's "My Last Duchess," on page 812 and Alfred, Lord Tennyson's "Ulysses," on page 779.

**DRAMATIC POETRY**   See *Poetry.*

**DYNAMIC CHARACTER**   See *Character.*

**ELEGY**   An *elegy* is a solemn and formal lyric poem about death. It may mourn a particular person or reflect on a serious or tragic theme, such as the passing of youth, beauty, or a way of

life. See Thomas Gray's "Elegy Written in a Country Churchyard," on page 586.
See *Lyric Poem.*

**EMBLEMATIC IMAGE**   An *emblematic image* is a symbolic figure or shape presented through the arrangement of the lines of a poem. For example, George Herbert's "Easter Wings," on page 412, is shaped like a pair of wings.
See *Concrete Poem.*

**END RHYME**   See *Rhyme.*

**END-STOPPED LINE**   An *end-stopped line* of poetry concludes with a break in the meter and in the meaning. This pause at the end of a line often is punctuated by a period, comma, dash, or semicolon. These lines from "Away, Melancholy," by Stevie Smith, are end-stopped:

> Are not the trees green,
> The earth as green?
> Does not the wind blow,
> Fire leap and the rivers flow?
> Away melancholy.

See *Run-on Line.*

**EPIC**   An *epic* is a long narrative poem about the adventures of gods or of a hero. *Beowulf,* on page 24, is a *folk epic,* one that was composed orally and then passed from storyteller to storyteller by word of mouth. The ancient Greek epics attributed to Homer—the *Iliad* and the *Odyssey* —are also folk epics. The *Aeneid,* by the Roman poet Virgil, and *The Divine Comedy,* by the Italian poet Dante Alighieri, are examples of literary epics from the Classical and Medieval periods, respectively. John Milton's *Paradise Lost,* a selection from which appears on page 449, is also a literary epic. Milton's goal in creating *Paradise Lost* was to write a Christian epic similar in form and equal in value to the great epics of antiquity. Because of an epic's length and seriousness of theme, it presents an encyclopedic portrait of the culture in which it was produced. One can learn a great deal about ancient Greece by reading Homer and a great deal about thirteenth- and fourteenth-century Italy by reading Dante.
See *Epic Convention.*

**EPIC CONVENTION**   An *epic convention* is a traditional characteristic of epic poems. These characteristics include an opening statement of the theme; an appeal for supernatural help in telling the story; a beginning *in medias res* (Latin: "in the middle of things"), long lists, or catalogs, of people and things; accounts of past events; and descriptive phrases such as kennings, Homeric similes, and Homeric epithets.
See *Catalog, Epic, Epithet,* In Medias Res, *Invocation,* and *Kenning.*

**EPIGRAM**   An *epigram* is a brief, pointed statement in prose or in verse. The concluding couplet in an English sonnet may be epigrammatic. An essay may be written in an *epigrammatic style,* one that is characterized by frequent use of epigrams.

**EPIGRAPH**   An *epigraph* is a quotation that appears at the beginning of a literary work, as is illustrated by Rainer Maria Rilke's lines at the beginning of Margaret Drabble's "A Voyage to Cythera," on page 1276. An epigraph generally introduces a motif or a theme that is developed in the work itself.

**EPIPHANY**   *Epiphany* is a term introduced by James Joyce to describe a moment of revelation or insight in which a character recognizes some truth. In Joyce's "Araby," the boy's epiphany comes at the end of the story, on page 987, when he recognizes the falsity of his dream.

**EPITAPH**   An *epitaph* is an inscription written on a tomb or burial place. In literature, epitaphs also include serious or humorous lines written as if they were intended for such use. Examples are the epitaph at the end of Thomas Gray's "Elegy

Written in a Country Churchyard," which appears on page 586, and this epitaph for Sir Isaac Newton, written by Alexander Pope:

Nature and Nature's laws lay hid in night:
God said, Let Newton be! and all was light.

**EPITHET**   An *epithet* is a word or phrase that states a characteristic quality of some person or thing. A.E. Housman uses epithets such as "golden friends" and "lightfoot lad" in "With Rue My Heart Is Laden," on page 854. Homeric epithets, such as "wide-wayed city," "clear-voiced heralds," and "high-hearted princes" in the *Iliad,* were common in classical epics and in later imitations of classical epics.
See *Epic Convention.*

**ESSAY**   An *essay* is a short, nonfiction work about a particular subject. Essays are of many types but may be classified by tone or style as formal or informal.

An essay may also be classed by its main purpose as descriptive, narrative, expository, argumentative, or persuasive.

**EXACT RHYME**   See *Rhyme.*

**EXEMPLUM**   An *exemplum* is a short tale or anecdote with a moral, especially one used in a medieval sermon. Geoffrey Chaucer's "The Pardoner's Tale," on page 159, illustrates the moral that "love of wealth is the root of all evil."

**EXPOSITION**   *Exposition* is writing or speech that explains, informs, or presents information. Types of exposition include analysis, classification, comparison and contrast, definition, and exemplification.

In the plot of a story or drama, the *exposition* is the part of the work that introduces the characters, the setting, and the basic situation. For example, in William Shakespeare's *A Midsummer Night's Dream,* the first scene introduces the lovers and their problems, locates the action in the palace at Athens near a wood, and establishes the light mood of a romantic comedy.
See *Forms of Discourse* and *Plot.*

**EXPRESSIONISM**   *Expressionism* was an artistic movement early in the twentieth century. The Expressionists emphasized the inner experiences of individuals rather than objective external realities. This movement influenced many dramatists and poets, including T.S. Eliot, whose poem "The Hollow Men," appears on page 1063.

**EXTENDED METAPHOR**   See *Metaphor.*

**FABLE**   A *fable* is a brief story, usually with animal characters, that teaches a lesson, or moral. The earliest extant fables are those attributed to Aesop, a Greek writer of the sixth century B.C. In modern times fables are popular both as nursery tales and as vehicles for satire. In his novella *Animal Farm,* George Orwell adapted the fable form for use in a satirical allegory about the Russian Revolution and its aftermath.

**FALLING ACTION**   The *falling action* is all of the action that takes place after the climax in a literary work. During this time, the conflict is resolved and the suspense decreases.
See *Plot* and *Rising Action.*

**FANTASY**   *Fantasy* is highly imaginative writing that contains elements not found in real life. Elizabeth Bowen's "The Demon Lover," on page 994, is a fantasy. Writers use fantasies to entertain readers and sometimes to make serious points about reality.

**FARCE**   *Farce* is a kind of comedy that features physical horseplay, stereotypical characters, and absurd plots, often ones involving mistaken identities and recognition scenes. The writer of a farce uses exaggeration, irony, and witty dialogue to move his or her audience to laughter. A farce may be a complete play or a scene used for contrast or comic relief within a serious work.

**FICTION**  *Fiction* is a prose writing that tells about imaginary characters and events. Some writers of fiction base their stories on real people and events, while others rely solely on their imaginations.
See *Narration, Nonfiction,* and *Prose.*

**FIGURATIVE LANGUAGE**  *Figurative language* is writing or speech not meant to be interpreted literally. Poets and other writers use figurative language to create vivid word pictures, to make their writing emotionally intense and concentrated, and to state their ideas in new and unusual ways that satisfy readers' imaginations.
See *Figure of Speech.*

**FIGURE OF SPEECH**  A *figure of speech* is an expression or a word used imaginatively rather than literally. Among the types of figurative language are antithesis, apostrophe, hyperbole, irony, metaphor, metonymy, oxymoron, paradox, personification, simile, synecdoche, and understatement.
See *Figurative Language.* See also the entries for individual figures of speech.

**FIRST-PERSON POINT OF VIEW**  See *Point of View.*

**FLASHBACK**  A *flashback* is a section of a literary work that interrupts the sequence of events to relate an event from an earlier time. The writer may present the flashback as a character's memory or recollection, as part of an account or story told by a character, or as a dream or daydream. For example, in Elizabeth Bowen's ''The Demon Lover,'' on page 994, Mrs. Drover remembers saying farewell to her fiancé twenty-five years earlier. Writers use flashbacks to show what motivates a character and to supply background information in a dramatic way.
See *Foreshadowing.*

**FLAT CHARACTER**  See *Character.*

**FOIL**  A *foil* is a character who provides a contrast to another character, thus intensifying the impact of that other character. For example, Banquo and Duncan act as foils for the ambitious and tyrannical Macbeth.

**FOLK BALLAD**  See *Ballad.*

**FOLKLORE**  *Folklore* includes the stories, legends, myths, ballads, riddles, sayings, and other traditional works produced orally by illiterate or semi-literate peoples. Folklore influences written literature in many ways, as is suggested by the beheading contest in *Sir Gawain and the Green Knight,* on page 170, and the fiancé in Elizabeth Bowen's ''The Demon Lover,'' on page 994.

**FOLK TALE**  A *folk tale* is a story composed orally and then passed from person to person by word of mouth. Many of Chaucer's stories were based on folk tales.
See *Folklore.*

**FOOT**  See *Meter.*

**FORESHADOWING**  *Foreshadowing* is the use, in a literary work, of clues that suggest events that have yet to occur. Writers use foreshadowing to create suspense or to prepare the audience for the eventual outcome of events.
See *Flashback.*

**FORM**  The *form* of a literary work is its structure, shape, pattern, organization, or style—the way it is made. A work's form is often distinguished from its *content*—what it is about.

**FORMS OF DISCOURSE**  The *forms of discourse* are the main types of writing—description, narration, exposition, and persuasion or argumentation. Each has a different purpose and may be a writer's main emphasis. Often, however, the forms of discourse are used together to support each other. For instance, a narrative may include description, or an argument may begin with exposition.

See *Argumentation, Description, Exposition, Narration,* and *Persuasion.*

**FREE VERSE**   *Free verse* is poetry not written in a regular rhythmical pattern, or meter. Instead of having metrical feet and lines, free verse has a rhythm that suits its meaning and that uses the sounds of spoken language in lines of different lengths. Free verse has been widely used in twentieth-century poetry. An example is "The Galloping Cat," by Stevie Smith:

> All the same I
> Intend to go on being
> A cat that likes to
> Gallop about doing good
> So
> Now with my bald head I go,
> Chopping the untidy flowers down, to and fro.

**GOTHIC**   *Gothic* is a term used to describe literary works that make extensive use of primitive, Medieval, wild, mysterious, or natural elements. Gothic elements offended eighteenth-century Neoclassical writers but appealed to the Romantic writers who followed them. *Gothic novels,* such as Mary Wollstonecraft Shelley's *Frankenstein,* a selection from which appears on page 734, are often set in gloomy castles where horrifying, supernatural events take place.

**HEPTAMETER**   See *Meter.*

**HEPTASTICH**   See *Stanza.*

**HERO/HEROINE**   A *hero* or *heroine* is a character whose actions are inspiring or noble. Often heroes struggle to overcome foes or to escape from difficulties. The most obvious examples of heroes and heroines are the larger-than-life characters in myths and legends, ones like Beowulf or Odysseus. However, more ordinary characters can, and often do, perform heroic deeds.

**HEROIC COUPLET**   See *Couplet.*

**HEXAMETER**   See *Meter.*

**HOMERIC EPITHET**   See *Epithet.*

**HYPERBOLE**   A *hyperbole* is a deliberate exaggeration or overstatement. In "On Monsieur's Departure," Queen Elizabeth I used this figure of speech:

> I grieve and dare not show my discontent,
> I love and yet am forced to seem to hate,
> I do, yet dare not say I ever meant,
> I seem stark mute but inwardly to prate.
>   I am and not, I freeze and yet am burned,
>   Since from myself another self I turned.

Of course, Queen Elizabeth was not turned by love into another person, she was not mute or burned, and she did not act in total opposition to her true feelings. Such excessive claims are examples of hyperbole. In Oscar Wilde's *The Importance of Being Earnest,* Algernon's claims likewise illustrate hyperbole:

> ALGERNON: I really don't see anything romantic in proposing. It is very romantic to be in love. But there is nothing romantic about a definite proposal. Why, one may be accepted. One usually is, I believe. Then the excitement is all over. The very essence of romance is uncertainty. If ever I get married, I'll certainly try to forget the fact.

As these examples suggest, hyperbole may be used for heightened seriousness or for comic effect.

See *Figurative Language.*

**IAMB**   See *Meter.*

**IAMBIC PENTAMETER**   See *Meter.*

**IMAGE**   An *image* is a word or a phrase that

appeals to one or more of the five senses—sight, hearing, touch, taste, or smell. In a famous essay on Hamlet, T.S. Eliot explained how a group of images can be used as an "objective correlative." By this phrase Eliot meant to suggest that a complex emotional state can be suggested by images that are carefully chosen to evoke this state.
See *Imagery.*

**IMAGERY**    *Imagery* is the descriptive language used in literature to re-create sensory experiences. The following lines from William Collins's "Ode to Evening," show how a poet can use imagery to appeal to several senses:

> Now air is hushed, save where the weak-eyed
>     bat,
> With short shrill shrieks flits by on leathern
>     wing,
> Or where the beetle winds
> His small but sullen horn,
> As oft he rises 'midst the twilight path,
> Against the pilgrim borne in heedless hum.

These lines describe the sounds, sights, and movements of evening, just as if a reader were out walking with the poem's speaker. Imagery can enrich writing by making it more vivid, setting a tone, suggesting emotions, and guiding a reader's reactions.

**INCITING INCIDENT**    See *Plot.*

**INCONGRUITY**    An *incongruity* is a juxtaposition of incompatible or opposite elements. For example, sometimes a writer's style and subject may be incongruous, as in Alexander Pope's *The Rape of the Lock,* on page 548. Pope uses the formal language and conventions of epic poetry, but his subject is only the social battle surrounding a lock of hair. When a writer talks about something trivial in formal language, the exaggeration and surprise of the incongruity may create a comic or humorous effect.

**INCREMENTAL REPETITION**    *Incremental repetition,* used in ballads and in other oral poetry, is the technique of repeating a line or a stanza with slight but significant changes. Incremental repetition is used in the ballad "Lord Randal":

> "O where have you been, Lord Randal, my son?
> O where have you been, my handsome young
>     man?—
> "I have been to the greenwood; O make my
>     bed soon,
> For I'm weary with hunting, and fain would lie
>     down."

Each stanza uses this question-and-answer pattern, supplying and repeating details that add to the story and increase suspense.
See *Ballad.*

**INDIRECT CHARACTERIZATION**    See *Characterization.*

**IN MEDIAS RES**    The phrase *in medias res,* Latin for "in the middle of things," is a storytelling method used in epic poems and in other narratives. When a writer begins *in medias res,* the story starts in the middle, jumping right into the action. The background and the initial events are introduced later by means of one or more flashbacks. John Milton's *Paradise Lost,* like the great epics of classical antiquity, follows this pattern. Milton's epic begins with Satan and the fallen angels on the burning lake in Chaos. Not until Books V and VI does Raphael tell Adam about the great battle that occurred just before those angels fell from heaven.
See *Epic Convention.*

**INTERNAL RHYME**    See *Rhyme.*

**INVERSION**    An *inversion* is a reversal or change in the regular word order of a sentence. For instance, Anne Killigrew begins the poem

"Upon the Saying That My Verses Were Made by Another" in this way:

> Next Heaven, my vows to thee, O sacred Muse!
> I offered up, nor didst thou them refuse.

These lines reverse the usual subject-verb-object order, "I offered up my vows to thee," and the usual negative construction, "nor didst thou refuse them." Poets, in particular, use inversion to emphasize words and sometimes to fit them to the meter of a poem.

**INVOCATION**   An *invocation* is an appeal to a Muse or to another divine being for help in writing the poem. In ancient Greece and Rome, writers often began their works by calling for the aid of the Muses, who were the nine daughters of Apollo responsible for the various arts. In *Paradise Lost,* on page 449, John Milton appeals to his "Heavenly Muse," the Holy Spirit of the Christian trinity.
See *Epic Convention.*

**IRONY**   *Irony* is the general name given to literary techniques that involve surprising, interesting, or amusing contradictions. In *verbal irony,* words are used to suggest the opposite of their usual meaning. In *dramatic irony,* there is a contradiction between what a character thinks and what the reader or audience knows to be true. In *irony of situation,* an event occurs that directly contradicts the expectations of the characters, the reader, or the audience.

**IRONY OF SITUATION**   See *Irony.*

**JOURNAL**   A *journal* is a daily autobiographical account of events and personal reactions. Daniel Defoe adapted this form to fictional use in his *A Journal of the Plague Year,* an excerpt from which appears on page 514.
See *Diary.*

**KENNING**   A *kenning* is a metaphorical phrase, used in Anglo-Saxon poetry to replace a concrete noun. In "The Seafarer," on page 17, the cuckoo is called "summer's sentinel" and the sea "the whale's home."
See *Anglo-Saxon Poetry* and *Epic Convention.*

**LEGEND**   A *legend* is a widely told story about the past, one that may or may not have a foundation in fact. A legend often reflects a people's identity or cultural values, generally with more historical truth and less emphasis on the supernatural than in a myth. English legends include the stories of King Arthur, of Robin Hood, and of other folk heroes.
See *Myth.*

**LIMITED POINT OF VIEW**   See *Point of View.*

**LITERARY BALLAD**   See *Ballad.*

**LITERARY CRITICISM**   *Literary criticism* is the art of analyzing, interpreting, and evaluating literary works. There are many different types, or schools, of literary criticism, as follows:
1. *Impressionistic* or *Reader-Response Criticism* deals with the subjective responses of individual readers.
2. *Biographical* or *Historical Criticism* deals with details of literary history as these relate to particular works.
3. *Archetypal Criticism* deals with universal patterns of meaning or symbolism believed to be part of the biological or cultural heritage of humankind as a whole.
4. *Psychological Criticism* interprets texts based on concepts derived from any of a number of psychological models, such as the Gestalt Model of perception or the Freudian model of personality.
5. *Linguistic Criticism* applies to literary criticism borrowed from the scientific study of language.
6. *Moral* or *Ethical Criticism* evaluates literary works based on the moral or ethical mes-

sages that they convey. *Political Criticism* is a type of moral or ethical criticism.

7. The so-called *New Criticism* concentrates on the characteristics or qualities of literary works themselves, apart from any extra-textual material such as information about authors' lives or literary movements.

8. *Reconstructionist Criticism* views the literary text as an occasion for a creative act in which the reader in effect makes a new text by virtue of what he or she brings to it.

**LYRIC POEM**   A *lyric poem* is a poem that expresses the observations and feelings of a single speaker. Unlike a narrative poem, it presents an experience or a single effect, but it does not tell a full story. Types of lyrics include the elegy, the ode, and the sonnet. The lyric flourished in the songs and sonnets of the Renaissance, was revived by the Romantic poets, and has remained the most common poetic form during the nineteenth and twentieth centuries. Alfred, Lord Tennyson; Robert Browning; Elizabeth Barrett Browning; Matthew Arnold; William Butler Yeats; T.S. Eliot; W.H. Auden; Dylan Thomas, and Stevie Smith—all were great writers of lyric poems.

**MAJOR CHARACTER**   See *Character.*

**MEMENTO MORI**   *Memento mori* is a Latin phrase meaning "remember that you must die." Many great literary works have been written on the *memento mori* theme, including Marvell's "To His Coy Mistress," on page 418, and Gray's "Elegy Written in a Country Churchyard," on page 586.

**METAPHOR**   A *metaphor* is a figure of speech in which one thing is spoken of as though it were something else, as in "death, that long sleep." Through this identification of dissimilar things, a comparison is suggested or implied. Emily Brontë uses the following metaphor in the second stanza of her poem "Remembrance": "my thoughts no longer hover...resting their wings." The metaphor suggests similarities between the speaker's thoughts and the wings of a bird.

An *extended metaphor* is one that is developed at length and that involves several points of comparison. Elizabeth Daryush uses extended metaphor in "November Sun":

> His face is pale and shrunk, his shining hair
>    Is prison-shorn;
> Trailing his grey cloak, up the short dark
>    stair
>  He creeps each morn,
>
> Looks out to his lost throne, to the
>    noon-height
>    Once his, then turns
> Back to the alien dungeon, where all night
>    Unseen he burns.

This poem metaphorically describes the November sun as a royal prisoner.

A *mixed metaphor* occurs when two metaphors are jumbled together. For example, thorns and rain are illogically mixed in "The thorns of life rained down on him."

A *dead metaphor* is one that has been so overused that its original metaphorical impact has been lost. Examples of dead metaphors include "the foot of the bed" and "toe the line." See *Figurative Language.*

**METAPHYSICAL POETRY**   *Metaphysical poetry* is the term used to describe the works of such seventeenth-century English poets as Richard Crashaw, John Donne, George Herbert, Andrew Marvell, Thomas Traherne, and Henry Vaughan. The term was first used by Samuel Johnson in an attack on writers who fill their works with far-fetched conceits and who make poetry a vehicle for displays of learning. Characteristic features of metaphysical poetry include intellectual playfulness, argument, paradoxes, irony, elaborate and unusual conceits, incongruity, and the rhythms of ordinary speech. Examples of metaphysical poems in this text include

Donne's "Song," on page 398, and Marvell's "To His Coy Mistress," on page 418.

**METER**   The *meter* of a poem is its rhythmical pattern. This pattern is determined by the number and types of stresses, or beats, in each line. To describe the meter of a poem, you must *scan* its lines. *Scanning* involves marking the strongly stressed and weakly stressed syllables, as follows:

> Tween | that, when |the grave's | dark wall
> Did first | her form | retain,
> They thought their hearts could ne'er recall
> The light | of joy | again.
>   —Emily Brontë, "Song"

As you can see, each strong stress is marked with a slanted line (´) and each weak stress with a horseshoe symbol (˘). The weak and strong stresses are then divided by vertical lines into groups called *feet*. The following types of feet are common in English poetry:

1. *Iamb:* a foot with one weak stress followed by one strong stress, as in the word "afraid"
2. *Trochee:* a foot with one strong stress followed by one weak stress, as in the word "heather"
3. *Anapest:* a foot with two weak stresses followed by one strong stress, as in the word "disembark"
4. *Dactyl:* a foot with one strong stress followed by two weak stresses, as in the word "solitude"
5. *Spondee:* a foot with two strong stresses, as in the word "workday"
6. *Pyrrhic:* a foot with two weak stresses, as in the last foot of the word "unspeak|ably"
7. *Amphibrach:* a foot with a weak syllable, one strong syllable, and another weak syllable, as in the word "another"
8. *Amphimacer:* a foot with a strong syllable, one weak syllable, and another strong syllable, as in "up and down"

A line of poetry is described as *iambic, trochaic, anapestic,* or *dactylic* according to what kind of foot appears most often in the line.

Lines are also described in terms of the number of feet that occur in them, as follows:

1. *Monometer:* verse written in one-foot lines:

> Sound the Flute!
> Now it's mute.
> Birds delight
> Day and Night.
>   —William Blake, "Spring"

2. *Dimeter:* verse written in two-foot lines:

> O Rose | thou art sick.
> The invis | ible worm,
> That flies | in the night
> In the how | ling storm:
> Has found | out thy bed
> Of crim | son joy:
> And his dark | secret love
> Does thy life | destroy.
>   —William Blake, "The Sick Rose"

3. *Trimeter:* verse written in three-foot lines:

> I went | to the Gard | en of Love
> And saw | what I nev | er had seen:
> A Chap | el was built in the midst,
> Where I used | to play | on the green.
>   —William Blake, "The Garden of Love"

4. *Tetrameter:* verse written in four-foot lines:

> I wand | er thro' | each chart | er'd street,
> Near where | the chart | er'd Thames | does
>   flow
> And mark | in ev | ery face | I meet
> Marks of | weakness, | marks of | woe.
>   —William Blake, "London"

5. *Pentameter:* verse written in five-foot lines:

> And we | are put | on earth | a litt | le space,
> That we | may learn | to bear | the beams | of
>   love
>   —William Blake, "The Little Black Boy"

A six-foot line is called a *hexameter.* A line with seven feet is a *heptameter.*

A complete description of the meter of a line tells both how many feet there are in the line and what kind of foot is most common. Thus the stanza from Emily Brontë's poem, quoted at the beginning of this entry, would be described as being made up of alternating iambic tetrameter and iambic trimeter lines. Poetry that does not have a regular meter is called *free verse*.

**METONYMY**   *Metonymy* is a figure of speech that substitutes something closely related for the thing actually meant. In the opening line of "The Lost Leader," Robert Browning says, "Just for a handful of silver he left us," using silver to refer to money in the form of a government grant. Browning's reference to silver is also an allusion to the handful of silver that Judas earned for betraying Christ in the Bible.
See *Figurative Language.*

**MINOR CHARACTER**   See *Character.*

**MIRACLE PLAY**   See *Drama.*

**MIXED METAPHOR**   See *Metaphor.*

**MOCK EPIC**   A *mock epic* is a poem about a trivial matter written in the style of a serious epic. The incongruity of the style and the subject matter produces comic effects. Alexander Pope's *The Rape of the Lock,* on page 548, is a mock epic.
See *Epic* and *Epic Convention.*

**MONOLOGUE**   A *monologue* is a speech or performance given entirely by one person or by one character.
See *Dramatic Monologue* and *Soliloquy.*

**MOOD**   *Mood,* or atmosphere, is the feeling created in the reader by a literary work or passage. The mood may be suggested by the writer's choice of words, by events in the work, or by the physical setting. Nadine Gordimer begins "The Train from Rhodesia," on page 1260, with a mood-evoking description of the brick, mud, and tin buildings at the hot, sandy train station. Everyone there—the stationmaster, his wife, the native vendors, and the children—awaits the train, the only relief expected in this inactive and restricted environment.

See *Setting* and *Tone.*

**MONOMETER**   See *Meter.*

**MORALITY PLAY**   See *Drama.*

**MOTIF**   A *motif* is a recurring literary convention or an element that is repeated within a literary work. For example, Titania and Bottom in William Shakespeare's *A Midsummer Night's Dream* exemplify a motif from folklore—the mortal enchanted by a fairy lover. D.H. Lawrence, in "The Rocking-Horse Winner," on page 974, repeats the motif of luck throughout his story. Whether a motif is part of the literary tradition or is an author's own invention, it generally unifies a work and adds to its theme.

**MOTIVATION**   A *motivation* is a reason that explains or partially explains a character's thoughts, feelings, actions, or speech. Characters may be motivated by their physical needs; by their wants, wishes, desires, or dreams; or by their beliefs, values, and ideals. Effective characterization involves creating motivations that make characters seem believable.
See *Character.*

**MYTH**   A *myth* is a fictional tale, originally with religious significance, that explains the actions of gods or heroes, the causes of natural phenomena, or both. Allusions to characters and motifs from Greek, Roman, Norse, and Celtic myths are common in English literature. In addition, mythological stories are often retold or adapted, as George Bernard Shaw's *Pygmalion,* on page 1109, illustrates. Pygmalion was a character from Greek mythology who created a beautiful sculpture of a woman and then fell in love with his own creation.
See *Legend.*

**NARRATION**   *Narration* is writing that tells a story. The act of telling a story is also called

*narration.* The *narrative,* or story, is told by a storyteller called the *narrator.* Narration is one of the major forms of discourse and appears in many guises. Biographies, autobiographies, journals, reports, novels, short stories, plays, narrative poems, anecdotes, fables, parables, myths, legends, folktales, ballads, and epic poems are all narratives, or types of narration.
See *Forms of Discourse.*

**NARRATIVE**   See *Narration.*

**NARRATIVE POEM**   A *narrative poem* tells a story in verse. Three traditional types of narrative poems include ballads, such as "Sir Patrick Spens" and "Barbara Allan"; epics, such as *Beowulf;* and metrical romances, such as *Sir Gawain and the Green Knight.* Other narrative poems in this text include the selection from Spenser's *The Faerie Queene,* on page 244; the selection from Milton's *Paradise Lost,* on page 449; Coleridge's "The Rime of the Ancient Mariner," on page 660; and Tennyson's "The Lady of Shalott," on page 786.

**NARRATOR**   See *Narration.*

**NATURALISM**   *Naturalism* was a literary movement among writers at the end of the nineteenth century and during the early decades of the twentieth century. The Naturalists, influenced by the theories of Social Darwinists like Sir Herbert Spencer, tended to view people as hopeless victims of immutable natural laws. Important Naturalist writers included the Norwegian playwright Henrik Ibsen and the French novelist Emile Zola.
See *Realism.*

**NEOCLASSICISM**   *Neoclassicism* was a literary movement during the Restoration and the eighteenth century in which writers turned to classical Greek and Roman literary models and standards. Like the ancient Greeks, the Neo-classicists stressed reason, order, harmony, restraint, correctness, and decorum. The way these qualities took literary form is illustrated by the balanced and controlled heroic couplet, perfected by John Dryden and Alexander Pope. Much Neoclassical literature dealt with themes related to proper and tasteful human conduct. The most popular literary forms of the day—essays, letters, early novels, epigrams, parodies, and satires—reflected this emphasis on society as subject matter. Just as the Neoclassicists rejected the individualism and extravagance of the Renaissance in favor of classical restraint, so the nineteenth-century Romantics rejected Neoclassicism in favor of imagination, emotion, and the individual.
See *Classicism* and *Romanticism.*

**NONFICTION**   *Nonfiction* is prose writing that presents and explains ideas or that tells about real people, places, objects, or events.
See *Fiction.*

**NOVEL**   A *novel* is a long work of fiction. A novel often has a complicated plot, many major and minor characters, a significant theme, and several settings. Novels can be grouped in many ways based on the historical periods in which they are written (such as Romantic or Victorian), on the subjects and themes that they treat (such as Gothic or regional), on the techniques used in them (such as stream of consciousness), or on their debts to literary movements (such as Naturalism or Realism). Among early novels were Samuel Richardson's works *Pamela* and *Clarissa Harlowe,* and Henry Fielding's *Tom Jones.* Other classic English novels include Jane Austen's *Pride and Prejudice,* Sir Walter Scott's *Waverley,* Charles Dickens's *David Copperfield,* and George Eliot's *The Mill on the Floss.* Major twentieth-century novelists include James Joyce, Virginia Woolf, D.H. Lawrence, Henry James, Graham Greene, and Patrick White. A *novella* is not as long as a novel but is longer than a short story. See, for example, Joseph Conrad's novella *Heart of Darkness.*

**OBJECTIVE CORRELATIVE**    See *Image.*

**OCTAVE**    See *Stanza.*

**ODE**    An *ode* is a long, formal lyric poem with a serious theme. It may or may not have a traditional structure with three alternating stanza patterns called the *strophe,* the *antistrophe,* and the *epode.* An ode may be written for a private occasion, as was John Keats's "Ode to a Nightingale," on page 721, which was written about a bird nesting near a friend's home. On the other hand, an ode may be prepared for a public ceremony, as was John Dryden's "A Song for St. Cecilia's Day," on page 499, which was performed in 1687 at an annual festival. Odes often honor people, commemorate events, respond to natural scenes, or consider serious human problems.
See *Lyric.*

**OMNISCIENT POINT OF VIEW**    See *Point of View.*

**ONOMATOPOEIA**    *Onomatopoeia* is the use of words that imitate sounds. Examples of such words are *buzz, hiss, murmur,* and *rustle.* Seamus Heaney uses onomatopoeia in "Churning Day" to suggest the sounds of making butter:

> My mother took first turn, set up rhythms
> that slugged and thumped for hours. Arms
>     ached.
> Hands blistered. Cheeks and clothes were
>     splattered
> with flabbymilk.

Onomatopoeia is used to create musical effects and to reinforce meaning, especially in poetry.

**ORAL TRADITION**    *Oral tradition* is the passing of songs, stories, and poems from genera-

tion to generation by word of mouth. Among the many materials composed or preserved through oral tradition in Great Britain are *Beowulf,* on page 24, and the folk ballads on pages 104–114. In his *Morte d'Arthur,* Sir Thomas Malory drew on written French sources and on Arthurian legends from the oral tradition. Edmund Spenser drew on the same sources when composing *The Faerie Queene.* Shakespeare drew on materials from the oral tradition to create the *sprites* and *fairies* of *A Midsummer Night's Dream.* Folk epics, ballads, myths, legends, folktales, folk songs, proverbs, nursery rhymes—all such products of the oral tradition were originally spoken or sung rather than written down.
See *Ballad, Folklore, Legend,* and *Myth.*

**OTTAVA RIMA**    *Ottava rima* is a stanza with eight iambic pentameter lines that rhyme *abababcc.* Lord Byron used this stanza for his *Don Juan,* a selection from which appears on page 697. William Butler Yeats was fond of this stanza form and used it in a number of his finest poems, including "Sailing to Byzantium," on page 1036.

**OVERSTATEMENT**    See *Hyperbole.*

**OXYMORON**    *Oxymoron* is a figure of speech that fuses two contradictory or opposing ideas. An oxymoron, such as "freezing fire" or "happy grief," thus suggests a paradox in just a few words. In Book I of *Paradise Lost,* Milton uses the oxymoron "darkness visible" to describe the pit into which Satan and the other rebellious angels have been thrown.
See *Figurative Language* and *Paradox.*

**PARADOX**    A *paradox* is a statement that seems to be contradictory but that actually presents a truth. In "Love's Growth," John Donne presents the following paradox:

> Methinks I lied all winter, when I swore
> My love was infinite, if spring make it more.

Because a paradox is surprising or even shocking, it draws the reader's attention to what is being said.

See *Figurative Language* and *Oxymoron.*

**PARALLELISM**   *Parallelism* is the repetition of a grammatical pattern. Stevie Smith uses parallel infinitive verbs in the first stanza of her poem "Is It Wise?":

> Is it wise
> To hug misery
> To make a song of Melancholy
> To weave a garland of sighs
> To abandon hope wholly?
> No, it is not wise.

Parallelism is used in poetry and in other writing to emphasize and to link related ideas.

**PARODY**   A *parody* is a humorous, mocking imitation of a literary work. The play-within-the-play in William Shakespeare's *A Midsummer Night's Dream* parodies the poor performances and versions of classical tales that were current in Shakespeare's day.

**PASTORAL**   A literary work is *pastoral* if it deals with the pleasures of a simple, rural life or with escape to a simpler place and time. The tradition of pastoral literature began in ancient Greece with the poetic idylls of Theocritus. Theocritus wrote about the simple lives of shepherds and goatherds. The Roman poet Virgil also wrote a famous collection of pastoral poems, the *Eclogues,* in imitation of Theocritus. Virgil's characters were, like Theocritus's, idealized rustics.

During the European Renaissance, pastoral writing became quite popular. One famous example of the genre is *The Countess of Pembroke's Arcadia,* by Sir Phillip Sidney. Another example is Christopher Marlowe's "The Passionate Shepherd to His Love," on page 230.

Today the term *pastoral* is commonly applied to any work in which a speaker longs to escape to a simpler, rural life. By this definition both William Wordsworth's "The World Is Too Much with Us," on page 657, and William Butler Yeats's "The Lake Isle of Innisfree," on page 1027, are pastoral poems.

**PATHOS**   *Pathos* is the quality in a literary work that arouses feelings of pity, sorrow, or compassion in readers or in an audience. In *Macbeth,* the murdering of Macduff's family is a source of pathos, causing the audience to feel great sympathy for Macduff.

**PENTAMETER**   See *Meter.*

**PERSONIFICATION**   *Personification* is a type of figurative language in which a nonhuman subject is given human characteristics. Percy Bysshe Shelley used personification in these lines from "To Night":

> Swiftly walk o'er the western wave,
>   Spirit of the Night!
> Out of the misty eastern cave
> Where, all the long and lone daylight
> Thou wovest dreams of joy and fear,
> Which make thee terrible and dear,
>   Swift be thy flight!

Effective personification of things or ideas makes them seem vital and alive, as if they were human.

See *Figurative Language* and *Metaphor.*

**PERSUASION**   *Persuasion* is writing or speech that attempts to convince the audience to take some action or to adopt some opinion. Persuasion is one of the major forms of discourse and is used in advertising, in editorials, in sermons, in political speeches, and in other such writings. Some people use the terms *persuasion* and *argument* synonymously. Others use *persuasion* to refer to works that appeal to the emotions and *argument* to refer to works that appeal to reason. See *Forms of Discourse.*

**PETRARCHAN CONCEIT**  See *Conceit*.

**PETRARCHAN SONNET**  See *Sonnet*.

**PLOT**  *Plot* is the sequence of events in a literary work. The two primary elements of any plot are characters and a conflict. Most plots can be analyzed into most or all of the following parts:

1. The *exposition* introduces the setting, the characters, and the basic situation.
2. The *inciting incident* introduces the central conflict.
3. During the *development,* the conflict runs its course and usually intensifies.
4. At the *climax,* the conflict reaches a high point of interest or suspense.
5. At the *resolution,* the conflict is ended.
6. The *denouement* ties up loose ends that remain after the resolution of the conflict.

There are many variations on the standard plot structure. Some stories begin *in medias res* (''in the middle of things''), after the inciting incident has already occurred. In some stories the expository material appears toward the middle, in flashbacks. In many stories there is no denouement. Occasionally, though not often, the conflict is left unresolved.

**POETRY**  *Poetry* is one of the three major types, or genres, of literature, the others being prose and drama. Poetry defies simple definition because there is no single characteristic that is found in all poems and not found in all non-poems. In other words, poems are what philosophers of language call an ''ill-defined set.''

Often poems are divided into lines and stanzas. Many poems employ regular rhythmical patterns, or meters. However, some poems are written out just like prose, and some are written in free verse. Most poems make use of highly concise, musical, and emotionally charged language. Many also make use of imagery, figurative language, and special devices of sound such as rhyme.

Types of poetry include narrative poetry (ballads, epics, and metrical romances), dramatic poetry (dramatic monologues and dramatic dialogues), lyrics (sonnets, odes, elegies, and love poems), and concrete poetry.

**POINT OF VIEW**  *Point of view* is the perspective, or vantage point, from which a story is told. If a character within the story tells the story, then it is told from the *first-person* point of view. If a voice from outside the story tells it, then the story is told from the *third-person* point of view. If the knowledge of the storyteller is limited to the internal states of one character, then the storyteller has a *limited* point of view. If the storyteller's knowledge extends to the internal states of all of the characters, then the storyteller has an *omniscient* point of view. The point of view from which a story is told determines what view of events will be presented.

**PROSE**  *Prose* is the ordinary form of written language and one of the three major types of literature. Most writing that is not poetry, drama, or song is considered prose. Prose occurs in two major forms: fiction and nonfiction.

**PROTAGONIST**  The *protagonist* is the main character in a literary work. In D. H. Lawrence's ''The Rocking-Horse Winner,'' on page 974, the protagonist is Paul.
See *Antagonist* and *Character*.

**PSALM**  A *psalm* is a song or hymn of praise, especially one included in the Book of Psalms in the Bible.

**PUN**  A *pun* is a play on words. A pun may involve using a word or a phrase that has two different meanings or it may involve using two different words or phrases with the same sound, as in *sun* and *son*. The title of George Herbert's poem ''The Collar'' is a pun that suggests both the clerical collar of an Anglican minister and "choler," or anger, the emotion expressed at the beginning of the poem but calmed by God's call to the poem's speaker. Puns are often humorous but may serve serious purposes as well, as the example from Herbert shows.

**PYRRHIC**  See *Meter.*

**QUATRAIN**  See *Stanza.*

**REALISM**  *Realism* is the presentation in art of the details of actual life. Another term for Realism, one that derives from Aristotle's *Poetics,* is *mimesis,* the Greek word for "imitation." During the last part of the nineteenth century and the first part of the twentieth, Realism enjoyed considerable popularity among writers in the English-speaking world. Nowhere, perhaps, was Realism more evident than in the novel. Novels often dealt with grim social realities and often presented realistic portrayals of the psychological states of characters. Realism also had considerable influence on theater in the early Modern Era. During the first part of this century, for example, the most common sort of stage setting was that in which a room was presented as though one wall had been removed and the audience were peering inside.

**REFERENTIAL MEANING**  See *Denotation.*

**REFRAIN**  A *refrain* is a regularly repeated line or group of lines in a poem or song. See, for example, the refrain "Lord, have mercy on us!" in Thomas Nashe's "A Litany in Time of Plague," on page 250.

**REGIONALISM**  *Regionalism* is the tendency to confine one's writing to the presentation of materials drawn from a particular geographical area. George Eliot, for example, tended to set her tales in the English Midlands. The Brontës wrote about Yorkshire. Thomas Hardy wrote about Dorset and Wessex. D. H. Lawrence wrote about Nottinghamshire. A Regionalist writer presents the distinct culture of an area, including its speech, customs, landscape, and history.

**REPETITION**  *Repetition* is the use, more than once, of any element of language—a sound, a word, a phrase, a clause, a sentence, a grammatical pattern, or a rhythmical pattern. Alliteration, assonance, consonance, meter, parallelism, refrains, and rhyme are all types of repetition.

**RESOLUTION**  See *Plot.*

**RHYME**  *Rhyme* is the repetition of sounds at the ends of words. *End rhyme* occurs when the rhyming words are repeated at the ends of lines. *Internal rhyme* occurs when the rhyming words fall within a line. *Exact rhyme* is the use of identical rhyming sounds, as in *love* and *dove. Approximate,* or *slant rhyme,* is the use of sounds that are similar but not identical, as in *prove* and *glove.*

**RHYME SCHEME**  A *rhyme scheme* is a regular pattern of rhyming words in a poem or stanza. To indicate a rhyme scheme, one assigns each final sound in the poem or stanza a different letter. Consider, for example, how the following lines from Charlotte Brontë's "On the Death of Anne Brontë" have been marked:

| There's little joy in life for *me,* | *a* |
| And little terror in the *grave;* | *b* |
| I've lived the parting hour to *see* | *a* |
| Of one I would have died to *save.* | *b* |

The rhyme scheme of this stanza is *abab.*

**RHYTHM**  See *Meter.*

**RISING ACTION**  The *rising action* is that part of a plot that leads up to the climax. During the rising action, suspense increases as the complications of the conflict develop.
See *Falling Action* and *Plot.*

**ROMANCE**    A *romance* is a story that presents remote or imaginative incidents rather than ordinary, realistic experience. The term *romance* was originally used to refer to medieval tales of the deeds and loves of noble knights and ladies. These early romances, or tales of chivalry and courtly love, are exemplified by *Sir Gawain and the Green Knight,* on page 170, and by Malory's *Morte d'Arthur,* on page 91. During the Renaissance in England, many writers drew heavily on the romance tradition. One such writer was Edmund Spenser, whose *The Faerie Queene* combines elements of romance and elements of the epic. From the eighteenth century on, the term *romance* has been commonly used to describe sentimental novels about love.

**ROMANTIC COMEDY**    See *Comedy.*

**ROMANTICISM**    *Romanticism* was a literary and artistic movement of the eighteenth and nineteenth centuries. In reaction against Neoclassicism, the Romantics emphasized imagination, fancy, freedom, emotion, wildness, the beauty of the untamed natural world, the rights of the individual, the nobility of the common man, and the attractiveness of pastoral life. Important figures in the Romantic movement included William Wordsworth; Samuel Taylor Coleridge; Percy Bysshe Shelley; John Keats; and George Gordon, Lord Byron.

**ROUND CHARACTER**    See *Character.*

**RUN-ON LINE**    A *run-on line* is one that does not contain a pause or a stop at the end. A run-on line ends in the middle of a statement and of a grammatical unit, and the reader must therefore read the next line to find the end of the statement and the completion of the grammatical unit. The beginning of Molly Holden's "The

Double Nature of White" illustrates the run-on line:

> White orchards are the earliest, stunning
> the spirit resigned to winter's black, white thorn
> sprays first the bare wet branches of the
>     hedge.

See *End-Stopped Line.*

**SATIRE**    *Satire* is writing that ridicules or holds up to contempt the faults of individuals or of groups. A satirist may use a sympathetic tone or an angry, bitter tone. Some satire, like Jonathan Swift's *Gulliver's Travels,* an excerpt from which appears on page 520, is written in prose. Other satire, such as Henry Reed's "The Naming of Parts," on page 1094, is written in poetry. Although a satire is often humorous, its purpose is not simply to make readers laugh but also to correct, through laughter, the flaws and shortcomings that it points out.

**SCANSION**    *Scansion* is the process of analyzing the metrical pattern of a poem.
See *Meter.*

**SCENE**    See *Drama.*

**SESTET**    See *Stanza.*

**SETTING**    The *setting* of a literary work is the time and place of the action. A setting can serve many different purposes. It can provide a backdrop for the action. It can be the force that the protagonist struggles against and thus the source of the central conflict. It can also be used to create a mood, or atmosphere. In many works the setting symbolizes some point that the author wishes to emphasize. Much of Emily Brontë's novel *Wuthering Heights,* which is discussed on pages 898–901, is set in the house named in the novel's title. When Lockwood visits this house at the beginning of the story, he finds it standing on a cold hilltop on the moors, built to

withstand the north wind and inhabited by fierce dogs and unsociable people. This setting creates a specific mood and suggests, symbolically, the wild emotional history of the past inhabitants of the house.
See *Mood* and *Symbol.*

**SHAKESPEAREAN SONNET**　See *Sonnet.*

**SHORT STORY**　A *short story* is a brief work of fiction. The short story resembles the longer novel but generally has a simpler plot and setting. In addition, a short story tends to reveal character at a crucial moment rather than to develop it through many incidents.

**SIMILE**　A *simile* is a figure of speech that compares two dissimilar things by using a key word such as *like* or *as.* Christina Rossetti uses similes in her poem "Goblin Market" to describe two sisters:

> Like two blossoms on one stem,
> Like two flakes of new-fallen snow,
> Like two wands of ivory
> Tipped with gold for awful kings.

By comparing dissimilar things, the writer of a simile shocks the reader into appreciation of the qualities of the things being compared. Thus a simile makes a description more vivid and memorable.
See *Figurative Language.*

**SLANT RHYME**　See *Rhyme.*

**SOLILOQUY**　A *soliloquy* in a play or prose work is a long speech made by a character who is alone and who thus reveals his or her private thoughts and feelings to the audience or reader. William Shakespeare's Act III of *Macbeth* opens with a soliloquy in which Banquo speculates on what Macbeth has done to fulfill the prophecy of the witches.
See *Monologue.*

**SONNET**　A *sonnet* is a fourteen-line lyric poem focused on a single theme. Sonnets have many variations but are usually written in iambic pentameter, following one of two traditional patterns.

The *Petrarchan* or *Italian sonnet* is divided into two parts, the eight-line octave and the six-line sestet. The octave rhymes *abba abba,* while the sestet generally rhymes *cde cde* or uses some combination of *cd* rhymes. The two parts of the Petrarchan sonnet work together. The octave raises a question, states a problem, or presents a brief narrative, and the sestet answers the question, solves the problem, or comments on the narrative.

The *Shakespearean* or *English sonnet* has three four-line quatrains plus a concluding two-line couplet. The rhyme scheme of such a sonnet is usually *abab cdcd efef gg.* Each of the three quatrains usually explores a different variation of the main theme. Then the couplet presents a summarizing or concluding statement.
See *Lyric* and *Sonnet Sequence.*

**SONNET SEQUENCE**　A *sonnet sequence* is a series or group of sonnets written to one person or on one theme. Although each sonnet can stand alone as a separate poem, the sequence lets the poet trace the development of a relationship or examine different aspects of a single subject. Examples of sonnet sequences are Sir Philip Sidney's *Astrophel and Stella,* Edmund Spenser's *Amoretti,* and Elizabeth Barrett Browning's *Sonnets from the Portuguese.*
See *Sonnet.*

**SPEAKER**　The *speaker* is the imaginary voice assumed by the writer of a poem. In other words, the speaker is the character who tells the poem.

This character often is not identified by name. The title of William Blake's poem "The Chimney Sweeper" identifies the speaker, a child who gives this account of his life:

> When my mother died I was very young,
> And my father sold me while yet my tongue
> Could scarcely cry "'weep! 'weep! 'weep!
>    'weep!"
> So your chimneys I sweep and in soot I sleep.

Although this speaker matter-of-factly accepts his life, the poem is ironic because the poet expects readers to have a different view of the child's situation. Recognizing the speaker and thinking about his or her characteristics is often central to interpreting a lyric poem.
See *Point of View.*

**SPENSERIAN STANZA** The *Spenserian stanza,* invented by Edmund Spenser for use in *The Faerie Queene,* has nine iambic lines rhymed *ababbcbcc.* All the lines are pentameters except the last, which is a hexameter or alexandrine. This close-knit rhyme scheme unifies the stanza, and the final line provides a dignified summary. This stanza form is used in George Gordon, Lord Byron's *Childe Harold's Pilgrimage,* on page 692, and in poems by William Wordsworth, John Keats, Percy Bysshe Shelley, and Alfred, Lord Tennyson.
See *Alexandrine.*

**SPONDEE**   See *Meter.*

**SPRUNG RHYTHM** *Sprung rhythm* is the term used by Gerard Manley Hopkins to describe the idiosyncratic meters of his poems. Discovering the underlying metrical pattern of a poem written in sprung rhythm is difficult if not impossible. The rhythm is quite varied and contains such violations of traditional metrical rules as several strong stresses in a row or feet containing more than two weak stresses. The following lines from

Gerard Manley Hopkins's "Spring" illustrate sprung rhythm:

> What is all this juice and all this joy?
> A strain of the earth's sweet being in
>    the beginning
> In Eden garden.—Have, get, before it
>    cloy,
> Before it cloud, Christ, lord, and sour
>    with sinning,
> Innocent mind and Mayday in girl and boy

**STAGE DIRECTIONS** *Stage directions* are notes included in a drama to describe how the work is to be performed or staged. Stage directions are usually printed in italics and enclosed within parentheses or brackets. They may mention how the characters should speak or move, what the costumes or scenery should look like, how the set should be arranged, what lighting should be used, and so on.

**STANZA** A *stanza* is a group of lines in a poem, considered as a unit. Many poems are divided into stanzas that are separated by spaces. Stanzas often function just like paragraphs in prose. Each stanza states and develops a single main idea.

Stanzas are commonly named according to the number of lines found in them, as follows:
1. *Couplet:* a two-line stanza
2. *Tercet:* a three-line stanza
3. *Quatrain:* a four-line stanza
4. *Cinquain:* a five-line stanza
5. *Sestet:* a six-line stanza
6. *Heptastich:* a seven-line stanza
7. *Octave:* an eight-line stanza
See *Sonnet* and *Spenserian Stanza.*

**STATIC CHARACTER**   See *Character.*

**STEREOTYPE**   See *Character.*

**STOCK CHARACTER**   See *Character.*

**STREAM OF CONSCIOUSNESS** *Stream of consciousness* is a narrative technique that presents thoughts as if they were coming directly from a character's mind. Instead of being arranged in chronological order, the events in a stream-of-consciousness narrative are presented from the character's point of view, mixed in with the character's ongoing feelings and memories. Developed by writers such as James Joyce and Virginia Woolf, stream-of-consciousness writing is used to reveal a character's complex psychology and to present it in realistic detail.
See *Point of View.*

**STYLE**  A writer's *style* is his or her typical way of writing. Determinants of a writer's style include his or her formality, use of figurative language, use of rhythm, typical grammatical patterns, typical sentence lengths, and typical methods of organization. John Milton is noted for a grand, heroic style that contrasts with John Keats's rich, sensory style and with T.S. Eliot's allusive, ironic style.
See *Diction.*

**SUBPLOT**  A *subplot* is a second, less important plot within a story or play. One subplot in William Shakespeare's *A Midsummer Night's Dream* deals with the presentation of a play by Bottom and his fellows. Another deals with the quarrel between Titania and Oberon. A subplot may add to, reflect, vary, or contrast with the main plot.
See *Plot.*

**SUSPENSE**  *Suspense* is a feeling of growing curiosity or anxious uncertainty about the outcome of events in a literary work. Writers create suspense by raising questions in the minds of their readers.

**SYMBOL**  A *symbol* is anything that stands for or represents something else. Thus a flag is a symbol of a country, a group of letters can symbolize a spoken word, a spoken word can symbolize an object, a fine car can symbolize wealth, and so on. In literary criticism a distinction is often made between *traditional* or *conventional symbols*—ones that are part of our general cultural inheritance—and *personal symbols*—ones that are created by particular authors for use in particular works. For example, the lamb in William Blake's poem "The Lamb" is a conventional symbol for peace, gentleness, and innocence, one that Blake inherited from the Bible and from the pastoral tradition. However, the tiger in Blake's poem "The Tiger" is not a conventional or inherited symbol. Blake created this symbol of evil specifically for this poem.

Conventional symbolism is often based on elements of the natural world. For example, youth is often symbolized by greenery or springtime, middle age by summer, and old age by autumn or winter. Death is often symbolized by darkness or cold. The sun is often used as a symbol of power or authority. Roses are symbols of love and beauty. Doves are symbols of peace. Foxes are symbols of craftiness, and owls of wisdom.

Conventional symbols are also sometimes borrowed from the spheres of religion and politics. For example, a cross may be a symbol of Christianity or the color red a symbol of Marxist ideology.

**SYMBOLISM**  *Symbolism* was a literary movement of nineteenth-century France. The Symbolist writers reacted against Realism and stressed, instead, the importance of suggestion and evocation of emotional states, especially by means of symbols corresponding to these states. The Symbolists were also quite concerned with using sound to achieve emotional effects. Important Symbolist writers included Stéphane Mallarmé, Paul Verlaine, and Arthur Rimbaud. English writers who were influenced by the Symbolist movement included William Butler Yeats and T. S. Eliot.

**SYNECDOCHE** *Synecdoche* is a figure of speech in which a part of something is used to stand for the whole. In the preface to his long poem entitled *Milton,* William Blake includes these lines: "And did those feet in ancient time/ Walk upon England's mountains green?" The feet, of course, stand for the whole body, and "England's mountains green" stand for England generally.
See *Figurative Language.*

**TERCET**   See *Stanza.*

**TERZA RIMA**   *Terza rima* is a three-line stanza pattern with interlocking rhymes that connect stanza to stanza. The middle line of one tercet rhymes with the first and last lines of the next so that *aba* is followed by *bcb, cdc, ded,* and so on. "The Triumph of Life," by Percy Bysshe Shelley, illustrates this pattern:

| | |
|---|---|
| As in that trance of wondrous thought I lay | *a* |
| This was the tenour of my waking dream, | *b* |
| Methought I sat beside a public way | *a* |
| Thick strewn with summer dust, and a great stream | *b* |
| Of people there was hurrying to and fro | *c* |
| Numerous as gnats upon the evening gleam | *b* |

As the name suggests, *terza rima* is an Italian verse form. The form was made famous by Dante Alighieri, who used it in his *The Divine Comedy.* Terza rima is a difficult form because of the rhymes required, but it has been used successfully by Sir Thomas Wyatt, Lord Byron, Robert Browning, and William Butler Yeats.

**TETRAMETER**   See *Meter.*

**THEME**   The *theme* is a central idea, concern, or purpose in a literary work. In an essay the theme might be directly stated in what is known as a thesis statement. In a serious literary work, the theme is usually expressed indirectly rather than directly. A light work, one written strictly for entertainment, may not have a theme.

**THIRD-PERSON POINT OF VIEW**   See *Point of View.*

**TONE**   The *tone* of a literary work is the writer's attitude toward the readers and toward the subject. A writer's tone may be formal or informal, friendly or distant, personal or pompous. For example, William Hazlitt's tone in his essay on Macbeth, on page 748, is earnest and respectful, while James Boswell's tone in *The Life of Samuel Johnson,* which begins on page 576, is familiar and engaging.
See *Mood.*

**TRAGEDY**   *Tragedy* is a type of drama or literature that shows the downfall or destruction of a noble or outstanding person, traditionally one who possesses a character weakness called a *tragic flaw.* Macbeth, for example, is a brave and noble figure led astray by ambition. The *tragic hero,* through choice or circumstance, is caught up in a sequence of events that inevitably results in disaster. Because the protagonist is neither a wicked villain nor an innocent victim, the audience reacts with mixed emotions—both pity and fear, according to the Greek philosopher Aristotle, who defined tragedy in his famous work, the *Poetics.* The outcome of a tragedy, in which the protagonist is isolated from society, contrasts with the happy resolution of a comedy, in which the protagonist makes peace with society.
See *Comedy* and *Drama.*

**TRIMETER**   See *Meter.*

**TROCHEE**   See *Meter.*

**UNDERSTATEMENT**   *Understatement* is the literary technique of saying less than is actually

meant, generally in an ironic way. An example of understatement is the description of a flooded area as "slightly soggy."
See *Figurative Language.*

**VERBAL IRONY**   See *Irony.*

**VERNACULAR**   *Vernacular* is the ordinary language of the people living in a particular region. Instead of using more formal literary language, writers may use vernacular to create realistic characters or to approach readers informally. See *Dialect.*

**VILLANELLE**   A *villanelle* is a nineteen-line French verse form. It has two refrains formed by repeating line 1 in lines 6, 12, and 18 and by repeating line 3 in lines 9, 15, and 19. The three lines in each of the first five stanzas rhyme *aba.* The final quatrain rhymes *abaa.* An example of a villanelle in this text is Dylan Thomas's "Do Not Go Gentle into That Good Night," on page 1102.

# HANDBOOK OF CRITICAL THINKING AND READING TERMS

**ABSTRACT** *adj.* Anything that is not concrete or definite is *abstract.* A building is concrete because its details can be perceived by the senses. A set of blueprints is abstract because most of these details are left out. Words and the ideas that they represent can also be abstract. Examples of abstract words include *love, truth, history, realism, courage, nature,* and *society.*

People can make abstract ideas clear by using specific examples and illustrations. Suppose, for instance, that a novelist wants to communicate the abstract idea of a society. To do so, he or she might create characters representing a cross section of ethnic, economic, and political backgrounds: a coal miner, an immigrant, a pop star, a farmer, an aristocrat, and a labor leader. The novelist might make this depiction seem realistic by including many specific details and allusions to actual places, styles of clothing, customs, and historical events.

Another way to express abstract ideas clearly is to use symbols and figures of speech. For example, in the poem "Do Not Go Gentle into That Good Night," on page 1102, Dylan Thomas uses a concrete image—light—as a symbol for an abstraction—life.

**ANALOGY** *n.* An *analogy* is a comparison that explains one subject by pointing out its similarities to another subject. Writers often use analogies to explain the unfamiliar in familiar terms. For example, a writer might explain the organization of a theatrical troupe by comparing it to the organization of a baseball team. An analogy is possible only when the two items being compared have elements or characteristics in common. Writers use a number of techniques to state or to suggest analogies, including metaphor, simile, and extended metaphor.

Whenever you read or hear an analogy, ask yourself what characteristics the two things being compared have in common. Whenever you create an analogy, make sure that the two things being compared do in fact share common elements or characteristics. Avoid false analogy—the fallacy of assuming that two things are similar in one respect simply because they are similar in another respect.

**ANALYSIS** *n.* *Analysis* is the process of studying a whole by examining its parts. When you analyze something, follow these steps: First, break the thing down into its parts. Next, study the properties and functions of the parts. Then, look for relationships among the parts and between each part and the whole. For example, you might analyze the plot of a short story into the exposition, the inciting incident, the development, the climax, the resolution, and the denouement. After breaking the events of the story down into these parts, you would then study each part and think about how each part advances the action and contributes to the whole.

There are many different types of analysis. A *functional analysis* is one in which a thing is broken down into parts and then the functions of each part are studied. A *cause-and-effect analysis* is one in which a series of events is broken down into separate events that are then identified as causes or effects.

**ARGUMENT** *n.* An *argument* is a set of logically-related statements consisting of a conclusion and one or more premises. The premises are the reasons for accepting the conclusion. For example, you might argue in a paper that Macbeth, the protagonist in Shakespeare's tragedy, is essentially a good man who is tempted by ambition to commit acts that he knows to be wrong. To support this argument, you might present the following evidence from the play:

1. Before committing the murder, Macbeth thinks aloud about the duty that he owes to Duncan and about the great evil involved in killing one's king, one's kinsman, and one's guest.
2. Macbeth has such a guilty conscience that he is driven to have hallucinations, seeing first a bloody dagger in the air and then the ghost of Banquo.
3. At the end of the play, in the "Tomorrow" soliloquy, Macbeth reveals that life has become completely meaningless for him.

Whenever you state an interpretation or an evaluation of a literary work, you should support your statement with reasons drawn from the work itself.

The term *argument* is also used to refer to a brief summary, or synopsis, of a literary work. Thus a summary of the plot of *Paradise Lost* might be described as presenting "the argument of the poem."

See *Conclusion, Deduction, Evidence, Induction, and Inference.*

**BANDWAGON**    See *Propaganda Technique.*

**BEGGING THE QUESTION**    See *Logical Fallacy.*

**CATEGORIZATION** *n.*    *Categorization* is the process of placing objects or ideas into groups. These groups may be called classes or categories. Categorization is always done according to some shared property or characteristic. For example, one might place Coleridge's "The Rime of the Ancient Mariner," on page 660, and Tennyson's "The Lady of Shallot," on page 786, into the same category because these poems share two important characteristics: Both tell stories, and both deal with extraordinary or supernatural events.

To categorize something, follow these steps:
1. Observe the characteristics of the thing to be categorized.

2. Think of other things that have the same characteristics.
3. Find or create a name for the group of things with the shared characteristic.

Categorization is a useful tool for organizing information. Information about literary works is organized by categorizing works into groups called *genres.* The major genres of literature are prose, poetry, and drama. Prose can be divided into the subcategories of fiction and nonfiction; poetry into the subcategories of lyric, narrative, dramatic, and epic poetry; and drama into the subcategories of comedy, serious drama, tragedy, melodrama, and farce.

**CAUSE AND EFFECT** *n. phrase*    When one event precedes and brings about another event, the first is said to be a *cause* and the second an *effect.* A *sufficient cause* is one that, by itself, is enough to bring about the effect. A *necessary cause* is one that is required in order to bring about an effect but that may or may not be sufficient to bring about the effect.

Cause-and-effect relationships are extremely important in literary study. The plot of a story, for example, is a series of events related by cause and effect. One event causes the next, which causes the next, and so on to the end of the story. Literary history often involves tracing the forces that caused the writer to produce particular works. Such forces might include the author's personal experiences and reading or the social, political, and cultural circumstances in which the author wrote.

The act of reading also involves cause and effect. Particular aspects of the text—the imagery or tone, for example—cause certain reactions in the reader. To understand the work, the reader must account for these reactions by determining what aspects of the text caused them.

**CIRCULAR REASONING**    See *Logical Fallacy.*

**COMPARISON** *n.*    *Comparison* is the process

of observing and pointing out similarities. For example, a comparison of Samuel Pepys and James Boswell might note that each author possessed an excellent eye for detail, that each was a skillful storyteller, and that each displayed a love for social life.

See *Contrast.*

**CONCLUSION** *n.*  A *conclusion* is anything that follows reasonably from something else. In an argument, the conclusion is a statement that follows from supporting facts and reasons. In a literary work, the conclusion is the final part, or ending, of the work.

**CONTRAST** *n.*  *Contrast* is the process of observing and pointing out differences. If, for example, you were to contrast writers of the Neoclassical and Romantic eras, you might point out the following differences:

1. Politics: The Neoclassicists were conservatives; the Romantics were liberals or radicals.
2. Style: The Neoclassicists used harmonious, ordered, stylized language; the Romanticists used language modeled on ordinary speech or language that was grand, heroic, and exuberant.
3. Social or ethical stance: The Neoclassicists stressed acceptable social norms; the Romanticists stressed the freedom of the individual.
4. Attitude toward nature: The Neoclassicists loved nature when it was controlled and ordered, as in a garden; the Romanticists loved nature in its uncontrolled, wild state.

See *Comparison.*

**DEDUCTION** *n.*  *Deduction* is a form of argument in which the conclusion has to be true if the premises are true. Consider the following arguments:

Major premise:  People living in the eighteenth century had no experience of electric lights, automobiles, computers, or airplanes.

Minor premise:  Dr. Johnson lived in the eighteenth century.
Conclusion:  Dr. Johnson had no experience of electric lights, automobiles, computers, or airplanes.

Major premise:  All sonnets have fourteen lines.
Minor premise:  Andrew Marvell's "To His Coy Mistress" has forty-six lines.
Conclusion:  Andrew Marvell's "To His Coy Mistress" is not a sonnet.

If you accept the premises of these arguments, then you must also accept their conclusions. Therefore, these arguments are deductions.

See *Generalization, Induction,* and *Inference.*

**DEFINITION** *n.*  *Definition* is the process of explaining the meaning of a word or a phrase. Definition is essential to communication because it establishes agreed-upon meanings for words.

The simplest type of definition, *ostensive definition,* involves pointing to something and saying its name. If, for example, you point to an object and say, "typewriter," you are giving an ostensive definition of the word *typewriter.* The word is defined by the observable characteristics of the object that is referred to.

Another common type of definition is the kind found in dictionaries, *lexical definition.* Lexical definition uses words to explain the meanings of other words. Some common types of lexical definition are definitions by synonym, by antonym, by example, and by genus and differentia.

In a *definition by synonym,* one uses a word or a phrase that has the same meaning as the word being defined: A *drama* is "a play."

In a *definition by antonym,* one uses a word or a phrase with an opposite meaning along with a negation such as *no* or *not: Free verse* is "poetry that does not have a regular meter."

*In a definition by example,* one lists things to which the term being defined applies: *Epic poems* include Homer's *Iliad* and *Odyssey,* Virgil's

*Aeneid,* Dante's *The Divine Comedy,* and Milton's *Paradise Lost.*

In a *genus and differentia* definition, one places the thing to be defined into a general category, or *genus,* and then one shows how the thing being defined differs from other things in the general category:

To be defined: Epic
Genus, or category: narrative poem
Differentia: long
          about the adventures of heroes or gods
Definition: An *epic* is "a long narrative poem about the adventures of heroes or gods."

Whenever you use words that your audience may not understand, define these words. Use the methods of lexical definition explained here.

## EITHER/OR FALLACY    See *Logical Fallacy.*

## EVALUATION *n.*    *Evaluation* is the process of making a judgment about the quality or value of something. When you make an evaluation of a work of literature, bear in mind these guidelines:

1. Make your evaluation specific. An evaluation such as "I hated it" or "It's a wonderful book" is too vague.
2. Base your evaluation on a clear standard, or criterion, of judgment.
3. Support your evaluation with evidence drawn from the work.

For more information on criteria for evaluation, see the lesson on Evaluating a Literary Work, on page 1370.
See *Opinion* and *Judgment.*

## EVIDENCE *n.*    *Evidence* is factual information presented to support an argument. When you write or speak about literature, the evidence that you use to support your statements will be details drawn from literary works. For example, consider the statement "The Old Man in Chaucer's 'The Pardoner's Tale' is Death personified." To support this interpretation you might provide the following evidence: The Old Man is described as being extremely aged, the Old Man possesses a ghostlike appearance, and the three young revellers are killed shortly after meeting the Old Man.

## FACT *n.*    A *fact* is a statement that can be proved true or false by evidence. For example, the following facts are true by definition:

A *dollar* is equal to one hundred cents.
A *conceit* is an extravagant or farfetched metaphor.

The following facts are true by observation:

"Barbara Allan" and "Sir Patrick Spens" are both ballads.
Some lyric poems are very short, and some are quite long.

When you write or speak about a literary work, use facts from the work to support the assertions that you make.
See *Opinion.*

## FALSE ANALOGY    See *Logical Fallacy.*

## GENERALIZATION *n.*    A *generalization* is a statement that applies to more than one thing. The following statements are generalizations:

Elizabethan poetry often praised Queen Elizabeth I.
Samuel Johnson's works contain many examples of the technique known as parallelism.

The first statement applies to more than one Elizabethan poem and the second to more than one of Samuel Johnson's works.

*Deductive arguments* often begin with generalizations. Consider the following deductive argument:

Premise: (generalization) Novels are written in prose.
Conclusion: Mary Shelley's novel *Frankenstein* is written in prose.

*Inductive arguments* often end with generalizations. Consider the following inductive argument:

> Premise: Tennyson's "The Splendor Falls" rhymes.
> Premise: Tennyson's "Crossing the Bar" rhymes.
> Premise: Tennyson's "The Lotos-Eaters" rhymes.
> Conclusion: (generalization) Many of Tennyson's poems rhyme.

When making generalizations, be careful to avoid overgeneralization, or making statements that are too broad. For example, the statement "All of Tennyson's poems rhyme" is too broad because some of his poems, such as "Ulysses," do not rhyme. To avoid overgeneralization, use qualifiers, or words that limit statements. Some common qualifiers include *a few, some, many,* and *most.*
See *Deduction, Induction,* and *Stereotype.*

**INDUCTION** *n.* *Induction* is a form of argument in which the conclusion is probably but not necessarily true. For example, if you read several comic plays and notice that each ends with a marriage, you might conclude that "All comedies end with marriages." However, you could not be certain of the truth of this statement unless you had read all the comedies ever written.

Most of what people know about the world is learned by induction. Each individual generalizes, based on his or her limited experience. Thus a small child sees several objects with wheels, each of which is called a car, and the child thus generalizes that all wheeled objects are cars. Eventually, the child will learn to limit this inductive generalization based on additional information.

Literary study often involves using induction. After you have read several works by one author or several works written in a particular period, you might, for example, make generalizations about the author or about the period. Remember, however, that such generalizations are sub-

ject to error and should be qualified by words and phrases such as *probably* or *most likely.*
See *Deduction, Generalization,* and *Inference.*

**INFERENCE** *n.* An *inference* is any logical or reasonable conclusion based on known facts or accepted premises. The conclusions of both deductive and inductive arguments are inferences. Reading actively involves continually making inferences based on details presented in the work being read.
See *Conclusion, Deduction,* and *Induction.*

**INTERPRETATION** *n.* *Interpretation* is the process of determining the meaning or significance of speech, writing, art, music, or actions. The interpretation of a literary work involves many different processes. These include the following:
1. Reading carefully and actively and responding to each new detail
2. Examining one's own responses to the work and identifying the details that create these responses
3. Being alert to patterns and relations that emerge during the reading of the work
4. Analyzing the work into its parts, studying these parts, and determining how the parts relate to one another and to the whole
5. Pulling together one's observations about the work to make generalizations about the significance, or meaning, of the work as a whole.

Interpretation usually aims at making clear the central theme of a work. For example, an interpretation of Percy Bysshe Shelley's "Ozymandias," on page 702 might read as follows: "'Ozymandias' is a poem about the vanity of worldly pretension." Of course, any such interpretation must be supported by evidence from the work. A sound interpretation is one that accounts for all the important parts of a work and that is not contradicted by any part of the work.
See *Analysis.*

**JUDGMENT** *n.* A *judgment* is a statement about the quality or value of something. A sound

judgment of a literary work is one that is based on evidence derived from careful reading and thoughtful analysis.
See *Evaluation* and *Opinion*.

**LOADED WORDS**  See *Propaganda Technique*.

**LOGICAL FALLACY** *n. phrase*  A *logical fallacy* is an error in reasoning. In the attempt to make persuasive arguments, people often fall into such errors. The following logical fallacies are quite common:

1. *Begging the question:* This fallacy occurs when someone assumes the truth of the statement to be proved without providing any evidence to support the statement. For example: "Of course, everyone knows that contemporary poetry is obscure." (No evidence is given to support the claim.)
2. *Circular reasoning:* This fallacy occurs when the evidence given to support a claim is simply a restatement of the claim in other words. For example: "Wordsworth should be considered a nature poet because he wrote poems about nature." (The second part of the sentence simply restates the claim made in the first part.)
3. *Either/or fallacy:* This fallacy occurs when someone claims that there are only two alternatives when there are actually more. For example: "William Blake was either a madman or a confused mystic." (The statement ignores a third possibility—that Blake was a sane but highly idiosyncratic writer who invented his own elaborate code, or symbol system, in which to express his ideas.)
4. *False analogy:* This fallacy occurs when someone falsely assumes that two subjects are similar in one respect just because they are similar in some other respect. For example: "The English people and the American people speak the same language. Therefore, their cultures must be alike." (The false assumption is made that because these peoples are similar in one respect they are similar in all respects.)
5. *Overgeneralization:* This fallacy occurs when someone makes a statement that is too broad or too inclusive. For example: "The Victorians were imperialists." (This statement is only partially true, for some British citizens of the Victorian Age opposed the government's imperialistic colonial policies.)
6. *Post hoc, ergo propter hoc:* (a Latin phrase meaning "After this, therefore because of this") This fallacy occurs when someone falsely assumes that an event is caused by another event simply because of the order of the events in time. For example: "After adopting the Christian religion, the Anglo-Saxons were defeated by the Normans. Therefore, the adoption of Christianity must have led to the Anglo-Saxon defeat." (This argument is, of course, completely fallacious. The adoption of Christianity took place long before the Norman invasion, and the Normans themselves were Christians. The defeat was actually due to other factors such as the divisiveness among the Anglo-Saxons, the surprise nature of the invasion, and the superiority of the Norman soldiers.)

When you do persuasive writing or speaking, try to avoid these logical fallacies. Also be on guard against these fallacies in other people's writing and speech.

**MAIN IDEA** *n. phrase*  The *main idea* is the central point that a speaker or writer wants to communicate. Sometimes, as in the thesis statement of an essay, the main idea is stated directly. However, often the main idea of a literary work is implied. The reader must identify the main idea based on clues provided by other elements of the work.
See *Purpose*.

**OBJECTIVE** *adj.*  Something is *objective* if it has to do with a reality that is independent of any

particular person's mind or personal, internal experiences. Statements of fact are objective because anyone can, at least in principle, verify them. Statements of opinion, on the other hand, are not objective because they express an individual's personal feelings and impressions. However, statements of opinion can be supported by objective facts. When you write about a literary work, you should strive to be objective. That is, you should support your statements with factual evidence that other people can verify by reading the work themselves.
See *Subjective*.


**OPINION** *n.*   An *opinion* is a statement that can be supported by facts but that is not itself a fact. Opinions may be judgments, predictions, or statements of policy or obligation. The following are opinions:

Judgment: William Butler Yeats is the greatest poet of the twentieth century.
Prediction: Third World writers will play an increasingly prominent role in the literature of the late twentieth and early twenty-first centuries.
Obligation: We must continually affirm the value of a literary education.

Whenever you express an opinion, you should support it with facts and with reasoned arguments.
See *Fact, Judgment,* and *Prediction.*


**OVERGENERALIZATION**   See *Logical Fallacy.*


**PARAPHRASE** *n.*   A *paraphrase* is a restatement in different words. When writing about literature, paraphrase can be used to support an interpretation or an analysis when the exact words of the original are not essential to the argument. However, when paraphrasing, be careful not to alter the meaning of the original. Simply translate what the writer said into equivalent words of your own.

**POST HOC, ERGO PROPTER HOC**   See *Logical Fallacy.*


**PREDICTION** *n.*   *Prediction* is the act of making statements about the future. An active reader continually makes and tests predictions on the basis of details presented in the work being read. For example, while reading about the Lilliputians' adoption of Lemuel Gulliver, on page 520, you might predict that these tiny people will put the giant Gulliver to military use. Gulliver's size in comparison to his hosts' makes this an obvious possibility, one that the story confirms.

Authors often supply hints or clues as to what will happen later in their works. This technique of providing clues to later events is called *foreshadowing,* and foreshadowing is one of the reasons why prediction of events in a literary work is possible. Often, of course, readers simply base their predictions on expectations related to the genre of the work being read or on general knowledge about how people, and thus characters, react in certain situations.

Sometimes an author will intentionally mislead readers into making predictions that later prove false. This technique, often used in mystery and detective fiction, makes possible the occurrence of surprise endings.
See *Opinion.*


**PROBLEM SOLVING** *n. phrase*   *Problem solving* is the process by which a person comes up with a solution to some difficulty. The following are some general guidelines for solving any sort of problem:
1. State the problem as precisely as possible.
2. Identify your goal.
3. Identify the differences between the goal state (the situation that will exist when the problem is solved) and the initial state (the situation that exists at the beginning of your work on the problem).
4. Take steps to reduce the differences between the goal state and the initial state.

The following rules of thumb, or *heuristics,* are useful for solving many types of problems.

1. Break the problem down into parts and solve the parts separately.
2. Think of similar problems that you have solved before and see whether the same solutions can be used.
3. Draw a diagram or sketch to clarify the problem.
4. Make a pros-and-cons chart.
5. Use brainstorming, freewriting, clustering, and other general thinking strategies to generate possible solutions.
6. Restate the problem in various ways or from several points of view.
7. Define any key terms or concepts related to the problem.
8. Examine your ideas about the problem to see whether they are too rigid. See if there aren't new ways of conceiving the problem and its solution.
9. Ask yourself "What if" questions to generate possible solutions.
10. Ask someone to help you with parts of the problem that are especially difficult.
11. Use means/ends analysis. That is, at each point in your work toward solving the problem, pause to determine whether you are advancing toward a solution.

Use these techniques or strategies to solve the many types of problems that you encounter in everyday life, including problems related to writing and to interpreting works of literature.

**PROPAGANDA TECHNIQUE** *n. phrase*    A *propaganda technique* is an improper appeal to emotion used for the purpose of swaying the opinions of an audience. The following propaganda techniques often appear in persuasive writing and speech.

1. *Bandwagon:* This technique involves encouraging people to think or act in some way simply because other people are doing so. For example: "Everyone's reading this new thriller. You should, too."
2. *Loaded words:* This technique involves using words with strong positive or negative connotations. Name-calling is an example of the use of loaded words. So is any use of words that are charged with emotional associations. For example: "I detest Kipling because his writings are *undemocratic.*"
3. *Snob appeal:* This technique involves making a direct or implied claim that one should act or think in a certain way because of the high social status associated with the action or thought. For example: "All really sophisticated readers appreciate Alexander Pope."
4. *Vague, undefined terms:* This technique involves promoting or challenging an opinion by using words that are so vague or so poorly defined as to be almost meaningless. For example: "Librarians shouldn't be allowed to purchase *awful* books like these."

Try to avoid propaganda techniques in your own speech and writing, and be on guard against these techniques in the speech and writing of others.

**PURPOSE** *n.*    The *purpose* is the goal, or aim, of a literary work. Works are often classified as narrative, descriptive, expository, or persuasive, based on their purposes. A narrative work tells a story. A descriptive work portrays a person, place, or thing. An expository work explains something or provides information. A persuasive work attempts to move an audience to adopt some opinion or to take some action. Many works combine these purposes. For example, a narrative work may also be, in places, descriptive, or a persuasive work may be, in places, expository.

Of course, most works also have more specific purposes. For example, Milton claimed that the purpose of *Paradise Lost,* an excerpt from which appears on page 449, was "to justify

God's ways to man." When used in this specific sense, the word *purpose* is equivalent to *theme.*

**REASON** *n.*    A *reason* is a statement made in support of some conclusion. The term *reason* is also used as a verb to signify the human ability to think logically and rationally.

**SNOB APPEAL**    See *Propaganda Technique.*

**SOURCE** *n.*    A *source* is anything from which ideas and information are taken. Some books, such as dictionaries, encyclopedias, atlases, almanacs, and biographies are specifically designed to be used as sources. Other types of sources include interviews with people, magazine articles, computerized information services, booklets, television programs, films, and recordings. Of course, every writer draws on at least one other very important source—his or her own experiences.

There are two basic types of sources, primary and seconary. A *primary source* is a first-hand account. Conversations, speeches, legal documents, and letters are examples of primary sources. *Secondary sources* are accounts or compilations written or prepared by people who are not eyewitnesses. A recent biography of Samuel Johnson would be a secondary source about Johnson's life. A collection of Johnson's letters would be a primary source. Boswell's *Life of Samuel Johnson,* an excerpt from which appears on page 576, is a primary source for some facts and a secondary source for others.

Whenever you gather information for use in a speech or in a paper, make sure that your sources are unbiased, up-to-date, authoritative, and reliable. Also make sure that you credit your sources properly by means of footnotes, endnotes, or in-text references.

**STEREOTYPE** *n.*    A *stereotype* is a fixed or conventional notion or characterization. Examples of stereotypical characters include the absent-minded professor, the suffering artist, the backroom politician, and the mad scientist. Although writers occasionally use stereotypes when they haven't the space to develop complete, rounded characters, good writers generally avoid stereotyping. Of course, in everyday life stereotyping leads people to make false assumptions about other people and groups of people. Stereotyping occurs because of the unfortunate human tendency to overgeneralize. See *Generalization.*

**SUBJECTIVE** *adj.*    Something is *subjective* if it is based on personal reactions or emotions rather than on some objective reality. A reader's reaction to a work of literature is, therefore, subjective. However, this subjective reaction can be supported by means of objective evidence drawn from the work. See *Objective.*

**SUMMARIZE** *v.*    To *summarize* something is to restate it briefly in other words. Generally, one summarizes long works and paraphrases short passages. When writing about literary works, you may sometimes find it useful to summarize events from literary history, positions taken by critics, or events in the works themselves. Always make sure that your summary is an accurate reflection of the original. In particular, make sure not to give more or less weight to particular parts than was given in the material that you are summarizing.

**VAGUE, UNDEFINED TERMS**    See *Propaganda Technique.*

# GLOSSARY

## READING THE GLOSSARY ENTRIES

The words in this glossary are from selections appearing in your textbook. Each entry in the glossary contains the following parts:

**1. Entry Word.** This word appears at the beginning of the entry, in boldface type.

**2. Pronunciation.** The symbols in parentheses tell how the entry word is pronounced. If a word has more than one possible pronunciation, the most common of these pronunciations is given first.

**3. Part of Speech.** Appearing after the pronunciation, in italics, is an abbreviation that tells the part of speech of the entry word. The following abbreviations have been used:

**n.** noun **p.** pronoun **v.** verb
**adj.** adjective **adv.** adverb **conj.** conjunction

**4. Definition.** This part of the entry follows the part-of-speech abbreviation and gives the meaning of the entry word as used in the selection in which it appears.

## KEY TO PRONUNCIATION SYMBOLS USED IN THE GLOSSARY

The following symbols are used in the pronunciations that follow the entry words:

| Symbol | Key Words | Symbol | Key Words |
|---|---|---|---|
| a | asp, fat, parrot | b | bed, fable, dub |
| ā | ape, date, play | d | dip, beadle, had |
| ä | ah, car, father | f | fall, after, off |
| | | g | get, haggle, dog |
| e | elf, ten, berry | h | he, ahead, hotel |
| ē | even, meet, money | j | joy, agile, badge |
| | | k | kill, tackle, bake |
| i | is, hit, mirror | l | let, yellow, ball |
| ī | ice, bite, high | m | met, camel, trim |
| | | n | not, flannel, ton |
| ō | open, tone, go | p | put, apple, tap |
| ô | all, horn, law | r | red, port, dear |
| o͞o | ooze, tool, crew | s | sell, castle, pass |
| oo | look, pull, moor | t | top, cattle, hat |
| yo͞o | use, cute, few | v | vat, hovel, have |
| yoo | united, cure, globule | w | will, always, swear |
| oi | oil, point, toy | y | yet, onion, yard |
| ou | out, crowd, plow | z | zebra, dazzle, haze |
| u | up, cut, color | ch | chin, catcher, arch |
| ur | urn, fur, deter | sh | she, cushion, dash |
| | | t‌h | thin, nothing, truth |
| ə | a in ago | t‍h | then, father, lathe |
| | e in agent | zh | azure, leisure |
| | i in sanity | ŋ | ring, anger, drink |
| | o in comply | ' | [indicates that a |
| | u in focus | | following l or n is a |
| ər | perhaps, murder | | syllabic consonant, as in |
| | | | able (ā' b'l)] |

This pronunciation key is from *Webster's New World Dictionary,* Second College Edition. Copyright © 1986 by Simon & Schuster. Used by permission.

## A

**abasement** (ə bās' mənt) *n.* Condition of being put down or humbled

**abash** (ə bash') *v.* To make ashamed or ill at ease

**abate** (ə bāt') *v.* To lessen; to put an end to

**abhorred** (əb hôrd') *adj.* Something that is regarded with horror or loathing

**abjure** (əb joor') *v.* To vow to give up; repudiate

**ablution** (ab lo͞o' shən) *n.* Washing or cleansing of the body

**abstract** (ab' strakt) *n.* Brief summary stating main points

**acanthus** (ə kan' t‌həs) *n.* Thistlelike plant

**accede** (ak sēd') *v.* (With to) To yield to; agree upon

**accursed** (ə kur' sid) *adj.* Hateful

**acrid** (ak' rid) *adj.* Sharp; bitter

**adamantine** (ad' ə man' tēn) *adj.* Unbreakable

**adjure** (ə joor') *v.* To appeal to earnestly

**advert** (ad vurt') *v.* To call attention

**affectation** (af' ek tā' shən) *n.* Pretense

**affected** (ə fek' tid) *adj.* In a manner not true to the person

**affliction** (ə flik' shən) *n.* State of pain or misery, pain; suffering

**aggrandizement** (ə gran' diz mənt) *n.* Increase in power

**alacrity** (ə lak' rə tē) *n.* Willingness

**allure** (ə loor') *v.* To entice; charm; induce

**amaranth** (am' ə rant‌h') *n.* Imaginary flower that never fades or dies

**amass** (ə mas') *v.* To gather together

**amity** (am' ə tē) *n.* Peaceful relations

**anarchy** (an' ər kē) *n.* Absence of government; confusion, disorder, and violence

**anglophobia** (aŋ glə fō' bē ə) *n.* Hatred or fear of England or things English

**animadversion** (an' ə mad vur' zhən) *n.* Unfavorable comment

**anointed** (ə noint' id) *adj.* Declared sacred

**anterior** (an tir' ē ər) *adj.* At or toward the front

**antiquity** (an tik' wə tē) *n.* Ancient times

**apace** (ə pās') *adv.* Swiftly: with speed

**aperture** (ap' ər chər) *n.* An opening

**apostate** (ə päs' tāt') *adj.* Denying former religious conviction

**apothecary** (ə pät‌h' ə ker ē) *n.* A pharmacist or druggist; person who formerly prepared drugs

**apparition** (ap' ə rish' ən) *n.* A ghost

**appendage** (ə pen' dij) *n.* Something added on

**application** (ap' lə kā' shən) *n.* A specific act or case

**apprehension** (ap rə hen' shən) *n.* Fear, concern

**appropriate** (ə prō' prē āt') *v.* To borrow without giving credit

**arbiter** (är' bə tər) *n.* Judge, umpire

**arboreal** (är bôr' ē əl) *adj.* Situated near or among trees

**ardor** (är' dər) *n.* Great warmth or intensity of passion, emotion, desire and so forth

**armament** (är' mə mənt) *n.* Arms, weapon

**ascendancy** (ə send' ən sē) *n.* A major or dominating influence

**aspire** (ə spīr′)  *v.* To be ambitious

**asperity** (as per′ ə tē)  *n.* Ill temper; irritability

**asphodel** (as′ fə del′)  *n.* Plant with yellow or white lilylike flowers

**assay** (a sā′)  *v.* To try, attempt; prove or test

**assiduity** (as ə dyōō′ ə tē)  *n.* Diligence

**assignation** (as′ ig nā′ s/hən)  *n.* An appointment to meet

**asunder** (ə sun′ dər)  *adv.* Apart; in separate directions

**atrophy** (a′ trə fē)  *v.* To waste away

**augment** (ôg ment′)  *v.* To make greater; enlarge

**august** (ô gust′)  *adj.* Inspiring awe and reverence

**austere** (ô stir′)  *adj.* Having a stern personality or appearance; somber

**avarice** (av′ ər is)  *n.* Greed

**aver** (ə vur′)  *v.* To state to be true

**avocation** (av′ ə kā′ s/hən)  *n.* Something that calls one away or distracts from something

**avouch** (ə vouch′)  *v.* To assert positively; affirm

**avow** (ə vou′)  *v.* To swear

**awe** (ô)  *n.* Fear mixed with great respect

**azurous** (az′ ər əs)  *adj.* Purple-blue

**B**

**baleful** (bāl′ fəl)  *adj.* Of or with evil intent

**balm** (bäm)  *n.* Anything healing or soothing

**balustrade** (bal′ ə strād′)  *n.* A railing supported by small pillars of stone or wood

**baneful** (bān′ fəl)  *adj.* Full of harm; destructive

**barbarous** (bär′ bər əs)  *adj.* Primitive; uncivilized

**barrow** (bar′ ō)  *n.* Heap of earth or rocks marking a grave

**Beelzebub** (bē el′ zə bub′)  *n.* Traditionally, the chief devil, or Satan

**beget** (bi get′)  *v.* To bring into being

**belie** (bi lī′)  *v.* To prove false; contradict

**benison** (ben′ ə z′n)  *n.* Blessing; benediction

**bent** (bent)  *adj.* Determined; resolved

**beseech** (bi sēch′)  *v.* To ask earnestly; entreat; implore

**betokeneth** (bi tō′ k′n et/h)  *v.* To be a sign of; to indicate

**blasphemous** (blas′ fə məs)  *adj.* Disrespectful of God; impious

**blight** (blīt)  *n.* Condtion of withering

**blithe** (blīt/h)  *adj.* Cheerful

**boatswain** (bō′ s′n)  *n.* Warrant officer or petty officer in charge of a ship's deck crew, rigging, and anchors

**bole** (bōl)  *n.* Tree trunk

**boon** (bōōn)  *n.* Something good or pleasant that is given, as a blessing

**brazen** (brā′ z′n)  *adj.* 1. Made of brass; 2. bold; shameless

**burnished** (bur′ nis/hd)  *adj.* Made shiny by daily use

**C**

**caitiff** (kāt′ if)  *n.* Evil person

**canker** (kaŋ′ kər)  *n.* Ulcer-like sore on the lips or in the mouth

**cant** (kant)  *n.* Insincere talk

**caprice** (kə prēs′)  *n.* A tendency to act on whim

**careen** (kə rēn)  *v.* To lean to one side

**career** (kə rir′)  *v.* To move swiftly forward

**carriage** (kar′ ij)  *n.* A way of bearing oneself; deportment

**casement** (kās′ mənt)  *n.* A window that is hinged at the sides

**castigation** (kas′ tə gā s/hən)  *n.* A punishment

**cataract** (kat′ ə rakt′)  *n.* A waterfall

**cavil** (kav′ ′l)  *v.* To raise trivial objections

**certitude** (sur′ tə tōōd)  *n.* A certainty

**chaffinch** (chaf′ finch′)  *n.* Small European songbird

**chary** (cher′ ē)  *adj.* Not giving freely

**chaste** (chāst)  *adj.* Pure; untainted; unblemished

**chastise** (chas tīz′)  *v.* To condemn sharply; scold

**chide** (chīd)  *v.* To scold; rebuke

**chimerical** (ki mir′ i k′l)  *adj.* Imaginary; unreal

**choleric** (käl′ ər ik)  *adj.* Easily provoked to anger

**chrysalis** (kris′ əl əs)  *n.* A cocoon of a butterfly

**churl** (churl)  *n.* 1. *same as* ceorl; farm laborer; peasant: 2. Surly, ill-bred person; boor

**circumscribe** (sur′ kəm skrīb′)  *v.* To limit; confine

**circumspection** (sur′ kəm spek′ s/hən)  *n.* Caution

**clamorous** (klam′ ər əs)  *adj.* Noisy

**cleave** (klēv)  *v.* Split apart

**cloyed** (kloid)  *adj.* Made sick by an overdose

**cluster** (klus′ tər)  *n.* A group, gathering; bunch, as of grapes for wine

**cockle** (käk′ ′l)  *n.* An edible shellfish with two heart-shaped shells

**colonnade** (käl′ ə nād′)  *n.* A series of columns set at regular intervals

**colossal** (kə läs′ ′l)  *adj.* Enormous

**compact** (kəm pakt′)  *v.* To put together

**complaisance** (kəm plā′ z′ns)  *n.* A desire to be agreeable

**compose** (kəm pōz′)  *v.* To get oneself together emotionally; calm

**compound** (käm′ pound)  *v.* To join; combine

**compunctious** (kəm punk′ s/həs)  *adj.* Sorrowful; regretful

**conciliatory** (kən sil′ ē ə tôr′ ē)  *adj.* Agreeable

**condone** (kən dōn′)  *v.* To approve; authorize

**conflagration** (kän′ flə grā′ s/hən)  *n.* A great fire

**conjecture** (kən jek′ chər)  *v.* To guess

**constant** (kän′ stənt)  *adj.* Faithful; unchanging; unceasing

**constitution** (kän′ stə tōō′ s/hən)  *n.* Makeup (of a person)

**consummation** (kän′ sə mā′ s/hən)  *n.* State of fulfillment or completion

**consumed** (kən sōōm′d)  *adj.* Overtaken, overwhelmed

**contention** (kən ten′ s/hən)  *n.* A controversy; dispute

**contentious** (kən ten′ s/həs)  *adj.* Of questionable validity

**contretemps** (kōn′ trə tän′)  *n.* An awkward mishap

**contrite** (kən trīt′)  *adj.* Willing to repent or atone

**conviction** (kən vik′ s/hən)  *n.* A belief in something meaningful, such as a creed

**convulse** (kən vuls′)  *v.* To shake; move violently

**coomb** (kōōm)  *n.* A deep, narrow valley

**copious** (kō′ pē əs)  *adj.* Abundant, plentiful

**coquet** (kō ket′)  *v.* To flirt

**corporeal** (kôr pôr′ ē əl)  *adj.* Of the body

**countenance** (koun′ tə nəns) *n.* A face

**coupe** (kōō pā′) *n.* A closed carriage with seats on one side

**courtier** (kôr′ tē ər) *n.* An attendant at a royal court

**covenant** (kuv′ ə nənt) *n.* A solemn, binding agreement

**coveted** (kuv′ it əd) *v.* Wanted eagerly

**covetousness** (kuv′ it əs nəs) *n.* Greediness

**cowed** (koud) *adj.* Made to feel timid or fearful

**coy** (koi) *adj.* Unwilling to make a commitment, *not* the modern sense of "pretending to be shy."

**credulity** (krə dōō′ lə tē) *n.* Tendency to believe too readily

**crimp** (krimp) *v.* To shape; crease

**cryptogram** (krip′ tə gram) *n.* A coded message

**cur** (kʉr) *n.* A dog of mixed breeds

**curb** (kʉrb) *n.* Chain or strap around a horse's lower jaw attached to the bit to check the horse

**curlew** (kʉr′ lōō) *n.* Large, brownish wading bird with long legs

**cynical** (sin′ i k'l) *adj.* Distrustful; sneering


**D**

**dah** (dä) *n.* A knife

**dais** (dā′ is) *n.* A platform

**dale** (dāl) *n.* A hollow; valley

**dappled** (dap′ 'ld) *adj.* Speckled; having more than one color

**dauntless** (dônt′ lis) *adj.* Fearless

**decamp** (di kamp′) *v.* To leave suddenly

**decrepitude** (di krep′ ə tōōd) *n.* State of being old and broken down

**deference** (def′ ər əns) *n.* Courtesy

**degree** (di grē′) *n.* Social class

**deign** (dān) *v.* To condescend; lower oneself

**deleterious** (del′ ə tir′ ē əs) *adj.* Harmful to health; injurious

**demesne** (di mān′) *n.* The lands of an estate

**deride** (di rīd′) *v.* To make fun of; ridicule

**derisive** (di rī′ siv) *adj.* Mocking

**descant** (des kant′) *v.* To talk at length

**desist** (di zist′) *v.* To stop

**desolate** (des′ ə lit) *adj.* Deserted; forlorn

**despoil** (di spoil′) *v.* To take away one's possessions

**despotic** (de spät′ ik) *adj.* Tyrannical

**destitute** (des′ tə tōōt) *adj.* Lacking

**desultory** (des′ 'l tôr ē) *adj.* Passing from point to point aimlessly

**didactic** (dī dak′ tik) *adj.* Instructive

**diffidence** (dif′ ə dəns) *n.* Shyness; hesitation

**diffusive** (di fyōō′ siv) *adj.* Spread out

**dirge** (dʉrj) *n.* A song of mourning

**disabused** (dis′ ə byōōzd′) *adj.* Freed from false ideas

**discourse** (dis kôrs′) *v.* To talk about; discussing

**discreet** (dis krēt′) *adj.* Wise; prudent

**discursive** (dis kʉr′ siv) *adj.* Reaching conclusions by a series of logical steps, as opposed to intuition

**dispensation** (dis pən sā′ shən) *n.* Religious system or belief

**distemper** (dis tem′ pər) *n.* Infectious disease, in this case the plague

**divers** (dī′ vərz) *adj.* Varied; having many parts (archaic spelling)

**diversion** (də vʉr′ zhən) *n.* A pastime; amusement

**divination** (div′ ə nā′ shən) *n.* A clever guess

**divining** (də vīn′ iŋ) *adj.* Guessing; intuitive

**doleful** (dōl′ fəl) *adj.* Filled with sadness

**dominion** (də min′ yən) *n.* A place of rule; home territory

**dotage** (dōt′ ij) *n.* Second childhood, state of senility

**doughty** (dout′ ē) *adj.* Brave

**dower** (dou′ ər) *n.* A gift

**dowry** (dou′ rē) *n.* The property that a woman brings to her husband at marriage

**drear** (drir) *adj.* Dreary; melancholy

**dregs** (dregz) *n.* Sediment of liquids

**dryad** (drī əd) *n.* In classical mythology, a wood nymph

**dudgeon** (duj′ ən) *n.* Angry resentment; rage

**dulcimer** (dul′ sə mər) *n.* Musical instrument with metal strings which produce sounds when struck by two small hammers

**dun** (dun) *adj.* Dull grayish brown

**dunt** (dunt) *n.* Heavy, dull-sounding blow


**E**

**eglantine** (eg′ lən tīn) *n.* Sweetbrier or honeysuckle

**elocution** (el′ ə kyōō′ shən) *n.* The art of public speaking

**elongated** (i lôŋ′ gāt id) *adj.* Lengthened; stretched

**eloquent** (el′ ə kwənt) *adj.* Very expressive

**empyreal** (em pir′ ē əl) *adj.* Referring to the indestructible substance of which Heaven, or the empyrean, is composed

**encomium** (en kō′ mē əm) *n.* The formal expression of praise or tribute

**encumber** (in kum′ bər) *v.* To weigh down with a load

**engender** (in jen′ dər) *v.* To bring into being; cause to exist

**enisled** (in īld′) *adj.* Isolated, as if placed on an island

**entreat** (in trēt′) *v.* To beg; plead

**envisage** (en viz′ ij) *v.* To form a mental picture of; imagine

**equipage** (ek′ wə pij) *n.* Horses and carriages

**equivocate** (i kwiv′ ə kāt′) *v.* To tell falsehoods

**escritoire** (es′ krə twär′) *n.* An ornamental writing desk or table

**eternize** (i tʉr′ nīz) *v.* To make everlasting

**evanescence** (ev′ ə nes′ 'ns) *n.* Gradual disappearance, especially from sight

**even** (ē′ vən) *adj.* Parallel; on the same level with; conforming to

**exact** (ig zakt′) *v.* To demand; compel

**exorciser** (ek′ sôr sīz′ ər) *n.* A sorcerer; magician

**expanse** (ik spans′) *n.* A wide, continuous stretch, as of land

**expedient** (ik spē′ dē ənt) *n.* Device used in an emergency

**expiate** (ek′ spē āt′) *v.* To make amends for; atone for; forgive; absolve

**expostulate** (ik späs′ chə lāt′) *v.* To reason earnestly with

**extradition**   (eks′ trə dish′ ən)   *n.* The release of an accused person into the custody of one state by another state

**F**

**faceted**   (fas′ ə tid)   *adj.* Having many sides
**fathom**   (fath′ əm)   *n.* A unit of measure for the depth of water; a fathom is six feet
**fastidious**   (fas tid′ ē əs)   *adj.* Hard to please
**feign**   (fān)   *v.* To pretend
**felicity**   (fə lis′ ə tē)   *n.* An apt expression or thought
**fen**   (fen)   *n.* Marsh or bog
**fettered**   (fet′ ər′d)   *adj.* Chained; confined
**fickle**   (fik′ ′l)   *adj.* Unfaithful
**firmament**   (fur′ mə mənt)   *n.* Sky, viewed poetically as a solid arch or vault
**firth**   (furth)   *n.* The narrow arm of a sea
**fleur-de-lys**   (flur′ də lēz′)   *n.* An emblem resembling a lily or iris
**fluency**   (floo′ ən sē)   *n.* Easy flow; smoothness
**fold**   (fōld)   *n.* Pen in which to keep sheep
**folly**   (fäl′ e)   *n.* A foolish action or belief
**foment**   (fō ment′)   *v.* To stir up; incite
**fond**   (fänd)   *adj.* Archaic: Foolish, not the modern sense of having affection for someone or something
**foreshortened**   (fôr shor′ t′nd)   *adj.* Narrowed by observer's angle of vision
**forethink**   (fôr think′)   *v.* To foretell; predict
**forlorn**   (fər lôrn′)   *adj.* Unhappy; in a pensive mood
**former**   (fôr mər)   *adj.* Earlier; coming before
**fret**   (fret)   *v.* To eat away
**frolic**   (fräl′ ik)   *adj.* Merry
**furbished**   (fur′ bishd)   *adj.* Brightened; polished
**furlong**   (fur′ loŋ)   *n.* A unit for measuring distance; a furlong is equal to one eighth of a mile
**fustian**   (fus′ chən)   *n.* A coarse cotton cloth

**G**

**gaiters**   (gāt′ ərz)   *n.* Cloth coverings for the instep and lower leg
**gall**   (gôl)   *n.* Something bitter or distasteful
**galled**   (gôld)   *adj.* Injured or made sore by rubbing or chafing
**gang**   (gaŋ)   *v.* To go or walk (Scot.)
**garnished**   (gär′ nisht)   *adj.* Decorated; trimmed
**garrulous**   (gar′ ə ləs)   *adj.* Tending to talk continuously
**gaudy**   (gôd′ ē)   *adj.* Showy in a tasteless way
**gaunt**   (gônt)   *adj.* Thin
**genial**   (jēn′ yəl)   *adj.* Kindly, cordial
**gesticulate**   (jes tik′ yə lāt′)   *v.* To communicate excitedly by gestures
**gigantified**   (jī gan′ tə fīd)   *adj.* Made to seem much larger
**gisarme**   (gi zärm′)   *n.* A battle-ax
**glean**   (glēn)   *v.* To pick from, as crops
**glen**   (glen)   *n.* A valley
**gowden**   (gou′ d′n)   *adj.* Golden
**grace**   (grās)   *n.* God's favor or approval
**grate**   (grāt)   *n.* Frame of metal bars used as a partition
**gratuitous**   (grə too′ ə təs)   *adj.* Undeservedly or without reason
**guerdon**   (gur′ d′n)   *n.* A reward
**guile**   (gīl)   *n.* Artful trickery; cunning

**H**

**habitation**   (hab′ ə tā′ shən)   *n.* A home; dwelling
**habituate**   (hə bich′ oo wāt′)   *v.* To accustom to; to make used to
**haft**   (haft)   *n.* Handle of a weapon or tool
**haggard**   (hag′ ərd)   *adj.* Having a worn, gaunt, or wild look
**halcyon**   (hal′ sē ən)   *adj.* Calm
**halter**   (hôl′ tər)   *n.* Rope for hanging; hangman's noose
**haply**   (hap′ lē)   *adv.* By chance
**harbinger**   (här′ bin jər)   *n.* A forerunner
**harmonious**   (här mō′ nē əs)   *adj.* In a manner that is in accordance
**harry**   (har′ ē)   *v.* To harass
**hauberk**   (hô′ bərk)   *n.* A coat of armor
**haughty**   (hôt′ ē)   *adj.* Lofty
**headrig**   (hed′ rig)   *n.* The part of a plow that turns over the soil; moldboard
**health**   (helth)   *n.* A wish for happiness, as in drinking a series of toasts
**heraldic**   (hə ral′ dik)   *adj.* Resembling an English coat of arms
**hermitage**   (hur′ mit ij)   *n.* A retreat suitable for meditation; originally, a hermit's dwelling
**hew**   (hyoo)   *n.* Color; hue
**hoary**   (hôr′ ē)   *adj.* White or gray with age
**hobnailed**   (häb′ nāld)   *adj.* Studded with nails to prevent wear or slipping
**husbandry**   (huz′ bən drē)   *n.* Farming

**I**

**ignominy**   (ig′ nə min′ ē)   *n.* Humiliation; dishonor; disgrace
**illimitable**   (i lim′ it ə b′l)   *adj.* Without limit or bounds; immeasurable
**illumine**   (i loo′ min)   *v.* To light up
**imminent**   (im′ ə nənt)   *adj.* Likely to happen soon
**impaired**   (im perd′)   *v.* Diminished
**imperiously**   (im pir′ ē əs lē)   *adv.* Arrogantly
**impertinence**   (im pur′ t′n əns)   *n.* Rudeness
**imperturbable**   (im′ pər tur′ bə b′l)   *adj.* Calm; not easily ruffled
**impetuous**   (im pech′ oo wəs)   *adj.* Given to rash or hasty action; doing things on the spur of the moment; tending to act impulsively, without thinking
**impious**   (im′ pē əs)   *adj.* Disrespectful; irreverent, ungodly
**importune**   (im′ pôr toon′)   *v.* To press with frequent requests; ask insistently
**importuning**   (im pôr toon′ iŋ)   *v.* Begging, urging
**imprecation**   (im′ prə kā′ shən)   *n.* A curse
**impressionistic**   (im presh′ ə nis′ tik)   *adj.* Conveying a quick, overall picture
**impudence**   (im′ pyoo dəns)   *n.* The quality of being rash or contrary
**inarticulate**   (in′ är tik′ yə lit)   *adj.* Not able to speak
**incessant**   (in ses′ ′nt)   *adj.* Never ceasing
**incitement**   (in sīt′ mənt)   *n.* A cause to perform; encouragement
**inconstancy**   (in kän′ stən sē)   *n.* A contradiction; fickleness; changeableness

**incorrigible**  (in kôr′ i jə b′l)  *adj.* Not capable of being corrected or of behaving better

**inculcate**  (in kul′ kāt)  *v.* To impress upon the mind by frequent repetition

**indissoluble**  (in′ di säl′ yoo b′l)  *adj.* Not able to be dissolved or undone

**inexorable**  (in ek′ sər ə b′l)  *adj.* Ongoing, with no sign of stopping

**infirmity**  (in fur′ mə tē)  *n.* Physical or mental defect; illness

**ingenuous**  (in jen′ yoo wəs)  *adj.* Naive; simple

**inglorious**  (in glôr′ ē əs)  *adj.* Little-known

**inimical**  (in im′ i k′l)  *adj.* Hostile; unfriendly

**iniquity**  (in ik′ wə tē)  *n.* Wickedness

**innumerable**  (in noo′ mər ə b′l)  *adj.* Too many to count

**inordinate**  (in ôr′ d′n it)  *adj.* Beyond reasonable limits

**inquisition**  (in′ kwə zish′ ən)  *n.* Any investigation that violates the privacy or rights of individuals

**insipid**  (in sip′ id)  *adj.* Not exciting or interesting; dull, lifeless

**intemperance**  (in tem′ pər əns)  *n.* Lack of restraint

**intermit**  (in tər mit′)  *v.* To stop for a time

**intimation**  (in′ tə mā′ shən)  *n.* A hint

**inventory**  (in′ vən tôr′ ē)  *n.* A list of possessions

**invincible**  (in vin′ sə b′l)  *adj.* Unconquerable

**irascibly**  (i ras′ ə b′lē)  *adv.* Irritably

**irremediable**  (ir i mē′ dē ə b′l)  *adj.* Incurable; incapable of being remedied

**irrepressible**  (ir′ i pres′ ə b′l)  *adj.* Not able to be restrained

**isthmus**  (is′ məs)  *n.* A narrow strip of land, with water on each side, connecting two larger land masses

**J**

**japonica**  (jə pän′ i kə)  *n.* A spiny plant with pink or red flowers

**jocund**  (jäk′ ənd)  *adj.* Cheerful; pleasant; jovial

**judicious**  (joo dish′ əs)  *adj.* having or showing good judgment

**K**

**keen**  (kēn)  *adj.* Having a sharp edge or point

**ken**  (ken)  *n.* The range of sight or knowledge

**ketch**  (kech)  *n.* A two-masted sailing vessel

**kindred**  (kin′ drid)  *n.* Relatives; relations

**knave**  (nāv)  *n.* A scoundrel; cheater

**knell**  (nel)  *n.* The sound of a bell, especially one rung slowly, as at a funeral

**kraal**  (kräl)  *n.* A fenced-in enclosure for cattle or sheep

**L**

**laboriously**  (lə bôr′ ē əs lē)  *adv.* In a manner involving much hard work

**laden**  (lād′ ′n)  *adj.* Burdened; weighed down

**lament**  (lə ment′)  *v.* To mourn; wail; bemoan

**lamentable**  (lam′ ən tə b′l)  *adj.* Distressing

**languid**  (laŋ′ gwid)  *adj.* Slow, lacking energy

**languish**  (laŋ′ gwish)  *v.* To become weak or sickly looking

**languor**  (laŋ′ gər)  *n.* Weakness, fatigue

**largess**  (lär jes′)  *n.* Generous gift

**largesse**  (lär′ jes)  *n.* A nobility of spirit

**lark**  (lärk′)  *v.* To play around

**laryngoscope**  (lə riŋ′ gō skōp′)  *n.* An instrument for examining the throat

**lay**  (lā)  *n.* A short poem to be sung

**leviathan**  (lə vī′ ə thən)  *n.* A great sea monster

**lexicographer**  (lek′ sə käg′ rə fər)  *n.* One who compiles a dictionary

**liege**  (lēj)  *n.* A lord or king

**lintel**  (lin′ t′l)  *n.* A beam over a door

**litany**  (lit′ ′n ē)  *n.* A form of prayer in which a congregation repeats a fixed response

**loath**  (lōth)  *adj.* Reluctant; unwilling

**lucrative**  (loo′ krə tiv)  *adj.* Profitable

**luminescent**  (loo mə nes′ ′nt)  *adj.* Giving out light without much heat

**lyric**  (lir′ ik)  *n.* A poem, one of the major categories of poetry; in classical literature, a song accompanied by a lyre

**M**

**madrigal**  (mad′ ri gəl)  *n.* A song with parts for several voices with no musical accompaniment

**magnanimous**  (mag nan′ ə məs)  *adj.* Generously forgiving

**mahout**  (mə hoot′)  *n.* An elephant keeper and rider

**mail**  (māl)  *n.* A flexible body armor made of metal

**maize**  (māz)  *n.* Corn

**malevolence**  (mə lev′ ə ləns)  *n.* Ill will; spitefulness

**malign**  (mə līn′)  *v.* To speak evil of; defame

**malignity**  (mə lig′ nə tē)  *n.* A strong desire to harm others; deadliness

**manifold**  (man′ ə fōld′)  *adj.* Of many kinds; varied

**mead-hall**  (mēd′ hôl)  *n.* A banquet hall; mead is a beverage made from fermented honey and water

**measure**  (mezh′ ər)  *n.* A quantity, dimension, size

**megalith**  (meg′ ə lith′)  *n.* A huge stone, especially one used in prehistoric monuments

**melancholy**  (mel′ ən käl′ ē)  *n.* Sadness; lowness of spirit

**mendacity**  (men das′ ə tē)  *n.* Lying

**mesmerism**  (mez′ mər iz′m)  *n.* Hypnotism

**mestizo**  (mes tē′ zō)  *adj.* Of Spanish and Indian parentage

**metaphysical**  (met ə fiz′ i k′l)  *adj.* Very abstract

**mettlesome**  (met′ ′l səm)  *adj.* High-spirited

**minion**  (min′ yən)  *n.* Attendant or agent

**miscreant**  (mis′ crē ənt)  *n.* A villan

**misanthropist**  (mis an′ thrə pist)  *n.* One who hates or mistrusts others

**modish**  (mōd′ ish)  *adj.* Fashionable

**moleskin**  (mōl′ skin)  *n.* Work clothes made from strong, twilled cotton fabric

**molt**  (mōlt)  *v.* Cast off; shed, as skin or feathers

**moly**  (mō′ lē)  *n.* In classical mythology, an herb of magic powers; European wild garlic

**moorline**  (moor′ līn)  *n.* The horizon where open, rolling wasteland meets the sky

**morosely**  (mə rōs′ lē)  *adv.* Sullenly; in bad humor

**mortification**  (môr′ tə fi kā′ shən)  *n.* A feeling of great shock and upset

**multitudinous**  (mul′ tə tood′ ′n əs)  *adj.* Existing in great numbers

**munificence**  (myoo nif′ ə s′ns)  *n.* Great generosity

**myriad**  (mir′ ē əd)   *n.* Ten thousand; a great number of things

**myrrh**  (mʉr)   *n.* A plant that produces a fragrant gum resin used in making incense and perfume

## N

**nativity**  (nə tiv′ ə tē′)   *n.* A birth, especially in regard to place and time

**nunnery**  (nun′ ər ē)   *n.* A convent, a dwelling place for nuns

**nymph**  (nimf)   *n.* In classical mythology, a minor nature goddess usually shown as a lovely young girl

## O

**obdurate**  (äb′ door ət, äb′ dyoor ət)   *adj.* Hardened against what is good or moral; stubborn, unyielding

**obliquely**  (ə blēk′ lē)   *adv.* At a slant; indirectly

**obliterate**  (ə blit′ ə rāt)   *v.* to destroy utterly

**obstinacy**  (äb′ stə nə sē)   *n.* Stubbornness

**ode**  (ōd)   *n.* A poem of varying line lengths and usually several stanzas, often addressed to someone; in classical literature, a poem to be sung, usually in praise of someone

**odious**  (ō′ dē əs)   *adj.* Exciting repugnance or aversion; abhorrent; hateful; offensive; disgusting

**officious**  (ə fish′ əs)   *adj.* Overly eager to please (obsolete meaning); offering unnecessary advice or services

**ope**  (ōp)   *v.* To open

**opiate**  (ō′ pē it)   *n.* Something that brings on relaxation or sleep

**oppress**  (ə pres′)   *v.* To burden

**oracle**  (ôr′ ə k′l)   *n.* In classical antiquity, the shrine in which a god spoke through a priest or priestess

**orderly**  (ôr′ dər lē)   *n.* A soldier assigned to carry out orders of a superior

**ordure**  (ôr′ jər)   *n.* Waste matter; excrement

**ostentation**  (äs′ tən tā′ shən)   *n.* A showy display

**overplus**  (ō′ vər plus′)   *n.* A surplus, abundance; enough over for others

**overscrupulous**  (ō′ vər skroo′ pyə ləs)   *adj.* Overly concerned about details

## P

**pallor**  (pal′ ər)   *n.* An unnatural lack of color; paleness

**palpable**  (pal′ pə b′l)   *adj.* Capable of being touched or felt

**panegyric**  (pan′ ə jir′ ik)   *n.* A speech giving praise

**parapet**  (par′ ə pit)   *n.* A low wall or railing

**parley**  (pär′ lē)   *n.* A discussion

**parquet**  (pär kā′)   *n.* A flooring of inlaid woodwork in geometric forms; wooden floors

**passé**  (pa sā′)   *adj.* Stale

**pastoral**  (pas′ tər al)   *adj.* Pertaining to country life

**patron**  (pā′ trən)   *n.* One who gives financial aid to an artist or writer

**penetrailia**  (pen′ ə trā′ lē ə)   *n.* The innermost parts

**penitent**  (pen′ ə tənt)   *adj.* Feeling or showing sorrow for one's misdeeds or sins

**penury**  (pen′ yə rē)   *n.* Poverty

**perchance**  (pər chans′)   *adv.* Perhaps, possibly

**peremptorily**  (pə remp′ tə ri lē)   *adv.* Decisively; without showing cause

**perfidious**  (pər fid′ ē əs)   *adj.* Disloyal; treacherous

**perfidiousness**  (pə fid′ ē əs nis)   *n.* The betrayal of trust

**perfunctorily**  (pər funk′ tə ri lē)   *adv.* Carelessly

**periwig**  (per′ ə wig′)   *n.* A type of wig often worn by men during the seventeenth and eighteenth centuries

**pernicious**  (pər nish′ əs)   *adj.* Causing serious injury; deadly; evil; wicked

**perpetual**  (pər pech′ oo wəl)   *adj.* Constant, unending

**persistent**  (pər sis′ tənt)   *adj.* Continuing

**perturbation**  (pur′ tər bā′ shən)   *n.* A disorder

**peruke**  (pə rook′)   *n.* A wig

**perversity**  (pər vur′ sə tē)   *n.* State of being wicked or wrong

**perverted**  (pər vur′ tid)   *adj.* Distorted; corrupted

**pestilence**  (pes′ t'l əns)   *n.* A highly contagious disease, such as plague

**petulance**  (pech′ oo ləns)   *n.* Insolent behavior; peevishness; moodiness

**phantasm**  (fan′ taz'm)   *n.* A supernatural form or shape

**phlegm**  (flem)   *n.* Sluggishness

**phoenix**  (fē′ niks)   *n.* A fabled bird of Arabia said to consume itself by fire every five hundred years and to rise renewed from its own ashes

**phosphorescence**  (fäs′ fə res′ 'ns)   *n.* The property of shining in the dark

**physiognomy**  (fiz′ ē äg′ nə mē)   *n.* Facial features thought to reveal character or disposition

**piazza**  (pē az′ ə)   *n.* An open public square

**piety**  (pī′ ə tē)   *n.* Devotion

**pike**  (pīk)   *n.* A voracious freshwater fish

**pince-nez**  (pans′ nā′)   *n.* Eyeglasses without sidepieces, held in place by springs gripping the bridge of the nose

**pirouette**  (pir′ oo wet′)   *v.* To dance or whirl on one foot

**pithead**  (pit′ hed)   *n.* The top of a mining pit or coal shaft

**plagiarism**  (plā′ jə riz'm)   *n.* The passing off of another's work as one's own

**platitude**  (plat′ ə tood′)   *n.* A statement lacking originality

**plebian**  (pli bē′ ən)   *adj.* Common; ordinary

**plutocracy**  (ploo täk′ rə sē)   *n.* The wealthy governing class

**poke**  (pōk)   *n.* An overhanging projection, such as the brim on a woman's poke bonnet

**portal**  (pôr′ t'l)   *n.* A door; gateway

**posy**  (pō′ zē)   *n.* A bouquet

**prate**  (prāt′)   *n.* To talk much and foolishly

**prau**  (prau)   *n.* A swift Malayan boat with a large sail

**prebendary**  (preb′ ən der′ ē)   *n.* In the Church of England, honorary clergyman

**precedency**  (pres′ ə dən sē)   *n.* Priority because of rank

**precipitate**  (pri sip′ ə tit)   *adj.* Steep

**predominance**  (pri däm′ ə nans)   *n.* Superiority

**preferment**  (pri fur′ mənt)   *n.* An advancement in rank

**pregnant**  (preg′ nənt)   *adj.* Full of ideas; inventive

**premonition**  (prē mə nish′ ən)   *n.* A warning in advance

**premonitory**  (pri män′ ə tôr′ ē)   *adj.* Giving warning beforehand

**presume** (pri zōōm′) *v.* To suppose
**presumptuous** (pri zump′ choo wəs) *adj.* Unduly confident or bold
**pretence** (pri tens′) *n.* A claim (British spelling)
**pretension** (pri ten′ shən) *n.* A claim to a rank or class
**pretentious** (pri ten′ shəs) *adj.* Making false claims
**preternatural** (prēt′ ər nach′ ər əl) *adj.* Outside the natural or normal order
**prevarication** (pri var ə kā′ shən) *n.* An evasion of truth
**prime** (prīm) *n.* The best stage or time; most mature period
**pristine** (pris′ tēn) *adj.* Pure; untouched; unspoiled
**prodigal** (präd′ i gəl) *adj.* Addicted to wasteful expenditure
**prodigious** (prə dij′ əs) *adj.* Enormous; huge; impressive
**profuse** (prə fyōōs′) *adj.* Abundant, pouring out
**progeny** (präj′ ə nē) *n.* Offspring; a child
**promiscuously** (prə mis′ kyoo wəs lē) *adv.* Without care or thought
**promontory** (präm′ ən tôr′ ē) *n.* The land that juts out into a body of water; high point of land extending into the sea
**propagator** (präp′ ə gāt′ ər) *n.* One who causes something to happen or to spread
**prophesy** (präf′ ə sī) *v.* Predict
**prophetic** (prə fet′ ik) *adj.* Having the power to predict or foreshadow
**propitiate** (prə pish′ ē āt′) *v.* Ease the burden of; appease
**prostrate** (präs′ trāt) *adj.* Defenseless; in a prone or lying position
**protracted** (prō trak′ tid) *v.* Drawn out; prolonged
**providence** (präv′ ə dens) *n.* Divine forethought, guidance, and care; also, God
**provoking** (prə vōk′ iŋ) *adj.* Annoying, irritating
**prow** (prou) *n.* The front of a boat
**prudence** (prōōd′ 'ns) *n.* Care in avoiding errors; discretion
**puissant** (pyōō′ i sənt) *adj.* Powerful
**pulverous** (pul′ və rəs) *adj.* Crumbling
**pumice** (pum′ is) *n.* A volcanic rock

## Q

**quay** (kē) *n.* A wharf with facilities for loading or unloading ships

## R

**raiment** (rā′ mənt) *n.* Clothing
**Raj** (raj) *n.* Rule
**rapture** (rap′ chər) *n.* An expression of great joy
**ravish** (rav′ ish) *v.* To violate
**recompense** (rek′ əm pens′) *n.* A payment in return; reward
**reconcile** (rek′ ən sīl′) *v.* To make up with
**recreant** (rek′ rē ənt) *adj.* Cowardly
**rectify** (rek′ tə fī) *v.* To set right; correct
**refractory** (ri frak′ tər ē) *adj.* Hard to manage; stubborn
**refulgent** (ri ful′ jənt) *adj.* Shining; radiant
**remonstrance** (ri män′ strəns) *n.* A protest
**remonstrate** (ri män′ strāt) *v.* To object strongly

**repose** (ri pōz′) *v.* Lie back
**repository** (ri päz′ ə tôr ē) *n.* A center for accumulation and storage
**repudiation** (ri pyōō′ dē ā′ shən) *n.* A rejection; denial
**requiem** (rek′ wē əm) *n.* Dirge or mass for the dead; Musical composition or service honoring the dead
**respite** (res′ pit) *n.* A postponement; delay
**resplendently** (ri splen′ dənt lē) *adj.* Splendidly, gorgeously
**reticent** (ret′ ə s′nt) *adj.* Laid back; uncommunicative
**retort** (ri tôrt′) *n.* A comeback with a smart answer or wisecrack
**retreat** (ri trēt′) *n.* A period of retirement or seclusion for prayer, religious study, and meditation
**reverence** (rev′ ər əns) *n.* A great respect; deep respect or awe
**reverie** (rev′ ər ē) *n.* A daydream
**righteousness** (rī′ chəs nis) *n.* Doing what is fair and just
**rill** (ril) *n.* A little brook
**rime** (rīm) *n.* A white frost
**rioter** (rī′ ət ər) *n.* A loud, dissolute bully
**rostral** (räs′ trəl) *adj.* Having a beaklike projection, or rostrum, as at the prow of a ship
**rout** (rout) *n.* An overwhelming defeat
**rue** (rōō) *n.* Sorrow
**ruminate** (rōō′ mə nāt) *v.* To think over; meditate
**rummage** (rum′ ij) *v.* To search by thoroughly examining

## S

**sacramented** (sak′ rə ment id) *adj.* Having the properties of religious rites or rituals
**sagacity** (sə gas′ ə tē) *n.* Wisdom: judgment
**salient** (sāl′ yənt) *adj.* Striking; easily noticeable
**salver** (sal′ vər) *n.* A tray usually used for the presentation of letters or visiting cards
**sampan** (sam′ pan) *n.* A small flat-bottomed boat with a cabin formed by mats
**sanguinary** (saŋ′ gwi ner′ ē) *adj.* Bloody
**sanguine** (san′ gwin) *adj.* Of cheerful temperament
**sarong** (sə rôŋ′) *n.* A long, brightly colored strip of cloth worn like a skirt
**satiety** (sə tī′ ə tē) *n.* State of being filled to excess
**saturnine** (sat′ ər nīn) *adj.* Sluggish or gloomy
**schism** (siz′ 'm) *n.* A division into groups or factions
**screed** (skrēd) *n.* A long, tiresome piece of writing
**scutcheon** (skuch′ ən) *n.* A coat of arms
**segmented** (seg′ ment id) *adj.* Separated into parts
**semblance** (sem′ bləns) *n.* Appearance; image
**senility** (si nil′ ə tē) *n.* Mental and physical decay due to old age
**sepulcher** (sep′ 'l kər) *n.* A tomb
**sequacious** (si kwā′ shəs) *adj.* *(Archaic.)* Tending to follow dutifully, in service of
**sequester** (si kwes′ tər) *v.* To keep apart from others
**Seraphim** (ser′ ə fim) *n.* The highest order of angels
**serrated** (ser′ āt əd) *adj.* Toothed or notched like a saw
**servile** (sur′ v′l) *adj.* Slavelike
**severance** (sev′ ər əns) *n.* State of being kept separate
**shard** (shärd) *n.* A fragment or broken pieces

**sheaf** (s/hēf)  *n.* A bundle of twigs or fibers

**sibilant** (sib' 'l ənt)  *adj.* Hissing

**signet** (sig' nit)  *n.* A seal

**sinecure** (sī' nə kyoor)  *n.* Any office or position that brings advantage but involves little or no work

**sinew** (sin' yōō)  *n.* Muscular power; force

**sinewy** (sin' yoo wē)  *adj.* Tough; vigorous; powerful

**sinuous** (sin' yōō əs)  *adj.* Winding, twisting; bending; curving in and out

**slagheap** (slag' hēp)  *n.* A pile of waste material from mining

**slumbrous** (slum' brəs)  *adj.* Peaceful, suggesting sleep

**sock** (säk)  *n.* The blade of a plow

**sojourn** (sō' jurn)  *v.* To stay for a while

**solace** (säl' is)  *n.* A comfort in grief or trouble; relief

**solicit** (sə lis' it)  *v.* Ask for, plead for

**solicitous** (sə lis' ə təs)  *adj.* Showing care or concern

**soliloquize** (sə lil' ə kwīz')  *v.* To talk to oneself

**somnambulist** (säm nam' byoo list)  *n.* A sleepwalker

**sophist** (säf' ist)  *n.* One who makes misleading arguments

**sordid** (sor' did)  *adj.* Unclean, dirty

**soiree** (swä rā')  *n.* Party held in the evening

**sophistry** (säf' is trē)  *n.* Clever but unsound reasoning

**sough** (sou)  *n.* A groan or sighing sound

**sovereign** (säv' rən)  *adj.* Supreme in power, rank, or authority

**specter** (spek' tər)  *n.* A ghost or ghost-like appearance

**spectral** (spek' trəl)  *adj.* Ghostly

**spendthrift** (spend' thrift')  *n.* A person who spends money wastefully or foolishly

**spent** (spent)  *adj.* Used up; gone

**splaying** (splā' iŋ)  *v.* Spreading

**sprightly** (sprīt' lē)  *adj.* Lively

**squalid** (skwäl' id)  *adj.* Miserably poor; wretched

**squire** (skwīr)  *n.* A country gentleman or landed proprietor

**stagnant** (stag' nənt)  *adj.* Standing still, as water

**stealthy** (stel' thē)  *adj.* In a quiet, secretive way; sly; furtive

**steep** (stēp)  *v.* To become saturated with

**stem** (stem)  *v.* To stop; dam up

**stile** (stīl)  *n.* A step or set of steps used in climbing over a fence or wall

**stoic** (stō' ik)  *n.* A person indifferent to pleasure or pain

**sublimity** (sə blim' ə tē)  *n.* The quality of being majestic or noble

**subordinate** (sə bôr' də nit)  *adj.* Beneath another in rank

**subtle** (sut' 'l)  *adj.* Cunning; ingenious

**succeed** (sək sēd)  *v.* To follow; come after

**succinct** (sək siŋkt')  *adj.* Belted (Archaic); terse

**suffuse** (sə fyōōz')  *v.* To fill

**sullen** (sul' ən)  *adj.* Gloomy; dismal

**sumpitan** (sump' ə tan)  *n.* A Malayan blowgun which discharges poisonous darts

**sundry** (sun' drē)  *adj.* Various; miscellaneous

**superfluity** (sōō' pər flōō' ə tē)  *n.* An excess

**supplant** (sə plant')  *v.* To take the place of; supersede

**suppliant** (sup' lē ənt)  *adj.* Beseeching prayerfully; imploring

**supplication** (sup' lə kā' s/hən)  *n.* The act of praying

**surfeit** (sur' fit)  *n.* Too much of something; an excess

**surmise** (sər mīz')  *v.* To guess, assume; to form an opinion from inconclusive evidence

**swaddling** (swäd' liŋ)  *adj.* Long, narrow bands of cloth wrapped around newborn babies

**swain** (swān)  *n.* A country youth

**switch** (swich)  *n.* A light whip

**sylvan** (sil' vən)  *adj.* Wooded

**symmetry** (sim' ə trē)  *n.* Beauty resulting from balance of form

**T**

**taffeta** (taf' i tə)  *n.* A fine silk fabric

**talent** (tal' ənt)  *n.* A Biblical unit of money; native ability

**tarry** (tar' ē)  *v.* To delay, linger, be tardy, abide; continue in the same condition

**tawdry** (tô' drē)  *adj.* Cheap; gaudy

**teeming** (tēm' iŋ)  *adj.* Filled to overflowing

**temperate** (tem' pər it)  *adj.* Exercising moderation and self-restraint

**tempest** (tem' pist)  *n.* A violent storm accompanied by rain; any violent commotion or tumult, an uproar

**tempestuous** (tem pes' choo wəs)  *adj.* Turbulent; violently stormy

**tenor** (ten' ər)  *n.* A general tendency or course

**terrestrial** (tə res' trē əl)  *adj.* Of this world; earthly

**thane** (thān)  *n.* In early England, a member of a class of freemen who held land of the king or a lord in return for military services

**thrall** (thrôl)  *n.* A slave; serf

**timorous** (tim' ər əs)  *adj.* Fearful; timid

**tincture** (tiŋk' chər)  *n.* A tint

**tithe** (tīth)  *n.* One tenth of a person's income, paid as a tax to support the church

**tor** (tôr)  *n.* A high, rocky hill; crag

**torrid** (tôr' id)  *adj.* Hot, scorching

**traffic** (traf' ik)  *n.* Business

**transcendence** (tran sen' dəns)  *n.* A rising above

**transfiguration** (trans fig yoo rā' s/hən)  *n.* A change in outward form or appearance

**transgress** (trans' gres)  *v.* To violate a law or command; overstep or break

**transient** (tran' s/hənt)  *adj.* A person who passes quickly through a place

**transitory** (tran' sə tôr' ē)  *adj.* Temporary; fleeting

**trefoil** (trē' foil)  *n.* Clover

**trellis** (trel' is)  *n.* A frame or crossed strips, usually of wood, used as a screen or support for climbing plants

**tremulous** (trem' yoo ləs)  *adj.* Trembling; timid

**tress** (tres)  *n.* A lock of human hair

**tryst** (trist)  *n.* A meeting

**tuft** (tuft)  *n.* A grouping of fibers such as hair or grass

**tumid** (tōō' mid)  *adj.* Swollen

**tumult** (tōō' mult)  *n.* Commotion, disturbance; uproar; noisy confusion

**tumultuous** (tōō mul' choo wəs)  *adj.* Disorderly; violent

**turbid** (tur' bid)  *adj.* Muddy or cloudy; confused

**turret** (tur' it)  *n.* A small tower projecting from a building

**twa** (twä)  *n.* Two (Scot.)

**U**

**uncanny** (un kan′ ē) *adj.* Mysterious; hard to explain

**unctuous** (uŋk′ choo wəs) *adj.* Oily

**ungenial** (un jēn′ yəl) *adj.* Unfriendly; characterized by bad weather

**unmitigable** (un mit′ i gə b′l) *adj.* Not able to be diminished in intensity

**unravished** (un rav′ is/hd) *adj.* Undisturbed, unspoiled

**unbraiding** (up brād′ iŋ) *n.* Stern words of disapproval for an action; scolding

**usurious** (yoo zhoor′ ē əs) *adj.* Lending money at a high rate of interest

**unsurped** (yoo surp′d′) *adj.* Wrongfully seized

**V**

**vain** (vān) *adj.* Foolish; worthless

**vair** (ver) *n.* A gray and white fur

**valance** (val′ əns) *n.* A decorative facing

**vale** (vāl) *n.* A valley

**vanity** (van′ ə tē) *n.* A trifle, knicknack, or other insignificant thing

**vaunt** (vônt) *v.* To speak boastfully

**vehemence** (vē′ ə məns) *n.* Strength of feeling and emotion

**vehement** (vē′ ə mənt) *adj.* Energetic, forceful

**veldt** (velt) *n.* Open, grassy country

**verdure** (vur′ jər) *n.* Green plants

**verge** (vurj) *n.* An edge, rim

**vestige** (ves′ tij) *n.* A trace; bit

**vestry** (ves′ trē) *n.* A church meeting room

**vexation** (vek sā′ s/hən) *n.* An annoyance

**vignettes** (vin yets′) *n.* Decorative designs or borderless pictures in a book

**vintage** (vin′ tij) *n.* A wine or nectar of high quality

**virago** (və rā′ gō) *n.* A scolding woman

**virtuous** (vur′ choo wəs) *adj.* Pure, righteous

**virulency** (vir′ yoo lən sē) *n.* Harmfulness

**visage** (viz′ ij) *n.* A person's face or facial expression

**vis-à-vis** (vē′ zə vē′) Face to face with

**viscous** (vis′ kəs) *adj.* Semifluid; sticky

**vizard** (viz′ ərd) *n.* A mask

**W**

**wan** (wän) *adj.* Sickly pale; (Archaic) gloomy, not the modern sense of sickly pale

**wane** (wān) *v.* To gradually become dimmer

**wanton** (wän′ t′n) *adj.* Luxuriant: said of vegetation; frisky; playful

**wantonness** (wän′ t′n nis) *n.* State of being reckless or undisciplined

**wanwood** (wän′ wood) *n.* A pale wood

**wax** (waks′) *v.* To grow, ripen

**weal** (wēl) *n.* A discolored ridge on the skin; blister

**whelk** (hwelk) *n.* A pimple

**wisteria** (wis tir′ ē ə) *n.* Vines of shrubs with clusters of bluish, white, pink, or purplish flowers

**wit** (wit) *n.* Intelligence, wisdom

**wrangle** (raŋ′ g′l) *v.* To argue noisily and angrily; bicker

**Y**

**yare** (yer) *adj.* Ready; prepared

**yoke** (yōk) *n.* A wooden contrivance joining the heads of two draft animals, such as oxen, to make them capable of pulling heavier loads

**ycladd** (i klad′) *pp.* Clothed, dressed

**yclept** (i klept′) *pp.* Called; named

**Z**

**zephyr** (zef′ ər) *n.* A gentle wind

# INDEX OF FINE ART

# INDEX OF SKILLS

## ANALYZING LITERATURE

## CRITICAL THINKING AND READING

## SPEAKING AND LISTENING

## STUDY AND RESEARCH

## THINKING AND WRITING

## UNDERSTANDING LANGUAGE

# INDEX OF TITLES BY THEMES

# INDEX OF AUTHORS AND TITLES

# ACKNOWLEDGMENTS (continued)

**Jonathan Clowes Ltd., London, on behalf of Doris Lessing (continued)**
sonal Voice: Essays, Reviews, Interviews by Doris Lessing. Copyright © 1957 by Doris Lessing. Reprinted by permission of Jonathan Clowes Ltd., London, on behalf of Doris Lessing.

**Jonathan Clowes Ltd., London, on behalf of Doris Lessing and Harper & Row, Publishers, Inc.**
"A Mild Attack of Locusts" from The Habit of Loving by Doris Lessing. Copyright © 1957 by Doris Lessing. Reprinted by permission.

**Doubleday, a division of Bantam, Doubleday, Dell Publishing Group, Inc.**
"The Lagoon" from Tales of Unrest by Joseph Conrad, Doubleday, Page & Company.

**Faber and Faber Ltd.**
"Days" from The Whitsun Weddings by Phillip Larkin. Copyright © 1960, 1961, 1962, 1964 by Phillip Larkin. "Sunday Morning" and "The Sunlight on the Garden" from The Collected Poems of Louis MacNeice by Louis MacNeice. Copyright © the Estate of Louis MacNeice 1966. Reprinted by permission of Faber and Faber Ltd.

**Farrar, Straus and Giroux, Inc. and Faber and Faber Ltd.**
"Taylor Street" from Selected Poems 1950-1975 by Thom Gunn. Copyright © 1957, 1958, 1961, 1967, 1971, 1973, 1974, 1975, 1976, 1979 by Thom Gunn. Published in London in Touch by Thom Gunn. "Follower," "Shore Woman," and excerpt from "Rite of Spring" from Poems 1965-1975 by Seamus Heaney. Copyright © 1966, 1969, 1972, 1975, 1980 by Seamus Heaney. "Follower" published in London in Death of a Naturalist by Seamus Heaney and "Shore Woman" published in London in Wintering Out by Seamus Heaney. "The Explosion" from High Windows by Philip Larkin. Copyright © 1974 by Philip Larkin. Reprinted by permission of the publishers.

**Harcourt Brace Jovanovich, Inc.**
Excerpt from "The Tragedy of King Richard the Second" from Shakespeare: The Complete Works, edited by G. B. Harrison, copyright 1948, 1952, 1968 by Harcourt Brace Jovanovich, Inc. Reprinted by permission of the publisher.

**Harcourt Brace Jovanovich, Inc. and Faber and Faber Ltd.**
"The Hollow Men," "Journey of the Magi," and "Preludes" from Collected Poems 1909-1962 by T. S. Eliot, copyright 1935, 1936 by Harcourt Brace Jovanovich, Inc.; copyright © 1964 by T. S. Eliot. Reprinted by permission of the publishers.

**Harcourt Brace Jovanovich, Inc., A. M. Heath & Company Ltd., the Estate of the Late Sonia Brownell Orwell, and Secker & Warburg Ltd.**
"Shooting an Elephant" from Shooting an Elephant and Other Essays by George Orwell, copyright 1950 by Sonia Brownell Orwell; renewed 1978 by Sonia Pitt-Rivers. Reprinted by permission.

**Harcourt Brace Jovanovich, Inc., The Hogarth Press Ltd., and the author's Estate**
"The Lady in the Looking Glass: A Reflection" from A Haunted House and Other Stories by Virginia Woolf, copyright 1944 by Harcourt Brace Jovanovich, Inc. and renewed 1972 by Harcourt Brace Jovanovich, Inc. and in England from The Complete Shorter Fiction of Virginia Woolf edited by Susan Dick, copyright © 1985 by Quentin Bell and Angelica Garnett. Reprinted by permission.

**Harper & Row, Publishers, Inc.**
"Woman" from The Works of Oliver Goldsmith edited by Peter Cunningham, Harper & Brothers. "The Horses" from New Selected Poems by Ted Hughes. Copyright © 1957, 1982 by Ted Hughes. Reprinted by permission of Harper & Row, Publishers, Inc.

**Harper & Row, Publishers, Inc., and Faber and Faber Ltd.**
"Hawk Roosting" from New Selected Poems by Ted Hughes. Copyright © 1959, 1982 by Ted Hughes. Published in London in The Hawk In the Rain by Ted Hughes. Excerpt from "Fourth of July" from Lupercal by Ted Hughes. Copyright © 1960 by Ted Hughes. Copyright renewal © 1988 by Ted Hughes. Reprinted by permission of the publishers.

**Alan W. Holden**
"Some Men Create" from To Make Me Grieve by Molly Holden, Chatto and Windus Ltd. Exclusive copyright Alan Holden.

**Henry Holt and Company, Inc.**
"Loveliest of trees, the cherry now," "To an athlete dying young," "When I was one-and-twenty," and "With rue my heart is laden" from The Collected Poems of A. E. Housman. Copyright © 1939, 1940, 1965 by Holt, Rinehart and Winston, Inc. Copyright © 1967, 1968 by Robert E. Symons. Reprinted by permission of Henry Holt and Company, Inc.

**Houghton Mifflin Company**
Lines from "Childe Harold's Pilgrimage" ("Apostrophe to the Ocean"), lines from "Don Juan," "She Walks in Beauty," and "So We'll Go No More A-Roving" reprinted from The Complete Poetical Works of Lord Byron. From "A Voyage to Brobdingnag" and from "A Voyage to Lilliput" reprinted from Gulliver's Travels and Other Writings by Jonathan Swift, edited by Louis A. Landa. Riverside Edition. Copyright © 1960 by Houghton Mifflin Company. Used by permission.

**Olwyn Hughes**
"Anniversary" and "Out" from The Magic Apple Tree by Elaine Feinstein. Copyright © 1971 by Elaine Feinstein. Reprinted by permission of Olwyn Hughes.

**Alfred A. Knopf, Inc.**
"The Demon Lover" copyright 1946 and renewed 1974 by Elizabeth Bowen. Reprinted from The Demon Lover and Other Stories by Elizabeth Bowen. "A Dill Pickle" copyright 1920 by Alfred A. Knopf, Inc. and renewed 1948 by John Middleton Murry. Reprinted from The Short Stories of Katherine Mansfield by Katherine Mansfield. Specified excerpt from Grendel by John Gardner. Copyright © 1971 by John Gardner. Reprinted by permission of Alfred A. Knopf, Inc.

**Little, Brown and Company, in association with The Atlantic Monthly Press**
"A Touch of Autumn in the Air" from The Collected Stories of

*Sean O'Faolain* by Sean O'Faolain. Copyright © 1962 by Sean O'Faolain. Reprinted by permission.

**Louisiana State University Press**
"A Birthday" reprinted from *The Complete Poems of Christina Rossetti*, Volume I, edited by R. W. Crump. Copyright © 1979 by Louisiana State University Press.

**Macmillan London Ltd.**
"A Song for St. Cecilia's Day" from *The Poetical Works of John Dryden* edited by W. D. Christie. "The Three Strangers" from *Wessex Tales* by Thomas Hardy.

**Macmillan Publishing Company**
"Ah, Are You Digging on My Grave?," "The Darkling Thrush," and "The Man He Killed" from *The Complete Poems of Thomas Hardy* edited by James Gibson (New York: Macmillan, 1978). This collection was published outside the U.S. by Macmillan (London) Ltd. in 1976. "The Lake Isle of Innisfree" and "When You Are Old"; "An Irish Airman Foresees His Death" and "The Wild Swans at Coole" copyright 1919 by Macmillan Publishing Company, renewed 1947 by Bertha Georgie Yeats; "The Second Coming" copyright 1924 by Macmillan Publishing Company, renewed 1952 by Bertha Georgie Yeats; "Sailing to Byzantium" copyright 1928 by Macmillan Publishing Company, renewed 1956 by Bertha Georgie Yeats; and "After Long Silence" copyright 1933 by Macmillan Publishing Company, renewed 1961 by Bertha Georgie Yeats. All poems reprinted with permission from *The Poems of W. B. Yeats: A New Edition,* edited by Richard J. Finneran (New York: Macmillan, 1983).

**The Marvell Press**
"Coming" by Philip Larkin is reprinted from *The Less Deceived* by Philip Larkin, by permission of The Marvell Press, England.

**Methuen & Company Ltd.**
"The Passionate Shepherd to His Love" and lines from *The Tragical History of the Life and Death of Dr. Faustus* from *Marlowe's Poems* edited by L. C. Martin. Lines from "An Essay on Man," "Canto III," and lines from "Canto V" reprinted from *The Poems of Alexander Pope* edited by John Butt. Published by Methuen & Co. Ltd., London.

**New American Library, a division of Penguin Books U.S.A. Inc.**
From *Beowulf* translated by Burton Raffel. Copyright © 1963 by Burton Raffel. From *The Tragedy of Macbeth* by William Shakespeare, edited by Sylvan Barnet. Copyright © 1963 by Sylvan Barnet. *The Tempest* by William Shakespeare, edited by Robert Langaum and Sylvan Barnet. Copyright © 1987 by Robert Langaum and Sylvan Barnet. Reprinted by arrangement with New American Library, a division of Penguin Books U.S.A. Inc., New York, New York.

**New Directions Publishing Corporation**
Lines from "In the Park," lines from "The Galloping Cat," and lines from "My Muse" from Stevie Smith, *The Collected Poems of Stevie Smith.* Copyright © 1972 by Stevie Smith. "Not Waving but Drowning" and "Pretty" from Stevie Smith, *The Collected Poems of Stevie Smith.* Copyright © 1972 by

Stevie Smith. Reprinted by permission of New Directions Publishing Corporation.

**New Directions Publishing Corporation and David Higham Associates Ltd.**
"Do Not Go Gentle into That Good Night," "Fern Hill," and "The Force That Through the Green Fuse Drives the Flower" from Dylan Thomas, *The Poems of Dylan Thomas.* Copyright 1939 by New Directions Publishing Corporation. Copyright 1945 by the Trustees for the Copyrights of Dylan Thomas. Copyright 1952 by Dylan Thomas. Published in London by J. M. Dent & Sons Ltd. Reprinted by permission.

**W. W. Norton & Company, Inc.**
Reprinted from *Sir Gawain and the Green Knight, A New Verse Translation* by Marie Borroff, by permission of W. W. Norton & Company, Inc. Copyright © 1967 by W. W. Norton & Company, Inc.

**Oxford University Press**
"The Wanderer" from *An Anthology of Old English Poetry,* translated by Charles W. Kennedy. Copyright 1960 by Oxford University Press, Inc.; renewed 1988 by Elizabeth D. Kennedy. Reprinted by permission of Oxford University Press.

**Oxford University Press, Inc. and A. P. Watt Ltd. on behalf of the Executors of the Estate of Robert Graves**
"Interruption," "One Hard Look," and "She Tells Her Love . . ." from *Collected Poems* by Robert Graves. Copyright © 1975 in this edition by Robert Graves. Reprinted by permission.

**Oxford University Press, England**
"A Poison Tree," "Holy Thursday," "Infant Sorrow," "The Human Abstract," "The Lamb," and "The Tiger" from *The Poetical Works of William Blake* edited by John Sampson. From "The Life of Samuel Johnson" in *Boswell's Life of Johnson* by James Boswell, edited by C. B. Tinker. From *Wuthering Heights* by Emily Brontë, edited by H. W. Garrod. "Sonnet 43" from *The Poetical Works of Elizabeth Barrett Browning,* Oxford Edition. "Kubla Khan" and "The Rime of the Ancient Mariner" from *The Poems of Samuel Taylor Coleridge.* "Easter Wings," "Man," and "Virtue" from *The Poems of George Herbert,* edited by Helen Gardner. "An Ode for Him" and "To the Virgins, to Make Much of Time" from *The Poems of Robert Herrick* edited by L. C. Martin. "God's Grandeur," "Hurrahing in Harvest," "Pied Beauty," and "Spring and Fall" from *Poems of Gerard Manley Hopkins,* 4th edition, edited by W. H. Gardner and N. H. MacKenzie. "Letter to Lord Chesterfield" from *The Letters of Samuel Johnson,* Volume I: 1719–1774, collected and edited by R. W. Chapman. "Dream Children: A Reverie" from *The Works of Charles Lamb* edited by Thomas Hutchinson. "To Althea" and "To Lucasta, On Going to the Wars" from *The Poems of Richard Lovelace* edited by C. H. Wilkinson. "Sonnet 31" and "Sonnet 39" from *The Poems of Sir Philip Sidney* edited by William A. Ringler, Jr. Lines from "The Faerie Queen," "Sonnet 1," "Sonnet 26," and "Sonnet 75" from *The Poetical Works of Edmund Spenser* edited by J. C. Smith and E. de Selincourt. From "Thoughts on Various Subjects" in *Satires and Personal Writings* by Jonathan Swift, edited by William Alfred Eddy. "Crossing the Bar," lines from "In

Memoriam A.H.H.," "Tears, Idle Tears," "The Lady of Shalott," "The Lotos-Eaters," lines from "The Princess' ("The Splendor Falls"), and "Ulysses" from *Alfred Tennyson: Poetical Works.*

**Pantheon Books, a division of Random House, Inc.**
From "The Preface" and from "A Dictionary of the English Language" by Samuel Johnson in *Johnson's Dictionary: A Modern Selection* edited by E. L. McAdam, Jr. and George Milne.

**Penguin Books Ltd.**
"The Nun's Priest's Tale" from *The Canterbury Tales* by Geoffrey Chaucer, translated by Nevill Coghill (Penguin Classics, Revised Edition, 1977), copyright © Nevill Coghill, 1951, 1958, 1960, 1975, 1977. Reprinted by permission of Penguin Books Ltd. From *A History of the English Church and People* by Venerable Bede, translated with an introduction by Leo Sherley-Price, revised by R. E. Latham (Penguin Classics, 1955, 1965, 1968), copyright © Leo Sherley-Price, 1955, 1965, 1968, copyright © R. E. Latham, 1968, pp. 37–40. "The Prologue" and 238 lines from "The Pardoner's Tale" from *The Canterbury Tales* by Geoffrey Chaucer, translated into modern English by Nevill Coghill (Penguin Classics, 1951, 1958, 1960), copyright © Nevill Coghill 1951, 1958, 1960, pp. 19–41, 268–274. Reprinted by permission of Penguin Books Ltd.

**Peters Fraser & Dunlop Group Ltd.**
"A Voyage to Cythera" by Margaret Drabble, published in *Mademoiselle* Magazine, December 1967. Reprinted by permission of the Peters Fraser & Dunlop Group Ltd.

**Kathleen Raine**
Lines from "In the Beck" from *The Collected Poems of Kathleen Raine* by Kathleen Raine. © Copyright 1956 by Kathleen Raine. Reprinted by permission of the author.

**Random House, Inc.**
from *Jane Eyre* by Charlotte Brontë. "Holy Sonnet 10," "Holy Sonnet 14," "Meditation 17," and "Song" from *Complete Poetry and Selected Prose of John Donne* by John Donne, edited by John Hayward. Excerpt from "Chard Whitlow" from *Parodies,* edited by Dwight Macdonald. Copyright 1960 by Dwight Macdonald.

**Random House, Inc. and Faber and Faber Ltd.**
"In Memory of W.B. Yeats" and "Musée des Beaux Arts" copyright 1940 and renewed 1968 by W. H. Auden. Reprinted from *W. H. Auden: Collected Poems* by W. H. Auden, edited by Edward Mendelson. "What I Expected" copyright 1934 and renewed 1962 by Stephen Spender. Reprinted from *Collected Poems 1928–1985* by Stephen Spender. Reprinted by permission of the publishers.

**Routledge & Kegan Paul, Associated Book Publishers (U.K.) Ltd.**
"The Picture of Little T.C. in a Prospect of Flowers" and "To His Coy Mistress" from *The Poems of Andrew Marvell* edited by Hugh MacDonald. "For Doreen: A Voice from the Garden" from *Collected Poems 1950–1970* by Donald Davie. Copyright © Donald Davie 1972. Reprinted by permission.

**Simon & Schuster, Inc.**
"The Truth about George" from *The Most of P. G. Wodehouse* by P. G. Wodehouse. Copyright © 1960 by Pelham Grenville Wodehouse. Reprinted by permission of Simon & Schuster, Inc. Pronunciation key from *Webster's New World Dictionary*—Second College Edition. Copyright © 1984 by Simon & Schuster, Inc. Reprinted by permission.

**The Society of Authors on behalf of the Estate of Bernard Shaw**
*Pygmalion* by Bernard Shaw. Copyright 1913, 1914, 1916, 1930, 1941, 1944 George Bernard Shaw. Copyright 1957 The Public Trustee as Executor of the Estate of George Bernard Shaw. Reprinted by permission.

**The University of Chicago Press and Faber and Faber Ltd.**
Lines from "Positives" in *Positives: Verses* by Thom Gunn. Copyright © 1967 by Tom Gunn. Reprinted by permission of the publishers.

**University of Nebraska Press**
"The Seafarer" reprinted from *Poems From the Old English,* translated, with an introduction by Burton Raffel, by permission of University of Nebraska Press. Copyright © 1960, 1964, by the University of Nebraska Press.

**Viking Penguin Inc.**
"The Train from Rhodesia" from *Selected Stories* by Nadine Gordimer. Copyright 1952 by Nadine Gordimer. "Snake" from *The Complete Poems of D. H. Lawrence* edited by Vivian de Sola Pinto and F. Warren Roberts. Copyright © 1964, 1971 by Angelo Ravagli and C. M. Weekley, Executors of the Estate of Frieda Lawrence Ravagli. "The Rocking-Horse Winner" from *The Complete Short Stories of D. H. Lawrence,* Vol. III. Copyright 1933 by the Estate of D. H. Lawrence; copyright renewed © 1961 by Angelo Ravagli and C. M. Weekley, Executors of the Estate of Frieda Lawrence Ravagli. "The Schartz-Metterklume Method" from *The Complete Short Stories of Saki* by Saki (H. H. Munro). Copyright 1930, renewed © 1958 by The Viking Press, Inc. "Sonnet 29," "Sonnet 73," "Sonnet 116," and "Sonnet 130" from *William Shakespeare: The Complete Works* edited by Alfred Harbage. Copyright © 1969 by Penguin Books, Inc. Reprinted by permission of Viking Penguin Inc.

**Viking Penguin Inc., Jonathan Cape Ltd., and the Executors of the James Joyce Estate**
"Araby" from *Dubliners* by James Joyce. Copyright 1916 by B. W. Huebsch. Definitive text copyright © 1967 by the Estate of James Joyce. Reprinted by permission.

**Viking Penguin Inc. and John Johnson Ltd.**
"The Distant Past" from *Angels at the Ritz and Other Stories* by William Trevor. Copyright © 1973 by William Trevor. Reprinted by permission.

**Viking Penguin Inc. and Laurence Pollinger Ltd.**
"Across the Bridge" from *Nineteen Stories* by Graham Greene. Copyright 1947, renewed © 1975 by Graham Greene. Published in London in *Collected Stories* by Graham

Greene by William Heinemann, Ltd. and The Bodley Head Ltd. Reprinted by permission.

**Viking Penguin Inc. and George Sassoon**
"Wirers" from *The Colleted Poems of Siegfried Sassoon* by Siegfried Sassoon. Copyright 1918 by E. P. Dutton Co. Copyright renewed 1946 by Siegfried Sassoon. Reprinted by permission.

**Wallace & Sheil Agency, Inc. and Tessa Sayle Agency, London**
"The Fiddle" from *The Second Chance and Other Stories* by Alan Sillitoe. Copyright © 1981 by Alan Sillitoe.


*Note:* Every effort has been made to locate the copyright owner of material reprinted in this book. Omissions brought to our attention will be corrected in subsequent editions.

# ART CREDITS

Cover and Title Page: *The Sisters,* 1900, Ralph Peacock, The Tate Gallery, London, Art Resource (N1772); **p. 1:** Bayeux Tapestry: Norman Cavalry Charge at the Shieldwall at the Battle of Hastings, The Granger Collection; **p. 3:** Religious Ceremony of the Druids, Forrest C. Crooks, Three Lions; **pp. 4, 5:** Stonehenge, D. E. Szymanski/D.P.I.; St. Augustine, Giuseppe Ribera/Three Lions; A Viking Sword, Viking, X Century, Sword, Iron, copper and silver, the Metropolitan Museum of Art, Rogers Fund, 1955, Copyright © 1980/87 by The Metropolitan Museum of Art; Danes Attacking a British Town, English ms., illumination c. 1130, The Granger Collection; Buddha Addressing a Disciple, The Granger Collection; The Coronation of William the Conqueror, ms. illumination c. 1470, The Granger Collection; A Roman Town After the Fall of the Empire, Roman Town at the Foot of the Alps After the Conquest by the Gauls, Octave Penguilly-L'Haridon, Three Lions; Charles Martel Battling the Moors, The Granger Collection; King Charlemagne, jeweled gold reliquary bust, c. 1350, Domschatz, Aachen, The Granger Collection; **p. 6:** Insignia of the Roman Civil Governor in Charge of the Five British Provinces, early 15th-century copy of a page from the now-lost Notitia Dignitatum Utriusque Imperii, a 4th-century list of the symbols of their provinces, The Granger Collection; **p. 8:** Saxons, Jutes, and Angles Arriving in Britain by Sea, English manuscript illumination, The Granger Collection; **p. 9:** An English Monk Exactly Contemporary with Bede, illumination from an early 8th-century Northumbrian codex, The Granger Collection; **p. 10:** The 9th-Century Oseberg Viking Ship, The Granger Collection; **p. 11:** Alfred the Great Acknowledged as King by All Men of England, 871 A.D., Three Lions; Page from an Early 12th-Century Manuscript of the *Anglo-Saxon Chronicle* Describing the Norman Conquest, The Granger Collection; **p. 12:** The Bayeux Tapestry: Edward the Confessor Speaks to Harold of Wessex, The Granger Collection; **p. 14:** A Page from the Caedmon Manuscript, c. 1000, The Granger Collection; **p. 18:** Ships with Three Men, Fish, ms. Ashmole 1511, folio 86 verso, Bodleian Library, Oxford; **p. 20:** (detail), see credit for p. 18; **p. 22:** Statens Historiska Museet, Stockholm, Werner Forman Archive; **p. 25:** The Dragon for "The High Kings," George Sharp; **p. 28:** Arthur Going to Avalon for "The High Kings"

(detail), George Sharp; **p. 34:** The So-Called "Sigurd's Helmet," Statens Historiska Museet, Stockholm, Werner Forman Archive; Coins Depicting Viking Longships, Statens Historiska Museet, Stockholm, Werner Forman Archive; The Gokstad Ship, Viking Ships, Museum, Bygdøy, Oslo, Werner Forman Archive; **p. 35:** Head of Carved Post from the Ship Burial at Oseberg, Werner Forman Archive; Helmet, Statens Historiska Museet, Stockholm, Werner Forman Archive; Golden Horns, National Museet Copenhagen, photo by Lennard Larsen; **p. 41:** *Slaying of a Bull on the base of a Cauldron, 100 B.C.,* Werner Forman Archive/National Museum, Copenhagen; **p. 42:** *Handle fixture of a bucket,* Celtic/Viking, Werner Forman Archive; **p. 43:** *Detail of a dragon head on the Mammen horse collar,* Viking, 10th century, Werner Forman Archive; **p. 44:** *Gilt-bronze winged dragon—bridal mounting,* 8th century, Werner Forman Archive/Statens Historiska Museet, Stockholm; **p. 47:** *Gilt silver brooch,* Viking migration period, Werner Forman Archive/Statens Historiska Museet, Stockholm; **p. 48:** *Silver pendant showing the helmet of the Vendel,* Viking 10th century, Werner Forman Archive/Statens Historiska Museet, Stockholm; **p. 49:** *The Oseberg Ship,* Viking, c. A.D. 850, Werner Forman Archive/Viking Ship Museum, Bygdøy, Oslo; **p. 53:** *Beowulf,* ms. page, The British Museum/The Bettmann Archive (p. 3955) (7779); **p. 55:** "Grendel" Frontispiece from *Beowulf,* 1908, Pattern Wilson, The British Library; **p. 57:** *Serra flying over a boat,* illumination from an English bestiary, c. 1185, The Granger Collection; **p. 59:** *Sutton Hoo Ship Burial,* A.D. 7th century, The Granger Collection; **p. 62:** (detail) and **p. 65:** Cotton ms. Tiberius C. II Folio 5 Verso, Page of Bede's History, The British Library; **p. 66:** Monks, ms. University College, 165 piii, Bodleian Library, Oxford; **p. 69:** *The Anglo Saxon Chronicle* (Ms. Cott TIB B1. Fol 132), The British Museum; **p. 72:** Pilgrims to Canterbury: Detail of an English illuminated manuscript, c. 1400, The Granger Collection; **p. 74:** Bayeux Tapestry: Duke William Encourages His Men at Hastings by Raising His Helmet, The Granger Collection; **p. 75:** A bailiff supervising the harvest (the month of August): Manuscript illumination, English, early 14th century, The Granger Collection; **pp. 76, 77:** The Murder of Thomas Becket, illumination from an English psalter, c. 1200, The Granger Collection; King John Signs the Magna Carta, The Granger Collection; Pope Gregory IX, mosaic head from the Old Basilica of St. Peter, The Granger Collection; The Siege of Jerusalem During the First Crusade, late 13th-century French ms. illumination, The Granger Collection; Roger Bacon, mid-15th-century Italian ms. illumination, The Granger Collection; Genghis Khan, Chinese silk album leaf, Yuan Dynasty; Manuscript of the Song of Roland, Anglo-Norman text from a 12th-century English ms., The Granger Collection; Twelfth-century Chess Piece, The Granger Collection; **pp. 78, 79:** François Villon (1431–after 1463), colored woodcut from the Grand Testament de Maitre François Villon, Paris, 1489, The Granger Collection; Printer's Device Used by Caxton, The Granger Collection; Marco Polo Entering Peking, 14th-century miniature from the Livre de Merveilles, The Granger Collection; Joan of Arc at the Coronation of Charles VII, canvas, 1854, by J. A. D. Ingres, The Granger Collection; Johann Gutenberg Printing First Bible, The Granger Collection; Black Death Sweeps Through England, Fear of plague in house of Fitzeisulf (detail) Trinity Chapel window, Canterbury Cathedral, 14th century, The Granger Collection; Canterbury Tales, The beginning of the prologue to Chaucer's Canterbury Tales, a 15th-century ms. page, The Granger Collection; *Battle During the Hundred Years' War, Battle of Poitiers*, Eugene Delacroix, Three Lions; **p. 81:** King John signing Magna Carter at Runnymede, 15th June 1215, colored engraving, 18th century, The Granger Collection; Four Kings of England depicted on a page of a 13th-century manuscript, The Granger Collection; **p. 82:** Funeral of plague victim in House of Fitzeisulf Trinity Chapel Window, Canterbury Cathedral, 14th century, The Granger Collection; **p. 83:** King Henry VII of England, panel, 1505, by Michiel Sittow, The Granger Collection; **p. 84:** *Sir Galahad,* 1864 (watercolor), Dante Gabriel Rossetti, The Granger Collection; **p. 85:** Johann Gutenberg examining the first proof his printed Bible from his press at Mainz, after the painting by J. L. G. Ferris (detail), The Granger Collection; **p. 86:** A page from the Lansdowne ms of Geoffrey Chaucer's *Canterbury Tales,* The Granger Collection; **p. 87:** *Robin Hood,* 1852, Richard Dadd, Yale Center for British Art, Paul Mellon Collection; **p. 94:** The Nine Heroes Tapestries, Christian Heroes: Arthur with Three Cardinals, Detail: Arthur, upper half, probably Nicolas Bataille, Paris, The Metropolitan Museum of Art, The Cloisters Collection, Munsey Fund, 1932, © Copyright 1985 by the Metropolitan Museum of Art, **p. 104:** Medieval Baron Dining, from *Breviarium Grimari,* 15th century, The Bettmann Archive; **p. 112:** *Veronica Veronese,* Dante Gabriel Rossetti, Delaware Art Museum, Samuel and Mary Bancroft Memorial Collection; **p. 114:** Geoffrey Chaucer, unknown artist, The Granger Collection; **p. 118:** The Tabard Inn, Arthur Szyk for *The Canterbury Tales,* The George Macy Companies; **p. 121:** The Yeoman, Arthur Szyk for *The Canterbury Tales,* The George Macy Companies; **p. 123:** The Monk, Arthur Szyk for *The Canterbury Tales,* The George Macy Companies; **p. 126:** The Student, Arthur Szyk for *The Canterbury Tales,* The George Macy Companies; **p. 130:** The Wife of Bath, Arthur Szyk for *The Canterbury Tales,* The George Macy Companies; **p. 143:** *English Travelers Setting Forth from Chaucer's Canterbury Tales,* Trustees of the British Library, (Roy 18.0.11 f.148 detail); **p. 146:** *Woman Feeding Chicken,* (Cod. ser. nov. 2644, fol. 65) Italian manuscript, Osterreichische National Bibliothek, Bild-archiv und Portrat-sammlung; **p. 151:** *The Nun's Priest* from *The Canterbury Tales* by Chaucer, The Huntington Library, San Marino, California; **p. 153:** *Chaucer reciting Troilus and Cressida before a court gathering (frontpiece),* Corpus Christi College; **p. 154:** *Chaucer's Canterbury Pilgrims,* 1810, William Blake, The Huntington Library, San Marino, California; **p. 162:** The Pardoner, Arthur Szyk for *The Canterbury Tales,* The George Macy Companies; **p. 166:** *World Map: Cathay and the Empire of the Great Khan,* 1459, Mauro, Biblioteca Nazionale Marciana, Venice/E. T. Archive; **p. 167:** *A Medieval View of the Universe,* © Ronald Sheridan, Ancient Art and Architecture Collection; **p. 171:** From *The Romance of King Arthur and His Knights of the Round Table,* Arthur Rackham, Weathervane Books; **p. 177:** Sir Gawain and the Green Knight, ms Douce 199, folio 157 verso, The Bodleian Library, Oxford; **p. 183:** Gawain Receiving the Green Girdle, woodcut by Fritz Kredel from Gardner, *The Complete Works of the Gawain Poet* © 1965, The University of Chicago; **p. 194:** *The Old Man and Death,* c. 1774, Joseph Wright of Derby, Wadsworth Atheneum, Hartford, Ella Gallup Sumner and Mary Catlin Sumner Collection, © Wadsworth Atheneum; **p. 196:** *Bayeux Tapestry/The Normans Attack the English,* Michael Holford; **p. 197:** Begining of the prologue to *Canter-*

*bury Tales,* 15th century ms. page, The Granger Collection; **p. 200–01:** *Queen Elizabeth and Sir Walter Raleigh,* Charles Edouard Boutibonne, Three Lions; **p. 203:** *Mona Lisa,* Leonardo da Vinci, Three Lions; **pp. 204–05:** *Sir Thomas More with His Family,* The Granger Collection; *Queen Elizabeth I,* The Granger Collection; *Copernicus's Treatise of Astronomy,* The Granger Collection; *The Last Supper,* Leonardo Da Vinci, Three Lions; *Columbus Sets Sail from Spain,* The Granger Collection; *English Navy Attacking Spanish Armada,* The Granger Collection; London, c. 1558, The Granger Collection; Francisco Pizarro, The Granger Collection; **pp. 206–07:** Globe Theatre, The Granger Collection; *Galileo,* The Granger Collection; *The Pilgrims Land at Plymouth Rock,* The Granger Collection; *Cervantes,* The Granger Collection; Engraving of William Shakespeare by Martin Droeshout on title page of the First Folio, 1623, The Granger Collection; Pieter Bruegel the Elder, *Wedding Dance in the Open Air,* Panel, 1566, The Granger Collection; *Akbar the Great,* Indian Mughal miniature by Manohar, c. 1600, The Granger Collection; **p. 208:** *Portrait of Erasmus,* Hans Holbein, National Gallery, Parma, Scala/Art Resource; **p. 209:** Martin Luther Fastening His 95 Theses on the Door of All Saints Church, Wittenburg, Germany, on 31 October, 1517, 19th-century engraving, The Granger Collection; **p. 210:** *King Henry VII of England,* Hans Holbein, The Granger Collection; **p. 211:** *Queen Elizabeth I of England,* c. 1588, by or after George Gower, The Granger Collection; **p. 212:** Queen Elizabeth I Knighting Francis Drake on Board the *Golden Hind* at Deptford, 4 April 1581, 19th-century engraving, The Granger Collection; The Launching of Fire ships Against the Spanish Armada, National Maritime Museum, Greenwich, England; **p. 214:** *Sir Walter Raleigh,* N. Hilliard, Three Lions; **p. 215:** *William Shakespeare,* artist unknown, Three Lions; **p. 216:** Title Page of the First Edition of the King James Bible, London, 1611, The Granger Collection; **p. 219:** *View of a Park, with Huntsmen and Deer,* Peter Tillemans, Victoria & Albert Museum Trustees; **p. 220:** The Granger Collection; **p. 222:** Sir Philip Sidney (detail), c. 1576, unknown artist, by courtesy of the National Portrait Gallery, London; **p. 225:** *Shepherds Under a Full Moon,* Samuel Palmer, c. 1830, © Ashmolean Museum, Oxford; **p. 228:** The Granger Collection; **p. 230:** The Hireling Shepherd, William Holman Hunt, The Manchester City Art Galleries; **p. 236:** *Sir Walter Raleigh* (detail), unknown artist, The Granger Collection; **p. 241:** *Portrait of an Unknown Man,* Nicholas Hilliard, Victoria & Albert Museum Trustees; **p. 242:** The Granger Collection; **p. 248:** New York Public Library, Picture Collection; **p. 252:** *William Shakespeare,* unknown artist, by courtesy of the National Portrait Gallery, London; **p. 256:** *The Sonnet,* William Mulready, Victoria & Albert Museum Trustees; **p. 263:** *The Woodcutter Courting the Milkmaid,* Thomas Gainsborough, Woburn Abbey, by kind permission of the Marquess of Tavistock, and the Trustees of the Bedford Estates; **p. 267:** The Granger Collection; **p. 272:** *The Three Witches,* Henry Fuseli, Courtauld Institute Galleries, London (Witt Collection No. 4533); **p. 277:** *Macbeth and the Witches,* Clarkson Stanfield, Leicestershire Museums, Art Galleries and Records Service; **p. 287:** *Scene from Macbeth,* Cattermole, from the art collection of the Folger Shakespeare Library; **p. 293:** *Ellen Terry as Lady Macbeth,* 1889, John Singer Sargent, The Tate Gallery, on loan to the National Portrait Gallery, London; **p. 298:** *Lady Macbeth Seizing the Daggers,* Henry Fuseli, The Tate Gallery, London; **p. 310:**

Wood engraving after Sir John Gilbert, The Granger Collection; **p. 325:** Macbeth and the Witches, engraved by Thew after Reynolds, Royal Academy of Arts, London; **p. 328:** Wood engraving after Sir John Gilbert, The Granger Collection; **p. 340:** *Mrs. Siddons as Lady Macbeth*, Garrick Club/G. H. Harlow; **p. 352:** *Delacroix as Hamlet*, Delacroix, Paris, Louvre/Giraudon/Art Resource (CFL 2050) (617P6); **p. 353:** *Ophelia, 1852,* Sir John Everett Millais, The Tate Gallery, London/Bridgeman/Art Resource (2078) (617P7); **p. 354:** *Hamlet and Horacio,* Delacroix, Paris, Louvre/Giraudon/Art Resource (LAC46564) (617P5) **p. 355:** *The Play Scene in Hamlet,* Exh1842, Daniel Maclise, The Tate Gallery, London/Art Resource (N422) (617P10); **p. 356:** *Francis Bacon* (detail), John Vanderbank, 1731 copy of painting c. 1618, by courtesy of the National Portrait Gallery, London; **p. 360:** "The Cosmographical Glasse," London, 1559 (p. 50), from William Cuningham, The Huntington Library at San Marino, California; **p. 365:** King James Bible, 1611, title page of the New Testament, by permission of the Folger Shakespeare Library; **p. 369:** Letters Patent from Elizabeth I to Francis Drake, 1687, E. T. Archive; **pp. 372–73:** *The Thames at Westminster Stairs,* 1631 or 1637, Claude de Jongh, c. 1631 or 1637, Yale Center for British Art, Paul Mellon Collection; **pp. 376–77:** *Francis Bacon,* John Vanderbank, 1731 copy of painting, c. 1618, by courtesy of the National Portrait Gallery, London; *Execution of King Charles I of England, 30 January 1649,* contemporary painting by "Weeson," The Granger Collection; John Milton, engraved from an original by William Faithorne, The Bettmann Archive; *The Night Watch,* Rembrandt van Rijn, Three Lions; *Covent Garden Market,* Three Lions; *New Amsterdam,* The Granger Collection; *Molière at Extreme Left with French and Italian Comedians,* oil attributed to Verio, 1670, The Granger Collection; *King Louis XIV,* canvas by Hyacinthe Rigaud, The Granger Collection; *Andrew Marvell,* oil on canvas, c. 1655–60 by an unknown artist, The Granger Collection; **p. 378:** *Portrait of Charles I,* Anthony Van Dyck, The Louvre, Paris, Art Resource; **p. 380:** *The Execution of King Charles I of England at Whitehall, London, January 30, 1649,* colored woodcut from contemporary balladsheet, The Granger Collection; **p. 382:** *Oliver Cromwell,* Sir Peter Lely (Peter Van der Faes), Firenze, Galleria Palatina, Art Resource; **p. 383:** *Ben Jonson,* The Granger Collection; **p. 385:** *John Donne,* The Granger Collection; **p. 387:** *George Herbert,* The Granger Collection; **p. 392:** *Shakespeare and Ben Jonson at Chess,* Karel van Mander, photo courtesy of William M. deHeyman, Philadelphia, Pennsylvania; **p. 395:** *Greenwich Palace from the Northeast with a Man-of-War at Anchor* (detail), c. 1630, National Maritime Museum; **p. 396:** *John Donne,* oil on canvas after Isaac Oliver, The Granger Collection; **p. 401:** *Sir Thomas Aston at the Deathbed of His Wife,* John Souch, Manchester City Art Galleries; **p. 408:** *George Herbert,* The Granger Collection; **p. 411:** *The Milkmaid,* Myles Birket Foster, Victoria & Albert Museum Trustees, Bridgeman/Art Resource; **p. 416:** *Andrew Marvell,* oil on canvas, c. 1655–60, unknown artist, The Granger Collection; **p. 422:** *Ben Jonson,* oil on canvas (detail), after Abraham van Blyenberch, The Granger Collection; **p. 427:** *Marriage à la Mode IV: The Countess's Morning Levée* (detail), William Hogarth, National Gallery, London; **p. 428:** New York Public Library Picture Collection; **p. 433:** *Three Ladies Adorning a Term of Hymen,* 1773, Sir Joshua Reynolds, The Tate Gallery, London; **p. 434:** (top) *Sir John Suckling,* Anthony Van Dyck, The Granger Collection; (bottom) *Richard Lovelace,* The Granger Collection; **p. 436:** Boucher, François, *The Interrupted Sleep,* The Metropolitan Museum of Art, The Jules Bach Collection 1949, © Copyright 1984 by The Metropolitan Museum of Art; **p. 437:** *Fair Is My Love* (detail), Edwin A. Abbey, The Harris Museum and Art Gallery, Preston; **p. 438:** Edward Burne-Jones, *Going to the Battle,* 1858, Fitzwilliam Museum, Cambridge; **p. 441:** *The Farrier's Shop,* c. 1620–87, Gael Barend, Guildhall Art Gallery, London, Bridgeman/Art Resource; **p. 442:** *John Milton,* c. 1629, detail of painting by an unknown artist, The Granger Collection; **p. 454:** *Paradise Lost,* 1688, angels/devil/death figures, John Milton, from the British Library; **p. 459:** *The Garden of Eden,* Erastus S. Field, Superstock; **p. 460:** John Bunyan, The Granger Collection; **p. 463:** Pilgrim's Progress (angels, pilgrim, knight figures), John Bunyan, The British Library; **p. 466:** *Captain John Smith (1580–1631): detail from Smith's Map of Virginia, 1616,* The Granger Collection; **pp. 470–71:** Morville Hall, Shropshire, John Inigo Richards, Roy Miles Fine Paintings, London, Bridgeman/Art Resource; **p. 474–75:** Palace at Versailles, Painting by Pierre Patel, The Granger Collection; The Syndics, Rembrandt, Three Lions; Samuel Pepys, painting by John Hayls, 1666, The Granger Collection; The Great Fire of London, 1666 Contemporary painting, Dutch School, The Granger Collection; John Locke (1632–1704), detail of oil on canvas, 1704, after Sir G. Kneller, The Granger Collection; La Salle Received in the Village of the Caddo Indians, May 1686, oil on canvas by George Catlin, The Granger Collection; Major Port for Trade with China, Portuguese colony of Macao, colored engraving, 1598, The Granger Collection; Johann Sebastian Bach, Gustav Zerner, Three Lions; **pp. 476–77:** Illustration from Gulliver's Travels, The Granger Collection; The American Revolution Begins, The Granger Collection; *Robert Burns (1759–96),* oil on panel by Alexander Nasmyth, The Granger Collection; James Boswell talking to Samuel Johnson 'till near two in the morning', satirical caricature etching by Thomas Rowlandson, 1786, The Granger Collection; *Captain Cook Explores the South Pacific,* painting by William Hodges, The Granger Collection; The Storming of the Bastille, Gouache by Claude Cholat, an eyewitness, The Granger Collection; Benjamin Franklin, with his lightning detector, English mezzotint, 1763, by Edward Fisher, The Granger Collection; The Boston Tea Party, The Granger Collection; *W. A. Mozart (1756–91),* posthumous portrait by Johann Peter Krafft, The Granger Collection; **p. 474:** *Queen Anne and the Knights of the Garter, 1713,* Peter Angelis, The Granger Collection; **p. 479:** *King George III of England, c. 1760,* Allan Ramsay, The Granger Collection; **p. 488:** *A Philosopher Lecturing on the Orrery,* Joseph Wright of Derby, Derby Art Gallery; **p. 483:** *The Rake's Progress: No. 5, The Marriage,* William Hogarth, The Granger Collection; **p. 486:** *Sir Isaac Newton, c. 1726,* Attributed to John Vanderbank, The Granger Collection; **p. 491:** *The Election—The Polling,* William Hogarth, Sir John Soane's Museum, London, Bridgeman/Art Resource; **p. 492:** *John Dryden* (detail), J. Maubert, by courtesy of the National Portrait Gallery, London; **p. 495:** *Shakespeare and his Contemporaries,* John Faed, From the Collection of Mr. and Mrs. Sandor Korein; **p. 500:** *The Music of a Bygone Age,* John Melhuish Strudwick, The Pre-Raphaelite Trust, Bridgeman/Art Resource; **p. 504:** *Samuel Pepys (detail) c. 1695,* John Closterman, The Granger Collection; **p. 508:** *The Great Fire of London, 1666,* The Museum of London; **p. 511:** *Conversa-*

tion in a Park, Thomas Gainsborough, The Louvre, Paris, Giraudon/Art Resources; **p. 512:** The Bettmann Archive; **p. 514:** Journal of the Plague Year: The Dead Cart, The British Library; **p. 518:** *Jonathan Swift,* Charles Jervas, The Granger Collection; **p. 522:** Illustration by Willy Pogany, The Donnell Library Children's Room, The Research Libraries, New York Public Library, Astor, Lenox and Tilden Foundations; **p. 526:** Illustration by Willy Pogany, The Donnell Library Children's Room, The Research Libraries, New York Public Library, Astor, Lenox and Tilden Foundations; **pp. 532, 533, 534, 535:** Illustrations from *Robinson Crusoe,* 1920, N. C. Wyeth, The Granger Collection; **p. 536:** *Joseph Addison* (detail), Sir Geoffroy Kneller, The Granger Collection; *Sir Richard Steele (detail), 1712,* Jonathan Richardson, The Granger Collection; **p. 542:** St. Edmund's Chapel, Westminster Abbey, John Fulleylove; **p. 546:** *Alexander Pope (detail) c. 1738–43,* William Hoare, The Granger Collection; **p. 549:** *The Barge,* 1895–6, From *The Rape of the Lock,* Smithers, 1896, from *The Best of Beardsley,* collected and edited by R. A. Walker, copyright © 1948 by The Bodley Head, published in the USA by Excalibur Books, plate 63; **p. 552:** The Rape of the Lock, 1895–6, from The Rape of the Lock, Smithers, 1986, from The Best of Beardsley, collected and edited by R. A. Walker, copyright © 1948 by The Bodley Head, published in the USA by Excalibur Books, plate 64; **p. 557:** The Battle of the Beaux and Belles, Aubrey Beardsley, The Barber Institute of Fine Arts, The University of Birmingham; **p. 563:** Oliver Goldsmith, James Boswell, and Samuel Johnson At The Mitre Tavern, Nineteenth-century colored engraving, The Granger Collection; **p. 564:** *Samuel Johnson (detail) 1756,* Sir Joshua Reynolds, The Granger Collection; **p. 574:** *James Boswell (detail) 1785,* Sir Joshua Reynolds, The Granger Collection; **p. 577:** Johnson and Boswell, © The Trustees of the British Museum; **p. 583:** *Haymakers, 1785,* George Stubbs, The Granger Collection; **p. 584:** *Thomas Gray (detail) 1748,* J. G. Eccardt, The Granger Collection; **p. 592:** *Oliver Goldsmith (detail) c. 1770* Studio of J. Reynolds, The Granger Collection; **p. 594:** *Robert Burns,* A. Nasmyth, National Portrait Gallery, London; **p. 602:** *The River Dee Near Eton Hall,* Richard Wilson, The Barber Institute, The University of Birmingham; **p. 606:** *William Blake (detail) 1807,* Thomas Phillips, The Granger Collection; **p. 609:** From a manuscript of "The Lamb" by William Blake, Lessing J. Rosenwald Collection, Library of Congress, Washington, D.C.; **p. 610:** Blake, William, The Tyger, A page from Songs of Innocence and Experience, The Metropolitan Museum of Art, Rogers Fund, 1917, © 1984 by The Metropolitan Museum of Art; **p. 614:** From a manuscript of "A Poison Tree" by William Blake, Lessing J. Rosenwald Collection, Library of Congress, Washington, D.C.; **p. 617:** An Allegory of the Royal Society, Hollar, The Mansell Collection; **pp. 620–21:** *View in Hampshire,* Patrick Nasmyth Guild Hall Art Gallery, City of London, Bridgeman/Art Resource; **p. 622:** *Capture of the Bastille, July 14, 1789,* Claude Cholat, The Granger Collection; **pp. 624–25:** *William Wordsworth, (1770–1850),* oil on canvas 1842, by Benjamin Haydon, The Granger Collection; *Jane Austen,* The Granger Collection; 'The Meeting of Sir Walter Scott and Robert Burns', painting by C. M. Hardie, The Granger Collection; George Stephenson's Locomotive, The Granger Collection; Union Jack, The Granger Collection; Rosetta Stone, The Granger Collection; *Napoleon Bonaparte as First Consul,* J. A. Ingres, Three Lions; *Beethoven composing in his studio,* a late nineteenth-

century painting by Carl Schlosser, The Granger Collection; Robert Fulton's Steamboat, The Granger Collection; **pp. 626–27:** *John Keats Listening to the Nightingale on Hampstead Heath,* oil, c. 1845, by Joseph Severn, The Granger Collection; London in the 1820's, The Granger Collection; Charles Lamb, The Granger Collection; *The Grove, or Admiral's House, Hampstead,* oil on canvas, 1820 by John Constable, The Granger Collection; Liverpool-Manchester Railway, The Granger Collection; The Peterloo Massacre, The Granger Collection; The Last of the Mohicans, The Granger Collection; Savannah, the First Steamer to Cross the Atlantic, The Granger Collection; *Edgar Allan Poe,* Thomas C. Corner, Three Lions; **p. 628:** *The Battle of Trafalgar,* J. M. W. Turner, The Granger Collection; **p. 629:** (top) *Napoleon (The Campaign in France, 1814),* J. L. E. Meissonier, The Granger Collection; (bottom) *King William of England,* Sir Martin Archer Shee, The Granger Collection; **p. 630:** *Sketch for Hadleigh Castle, c. 1828–29,* John Constable, The Granger Collection; **p. 631:** *Rain, Steam and Speed—The Great Western Railway, Before 1844,* J. M. W. Turner, The Granger Collection; **p. 632:** *Portrait of Goethe,* Joseph Karl Steiler, Three Lions; **p. 633:** (top) *Calais Pier: An English Packet Arriving,* J. M. W. Turner, The Granger Collection; (bottom) *Samuel Taylor Coleridge,* Peter Vandyke, The Granger Collection; **p. 635:** *John Keats,* Joseph Severn, The Granger Collection; **p. 636:** *Sir Walter Scott/Abbotsford Family, 1804,* Sir David Wilkie, The Granger Collection; **p. 641:** *Salisbury Cathedral,* John Constable, Musea de Arte, São Paolo, Giraudon/Art Resource; **p. 642:** *William Wordsworth (detail) 1842),* Benjamin Haydon, The Granger Collection; **p. 645:** *Tintern Abbey,* J. M. W. Turner, Reproduced by Courtesy of the Trustees of the British Museum; **p. 650:** *Landscape With Rainbow,* Joseph Wright of Derby, Derby Art Collection; **p. 655:** *Cornfield by Moonlight,* Samuel Palmer, Reproduced by Courtesy of the Trustees of the British Museum; **p. 658:** *Samuel Taylor Coleridge* (detail), by Courtesy of the National Portrait Gallery, London; **pp. 663–73:** Engravings by Gustav Doré for The Rime of the Ancient Mariner, by Samuel Taylor Coleridge; **p. 687:** *Chinese Silk Album Leaf, Yuan Dynasty, Kublai Khan,* The Granger Collection; **p. 688:** *Lord Byron (detail),* William West, The Granger Collection; **p. 693:** *Shipwreck,* J. C. C. Dahl, Munich Neue Pinakothek/Kavaler, Kavaler/Art Resource; **p. 700:** *Percy Bysshe Shelley* (detail), A. Curran, The Granger Collection; **p. 705:** *Cirrus Cloud Study,* John Constable, Victoria & Albert Museum, Trustees; **p. 709:** *Cloud Study, 1821,* John Constable, Yale Center for British Art, Paul Mellon Collection; **p. 714:** *John Keats* (detail), Joseph Severn, The Granger Collection; **p. 717:** Frontispiece, Homer's Iliad and Odyssey, 1612, G. Chapman, The British Library; **p. 719:** *John Keats, 1821,* J. Severn, By Courtesy of the National Portrait Gallery, London; **p. 722:** *Small Bird on a Flowering Plum Branch,* The Goto Museum; **p. 727:** Greek Vase, terracotta c. 460 B.C., attributed to the Orchard Painter, Column Crater (called the "Orchard Vase"), Side A: Women Gathering Apples,The Metropolitan Museum of Art, Rogers Fund, 1907 © copyright 1984 by The Metropolitan Museum of Art; **p. 731:** *Fishermen Upon a Lee Shore,* J. M. W. Turner, The Iveagh Bequest, Kenwood, Bridgeman/Art Resource; **p. 732:** *Mary Shelley,* (detail) c. 1840, Richard Rothwell, By Courtesy of the National Portrait Gallery, London; **p. 735:** *A View of Chamonix and Mt. Blanc,* Julius Schnon von Caròlsfeld, Austrian Gallery, Vienna; **p. 739:** *Faust: Henry Irving as Mephistopheles,* c. 1885,

Theatre Museum/E. T. Archive; **p. 740:** *Charles Lamb* (detail), After Henry Hopper Meyer, By Courtesy of the National Portrait Gallery, London; **p. 746:** *William Hazlitt,* 1825, William Bewick, By Courtesy of the National Portrait Gallery, London; **pp. 752, 754, 755:** Illustrations from *Pride and Prejudice,* 19th century engraving, Hugh Thomson, The Granger Collection; **p. 757:** *Sir Walter Scott,* 1824, Sir Edwin Landseer, National Portrait Gallery, London/Jean-Loup Charmet; **pp. 760–61:** *Queen Victoria's Visit to Cherbourg,* Jules Achille Noel, Royal Academy, London, Bridgeman/Art Resource; **p. 762:** Painting of London's Crystal Palace, Done for the Great Exhibition of 1851, Reproduced by the courtesy of the Trustees of the British Museum; **pp. 764–65:** *Queen Victoria of England,* oil on canvas, 1838, by Sir George Hayter, The Granger Collection; *Charles Darwin in his greenhouse at Down House,* posthumous Russian painting, The Granger Collection; Charlotte Brontë, The Granger Collection; Charles Dickens, The Granger Collection; Battle from the Crimean War, The Granger Collection; Sepoy Mutiny, The Granger Collection; Karl Marx, The Granger Collection; Samuel F. B. Morse with his telegraph: mezzotint by John Sartain, The Granger Collection; Richard Wagner (1813–1883), oil by Franz von Lenback, The Granger Collection; **pp. 766–67:** Illustration, 1911, by N. C. Wyeth for Robert Louis Stevenson's *Treasure Island,* The Granger Collection; *Robert Browning,* Rudolph Lehman, Three Lions; Suez Canal, The Granger Collection; Alexander Graham Bell, The Granger Collection; The Mad Tea Party, colored engraving after the design by Sir John Tenniel for the first edition of Lewis Carroll's *Alice's Adventures in Wonderland,* 1865, The Granger Collection; The (First) Battle of Bull Run, 21 July 1861, lithograph, 1889, by Kurz & Allison, The Granger Collection; Anton Chekhov, The Granger Collection; *Marines Fight in the Boxer Rebellion Outside Peking Legation,* John Clymer, Three Lions; **p. 768:** *Warrington High Street,* T. Hesketh, Warrington Museum and Art Gallery, Bridgeman/Art Resource; **p. 769:** The Triumphs of the British Army and Navy, 1897, Commemorating the Diamond Jubilee of Queen Victoria, English lithograph, 1897, The Granger Collection; **p. 772:** Dudley Street, Seven Dials, London, 1872, Gustav Doré, The Granger Collection; **p. 773:** *Beata Beatrix, c. 1863,* Dante Gabriel Rossetti, The Granger Collection; **p. 774:** Alfred, Lord Tennyson, Caricature, 1871, Carlo Pellegrini, The Granger Collection; **p. 775:** *Bayswater Omnibus,* G. W. Joy, Museum of London; **p. 776:** Hyde Park Near Grosvenor Gate, 1842 (detail), Thomas Shotter Boys, Guildhall Art Gallery, Bridgeman/Art Resource; **p. 780:** Ulysses c. 1827, Jean-Auguste-Dominique Ingres, National Gallery of Art, Washington; Chester Dale Collection; **p. 783:** Fair, Quiet, and Sweet Rest (detail), Luke Fildes, Warrington Museum and Art Gallery, Bridgeman/Art Resource; **p. 784:** Baron Alfred Tennyson c. 1840, S. Laurence, By Courtesy of the National Portrait Gallery, London; **p. 787:** *The Lady of Shalott,* John Waterhouse, The Tate Gallery, London; **p. 795:** *The Bard,* John Martin, Yale Center for British Art, Paul Mellon Collection; **pp. 810–11:** *Nocturne: Grey and Gold—Chelsea Snow, 1876,* James McNeill Whistler, The Fogg Art Museum, Cambridge, Mass. Bequest—Grenville L. Winthrop; **p. 805:** Carved Gem of Light Brown Sardonyx, Roman 3rd to 2nd Century B.C., Ulysses Mourning for Home, Staatliche Museen zu Berlin; **p. 808:** *The Angry Sea* (detail), James McNeill Whistler, Courtesy of the Freer Gallery of Art, Smithsonian Institution, Washington, D.C.; **p. 810:** *Robert Browning,* M. Gordigiani, The Granger Collection; **p. 813:** *Portrait of a Lady (or Antea),* Parmagianino, Museo Nationale di Capodimonte, Naples; **p. 816:** *In Early Spring,* Inchbold, Ashmolean Museum, Oxford; **p. 819:** *Italian Ruins,* John Claude Nattes, Victoria & Albert Museum Trustees; **p. 824:** *Matthew Arnold* (detail) *1888,* G. J. Watts, By Courtesy of the National Portrait Gallery, London; **pp. 832:** *Thomas Hardy,* By Courtesy of the National Portrait Gallery, London; **p. 837:** *At the Window, 1960,* Jacob Kainen, 1979.83, oil on canvas $47\frac{7}{8} \times 59\frac{7}{8}$ ", National Museum of American Art, Smithsonian Institution, Gift of Mr. and Mrs. Wallace F. Holladay; **p. 840:** *Gerard Manley Hopkins,* A. E. Hopkins, By Courtesy of the National Portrait Gallery, London; **p. 843:** *Bird's Nest,* Ros W. Jenkins, Warrington Museum and Art Gallery, Bridgeman/Art Resource; **p. 844–45:** *Harvest Field with Gleaners, Haywood, Herefordshire, 1815,* George Robert Lewis, The Tate Gallery, London; **p. 847:** *A Mother and Child of the Isle of Wight c. 1849–51,* James Collinson, Yale Center for British Art, Paul Mellon Collection; **p. 848:** Alfred Edward Housman, F. Dodd, The Granger Collection; **p. 855:** *Temperantia* (detail) *1872,* Sir Edward Burne-Jones, Christie's, London, Bridgeman/Art Resource; **p. 856:** (top) *Elizabeth Barrett Browning, 1859,* Field Talfourd, The Granger Collection; (bottom) *Dante Gabriel Rossetti, 1847,* Self Portrait, The Granger Collection; **p. 859:** "Wey" Chintz, 1884, William Morris, The Granger Collection; **p. 860:** George Meredith, The Granger Collection; *Christina Rossetti,* D. G. Rossetti, By Courtesy of the National Portrait Gallery, London; *Rudyard Kipling,* (detail) *1899,* P. Burne-Jones, By Courtesy of the National Portrait Gallery, London; *Robert Louis Stevenson (Detail),* John Singer Sargent, The Taft Museum, Gift of Mr. and Mrs. Charles Phelps Taft; **p. 867:** *A Summer Day in Hyde Park,* John Ritchie, Museum of London; **p. 868:** Charles Dickens, The Granger Collection; **p. 872:** Two Tunnels, 1975, Guy Worsdell; **p. 877:** *Red Virginia Creeper,* Edvard Munch, Three Lions; **p. 880:** *Thomas Hardy,* By Courtesy of the National Portrait Gallery, London; **p. 884:** *Summer, Afternoon After a Shower,* (detail), John Constable, The Tate Gallery, London; **p. 887:** *Cottage and Pond, Moonlight,* Thomas Gainsborough, Victoria & Albert Museum Trustees; **p. 901:** Lithograph of Oscar Wilde from *Vanity Fair,* May 24, 1884, Ape (also known as "Singe"), The Mansell Collection; **p. 905:** *Suffragettes Expelled After Demonstrating at Westminster,* 1906, A. Beltrame, E. T. Archive (SOH/111/A); **p. 906:** *Disraeli and Queen Victoria* (cartoon), 1876, John Tenniel, The Granger Collection (4E524.14); **pp. 910–12:** *Big Ben, 1905–1906,* André Derain, Art Resource; *An English Rose,* Joseph Clark, Gallerie George, London, Bridgeman/Art Resource; **p. 913:** *A Star Shell, c. 1916,* Christopher Richard Wynne Nevinson, Tate Gallery London; **pp. 914–15:** *King Edward VII of England, Canvas by Sir Luke Fildes,* The Granger Collection; *King George V and Royal Family of England,* Canvas, 1913, by J. Lavery, The Granger Collection; 1908 Olympic Games, The Granger Collection; *Joseph Conrad (1857–1924),* oil on canvas 1923–24, by Walter Tittle, The Granger Collection; *Albert Einstein,* Frank Einzheimer, Three Lions; *Bombardment of Trenches,* watercolor, 1918, by Raoul Lespagne; *Flight of the Wright Brothers at Kitty Hawk,* The Granger Collection; Postcard Commemorating Discovery of North Pole, The Granger Collection; **pp. 916–17:** *Devastation, 1941: An East End Street, London,* Graham Sutherland, watercolor, 1941, The Granger Collection; *Winston Churchill (1874–1965),* oil on canvas, 1946, by Douglas

Chandor, The Granger Collection; *Conversation Piece (George VI of England with Family)*, Herbert James Gunn, Three Lions; *The Persistence of Memory, 1931*, Salvador Dali, The Granger Collection; *Mandolin and Guitar, 1924*, Pablo Picasso, The Granger Collection; *Dylan Thomas (1914–1953)*, oil on canvas, 1940, Rupert Shephard; Adolf Hitler, The Granger Collection; **p. 918:** *Over the Top (at Marcoing, December 1917)*, The Granger Collection; **p. 921:** *Ezra Pound, 1938–39*, Wyndham Lewis, The Granger Collection; **p. 923:** *The Artist's Garden at Durbins, c. 1915*, Roger Fry, Yale Center for British Art, Paul Mellon fund; **p. 925:** *Studland Beach (Detail)*, Vanessa Bell, The Tate Gallery, London; **p. 926:** *The Mud Bath*, David Bromberg, The Tate Gallery, London; **p. 937:** *Gardens in the Pound, Cookham, 1936*, Stanley Spencer, Collection, Leeds City Art Galleries; **p. 938:** *Joseph Conrad* (detail) *1923–24*, Walter Tittle, By courtesy of the National Portrait Gallery, London; **p. 956:** *Edward Morgan Forster, 1920*, Dora Carrington, By Courtesy of the National Portrait Gallery, London; **p. 959:** *The Newspaper*, Edouard Vuillard, The Phillips Collection, Washington, D.C.; **p. 961:** *The Conversation*, Hobson Pittman, The North Carolina Museum of Art, Raleight, N.C. Gift of the Artist; **p. 967:** *The Garden of Love*, Walter Richard Sickert, The Fitzwilliam Museum, Cambridge; **p. 972:** *D. H. Lawrence (detail) 1920*, Jan Juta, By Courtesy of the National Portrait Gallery, London; **p. 984:** *James Joyce (detail) 1935*, Jacques-Emile Blanche, The Granger Collection; **p. 986:** *St. Patrick's Close*, Walter Osborne, National Gallery of Ireland; **p. 995:** Holy Bush Hill, Hampstead, 1921, Ethelbert White; **p. 997:** *Ox House, Shaftesbury, 1932*, John R. Biggs; **p. 1019:** "Who controls the Past controls the Future," George Orwell, illustration by Richard Martin; **p. 1023:** *Houses of Parliament, Sunset, 1903*, Claude Monét, The Granger Collection; **p. 1024:** William Butler Yeats, Augustus Johns, The Granger Collection; **p. 1027:** *Old House (Ivy Cottage), Shoreham, 1831–32*, Samuel Palmer, Ashmolean Museum, Oxford; **p. 1031:** *Burning Airplane*, Photri; **p. 1038:** *D. H. Lawrence (detail) 1920*, Jan Juta, By courtesy of the National Portrait Gallery, London; **p. 1045:** Drawing of Tanks, World War I, Photri, Inc.; **p. 1048:** *Rupert Brooke 1911*, Clara Ewald, The Granger Collection; **p. 1050:** War Poster, Photri; **p. 1051:** *White Cup and Saucer, No. 1016*, Fantin-Latour, Fitzwilliam Museum, Cambridge; **p. 1054:** *T. S. Eliot (detail) 1888–1965*, Sir Gerald Kelly, National Portrait Gallery, Smithsonian Institution; **p. 1056:** *Bolton, 1938* (detail), William Coldstream, The National Gallery of Canada, Ottawa, Gift of the Massey Foundation, 1946; **p. 1068:** *Robert Graves, 1968*, J. Aldridge, The Granger Collection; **p. 1071:** *Sun, Wind, and Rain, 1845*, David Cox, The City Museum and Art Gallery, Birmingham; **p. 1081:** *The Fall of Icarus*, P. I. Bruegel, Musées Royeaux des Beaux-Arts de Belgique, Bruxelles; **pp. 1084–85:** *Old Thatched Summer House*, Lillian Stannard, Christopher Wood Gallery, London, Bridgeman/Art Resource; **p. 1099:** *The Magic Apple Tree, c. 1830*, Samuel Palmer, Fitzwilliam Museum, Cambridge; **p. 1103:** *Set design of Covent Garden for Pygmalion*, Donald Oenslager, Harvard Theater Collection; **p. 1104:** *George Bernard Shaw*, The Bettmann Archive; **pp. 1198–99:** *Papagena 1983*, Gillian Ayres, Private Collection, Photograph courtesy of The South Bank Center; **Time Line, 2nd spread** (between pp. 1201 and 1206): *Mao Tse-tung*, The Granger Collection; Martin Luther King, Jr., Gruerio/Three Lions; **p. 1206:** *Industrial Landscape*, L. S. Lowry, The Tate Gallery,

London; **p. 1208:** *Great Black-Backed Gull*, Douglas Anderson, Oscar and Peter Johnson Ltd., London, Bridgeman/Art Resource; **p. 1209:** *King's Cookham Rise, 1947*, Stanley Spencer, The Metropolitan Museum of Art, Purchase Lila Acheson Wallace Gift, 1981, © copyright 1986 by the Metropolitan Museum of Art; **p. 1225:** *The Identi-Kit Man*, Derek Boshier, The Tate Gallery, London; **p. 1242:** The Soothsayer from the Green Island, 1946, John Petts; **p. 1233:** *Knockalla Hills, Donegal*, Dan O'Neill, Ulster Museum, Belfast; **p. 1269:** *Hillside in Wales* (detail), L. S. Lowry, The Tate Gallery, London; **p. 1278:** *Shunters, 1965*, James Dolby; **p. 1291:** *Mount Fuji and Flowers, 1972*, David Hockney, The Metropolitan Museum of Art, Purchase Mr. and Mrs. Arthur Hays Sulzberger Gift, 1972, © copyright 1987 by The Metropolitan Museum of Art; **p. 1292:** *Philip Larkin (detail) 1984*, Humphrey Ocean, By courtesy of the National Portrait Gallery, London.

# PHOTOGRAPH CREDITS

**p. 247:** Bodego Bay, California, Pacific Ocean, © Peter Arnold; **p. 404:** Messerschmidt/Leo deWys, Inc.; **p. 545:** Photo by Rex Joseph; **p. 587:** Ian Berry/Magnum; **p. 596:** Alvin E. Staffan; Photo Researchers; **p. 703:** Diane Rawson, Photo Researchers; **p. 753:** Masterpiece Theater © BBC; **p. 830:** Thomas Hollyman/Photo Researchers; **p. 834:** Marshall Sklar/Photo Researchers; **p. 852:** Kees Van Den Berg/Photo Researchers; **p. 899:** Still from "Wuthering Heights," Laurence Olivier and Merle Oberon, Movie Still Archives; **pp. 902, 903:** Production stills from "The Importance of Being Earnest," 1977, Martha Swope; **p. 915:** Mohandas Gandhi, The Granger Collection; **p. 916:** Charles Lindbergh, The Granger Collection; **p. 917:** T. S. Eliot, The Granger Collection; **p. 941:** Dieter and Mary Plage; Bruce Coleman; **p. 950:** The Granger Collection; **p. 964:** The Granger Collection; **p. 992:** Alfred A. Knopf; **p. 1000:** The Granger Collection; **p. 1003:** ABBAS/Magnum; **p. 1010:** The Granger Collection; **p. 1013:** R. Dev/Photo Researchers; **pp. 1021, 1022:** Film stills from "1984," with Richard Burton and John Hurt, Photofest; **pp. 1028–29:** Dennis Stock/Magnum; **p. 1040:** Joe McDonald/Animals Animals; **p. 1044:** Siegfried Sassoon (detail) 1920, Bassano, By courtesy of the National Portrait Gallery, London; **p. 1074:** The Bettmann Archive/BBC Hulton; **p. 1082:** Louis MacNeice (detail) c. 1936, N. Coster, By courtesy of the National Portrait Gallery, London; **p. 1088:** (top) The Granger Collection; (bottom) Rollie McKenna; **pp. 1109, 1116, 1127, 1133, 1138, 1146–47, 1159, 1161, 1163, 1171, 1175, 1183, 1186:** Martha Swope; **pp. 1194, 1195:** Audrey Hepburn in "My Fair Lady," Warner Brothers, Movie Still Archives; **p. 1201:** Berlin Wall, P. Zachmann/Magnum; **Time Line 1st spread** (between pp. 1201 and 1206): Bruno Barbey/Magnum; Peter Marlow/Sygma; F. Scianna/Magnum; Peter Marlow/Sygma; Henri Cartier-Bresson/Magnum; Sygma; Ian Berry/Magnum Photos; Susan Meiselas/Magnum; Stuart Franklin/Sygma; Abbas/Magnum; **Time Line 2nd spread:** The Granger Collection; The Granger Collection; Erich Lessing/Magnum; Three Lions; Henri Cartier-Bresson/Magnum; Morath/Magnum; **p. 1207:** (top) Stuart Franklin/Sygma; (bottom) The Granger Collection; **p. 1211:** The Granger Collection; **p. 1216:** Nicholas Devore/Bruce Coleman; **p. 1223:** Mark

Gerson; **p. 1226:** Godfrey Graham; **p. 1232:** UPI/Bettmann Archive; **p. 1250:** Thomas Victor; **p. 1254:** Brian Brake/Photo Researchers; **p. 1258:** Thomas Victor; **p. 1266:** The Bettmann Archive/BBC Hulton; **p. 1274:** Thomas Victor; **p. 1287:** Photo by Rex Joseph; **pp. 1288, 1290:** Stills from Peter Brook's, "Lord of the Flies," Photofest; **p. 1295:** David Hurn/Magnum; **p. 1298:** Thomas Victor; **p. 1300:** Thomas Victor; **p. 1302:** Clem Haagner/Bruce Coleman; **p. 1306:** Stevie Smith (detail) 1970, Godfrey Argent, By Courtesy of the National Portrait Gallery, London; **p. 1310:** Layle Silbert; **p. 1314:** Thomas Victor; **p. 1318:** J. G. Ross/Photo Researchers; **p. 1320:** (top) Doreen Davie; (bottom) Alan Holden; **p. 1325:** Photos by Rex Joseph.

## ILLUSTRATION CREDITS

**pp. 7, 22, 1241, 1244, 1260:** The Art Source.